CASES AND MATERIALS ON MARINE INSURANCE LAW

CASES AND MATERIALS ON MARINE INSURANCE LAW

Susan Hodges, LLB, LLM, PhD
Lecturer, Department of Maritime Studies
and International Transport
University of Wales, Cardiff

with the assistance of
Roy Carlile, BSc, LLM

First published 1999 by Cavendish Publishing

Transferred to digital printing 2009
by Routledge-Cavendish
2 Park Square, Milton Park, Abingdon, Oxon, OX14 4RN

Simultaneously published in the USA and Canada
by Routledge-Cavendish
270 Madison Avenue, New York, NY 10016

Routledge-Cavendish is an imprint of the Taylor & Francis Group, an informa business

© Hodges, Susan 1999

All rights reserved. No part of this publication may be reproduced, stored in a retrieval system, or transmitted, in any form or by any means, electronic, mechanical, photocopying, recording, scanning or otherwise, except under the terms of the Copyright Designs and Patents Act 1988 or under the terms of a licence issued by the Copyright Licensing Agency, 90 Tottenham Court Road, London W1P 9HE, UK, without the permission in writing of the publisher.

Hodges, Susan
Cases and materials on marine insurance
1. Insurance, Marine – England 2. Insurance, Marine – Wales
I. Title

346.4'2'0862'0264

ISBN 1 85941 438 9

Publisher's Note
The publisher has gone to great lengths to ensure the quality of this reprint but points out that some imperfections in the original may be apparent.

In memory
of
my father

PREFACE

This book is the companion to the author's previous title, *Law of Marine Insurance*. It is, however, specifically structured so as to stand as a work of reference in its own right. To that end, the primary aim is to provide, within the confines of one volume, an easy and convenient means of accessing case law, statutory provisions and standard terms and conditions relevant to a policy of marine insurance. In particular, in producing this work, it is appreciated that not all students or practitioners of the law, at home or abroad, have access to comprehensive library facilities. Thus, a major objective is to spare the reader the inconvenience of having to refer, especially for the older cases, to law reports which may not be readily available.

The book is not intended as a mere compilation of case law, statutory provisions and contractual terms. The relationship between the Marine Insurance Act 1906, the Institute Clauses and case law is too complex to be presented without clarification. Each case, therefore, is considered in the light of statutory provisions and the specific contractual terms incorporated into the contract of insurance, and the difficult or controversial points of law discussed in some depth. Recent developments and problematical areas which have arisen in the law are also analysed in detail. The intention is to bridge the gap between text and reference book and, in this respect, certainly where marine insurance is concerned, it is believed that the format of this work is unique.

A particular feature of the book is the attention paid to layout and presentation. Each subject or topic of law is preceded by a brief introduction painting the background upon which the relevant cases and materials may lie. Whenever it is not self-evident, the relevance of each particular case to the law in question is emphasised and a summary of the facts and the decisions reached are clearly presented for ease of reading and consistency. Significant judicial extracts from the cases are then presented in the light of those facts and the legal effects discussed where necessary.

However, it is also recognised that only by examining case law spanning more than two centuries is it truly possible to trace the manner in which the law has evolved. Indeed, the Marine Insurance Act 1906 is a codification of previous case law and, therefore, an appreciation of those past authorities is not only an essential requirement to the understanding of the legal concepts generally, but also of paramount importance when wishing to gain an insight into the very construction of the sections within the Act.

Thus, whilst every effort has been made to ensure that recent high profile cases have been given maximum coverage, no apology is made for the inclusion of many of the older cases which have laid down the cardinal principles of marine insurance law, many of which remain relevant to this day. Indeed, the courts have not been averse to referring to the early cases for clarification of fundamental concepts.

It is hoped that the book will be found useful not only by postgraduate students of law, in-house lawyers, insurance brokers and claims adjusters, but also by other students and practitioners within the maritime industry who wish to have at hand a convenient source of cases and materials which may be difficult to obtain. With that in mind, particular attention has been paid to ensuring that the facts, together with the law, in all the cases highlighted are not only concise and comprehensive, but also eminently interesting and readable.

The law is stated as it stood on 1 January 1999.

Susan Hodges
Cardiff
March 1999

CONTENTS

Preface	*vii*
Table of Cases	*xix*
Table of Statutes	*xlvii*

1	**CONTRACT OF INDEMNITY**	**1**
	INSURANCE IS A CONTRACT OF INDEMNITY	1
	The indemnity is not necessarily perfect	2
	GAMING AND WAGERING CONTRACTS	3
	Assured has no insurable interest or expectation of acquiring such an interest	4
	DOUBLE INSURANCE, RIGHT TO CONTRIBUTION AND RETURN OF PREMIUM	8
	Double insurance and the right to contribution	9
	Over-insurance includes ppi policies	14
	Return of premium	15
	SUBROGATION	17
	Definition of subrogagtion	17
	No right of subrogation under a ppi policy	18
	Where the insurer pays for a total loss	19
	Where the insurer pays for a partial loss	25
	The insurer is limited to recovering the amount of the indemnification	26
	The assured is impliedly bound to mitigate the loss suffered by the insurer	26
	Subrogation brings about an equitable proprietary interest	27
	An insurer cannot exercise rights of subrogation against a co-assured	31
	An insurer cannot recoup gifts and voluntary payments	34
	The subrogation waiver clause	35
	Under-insurance: apportionment of moneys recovered from a third party wrongdoer	37
2	**INSURABLE INTEREST**	**39**
	INTRODUCTION	39
	DEFINITIONS OF INSURABLE INTEREST	40
	THE ASSURED	46
	Owner of a ship	46
	Owner of goods	50
	Owner of freight	59
	The insurer	62
	Mortgagor and mortgagee	65
	The interest of a shareholder	67
	Other persons with insurable interest	72

	WHEN INTEREST MUST ATTACH	76
	Lost or not lost	78
	An assignee	82
3	**SUBJECT MATTER INSURED**	**83**
	INTRODUCTION	83
	SHIP	85
	Hull policies (MAR 91 form) and the Institute Hulls Clauses	87
	GOODS	87
	The Institute Cargo Clauses (A), (B) and (C)	88
	Deck cargo and living animals	88
	Containers and packing materials	91
	Insurance on goods includes loss of the adventure	91
	MOVABLES	93
	FREIGHT	93
	Meaning of freight	94
	Freight payable by a third party	96
	PROFIT	112
	Profit on goods	113
	Profit on charter	114
	COMMISSION	115
	DISBURSEMENTS	116
	Disbursements incurred by a ships agent	117
	Disbursements – over-insurance by double insurance	118
	SEAMEN'S WAGES	119
	VENTURES UNDERTAKEN BY A COMPANY	120
	LIABILITY TO A THIRD PARTY	120
4	**TIME AND VOYAGE POLICIES**	**121**
	INTRODUCTION	121
	TIME POLICY	121
	A definite period of time	121
	The Navigation Clause	125
	The Continuation Clause	127
	The Termination Clause	128
	The Classification Clause	133
	VOYAGE POLICY	134
	Voyage policy on ship	134
	Voyage policy on goods	170
	MIXED POLICY	181

Contents

5	**VALUED AND UNVALUED POLICIES**	**185**
	VALUED POLICIES	185
	Introduction	185
	The agreed value is conclusive	186
	Excessive over-valuation	191
	Subject to the provisions of this Act	203
	UNVALUED POLICIES	206
	Insurable value	206
6	**UTMOST GOOD FAITH, DISCLOSURE AND REPRESENTATIONS**	**213**
	INTRODUCTION	213
	UTMOST GOOD FAITH	214
	Nature of the duty	214
	Utmost good faith	236
	End of the continuing duty to observe utmost good faith	240
	Avoidance of the contract	241
	DUTY OF DISCLOSURE UNDER s 18	246
	Nature of the duty	246
	REPRESENTATIONS	267
7	**WARRANTIES**	**269**
	INTRODUCTION	269
	NATURE OF A WARRANTY	270
	A warranty must be 'exactly complied with'	270
	A warranty need not be material to the risk	272
	There is no remedy for breach	273
	There is no defence for breach	274
	A promissory warranty is a promissory condition precedent	275
	Legal effects of breach of warranty	277
	EXPRESS WARRANTIES	282
	The form of a warranty	282
	Construction of warranties	299
	IMPLIED WARRANTIES	301
	The implied warranty of portworthiness	302
	The implied warranty of seaworthiness	303
	The implied warranty of cargoworthiness	325
	The implied warranty of legality	326

8	**THE CAUSE OF LOSS**	**335**
	INTRODUCTION	335
	The efficient or predominate cause	336
	ONE PROXIMATE CAUSE OF LOSS	341
	TWO OR MORE PROXIMATE CAUSES OF LOSS	342
	Proximate causes of equal efficiency	342
	Two or more proximate causes – no express exclusion in the policy	344
	Two or more proximate causes– one expressly excluded by the policy	345
	LOSS CAUSED BY APPREHENSION OF A PERIL	347
	SUBJECT TO THE PROVISIONS OF THIS ACT	349
	Section 39(5) – loss 'attributable to' unseaworthiness	349
	Section 55(2)(a) – loss 'attributable to' the wilful misconduct of the assured	354
	UNLESS THE POLICY OTHERWISE PROVIDES	357
	Caused by and arising from	357
	Attributable to and reasonably attributable to	357
	Consequences thereof	358
	Consequent on	360
9	**MARINE RISKS**	**363**
	INTRODUCTION	363
	PERILS OF THE SEAS	364
	Perils of the sea defined	364
	Unascertainable perils of the seas	384
	The Institute Cargo Clauses (B) and(C)	385
	Loss caused by preventative action	391
	FIRE AND EXPLOSION	392
	Fire	393
	Explosion	403
	VIOLENT THEFT BY PERSONS FROM OUTSIDE THE VESSEL	405
	Violent theft	405
	PIRACY	411
	Rioters from the shore	411
	Passengers who mutiny	412
	Piracy is indiscriminate and not politically motivated	413
	Piracy requires force	415
	ACCIDENTS IN LOADING	415
	ALL RISKS: THE ICC (A)	416
	Burden of proof	418

10 EXCLUDED LOSSES — 421

- INTRODUCTION — 421
- WILFUL MISCONDUCT OF THE ASSURED — 422
  - Meaning of wilful misconduct — 422
- DELAY — 433
- ORDINARY WEAR AND TEAR — 435
- ORDINARY LEAKAGE AND BREAKAGE — 437
- INHERENT VICE OR NATURE OF THE SUBJECT MATTER INSURED — 440
  - Inherent vice includes insufficient packing — 441
  - Unless the policy otherwise provides — 442
- RATS AND VERMIN — 444
- INSOLVENCY — 445
- DELIBERATE DAMAGE — 447

11 BURDEN AND STANDARD OF PROOF — 449

- INTRODUCTION — 449
- PROOF OF LOSS BY PERILS OF THE SEAS — 451
  - The plaintiff's burden of proof — 451
  - The defendant's burden of proof — 467
- PROOF OF LOSS BY FIRE — 474
  - Standard of proof for the defence of wilful misconduct of the assured — 476
- PROOF OF LOSS BY BARRATRY — 477
  - Onus of proof of complicity — 477
  - Standard of proof of complicity — 485

12 THE INCHMAREE CLAUSE — 489

- INTRODUCTION — 489
- CAUSED BY — 492
- BREAKAGE OF SHAFTS — 494
- LATENT DEFECT IN THE MACHINERY OR HULL — 495
  - Meaning of latent defect — 497
  - Latent defect and unseaworthiness — 500
- NEGLIGENCE OF MASTER OFFICERS CREW OR PILOTS — 502
  - Negligence or unseaworthiness? — 505
  - Negligence of master who is owner or a part-owner — 506
- NEGLIGENCE OF REPAIRERS OR CHARTERERS — 508
- BARRATRY — 509
  - Wrongful act — 510
  - The owner or, as the case may be, the charterer — 524
  - The innocent mortgagee — 530
- THE DUE DILIGENCE PROVISO — 532

13 THE 3/4THS COLLISION LIABILITY CLAUSE — 535
INTRODUCTION — 535
THE 3/4THS COLLISION LIABILITY CLAUSE — 537
    Collision — 538
    In consequence of — 540
    Vessel — 541
    By way of damages — 545
    Paid by the assured (pay to be paid rule) — 547
LEGAL COSTS — 550
EXCLUSIONS — 551
    Removal or disposal of obstructions, wrecks, cargoes or any other thing whatsoever – cl 8.4.1 — 551
    Pollution, contamination and damage to the environment – cl 8.4.5 — 553
THE SISTER SHIP CLAUSE — 554

14 WAR AND STRIKES RISKS — 557
INTRODUCTION — 557
    The f c and s clause — 558
    The Paramount and the Exclusion Clauses — 558
    Dual causes of loss – marine risk and war risk — 559
    The rule of proximate cause — 559
WAR RISKS — 561
    Clause 1.1: War civil war revolution rebellion insurrection, or civil strife arising therefrom, or any hostile act by or against a belligerent power — 562
    Clause 1.2: Capture seizure arrest restraint or detainment, and the consequence thereof or any attempt thereat — 569
    Clause 1.3: Derelict mines torpedoes bombs or other derelict weapons of war — 580
STRIKES RISKS — 581
    Clause 1.4: Strikers locked-out workmen or persons taking part in labour disturbances riots or civil commotions — 581
    Clause 1.5: Any terrorist or any person acting maliciously or from a political motive — 587
    Clause 1.6: Confiscation or expropriation — 587
EXCLUSIONS UNDER THE IWSC(H)(95) — 589
    Clause 5.1.2: Requisition and pre-emption — 589
    Clause 5.1.3: Capture seizure arrest … by or under the order of the government …of the country in which the vessel is owned or registered — 593

INSTITUTE WAR CLAUSES (CARGO) AND INSTITUTE STRIKES CLAUSES (CARGO)	594
The frustration clause	594

15 ACTUAL TOTAL LOSS — 599

INTRODUCTION	599
Notice of Claim and Tenders Clause	599
Prompt notice	599
Automatic discharge from liability	600
DEFINITION OF ACTUAL TOTAL LOSS	600
TYPES OF ACTUAL TOTAL LOSS	601
Where the subject matter is totally destroyed	601
Cease to be a thing of the kind insured	609
Irretrievably deprived thereof	613
ACTUAL TOTAL LOSS OF FREIGHT	617
Actual total loss of freight caused by an actual or constructive total loss of ship and/or goods	617
Actual total loss of freight caused by a loss of voyage or adventure	620
RECOVERY FOR A PARTIAL LOSS	621

16 CONSTRUCTIVE TOTAL LOSS — 623

DEFINITIONS OF CONSTRUCTIVE TOTAL LOSS	623
Section 60 is a complete definition	623
Loss of voyage or adventure	625
TYPES OF CONSTRUCTIVE TOTAL LOSS	629
Reasonable abandonment of the subject matter insured	629
Deprivation of possession of ship or goods	636
Damage to ship	644
Damage to goods	657
EFFECTS OF CONSTRUCTIVE TOTAL LOSS	658
Abandonment of subject matter insured	658
Notice of abandonment	660
ADEMPTION OF LOSS	668
The waiver clause	670

17 PARTIAL LOSS – 1 — 673

PARTICULAR AVERAGE LOSS	673
Introduction	673
PARTIAL LOSS OF A SHIP	675
Measure of indemnity	676
Repaired damage	678

Unrepaired damage	686
PARTIAL LOSS OF GOODS	704
A total loss of part of the goods	704
A partial loss of the whole or part of the goods	706
Part of the goods are partially damaged	709
Goods that are not identifiable	709
Computing the measure of liability	709
PARTIAL LOSS OF FREIGHT	710
Total loss of part of the cargo	711
Chartered freight – substituted cargo	712
Goods carried in a substituted ship	713
Measure of indemnity	715
18 PARTIAL LOSS – 2	**719**
SALVAGE, GENERAL AVERAGE AND SUE AND LABOUR	719
Introduction	719
SALVAGE CHARGES	721
Introduction	721
Definition of salvage charges	722
Salvage charges and sue and labour compared	729
Salvage charges and general average compared	732
Salvage and general average under the York-Antwerp Rules	733
GENERAL AVERAGE	734
Introduction	734
Definition of general average loss	735
SUE AND LABOUR	764
Introduction	764
Definition of sue and labour	764
Cargo insurance – duty under cl 16.2	778
Supplementary cover	780
Breach of the duty to sue and labour	782
When is the cut-off date for suing and labouring?	788
Is an express clause essential to a right of reimbursement?	789
No claim for salvage charges – no s/c	793

APPENDICES

1	Marine Insurance Act 1906	795
2	Marine Insurance (Gambling Policies) Act 1909	826
3	Third Parties (Rights Against Insurers) Act 1930	828
4	Lloyd's Marine Policy [Mar 91]	831
5	Institute of London Underwriters – Companies Marine Policy [Mar 91]	835
6	Institute Time Clauses Hulls (1995) [ITCH(95)]	839
7	Institute Voyage Clauses Hulls (1995) [IVCH(95)]	852
8	Institute Time Clauses – Hulls – Restricted Perils (1995)	863
9	Institute Additional Perils Clauses – Hulls (1995)	876
10	Institute Cargo Clauses (A) [ICC(A)]	877
11	Institute Cargo Clauses (B) [ICC(B)]	882
12	Institute Cargo Clauses (C) [ICC(C)]	887
13	Institute Time Clauses Freight (1995) [ITCF(95)]	892
14	Institute Voyage Clauses Freight (1995) [IVCF(95)]	900
15	Institute Dual Valuation Clause	906
16	Institute Warranties	907
17	Institute Malicious Damage Clause	908
18	Institute Theft, Pilferage and Non-delivery Clause	909
19	Institute War and Strikes Clauses Hulls – Time (1995) [IWSC(H)(95)]	910
20	Institute War Clauses (Cargo) (1982) [IWC(C)(82)]	913
21	Institute Strikes Clauses (Cargo) (1982) [ISC(C)(82)]	918
22	The York-Antwerp Rules 1994	922
23	Lloyd's Standard Form of Salvage Agreement 1995 [LOF 1995]	931

Index   941

TABLE OF CASES

AG v Adelaide Steamship Co Ltd, 'Warilda'
[1923] AC 292, HL 339, 423, 560, 561
AG v Glen Line Ltd and Liverpool and London
War Risks Insurance Association Ltd [1930] 37 LlL 55;
(1930) 36 Com Cas 1, HL 20, 26
Agenoria Steamship Co Ltd v Merchants' Marine
Insurance Co Ltd (1903) 8 Com Cas 212 ....683, 684
Aitchison v Lohre (1879) 4 App Cas 755, HL 3, 727–30, 769
Ajum Goolam Hossen & Co v Union Marine
Insurance Co [1901] AC 362, PC 384, 460
Allgemeine Gesellschaft Helvetia v
Administrator of German Property [1931] 1 KB 672 24
Allison v Bristol Marine Insurance Company
(1875) 1 App Cas 209, HL 59, 111
Allkins v Jupe (1877) 2 CPD 375 334
Almojil Establishment v Malayan Motor and
General Underwriters (Private) Ltd, 'Al-Jubail IV'
[1982] 2 Lloyd's Rep 637, Singapore CA 182
Alps, The [1893] P 109 ....105, 106
Alston v Campbell (1799) 4 Bro Parl Cas 476 66
Anderson v Royal Exchange Assurance Co (1805) 7 East 38 608
Anderson, Tritton and Co v
Ocean SS Co (1884) 5 Asp MLC 401 ....733, 743, 744
Angerstein v Bell (1795) 1 Park 54 166
Anghelatos v Northern Assurance Co, 'Olympia'
(1924) 19 LlL Rep 255, HL 433, 483
Anglis and Co v P and O Steam Navigation Co
[1927] 2 KB 456 308
Anonima Petroli Italiana SpA and Neste Oy v
Marlucodez Armadora SA, 'Filiatra Legacy'
[1991] 2 Lloyd's Rep 337, CA 486, 487
Anthony John Sharpe and Roarer Investments Ltd v
Sphere Drake Insurance plc, Minster Insurance Co Ltd
and EC Parker and Co Ltd, 'Moonacre'
[1992] 2 Lloyd's Rep 501 .... 42, 43, 45, 47, 49,
50, 72, 77
Antigoni, The [1991] 1 Lloyd's Rep 209 308
Apollinaris Co v Nord Deutsche Insurance Co
[1904] 1 KB 252 89
Aquacharm, The [1982] 1 Lloyd's Rep 7 308
Armar [1954] 2 Lloyd's Rep 95; [1954] AMC 1674 691

Asfar and Co v Blundell and Another [1896] 1 QB 123, CA 98, 114, 609–11, 619
Ashworth v General Accident Fire and Life Assurance
  Corporation [1955] IR 268, Supreme Court of Ireland 339, 341, 352–54
Astrovlanis Compania Naviera SA v Linard,
  'Gold Sky' [1972] 2 Lloyd's Rep 187 ....471, 766, 767, 783, 785
Athel Line Ltd v Liverpool and London War Risks
  Association Ltd [1946] 1 KB 117, CA 567
Athens Maritime Enterprises Corporation v
  Hellenic Mutual War Risks Association (Bermuda) Ltd,
  'Andreas Lemos' [1982] 2 Lloyd's Rep 483 ....406, 415, 584
Atlantic Maritime Co v Gibbon [1953] 2 Lloyd's Rep 294, CA 596
Atlantic Mutual Insurance Co v King [1918] 1 KB 307 568
Atwood v Sellar and Co (1879) 4 QBD 342 738
Australian Coastal Shipping Commission v
  Green [1971] 1 All ER 353 ....738, 739

Bah Lias Tobacco and Rubber Estates Ltd v
  Volga Insurance Co Ltd (1920) 3 LlL Rep 155 148
Ballantyne v MacKinnon [1896] 2 QB 455, CA 342, 344, 501, 727
Bamburi, The [1982] 1 Lloyd's Rep 312 ....348, 575, 579, 638,
                                                                      643, 670
Bank Line Ltd v Arthur Capel and Co [1919] AC 435 642
Bank of England v Vagliano [1891] AC 107 652
Bank of Nova Scotia v Hellenic Mutual War Risks
  Association (Bermuda) Ltd, 'Good Luck'
  [1988] 1 Lloyd's Rep 514; [1989] 2 Lloyd's Rep 238;
  [1991] 2 Lloyd's Rep 191, HL 133, 165, 213, 215, 220, 223,
                                                    224, 226, 244, 245, 275–79,
                                                             285, 287, 293, 299,
                                                                  318, 333, 490
Banque Financière de la Cité SA v Westgate Insurance
  Co Ltd [1987] 1 Lloyd's Rep 69; [1988] 2 Lloyd's Rep 513;
  [1990] 2 Lloyd's Rep 377, HL 214, 215, 222, 227,
                                                                 236, 238, 242–45
Banque Keyser Ullmann SA v Skandia (UK) Insurance
  Co Ltd and Others [1987] 1 Lloyd's Rep 69 ....214, 227
Banque Monteca and Carystuiaki and Another v
  Motor Union Insurance Co Ltd (1923) 14 LlL Rep 48 414
Barclay v Cousins (1802) 2 East 545 ....112, 113
Baring v Christie (1804) 5 East 398 290

Table of Cases

Barker v Janson (1868) LR 3 CP 303 ....187, 188, 604, 605
Bater v Bater [1951] P 35 ....476, 486, 487
Bates v Hewitt (1867) LR 2 QB 595 247
Baxendale v Fane, 'Lapwing' (1940) 66 LlL Rep 174 ....374, 503
Bean v Stupart (1778) 1 Dougl 11 ....283, 300
Beatson v Howarth (1741) 6 Term Rep 533 156
Becker, Gray and Co v London Assurance Corporation
   [1918] AC 101, HL 348, 349
Bedouin, The (1899) 7 Asp MLC 391 105
Bell v Bell (1810) 2 Camp 475 ....142, 145
Bell v Carstairs (1810) 2 Camp 543 507
Bell v Nixon (1816) Holt NP 423 601
Bennett SS Co v Hull Mutual SS Protection Society
   [1914] 3 KB 57, CA 544
Bensaude and Others v Thames and Mersey Marine
   Insurance Co Ltd [1897] AC 609, HL 360
Berger and Light Diffusers Pty Ltd v
   Pollock [1973] 2 Lloyd's Rep 442 ....200, 209, 263–65
Berk and Co v Style [1955] 2 Lloyd's Rep 383;
   [1955] 1 QB 180 ....91, 217, 441, 443, 773
Biccard v Shepherd (1861) 14 Moore 491 ....309, 310
Bill v Mason 169
Birkley v Presgrave (1801) 1 East 220 ....736, 738, 741
Birrell and Others v Dryer and Others
   (1884) 9 App Cas 345, HL 296–98, 301
Black King Shipping Corporation v Massie, 'Litsion Pride'
   [1985] 1 Lloyd's Rep 437 ....194, 213, 216, 217, 219–21,
                                                   223–25, 227, 230–32, 235,
                                                   237, 240, 241, 244,
                                                   252, 254, 663, 665
Blackburn v Liverpool, Brazil and River Plate Steam
   Navigation Co [1902] 1 KB 290 382
Blackett, Magalhaes and Colombie v National Benefit
   Assurance Co (1921) 8 LlL Rep 293, CA 326
Blackhurst v Cockell (1789) 3 Term Rep 360 291
Blane Steamships Ltd v Minister of Transport
   [1951] 2 Lloyd's Rep 155, CA 24
Board of Trade v Hain SS Co Ltd [1929] AC 534, HL 339
Boiler Inspection and Insurance Co of Canada v
   Sherwin-Williams Co of Canada [1951] AC 319, PC 404

Bolands Ltd v London and Lancashire Fire Insurance
Co Ltd [1924] 19 LlL Rep 1, HL 585
Bond Air Services Ltd v Hull [1955] 2 QB 417;
[1955] 1 Lloyd's Rep 498 286
Boon and Cheah v Asia Insurance Co Ltd
[1975] 1 Lloyd's Rep 452, Malaysian High Court 621
Booth v Gair (1863) 33 LJCP 99 .... 774, 775, 777
Bouillon v Lupton (1863) 15 CB (NS) 113 .... 160, 309, 310
Boyd v Dubois (1811) 3 Camp 133 401
Bradley v Newsom, Sons and Co [1939] AC 16 630
Brandeis Goldschmidt and Co v Economic Insurance Co Ltd
(1922) 38 TLR 609 .... 735, 759
Brigella, The (1893) PD 189 .... 734, 751
Britain SS Co v King, 'Petersham'; Green v British India
Steam Navigation Co Ltd, 'Matiana' [1921] 1 AC 99, HL 358, 567
British and Foreign Insurance Co Ltd v Wilson Shipping
Co Ltd [1921] 1 AC 188, HL 3, 697–99
British and Foreign Marine Insurance Co Ltd v
Samuel Sanday and Co [1915] 1 AC 650, HL 92, 93, 331, 574, 594,
596, 616, 626,
627, 629
British and Foreign Marine Insurance Co v
Gaunt [1921] 2 AC 41, HL 89, 90, 416, 417, 419, 441
British Dominions General Insurance Company Ltd v
Duder and Others, 'Katina' [1915] 2 KB 394 63
Britton v The Royal Insurance Co (1866) 4 F&F 905 .... 217, 232
Broadmayne, The [1916] P 64, CA 589–92
Brotherston v Barber (1816) 5 M&S 418 1
Brough v Whitmore (1791) 4 Term Rep 206 86
Brown v Fleming (1902) 7 Com Cas 245 91
Brown v Nitrate Producers SS Co (1937) 58 Lloyd's Rep 188 500
Buchanan v Faber, 'Queen Victoria' (1899) 4 Com Cas 223 .... 76, 77, 117
Buckeye State, The (1941) 39 F Supp 344 393
Burges v Wickham (1863) 3 B&S 669 307
Burnard v Rodocanachi (1882) 7 App Cas 333, HL 17, 26, 34
Burton v English (1883) 12 QBD 218 738
Busk v Royal Exchange Assurance Co (1818) 2 B&Ald 73 .... 397, 398
Butler v Wildman (1821) 3 B&Ald 398 389

Table of Cases

Byrant and May v London Assurance Corporation
  (1866) 2 TLR 591 387
Cambridge v Anderton (1824) 2 B&C 691 602
Canada Rice Mills Ltd v Union Marine and General
  Insurance Co Ltd (1940) 67 LlL Rep 549; [1941] AC 55 ....384, 391
Captain JA Cates Tug and Wharfage Co Ltd v
  Franklin Insurance Co [1927] AC 698, PC 604
Carisbrook SS Co Ltd v London and Provincial Marine
  and General Insurance Co Ltd (1901) 6 Com Cas 291 751
Carras v London and Scottish Assurance Corporation Ltd
  [1936] 1 KB 291, CA 101
Carter v Boehm (1766) 3 Burr 1905 ....213–15, 224, 247, 250
Case v Davidson (1816) 5 M&S 79 21
Castellain v Preston (1883) 11 QBD 380 ....1, 209, 692
Cator v Great Western Insurance Co of New York
  (1873) 8 LE 8 CP 552 ....390, 391
CCR Fishing Ltd and Others v Tomenson Inc and Others,
  'La Pointe' [1991] 1 Lloyd's Rep 89,
  Supreme Court of Canada 365, 367
Cepheus Shipping Corporation v Guardian Royal
  Exchange Assurance, 'Capricorn'
  [1995] 1 Lloyd's Rep 622 ....42, 51, 60–62, 77, 108, 110
Chandler v Blogg [1898] 1 QB 32 ....542, 543
Clan Line Steamers Ltd v Liverpool and London
  War Risks Association Ltd (1943) 73 LlL Rep 165 567
Clason v Simmonds (1741) 6 Term Rep 533 156
Cleveland Twist Drill Co (GB) Ltd v Union Insurance of
  Canton (1925) 2 LlL Rep 50, CA 409
Coast Ferries Ltd v Century Insurance Company of Canada
  and Others, 'Brentwood' [1973] 2 Lloyd's Rep 232, CA 506, 533
Colledge v Hardy (1851) 6 Exch 205 296
Cologan v London Assurance (1816) 5 M&S 447 659
Colonial Insurance Company of New Zealand v
  Adelaide Marine Insurance Company,
  'Duke of Sutherland' (1886) 12 AC 128, PC 53, 54
Coltman v Bibby Tankers Ltd, 'Derbyshire'
  [1986] 1 WLR 751 308
Commonwealth Smelting Ltd and Another v Guardian
  Royal Exchange Assurance Ltd [1984] 2 Lloyd's Rep 608 404

Commonwealth, The [1907] P 216, CA 37
Compania Maritima San Basilio SA v Oceanus Mutual
   Underwriting Association (Bermuda) Ltd, 'Eurysthenes'
   [1976] 2 Lloyd's Rep 171, CA 123, 128, 319, 320,
                                                                 322, 429, 430
Compania Martiartu v Royal Exchange Assurance
   Corporation, 'Arnus' [1923] 1 KB 650, CA 433, 454, 456, 466,
                                                                 468–70, 479–81
Compania Naviera Santi SA v Indemnity Marine
   Insurance Co Ltd, 'Tropaioforos' [1960] 2 LlL Rep 469 .... 433, 451, 467, 468, 483
Compania Naviera Vascongada v British and Foreign
   Marine Insurance Co Ltd, 'Gloria' (1936) 54 LlL Rep 35 .... 322, 433, 452,
                                                                 468, 470, 471
Constitution Insurance Co of Canada et al v Kosmopoulos
   et al (1987) 34 DLR (4th) 208, Supreme Court of Canada 43, 70
Container Transport International Inc and Reliance
   Group Inc v Oceanus Mutual Underwriting Association
   (Bermuda) Ltd (CTI case) [1982] 2 Lloyd's Rep 178;
   [1984] 1 Lloyd's Rep 476, CA 216, 219, 224, 236, 250,
                                                                 256, 257, 261,
                                                                 262, 264
Continental Illinois National Bank and Trust Co of Chicago
   and Xenofon Maritime SA v Alliance Assurance Co Ltd,
   'Captain Panagos DP' [1986] 2 Lloyd's Rep 470;
   [1989] 1 Lloyd's Rep 33, CA 233, 245, 400, 401, 431,
                                                                 433, 474–76, 482
Corfu Navigation Co and Bain Clarkson Ltd v Mobil
   Shipping Co Ltd, The Alpha [1991] 2 Lloyd's Rep 515 745
Cornfoot v Royal Exchange Assurance Corporation
   [1903] Com Cas 205; aff'd [1904] 9 Com Cas 80, CA 167
Cory v Burr (1883) 8 AC 393, HL 517, 522, 569, 570, 572
Cory v Patton (1874) LR 9 QB 577 .... 223, 253, 254
Costain-Blankevoort (UK) Dredging Co Ltd v
   Davenport, 'Nassau Bay' [1979] 1 Lloyd's Rep 395 .... 388, 537, 580
Court Line Ltd v R, 'Lavington Court'
   [1945] 78 LlL Rep 390, CA 630, 632, 633, 639
Covington v Roberts (1806) 2 Bos&PNR 378 747
Coxe v Employers' Liability Assurance Corporation Ltd
   [1916] 2 KB 629 357
Crouan v Stainer [1903] 1 KB 87 769
Cullen v Butler (1816) 5 M&S 461 378

Table of Cases

Currie and Co v Bombay Native
 Insurance Co (1869) LR 3 PC 72 ....782, 785

Dakin v Oxley (1864) 15 CBNS 646 98
Davidson and Others v Burnard (1868) LR 4 CP 117 373
De Hahn v Hartley (1786) 1 TR 343 ....267, 271
De Hart v Compania Anonima de Seguros,
 'Aurora' [1903] 2 KB 503, CA 761–64
De Monchy v Phoenix Insurance Co of Hartford and
 Another (1929) 34 LlL Rep 201, HL 437
De Vaux v Salvador [1836] 4 Ad&E 420 ....535, 682
Dean v Hornby (1854) 3 E&B 180 615
Delaney v Stoddart (1785) 1 Term Rep 22 159
Demetriades and Co v Northern Assurance Co,
 'Spathari' (1923) 17 LlL Rep 65, CA; aff'd
 (1924) 21 LlL Rep 265, HL 480
Denoon v Hone and Colonial Assurance Co
 (1872) LR 7 CP 431 96
Diamond, The [1906] P 282 394
Dickinson v Jardine (1868) LR 3 CP 639 756
Dino Services Ltd v Prudential Assurance Co Ltd
 [1989] 1 Lloyd's Rep 379, CA 407
Dixon v Sadler (1839) 5 M&W 405; (1841) 8 M&W 894 ....302, 305, 309–12,
                                                                  373, 507
Dixon v Whitworth (1880) 4 Asp MLC 326, CA 720, 731
Dodwell and Co Ltd v British Dominions General
 Insurance Co Ltd [1955] 2 LlL Rep 391 ....439, 440
Douglas v Scougal (1816) 4 Dow 269 275
Doyle v Dallas (1831) 1 M&Rob 48 ....594, 628, 651
Driscoll v Passmore (1798) 1 B &P 200 ....136, 137
Dudgeon v Pembroke (1877) 2 App Cas 284, HL 353
Duff v Mackenzie (1857) 3 CBNS 16 ....87, 705
Dyson and Others v Rowcroft (1802) 3 B&T 474 608

Eagle Star Insurance Co v Provincial Insurance plc
 [1993] 2 Lloyd's Rep 143, PC 12
Earle v Rowcroft (1806) 8 East 126 512
Edwards and Co Ltd v
 Motor Union Insurance Co Ltd [1922] 2 KB 249 18

Elcock v Thomson [1949] 2 All ER 381 690
Elder Dempster and Co v Paterson,
    Zochonis and Co [1924] AC 522 .... 305, 308, 326
Elfie A Issaias v Marine Insurance Co Ltd
    (1923) 15 LlL Rep 186, CA 433, 468, 478, 480–82,
                                                                   485–87, 524
Elliot v Wilson (1997) 4 Bro Parl Cas 470, PC 156, 157
Emperor Goldmining Co Ltd v Switzerland
    General Insurance Co Ltd [1964] 1 Lloyd's Rep 348,
    Supreme Court of New South Wales 789, 793
Enimont Supply SA v Chesapeake Shipping Inc,
    'Surf City' [1995] 2 Lloyd's Rep 242 35
Esso Petroleum Co Ltd v Hall Russell and Co
    [1988] 3 WLR 730, HL 17
Euro-Diam Ltd v Bathurst [1988] 2 All ER 23, CA 317, 328, 329
Everth v Hannam (1815) 6 Taunt 375 513

Fanti, The and The Padre Island [1990] 2 Lloyd's Rep 191, HL 548, 549
Farnworth v Hyde (1866) LR 2 CP 204 .... 634, 657
Farr v Motor Traders Mutual Insurance Society Ltd
    [1920] 3 KB 669, CA 273, 297
Field Steamship Co Ltd v Burr [1899] 1 QB 579, CA 681, 684
Field v Receiver of Metropolitan Police [1907] 2 KB 853 583–85
Fisk v Masterman (1841) 8 M&W 165 16
Fiumana Società di Navigazione v
    Bunge and Co Ltd [1930] 2 KB 47 308
Flint v Flemyng (1830) 1 B&Ad 45 .... 94, 99, 112
Foley v Tabor (1861) 2 F&F 663 307
Foley v United Marine Insurance Co of Sydney
    (1870) LR 5 CP 155 143
Forbes v Aspinall (1811) 13 East 326 .... 99, 204
Forder v Great Western Railway Co [1905] 2 KB 532 428
Forestal Land, Timber and Railways Co Ltd v
    Rickards, 'Minden' [1940] 4 All ER 96 .... 410, 571, 580
Forshaw v Chabert (1821) 3 Br&B 159 273
Foster v Driscoll [1929] 1 KB 470 328
Fracis, Times and Co v Sea Insurance Co (1896) Com Cas 229 329
France Fenwick and Co Ltd v The King [1927] 1 KB 458 .... 589, 591
France, Fenwick and Co v Merchants Marine Insurance
    Co Ltd [1915] 3 KB 290 .... 540, 541

Table of Cases

Francis v Boulton [1895] 1 Com Cas 217 611
Fraser Shipping Ltd v Colton and Others
 [1997] 1 Lloyd's Rep 586 ....154, 227, 263, 605, 609, 613
Friso, The [1980] 1 Lloyd's Rep 469 308
Fuerst Day Lawson Ltd v Orion Insurance Co Ltd
 [1980] 1 Lloyd's Rep 656 ....55, 81, 418
Furness Withy and Co v Duder [1936] 2 KB 461 545

Gambles v Ocean Marine Insurance Co of Bombay
 (1876) 1 Ex D 141, CA 181
Gandy v Adelaide Marine Insurance Co
 (1871) LR 6 QB 746..293, 294
Gaupen, The [1926] 24 LlL Rep 355...306
Gedge and Others v Royal Exchange Assurance
 Corporation [1900] 2 QB 214 ....280, 332, 333
Gee and Garnham Ltd v Whittall [1955] 2 LlL Rep 562 441
General Shipping and Forwarding Co and Another v
 British General Insurance Co Ltd (1923) LlL Rep 175 ....3, 198
George Cohen, Sons and Co v
 National Benefit Assurance Co Ltd 382
George Cohen, Sons and Co v Standard Marine
 Insurance Co (1925) 21 LlL Rep 30 ....324, 351, 606, 613, 641
Gibson v Small (1853) 4 HL Cas 352; (1853) 10 ER 499...............275, 303–05, 307,
                                                                       316, 319
Glafki Shipping Co SA v Pinos Shipping Co No 1,
 'Maira' (No 2) [1986] 2 Lloyd's Rep 12, HL 193
Glengate-KG Properties Ltd v Norwich Union Fire
 Insurance Society Ltd [1996] 2 All ER 487, CA 42
Gooding v White (1913) 29 TLR 312 196
Goole and Hull Steam Towing Co Ltd v Ocean
 Marine Insurance Co [1927] 29 LlL 242 ....3, 685, 686
Gordon v Rimmington (1807) 1 Camp 123 396
Goss v Withers (1758) 2 Burr 683..637
Goulstone v Royal Insurance Company (1858) 1 F&F 276 ....231, 232, 240
Graham Joint Stock Shipping Co Ltd v Merchants'
 Marine Insurance Co, The Ioanna (1923) 17 LlL Rep 44, HL 430, 530
Graham v Belfast and Northern Counties Ry Co
 [1924] All ER Rep 66 428
Grand Union Shipping Limited v London SS
 Owners' Mutual Insurance Association Ltd,
 'Bosworth' (No 3) [1962] 1 Lloyd's Rep 483 726

Grant, Smith and Co v Seattle Construction and
  Dry Dock Co [1920] AC 162, PC 376, 383
Gray and Another v Barr [1971] 2 Lloyd's Rep 1, CA 339, 341
Great Indian Peninsula Railway Co v
  Saunders (1862) 2 B&S 266 774–77
Green Star Shipping Co Ltd v London Assurance and
  Others [1933] 1 KB 378 .... 737, 758, 763
Green v Brown (1743) 2 Str 1199 .... 464, 466, 607
Greene v Pacific Mutual Insurance Co 570
Greenhill v Federal Insurance
  Company Ltd [1927] 1 KB 65, CA 248
Greenock Steamship Co v Maritime Insurance Co Ltd
  [1903] 1 KB 367; aff'd [1903] 2 KB 657, CA 155, 161, 281, 282,
                                                                    309, 314
Griffiths and Others v Bramley-Moore and
  Others (1878) 4 QB 70, CA 102, 711
Guarantee Co of North America v Aqua-land
  Exploration Ltd (1965) 54 DLR (2nd) 229; [1996] SCR 133 .... 43, 70

Haigh v De La Cour (1812) 3 Camp 319 .... 3, 192
Hall Bros SS Co v Young [1939] 1 KB 748, CA 545–47
Hall v Hayman [1912] 2 KB 5 649
Hallett v Wigram (1850) 9 CB 580 738
Hamilton v Mendes (1761) 2 Burr 1198 .... 637, 669
Hamilton, Fraser and Co v Pandorf and Co
  (1887) 12 App Cas 518 .... 366, 368, 382, 444, 492
Harris v Scaramanga (1872) LR 7 CP 481 .... 761, 762, 764
Hart v Standard Marine Insurance Co [1889] 22 QBD 499, CA 299
Helmville Ltd v Yorkshire Insurance Co Ltd,
  The Medina Princess [1965] 1 Lloyd's Rep 361 .... 682, 683, 687, 688,
                                                                690, 691, 694
Herring v Janson and Others (1895) 1 Com Cas 177 .... 192, 195, 196
Heskell v Continental Express and
  Another [1950] 1 All ER 1033 .... 342, 343
Hibernia Foods plc v McAuslin and General Accident
  Fire and Life Assurance Corporation plc, 'Joint Frost'
  [1998] 1 Lloyd's Rep 310 176
Hingston v Wendt (1876) 1 QBD 367 .... 674, 743
HL Bolton (Engineering) Co Ltd v TJ Graham and
  Sons Ltd [1957] 1 QB 159 251

Table of Cases

Hobbs v Hannam (1811) 3 Camp 93 ....525, 526
Hoff Trading Company v Union Insurance
  Society of Canton Ltd (1929) 45 TLR 466, CA 238, 248
Hogarth v Walker [1899] 2 QB 401 86
Home Insurance v Davila (1954) 212 D 2d 731 565
Hong Kong Fir Shipping Co v Kawasaki Kisen Kaisha
  [1962] 2 QB 26; [1961] 2 Lloyd's Rep 478 308
Hood v West End Motor Car Packing Co [1917] 2 KB 38, CA 88
Hore v Whitmore (1778) 2 Cowp 784 275
Hornal v Neuberger Products Ltd [1957] 1 QB 247, CA 476, 486–88
Horneyer v Lushington (1812) 15 East 46 169
Houghton v Empire Marine Insurance Co Ltd
  (1866) LR 1 Exch 206 ....141, 142, 149
Houstman v Thornton (1816) Holt NP 242 607
Hussain v Brown [1996] 1 Lloyd's Rep 627 278
Hutchins Brothers v Royal Exchange Assurance
  Corporation [1911] 2 KB 398, CA 444, 492, 493

Ikerigi Compania Naviera SA and Others v
  Palmer and Others, 'Wondrous' [1991] 1 Lloyd's Rep 400;
  aff'd [1992] 2 Lloyd's Rep 566, CA 95, 108, 574–76
Incorporated General Insurances Ltd v
  AR Shooter T/A Shooter's Fisheries, 'Morning Star'
  [1987] 1 Lloyd's Rep 401, SA CA 560
Inglis v Stock (1885) App Cas 263, HL 52, 56, 59
Inman Steamship Co Ltd v Bischoff (1882) 5 Asp MLC 6 105
Integrated Container Service Inc v British Traders
  Insurance Co Ltd [1984] 1 Lloyd's Rep 154, CA 445, 446, 770, 773,
                                                                          777, 783
Ionides v Pacific Fire and Marine
  Insurance Co (1871) LR 6 QB 674 ....252, 255
Ionides v Pender (1874) LR 9 QB 531, CA 3, 194, 202
Ionides v Universal Marine Insurance Co
  (1863) 14 CB (NS) 274 ....359, 578
Iredale and Another v China Traders Insurance Co
  [1900] 2 QB 519, CA 618
Irish Spruce, The [1976] 1 Lloyd's Rep 63 308
Irvin v Hine [1949] 1 KB 555 ....625, 642, 643, 684,
                                                                          688–91, 771
Irving v Manning (1847) 1 HL Cas 287 ....3, 185, 187, 646

Jackson v Union Marine Insurance (1873) 2 Asp MLC 435 .... 105, 106, 620
James Yachts Ltd v Thames and Mersey Marine
  Insurance Co Ltd [1977] 1 Lloyd's Rep 206 333
Jenkins v Heycock (1853) 8 Moore PC Cas 350 319
Joel v Law Union and Crown Insurance Company
  [1908] 2 KB 863, CA 249
John Anderson v James Farquhar Morice, 'Sunbeam'
  (1876) 1 App Cas 713; (1876) 3 Asp MLC 290, HL 45, 51, 52, 54–56, 80,
                                                                   81, 459, 461
Johnson v Sheddon (1802) 2 East 581 .... 707, 708
Jones v Nicholson (1854) 10 Exch 28 .... 528, 529
Joseph Watson and Son v Firemen's Fund Insurance
  Co of San Francisco [1922] 2 KB 355 .... 746, 752

Kacianoff v China Traders Insurance Co Ltd
  [1914] 3 KB 1121, CA 347, 349
Kaltenbach v MacKenzie (1878) 3 CPD 467, CA 659–61, 664–66
Kawasaki Kisen Kabushiki Kaisha of Kobe v
  Bantham Steamship Co Ltd [1939] 2 KB 544, CA 562
Kemp v Halliday (1866) 6 B&S 623; (1865) 34 LJQB 233 .... 648, 652, 654–56,
                                                                   737, 741
Kidston and Others v Empire Marine Insurance Co Ltd
  (1866) LR 1 CP 535 .... 713, 714, 720, 765, 770, 776
King v Victoria Insurance Co Ltd [1896] AC 250 26
Kingston v Phelps (1795) (cited) 7 Term Rep 165 .... 158, 159
Kleinwort v Shepard (1859) E&E 447 571
Knight of St Michael, The [1898] P 30 .... 395, 402
Knight v Faith (1850) 15 QB 509 .... 698, 702, 703
Kopitoff v Wilson (1876) 3 Asp MLC 163; (1876) 1 QBD 377 .... 305, 326
Koster v Innes (1925) Ry&Mood 334 .... 464, 465
Koster v Reed (1826) 6 B&C 19 .... 464, 465
Kulukundis v Norwich Union Fire Insurance
  Society Ltd [1937] 1 KB 1, CA 97
Kusel v Atkin, 'Catariba' [1997] 2 Lloyd's Rep 749 .... 687, 692, 694, 695
Kuwait Airways Corporation v Kuwait Insurance Co SAK
  [1996] 1 Lloyd's Rep 664 .... 641, 771, 788
Kynance Sailing Ship Co Ltd v Young (1911) 27 TLR 306 150

Table of Cases

La Fabrique de Produits Chimiques SA v
Large [1923] 1 KB 203 .... .406
Laing v Union Marine
Insurance Co (1895) 1 Com Cas 11 .... .164
Lakeland, The (1927) 28 LlL Rep 293 .... .433, 472, 473, 484
Lamb Head Shipping Co Ltd v Jennings, 'Marel'
[1992] 1 Lloyd's Rep 402; aff'd [1994] 1 Lloyd's Rep 624, CA .... .384, 453, 462
Lambert v Liddard (1814) 5 Taunt 480 .... .139, 140
Lane v Nixon (1866) LR 1 CP 412 .... .312
Langdale v Mason (1780) 2 Park on Insurance 965 .... .586
Lawther v Black (1900) 6 Com Cas 5 .... .117
Le Cheminant v Pearson (1912) 4 Taunt 367 .... .699
Le Roy v United Insurance Co (1811) 7 Johns 343 .... .208
Lee and Another v
Southern Insurance Co (1870) LR 5 CP 397 .... .781
Legal and General Assurance Society Ltd v
Drake Insurance Co Ltd [1992] 1 All ER 283, CA 11–13
Lek v Mathews (1927) 29 LlL Rep 141, HL .... .233, 240, 487
Lemar Towing Co v Fireman's Fund Insurance Co
[1973] AMC 1843 .... .490, 502, 505, 506
Lennard's Carrying Co Ltd v Asiatic Petroleum Co Ltd
[1915] AC 705 .... .251
Leon v Casey [1932] 2 KB 576, CA .... .224
Levin v Allnutt (1812) 15 East 267 .... .588
Levy v Assicurazioni Generali [1940] 3 All ER 427, PC .... .585
Lewis v Rucker (1761) 2 Burr 1167 .... .3, 185, 707
Leyland Shipping Co Ltd v Norwich Union Fire
Insurance Society Ltd [1918] AC 350, HL .... .336, 337, 339,
340, 346, 470, 479
~~Leyland Shipping Co Ltd v Norwich Union Fire Insurance Society Ltd [1918] AC 350, HL~~ ....
Liberian Insurance Agency Inc v Mosse
[1977] 2 Lloyd's Rep 560 .... .161, 162, 179, 217, 220,
227, 237, 282
Lidgett v Secretan (1870) LR 5 CP 190; (1871) LR 6 CP 616 .... .168, 186, 188, 701
Lind v Mitchell (1928) 45 TLR 54, CA .... .502, 632, 786
Lishman v Northern Marine Insurance Co (1875) LR 10 CP 179 .... .223, 253

Liverpool and London War Risks Association Ltd v
   Ocean SS Co Ltd, 'Priam' [1947] AC 243, HL 359
Livie v Janson (1810) 12 East 648 ....697, 698, 702
Livingstone, The (1904) 130 Fed 746 26
Lloyd Instruments Ltd v Northern Star Insurance
   Co Ltd, 'Miss Jay Jay' [1985] 1 Lloyd's Rep 264;
   [1987] 1 Lloyd's Rep 32, CA 307, 344, 346, 353, 354, 380–83,
                                                                       435, 443, 490, 500
Lockyer v Offley (1786) 1 TR 252 ....170, 517, 519, 703
Loders and Nucoline Ltd v Bank of New Zealand
   (1929) 33 LlL Rep 70 ....3, 189, 199, 203
London and Provincial Process Ltd v
   Hudson [1939] 3 All ER 857 ....370, 445
London County Commercial Reinsurance
   Office Ltd, Re [1922] 2 Ch 67 ....6, 7
Lonrho Exports Ltd v Export Credits Guarantee
   Department [1996] 4 All ER 673 30
Louis Dreyfus and Co v
   Tempus Shipping Co [1931] AC 726, HL 308
Lucena v Craufurd (1806) 2 B&P (NR) 269, HL 40, 45, 52, 70–72,
                                                                       75, 81
Lysaght v Coleman [1895] 1 QB 49 91

M'Cowan v Baine and Johnson and Others,
   'Niobe' [1891] AC 401, HL 538, 539
M'Dougle v Royal Exchange Assurance Co (1816) 4 Camp 283 386
MacBeth and Co Ltd v
   Maritime Insurance Co Ltd [1908] AC 144, HL 648–50
McFadden v Blue Star Line [1905] 1 KB 697 ....307, 310
McIver and Co v Tate Steamers Ltd [1903] 1 KB 362 308
McSwiney v Royal Exchange Assurance Co (1849) 14 QB 633 ....69, 113
Macaura v Northern Assurance Co Ltd (1925) 21 LlL Rep 333;
   [1925] AC 619 ....45, 47, 49, 67,
                                                                       70–72, 120
Mackenzie v Whitworth (1875) 1 Ec D 36, CA 84
Magnus and Others v Buttemer (1852) 11 CB 876 387
Main, The [1894] P 320 204
Makedonia, The [1962] 1 Lloyd's Rep 316 308

Table of Cases

Manchester Liners Ltd v British and Foreign
    Marine Insurance Co Ltd [1901] 7 Com Cas 26 ....104, 110
Manifest Shipping and Co Ltd v Uni-Polaris Insurance
    Co Ltd and La Réunion Européenne, 'Star Sea'
    [1995] 1 Lloyd's Rep 651; [1997] 1 Lloyd's Rep 360, CA 221, 226, 227, 235, 236,
                                                                  238–41, 250, 251,
                                                                  322–24
Marc Rich and Co AG v Portman [1996] 1 Lloyd's Rep 430;
    [1997] 1 Lloyd's Rep 225, CA 265, 266
Margetts and Ocean Accident and Guarantee
    Corporation, Re [1901] 2 KB 57 ....544, 545
Maria, The (1937) 91 Fed Rep (2d) 819 308
Marine Insurance Co v China Transpacific SS Co,
    'Vancouver' (1886) 11 App Cas 573, HL 678
Marine Sulphur Queen, The [1973] 1 Lloyd's Rep 88 308
Maritime Insurance Co v Alianza Insurance Co of
    Santander (1907) 13 Com Cas 46 140
Marstrand Fishing Co Ltd v Beer, 'Girl Pat'
    [1937] 1 All ER 158 ....613, 614, 639–42
Martin Maritime Ltd v Provident Capital Indemnity
    Fund Ltd, 'Lydia Flag' [1998] 2 Lloyd's Rep 652 ....316, 508
Mary Thomas, The (1894) P 108, CA 757, 759, 762, 764
Mathie v Argonaut Marine Insurance Co Ltd
    (1925) 21 LlL Rep 145, HL 201
Mayor and Corporation of Boston v
    France Fenwick and Co Ltd (1923) LlL Rep 85 ....24, 25
Mentz Decker and Co v Maritime Insurance Co
    [1909] 1 KB 132 ....155, 162, 282
Merchants Marine Insurance Co v North of
    England Protection and Indemnity Association
    (1926) 32 Com Cas 165, CA 543
Merchants Trading Co v Universal Marine
    Insurance Co (1870) CP 431, CA 379
Meretrony and Dunlope (1783) (cited) 1 Term Rep 260 520
Meridian Global Funds Management Asia Ltd v
    The Securities Commission [1995] 3 All ER 918;
    [1995] 2 AC 500, PC 251, 252
Mersey Mutual Underwriting Association Ltd v
    Poland (1910) 15 Com Cas 205 ....302, 303

Meyer v Ralli (1876) CPD 358 772
Michalos (N) and Sons v Prudential Assurance Co Ltd,
   'Zinovia' [1984] 2 Lloyd's Rep 264 ....433, 451, 471, 481
Middlewood v Blakes (1797) 7 Term Rep 162 158
Miller v Law Accident Insurance Co [1903] 1 KB 712, CA 573
Mills v Roebuck, 'Mills Frigate'
   (1853) 4 HL Cas 352; (1853) 10 ER 499 275
Minett and Others v Anderson (1794) Peake 277 167
Montgomery and Co v Indemnity Mutual Marine
   Insurance Co [1902] 1 KB 734 ....749, 750
Montoya and Other v London Assurance Co
   (18521) 6 Exch 451 390
Moore v Evans [1918] AC 185 ....329, 636
Moran, Galloway and Co v Uzjielli and Others,
   'Prince Louis' [1905] 2 KB 555 ....72–74, 117
Morgan and Provincial Insurance Co, Re
   [1932] 2 KB 70, CA 297
Moss and Others v Smith and Another (1850) 9 CB 94 645
Motteaux v London Assurance
   Company (1739) 1 Atk 545 142
Mount v Larkins (1831) 8 Bing 108 ....146, 147

Nanfri, The [1978] 2 Lloyd's Rep 132, CA 103
Napier and Ettrick v Hunter, Lord Napier and Ettrick v
   RF Kershaw Ltd [1993] 1 All ER 385; [1993] AC 713, HL 27–31
National Benefit Assurance Co Ltd, Application of
   HL Sthyr, Re (1933) 45 LlL Rep 147 50
National Justice Compania Naviera SA v
   Prudential Assurance Co Ltd, 'Ikarian Reefer'
   [1993] 2 Lloyd's Rep 68; [1995] 1 Lloyd's Rep 455, CA 403, 433, 467, 475,
                                                                     476, 486, 487
National Oil Co of Zimbabwe (Private) Ltd v
   Sturge [1991] 2 Lloyd's Rep 281 565
National Oilwell (UK) Ltd v Davy Offshore Ltd
   [1993] 2 Lloyd's Rep 582 ....31, 42, 44, 46, 422,
                                                            426, 428, 430, 786
Nautilus SS Co, Re (1935) 52 LlL Rep 183, CA 547
Nautilus Virgin Charters Inc, Hilliard L Lubin and Aileen
   G Lubin v Edinburgh Insurance Co Ltd (1981) AMC 2082 ....522, 572

Naviera de Canarias SA v Nacional Hispanica
  Aseguradora SA, 'Playa de les Nieves' [1978] AC 853;
  [1977] 1 Lloyd's Rep 457, HL 106, 107, 283, 361
Nesbitt v Lushington (1792) 4 TR 783 411
Netherlands Insurance Co (Est 1845) Ltd v Karl Ljungberg
  and Co A/B [1986] 2 Lloyd's Rep 19, PC 771, 779, 790, 792, 793
New Hampshire Insurance Co v
  MGN Ltd [1997] LRLR 24, CA 225, 230, 231, 254
New South Wales Medical Defence Union Ltd v
  Transport Industries Co Ltd [1985] 4 NSWL 107 ....230, 231
Newcastle Fire Insurance Co v
  MacMorran and Co (1815) 3 Dow 255 272
Nicholson v Chapman (1793) 2 H Bl 254 ....721, 769
Niger Co Ltd v Guardian Assurance Co and Yorkshire
  Insurance Co (1922) 13 LlL Rep 75, HL 223, 224, 253, 254
Nishina Trading Co Ltd v Chiyoda Fire and Marine
  Insurance Co Ltd, 'Mandarin Star' [1969] 2 All ER 776 405
Noble Resources Ltd v George Albert Greenwood,
  'Vasso' [1993] 2 Lloyd's Rep 309 ....779, 785
North Atlantic Steamship Co Ltd v
  Burr (1904) 9 Com Cas 164 651
North Britain, The [1894] P 77 551–53
North British and Mercantile Insurance Co v London,
  Liverpool and Globe Insurance Co (1877) 5 Ch D 569, CA 9, 10
North of England Iron Steamship Insurance Association v
  Armstrong (1870) LR 5 QB 244 ....22, 26, 190
Northumbrian Shipping Co v E Timm and
  Son Ltd [1939] AC 397, HL 308, 310
Northwestern Mutual Life Insurance Co v
  Linard, 'Vainqueur' [1973] 2 Lloyd's Rep 275 ....427, 433, 472
Noten BV v Paul Charles Harding
  [1990] 2 Lloyd's Rep 283, CA 440
Nourse v Liverpool Sailing Ship Owners Mutual Protection
  and Indemnity Association (1879) 4 App Cas 755, CA 725, 726
NSW Leather Co Pty Ltd v Vanguard Insurance Co Ltd
  [1991] 105 FLR 381 ....56, 78, 81
Nutt v Bourdieu (1786) 1 Term Rep 323 ....512, 514, 525, 527

Oceanic Steam Navigation Co v Evans
(1934) 50 LlL Rep 1, CA 23, 24
Oceanic Steamship Co v Faber [1907] 13 Com Cas 28, CA 444, 492
Oppenheimer v Fry (1863) 3 B&S 873 749
Orakpo v Barclays Insurance Services and Another
[1995] 1 LRLR 443, CA 221, 233, 235,
238, 240, 246
Ougier v Jennings (1800) 1 Camp 505 148
Overseas Commodities Ltd v Style
[1958] 1 Lloyd's Rep 546 ....220, 227, 237, 271, 288

PCW Syndicates v PCW Reinsurers
[1996] 1 Lloyd's Rep 241, CA 250
Pacific Queen Fisheries v Symes, 'Pacific Queen'
[1963] 2 Lloyd's Rep 201 ....330, 331
Palamisto General Enterprises SA v Ocean Marine
Insurance Co Ltd, 'Dias' [1972] 2 Lloyd's Rep 60, CA 433, 467, 468, 471
Palmer and Another v Naylor and Others (1854) 10 Ex 382 412
Palmer v Blackburn (1822) 1 Bing 61 ....95, 207, 716
Palmer v Marshall (1832) 8 Bing 317 147
Pan American World Airways Inc v The Aetna
Casualty and Surety Co [1974] 1 Lloyd's Rep 207;
SDNY; [1975] 1 Lloyd's Rep 77 ....584, 585
Pan Atlantic Insurance Co Ltd v Pine Top Insurance
Co Ltd [1994] 2 Lloyd's Rep 427; [1995] 1 AC 501, HL 214, 219, 242, 256,
258, 260–64,
266–68
Panamanian Oriental Steamship Corporation v Wright,
'Anita' [1970] 2 Lloyd's Rep 365;
[1971] 2 All ER 1028, CA 109, 557, 576–78, 670
Papadimitriou v Henderson [1939] 64 LlL Rep 345 ....422, 423
Papayanni and Jeromia v Grampian Steamship Co Ltd
(1896) 1 Com Cas 448 745
Parente v Bayville Marine Inc and General
Insurance Co of America [1975] 1 Lloyd's Rep 333 500
Parfitt v Thompson (1844) 13 M&W 392 313
Parmeter v Cousins (1809) 2 Camp 235 ....142, 145
Parmeter v Todhunter (1808) 1 Camp 540 667
Pateras and Others v Royal Exchange Assurance,
'Sappho' (1934) 49 LlL Rep 400 ....433, 470

Table of Cases

Paterson v Harris (1861) 1 B&S 336 .... 69, 120
Pawson v Watson (1778) 2 Cowp 785 .... 267, 270, 283
Pelton SS Co v North of England Protection and
  Indemnity Association (1925) 22 LlL Rep 510 542
Pesquerias y Secaderos de Bacalao de Espana SA v
  Beer (1946) 79 LlL Rep 417 668
Petrofina (UK) Ltd and Others v Magnaload Ltd and
  Others [1983] 2 Lloyd's Rep 91 .... 32, 33
Phelps v Auldjo (1809) 2 Camp 350 152
Phyn v Royal Exchange Assurance Co (1798) 7 Term Rep 505 .... 515, 516
Pickup v Thames and Mersey Marine Insurance Co Ltd
  (1878) 3 QBD 594, CA 457, 461
Piermay Shipping Co SA v Chester,
  'Michael' [1979] 1 Lloyd's Rep 55;
  [1979] 2 Lloyd's Rep 1, CA 321, 433, 479, 482, 524
Pink v Fleming (1890) 25 QBD 396 .... 175, 336, 433
Piper v Royal Exchange Assurance (1932) 44 LlL Rep 103 .... 47, 197, 197
Pipon v Cope (1808) 1 Camp 434 .... 332, 523
Pitman v Universal Marine Insurance Co
  (1882) 9 QBD 192, CA 676, 677, 689, 692, 693
Planche v Fletcher (1779) 1 Doug KB 251 327
Polpen Shipping Co Ltd v Commercial Union
  Assurance Co Ltd [1943] 1 All ER 162 545
Polurrian Steamship Co Ltd v Young [1915] 1 KB 922, CA 637–43, 670
Pomeranian, The (1895) P 34 .... 770, 772
Popham and Willett v St Petersberg Insurance Co
  (1904) 10 Com Cas 31 .... 365, 366
Power v Whitmore (1815) 4 M&S 141 760–62
President of India, The [1963] 1 Lloyd's Rep 1 308
Price and Another v Maritime Insurance Co Ltd
  [1901] 2 KB 412, CA 712
Probatina Shipping Co Ltd v Sun Insurance Office Ltd,
  'Sageorge' [1974] 1 Lloyd's Rep 369, CA 432
Promet Engineering (Singapore) Pty Ltd v Sturge and
  Others, 'Nukila' [1997] 2 Lloyd's Rep 146, CA 496, 497
Provincial Insurance Co of Canada v
  Leduc (1874) LR 6 PC 224, PC 278, 279, 296
Prudent Tankers Ltd SA v Dominion Insurance Co Ltd,
  'Caribbean Sea' [1980] 1 Lloyd's Rep 338 .... 130, 131, 437, 443, 498
Pyman Steamship Co v Lords Commissioners
  of the Admiralty [1919] 1 KB 49, CA 728

Quebec Marine Insurance Co v Commercial Maritime
    Bank of Canada (1870) LR 3 PC 234, PC 274, 302, 311

R v Hampshire CC [1985] ICR 317 488
R v Secretary of State for the Home Department
    ex p Khawaja [1984] AC 74 488
Raisby, The (1885) 10 PD 114 .... 723, 724, 732, 733
Rankin v Potter (1873) LR 6 HL 83 .... 100, 618, 619, 658, 659,
                                                                663, 664, 711, 713
Read v Bonham (1821) 3 Brod&B 147 632
Reardon Smith Line Ltd v Black Sea and Baltic
    General Insurance Co [1939] AC 562, HL 157, 158
Redmond v Smith and Another (1844) 7 Man&G 457 .... 329, 330, 332
Regazzoni v KC Sethia (1944) Ltd [1958] AC 301, HL 327
Regina Fur Co Ltd v Bossom [1958] 2 Lloyd's Rep 425 468
Reid v Darby [1808] 10 East 143 650
Reinhart Co v Joshua Hoyle and Sons Ltd
    [1961] 1 Lloyd's Rep 346 .... 78, 79
Reischer v Borwick (1894) 2 QB 548, CA 336, 337, 339
Reisman v New Hampshire Fire Insurance Co 498
Republic of Bolivia v Indemnity Mutual Marine
    Insurance Co Ltd [1909] 1 KB 785, CA 413
Republic of China, China Merchants Steam Navigation
    Company Ltd and United States of America v
    National Union Fire Insurance Company of Pittsburgh,
    Pennsylvania, 'Hai Hsuan'
    [1958] 1 Lloyd's Rep 351, US CA 521, 571, 572
Rhesa Shipping Co SA v Herbert David Edmunds,
    'Popi M' [1985] 1 WLR 948; [1985] 2 Lloyd's Rep 1, HL 453, 454, 466, 469,
                                                                       471, 475
Rickards v Forestal Land, Timber and Railways Co Ltd;
    Robertson v Middows Ltd; Kann v WH Howard
    Bros and Co [1941] 3 All ER 62, HL 2, 152, 160, 595, 596,
                                                                624, 639, 667, 670
Rio Tinto Co Ltd v Seed Shipping Co Ltd (1926) 24 LlL Rep 316 306
Roberts v Anglo-Saxon Insurance Ltd (1927) 10 LlL Rep 313 297
Robertson v Ewer (1786) 1 Term Rep 127 .... 681, 682
Robertson v Petros M Nomikos Ltd [1939] AC 371, HL 623–25, 662
Robinson Gold Mining Co and Others v
    Alliance Insurance Co [1901] 2 KB 919 569

Roddick v Indemnity Mutual Marine Insurance Co Ltd
    [1895] 2 QB 380; aff'd [1895] 2 QB 380, CA 85, 117, 206
Rodocanachi v Elliott (1874) LR 9 CP 518 .... 92, 570, 625–27
Rosa and Others v Insurance Co of the State of Pennsylvania,
    'Belle of Portugal' [1970] 2 Lloyd's Rep 386 .... 398, 504, 505
Roselodge Ltd (formerly 'Rose' Diamond Products Ltd) v
    Castle [1966] 2 Lloyd's Rep 113 468
Rosetto v Gurney (1851) 11 CB 176 658
Ross v Hunter (1790) 4 Term Rep 33 .... 160, 515, 517
Roura and Forgas v Townend [1919] 1 KB 189 .... 661, 662, 788
Roux v Salvador (1836) 3 Bing NC 266 .... 600, 601, 610, 644
Ruabon Steamship Co Ltd v London Assurance
    [1900] AC 6, HL 679, 680
Russell v Provincial Insurance Co Ltd
    [1959] 2 Lloyd's Rep 275 .... 126, 292
Russian Bank for Foreign Trade v Excess Insurance Co Ltd
    [1918] 2 KB 123 .... 108, 361, 362
Ruys v Royal Exchange Assurance Corporation
    [1897] 2 QB 135 668

Safadi v Western Assurance Co (1933) 46 LlL Rep 140 174
Sailing Ship Blairmore Co Ltd v Macredie,
    'Blairmore' [1898] AC 593, HL 603, 604, 669–71
Sailing Ship Holt Hill Co v United Kingdom Marine
    Association [1919] 2 KB 789 647
Saloucci v Johnson 4 Dougl 224; cited 8 East 129 517
Samuel v Dumas (1928) 18 LlL Rep 211; [1923] 1 KB 592, CA 33, 34, 66, 345, 356,
                                                                 369, 370, 380, 381,
                                                                 384, 385, 401,
                                                                 431, 454, 484,
                                                                 525, 530–32
Sarpen, The [1916] P 306, CA 589–91
Sassoon (ED) and Co v Western Assurance Co
    [1912] AC 561, PC 377, 380
Scaramanga v Stamp (1880) 5 CPD 295 160
Schiffshypothekenbank Zu Luebeck AG v
    Norman Philip Compton, 'Alexion Hope'
    [1988] 1 Lloyd's Rep 311, CA 395, 396, 399, 400,
                                                                 431, 433, 475

Schloss Brothers v Stevens [1906] 2 KB 665 . . . . .407, 416, 418, 434
Scindia Steamships Ltd v The London Assurance
    [1937] 1 KB 636 . . . . .444, 492, 494
Scottish Metropolitan Assurance Co v Steward
    (1923) 15 LlL Rep 55 . . . . .121, 122
Scottish Shire Line Ltd v London and Provincial Marine
    and General Insurance Co Ltd [1912] 3 KB 51 . . . . .97, 99
Sea Insurance Co v Blogg [1898] 2 QB 398, CA 135
Shawe v Felton (1801) 2 East 109 169
Shell International Petroleum Co Ltd v
    Caryl Antony Vaughan Gibbs, 'Salem'
    [1982] 1 Lloyd's Rep 369; [1982] QB 946, CA 415, 482, 512–14, 524,
                                                                                                         525, 527, 528,
                                                                                                         532, 585
Simmonds v Cockell [1920] 1 KB 843 300
Simon v Gale, 'Cap Tarifa' [1957] 2 Lloyd's Rep 485; aff'd
    [1958] 2 Lloyd's Rep 1, PC 284, 286
Simon, Israel and Co v Sedgwick [1893] 1 QB 303, CA 137, 178
Simonds v White (1824) 2 B&C 805 . . . . .735, 760
Simpson Steamship Co Ltd v Premier Underwriting
    Association Ltd (1905) Com Cas 198;
    (1905) 10 Asp MLC 127 299
Simpson v Thomson (1877) 3 App Cas 279, HL 17, 21, 23, 554
Sipowicz v Wimble and Others, 'Green Lion'
    [1974] 1 Lloyd's Rep 593 . . . . .443, 497, 498
Skandia Insurance Co v Skoljarev [1979] 142 CLR 375,
    High Court of Australia 382, 427, 428,
                                                                                                         456, 461
Slattery v Mance [1962] 1 All ER 525 . . . . .399, 402, 433,
                                                                                                         474, 476
Small v United Kingdom Marine Mutual Insurance
    Association [1897] 2 QB 311, CA 369, 512, 525,
                                                                                                         530, 532
Smith and Others v Scott (1811) 4 Taunt 126 371
Smith Hogg and Co v Black Sea and
    Baltic Insurance Co [1940] AC 997 308
Smith v Chadwick (1884) 9 App Cas 187 266
Smith v Surridge (1801) 4 Esp 25 . . . . .146, 160
Soares v Thornton (1817) 7 Taunt 627 512525

xl

Table of Cases

Société Anonyme d Intermédiaires Luxembourgeois v
  Farex Cie [1995] LRLR 116, CA 225
Société Nouvelle d'Armement v Spillers and
  Bakers Ltd [1917] 1 KB 865 .... 742, 747
Soya GmbH Mainz Kommanditgesellschaft v White
  [1982] 1 Lloyd's Rep 136, CA; [1983] 1 Lloyd's Rep 122, HL 436, 442
Sparthari, The (1924) 21 LlL Rep 265 433
Spence and Another v Union Marine Insurance Co Ltd
  [1868] LRT 3 CP 427 .... 611, 612, 709
Spinney's (1948) Ltd v Royal Insurance Co
  [1980] 1 Lloyd's Rep 406 .... 563, 565, 567, 586
St Johns, The (1900) 101 Fed 469 26
St Macher, The (1939) 65 LlL Rep 119 544
St Paul Fire and Marine v McConnell
  [1993] 2 Lloyd's Rep 503; [1995] 2 Lloyd's Rep 116, CA 261, 264, 266
Standard Oil Co of New York v
  Clan Line Steamers Ltd [1924] AC 100 308
Stanley v Western Insurance Co (1868) LR 3 Ex 71 .... 392, 394
State of The Netherlands v Youell and
  Hayward and Others [1998] 1 Lloyd's Rep 236, CA 766, 767, 783,
                                                                      784, 787
State Trading Corporation of India Ltd v
  M Golodetz Ltd [1989] 2 Lloyd's Rep 277 .... 278, 280
Steamship 'Balmoral' Co Ltd v Marten [1902] AC 511, HL 191, 755
Steaua Romana, The; The Oltenia [1944] P 43 .... 589, 591
Steel v State Line SS Co (1877) 3 B&S 669;
  (1877) 3 App Cas 72, HL 305, 306
Steinman and Co v Angier Line Ltd [1891] 1 QB 619, CA 408
Stephen AP v Scottish Boatowners Mutual Insurance
  Association, 'Talisman' [1989] 1 Lloyd's Rep 535, HL 778
Stephens v Australasian Insurance Co (1872) LR 8 CP 18 212
Stirling v Vaughan (1809) 11 East 619 74
Stock v Inglis (1884) 12 QBD 564 58
Stone Vickers Ltd v Appledore Ferguson Shipbuilders Ltd
  [1992] 2 Lloyd's Rep 578 .... 32, 33, 42, 45, 46
Stott (Baltic) Steamers Ltd v Marten and Others
  [1916] AC 304, HL 377, 378, 415, 416
Stranna, The [1938] 1 All ER 458, CA 374

Stringer and Others v English and Scottish
   Marine Insurance Co Ltd (1869) LR 4 QB 676 .... 615, 644, 778
Subro Valour, The [1995] 1 Lloyd's Rep 509 308
Sutherland v Pratt (1843) 11 M&W 296 .... 78, 79
Svendsen v Wallace Bros (1885) 10 App Cas 404 738
Swain v Wall (1641) Rep Ch 149; (1941) 21 ER 534 12
Symington and Co v Union Insurance Society of
   Canton Ltd (1928) 34 Com Cas 23, CA 171, 389, 395

Tasker v Cunninghame (1819) 1 Bligh 87, HL 139, 151, 153
Tate and Sons v Hyslop (1885) 15 QBD 368, CA 255
Tatham, Bromage and Co v
   Burr Engineer [1898] AC 382, HL 551–53
Taylor v Curtis (1816) 6 Taunt 608 742
Taylor v Dunbar (1869) LR 4 CP 206 .... 389, 434
Taylor v Liverpool and Great Western Steam Co
   (1874) LR 9 QB 546 408
Tesco Stores Ltd v Brent LBC [1993] 2 All ER 718 251
Tesco Supermarkets Ltd v Nattras [1972] AC 153 251
Thames and Mersey Marine Insurance Co Ltd v
   Hamilton, Fraser and Co, 'Inchmaree'
   (1877) 12 AC 484, HL 365, 376, 378,
                                                                     489, 491
Thames and Mersey Marine Insurance Co Ltd v
   Van Laun and Co [1917] 2 KB 48, HL 155, 156, 163,
                                                                     164, 282
Thames and Mersey Marine Insurance Co v 'Gunford'
   Ship Co [1911] AC 529, HL 3, 14, 15, 118,
                                                                 119, 192, 193,
                                                              200–02, 207, 295
Thames and Mersey Marine Insurance Co v
   British and Chilean Steamship Co [1915] 2 KB 2;
   aff'd [1916] 1 KB 30, CA 26
Theodegmon, The [1990] 1 Lloyd's Rep 52 308
Theodorou v Chester [1951] 1 Lloyd's Rep 204 419
Thin v Richards [1892] 2 QB 141, CA 308, 309
Thomas (M) & Son Shipping Co Ltd v The London and
   Provincial Marine and General Insurance Co
   (1914) 30 TLR 595, CA 324, 325, 349, 352

Table of Cases

Thomas Cheshire and Co v Vaughan Brothers and Co
 [1920] 3 KB 240, CA 5, 7
Thomas v Tyne and Wear Steamship Freight Insurance
 Association [1917] 1 KB 938 .... 325, 350
Thompson v Hopper (1856) 6 E&B 937;
 (1858) EB&E 1038 .... 353–56, 422, 424,
 425, 427, 507
Thomson v Weems (1884) 9 App Cas 671 .... 272, 276
Thurtell v Beaumont (1824) 8 Moore CP 612 487
Torenia, The [1983] 1 Lloyd's Rep 210 308
Traders and General Insurance Association Ltd, Re
 (1921) 38 TLR 94 .... 437, 438
Tramp Shipping Corporation v Greenwich Marine Inc,
 'New Horizon' [1975] ICR 261, CA 582
Transthene Packaging Co Ltd v Royal Insurance (UK) Ltd
 [1996] LRLR 32 .... 233, 234, 238, 239,
 284–87, 301
Trinder, Anderson and Co v Thames and Mersey Marine
 Insurance Co [1898] 2 QB 114, CA 353, 355, 376, 398, 506
Troilus, The [1951] 1 Lloyd's Rep 467, HL 292
Tyrie v Fletcher (1777) 2 Cowp 666 .... 15, 16

Union Insurance Society of Canton Ltd v
 George Wills and Co [1915] AC 281, PC 211
Union Marince Insurance Co v Borwick [1895] 2 QB 279 539
United States Shipping v
 Express Assurance Corporation [1907] 1 KB 259 716
Usher v Noble (1810) 12 East 639 .... 210, 710
Uzielli and Co v Boston Marine Insurance Company
 (1884) 15 QBD 11, CA 62, 768

Vacuum Oil Co v Union Insurance Society of Canton
 (1925) 24 LlL Rep 188 .... 91, 634, 635, 664
Vallance v Dewar (1808) 1 Camp 508 148
Vallejo v Wheeler (1774) 1 Cowp 143 .... 510, 511, 516,
 525–27, 532
Vlassopoulos v British and Foreign Marine
 Insurance Co [1929] 1 KB 187 747
Vortigern, The [1899] P 40, CA 309

Wadsworth Lighterage and Coaling Co v
    Sea Insurance Co (1929) 15 Com Cas 1, CA 383, 436
Walker v Maitland (1821) 5 B&Ald 171 372
Waples v Eames (1745) 2 Str 1243 ....166, 169
Ward v Weir (1899) 4 Com Cas 216 ....115, 116
Waterman SS Corporation v United States SR and M Co 498
Way v Modigliani (1787) 2 Term Rep 30 ....136, 144
Wayne Tank and Pump Co Ltd v Employers Liability
    Insurance Corporation Ltd [1973] QB 57, CA 344, 345, 572
Wedderburn and Others v Bell (1807) 1 Camp 1 308
Weir and Co v Girvin and Co [1899] 1 QB 193, CA 98
Weir v Aberdeen (1819) 2 B&Ald 320 274
Weissburg v Lanb (1950) 84 LlL Rep 509 772
Wells v Owners of Gas Float Whitton No 2 [1897] AC 337 544
Western Assurance Company of Toronto v
    Poole, 'Edmund' [1903] 1 KB 376 ....64, 658, 676, 793
Westport Coal Co v McPhail [1898] 2 QB 130, CA 375
Whiting v New Zealand Insurance Co
    (1932) 44 LlL Rep 179 709
Williams v North China Insurance Co (1876) 1 CPD 757 205
Williams Brothers (Hull) Ltd v Namlooze Vennootschap
    WH Berghuys Kolenhandel (1915) 21 Com Cas 253 581
Williams v Atlantic Assurance Co Ltd [1932] 1 KB 81, CA 207, 209, 210
Wills and Sons v World Marine Insurance Company Ltd,
    'Mermaid' (1911) The Times, 14 March (reported as a
    note in [1980] 1 Lloyd's Rep 350) 495
Wilson and Another v Bank of Victoria (1867) LR 2 QB 203 741
Wilson and Sons Co v Owners of Cargo per 'Xantho'
    (1887) 12 App Cas 503, HL 365, 366, 371, 372, 376,
    377, 382, 535, 538
Wilson Brothers Bobbin Co Ltd v Green [1917] 1 KB 860 781
Wilson v Boag [1957] 2 Lloyd's Rep 564,
    Supreme Court of New South Wales 124, 182, 183, 298
Wilson v Jones (1867) LR 2 Exch 139 ....68, 120
Winter v Employers Fire Insurance Co
    [1962] 2 Lloyd's Rep 320 300

Table of Cases

Wolf v Archangel Maritime Bank and Insurance Co Ltd
 (1874) LR 9 QB 451 147
Wood v Associated National Insurance Co Ltd
 [1984] 1 Qd R 507; [1985] 1 Qd R 297 .... 422, 426, 427, 429
Woodrop-Sims (1815) 2 Dods 83 540
Woodside v Globe Marine Insurance Co Ltd [1896] 1 QB 105 .... 188, 700
Wooldridge v Boydell (1778) 1 Doug KB 16 .... 137, 156, 158
Woolf v Claggett (1800) 3 Esp 257 160
Wunsche Handelsgesellschaft International mbH v
 Tai Ping Insurance Co Ltd and Another
 [1998] 2 Lloyd's Rep 8, CA 172

Xenos v Fox [1869] LR 4 CP 665 .... 550, 551

Yamatogawa, The [1990] 2 Lloyd's Rep 39 308
Yasin, The [1979] 2 Lloyd's Rep 45 33
Yorkshire Dale SS Co Ltd v Minister of War Transport,
 The Coxwold (1942) 73 LlL Rep 1, HL 339, 340, 559, 567
Yorkshire Insurance Co Ltd v Campbell [1917] AC 218, PC 287
Yorkshire Insurance Co v Nisbet Shipping Co Ltd
 [1961] 1 Lloyd's Rep 479 .... 19, 20, 26–28
Yorkshire Water Services Ltd v Sun Alliance and London
 Insurance plc and Others [1997] 2 Lloyd's Rep 21, CA 790, 791

Zamora, The [1916] 2 AC 77, PC 592

TABLE OF STATUTES

Admiralty Court Act 1840—
  s 6 73
Commonwealth Marine
  Insurance Act, No 11 1909—
  s 35(3) 212
Emergency Powers Act 1920 591
Finance Act 1901 123
Finance Act 1959 122
Gaming Act 1845—
  s 18 43
Marine Insurance Act 1745 295
Marine Insurance Act 1906 .... 4, 7, 8, 15,
    19, 25, 79, 88,
    90, 92, 152, 242,
    243, 260, 262, 269,
    332, 351, 353, 359,
    385, 392, 401, 405,
    410, 428, 509, 535,
    583, 599, 626–28,
    648–50, 723, 733,
    735, 746, 795
  ss 1–21 795
  ss 1–3 799
  s 1 .... 1, 123
  s 2(1) 170
  s 3 .... 83, 326, 557, 569
  s 3(1) 123, 535
  s 3(1)(b) 112
  s 3(2)(a) 93
  s 3(2)(b) 59, 94, 109, 115, 119
  s 3(2)(c) 120, 123, 535
  ss 4–8 800
  s 4 .... 8, 18, 39, 43, 295
  s 4(1) 3, 4, 14
  s 4(2) 4
  s 4(2)(a) 4, 76
  s 4(2)(b) 5, 6
  s 5 .... 39, 40, 44, 47
  s 5(1) 44
  s 5(2) 4, 39, 40, 44, 46,
    56, 62, 72
  s 6 .... 47, 61, 77, 79
  s 6(1) 5, 40, 76

Marine Insurance Act 1906 (Cont'd)—
  s 6(2) 76, 78
  s 7 .... 39, 51
  s 8 39
  ss 9–16 801
  s 9 62
  s 10 75
  s 12 .... 59, 79
  s 12(2) 80
  s 14(1) 65
  s 14(3) 46
  s 15 .... 82, 215
  s 16 206
  s 16(1)–(3) 207, 212
  s 16(1) 691
  s 16(2) 715
  s 16(3) 209, 710
  s 16(4) 212, 710
  ss 17–20 213
  ss 17–18 802
  s 17 ...... 78, 194, 213–20, 222–25, 227,
    229, 236, 237, 240, 241, 243,
    245, 246, 252–54, 788
  s 18 .... 78, 194, 214, 219, 222, 224,
    225, 228, 229, 237, 241,
    242, 246, 247, 250–54,
    257, 258, 264, 270
  s 18(1) 84, 263
  s 18(2) 256–59, 267
  s 18(3)(b) 197, 198
  ss 19–21 803
  s 19 .... 219, 237
  s 20 .... 194, 214, 241, 246,
    258, 262
  s 20(1) 263, 267, 271
  s 20(2) 259, 267
  s 20(4) 267
  s 21 252
  ss 22–49 796
  ss 22–26 804
  ss 23, 25 123
  s 25(1) 121, 122, 123,
    128, 134, 181

xlvii

Marine Insurance Act 1906 (Cont'd)—
s 25(2) 122
s 26 .... 47, 617
s 26(1) 83, 97
ss 27–31 805
s 27(2) 185
s 27(3) 2, 186, 189–91, 199,
203, 676, 690,
692, 693
s 27(4) 3, 26, 185, 646,
647, 689, 692
s 28 206
s 29(1) 211
s 29(3) 211, 212
s 29(4) 189, 199, 203, 211
ss 32–34 806
s 32(1) 9
s 32(2)(a)–(d) 8
ss 33–41 285
s 33(1) 269, 289
s 33(3) 165, 270, 272, 277,
280, 332, 333
s 34(1) 274, 275
s 34(2) 273
s 34(3) 278, 280, 333
ss 35–39 807
s 35(1) 269, 282, 283, 289
s 35(2) 282
s 35(3) 333
s 36 289
s 36(1), (2) 290
s 38 .... 289, 291
s 39 .... 301, 489
s 39(1) 183, 281, 303, 311,
312, 315, 489
s 39(2) 301,. 302, 422
s 39(3) 309
s 39(4) 305, 306, 319
ss 39(5) 123, 183, 250, 293,
303, 319, 320, 324, 335,
345, 349, 350, 353,
354, 357, 425 ,426,
429, 490, 501

Marine Insurance Act 1906 (Cont'd)—
ss 40–45 808
s 40(1) 311, 325
s 40(2) 281, 302, 311,
315, 325, 326
s 41 .... 302, 326, 328,
329, 331–33
s 42 .... 146, 147
s 42(1) 141, 146, 147,
149
s 42(2) 147, 148, 154
s 43 333
s 44 .... 137, 151
s 45 152–55
s 45(1) 151, 152
s 45(2) 153
ss 46–49 809
s 46 147
s 46(1) 155, 161
s 46(2) 156
s 46(3) 158
s 48 .... 146, 147, 164,
173, 174
s 49 164
s 49(1) 160, 164, 165
ss 50–78 797
ss 50–53 810
s 50 .... 82, 215
s 50(1) 82
s 50(2) 65
s 51 .... 40, 82
ss 54–57 811
s 55 .... 357, 360, 421,
560, 578
s 55(1) 107, 335, 347, 349,
359, 361, 421
s 55(2) 363, 421, 434
s 55(2)(a) 324, 335, 349, 354,
358, 364, 369, 372, 375, 392,
396, 398, 421, 422, 426,
429–31, 452, 475, 490,
502, 524, 538, 783,
784, 786–88

xlviii

Marine Insurance Act 1906 (Cont'd)—
s 55(2)(b) 165, 175, 421, 422,
433, 435, 772,
787
s 55(2)(c) 383, 384, 393, 421,
422, 435–37, 440, 443,
444, 489, 494,
500, 538
ss 56–60 615
s 56 368
s 56(1) 599, 625, 673, 674
s 56(2) 599
s 56(4) 621
s 56(5) 611, 709
s 57 . . . . .625, 659
s 57(1) 600, 605, 613, 617
ss 58–62 812
s 58 . . . . .449, 466
s 59 772
s 60 . . . . .92, 623–25, 629,
631, 659
s 60(1) 630, 632–34, 637,
641, 650, 657,
658
s 60(2) 641, 656
s 60(2)(i) 579, 628, 632, 636,
640, 644, 651,
654, 657
s 60(2)(i)(b) 643, 658
s 60(2)(ii) 633, 644, 655–57
s 60(2)(iii) 658
s 61 . . . . .25, 633, 658,
662, 676
s 61(2)(a) 427
s 62 . . . . .662, 664
s 62(1) 658
s 62(2) 667
s 62(3) 666
s 62(5) 667
s 62(7) 663, 664
s 62(9) 663
s 63 . . . . .20, 21, 813
s 63(1) 20, 21

Marine Insurance Act 1906 (Cont'd)—
s 63(2) 20–22
s 64 813
s 64(1) 674, 719, 720
s 64(2) 675, 719, 720, 764
ss 65–67 814
s 65(1) 673, 675, 719,
722, 727
s 65(2) 675, 722, 729
s 66 . . . . .655, 735, 737, 759
s 66(1) 738
s 66(2) 736, 743, 747
s 66(3) 740
s 66(4) 754, 757, 759
s 66(5) 759
s 66(6) 752
s 66(7) 750
s 67(1) 209
ss 68–71 815
s 69 . . . . .677, 685, 687,
692, 696
s 69(1) 678, 685, 691
s 69(2) 678, 686, 691
s 69(3) 686–91, 694–96
s 70 715
s 71 709
s 71(1), (2) 706
s 71(3) 706, 707, 710
s 71(4) 708
ss 72–74 816
s 72(1) 704
ss 75–78 817
s 76(1) 705, 720
s 76(2) 713, 720, 731, 774
s 77(1) 694, 696
s 77(2) 688, 697, 701
s 75(2) 189, 199, 203
s 76(2) 676
s 78 . . . . .675, 777, 779, 780,
787, 789
s 78(1) 713, 780, 789
s 78(3) 764, 772

Marine Insurance Act 1906 (Cont'd)—
    s 78(4) 764, 766–68, 771,
                        777, 778, 783–87,
                        789, 790, 793
    ss 79–94 798
    ss 79–82 818
    s 79 ....19, 21
    s 79(1) 19, 20
    s 79(2) 25
    ss 80, 82–84 9
    s 83 819
    s 84 ....16, 819
    s 84(1) 7, 16
    s 84(2), (3) 16
    s 84(3)(a) 5
    s 84(3)(f) 9, 16
    s 84(4) 790
    ss 85–90 820
    s 88 .... 599, 642, 666
    s 90 ....93, 94, 112
    ss 91–94 821
    s 91(2) 92, 263,
                        625–27, 652
    s 92 7
    Sched 1 ....88, 501, 821–25
    Sched 2 ....79, 825

Marine Insurance (Gambling
    Policies) Act 1909 ....4, 5, 7,
                                826, 827
Merchant Shipping Act 1854 724
Merchant Shipping Act 1894 ....726, 727
    s 502 394
    s 544 ....724, 725
    s 557 590
    s 742 ....503, 504, 544
Public Order Act 1986 583
    s 10(2) 583
Road Traffic Act 1991 13
Sale of Goods Act 1979 35
Stamp Act 1891 123
Supreme Court Act 1981—
    s 20(2)(m), (p) 73
Third Party (Rights Against
    Insurers) Act 1930 547–49,
                                828–30
    s 1(1), (3) 549

CHAPTER 1

CONTRACT OF INDEMNITY

INSURANCE IS A CONTRACT OF INDEMNITY

The basic principle of a contract of insurance is that the indemnity recoverable from the insurer is the pecuniary loss suffered by the assured under that contract. Thus, s 1 of the Marine Insurance Act 1906,[1] in defining marine insurance, confirms that the contract is, first and foremost, a contract of indemnity:

> A contract of marine insurance is a contract whereby the insurer undertakes to indemnify the assured, in a manner and to the extent thereby agreed, against marine losses, that is to say, the losses incident to a marine adventure.

In order that the fundamental principle of indemnity is upheld, other concepts and rules have become established in insurance law; these include double insurance, the right to contribution, return of premium and subrogation, all of which are discussed in the course of this chapter.

The philosophy behind insurance and indemnification was summed up in the early case of *Brotherston v Barber* **(1816) 5 M&S 418**, where an insured ship was captured by an American privateer and then re-captured by a Royal Navy ship. Although the claimant, on hearing of the initial capture, claimed for a total loss, the court ruled that he could only be indemnified for a partial loss, as the ship had been re-captured.

> **Abbott J:** [p 425] ... But, the great principle of the law of insurance is that it is a contract for indemnity. The underwriter does not stipulate, under any circumstances, to become the purchaser of the subject matter insured; it is not supposed to be in his contemplation: he is to indemnify only. This being the principle, it seems to me that any practice or doctrine which is calculated to break in upon it ought to be narrowly watched.

Similarly, Brett LJ was moved to reiterate the fundamental concept of insurance in *Castellain v Preston* **(1883) 11 QBD 380, CA,** where a house was damaged by fire whilst it was in the process of being sold. The vendors not only received an indemnity from their insurers, but also, later, despite the fire, the full amount of the purchase money from the buyers. Not unreasonably, the underwriters sought from the vendors a return of the payment they had made to them on the basis that they, the vendors, had, in fact, suffered no pecuniary loss. In this, the insurers were successful.

---

1 See Appendix 1.

Brett LJ: [p 386] ... The very foundation, in my opinion, of every rule which has been applied to insurance law is this, namely, that the contract of insurance contained in a marine or fire policy is a contract of indemnity, and of indemnity only, and that this contract means that the assured, in case of a loss against which the policy has been made, shall be fully indemnified, but shall never be more than fully indemnified. That is the fundamental principle of insurance, and if ever a proposition is brought forward which is at variance with it, that is to say, which either will prevent the assured from obtaining a full indemnity, or which will give to the assured more than a full indemnity, that proposition must certainly be wrong.

And, in *Rickards v Forestal Land, Timber and Railways Co Ltd* **[1941] 3 All ER 62, HL**, where goods aboard a German vessel were lost at the outset of the Second World War, when the ship was scuttled in order to avoid capture, Lord Wright had occasion to consider the purpose of a contract of insurance and the part the Act had to play in the construction of that contract.

Lord Wright: [p 76] ... The Act is merely dealing with a particular branch of the law of contracts – namely, those of marine insurance. Subject to various imperative provisions or prohibitions and general rules of the common law, the parties are free to make their own contracts and to exclude or vary the statutory terms. The object both of the legislature and of the courts has been to give effect to the idea of indemnity, which is the basic principle of insurance, and to apply it to the diverse complications of fact and law in respect of which it has to operate. In this way, the law merchant has solved, or sought to solve, the manifold problems which have been presented by insurances of maritime adventures.

The indemnity is not necessarily perfect

Whilst the overriding principle of insurance is that of indemnification for losses sustained, the courts accept the fact that, because there must be an element of freedom for the parties to the insurance to contract on whatever terms they deem fit, in many instances, the indemnity is unlikely to be perfect. This is largely attributable to the fact that both the common law and s 27(3) of the Act endorse the fact that the value fixed by the policy is conclusive of the insurable value of the subject matter insured. This allows the parties the freedom to set the value of the subject matter insured at whatever figure they so wish. Provided that any over-valuation is not so excessive as to offend the cardinal principle of the duty to observe utmost good faith, the law of non-disclosure of a material fact, and of misrepresentation and the rule against wager, the courts are obliged to uphold the value fixed in the policy as conclusive. It is, of course, difficult at any given time to gauge the value of any subject matter with precision, but gross or exorbitant over-valuation could be construed as evidence of fraud.[2] That the principle of indemnity is not perfect is illustrated in the case of *Irving v Manning*, below.

Irving v Manning (1847) 1 HLC 287

In a valued policy of insurance, the agreed value of a vessel, *General Kyd*, was put at £17,500. When *General Kyd* was severely damaged by storms, she was deemed a constructive total loss, because it was estimated that the cost of repairs would have amounted to £10,500, whilst her marketable value, on being repaired, was only £9,000.[3] Thus, the assured was indemnified to the value of £17,500, when the true value of the ship was only £9,000.

> **Patteson J:** [p 307] ... A policy of assurance is not a perfect contract of indemnity. It must be taken with this qualification, that the parties may agree beforehand in estimating the value of the subject assured, by way of liquidated damages, as indeed they may in any other contract to indemnify.

In ***Goole and Hull Steam Towing Co Ltd v Ocean Marine Insurance Co* [1927] 29 LlL Rep 242**, McKinnon J noted that: [p 244] '... the real question in the case is: what is the measure of indemnity that, by the convention of the bargain, has been promised to the assured? That may in some cases be less than an ideal pecuniary indemnity, in some cases it may be more.'[4]

However, although it is conceded that a contract of indemnity is not always perfect, the principle of indemnification for actual pecuniary loss remains in the forefront of the minds of judges. This was confirmed by Lord Sumner, in *British and Foreign Insurance Co Ltd v Wilson Shipping Co Ltd* [1921] 1 AC 188, HL, who observed that: [p 214] '... In practice, contracts of insurance by no means always result in a complete indemnity, but indemnity is always the basis of the contract.'

GAMING AND WAGERING CONTRACTS

The Act, in s 4(1), states that:
> Every contract of marine insurance by way of gaming or wagering is void.

---

2   See, eg, *Lewis v Rucker* (1761) 2 Burr 1167; *Haigh v De La Cour* (1812) 3 Camp 319; *Ionides v Pender* (1874) LR 9 QB 531; *Thames and Mersey Marine Insurance Co v 'Gunford' Ship Co* [1911] AC 529, HL; *General Shipping and Forwarding Co and Another v British General Insurance Co Ltd* (1923) LlL Rep 175; and *Loders and Nucoline Ltd v Bank of New Zealand* (1929) 33 LlL Rep 70. For a fuller discussion of the legal effects of excessive over-valuation, see Chapter 5, p 191.

3   Under common law and s 27(4), when deciding whether a ship is or is not a constructive total loss, the cost of repairs must be compared with the market, not the insured value of the ship. However, cll 19.1 and 17.1 of the ITCH(95) and IVCH(95) respectively have provided that the insured value shall be taken as the repaired value. See Chapter 16, p 647.

4   See, also, *Aitchison v Lohre* (1879) 4 App Cas 755.

Although the Act, in itself, does not specify that the effecting of a gaming or wagering contract of insurance is illegal, only that it is void, attention is also drawn to the Marine Insurance (Gambling Policies) Act 1909,[5] which is also relevant. The 1909 Act affirms that:

(1) If:
   (a) any person effects a contract of marine insurance without having any *bona fide* interest, direct or indirect, either in the safe arrival of the ship in relation to which the contract is made, or in the safety or preservation of the subject matter insured, or a *bona fide* expectation of acquiring such an interest; or
   (b) any person in the employment of the owner of a ship, not being a part owner of the ship, effects a contract of marine insurance in relation to the ship, and the contract is made 'interest or no interest', or 'without further proof of interest than the policy itself', or 'without benefit of salvage to the insurer', or subject to any other like term,
   the contract shall be deemed to be a contract by way of gambling on loss by maritime perils, and the person effecting it shall be guilty of an offence ...

Thus, despite the Marine Insurance Act 1906 stating, in s 4(1), that a gaming or wagering contract of insurance is merely void, under the Marine Insurance (Gambling Policies) Act 1909 it is also a criminal offence to effect insurance when the assured has no insurable interest in the adventure.

There are, essentially, two forms of gaming and wagering contracts contemplated by s 4(2) of the 1906 Act, namely:

(a) policies where the assured has no insurable interest or expectation of acquiring such an interest; and
(b) 'honour' or 'ppi' (policy proof of interest) policies.

Assured has no insurable interest or expectation of acquiring such an interest

Section 4(2)(a) of the Act states that:

A contract of marine insurance is deemed to be a gaming or wagering contract:
(a) where the assured has not an insurable interest as defined by this Act, and the contract is entered into with no expectation of acquiring such an interest ...

In defining 'insurable interest,' s 5(2) stipulates that a person having an insurable interest would be one who '... may benefit by the safety or due arrival of insurable property, or may be prejudiced by its loss, or by damage thereto, or by the detention thereof, or may incur liability in respect thereof'.

---

5   See Appendix 2.

Notably, that insurable interest is only relevant '... at the time of the loss, though he need not be interested when the insurance is effected ...'.[6]

The premium, with respect to a policy which is void, is, under s 84(3)(a) of the Act, only returnable if '... there has been no fraud or illegality on the part of the assured ...'.[7]

'Honour' or 'ppi' policies

A 'ppi' policy (policy proof of interest), often referred to as an 'honour'[8] policy, is also deemed to be a gaming or wagering contract by the Act when it confirms, in s 4(2)(b), that:

> A contract of marine insurance is deemed to be a gaming or wagering contract:
>
> (b) where the policy is made 'interest or no interest', or 'without further proof of interest than the policy itself', or 'without benefit of salvage to the insurer', or subject to any other like term,
>
> provided that, where there is no possibility of salvage, a policy may be effected without benefit of salvage to the insurer.

It is emphasised that this sub-section is aimed directly at the wording contained within a contract of insurance. It is immaterial, when such words as 'interest or no interest', 'without further proof of interest than the policy itself', 'without benefit of salvage to the insurer', or any other like term, are used, whether the assured has or has not an insurable interest in the subject matter insured. Just the use of the words themselves, or any other like term, is sufficient to render the contract void. This was particularly well illustrated in the case of *Cheshire and Co v Vaughan Brothers and Co*, below.

Thomas Cheshire and Co v Vaughan Brothers and Co [1920] 3 KB 240, CA

The plaintiffs were the owners of warehouses at Liverpool, Birkenhead and Newport, where they were in the habit of storing nitrate of soda. At the time, the First World War was in progress, and the British Government controlled all shipments of nitrate from South America. When the plaintiffs anticipated a shipment of nitrate from South America, they reserved space in their warehouses and instructed their brokers to effect a policy of insurance (ppi) with the defendants on anticipated profits; the policy to cover marine and war risks, and the risk of the cargo of nitrate being diverted to another port by the Government. At the time the policy was effected, the insurers were not made aware of the real risk of the shipment being diverted by the Government. So,

---

6   Unless the subject matter is insured 'lost or not lost': see s 6(1).
7   The gaming or wagering policy is rendered illegal by the Marine Insurance (Gambling Policies) Act 1909.
8   A 'ppi' policy is often referred to as an 'honour' policy, because it relies on the insurer to honour the contract of insurance, even though it has no standing in law.

when the shipment of nitrate was diverted by the Government and the plaintiffs claimed on their policy, the insurers refused payment on the basis that the policy had attached to it a slip which stated that the policy was made 'without further proof of interest than the policy itself', thereby making the contract void by s 4(2)(b) of the Marine Insurance Act 1906.

The Court of Appeal upheld the decision of the trial judge, and ruled that the policy amounted to a ppi policy and was, therefore, void.

> **Bankes LJ:** [p 248] ... The second point [raised by counsel for the plaintiffs] is that this policy is not within s 4(2)(b). The section speaks of contracts of marine insurance being deemed to be gaming or wagering contracts where the policy is made 'interest or no interest', etc. The contention is that, as the plaintiffs had an insurable interest, the section does not apply. It seems to me that the language of the section does not permit of that construction. The section is drawn for the purpose, as it seems to me, of excluding any inquiry into the question whether or not an insurable interest exists. Sub-section 2(b) is directed to the form of the instrument and, if it is directed to the form, it must include everything which forms part of the instrument, whether it is pasted on or pinned on. In my opinion, when the section says that a contract of marine insurance is to be deemed a gaming or wagering contract where the policy is made 'interest or no interest', or subject to any other like term, it makes void a contract where the instrument contains one of those objectionable clauses.
>
> **Scrutton LJ:** [p 254] ... The argument, if I understand it rightly, is that sub-s 2 means that the contract is *prima facie* deemed to be a gaming and wagering contract, but that inference may be rebutted by showing that the assured had either an insurable interest or an expectation of acquiring one. That is, in effect, to read cl (a) of sub-s 2 into cl (b). I see no ground for cutting down the section in that way. It seems to me Parliament has said that, if this clause is in the policy, it is to be deemed to be a gaming and wagering policy, because it is a gaming and wagering clause.

Nor is it of any consequence whether a ppi clause, once attached to the policy, has since been detached, as was shown in *Re London County Commercial Reinsurance Office Ltd*, below.

Re London County Commercial Reinsurance Office Ltd [1922] 2 Ch 67

A reinsurance company was being wound up and a committee of creditors was appointed. The liquidator, whilst investigating claims against the company, noted that there were outstanding claims made under ppi policies amounting to £97,538; these included some marine policies. The issue before the court was whether the policies, which included ppi slips, were valid under the Act; in particular, those policies where the ppi slips had become detached.

The court ruled that the policies were void. The fact that the ppi slips had become detached was immaterial; the real issue was whether they were part of the policy when the contract was entered into.

> **Lawrence J:** [p 81] ... In my judgment, there is no difference between the policies which still have the ppi clause attached to them and those from which the ppi clause has been detached. It is not necessary to consider what course the court would have adopted if, before the policies had been brought to its attention, the ppi clause had been detached, and neither of the litigating parties had raised the point that such a clause had ever formed part of the policies, because, in the present case, evidence has been adduced on behalf of the liquidator which proves clearly that the ppi clause was attached to all the policies when they were signed and handed to the assured. In my judgment, the proper time to judge whether these policies are valid or void is at the time when they are issued. The subsequent tearing off of the ppi clause by the assured (even though it was done with the permission of the insurers) cannot, in my opinion, have the effect of rendering the policies valid if they were null and void when they were issued.

However, it is emphasised that, under the 1906 Act, ppi policies are not, in themselves, illegal; they are simply void. Thus, under s 84(1), provided that there has been '... no fraud or illegality on the part of the assured or his agents, the premium is thereupon returnable to the assured'.[9] This was confirmed by Lawrence J, in *Re London County Commercial Reinsurance Office Ltd* **[1922] 2 Ch 67**, cited above.

> **Lawrence J:** [p 85] ... There remains to be considered the question whether the claimants under these policies are entitled to the return of the premiums which they have paid. Having regard to the fact that the Act 19 Geo 2, c 37, which rendered marine policies effected by way of gaming or wagering illegal, was repealed by s 92 of the Act of 1906, and that the latter Act merely renders such policies void, I am of opinion that the claimants are entitled to prove for the amount of the premiums paid by them in respect of these policies. It is admitted that the original assured, and therefore the reassured, had an insurable interest in the subject matter and that there was no fraud or illegality on the part of the assured or reassured or their agents. In these circumstances, I am of opinion that, as the consideration for the payment of the premiums has totally failed, s 84(1) of the Act of 1906 applies and the premiums are returnable by the company. In my judgment, therefore, the liquidator ought to admit the claimants under these policies as creditors in respect of the premiums paid by them.

Perhaps the philosophy behind ppi policies and the problems which arise under such policies were best illustrated by Scrutton LJ, in *Thomas Cheshire and Co v Vaughan Brothers and Co* **[1920] 3 KB 240, CA**, cited above.

> **Scrutton LJ:** [p 252] ... For many years, there has been an unfortunate conflict between the statute law and the practice of businessmen. It has been extremely common to place in policies a ppi clause providing that there shall be no necessity to prove the amount of loss, although all the time there was a statute

---

9   However, if the assured has no insurable interest in a ppi policy, he would be guilty of an offence under the Marine Insurance (Gambling Policies) Act 1909, and the premium would not then be returnable under s 84(1) of the MIA 1906.

which said that such a clause was either illegal or null and void. It is unfortunate that that practice has prevailed, because while, on the one hand, there are undoubtedly cases where there is a real loss, but it is difficult to prove its exact amount, and it is convenient in a business sense to have it assessed beforehand, on the other hand, there is no doubt that cases of deliberate attempts to get insurance money where there is no insurable interest, and cases of over-valuation on the chance of a loss, are rendered possible by the continued insertion of a ppi clause. Apart from the fact that the clause facilitates fraud, as it does in many cases, a practice has arisen with regard to it which places judges in great difficulty. It is the duty of judges, if they know that a policy has that clause on it, to treat it as null and void under the Act, and a practice has grown up of deceiving the court by parties tearing off the clause which they have put on the policy in the hope that the court will not know that there is such a clause and will give effect to the policy ... that is the practice, and the only thing to be said to businessmen who carry on business in that way is that, if they persistently enter into contracts which are null and void under a statute, they must not complain if the courts obey the statute rather than their commercial practice.

Without benefit of salvage to the insurer

'Without benefit of salvage' is a term used in marine insurance law to signify that there is nothing capable of being abandoned to the insurer. That is, the assured has no property in the adventure which could be salvaged for the benefit of the insurer. This could be interpreted as the assured having no insurable interest in the adventure, therefore rendering the policy a gaming or wagering policy.

However, the Act recognises the fact that it is possible for an assured to have a type of insurable interest in the adventure which could not be abandoned to an insurer. Such would be the case when 'commissions' or 'anticipated profits' on a voyage are insured and the Act makes provision for such insurable risks by stating, at the end of s 4, that '... where there is no possibility of salvage, a policy may be effected without benefit of salvage to the insurer'.

DOUBLE INSURANCE, RIGHT TO CONTRIBUTION AND RETURN OF PREMIUM

The basis of insurance is that of indemnification for pecuniary losses incurred: this would preclude profit making by an assured through over-insurance by double insurance.[10] Equally, on the same principle, when there is over-insurance by double insurance, each insurer must bear his share of any loss by

---

10   See s 32(2)(a)–(d).

way of a 'contribution' proportionate to the amount for which he is liable under the contract.[11] And, should any insurer pay more than his proportion of the loss, he is entitled to recover from the other insurers their proportion of the loss by way of the right to contribution.[12]

With respect to any return of premium, the Act, in ss 82–84, enumerates the conditions under which the return of any premium or proportion of that premium is applicable, including a specific provision for over-insurance by double insurance. Under this provision, in keeping with the principle of indemnity, an insurer may be liable to return to the assured a proportion of the full premium because, on account of the double insurance, the risk insured amounts to less than that for which that full premium was paid.[13]

Double insurance and the right to contribution

Over-insurance by double insurance and the right to contribution are so interdependent that they are inseparable. With respect to over-insurance by double insurance, s 32(1) of the Act states:

> Where two or more policies are effected by or on behalf of the assured on the same adventure and interest or any part thereof, and the sums insured exceed the indemnity allowed by this Act, the assured is said to be over-insured by double insurance.

And, with regard to any right to contribution arising out of over-insurance by double insurance, s 80 of the Act affirms that:

> (1) Where the assured is over-insured by double insurance, each insurer is bound, as between himself and the other insurers, to contribute rateably to the loss in proportion to the amount for which he is liable under his contract.
>
> (2) If any insurer pays more than his proportion of the loss, he is entitled to maintain an action for contribution against the other insurers, and is entitled to the like remedies as a surety who has paid more than his proportion of the debt.

However, it is emphasised that, as the Act states in s 32(1), over-insurance by double insurance and any contributions resulting from such, are only applicable to two or more policies of insurance which are effected on the same subject matter by or on behalf of the same person. It does not apply when different persons insure the same subject matter in respect of different rights. Mellish LJ was careful to point this out in *North British and Mercantile Insurance Co v London, Liverpool, and Globe Insurance Co*, below.

---

11 See s 80(1).
12 See s 80(2).
13 See s 84(3)(f).

North British and Mercantile Insurance Co v London, Liverpool, and Globe Insurance Co (1877) 5 Ch D 569, CA

A quantity of grain, owned by Rodocanachi and Co, was stored in the warehouse of another company, Barnett and Co. The grain was insured by both companies with different underwriters. When a fire broke out and destroyed the grain, Barnett and Co, the warehouse owners, were indemnified in full by the plaintiffs, North British and Mercantile Insurance Co who, in turn, claimed that the defendants, the insurers of Rodocanachi and Co, were liable for a contribution to the claim which had already been settled in full.

The Court of Appeal, in affirming the decision of the lower court, ruled that the defendants, the insurers of Rodocanachi and Co, were not liable to contribute towards the indemnity already settled by the plaintiffs, North British Insurance Co. This was because, although the subject matter of insurance was the same with respect to both underwriters, the assured under the respective policies were different. Mellish LJ distinguished the right to contribution from the right of subrogation.

> **Mellish LJ:** [p 583] ... Now I do not know of any English cases on the subject of contribution as applied to fire policies; but I can see no reason why the principle in respect of contribution should not be exactly the same in respect of fire policies as they are in respect of marine policies, and I think if the same person in respect of the same right insures in two offices, there is no reason why they should not contribute in equal proportions in respect of a fire policy as they would in the case of a marine policy. The rule is perfectly established in the case of a marine policy that contribution only applies where it is an insurance by the same person having the same rights, and does not apply where different persons insure in respect of different rights. The reason for that is obvious enough. Where different persons insure the same property in respect of their different rights they may be divided into two classes. It may be that the interest of the two between them makes up the whole property.
>
> ... But then there may be cases where, although two different persons insured in respect of different rights, each of them can recover the whole, as in the case of a mortgagor and a mortgagee. But wherever that is the case, it will necessarily follow that one of these two has a remedy over against the other, because the same property cannot in value belong at the same time to two different persons ... I think whenever that is the case, the company which has insured the person who has the remedy over succeeds to his right of remedy over, and then it is a case of subrogation.

In 1992 and 1993, two significant insurance cases concerning the right to contribution, neither of them marine insurance cases, but nonetheless relevant, came before the Court of Appeal and the Judicial Committee of the Privy Council respectively. Effectively, the issue before the courts in both instances was whether a co-insurer could, by a provision within the contract of insurance, exclude his liability to contribute to a loss.

That the right to contribution is founded in equity rather than contract is well established, and it was accepted, in the case of *Legal and General Assurance Society Ltd v Drake Insurance Co Ltd*, below, that the equitable right to contribution could be varied or excluded by contract, even between the assured and the insurer. However, in the case in question, Lloyd LJ was of the opinion that the clause on notification of claim[14] was not one which could modify or exclude the equitable right to contribution.

Legal and General Assurance Society Ltd v Drake Insurance Co Ltd [1992] 1 All ER 283, CA

Two insurance companies insured the same driver under standard private car policies. Both policies provided that immediate written notice had to be given of an event which might give rise to a claim, observance of which was a condition precedent to liability, and that if there was 'any other insurance covering the same loss' when the claim arose, the insurers would not pay or contribute more than their rateable proportion. When the insured driver injured a pedestrian, the plaintiffs (Legal and General) settled the claim without knowing that the assured had taken up another policy of insurance. When the plaintiffs learned about the other policy, they sought a 50% contribution from the other insurer, the defendants (Drake Insurance). However, Drake Insurance refused to contribute, on the basis that they had a good defence to any claim under their policy, as the driver had been in breach of a condition precedent in not having given notice of claim within the stipulated period.

The Court of Appeal (Ralph Gibson LJ dissenting) ruled that the right to contribution was not defeated by the failure of the assured to notify the co-insurer of a potential claim, albeit such failure constituted a breach of a condition under the policy. The plaintiffs were held to have had an undoubted right to contribution in equity against the defendant for half the amount for which the claim was settled. It was held that the right to contribution accrued on the date of loss; and as the breach of the condition precedent must necessarily occur after the date of loss – by which time the right to contribution had already accrued – the plaintiff was entitled to a 50% contribution from the defendant.

> **Lloyd LJ:** [p 287] ... It may be said that the distinction between breach of condition prior to the loss and breach of condition subsequent to the loss is a narrow one. So it may be. But the difference is crucial. For it is at *the date of the loss* that the co-insurer's right to contribution, if any, accrues. [Emphasis added.]

---

14 It is noted that there is a 'Notice of Claim and Tenders' Clause in both the ITCH(95) and the IVCH(95), cll 13 and 11 respectively, which is discussed in Chapter 15, p 599.

It is often said that, though the right to contribution is founded in equity, yet it may be varied or excluded by contract. As long ago as 1641, in *Swain v Wall* Rep Ch 149, 21 ER 534, it was held that the right of contribution could be modified by contract between the co-obligers. But it can also be modified or excluded by contract between the assured and the insurer, in this sense, that the policy may limit the amount of the insurer's liability, or may provide, typically, that the insurer should not be liable beyond his rateable proportion of the loss. But, a provision requiring the assured to give notice of claim does not, in my opinion, modify or exclude the equitable right to contribution in the same sense.

Nourse LJ: [p 291] ... There being no contract between the two insurers, the right of contribution depends, and can only depend, on an equity which requires someone who has taken the benefit of a premium to share the burden of meeting the claim.

Why should that equity be displaced simply because the assured has failed to give the notice which is necessary to make the other insurer liable to *him*? At the moment of the accident, either insurer could have been made liable for the whole of the loss. Why should he who accepts sole liability for settling the claim be deprived of his right to contribution, by an omission on the part of the assured over which he has no control? As between the two insurers the basis of the equity is unimpaired. He who has received a benefit ought to bear his due proportion of the burden.

While accepting that a line must be drawn somewhere, I am of the opinion that a denial of the right to contribution in circumstances such as these would be unduly restrictive and indeed inequitable. An attempt to state, in general terms, where the line ought to be drawn is neither necessary nor desirable. For present purposes it is enough to say that it ought not to be drawn so as to exclude the right to contribution in a case where, at the moment of the accident, each insurer is potentially liable for the whole of the loss.

The issue of contribution arose again in *Eagle Star Insurance Co v Provincial Insurance plc*, below, where the Privy Council expressed its disagreement with the stand and reasoning taken in the *Legal and General* case that, for the purposes of contribution between co-insurers, there was a special cut-off point, viz, at the time of loss, at which the position is to be judged.

Eagle Star Insurance Co v Provincial Insurance plc [1993] 2 Lloyd's Rep 143, PC

A Mr Simms, who suffered injuries as a result of a road accident, brought proceedings and obtained judgment against the negligent driver, a Mr O'Reilly. But, as Mr O'Reilly failed to meet the judgment, he brought proceedings against Mr O'Reilly's insurer, Eagle Star, and the repairer's insurer, Provincial, under the Road Traffic Act, which provided, *inter alia*, that an insurer was bound to meet an injured person's claim when the driver responsible failed to do so. The policies issued by Eagle Star and by Provincial both contained a condition under which the company was not liable to contribute more than its rateable proportion of any loss, damage or expense.

The accident was never reported to Provincial, and under the terms of their policy, they were entitled to repudiate liability.[15] Eagle Star contended that they were entitled to be indemnified by Provincial, because they were not at risk, having cancelled their policy before the accident.[16] Provincial claimed that it was entitled to a 50% contribution from Eagle Star. Thus, the present action was concerned with the right to contribution between the two insurance companies, both of which were under a statutory liability to meet the injured person's claim when the driver responsible failed to do so.

The Privy Council ruled that both insurance companies had to contribute equally to the loss, because they were both statutorily liable to a third party claim.

> **Lord Woolf:** [p 147] ... [referring initially to the *Legal and General* case] On an appeal from the decision at first instance that Legal and General were entitled to 50% contribution, the Court of Appeal (by a majority of Lloyd and Nourse LJJ, Ralph Gibson LJ dissenting) held that where an assured had effected insurance with two different insurers to cover the same loss, the right of one insurer to contribution from a second insurer as to the costs of meeting a claim accrued at the time of the loss. Therefore, even if Drake Insurance Co were entitled to establish that their cover had lapsed because of late notification, the cover would not have lapsed until after the loss, and accordingly, the right of Legal and General to contribute was not affected.
>
> [p 148] ... Lloyd LJ acknowledges that:
>
>> ... it is often said that, though the right to contribution is founded in equity, yet it may be varied or excluded by contract.
>
> Lloyd LJ then accepted that, for the purpose of contribution, the assured and the insurer by contract can limit the amount of the insurer's liability or provide that the insurer should not be liable beyond his rateable proportion. However, Lloyd LJ distinguishes a provision requiring the assured to give notice of claim because it does not:
>
>> ... modify or exclude the equitable right to contribution in the same sense.
>
> Approaching the issue as a matter of principle, in a case such as the present, where both insurers are required to indemnify a third party by statute, there can only from a practical point of view be two solutions to the question of contribution: either the insurers should contribute in accordance with their respective statutory liabilities so that, if they are statutorily equally liable, they will so share the loss; or contribution is determined in accordance with the extent of their respective liabilities to the person insured under the separate contracts of insurance. Of the two alternatives, the contractual approach is the more appropriate, since the extent of their respective liabilities to the person insured will indicate the scale of the double insurance.

---

15 The contractual condition in the Provincial insurance policy was a notice of claim requirement similar to that which had been the issue in the *Legal and General* case.

16 But, due to an administrative error, the policy was never cancelled, and Eagle Star remained liable to a third party (Mr Simms) under the Road Traffic Act.

If the contractual approach is adopted, then there can be no justification for departing from the contractual position by creating, for the purposes of contribution between the co-insurers, a special cut-off point which requires the position to be judged at the date of the loss. Having such a cut-off point could produce results which do not reflect the contractual situation so far as liability to the insured is concerned. Looking at the issue from the insurer's and insured's standpoint, it makes no difference if an insurer defeats a claim by relying on action taken before or after the loss has occurred. If both insurers are liable at least in part to the person insured, then they should contribute to their statutory liability in accordance with their respective liability to the person insured for the loss. While this could have the result that the action of a person insured in relation to one insurer can affect the rights of contribution of the other insurer, this is an inevitable consequence of one insurer being able to take advantage of any limitation of his contractual liabilities on the question of contribution. However, before suggesting this could be unfair, it has to be remembered that it is unlikely that the existence of the other insurer would have been known at the time that the contract of insurance was made.

[p 149] ... Halsbury accurately states [the condition which] must be satisfied before a right of contribution can arise. The condition is that:

> ... each policy must be in force at the time of the loss. There is no contribution if one of the policies has already become void or the risk under it has not yet attached; the insurer from whom contribution is claimed can repudiate liability under his policy on the ground that the assured has broken a condition.

In this case, therefore, both insurers are in the same position. They were both under a statutory liability in relation to the claim of the third party but they both would have been entitled to repudiate liability to the insured person. No distinction should be made in relation to their respective positions and accordingly they should each contribute equally to the amount payable to Mr Simms.

Over-insurance includes ppi policies

Although a ppi policy is rendered void by s 4(1) of the Act, it can, nevertheless, be adjudged to be a form of over-insurance. This is because, if both a marine policy and a ppi policy are effected upon maritime property and, in the event of a loss, the insurer chooses to 'honour' the ppi policy, the indemnity, when added up under both policies, would amount to over-insurance. This issue arose in the case of *Thames and Mersey Marine Insurance Co Ltd v 'Gunford' Ship Co Ltd*, below.

Thames and Mersey Marine Insurance Co Ltd v 'Gunford' Ship Co Ltd [1911] AC 529, HL

Gunford was grossly over-insured, not only by the over-valuation[17] of the subject matter insured, but also by additional ppi policies.

The House of Lords ruled that the underwriters were not liable for the loss, because the assured's failure to inform the insurers of the over-insurance amounted to the non-disclosure of a material fact.

> **Lord Alverstone CJ:** [p 536] ... Some distinction was attempted to be made between over-valuation and over-insurance, but, in as much as all the policies were valued policies, the question becomes immaterial. There was, on the evidence, over-valuation to the extent of £11,100, without taking into consideration the difference between the declared value, £18,500, and the actual value, £9,000. Apart, then, from evidence in the particular case, it seems to me that the statement of the above facts is sufficient to show that, looking to the provisions of the Act of 1906, the circumstances above stated were material as being those which would influence the judgment of a prudent insurer in fixing the premium or determining whether he would take the risk.
>
> **Lord Robson:** [p 549] ... They [the plaintiffs] proceeded, however, to effect a valued policy for £4,600 on 'disbursements'. A list of the payments comprised under this head was put in by the plaintiffs, and amounted to £5,280 as against a total chartered freight of £4,790. So far as these payments consisted of current working expenses necessary to earn freight, they were covered by the insurance on the gross freight, and so far as they consisted of repairs, outfit, and insurance premium on hull, they would ordinarily be included in the policy on ship and materials.
>
> This policy was, therefore, an over-insurance by double insurance. The plaintiffs could not legally avail themselves of it to enforce recovery of any sum in excess of the indemnity allowed by law, but this was a 'ppi' or 'honour' policy, that is, it was made 'without further proof of interest than the policy itself'. In other words, it was a wager, and it is well known that the sums insured under such policies are, under ordinary circumstances, paid with the same regularity as if they were legally due.

Return of premium

As long ago as 1777, Lord Mansfield laid down the two general rules applicable to the return of premium, in *Tyrie v Fletcher*, below.

Tyrie v Fletcher (1777) 2 Cowp 666

A 12 month time policy of insurance, warranted 'free from captures and seizures by the Americans', was effected upon the ship *Isabella*. When *Isabella* was captured by an American privateer only two months into the currency of

---

17 On the issue of excessive over-valuation, this case is discussed in Chapter 5, pp 193 and 200.

the policy, a loss for which the insurers bore no liability, the plaintiff sought to recover the premium for the outstanding 10 months, on the basis that the risk had ceased at the moment of capture. In ruling against the plaintiff, the court clarified the position regarding return of premium.

> **Lord Mansfield:** [p 668] ... This case is stript of every authority. There is no case or practice in point; and, therefore, we must argue from the general principles applicable to all policies of insurance. And I take it, there are two general rules established, applicable to this question: the first is, that where the risk has not been run, whether its not having been run was owing to the fault, pleasure, or will of the insured, or to any other cause, the premium shall be returned: because a policy of insurance is a contract of indemnity. The underwriter receives a premium for running the risk of indemnifying the insured, and whatever cause it be owing to, if he does not run the risk, the consideration, for which the premium or money was put into his hands, fails, and therefore he ought to return it ... Another rule is, that if that risk of the contract of indemnity has once commenced, there shall be no apportionment or return of premium afterwards. For though the premium is estimated, and the risk depends upon the nature and length of the voyage, yet, if it has commenced, though it be only for 24 hours or less, the risk is run; the contract is for the whole entire risk, and no part of the consideration shall be returned:

The two general rules for return of premium laid down by Lord Mansfield now provide the basis of the provisions contained within s 84 of the Act. Section 84(1) relates to the first rule spelled out by Lord Mansfield in *Tyrie v Fletcher*, whilst s 84(2) is concerned with the second. Section 84(3), on the other hand, merely promulgates a list of examples which may be applicable to either s 84(1) or s 84(2).

Notably, s 84(3)(f) makes specific reference to over-insurance by double insurance when it states:

> Subject to the foregoing provisions, where the assured has over-insured by double insurance, a proportionate part of the several premiums is returnable:
>
>> provided that, if the policies are effected at different times, and any earlier policy has at any time borne the entire risk,[18] or if a claim has been paid on the policy in respect of the full sum insured thereby, no premium is

---

18 This specific provision follows the ruling in *Fisk v Masterman* (1841) 8 M&W 165, where policies of insurance were issued on 12 April on a cargo of cotton aboard the ship *Bradshaw* when she was known to be overdue. One day later, on 13 April, further policies were effected on the cotton, although, by this time, the ship was known to be safe. As the cargo was now over-insured by double insurance, the owners of the cargo sought a return of premium. However, the court ruled that there was to be a return of premium only on those policies issued on 13 April; those policies issued on 12 April had, for a time, borne the whole risk. *Per curiam*, 'the judgment must be for the plaintiff to have a return of the premium to the amount of the over-insurance, to which the underwriters subscribed the policies on 13 April are to contribute rateably, in proportion to the sums insured by them respectively on that day – the amount of over-insurance to be ascertained by taking into account all the policies, but no return of premium to be made in respect of the policies effected on 12 April'.

returnable in respect of that policy, and when the double insurance is effected knowingly by the assured, no premium is returnable.

SUBROGATION

Definition of subrogation

Lord Blackburn summed up the principle of subrogation in clear terms in the case of **Burnard v Rodocanachi (1882) 7 App Cas 333, HL**, cited later in the chapter,[19] where cargo was destroyed by the Confederate cruiser *Alabama* during the American Civil War.

> **Lord Blackburn:** [p 239] ... The general rule of law (and it is obvious justice) is that where there is a contract of indemnity (it matters not whether it is a marine policy, or a policy against fire on land, or any other contract of indemnity) and a loss happens, anything which reduces or diminishes that loss reduces or diminishes the amount which the indemnifier is bound to pay; and if the indemnifier has already paid it, then, if anything which diminishes the loss comes into the hands of the person to whom he has paid it, it becomes an equity that the person who has already paid the full indemnity is entitled to be recouped by having that amount back.

Thus, strictly, subrogation is a process in insurance law whereby an insurer, having indemnified an assured, has transferred to himself all the rights and remedies of the assured with respect to the subject matter as from the time of the casualty. However, those rights and remedies brought about by way of subrogation, may only be acted upon in the name of the assured who has been indemnified.[20]

This whole concept was particularly well illustrated by the Lord Chancellor, Lord Cairns, in **Simpson v Thomson (1877) 3 App Cas 279, HL**, where two ships, belonging to the same owner, were in collision, and one of the ships was totally lost. The insurer paid an indemnity to the shipowner for that total loss. Having paid the indemnity, the insurer then sought, by way of subrogation, to be included with the owners of the cargo which had been destroyed, in the distribution of the fund lodged in the court by the owner of the other colliding vessel who was, of course, the very same person whom the insurer had previously indemnified.

---

19 See below, p 34.
20 See *Esso Petroleum Co Ltd v Hall Russell and Co* [1988] 3 WLR 730, HL, *per* Lord Jauncey of Tullichettle: [p 748] '... My Lords, the foregoing authorities leave me in no doubt as to the existence of a general rule in both English and Scots law that where an indemnifier is subrogated to the rights of someone whom he has indemnified he can only pursue those rights in the name of that person.'

The House of Lords ruled that the insurer, in the circumstances, had no right to be a claimant to any part of the fund because, as he was acting in the name of the assured, he was in fact taking action against himself.

The Lord Chancellor: [p 284] ... where one person has agreed to indemnify another, he will, on making good the indemnity, be entitled to succeed to all the ways and means by which the person indemnified might have protected himself against or reimbursed himself for the loss. It is on this principle that the underwriters of a ship that has been lost are entitled to the ship *in specie* if they can find and recover it; and it is on the same principle that they can assert any right which the owner of the ship might have asserted against a wrongdoer for damages for the act which has caused the loss. But this right of action for damages they must assert, not in their own name but in the name of the person insured, and if the person insured be the person who has caused the damage, I am unable to see how the right can be asserted at all.

No right of subrogation under a ppi policy

There is no right of subrogation with respect to a ppi policy of insurance; such an insurance, though regularly honoured by insurers, being 'void' in law.

Edwards and Co Ltd v Motor Union Insurance Co Ltd [1922] 2 KB 249

The plaintiffs, who were the owners of a vessel, which was sunk after a collision with another vessel, had insured the chartered freight with the defendants under a ppi policy. The insurers, having honoured the policy and indemnified the assured, acting in the name of the assured, then found themselves excluded from a fund deposited with the court by the owners of the other colliding vessel.

McCardie J: [p 255] ... If, then, the right of subrogation rests upon payment under a contract of indemnity, how does the matter stand when the policy of insurance is an honour policy only? In my opinion, such a policy is not a contract of indemnity at all. It is the negation of such a contract ... I think that Parliament has placed a ppi policy on much the same footing as a wager on a horse race. In substance it is a mere bet. The insurer agrees to pay on the occurrence of a given event, irrespective of the actual interest or loss of the assured. It is none the less a bet in substance, because the wagering parties may have clothed the wager with certain conditions. Section 4 of the Act of 1906 cannot be defeated by a mere device of phrases. If, then, the policy before me is to be deemed a mere wager and not a contract of indemnity, it follows that there is no juristic scope for the operation of the principle of subrogation. The essential basis of subrogation is wholly absent.

There is also the further point – namely, that by s 4 of the Act of 1906 the present policy is void. It is destitute of all legal effect between the parties. If so, it cannot operate as if it were a valid bargain carrying with it the legal and equitable results and the body of jural remedies which ordinarily flow from an insurance indemnity contract. Legal proceedings to enforce subrogative rights cannot be based on a document which is stricken with sterility by Act of Parliament.

Finally, because the issues involved are different, the right of subrogation under the Act is specifically divided into the two types of loss: total and partial.

Where the insurer pays for a total loss

Section 79(1) of the Act states:

> Where the insurer pays for a total loss, either of the whole, or in the case of goods of any apportionable part, of the subject matter insured, he thereupon becomes entitled to take over the interest of the assured in whatever may remain of the subject matter so paid for, and he is thereby subrogated to all the rights and remedies of the assured in and in respect of that subject matter as from the time of the casualty causing the loss.

There are two distinct elements to s 79(1), namely:

(a) the right to take over the interest of the assured in whatever may remain of the subject matter paid for; and

(b) the rights and remedies of the assured in respect of the subject matter by way of subrogation.

The first limb is concerned with the proprietary rights of the insurer in the event of abandonment being accepted, and the second relates to the right and remedies conferred upon the insurer by way of subrogation after the assured has been indemnified. In the case of *Yorkshire Insurance Co v Nisbet Shipping Co Ltd* [1961] 1 Lloyd's Rep 479, Diplock J was careful to differentiate between the 'two distinct matters', to use his words, contained within s 79(1).

Subrogation includes 'proprietary rights'

Yorkshire Insurance Co v Nisbet Shipping Co Ltd [1961] 1 Lloyd's Rep 479

The owner of a British ship, totally lost after a collision with a Canadian warship, was indemnified by the insurers for a total loss. Some years later, the owners, with the consent of the insurers, succeeded in recovering considerably more from the Canadian Government than the indemnity originally paid by the insurers, because of an advantageous change in the rate of exchange. The insurers claimed they were entitled to the full amount under subrogation, but the court ruled that, under the principle of indemnity, they were only entitled to the same amount as they had paid out originally.

> **Diplock J:** [p 482] ... I turn first, as is my duty, to the Marine Insurance Act, 1906, s 79 of which deals with the rights of the insurer on payment ... It is to be noted that the sub-section, which comes into operation only upon payment for the total loss by the insurer, deals with two distinct matters: (1) the interest of the assured in the subject matter insured, and (2) the rights and remedies of the assured in and in respect of that subject matter. The former, the insurer, is

entitled, although not bound, to take over; if he does, the whole interest of the assured in the subject matter insured is transferred to him. To the rights and remedies of the assured in respect of the subject matter insured, with which alone I am concerned in this case, the insurer is 'subrogated as from the time of the casualty causing the loss'.

It is emphasised that, when considering the proprietary rights of the assured which are transferred to the insurer in the event of the insurer accepting abandonment, s 79(1) of the Act should be read in conjunction with s 63, the 'effect of abandonment'.[21] Notably, both ss 79(1) and 63(1) refer pointedly to the fact that the insurer is not bound to 'take over the interest of the assured'. It is nothing more than an entitlement, which the insurer may or may not elect to take advantage of, depending on the circumstances.

Diplock J alluded to this in the *Nisbet* case, above, but, in the earlier case of *AG v Glen Line Ltd*, below, Atkin LJ went into considerably more detail on the issue. Lord Atkin also clarified the issue regarding freight being earned, as referred to in s 63(2), and further pointed out that, whilst the right of subrogation accrued after indemnification, proprietary rights exist as from a valid abandonment.

AG v Glen Line Ltd and Liverpool and London War Risks Insurance Association Ltd [1930] 37 LlL Rep 55, HL

The British vessel *Glenearn* was in Hamburg at the outset of the First World War; she was detained in Germany throughout the duration of the hostilities and the war risks insurer settled the claim for total loss with the owners. However, the ship had been reinsured with the British Government on the basis of 80% liability, against the war risks insurer's liability of 20%. When, after the war was over, the owners of *The Glenearn* were compensated for their loss by the German authorities, the British Government claimed that the sum recovered should be paid to themselves and the war risks insurer on the said 80:20 basis. Both the war risks insurer and Glen Line Ltd disagreed.

The House of Lords ruled that neither the British Government nor the war risks insurer had any right to the compensation, which was 'personal' to the shipowner, in that it was for loss of earnings during the years of detention. In his summing up, Lord Atkin analysed s 79(1), affirmed its relationship with

---

21 Section 63(1) of the Act states: 'Where there is a valid abandonment, the insurer is entitled to take over the interest of the assured in whatever may remain of the subject matter insured, and all proprietary rights thereto.'

s 63(1), discussed the earning of freight[22] and pointed out the difference between proprietary rights and subrogation.

Atkin LJ: [p 61] ... On a valid abandonment the insurer becomes no doubt entitled to proprietary rights incidental to the subject matter insured as from the time of the loss. He is put in the same position as though the subject matter insured was assigned to him by way of sale immediately after the event which constitutes the loss. He has no rights until the loss, and he takes over 'whatever may remain' of the subject matter insured. Thus, on abandonment of the ship, he is entitled to the property in the ship, and if it is used after he has acquired the property, he is entitled to the profits of such use. Therefore, if the ship so abandoned proceeds to earn freight in respect of the voyage on which she was abandoned, the insurer as owner of the vessel becomes entitled to the freight, which has only become payable on the hypothesis by his vessel completing the voyage and delivering the cargo at the port of discharge (*Case v Davidson* (1816) 5 M&S 79). But a right to sue a wrongdoer for a wrongful act which causes a loss which gives rise to an abandonment appears to be something quite different from the proprietary rights incidental to the ship which pass on abandonment.

If one treats the insurer by analogy as a purchaser after the marine peril had taken effect, it is plain that the sale by itself would not pass the right to sue, which would remain in the vendor. The fact is that confusion is often caused by not distinguishing the legal rights given by abandonment (s 63) from the rights of subrogation (s 79). No one doubts that the underwriter on hull damaged by collision and abandoned as a constructive total loss is entitled to the benefit of the right of the assured to sue the wrongdoer for the damage to hull. But he derives his right from the provisions of s 79, whereby he is subrogated to 'all rights and remedies of the assured in and in respect of the subject matter', very different words from 'all proprietary rights incidental thereto'. And it is to be noted that, in respect of abandonment, the rights exist on a valid abandonment, whereas in respect of subrogation, they only arise on payment.

Notes

Section 63(2) of the Act states:

Upon the abandonment of a ship, the insurer thereof is entitled to any freight in course of being earned, and which is earned by her subsequent to the casualty causing the loss, less the expenses of earning it incurred after the

---

22 On the issue of freight, on a valid abandonment, only the as yet 'unearned freight' passes to the insurer, as was pointed out in *Simpson v Thomson* (1877) 3 App Cas 279, HL, where Lord Blackburn stated: [p 292] '... The right to receive payment of freight accruing due but not earned at the time of the disaster is one of those rights so incident to the property in the ship, and it therefore passes to the underwriters because the ship has become their property, just as it would have passed to a mortgagee of the ship who, before the freight was completely earned, had taken possession of the ship ... This is at times very hard upon the insured owner of the ship; he can, however, avoid it by claiming only for a partial loss, keeping the property in himself, and so keep the right to earn the accruing freight.'

casualty; and, where the ship is carrying the owner's goods, the insurer is entitled to a reasonable remuneration for the carriage of them subsequent to the casualty causing the loss.

The Freight Waiver Clause (cl 20 of the ITCH(95) and cl 18 of the IVCH(95)) overrides s 63(2) when it states:

> In the event of total or constructive total loss, no claim to be made by the Underwriters for freight whether notice of abandonment has been given or not.

Abandonment not accepted – who owns the property?

An insurer is entitled, but not bound, to take over property abandoned by an assured; this will engender problems when the insurer refuses, impliedly or expressly, to accept the abandoned property. Who, therefore, in such circumstances, owns the abandoned property? Is ownership of the property transferred to the insured by way of automatic transfer, or does it still remain with the assured? Is it, having been abandoned to the whole world, *res nullius*, belonging to no one?

Ownership of the property passes to the insurer by automatic transfer?

Unlike under the Act, where proprietary rights are strictly separated from rights and remedies under subrogation, in the earlier pre-statute cases, the prevailing view appears to have been that, as soon as the insurer indemnified the assured for a total loss, the proprietary rights in the subject matter insured as well as the right of subrogation passed *automatically* to the insurer.

This was well illustrated in the case of **North of England Steamship Insurance Association v Armstrong (1870) LR 5 QB 244,** where the insurers of a vessel indemnified the assured owners of a vessel for a total loss after a collision with another ship. When, later, the assured succeeded, in the Admiralty Court, in recovering a large sum by way of damages from the owners of the other colliding ship, the insurers successfully sued the assured for that money on the basis that it belonged to them by way of subrogation. However, on the issue of who owned the wreck, Cockburn CJ was in no doubt that it had automatically passed to the insurers after payment of the indemnity.

> **Cockburn CJ:** [p 248] ... Now, I take it to be clearly established, in the case of a total loss, that whatever remains of the vessel in the shape of salvage, or whatever rights accrue to the owner of the thing insured and lost, they pass to the underwriter the moment he is called upon to satisfy the exigency of the policy, and he does satisfy it.

And, similarly, in yet another early case, that of **Simpson v Thomson (1877) 3 App Cas 279, HL**, cited earlier,[23] where two ships belonging to the same owner collided and one of the ships was totally lost, Lord Blackburn stated:

> [p 292] ... I do not doubt at all that, where the owners of an insured ship have claimed or been paid as for a total loss, the property in what remains of the ship, and all rights incident to that property, are transferred to the underwriters as from the time of the disaster in respect of which the total loss is claimed for and paid.

Ownership of the property remains with the assured?

The prevailing modern and logical view is that, when an underwriter refuses to take over the insured subject matter after a total loss, the ownership of the property remains with the assured. This was the approach taken by Greer LJ in *Oceanic Steam Navigation Co v Evans*, below, although, in this instance, his reasoning was helped by the actions of the shipowner after the casualty.

Oceanic Steam Navigation Co v Evans (1934) 50 LlL Rep 1, CA

The plaintiffs were the owners of the steamship *Celtic*, which was wrecked near the entrance to Cork harbour. The insurers refused to take over the wreck because of the dangerous position in which it lay. Thus, the owners, anticipating liabilities to the Cork Harbour Authority, employed a Danish firm to remove the wreck and then effected an insurance with the defendants against any claims that may be made by the Cork Harbour Authority as a result of anything done or omitted to be done with respect to the wreck removal. The Danish wreck removers failed under their contract, and the Cork Harbour Authority finally removed the wreck under statutory powers, the cost of which fell upon the plaintiffs who, in turn, claimed upon their policy of insurance.

The Court of Appeal ruled that the plaintiffs should be indemnified under the policy and, in the process of reaching their decision, considered the ownership of the wreck.

> **Greer LJ:** [p 2] ... It was alleged by the owners of *Celtic* that she was a constructive total loss, and they desired to put themselves in their right position to claim on that basis by giving notice of abandonment, that is to say, the owners offered to abandon what remained of the vessel, in the position in which she was, to the insurers on hull. The insurers on hull, I suppose, thinking that they might be incurring some responsibility, with the wreck in the position in which it was, somewhat dangerous to those who desired their ships to enter Cork harbour, refused to accept abandonment. It does not follow that, because notice of abandonment is given to an insurer, therefore the vessel, which may have some value, is abandoned to all the world, so that it has no

---

23 See above, p 17.

owner at all, and becomes what lawyers prefer to describe, using the Latin language, as *res nullius*. I do not think in this case we can find that there was an abandonment of this ship in that sense. I think Mr Miller [for the insurers] was quite right in saying that something very short of that was proved. The way they behaved afterwards, in securing some profit out of the remains of this great vessel, seems rather to indicate that they had not abandoned her to all the world, and still regarded themselves as owners able to sell the opportunity to recover such of this vessel as was worth recovering to a salvor or a person undertaking to remove wreck.

And, in *Blane Steamships Ltd v Minister of Transport*, below, Cohen LJ had little doubt that, when the insurer declined to take over the property after indemnifying the assured, the ownership remained with the assured. Cohen LJ, in his summing up, referred with approval to the approach taken in *Oceanic Steamship Navigation Co v Evans* by Greer LJ, and disapproval to the approach taken by Bailhache J in *Mayor and Corporation of Boston v France, Fenwick and Co Ltd*, below.

Blane Steamships Ltd v Minister of Transport [1951] 2 Lloyd's Rep 155, CA

The vessel *Empire Gladstone* was time chartered by Blane Steamships Ltd from the Ministry of Transport, but went aground on the Australian coast, south of Sydney, and was abandoned to insurers as a constructive total loss. Under the terms of the charterparty, the charterers had been obliged to insure the ship. The insurers paid for a constructive total loss, but refused to take over the wreck. As the charterers still wished to buy the vessel under an option to purchase contained in the charterparty, they claimed that they were entitled to the indemnity and not the Minister of Transport.

The Court of Appeal ruled against the charterers and, not unnaturally, after the refusal by the insurers to take over the ship, the issue of ownership was raised.

> **Cohen LJ:** [p 163] ... There is, however, one other point to which I ought to allude. Mr Scott Cairns [for the minister], in the course of his argument as to the effect of a notice of abandonment, referred to and relied on a statement in s 1213 on p 1114 of the 13th edition of Arnould on Marine Insurance to the effect that, if notice of abandonment is given, but not accepted, the property becomes *res nullius*. That statement was stated in the Note to be based on a decision of Bailhache J, in *Mayor and Corporation of Boston v France, Fenwick and Co* (1923) 15 LlL Rep 85, and reference was made in that Note to two other cases. The decision of Bailhache J undoubtedly supports the statement, but the cases of *Allgemeine Gesellschaft Helvetia v Administrator of German Property* [1931] 1 KB 672, p 687, and *Oceanic Steam Navigation Company Ltd v Evans* (1934) 50 LlL Rep 1, p 3, do not do so.
>
> The first-mentioned case seems irrelevant, and the second case, far from supporting it, contains a statement by Greer LJ on p 3 which is inconsistent with it. Greer LJ said:

It does not follow that, because notice of abandonment is given to an insurer, therefore the vessel, which may have some value, is abandoned to all the world, so that it has no owner at all, and becomes what lawyers prefer to describe, using the Latin language, as *res nullius*.

That expression of opinion was *obiter*, and it is not necessary for me to reach a conclusion on the matter, but the view expressed by Bailhache J seems to me difficult to reconcile (a) with the option given to the assured, by s 61 of the Marine Insurance Act 1906, to treat the loss as a partial loss, and (b) with the doctrine of ademption of loss explained in Chalmers, *Marine Insurance Act*, 4th edn, 1906, p 89. My inclination, therefore, is to prefer the opinion expressed by Greer LJ to that of Bailhache J.

'Res nullius' – it is abandoned to the world?

The concept that, when there is no acceptance of abandonment by an insurer, the subject matter insured no longer belongs to anybody, and is, in fact, abandoned to the world, is difficult to accept as a practical solution and appears to have garnered little support. Nevertheless, this proposition was put forward as an alternative approach in the case of **Mayor and Corporation of Boston v France, Fenwick and Co Ltd (1923) 15 LlL Rep 85.** In this instance, the insurers had refused to accept the abandoned property and the plaintiffs, the port of Boston in Lincolnshire, sought to recover from the shipowner expenses which they had incurred when removing the wreck of the steamship *Lockwood* from the River Witham.

> **Bailhache J:** [p 91] ... I have refrained from expressing any opinion as to whether a valid notice of abandonment unaccepted by underwriters, while it divests the owner of his property in the wreck, at the same time automatically transfers the property to the underwriters. I will only say that there is a good deal to be said against this view in favour of the wreck in such circumstances becoming a *res nullius*. The point does not call for direction, and I will leave it.

Where the insurer pays for a partial loss

The only right is subrogation

As the issue of abandonment cannot arise in the case of a partial loss, there is no prospect to the insurer of acquiring any proprietary rights. This is confirmed by s 79(2) of the Act, which states:

> Subject to the foregoing provisions, where the insurer pays for a partial loss, he acquires no title in the subject matter insured, or such part of it as may remain, but he is thereupon subrogated to all rights and remedies of the assured in and in respect of the subject matter insured as from the time of the casualty causing the loss, in so far as the assured has been indemnified, according to the Act, by such payment for the loss.

As with a total loss, the right of subrogation is only bestowed upon the insurer after the assured has been indemnified. But, in the event of a partial loss, the only rights and remedies conferred on the insurer are in respect of that portion of the loss for which the insurer has indemnified the assured. The insurer has no proprietary rights in any part of the subject matter remaining.

The insurer is limited to recovering the amount of the indemnification

It is now well established in insurance law that, in any action instituted by an insurer by way of subrogation, the maximum sum which he may recover is the amount by which he has indemnified the assured.[24]

In *Thames and Mersey Marine Insurance Co v British and Chilean Steamship Co* **[1915] 2 KB 24, aff'd [1916] 1 KB 30, CA**, a vessel was sunk after a collision with another ship and was totally lost. Having indemnified the assured for a total loss, the insurer was held to be entitled to recover from the assured the whole amount for which the other ship was deemed liable by the Admiralty Court, but only because that sum amounted to less than the indemnity paid by the insurer.

> **Scrutton J:** [p 32] ... as the amount recovered by the assured did not exceed the amount paid by the underwriters on the policy, the underwriters were entitled to recover from the assured the whole of the amount recovered by them in the Admiralty action, notwithstanding that it was based upon a value which was higher than that agreed in the policy.[25]

The assured is impliedly bound to mitigate the loss suffered by the insurer

In *Yorkshire Insurance Co Ltd v Nisbet Shipping Co Ltd* **[1961] 1 Lloyd's Rep 479**, cited earlier, where a collision occurred between a British vessel and a Canadian warship, Diplock J analysed the whole doctrine of subrogation. The

---

24   In the old case of *North of England Iron Steamship Insurance Association v Armstrong* (1870) LR 5 QB 244, the court was of the opinion that, after payment for a total loss, the insurer was entitled to *everything* he could recover by way of subrogation. The reasoning in this case on the issue of subrogation has been the subject of much disapproval in many other cases and must be considered as flawed: see *Yorkshire Insurance Co v Nisbet Shipping Co Ltd* [1961] 1 Lloyd's Rep 479, where Diplock J (pp 485–86) confirmed the present view and cited the following authorities in support: *Burnard v Rodocanachi* (1882) 7 App Cas 333, p 339; *King v Victoria Insurance Co Ltd* [1896] AC 250, p 256; *AG v Glen Line Ltd* (1930) 36 Com Cas 1, p 13; *The St Johns* (1900) 101 Fed 469, p 474; and *The Livingstone* (1904) 130 Fed 746.

25   Both the lower court and the Court of Appeal ruled that the damages recoverable from the other colliding ship (5/12ths of the total) should be based upon the real value of the assured's vessel, and not the value agreed in the policy. This is, of course, the position under s 27(4) and common law, but not under the ITCH(95) or the IVCH(95).

judge confirmed that the limit recoverable by an insurer by way of subrogation was the value of the indemnity, and that there was an implied term in a contract of insurance that an assured was, whenever it was in his power, duty bound to reduce the amount of the loss indemnified by the insurer.

> **Diplock J:** [p 483] ... In my view, the doctrine of subrogation in insurance law requires one to imply in contracts of marine insurance only such terms as are necessary to ensure that, notwithstanding that the insurer has made payment under the policy, the assured shall not be entitled to retain, as against the insurer, a greater sum than what is ultimately shown to be his actual loss ... Thus, if after payment by the insurer of a loss, that loss, as a result of an act of a third party, is reduced, the insurer can recover from the assured the amount of the reduction, because that is the amount which he, the insurer, has overpaid under the contract of insurance. This sum he can recover at common law, without recourse to equity, as money had and received (see Bullen and Leake, 3rd edn, p 187). It is immaterial in what way the loss has been reduced, or whether it has been reduced after the casualty but before the actual date of payment; if the insurer has paid more than the actual loss, he can recover from the assured, as money had and received, the amount of the overpayment.
>
> It is also an implied term of the contract that, if it is within the power of the assured to reduce the amount of the loss for which he had received payment from the insurer, by exercising remedies against third parties, he must do so on being indemnified by the insurer against the costs involved. Since such remedies are personal to the assured, they must be exercised in his own name. As the common law provides no method by which a person can be compelled to bring legal proceedings against another, recourse was needed by the insurer before the Judicature Acts to Chancery to compel the assured to allow his name to be used for legal proceedings against third parties in order to reduce the loss. But the duty of the assured to take proceedings to reduce his loss and the correlative right of the insurer to require him to do so was a contractual duty. The remedy for its breach, by compelling the assured to allow an action to be brought in his name, was an equitable remedy in aid of rights at common law, and was alternative to the common law remedy of recovering damages for the breach of the duty.

Subrogation brings about an equitable proprietary interest

In the following important case, *Napier and Ettrick v Hunter*, the comments of Lord Diplock in the *Nisbet Shipping* case regarding the issue of subrogation were considered and expanded upon by the House of Lords. Their Lordships ruled that, under the doctrine of subrogation, an insurer has an enforceable equitable proprietary lien on any damages recovered by an assured from a third party wrongdoer.

Napier and Ettrick v Hunter and Others [1993] 1 All ER 385, HL[26]

This was an action by Lloyd's 'names' against their stop-loss insurers. The 'names' had effected stop-loss policies of insurance which were designed to provide indemnity for them (the 'names') in the event of losses in the insurance market in excess of a certain amount and up to a fixed maximum amount. As a result of the negligence of the Outhwaite syndicate's managing agents, many insurance policies underwriting claims for asbestosis had been issued without adequate reinsurance cover, with the result that many 'names' suffered catastrophic losses and claimed upon their stop-loss policies. These claims were met by the stop-loss insurers. Subsequently, the 'names' had also brought actions against their agents (of Outhwaite), claiming damages for negligence. Those actions were settled by way of a payment of £116 m (the settlement moneys) which was held on behalf of, *inter alia*, the 'names'. The stop-loss insurers averred that, under the principle of subrogation, they had an equitable proprietary interest in the names' share of the settlement moneys to the extent of the claims they (the stop-loss insurers) had met.

The House of Lords ruled that the stop-loss insurers had (to the extent they had reimbursed the 'names') an equitable proprietary lien or charge in their favour in the settlement moneys, which could be enforced. Thus, the 'names' could not receive any money from the settlement fund until the stop-loss insurers had first been fully reimbursed in respect of the money they had paid out to the 'names' under the stop-loss policies. In coming to their decision, the House considered the whole issue of subrogation and rights in equity.

> **Lord Templeman:** [p 395d] ... Lord Diplock [in the *Nesbit Shipping* case], far from deciding that a court of equity could not lend its aid to compel the assured to direct that the insurer be recouped under the doctrine of subrogation out of the damages recovered from the wrongdoer, equated the right of the insurer to that of the assignee of an equitable interest, a right which equity will, of course, enforce.
>
> It may be that the common law invented and implied in contracts of insurance a promise by the insured person to take proceedings to reduce his loss, a promise by the insured person to account to the insurer for moneys recovered from a third party in respect of the insured loss and a promise by the insured person to allow the insurer to exercise in the name of the insured person rights of action vested in the insured person against third parties for the recovery of the insured loss if the insured person refuses or neglects to enforce those rights of action. There must also be implied a promise by the insured person that, in exercising his rights of action against third parties, he will act in good faith for the benefit of the insured person so far as he has borne the loss and for the benefit of the insurer so far as he has indemnified the insured person against the insured loss. My Lords, contractual promises may create equitable

---

26 Hereinafter referred to as the *Lord Napier* case.

interests. An express promise by a vendor to convey land on payment of the purchase price confers on the purchaser an equitable interest in the land. In my opinion, promises implied in a contract of insurance with regard to rights of action vested in the insured person for the recovery of an insured loss from a third party responsible for the loss confer on the insurer an equitable interest in those rights of action to the extent necessary to recoup the insurer who has indemnified the insured person against the insured loss.

[p 397a] ... I am not prepared to treat authorities which span over two centuries in a cavalier fashion. The principles which dictated the decisions of our ancestors and inspired their references to the equitable obligations of an insured person towards an insurer entitled to subrogation are discernible and immutable. They establish that such an insurer has an enforceable equitable interest in the damages payable by the wrongdoer. The insured person is guilty of unconscionable conduct if he does not provide for the insurer to be recouped out of the damages awarded against the wrongdoer. Equity will not allow the insured person to insist on his legal rights to all the damages awarded against the wrongdoer and will restrain the insured person from receiving or dealing with those damages so far as they are required to recoup the insurer under the doctrine of subrogation.

Where the insured person has been paid policy moneys by the insurer for a loss in respect of which the insured person recovers damages from a wrongdoer, the insured person is guilty of unconscionable conduct if he does not procure and direct that the sum due to the insurer shall by way of subrogation be paid out of the damages.

It is next necessary to consider how equity copes with such unconscionable conduct ... In order to protect the rights of the insurer under the doctrine of subrogation, equity considers that the damages payable by the wrongdoer to the insured person are subject to an equitable lien or charge in favour of the insurer. The charge is imposed by equity because the insurer, once he has paid under the policy, has an interest in the right of action against the wrongdoer and an interest in the establishment, quantification, recovery and distribution of the damages awarded against the wrongdoer.

[p 398g] ... Since drafting this speech I have read in draft the speech to be delivered by my noble and learned friend Lord Goff of Chieveley. He agrees that the doctrine of subrogation conveys on the insurer an equitable proprietary lien or charge on the moneys recovered by the insured person from a third party in respect of the insured loss. I agree that, in the circumstances, it is not now necessary to decide whether the equitable lien or charge attaches also to the rights of action vested in the insured person to recover from a third party. I have expressed the view that the doctrine of subrogation does apply in those circumstances, but in any future case, if the point becomes material, that view may require reconsideration in the light of further research.

Lord Goff of Chieveley: [p 403b] ... There is one particular problem to which I wish to refer, although, as I understand it, it does not fall to be decided in the present case. Does the equitable proprietary interest of the insurer attach only to a fund consisting of sums which come into the hands of the assured in reduction of the loss paid by the insurer? Or does it attach also to a right of action vested in the assured which, if enforced, would yield such a fund? The point is not altogether easy. I can see no reason in principle why such an interest should not be capable of attaching to property in the nature of a chose in action.

The *Lord Napier* case, above, having established the equitable proprietary rights of an insurer under subrogation, was not called upon to consider the equitable proprietary rights of the insured when an insurer, by way of subrogation, recovers more than the amount he had indemnified the insured. This very issue, the other side of the coin, was raised in *Lonrho Exports Ltd v Export Credits Guarantee Department*, below.

Lonrho Exports Ltd v Export Credits Guarantee Department [1996] 4 All ER 673

The plaintiffs, Lonrho, having exported goods to Zambia, were owed a great deal of money because of the state of the economy in Zambia in 1975, coupled with foreign exchange restrictions. However, Lonrho had entered into export credit agreements with the defendant, Export Credits Guarantee Department (ECGD), under which ECGD had agreed to reimburse them 95% of the amount of any losses arising under its contracts of sale with buyers in specified contracts by reason of, *inter alia*, 'political events, or economic difficulties ...'. After ECGD had indemnified the plaintiffs for their loss, they recovered a sum of money from the Zambian Government, which money was then placed in a fund. The plaintiffs then claimed that the fund held by ECGD owed them their uninsured losses (the outstanding 5%) and the interest on that sum.

In the course of his judgment, Lightman J took time to explain the general principle of subrogation to the effect that, where an insurer recovers, by way of subrogation, a sum of money greater than what he has paid out to the assured, he (the insurer) holds the balance on trust for the assured, who has an equitable proprietary interest in the money. However, the court ruled that, as the money received by ECGD was, in the circumstances, the absolute property of the State and was, therefore, not recoverable by the plaintiffs under the terms of the credit export agreement, the plaintiff's claim must fail.

Lightman J: [p 690e] ... The general law on the rights of the insurer in respect of recoveries is authoritatively stated in the decision of the House of Lords in *Lord Napier and Ettrick v Hunter, Lord Napier and Ettrick v RF Kershaw Ltd* [1993] 1 All ER 385, [1993] AC 713. The insured, who has been indemnified in whole or in part by the insurer, retains the right to enforce any cause of action against the party who occasioned the loss, but the insurer has the right in the name of the insured to enforce that cause of action. If the insured obtains any recoveries, the insurer has an equitable lien on those recoveries to secure the amount due to the insurer from such recoveries, but subject to that lien, the recoveries belong beneficially to the insured. The question raised in this case concerns the situation where the insurer obtains recoveries which exceed the sum which he is entitled to recoup himself and whether he holds the balance on trust for the insured or is merely liable to pay over to the insured a sum equal to the balance, either as debt or as moneys had and received. I have been told by counsel that there is no authority or textbook affording guidance on this question. If this is so, this is a remarkable lacuna, for the situation is one which must be met with in practice.

So far as there is absent any authoritative guidance, recourse must be had to principle. The significant facts in such a situation are that: (a) the cause of action or right to recover belongs beneficially and (unless assigned) at law to the insured; (b) the insurer is entitled through the medium of the insured to enforce the cause of action to settle his recoupment; (c) whilst the House of Lords, in *Lord Napier and Ettrick v Hunter*, left open whether the insurer has an equitable charge on the cause of action, he has an equitable lien on the recoveries. In short, the insurer enforces a cause of action belonging beneficially to the insured for the joint benefit of the insured and the insurer and, in the fruit of that endeavour, the insurer has only a limited interest. The applicable principles in this situation lie in the law of mortgages, which provides that a chargee who, in exercise of his rights as a security holder, obtains a payment of realisation exceeding his debt (for example, by sale of the charged property) holds the surplus recoveries on trust for the mortgagor (see, for example, *Snell's Equity*, 29th edn, 1990, p 416). As it seems to me, by parity of reasoning, the insurer holds the surplus recoveries on trust for the insured. The moneys in the hand of the insurer belong to the assured, subject only to the right of the insurer to retain the sum secured in his own favour. He is duty bound to divide up the moneys in his hands between the assured and himself in the shares reflecting their respective entitlement and to hold the insured's entitlement on trust for the insured ... Equity has intervened to lend assistance to the insurer, not to deny the insured his equitable proprietary title to recoveries.

An insurer cannot exercise rights of subrogation against a co-assured

As a general rule, there can be no right of subrogation conferred on an insurer who has paid a claim and wishes to take up the rights and remedies of one co-assured against another co-assured, unless the other co-assured is guilty of wilful misconduct or is not covered by the policy against the risk under which the indemnity was paid. This was confirmed by Colman J, in *National Oilwell (UK) Ltd v Davy Offshore Ltd*, below.

National Oilwell (UK) Ltd v Davy Offshore Ltd [1993] 2 Lloyd's Rep 582

Under an agreement in 1988, one company, National Oilwell (NOW), had contracted to supply engineering equipment to another, Davy Offshore (DOL) in order to build an oil production platform for use in the North Sea. However, a dispute had grown up between the companies over quality of workmanship which, in turn, had resulted in invoices totalling in excess of £13 m for work done by NOW being unpaid. As previously, DOL had effected a Builders All Risks policy of insurance on the whole project, for which DOL had been indemnified under the policy for losses caused by the defective equipment supplied by NOW. When NOW sued DOL over the unpaid invoices, the insurers, by way of subrogation, in the name of DOL, counterclaimed for their losses.

On the issue of co-insurance, it was common ground that NOW was a party to the insurance effected by DOL, and the court was in no doubt that an insurer could not exercise rights of subrogation in the name of one co-assured against another co-assured unless the other co-assured was guilty of wilful misconduct, or was not covered by the policy against the risk under which the indemnity was paid. To allow an insurer to exercise such a right of subrogation would be a breach of an implied term in the policy; moreover, such a right is excluded by the principles of circuitry of action.

Colman J: [p 613] ... The explanation for the insurer's inability to cause one co-assured to sue another co-assured is that, in as much as the policy on goods covers all the assureds on an all risks basis for loss and damage, even if caused by their own negligence, any attempt by an insurer, after paying the claim of one assured, to exercise rights of subrogation against another would, in effect, involve the insurer seeking to reimburse a loss caused by a peril (loss or damage even if caused by the assured's negligence) against which he had insured for the benefit of the very party against whom he now sought to exercise rights of subrogation. That party could stand in the same position as the principal assured as regards a loss caused by his own breach of contract or negligence. For the insurers who had paid the principal assured to assert that they were now free to exercise rights of subrogation and thereby sue the party at fault would be to subject the co-assured to a liability for loss and damage caused by a peril insured for his benefit. As I said in *Stone Vickers*, it is necessary to imply a term into the policy of insurance to avoid this unsatisfactory possibility. The implication of such a term is needed to give effect to what must have been the mutual intention (on this hypothesis) of the principal assured and the insurers, as to the risks covered by the policy. On this basis, the purported exercise by insurers of rights of subrogation against the co-assured would be in breach of such a term and would, accordingly, provide the co-assured with a defence to the subrogated claim in the manner which I explained in the passage cited from my judgment.

[p 614] ... For these reasons I am firmly of the view that the conclusion arrived at by Lloyd J, in *Petrofina*, was right: an insurer cannot exercise rights of subrogation against a co-assured under an insurance on property in which the co-assured has the benefit of cover which protects him against the very loss or damage to the insured property which forms the basis of the claim which underwriters seek to pursue by way of subrogation. The reason why the insurer cannot pursue such a claim is that to do so would be in breach of an implied term in the policy and, to that extent, the principles of circuity of action operate to exclude the claim.

[p 616] ... if DOL's claim on NOW includes losses attributable to NOW's wilful misconduct, such could not provide NOW with the basis of any claim on insurers, first because the policy does not insure such claims, and secondly, because the putting forward of such claims would be fraudulent and would discharge the insurers from all liability relating to such losses. Accordingly, if insurers then proceeded to pay DOL in respect of such losses and purported to exercise rights of subrogation against NOW, that exercise of rights of subrogation would fall outside the scope of the term which I have held to be implied in the policy preventing the making of subrogated claims against a co-assured in respect of losses covered for the benefit of that co-assured. This would not be the case of an insurer trying to use rights of subrogation to recoup a loss insured for the benefit of a co-assured. In this case, the co-assured could not have claimed under the policy in respect of those losses and therefore the whole basis of the subrogation defence would have gone.

Notes

It can now be safely asserted that, in the case of joint insurance, there is a 'fundamental rule' that an insurer cannot exercise a right of subrogation against one of the co-assured in the name of the other. The problem which is likely to arise in each case is one of fact, namely, whether the parties are, in fact, co-assured. Whether the relationship be one of bailor and bailee (see *The Yasin* [1979] 2 Lloyd's Rep 45); contractor and sub-contractor (see *Petrofina (UK) Ltd and Others v Magnaload Ltd and Others* [1983] 2 Lloyd's Rep 91 and *Stone Vickers Ltd v Appledore Ferguson Shipbuilders Ltd* [1992] 2 Lloyd's Rep 578, CA; or shipowner and mortgagee (see *Samuel v Dumas* (1928) 18 LlL Rep 211, HL) the first question for determination is, what is the relationship of the relevant parties under the policy: are their interests in the policy so 'inseparably connected' as to make them co-assured?

In *The Yasin*, as the defendants, who were the shipowners, were unable to demonstrate to the satisfaction of the court that they and the cargo-owners were co-assured under the policy, it was unnecessary for the court to proceed to the second stage of the inquiry pertaining to the legitimacy of the exercise of the right of subrogation by the cargo insurers.

Similarly, in *Stone Vickers*, the Court of Appeal, which overturned the decision of the court of first instance, found on the evidence and construction of the policy that the plaintiffs and the defendants, the subcontractors and the contractor of a shipbuilding contract respectively, were not co-assured. On the other hand, in *Petrofina*, Lloyd J held that, as the contractors and subcontractors engaged on a common enterprise under a building contract were co-assured, the fundamental rule of law, that insurers can never sue one co-assured in the name of another, applied.

The issue of whether an insurer, who has indemnified an innocent mortgagee for a loss, could, by way of subrogation, bring an action against the shipowner in order to recoup his loss, was discussed in *Samuel v Dumas*

(1928) 18 LlL Rep 211, HL, by Viscount Cave, p 214. If the mortgagee and the shipowner were jointly insured and their interests are 'inseparably connected', the misconduct of one was, according to Viscount Cave, sufficient to contaminate the whole insurance. The converse position is that, if 'there is no difficulty in separating the interests of the mortgagee from that of the owner, and if the mortgagee should recover on the policy, the owner will not be advantaged, as the insurers will be subrogated as against him to the rights of the mortgagee'.

An insurer cannot recoup gifts and voluntary payments

Gifts and voluntary payments lie outside what an insurer may recoup from an insured who has been indemnified for a loss: this is because such gifts and voluntary payments are 'not given with the intention of reducing the loss'. In **Burnard v Rodocanachi (1885) 7 App Cas 333, HL**, insured cargo was lost during the American Civil War when it was destroyed by the Confederate cruiser *Alabama*. The underwriters indemnified the cargo-owners for their loss, but, as the United States Government also paid compensation to the cargo owners, the insurers claimed, on the basis of subrogation, that they were entitled to the compensation.

However, the House of Lords ruled that the insurers were not entitled to the compensation, because the compensation paid by the United States Government to the cargo-owners was a voluntary gift, not a payment made to reduce the loss.

> **Lord Blackburn**: [p 341] ... In the present case, the Government of the United States did not pay it [the compensation] with the intention of reducing the loss. Lord Coleridge [at the Court of Appeal] says in his judgment, and says very truly, that the Government of the United States cannot by any action of theirs deprive a man, suing in this country, of any right which he has. I quite agree in that; but I think that Lord Coleridge, if he had taken the same view as I do of the matter, would have seen that an Act of Congress of the United States might effectively prevent any such right arising. If, once the right had vested to recover any such sum, of course an Act of Congress could not take it away; but when Congress in express terms say, 'We do not pay the money for the purpose of repaying or reducing the loss against which the insurance company have indemnified, but for another and a different purpose', it effectively prevents the right rising. Bramwell LJ, in his judgment, has used the phrase, 'It was not given as salvage'. I should, myself, prefer to use my own phrase expressing the same idea, and to say that it was not paid in such a manner as to reduce the loss against which the plaintiffs had to indemnify the defendants; it is the same thing, but rather differently expressed.

The subrogation waiver clause

It is a common feature in the oil industry for oil companies, through subsidiaries, also to own the tankers which transport their oil. In such circumstances, if a loss takes place at sea and the cargo-owner claims on his policy of insurance for that loss, the cargo-owner's insurer, on payment, would have bestowed on him, by way of subrogation, the right to pursue the carrier for redress. In a roundabout way, the same company would have stood the loss.

Furthermore, given the circumstance where the carrier and a seller of a cargo are fundamentally one and the same, the similar problem could arise where a cargo is sold CIF.[27] Many oil cargoes are sold CIF where, although the risk passes on shipment, the buyer still has the option of rejecting the documents if they are not in order, thereby avoiding payment. Should the CIF buyer reject the documents, for whatever reason, and the cargo is lost, the loss falls upon the seller. If the seller then claims on his policy for that loss, again, the seller's insurer could, after payment, pursue the carrier-cum-seller by way of subrogation.

Thus, where a company has, at any stage, a vested interest in both the cargo and the carriage of the cargo, it makes good commercial sense, when insuring the shipment, to employ, in the policy of insurance, a 'subrogation waiver clause'. Such a clause, in the event of a loss during the sea transit, would prevent the insurer, after having indemnified the assured, from pursuing (using his rights under subrogation) against the carrier.

However, in the *Surf City* case, below, where a 'subrogation waiver clause' was employed, the court confirmed that the said clause was not only applicable to the original assured (the CIF seller), but was also applicable to an assignee of the policy (the CIF buyer).

Enimont Supply SA v Chesapeake Shipping Inc, 'Surf City' [1995] 2 Lloyd's Rep 242

In February 1990, one day out of Kuwait, the tanker *Surf City*, which was carrying a cargo of naptha and gas oil, exploded and caught fire. The fire was brought under control by the salvors operating under Lloyd's form. Gulf Insurance indemnified Enimont, the CIF buyers of part of the cargo of naptha, for their loss and then sought, by way of subrogation, to recover their loss from Chesapeake Shipping, the owners of *Surf City*. Chesapeake Shipping

---

27 Cost, insurance and freight. The seller arranges the contract of carriage, insures the goods and pays the freight. The documents (bill of lading, certificate of insurance, invoice, customs requirements, etc) are then passed to the buyer who, on acceptance, must then pay for the goods. The buyer may reject those documents if they if they do not conform with the description in the contract or the requirements of the Sale of Goods Act 1979.

contended that Gulf Insurance had no rights of subrogation, because of a term in the policy of insurance, cl 6 of the Bulk Oil Clauses (dated January 1962), which stated: 'It is agreed that no right of subrogation except through general average, shall lie against any vessel ... on which cargo hereby insured is being carried ... belonging in part or in whole to a subsidiary and/or affiliated company.'[28] Gulf Insurance accepted that cl 6 precluded them from claiming against the original assured, the CIF sellers, but contended that, as Enimont were CIF buyers, they were not a party to the original insurance, and as they were assignees to the policy of insurance, cl 6 did not apply.

The court ruled that Chesapeake Shipping were entitled to rely on the right of subrogation waiver clause, because cl 6 applied not only to the original assured, the CIF seller, but also to the CIF buyer to whom the policy had been assigned.

> **Clarke J:** [p 246] ... A shipper who sells cargo CIF and who regularly arranges the carriage of such cargo on vessels owned by companies which are part of his group will naturally wish to ensure that if the cargo is lost in circumstances in which, for some reason, the buyer rejects the documents, he will be able to recover from his insurer without the insurer being able to claim the money back from his subsidiary as owner of the carrying ship.
>
> ... It does not seem to me to follow from those considerations that because the assured's subsidiary will be protected where the assured is paid under the policy, the clause means that it is not to be protected where the insurer pays the CIF buyer and not the original insured.
>
> [p 247] ... The insured CIF seller will naturally wish to protect vessels owned by his subsidiary. As I see it, he will wish to do so whether the insurer pays him or his buyer. In both cases his interest will be the same, namely, the protection of vessels within his group which he is using to carry the cargo. That interest does not cease just because the documents are negotiated to the buyer. Some of the clauses which form part of the Bulk Oil Clauses expressly refer to the assured, while some do not. But, they all seem to me to be concerned with the rights of the assured. Thus, on its face, cl 6 seems to me to protect subsidiaries of the assured.
>
> The question then arises whether, on the true construction of the clause, that protection is lost when the documents are delivered to a CIF buyer. In my judgment, there is nothing in the wording of cl 6 which leads to that conclusion. However, Mr Teare [for the plaintiffs, Gulf Insurance] submits that the effect of delivery of the insurance policy to the buyer is to assign the benefit of the waiver to the buyer, and that thereafter only the assignee is entitled to the benefit of the waiver of the right of subrogation in cl 6 and not the original assured: and then only if the assignee is paid under the policy.
>
> ... I am unable to accept that submission. However, it does not follow that, when the documents are tendered to the buyer and the beneficial interest in

---

28 It would appear that there is no subrogation waiver clause in the current version of the Institute Bulk Oil Clauses (1/2/83).

the policy is assigned, at least in part, to the buyer, the original assured loses the benefit of cl 6 ... there is nothing in the wording of the clause that supports the conclusion that he does. Moreover, for the reasons I have given, there is no good reason why the original assured should surrender the protection offered to the carrying ship owned by his subsidiary when the documents are transferred.

The same is, I think, true if the matter is viewed from the point of view of the insurer. The clause shows that the insurer is willing to waive his rights against the carrying ship where a CIF buyer procures the carriage in a vessel owned by a company in his group. I see no good commercial reason why he should not be willing to do so throughout the carriage. It makes no commercial sense to say that the waiver applies only so long as the loss is sustained by the assured and not when it is sustained by the buyer.

Under-insurance: apportionment of moneys recovered from a third party wrongdoer

Where an assured is under-insured, he is said to be his own insurer for the amount of that under-insurance. If moneys are then recovered from a third party wrongdoer, these moneys must, under marine insurance law, be apportioned between the insurer and the assured as a proportion of their insurance liability to the sum recovered. This concept was particularly well illustrated in *The Commonwealth* [1907] P 216, CA, below.

The Commonwealth [1907] P 216, CA

A schooner, *Welsh Girl*, was run down by the steamship *The Commonwealth*, and was totally lost. *Welsh Girl* was valued at £1,350, but was only insured for £1,000. After the insurers had paid the owners of *Welsh Girl* the £1,000 indemnity, they pursued the owners of *The Commonwealth* by way of subrogation, recovered £1,000, and contended that they, the insurers, were entitled to the whole sum.

The Court of Appeal ruled that, as the value of *Welsh Girl* was £1,350 and the underwriters were only liable for £1,000, the owners of *Welsh Girl* were self-insured for the remaining £350. Thus, the apportionment of the sum recovered from the third party should be 350/1,350ths to the owners and 1,000/1,350ths to the underwriters.

Sir Gorrell Barnes: [p 223] ... It seems to me, however, that when the underwriter pays the assured, he is subrogated to his rights having regard to the risk he has taken – that is to say, in the present case, when the assured's name is used for the purpose of enforcing an action against a wrongdoer, the remedy is sought for the underwriter to the extent to which he had insured, and for the assured to the extent to which he had left himself uninsured. That being so, it seems logically to follow that, when the money which is recovered in hand, it ought to be divided in proportion to the respective interests. That seems to me reasonable in principle, and, although there is no authority for it, it also seems to me to be analogous to the case of salvage where there is abandonment. That being so, it follows that the proportions which ought to be recovered in a case of this kind are easily ascertained; £1,000 was recovered from the wrongdoer, partly for the owner and partly for the underwriter, and, therefore, the proportion becomes 350/1350ths in the one case and 1000/1350ths in the other.

Notes

It is emphasised that, in the case of under-insurance, when calculating the apportionment of moneys recovered from a third party wrongdoer, any 'excess' (deductible) for which the assured was liable before the insurer himself became liable under the policy is to be totally ignored.[29]

References and further reading

Parks, AL, 'Marine insurance principles: contracts formation and interpretation' [1977] The Maritime Lawyer 127

Thomas, RT, 'Perspectives on the contract of marine insurance', in *The Modern Law of Marine Insurance*, 1996, London, LLP, p 1

---

29 Other forms of insurance use a 'top down' or 'recover down' layer system of apportionment. For more information on this issue, see Merkin, R, *Annotated Marine Insurance Legislation*, 1997, London: LLP, Chapter 7, p 58.

CHAPTER 2

INSURABLE INTEREST

INTRODUCTION

The law of insurable interest is set out in general terms in s 5 of the Marine Insurance Act 1906. The main requirement of insurable interest is, it would appear, to stamp out wagering contracts. It is also linked to the fact that a contract of marine insurance is a contract of indemnity; thus, an assured must first show that he has suffered a loss before he can put in a valid claim under the policy. A person can only suffer a loss if he has an interest in the subject matter insured; if he has no interest in the subject matter insured, he suffers no loss, and the contract of insurance is effectively a gamble or a wager, and, therefore, void under s 4 of the Act.

To have an insurable interest the assured must be 'interested' in a marine adventure. In the language of s 5(2), '... a person is interested in a marine adventure where he stands in any legal or equitable relationship to the adventure or to any insurable property at risk therein'. That this covers a wide range of persons is obvious: it includes the owner of the insurable property, a mortgagee and even an insurer. Apart from these three main classes, there are also other persons who might have an insurable interest in the subject matter insured, such as agents, executors, lien holders and trustees. The general principles applicable are the same in all cases.

The concept of insurable interest is broad; a person does not have to have a whole interest in the subject matter insured. The Act provides that limited forms of interest are also insurable, such as a partial interest (s 8), and a contingent or defeasible interest (s 7). The latter are interests the acquisition of which depends upon certain contingencies; for instance, a buyer may reject the goods on arrival if he is not satisfied with their condition, in which case the property in the goods reverts to the seller. The main problem with insurable interest concerns the time at which the interest must attach; as a general rule, the assured must, *at the time of the loss*, have an insurable interest in the subject matter insured. In contracts of international sale of goods, it is not always easy to ascertain at any given time whether the property has in fact passed from seller to buyer.

The law recognises certain exceptions to the general rule that the assured must have an insurable interest at the time of the loss. First, if the policy offers cover on a 'lost or not lost' basis, then the assured is, according to the proviso to s 6(1)[1] permitted to recover under the policy even though the loss was sustained before the insurance was effected. This exception operates to protect an assured who might have purchased goods without knowing whether or not they have already been lost at sea. Secondly, an assignee of a policy can acquire an interest in the subject matter insured even though the policy was assigned to him only after the loss, provided, of course, that the assignor himself had, at the time of assignment, an interest to assign.[2]

DEFINITIONS OF INSURABLE INTEREST

Section 5 of the Act defines 'insurable interest' as follows:
(1) Subject to the provisions of this Act, every person who is interested in a marine adventure.
(2) In particular, a person is interested in a marine adventure where he stands in any legal or equitable relation to the adventure or to any insurable property at risk therein, in consequence of which he may benefit by the safety or due arrival of insurable property, or may be prejudiced by its loss, or by damage thereto, or by the detention thereof, or may incur liability in respect thereof.

The most comprehensive of judicial pronouncements on the subject of insurable interest before the Act were delivered by Lord Eldon and Lawrence J, in *Lucena v Craufurd*, below. It would appear that the sentiments of Lord Eldon have been incorporated in the definition provided in s 5(2) of the Act, to the effect that the assured must stand in some relationship recognised by law to the subject matter insured.

Lucena v Craufurd (1806) 2 B&P (NR) 269, HL

The assured were the Commissioners of Admiralty, whose duty was, under statute, to take care of Dutch vessels and cargoes 'which had been or might be thereafter detained in or brought into the ports of the United Kingdom'. Before the commission was issued, certain Dutch vessels and their cargoes had been seized by order of the British Government for the purpose of being brought to England. After the commission was issued, the Commissioners insured these ships and their cargoes. The ships were lost during their voyage

---

1 The proviso reads: 'Provided that where the subject matter is insured "lost or not lost", the assured may recover although he may not have acquired his interest until after the loss, unless at the time of effecting the contract of insurance the assured was aware of the loss, and the insurer was not.'

2 Marine Insurance Act 1906, s 51: 'Where the assured has parted with or lost his interest in the subject matter insured, and has not, before or at the time of so doing, expressly or impliedly agreed to assign the policy, any subsequent assignment of the policy is inoperative: provided that nothing in this section affects the assignment of a policy after loss.'

to England. The Commissioners then sought to recover under the policy. The insurer's defence was that the Commissioners had no insurable interest in the ships at the time of loss.

The House of Lords upheld the insurer's defence on the basis that the Commissioners' duty was to take care of the ships only *after* their arrival. Since the ships had not yet arrived in England at the time of loss, the Commissioners did not have an insurable interest. A panel of judges was summoned to advise the House on the issues raised; notably, Lawrence J offered his perception, sometimes referred to as 'the moral certainty' or the 'factual expectancy' test, of what constitutes 'insurable interest'.

Chambre J: [p 298] ... To constitute an interest, such as that which in the declaration is averred to be vested in the plaintiffs as Commissioners under the Act, I presume it must be necessary to show that the ships and goods at the time of the sailing, or at least before or at the times of the losses, had become the objects of the plaintiff's commission. If they were not the objects of their commission, I have no conception in what way they could have an interest in them as Commissioners.

Lawrence J: [p 300] ... It is first to be considered what that interest is, the protection of which is the proper object of a policy of assurance. And this is to be collected from considering what is the nature of such contract.

[p 301] ... that insurance is a contract by which the one party in consideration of a price paid to him adequate to the risk, becomes security to the other that he shall not suffer loss, damage, or prejudice by the happening of the perils specified to certain things which may be exposed to them.

[p 302] ... That a man must somehow or other be interested in the preservation of the subject matter exposed to perils, follows from the nature of this contract, when not used as a mode of wager, but as applicable to the purposes for which it was originally introduced; but to confine it to the protection of the interest which arises out of property, is adding a restriction to the contract which does not arise out of its nature ... A man is interested in a thing to whom advantage may arise or prejudice happen from the circumstances which may attend it ... And whom it importeth, that its condition as to safety or other quality should continue: interest does not necessarily imply a right to the whole, or a part of a thing, nor necessarily and exclusively that which may be the subject of privation, but the having some relation to, or concern in the subject of insurance, which relation or concern by the happening of the perils insured against may be so affected as to produce a damage, detriment, or prejudice to the person insuring: and where a man is so circumstanced with respect to matters exposed to certain risks or dangers, as to have *a moral certainty of advantage or benefit* [emphasis added], but for those risks or dangers he may be said to be interested in the safety of the thing. To be interested in the preservation of a thing is to be so circumstanced with respect to it as to have benefit from its existence, prejudice from its destruction. The property of a thing and the interest devisable from it may be very different: of the first, the price is generally the measure, but by interest in a thing every benefit and advantage arising out of or depending on such thing, may be considered as being comprehended.

Lord Eldon: [p 318] ... Accordingly, the power of the Commissioners is expressly limited to ships and goods that have actually come, or been brought into the ports of Great Britain ... and it appears to me ... that there is nothing in this Act of Parliament which touches the prerogative while the ships and cargoes were at sea ...

[p 321] ... Since the 19 Geo 2, it is clear that the insured must have an interest, whatever we understand by that term. In order to distinguish that intermediate thing between a strict right, or a right derived under a contract, and a mere expectation or hope, which has been termed an insurable interest, it has been said in many cases to be that which amount to a moral certainty. I have in vain endeavoured, however, to find a fit definition of that which is between a certainty and an expectation; nor am I able to point out what is an interest unless it be a right in the property, or a right derivable out of some contract about the property, which in either case may be lost upon some contingency affecting the possession or enjoyment of the party.

[p 323] ... That expectation, though founded upon the highest probability, was not interest, and it was equally not interest, whatever might have been the chances in favour of the expectation.

[p 324] ... If moral certainty be a ground of insurable interest, there are hundreds, perhaps thousands, who would be entitled to insure. First, the dock company, then the dock master, then the warehouse keeper, then the porter, then every other person who to a moral certainty would have anything to do with the property, and of course get something by it.

Notes

It can be seen from the above that Lawrence J had adopted a wide and most liberal approach, whilst Lord Eldon, a narrow and more legalistic approach to the term. It is pertinent to note that, recently, the ambit of the concept of 'insurable interest' had occasion to be looked at afresh in a trilogy of successive cases, the most notable of which is the *Moonacre* case, below, all of which were presided over by the same judge.[3] Though these cases were not concerned with a hull policy of insurance, nevertheless, the statements made by Colman J are significant, for they provide us with a better insight into how the law of insurable interest could be developed. A hint of recognition of a much more flexible and wider interpretation of the notion can be gleaned from the language used by Colman J. Whether the legal principle so expressed (in somewhat generous terms) is indicative of the beginning of a new trend in this area of law is, of course, yet to be confirmed: in this country, the precise scope of the concept awaits judicial confirmation from higher authority.[4] It

---

[3] See *Stone Vickers Ltd v Appledore Ferguson Shipbuilders Ltd* [1991] 2 Lloyd's Rep 288 and *National Oilwell (UK) Ltd v Davy Offshore Ltd* [1993] 2 Lloyd's Rep 582.

[4] In *Cepheus Shipping Corpn v Guardian Royal Exchange Assurance plc, 'Capricorn'* [1995] 1 Lloyd's Rep 622, Mance J gave a restrictive interpretation to the term: see below, p 61. See, also, *Glengate-KG Properties Ltd v Norwich Union Fire Insurance Society Ltd* [1996] 2 All ER 487, CA, a non-marine case.

appears that, in Canada[5] and the USA, the wider test of Lawrence J is now preferred.

Chalmers observes and warns: 'The definition of "insurable interest" has been continuously expanding, and *dicta* in some of the older cases, which would tend to narrow it, must be accepted with caution.'[6] The same sentiments are expressed in Arnould as follows: 'The legal conception of insurable interest has been continuously expanding, and possibly the court may, on some future occasion, continue this procession of expansion ...'[7]

Anthony John Sharp and Roarer Investments Ltd v Sphere Drake Insurance plc, Minster Insurance Co Ltd and EC Parker and Co Ltd, 'Moonacre' [1992] 2 Lloyd's Rep 501

Insurance was taken out for the motor yacht *Moonacre* which, for all intents and purposes, was owned by a Mr Sharp. But for tax purposes, a company, Roarer Investments, incorporated in Gibraltar, was registered as owner of *Moonacre*. Mr Sharp was then given power of attorney by the registered company to sail and manage the vessel, and he was also named as the assured in the contract of insurance. During the policy, whilst the single crewman employed on board *Moonacre* was away, she caught fire at her moorings and became a constructive total loss. When the assured, Mr Sharp, sought to recover under the policy, the insurers declined payment on the grounds, *inter alia*, that Mr Sharp did not possess any insurable interest in *Moonacre*.

The court ruled that Mr Sharp did, in fact, have an insurable interest in the yacht.

> **Deputy Judge Colman QC:** [p 509] ... Before considering these submissions in detail, it is helpful to keep in mind the purpose behind the requirement that the assured should have an insurable interest in the insured property before he is permitted to recover under a marine policy. By the beginning of the 18th century, a contact of marine insurance could be enforced at common law by the assured notwithstanding he had no personal interest in the subject matter of the insurance, that is to say, even if he stood neither to lose nor to gain from the success or failure of the adventure or the loss or survival of the insured property. These contracts were, in substance, wagering contracts. It was only by a 1745 Act (19 Geo 2 c 37) that such contracts were declared to be null and void in respect of British ships and their cargoes ... The Gaming Act 1845, s 18, had the effect of making void all contracts of insurance which were wagers by reason of the assured's lack of interest in the subject matter of the policy. Eventually, by s 4 of the Marine Insurance Act 1906, it was provided: (1) Every contract of marine insurance by way of gaming or wager is void ...

---

5 See *Constitution Insurance Co of Canada et al v Kosmopoulos et al* (1987) 34 DLR (4th) 208, Supreme Court of Canada, discussed below, p 70. Cf *Guarantee Co of North America v Aqua-land Exploration Ltd* (1965) 54 DLR (2nd) 229; [1966] SCR 133.
6 Chalmers, D, *Marine Insurance Act 1906*, 10th edn, 1993, London: Butterworths, p 11.
7 Arnould, J, *Law of Marine Insurance and Average*, 16th edn, 1981, London: Sweet & Maxwell, Vol 1, para 362.

[p 510] ... Accordingly, the essential question to be investigated in those cases which, since 1745, have been concerned to test the existence of an insurable interest, has been whether the relationship between the assured and the subject matter of the insurance was sufficiently close to justify his being paid in the event of its loss or damage, having regard to the fact that, if there were no or no sufficiently close relationship, the contract would be a wagering contract.

[p 510] ... Neither the words of any statute since 1845 nor any judicial pronouncement suggest that there should be a category of contracts of insurance which were not wagering contracts but which, on account of the absence of an 'insurable interest', should not be enforceable. Accordingly, in approaching the construction and application of s 5 of the Marine Insurance Act it is, in my judgment, right to proceed on the assumption that, provided the assured has sufficient interest in the subject matter of the insurance to prevent his contract being a wagering contract, he is entitled to enforce that contract.

The starting point for consideration of the meaning of 'insurable interest' under s 5(1) is, clearly, s 5(2). This does not provide an exhaustive definition, but it does identify three characteristics which the presence of an insurable interest would normally require: (a) the assured may benefit by the safety or due arrival of insurable property or be prejudiced by its loss or damage or in respect of which he may incur liability; (b) the assured stands in a legal or equitable relation to the adventure or to any insurable property at risk in such adventure; (c) the benefit, prejudice or incurring of liability referred to at (a) must arise in consequence of the legal or equitable relation referred to at (b).

... That which brings about the benefit to the assured from the safety or due arrival of the property and that which brings about the possibility of his prejudice from its loss, damage or detention or his incurring liability in respect of such property must, therefore, be the 'legal or equitable relation' to the adventure or property in which the assured stands. That must involve an investigation of whether there have been conferred on him any rights recognised by law or in equity or imposed on him any obligations so recognised in respect of the adventure or the insured property the enjoyment of which rights may be lost or interfered with or the performance of which obligations may be brought about or rendered more onerous by the incidence of an insured peril.

Later, Colman J (as he became) was afforded further opportunity to discuss the matter in *National Oilwell (UK) Ltd v Davy Offshore Ltd* **[1993] 2 Lloyd's Rep 582**[8] (hereinafter referred to as *NOW v DOL*). This time, he extended the definition of insurable interest to cover a case in which the assured was not in possession of property, but his relation to it was such that he may incur liability in respect of the property being damaged. *NOW v DOL* was concerned with a dispute relating to defective equipment supplied by NOW. Whilst NOW sought to recover in respect of unpaid invoices, DOL counterclaimed, *inter alia*, that the plaintiffs (NOW) had no insurable interest

---

8   The full facts of the case are recited above, Chapter 1, p 31.

in any of the insured property after they had been delivered to DOL. Not surprisingly, Colman J, relying on the *Moonacre* case, ruled that NOW had an insurable interest by reason of their potential liability in respect of loss or damage in the equipment.

Colman J: [p 611] ... There is, in my judgment, in particular no reason in principle why such a supplier should not, and every commercial reason why he should, be able to insure against loss or damage to property involved in the common project not owned by him and not in his possession. The argument that, because he has no possessory or proprietary interest in the property, he can have no insurable interest in it and that his potential liability in respect of loss of or damage to it is insufficient to found such an insurable interest, is, in my judgment, misconceived. That the presence of such an interest in the proper insured is unnecessary to found an insurance interest was a point which arose in *Moonacre* [1992] 2 Lloyd's Rep 501, where the issue was whether the plaintiff had an insurable interest in a yacht of which he was not the registered owner, or the bailee or the charter, but which he merely sailed under a power of attorney from the registered owner. I rejected the submissions on behalf of underwriters that he had no insurable interest and I endeavoured to explain that, in order to establish a sufficient relation to the property in question, having regard to the decisions in *Lucena v Craufurd* [1806] 2 B&P (NR) 269, *John Anderson v James Farquhar Morice* (1876) 1 App Cas 713 and *Macaura v Northern Assurance Co Ltd* (1925) 21 LlL Rep 333; [1925] AC 619, it might in some cases be unnecessary to establish that the assured had any proprietary legal or equitable interest in the goods: see pp 510–13.

The suggestion that there cannot, as a matter of law, be an insurable interest based merely on potential liability arising from the existence of a contract between the assured and the owner of property or from the assured's proximate physical relationship to the property in question, is, in my judgment, to confine far too narrowly the requirements of insurable interest. There is nothing in the authorities which prevents such a relationship to the property from giving rise to an insurable interest in the property for the purposes of an insurance on property. In *Stone Vickers v Appledore Ferguson Shipbuilders, supra*, I sought to explain the identification of an insurance interest in such multi-participant projects in the passage at p 301 already cited.

It is no doubt true that the conventional means of obtaining in the marine insurance market protection against such liability for property damage is to take out a liability policy, and for the purposes of such policy there is no question that the assured would have an insurable interest in his potential liability. But the fact that he has an insurable interest for that kind of risks does not lead to the conclusion that he cannot have an insurable interest in the property itself for the purpose of a policy on property risks. The fact that the market does not offer such policies is neither here not [sic] there. What matters is whether, if such a policy were effected, the assured would have a sufficient relationship with the subject matter to give rise to an insurable interest. In my judgment, he would.

Notes

In the third case presided over by Deputy Judge Colman (as he then was), *Stone Vickers Ltd v Appledore Ferguson Shipbuilders Ltd* [1991] 2 Lloyd's Rep 288, which he referred to in *NOW v DOL*, there was no need for any discussion on the law of insurable interest because, as the judge had little doubt that the subcontractors (the plaintiffs), responsible for the construction and the supply of equipment, had sufficient interest in the whole contract to be entitled to be regarded as a co-assured. However, on appeal,[9] the court, on the evidence and construction of the policy, found otherwise: as the subcontractors were not intended to have the benefit of the insurance, they could not be considered as a co-assured of the policy for builders' risks subscribed by the main contractor.

THE ASSURED

It is of utmost importance to determine the persons who stand in 'any legal or equitable relationship to the adventure or to any insurable property at risk therein,' as stated in s 5(2). The Act recognises the shipowner, the mortgagee and the insurer as obvious examples of persons who have legal rights in the property and, thus, an insurable interest. Besides these categories, there are other persons recognised by case law to have an insurable interest, such as captors and agents who might accrue a benefit from the preservation of the subject matter insured. All these people are the 'assured' under the policy, and will be entitled to be indemnified should they sustain a loss.

Owner of a ship

The owner of a ship is, of course, entitled to insure her for her full value. He is thus allowed to recover for any loss or damage to his ship, notwithstanding that a third party may have agreed to indemnify him for the loss.[10] The difficulty sometimes arises in ascertaining who, at any given time, the true owner of the vessel is, especially when there is a sale, and property changes hands. The following case is an example of a dispute arising as to the ownership of the vessel with regard to passing of property.

---

9   [1992] 2 Lloyd's Rep 578, CA. The main issue, in both the court of first instance and on appeal, was concerned with the application of the fundamental rule that an insurer cannot exercise his right of subrogation against a co-assured. As the Court of Appeal had, on the evidence and construction of the policy, found that the plaintiffs (the subcontractors) were not a co-assured, the said fundamental rule did not apply. For a further discussion of this rule, see Chapter 1, p 32.

10 See Marine Insurance Act 1906, s 14(3): the owner of insurable property has an insurable interest in respect of the full value thereof, notwithstanding that some third person may have agreed, or be liable, to indemnify him in case of loss.

Piper v Royal Exchange Assurance (1932) 44 LlL Rep 103

The assured bought a yacht in Norway 'as she lies'. The yacht was to be delivered to England and was, until her arrival, at the risk of the seller. On the voyage to England, the vessel sustained some damage. The buyer claimed upon the policy, and was indemnified for the loss.

The court ruled that, since the risk was on the seller during the voyage, the buyer had no insurable interest at the time of loss. The underwriters, therefore, having paid under a mistake of fact, were entitled to recoup the amount they had paid to the assured buyer.

> **Roche J:** [p 116] ... Now, in those circumstances the underwriters say: 'We insured the plaintiff through the broker on the basis that he had an interest, and we paid him on the basis that he had an interest, and he had not, and in those circumstances we claim the recovery back of the sum which we paid in settlement of this particular average claim.'
>
> In my judgment, the underwriters are so entitled. The matter depends now as regards interest upon the Marine Insurance Act 1906, and ss 5 and 6 deal with the question of interest, with its attachment; and there are some other sections following upon that which deal with other topics of interest. Section 26 deals with the designation of the subject matter. I need not read these sections; they have been read and re-read in the course of the argument. Suffice it to say that, in my judgment, the plaintiff had no interest here. It is unnecessary to decide, but it is probable that he had an interest, not in the ship itself, but in its arrival, which might have been insured and constituted an insurable contingent interest, but I think it ought to have been so described, and this is just one of those matters of interest which requires to be defined, because it is necessary still to define the subject matter insured, although it is not necessary to specify the nature and extent of the injuries of the subject matter insured.

A person with power of attorney

In *Moonacre* **[1992] 2 Lloyd's Rep 501**, the facts of which have been cited earlier,[11] Deputy Judge Colman QC had to consider the point of whether a person who has been given power of attorney to sail and manage a yacht had an insurable interest in her. The judge dealt with the issue in the following manner.

> **Deputy Judge Colman QC:** [p 512] ... The insurers pray this case [referring to *Macaura v Northern Assurance Co Ltd*][12] in aid as an illustration of the proposition that even if the assured is a bailee of the goods, if he has no responsibility for them or beneficial right in respect of them he has no insurable interest in them. They contend that Mr Sharp was a mere licensee of the vessel and not even a bailee – having no responsibility for its safety,

---

11 See above, p 43.
12 (1925) 21 LlL Rep 333, HL. This case is further discussed in depth below, p 67.

because such a duty would be inconsistent with his purpose of insulating himself as completely as possible from the vessel for tax purposes ...

Let it be assumed that Mr Sharp was indeed no more than a licensee and further that he was subject to no duty of care in relation to the vessel, can it be said that he is in no materially different relation to the vessel from that of Mr Macaura to the timber? Such a submission entirely overlooks the fact that by the two powers of attorney Roarer had conferred on Mr Sharp authority to enjoy the use of the vessel exclusively for his own purposes. That was a valuable benefit which would be lost if the vessel were lost. The legal relation in which he stood to the vessel was that, for as long as the powers of attorney remained, he was entitled to use it for his own purposes and to exercise over it such control as he saw fit. His powers were such that he could even abandon it to the insurers in the event of a constructive total loss; a relation to the goods sometimes considered decisive on the issue of title to sue ...

... In my judgment, Mr Sharp, by reason of the powers of attorney, stood in a legal relationship to the vessel in consequence of which he would benefit from the preservation of the vessel and, if the vessel were lost or damaged, he would suffer loss of a valuable benefit. I therefore hold that he had an insurable interest in the vessel.

[p 513] ... Although, no doubt, the authority given to a master in respect of his ship and the terms on which the owners employ him will not normally give rise to the passing of possession, that is not impossible. In any event, the terms on which Mr Sharp was appointed skipper and the powers vested in him are so fundamentally different from the terms normally to be expected that Mr Sharp stands in a quite different relationship to his vessel from that relationship normally found in the articles of employment of a master. Moreover, as I have already held, the existence of an insurable interest does not depend in this case on whether there was a relationship of bailment. If, however, this is not right, I consider that, given the wide terms of the powers of attorney, the master was given such degree of control as to amount to the passing of possession of the vessel in this case and was accordingly its bailee ... That said, the terms of the bailment in this case are such that they conferred on the bailee a valuable benefit and the risk of loss of that benefit could quite properly found an insurable interest in the vessel itself.

I express no concluded view on the question whether, having regard to the terms on which Mr Sharp controlled the vessel, he was under any personal duty to Roarer to exercise reasonable care over the vessel and her operation. If there were such a duty of care, clearly, Mr Sharp could insure the vessel against marine perils and if the vessel were lost and even though he had incurred no such liability, he would be entitled as against the insurers to recover the value of the vessel and hold it as trustee for Roarer ... My provisional view is that Mr Sharp did owe a duty to Roarer to exercise reasonable care over the management and navigation of the vessel, and that on these grounds alone, he would have had an insurable interest in her.

... If, as I have held, Mr Sharp had an insurable interest in the vessel, he could sue on the policy, and it is unnecessary to decide whether Roarer was interested in the policy and could sue on it. However, in case this matter goes further, I shall set out my conclusions on this issue.

[p 514] ... Did Mr Sharp have the authority of Roarer to act as its agent to enter into a contract of insurance? I am unable to accept the plaintiffs' submissions on this point ... The express authority which Roarer gave to Mr Sharp to purchase the vessel and register it in the company's name as evidenced by his solicitors' attendance ... gave rise to no such implication of authority. Those documents evidence express authority confined to two functions only – purchase and registration. There is no basis upon which it can be reasonably suggested that Mr Sharp was additionally, by implication, thereby authorised to create privity of contract between the company and insurers.

[p 515] Can Roarer rely on ratification of the contract? In my judgment, the plaintiffs were not entitled to ratify the contract. The policy entered into by Mr Sharp was not a contract in the name of Roarer, but in his own name. It was not even a policy entered into in his own name and for the benefit of an additional class of persons 'for their respective rights and interests' ... Where the agent has not purported to create privity of contract, he has not done any act for which he lacked authority. His uncommunicated intention to bind the principal is irrelevant. There was, therefore, nothing capable of ratification in the present case. Once the proposal had been made in the name of Mr Sharp alone and the policy issued only in his name, the parties to the contract were fixed and confined to those in whose names the contract was expressed to be made, namely, Mr Sharp and the insurers.

... In my judgment, Roarer was neither a party to the initial contract of insurance ... nor to the renewal policy ... and accordingly, has no title to sue in respect of the loss of *Moonacre*.

Notes

Deputy Judge Colman QC also considered the position of a bailee or a licensee with respect to insurable interest. In support of the proposition that the mere existence of a bailment may not be enough to give rise to an insurable interest, he referred to the case of *Macaura v Northern Assurance Company Ltd* (1925) 21 LIL Rep, HL.[13] That case involved the sale of timber to a company of which the assured was the sole shareholder, and also a substantial creditor. When the timber was destroyed by fire, the assured claimed under the policy. The House of Lords ruled, *inter alia*, that he may have been the bailee of the timber, but he had no liability and owed no duty to the company in respect of the safe custody of the timber. The assured's relation and responsibility was to the company alone, and not to the company's property.

---

13 For a fuller discussion of this case, see below, p 67.

In the view of Deputy Judge Colman QC, the test appears to be whether the assured has any beneficial rights in the subject matter insured. And, as the assured had rights and obligations in *Moonacre*, he was held to have an insurable interest in her. Regarding the position of a licensee, Deputy Judge Colman did not find it necessary to elaborate if and when a licensee might have an insurable interest, as the assured, Mr Sharp, had two powers of attorney, which was sufficient to establish a legal relationship with *Moonacre*.

Owner of goods

An owner of goods will naturally have an insurable interest in his goods. However, property might change during the currency of the policy, and in such an event it is not always easy to pinpoint who the owner of the goods is at the time of loss. A great deal hinges upon the terms of the particular contract of sale which determines the time of the passing of property.

Re National Benefit Assurance Co Ltd, Application of HL Sthyr (1933) 45 LlL Rep 147

A claim was made by the seller, with respect to the loss of goods, upon a policy of marine insurance which purported to insure goods shipped from the UK to Russia. The insurers declined payment on the ground, *inter alia*, that the seller did not have an interest in the goods, as he had already consigned them to a Mr Vitouchnovsky, and thus had parted with the property in the goods.

The court ruled that the seller did, in fact, have an insurable interest, as the sale was not an outright sale, but conditional on the arrival of the goods.

> **Maugham J:** [p 151] ... Then remains the more serious question as to whether there was not an out and out sale to Mr Vitouchnovsky and the present claimant is unable to make a valid claim. In that matter, there is this difficulty, that all the documents which were in existence at the time, or practically all of them, have been destroyed and the records of the Russo-Scandinavian Bank have been taken over by the People's Bank and there is some difficulty in ascertaining the facts ... the sale was conditional on the goods reaching Rostoff-on-Don. I think that, taking into consideration what took place when the State Bank took possession, I should be quite wrong in coming to the conclusion that the property passed before the goods reached Rostoff-on-Don. Accordingly, although it is a serious point, I must come to the conclusion which is consistent with my view of the business probabilities of the time, that the goods were not sold outright to Mr Vitouchnovsky and that the consignors were entitled to a claim on the goods.

Contingent and defeasible interests in goods

By virtue of s 7, a contingent and defeasible interest are insurable.[14] In terms of insurance of goods, these words simply mean that the interest is not 'fixed' or, in a manner of speech, stable, in the sense that it does not remain with one person throughout the policy, and may revert from the buyer to the seller and vice versa because of certain events. For instance, whilst property may have passed to the buyer, he may choose to reject the goods, in which case the property and interest in the goods will revert to the seller. Likewise, if the seller does not get paid, he can recall the property in the goods and thus 'defeat' the interest of the buyer. In this sense, the interests of both buyer and seller are dependent on the happening of certain contingencies.

Anderson v Morice (1876) 3 Asp MLC 290, HL

In a contract of sale on the terms 'bought for account of A, of B and Co, the cargo of new crop Rangoon rice *per Sunbeam*', the buyer insured the rice 'at and from' Rangoon to the UK, 'as interest may appear'. The ship proceeded to Rangoon and, after the greater part of the rice had been shipped, she suddenly sank and the rice already shipped was lost. The buyer sought to recover under the policy.

The House of Lords ruled that the buyer had no insurable interest, as the rice was not at his risk at the time of the loss.

> **Lord Chelmsford:** [p 291] ... The question to be determined upon this appeal is one of some difficulty, and it has given rise to a great diversity of judicial opinion. It may be thus shortly stated: whether the appellant, under a contract for the purchase of cargo of rice to be shipped on board a vessel called *Sunbeam*, had any property in the rice, or had incurred any risk in respect of it so as to give him an insurable interest at the time of the total loss of the vessel and cargo.
>
> Having regard to the terms of the contract for the purchase of the rice, it is clear, to my mind, that if the intention of the parties is to be collected from that document alone, no interest in the rice passed to the buyers till the cargo was completed, for payment was to be made only when the loading was finished ...

---

14 A shipowner may, of course, insure a ship's physical capacity to earn charter freight. Such a contingent interest in freight, though insurable, has its limits: it is contingent upon the vessel being deployed, as opposed to a mere intention to trade or to earn freight: see *Cepheus Shipping Corpn v Guardian Royal Exchange Assurance plc, 'Capricorn'* [1995] 1 Lloyd's Rep 622, discussed below, p 60. A further illustration of a contingent interest is reinsurance, namely when an insurer takes out a policy of insurance in respect of a part or the whole of the risk which he has agreed to bear. In such a case, the original insurer becomes the assured and the re-insurance company becomes the insurer, who has to indemnify the original insurer should he suffer a loss. As the insurable interest of the original insurer is dependent upon a claim being settled on the original assured, that insurable interest is said to be contingent: see below, p 60.

... But it seems to me clear that, unless a change was produced in the rights and liabilities of the plaintiffs under the contract by their undertaking the insurance, they could have had no interest in the rice until a complete cargo had been shipped. But, although this was their position in relation to the contract itself, they had a contingent benefit which might accrue to them from the completion of the cargo on board *Sunbeam*, and its safe delivery. This contingent benefit was one on expected profits, and, although it would not be protected by an insurance on the rice (*Lucena v Craufurd* (1806) 2 B&P (NR) 269), yet the plaintiffs having that contingent interest in the safety of the cargo, might not be indisposed to take upon themselves an insurance against its loss, more especially as they would have an interest in the rice itself at Rangoon as soon as the cargo should be completed. The question is, did this insurance throw the risk of the loss of the rice upon them?

[p 292] ... Did they, by undertaking it, impliedly agree with the vendors that, if the rice was destroyed after any part had been shipped on board *e Sunbeam*, the loss should be theirs? ... If this was really their undertaking, every bag of rice shipped on board *Sunbeam* was at their risk, and the loss of it must have fallen upon them. But the Court of Common Pleas held that, as the plaintiffs would not, if the ship had sailed and arrived with what was on board of her when she sank, have been obliged to accept what was on board, they were not bound to pay for the rice which was on board and lost when the ship sank; from which it would seem to follow that the plaintiffs were not exposed to any risk of loss before a complete cargo had been shipped on board *Sunbeam*.

... There being, therefore, conflicting evidence of intention as to the interest in the rice passing to the purchasers or remaining in the vendors, the effect of the written contract being that the interest was to continue in the vendors until the completion of the cargo, and the consent of the purchasers to insure not shifting the property during the loading and before the cargo was complete, and it being at the utmost an indication of intention to assume the risk, I think your Lordships should not look out of the contract, but determine the rights and the liabilities of the parties by it alone. It was not disputed that, by the terms of the contract, the plaintiffs were not bound to take less than a complete cargo of rice, and that they had an option either to accept or reject a part cargo. If they had exercised this option by accepting what was on board before *Sunbeam* sank as a fulfilment of the contract on the part of the vendors, they would have had an insurable interest in the rice at the time of the loss.

Inglis v Stock (1885) App Cas 263, HL

By two contracts, Drake and Co sold to one Beloe and to the respondent (plaintiff below) respectively 200 tons (or 2,000 bags) each of sugar to be shipped FOB Hamburg, payment in cash in London on exchange for bills of lading. By a separate contract, Beloe resold his 200 tons of sugar to the respondent, who then took up a floating policy upon 'any kind of goods and merchandises', and duly declared his interest in respect of this cargo. To fulfil these contracts of sale, 390 tons (10 tons short) were shipped in bags on board *City of Dublin*. The ship sailed from Hamburg for Bristol and was lost. After receiving news of the loss, Drake and Co allocated 200 tons to Beloe's contract and 190 tons to the respondent's contract. The issue before the court was whether the respondent had, at the time of the loss, an insurable interest in the 390 tons of sugar.

The House of Lords ruled that the sales being 'FOB Hamburg', the sugar was, after shipment, at the risk of the respondent; he, therefore, had an insurable interest in the sugar and the underwriter was liable for the loss.

Earl of Selborne LC: [p 266] ... The quantity actually put on board *City of Dublin* at Hamburg was only 3,900 bags, or 390 tons. As to this, I think it is enough to say that, if the plaintiff would have had an insurable interest in 4,000 bags, under the circumstances of the case, he had, in my opinion, such an interest though the quantity was short by 10 tons.

... But no particular bags were then set apart or marked as applicable to the one contract more than the other; it was thought sufficient by Drake and Co, or their agents, to leave this to be done when the bills of lading came forward.

[p 268] ... The goods were, by the act of the vendors, separated from the bulk of all other goods belonging to them; they were shipped 'free on board' in what (for that purpose) was the purchaser's ship, under two contracts so to deliver them; in both which contracts ... the plaintiff was then ... solely interested. I cannot infer, from any part of the evidence, that, in so shipping them indiscriminately, the vendors intended to break, instead of fulfilling, their contract, and to take upon themselves (contrary to those contracts) the subsequent risk of loss ...

Lord Blackburn: [p 274]... I am quite unable to perceive why an undivided interest in a parcel of goods on board a ship may not be described as an interest in goods just as much as if it were an interest in every portion of the goods. No authority was cited in order to show that it was not so, and I can see no reason for it. Then, that being so, of course it follows that there is no defence at all, and this is my opinion.

Colonial Insurance Company of New Zealand v Adelaide Marine Insurance Company (1886) 12 AC 128, PC

Pursuant to a contract of sale, a cargo of wheat was to be shipped from New Zealand to England. The buyer took out an insurance policy providing cover for 'wheat cargo now on board or to be shipped' in the ship *Duke of Sutherland*. After commencement of loading, but before the whole cargo was loaded, both ship and cargo were lost by perils of the sea. On an action by the buyers upon the policy, the insurers contended that the buyers did not, at the time of loss, have an insurable interest on the wheat insured.

The court ruled that the buyers' risks commenced as and when any portion of the cargo of wheat was loaded on board.

Sir Barnes Peacock: [p 136] ... In *Anderson v Morice* ... Anderson agreed ... to purchase the cargo of new crop Rangoon rice *per Sunbeam* ... and freight, expected to be March shipment, payment by seller's draft on purchaser at six months' sight with documents attached. The cargo to be purchased in that case was an entire thing, and was not in existence at the time when the contract was entered into, and would not be in existence until the whole cargo should be put on board.

In the present case, the vendors did not sell a particular cargo on board a ship chartered by them, but merely offered to supply a cargo of wheat for *Duke of Sutherland* ... on board at Timaru. No time or mode was fixed for payment, and nothing was said as to the place to which the cargo, when supplied and put on board, was to be carried, or to the effect that the sellers were to have anything to do with bills of lading or other shipping documents. The purchasers accepted the offer, they themselves being the charterers of *Duke of Sutherland*, whereas in *Anderson v Morice* ... the firm who agreed to sell the cargo of rice by *Sunbeam* were themselves the charterers of that vessel, and were to receive freight for the carriage of the rice, such freight being included in the purchase money. In putting the rice on board *Sunbeam* the seller were not delivering it to Anderson, but were putting it on board a vessel, of which they were the charterers, for the purpose of completing the cargo which they had agreed to sell. The master of *Sunbeam* received it on their account, and not on account of the purchasers. The purchasers' right was to depend on the shipping documents, which were to be under the direction of the sellers. In the present case, in putting the wheat on board *Duke of Sutherland*, the contractors were delivering it to the purchasers in pursuance of their contract to put it free on board, the master of the vessel which had been chartered by them being their agent to receive it on their account. The shipowners received it under the charterparty, by which they bound themselves to load from the charterers a full and complete cargo, and to proceed with it, etc, as ordered by the charterers or their agents. The sellers had nothing to do with the wheat or the destination thereof after it was on board, and by putting it on board they did not render themselves liable to the owners of the ship for freight, demurrage, commission, or any other charges provided for by the charterparty. The master would not have been justified in returning to the sellers any portion of the wheat without the authority of the purchasers, who were entitled under the charterparty to have bills of lading signed for it as directed by them according to the terms stipulated by the charterparty ... By the charterparty, the cargo was to be brought to and taken from alongside at merchant's risk and expense. By the vendors' contract, they were to put it free on board for the charterer, and when put on board, the master would receive it for the purchasers and hold it for them.

[p 138] ... In the present case, if no loss had happened, and the sellers, without lawful excuse, had neglected to supply a complete cargo, the purchasers must have paid for the wheat which had been put on board, unless they returned it. If the sellers had completed the cargo, the purchasers must have paid for the whole. In either case they had, at the time of the loss, an interest in the part which had been put on board. In the one case, that they

might be able to return it to excuse them from payment for it in the event of their electing to put an end to the contract in case of the non-completion of the supply; in the other, that they might have the goods for which they would be obliged to pay.

[p 140] ... In the present case, there was a sale, a delivery, and a receipt by the purchasers of the wheat which was put on board. The charterers, and not the contractors, would have been liable to the shipowners for the freight if the wheat had been carried to its destination.

Their Lordships are of opinion that the delivery of the wheat from time to time was a delivery to the purchasers, that it vested in them the right of possession as well as the right of property, and that at the time of the loss it was at their risk. The right which they had to return the wheat which had been delivered, in the event of the sellers neglecting, without lawful excuse, to complete the supply, did not prevent them from having an insurable interest. The interest in this case was defeasible, not by the vendors, but at the option of the vendees in the event of the vendors not completing the contract.

Notes

As can be seen, *Anderson v Morice* was distinguished on facts. In *Anderson v Morice*, the nature of the contract of sale, though also FOB, was such as to allow the passing of property and risks to the buyer only when the *whole* of the cargo was loaded on board.

It should be remembered that there is another matter, namely, that of attachment of risk, which has to be considered before any question on the passing of property becomes relevant. This was demonstrated in the case of **Fuerst Day Lawson Ltd v Orion Insurance Co Ltd [1980] 1 Lloyd's Rep 656**, where a cargo of drums of scented oil insured 'lost or not lost' against 'all risks' was found on arrival to contain water with slight traces of oil. On the evidence, Mocatta J found that any substitution of oil by water was likely to have taken place before shipment. And, as the plaintiffs (the assured) could not prove, on the balance of probabilities, that the oil in drums that they had agreed to buy had ever started on their journey, the risk under the policy never attached. As this alone was sufficient to dismiss the plaintiffs' case, there was no need for the judge to consider any question relating to the passing of property. Nevertheless, Mocatta J's comments on the subject are enlightening:

> **Mocatta J:** [p 664] ...The goods were clearly at the risk of the sellers prior to shipment and ... had the drums under a particular contract met with an accident during the transfer to the godowns and their contents been destroyed by fire or otherwise, the plaintiffs would not have had to pay for them, since no bills of lading could have been issued on them. The defendants argued that in such circumstances the plaintiffs would have had no insurable interest in the goods, though the position would have been different if the plaintiffs, instead of insuring on goods, had insured expressly against loss of profits or against the sellers' default in shipment.

Even more revealing was the judge's response to the finer points of law raised by counsel for the plaintiffs, to the effect that the definition of insurable interest in s 5(2) is 'very wide', that *Anderson v Morice* was no longer good law since the passing of s 5(2) of the Act, and that, under the 'lost or not lost' clause, an assured may recover although he may have acquired his interest only after the loss. Save for acknowledging that they 'clearly raise points of some difficulty,' he had left them for another day.

The passing of risks under an FOB contract of sale, and the effect it has upon the insurable interest of an assured (a buyer) under a policy of insurance, were examined in the Australian case of *NSW Leather Co Pty Ltd v Vanguard Insurance Co Ltd* [1991] 105 FLR 381, below. The Supreme Court had to consider two main issues: first, whether a buyer (on FOB terms) had an insurable interest in the goods *at the time of loss* when the containers in which they were packed were broken into before they were loaded on board ship. In such a circumstance, the old authorities of *Inglis v Stock* and, in particular, *Anderson v Morice* have clearly established that, before the goods cross the ship's rail, the risks and property in them remained with the seller. Secondly, the court also had to decide the effect the 'lost or not lost' clause had upon the claim; this point is discussed later.[15]

NSW Leather Co Pty Ltd v Vanguard Insurance Co Ltd [1991] 105 FLR 381, Supreme Court of New South Wales

Under a contract of sale on FOB terms, quantities of leather purchased by the plaintiff were loaded into containers for shipment to Sydney. However, prior to shipment, the containers were broken into and the bulk of the leather was stolen; fresh seals were then fraudulently attached to the containers. The buyer, having paid for the goods without knowing of the theft, sought to recover under the insurance policy after he was aware of the loss. The goods were insured warehouse to warehouse and on a 'lost or not lost' basis.

The Supreme Court ruled that, at the time of loss, the buyer did not have an insurable interest in the goods. However, by reason of the 'lost or not lost' clause, they were entitled to claim under the policy for they had acquired their insurable interest *after* the loss.

> **Handley JA:** [p 387] ... We were also referred to the decisions in *Anderson v Morice* ... and *Stock v Inglis* ... These decisions establish that a buyer under an FOB contract has an insurable interest in the goods when they are at his risk, and this occurs from the moment he becomes liable to pay the price, notwithstanding any subsequent loss or damage to the goods ...
>
> [p 389] ... The policy in the present case was on 'goods and/or merchandise' and was limited to such goods, etc, 'in which [the insured] have an insurable interest'. In my opinion, and subject to the lost or not lost clause, this policy on

---

15   See, also, below, p 78.

goods did not cover the appellant in respect of these goods before the risk passed to it when they were loaded on board and did not cover it against the financial risks it incurred when it paid cash against documents.

The appellant was not at risk, except as to anticipated profits, if the goods had been stolen while in transit from the interior, or from the freight consolidators' depot prior to packing the containers, or if the goods, or the loaded containers, had been destroyed by fire prior to loading. In such cases, the appellant would presumably have become aware of the loss, and the carrier would not have issued any bill of lading for the goods. However, and what is of critical importance, the appellant would not have been under any liability to pay for the goods.

[pp 389–90] ... In my opinion, the existence of cover or otherwise under the present policy (apart from the lost or not lost clause) cannot depend on whether the appellant became aware of the loss before or after it was asked to pay for the goods. If the appellant was insured under this policy in respect of the risk of these surreptitious thefts, it would also have been insured against the risks of fire and blatant theft on land. However, the latter conclusion is denied by long settled authority. Moreover, in my opinion, the risk the appellant faced from surreptitious thefts was not a risk that it would be liable under its contract to pay for stolen goods, but the risk that it would be deceived into paying for stolen goods although it was not liable to do so. This is an entirely different risk, and not one which is covered by the policy in the present form.

This analysis also leads to the conclusion that the loss suffered by the appellant in this case was not a loss of goods. A buyer under an FOB contract who is bound to pay cash against documents may reject the documents if they do not conform to the contract. It also has a right to reject the goods themselves after they have been inspected on arrival ...

Accordingly, if the existence of the thefts had been discovered in time, the appellant could have rejected the shipping documents and declined to pay the price. Having accepted and paid for the shipping documents, the appellant still had the right to reject the goods and recover the price when it inspected the containers on arrival and learned the true situation. Understandably, perhaps, the appellant elected not to reject the goods, but it retained the right to sue the seller for damages for short delivery.

Undoubtedly, the appellant has suffered a loss in each case, but the losses are consequential on the seller's breaches of contract to ship the full quantity of leather. The appellant had an insurable interest in its contracts, but ... the policy it required to cover its losses was not a policy on goods, but one in the nature of a guarantee of the seller's obligation to deliver.

[p 392] ... The respondent contended that the appellant still cannot recover, because it suffered no loss. The appellant was not at risk when the goods were stolen. However, it suffered financial loss because of the prior loss of the goods, and this is sufficient. The fact that it had contractual remedies against the seller is no answer.

Since the appellant was not at risk in respect of the goods prior to loading, it follows that it can derive no direct assistance from the warehouse to warehouse clause.

[pp 392–93] ... The respondent further contended that the appellant could not recover under the clause because it never acquired an insurable interest in the stolen goods. The argument was that the property in the stolen goods never passed, because the goods were not shipped. Accordingly, so it was submitted, the only goods in which the risk or the property passed were those remaining in the containers. Counsel for neither party was able to refer the court to any authority directly in point and accordingly during argument the question was considered on principle. On this basis, in my opinion, the court should hold that property in the stolen goods passed to the appellant at the time and in the manner in which it would have passed had the containers not been pilfered.

Notes

As can be seen, a good deal hinges upon the nature of the contract of sale and the shipping arrangements agreed between a seller and a buyer. To overcome such problems likely to be encountered by a buyer, it would appear that a buyer would be well advised to subscribe to a policy, as suggested by Handley JA, not on goods, but on anticipated profits, or one in the nature of a guarantee of the seller's obligation to deliver.

Arnould,[16] on noting that the conception of insurable interest has been 'continuously expanding', had hopes that the courts, in continuation of this process of expansion, would 'hold that the existence of a contract of freight in itself gives an insurable interest in the freight'. There is no reason why the same should not hold true in a contract for the purchase of goods.

Further, should a court be in any way in doubt, it may perhaps be useful for it to be reminded of the words uttered by Brett MR, in the Court of Appeal in *Stock v Inglis* **(1884) 12 QBD 564**, that it should lean in favour of an insurable interest, so as to ensure that insurers will not be able so easily to escape from honouring their liabilities under the policy.

Brett MR: [p 571] ... In my opinion it is the duty of a court always to lean in favour of an insurable interest, if possible, for it seems to me that after underwriters have received the premium, the objection that there was no insurable interest is often, as nearly as possible, a technical objection, and one which has no real merit, certainly not as between the assured and the insurer. Of course, we must not assume facts which do not exist, nor stretch the law beyond its proper limits, but we ought, I think, to consider the question with a mind, if the facts and the law will allow it, to find in favour of an insurable interest.

---

16 *Op cit*, Arnould, fn 7, Vol 1, para 326.

Partial interest in goods

A partial interest of any nature is also insurable by virtue of s 8. Thus, the buyer of an undivided part of goods in a bulk cargo has an insurable interest in respect of the quantity of goods belonging to him. In *Inglis v Stock* (1885) App Cas 263, HL, discussed above, Lord Blackburn said: [p 274] 'I am quite unable to perceive why an undivided interest in a parcel of goods on board a ship may not be described as an interest in goods just as much as if it were an interest in every portion of the goods. No authority was cited in order to show that it was not so, and I can see no reason for it.'

Owner of freight

Freight may be divided into three broad categories: ordinary or bill of lading freight, charterparty freight and advance freight.[17] The Act specifically provides, in s 12, that in the case of an advanced freight, 'the person advancing the freight has an insurable interest, in so far as such freight is not repayable in case of loss'. No mention is specifically made of ordinary or chartered freight, save that s 3(2)(b) states that '... there is a marine adventure where the earning or acquisition of any freight ... is endangered by the exposure of insurable property to maritime perils'. Thus, the insurable interest lies with the person who is to benefit from the acquisition of the freight.

Section 12 of the Act has clarified in no uncertain terms that, in the case of advance freight, the interest lies with the person who has prepaid the freight. The *locus classicus* on the subject is **Allison v Bristol Marine Insurance Company (1875) 1 App Cas 209, HL**, where the House of Lords held that the charterer, and not the shipowner, had an insurable interest in the advance freight: as he had prepaid half of the freight, he bore the risk for that half. The shipowner, on the other hand, had an insurable interest in the other half of the freight which was at risk by perils of the sea.[18]

> **Lord Hatherley:** [p 235] ... The two points to be considered are, first, what is the insurance that has been effected by the policy and the subject matter thereby insured; and we are led, in the consideration of that point, to the farther question as to what was the contract between the insurer and the person with whom he bargained, as the charterer of the ship, in order to ascertain what were the perils of the sea against which the assured desired so to protect himself.
>
> [pp 235–36] ... Now, my Lords, we must bear in mind in this inquiry, in the first instance, that if there be any question of doubt (I think in truth we shall

---

17 See Chapter 3, p 96, on the types of freight which may constitute the subject matter of a marine policy of insurance.
18 For a further discussion of this case in the context of advance freight as a subject matter of insurance, see Chapter 3, p 111.

find there is none) as to what the subject matter of insurance is, then on principle it is to be held in all cases that in respect of which the insurance is made is that which is capable of being a subject matter of insurance, namely, that which is at risk; and that in regarding the contract of insurance, we must not assume, and we cannot in any way consistently with law assume, that the assured is endeavouring to effect a policy upon that which is at no risk whatever. Next, when we come to look at the contract itself, it being a contract of freight, we have to remember that from a very early period ... it has been settled in our maritime law that prepaid freight cannot be recovered back. I think, when we consider these two points, that on the one hand that is to be taken as insured which is at risk, and on the other hand that prepaid freight cannot be recovered back, we shall be led very easily and safely to the solution of the difficulty which appears to have arisen in the case before us.

Contingent or defeasible interest in freight

As in the case of insurance on goods,[19] it is also possible for an assured to have a contingent or defeasible interest in charterer freight. The concept was put to the test recently, in the *Capricorn* case, below, where an assured of a policy on loss of charter hire endeavoured to push the limits of the notion of insurable interest to the extreme.

Cepheus Shipping Corporation v Guardian Royal Exchange Assurance, 'Capricorn' [1995] 1 Lloyd's Rep 622

The plaintiffs, owners of the reefer vessel *Capricorn*, effected a 'loss of hire' policy of insurance, covering six vessels for differing six month periods at agreed daily rates. The policy 'interest' was described as: 'Loss of earnings and/or expenses and/or hire and was ... to pay up to 60 days each accident or occurrence ... whether vessel chartered or unchartered.' *Capricorn* had been chartered to the Blue Star Line, but, by May 1986, she had been released from the charter. One week after coming off charter, it was discovered that one of *Capricorn*'s generators had been damaged by an insured peril, the negligence of the crew in using an incorrect spanner. *Capricorn* sailed to Falmouth, where the generator was repaired, and the plaintiffs then claimed on their insurers for 60 days' loss of time, on the basis that the policy was simply on the vessel's earning capacity, regardless of her actual or prospective engagements. The insurer's defence, *inter alia*, was that the plaintiffs had no insurable interest at the time of loss.

The court ruled that the plaintiffs could not recover under their policy of insurance covering loss of hire. Besides the matter of causation,[20] Mance J also

---

19 See above, p 51.
20 This aspect of the case, that the loss of earning capacity is a subject matter of insurance under a policy of loss of charter hire, is discussed in Chapter 3, p 110.

ruled in favour of the insurer on the point that the interest of the plaintiffs was too tenuous and speculative in nature to be capable of supporting an 'insurable interest' as understood by the Act.

Mance J: [p 634] ... In summary, market conditions in May 1986 were such, in my judgment, as to make it virtually inevitable that Blue Star would not exercise their off-season option and the plaintiffs would have known this. The plaintiffs decided that the vessel would, on this basis, be laid up, and they booked a lay up berth for the off-season accordingly. *Capricorn* would have gone into lay up in Falmouth, damage or no damage. Further, market conditions never changed or improved to any extent which could or would have led the plaintiffs to consider reactivating *Capricorn* before she was in fact ready to sail in October 1986. The plaintiffs' intention throughout the off-season was, and would irrespective of the damage repairs have been, that the vessel should remain laid up at the King Harry Reach lay up berth.

[p 638] ... The underlying principle of this insurance remains that of indemnity. In my judgment, the plaintiffs' case conflicts with that principle. It is no answer to say in general terms that the defendants have received premium for six months' cover. Premium is commonly computed on a broad basis, which may not, in all circumstances, precisely reflect exposure which may or does materialise. The subject matter of the policy is loss of trading income, and the policy and its references to the vessel's earning capacity, in my judgment, contemplate a loss involving a vessel with an earning capacity which was intended to be and would have been deployed in trade, for whatever she might thereby earn.

[p 641] ... I have not so far addressed the problems of insurable interest or value, which the defendants suggest that the claim also raises ... the present policy is not on its face one which the parties made for other than ordinary business reasons; it does not bear the hallmarks of wagering or the like. If underwriters make a contract in deliberate terms which covers their assured in respect of a specific situation, a court is likely to hesitate before accepting a defence of lack of insurable interest. Under s 6 of the Marine Insurance Act, the plaintiffs' insurable interest in the subject matter insured (here freight or other income from trading) must have existed at the time of the *loss*, though no such interest need exist when the insurance is effected.

[pp 641–42] ... In the present case, the loss of earnings which the insurance contemplated would have been sustained over the early months of the off-season period; it was common ground that questions of insurable interest fall thus to be considered on a continuing or day by day basis. But, even at the date of the accident, it was, to all intents and purposes, clear that Blue Star would not exercise their off-season option and the plaintiffs' intention was, on that basis, to lay her up. The vessel was thereafter laid up. The only difference made by the accident was that steps had to be taken during lay up to repair her. The plaintiffs seek to find a continuing and sufficient insurable interest on a day to day basis in the possibility that the market might improve during the off-season and in what they asserted to be the plaintiffs' intention to trade [the vessel] if the market improved sufficiently. They say that this was an insurable interest which the parties embraced, and valued, by their agreed valuation of the subject matter insured. In fact, as I have held, the plaintiffs' actual intention throughout was and would (irrespective of the damage repairs) have been that the vessel should remain in lay up at the King Harry Reach. I am ready to assume that, had the market improved substantially and the vessel been no longer under repair, they would have reconsidered their intention to continue the lay up. But the market never did improve significantly, and prospect that it might was never more than remote. If permissible at all, the plaintiffs' suggested insurable interest constitutes a novel and extended insurable interest, involving a substantial element of speculation with respect to the state of the market and/or the owners' intentions. I do not find it necessary to decide that parties may never agree on or value such an insurable interest. But there appears to me a distinct unlikelihood about their so doing to which I have already alluded in the context of construction.

Notes

Another way of resolving the problem in the *Capricorn* case is to say that the insurable property, namely charter hire, was, in the words of s 5(2) of the Act, never 'at risk', for the plaintiffs had neither intended to trade the vessel, nor were market conditions such as to allow an inference to be drawn that they would have traded. Though the concept of insurable interest is capable of expansion, Mance J was not, in this instance, prepared to extend its parameters.

The insurer

With regard to the insurer, s 9 of the Act has made it clear that there is an insurable interest on his part and he may reinsure his liabilities as an insurer. It has to be borne in mind that, since reinsurance is also a contract of indemnity, the insurer cannot be indemnified for more than his share of the loss.

Uzielli and Co v Boston Marine Insurance Company (1884) 15 QBD 11, CA

The owners of a ship insured her for 12 months under an ordinary Lloyd's policy containing a suing and labouring clause. The underwriters of the Lloyd's policy reinsured themselves with a French company (Uzielli and Co), which reinsured itself with the defendants, Boston Marine Insurance Company. The policy underwritten for the French company by the defendants for £1,000 bound them (the defendants) to pay as might be paid on the original policy; it was to cover the risk of total loss only, and also contained a suing and labouring clause. During the currency of the policy, the ship was damaged, and rendered a constructive total loss. The underwriters of the ship settled the damage with the owners at 88%, but due to additional charges in floating the ship, the loss represented 112%. The French reinsurers, who became liable to the original insurer, brought an action on their policy to recover that sum from their insurer, the defendants.[21]

The court ruled that the plaintiffs' reinsurers were not entitled to be indemnified for more than £1,000, as they, in turn, had only re-insured themselves to the extent of that sum.

Brett MR: [pp 16–17] ... It is a reinsurance policy effected by reinsurers; but, after all, it is a policy on the ship. What was the interest of the real plaintiffs, the reinsurers, in the ship? They were not owners, and, therefore, they had none as owners. But they have an insurable interest of some kind, and that insurable interest is the loss which they might or would suffer under the policy, upon which they themselves were liable. What does this loss amount to? It might be more than the real plaintiffs' share in the full value of the ship, because of the sue and labour clause: they might have to pay more than their share in the full value of the ship under the suing and labouring clause: their liability might include not only their share in the full value of the ship, but what might be charged to them under the suing and labouring clause. Therefore, if the reinsurers insured the ship to the full amount of her value and more, I should say that it would not be a case of over-insurance, and that is because of the operation of the suing and labouring clause. That is the nature of the plaintiffs' interest. Therefore, the real plaintiffs might have insured for more than their share in the full value of the ship; but they have insured only to the extent of £1,000, and they cannot recover on the policy more than they have insured for: all that they can recover is £1,000. It is simply a policy on the ship to the extent of £1,000.

Cotton LJ: [p 18] ... I agree that the policy is a contract of insurance upon the ship: it is a reinsurance upon the policy issued by the French company to pay as they shall pay, but to cover a total loss only. The insurance is effected by those who are not owners, but by those who are liable in respect of the ship. What is the extent of the defendants' liability? The original insurers are liable in respect of the loss of the ship; but the defendants' liability on the policy is limited to the extent of £1,000, and that is all which they can be properly called upon to pay on the policy. They are liable to this extent by reason of the total loss which has occurred.

British Dominions General Insurance Company Ltd v Duder and Others [1915] 2 KB 394

The plaintiffs, who had insured *Katina*, reinsured her with the defendants against total and/or constructive total loss only. The reinsurance policy did not contain the 'to pay as may be paid thereon' clause. During the currency of the policy, *Katina* stranded, and her owners gave a notice of abandonment, claiming that she was a constructive total loss. The insurers declined to accept the notice of abandonment and, in an action by the owners, a compromise was

---

21 The question of whether an original insurer may be regarded as the 'factors, servants or assigns' of a reinsurer for the purpose of suing and labouring was the main issue in this case. This point is discussed in Chapter 18, p 768.

reached by which the plaintiffs paid the owners a sum representing 66% of the loss. The insurers then sought to recover from the defendants that sum on the reinsurance policy.

The court ruled that the plaintiffs' insurers were entitled only to 66%, not 100% of the loss: thus, the defendant reinsurers were allowed to enjoy the benefit of the compromise made between the plaintiffs and the owners.

> **Buckley LJ:** [p 400] ... A contract of insurance and a contract of reinsurance are independent of each other. But a contract of reinsurance is a contract which insures the thing originally insured, namely, the ship. The reinsurer has an insurable interest in the ship by virtue of his original contract of insurance. The thing insured, however, is the ship, and not the interest of the reinsurer in the ship by reason of his contract of insurance upon the ship.
>
> [p 403] ... I regret to have come to the conclusion that the defendants, who would have nothing to do with the compromise, are nevertheless entitled to the benefit of it. But it seems to me that, as a matter of legal right, the plaintiffs cannot, even in such a state of facts as this, make a profit out of the reinsurance. For these reasons, I think that the appeal must be allowed. The plaintiffs are, however, entitled to indemnity, and this is not necessarily confined to the 66%. They are entitled to such further sum, if any, as is required to give them an indemnity. The costs, for instance, of obtaining the compromise at 66% should be added to the 66%. I shall be prepared to hear anything that may be said as to the proper terms of an inquiry to ascertain what such further sum would be.

Western Assurance Company of Toronto v Poole [1903] 1 KB 376

The plaintiffs, who had insured the ship *Edmund*, reinsured her with the defendants. Though the original policy between the shipowner and the plaintiffs was for a partial as well as a total loss, the reinsurance was for a total or constructive total loss only. The reinsurance policy contained the following clauses: 'Being a reinsurance subject to the same clauses and conditions as the original policy and to pay as may be paid thereon' and 'No claim to attach to this policy for salvage charges'.[22] During the course of the insured voyage, the ship stranded and suffered damage. Even though the cost of repairs exceeded the agreed value of the ship in the policy, the owners elected not to give notice of abandonment, but to claim only for a partial loss. The owners finally recovered from their insurers 107% of the value of the ship, that sum being made up partly of the expense of repairs and partly of the expense of floating her. The plaintiff insurers then sued their reinsurers for the full amount underwritten by them as in respect of a constructive total loss.[23]

---

22 The reinsurance policy also contained in print the usual undertaking by the insurers to contribute to suing and labouring charges and the clause 'No claim to attach to this policy for salvage charges'. Bigham J's judgment on the effect of these clauses is examined in Chapter 18, p 793.

23 Bigham J also considered in depth what constitutes a constructive total loss: his words on this subject can be found in Chapter 16, pp 658 and 659.

The court ruled that the plaintiffs' insurers were not entitled to recover from the reinsurance company as for a constructive total loss, the reasoning being that, since no notice of abandonment had been tendered by the shipowner, his claim was only for a partial loss. And, as the subscription under the reinsurance policy was for a total loss only, the plaintiffs were barred from recovering for a constructive total loss.

Bigham J: [p 383] ... The first question is whether there has been any constructive total loss within the meaning of the contract sued on. It is quite a common practice for an insurer against total and partial loss to reinsure the risk of total loss while keeping himself uncovered as to partial loss. Of course he does this at a premium much lower than that which he himself receives for the double risk, and in the event of the insured vessel sustaining damage by the perils insured against, it is very much to his interest that the damage should be sufficiently serious to constitute a constructive total loss, for in that event only can he get his loss recouped by his reinsurer, and secure his profit, namely, the difference between the two premiums. So, in the present case, the plaintiffs are anxious to make that which the shipowner treated as a partial loss under the original policy a total loss under the reinsurance policy. But can they? I think not. What the defendant promised by his contract was to indemnify the plaintiffs if they were called upon to pay a constructive total loss.

[p 384] ... Of course, the owner is not compellable to give any notice of abandonment; there is nothing in his policy which obliges him to divest himself of his property in the ship; and this is true whatever the extent of the damage may be. He can always keep his ship and claim for a partial loss, even though the cost of repairs may amount to 100% of the insured value. But if he elects to take this course, his claim is a claim for a partial loss only.

[p 390] ... The fact is that this policy is an indemnity against total or constructive total loss only, and against nothing else; and such a loss has not happened. The plaintiff's claim, therefore, wholly fails.

Mortgagor and mortgagee

As to the insurable interest of mortgagor and mortgagee, s 14(1) provides that:

> Where the subject matter insured is mortgaged, the mortgagor has an insurable interest in the full value thereof, and the mortgagee has an insurable interest in respect of any sum due or to become due under the mortgage.

A mortgagee has an insurable interest whether he sues as an original assured or as an assignee of a policy. In the case of the latter, the mortgagee's rights are wholly dependent upon the rights of the assignor. The shipowner, as an assignee, cannot acquire any better rights than the assignor.[24]

---

24 See Marine Insurance Act 1906, s 50(2).

It must be pointed out that even an unregistered mortgage confers an insurable interest upon the mortgagee; this is because of his equitable relationship to the subject matter insured. The principle has been long settled[25] by the celebrated case of *Samuel v Dumas*, below.

Samuel v Dumas (1924) 18 LlL Rep, HL

A ship was scuttled with the connivance of her owners, but without any connivance or complicity on the part of the mortgagee. When the innocent mortgagee sought to claim under the insurance policy, the issue arose as to whether or not he had an insurable interest. It was argued that, as the mortgage was not registered, the mortgagee had no insurable interest upon which to prefer a claim.

The court ruled that whether the mortgage be registered or not, the mortgagee had an insurable interest. The claim, however, failed on other grounds, namely, the loss was not caused by an insured peril, as scuttling is not a peril of the seas.[26]

> **Viscount Cave:** [p 213] ... First, it is said that, as *Gregorios* was a Greek ship at the time of her loss and neither the ship nor the mortgage upon her had then been registered in Greece, the mortgagee had no valid security upon the ship and so had no insurable interest. Upon this point, I accept the finding of the learned trial judge that before you can have a valid mortgage on a Greek ship under Greek law the ship and the mortgage must be registered in Greece, and the mortgage must be for a specific sum, and not merely for the balance of a current account, and that these conditions were not complied with; but, nevertheless, I agree with his view that the mortgagee in this case had an insurable interest ... In the present case, the appellant held a British mortgage on the ship and a deed of covenant, which recited an agreement by the owner to deliver to the mortgagee a 'formal first mortgage of the said steamship duly executed and registered in Greece', and contained a covenant by him to 'take such steps as might be necessary to effect the complete registration of the said steamship as a Greek steamship'; and he was entitled in equity to enforce these agreements. This being so, I think it impossible to say that he was not interested in the adventure within the meaning of the above section; and if so, he clearly had an insurable interest to the extent of the sum secured by the mortgage.

Alston v Campbell (1799) 4 Bro Parl Cas 476

A Mr Caldwell, the sole owner of a ship, insured her with the defendant. Later he made an absolute assignment of his ship to a Mr M'Allister. When the ship was afterwards lost, Mr Caldwell brought an action to recover under the policy. The underwriters declined payment, on the basis that he had no insurable interest, having 'sold' his ship prior to the loss.

---

25 See, also, *Alston v Campbell* (1799) 4 Bro Parl Cas 476.
26 The ruling of the House that scuttling is not a peril of the sea is discussed in Chapter 9, p 369.

The court ruled that the owner had an insurable interest in the ship at the time of the loss – the real transaction being no more than a pledge or security for the mortgage debt.

Lord Gardenstone: [p 481] ... The appellant [insurers] therefore thought proper to appeal from all the interlocutors, insisting that the policy was void for want of interest, Mr Caldwell having sold the vessel by a deed of sale to Mr M'Allister.

[pp 481–82] ... On the other side it was said that, although it may otherwise appear upon the face of the instrument executed by Caldwell, yet there was no absolute or immediate transfer of the property in the ship for value paid or agreed upon; nor could that be meant under the circumstances of this case. The real transaction was no more than a pledge or security lodged with M'Allister, the value whereof would of course be allowed to Caldwell, when it was made effectual, or the proceeds were actually in M'Allister's hands; but, till then, his demand against Caldwell remained as before. As, therefore, the loss of the ship in the interval must have been sustained by Caldwell, an interest subsisted in him sufficient to warrant him in insuring her.

The interest of a shareholder

It is well established under English law that a shareholder in a company does not possess any proprietary rights in the assets of the company in which he holds the shares. The leading authority on this issue is the non-marine insurance case of *Macaura v Northern Assurance Co Ltd*, below.

Macaura v Northern Assurance Co Ltd [1925] AC 619, HL

The owner of a large estate in Ireland agreed to sell the timber on his estate, felled or standing, to a Canadian timber company for £27,000; the purchase price was paid by way of shares in the timber company. The estate owner then insured all the timber on his estate with the defendants. Two weeks later, the larger part of the timber was destroyed by fire and the assured, the estate owner, claimed on his policy of insurance.

The House of Lords ruled that the assured, either as creditor or shareholder in the timber company, had no insurable interest in the timber and, therefore, could not recover on his policy of insurance.[27]

Lord Buckmaster: [p 626] ... As a creditor, his position appears to me quite incapable of supporting the claim. If his contention were right, it would follow that any person would be at liberty to insure the furniture of his debtor, and no such claim has ever been recognised by the courts.

---

27 See Chapter 3, p 120, where this case is also discussed in the context that a shareholder may insure the *ventures* undertaken by the company in which he owns the shares, but not the assets or property owned by the company.

... Now, turning to his position as shareholder, this must be independent of the extent of his share interest. If he were entitled to insure holding all the shares in the company, each shareholder would be equally entitled, if the shares were all in separate hands. Now, no shareholder has any right to any item of property owned by the company, for he has no legal or equitable interest therein. He is entitled to a share in the profits while the company continues to carry on business and a share in the distribution of the surplus assets when the company is wound up. If he were at liberty to effect an insurance against loss by fire of any item of the company's property, the extent of his insurable interest could only be measured by determining the extent to which his share in the ultimate distribution would be diminished by the loss of the asset – a calculation almost impossible to make. There is no means by which such an interest can be definitely measured and no standard which can be fixed of the loss against which the contract of insurance could be regarded as an indemnity.

Insurable interest in the ventures of a company

A shareholder, though he may not have any proprietary rights in the assets of a company, has, as was illustrated in *Wilson v Jones*, below, an insurable interest in the 'ventures' which that company may wish to undertake. The only prerequisite laid down by the court was that the subject matter of the insurance (the venture) should be clearly and properly defined.

Wilson v Jones (1867) LR 2 Exch 139

The plaintiff, as a shareholder in Atlantic Telegraph Company, effected a policy of insurance with the defendants, to cover against losses which the company might incur in the event of the cable laying operation across the Atlantic being a failure. The policy contained the following words: '... it is hereby understood and agreed that this policy ... shall cover every risk and contingency attending the conveyance and successful laying of the cable ...' The attempt to lay the cable failed, and the plaintiff claimed on his policy of insurance. The underwriters rejected the claim, and questioned the subject matter of the insurance as well as the insurable interest of the assured.

The court in the Exchequer Chamber ruled that the insurers were liable under the policy. As the plaintiff's insurable interest was not on the cable itself, but on the laying of the cable, it was held that he had an interest in the profits to be derived from the success of the adventure.

Willes J: [p 145] ... The first question therefore is, what was the subject matter insured? Is it, as has been contended, an insurance on the cable, or is it an insurance of the plaintiff's interest in a share of the profits to be derived from the cable which was to be laid down? In one sense, indeed, it is an insurance on the cable; that is, it affects the cable, as an insurance on freight affects the ship. The state of the ship and freight are so connected that it is impossible that they should be dissevered, except in cases where the loss of freight is effected by the loss of the goods only, in which case it might equally be said that the insurance on freight is an insurance on the goods. But except in that sense, it will appear, when the language of the policy is examined, that the insurance is an insurance, not on the cable, but on the interest which the plaintiff had in the success of the adventure.

[p 147] ... The present policy is evidently framed with skill and under good advice ... I am more fortified in this conclusion as to what is the subject matter insured, from the difficulty of suggesting any other construction of the policy, except that it is an insurance on the cable, which, for the reasons before mentioned, is not a rational construction.

Blackburn J: [p 151] ... He [the assured] was interested in a company which was about to lay down a cable across the Atlantic. If that event happened, there can be no doubt that the owner of shares in the company would be better off; if it did not happen, there can be no doubt his position would be worse. It follows, then, equally without doubt, that if by proper words the parties have entered into a contract of insurance for that interest, the policy is good. Now, if they had stopped at the word cable, the plaintiff's interest would not have been correctly or sufficiently described, according to the principle of the case *McSwiney v Royal Exchange Assurance Co*.[28] Neither if they had said that it was a cable as shipped on board *Great Eastern* [the ship laying the cable], would it have been a sufficient description. But, here, they have used words as to which I will only say, that no one who looks at them fairly, and reads them in connection with the circumstances, can fail to see that the intention of the parties would be frustrated by such a construction as is contended for by the defendant [the insurer].

Six years earlier, there had been another case of a claim on an insurance policy effected by a shareholder in Atlantic Telegraph Company, namely, **Paterson v Harris (1861) 1 B&S 336**. In this instance, the plaintiff, who was a major shareholder in Atlantic Telegraph Company, had effected a policy of insurance, and claimed that the subject matter of the insurance was his share in the company's venture, not the cable itself.

Although, in the event, the plaintiff shareholder was unsuccessful in his claims, because the losses did not fall within the cover of the policy, the court seemed to give credence to the fact that a shareholder could insure his interests in the company's activities. It is suggested that, as was the case in *Wilson v Jones* some years later, cited above, the court was trying to differentiate between the subject matter of the insurance being the venture rather than items of property owned by the company.

Cockburn CJ: [p 351] This is an action on a policy of insurance of a novel and somewhat remarkable character; being a policy on the plaintiff's share in a

---

28 *McSwiney v Royal Exchange Assurance Co* (1849) 14 QB 633, which is also concerned with profits on an adventure, is discussed in Chapter 3, p 113, where the principle referred to by Blackburn J is clearly illustrated.

company called Atlantic Telegraph Company ... The policy was in the ordinary form of marine insurance, with the addition of a special agreement contained in a memorandum annexed to the policy that the insurance should 'cover and include the successful working of the cable when laid down'.

[p 355] ... Now, it is obvious that the share in the company itself was never capable of being put on board ships or steamers; nor was it directly liable to be lost in consequence of the maritime risks ... It appears to us, therefore, that, on the true construction of this policy, the underwriters contract to indemnify the owner of that share against any losses arising to his interest in the cable, which interest is, by agreement, valued at £1,100.

Notes

In this connection, it would be helpful to be aware of the direction in which Canadian (and American) law has advanced. Further, in the light of the recent developments evident in this area of English law, in particular, the 'push' on the frontier of the concept of insurable interest, one would be ill-advised not to be familiar with the Canadian approach, as illustrated in *Constitution Insurance Co of Canada et al v Kosmopoulos et al*, below, albeit a non-marine case.

Constitution Insurance Co of Canada et al v Kosmopoulos et al (1987) 34 DLR (4th) 208, Supreme Court of Canada

Mr Kosmopoulos, the sole shareholder and director of a company, obtained insurance in his own name on the assets of his company. As a result of a fire, the assets of the company suffered smoke and water damage. He then brought an action under the policy, to which the insurers denied liability, on the ground that he had no insurable interest in the assets of the company.

The Supreme Court of Canada held that he had sufficient relation to or concern in the subject matter of the insurance to confer upon him an insurable interest. The court chose not to apply the rule in the *Macaura* case.[29] To ease itself out of a predicament, the court employed the device of the lifting of the corporate veil. The cases of *Lucena v Craufurd* and *Macaura* were examined in detail.

McIntyre J: [p 210] ... Modern company law now permits the creation of companies with one shareholder. The identity then between the company and the sole shareholder and director is such that an insurable interest in the company's assets may be found in the sole shareholder. This approach fits well with *Lucena v Craufurd* without opening the concept of insurable interest to indefinable limits.

---

29 Cf *Guarantee Co of North America v Aqua-land Exploration Ltd* (1965) 54 DLR (2d) 229 where, earlier, the Supreme Court, by a three to two majority held that a plaintiff, who lent money to the builders of a marine drilling tower and had safeguarded his loan by taking out an insurance policy on the tower, had no insurable interest in the tower. On this occasion, the court relied heavily on Lord Eldon's restrictive approach and the *Macaura* principle.

Wilson J: [p 218] ... A broadening of the concept of insurable interest would, it seems to me, allow for the creation of more socially beneficial insurance policies than is the case at present with no increase in risk to the insurer. I therefore find both of Lord Eldon's reasons for adopting a restrictive approach to insurable interest unpersuasive.

The difficulty of measuring the loss suffered by an individual shareholder should not, in my view, prevent a broadening of the definition of insurable interest. Modern company statutes ... require courts in certain circumstances to value shares. The task is obviously not considered impossible.

[p 221] ... Three policies have been cited as underlying the requirement of an insurable interest ... They are (1) the policy against wagering under the guise of insurance; (2) the policy favouring limitation of indemnity; and (3) the policy to prevent temptation to destroy the insured property. Does the implementation of these policies require the restrictive approach to insurable interest reflected in *Macaura*?

[p 222] (1) *The policy against wagering*

... I think it is probably easy to overestimate the risk of insurance contract being used in today's world to create a wagering transaction. There seem to be many more convenient devices available to the serious wagerer.

If wager should be a major concern in the context of insurance contracts, the current definition of insurable interest is not an ideal mechanism to combat this ill.

[p 223] ... I ... find, therefore, that the restrictive definition of insurable interest set out in *Macaura* is not required for the implementation of the policy against wagering.

[p 223] (2) *Indemnification for loss*

The public policy restricting the insured to full indemnity for his loss is not consistent with the restrictive definition of insurable interest set out in *Macaura* ...

[p 224] (3) *Destruction of the subject matter*

It has also been said that if the insured has no interest at all in the subject matter of the insurance, he is likely to destroy the subject matter in order to obtain the insurance money. But it is clear that the restrictive definition of insurable interest does not necessarily have this result ... If Lawrence J's definition of insurable interest in *Lucena v Craufurd* were adopted, this moral hazard would not be increased. Indeed, the moral hazard may well be decreased because the subject matter of the insurance is not usually in the possession or control of those included within Lawrence J's definition of insurable interest, that is, those with a pecuniary interest only.

[p 225] ... I have already noted that, while in the case of a single shareholder corporation, courts are unlikely to lift the corporate veil for the benefit of that single shareholder, they have been willing to lift the corporate veil 'in the interests of third parties who would otherwise suffer as a result of that choice': Gower ... p 138.

In summary, it seems to me that the policies underlying the requirement of an insurable interest do not support the restrictive definition: if anything, they support a broader definition than that set out in *Macaura*.

While *Macaura* continues as the law in the United Kingdom ... and in Australia and New Zealand ... many jurisdictions in the United States have abandoned the restrictive definition of insurable interests in favour of the 'factual expectancy test' ...

[p 227] ... No material has been referred to us by counsel to show that these developments in the United States have led to insoluble problems of calculation, difficulties in ascertaining insurable interests, wagering, over-insurance or wilful destruction of property. Indeed, the commentators both in the United States and Canada seem to be uniformly in favour of the adoption of the factual expectancy test for insurable interest and the rejection of the test set out by the House of Lords in *Macaura* ...

In my view, there is little to commend the restrictive definition of insurable interest ... I think *Macaura* should no longer be followed.

[p 228] Mr Kosmopoulos, as a sole shareholder of the company, was so placed with respect to the assets of the business as to have benefit from their existence and prejudice from their destruction. He had a moral certainty of advantage or benefit from these assets but for the fire. He had, therefore, an insurable interest in them capable of supporting the insurance policy and is entitled to recover under it.

Notes

The Canadian court's analysis and acceptance of the wider approach of Lawrence J in *Lucena v Craufurd* are commendable. But it has to be emphasised that, under English law, the restrictive rule of Lord Eldon still applies which, though stirred by Colman J in the *Moonacre*, case had not been shaken.

Other persons with insurable interest

As mentioned earlier, the wording of s 5(2) is indeed wide enough to accommodate a host of persons who might have an insurable interest. The Act does specify certain classes of people with insurable interest, but they are by no means exhaustive. There are also others who are likely to benefit from the preservation of the subject matter insured, such as a ship's agent, captors and the lender of money on bottomry and respondentia.

A ship's agent

Moran, Galloway and Co v Uzielli and Others [1905] 2 KB 555

The agents (plaintiffs) in the UK had advanced moneys over a number of years to the owners of a foreign ship, *Prince Louis*. The agents had also effected a policy of insurance on disbursements against total and constructive total loss caused by, amongst other things, perils of the sea. When *Prince Louis* arrived at Cardiff and discharged her cargo of timber from Vancouver, the freight was paid to the plaintiffs, as agents for the owners. However, when *Prince Louis* was making ready to load her next cargo, she was found to have been severely damaged by bad weather, which she had experienced during her voyage from Vancouver, and deemed to be a constructive total loss. The agents retained the freight which they had a lien upon and then claimed on their policy of insurance on disbursements. The question before the court was whether an agent of a ship had an insurable interest in the ship.

The court ruled that the agents did have an insurable interest in the ship, not because they drew any benefit from the safe arrival of the ship, but because they had a right of action *in rem* against the ship under s 6 of the Admiralty Court Act 1840.[30]

> **Walton J:** [p 558] ... Before proceeding further, I may point out that, in the case of an ordinary shipowner's policy on disbursements, no questions arise such as have to be considered in the present case. In such cases, the disbursements represent expenditure by the shipowner either on his ship or for the purpose of earning his freight, and such policies are in the nature of insurances of the shipowner, either upon his ship or upon his freight.
>
> [p 559] ... The question which has to be determined in this action is whether the plaintiffs have lost by perils of the sea anything in which they had at the time of loss an insurable interest, and, if so, what was the amount of such loss. ... The plaintiffs' interest was in respect of their advances, and it has been admitted that such interest is sufficiently described in the policy as 'disbursements' ... What, then, was the plaintiffs' interest? They clearly had an interest in the debt which was due to them on account of their disbursements, or, in other words, in their legal right as creditors of the shipowners. But this legal right was in no sense dependent on the safe arrival of the ship. It remained the same whether the ship was lost or not. It was not, and was not capable of being, exposed to the perils insured against. It was never at risk under the policy. It was not lost ... I think, therefore, that the fact that the plaintiffs were interested in the debt merely as a debt did not give them any insurable interest ... There was no evidence before me to show that the debt may not still be recoverable from the shipowners. The plaintiffs' case in this respect cannot be put higher, I think, than this, that the recovery of the debt was rendered less certain and more difficult by the loss of the ship.
>
> [p 562] ... In so far as the plaintiffs' claim depends upon the fact that they were ordinary unsecured creditors of the shipowners for an ordinary unsecured debt, I am satisfied that it must fail. The probability that if the debtor's ship should be lost he would be less able to pay his debts does not, in my judgment, give to the creditor any interest, legal or equitable, which is dependent upon the safe arrival of the ship. In such a case, all that the creditor has, all that he

---

30 See, now, Supreme Court Act 1981, s 20(2)(m) and (p).

can lose by the loss of the ship, is an expectation. I do not think that the creditor of the shipowner has an insurable interest in all the shipowner's property which is exposed to maritime risks.

[pp 562–63] ... But a further, and to my mind much more difficult, point remains to be considered. It is said that the plaintiffs in the present case had more than an expectation, because they had the right, under the Admiralty Court Act 1840, to proceed *in rem* for the recovery of the amount owing to them.

... If the ship was lost, the right to obtain this security on *Prince Louis* was gone. Was this a real risk which underwriters may be asked, in consideration of an adequate premium, to undertake? And if they do undertake it, is the contract a binding contract? There is no doubt, to my mind, as to the reality of the risk. The foundation of the rules as to insurable interest is that the contract of marine insurance is essentially a contract of indemnity. Unless the assured is exposed to a risk of real loss by the perils insured against, the contract is not a contract of indemnity, but is a mere wagering contract, and cannot be enforced. I am satisfied that a contract such as I have indicated, and such as is contained in the policy now in question (in so far as it extends to cover the plaintiffs' interest in respect of necessaries), is not a wagering contract, and is a contract by which the plaintiffs were protected from the risk of a real loss.

[p 564] ... I think there is a distinction between the position of a creditor for an ordinary debt who has no right to arrest the property of his debtor except after judgment, under a writ of execution, and the position of the plaintiffs in this case. To hold that there was an insurable interest in this case will not offend against the principles of the rules as to insurable interest, or against any decision of our courts. To hold that there would be no insurable interest would, I think, be to impose an unnecessary fetter upon business which seems to me very ordinary and reasonable business, in no way tainted by the vice of wagering or gaming. Therefore I hold that, to the extent to which the plaintiffs' claim for disbursements was a claim for necessaries within 3 & 4 Vict C 65, s 6, they had an insurable interest.

Captors

Stirling v Vaughan (1809) 11 East 619

A vessel, later named as *Prize No 3*, was captured by the plaintiffs from the Spanish and insured for the voyage to England from Montevideo. During the voyage, the vessel was lost by perils of the sea and the issue before the court was whether the captors, before there had been any official condemnation of the vessel by the Court of Admiralty, had an insurable interest in her.

The court ruled that the captors had an insurable interest in the ship, and the insurers were liable under the policy.

Lord Ellenborough CJ: [p 629] ... The captors have the actual possession of the subject matter of insurance by the grant of the King, the only person in the kingdom who could contest the title with them. They have the possession, with a partial right of disposing of the thing immediately, liable indeed to have their right devested by a sentence of restoration. But what difference is there between the right of the captors and of the Crown itself in these respects? The assignees of the Crown, as they may be styled, must stand in the same situation in this respect as the Crown itself. This is not like insuring a mere expectation, nor like the case of the Dutch Commissioners, who had no interest in the ships insured till they came within the ports of the realm. But these captors had a present possession and a right to maintain trespass against any person attempting to take the prize from them. Even with respect to captors in general; supposing the prize not to have been acquired tortiously, but *jure belli*, I should think that in respect of such their lawful possession and special property, they might insure; but it is not necessary in this case to decide that general point, because here the captors had a more perfect right; they had not only a right of possession, but a right of property as far as the Crown had the power of granting it, liable only to be dispossessed by the release of the Crown before condemnation or by sentence of restoration.

Bayley J: [p 632] ... The captors have the possession of it, and they are liable in damages to the original owners if the capture has been irregularly made: and there have been many cases where, though the capture was properly made under the circumstances, yet the captors were decreed to restore the ship and cargo, in whole or in part: they, therefore, ought to be in a condition to restore the value in case of loss, if ultimately they should be directed by the Court of Admiralty so to do. The interest in the prize is so far vested in the captors, that in case of the death of any of them before condemnation, his share when condemned goes to his representatives. The case of a consignee of goods is not so strong as that of a captor in favour of an insurable interest. He has no present possession of, he may have no beneficial interest in, the goods; and in case of his death, his lien on the consignment is lost. On reading the note of what fell from Lord Eldon in the House of Lords upon the case of *Lucena v Craufurd*, it appears to me that his Lordship considered that captors would have an insurable interest upon the ground on which he put their claim.

Bottomry and respondentia

In the old days, in cases of utmost necessity when money was needed for the ship, the master used to put the ship (the bottom) as security for a loan. Naturally, the person who advances the loan has an insurable interest in the ship, in accordance with s 10 of the Act. The term 'respondentia' refers to advances made in respect of cargo. Both forms of such security, however, have nowadays become obsolete.

WHEN INTEREST MUST ATTACH

That the assured must have an insurable interest before he is permitted to recover for a loss is established law. The cardinal rule in marine insurance, however, is that this interest must have attached *at the time of the loss*, otherwise he is not entitled to be indemnified.[31] This, however, does not mean that the assured should necessarily have an insurable interest at the time when the policy was effected; this is clarified by s 4(2)(a), read with s 6(1) of the Act. Section 4(2)(a) states:

> A contract of marine insurance, is deemed to be a gaming or wagering contract:
>
> (a) where the assured has not an insurable interest as defined by this Act, and the contract is entered into with no expectation of acquiring such an interest ...

Section 6(1) states:

> (1) The assured must be interested in the subject matter insured at the time of the loss though he need not be interested when the insurance is effected ...
>
> (2) ...
>
> (3) Where the assured has no interest at the time of the loss, he cannot acquire interest by any act or election after he is aware of the loss.

The ICC, cl 11.1, reiterates thus:

> In order to recover under this insurance the Assured must have an insurable interest in the subject matter insured at the time of the loss.

Buchanan v Faber (1899) 4 Com Cas 223

The steamship *Queen Victoria* grounded and was damaged near Port Elizabeth in South Africa. After she was got off the reef, the plaintiffs, who were insurance brokers, effected a policy on disbursements to cover their own interests, the commissions they expected to earn, as well as the interests of the managing owners for the short voyage to Cape Town for permanent repairs. However, the weather worsened, and *Queen Victoria* was wrecked and became a total loss. The plaintiffs claimed on their policy of insurance, but the insurers refused payment on the basis that the ship was never seaworthy for the voyage.

The court ruled that the plaintiffs could not recover on their policy because *Queen Victoria* was unseaworthy. Bigham J, however, briefly touched upon the question of insurable interest.

---

31 See Marine Insurance Act 1906, s 6(2).

Bigham J: [p 226] ... It is not necessary for me to deal with the question whether the plaintiffs had any insurable interests; but I think they had none. They had nothing more than a hope that, if the vessel lived, they might continue to earn their commissions and brokerage. No contract between Messrs Dunlop [the managing owners] and the owners was produced to show that they had a permanent right to be employed as managing owners. Every ship's husband and insurance broker has a right to entertain a similar hope, perhaps not so likely to be realised, but in its character the same. If, however, the plaintiffs had an insurable interest, the word 'disbursements' was quite sufficient to describe it. It is well understood at Lloyd's to be a compendious term used to describe any interest which is outside the ordinary and well known interests of 'hull', 'machinery', 'cargo', and 'freight'.

Notes

The case of *Buchanan v Faber* was commented on by Deputy Judge Colman QC, in *Moonacre* **[1992] Lloyd's Rep 501**, discussed earlier, as follows:[32]

Deputy Judge Colman QC: [pp 510–11] ... The requirement for the existence *at the time of the loss* [emphasis added] of rights in respect of the adventure or property recognised by law or in equity is exemplified by the cases, such as *Buchanan v Faber* (1899) 4 Com Cas 223, where the benefit to the assured from the preservation of the property arises only from the possibility that the assured will *in future* make a contract which, if the goods survive, will or may confer benefits on him. In such cases, the only relationship between the assured and the property is an expectation or possibility of the future acquisition of a closer relationship giving rise to rights dependent upon the preservation of the property. The mere hope of a future relationship does not take the assured out of the realms of wager into the area of indemnifiable risk. Once one can establish the existence at the time of the loss of rights enjoyed by the assured in respect of the insured property and that if it is lost or damaged such rights will or may be less beneficial, an insurable interest exists, regardless of the precise nature of the rights or the means by which they have been acquired. There then can be said to exist a risk of loss against which the assured can, consistently with the law against wagering contracts, ask to be indemnified.

In *Capricorn* [1995] 1 Lloyd's Rep 622, discussed earlier in the chapter, Mance J also stressed the significance of the requirement that the assured must have an insurable interest at the time of loss. He said: [p 641] '... Under s 6 of the Marine Insurance Act, the plaintiffs' insurable interest in the subject matter insured (here freight or other income from trading) must have existed at the time of the *loss* though no such interest need exist when the insurance is effected.'

---

32 See above, p 43.

Lost or not lost

In times past, when communications were poor, a buyer was often at risk of having bought goods which had already been lost at sea. However, he could overcome the general principle that an assured must have acquired an insurable interest *at the time of loss* by incorporating a 'lost or not lost' clause into the insurance policy. The purpose of the clause is to protect a buyer by permitting him to recover on the policy, even though he may have only acquired his interest *after* the loss. The assured buyer, however, would be barred from recovery if he was aware of the loss and the insurer was not, in accordance with the proviso of s 6(2). As to the position of the cargo-owner, cl 11.2 of the ICC echoes the principle of the proviso in s 6(2):

> Subject to 11.1 above, the Assured shall be entitled to recover for insured loss occurring during the period covered by this insurance, notwithstanding that the loss occurred before the contract of insurance was concluded, unless the Assured were aware of the loss and the Underwriters were not.

The same is repeated in r 1 of the Rules for Construction of the Act:

> Where the subject matter is insured 'lost or not lost', and the loss occurred before the contract is concluded, the risk attaches unless, at such time, the assured was aware of the loss, and the insurer was not.

Needless to say, if the assured was aware of the loss and the insurer was not, the assured would be barred from recovery also on the grounds of a breach of the duty to observe utmost good faith under s 17, and of non-disclosure of a material circumstance under s 18 of the Act.

The problems associated with a 'lost or not lost' clause were recently highlighted in *NSW Leather Co Pty Ltd v Vanguard Insurance Co Ltd* **[1991] 105 FLR 381**, the facts of which have already been cited in full earlier.[33] Though the 'lost or not lost' clause has, it would appear, fallen into disuse, nevertheless, the issues raised in the said case are pertinent in so far as they relate to the question of insurable interest. Further, there is, of course, nothing in law to prevent a buyer today from insuring his goods on a 'lost or not lost' basis. As the only two English cases on the 'lost or not lost' clause, namely, *Sutherland v Pratt* (1843) 11 M&W 296 and *Reinhart Co v Joshua Hoyle and Sons Ltd* [1961] 1 Lloyd's Rep 346, are discussed in the *NSW Leather* case, they will not be examined separately. On the application of the 'lost or not lost' clause, Handley JA's judgment reads as follows:

> **Handley JA:** [pp 390 and 391] ... In the present policy, the [lost or not lost] clause was part of the printed form. The policy also included a typewritten schedule which provided expressly that the policy was on goods in which the assured had an insurable interest. The defendant [insurer] argued at the trial that the typewritten schedule was inconsistent with and prevailed over the

---

33 See above, p 56.

printed clause. The trial judge rejected this submission and so do I. There is no inconsistency between these provisions.

It is now clear that this clause operates in two quite distinct ways. The first is dealt with in r 1 of the second Schedule to the Marine Insurance Act, which provides:

> Where the subject matter is insured 'lost or not lost', and the loss has occurred before the contract is concluded, the risk attaches unless, at such time, the assured was aware of the loss, and the insurer was not.

An assured with an existing insurable interest in a marine adventure may therefore insure that interest and recover, although at the time, unknown to both parties, its subject matter had already been lost or damaged. This effect of the clause is not relevant, because here, the open policy had been issued several years before the thefts.

However, the clause also operates in a quite different manner. This is covered by s 12 [our s 6] which provides, so far as relevant:

> (1) The assured must be interested in the subject matter insured at the time of loss ... provided that where the subject matter is insured 'lost or not lost', the assured may recover although he may not have acquired his interest until after the loss ...
>
> (2) Where the assured has no interest at the time of the loss, he cannot acquire interest by an act or election after he is aware of the loss.

... An insured who acquires an insurable interest in a marine adventure after a loss is entitled to recover, provided that loss then falls on him and there is an appropriately worded policy.

... The court was referred to *Sutherland v Pratt* ... and *Reinhart Co v Joshua Hoyle and Sons Ltd* ... which appear to be the only relevant English decisions. In *Sutherland v Pratt* ... the plaintiff sued on a marine policy effected on his behalf on cotton consigned from Bombay to London which had been pledged to him to secure an advance. Unknown to the parties, the cotton had already been damaged when it was pledged to the plaintiff. When sued on the policy, the underwriter pleaded that the loss had occurred prior to the plaintiff acquiring his interest, but this was held to be no answer. Parke B (pp 311–12) said:

> ... the simple question is, whether it is any answer to an action on a policy on goods (lost or not lost) that the interest in them was not acquired until after the loss. We are of the opinion that it is not. Such a policy is clearly a contract of indemnity against all past, as well as all future losses, sustained by the assured, in respect to the interest insured. It operates just in the same way as if the plaintiff having purchased goods at sea, the defendant, for a premium, had agreed that if the goods had at the time of the purchase sustained any damaged by perils of the sea, he would make it good.

In *Reinhart Co v Joshua Hoyle and Sons Ltd* ... the parties were the seller and buyer under a C&F contract for the sale of Mexican cotton to the United Kingdom ... Pearson J referred to *Sutherland v Pratt* and the corresponding provision in the Marine Insurance Act 1906 (UK) and, not surprisingly, held (p 489) '... it is possible for an assured to be insured in respect of a loss which happened before he acquired his insurable interest' ... In the result, he held that the buyers were covered under the policy for damage sustained by the cotton before it was loaded on board.

... Accordingly, subject to two remaining matters, the appellant is entitled to invoke the lost or not lost clause in respect of the losses through theft which occurred prior to it acquiring its insurable interest in these goods.

This conclusion is consistent with the decision of the higher courts in *Anderson v Morice*. There, the plaintiff, having taken up the shipping documents after loss with knowledge of the facts, was held not entitled to recover under the policy. The lost or not lost clause was not referred to either in the arguments or in the judgment in any court, but it is evident that the effect of the decision is embodied in s 12(2).

The respondent contended that the appellant still cannot recover, because it suffered no loss. The appellant was not at risk when the goods were stolen. However, it suffered financial loss because of the prior loss of the goods, and this is sufficient. The fact that it has contractual remedies against its seller is no answer ... Here, the appellant suffered loss because the goods had previously been stolen and the lost or lost not clause entitled it to recover for the earlier thefts, although it suffered no loss when they occurred.

[pp 392–93] ... The respondent further contended that the appellant could not recover under the clause because it never acquired an insurable interest in the stolen goods. The argument was that the property in the stolen goods never passed, because the goods were not shipped. Accordingly, so it was submitted, the only goods in which the risk or the property passed were those remaining in the containers. Counsel for neither party was able to refer the court to any authority directly in point and accordingly, during argument, the question was considered on principle. On this basis, in my opinion, the court should hold that property in the stolen goods passed to the appellant at the time and in the manner in which it would have passed had the containers not been pilfered.

[p 393] The sellers had contracted to sell the goods, the containers thought to contain such goods had been loaded on board and the appellant had paid the price ... On principle, it seems to me that these parties intended the property in the goods, which unknown to them had been stolen, to pass to the buyer under their contracts. The only question can be whether the theft of the goods prior to their delivery frustrated or defeated the parties' contractual intention. I can see no reason why the law should defeat the parties' intention in such a case. The buyer, of course, was entitled to reject the goods on arrival, and thus re-vest title in the seller, but this tends to confirm the conclusion that the property in all the goods had previously passed to the buyer.

During argument, members of the court put to counsel for the respondent a hypothetical example relating to a vintage car sold on FOB terms stolen from its container prior to shipment with the theft not discovered until arrival. If the stolen car was later recovered, could the seller refund the price and retain the car against the buyer, perhaps after it had risen in value? Counsel for the respondent submitted that the seller was entitled to do so. In my judgment the question answers itself. The property in the stolen car would have passed under the contract, at the latest on payment of the price, and provided the contract remained on foot, the property would be with the buyer.

[p 394] ... The appellant is therefore entitled to succeed under the lost or not clause in the policy.

Notes

Even though the case is Australian, and therefore does not bind English courts, it is, nonetheless, a decision of considerable interest. It has raised a few obscure points and has left several questions unanswered. It is common ground that, under the terms of an FOB contract, the goods are at the risk of the seller up to the point of shipment. On this basis, the risks were borne by the seller when the goods were stolen. Thus, the decision of the court that the plaintiff, the buyer, did not have an insurable interest at the time when the goods were stolen, is in accord with established legal principles laid down in *Anderson v Morice*.[34]

Having said that, the court would then like us to assume for the purpose of the 'lost and not lost' clause that property had passed to the buyer on the shipment of what was effectively empty containers. In so imagining, the court was able to satisfy itself that the buyers had acquired an interest *after* the loss, and were able to recover under the said clause. The court was prepared to premise its decision on something which *would*, in the normal course of events, happen. The prickly question is, can a buyer acquire interest in non-existent goods? Handley JA, p 393, was clear in his mind that the buyer may even reject the goods on arrival and thus re-vest the title in the seller. Indeed, the same issue arises, can a buyer reject goods which do not arrive at their intended destination?

It is suggested that perhaps a far less contrived solution to the conflict is to keep apart the law of passing risks and property in a contract of sale from that of insurable interest in marine insurance. Should the liberal approach of Lawrence J, in *Lucena v Craufurd*, be applied, there would be no reason why a buyer should not be regarded as having an insurable interest in the goods at the time of loss, provided, of course, that a valid contract of sale has been entered into; his concern or relationship, or 'a moral certainty of advantage or benefit', in the goods should be sufficient to afford him an insurable interest. His relationship with the goods is not, by any stretch of imagination, speculative, or one of mere expectation, it is real and a 'factual expectancy'.

---

34 The court could not, in this case, go the other way by applying the principle in *Fuerst Day Lawson Ltd v Orion Insurance Co Ltd* [1980] 1 Lloyd's Rep 656, that the risk under the policy never attached because the goods that were shipped were not the goods which were insured. In the *NSW Leather* case, the policy was from warehouse to warehouse, and the insured goods packed in containers were stolen *after* the risk under the policy had attached at the warehouse.

An assignee

The other exception to the rule that an assured must have an insurable interest at the time of loss is to be found in the case of an assignee of a policy. By s 50(1), a policy may be assigned either before or after the loss. Thus, an assignee who has acquired his interest after a loss is entitled to recover under the policy even though he has no interest at the time of loss. The only prerequisite is that the assignor must, at the time of the assignment, have an interest to assign. This is perfectly logical, for a man cannot give or assign what he does not possess.[35]

---

35 See Marine Insurance Act 1906, ss 15, 50 and 51.

CHAPTER 3

SUBJECT MATTER INSURED

INTRODUCTION

Section 3 of the Marine Insurance Act 1906 declares that every 'lawful marine adventure' may be insured, and the section then goes on to consider what may constitute a 'marine adventure':

(1) Subject to the provisions of this Act, every lawful marine adventure may be the subject of a contract of marine insurance.

(2) In particular, there is a marine adventure where:

    (a) any ship goods or other movables are exposed to maritime perils. Such property is in this Act referred to as 'insurable property';

    (b) the earning or acquisition of any freight, passage money, commission, profit, or other pecuniary benefit, or the security for any advances, loan, or disbursements, is endangered by the exposure of insurable property to maritime perils;

    (c) any liability to a third party may be incurred by the owner of, or other person interested in or responsible for, insurable property, by reason of maritime perils.

Thus, in keeping with s 3 of the Act, the following subject matter are insurable under a marine policy of insurance:

(a) ship;
(b) goods;
(c) movables;
(d) freight;
(e) profits;
(f) commissions;
(g) disbursements;
(h) wages;
(i) ventures undertaken by a company;
(j) third party liability.

The only stipulation made by the Act with respect to the nature of the subject matter insured is that it should be 'designated with reasonable certainty' in the marine policy. To this effect, s 26(1) of the Act states:

The subject matter insured must be designated in a marine policy with reasonable certainty.

Failure to designate the subject matter in the policy with reasonable certainty could be construed as non-disclosure of a material circumstance.[1]

However, it is emphasised that, whilst the subject matter within the policy must be designated with reasonable certainty, there is no requirement for the assured to indicate the nature and extent of his interest in the policy. Thus, it is not necessary in the case of reinsurance for the policy to stipulate that it is in fact a policy of reinsurance. This was well illustrated in *Mackenzie v Whitworth*, below.

Mackenzie v Whitworth (1875) 1 Ex D 36, CA

A cargo of cotton was insured by American underwriters for a voyage from New Orleans to Revel (now Tallin) in Estonia. The American underwriters then reinsured a portion of the cotton without disclosing the fact that the policy was in fact a policy of reinsurance. When the American underwriters came to claim on their policy of reinsurance, the reinsurers refused to pay, asserting that they had not been informed that the policy was one of reinsurance.

The Court of Appeal, however, ruled that, although the reinsurers had not been informed that the policy was one of reinsurance, it did not amount to the concealment of a material fact.

> **Blackburn J:** [p 40] ... A description of the subject matter of insurance is required both from the nature of the contract and from the universal practice of insurers. It is generally described very concisely as being so much 'on ship', 'on goods', 'on freight', 'on profits on goods', 'on advances on coolies', 'on emigrant money', and many other examples might be given. And, if no property which answers the description in the policy be at risk, the policy will not attach, though the assured may have other property at risk of equal or greater value. The reason being, that the insurers have not entered into a contract to indemnify the assured for any loss on that other property.
>
> [p 42] ... In all cases where the peculiar nature of the interest alters the risk, it may be properly said that such interest is the subject matter of the insurance; and at all events there is great force in the argument that the nature of that interest should be stated. But in the case now before us, the nature of the interest of the parties assured in the cotton does not in the slightest degree vary the nature of the risk ... The subject matter of insurance, viz, the cotton, is fully described, and there is no apparent reason which would make it just to require the nature of the interest to be described. Still, if there were a series of decisions determining that in such a case, or in cases analogous to it, a description was required beyond what would seem to us reasonable, we would be unwilling to disturb the established practice. But we do not find any such decisions.

---

1   See Marine Insurance Act 1906, s 18(1): 'Subject to the provisions of this section, the assured must disclose to the insurer, before the contract is concluded, every material circumstance which is known to the assured ...'

SHIP

What constitutes a 'ship' is determined by r 15 of the Rules for Construction, which states:

> The term 'ship' includes the hull, materials and outfit, stores and provisions for the officers and crew, and, in the case of vessels engaged in a special trade, the ordinary fittings requisite for the trade, and also, in the case of a steamship, the machinery, boilers, and coals and engine stores, if owned by the assured.

It is to be noted that a policy on 'ship' is an insurance of more than just the hull; it includes materials and stores necessary for the prosecution of the voyage as well as the engine room machinery, coals and stores. It does not, however, include stores for passengers.

Thus, an insurance policy on a 'ship' is much more comprehensive than an insurance on 'hull and machinery', as was illustrated in *Roddick v Indemnity Mutual Marine Insurance Co Ltd*, below.

Roddick v Indemnity Mutual Marine Insurance Co Ltd [1895] 2 QB 380, CA

The plaintiff owners of the steamship *Oxenholme* insured her 'hull and machinery' with the defendants under a time policy of insurance which contained a warranty that £5,000 was to be uninsured. As the ship was valued at £10,000, the plaintiffs effected hull and machinery policies to the extent of £5,000 and no more. However, the plaintiffs effected further ppi policies[2] on disbursements made on coals, stores and expenses totalling £2,600. When *Oxenholme* was lost, and the plaintiffs claimed on their insurance, the insurers refused payment, on the basis that the plaintiffs had exceeded the £5,000 warranty when they insured the disbursements.

The Court of Appeal, in affirming the decision of the trial judge, ruled in favour of the plaintiff owners. The ppi policies on disbursements did not relate to the hull and machinery policies and, therefore, there was no breach of the warranty.

> **Lord Esher MR:** [p 384] ... The defendant company have departed from the use of the word 'ship', and have used instead of it another term – 'hull and machinery' – and we have to construe those words. The 'hull' of a ship is a well known term. If you were to tell a sailor that the 'hull' of his ship included the provisions on board, he would be very much surprised; and so he would if he were told that the provisions were part of the 'machinery' of the ship. Taking the words 'hull and machinery' in their ordinary natural sense, it is perfectly clear what they mean. Has it then been proved that these words have, as between assurer and assured, universally acquired a meaning different from their natural meaning? In my opinion, the learned judge was

---

2 Policy proof of interest. The purpose of these 'honour' policies, which have no standing in law, is explained in Chapter 1, p 5.

quite right in holding that this had not been proved. I am satisfied that the words 'hull and machinery' cannot be taken as including those things which are covered by the 'disbursement' policies. It follows that the defence of breach of warranty cannot be maintained, and the learned judge was right in so holding.

> **AL Smith LJ:** [p 386] ... What is the ordinary meaning of an insurance upon the 'hull and machinery' of a steamship? Does it cover the coal on board, or the provisions and stores? I think it clear that it does not. It was ingeniously argued that 'hull and machinery' in the case of a steam vessel means the ship, and that there is authority for saying that the word 'ship' covers 'coal and stores'. In *Brough v Whitmore*, the insurance was upon the 'ship' and the 'furniture' of the ship, and it was held that the policy covered provisions for the use of the crew ... Here, however, the words used are 'hull and machinery', not 'ship', and in my opinion, the judgment of the learned judge was right.

The above case, where only the hull and machinery were insured, should be compared with *Hogarth v Walker*, below.

Hogarth v Walker [1899] 2 QB 401

A vessel employed continuously in the Black Sea grain trade was insured under a policy on 'ship and furniture'. When the vessel collided with a pierhead and severely damaged her bow section, where a large number of dunnage mats[3] and separation cloths were stowed, the owners of the ship claimed on their policy for the loss of the dunnage mats and separation cloths which had floated away. The underwriters defended the action, on the basis that the dunnage mats and separation cloths were not covered by the policy.

The court ruled that the owners could recover under the policy because the insurance was on 'ship and furniture'.

> **Bigham J:** [p 402] ... In my opinion, the plaintiffs are entitled to succeed. The question is whether an ordinary Lloyd's time policy on ship, the ship being engaged in the grain trade, covers separation cloths and dunnage mats. It seems clear that, under the ordinary circumstances of that trade, the use of such cloths and mats would be necessary for the proper carriage of the cargo, and that if the ship went to sea without them, she would be unseaworthy. Therefore, they must be regarded as forming part of her furniture. I can see no distinction between them and movable bulkheads, which it was admitted by the defendants would form part of the ship's furniture. Both are intended for the same purpose – namely, to separate one part of the cargo from another.

---

3   Dunnage mats, or raffia mats, are mats made from the leaves of palm trees which are placed between the grain and the ship's bulkheads and sides to prevent the grain being damaged by condensation. They are also used for separating portions of cargo.

Hull policies (MAR 91 form) and the Institute Hulls Clauses

There are two standard sets of Institute Hulls Clauses which may be employed with, and only with, the current Lloyd's Marine Policy (MAR 91)[4] and the Institute of London Underwriting Companies Marine Policy Form (MAR 91).[5]

The standard hull policies are:[6]

(a) the Institute Time Clauses Hulls, 1/11/95 (ITCH(95));[7]

(b) the Institute Voyage Clauses Hulls, 1/11/95 (IVCH(95)).[8]

All the Institute Clauses are unreservedly subject to English law and practice,[9] but it should be noted that the ITCH(95) and the IVCH(95) are less favourable to the assured than the 1983 Clauses.[10]

GOODS

'Goods' are defined in the first part of r 17 of the Rules for Construction thus:

> The term 'goods' means goods in the nature of merchandise, and does not include personal effects or provisions and stores for use on board.

Goods, therefore, are restricted to those goods which are merchantable in the way of trade; ship's provisions and stores as well as personal effects[11] are excluded under the definition.

---

4 See Appendix 4.
5 See Appendix 5.
6 A range of other Institute Hulls Clauses are available with specialised cover: the ITCH(95) – Restricted Perils (see Appendix 8); the Institute Additional Perils Clauses – Hulls 1995 (see Appendix 9); the ITCH(95) – Total Loss, General Average and 3/4ths Collision Liability (including Salvage, Salvage Charges and Sue and Labour); the ITCH(95) – Total Loss Only; the ITCH(95) – Disbursements and Increased Value (Total Loss only, including Excess Liabilities); and the ITCH(95) – Excess Liabilities.
7 See Appendix 6.
8 See Appendix 7.
9 On the question of jurisdiction, see Mandaraka-Sheppard, A, 'Hull and time clauses: marine perils in perspective', in *The Modern Law of Marine Insurance*, 1996, London: LLP, pp 49–54.
10 As all the 1983 Clauses will soon be (if they have not already been) phased out of use, they will not be used as the basis for discussion.
11 The leading authority on personal effects is the case of *Duff v Mackenzie* (1857) 3 CBNS 16. This case is discussed in Chapter 17, p 705.

The Institute Cargo Clauses (A), (B) and (C)

Goods may be insured under the Institute Cargo Clauses (A), (B) and (C).[12] Whereas the ICC (B) and (C) provide cover for enumerated perils, the ICC (A) provides 'all risks' cover and, because of this, has the added and important advantage of making the burden of proof placed upon a claimant less rigorous. Unlike the ICC (B) and (C), under the ICC (A), the claimant does not have to show how the loss occurred, only that it did occur. It then falls upon the insurer to prove that the loss fell within one of the exceptions in the policy for which he is not liable.

Deck cargo and living animals

The second part of r 17 of the Rules for Construction affirms that:

> In the absence of any usage to the contrary, deck cargo and living animals must be insured specifically, and not under the general denomination of goods.

Thus, the Act confirms that, because of the special nature and hazards which are commensurate with the carriage of deck cargo and living animals, they must be specifically insured as such unless there is 'usage to the contrary'.

The importance of complying with r 17 was illustrated in the case of *Hood v West End Motor Car Packing Co* **[1917] 2 KB 38, CA**, where the plaintiff instructed the defendants, who specialised in the packing of cars, to forward his motor car from London to Messina in Sicily. In the event, the car was carried on deck without the insurers' knowledge, and when it arrived at Messina, it was found to be damaged beyond repair. As the insurers refused to pay the claim, the plaintiff sued the defendants.

The Court of Appeal ruled that the risk of carrying a car on deck was not covered by the insurance policy and the defendants, who had agreed to insure the car as part of the contract with the plaintiff, were liable.

> **Scrutton LJ:** [p 47] ... Upon the true construction of the documents, I think that the defendants undertook the latter obligation, namely, to procure a policy against all risks except war risks. The next question is, have they performed that obligation? They shipped the car on deck. In the body of the policy it is stated that the insurance was 'on motor car', not stating that the car was to be carried on deck. By the old law before the Marine Insurance Act 1906, and now by r 17 of the Rules for Construction of Policy in Sched I to the Act, in the absence of any usage to the contrary, cargo carried on deck must be insured specifically. The defendants, therefore, have not procured a policy in terms covering a motor car carried on deck against all marine risks.

---

12 See Appendices 10, 11 and 12, respectively.

Is r 17 applicable to deck cargoes carried on inland voyages?

This question was raised in *Apollinaris Co v Nord Deutsche Insurance Co*, below. The issue of whether the general rule contained in r 17 regarding deck cargoes was inapplicable to all inland voyages was left open. However, Walton J was 'by no means satisfied' that the rule should apply to inland voyages by canal or river. This is not an unreasonable supposition, as the rationale that there is an increase in hazard when goods are carried on deck on sea voyages applies with much less force in the case of inland voyages.[13]

Apollinaris Co v Nord Deutsche Insurance Co [1904] 1 KB 252

The plaintiffs insured a variety of goods with the defendants against all risks for a voyage from London to Amsterdam and thence up the River Rhine to Neuenahr. On arrival at Amsterdam, the goods were transhipped and stowed on the deck of a Rhine steamer in readiness for the canal and river passage. However, a fire broke out, and many of the goods were destroyed. When the plaintiffs claimed on their policy of insurance, the insurers refused to pay, on the basis that they, the insurers, had not been notified that the goods were to be carried on deck.

The court ruled that, as it was common practice for goods to be stowed on the deck of Rhine steamers and, therefore, as the goods need not be specifically insured, the insurers were liable under the policy.

> **Walton J:** [p 261] ... the same gentleman [a Dutch lawyer] who proved the Dutch law also proved that deck cargoes are very commonly carried on the Rhine steamers, and I understood from his evidence that the usual form of bill of lading used by the Rhine steamers gives express liberty to stow cargo on deck ... I have come to the conclusion that it is, and has been for many years, the practice and usage to carry deck cargoes on Rhine steamers plying from Amsterdam ... The fact that the shipowners undertake a greater liability for cargo on deck than for cargo carried under deck does not appear to me to affect the question as between the assured and the underwriters.
>
> [p 262] ... I am by no means satisfied that the rule [referring to r 17] which exempts underwriters from liability for the loss of deck cargo applies to inland voyages by canal or river. I am satisfied that it does not apply to an inland voyage by canal and river plainly contemplated by the policy, on which voyage it is and has been for many years the practice and usage for steamers and other vessels to carry cargoes on deck.

Meaning of usage to the contrary

That the word 'usage' refers to the usage in a particular trade, and not to the usage in insurance, was confirmed by the House of Lords in *British and Foreign Marine Insurance Co v Gaunt*, below.

---

13 See Arnould, J, *Law of Marine Insurance and Average*, 16th edn, 1981, London: Sweet & Maxwell, Vol 1, para 308.

British and Foreign Marine Insurance Co v Gaunt [1921] 2 AC 41, HL

Under an all risks policy of insurance, a consignment of wool from Chile to Bradford in England was damaged by water. It transpired that, before being loaded into the ocean going ship at Punta Arenas, in southern Chile, the wool had been carried on the decks of local steamers without the insurers being notified. The insurers therefore rejected the claim on the policy of insurance made by the plaintiffs.

The House of Lords ruled that the insurers were liable under the policy because the method of transportation by local steamers was common usage in the trade. However, Viscount Finlay, in his speech, analysed r 17 in depth.

Viscount Finlay: [p 53] ... The construction of this rule [r 17] has given rise to a great deal of controversy, and it is now necessary that we should endeavour to settle this vexed question of construction. Rule 17 is very oddly worded, but it appears to me that, on its true reading, it leaves the law as to insurance of deck cargo very much as it was before the Marine Insurance Act was passed.

The rule prescribes that deck cargo and living animals must be insured specifically in the absence of any usage to the contrary. What is the meaning of the provision that deck cargo and living animals 'must be insured specifically?' I think 'specifically' in this connection means 'as such'. In the case of deck cargo there must, in addition to the ordinary description of the goods, be an intimation in the policy that the goods are to be carried on deck, by inserting 'for carriage on deck', or other similar words. In the case of 'living animals', the description must convey an intimation that the animals are alive and not mere carcasses, that is, if there is any ambiguity in the description, there must be added to it the word 'live,' or some equivalent expression.

There are, of course, special risks attached to deck cargo and live animals, and the rule is, I think, intended to secure that the underwriter must have express information of the existence of such risks 'in the absence of any usage to the contrary'.

What is the meaning of these words as to usage which are prefixed to the second part of r 17? In the case of deck cargo, I think that these words would be satisfied by proof of a usage in a particular trade, or generally, to carry on deck goods of a particular kind. The underwriter is bound to know of the existence of such usages, and the description of particular goods as of the class to which such a usage applies gives him the information that the goods will or may be carried on deck. If there is such a usage, there is no reason for requiring a statement that goods which fall within it are, in fact, to be carried on deck, as the mere description of the goods gives the necessary information. Such a usage may be fairly described as 'a usage to the contrary'. I cannot adopt the appellants' contention that the usage must be a usage not in the carrying trade with regard to such goods, but in the insurance world with reference to the manner in which they are to be described for insurance purposes. Such a usage as to insurance may, of course, grow up in any trade in which deck carriage of certain articles prevails, and if such a usage in the business of insurance has grown up it will be a usage to the contrary. But, in my opinion, no such usage in the business of insurance is necessary to dispense with the specific description of deck cargo as such. Any such construction of r 17 would bring it into acute conflict with the law as to insurance of deck cargo as it existed up to 1906, and is not, in my opinion, warranted by the wording of the rule.

In the case of 'living animals', the words 'in the absence of any usage to the contrary' may have been introduced to guard against the conceivable case that in a particular trade in which the goods carried were almost exclusively live cattle or sheep, there might be a usage that such livestock should be merely described as 'goods'. The contingency is not a very probable one, but Parliament, if it considered the wording of this rule, may have thought that to provide against any possible usage to the contrary could do no harm and might conceivably be useful.

The concluding words of the paragraph that deck cargo and livestock are not to be insured simply as goods appear to be quite unnecessary, but do not militate against the construction of the paragraph which I disposed to adopt.

As both the Master of the Rolls and Atkin LJ point out, there was abundant evidence of a usage that in this trade bales of wool should be carried on deck. The 'usage to the contrary' was therefore established, and there was no necessity to ensure [insure] the bales specifically as for carriage on deck.

Containers and packing materials

Unfortunately, the statutory definition of 'goods' provided by r 17 of the Rules for Construction has failed to clarify whether containers and packing materials, usually essential to the safe carriage of goods, may be considered as part of those goods and, therefore, covered by the policy of insurance.

A general test appears to be that where the containers or packing materials are supplied by the owner of the goods and may also be considered, for practical purposes, as an integral part of the goods, then the containers and packing materials should be included within the cover provided by the policy of insurance.[14] Much, therefore, depends upon a question of construction of the policy.

Insurance on goods includes loss of the adventure

When goods are insured, they are insured not only against physical loss or damage, but also for a loss brought about by the loss of the voyage or adventure which has prevented the goods from reaching their destination. That is, even though the goods remain physically intact and are still within the

---

14　See *Lysaght v Coleman* [1895] 1 QB 49; *Brown v Fleming* (1902) 7 Com Cas 245; *Vacuum Oil Co v Union Insurance Society of Canton* (1925) 24 LlL Rep 188; and *Berk v Style* [1955] 2 Lloyd's Rep 383.

control and possession of the assured, the insurers may be liable for the loss of the voyage or adventure provided that the loss of the voyage or adventure was brought about by a peril insured against.

This concept, where goods are concerned, that there can be a loss brought about by the loss of the venture itself is not new.[15] Under common law, the concept was well established,[16] but it was not until the case of *British and Foreign Marine Insurance Co Ltd v Samuel Sanday and Co*, below, came before the House of Lords that it was confirmed that the doctrine of loss of venture also applied to the Act.

British and Foreign Marine Insurance Co Ltd v Samuel Sanday and Co [1915] 1 AC 650, HL

A British firm of corn merchants shipped two consignments of linseed and wheat aboard the British steamships *St Andrew* and *Orthia* from Argentina to Hamburg. Before the ships reached Hamburg, hostilities broke out between Germany and Great Britain and both vessels were ordered into British ports. The cargo-owners warehoused their goods and served notice of abandonment on their insurers.

The House of Lords, affirming the decisions of both the lower courts, ruled that there was a total loss of the adventure itself caused by the restraint of princes, a peril insured against. Therefore, the cargo-owners could recover under their policy of insurance.

> **Earl Loreburn:** [p 656] ... The first question is whether the old rule still prevails, that upon an insurance on goods, substantially in the words of these policies, the frustration of the adventure by an insured peril is a loss recoverable against underwriters, though the goods themselves are safe and sound.
>
> [p 657] ... The words of this policy have for generations been understood and held by judges to designate not merely the goods, but also the adventure. So far from abrogating this designation of subject matter, I should have thought the Act took pains to preserve it and others like it.
>
> **Lord Wrenbury:** [p 673] ... If, then, in marine insurance, a policy on goods means by usage a policy on the safe arrival of goods, that meaning is by s 26 preserved. Section 60 is as to constructive total loss, and sub-s 2(iii) provides that, in the case of damage to goods, there is a constructive total loss when the cost of repairing the damage *and forwarding the goods to their destination* would exceed their value on arrival. Lastly, s 91(2) enacts that the rules of the common law, including the law merchant, save in so far as they are inconsistent with the express provisions of this Act, shall continue to apply to contracts of marine insurance.
>
> My Lords, these provisions seem to me ample to support the conclusion at which I have arrived, that the Act of 1906 has not altered but has preserved the

---

15   The concept of 'loss of voyage' also applies to policies on freight and profits, but not to a policy on ship. See *op cit*, Arnould, fn 13, Vol 2, para 1186.
16   See *Rodocanachi v Elliott* (1874) LR 9 CP 518, discussed in Chapter 16, p 626.

law upon this point as it stood before 1906, and that law was that, under a policy on goods at and from a port to a port, the venture, and not the goods merely, was the subject matter insured.

The Institute War Clauses (Cargo) – the frustration clause

Following the House of Lords' decision in the *Sanday* case, above, where insurers were held to be liable, under a policy on goods, for the loss of the venture itself because it was caused by the restraint of princes, an insured peril, a frustration clause was introduced into the Institute War Clauses (Cargo)[17] to ensure that insurers are now excepted from such liability. Clause 3.7 of the Institute War Clauses (Cargo) states:

> In no case shall this insurance cover ... any claim based upon loss of or frustration of the voyage or adventure.

MOVABLES

The term 'movables' is defined by s 90 of the Act thus:

> 'Movables' means any movable tangible property, other than the ship, and includes money, valuable securities, and other documents:

That 'movables' are insurable under a policy of marine insurance is confirmed by s 3(2)(a) of the Act; the only proviso being that such movables '... are exposed to maritime perils'.

FREIGHT

The subject of 'freight' can be confusing because, primarily, the payment of freight is concerned with contracts of carriage, not marine insurance. However, freight is also an insurable subject matter and, therefore, relevant to marine insurance. Thus, where freight is concerned, contracts of carriage and contracts of insurance, though separate issues, are closely related.

Freight may be insured under a policy incorporating the Institute Time Clauses – Freight (1995) (ITCF(95))[18] or the Institute Voyage Clauses – Freight (1995) (IVCF(95)).[19]

---

17 See Appendix 20.
18 See Appendix 13.
19 See Appendix 14.

Meaning of freight

Section 90 of the Act and r 16 of the Rules for Construction employ precisely the same words when they define 'freight' thus:

> The term 'freight' includes the profit derivable by a shipowner from the employment of his ship to carry his own goods or movables, as well as freight payable by a third party, but does not include passage money.

And, as s 3(2)(b) of the Act affirms, freight is insurable under a policy of marine insurance provided that the freight '... is endangered by the exposure of insurable property to maritime perils'.

Thus, because freight is intangible, in that it is money earned by the employment of the ship, the earning of that freight can only be a risk insured if the insurable property earning that freight is exposed to maritime perils.

What may be insured as freight and, furthermore, when a policy on freight attaches, was clarified long ago in the old case of *Flint v Flemyng*, below. Lord Tenterden confirmed that: (a) a shipowner was entitled to insure the freight due from a third party who charters the whole ship; (b) a shipowner was entitled to insure the freight payable by a third party who puts specific quantities of goods aboard the ship; and (c) a shipowner was entitled to insure as freight the increase in value of his own goods brought about by them being carried in his own ship.

However, for the insurer to be liable for a loss of freight, there must be some proof that the freight would have been earned. That is, the goods must have either have been placed on board the ship or there be in existence a contract of carriage relating to those goods.

Flint v Flemyng (1830) 1 B&Ad 45

The freight on the ship *Hope* was insured by the plaintiff with the defendant insurers for a voyage at and from Madras to London. The cargo comprised some 25 tons of redwood, which the master had purchased on behalf of his owner, 122 tons of saltpetre, for which the ship was contracted to carry, and a further 90 tons of light goods, for which there was no written contract of carriage, only a verbal undertaking. Before any of the cargo was loaded, *Hope* was lost by a peril insured against and the plaintiff claimed on his policy of insurance. The question before the court was: on which items of cargo could the policy on freight be held to have attached?

The court ruled that the insurers were liable for the freight on the redwood and saltpetre, but were only liable for the freight on the light goods if the contract of carriage could be found.

> **Lord Tenterden CJ:** [p 48] ... If it be a necessary ingredient in the composition of freight, that there should be a money compensation paid by one person to another, the benefit accruing to a shipowner from using his own ship to carry

his own goods is not freight. But if the term freight, as used in the policy of insurance, import the benefit derived from the employment of the ship, then there has been a loss of freight. It is the same thing to the shipowner whether he receives the benefit of the use of his ship by a money payment from one person who charters the whole ship, who from various persons who put specific quantities of goods on board, or from persons who pay him the value of his own goods at the port of delivery, increased by their carriage in his own ship.

... Then, as to the other point, to recover upon a policy on freight, the assured must prove that, but for the intervention of some of the perils insured against, some freight would have been earned, either by showing that some goods were put on board, or there was some contract for doing so ... The defendant, therefore, is entitled to a new trial upon that ground, but he must, at all events, have a verdict against him for the amount of the freight on the redwood and saltpetre. It would, therefore, be advisable for the defendant to pay to the plaintiff the costs of this action and the freight of the redwood and saltpetre, and that he should undertake to pay the freight of the light goods, if, on reference to an arbitrator, it shall be found that there was a contract to ship those goods.

Gross or net freight?

That the freight insured under an open policy is the gross freight and not the net freight was established in the old case of ***Palmer v Blackburn* (1822) 1 Bing 61**, where a vessel was lost on a voyage from the East Indies to London. When the plaintiff claimed on his policy on freight for the full amount, the insurers contended that their liability only amounted to the net freight – the amount that would have been payable by the cargo interests, less the charges the plaintiffs would have incurred in the event of the safe arrival of the ship (seamen's wages, pilotage, light dues, tonnage duty and dock dues).

> **Dallas CJ** *dubitante*: [p 61] ... The general principle of insurance, that the insured shall, in case of a loss, recover no more than an indemnity, may be controlled by a mercantile usage clearly established to the contrary: and usage, that the loss in an open policy on freight shall be adjusted on the gross, and not on the net amount of the freight, is a legal usage.

And, in ***Ikerigi Compania Naviera SA v Palmer, 'Wondrous'* [1991] 1 Lloyd's Rep 400; aff'd [1992] 2 Lloyd's Rep 566, CA,** where a vessel was detained in Iran because of the non-payment of port dues and freight tax, at first instance, Hobhouse J had reason to consider the concept of freight.[20]

> **Hobhouse J:** [p 417] ... Freight insurance is concerned with the earnings or potential earnings of the vessel, not with the expenses of earning those sums. It is not concerned as such with the fact that the voyage took longer, nor with the fact that the costs of performing it were higher than expected. Save possibly in

---

20 Loss of hire as a subject matter of insurance is discussed below, p 105.

special situations such as general average, it is a gross, not a net concept; it is not a profits insurance, but has as its underlying concept that part of the value of a vessel or of a voyage or other adventure as its capacity to earn freights.

Passage money

Passage money, the money earned by carrying passengers, must be insured separately and may not be insured as freight. This was confirmed in *Denoon v Home and Colonial Assurance Co*, below.

Denoon v Home and Colonial Assurance Co (1872) LR 7 CP 431

After the failure of a charterparty, whereby the vessel *Sandringham* was to have carried a cargo from Calcutta to London, the master procured alternative employment for the ship by sailing to Mauritius with a cargo of rice and 360 coolies. The plaintiff owner of *Sandringham* had the policy on freight altered, but failed to convey to the insurers that only the freight on the rice was to be insured and that the policy did not include the passage money payable by the coolies on arrival at Mauritius. When *Sandringham* arrived off Mauritius, she was wrecked, and the cargo of rice totally lost, together with the freight payable. When the plaintiff claimed on his policy of insurance for the total loss of freight, the insurers contested the claim by claiming there was only a partial loss, as the passage money payable by the coolies must be included in the term 'freight' used in the policy.

The court ruled that the term 'freight' did not include passage money and, consequently, there was a total loss of the freight insured under the policy.

> **Willes J:** [p 347] ... Evidence was given on both sides to prove a customary use of the word 'freight' in the particular trade; but this evidence was insufficient to make out a binding usage either way. It appears, however, that the most frequent course is to describe passage money by a distinguishing term, and not merely as freight; and it was proved that, for insurance purposes, there is a distinction between freight and passage money, because the premium for the latter, upon a voyage from Calcutta to Mauritius, is generally less than that for the former; so that, as a matter of business, the not mentioning the subject upon the occasion of the insurance would indicate that the freight was probably intended to refer to merchandise.

Freight payable by a third party

There are essentially two types of freight which may be earned by a ship with respect to a third party, namely:

(a) ordinary freight, often referred to as 'bill of lading freight'; and

(b) chartered freight.

The Act only refers to 'freight' in general terms and does not differentiate between the two types of freight, namely, 'ordinary' and 'chartered'.[21] However, this does not appear to have been considered by the courts to be in contravention of s 26(1), which stipulates that the subject matter insured must be designated with reasonable certainty.

Indeed, the form of policies on freight was an issue bemoaned by Scott LJ in *Kulukundis v Norwich Union Fire Insurance Society* **[1937] 1 KB 1, CA**, where the assured claimed for a total loss of freight on a policy covering a voyage from Liverpool to the west coast of South America and back. Nevertheless, despite his criticism, the judge was prepared to construe the words as he thought the parties intended.

> **Scott LJ:** [p 34] ... The archaic words of our ancient form of marine policy, set out in the Schedule to the Act, and embodied in the policy sued on, afford little guidance in the way of description or explanation as to the circumstances which the insurer agrees shall constitute a loss for which he has to pay. Indeed the statutory form is inapt to cover freight at all, although it is habitually used by Lloyd's for insurance of freight by adding written or typed words to the printed form, regardless of grammar, so as to bring in that subject matter. The policy in the present case is not wholly in the statutory form; it is entitled as a 'cargo and freight' policy, and it excludes the usual words of hull insurance; but it is very nearly in common form, and certainly contains nothing to indicate a different construction to that of the statutory form with the words 'on chartered freight and/or freight' added in ink or type in such a place as to show that that was to be the subject matter of the insurance. There is, however, at this stage of English legal history, no room for doubt that the primary bargain intended by the policy before us is simply this: 'We the insurers agree that if the assured suffers a total loss of his chartered freight by perils of the sea, we will pay him the whole sum insured.'

Ordinary freight

'Ordinary freight' is the remuneration earned by a carrier, be he shipowner or charterer, for the transportation of goods belonging to another party. It is often referred to as 'bill of lading freight', in order to distinguish it from chartered freight; the contract of affreightment is between the carrier and a cargo-owner and, thus, is evidenced by a bill of lading rather than a charterparty.

A short, but precise, definition of 'ordinary freight' was postulated by Hamilton J in *Scottish Shire Line Ltd v London and Provincial Marine and General Insurance Co Ltd* **[1912] 3 KB 51**, where a general ship was incapacitated by a peril insured against and was unable to earn freight on cargoes which she had contracted to carry from Australia to the UK. The

---

21 Nor do the Institute Freight Clauses, the ITCF(95) and the IVCF(95), differentiate between 'ordinary' and 'chartered' freight.

judge was, in fact, making a comparison between 'ordinary' and 'chartered' freight: [p 65] '... bill of lading freight is *prima facie* the shipowner's own contracted remuneration for the carriage of goods in his own ship by his own servants.'

Whilst payment for ordinary freight is normally made on delivery, there is nothing to prevent the parties to the contract of affreightment making other arrangements as to the payment of freight, as was illustrated in **Weir and Co v Girvin and Co [1899] 1 QB 193, CA**. In this instance, a fire broke out aboard a vessel whilst she was loading cargo and the portion loaded was destroyed. Although the case was concerned with advance freight, the court saw fit to consider the general character of freight.

> **Lord Russell CJ:** [p 196] ... Freight is a payment to be made to the ship for carriage and delivery, and until there has been carriage and delivery, the shipowner is not under ordinary circumstances entitled to demand freight at all. The parties may, of course, make a special agreement if they choose. They may stipulate that the whole freight, or some portion of it, is to be paid the moment the cargo is put on board, or when the ship sails, or at any other time they please. But they must do so in language showing clearly that the ordinary obligation of the shipper is altered.

However, under normal circumstances with a contract of affreightment, it is well established that the payment of freight must be made on delivery even when the cargo is short delivered or damaged.[22] Nevertheless, freight is not payable when cargo is delivered in such a state that the nature of the cargo has been altered and has lost its merchantable character. The leading authority on this issue is undoubtedly the case of *Asfar v Blundell*, below.[23]

Asfar and Co v Blundell and Another [1896] 1 QB 123, CA

The plaintiffs chartered the vessel *Govino* for a voyage from the Persian Gulf to London and insured the profit on charter with the defendants. When *Govino* arrived in the Thames with a mixed cargo, including dates, she was in collision with another vessel and sank. Although she was later raised, the dates were deemed unfit for human consumption and were sold to be distilled into spirits. The plaintiffs, having paid the chartered freight, claimed from their insurers for the loss of profits brought about by the non-delivery of the dates.

The Court of Appeal ruled that there had been a total loss of the consignment of dates and the plaintiffs were entitled to recover the difference between the chartered freight and the total amount of bill of lading freight that would have been received had the whole cargo, including the dates, been delivered in London.

---

22 See *Dakin v Oxley* (1864) 15 CBNS 646.
23 Also discussed, in relation to an actual total loss, in Chapter 15, p 610.

Lopes LJ: [p 130] ... The first point taken was that there was no total loss of the dates. But the facts show that they had been submerged for two days, and that when they were again seen they were a mixture of date pulp and sewage and were in a state of fermentation and putrefaction; they had clearly lost any merchantable character as dates. In my judgment, it is idle to suggest that there was not a total loss of the dates, and that the plaintiffs were not entitled to recover as for a total loss of their freight.

Furthermore, as briefly pointed out earlier,[24] an assured of freight, ordinary or chartered, may not recover under a policy on freight unless the assured can prove that some freight would have been earned. Such proof is provided by either the cargo being loaded or there being in existence a contract of affreightment. This was established long ago by Lord Ellenborough in *Forbes v Aspinall* **(1811) 13 East 326**, where a vessel was lost before she could load a return cargo which she was seeking by means of bartering the outward cargo. Because the cargo was neither contracted for nor loaded, the policy on freight could not attach, as there was no proof that the freight would have been earned.

Lord Ellenborough: [p 325] ... An insurance upon freight has no reference to the hull of the ship, or to its outfit for the voyage; both of which are protected by insurance upon the ship; but its sole object is to protect the assured from being deprived, by any of the perils insured against, of the profit he would otherwise earn by the carriage of goods. To recover, therefore, in any case upon a policy on freight, it is incumbent on the assured to prove that, unless some of the perils insured against had intervened to prevent it, some freight would have been earned; and where the policy is open, the actual amount of the freight, which would have been so earned, limits the extent of the underwriter's liability. In every action upon such a policy evidence is given, either that goods were put on board, from the carriage of which freight would result, or that there was some contract, under which the shipowner, if the voyage were not stopped by the perils insured against, would have been entitled to demand freight.

Chartered freight

Hamilton J may again be turned to for a short, but concise, definition of 'chartered freight' which he had advanced in *Scottish Shire Line Ltd v London and Provincial Marine and General Insurance Co Ltd* **[1912] 3 KB 51**, cited earlier.[25] His definition reads as follows: [p 65] '... Chartered freight is the remuneration paid to the shipowner by another who hires his ship or part of it, generally with an added contract that the shipowner's captain shall sign bills of lading for the charterer's benefit.'

---

24 See *Flint v Flemyng* (1830) 1 B&Ad 45, discussed above, p 94.
25 See above, p 97.

However, the chartered freight which may be insured is that freight which is expected to be earned under a contract of affreightment, namely, a charterparty. But, as charterparties may be in the form of either voyage or time, each must be considered separately.

Voyage chartered freight

When a vessel is chartered for a voyage, the shipowner may elect to insure the money that the ship would earn under the charterparty as 'chartered freight'. Should the charterparty then not be performed, the shipowner's loss of chartered freight would be recoverable under the policy, provided that the cause of the loss of freight was by a peril insured against.

It follows, then, that as a voyage charterparty may include a sea passage in ballast to the port of loading, if the freight payable under the charterparty is then insured, the policy attaches from the outset of the charter and there is no requirement for there to be cargo on board a vessel for the risk under the policy to attach.

The position with respect to the insurance of chartered freight was particularly well summed up by Brett J, in *Rankin v Potter*, below.[26] In this instance, the chartered vessel was damaged before she could load her chartered cargo, but the court held that the insurers were still liable for the resulting total loss of chartered freight.

Rankin v Potter (1873) LR 6 HL 83

The plaintiffs (respondents) were the mortgagees in possession of the vessel *Sir William Eyre* which, whilst on its outward passage to New Zealand, was chartered to sail afterwards to Calcutta to load a cargo for Liverpool or London; the chartered freight for the whole voyage was then insured with the defendants (appellants). When *Sir William Eyre* arrived at Calcutta, she was surveyed because of a grounding that had taken place previously and it was found that the cost of repairs would have exceeded her value. The plaintiffs claimed for a total loss of freight occasioned by perils of the sea, but the underwriters refused payment, on the basis that the shipowner had become bankrupt and it was that which had caused the charterer to withdraw from the charter.

The appeal was dismissed, and the court ruled that there was a total loss of freight occasioned by a peril of the sea, and the insurers were liable under the policy on freight.

> **Brett J:** [p 103] ... Another form of policy on freight, not unusual, but not so frequent as a policy on freight in general terms, is a policy insuring 'chartered freight'. In such policies, the voyage insured commences usually at or from the

---

26 Also discussed in a different context in Chapter 15, p 618.

port of sailing on the voyage described in the charterparty, or on or at the commencement of the voyage the ship must make to reach that port; but in both cases the voyage insured usually covers also the whole voyage to be sailed under the charterparty. Such a policy attaches earlier than a policy on freight in general terms; it attaches before any goods are on board the ship. If the ship be lost or damaged, or the cargo lost after the goods are on board, the same circumstances must arise and the same considerations apply as have been related and treated of in the case of a policy on freight in general terms.

... The questions raised are, whether there is any loss of freight by a peril insured against, and if so, is that loss a total loss? The ship was damaged during the voyage insured; it was damaged by a peril insured against. Unless the damages to the ship should be wholly, or sufficiently repaired, the insured freight could not be earned. If the damage to the ship could not be sufficiently repaired to enable the assured to earn the charter freight by carrying goods on board that ship, it seems to me that the damage to the ship caused by a peril insured against, during the voyage insured, is the cause of the loss of the earning the chartered freight by that ship. Loss of freight by reason of such damage to the ship caused by such a peril, is a loss against which, according to the interpretation put upon the policy at the commencement of this opinion, the underwriter on this policy on freight has, in terms, agreed to indemnify the assured.

Similarly, in *Carras v London and Scottish Assurance Corporation Ltd* [1936] 1 KB 291, CA, a vessel was chartered to sail to Valparaiso to load a cargo of nitrate. Whilst proceeding through the Straits of Magellan, the vessel stranded and was eventually abandoned to the hull insurers. Although the ship had not yet reached the port of loading, the court ruled that the insurers of the chartered freight were liable, because the performance of the charterparty and the earning of the freight was prevented by a peril insured against.

Lord Wright MR: [p 299] ... The earning of freight under a charterparty of a specific vessel depends on the continued existence of that vessel as a cargo carrying vessel, at least in a case like the present where no cargo is on board and the vessel is on her way to the port where she should be tendered to the charterers. If, therefore, the ship is lost or destroyed, the performance of the charterparty and the earning of the freight is prevented; if that is due to perils of the sea, the shipowner is relieved from liability in damages to the charterers by the usual exception of perils of the sea in the charterparty.

[p 303] ... the assured is irretrievably deprived of any possibility of earning the insured freight. What is insured under the freight policy is not a chattel like a ship or a cargo; it is, even in the case of chartered freight, as in the present case, which is the most definite type of insurable interest in freight, merely a chose in action, a right of earning freight under the charter; *a fortiori* where there is merely an expectancy of earning freight, though enough to constitute an insurable interest.

Greene LJ: [p 315] ... By the freight policy the shipowner effected an insurance of the freight payable under the charterparty against the risk of loss by perils of the sea. The subject matter of the insurance is a chose in action – viz, the contractual right to receive the freight from the charterer under the charterparty. If that right is lost through a peril of the sea, the underwriters are liable as on a total loss. In considering whether or not there has been such a loss of the right to receive freight through a peril of the sea, it is necessary to determine, in the first place, whether or not as between charterer and shipowner the right to receive the freight has been lost by peril of the sea.

However, if the terms of a charterparty are such that the freight payable is consequent on the condition of the cargo on delivery, there is nothing to prevent the shipowner insuring just that proportion of the freight which is at risk, as was the case in *Griffiths v Bramley-Moore*, below. In this instance, the shipowner only insured that proportion of the freight which would not be paid by the charterer if the cargo arrived sea-damaged.

Griffiths and Others v Bramley-Moore and Others (1878) 4 QB 70, CA

The plaintiff shipowners entered into a charterparty which included the clause: 'If any portion of the cargo be delivered sea-damaged, the freight on such sea-damaged portion to be two-thirds of the above rate ...' The plaintiffs then insured the chartered freight with the defendants under a policy of insurance which provided cover for: '... only the one-third loss of freight in consequence of sea-damage as per charterparty ...' During the performance of the charterparty, sea damage occurred and one-third of the freight payable under the charterparty was deducted by the charterers. The plaintiffs then claimed on their policy of insurance for a total loss of the one-third of the freight not payable under the charterparty.

> The court ruled that the plaintiffs could recover on their policy as claimed.
>
> **Brett LJ:** [p 73] ... the question is whether the subject matter of the insurance is the whole charterparty freight or only a part of it ... there is a provision in the charterparty that 'if any portion of the cargo be delivered sea-damaged, the freight on such sea-damaged portion to be two-thirds of the above rate'. Well then, if any portion of the cargo is delivered sea-damaged, there is a loss under the charterparty, and that loss is a loss of a portion of the freight on that portion of the cargo delivered sea-damaged, and that loss is one-third. Then, turning from that clause in the charterparty back to the policy to see what is the subject matter of insurance, we find it is the loss – the one-third loss accrued on the charterparty under and by virtue of the clause I have read. That is the subject matter of insurance, and there is no other. The subject matter of the insurance is 'the loss of freight in consequence of sea-damage, mentioned in the charterparty'.
>
> [p 74] This policy, and some others of a similar kind, are peculiar and exceptional, as it seems to me, in this, that although the subject matter of insurance is accurately defined or described, it or the quantity of it is not ascertained until the loss has occurred. The subject matter, though defined in the policy, is not completely ascertained till the loss. The only peril is the peril by sea damage; the only thing insured is one peculiar loss caused by such peril; it seems to me to follow that the only loss that could be recovered under this

policy is a total loss. The subject matter of insurance being a loss on the cargo which receives sea damage, there can be no loss in this case but a total loss, and if there is a total loss, then the underwriter is liable to the full amount of his subscription.

Time freight or time charter hire

'Time freight' is the remuneration made to a shipowner by a charterer for the use of his ship for a particular period of time. However, under a time charterparty, time freight is usually referred to as 'time charter hire', which readily distinguishes freight earned under a time charterparty from freight earned under a voyage charterparty. This was discussed in *The Nanfri*, below, where Lord Denning acceded to the fact that, in modern times, payments due under a time charter are now described as 'hire', in recognition of the fact that a time charter is very different from a voyage charter.

The Nanfri [1978] 2 Lloyd's Rep 132, CA

The charterers of three vessels deducted sums of money from the costs of hire of those vessels; in the case of *The Nanfri*, for loss of speed. As the owners then instructed the masters of their vessels to refuse to sign bills of lading, the charterers then informed the owners that the charterparty was terminated.

The dispute reached the Court of Appeal, where it was adjudged that the charterers were within their rights to deduct the sums of money from the cost of hire. Lord Denning, however, saw good reason to distinguish the fact that payments made under a time charter usually amounted to payments for 'hire', whilst payments under a voyage charter were payments by way of 'freight'.

Lord Denning MR: [p 139] ... On 1 September 1977, the monthly hire due on all three vessels together was $540,000. The charterers deducted $109,000 for various reasons, of which they have detailed justifications. On 13 September 1977, the owners agreed that these deductions were justified save for $38,000. So all was paid except $38,000 – that is, about 7%. The owners contested these deductions. They did so on the ground that:

> ... the charterers were not entitled to make any deduction from hire by way of off-hire or set off (even if the same was in fact due to the charterers) unless prior to such deduction either the owners had accepted the validity thereof or it was supported by vouchers signed by the master or a proper tribunal had pronounced on its validity.

The contention was founded on the proposition that hire payable under a time charterparty is in the same position as freight payable under a voyage charterparty: and that under a settled rule of law, freight is payable in full without deduction. Even if cargo is short delivered, or delivered damaged, there can be no deduction on that account.

... At one time, it was common to describe the sums payable under a time charterparty as 'freight'. Such description is to be found used by judges and textbook writers of great distinction. But in modern times, a change has come about. The payments due under a time charter are usually now described as 'hire' and those under a voyage charter as 'freight'. This change of language corresponds, I believe, to a recognition that the two things are different. 'Freight' is payable for carrying a quantity of cargo from one place to another. 'Hire' is payable for the right to use a vessel for a specified period of time, irrespective of whether the charterer chooses to use it for carrying cargo or lays it up, out of use. Every time charter contains clauses which are quite inappropriate to a voyage charter, such as the off-hire clause and the withdrawal clause. So different are the two concepts that I do not think the law as to 'freight' can be applied indiscriminately to 'hire'. In particular, the special rule of English law whereby 'freight' must be paid in full (without deductions for short delivery or cargo damage) cannot be applied automatically to time charter 'hire'. Nor is there any authority which says that it must.

Manchester Liners Ltd v British and Foreign Marine Insurance Co Ltd [1901] 7 Com Cas 26

The owners of a vessel under time charter to the Admiralty effected a policy on 'chartered or hire money' with the defendant insurers. When the ship was discharged from service by the Admiralty because of a mechanical defect, the plaintiffs claimed on their policy for their loss. Counsel for the shipowners argued that, under a policy covering 'chartered or hire money', the subject matter of the insurance was not just the freight or hire money payable under a contract of affreightment, but also the interest which the shipowner has in the use of his ship.

The court ruled that the insurers were not liable under the policy, because the subject matter of the insurance was 'hire' payable under a contract, and the loss of hire had not been caused by a peril insured against, but rather by the Admiralty's right under the charterparty to discharge the vessel should she become defective. Walton J was in no doubt that the subject matter of insurance under 'time charter hire' was in the nature of freight payable under contract.

> **Walton J:** [p 32] ... The defendants [insurers] contend that the subject matter of the insurance was hire money to be earned under a contract in the nature of a time charterparty; that the only hire money at risk on 5 April was the freight payable under the charterparty of 14 December; and that there was no loss of such freight by the perils insured against. On the other hand, Mr Carver, on behalf of the plaintiffs [the shipowners], contended that the subject matter of the insurance was not limited to freight or hire money payable under a contract, but included or covered the interest of the shipowner in the interest of his ship, entirely independent of any particular contract for the payment of freight or hire. It seems to me clear that a shipowner has an interest in the use of his ship, and that he may insure himself against the loss which he may undoubtedly suffer from being deprived of its use by perils of the sea or other causes. But, in cases of this kind, it is not enough to consider what interest the shipowner had and against what losses he might lawfully have insured himself; the true question must be whether the interest in respect of which he

claims to be insured, and the loss against which he claims to be indemnified, were in fact covered by the terms of the policy which he effected and upon which he sues. In the present case, the subject matter of the policy is 'chartered or hire money', and, in my judgment, this means 'hire money' in the nature of freight payable under a contract. I do not think that it is enough for the plaintiffs, in order to entitle them to succeed in this action, to show that they were interested in the use of their ship, and that they were deprived of such use for 14 or 15 days by a peril insured against.

Loss of hire

Hire payable under a time charter is for a period of time, regardless of whether the vessel has or has not any cargo on board. Any loss of time brought about by the ship not being fit to perform the services required under the terms of the time charter is generally at the expense of the shipowner. This is normally provided for in the 'off-hire' clause contained in the time charterparty. Should an event stipulated in the said clause cause the vessel to be off-hire, the charterer is entitled to make the necessary deduction from the amount of hire he has to pay to the shipowner. Whether this sum is recoverable by the shipowner from his insurer is governed by the terms of the policy.

Under common law, before the introduction of the 'loss of time' clause into a time policy on freight, a freight insurer was liable under the policy for any hire lost due to the ship being withdrawn from the charterer by reason of her not being capable of performing the services immediately required of her; and provided that the incapacity was caused by a peril insured against, the loss of hire suffered by the shipowner was recoverable from the freight insurer. This was highlighted in *The Alps*, below.[27]

The Alps [1893] P 109

The steamship *The Alps* was time chartered at a monthly rate of £425 and a clause in the charterparty stated: '... in the event of loss of time from ... want of repairs ... preventing the working of the vessel for more than 24 hours ... the payment of hire shall cease ...' The plaintiff owners then insured the time chartered freight with the defendants for 12 months. The policy covered loss caused by the usual perils, but did not incorporate a loss of time clause. Whilst loading in New York, *The Alps* was damaged by fire and, as she was off-hire for 13 days undergoing repairs, the plaintiffs repaid the charterer for the time lost under the charter and then claimed under their policy of insurance on freight. The insurers refused to pay the claim, contending that the proximate cause of the loss was not by fire, a peril insured against, but a loss under the contract of affreightment (the charterparty).

---

27 See, also, *Jackson v Union Marine Insurance* (1873) 2 Asp MLC 435; *Inman Steamship Co Ltd v Bischoff* (1882) 5 Asp MLC 6; and *The Bedouin* (1899) 7 Asp MLC 391, which have all reiterated the same principle.

The court ruled that the underwriters were liable under the policy. As the loss suffered by the plaintiffs was the loss of hire, and that loss of hire had been brought about by fire, a peril insured against, the insurers were liable under the policy on freight.

> **Gorrell Barnes J:** [p 118] ... The inefficiency of this vessel was admittedly due to fire, one of the perils insured against. It has been expressly stipulated in the charterparty that, in the event of loss of time from want of repairs, the hire should cease to be payable so long as the vessel was incapable from that cause of efficiently performing her service. It is a case of cesser, or loss of freight, through a peril insured against. The counsel for the defendants urges that many other causes might produce want of repairs. Yes; but only certain perils are insured against, one of which is fire, and it seems to me that, having regard to the judgments I have referred to, and the principles they seem to indicate, and also to the case of *Jackson v Union Marine Insurance Co*, the true view to take of an insurance such as this, applied to a very ordinary form of charterparty, containing a very ordinary and usual clause, is that it casts upon the underwriters the risk of loss of freight when that clause is put into operation through the immediate action of the perils insured against.

The Loss of Time Clause

To overcome such a liability as was imposed upon the insurer by the ruling in *The Alps*, the current version of the ITCF(95) has incorporated the Loss of Time Clause, cl 15, which reads as follows:[28]

> This insurance does not cover any claims consequent on loss of time whether arising from a peril of the sea or otherwise.

The leading authority on the clause has to be the *Playa de las Nieves* case, below.

Naviera de Canarias SA v Nacional Hispanica Aseguradora SA, 'Playa de las Nieves' [1978] AC 853, HL

The plaintiffs, Spanish shipowners, insured their fleet of vessels with the defendant Spanish insurers, and included in this cover was a policy for freight, which was in the form of the Institute Time Clauses – Freight. Clause 8 in this policy for freight exempted the insurers from liability for 'any claim consequent on loss of time whether arising from a peril of the sea or otherwise'. The plaintiffs chartered one of their vessels under a time charter which contained an 'off-hire' clause. One day after *Playa de las Nieves* was delivered to the charterers, she suffered a machinery breakdown which resulted in a stranding. Although *Playa de las Nieves* was eventually salved, the plaintiffs incurred a loss due to her being off-hire and, therefore, sought to make good their loss from their insurers.

---

28 IVCH(95), cl 11.

The House of Lords, in reversing the decision of the Court of Appeal, ruled that the insurers were not liable, as cl 8 in the freight policy exempted a claim consequent on loss of time.

Lord Diplock: [p 879] ... The time charter clause in the Institute Time Clauses – Freight postulates a chain of events, viz (1) the occurrence of a peril insured against, resulting in (2) loss of time, resulting in (3) loss to the assured of freight which he would have earned from the use or hire of his vessel. In the context of a vessel engaged under a time charter, the expression 'loss of time' must include a period during which the vessel is prevented from, or delayed in, performing the service for which she has been chartered. A similar reference to such a period as being 'time lost' is to be found in the off-hire clause in other standard forms of time charter. So, where an off-hire clause provides that hire shall not be payable during any period during which the vessel is prevented from full working, I do not see how the ensuing loss of freight by the shipowner could be more appropriately described than as 'consequent on loss of time'.

[p 880] ... My Lords, in the absence of any direct authority to suggest that some esoteric meaning peculiar to marine insurance is to be substituted for what seems to me to be the plain and ordinary meaning of the time charter clause, the citation and critical analysis of cases dealing with the application of the clause to cases where adventures under voyage charters have ended prematurely or with matters even more remote from off-hire under time charters, in my view, serve only to prolong and obfuscate the argument.

[p 881] ... In the instant case, the dominant and effective cause of the loss of hire while *Playa de las Nieves* was being repaired was the breakdown of machinery and the stranding which made the repairs necessary. As a proposition of marine insurance law, this may be unexceptionable and would be relevant to the question whether the loss of hire was caused by a peril insured against – as it must have been if there were to be any loss upon which the time charter clause as an exceptions clause could bite. The next step in the respondents' [shipowners'] argument is that in the time charter clause itself 'consequent on' means 'caused by', which requires one to look for the proximate cause of the loss of hire for which the claim is made. The dominant and effective cause was the peril insured against, viz, breakdown of machinery and stranding. Therefore, it was the breakdown and stranding on which the loss of hire was consequent, and not the loss of time.

My Lords, the fallacy in this argument is that we are not concerned in the instant case with whether the loss of hire was 'proximately caused' by a peril insured against in the sense in which that expression is used in s 55(1) of the Marine Insurance Act 1906. What we are concerned with is the construction of an exceptions clause which does not even use the word 'cause'. It contemplates a chain of events expressed to be either 'consequent on' or 'arising from' one another. It expressly makes the operation of the clause dependent upon the presence in the chain of an intermediate event (viz, loss of time) between the loss for which the claim is made (viz, loss of freight) and the event which in insurance law is the 'proximate cause' of that loss (viz, a peril insured against). The intermediate event, 'loss of time', is not in itself a peril, though it may be the result of a peril. That is why the words 'whether arising from a peril of the sea or otherwise' are not mere surplusage, as was suggested *obiter* by Bailhache J in *Russian Bank for Foreign Trade v Excess Insurance Co Ltd* [1918] 2 KB 123, p 127. They are there to make it plain that the clause is concerned with an intermediate event between the occurrence of a peril insured against and the loss of freight of which the peril was, in insurance law, the proximate cause.

Insurance for loss of hire

A freight insurer, by reason of the Loss of Time Clause in the ITCF(95) is excepted from liability for any loss of hire sustained by the assured because of the operation of the off-hire clause. Should the owner of a time chartered vessel wish to cover for such a loss, he must either take out a special policy of insurance which specifically provides cover for time whilst the vessel is off-hire, or negotiate for the deletion of the Loss of Time Clause, in which case a reversion to the position under common law would arise.

Ordinarily, insurance for 'loss of hire' only covers the periods of time when the vessel is actually on charter, and then only if the off-hire is caused by a peril insured against under the freight policy. As can be seen from the *Capricorn* case, below, even the inclusion of the words *'whether chartered or unchartered'* into a loss of hire policy of insurance did not assist the shipowner in the specific circumstances of the case: the court adjudged the loss of earning to have been brought about merely by the vessel being off-hire, and not by an insured peril.

In the *Wondrous* case, below, the general philosophy behind loss of hire insurance was discussed by Hobhouse J in the court of first instance.

Ikerigi Compania Naviera SA and Others v Palmer and Others, 'Wondrous' [1991] 1 Lloyd's Rep 400; [1992] 2 Lloyd's Rep 566, CA

The plaintiffs chartered their vessel *Wondrous* to an Iranian company to carry a full cargo of 30,000 tons of molasses from Bandar Abbas in Iran to North European or Mediterranean ports. The plaintiffs then effected insurance policies with the defendants including loss of hire; the loss of hire policy incorporated war risks. On arriving at Bandar Abbas, *Wondrous* was delayed from sailing for 18 months because the charterers were unable to pay the port dues and freight tax. When *Wondrous* did eventually sail with her cargo for Denmark, she first had to be towed to another port to repair her engines, which had become inoperable; the overall losses were considerable. The plaintiffs claimed on their policy for loss of hire, but the underwriters refused payment.

The Court of Appeal affirmed the decision of the lower court and ruled that the insurers were not liable under the loss of hire policy. However, at first instance, Hobhouse J analysed the function of the 'loss of hire' policy; in particular, the judge pointed out that, although the insurable property at risk was the ship itself (s 3(2)(b) of the Marine Insurance Act 1906), it was not necessary for that property at risk, the ship, to be damaged for the insurers to be liable under the loss of hire policy. The subject matter of insurance remained the 'earning capacity' of the vessel.

Hobhouse J: [Court of first instance, p 415] ... The first matter that the plaintiffs need to prove is that there was a loss for the purposes of these policies. The relevant criterion is that the vessel be 'prevented from earning hire or reward' (or 'deprived of her earning capacity') ... I consider that the vessel was deprived of her earning capacity within the meaning of the phrase used in these policies from 14 August 1987 to 17 October 1988. During this period, she was not prosecuting any voyage and not earning any freight either under the charterparty or the bills of lading. She had cargo on board, but she was not doing anything with it to enable her to earn any reward.

... The next question is whether this loss was caused by a peril insured against under the policy. The plaintiffs' case, as previously mentioned, was that all they need show was that there was a 'restraint or detention' of the vessel. I accept their submission that the fact that the detention was under the ordinary laws not fatal to their case (*The Anita* [1970] 2 Lloyd's Rep 365) ...

[pp 415–16] But it was still necessary for the plaintiffs to show that the detention was fortuitous ... For the purposes of the law of insurance, in the absence of an express agreement to the contrary, a policy would not be construed as covering the ordinary consequences of voluntary conduct of the assured arising out of the ordinary incidents of sailing; it is not a risk. By this criterion, I consider that, on any law, it is not correct to characterise the period of detention to 30 September 1987 as fortuitous.

[p 416] ... The defendants' [insurers'] argument has two parts. First, they submit that the 'risks enumerated' means risks 'of loss or damage to the vessel caused by ...'; in other words, it is only if there is a loss of the vessel or damage to the vessel that there can be a claim for loss of hire. I consider that this argument does not have sufficient regard to the actual phraseology of cl 1, or to the fact that the subject matter of a hull policy is the ship, but the subject matter of these policies is 'loss of hire and/or earnings and/or anticipated hire'. Whilst it is fair to construe the policies as requiring that the peril shall operate on the subject matter through the vessel, it is quite another matter to construe them as requiring that there shall have been a loss of or damage to the vessel as well. That additional requirement is not part of a loss of hire cover. It is not a description of a peril; it is in the hull clauses as part of the wording of a hull policy.

... The unacceptability of this argument of the defendants in relation to the present contract is demonstrated by the facts of this case; that a vessel may well be prevented from earning hire by being detained is obvious; that she will actually be damaged by detention is not only unlikely, but is almost certainly commercially irrelevant to a loss of hire cover limited to 104 days' detention.

A 'loss of hire' policy of insurance was again the issue in *Cepheus Shipping Corporation v Guardian Royal Exchange Assurance, 'Capricorn'* **[1995] 1 Lloyd's Rep 622**, discussed earlier in relation to insurable interest.[29] The court ruled that the plaintiffs could not recover under their policy of insurance covering loss of hire because the purpose of a 'loss of hire' policy was to provide cover against loss of trading income should that trading income be terminated by a peril insured against. But, in this instance, the loss of earning was not caused by the generator being damaged by a peril insured against, but by the vessel already being laid up. During his deliberations, Mance J referred to Walton J's reasoning in the case of *Manchester Liners Ltd v British and Foreign Marine Insurance Co Ltd* (1901) 7 Com Cas 26, cited earlier.[30]

> **Mance J:** [p 638] ... I was referred to a number of authorities on loss of earnings insurance ... In *Manchester Liners v British and Foreign Marine Insurance Co* (1901) 7 Com Cas 26, the issue was whether the policy language:
>
> > ... covered the interest of the shipowner in the use of his ship, entirely independent of any particular contract for the payment of freight or hire [see p 33].
>
> This turned on the true construction of the policy, as Walton J went on to emphasise:
>
> > It seems to me clear that a shipowner has an interest in the use of his ship, and that he may insure himself against the loss which he may undoubtedly suffer from being deprived of its use by perils of the sea or other causes. But in cases of this kind, it is not enough to consider what interest the shipowner had and against what losses he might lawfully have insured himself; the true question must be whether the interest in respect of which he claims to be insured, and the loss against which he claims to be indemnified, were in fact covered by the terms of the policy which he effected and upon which he sues.
>
> The language of the policy in that case covered 'chartered or hire money', which Walton J interpreted as meaning hire money in the nature of freight payable under a contract. The policy was thus conspicuously not on 'chartered or unchartered' terms. But it is worth noting that Walton J described the interest of a shipowner 'in the use of his ship' as clear. It is the inability to use or deploy the earning capacity of a vessel which is the rationale for insurance of earnings.

Advance freight

Ordinary or chartered freight may be paid in advance. Once paid, advance freight cannot be recovered. In such circumstances, because the risk is now borne by the owner of the goods in the case of ordinary freight, or the

---

29 See Chapter 2, p 60.
30 See above, p 104.

charterer in the case of chartered freight, and not the shipowner, it is for the owner of the goods or the charterer to insure the freight. The position regarding advance freight was particularly well summed up by Lord Hatherley, in *Allison v Bristol Marine Insurance Co Ltd*, below.[31]

Allison v Bristol Marine Insurance Co Ltd (1875) 1 App Cas 209, HL

A vessel was chartered to sail from Greenock to Bombay with half of the freight being paid in advance, the other half being paid on right delivery. The shipowner insured the half of the freight which was payable on delivery. As the vessel was lost before entering Bombay harbour and only half of the cargo of coal was delivered, the shipowner claimed for a total loss on his policy on freight, even though he had already received the advance freight for half of the cargo. The insurers contested the claim.

The House of Lords ruled that the policy on half the freight payable on delivery, effected by the shipowner, was completely separate from the advance freight already received, and the shipowner was entitled to recover for a total loss of the half of the freight that would have been paid on delivery. The House considered the significance of advance freight.

> **Lord Hatherley:** [p 237] ... What would ordinarily be the risk of the shipowner with regard to the freight so prepaid is transferred in this way to the charterer, and the shipowner has the money in pocket; and having the money in pocket, and seeing that it cannot be recovered back, he is assured of that – that is at no risk. Whatever loss happens at sea, he retains that money; and therefore, if there be a total loss of the whole cargo, the loss in respect of this prepayment of freight falls upon the person who has so prepaid it. Consequently, a custom seems to have grown up of allowing a sum by way of insurance, in order to compensate the person making this prepayment for the risk he thereby runs, in as much as he cannot recover it back again if there be a total loss of cargo.
>
> That being so, my Lords, you find this state of things; as to a moiety of this freight the shipowner is quite safe; he cannot want to insure it, he has got it. But as to the other moiety, he is not safe as regards the perils of the sea, because if there should be a total loss, and if he should not be able to deliver any part of the goods, then he would get no more freight. He has got one moiety safe in his pocket; the other moiety is that which is at risk, and that he can insure. Therefore, when you look at the contract of insurance in this case, which we have here before us, and ask as to which of the moieties of freight the insurance is effected, the answer must be the shipowner has effected the insurance upon the unpaid moiety, which may be lost entirely to him. He cannot effect an insurance upon that which is at no risk; therefore he must be taken to have done that which only he rightly could do, namely, to have insured against that which is at risk – the other moiety of the freight, which may be lost to him in consequence of the perils of the sea.

---

31 The question of who has the insurable interest in advance freight was also discussed in this case: see Chapter 2, p 59.

Owner's trading freight

Owner's trading freight is the money earned by a shipowner for carrying his own goods. It is, however, emphasised that the freight insurable is the 'profit' that the shipowner would earn by carrying his own goods. This is confirmed by the statutory definition contained within s 90 of the Act and r 17 of the Rules for Construction, both of which state: 'The term "freight" includes the profit derivable by a shipowner from the employment of his ship to carry his own goods or movables ...'

That insurable profit by way of owner's trading freight is the difference in value in the goods as loaded as compared with the value of the goods when discharged at the port of delivery. This was confirmed long ago in the case of *Flint v Flemyng* **(1830) 1 B&Ad 45**, cited above, p 94, where a vessel was lost at Madras before any cargo was loaded and the policy on freight was held to have attached when any cargo was either loaded or there was a valid contract of affreightment in evidence.

> **Bayley J:** [p 49] ... I am not aware that it has ever been decided that a party is entitled to recover, upon a policy of insurance on freight, for a loss accruing to him by reason of his having been deprived of the means of carrying his own goods in his own ship, but I have no doubt whatever that he is. Whether the shipowner carry his own goods or the goods of another person, is immaterial to him. In either case he has to pay the whole expense of the ship, of provisions, and of wages; he may fairly expect to reimburse himself out of the profit he may derive from carrying goods being his own property, or that of others, and he may insure that profit under the name of freight, whether it accrue from the price paid for the carriage of the goods of others, or from the additional value conferred on his own goods by their carriage.

PROFIT

It has long been accepted in marine insurance law that the 'profit' which may reasonably be expected to be earned by a shipowner or a charterer when undertaking a maritime adventure may be insured. This is confirmed by s 3(1)(b) of the Act; the only proviso being that, as with freight, the 'insurable property' (the ship, goods or movables) must be exposed to maritime perils; otherwise, there would be no risk to insure. An early example of the insurance of profit is provided by the case of *Barclay v Cousins*, below, where Lawrence J advanced the philosophic reasons why profit should be an insurable interest.

Barclay v Cousins (1802) 2 East 545

An insurance was effected by the plaintiff on the profits of £2,000 which were expected to be made by the brig *Jonah* on a voyage from Barbados to the west coast of Africa and back. After arriving in Africa, *Jonah* loaded 30 slaves, but, on sailing, was captured by French frigates and then used to transport English prisoners to Sierra Leone. In Sierra Leone, the remainder of the outward cargo and the 30 slaves were sold. *Jonah* finally arrived back in Barbados under a new master with the English prisoners of war, and the Admiralty Court awarded the master and crew one-eighth of the proceeds of the voyage and the value of the cargo which had been on board at the time of her capture. The plaintiff claimed on his policy of insurance for the loss of the expected profits.

The court ruled that the plaintiff was entitled to be indemnified under the policy on profits.

Lawrence J: [p 546] ... The case states that the insured shipped on board the ship Jonah a cargo of goods to be carried on a trading voyage; so that it appears that he had an interest in the profits to arise from a cargo which was liable to be affected by the perils insured against. And the question is, if on an insurance made on the profits to arise from such cargo the plaintiff can recover. As insurance is a contract of indemnity, it cannot be said to be extended beyond what the design of such species of contract will embrace, if it be applied to protect men from those losses and disadvantages, which but for the perils insured against the assured would not suffer: and in every maritime adventure the adventurer is liable to be deprived not only of the thing immediately subjected to the perils insured against, but also of the advantages to arise from the arrival of those things at their destined port. If they do not arrive, his loss in such case is not merely that of his goods or other things exposed to the perils of navigation, but of the benefits which, were his money employed in an undertaking not subject to the perils, he might obtain without more risk than the capital itself would be liable to: and if when the capital is subject to the risks of maritime commerce it be allowable for the merchant to protect that by insuring it, why may he not protect those advantages he is in danger of losing by their being subjected to the same risks? It is surely not a proper encouragement of trade to provide that merchants in case of adverse fortune should not only lose the principal adventure, but that that principal should not in consequence of such bad fortune be totally unproductive; and that men of small fortunes should be encouraged to engage in commerce by their having the means of preserving their capitals entire, which would continually be lessened by the ordinary expenses of living, if there were no means of replacing that expenditure in case the returns of their adventures should fail.

Profit on goods

Insurance on the 'profit on goods' is entirely separate from the insurance on the goods themselves, as was shown in the case of ***M'Swiney v Corporation of the Royal Exchange Assurance* (1849) 14 QB 633**, where the plaintiff insured the profit to be made on 6,000 bags of rice being shipped from Madras to London. In this instance, the plaintiff had bought the rice in Madras for 19s per cwt and had contracted to sell the rice in London for £1 0s 6d per cwt.

When part of the cargo had been loaded in Madras, the vessel was so damaged by severe weather that she was unable to undertake the voyage, and the plaintiff claimed on his policy of insurance for loss of expected profit.

The court ruled that the underwriters were liable under the policy, because the loss had been occasioned by a peril insured against. There was an insurable interest in the expected profit because: (a) the goods were ready to be shipped under a valid contract; and (b) there was a legal certainty that the profit would be made if the goods arrived in London.

Lord Denman CJ: [p 645] ... where there is a legal certainty that profit will be made if goods arrive, and that the goods are ready to be shipped under a valid contract, there is an insurable interest; and that, if the loss arises from a peril insured against, such as the perils of the sea, the underwriters are responsible. The risk of loss of profits attached when the vessel was at Madras, ready to take in her cargo, and having actually begun to take it in; and the loss occurred by the ship being blown off and sustaining too much damage to take in all the cargo, which was a peril of the sea. Upon the whole, we are of opinion that the plaintiff is entitled to our judgment.

Profit on charter

The charterer of a ship may employ the chartered vessel as a general ship, or subcharter the ship to another party. The profit that the charterer then expects to earn is the difference between what he, the charterer, has paid the shipowner to charter the vessel and that sum of money he would expect to receive from shippers or from the subcharterer. If that profit on charter is then insured, the subject matter of insurance is not the freight, it is the difference between chartered freight paid by the charterer and the freight he would expect to receive under bills of lading or under a subcharter.

The insurance of the 'profit on charter' was a major issue in the case of *Asfar v Blundell* **(1895) 1 QB 123, CA**, cited in full earlier in the chapter.[32] In this instance, the plaintiff chartered a vessel by way of a lump sum for £3,900 and expected in return £4,690 by way of bills of lading freight. The plaintiff then insured his 'profit on charter' with the defendant insurers; the policy was warranted free from average. However, on arriving in London, the chartered vessel was involved in a collision with another vessel and was sunk, with the result that a consignment of dates was deemed a constructive total loss with no freight being payable.

The plaintiff claimed under his policy for the loss of 'profit on charter' and the court awarded him £790, the difference between the charter freight and the expected bills of lading freight.

---

32 See, also, Chapter 15, p 610.

Lord Esher: [p 128] ... Let us now consider what was the subject matter of the insurance. The plaintiffs had chartered a ship in such a form that until she arrived at her destination they were to have the whole of her carrying power and capacity, paying to the owners an agreed sum as chartered freight. The plaintiffs were then, through their captain, to collect cargo and give bills of lading in respect of it, and their profit would depend upon whether they received more for the bills of lading freight than they paid as chartered freight, the difference between the two being their profit. That was their speculation; and if by reason of the perils of the sea they were prevented from getting a larger sum as bills of lading freight than they were paying as chartered freight, they would get no profit from their venture. I may say that it is as nearly certain as possible in business that the chartered freight in such a case as the present would be a lump sum; it is the ordinary practice to stipulate for a lump sum freight. It must be taken, therefore, that in this case there was a lump freight or chartered freight and the sum eventually earned as bills of lading freight, which is payable ordinarily at the port of destination. There was here a total loss of the bill of lading freight on these dates; and that being so, there was no profit on the venture, the profit being the difference between the chartered freight and the bills of lading freight, which difference wholly disappeared with the loss of the freight on these dates. There was, therefore, a total loss of the subject matter of insurance. The case was put on behalf of the defendants [insurers] as though the subject matter of the insurance had been the freight on the goods themselves – in which case, the warranty against average loss might have applied; the contention, however, has no application to the facts of the present case, where the subject matter of insurance was the difference between the two freights, which difference was totally lost.

COMMISSION

Commission is that sum of money which an agent or other third party may rightfully expect to receive for services rendered. If an agent or third party stands to gain by the safety or due arrival of the ship at her intended destination, there is no reason why he should not insure that commission under a policy of marine insurance. Thus, under s 3(2)(b) of the Act, commissions are insurable provided that the insurable property (ship, goods or movables) is exposed to maritime perils.

Conversely, as a shipowner may be liable to pay a commission under the terms of a contract of affreightment, this liability to pay a commission is also insurable, as was illustrated in the carriage of goods by sea case of *Ward v Weir*, below.

Ward v Weir (1899) 4 Com Cas 216

The vessel *David Morgan* was owned by the defendants, Andrew Weir and Co, and chartered to the plaintiffs. The charterparty provided that *David Morgan*, presently at Philadelphia, should sail to Japan and, having discharged there, proceed to British Columbia and there load a cargo for London. The charterparty also contained the following clause: 'A commission of 3¾% shall be paid to charterers and 1% to James McMillan [the owner's broker] on amount of this charter in US gold coin on the completion of loading, or should the vessel be lost.' *David Morgan* was lost on passage from Philadelphia to Japan, but the shipowners refused to pay the commission, because, they contended, the charterparty did not come into operation until the ship discharged her cargo in Japan and, therefore, no commissions were due.

The court ruled that the contract of affreightment, the charterparty, was effective from the day of its execution and the voyage to Japan was an important aspect of the charterparty. Therefore, as the charterparty was in operation, the shipowner was liable for the commissions. In passing his judgment, Matthew J clearly felt that the commissions could have been insured by the shipowner.

> **Matthew J:** [p 221] ... It appears to me to be clear, upon the proper construction of this charterparty, that the ship was bound to go to Japan, and that the charterparty became efficient from the date of its execution. It was very important both to the charterers and to the shipowners that it should be known where the ship was at the time the charterparty was entered into, and it was a material part of the contract that the ship should be at Philadelphia, and that she should proceed to Japan to discharge cargo there with a view to performing the other obligations under the charterparty.
>
> [p 222] ... It is quite clear too, to my mind, that in this case, the shipowners could have insured this commission, if they were minded so to do, and there is no hardship resulting from the construction which I place upon the charterparty. In my opinion, the commission is payable to the charterers, and therefore they are entitled to recover in this action.

DISBURSEMENTS

There is no definition of the word 'disbursements' in the Act, but, in general terms, disbursements, with respect to marine insurance, is the money expended on the insurable property '... the benefit of which will be lost or the object of which will be frustrated by marine perils ...'.[33] Therefore, the question arises, what type of expenditure may rightly be called a 'disbursement' and thereby be insured?

---

33 *Op cit*, Arnould, fn 13, Vol 2, para 325.

In *Roddick v Indemnity Mutual Marine Insurance Co Ltd* [1895] 1 QB 837; aff'd by CA [1895] 2 QB 380, cited earlier in the chapter,[34] the court decided that the hull policy did not include expenditure on fuel, engine room and deck stores; such items rightfully being disbursements and insurable as such.[35]

Kennedy J: [Court of first instance, p 837] ... he [the shipowner] intended in effecting these honour policies for £2,600 to cover certain disbursements, amounting to about £2,583 for coals, stores, and expenses which he had made in respect of the ship in view of her proceeding from the United Kingdom to the coast of South America, and afterwards trading there as warranted by him in his 'hull and machinery' policies. The figures of these disbursements were as follows:

About £1,487 expended on coal

" £ 318 engine room and deck stores

" £ 462 provisions and cabin stores

" £ 191 port expenses at Newport and advances

" £ 395 premiums.

Lord Esher MR: [Court of Appeal, p 384] ... I am satisfied that the words 'hull and machinery' cannot be taken as including those things which are covered by the disbursement policies.

Ordinarily, an expenditure by way of disbursements is one made on insurable property which lies outside the cover provided by the hull and machinery, cargo or freight policies of insurance. This was confirmed by Bigham J, in the case of *Buchanan v Faber* (1899) 4 Com Cas 223, discussed earlier,[36] where a policy on disbursements had been effected by a ship's agent.

Disbursements incurred by a ship's agent

The insurance of 'disbursements' is normally undertaken by a shipowner in order to cover the necessary expenditures incurred in maintaining and operating his ship. However, policies of insurance on 'disbursements' are, as was seen in *Buchanan v Faber*, above, occasionally effected by ship's agents. The general view appears to be that an agent, under normal circumstances, has no right in law to effect an policy on disbursements, because he has no insurable interest in the ship. However, a different stance was taken in *Moran v Uzielli* [1905] 2 KB 555, discussed earlier,[37] because the agent had advanced

---

34 See above, p 85.

35 In *Lawther v Black* (1900) 6 Com Cas 5, the court held that the cost of 'dry docking and painting' could be included in disbursements, and in *Moran v Uzielli* [1905] 2 KB 555, disbursements were held to include 'necessaries supplied to a ship'.

36 See Chapter 2, p 76, for the facts of the case and for a discussion of the nature of the insurable interest of an agent (eg, brokers and managing owners).

37 See Chapter 2 , p 72.

moneys to the shipowner and, therefore, had an insurable interest in the ship because of his right to institute an action in rem against that ship.

Disbursements – over-insurance by double insurance

A major problem with the insurance of disbursements is the distinct possibility of over-insurance by double insurance. Many of the normal operating expenses incurred, for example, in earning freight could quite easily also be insured as disbursements, thereby resulting in over-insurance by double insurance.

Such was the case in *Thames and Mersey Marine Insurance Co Ltd v 'Gunford' Ship Co Ltd* [1911] AC 529, HL, where a vessel was grossly over-insured to the amount of £35,800 when the property at risk only amounted to £14,000. Included in this amount was insurance to the value of £5,500 on freight and a further £11,100 on disbursements by way of two ppi policies.[38] Many of the expenses insured under the disbursements policies duplicated the expenses normally associated with expenditures made in earning the freight. When the vessel was lost, the owners claimed upon all their policies.

The House of Lords ruled that the owners could not recover on their policies because their failure to inform the insurers of the over-insurance amounted to a non-disclosure of a material fact, which would have influenced the insurers in accepting the risk and setting the premiums.

> **Lord Shaw of Dunfermline:** [p 542] ... My Lords, much more serious considerations, however, follow. There were insurances on freight to the extent of £5,500, and insurances on disbursements to the extent of £4,600. The latter policies, those on disbursements, were ppi policies. They were bound to be so, because, in point of fact, as was admitted in arguments for the respondents [shipowners], the disbursements were the very things which had been already accounted for in the freight, and when the ship became a wreck, the payment on these policies was not to be a payment of indemnity, but a present to the assured of this sum of money, a present falling to be made in the event of the wreck and loss of the vessel.
>
> The story, however, does not stop there. There were also insurances on disbursements on behalf of Briggs [the Gunford Ship Co manager]. These were time policies current during the voyage to an amount of no less than £6,500. Briggs had made advances on the bank on behalf of the company, and he was in other ways deeply involved as a creditor. Any payments made under these insurances would, again, not be payments to indemnify Briggs for loss, but be of the nature also of presents, presents made on the issue of a gamble upon the life of the vessel, the issue to be favourable to Briggs when the vessel was lost.

---

38 Policy proof of interest or 'honour' policies: see Chapter 1, p 15.

My Lords, it needs no words of mine to point out that property at sea and the lives of seamen stand in the greatest peril if business of that character obtains the sanction of law.

The Disbursements Warranty Clause

It was clearly shown in the *Gunford* case, above, that when insuring disbursements, it is all to easy to over-insure by double insurance. The Institute Hulls Clauses – Time and Voyage, now incorporate a Disbursements Warranty Clause, which warrants that disbursements may now only be insured up to 25% of the value in the policy.[39]

The Institute Time Clauses – Hulls Disbursements and Increased Value (total loss only, including excess liabilities)

Disbursements may be insured under the above Institute Hulls Disbursements Clauses. Traditionally, disbursements policies are underwritten 'free from average' and, thus, settlement under the policy only takes place if payment has been made under the hulls policy for a total loss, actual or constructive.

SEAMEN'S WAGES

A seaman would suffer a pecuniary loss, namely, the loss of wages if the ship upon which he is employed is so damaged by maritime perils as to be unable to perform the voyage. There is nothing to prevent the master or any member of the crew from insuring their wages; this is in fact sanctioned by s 11 of the Act, which states:

> The master or any member of the crew of a ship has an insurable interest in respect of his wages.

Furthermore, as a seaman's wages may be considered as a 'pecuniary benefit', s 3(2)(b) of the Act allows for the insurance of such, provided that the subject matter insured is exposed to maritime perils; otherwise there is no risk to insure.

---

39 See the ITCH(95), cl 22 and the IVCH(95), cl 20. For a fuller discussion of the Disbursements Warranty Clause, see Chapter 7, p 294.

VENTURES UNDERTAKEN BY A COMPANY

As was seen earlier, a shareholder in a company has no insurable interest in the assets of the company in which he holds shares.[40] As such, according to *Macaura v Northern Assurance Co Ltd* [1925] AC 619, HL, he cannot take out a policy on the assets of the company. However, in the cases of *Paterson v Harris* (1861) 1 B&S 336 and, in particular, *Wilson v Jones* (1867) LR 2 Exch 139, the courts were prepared to acknowledge the fact that a shareholder has an insurable interest in the ventures of the company and, therefore, may insure the risks involved in such ventures.[41]

LIABILITY TO A THIRD PARTY

A shipowner may incur liability by causing injury or damage to persons or property belonging to a third party. Provision is made under the Act for insurance to be effected against such third party liability. Section 3(2)(c) affirms that:

> In particular, there is a marine adventure where:
>
> ... any liability to a third party may be incurred by the owner of, or other person interested in or responsible for, insurable property, by reason of maritime perils.

The most obvious example of third party liability which a shipowner may incur is collision damage to another ship. Such liability is specifically covered by the Institute Hulls Clauses – Time and Voyage, by way of the '3/4ths Collision Liability Clause'.[42]

References and further reading

Bennett, HN, 'The new Institute Time Clauses Hulls' [1996] LMCLQ 305

George, A, 'The new Institute Cargo Clauses' [1986] LMCLQ 438

Koh, PSK, 'Insurable risks and the new Institute Cargo Clauses' [1988] JBL 287

Leloir, N, 'The Lloyd's marine policy and the Institute Cargo Clauses' [1985] JBL 288

O'May, DR, 'The new marine policy and Institute Clauses' [1985] LMCLQ 191

---

40 See Chapter 2, p 67.
41 This area of law is discussed in depth in Chapter 2, p 68.
42 See cl 8 of the ITCH(95) and cl 6 of the IVCH(95); for further discussion on third party liability for collision damage, see Chapter 13.

CHAPTER 4

TIME AND VOYAGE POLICIES

INTRODUCTION

Section 25(1) of the Act states:

> Where the contract is to insure the subject matter at and from, or from one place to another or others, the policy is called a 'voyage policy', and where the contract is to insure the subject matter for a definite period of time, the policy is called a 'time policy'. A contract for both voyage and time may be included in the same policy.

Thus, the Act provides for a contract of marine insurance to be in the form of:

(a) a time policy;

(b) a voyage policy; or

(c) a mixed policy (both time and voyage).

However, whilst it is the Act which lays down the statutory framework governing such policies of insurance, it is the Institute Clauses which determine the terms and conditions by which the parties to the insurance are governed.

TIME POLICY

A definite period of time

The Act, in s 25(1), defines a 'time policy' as a policy '... where the contract is to insure the subject matter for a definite period of time ...'. Ordinarily, the cover provided by the insurance will commence at a time and date specified by the policy and terminate at another time and date designated by the policy.

Should, however, only the date of commencement and the date of termination of cover be stipulated by the policy, the actual time on those respective dates not being specified, the policy is said to run from 0000 hours on the day of commencement to 2400 hours on the day of termination. This was confirmed in the case of *Scottish Metropolitan Assurance Co v Steward*, below.

Scottish Metropolitan Assurance Co v Steward (1923) 15 LIL Rep 55

A voyage policy of insurance was reinsured by the plaintiffs with the defendants whereby the steamship *Earlshaw* was covered against marine losses 'from 20 September 1922, inclusive, to noon 20 February 1923'. When *Earlshaw* was actually lost at 7.30 pm on 20 September 1922, after being found abandoned in the North Sea, the insurers questioned whether the risk had attached at the time of the loss.

The court ruled that the insurers were liable for the loss. It was the duty of the court to try and interpret the words in the contract of insurance in accordance with intention of the parties to that contract and, when only the dates and not the times were given to indicate the commencement and termination of the policy, the whole of those dates were to be included in the cover.

> **Rowlatt J:** [p 409] ... As to the effect of fixing a period from a named day, it was clear that there was no technical rule of construction to be applied; the words must be construed in accordance with the intention of the parties as it could be gathered from the circumstances of the case ... according to the ordinary construction of the English language, when two days were mentioned as the dates on which a period began and ended, both those days were included in that period. People only mentioned days with which they were actually concerned; for example, if it was said that the court sat from Monday to Friday in each week, or that the year ran from 1 January to 31 December, the days at each end of the period were included ... this insurance expressed to run from 20 September included 20 September, and the risk had, therefore, attached before the vessel sank.

Although the majority of time policies are underwritten for 12 month periods, there is no longer any statutory limit to the time period over which the policy may provide cover.[1]

Time policy containing an extension clause

One of the issues which arose in the *Eurysthenes*, case, below, was whether a policy of insurance which provided cover from a certain date, but did not contain a 'definite' termination date, was, in fact, a time policy within the meaning of s 25(1). Counsel for the shipowners submitted that the policy could not be a time policy because, once the policy had attached, it only terminated after notice was given by either the assured or the P & I Club; there was no actual date of termination. In the context of the case, this was an important point which was, however, rejected by the Court of Appeal.

---

1 The 12 month time limit previously imposed by s 25(2) was repealed by the Finance Act 1959.

Compania Maritima San Basilio SA v Oceanus Mutual Underwriting Association (Bermuda) Ltd, 'Eurysthenes' [1976] 2 Lloyd's Rep 171, CA

The plaintiffs entered their vessel *Eurysthenes* with the defendant P & I Club to be covered for class 1 risks. The Club rules stated: [r 9] '... the ship shall be deemed to be entered in the Association from the time stated in the certificate and such entry shall continue from Policy year to year unless notice to the contrary be given ...'; and [r 17] 'A Member may terminate the entry of an entered ship by giving to the managers not less than two months' notice in writing ... and the Association may at any time discontinue the insurance of a Member ... by giving him seven days' notice in writing ...'. *Eurysthenes* stranded on a voyage from the USA to the Philippines. The P & I Club contended that *Eurysthenes* was unseaworthy and, as the owners were privy to that unseaworthiness under s 39(5), the insurers were not liable.[2] The owners put forward the argument that s 39(5) did not apply, because the policy in question was not a true time policy as defined by s 25(1). Both the shipowners and the P & I Club sought guidance from the court as to their positions under the policy.

The Court of Appeal ruled that the policy was, in fact, a time policy; there were only two types of marine policy – time or voyage, or a combination of both.

> **Roskill LJ:** [p 180] ... Mr Mustill [for the shipowners] accepted that the club cover was a contract of marine insurance within s 1 of the 1906 Act, and that there was here a marine adventure within s 3(1) and (2)(c) of that Act which was properly the subject of a contract of marine insurance. But he sought to argue that s 25(1) did not create a statutory dichotomy between time policies and voyage policies, notwithstanding that that sub-section allows a policy of marine insurance to include a contract both for voyage and for time. There was room, he argued, for a contract of marine insurance which was neither a voyage nor a time policy nor a combination of the two ... Therefore, it was said that this was not a 12 months' policy, nor was it a policy for a 'definite' period, because there were so many events which might either extend or abridge its duration.
>
> [p 181] ... It seems to me plain ... that whether one looks at this matter simply as one of the construction of s 25 of the 1906 Act, coupled with s 23 of that Act, or more elaborately as one of the construction of those sections against the background of the revenue legislation enacted in the Stamp Act 1891, as amended by the Finance Act 1901, there is a clear statutory dichotomy between time and voyage policies, a combined time and voyage policy being also permitted. In short, a policy of marine insurance must be one or the other or both, but it cannot be something else.
>
> ... I am, therefore, clearly of the view that a policy for a period of time and not for a voyage does not cease to be a time policy as defined merely because that period of time may thereafter be extended or abridged pursuant to one of the

---

2   The defence of unseaworthiness under s 39(5) is discussed in Chapter 7, p 319.

policy's contractual provisions. The duration of the policy is defined by its own terms and is thus for a 'definite period of time'. In my view, the word 'definite' was added to emphasise the difference between a period of time measured by time and a period of time measured by the duration of a voyage.

Time policy with a geographical limit

A geographical limitation placed upon a time policy does not change that time policy into a mixed policy. The policy remains fundamentally a time policy, even though it only covers voyages within the prescribed geographical limits.

In *Wilson v Boag* **[1957] 2 Lloyd's Rep 564**, the plaintiff owner of a motor launch insured her for four months on the basis that the policy provided cover for losses incurred within a 50 mile radius of Port Stephens. When a loss occurred within that 50 mile radius, but on a voyage intended to go as far as Sydney, 90 miles away, the insurers refused payment, contending that the policy was both a time policy and a voyage policy (mixed), and the cover only extended to voyages undertaken within the prescribed geographical limits.

The Supreme Court of New South Wales ruled that the policy was a time policy only and, as the loss occurred within the prescribed geographical limit of 50 miles, the insurers were liable.

> **Supreme Court of New South Wales:** [p 565] ... The plaintiff contends that, on the true construction of the policy, the launch was covered if a loss by a peril insured against occurred within the limits of the area set by the policy ... and that at the time of the loss it was proceeding within that area to a destination outside it is irrelevant. The defendant contends that the policy is a 'mixed policy', that is to say, that it is both a time and voyage policy; that the only 'voyages' covered by the policy are those made within the prescribed perimeter; and that a 'voyage' embarked upon and designed to take the launch outside that perimeter was not within the policy even though the loss may have occurred while the launch was still within the defined geographical area. If the policy is a time and voyage policy, then it would not attach to a voyage embarked upon for the purposes of taking the launch to Sydney, even if the loss was sustained at a time when the launch in the course of its journey was within the geographical limit described in the policy.
>
> ... On the whole, we are of opinion that the policy here in question should not be construed as a voyage policy attaching only to voyages intended to begin and end within the perimeter and to remain wholly within it. It is to be regarded rather as a time policy in which is contained a limitation of the liability of the insurer to loss sustained while the launch is within a defined geographical area. We think that the policy covers loss occurring within the perimeter even though the launch was then in the course of proceeding to a point outside it. That seems to us to be the natural meaning to be given to the relevant words.
>
> There appear to be no reported cases precisely in point, and to apply the rules of law relating to commercial voyage policies to this case seems to us to be

somewhat unreal, and not to be warranted by anything to be found in the terms of the contract.

The Navigation Clause

The Navigation Clause, cl 1 of the ITCH(95), is identical to the equivalent Navigation Clause contained within the IVCH(95), except for cl 1.5, the 'Scrapping Voyage Clause', which is only relevant to a time policy of insurance.

The purpose of the Navigation Clause is to confirm expressly that cover is provided for those less usual seaborne operations which may be considered to fall outside normal practice.

At all times

The first part of cl 1.1 states:
> The Vessel is covered subject to the provisions of this insurance at all times and has leave to sail or navigate with or without pilots, to go on trial trips and to assist and tow vessels or craft in distress ...

Thus, the Clause confirms that cover is provided by the policy *at all times* whilst the insured vessel:

(a) sails or navigates with or without pilots;

(b) goes on trial trips; and

(c) assists and tows vessels or craft in distress.

Towage and salvage warranty

Having established those marine operations under which the policy remains in force, the second part of cl 1.1 confirms, by way of a warranty, those towage and salvage operations which are or are not covered by the policy:

> ... but it is warranted that the Vessel shall not be towed, except as is customary or to the first safe port or place when in need of assistance, or undertake towage or salvage services under a contract previously arranged by the Assured and/or Owners and/or Managers and/or Charterers. This Clause 1.1 shall not exclude customary towage in connection with loading and discharging.

That is, it is warranted that the vessel shall not:

(a) be towed, except as is customary or to the first *safe* port or place when in need of assistance;[3] or

---

3 Not the nearest port, but the nearest *safe* port.

(b) undertake towage or salvage operations under a contract previously arranged by the assured and/or owners and/or managers and/or charterers.

But the warranty does not apply when the vessel is engaged in 'customary towage in connection with loading and discharging'.

Clause 1.2 of the Navigation Clause then goes on to qualify the conditions laid down in cl 1.1. Clause 1.2 states:

> This insurance shall not be prejudiced by reason of the Assured entering into any contract with pilots or for customary towage which limits or exempts the liability of the pilots and/or tugs and/or towboats and/or their owners when the Assured or their agents accept or are compelled to accept such contracts in accordance with established local law or practice.

The Clause thus recognises the fact that some pilotage and towage contracts must be entered into in accordance with local law and practice; in particular where such contracts limit or exempt the liability of pilots, tugs and tug owners. In such circumstances, cl 1.2 ensures that the insurance cover remains in force.[4]

The use of helicopters

Clause 1.3 acknowledges that, with many modern marine operations, helicopters are utilised to transport personnel, supplies and equipment to and from a vessel. Thus, cl 1.3 states:

> The practice of engaging helicopters for the transportation of personnel, supplies and equipment to and/or from the Vessel shall not prejudice this insurance.

Trading operations entailing loading and discharging operations at sea

In the event of loading and discharging operations taking place at sea between two vessels, the ships would have to be 'ranged' alongside each other. Not surprisingly, such practice greatly increases the risk of contact and collision damage being sustained by either or both of the vessels.

Thus, because of the hazardous nature of the operation and the attendant increase in risk, cl 1.4, often referred to as the 'Ranging Clause', confirms that such 'trading'[5] operations are not covered by the policy unless the vessels being loaded from or discharged into are 'harbour or inshore craft'. Further, in

---

4 Where towage is concerned, the main criterion is whether the towage is customary or not. See *Russell v Provincial Insurance Co Ltd* [1959] 2 Lloyd's Rep 275; this case is discussed in detail in Chapter 7, p 291.

5 The word 'trading' implies regular usage. Thus, it is presumed that transhipment in the case of an emergency or on a one-off basis is still covered; cl 1.4 not being applicable.

recognition of the fact that transhipment is now a feature of modern sea-going operations, underwriters are prepared to undertake such risks provided that previous notice is given and the amended terms of cover and any additional premium is agreed. To this effect, cl 1.4 affirms:

> In the event of the Vessel being employed in trading operations which entail cargo loading or discharging at sea from or into another vessel (not being a harbour or inshore craft), no claim shall be recoverable under this insurance for loss of or damage to the Vessel or liability to any other vessel arising from such loading or discharging operations, including whilst approaching, lying alongside and leaving, unless previous notice that the Vessel is to be employed in such operations has been given to the Underwriters and any amended terms of cover and any additional premium required by them have been agreed.

It is emphasised that the Clause excludes cover not only to the insured ship itself, but also liability for any damage caused to the other vessel. Thus, in such circumstances, it must be presumed that, in the event of any collision damage occurring between the two ships engaged in transhipment at sea, whether approaching, moored or leaving, the 3/4ths Collision Liability Clause,[6] would be ineffective.

The Continuation Clause

Clause 2 of the ITCH(95), the Continuation Clause, states that:

> Should the Vessel at the expiration of this insurance be at sea and in distress or missing, she shall, provided notice be given to the Underwriters prior to the expiration of this insurance, be held covered until arrival at the next port in good safety, or if in port and in distress until the vessel is made safe, at a pro rata monthly premium.

Thus, provided that notice is given to the underwriter *prior to the expiration of the insurance*, the vessel is held covered even though she is:

(a) at sea and in distress or missing – in which case, the vessel is held covered until arrival at the next port in good safety; or

(b) in port and in distress – in which case, the vessel is held covered until she is made safe.

However, the fact that the vessel may be held covered under the Continuation Clause, thereby extending the period of insurance, does not mean that the policy is anything other than a time policy within the meaning of s 25(1) of the Act. Reference to this was made by Lord Denning in the case of *Compania*

---

6   The 3/4ths Collision Liability Clause is discussed in Chapter 13.

Maritima San Basilio SA v Oceanus Mutual Underwriting Association (Bermuda) Ltd, 'Eurysthenes' **[1976] 2 Lloyd's Rep 171, CA**, the facts of which were cited earlier.[7]

Lord Denning MR: [p 177] ... Mr Mustill [for the shipowners] stressed the word 'definite' in s 25. This means, I think, that the period must be specified. But it is, I think, sufficiently specified if it specifies a stated period, even though that period is determinable on notice, and even though the assurance will be renewed or continued automatically at the end of the period, unless determined; or will continue under a continuation clause. This is supported by the fact that, in an ordinary time policy, the Institute Time Clauses (Hulls) include a continuation provision in cl 4 [now cl 2], but that does not prevent the policy being a time policy.

The Termination Clause

Automatic termination

A time policy of insurance will, under normal circumstances, expire on the date specified in that policy. However, 'unless the underwriters agree to the contrary in writing', a time policy of insurance will terminate *automatically* should any of the conditions laid down in cl 5, the Termination Clause, not be met. The importance of the Clause lies in the fact that it is prefaced with a paramount clause, in bold print, declaring:

This Clause 5 shall prevail notwithstanding any provision whether written typed or printed in this insurance inconsistent therewith.

The significance of the words 'automatic termination' in cl 5.1 is that, unlike the breach of a promissory warranty which a breach of cl 4, the Classification Clause, amounts to, there is no question of the breach being waived by the insurers; the contract of insurance is *automatically* terminated.

The Termination Clause is in two parts: the first part deals with 'classification', and the second with 'change of ownership or flag' and related matters. It is emphasised that cl 5, the Termination Clause, must be read in conjunction with cl 4, the Classification Clause, discussed below.[8] As will be seen, there is a degree of overlap between these two Clauses on matters pertaining to classification societies and maintenance of class.

---

7   See above, p 123.
8   See below, p 133.

Classification

Clause 5.1 of the ITCH(95) confirms that:

> Unless the Underwriters agree to the contrary in writing, this insurance shall terminate automatically at the time of ...
>
> change of the Classification Society of the Vessel, or change, suspension, discontinuance, withdrawal or expiry of her Class therein, or any of the Classification Society's periodic surveys becoming overdue unless an extension of time for such survey be agreed by the Classification Society, provided that if the Vessel is at sea, such automatic termination shall be deferred until arrival at her next port. However, where such change, suspension, discontinuance or withdrawal of her Class or where a periodic survey becoming overdue has resulted from loss or damage covered by Clause 6 of this insurance or which would be covered by an insurance of the Vessel subject to current Institute War and Strikes Clauses Hulls – Time, such automatic termination shall only operate should the Vessel sail from her next port without prior approval of the Classification Society or in the case of a periodic survey becoming overdue without the Classification Society having agreed an extension of time for such survey ...

Thus, unless the underwriters agree to the contrary in writing, the insurance will terminate automatically at the time of:

(a) change of the Classification Society of the vessel; or

(b) change, suspension, discontinuance, withdrawal or expiry of her class therein; or

(c) any of the Classification Society's periodic surveys becoming overdue, unless an extension of time for such survey be agreed by the Classification Society.

Change of classification society

Clause 5.1, the Termination Clause provides for an automatic termination of the policy in the event of a 'change of the Classification Society of the Vessel'. In this connection, there is a degree of overlap between cl 4.1.1 of the Classification Clause and cl 5.1, the Termination Clause.

But, as the Termination Clause is expressly confirmed as prevailing over other provisions in the insurance, there must be 'automatic termination' of the insurance in the event of a change of classification society or a failure to maintain class, unless, of course, the underwriters agree to the contrary in writing. The only other proviso made by cl 5.1 with regard to automatic termination is that: '... if the vessel is at sea, such automatic termination shall be deferred until arrival at her next port.'[9]

---

9   Clause 4.2 contains a similar proviso: '... If the vessel is at sea at such date the Underwriters' discharge from liability is deferred until arrival at her next port.'

Change, suspension, discontinuance, withdrawal or expiry of class

Again, a degree of overlap can be seen here, in that cl 5.1, the Termination Clause, has also concerned itself specifically with 'change, suspension, discontinuance, withdrawal or expiry' of Class. Clause 4.1 is, however, couched in more general terms, that 'her class within that Society be maintained'. Though it is expressly stated that its breach will result in discharging the insurer from liability, nevertheless, as described earlier, the paramount clause in the Termination Clause will take precedence and the contract will be automatically terminated.

However, cl 5.1 offers a reprieve in its proviso, that termination of the policy will not operate:

> ... where such change, suspension, discontinuance, withdrawal or expiry of her class has resulted from loss or damage covered by Clause 6 of this insurance or which would be covered by an insurance of the Vessel subject to current Institute War and Strikes Clauses Hulls – Time ...

But, termination will automatically take place 'should the Vessel sail from her next port without prior approval of the Classification Society ...'.

So, what is meant by a 'withdrawal' of class or a failure to maintain class? This issue was considered in the *Caribbean Sea* case, below.

Prudent Tankers Ltd SA v Dominion Insurance Co Ltd, 'Caribbean Sea' [1980] 1 Lloyd's Rep 338

The tanker *Caribbean Sea* was insured under a policy incorporating the American Institute Hulls Clauses and classified by Bureau Veritas. When she sank in fair weather conditions whilst on a voyage from the Panama Canal to Tacoma, because of the circumstances surrounding the loss, the issue of classification arose. The insurers contended that they were not liable under the policy, because a previous minor grounding had invalidated her class.

A ship's class, the court decided, could only be withdrawn by the classification society if the ship had not been kept in proper condition or had not been subjected to surveys as required under the classification society's rules. On confirmation of the rules laid down by way of a letter from the classification society regarding class, the court differentiated between 'loss of validity of the classification certificate' and 'withdrawal of class'.

> **Robert Goff J:** [p 349] ... M Ollivier, head of the relevant department of Bureau Veritas, wrote as follows on 7 June 1979:
>
>> The Society's Rules differentiate between the loss of validity of the classification certificate, which is an automatic consequence of the omission of the owner to fulfil his obligations towards the Society, and the withdrawal of class, which requires a positive act from the Society.
>>
>> After a grounding and in order to revalidate the classification certificate, the owner or his representative must, in conformity with regulation 2–14.11 (1977 Rules), call in a surveyor.

When *Caribbean Sea* was on transit in the Panama Canal and stopped at Cristobal and Balboa in May 1977, the Society did not have a surveyor in the area. In the absence of a BV surveyor, the ship's captain should have, in conformity with regulation 2–14.14, notified BV Head Office in Paris of the grounding. At that time, the Society had a surveyor available for survey at Tacoma.

... In the case of *Caribbean Sea*, apart from the automatic invalidation of the classification certificate rendering the class position irregular (if the vessel grounded in the Maracaibo Canal on 20 May 1977), the Society has no knowledge of any other circumstances which would have affected the class position of the vessel at the date of her loss.

It is clear from this letter that, on the interpretation placed by Bureau Veritas on their own rules, and on the application of these rules to the events which occurred, the ship's *class* was not, in fact, affected. It follows, in my judgment, that for this reason alone, the underwriters are unable to say that the ship's *class* was changed, cancelled or withdrawn, and accordingly, their argument based on the hull clauses fails. But even if I am wrong in this conclusion and I have to decide the point as a matter of the construction which I myself would place upon r 2–14, I would reach the same conclusion. The words of 2–14.11 are, in my judgment, plain. They state that 'the classification *certificate* loses its validity'. I can see no reason why I should give these words any other than their natural and ordinary meaning. As M Ollivier states, the rules themselves distinguish between the classification certificate, and the ship's actual class.

... The rule therefore refers expressly to r 2–14, and provides that, if the ship has not been subjected to the surveys as required by that rule, her class *may be* withdrawn. Now if the underwriters' submission was correct, that rule would be nonsensical, because on their argument, the vessel's class would already have automatically 'lost its validity' by virtue of the grounding or damage; if that were so, it would be otiose, indeed inconsistent, to provide that, in the event of a failure to subject the ship to a survey following such grounding or damage the vessel *may* lose her class. For this reason alone, I can see no reason why I should depart from the natural and ordinary meaning of the words of r 2–14.11; and it follows once again that there was, by virtue of the grounding, no change, cancellation or withdrawal of the ship's class, and the underwriters' argument fails.

Periodic survey becoming overdue

An 'automatic termination' of the contract of insurance would arise should any requirement by the Classification Society to undertake periodic surveys not be adhered to. The only exception to the rule is, as in the case of a 'change, suspension, discontinuance, withdrawal or expiry of class', where 'a periodic survey becoming overdue has resulted from loss or damage covered by Clause 6 or which would be covered by an insurance of the Vessel subject to current Institute War and Strikes Clauses Hulls – Time'. But, 'should the Vessel sail from her next port ... without the Classification Society having agreed an extension of time for such survey, the policy will terminate automatically'.

Change of ownership or flag

Clause 5.2 of the Termination Clause states that:

> Unless the Underwriters agree to the contrary in writing, this insurance shall terminate automatically at the time of:
>
> > ... any change, voluntary or otherwise, in the ownership or flag, transfer to new management, or charter on a bareboat basis, or requisition for title or use of the Vessel, provided that, if the Vessel has cargo on board and has already sailed from her loading port or is at sea in ballast, such automatic termination shall if required be deferred, whilst the Vessel continues her planned voyage, until arrival at final port of discharge if with cargo or at port of destination if in ballast. However, in the event of requisition for title or use without the prior execution of a written agreement by the Assured, such automatic termination shall occur 15 days after such requisition whether the Vessel is at sea or in port.

The primary purpose of cl 5.2 of the Termination Clause is to protect the insurer from changes in the vessel's status with respect to:

(a) any change in the ownership;

(b) any change in the flag;

(c) transfer to new management;

(d) charter on a bareboat basis; or

(e) requisition for title or use,

all of which would materially alter the risks insured.

But, if required, the 'automatic termination' may be deferred until arrival at the final port of discharge, if the vessel has cargo on board and has already sailed from her loading port. Similarly, it may also be deferred to the port of destination, if the vessel is in ballast and has already sailed.

With respect to a 'requisition' which takes place without the prior execution of a written agreement to that requisition by the assured, termination shall occur 15 days after the requisition, regardless of whether the vessel is at sea or in port. The corollary of this is that, should the vessel be requisitioned 'with' the prior execution of a written agreement by the assured, there would be no period of grace, and the policy would terminate as from the time of that agreement.

Return of premium

The Termination Clause, cl 5, of the ITCH(95) concludes with a reference to return of premium in the event of 'automatic termination', when it states:

A pro rata daily return of premium shall be made provided that a total loss of the Vessel, whether by insured perils or otherwise, has not occurred during the period covered by this insurance or any extension thereof.

That is, unless there has been a total loss of the insured vessel, whether or not that loss has been caused by a peril insured against, there will be a pro rata return of premium.

The Classification Clause

Clause 4.1 of the Classification Clause states:[10]

    4.1 It is the duty of the Assured, Owners and Managers at the inception of and throughout the period of this insurance to ensure that:

        4.1.1 the Vessel is classed with a Classification Society agreed by the Underwriters and that her class within that Society is maintained;

        4.1.2 any recommendations requirements or restrictions imposed by the Vessel's Classification Society which relate to the Vessel's seaworthiness or to her maintenance in a seaworthy condition are complied with by the dates required by that Society.

Clause 4.2 of the Classification Clause then goes on to spell out the effect of a breach of any of the conditions contained within cl 4.1, when it affirms:

    4.2 In the event of any breach of the duties set out in Clause 4.1 above, unless the Underwriters agree to the contrary in writing, they will be discharged from liability under this insurance as from the date of the breach provided that if the Vessel is at sea at such date the Underwriters' discharge from liability is deferred until arrival at her next port.

For all intents and purposes, the duties imposed by cl 4.1 are warranties, the breach of which should now, in the light of the *Good Luck* case on promissory warranties, *automatically* discharge the insurer from liability.[11]

The conditions set out in cl 4.1.1 of the Classification Clause are complementary to, and in some respects mirror, the classification conditions laid down under the Termination Clause, cl 5, discussed earlier.[12] However, by reason of the paramount clause incorporated into the Termination Clause, it must be remembered that the latter will have precedence over the Classification Clause and any breach with respect to classification, without agreement from the underwriters in writing, must bring about an 'automatic termination' of the contract of insurance.

---

10   The IVCH(95) also has a Classification Clause, cl 3, but not a Termination Clause. Thus, much of the discussion here on the Classification Clause is also relevant to a voyage policy incorporating the IVCH(95): see below, p 165.

11   For a discussion of the legal effects of a breach of a promissory warranty, see Chapter 7.

12   See above, p 129.

Though there is a degree of overlap between cl 4.1.1 (on classification) and cl 5 (the Termination Clause), cl 4.1.2, on the subject of seaworthiness, is, however, not covered by the Termination Clause. Regarded as the most significant provision of the Classification Clause, cl 4.2 is by no means to be read as introducing a warranty of seaworthiness into a time policy: its scope is confined specifically to 'recommendations, requirements or restrictions' imposed by the vessel's Classification Society on matters relating to the vessel's seaworthiness and her maintenance in a seaworthy condition. It is the failure to comply with such recommendations, etc, that constitutes a breach of the clause. Whether the vessel is, or is in fact not, rendered unseaworthy by reason of the failure to comply is beside the point.

It is to be noted that cl 4.2 – stipulating the effect of discharge from liability – is applicable only to a breach of cl 4.1. The legal consequences of a breach of cl 4.3, for a failure to report 'any incident condition or damage in respect of which the Vessel's Classification Society *might* make recommendations as to repairs or other action', and of cl 4.4, for 'failure on the part of the Assured to provide the necessary authorisation so as to enable the Underwriters to approach the Classification Society directly for information and/or documents', are not stated.

VOYAGE POLICY

A voyage policy of insurance, whether it be on ship, goods or freight, is defined by s 25(1) of the Act in the following terms:

> Where the contract is to insure the subject matter at and from, or from one place to another or others, the policy is called a 'voyage policy'...

Whilst it is accepted that most ships are now insured under time policies of insurance, for practical reasons, there is nothing to prevent a voyage policy on ship being effected, particularly in the event of one-off voyages. However, there are many old constraints and problems, associated with voyage policies, which do not apply to time policies.

Goods, on the other hand, are almost invariably insured under voyage policies and, because of their importance, will be dealt with separately.

Voyage policy on ship

Over the years, a major issue associated with voyage policies has been that of determining when the policy 'attaches' and 'terminates'. Section 25(1) describes a voyage policy as a policy where the contract is to insure the subject matter 'at and from' or 'from' one place to another. Furthermore, unless the policy provides otherwise, the words 'from' or 'at and from' must have the meaning given to them by rr 2 and 3 of the Rules for Construction contained within the Act.

The policy attaches 'from' a particular place

Rule 2 of the Rules for Construction states:
> Where the subject matter is insured 'from' a particular place, the risk does not attach until the ship starts on the voyage insured.

Where a voyage policy is characterised as being 'from' a particular port or place, for the policy to attach, the vessel must have left her moorings or broken ground with the intention of starting upon the actual voyage insured. Simply moving from moorings to an anchorage in readiness to sail is not to be construed as the commencement of the insured voyage, as was shown in *Sea Insurance Co v Blogg*, below.

Sea Insurance Co v Blogg [1898] 2 QB 398, CA

This was a claim on a reinsurance policy on goods where a vessel was lost on a voyage from Newport News, Virginia, to London. The policy had been underwritten to attach on or after 1 March 1896. Late on 29 February 1896, the steamship *Masacoit* completed her loading at the wharf at Newport News and the master then moved her from the wharf to an anchorage in the James River in readiness for departure in the morning. Evidence was provided to show that the master had moved the ship in order to stop his crew going ashore and getting drunk. The following morning, 1 March, the *Masacoit* sailed for London and was lost. When the insurers claimed on their policy of reinsurance, the reinsurers refused payment, on the basis that the voyage had commenced on 29 February and, therefore, the policy had not, in compliance with the policy attached 'on or after 1 March'.

The Court of Appeal upheld the decision of the trial judge and ruled that the reinsurers were liable under the policy. The moving of the ship on the night of 29 February was not intended to be the commencement of the insured voyage; the voyage did not actually commence until the following morning, 1 March.

> **AL Smith LJ:** [p 400] ... I think that the evidence is conclusive that it was not the intention that the ship should sail when she was moved from the quay that night, but the intention merely was that she should move out into the stream for the night, and should not start on her voyage till the next morning. She was only moved a short distance, namely, about 500 yards, from the wharf in order that the crew might not be able to go ashore and get drunk, and there was no intention of then commencing the voyage.

Alteration of port of departure – s 43

Not surprisingly, if a vessel departs on her insured voyage from a port other than that named in the policy, the risk does not attach. This is confirmed by s 43 of the Act, which states:

> Where the place of departure is specified by the policy, and the ship, instead of sailing from that place, sails from any other place, the risk does not attach.

Section 43 is based upon the principle laid down in the old case of *Way v Modigliani*, below.

Way v Modigliani (1787) 2 Term Rep 30

The vessel *Polly* was insured: '... at and from 20 October 1786, from any ports in Newfoundland to Falmouth.' On 1 October 1786, *Polly* left Newfoundland to fish on the Grand Banks, from whence she departed for England on 17 October with her catch of fish. *Polly* was lost on the voyage to Falmouth. When the policy was claimed upon, the court ruled that the insurance had never attached.

> **Buller J:** [p 32] ... the policy never attached at all. Where a policy is made in such terms as the present to insure a vessel from one port to another, it certainly is not necessary that she should be in port at the time when it attaches, but then she must have sailed on the voyage insured, and not on any other.

The above case should be compared with *Driscoll v Passmore*, below, where the question before the court was whether a 'leg' of an overall round voyage could be considered as a separate insurable voyage rather than as a part of the whole. The insurers of the freight to be earned on the leg on which the loss occurred denied liability for that loss, because, they contended, the ship had sailed from the wrong port on the previous leg.

Driscoll v Passmore (1798) 1 B&P 200

The vessel *Timandra* was insured under three policies covering a round voyage from Lisbon to Madeira, thence to Saffi in Africa and back to Lisbon. The policy in question was a policy on freight covering the return voyage from Saffi to Lisbon. When *Timandra* arrived at Madeira, the crew refused to sail to Saffi, because of the presence of Moorish cruisers in the area. Thus, the captain brought *Timandra* back to Lisbon before sailing direct to Saffi. *Timandra* was captured on her return voyage from Saffi to Lisbon. The insurers of the voyage from Saffi to Lisbon refused to pay for the loss because, they contended, the voyage which had been insured was part of a voyage from Madeira to Saffi and back to Lisbon, not from Lisbon to Saffi and back. The latter being a new voyage, therefore, the insurance never attached.

The court ruled that the insurers were liable for the loss; the voyage insured was separate from the voyage as a whole, and that part of the voyage had, in substance, been performed.

Eyre CJ: [p 203] ... It has been argued in support of the rule, that the voyage insured was the third branch of a specific voyage, specifically described in the policy; but I take the voyage insured to be a voyage from Saffi to Lisbon only. ... The voyage from Saffi to Lisbon might have been performed with as much ease after the circuitous voyage had taken place (unless a Spanish war had broken out) as in the direct course originally proposed. On what principle then can the underwriters be discharged? The voyage has, in substance, been performed: the ship was diverted from her intended course by circumstances for which no one was to blame, and having arrived at Saffi, took in the cargo which was the original object of the insurance

Sailing for a different destination – s 44

Where a vessel sails 'from' the agreed place of departure to a place or port other than that specified in the policy, the risk does not attach. To this effect, s 44 of the Act states:

> Where the destination is specified in the policy, and the ship, instead of sailing for that destination, sails for any other destination, the risk does not attach.

Section 44 is based upon the ruling in the old case of *Wooldridge v Boydell*, below.

Wooldridge v Boydell (1778) 1 Doug KB 16

The vessel *Molly* was insured for a voyage from Maryland to Cadiz. In reality, it was suspected that *Molly* was engaged in supplying the American army during the War of Independence and was actually bound for Boston. In the event, *Molly* left Maryland under papers for Falmouth and was captured in the Chesapeake Bay. The fact that her loss occurred before a different course could be set for Falmouth, rather than Cadiz, made no difference, because, where the port of destination was changed, the risk never attached.

> **Lord Mansfield:** [p 17] ... The policy, on the face of it, is from Maryland to Cadiz, and therefore purports to be a direct voyage to Cadiz. All contracts of insurance must be founded on truth, and the policies framed accordingly ... Here, was the voyage ever intended for Cadiz? There is not sufficient evidence of the design to go to Boston, for the court to go upon. But some of the papers say to Falmouth and a market, some to Falmouth only. None mention Cadiz, nor was there any person in the ship, who ever heard of any intention to go to that port ... In short, that was never the voyage intended, and, consequently, is not what the underwriters meant to insure.

Simon, Israel and Co v Sedgwick [1893] 1 QB 303, CA

Goods specifically insured for a voyage from Bradford to Madrid via '... any port in Spain this side of Gibraltar', were lost when they were carried in a ship bound for Cartagena, the other side of Gibraltar.

The court held that the policy had not attached.

Lindley LJ: [p 306] ... The plaintiffs say that, upon the true construction of this policy, this is a policy from Bradford to Madrid. If it is, then I think it is not denied by their opponents that the underwriters would be liable. But it is contended that this is not a policy from Bradford to Madrid; and, on consideration, I have come to the conclusion that the view of the underwriters is right. We must ask ourselves what is the voyage that includes the risks to which I have alluded – the risks printed in type? ... The starting point is that the goods were insured from Liverpool to some place this side of Gibraltar. They never were on that voyage; and, that being the case, you cannot extend the policy to cover the risks not included in the voyage for which these goods were insured. That appears to me to be the short answer, and the conclusive answer, to the plaintiffs' argument. In other words, this policy is not a policy from Bradford to Madrid; and the plaintiffs are unable, by reason of the blunder which has been committed, to bring themselves within the risks which are included in a voyage for which these goods were insured. I think the view taken by the learned judge is right, and that this policy never attached, and, that being so, the memorandum about deviation, or change of voyage, does not affect the question.

The policy attaches 'at and from' a particular place

A ship may be insured under a voyage policy of insurance which specifies that the risk attaches 'at and from' a particular port or place. The significance of the words 'at and from' are spelt out by r 3 of the Rules for Construction, which states:

(a) where a ship is insured 'at and from' a particular place, and she is at that place in good safety when the contract is concluded, the risk attaches immediately;

(b) if she be not at that place when the contract is concluded, the risk attaches as soon as she arrives there in good safety, and, unless the policy otherwise provides, it is immaterial that she is covered by another policy for a specified time after arrival.

However, there is a third scenario, not contemplated by the Act, namely, where the ship has already sailed from the named port at the time the contract is concluded.

Thus, with respect to attachment of risk, there are three situations which may arise at the time the contract is concluded:

(a) the ship is already at the named port;

(b) the ship is not yet at the named port; or

(c) the ship has already sailed from the named port.

The significance of the word 'at' and the words 'good safety' will also be considered.

The ship is already at the named port

If the ship is already at the port named in the policy, the policy cannot attach if the ship is at the specified port for purposes other than the voyage insured. However, once the ship is deemed to be 'preparing' for the voyage insured and is in 'good safety' at the port named in the contract, the policy will attach. This was clearly illustrated in the case of *Lambert v Liddard*, below.

Lambert v Liddard (1814) 5 Taunt 480

The ship *Lion* was insured under a voyage policy at and from Pernambuco or other ports in Brazil to London. When *Lion*, which had previously been engaged as a privateer, arrived near Pernambuco, an officer was dispatched ashore to inquire into the availability of cargo. On hearing there was no cargo available, *Lion* sailed for St Salvador, a Brazilian port 600 miles to the north, in order to secure an alternative cargo, but, whilst on passage, she was lost. When the plaintiff claimed on his policy of insurance, the insurers refused payment, contending that the ship had not put into any port in Brazil and, therefore, the policy had never attached.

The court ruled that the insurers were liable as the policy had attached when *Lion* arrived off Pernambuco in preparation for the voyage insured.

> **Chambre J:** [p 487] ... The ship had finished her cruise [as a privateer], and was preparing for her voyage to England. What preparation was she to make? She was not coming in ballast to England; she was to get a cargo. She goes to Pernambuco; she inquires there for a cargo, and does not obtain one; but can it be said, that while she was so employed, she was not preparing? She went thither for the very purpose of preparing. Not getting a cargo there, she goes to another part of the coast for the same purpose. The policy attached at Pernambuco, and there was no subsequent deviation, she had a right to go to any of the other ports, to perfect her cargo, I therefore think the rule must be discharged.

In similar vein, the House of Lords referred to the above case when reaching their decision in *Tasker v Cunninghame*, below.

Tasker v Cunninghame (1819) 1 Bligh 87, HL

The vessel *Henrietta* was insured for a voyage 'at and from' Cadiz to the Clyde; the destination later being altered to Liverpool with the consent of the insurers. The purpose of the voyage was to sail to Liverpool and load salt for a fishery in Newfoundland. However, salt became available at Cadiz and, without informing the insurers, it was decided that *Henrietta* should load the salt at Cadiz and then sail direct to Newfoundland. Some eight days after the change of destination, *Henrietta* stranded in Cadiz harbour after a storm, and she was later totally lost when French troops set fire to her. The insurers refused to settle the claim because the intended voyage had been abandoned.

The House of Lords ruled that the insurers were not liable under the policy; once the insured voyage was abandoned, the policy was no longer in force.

House of Lords: [p 103] ... The Lords found (7 July 1819) that the voyage ought to be considered as having been abandoned before the loss of the vessel – and the interlocutors were reversed.

Upon the question, when a risk commences under the word 'at', the case of *Lambert v Liddard* (1814) 5 Taunt 480, makes the nearest approach to the case reported. In *Lambert v Liddard*, it was held that the risk had commenced upon the ground that the ship had *prepared for the voyage*, by inquiring for a cargo. Where the contract is, that the beginning of the adventure shall be 'immediately *from* and after the arrival of 'the ship at', etc; or 'from the departure', the difficulty is removed. In the common case where it is 'at and from', etc, without any special words to restrict the meaning of the word 'at', the beginning to load the cargo, or preparing for the voyage, seem to be the principal circumstances to determine the commencement of the risk.

It should be noted that the words 'at and from' may have a wide or narrow meaning, depending on the context in which they are used. If, for example, a ship is insured 'at and from' Japan, the policy would attach whenever the ship arrived in good safety anywhere in Japan, provided that she was preparing for the insured voyage. But, if the ship is insured 'at and from' Tokyo, the policy could only attach when the ship actually arrived in Tokyo itself, in good safety and preparing for the voyage insured.

This very point was the issue in the case of *Maritime Insurance Co v Alianza Insurance Co of Santander*, below.

Maritime Insurance Co v Alianza Insurance Co of Santander (1907) 13 Com Cas 46

This was a case involving reinsurance. The plaintiffs, the original insurers of the vessel *Dumfriesshire*, underwrote a voyage policy 'at and from a port in New Zealand to Nehoue, New Caledonia and while there and thence to Grangemouth'. The plaintiffs then effected a policy of reinsurance with the defendants, which only provided cover for part of the original risk, namely, 'at and from 1 July 1904, until 31 August 1904 ... whilst at port or ports, place or places in New Caledonia'. *Dumfriesshire* struck the reef surrounding New Caledonia, about 10 miles from the mainland, and suffered damage. The reef was considered as being geographically part of New Caledonia. After settling the claim on the original insurance, the plaintiffs sought to recover their loss under the policy of reinsurance. The reinsurers refused payment.

The court ruled that the plaintiffs could not recover under the policy of reinsurance. The words 'port or ports, place or places' limited the attachment of the cover to a port or place in New Caledonia. A reef, which surrounded the island, could not be construed to mean a 'port' or 'place' as described in the policy, which, therefore, had not attached at the time of the loss.

Walton J: [p 49] ... If the reinsurance had been against losses occurring whilst the vessel was 'at' New Caledonia, it may be that the defendants would be liable. I think that would be so if the reef was in New Caledonia. But the policy is not against losses occurring whilst 'at' New Caledonia. The words used are different – 'at port or ports, place or places in New Caledonia'. Is the effect the same? I have come to the conclusion it is not.

[p 50] ... I do not wish to attempt an exhaustive interpretation, but it seems to me that the word 'place' means some place at which the vessel has arrived to load, or maybe to discharge, or to take coal, or to repair, or even to shelter – a place at which the vessel is for some purpose, not a place at which she happens to be in passing. As the loss did not occur, within the meaning of the policy, at a 'port or ports, place or places in New Caledonia', there must be judgment for the defendants.

Ship not at named port

In accordance with r 3(b) of the Rules for Construction, a ship need not be at the named port at the time the contract of insurance is concluded; the policy attaching later, at the time when the ship arrives at the named port in good safety. In addition to r 3(b), the first part of s 42(1) of the Act also confirms that:

> Where the subject matter is insured by a voyage policy 'at and from' or 'from' a particular place, it is not necessary that the ship should be at that place when the contract is concluded.

It is emphasised that, where the contract of insurance is concluded before the vessel is at the named port, the policy attaches at 'the first arrival' of the vessel in good safety within the 'geographical limits' of that named port. This was illustrated in the case of *Houghton v Empire Marine Insurance Co Ltd*, below.

Houghton v Empire Marine Insurance Co Ltd (1866) LR 1 Exch 206

The vessel *Urgent* arrived at Havana, but, having entered the harbour, grounded and sustained damage when she fouled the anchor of another ship. The insurers claimed they were not liable under the policy because *Urgent* had not been in good safety when the damage occurred and, that being so, the policy on the previous voyage had not terminated, as the requirement for termination was that the ship should have arrived at the port of destination and be moored there in good safety for 24 hours.

The court ruled that the insurers were liable, as the policy had attached as soon as *Urgent* arrived 'geographically within the harbour' of Havana. The meaning of 'good safety' at the commencement of the risk was not the same as that for the termination of the risk,[13] and, furthermore, it was irrelevant that the previous policy was still in force.

---

13 See below, p 166.

Channel B: [p 209] ... It appears that *Urgent* having arrived off Havana, the captain engaged the services of a steam tug and a pilot for the purpose of taking her to a clear anchorage. She was towed into the harbour, past the point where she ultimately discharged her cargo, to a point at the head of the harbour, called the Regla Shoal. There she grounded, and received damage from the anchor of another ship. In my opinion, she was at that time at Havana, and, consequently, the risk under the policy had attached. The damage occurred *at* Havana, geographically speaking, and there is nothing which, to my mind, shows that the parties, at the time this policy was underwritten, contemplated any other meaning of the word '*at*'. All the limitation which the law appears ever to have imposed as to the time of commencement of the risk in such a case is, that the ship should arrive at the port *at* which she is insured in a state of sufficient repair or seaworthiness to be enabled to be there in safety: see *Parmeter v Cousins*, and *Bell v Bell*,[14] in the latter of which cases the ruling of Lord Ellenborough CJ, at *Nisi Prius*, was upheld by the court in Blanc. Here, however, there seems to be no doubt that the ship was really within the harbour in good safety, and the loss occurred from a peril in the harbour, and in no way from any injuries she had received before her arrival. The ship being insured while at Havana is evidently, in the absence of any provision to the contrary, insured all the time she is there, and therefore the risk commences on her first arrival, as put by Lord Hardwicke in *Motteaux v London Assurance Company*.[15]

Unless, therefore, we can say that her first arrival at the port is when she cast anchor there, instead of when she enters the port, our judgment must be for the plaintiffs. In many cases, the nature of the port may be such that the two events may be identical. There may be nothing to show the arrival till the vessel casts anchor. But here we have evidence as to the port of Havana which is sufficient, in my judgment, to show that the arrival was before casting anchor. It has been argued that the first arrival, which must be no doubt in good safety, must be identical with the mooring in good safety usually named in outward policies. But I think we cannot construe the terms of one contract by reference to those of another not referred to in it. And it is clear that there is no usage that the duration of the outward and homeward policies should not overlap, because the outward policy usually extends to 24 hours after the vessel is moored in good safety. During those 24 hours, there is no question that there is double insurance, and, therefore, I see no ground for saying that the parties contracted subject to any usage that such a policy would not attach until the previous one had determined ... if ... they had chosen to make the risk date from the vessel being moored in safety, they would have done so; but, as it stands, it is from the first arrival, which, as a matter of fact, I think to be on her entering the port. My judgment is, therefore, for the plaintiffs, that the rule be discharged.

---

14 These cases are discussed later in the chapter, under the heading of 'good safety'.

15 In *Motteaux v London Assurance Co* (1739) 1 Atk 545, Lord Hardwicke stated: '... It was doubted whether the words "at and from Bengal" meant the first arrival of the ship at Bengal ... it was agreed the words "first arrival" were implied and always understood in policies.'

Pigott B: [p 211] ... The sole question is whether the policy had attached. I am of opinion that it had. I agree with the plaintiff's counsel, that the language used by the parties ought to have a plain construction, and that as the ship had arrived geographically within the harbour of Havana, and was in good safety there before the injury was received, the risk then commenced.

It is emphasised that the principles relating to the attachment of risk are the same whether the policy is on ship or freight. In *Foley v United Marine Insurance Co of Sydney*, below, the insurers put forward the argument that, because the policy was on freight, the risk could not attach until the vessel had fully discharged her previous cargo and was in readiness to receive the cargo for the voyage under which the freight was insured.

Foley v United Marine Insurance Co of Sydney (1870) LR 5 CP 155

The plaintiff owner of the ship *Edmund Graham* chartered her to the agents of a merchant for a voyage from Mauritius to Akyab in Burma; there to await orders to load a cargo of rice for Europe. The plaintiff insured the freight to be earned under the charterparty with the defendants. Whilst *Edmund Graham* was discharging her outward cargo in Mauritius, she was wrecked by a violent hurricane. The plaintiff claimed on his policy on freight, but the insurers refused payment on the basis that the cargo from the previous voyage had not been fully discharged and, therefore, the voyage on which the freight had been insured had not yet commenced. Thus, the insurers contended, the policy on freight had not attached.

The court ruled that the policy on freight had attached when the ship arrived at Mauritius. The fact that the ship still had cargo on board from a previous voyage when she was wrecked did not mean that the risk on the policy on freight covering the next voyage had not attached. Therefore, the insurers were liable for the loss of freight.

Lush J: [p 163] ... The question, when did the risk upon this policy attach? The ship was chartered to proceed from Calcutta to Mauritius, and, having discharged her cargo there, was to go to the rice ports and there load a cargo of rice for the United Kingdom, for a certain freight payable on delivery. The policy describes the risk to be 'at and from Mauritius to rice ports, and at and thence to a port of discharge in the United Kingdom'; and the interest insured is 'chartered freight, valued at £1,150'. The vessel was lost after her arrival at Mauritius, and after part of her cargo had been discharged, but before the residue was unshipped. Mr Quain [for the insurers] contends that the word 'at' is to receive some qualification; and that, because at the time of her loss the vessel was not in a state of complete readiness to proceed at once to Akyab, the risk intended to be covered by the policy had not attached. He has cited no authority on that position; and I am at a loss to discover any principle upon which it can be sustained. The vessel was at Mauritius, and in the course of prosecuting the voyage described in the charterparty.

[p 164] Mr Quain admits that if the entire cargo had been discharged, the loss would have been a loss within the terms of the policy. I must confess I do not

see why the ship was not as much engaged in the prosecution of her voyage as if she had actually left Mauritius. What she was doing was preparatory to her voyage to Akyab. I think the chartered freight on that voyage was clearly an insurable interest, and that the plaintiff had been prevented from earning it by one of the perils against which the policy was intended to insure him.

Ship already sailed from named port

The Act makes no provision to cover the situation where a contract of insurance is concluded after the vessel has already sailed from the named port. However, there is nothing in law to prevent a shipowner from taking up a policy, after the vessel had sailed, to provide cover retrospectively to the commencement of the voyage.

Indeed, there appears to be no practical purpose in wishing to provide such cover when a mixed policy would suffice. That is, the vessel having sailed from the named port at a certain date, a policy could then be underwritten for the voyage on the basis that the risk under the policy would attach on a date fixed by the policy.

This was in fact the nature of the policy in **Way v Modigliani (1787) 2 Term Rep 30**, cited earlier in the chapter,[16] where the vessel *Polly* was insured '... at and from 20 October 1786, from any ports in Newfoundland to Falmouth'. *Polly* had, in fact, left Newfoundland some 19 days earlier, on 1 October 1786. Nevertheless, the court confirmed that there was no reason why the policy should not attach just because the insured vessel was not in port at the time of the attachment. Buller J said: [p 32] '... Where a policy is made in such terms as the present to insure a vessel from one port to another, it certainly is not necessary that she should be in port at the time when it attaches.'

Good safety

When a voyage policy of insurance is stated to be 'at and from' a port or place named in the contract, there is a requirement that the ship must be in a state of 'good safety'[17] when she arrives 'at' that port or place named before the risk under the policy can attach. This is specified in r 3(a) and (b) of the Rules for Construction.[18]

---

16 See above, p 136.
17 A voyage policy could well specify, as in the SG policy, that the ship be in 'good safety' (for any stipulated period) before the risk under the policy can terminate. It would appear from past cases that the concept of 'good safety' is for the purpose of termination of risk different from that for the commencement of risk: see below, p 166.
18 See above, p 138.

Good safety means physical good safety

The requirement of 'good safety' must not be confused with seaworthiness. In the old case of *Parmeter v Cousins*, below, Lord Ellenborough confirmed that for a ship to be in 'good safety' at the commencement of the voyage insured, she must be in such a condition as to enable her 'to lie in reasonable security': she need not be seaworthy, but she must be better than a wreck.

Parmeter v Cousins (1809) 2 Camp 235

The plaintiff effected a policy of insurance on ship and freight for a voyage 'at and from St Michaels, or all or any of the Westward Islands, to England'. On the outward voyage, the ship was so damaged by bad weather that when she arrived at St Michaels, she was leaking so badly that the pumps had to be manned continuously and she was totally unfit to receive any cargo. In fact, the bad weather continued and, 24 hours after the ship anchored at St Michaels, she was blown out to sea and wrecked. Nevertheless, the plaintiff claimed on his policy of insurance on the basis that the vessel had arrived 'at' the port or place specified in the policy.

The court ruled that the vessel never was in 'good safety' and the policy on ship and freight for the homeward voyage never attached.

> **Lord Ellenborough:** [p 237] What we have to consider here is, whether the underwriters on this ship, at and from St Michael's to England, be liable for a loss happening in the manner that had been described? I am clearly of opinion that they are not. To be sure, while the ship remains at the place, a state of repair and equipment may be sufficient, which would constitute unseaworthiness after the commencement of the voyage. But while in port, she must be in such a condition as to enable her to lie in reasonable security till she is properly repaired and equipped for the voyage. She must have once been at the place in good safety. If she arrives at the outward port so shattered as to be a mere wreck, a policy on the homeward voyage never attaches. Such is the present case. I do not remember any one like it; but the principles on which it must be decided are perfectly well established.

And, in the other significant early case of *Bell v Bell*, below, Lord Ellenborough confirmed that 'good safety' at the commencement of the voyage insured only meant good 'physical' safety from the perils insured against. 'Good safety' at the commencement of the voyage did not include good political safety.

Bell v Bell (1810) 2 Camp 475

The plaintiff insured the ship *Rising Sun* and the freight to be earned by that vessel under a policy, underwritten by the defendants, for a voyage 'at and from' Riga, on the Baltic, to the UK. *Rising Sun* arrived safely at Riga, on the Baltic, but was then seized by the Russian Government and condemned before she could discharge her outward cargo. When the plaintiff claimed on his policy of insurance, the insurers refused payment, on the basis that the policy could not have attached, as the seizure of the ship meant that she had not been in good safety.

The court ruled that the policy had attached and the insurers were liable. For the ship to be in 'good safety' at the commencement of the voyage insured, it was sufficient for her to in good 'physical' safety; there was no requirement for her to be in good political safety.

> **Lord Ellenborough:** [p 478] ... The safety required to give a good commencement to the risk on the ship, is a physical safety from the perils insured against, and not a freedom from political danger.

Implied condition as to commencement of risk

The above implied condition applies to voyage policies whether they are designated 'at and from' or 'from' a port or place specified in the policy. To that effect, s 42(1) of the Act states that:

> Where the subject matter is insured by a voyage policy 'at and from' or 'from' a particular place ... there is an implied condition that the adventure shall be commenced within a reasonable time, and that if the adventure is not so commenced the insurer may avoid the contract.

First and foremost, s 42(1) should not be confused with s 48 of the Act, for the former is directed specifically to the commencement of the voyage insured, whereas the latter[19] is concerned with the prosecution of the insured voyage 'throughout its course'.

The primary reason why delay in the commencement of the insured voyage[20] is of utmost concern to an underwriter is that any such delay may result in a seasonal variation in the weather which could 'vary' the risks insured. For this reason, it was thought that, if the risks were varied, that alone should be sufficient to permit the insurer to avoid the policy, if he so wishes.

In some of the earlier cases,[21] it was also thought that, if the cause for the delay was reasonable, such as one of necessity, then, this may be pleaded by the assured as a defence to a breach of the implied condition. This, however, is not the current law on the subject as, save for consent and waiver, s 42 does not allow a plea of lawful excuse.

---

19 Section 48 of the Act states: 'In the case of a voyage policy, the adventure insured must be prosecuted throughout its course with reasonable dispatch, and, if without lawful excuse it is not so prosecuted, the insurer is discharged from liability as from the time when the delay became unreasonable.'

20 A delay in the commencement of the insured voyage may occur in two distinct ways: the insured voyage may, in an 'at and from' policy, be delayed *after* the policy has attached 'at' that particular place, or the previous voyage may have become protracted with the knock-on effect causing a delay in the attachment of the policy, whether the policy be 'at and from' or 'from' a particular place.

21 Such as *Smith v Surridge* (1801) 4 Esp 25 and *Mount v Larkins* (1831) 8 Bing 108.

There is no defence of 'lawful excuse' in s 42

It is to be noted that both s 46, which deals with deviation, and s 48, which is concerned with delay arising during the course of the voyage, may be defended by a plea of 'lawful excuse'. No such provision of lawful excuse is contained within s 42 of the Act. Therefore, it must be presumed that, with respect to delay at the commencement of the insured voyage, no such defence is available to the assured. The only defences available to him are those set out in s 42(2):

> The implied condition may be negatived by showing that the delay was caused by circumstances known to the insurer before the contract was concluded, or by showing that he waived the condition.

Thus, it would appear that no consideration may be given to the cause of the delay. The section is not concerned with whether the delay has increased the risks, for any variation of risks would infringe s 42(1). This omission of the defence of 'lawful excuse' in s 42 appears to be founded upon the case of *De Wolf v Archangel Maritime Bank and Insurance Co Ltd*, below.[22] Blackburn J was in disagreement with the reasoning in earlier cases; in particular, the opinion voiced by Tindal CJ in *Mount v Larkins*, that an underwriter remained liable under the policy if the unreasonable delay to the commencement of the voyage insured was brought about by necessity. The judge was categorical that it was immaterial to the underwriter whether the unreasonable delay to the commencement of the voyage was brought about by fault or misfortune. Section 42 would appear to confirm this reasoning.

De Wolf v Archangel Maritime Bank and Insurance Co Ltd (1874) LR 9 QB 451

A policy of insurance, dated 13 July 1872, was effected by the plaintiffs with the defendants upon the vessel *Florence Chapman* for a voyage from Montreal to Montevideo. In the event, *Florence Chapman* did not arrive at Montreal until 30 August 1872. The underwriters contended that, as the delay effectively altered the risk insured from a summer voyage to a winter voyage, the policy did not attach. The court concurred with this argument.

> **Lord Blackburn:** [p 455] ... The case, however, that comes nearest to the present is that of *Mount v Larkins*. ... The ground on which the judgment delivered by Tindal CJ in *Mount v Larkins* is based, is that:
>
>> the underwriter has as much right to calculate upon the outward voyage, on which the ship is then engaged, being performed in a reasonable time, and without unnecessary delay, in order that the risk may attach, as he has that the voyage insured shall be commenced within a reasonable time, after the risk has attached. In either case, the effect is the same, as to the underwriter, who has another risk substituted instead of that which he has insured against; and in both cases, the alteration is occasioned *by the wrongful act of the assured himself.*

---

22 See, also, *Palmer v Marshall* (1832) 8 Bing 317.

This may be relied on as an expression of opinion that the delay, if *necessary*, would not discharge the underwriters. It may be so, where the fact that the vessel is on a preliminary voyage is known and communicated to the underwriter, so as to make the basis of the contract; and it seems to have been understood by Tindal CJ, that the principle on which the cases of *Vallance v Dewar* and *Ougier v Jennings* were decided was on the ground of notice. He says in both those cases:

> It is admitted that a delay in the commencement of the risk, by the interposition of an immediate voyage not communicated to the underwriters, would discharge the policy, unless such intermediate voyage was one which was made usually and according to the course of the trade in which the ship was then engaged, which would be equivalent to notice to the underwriters.

We need not, in the present case, decide how that is, for there was no communication made to the underwriters as to where the ship was at the time when the policy was made. And we think it, under such circumstances, not material whether the delay which varies the risk was occasioned by the fault or the misfortune of the assured. In either case, the risk is equally varied.

[p 457] ... We think, at all events, in the absence of a representation [to the underwriters], that in a policy 'at and from a port' it is an implied understanding that the vessel shall be there within such a time that the risk shall not be materially varied, otherwise the risk does not attach.

The implied condition may be negatived

Section 42(2) of the Act allows for the implied condition that a voyage must be commenced within a reasonable time after the contract has been concluded to be 'negatived' if:

(a) the delay was caused by circumstances known to the insurer before the contract was concluded; or

(b) the insurer waives the implied condition.

In *Bah Lias Tobacco and Rubber Estates Ltd v Volga Insurance Co Ltd*, below, the insurers were held to be liable under the policy even though there was an unreasonable delay in the commencement of the venture; by accepting an additional premium, the insurers had impliedly waived the implied condition.

Bah Lias Tobacco and Rubber Estates Ltd v Volga Insurance Co Ltd (1920) 3 LIL Rep 155 and 202

The plaintiffs insured the tobacco crop at their estate in Sumatra against various risks with the defendants under a voyage policy of insurance 'at and from ports and/or places ... in Sumatra to London and/or ports ... in Holland'. The insurance included cover against loss or damage caused by fire occurring prior to shipment. The policy was dated June 1917. In July 1918, a fire destroyed a portion of the crop which was stored in the plaintiffs' barns. The plaintiffs claimed on their policy of insurance on the basis that the risk attached as soon as the tobacco was stored in the barns on their plantation. The insurers contended that there had been an unreasonable delay in the commencement of the venture. The plaintiffs countered by alleging that the insurers knew of the delay because they, the plaintiffs, had paid an additional premium soon after the fire had occurred; the payment of an additional premium being the traditional method in such shipments of tobacco of keeping the policy alive.

Shearman J ruled that the insurers were liable under the policy. By accepting the extra premium, the insurers could not rely on the defence of unreasonable delay: they had impliedly waived the breach.

Legal effect of breach

Section 42(1) of the Act confirms that, if the adventure is not commenced within a reasonable time after the contract is concluded '... the insurer may avoid the contract'. Thus, unless the assured can demonstrate that the delay was caused by circumstances known to the insurer or that the insurer had waived the implied condition, the insurer may elect to avoid the contract.

Overlapping of policies

It is not unusual for the cover provided by one policy to overlap with the cover provided by another policy. That is, a policy on an outward voyage may not have terminated before the policy covering the homeward voyage attaches.

This was recognised long ago in the case of **Houghton v Empire Marine Insurance Co (1866) LR 1 Exch 206**, cited earlier,[23] where it was argued by the insurer of a homeward bound ship for a voyage 'at and from Havana to Greenock' that the policy had not attached, because the policy on the outward voyage had not terminated. Channel B was of the opinion that, if the underwriters wished to ensure that there was no such overlapping of policies, it was for them to stipulate such in the contract.

> **Channel B:** [p 210] ... it is clear that there is no usage that the duration of the outward and homeward policies should not overlap, because the outward policy usually extends to 24 hours after the vessel is moored in good safety. During those 24 hours there is no question that there is double insurance, and therefore, I see no ground for saying that the parties contracted subject to any usage that such a policy would not attach until the previous one had determined ... if ... they had chosen to make the risk date from the vessel being moored in safety, they would have done so ...

---

23 See above, p 141.

Risk to commence from expiration of previous policy

Recognising the danger of the overlapping of policies and double insurance, the underwriters of a voyage policy in *Kynance Sailing Ship Co Ltd v Young*, below, ensured that their policy did not attach until the previous policy had terminated by utilising the term 'Risk to commence from expiration of previous policy' in the contract of insurance.

Kynance Sailing Ship Co Ltd v Young (1911) 27 TLR 306

The vessel *Kynance* was chartered to carry a cargo of coal from Newcastle, New South Wales to Valparaiso. The plaintiffs then insured the ship with the defendant insurers for the said voyage 'to port or ports, place or places ... in any order or rotation on the west coast of South America and while in port for 30 days after arrival'. Under a second charterparty, *Kynance* was to proceed to Tocopilla, South America, to load a nitrate cargo for Europe. The plaintiffs then insured the second voyage with the same insurers 'at and from Valparaiso and/or port or ports and/or place or places in any order or rotation on the west coast of South America' to European ports. But, in addition, the second policy stated 'Risk to commence from expiration of previous policy'. After *Kynance* had discharged most of her cargo of coal at Valparaiso, she proceeded to Tocopilla, with the agreement of the charterers, with 800 tons of coal remaining on board acting as ballast, but was lost on the short voyage. When the plaintiffs claimed on their first policy, the insurers refused payment on the basis that the risk had ended at Valparaiso where all the cargo under the charterparty was originally to have been discharged.

The court ruled that the insurers were liable under the first policy, because the risk had not terminated at Valparaiso; the policy covered ports on the west coast of South America, and not just Valparaiso. The express clause – that 'risk to commence from the expiration of the previous policy' – prevented the attachment of the second policy.

> **Scrutton J:** [p 307] ... There has grown up a well known course of trade for ships which bring home nitrate from the west coast of South America. It suits them to make their outward voyage from the United Kingdom to some place in the East, then to proceed to Newcastle (NSW), take coal from there to the west coast of South America and to discharge it at various ports on that coast, and then to proceed to certain other ports to load nitrate for the United Kingdom. Various forms of words, more or less obscure, have been devised to cover various parts of that round voyage or adventure.
>
> ... At the time the accident happened, the vessel was proceeding to Tocopilla, for, amongst other purposes, the discharge of 800 tons or 900 tons of coal which, from the cargo-owner's point of view, was part of the original cargo and was to be discharged as cargo. *Prima facie*, therefore, Tocopilla is a port of discharge ... Why is it not to be treated as a place of discharge within the policy? If I correctly followed Mr Scott's argument [for the insurers] it was

this: Tocopilla was not a place of discharge under the charter ... In fact, as I have found, the two parties to the charterparty varied the mode of its performance by agreeing that instead of discharging at one port, as originally provided in the charter, they should discharge the original cargo at two ports.

[p 308] ... It is clear to me in this case that the policy was taken out to cover such adventure to the west coast of South America as, at the time of carrying it out, the charterer and the shipowner agreed upon ... I come to the conclusion that the plaintiffs' claim under the first policy is well founded, and there will be judgment for the plaintiffs ...

Change of voyage

As a 'change of voyage' could alter the risk insured, an underwriter is allowed to discharge himself from liability should such a change of voyage take place. To this effect, s 45(1) of the Act defines a 'change of voyage' in the following terms:

> Where, after the commencement of the risk, the destination of the ship is voluntarily changed from the destination contemplated by the policy, there is said to be a change of voyage.

As s 45(1) is unqualified, it would not be unreasonable to assume that 'change of voyage' is applicable to any voyage policy, be it on ship, cargo or freight.

The underlying reasoning why a 'change of voyage' should discharge an insurer from liability under the policy was summed up in the early case of *Tasker v Cunninghame* (1819) 1 Bligh 87, HL, cited in full earlier.[24] In this instance, a vessel in Cadiz harbour was lost soon after it had been decided to load a cargo of salt at Cadiz rather than Liverpool. The underwriters were held not liable because, at the time of the loss, the voyage underwritten by the insurers, being 'at and from' Cadiz to Liverpool, had, in fact, been altered by the assured's agent to a direct voyage to Newfoundland.

> **Lord Chancellor:** [p 100] ... When a ship is insured *at* and from a given port, the probable continuance of the ship in that port is in the contemplation of the parties to the contract. If the owners, or persons having authority from them, change their intention, and the ship is delayed in that port for the purpose of altering the voyage and taking in a different cargo, the underwriters run an additional risk if such a change of intention is not to affect the contract.

It is emphasised that a 'change of voyage should not be confused with a 'change of destination' as contemplated by s 44, which has already been discussed.[25] A 'change of destination' occurs when the ship sails to a destination other than that specified in the policy. When a different adventure is undertaken from the outset, the policy never attaches.

---

24 See above, p 139.
25 See above, p 137.

A 'change of voyage,' on the other hand, is where the risk has already attached and the voyage contemplated by the policy of insurance is then voluntarily altered by the assured 'after the commencement of the risk'. Section 45(1), therefore, confirms that, for there to be a 'change of voyage,' the change must have been made:

(a) voluntarily; and

(b) after the commencement of the risk.

Voluntarily changed

For there to be a 'change of voyage' as contemplated by s 45(1), the voyage must have been changed voluntarily. A voyage which has had to be changed through force of necessity would not discharge an insurer from liability under the policy.

This was clearly illustrated by Lord Porter in the well known case of **Rickards v Forestal Land, Timber and Railways Co Ltd [1941] 3 All ER 62, HL**, where cargo was lost to British merchants when the three German ships (*Minden, Wangoni* and *Halle*) carrying that cargo came under the control of the German Government at the outbreak of the Second World War. *Halle*, the subject of the extract from Lord Porter's speech, altered her planned voyage before eventually being scuttled in order to avoid capture by the French navy. In the event, the court confirmed that, as the change of voyage made by *Halle* had not been made voluntarily, s 45 of the Act was not applicable.

> **Lord Porter:** [p 96] ... The master's act was both necessitated by moral force and reasonably necessary for the safety of the ship, which, unless such steps were taken, might well have fallen into the hands of the British Navy. It is said, however, that, in addition to, or instead of, deviating, the master at some stage changed his voyage. I do not think that he did in the sense in which those words are used in the Marine Insurance Act 1906. Change of voyage is now defined in s 45 of the Act as occurring when, after the commencement of the risk, the destination of the ship is voluntarily changed from the destination contemplated by the policy. There was no voluntary change in the case of *Minden*. The master was acting, not on his own initiative, but on the orders which, to use the words of Lord Ellenborough in *Phelps v Auldjo*, morally as a good subject he ought not to have resisted. The same considerations apply to *Halle*. As I have said, I cannot find any authorisation for deviating or changing the voyage in the contract of affreightment, but, as the master's action was by circumstances beyond his and his employer's control, and was involuntary, the deviation was excusable, and the voyage was not changed within the provisions of s 45 of the Act.

After the commencement of the risk

A 'change of voyage' can only arise after the commencement of risk. Thus, in an 'at and from' policy, the risk has first to attach 'at' the particular port or place before a 'change of voyage' can occur. As such, the change can only be made whilst the vessel is 'at' the port or place specified by the policy, or after the vessel has sailed on her insured voyage. In the case of a policy 'from' a named port or place, a change of voyage can only arise after the vessel has sailed from that named port or place for its intended destination.

As from the time the determination to change it is manifested

Section 45(2) of the Act spells out not only the legal consequences of a 'change of voyage', but also, what constitutes such a change in law:

> Unless the policy otherwise provides, where there is a change of voyage, the insurer is discharged from liability as from the time of change, that is to say, as from the time when the determination to change it is manifested; and it is immaterial that the ship may not in fact have left the course of voyage contemplated by the policy when the loss occurs.

Notably, a ship need not have actually left the course of the insured voyage for there to have been a 'change of voyage' as contemplated by s 45. A 'change of voyage' is considered to have taken place from the time the 'determination to change it is manifested', as the Lord Chancellor stated, in ***Tasker v Cunninghame*** **(1819) 1 Bligh 87, HL**, cited earlier,[26] where a vessel insured 'at and from' Cadiz to Liverpool changed her voyage in order to go direct to Newfoundland.

> **Lord Chancellor:** [p 102] ... Undoubtedly, a mere meditated change does not affect a policy. But circumstances are to be taken as evidence of a determination, and what better evidence can we have, than that those who were authorised had determined to change the voyage. In my opinion the voyage was abandoned.

Change of Voyage Clause

Section 45(2) of the Act is introduced with the words 'Unless the policy otherwise provides' – thereby giving the parties to the insurance the freedom to contract, with respect to change of voyage, in a manner in which they please.

Thus, taking advantage of the provision in s 45(2), which allows the parties to contract freely, the IVCH(95) contains a 'held covered' clause, which overrides s 45 should a change of voyage take place. Clause 2, the Change of Voyage Clause, of the IVCH(95) states:

> Held covered in case of deviation or change of voyage or any breach of warranty as to towage or salvage services, provided notice be given to the Underwriters immediately after receipt of advices and any amended terms of cover and any additional premium required by them be agreed.

---

26 See above, p 139.

Interestingly, a case primarily concerned with the Change of Voyage Clause came before the courts as recently as 1997. In *Fraser Shipping v Colton*, three of the issues which arose were: (a) the nature of the loss;[27] (b) the duty of an assured to notify an insurer, after a change of voyage, of all the material circumstances which may alter the risk;[28] and (c) the effect of a late acceptance by an insurer of notification of a change of voyage.

Fraser Shipping Ltd v Colton and Others [1997] 1 Lloyd's Rep 586

The plaintiffs, who sold their semi-submersible heavy lift vessel *Shakir III* to a Chinese company for demolition, had also contracted with a tug company to tow the vessel from Jebil Ali to Wuson (Shanghai) or Huang Pu. When *Shakir III* was insured by the plaintiffs with the defendants under a valued policy, which incorporated the Institute Voyage Clauses Hulls – Total Loss Only, the policy only provided cover '... until safe arrival at Shanghai outer anchorage plus seven days, in single tow of approved Tug and for break-up'. No mention of Huang Pu was made in the policy. The said policy also contained a Change of Voyage Clause.

On 19 May, the tug departed Jebil Ali. In the event, on 25 May 1993, *Shakir III* was ordered to be towed to Huang Pu and not Shanghai, but the plaintiffs did not inform the insurers of the change of voyage until *Shakir III* had actually arrived at Huang Pu on 25 June 1993, by which time the anchorage there was known to be dangerous because of the proximity of a typhoon. When the plaintiffs eventually informed the insurers of the change of voyage, no mention was made of the adverse conditions at Huang Pu, nor of the fact that *Shakir III* had already been involved in a minor collision with a Chinese merchant ship. When the typhoon struck, the towlines broke and *Shakir III* was swept 45 miles away and stranded on an island. The plaintiffs claimed on their policy, but the insurers refused payment.

The court held, *inter alia*, that the acceptance by the insurers of the late notice of change of voyage did not amount to a waiver of their rights under s 45 of the Marine Insurance Act. Moreover, as the notice tendered was not 'immediate', the assured was not held covered by the Change of Voyage Clause.

> **Potter LJ:** [p 593] ... (4) *Are the defendants discharged from liability under the policy by virtue of s 45 of the MIA?*
>
> Section 45(2) of the MIA states:
>
>> Unless the policy otherwise provides, where there is a change of voyage, the insurer is discharged from liability as from the time of change, that is to say, as from the time when the determination to change it is manifested ...

---

27 The point as to whether the loss was an actual total loss is discussed in Chapter 15, p 605.

28 The issue of non-disclosure of material facts is discussed in depth in Chapter 6, p 227.

By reason of the incorporation of the Institute Voyage Clauses, the policy 'otherwise provided' to the extent of a limited 'held covered' extension in the event of a change of voyage:

> ... provided notice be given to the underwriters immediately after request of advices.

The plaintiffs concede that the notice which they first gave on 25 June 1993 was not immediate, because the change of voyage had occurred when the plaintiff ordered the tug to Huang Pu on 28 May. However, they assert waiver on the part of the defendants by reason of their scratching the endorsement of 25 June.

[p 594] ... (5) *Did the defendants waive their right to rely on s 45 of the MIA by scratching the endorsement of 25 June 1993?*

It is the plaintiffs' case that the defendants waived compliance with the 'immediate notice' condition by agreeing the change of voyage endorsement in the knowledge that it was late ...

The plaintiffs' fall back position is that, even if the underwriters were not shown the fax, waiver should be inferred because they failed to ask any elucidatory questions in circumstances where they should have done so ... However, there was nothing on the endorsement which provided the means of knowing that the change of voyage notification was late without the asking of further questions. Proof of waiver depends upon proof of such knowledge. I am not satisfied that the defendant underwriters either knew, or by reason of what they were shown, had the means of knowing that the change of voyage notification was late. Accordingly, the plea of waiver fails.

Notes

To ensure that he is covered by the policy, the assured has to tender notice to the underwriters 'immediately after receipt of advices'. As was held in *Greenock Steamship Co v Maritime Insurance Co Ltd* [1903] 2 KB 657, discussed earlier,[29] such a notice, provided that it is given within a reasonable period of time, may be given even after a loss.[30]

Deviation

An act of deviation would obviously vary the risk insured by the policy. To this end, s 46(1) of the Act lays down the general rules regarding deviation and the legal effects of such when it states:

> Where a ship, without lawful excuse, deviates from the voyage contemplated by the policy, the insurer is discharged from liability as from the time of

---

29 This case is discussed below, p 161, and in full in Chapter 7, p 281.
30 See, also, *Mentz Decker and Co v Maritime Insurance Co* [1909] 1 KB 132, and *Thames and Mersey Marine Insurance Co Ltd v Van Laun and Co* [1917] 2 KB 48, HL, discussed below, pp 162–64.

deviation, and it is immaterial that the ship may have regained her route before any loss occurs.

Deviation should not be confused with a change of voyage, described earlier. Unlike a change of voyage, with deviation, the intention is always to return to that prescribed course and complete the insured voyage, even though the ship has left the prescribed course.

The issue of deviation was probably best summed up by Lord Mansfield in **Wooldrige v Boydell (1778) 1 Doug KB 16**, cited earlier,[31] where the vessel *Molly* was captured during the American War of Independence, suspected of carrying supplies for the American army whilst purporting to be on a voyage from Maryland to Cadiz. The case turned on whether *Molly* intended merely to deviate or change her voyage.

> **Lord Mansfield:** [p 18] ... Deviations from the voyage insured arise from afterthoughts, after-interest, after-temptation; and the party who actually deviates from the voyage described, means to give up his policy. But a deviation merely intended, but never carried into effect, is as no deviation. In all the cases of that sort, the *terminus a quo*, and *ad quem*, were certain and the same.

And, in similar vein, in the case of **Thames and Mersey Marine Insurance Co Ltd v Van Laun and Co [1917] 2 KB 48, HL**, where a vessel carrying livestock to China from Australia had to put into an alternative port because her port of destination, Taku, was said to be blocked by ice, the court had to consider whether the action amounted to a deviation or a change of voyage (or delay).

> **Lord Davey:** [p 53] ... It is often a nice question on the facts whether an interruption of the voyage amounts to a deviation only or is a change of voyage. The usual test is whether the ultimate terminus *ad quem* remains the same.

The course of the voyage

Section 46(2) of the Act amplifies the meaning of deviation when it affirms:

There is a deviation from the voyage contemplated by the policy:

(a) where the course of the voyage is specifically designated by the policy, and that course is departed from; or

(b) where the course of the voyage is not specifically designated by the policy, but the usual and customary course is departed from.

Thus, if the course of the voyage is 'specifically designated,' that course must be strictly complied with. This was the issue in *Elliot v Wilson*,[32] below.

---

31 See above, p 137.
32 See, also, *Clason v Simmonds* (1741) cited in *Beatson v Howarth* 6 Term Rep 533: '... it was sworn by several captains to be their opinion (but the Ch J did not say anything to this point) that the going no further in the Streights than Leghorn, and then returning back again, was a determination of the insurance at Leghorn, and the insurers discharged from the loss that happened afterwards.'

Although this case is a leading authority on the rule of strict compliance, and also that, once a deviation has occurred, the insurer is irreversibly discharged from liability under the policy, the summary contains little in the way of text to illustrate the reasoning behind the verdict. Thus, only the facts and text relating to those facts are reproduced.

Elliot v Wilson (1776) 4 Bro Parl Cas 470, PC

A cargo of tobacco aboard the vessel *Kingston* was insured for the short voyage from the Carron wharf, on the Firth of Forth, to Hull, with liberty to call at Leith. During the course of the voyage, *Kingston* put into the small port of Morrison's Haven, about six miles east of Leith, and although she safely regained her course, she was later wrecked in a gale off Holy Island, Northumberland.

The court ruled that, because of the deviation into the unauthorised port of Morrison's Haven, the underwriters were discharged from liability under the contract. Furthermore, the fact that the vessel regained her course after the deviation did not mean that the risk could re-attach; the discharge of the insurer from liability was irreversible.

> [p 475] ... An express allowance to call at one port being given, the vessel passed it and touched at another, only six miles farther down the river, and in the course of the voyage insured. The alleged deviation was singly the act of entering Morrison's Haven; for the vessel's sailing close by it never would have been so termed, so near was it to the direct course of the voyage ... The risk was not greater, as it is allowed by every person acquainted with the coast, that Morrison's Haven is even a safer and more accessible harbour than Leith; and in fact no damage was sustained by the deviation, the vessel having regained the direct course to Hull, and being wrecked after proceeding in it several leagues.

But, if the course is 'not specifically designated' by the policy, the usual and customary course should be followed. This principle was particularly well illustrated by the case of *Reardon Smith Line Ltd v Black Sea and Baltic General Insurance Co Ltd*, below. Although the case is one of carriage of goods by sea, the principles involved are equally applicable to insurance law.

Reardon Smith Line Ltd v Black Sea and Baltic General Insurance Co Ltd [1939] AC 562, HL

The owners of the vessel *Indian City* chartered her to the Russian State Trading Corporation for a voyage from Poti, on the Black Sea, to Sparrow's Point, in the USA. The conditions of the charterparty were that *Indian City* should burn oil and proceed with all convenient speed and by the direct geographical route. After loading her cargo at Poti, the master of *Indian City* was directed by his owners to put into Constanza to refuel. Constanza was not on the direct geographical route. However, whilst entering Constanza, *Indian City* ran aground and, after effecting temporary repairs, changed her destination to

Rotterdam because of her condition. As a result, the shipowner incurred a considerable general average expenditure and, in this action, sought to recover the general average contribution owed by the charterers from an insurance company who had guaranteed to pay any general average contributions due in respect of the cargo. The insurance company refused to pay any such general average contribution because, they contended, *Indian City* had deviated from the agreed course of the voyage.

The House of Lords ruled that the insurers were liable for the general average contribution in respect of the cargo. The refuelling stop at Constanza, although not on the direct geographical route, was on the usual and customary course used by ships in the trade.

> **Lord Porter:** [p 584] ... The law upon the matter is, I think, reasonably plain, though its application may from time to time give rise to difficulties. It is the duty of a ship, at any rate when sailing upon an ocean voyage from one port to another, to take the usual route between those two ports. If no evidence be given, that route is presumed to be the direct geographical route, but it may be modified in many cases for navigational or other reasons, and evidence may always be given to show what the usual route is, unless a specific route be prescribed by the charterparty or bill of lading ... In some cases, there may be more than one usual route ... Similarly, the exigencies of bunkering may require the vessel to depart from the direct route, or at any rate compel her to touch at ports at which, if she were proceeding under sail, it would be unnecessary for her to call.
>
> It is not the geographical route but the usual route which has to be followed, though in many cases the one may be the same as the other. But the inquiry must always be, what is the usual route, and a route may become a usual route in the case of a particular line though that line is accustomed to follow a course which is not that adopted by the vessels belonging to other lines or to other individuals. It is sufficient if there is a well known practice of that line to call at a particular port.

The intention to deviate is immaterial

Unlike change of voyage, the 'intention to deviate' is immaterial and, to this effect, s 46(3) of the Act states:

> The intention to deviate is immaterial; there must be a deviation in fact to discharge the insurer from his liability under the contract.

Section 46(3) is based upon the ruling in the old case of *Wooldridge v Boydell* (1778) 1 Doug KB 16, cited earlier, where Lord Mansfield observed: [p 18] '... But a deviation merely intended but never carried into effect, is as no deviation.'

This principle, that a deviation intended but not carried out is no deviation, was highlighted in the case of *Kingston v Phelps* (1795) where the judgment of Lord Kenyon was later cited in *Middlewood v Blakes* (1797) 7 Term Rep 162.

[p 165] ... In the last case [*Kingston v Phelps*], the insurance was from Cork to London, the captain sailed with an intention of touching at Weymouth on his way, but before he had actually deviated for that purpose, a violent storm arose, and he was ultimately driven by stress of weather into the very port of Weymouth; Lord Kenyon said that the underwriter was bound notwithstanding the intention to deviate inasmuch as the actual deviation arose ultimately from inevitable necessity, and not from choice; and the plaintiff recovered.

Without lawful excuse

The general rule is that, where a deviation is not voluntary but is made out of necessity, the insurer remains liable under the policy, as was shown in *Delaney v Stoddart*, below.

Delaney v Stoddart (1785) 1 Term Rep 22

The plaintiff insured his vessel *Friendship* and the freight to be earned by her with the defendants for a voyage 'at and from St Kitts to London', warranted to sail in convoy. When *Friendship* weighed anchor at St Kitts to move into the harbour to load, she was blown out to sea by adverse winds and was obliged to put into St Eustatia. Although *Friendship* tried to return to St Kitts, she was prevented by the weather, and eventually loaded a cargo in St Eustatia before sailing and joining the convoy as warranted. On the voyage to London, *Friendship* foundered at sea, and the insurance was claimed upon.

The court ruled that the insurers were liable under the policy. The deviation was a necessity brought about by stress of weather. Furthermore, Lord Mansfield pointed out that where a vessel is forced to deviate, 'she is not obliged to return back to the point from whence she was driven'.

> **Lord Mansfield:** [p 25] ... The great question is, whether there was a deviation? And that depends on the evidence. If a storm drive a ship out of her voyage into any port, and being there, she does the best she can to get to her port of destination, she is not obliged to return back to the point from whence she was driven; but here the witnesses say, she tried to get back to St Kitts, and could not; and it is a much easier navigation to go directly from St Eustatia to London, than go back to St Kitts first. And as to the taking in the cargo at St Eustatia, I do not find that the ship lost any time by it. Every thing should be imputed to the storm which was in reality done and occasioned by it. This is the only point on which I had any doubt; and it required some consideration. It was a question which was proper to be left to the jury, whether this was the same voyage or not; and they have determined it.
>
> **Ashhurst J:** [p 25] ... This ought to be considered as the same voyage insured. Wherever a ship is driven by stress of weather out of her own port into another, that shall not be considered as a deviation. Here the ship was forced by stress of weather to go to St Eustatia, and being there, she endeavoured several times to get back to St Kitts, but without effect. In fact it was better for the parties that the cargo should be completed at St Eustatia. Her continuing

at St Eustatia rather diminished the risk than otherwise; because, if she had gone back to St Kitts, it would have taken a longer time. If then everything was done that could be done under such circumstances for the benefit of the adventure, this shall not vacate the policy.

Lawful excuses for deviation and delay – s 49(1)

Section 49(1) of the Act catalogues a number of reasons under which a 'deviation' or 'delay' in prosecuting the voyage would be excused. All of these excuses were based upon or derived from previous cases under common law, which have now been incorporated into the Act. Thus, s 49(1) states:

Deviation or delay in prosecuting the voyage contemplated by the policy is excused:

(a) where authorised by any special terms in the policy;[33] or

(b) where caused by circumstances beyond the control of the master and his employer;[34] or

(c) where reasonably necessary in order to comply with an express or implied warranty;[35] or

(d) where reasonably necessary for the safety of the ship or subject matter insured;[36] or

(e) for the purpose of saving human life, or aiding a ship in distress where human life may be in danger;[37] or

(f) where reasonably necessary for the purpose of obtaining medical or surgical aid for any person on board the ship;[38] or

(g) where caused by the barratrous conduct of the master or crew, if barratry be one of the perils insured against.[39]

---

33 Eg, a liberty to deviate clause.
34 See *Rickards v Forrestal Land, Timber and Railway Co Ltd* [1942] AC 50, HL, where German ships were forced to deviate from the voyages insured because they came under the control of the German Government at the outbreak of the Second World War.
35 See *Bouillon v Lupton* (1863) 15 CB (NS) 113, where a delay was incurred to ensure that vessels leaving the River Rhone were seaworthy for the voyage across the Mediterranean.
36 See *Smith v Surridge* (1801) 4 Esp 25, where a delay was incurred carrying out repairs to the ship and awaiting sufficient depth of water to clear the bar at Pillaw.
37 See *Scaramanga v Stamp* (1880) 5 CPD 295, where the vessel *Arion* deviated to assist another vessel in distress and save human life. However, in this instance the deviation was held to be unjustified, because it included a tow to port during which *The Arion* stranded.
38 See *Woolf v Claggett* (1800) 3 Esp 257, where a Danish vessel diverted into Plymouth for medicines and remained there for 14 days. However, on the facts of the case, the deviation was held to be unjustified.
39 See *Ross v Hunter* (1790) 4 Term Rep 33, where the master of the vessel *Live Oak* deviated to Havana for his own purposes, during which deviation, the ship and cargo were lost.

Legal effect of deviation

Section 46(1) of the Act states that:

> Where a ship ... deviates from the voyage contemplated by the policy, the insurer is discharged from liability as from the time of deviation ...

It is to be noted that the effects of s 46(1) may well be displaced if the policy incorporates a 'held covered' provision. Such a provision can be found in cl 2 of the IVCH(95), the Change of Voyage Clause.

Held covered

The Change of Voyage Clause, cl 2 of the IVCH(95), states:

> Held covered in case of deviation or change of voyage or any breach of warranty as to towage or salvage services, provided notice be given to the Underwriters immediately after receipt of advices and any amended terms of cover and any additional premium required by them be agreed.

So, how does a 'held covered' clause apply in practice?[40] In *Greenock Steamship Co v Maritime Insurance Co Ltd* **[1903] 1 KB 367**, the 'held covered' clause was adjudged to apply even though the assured was unaware that a warranty, in this instance seaworthiness, had been breached.[41] The court ruled that, in applying the 'held covered' clause, the insurer was entitled 'to exact a new premium commensurate with the added risk'. As a result, the insurers were held not liable under the policy, because the court calculated that, at the time of the breach of the warranty of seaworthiness, the extra premium payable by the assured would have amounted to at least as much as the loss being claimed.[42]

> **Bigham J:** [p 374] ... What, then, is the operation of the clause? In my opinion, it [the 'held covered' clause] entitles the shipowner, as soon as he discovers that the warranty has been broken, to require the underwriter to hold him covered. It also entitles the underwriters to exact a new premium commensurate with the added risk. But what is to happen if the breach is not discovered until a loss has occurred? I think even in that case the clause still holds good, and the only open question would be, what is a reasonable premium for the added risk? To answer this, the parties must assume that the breach was known to them at the time it happened, and must ascertain what

---

40   For an in depth analysis of the application of a 'held covered' clause, see, also, *Liberian Insurance Agency Inc v Mosse* [1977] 2 Lloyd's Rep 560. As this case is concerned with a 'held covered' clause incorporated into a policy of insurance on cargo, it is dealt with in some depth below, p 179.

41   The *Greenock* case is discussed in full in Chapter 7, p 314, where the law relating to cover under a 'held covered' clause for breach of the implied warranty of seaworthiness in a voyage policy is examined.

42   The Change of Voyage Clause, it is to be noted, does not provide cover for a breach of the implied warranty of seaworthiness; only a breach of a warranty as to 'towage or salvage services' are held covered.

premium it would then have been reasonable to charge. If they cannot do it by agreement, they must have recourse to a court of law.

All 'held covered' clauses contain a condition that the assured will provide the underwriters with notice of any deviation or other default held covered under the policy within a certain time period of receiving advices. The clause may stipulate that the notice must be given 'immediately' or 'promptly' or 'within a reasonable time' or may simply require the assured to provide 'due notice'. Needless to say, the courts are often called upon to interpret the meaning of words such as 'immediate' or 'prompt'.[43]

In the case of *Mentz, Decker v Maritime Insurance Co*, below, the insurers only required 'due notice' under the held covered clause. In this instance, a vessel deviated twice before being lost, the first occasion being unknown to the assured. Nevertheless, Hamilton J was of the opinion that the notice finally given to the underwriters by the assured on finally receiving advices, months after the event, was sufficient to satisfy the term 'due notice'.

Mentz, Decker and Co v Maritime Insurance Co [1909] 1 KB 132

The plaintiffs, who were the owners of the vessel *Viduco*, insured the commissions on the ship with the defendants. The policies contained a held covered clause, which stated that any deviation was held covered at a premium to be arranged 'provided due notice be given by the assured on receipt of advice of such deviation'. After two barratrous deviations by the master, *Viduco* was lost. The plaintiffs notified the insurers of the second deviation as soon as they were aware that the ship had been lost, but did not inform the insurers of the first deviation for some months as they had no knowledge of it at the time of the loss and, when they did hear of it, they thought it immaterial in the circumstances. The defendants refused to indemnify the plaintiffs for their loss contending, *inter alia*, that the policy had not been held covered, as 'due notice' had not been given.

The court ruled that the notice given after the loss was sufficient to satisfy the proviso. However, Hamilton J considered the implications of the held covered clause, in particular, the meaning of 'due notice'.

Hamilton J: [p 134] ... As there has been an argument upon the deviation clause, I think I ought to state my opinion as to its meaning ... I agree that it is impossible to construe the clause as giving an option to the assured to be covered or not as he chooses, but I think that, in the event of the ship arriving safely, the assured would be bound to give the notice and the underwriter would be entitled to his premium. On the other hand, I do not think the words 'due notice' can be read as meaning that no notice is to be considered as 'due'

---

43 See *Liberian Insurance Agency v Mosse* [1977] 2 Lloyd's Rep 560, where the 'held covered' clause on a policy on goods contained the word 'prompt'. This case is discussed in detail below, p 179, where Donaldson LJ was of the opinion that the word 'prompt' should not be taken as meaning 'within a reasonable time'.

unless it is given at a time when the underwriter can still protect himself by reinsurance. I think the clause must be read as an agreement to hold the assured covered subject to a proviso which is satisfied by the giving of such a notice as the assured could give after advice of the deviation, and that, there being nothing practicable to be done on the receipt of the notice under the circumstances of the present case, the notice was given sufficiently early at the time when it was in fact given.

But, what may be considered a 'reasonable time' in which to give notice of a deviation under a 'held covered clause?' The question was largely answered in the case of *Thames and Mersey Marine Insurance Co Ltd v Van Laun*, below. Not unexpectedly, the House of Lords decided that a 'reasonable time' must be dependent upon the circumstances in the case.

Thames and Mersey Marine Insurance Co Ltd v Van Laun and Co [1917] 2 KB 48, HL

The respondents chartered a steamer to transport livestock from Australia to China, and then insured the shipments under two voyage policies, both of which incorporated 'held covered' clauses. The policy effected in Liverpool required that, in the event of deviation '... notice [is] to be given ... immediately after the receipt of advices', but the policy underwritten in London only required the notice to be given, in the event of deviation, in 'a reasonable time'. However, on 4 December 1900, the purchasers of the livestock, the German Government, refused to take delivery and, furthermore, on 16 December, the chartered steamer had to put into the port of Wei-hai-wei because the port of destination, Taku, was said to be blocked by ice. On 25 December, still awaiting orders, the master sailed to Chefoo to obtain water and finally arrived at Shanghai on 16 January, by which time the livestock were in such poor condition, they had to be taken out to sea and slaughtered. The insurers, however, received no notification of deviation until 31 December and, later, refused the pay the resulting claim.

The House of Lords, in reinstating the decision of Kennedy J at first instance, ruled that the notice of the delay or deviation to the insurers, in both instances, had not been made in a reasonable time considering the circumstances. Therefore, the respondents, the charterers, could not avail themselves of the 'held covered' clauses in the policies.

> **Lord Halsbury LC:** [p 51] ... In the Liverpool policy, it is provided that in case of deviation or change of voyage the assured are to be held covered, provided notice be given and any additional premium required be agreed immediately after the receipt of advices. On 17 December, the plaintiffs knew that the port of discharge, Taku, was closed, and that the ship was waiting at Wei-hai-wei, and it was not until the last day of the year that the plaintiffs' agent gave any notice at all. I certainly find as a fact that the condition was not complied with so as to cure the deviation.

In respect of the London policy, the language is not the same, but I agree with Kennedy J [at first instance], and so find as a fact, that the notice was not given within a reasonable time, and that it is an implied term of the provision that reasonable notice should be given and that it is not competent to the assured to wait as long as he pleases before he gives notice and settles with the underwriter what extra premium can be agreed upon. I take Kennedy J's view. I adopt his language where he says: 'Reasonableness in such a matter as to the time of giving a notice depends, of course, upon the particular circumstances of the case. Here the subject matter of the insurance was cattle on shipboard, in the winter season of a coast where, except at a few places, neither water nor fodder could easily be obtained only at serious risk, as the events have proved, of infection from disease. Every day of delay diminished the supply of both food and water, and helped to fill the cattle-pens with manure, creating a state of things which both weakened the health of the cattle and disabled with sickness the cattle-men whose duty it was to attend the animals ... I have come to the conclusion that no tribunal could hold upon these facts that the plaintiffs fulfilled the obligation ... "Reasonable time" in such circumstances surely must be comprised within much narrower limits than those of any such protracted period.'

But, a held covered clause is not applicable when an assured has, even before the conclusion of the contract, intended to deviate from the insured voyage. In *Laing v Union Marine Insurance Co* (1895) 1 Com Cas 11, it was held that the assured could not rely on the held covered clause, as the contract of insurance underwritten by the insurers did not correspond to the voyage actually undertaken by the assured, with the result that, when a loss occurred, the shipowners were not able to recover on their policy. Moreover, the assured were also guilty of non-disclosure of a material fact, namely, the intention to call at the port of Hongay, which was well known to be hazardous.

Delay in voyage

Section 48 of the Act states:

In the case of a voyage policy, the adventure insured must be prosecuted throughout its course with reasonable dispatch, and if without lawful excuse it is not so prosecuted, the insurer is discharged from liability as from the time when the delay became unreasonable.

The effects of deviation and delay can sometimes be so similar as to be indistinguishable, and for that reason, the excuses for deviation under s 49(1) of the Act are equally applicable to 'delay'.[44]

This similarity in effect was clearly illustrated in the case of ***Thames and Mersey Marine Insurance Co Ltd v Van Laun and Co* [1917] 2 KB 48, HL**, cited above, where livestock had to be slaughtered when the vessel carrying them deviated and was delayed because the port of destination was blocked by ice.

---

44 The lawful excuses for deviation and delay in s 49 are recited above, p 160.

Lord Davey: [p 53] ... Kennedy J held that there was a deviation (if not as to the course of navigation on the voyage insured) as to the time in which the voyage ought to have been completed.

Legal effect of delay

With respect to 'delay', there is no provision made within the IVCH(95) to hold covered the subject matter insured should such a delay occur: cl 2 of the IVCH(95), the Change of Voyage Clause, does not cover delay. Thus, the position regarding delay is wholly governed by s 48 of the Act, in conjunction with s 49(1).

However, s 55(2)(b) of the Act states:

> Unless the policy otherwise provides, the insurer on ship or goods is not liable for any loss proximately caused by delay, although the delay be caused by a peril insured against ...

Thus, as s 55(2)(b) is prefixed by the phrase 'unless the policy otherwise provides', there is nothing to prevent an assured of ship or cargo specifically insuring against a loss proximately caused by delay, should he so wish.[45]

The Classification Clause

The IVCH(95) has a Classification Clause, cl 3, which is identical to that (cl 5) in the ITCH(95). As discussed earlier, the insurer will, under cl 3, be discharged from liability in the event of a change of Classification Society, a failure to maintain class and a failure to comply with any recommendations, requirements or restrictions that may be imposed by the vessel's Classification Society which relate to the vessel's seaworthiness and to her maintenance in a seaworthy condition. However, it is emphasised that, as there is no Termination Clause (or its equivalent) in the IVCH(95), there is no question, as in the case of ITCH(95), of an automatic termination of the policy. As the Classification Clause is perceived as a warranty, it can, as with any promissory warranty, only bring about an automatic[46] discharge of the insurer from further liability under the policy.

Termination of insurance

As was seen,[47] a ship has to be in a state of 'good safety' before the risk under a policy can attach: this is stipulated by r 3 of the Rules for Construction. There is, however, no corresponding provision for the termination of the risk.

---

45 See Chapter 10, p 433.
46 In the light of *'Good Luck'* [1991] 2 Lloyd's Rep, 191, HL, 'discharge' in s 33(3) of the Act should now be read to mean 'automatic' discharge. For a deeper study of the legal effects of a breach of a promissory warranty, see Chapter 7.
47 See above, p 144.

It is observed that the old SG policy, which has now, of course, fallen into disuse, expressly declared that the risk will only terminate when the vessel 'hath moored at anchor 24 hours in good safety'. This requirement has, over the years, generated a body of case law offering judicial explanations of the term, and of how it is to be applied for the purpose of determining when the risk under a policy is to terminate.

As the format of the Institute Clauses is different,[48] it would not be unreasonable to assume that, unless the policy expressly provides, the insured vessel does not, on her arrival at the final port of destination, have to be in any condition of 'good safety' (for any length of time) for the policy to come to an end. But, should the parties choose to incorporate a 'good safety' clause into their policy, then, reference to past case law may be invaluable in order to determine the meaning of the term. One would have thought that, as the same expression is also used for the commencement of risk, the same meaning should be awarded to the term when applied to termination. This, however, is clearly not the case, for in the context of termination, the term 'good safety' is much wider, covering both physical and political good safety.

'Good safety' means both physical and political good safety

In a voyage policy of insurance containing a good safety clause, the normal requirement under common law is for the vessel to have arrived at the port of destination, be anchored or moored in the usual area for 24 hours in good safety and ready to discharge her cargo.[49] An early example of this requirement was the old, but often quoted, case of *Waples v Eames*, below, where the court decided that a ship lying in the quarantine area was not in 'good safety' within the meaning of the term.

Waples v Eames (1745) 2 Str 1243

The vessel *Success* was insured 'at and from Leghorn to the Port of London, and till there moored 24 hours in good safety'. On arriving at London, *Success* moored briefly, but was almost immediately ordered to leave and serve a period of time in quarantine. On news of this, the crew deserted, and it was some three weeks before she could be sailed to the quarantine area. Before the quarantine was completed, *Success* caught fire and was burned. The plaintiff claimed on his policy of insurance, but the insurers contended that the policy had terminated, the ship having been moored 24 hours in good safety.

The court ruled that *Success* never was in good safety before the loss occurred, and the insurers were liable under the policy. Whilst the ship was in the quarantine area, she was not in the usual place where ships moored, and

---

48 As the parties have to insert in the MAR 91 Form the particulars of the voyage.
49 But, where a vessel is moored in an area where she cannot discharge her cargo, but is nonetheless in an area where a ship would usually moor, she would be considered to be in 'good safety': see *Angerstein v Bell* (1795) 1 Park 54.

she had no opportunity to discharge her cargo. Therefore, the policy was still intact.

> [p 1244] ... it was ruled that, though the ship was so long at her moorings, yet she could not be said to be there in good safety, which must mean the opportunity of unloading and discharging, whereas here she was arrested within the 24 hours, and the hands having deserted, and the regency taken time to consider the petition, there was no default in the master or owners.

Further, in *Minett v Anderson*, below, it was shown that, for a ship to be in 'good safety', she not only had to be in physical good safety, but also in 'political' good safety.

Minett and Others v Anderson (1794) Peake 277

The vessel *Hercules* was insured for a voyage from Bilbao to Rouen '... until she is 24 hours moored in good safety there'. When *Hercules* arrived at Rouen, the ship was detained as a prize and the crew interned as prisoners of war. The court ruled that the insurers were liable under the policy because the ship was never in 'good safety' within the meaning of the term.

> **Lord Kenyon**: [p 278] ... She could not be said to be 24 hours, or a minute moored in good safety, as far as relates to these plaintiffs; for immediately she entered the port she was, to all intents and purposes, captured by the French. Verdict for the plaintiffs.

However, a question which has to be asked is: if a ship has to be moored in good safety for 24 hours or a set number of days for the risk to terminate, from what point in time should the period be measured? This very issue was raised in the case of *Cornfoot v Royal Exchange Assurance Corporation*, below.

Cornfoot v Royal Exchange Assurance Corporation [1903] Com Cas 205; aff'd CA [1904] 9 Com Cas 80

The vessel *Inchcape Rock* was insured for a voyage from 'Portland Oregon by any route to Algoa Bay, and for 30 days in port after arrival however employed'; the usual '24 hours' had been deleted and replaced by the 30 day period. The vessel arrived and was in good safety at Algoa Bay at 11.30 am on 2 August 1902. But, at 4.30 pm on 1 September 1902, the ship was wrecked by a gale which drove her ashore. Counsel for the plaintiff shipowner contended that the insurers were liable under the policy, because the 30 days should be taken to be 30 consecutive calendar days which ran from the midnight following the time of arrival.

The court, however, decided that the time ran in consecutive 24 hour periods measured from the actual time of the ship's arrival and, therefore, the insurers were not liable, as the policy had terminated.

> **Bigham J**: [p 208] ... No doubt, in some cases, the word 'day' means a period of 24 hours starting from midnight and ending at midnight. That is a calendar

day – a Monday or a Tuesday. But did the parties to this contract use the word in that sense? I think clearly not. The risk was to be a continuing risk. It was not to stop at 11.30 on the morning of 2 August and then to revive at midnight. It was to run continuously from 11.30 am on 2 August until the expiration of 30 days, and no longer. To interpret the contract in the way contended for by the plaintiff would have had the effect either of imposing on the defendants a longer risk than they bargained to undertake or of relieving them from liability during the hours from 11.30 am on 2 August until midnight. Neither party intended to make such a contract. It follows, therefore, that the 30 days mentioned in the policy must be taken to mean 30 consecutive periods of 24 hours beginning at the time of the ship's mooring in the bay.

... I am, however, quite satisfied, notwithstanding some of the *viva voce* evidence, that the ship was an arrived ship within the meaning of the policy by 11.30 am, and was then ready to discharge, and this was what the jury meant to find, and did find, in answer to my questions. There must be judgment for the defendants, with costs.

Undoubtedly, the leading authority on 'good safety' is the case of *Lidgett v Secretan*, below.[50] A substantial quantity of text is reproduced from the reasoning of Bovill CJ, because of the thoroughness with which the judge analysed the issue and consulted previous case law. Of particular interest is the fact that the judge never used the term 'political safety'. Instead, he preferred to define the meaning of 'good safety' in more general terms. That is, for a ship to be in 'good safety', she should not only exist as a ship, but should be in 'the possession and control of her owners'.

Lidgett v Secretan (1870) LR 5 CP 190

The sailing vessel *Charlemagne* was insured for a voyage 'at and from London to Calcutta, and for 30 days after arrival ... until she hath moored at anchor 24 hours in good safety'. On the voyage, *Charlemagne* struck a reef and, although she eventually arrived at Calcutta on 28 October 1866, she had sustained such damage that she had to be pumped out continuously throughout the remainder of the voyage and whilst the cargo was being discharged. Later, *Charlemagne* was taken into dry dock but, whilst there, she was destroyed by fire on 5 December 1866. The issue was whether the ship had ever in fact been moored in good safety.

The court ruled that, as *Charlemagne* had been moored for more than 24 hours as a ship and not a mere wreck, she had been moored in good safety for more than the requisite 24 hours. As the loss by fire had then occurred more

---

50 It must be pointed out that there are two cases under the name of *Lidgett v Secretan*, the citations being different, but the litigants and the facts in both cases are the same, only the basis of the claims being different. The case now cited is the earlier case. See, also, *Lidgett v Secretan* (1871) LR 6 CP 616.

than 30 days after her being moored in good safety for 24 hours,[51] the insurers were not liable because the risk had terminated.

Bovill CJ: [p 198] ... Assuming, then, that the 30 days are to be reckoned from the time of the ship being moored for 24 hours in good safety, the question arises, what is the meaning of those words in such a policy.

We are of opinion that the meaning is not, as has been contended, that the moorings are safe, but that the words refer to the ship being in safety. The words cannot mean that the vessel is to arrive without any damage or injury whatever from the effects of the voyage; otherwise, the loss of a mast, or even a spar, a sail, or a rope though the vessel was perfectly fit to keep not only the river but the sea, would, contrary to all the ordinary meaning of language, prevent her from being considered as in safety. So, on the other hand, the words would not, in our opinion, be satisfied by the vessel arriving and being moored in a sinking state or as a mere wreck, or by a mere temporary mooring.

We think also that the mere liability to damage, whether partial or total, during the 24 hours, by the occurrence of some or all of the perils insured against, cannot prevent the running of the 24 hours, because the extension of the period of risk for 24 hours after having moored in good safety clearly implies that, notwithstanding the safety intended, the ship is liable to partial or total loss by the occurrence of a peril insured against.

The American decision upon that point, of *Bill v Mason*, proceeded on the ground that, although the ship was, during 24 hours after being moored, liable to damage or total loss, she was not in fact either lost or in that case even damaged. Where, on the other hand, a ship arrived in port in a sinking state, and, on being moored, was obliged to be lashed to a hulk in order to keep her afloat until the people on board were landed, and where she sunk on being moved towards the shore, it was held that she was not moored in safety, because the court considered that she in fact arrived as a wreck, and not as a ship: *Shawe v Felton*. So, where a vessel arriving in a hostile port with simulated papers had her papers immediately taken and her hatches sealed down by the officers of government, although she was not formally condemned until afterwards, it was held that she had not been moored in safety for 24 hours, because she was in effect within the 24 hours taken from her owners by the foreign government: *Horneyer v Lushington*. Nor was a vessel which had been for a short period moored to a wharf, but within 24 hours was ordered into quarantine, and whilst there, but more than 24 hours after the original temporary mooring, was lost by a peril insured against, considered to have moored in good safety, because, as it would seem, she had not, before the loss in respect of which the claim was made been finally moored at the ordinary place of mooring: *Waples v Eames*.

Where a vessel, after being moored, remained in actual safety as a ship for 24 hours, and so that during those 24 hours her owners had complete and

---

51 The court did not have to decide whether the 30 days accrued from the time of arrival at Calcutta or from the time after the 24 hours in good safety had expired, because the time of the loss was well beyond the 30 days required in the latter case anyway.

undisturbed possession of her, but afterwards she was seized in consequence of the master having smuggled before her arrival, it was held that the terms of the policy were satisfied, and that the loss by the seizure was a loss after the termination of the risk: *Lockyer v Offley*.

[p 200] ... In the present case, the vessel, though considerably damaged and leaky, and with one compartment full of water, existed as a ship at the time of her arrival, and she was able to keep afloat and did keep afloat as a ship for more than 24 hours after being moored, by exerting the means within the power of the captain. She arrived and moored at the ordinary place for unloading, and was so moored as a ship in the possession or control of her owners for more than 24 hours; and she remained as a ship and in possession of her owners for more than 30 days after the lapse of the 24 hours before described, and until the time of the fire by which she was totally lost.

If the underwriters are liable beyond 30 days from her being so moored for 24 hours, it is difficult under such circumstances to see when the liability is to end. We think the only safe rule in this case is to hold that, after the expiration of 30 days from the arrival and mooring of the vessel, and her having remained as a vessel, and in the possession or control of her owners, though not sound, for 24 hours, the underwriters were not responsible. We are, therefore, of opinion that there was not a total loss within the period of risk covered by this policy, and that our judgment should be for the defendant.

Voyage policy on goods

Goods are almost invariably insured under voyage policies incorporating either the ICC (A), (B) or (C). Furthermore, because contracts of affreightment are usually by way of combined transport, involving more than one mode of carriage, the insurance of such must accommodate both the sea transport and the land transport phases of the overall voyage.

Thus, a voyage policy on goods is extended to cover carriage by land or inland waterway provided that such carriage is *incidental* to the sea voyage. To this effect, s 2(1) of the Act states:

> A contract of marine insurance may, by its express terms, or by usage of trade, be extended so as to protect the assured against losses on inland waters or on any land risk which may be incidental to the sea voyage.

However, as s 2(1) of the Act only makes the general provision for a contract of marine insurance to include transportation by land and inland waterway, reliance is placed upon the ICC to lay down the terms and conditions pursuant to that contract. Those terms and conditions are to be found in three clauses contained within the ICC, all of which come under the heading of 'Duration', namely:

(a) cl 8 – the Transit Clause (or warehouse to warehouse clause);

(b) cl 9 – the Termination of Contract of Carriage Clause; and

(c) cl 10 – the Change of Voyage Clause.

Attachment of insurance

Clause 8.1 of the ICC states:

> This insurance attaches from the time the goods leave the warehouse or place of storage at the place named herein for the commencement of the transit, continues during the ordinary course of transit ...

It is emphasised that the insurance only attaches when the goods *leave* the warehouse or place of storage. Thus, there is no cover whilst the goods are actually being stored *at* the place named therein. In its choice of words, cl 8.1 is carefully constructed to ensure that liability does not fall upon the insurer *before* the transit from the warehouse or place of storage actually commences.

Symington and Co v Union Insurance Society of Canton Ltd (1928) 34 Com Cas 23, CA

The cargo-owner, a cork grower, was in the habit of storing his cork in an inland warehouse and then sending small quantities at a time to the port of Algeciras to await shipment. Some of that cork was lying on the jetty at Algeciras, awaiting shipment, when a fire broke out some distance away. In order to prevent the fire spreading, the authorities threw some of the cork into the sea and doused the rest with water. The policy covering the shipment of the cork contained a warehouse to warehouse clause which stated that the insured goods were covered: '... from the time of leaving the shipper's or manufacturer's warehouse during the ordinary course of transit ... until safely deposited in consignee's or other warehouse at destination ...'

When the plaintiff claimed on his policy of insurance, the Court of Appeal ruled that the insurers were liable, because the fire occurred in the 'ordinary course of transit' from warehouse to warehouse.

> **Scrutton LJ:** [p 34] ... Now, in my judgment, one has to read No 6 of the Institute Cargo Clauses as an extension of the insurance beyond which it would be if one had to read the policy only without the attached clause, and I read it as meaning that the further period to be covered in respect of fire, amongst other things, is the period of time and also the operation which takes place, when the goods are coming from the shipper's or the manufacturer's warehouse during the ordinary course of transit until on board the vessel; and it is conceded that if the warehouse were in the port of loading, the transit, however far the distance might have been from the warehouse to the ship, would have been covered by this clause extending the insurance. Now it seems to me that there is nothing in the clause which limits that extended insurance to the distance between the warehouse which is in the port of loading and the ship but excludes the warehouse some miles distant from the port of loading; and I am of opinion that the learned arbitrator was not wrong in concluding that the insurance covered the goods while they were on a stage in the transit from the manufacturer's or shipper's warehouse to the ship.

A particularly interesting issue was raised in the *Wunsche* case, below. That issue was whether an ex-factory marine insurance policy on goods could attach retrospectively to a time before the goods had been appropriated.

Wunsche Handelsgesellschaft International mbH v Tai Ping Insurance Co Ltd and Another [1998] 2 Lloyd's Rep 8, CA

The plaintiffs, Wunsche, were CIF buyers of canned mushrooms and asparagus and were also the assignees to the policies of insurance covering the shipments from China to Hamburg. The canned goods were originally packed into cartons at plants in mainland China before being sent by rail or truck to Shenzhen, where the cartons were put into containers. The containers were then transported by barge or truck to Hong Kong, where they were loaded on board ocean-going vessels. The insurances, ex-factory to warehouse, were mostly effected retrospectively, the day before the containers were loaded aboard the ocean-going vessels at Hong Kong.

On arrival in Hamburg, the canned goods were found to be rusted and dented, and pilferage had taken place. It was established that most of this damage and loss had occurred before the goods had been put into containers at Shenzhen. The plaintiffs claimed on their ex-factory policies of insurance, but the insurers refused payment, on the basis that the goods were only appropriated at Shenzhen when they were put into the containers and, therefore, the policies only attached at that time. Any loss prior to that time, the insurers contended, was not covered by the policies.

The Court of Appeal, in affirming the decision of Moore-Bick J at first instance, ruled that the insurers were liable under the contract for the damage sustained by the canned goods. However, one of the issues raised was whether goods which had actually been lost (pilfered) could be appropriated to a contract of insurance. The court concluded that goods not in existence could not be appropriated to the contract, but there was no reason why goods actually appropriated to the contract could not, by agreement, be covered from an earlier date.

> **Waller LJ:** [p 12] ... When the goods left the factories, they had not been appropriated to a particular contract or shipment, and obviously not thus to any particular contract of insurance. The contention of Wunsche is that once the contract of insurance was made in relation to a specific parcel of goods, and once that parcel had been appropriated to the contract, the insurers became liable for any loss or damage which had occurred prior to that appropriation. The contention of the insurers is that the concept of goods being covered prior to some appropriation of the goods to the contract is a radical departure from anything recognised in previous authority.
>
> [p 14] ... At one time, I thought that there would be an illogicality if it had to be conceded that the cover did not provide recovery for lost goods, but did for damaged goods. However, it seems to me that in fact there is not any illogicality. The insureds were making a good contract of insurance by

reference to goods as described in the contract, and as appropriated at that moment or shortly thereafter. That contract covered 'loss damage liability or expense to the extent and in the manner herein provided'. Basically, goods that did not exist could not be appropriated to the contract. There is no reason, however, why it should not be agreed that, in relation to the goods appropriated to the contract, the insurance should cover those goods from some earlier date. It is not because the assured for some reason cannot recover for lost goods, it is simply that goods already lost were not covered. Difficult questions might arise if the 'goods' were the cartons as appropriated and tins were missing from the carton, or if the goods had in fact at all times been in containers, but once again, if at the time of appropriation a whole carton was missing or a whole container had been lost (apart from obvious points about knowledge), there would be no reason why the contract of insurance should not provide cover simply for the goods appropriated, but not unappropriated goods, that is, missing cartons or containers.

As will now be apparent, I take the view that the judge was right on this aspect as well, and that having formed the view that he did about the meaning of the 'ex-factory' terms and the 'contractual context', including the moment in time when the contract was being made, his conclusion was the only logical one.

Circumstances when the insurance remains in force

Clause 8.3 of the ICC states that:

> This insurance shall remain in force (subject to termination as provided for above and to the provisions of Clause 9 below) during delay beyond the control of the Assured, any deviation, forced discharge, reshipment or transhipment and during any variation of the adventure arising from the exercise of a liberty granted to shipowners or charterers under the contract of affreightment.

Thus, subject to termination and the provisions of cl 9 (the Termination of Contract of Carriage Clause), under cl 8.3, the insurer agrees to maintain cover in the event of:

(a) delay beyond the control of the assured;

(b) any deviation;

(c) any forced discharge, reshipment or transhipment; and

(d) any variation of the adventure (arising from the exercise of a liberty granted to shipowners or charterers under the contract of affreightment).

Delay beyond the control of the assured

A cargo-owner rarely has control over the performance of the voyage under which his goods are shipped. Thus, because of the drastic effects of delay under s 48 of the Act which, in the absence of lawful excuse, discharges the insurer from liability as from the time the delay became unreasonable, the cargo-owner needs protection from a delay brought about by circumstances beyond his control. To this effect, cl 8.3 of the ICC provides that protection by overriding s 48 of the Act, but only when the delay is beyond the control of the assured.

Thus, under cl 8.3, subject to normal termination and the provisions contained within cl 9 (the Termination of Contract of Carriage Clause), the cargo-owner is covered for any delay beyond his own control. Conversely, if a delay occurs because of circumstances within the control of the cargo-owner, cover would be terminated. This is confirmed by cl 18 of the ICC which, it is emphasised, is not just confined to the sea voyage as is s 48 of the Act. Clause 18 affirms:

> It is a condition of this insurance that the Assured shall act with reasonable despatch in all circumstances within their control.

Safadi v Western Assurance Co (1933) 46 LlL Rep 140

Bales of cotton in transit from Manchester to Damascus were destroyed by fire whilst they were delayed in the Customs House at Beirut. The reason for the delay was suggested as being civil unrest between Beirut and Damascus but, in reality, it turned out that the goods had not been released from the Customs House because nobody had paid for them. When Mr Safadi claimed on his policy of insurance, the insurers refused payment because, they contended, the delay had not been beyond the control of the assured.

> The court concurred with the insurers and ruled in their favour.
>
> **Roche J:** [p 142] ... I am satisfied that, although there may have been some danger of the rebels trying to get goods such as these cotton goods, that was not a real danger and it was not one which was influencing Messrs Sabeh and Kahaleh [Mr Safadi's business partners]. The truth is that they left the goods in the Customs House at Beirut because they did not want to pay for them. They had got credit and they chose to extend the credit.
>
> [p 143] ... this delay in the Customs House at Beirut did not, in my view of the facts, arise from any circumstances beyond the control of the assured, but arose from the deliberate desire and intention of Messrs Sabeh and Kahaleh to leave the goods there as long as it was commercially convenient to themselves to do so.
>
> There is this further matter to be borne in mind. There is a good deal of doctrine and authority to the effect that you cannot apply language such as 'causes or circumstances and matters beyond the control of the assured' to excuse performance when those causes and circumstances and matters are represented by causes and circumstances and matters in existence and known to be in existence by the person relying upon them at the time he makes the contract from the performance of which he seeks to be excused. Those circumstances as to the state of war and the operation of the Druses [rebels] were known to everybody at the time these policies were taken out and at the time these goods were sent forward and the documents representing them

were sent forward ... That is sufficient to dispose of this case and to result in judgment for the defendant company [the insurers].

Loss proximately caused by delay

Whilst cl 8.3 of the ICC allows for the insurance cover to remain in place in the event of there being a delay beyond the control of the assured, it should be borne in mind that there is no recovery, under insurance law, for a loss proximately caused by delay. This is confirmed by s 55(2)(b)[52] of the Act and cl 4.5 of the ICC. The latter states:

> In no case shall this insurance cover ...
>
> loss damage or expense caused by delay, even though the delay be caused by a risk insured against (except expenses payable under Clause 2 above).[53]

The principle in law of no recovery for loss proximately caused by delay was confirmed long ago in *Pink v Fleming* (1890) 25 QBD 396, where the court ruled that, as it was the delay (in the additional handling of the cargo) which was the proximate cause of the loss, not the collision, there was no recovery under the policy.[54]

Deviation, forced discharge, reshipment, or transhipment and any variation of the adventure

Unlike a shipowner, a cargo-owner usually has no control over any *'deviation, forced discharge, reshipment or transhipment and ... any variation of the adventure* arising from the exercise of a liberty granted to shipowners or charterers under the contract of affreightment'. Thus, the insurer agrees that the insurance remains in force subject to normal termination and the provisions contained within cl 9, the Termination of Contract of Carriage Clause. There is no requirement for any notice to be given to the insurer or any additional premium to be agreed.

Termination of insurance

Normal termination

Under normal circumstances, the insurance terminates in a manner as laid down by cll 8.1.1 to 8.1.3 of the ICC. These clauses state:

---

52 Section 55(2)(b) of the Act states: 'Unless the policy otherwise provides, the insurer on ship or goods is not liable for any loss proximately caused by delay, although the delay be caused by a peril insured against'; cl 4.5 of the ICC ensures that the policy does not otherwise provide.

53 The only exception to a claim under the head of delay lies in cl 2 of the ICC, where the insurer will undertake to compensate a cargo-owner for any general average contributions becoming due because of delay.

54 See Chapter 10, p 433, where delay as an excluded loss is further discussed.

8.1 This insurance ... terminates either:

    8.1.1 on delivery to the Consignees' or other final warehouse or place of storage at the destination named herein;

    8.1.2 on delivery to any other warehouse or place of storage, whether prior to or at the destination named herein, which the Assured elect to use either:

        8.1.2.1 for storage other than in the ordinary course of transit; or

        8.1.2.3 for allocation or distribution; or

    8.1.3 on the expiry of 60 days after completion of discharge overside of the goods hereby insured from the oversea vessel at the final port of discharge,

    whichever shall first occur.

The issue of termination arose in the *Joint Frost* case, below, only in this instance, the express provision was that the policy was to terminate 30 days after final discharge at the port of discharge.

Hibernia Foods plc v McAuslin and General Accident Fire and Life Assurance Corporation plc, 'Joint Frost' [1998] 1 Lloyd's Rep 310

The plaintiffs insured cargoes of meat products with the defendants under 12 month time policies of insurance. The policy covering the shipment aboard the vessel *Joint Frost* included cover against marine risks, including the EC export refunds and subsidies payable on sale. The policy also incorporated the Institute Frozen Meat Clauses, which stated that: 'This policy terminates ... on the expiry of 30 days ... after the final discharge of the goods ... at the port of discharge.' *Joint Frost* discharged her cargo into a cold store at Port Said, Egypt, in September 1993. In October 1993, the Egyptian authorities rejected about 400 tonnes of the meat, which was returned to Ireland in July 1994, where, on arrival, 92 tonnes was declared unfit for human consumption and sold as cattle food. The plaintiffs claimed on their policy of insurance for the loss, but the insurers refused payment, contending that that the 92 tonnes of meat had been spoiled in the cold store at Port Said in January 1994 because of poor temperature control and, therefore, the loss had occurred long after the policy covering carriage in *Joint Frost* had expired 30 days after discharge.

The court ruled that the insurers were not liable, as the policy had expired 30 days after the discharge from the vessel.

    Tuckey J: [p 313] ... Both the meat itself and the export refund were insured by the same clause against the same risks, so one would expect the duration of the cover to be the same. Those risks were in the nature of marine risks and one would expect the cover to terminate shortly after the marine adventure. This is what the policy provided for, in my judgment.

    ... The insurance provided by the defendants to the plaintiff under the policy terminated 30 days following completion of discharge of the vessel on 3 October 1993. It follows that the answer to the question ... 'Are the plaintiffs entitled to recover under the policy for export refund or subsidy lost in respect of the condemned cargo?' must be 'No'.

Premature termination

Termination of the contract of insurance may occur for reasons outside those envisaged by cll 8.1.1 to 8.1.3. The ICC contain specific provisions which allow for the contract to be terminated prematurely, because the risks under the policy have been altered. The three clauses in the ICC which deal with premature termination are:

(a) cl 8.2 – Change of final destination (after discharge at final port of discharge);

(b) cl 9 – Termination of Contract of Carriage Clause; and

(c) cl 10 – Change of Voyage Clause.

Change of final destination – cl 8.2

Clause 8.2 of the ICC states:
> If, after discharge overside from the oversea vessel at the first port of discharge, but prior to termination of this insurance, the goods are to be forwarded to a destination other than that to which they are insured hereunder, this insurance, whilst remaining subject to termination as provided for above, shall not extend beyond the commencement of transit to such other destination.

It is emphasised that cl 8.2 is limited in scope and only applies where the cargo has been discharged at the final port of discharge (the sea carriage having been completed) and the destination of the goods is then altered.

Effectively, cl 8.2 is stating that any change of destination after the sea carriage is completed is not covered by the policy. This is entirely logical because, should such a change of destination occur, the nature of the risk originally insured would have been altered.

Termination of Contract of Carriage Clause – cl 9

Clause 9 of the ICC states:
> If, owing to circumstances beyond the control of the Assured, either the contract of carriage is terminated at a port or place other than the destination named therein or the transit is otherwise terminated before delivery of the goods as provided for in Clause 8 above, then this insurance shall also terminate unless prompt notice is given to the Underwriters and continuation of cover is requested when the insurance shall remain in force, subject to an additional premium if requested by the Underwriters, either:
>
> 9.1 until the goods are sold and delivered at such port or place, or, unless otherwise specially agreed, until the expiry of 60 days after arrival of the goods hereby insured at such port or place, whichever shall first occur;

or

9.2 if the goods are forwarded within the said period of 60 days (or any agree extension thereof) to the destination named herein or to any other destination, until terminated in accordance with the provisions of Clause 8 above.

Thus, in essence, cl 9 is saying that if, owing to circumstances beyond the control of the assured:

(a) the contract of carriage is terminated at a port or place other than the destination named; or

(b) the transit is otherwise terminated before delivery of the goods as provided for in cl 8 above,

then this contract of insurance is terminated unless prompt notice is given to the underwriter and continuation of cover is requested (*when the insurance shall remain in force*), subject to an additional premium, if required. Given those circumstances, the insurance will then remain in force under the conditions laid out by cll 9.1 and 9.2.

The inclusion of the words 'when the insurance shall remain in force' is problematical. The words suggest that cover may only be continued if the request for such continuation is made whilst the insurance is still in force. That is, cl 9 cannot be applied retrospectively. This interpretation of the clause could, if applied strictly, make the clause quite restricted in its use.

It is apparent that the purpose of cl 9 is to provide cover for an assured of goods where, for whatever reason, be it hostilities or damage suffered by a carrying ship, the contract of carriage cannot be fulfilled and the goods have to be forwarded by alternative means. Notably, from the wording, the clause would appear to apply not only to the sea transit, but to any mode of transport.

Change of Voyage Clause – cl 10

Clause 10 of the ICC is a 'held covered' clause which ensures that the policy remains in force when the destination of the goods is changed by the assured, provided that 'prompt' notice be given to the underwriters and the premium and conditions of the insurance re-arranged. Clause 10 states:

Where, after attachment of this insurance, the destination is changed by the Assured, held covered at a premium and on conditions to be arranged subject to prompt notice being given to the Underwriters.

Notably, cl 10 may only be relied upon 'after the policy has attached'. A particularly good example of a policy never attaching was that of *Simon, Israel and Co v Sedgwick* **[1893] 1 QB 303, CA**, where goods were sent from Bradford to Madrid via Cartagena, to the east of Gibraltar, rather than via the west coast of Spain, 'this side of Gibraltar', as specified in the policy. As the insured voyage was never, in fact, undertaken, the policy did not attach.[55]

> **AL Smith LJ:** [p 309] ... This policy begins by stating that the plaintiffs are insured at and from the Mersey to the west coast of Spain, this side of Gibraltar, and at and from the west coast of Spain to any places in the interior of Spain. Now, that is the voyage which is contemplated in this policy – at and from the Mersey (leaving out London) to the west coast of Spain, and from the west coast of Spain to the interior of Spain. Then how does the policy go on? When you get what the voyage is, then come the risks which are to be included in that voyage; and, as I read the policy, when you once get the goods upon the voyage in question, then the risk which the underwriter undertakes is the risk from the warehouse to the ship in this country, during the voyage, and from the ship to the warehouse in the other country. But unless you get the goods started upon or allocated by contract, as Bowen LJ says – and I adopt that phrase – to the insured voyage, in my judgment, this policy does not attach

In 1977, a case, *Liberian Insurance Agency Inc v Mosse*, below, came before the court which has helped to throw more light on the working of a 'held covered' clause with respect to an insurance on goods. Donaldson J (as he then was) considered at depth the meaning of the words 'reasonable' and 'prompt' in relation to the time that notice should be given to an underwriter in order to take advantage of the 'held covered clause'. Furthermore, most helpfully, the judge summarised the application and relevance of the 'held covered clause'.

Liberian Insurance Agency Inc v Mosse [1977] 2 Lloyd's Rep 560

The plaintiffs, as agents for a third party, insured a consignment of enamelware (cups and plates) with the defendant insurers under a voyage policy from Hong Kong to Monrovia. The policy incorporated the ICC (A), cl 4 of which stated: 'Held covered at a premium to be arranged in case of change of voyage or of any omission or error in the description of the interest vessel or voyage.' There was also a requirement for the assured, on 'becoming aware of an event which is held covered ... to give prompt notice to the underwriters'. When the consignment arrived in Monrovia, it was found that some of the enamelware was missing, but a large proportion was damaged. On inspecting the goods, surveyors found that they did not match the description in the insurance; the quality was very poor and, in many cases, the goods had been packed in cartons instead of wooden boxes. Thus, the issue before the court was whether the 'held covered' clause was applicable where the goods were so obviously not as described.

The court ruled that the plaintiffs could not rely on the 'held covered' clause, because the clause only applied when the premium to be arranged would be a 'reasonable commercial rate' and no underwriter, given the present circumstances, would have quoted a reasonable commercial rate

---

55 See above, p 137.

unless he was protected by an fpa clause. Donaldson J not only considered the meaning of 'prompt notice', but also summarised the application of a 'held covered' clause.

Donaldson J: [p 566] ... If the assured is to take advantage of the held covered clause, he must give notice to the underwriters expressly or impliedly seeking cover in accordance with the clause within a reasonable time of learning of the change of voyage or of the omission or error in the description. What time is reasonable will depend upon all the circumstances. Thus, if the assured learns the true facts while the risk is still current, a reasonable time will usually be a shorter period than if this occurs when the adventure has already ended. If the assured learns the true facts when the insured property is in the grip of a peril, which is likely to cause loss or damage, a reasonable time will be very short indeed.

It may be objected that it is unfortunate to use the words 'prompt notice' when what is meant is notice within a reasonable time. However, in the context of a clause which may impose upon underwriters, and directly upon reinsuring underwriters, risks which they have never specifically accepted, I do not think that notice which is other than prompt could ever be said to be given within a reasonable time. In my judgment, the use of the word 'prompt' is not only justifiable, but also desirable in explanation of the obligation which is implicit in the clause itself.

[p 568] ... In my judgment, the clause [held covered clause] only applies if the assured, on the basis of an accurate declaration of all the facts affecting the risk but excluding knowledge of what was to happen in the event, could have obtained a quotation in the market at a premium which could properly be described as 'a reasonable commercial rate'. This can be relatively high if the risk is high, but it will not be in the same class as, for example, rates of premium for reinsurance cover after a casualty has in fact occurred. Still less will it approach 100% of the sum insured.

I can summarise the application of the held covered clause as follows:

(1) the assured seeking the benefit of the clause must give prompt notice to the underwriters of his claim to be held covered as soon as he learns of the facts which render it necessary for him to rely upon the clause;

(2) it is no obstacle to the operation of the clause that it will defeat underwriters' right to avoid the contract for non-disclosure or misdescription;

(3) the assured cannot take advantage of the clause if he has not acted in the utmost good faith;

(4) the clause does not contemplate any alteration in the terms of the insurance other than in respect of premium;

(5) the clause only applies if the premium to be arranged would be such as could properly be described as a reasonable commercial rate.

In the present case, the evidence is clear. No underwriter knowing that this was an end of production consignment of enamelware containing a variety of qualities including a high proportion of seconds and that a significant proportion of the cargo was packed in export cartons would have quoted a reasonable commercial rate of premium on all risks terms, unless he was protected by a free from particular average (fpa) warranty. Furthermore, neither ATC [African Trading Co, the owners of the goods] nor LIA [Liberian Insurance Agency, agents of ATC] on its behalf ever put the full facts before underwriters and sought the protection of the clause. All that happened was that the fact that part of the consignment was in cartons was revealed incidentally in the course of a survey report.

The claim to take advantage of the held covered clause therefore fails and underwriters were, in my judgment, entitled to repudiate all liability under the policy.

MIXED POLICY

The last limb of s 25(1) of the Act confirms that:

A contract for both voyage and time may be included in the same policy.

Thus, a policy may not only provide cover for a specific voyage, but there may also be included in the insurance a time element which ensures the cover extends beyond the time when a voyage policy would normally terminate. Such was the case in *Gambles v Ocean Marine Insurance Co of Bombay*, below.

Gambles and Others v Ocean Marine Insurance Co of Bombay (1876) 1 Ex D 141, CA

A vessel was insured 'at and from the port of Pomaron to Newcastle on Tyne, and for 15 days whilst there after arrival'. Having arrived at Newcastle on 4 December, the ship completed the discharge of her cargo and then moved to another berth to load coal for another separate voyage. On 16 December, the vessel was damaged in a storm, and the policy claimed upon on the basis that the insurance was still in force, as 15 days had not elapsed since arrival.

The Court of Appeal ruled that the policy was in fact a mixed policy, whereby a time policy had been grafted onto a voyage policy and, therefore, the insurers were liable.

Lord Cairns LC: [p 143] The question appears to me to be this, is this purely a voyage policy? Undoubtedly, so far as regards the transit of the ship from Pomaron to Newcastle on Tyne, it is a voyage policy, and I will assume that as regards the conduct of the ship during that period it is to be judged of as the conduct of any ship subject to a voyage policy ought to be judged of. But then, it appears to me that unless these words 'for 15 days whilst there' – that is, at Newcastle – 'after arrival', have obtained some peculiar mercantile meaning by usage or otherwise (which is not contended), there arises after the voyage is completed an addition to, an excrescence upon, the voyage policy in the shape of a stipulation which carries the persons interested in the ship safely over a further period of 15 days, and that as to that it is not a voyage policy, but a time policy. There is, therefore, a stipulation for a voyage, and engrafted upon that a further period of 15 days during which the loss of the ship is insured against ... The appellants are therefore entitled to recover.

But a 'mixed' policy may also be a time policy with the constraints of a voyage policy grafted upon it. In the Australian case of *Wilson v Boag* **[1957] 2 Lloyd's Rep 564**, a motor launch was insured for four months, but the policy only covered loss within a 50 mile radius of Port Stephens. On this occasion, when a loss occurred within the 50 mile radius, but during a voyage extending beyond that radius, the court held that the policy remained a time policy with a condition that the insurer was not liable for any losses sustained outside that 50 mile radius.[56] The significance of the decision was that the court, in construing the policy, endeavoured to ascertain the intentions of the parties when the contract of insurance was drawn up.

> **Supreme Court of New South Wales:** [p 565] ... We think that the policy covers loss occurring within the perimeter even though the launch was then in the course of proceeding to a point outside it. That seems to us to be the natural meaning to be given to the relevant words. There appear to be no reported cases precisely in point, and to apply the rules of law relating to commercial voyage policies to this case seems to us to be somewhat unreal, and not to be warranted by anything to be found in the terms of the contract.

The importance of determining, with a mixed policy, whether or not it is essentially a voyage policy or a time policy was underlined in the *Al-Jubail IV* case, below, where the issue was one of seaworthiness. In reaching its decision, the Singapore Court of Appeal referred to *Wilson v Boag*, and applied the same logic, when construing the policy, of ascertaining the intention of the parties to the contract.

Almojil Establishment v Malayan Motor and General Underwriters (Private) Ltd, 'Al-Jubail IV' [1982] 2 Lloyd's Rep 637, Singapore CA

The respondents, who were engaged in the construction of offshore installations in Saudi Arabia, bought the coastal defence vessel *Al-Jubail IV* from Singapore Shipping Industries (SSI) to be used to carry personnel to and from platforms at sea. SSI arranged delivery of the vessel to the respondents, and also effected a policy of insurance on the hull of *Al-Jubail IV* on behalf of the respondents. Although the policy was a time policy, the 12 month period of cover did not commence until the vessel left Singapore for the Persian Gulf. Furthermore, the insurers had insisted on a condition survey being carried out before *Al-Jubail IV* sailed.

On the voyage across the Indian Ocean, *Al-Jubail IV* was lost and the respondents claimed on their policy of insurance, contending that the policy was not a voyage policy and, therefore, there was no implied warranty of

---

56 This case is also discussed in Chapter 7, p 298.

seaworthiness. The insurers refused payment on the basis that the policy was essentially a voyage policy, and (a) the vessel had not been seaworthy when she sailed, and (b) the warranted condition survey had not been carried out by an approved surveyor.

The Singapore Court of Appeal ruled that the insurers were not liable. The policy was a mixed policy and, as the assured had possession and control of the vessel before she left Singapore, the policy had all the attributes of a voyage policy and, therefore, there was an implied warranty that the vessel be seaworthy at the commencement of the voyage. Furthermore, the condition survey had not been carried out by an approved surveyor.

Lai J: [p 640] ... the court [in *Wilson v Boag*] declined to apply the rules of law relating to commercial voyage policies as to do that had seemed to them 'to be unreal'. The substance of the transaction was looked at and effect was given to it. We would do likewise.

In construing this policy and ascertaining the intention of the parties, we look at the whole policy and the terms used in it for their plain, ordinary and popular sense. We also look at all the surrounding circumstances known to the parties at the time the contract of insurance was made ... We are accordingly of the opinion that the policy here in question is not a time policy *simpliciter*, but is a 'mixed policy' affording a cover of 12 months and attaching as from and on the voyage from Singapore to the Persian Gulf.

... We now turn to the second branch of the respondent's argument against implying a warranty of seaworthiness by the respondent. Counsel submitted that, even if this is a 'mixed policy', the implication of the warranty of seaworthiness does not automatically follow. A mixed policy is neither a voyage policy nor a time policy. Accordingly, neither sub-s 39(1) nor sub-s 39(5) of the Act applies.

... Why was the warranty of seaworthiness implied in the past in the case of voyage policies? The principal reason was that an assured was usually in control and possession of a vessel before a vessel embarked on a voyage and was able to do something about and comply with any obligation as regards the seaworthiness of the vessel. So the warranty of seaworthiness was implied in voyage policies and legislative expression was given to it by sub-s 39(1) of the Act.

In this case, the respondent, as the assured, was in possession and control of the vessel before it left Singapore and began what would clearly be the most turbulent part of its life in the 12 month period. This part of the cover was between two termini and the policy so far as the delivery voyage was concerned had all the attributes of a voyage policy. In these circumstances, the answer to an officious bystander's question whether the assured warrants the seaworthiness of the vessel must be a categorical affirmation.

[p 641] ... We are, in the circumstances, of the opinion that the vessel was not seaworthy and the respondent was in breach of the warranty of seaworthiness.

[p 642] ... For the appellants [insurers] it was also submitted, and we accept the submission, that the expression 'approved surveyor' means a surveyor

approved by underwriters in Singapore. This is the reasonable construction. There is no evidence that either Vesuna [the surveyors used] or the Maritime Inspection Corporation were approved by underwriters in Singapore generally.

CHAPTER 5

VALUED AND UNVALUED POLICIES

VALUED POLICIES

Introduction

The Act, in s 27(2), provides the definition of a valued policy in the following terms:

> A valued policy is a policy which specifies the agreed value of the subject matter insured.

The purpose of a valued policy was considered in the old case of **Lewis v Rucker (1761) 2 Burr 1167**, where hogsheads of sugar were insured under valued policies of insurance for a voyage from the West Indies to Hamburg. When, on arrival at Hamburg, the hogsheads were found to be damaged by seawater, the owner of the goods claimed on his policy and the court was obliged to consider the significance of a valued policy which, at the time, was thought by many to be a means of effecting a wagering policy.

> **Lord Mansfield:** [p 1171] ... A valued policy is not to be a considered a wager policy, or like 'interest or no interest' ... The only effect of the valuation is fixing the amount of the prime cost; just as if the parties admitted it at the trial: but, in every argument, and for every other purpose, it must be taken that the value was fixed in such a manner as that the insured meant only to have an indemnity.

And, in *Irving v Manning* **(1847) 1 HL Cas 287**, an ex-East Indiaman, *General Kydd*, was insured under a valued policy for a voyage from China to Madras when she was severely damaged by heavy weather. Two issues were resolved: (a) in determining whether she was or was not a constructive total loss, the significant value for verifying such a loss was the market value of the ship or the value specified in the policy;[1] (b) the measure of indemnity was the sum agreed at the time the policy was effected.

> **Patteson J:** [p 305] ... By the terms of it, the ship, etc, for so much *as concerns the assured, by agreement* between the assured and the assurers, are and shall be rated and valued at £17,500, and the question turns upon the meaning of these words.

---

1 Under s 27(4) of the Act and common law, when determining whether a vessel is or is not a constructive total loss, the cost of repairs is to be compared with the market value of the vessel after she has been repaired. Under the Institute Hulls Clauses, the insured value is to be taken for the purpose of comparison: see the ITCH(95), cl 19.1 and the IVCH(95), cl 19.1 and cl 17.1. This aspect of the law is discussed in Chapter 16, p 646.

Do they, as contended for by the plaintiff in error, amount to an agreement that, for all purposes connected with the voyage, at least for the purpose of ascertaining whether there is a total loss or not, the ship should be taken to be of that value, so that when a question arises whether it would be worth while to repair, it must be assumed that the vessel would be worth that sum when repaired? Or do they mean only, that for the purpose of ascertaining the amount of compensation to be paid to the assured, when the loss has happened, the value shall be taken to be the sum fixed, in order to avoid disputes as to the *quantum* of the assured's interest?

We are all of the opinion that the latter is the true meaning; and this is consistent with the language of the policy, and with every case that has been decided upon valued policies.

Finally, in **Lidgett v Secretan (1871) LR 6 CP 616**, a vessel, which was insured under two valued policies of insurance, was lost after a fire consumed her whilst she was in dry dock undergoing repairs to damage caused by a previous grounding. In the course of his reasoning, Willes J considered the overall significance of a valued policy and why such a policy could be advantageous to both the assured and the insurer. The judge also pointed out the problems which are inherent in valued policies, but suggested that they were a necessity to the shipping industry.

> **Willes J:** [p 627] ... The second point arises upon the second policy, and is one of great importance, and one which has been the subject of much discussion and criticism both by lawyers and legislators; and yet nobody has been able to improve upon the practice as to valued policies which has been recognised and adopted by shipowners and underwriters, and has, at least amongst honest men, the advantage of giving the assured the full value of the thing insured, and of enabling the underwriters to obtain a larger amount of profit. It saves them both the necessity of going into an expensive and intricate question as to the value in each particular case ... Of course, if the sum inserted as the value of the ship were so outrageously large as to make it plain that the assured intended a fraud on the underwriters, the latter would have their remedy. So, if a jury should think the real intention was a wager on the value of the ship. There are many questions why this system of valuation – though unquestionably often resorted to for the purpose of evading the law against wagering policies – is useful. Ships are often insured whilst on a distant voyage, and when their exact condition or value cannot be known or ascertained. It is manifestly important that the owner should be able to insert a fair sum as to the value of the vessel, treating her as sound, though she may at the time have sustained damage even to the extent of what may ultimately turn out to be a total loss, that being in fact one of the perils insured against.

The agreed value is conclusive

Section 27(3) of the Act confirms that the value fixed by the policy is conclusive of the value of the subject matter 'intended' to be insured when it states:

Subject to the provisions of this Act, and in the absence of fraud, the value fixed by the policy is, as between the insurer and assured, conclusive of the insurable value of the subject intended to be insured, whether the loss be total or partial.

The Act specifically uses the words 'intended to be insured' to signify that the value fixed by the policy is the figure agreed at the time the contract is made, before the policy attaches. In so doing, the Act recognises that there may be a lapse of time between the conclusion of the contract and the attachment of the policy, with the result that the value of the subject matter may be quite different at those points in time.

This was noted long ago, in **Barker v Janson (1868) LR 3 CP 303**, where a vessel, *Sir William Eyre*, was insured under a valued time policy of insurance for £6,000. Although, at the time of the effecting of the policy and unknown to the assured, the ship had already met with a serious accident, the value fixed by the policy was considered by the court to be conclusive.

Montague Smith J: [p 307] ... A thousand things might lessen the value of a vessel between the time of the policy being made and the time of its attaching, such as natural decay, worms, or the ship becoming a drug in the market; and all the evils intended to be avoided by this kind of policy would arise again.

However, early in the 19th century there had been some concern over valued policies being nothing more than a convenient way of effecting a wagering policy. Added to this, the law as to the measure of indemnity under a valued policy had not been clearly settled by the courts.

When this vexed issue, concerning whether the sum agreed under a valued policy was conclusive, was eventually clarified in the case of ***Irving v Manning* (1847) 1 HL Cas 287**, Lord Campbell could hardly contain his pleasure at finally seeing it being resolved. In this instance, the ship *General Kydd* was insured under a valued policy of insurance for £17,500. When she was severely damaged by bad weather on a voyage from China to Madras, the court was faced with determining whether she was or was not a constructive total loss, and what the measure of indemnity was.

The House of Lords ruled that the valuation fixed by the policy was conclusive of the amount recoverable under the policy in the event of a loss. However, at the time, under the common law, the valuation had nothing to do with determining whether the ship was or was not a constructive total loss.[2]

Lord Campbell: [p 307] ... My Lords, I am extremely glad that a question which has agitated Westminster Hall for the last 30 years is at last solemnly decided by a judgment of your Lordships. It is a question of great importance

---

[2] It has to be emphasised that this ruling took place under the common law where the cost of repairs was to be compared with the repaired market value when determining whether a vessel was a constructive total loss. Cf the ITCH(95), cl 19.1 and the IVCH(95), cl 17.1, where the cost of repairs is to be compared with the insured value.

to the commerce of this country. I entirely concur in the opinion expressed by my noble and learned friend upon this subject.

My Lords, it appears to me that on the just construction of this contract, the plaintiff was entitled to recover the sum which the jury has awarded him. If you look at the contract, it seems to me that it was definitely determined that, for all purposes, the value of the ship would be taken at the sum of £17,500. There was nothing illegal in this contract; we have only to put a construction upon it, and if it be a just construction, and there is neither any rule of common law nor any statute to prevent the construction being carried into effect, we are bound to give effect to it, and to pronounce in favour of the plaintiff below. I repeat that I rejoice that this question, which has so long agitated Westminster Hall, is now for ever set at rest, and is satisfactorily decided.

That, with a valued policy of insurance, the value fixed in the policy is binding on the parties, has been confirmed many times by the courts.[3]

Woodside v Globe Marine Insurance Co Ltd [1896] 1 QB 105

The vessel *Bawnmore* was insured under a valued time policy of insurance for £20,000. During the currency of the policy, she was driven ashore on the coast of Oregon and stranded; some 36 hours later, she was completely destroyed by fire.

The court ruled that the plaintiffs could recover for the full amount insured under the policy. Mathew J summed up the law with respect to valued policies of insurance on both ship and goods.

> **Mathew J:** [p 107] Whether the subject matter of insurance be ship or goods, the valuation is the amount fixed by agreement at which, in case of loss, the indemnity is to be calculated. Where goods are assured, the valuation may be low when the policy attaches; but the value to the owner may be enhanced when the goods have nearly reached their destination by the expenses of transit, etc. Yet the valuation is binding. And, again, if the valuation be high, but the goods are depreciated in value from fall of market or other causes for which the underwriter is not liable, the valuation cannot be opened.
>
> In the case of a ship, in the same way, the vessel may, from many causes, be worth much less at the time of the loss than the agreed value; but the valuation determines the amount of the underwriter's liability.

---

3   In *Barker v Janson* (1868) LR 3 CP 303, Bovill CJ stated: [p 306] '... In this case, both parties have agreed upon a time policy ... and have further agreed that, whatever its condition may have been at the time the policy attached, they will treat the value of the vessel as of a certain amount.' And, in *Lidgett v Secretan* (1871) LR 6 CP 616, Montague Smith J affirmed: [p 631] '... It seems to me that it would be contrary to the principle upon which the practice of making valued policies is based, if any of the circumstances [damage sustained before the policy attached] could be taken into consideration in order to open the valuation.'

The introduction of the Act in 1906 has in no way made the sum fixed in a valued policy of insurance less binding on the parties. This was confirmed in the interesting case of *Loders and Nucoline Ltd v Bank of New Zealand*, below, where the issue was whether, under a CIF contract of sale, the insurance covering the goods should also have covered the freight payable on those goods.

Loders and Nucoline Ltd v Bank of New Zealand (1929) 33 LlL Rep 70

The Bank of New Zealand, the defendants, sold 300 tons of copra to Messrs Fischel and Co who, then, sold the same consignment of copra to Messrs Loders and Co. The sale was on CIF terms. However, the ship carrying the copra caught fire whilst she was at Fiji, and both ship and cargo were totally lost, with the result that there was no freight payable on the copra at the intended port of destination. The plaintiffs, Loders and Co, as assignees to the policies of insurance, claimed against the underwriters, but the sum paid out only amounted to the value of the copra and did not include the freight. The plaintiffs then sued the Bank of New Zealand for the freight, which should have been insured as part of the gross price of the copra under a CIF contract of sale.

The court ruled in favour of the plaintiffs, Loders and Co, the purchasers of the copra. As the sale was CIF, the policies of insurance should have covered the cost of the freight and, therefore, the bank was liable to the plaintiffs for a sum amounting to the freight which would have been payable.

> **Wright J:** [p 75] ... I think the sellers [Bank of New Zealand] were wrong in this contention, and I think that the insurance company would have been bound to pay the insured value in the event of a total loss if the policies had been, as they ought to have been, policies on copra valued at whatever the amount is, £27 plus 5%. First of all, the policy would have been a valued policy, and I think that it is of primary importance in the law of marine insurance that the valuation in a policy should be treated as something binding and conclusive; but, in any case, the law is now very well established that the valuation cannot be reopened. I believe that can be stated categorically and without any qualification at all, because the only qualification which is found in the Act is, I think, on its true construction, not a qualification of that sort, but a reminder of another rule, which again is of essential importance in marine insurance.
>
> I need not refer to the earlier cases about valued policies. It has been laid down over and over again that the valuation in a policy cannot be reopened; but s 27(3) of the Marine Insurance Act 1906 says this:
>
>> Subject to the provisions of this Act, and in the absence of fraud, the value fixed by the policy is, as between the insurer and assured, conclusive of the insurable value of the subject intended to be insured, whether the loss be total or partial.
>
> [p 76] ... The words qualifying s 27(3), namely, 'subject to the provisions of this Act', may perhaps refer to ss 29(4) and 75(2), as the learned editor (Chalmers)

points out, and the words 'in the absence of fraud' do not, in my judgment, mean that the value as such can be reopened. They are simply a warning that if there is fraud, not only the valuation, but the whole of the policy may be reopened and avoided.

[p 77] ... There is no foundation at all for saying here that, under such a policy, assuming it to have been taken out, the insured value would have been notionally split up or that part of the value which might be said to be attributable to freight can be separated from some other parts of the value which it was said ought to be attributed to the goods. The insurance would have been on, and ought to have been on, a single indivisible value per ton, on a single and indivisible subject matter of insurance, 100 tons of copra on each policy; and, that being so, if the buyers had, as I hold they ought to have had, those policies, they could not have failed to recover the total amount under those policies; and, therefore, in my judgment the arbitrators were quite right in awarding to the buyers the amount that they had awarded, namely, the difference between the amount recoverable under the then policies and the amount that would have been recovered under the policies if they had been in the proper form.

The agreed value is also binding on the assured

Section 27(3) of the Act confirms that, under a valued policy, the sum by the policy is '... as between the insurer and assured, conclusive ...'. That is, not only is the insurer bound by the valuation, but also the assured. Thus, if an assured is indemnified by the insurer to the amount agreed in the policy and he, the assured, then succeeds in a claim against a third party, the insurer has the right, by way of subrogation, to recover that money from the assured.[4]

Such was the case in **North of England Iron Steamship Insurance Association v Armstrong** (1870) LR 5 QB 244, where a vessel sank after a collision with another ship and was totally lost. As the sunken vessel had been insured under a valued time policy of insurance, the insurers indemnified the owners to the extent of £6,000, the sum fixed by the policy. Later, the insurers sought to recover over £5,000 from the owners when they, the owners, were awarded that sum by the Admiralty Court from the other colliding vessel. In this, the insurers were successful.

Lush J: [p 250] ... If each of the parties agrees that a certain sum shall be deemed to be the value of the thing insured, the underwriter, in the case of a total loss, is not to be at liberty to say the thing is not worth so much; he is bound to pay the amount fixed upon, whether it is the proper amount or not. And, on the other hand, the assured is not at liberty to say it is worth more; he is bound by that amount.

Furthermore, should an assured claim upon a valued policy of insurance, the indemnity he is entitled to receive can only be based upon the valuation fixed

---

4   On the issue of subrogation, see Chapter 1, p 17.

in the policy, regardless of the true value of the subject insured. In *Steamship 'Balmoral' Co Ltd v Marten* [1902] AC 511, HL, the vessel *Balmoral*, after suffering a fractured tail shaft in heavy weather, received assistance by way of a tow to London. Although, in the ensuing salvage action, the amount to be paid by the owners of *Balmoral* in general average was based on the 'true' value of the ship, the indemnity paid by the insurers was based upon the 'insured' value of the vessel, which was considerably less.

Thus, as *Balmoral*'s true value was £40,000 and her insured value was £33,000, the insurers were only liable for 33/40ths of the claim made upon them by the assured.

> **Lord Shand:** [p 515] ... The policy of insurance provides that the ship, for so much as concerns the assured, by agreement between the assured and assurers in this policy, is and shall be valued at, say, £33,000. In all questions of indemnity, therefore, the parties to the policy, insurers and insured, have agreed that, though the ship may in truth be much more valuable, her value is to be taken at £33,000 only. There is no exception.

Scrapping voyages – the value is the scrap value

The Institute Time Clauses Hulls incorporates a clause, namely cl 1.5, which is intended to provide specifically for what is termed a 'scrapping voyage'. Under a time policy of insurance on hull, should the insured ship undertake a voyage for the purpose of being broken up or be sold to be broken up, the value of the ship, in the event of loss or damage, is taken to be her scrap value, and not the value fixed by the policy. This rule applies, unless the underwriter is notified prior to the voyage, and the terms of cover, insured value and premium are refixed.

To this effect, cl 1.5 of the ITCH(95) states:

> In the event of the Vessel sailing (with or without cargo) with an intention of being: (a) broken up; or (b) sold for breaking up, any claim for loss of or damage to the Vessel occurring subsequent to such sailing shall be limited to the market value of the Vessel as scrap at the time when the loss or damage is sustained, unless previous notice has been given to the Underwriters and any amendments to the terms of cover, insured value and premium required by them have been agreed ...

Excessive over-valuation

In the absence of fraud

The Act, in s 27(3), makes specific reference to 'fraud' when it states that the sum fixed by a valued policy is conclusive only '... in the absence of fraud ...'.

However, excessive over-valuation does not necessarily imply a wager or fraud, for there are usually sound commercial reasons why, for example, a ship is valued under a policy for far more than its true value. It therefore falls upon the courts to be pragmatic on this issue, and distinguish between over-valuation for good reasons and over-valuation based on fraudulent practice.

Fraudulent over-valuation

The position with respect to fraudulent over-valuation was laid down long ago, in a clinical fashion, by Sir James Mansfield in the old case of *Haigh v de la Cour*, below.

Haigh v de la Cour (1812) 3 Camp 319

Goods were insured under a valued policy for £5,000 for a voyage from London to Pernambucco, in Brazil, aboard the ship *Maira*. In reality, the insurance had been effected by bankrupts, and the goods were worth nothing more than £1,400. The invoices were fictitious, the bills of lading had been altered and the bankrupts had placed an associate aboard, who ran away with the ship and sold the goods in the West Indies.

When the assignees to the policy laid claim for their loss, the court was in no doubt that the policy was rendered void.

> **Sir James Mansfield CJ:** [p 320] If the bankrupts intended from the beginning to cheat the underwriters, the assignees can recover nothing. The fraud entirely vitiates the contract.

But fraud, being a criminal offence, is not easy to prove. In the well known case of ***Thames and Mersey Marine Insurance Co Ltd v 'Gunford' Ship Co Ltd* [1911] AC 529, HL**, where a vessel was grossly over-insured and there were additional high value ppi policies effected on disbursements, the insurers made no attempt to defend themselves on the basis that the claim was fraudulent. Instead, they successfully contended that the owners were guilty of the non-disclosure of a material fact, in that they (insurers) had not been informed of the existence of other policies. Nevertheless, the court considered the likely effect of fraud.

> **Lord Shaw of Dunfermline:** [p 320] ... Had this over-valuation been tainted by fraud, the contract of insurance could not have been enforced. Where there is heavy over-valuation fraud is, a priori, not very far to seek. But fraud is not here pleaded.

Over-valuation for sound business reasons

As already suggested, over-valuation is often a commercial necessity, a fact recognised by the courts. Over-valuation of a ship by a shipowner may reflect his commitment to a mortgage and/or the cost of replacement,[5] rather than the real value of the ship itself. As Lord Robson has pointed out, in ***Thames***

---

5   On the subject of replacement value, see *Herring v Janson and Others* (1895) 1 Com Cas 177 discussed below, p 196.

and Mersey Marine Insurance Co Ltd v 'Gunford' Ship Co Ltd [1911] AC 529, HL, where the issue before the court was one of serious over-valuation, it is often to the benefit of the insurer that the insured property be over-valued.

> **Lord Robson:** [p 548] ... Although the contract of insurance is expressed to be a contract of indemnity, and the indemnity is properly based on market value at the time of the loss, yet the law allows the insured value to be agreed between the parties, and the agreed value is binding in the absence of fraud. There are often legitimate business reasons for this discrepancy between the selling value and the insured value, and it should not be assumed that it necessarily creates any actual conflict between duty and interest on the part of the shipowner in regard to the safety of the thing insured. The assured naturally aims at reinstatement rather than bare indemnity, and the insurer has also his own reasons for preferring that the values should be high, so long as they do not constitute a temptation of loss. In order that he may be saved the trouble of small claims, which are often of a doubtful character, he stipulates that the ship shall be warranted free from average under 3%, and where the total agreed value is high, the insurer's protection under this clause is increased. Again, in claims for constructive total loss, the higher the value, the more difficult it is for the assured to establish that the cost of repairs will exceed the repaired value, so as to entitle him to treat the vessel as lost and leave the wreck on the insurer's hands. The insurer is therefore willing to undertake the risk of a certain amount of over-valuation, relying, no doubt, on the character of the assured and also on the interest that the managing owners or managers have in preserving the ship as a source of business profit to themselves.

A particularly good example for over-valuing a ship for the best of commercial reasons can be found in the *Maira (No 2)* case, below.

Glafki Shipping Co SA v Pinos Shipping Co No 1, 'Maira' (No 2) [1986] 2 Lloyd's Rep 12, HL

The defendants, Pinos Shipping Co, were the owners of the vessel *Maira* which had been built in Japan in 1977. The money to pay for the vessel had been raised by way of two marine mortgages, the terms of which were that the ship should be insured for 130% of the mortgage debt. The management of *Maira* was entrusted to the plaintiffs, who insured the vessel for $10,000,000, the actual value at the time being $4,875,000. Ten days after the insurance was effected, *Maira* exploded and sank off the coast of Australia, and the insurers paid the resulting claim in full. However, the defendant owners of *Maira* contended that, under the terms of the management agreement, the ship should have been insured by the plaintiff ship managers for almost $12,000,000 – that sum representing 130% of the outstanding balances owed under the mortgages.

The House of Lords ruled that the plaintiff ship managers were liable to the owners for the sum of almost $2,000,000, as they had failed to insure the ship to the full value agreed under the management agreement.

Lord Brandon of Oakbrook: [p 17] ... Three parties, the Japanese bank as first mortgagees, the Greek bank as second mortgagees and the owners as payers of 30% of the price of the ship, all had interests which needed to be protected in the event of the ship being lost. It was manifestly the purpose of the composite transaction that the first two of these parties, the Japanese bank and the Greek bank, should be protected against the risk with an ample margin to spare, and that that margin, except to the extent that it might be absorbed by some special circumstances, should enure for the benefit of the third of the three parties, the owners.

Breach of duty to observe 'utmost good faith'

The principle of 'utmost good faith' contained in s 17 is the ethical doctrine upon which all contracts of insurance are based.[6] Thus, in order to comply with the doctrine of *uberrimae fidei* under s 17, the assured must observe utmost good faith not only before, but also after, the conclusion of the contract.[7] It falls upon an assured under s 18 to disclose any material circumstance before the conclusion of the contract, and, under s 20, not to make any material misrepresentation during the negotiations for the contract. As with the case of a breach of the duty to observe utmost good faith under s 17, a breach of ss 18 and 20 renders the policy voidable.

It is, therefore, emphasised that a court could well be persuaded to find an excessive over-valuation as evidence of fraud, upon which the insurer would be perfectly entitled to avoid the policy.

Non-disclosure of a material circumstance

In *Ionides v Pender*, below, the trial judge laid down a simple, but effective, test for deciding whether there was over-valuation and whether knowledge of that over-valuation was material to an underwriter. That test was adopted by Blackburn J, who then went further, by highlighting the problems associated with over-valuation, before laying down the general principles which were to be used for the purpose of determining whether a circumstance was or was not 'material' for the purpose of disclosure.

Ionides v Pender (1874) LR 7 QB 531, CA

The vessel *Da Capo* was chartered for a voyage to Vladivostok and the plaintiffs (charterers) effected a number of valued policies on the venture through brokers in Hamburg. The insurances on the goods, including profits, amounted to about £14,000 and, in addition, there was an insurance on commissions of £1,500, as well as a further policy for £1,000 covering safe

---

6   For a fuller discussion of the doctrine of utmost good faith, see Chapter 6.
7   See *Black King Shipping Corpn v Massie, 'Litsion Pride'* [1985] 1 Lloyd's Rep 437, discussed in Chapter 6, p 216.

arrival. In all, the plaintiffs stood to receive a very large sum if the venture was lost. When the ship was, in fact, lost in suspicious circumstances and the plaintiffs claimed upon their insurances, the underwriters refused payment on the basis that: (a) the loss of the vessel was not caused by a peril insured against; and (b) the plaintiffs had failed to disclose facts which were material to the underwriting of the policies, namely, the excessive over-valuation under several policies.

The Appeal Court affirmed the decision of the trial judge and ruled that the plaintiffs could not recover under the policies, because they had failed to disclose the fact that there was an excessive over-valuation. Blackburn J repeated the seven questions originally put by the trial judge to the jury, four of which were pertinent to the over-valuation.

> **Blackburn J:** [p 535] ... On this evidence, my Brother Hannen [the trial judge] proposed to ask the jury seven questions: first: whether the goods were really put on board? Secondly: were the valuations for insurance excessive? Thirdly: if excessive, were they so made with a fraudulent intent? Fourthly: whether fraudulent or not, was it material to the underwriter to know that the valuation was excessive? Fifthly: was it concealed from the underwriters? Sixthly: was the vessel lost by perils insured against? Lastly: did the assured know or intend that the vessel should be cast away? The counsel for the defendant admitted that the first question must be answered in favour of the plaintiffs. The other six questions were asked of the jury, who answered: that the valuations were excessive; that there was not sufficient evidence to show whether they were made with fraudulent intent; but that, whether fraudulent or not, it was material to the underwriter to know that they were excessive; and that that was concealed.
>
> [p 538] ... It is to be observed that the excessive valuation not only may lead to suspicion of foul play, but that it has a direct tendency to make the assured less careful in selecting the ship and captain, and to diminish the efforts which, in case of disaster, he ought to make to diminish the loss as far as possible, and cannot therefore properly be called altogether extraneous to the risks ... We agree that it would be too much to put on the assured the duty of disclosing everything which might influence the mind of an underwriter. Business could hardly be carried on if this was required. But the rule laid down in *Parsons on Insurance*, Vol I, p 495, that all should be disclosed which would effect the judgment of a rational underwriter governing himself by the principles and calculations on which underwriters do in practice set, seems to us a sound one ... and applying it to the present case, there was distinct and uncontradicted evidence that underwriters do, in practice, act on the principle that it is material to take into consideration whether the over-valuation is so great as to make the risk speculative.

In *Herring v Janson and Others*, below, Mathew J made use of the test put forward by Hannen J in the *Ionides* case. The judge pointed out that the true valuation of the subject matter was not its sale price, but its replacement value.

Herring v Janson and Others (1895) 1 Com Cas 177

A yacht, which was insured for £5,000, was destroyed by fire. The underwriters refused payment under the policy because, they contended, the vessel was over-insured and the plaintiffs were guilty of concealing her real value. The court ruled that there was no such over-valuation.

> **Mathew J:** [p 177] ... Valuation ought not to be lightly set aside, in as much as it is an agreement entered into for the specific purpose of preventing further dispute in case of a loss under the policy. The assured was not bound to value the yacht at what he would sell for. He was entitled to take into account what it would have cost him for necessary repairs and outfit of the vessel, and, further, what he would have to pay to replace her.
>
> I will quote to you what seems to me an accurate statement of the law, by one of our greatest commercial lawyers, the late Willes J:[8]
>
>> In the absence of proof that the value fixed by the contract is so exaggerated as to be a mere cloak for gambling, in representing more than any possible interest which the assured could have in the ship and outfit, or that the exaggeration was fraudulent with a view to cheat the underwriter, the latter is bound in case of total loss to pay the agreed sum. It is only where the over-valuation is so exaggerated as to show to the satisfaction of a jury that it must have been designed in order to obtain more than a just and complete indemnity that the insurance is void.
>
> [p 180] ... The following questions were then put to the jury:
>
> (1) Was the valuation of the vessel in the policy excessive?
>
> (2) If excessive, was the valuation made with a fraudulent intent?
>
> (3) If not made with a fraudulent intent, was it material for the underwriters to know what the vessel cost the assured?
>
> (4) Was the excessive valuation concealed from the underwriters?
>
> The jury answered all these questions in the negative, and judgment was entered for the plaintiff.

Since the passing of the Act, a number of well known cases concerning over-valuation have shown that the defence of 'non-disclosure' is equally potent under statute as it was under the common law. One such is now illustrated.

Gooding v White (1913) 29 TLR 312

A cargo of cloves was loaded aboard the barge *Horace and Willie* to be taken from Harwich to London. The barge sprang a leak and had to be beached. Part of the cargo was then jettisoned, and the remainder was returned to Harwich, where it was landed and dried. The cargo-owner claimed on his policy of insurance, but the insurers refused payment, contending that the cargo was

---

8   Approval was also passed upon an appraisal of over-valuation written by Willes J in the publication *Memorandum on Over-Insurance, Valued Policy, and Constructive Loss*, in 1867.

excessively over-insured at £5,000 and that 'the whole thing was a fraud from beginning to end'.

The court ruled in favour of the underwriters, for the assured had concealed a material fact.

> **Pickford J:** [p 312] ... To ascertain whether there was such an over-valuation as to alter the nature of the risk, his Lordship then examined the figures in great detail, and said that he had come to the conclusion that the cargo had been very much over-valued. He had the gravest doubts whether the cargo was worth half the £4,000 which was the figure one of the witnesses put upon it. It was unnecessary to say whether that over-valuation was effected for the purpose of defrauding the underwriters or was done with too enthusiastic an idea of the profits likely to be realised from the cargo. It was sufficient if there was, as he thought there was, such an over-valuation as ought to have been communicated to the underwriters, and as it had not been communicated, there was a concealment of a material fact which avoided the policy. On that ground, therefore, the action failed.

The insurer is presumed to know matters of common notoriety or knowledge – s 18(3)(b)

Section 18(3)(b) of the Act states:

> In the absence of inquiry, the following circumstances need not be disclosed, namely:
>
> Any circumstance which is known or presumed to be known to the insurer. The insurer is presumed to know matters of common notoriety or knowledge, and matters which an insurer, in the ordinary course of his business, as such, ought to know.

In *Piper v Royal Exchange Assurance*, below, where one of the issues was that of over-valuation, one of the points raised by the assured was that, under s 18(3)(b) of the Act, it was the business of the insurers to know the true value of the insured subject matter.

Piper v Royal Exchange Assurance [1932] 44 LlL Rep 103

The plaintiff bought the yacht *Atalanta II* from a Norwegian for £1,000, and insured her under three policies for a total of £2,500. The yacht was in poor condition and sustained minor damage whilst being sailed to England from Norway, for which loss the plaintiff was indemnified. However, at a later date, the yacht grounded on Buxey Sands, near Burnham-on-Crouch, and sustained yet more damage, but, in this instance, the insurers refused to pay their share of the total claim of £870. About a year later, the yacht suffered two fires and the damage was said to amount to £2,284. Again, the insurers refused to pay, claiming that the fires had been started deliberately, and the yacht was also fraudulently over-insured.

The court ruled that the plaintiff could recover for the damage sustained by the grounding because, at that time, the yacht was not over-valued, in that the plaintiff hoped to sell her for about £2,000. However, at the time of the fires, the yacht had deteriorated and was only worth half what she was insured for. Therefore, the plaintiff could not recover for the fire damage because the insurers should have been informed of the deterioration and the lessening in value. The court considered whether the insurers, in the ordinary course of their business, should have known the true value of the yacht.

> **Roche J:** [p 120] ... It remains to deal with the contention that the underwriters themselves knew of the facts, and that the case is, therefore, brought within s 18(3)(b) of the Marine Insurance Act 1906. With regard to that, various comments have been made, and perhaps I have made some of them, on the organisation of the defendants' business. The fact is that some things are known to one department which are not known to another, and some things were not known to people who were underwriting the later insurance which might well, under a better business organisation – which, I understand, has now been introduced – have been known to them, but they were not the facts which I have found ought to have been the subject matter of disclosure on this occasion. They knew from the reports which they had received, both from the voyage damage and in respect of the stranding damage, that there were defects in this ship which would affect her value ... what they did not know was of the progress of the deterioration on board the ship, evidenced by her manifest unsaleability ... I am not saying, and it was never contended on the part of the defendants, that those were facts which ought to have been disclosed *eo nomine* or specifically to the underwriters, but what was said was that this deterioration and these facts with regard to her value were matters which were known to the assured and were not known to the underwriters. I think that is true, and, therefore, I hold that the plaintiff is not saved by the provisions of s 18(3)(b) of the Marine Insurance Act 1906.

But, s 18(3)(b) did come to the aid of the owners of a small coaster which was over-valued in the case of *General Shipping and Forwarding Co v British General Insurance Co Ltd*, below. However, Bailhache J conceded that s 18(3)(b) was less likely to be of assistance to an owner of goods, because an underwriter is unlikely to have the necessary information regarding the true value of goods at his fingertips; and fraud on the valuation of goods is much easier to perpetrate.

General Shipping and Forwarding Co and Another v British General Insurance Co Ltd, 'Borre' (1923) 15 LlL Rep 175

The vessel *Borre* was insured by the plaintiffs with the defendants under a valued time policy for 12 months. *Borre* was valued at £5,000 and the defendants had underwritten a line for £2,000. Her value on the market was later estimated to be about £1,400. On a voyage from Liverpool to Bantry, in Ireland, *Borre* sprang a leak and sank near Anglesey. When the plaintiffs claimed on their policy of insurance, the underwriters refused payment on the basis that, *inter alia*, there had been non-disclosure of material facts, viz, over-valuation and the existence of ppi policies.

The court ruled that, although there was heavy over-valuation, it did not amount to fraud. Furthermore, the insurers should have been well aware of her actual value and, although the ship was over-valued, she was probably worth more to her owners than her actual market value. Therefore, the insurers were liable under the policy.

Bailhache J: [p 176] ... It is possible and quite likely that her value for the purposes of the trade which was being carried on by her owners and managers was very considerably in excess of £1,400, which was the sum she was worth in the open market. Making every allowance for that, the vessel was very considerably over-insured, probably to the extent of twice her value, whether one regards it as her market value or her value for the particular trade for which she was employed.

Now it is sought to reopen the valuation upon the ground of excessive insurance. In considering that, one must bear in mind that this was an insurance on hull and machinery and not an insurance of goods. One must bear in mind that the underwriter had at his hand in Lloyd's Register of Ships all the information about *Borre* that the owners had ... The defendants had been on the risk twice before; and on this third occasion, they increased their risk to £2,000. The underwriters were just as well able, in my judgment, to estimate what the market value of *Borre* was as were the people who owned her; and with all the information before them and the same possibilities of estimating her value, they chose to accept this valuation and to make a contract on these terms, and to take premiums on this valuation of £5,000.

Now they seek to upset it on the ground that it is an over-valuation so excessive as to entitle them to be off the risk. The matter is dealt with in s 27(3) of the Marine Insurance Act 1906. It begins by saying: 'Subject to the provisions of this Act'; but I am not aware of any provision of the Act which varies this provision:[9] 'and in the absence of fraud the value fixed by the policy is as between the insurer and assured conclusive of the insurable value ...' Now, where the subject matter of the case is goods, the matter is on a different footing. There, the underwriter has no means of knowing the value of the goods, except the statement of the assured. He has not, as in this case, all the information to his hand when he comes to insure goods; and it is much more easy to infer fraud from over-insurance of goods than from over-insurance of ships when both parties are in approximately the same position to know what the market value of the ship proposed to be insured is.

[p 177] ... In all the circumstances I have come to the conclusion that, though there was this heavy over-valuation, there was no fraud; and the attempt to be off risk on the ground of over-valuation fails.

---

9   But, see *Loders and Nucoline Ltd v Bank of New Zealand* (1929) 33 LlL Rep 70, *per* Wright J: [p 76] '... The words qualifying s 27(3), namely, "subject to the provisions of this Act", may perhaps refer to ss 29(4) and 75(2) ...'. This case is discussed in depth above, p 189.

Burden of proof over the 'materiality' of the over-valuation

In the case of *Berger and Light Diffusers v Pollock*, below, Kerr J pointed out that the burden of proving that the over-valuation was a material circumstance which ought to have been disclosed by the assured fell upon the insurers.

Berger and Light Diffusers Pty Ltd v Pollock [1973] 2 Lloyd's Rep 442

The plaintiffs' agents shipped four large steel injection moulds from Australia to England aboard the vessel *Paparoa*. The moulds were insured with the defendants, and valued at £20,000, but the policy, as was later shown, was not actually a valued policy. On arrival at London, the moulds were found to be badly rusted, the cause of which had been a leaking pipe in the hold in which the moulds had been stowed. When the plaintiffs claimed on their policy for a total loss, the insurers refused to settle the amount claimed on the basis, *inter alia*, that the moulds were over-valued.

The court ruled that the insurers were liable under the policy. However, the policy was actually an unvalued policy, not a valued one; the sum of £20,000 only represented the underwriters' maximum liability, and there was nothing in the policy specifying the value of the subject matter insured. Therefore, the plaintiffs could only recover £5,316, the actual value, including the freight and insurance premium, of the moulds when shipped from Australia. The issue of the burden of proving the materiality of the undisclosed circumstance, that is, the over-valuation, was considered.

> **Kerr J:** [p 463] ... The burden of establishing the materiality of undisclosed circumstances rests on the defendant [insurer] ...
>
> [p 465] ... Further, it must always be borne in mind that, in the absence of fraud, an excessive over-valuation is not itself a ground for repudiating a contract. Over-valuation is only one illustration of the general principle that insurers are entitled to avoid policies on the ground of non-disclosure of material circumstances. It must, therefore, always be shown that the over-valuation was such that, if it had been disclosed, it would have entitled the insurer to avoid the policy because it would have affected his judgment as a prudent insurer in fixing the premium or determining whether or not to take the risk.

Non-disclosure of additional insurance

If an assured effects a number of valued policies which, overall, results in excessive over-insurance, without informing the insurers of the existence of other policies covering the same subject matter, the courts may well consider that the assured has failed to disclose a material fact. This material fact could have influenced a prudent insurer in setting the premium and accepting the risk.

In **Thames and Mersey Marine Insurance Co Ltd v 'Gunford' Ship Co Ltd [1911] AC 529, HL**, the owners of a vessel had over-insured the ship, freight and disbursements under a number of policies. The House of Lords considered the effect of not disclosing the existence of all the policies to the respective insurers.[10]

> **Lord Loreburn LC:** [p 531] ... Now, my Lords, it is common ground that owners and agent between them (for I cannot discriminate) effected policies upon her hull, freight, and disbursements for £35,600, apart from Master's effects valued at £200. If the insurances be split up they are as follows: upon hull, £19,000; on freight, £5,500; the freight for the voyage being about £4,800, of which one-half had been paid in advance and was not at risk; on disbursements, £4,600, and additional on hull and disbursements (including debts of ship to her managing owners and others) against total loss, £6,500. The actual value of the hull was about £9,000 ... It was admitted that it would be a great deal better for the shareholders if the ship be lost.
>
> ... Accordingly I ask myself, in the language of the statute, would these circumstances influence the judgment of a prudent insurer in fixing the premium or determining whether he would take the risk? I can answer this question only in one way. In truth, the witnesses for the most part answered it in the same way.
>
> It is very possible that some underwriters do not ask, and do not expect to be told, what are the insurances, and that some underwriters gamble. But I do not believe that prudent underwriters would treat as immaterial such over-insurance and such large sums placed on disbursement as were effected in this case.

The *Gunford* case should be compared with *Mathie v Argonaut Marine Insurance Co Ltd*, below. In the former, the insurance amounted to a 'speculative risk', whilst, in the latter, the risk was never more than a 'business risk'. It was a question of fact, not law, and it was on that point that the House of Lords distinguished the two cases.

Mathie v Argonaut Marine Insurance Co Ltd (1925) 21 LlL Rep 145, HL

The respondent owners of the ship *Selene* dispatched her to Delagoa Bay to load a cargo of coal for Mauritius. Insurances were effected on freight for £6,000 and £4,000 on disbursements. By the time *Selene* reached Delagoa Bay, the market price of coal had plummeted, and so *Selene*'s owners purchased a cargo of coal on their own account, loaded it into *Selene* and sent her to Bombay. Additional premiums were paid on the freight and disbursements policies. However, the shipowners also insured the cargo of coal itself with other insurance companies, including the appellants, who had underwritten £1,500 of the total insurance on cargo. When the cargo of coal was lost on the voyage to Bombay, and the shipowners claimed on their policy with the appellant insurers, the insurers refused an indemnity, contending that the shipowner had not disclosed the existence of the other policies.

---

10 See Chapter 6.

The House of Lords ruled that the underwriters were liable under the policy. Lord Buckmaster referred back to the reasoning of Baihache J at first instance which Scrutton LJ, at the Court of Appeal, had approved. That reasoning was that there was only a duty to disclose existing policies if the difference between the insured value and the actual value would 'change the character of the risk from a business risk to a speculative risk'.

Lord Buckmaster: [p 146] ... It was essentially a question of fact which had to be determined by the evidence which was before the court; and in determining that question, the learned judge [Bailhache J] took the principle laid down in that case [*Ionides v Pender*][11] to which I have referred. He explained it in these words:

> As I understand it, in order to find out whether existing insurances ought to be disclosed when a fresh insurance is taken out, one has to consider this: of course one must take the figures, but one has to consider whether the discrepancy between the insured value and the actual insurable value is of such a nature as to change the character of the risk from a business risk to a speculative risk.

The learned judge thought, in the circumstances of this case, that no such change had been effected; and he accordingly held that the insurance company on whom the burden of proof lay had failed to discharge themselves of their duty. The Court of Appeal has approved of that judgment, Scrutton LJ stating that he thought it was not their duty to interfere with a judgment so reached unless it were established to their satisfaction that there were good grounds why the learned judge had been mistaken.

In considering questions of fact such as this, I regard that as a very wise and salutary rule. The judgment of a court should not be displaced, where its basis is the consideration of questions of fact and there is no question of law, except upon a strong case shown as to why the judgment should be overthrown. In this case, the principle of law has been accurately and carefully enunciated by the learned judge; and I see no reason to differ from the conclusion of fact which he reached. For these reasons, I think the appeal should be dismissed.

Lord Dunedin: [p 146] ... I think the vital difference between this case and the case of *Thames and Mersey Marine Insurance Co v 'Gunford' Ship Co* [1911] AC 529, is that there it was held that the risk was entirely speculative: but here, if these underwriters had been told about the Liverpool policy and had then asked the question 'How came you to insure freight for £6,000?' they would have been told: 'I insured it for £6,000 because that was the limit, seeing the value of the hull, to which I was entitled to go.' In other words, they would have been told that the transaction was a perfectly ordinary one. It does not seem to me that anything happened to change what was a perfectly usual and legitimate business transaction into a purely speculative one.

---

11 The general principles laid down by Blackburn J in *Ionides v Pender* (1874) LTR 7 QB 531, CA, on excessive over-valuation and when disclosure of such to the underwriter is relevant, are discussed above, p 194.

Lord Sumner: [p 146] ... The question is purely one of fact; and, being one of fact, it is a question of degree and is therefore pre-eminently one on which it would be inadvisable to interfere with the decision of the learned judge at the trial, although, of course, I recognise that his decision is subject to review through a decision on facts.

Subject to the provisions of this Act

Section 27(3) prefixes the rule, that the value fixed by the policy is conclusive as between the insurer and assured, with the words: 'Subject to the provisions of this Act ...' What, therefore, are the provisions of this Act?

In *Loders and Nucoline Ltd v Bank of New Zealand* **(1929) 33 LlL Rep 70,** referred to earlier,[12] where 300 tons of copra were sold CIF to buyers and the insurances on that cargo did not include the freight as they should have done, Wright J was of the opinion that the 'provisions of this Act' relevant to s 27(3) were ss 29(4) and 75(2). His exact words were: [p 76] '... The words qualifying s 27(3), namely, "subject to the provisions of this Act", may perhaps refer to ss 29(4) and 75(2) as the learned editor (Chalmers) points out.'

Floating policies – s 29(4)

Section 29(4) of the Act is specifically concerned with a floating policy where no declaration of value is made until after notice of loss or arrival of the ship or ships. Where such is the case, the policy must be treated as an unvalued policy. The effects of s 29(4) are, therefore, discussed later under the more appropriate heading of 'floating policies'.

Subject matter insured not at risk – s 75(2)

However, s 75(2) is of considerable importance when considering valued policies. The sub-section states:

> Nothing in the provisions of this Act relating to the measure of indemnity shall affect the rules relating to double insurance, or prohibit the insurer from disproving interest wholly or in part, or from showing that at the time of the loss the whole or any part of the subject matter insured was not at risk under the policy.

Whereas the first part of the sub-section confirms that nothing in the provisions of the Act shall affect the rules relating to double insurance or prevent the insurer from disproving insurable interest, the second part is specifically concerned with the measure of indemnity that is applicable when the whole or part of the subject matter insured is actually at risk. It is, therefore, this latter part of the sub-section which requires further analysis.

---

12 See above, p 189.

This issue, the measure of indemnity under a valued policy of insurance where only part of the subject matter is actually at risk, was raised long ago in *Forbes v Aspinall*, below.

Forbes v Aspinall (1811) 13 East 323

The plaintiffs effected a valued policy of £6,500 on the freight expected to be earned by the ship *Chiswick* on a voyage from Haiti to Liverpool. The expected cargo was to be procured by means of bartering the outward cargo. When *Chiswick* arrived at Haiti, only part of her homeward cargo, 55 bales of cotton, had been loaded before she was lost by a peril insured against. As the policy on freight was valued, the plaintiffs contended that they were entitled to an indemnity amounting to the full value stated in the policy. The insurers, on the other hand, claimed that they were only liable for the portion of the homeward cargo actually loaded, namely, the 55 bales of cotton.

The court ruled that the plaintiffs were only entitled to recover a proportion of the value fixed by the policy, as only that proportion of the freight had ever been at risk.

> **Lord Ellenborough:** [p 331] ... In a case therefore circumstanced as this is, where the valuation was with reference to freight upon a complete cargo; where a complete cargo, or anything like a complete cargo, never was in fact obtained, and for all that appears never might have been obtained; where there was no contract by any person to load a complete cargo, or pay dead freight, but the ship was a mere seeking ship; we cannot feel ourselves warranted in saying, that there has been a total loss by any peril insured against of that which the insurance was intended to cover, and which the valuation contemplated, viz, freight upon a complete cargo; but are obliged to pronounce, that no loss by the perils insured against is made out beyond the loss of freight upon part of a cargo only, viz, upon the 55 bales of cotton: that the assured are, therefore, not entitled to recover a total loss, but an apportionment only, according the measure of their actual loss.

Establishing the measure of indemnity under a policy on freight, where only a part of that freight is at risk when the loss occurs, can be quite complex, as was shown in the much later case of *The Main*, below.

The Main [1894] P 320

The plaintiffs effected a policy of insurance on freight with the defendants for £1,500 on freight totalling £5,500 to be earned by the vessel *The Main* on a voyage from New Orleans to Liverpool. However, when *The Main* eventually sailed, having been delayed by an accident, only part of the original cargo was loaded and the freight had dropped to £3,250, of which £952 had already been paid as advance freight. Thus, when *The Main* was lost during her sea passage, the total freight at risk at the time of the loss only amounted to £2,298. When the plaintiffs claimed on their insurers for the full £1,500 which they had underwritten, the insurers refused to meet the claim in full because, they contended, the total freight at risk no longer amounted to the same value as that which had been originally insured.

The court ruled that the valuation on the policy was binding. But, as the freight actually at risk was less than that which was insured, the insurers were only liable for a corresponding proportion of that freight. Thus, instead of being liable for £1,500, the defendants were only liable for £639.[13]

> **Gorrell Barnes J:** [p 328] ... though the assured may value that which he intended should be at risk upon the basis of a value which ultimately turns out to be erroneous, because of facts of which he had no knowledge at the time when he took out the policy, yet still, if the policy attaches, the amount which he has valued as that which is to be at risk is to be taken as conclusive and binding, although the amount which actually is at risk turns out to be very much less than was actually intended at the time of making the policy.
>
> I therefore hold that the plaintiffs are right in maintaining that the policy covered the freight at risk on the voyage in question, and that the valuation is binding on both parties with regard to what actually came at risk under the policy, and that amount is £5,500.
>
> The subordinate question in the case is: what amount the plaintiffs are entitled to recover? A sum of £952 3s 9d was paid in respect of freight before the ship sailed. It was paid, according to the admission of the parties, on the shipment of the goods to which the policy related and, therefore, that sum never came at risk upon the policy. The result is that the sum, out of the sum of £3,250 7s, was not at risk, and therefore the valuation of £5,500 must be reduced in proportion to the rule-of-three sum arrived at by the relationship of £952 to £3,250, as stated in the judgment of *Williams v North China Insurance Co*, and in the other cases cited. That, I understand from counsel it is agreed, would leave the sum of £3,889, as being the value of what was at risk, taking the valuation in the policy during this voyage, and as the sum of £3,250 has already been paid by other underwriters, the amount which is recoverable from the present defendants will be reduced to £639. That figure, if my view of this case is correct – and subject to the premium of £15 paid into court, and to the small addition of £4 7s 6d by way of return of a proportionate part of that premium – is the amount for which the parties are agreed judgment must be entered.

---

13 The calculation:
   Actual freight: £3,250   Advance freight: £952   Proportion = 29.3%
   Freight fixed by policy: £5,500 Proportionate advance freight (29.3% of £5,500) = £1,611
   Freight at risk as a proportion to the total amount fixed by the policy:
                              £5,500 – £1,611 = £3,889
   Sums recovered under other policies: £3,250
   Amount owed by defendant insurers   £ 639

UNVALUED POLICIES

An unvalued policy, often referred to as an 'open' policy, is defined by s 28 of the Act thus:

> An unvalued policy is a policy which does not specify the value of the subject matter insured, but, subject to the limit of the sum insured, leaves the insurable value to be subsequently ascertained, in the manner herein-before specified.

Unlike a valued policy, where the value is fixed by the policy, under an unvalued or open policy, the insurable value of the subject matter insured is only ascertainable by making reference to the relevant rules contained within s 16 of the Act. The amount arrived at is then subject to the limit set by the policy.

Insurable value

Section 16 of the Act explains the methods to be used in determining the insurable values of:

(a) ship;

(b) freight;

(c) goods or merchandise;

(d) any other subject matter.

The insurable value of ship

Section 16(1) of the Act states:

> In insurance on ship, the insurable value is the value, at the commencement of the risk, of the ship, including her outfit, provisions and stores for the officers and crew, money advanced for seamen's wages, and other disbursements (if any) incurred to make the ship fit for the voyage or adventure contemplated by the policy, plus the charges of insurance upon the whole.
>
> The insurable value, in the case of a steamship, includes also the machinery, boilers, and coals and engine stores if owned by the assured, and, in the case of a ship engaged in a special trade, the ordinary fittings requisite for that trade.

It should be noted that, when considering what constitutes a 'ship', s 16(1) should be read in conjunction with r 15 of the Rules for Construction. It should also be borne in mind that an insurance upon 'hull and machinery' is not as comprehensive a cover as that upon 'ship'. Hull and machinery does not include 'coals and engine stores'.[14]

---

14 See Chapter 3, p 85, where the relevant case of *Roddick v Indemnity Mutual Insurance Co Ltd* [1895] 2 QB 380, CA, is discussed.

It is further emphasised that s 16(1) confirms that that the 'insurable value' of a ship is based upon her value at the 'commencement of the risk'. Thus, under a voyage policy of insurance, further reference to the Rules for Construction (rr 2 and 3) must be made in order to determine when the policy actually attaches.[15]

The insurable value of freight

Section 16(2) of the Act affirms:

> In insurance on freight, whether paid in advance or otherwise, the insurable value is the gross amount of the freight at the risk of the assured, plus the charges of insurance.

That the freight insured is the 'gross' and not the net freight was established long ago, in the case of **Palmer v Blackburn (1822) 1 Bing 61**, where it was confirmed that, after the total loss of a ship, the freight for which the insurer was liable was to include 'the seamen's wages, pilotage, light dues, tonnage duty and dock dues'.

The practical sense in so adjusting a policy on freight as the 'gross' freight was summed up by Robson LJ in **Thames and Mersey Marine Insurance Co Ltd v 'Gunford' Ship Co [1911] AC 529, HL**.

> **Robson LJ:** [p 549] ... the insurance of gross instead of net freight is expressly allowed by our law, and is of great practical convenience in avoiding a troublesome, uncertain, and possibly litigious inquiry into working expenses.

The insurable value of goods and merchandise

Section 16(3) of the Act states:

> In insurance on goods and merchandise, the insurable value is the prime cost of the property insured, plus the expenses of and incidental to shipping and the charges of insurance upon the whole.

Thus, the 'insurable value' of goods or merchandise is the 'prime cost' plus the expenses of shipping those goods or merchandise as well as the cost of insurance on those goods or merchandise. But, what is meant by the words 'prime cost'? Much of the answer to that question was provided in the case of *Williams v Atlantic Assurance Co Ltd*, below.

Williams v Atlantic Assurance Co Ltd [1932] 1 KB 81, CA

Goods shipped aboard the vessel *Parthian* were insured under an open policy for a voyage from Alexandria to Liverpool; the goods were said to be worth £8,000, but there was no agreement on the value. *Parthian* and the goods in question were lost when the ship caught fire in Oran harbour, Algeria, in

---

15 See Chapter 4, p 135.

suspicious circumstances. To extinguish the fire, the port authorities sank the vessel. One of the issues before the court was what, in an unvalued policy on goods, was the 'prime cost' of those goods.

The court ruled that the 'prime cost' of the goods was the invoice or market value at or near the time of shipment or the time when the goods were first at risk. In this instance, the actual value of the goods was established as being no more than £250.

> **Scrutton LJ:** [p 90] ... 'Prime cost' would ordinarily mean the first cost of manufacturing and would, on the cardinal principle of insurance indemnity, refer to the state of the goods at or about the time of their first being at risk, the time of commencing the adventure. The underwriters would not pay on an open policy on goods for the loss of a profit or rise in the market price which was expected to be made or to occur in the future; nor would the assured recover for a loss which had already been made at the time of starting the adventure, because the market price had fallen heavily since the assured bought or manufactured the goods.
>
> [p 91] ... The United States have no statute, but that excellent writer, Mr Phillips, who I may say has probably been taken as one of the most authoritative writers on marine insurance, puts the matter thus. Section 1226 [3rd edn, 1853, Vol 2, p 39] says: 'The amount of insurable interest in goods is their market value at the time and place of the commencement of the risk. The best, though not conclusive, criterion of this interest, is the cost of the goods to the assured. This is the most satisfactory proof of the value, in case they are purchased near the time when the risk commences.' The first paragraph of s 1229 says: 'The amount of insurable interest is most frequently the invoice price. But stating a price in the invoice does not determine the amount of interest any further than as it is a proof of the actual cost.' The test is put in the Supreme Court of New York in *Le Roy v United Insurance Co* [(1811) 7 Johns 343, p 355] in this way:
>
>> The prime cost of the goods might not, in many cases, be a just rule of computation, as where they were not purchased with a view to an immediate exportation, and had remained on hand for a considerable length of time. But in matters of commerce, the plainest and simplest rules are always the best. And I should incline to think that, generally speaking, the prime cost would be the best rule by which to test the value of the subject. The prime cost is commonly the market price of the article. And as the shipment, in the usual course of business, is made soon after the purchase, the prime cost is, ordinarily, the real value of the subject.
>
> It has frequently been pointed out by great judges, and especially by Bowen LJ in *Castellain v Preston*: 'When there is a contract of indemnity no more can be recovered by the assured than the amount of his loss ... In all these difficult problems, I go back with confidence to the broad principle of indemnity. Apply that and an answer to the difficulty will always be found ... Apply the broad principle of indemnity, and you have the answer. The vendor cannot recover for greater loss than he suffers.'

Greer LJ: [p 102] ... I think the words 'prime cost' in that section mean the prime cost to the assured at or about the time of shipment, or at any rate at some time when the prime cost can be reasonably deemed to represent their value to the owner at the date of shipment ... I am disposed to think that the values as stated in the invoices should, in the absence of evidence justifying a finding of fraud, be taken to be the value at the time when Valsamis [the owner and shipper of the goods] acquired the goods towards the end of 1919, or the early part of 1920.

Slesser LJ: [p 107] ... The misrepresentation that the goods were worth £8,000, when in fact they were worth, as I find, at any rate not more than £250, is an over-valuation so gross that it is calculated to influence, and must in fact have influenced, the underwriter in taking the risk.

Notably, the only real concern raised in the *Williams* case, above, was about 'prime cost' being equated to the invoice price, the price at which the goods were purchased. The original cost or invoice price may not always represent the true value of the goods. Thus, the alternative method of establishing the 'prime cost' may be utilised, namely, the market price at or about the time of shipment or when the goods are first put at risk.

This very issue was clearly dealt with by Kerr J, in ***Berger and Light Diffusers Pty Ltd v Pollock* [1973] 2 Lloyd's Rep 442**, when injection moulds, shipped from Australia under what turned out to be an unvalued policy of insurance, were found to be water damaged on arrival in England.

Kerr J: [p 455] ... The starting point for assessing the sum, if any, which he [the plaintiff owner of the injection moulds] can recover, that is, the measure of indemnity, is to determine the insurable value of the moulds on the basis that this was an unvalued policy; see s 67(1) of the Marine Insurance Act 1906. In s 16(3), the insurable value of goods is defined as:

> ... the prime cost of the property insured, plus the expenses of and incidental to shipping and the charges of insurance upon the whole.

However, the words 'prime cost' require qualification. Where the assured is not the manufacturer and has bought the goods some time before the insured adventure commenced, their original cost may not give any reliable guidance to their value at the relevant time. Although their cost is no doubt a matter to be borne in mind, the function of the court in such cases is to assess what the true value was at the commencement of the adventure: see *Williams v Atlantic Assurance Co Ltd* [1933] 1 KB 81, in particular *per* Scrutton LJ, p 92, and Greer LJ, pp 102 and 103.

[p 455] ... I must therefore ask myself whether the plaintiff has established that these moulds had some reasonably ascertainable commercial value when they left Australia. If I am left with the clear impression on the evidence as a whole that the moulds had some commercial value, then I should not be deterred from trying to put some figure on it merely because the ascertaining of a precise value is a matter of difficulty. Courts are frequently faced with difficulty in assessing precise sums, but are not thereby deterred from reaching a conclusion. If they are left in such doubt that they find this impossible, then

the defendant must succeed, because the onus rests on the plaintiff; but subject to this, the court must simply do its best.

The same principle for determining the 'insurable value' of goods insured under an unvalued policy applies when there is a partial loss of those goods. Although, in the old case of *Usher v Noble*, below, Lord Ellenborough only took into consideration the 'invoice' price of the goods at the port of loading, it must be presumed that, following the rule laid down in *Williams v Atlantic Assurance Co Ltd*, cited above, the correct method of establishing the 'prime cost' is either the invoice price or the market value at or near the time of shipment or the time when the goods are first put at risk.

Usher v Noble (1810) 12 East 639

Some of the goods aboard the vessel *General Miranda* were lost when she stranded in the Thames close to the entrance to the West India Dock system. The goods had been insured under an unvalued policy of insurance, and the question before the court was the measure of indemnity.

The court ruled that the 'insurable value' of goods insured under an unvalued policy of insurance was the invoice price at the port of loading, plus insurance and commission. To then establish the measure of indemnity for a partial loss of those goods, the system to be used was the same as that under a valued policy. That is, the difference in value between the selling price of the undamaged goods as compared with the selling price of the damaged goods at the port of delivery, but this time expressed as a proportion of that 'insurable value' established at the port of loading.

> **Lord Ellenborough CJ:** [p 647] ... In the case of a valued policy, the valuation in the policy is the agreed standard: in case of an open policy, the invoice price at the loading port, including premiums of insurance and commission, is, for all purposes of either total or average loss, the usual standard of calculation resorted to for the purpose of ascertaining this value. The selling or market price at the port of delivery cannot be alone the standard; as that does not include premiums of insurance and commission, which must be brought into the account, in order to constitute an indemnity to an owner of goods who had increased the original amount and value of his risk by the very act of insuring. The proportion of loss is necessarily calculated through another medium, namely, by comparing the selling price of the sound commodity with the damaged part of the same commodity at the port of delivery. The difference between these two subjects of comparison affords the proportion of loss in any given case; that is, it gives the aliquot part of the original value, which may be considered as destroyed by the perils insured against, and for which the assured is entitled to be recompensed. When this is ascertained, it only remains to apply this liquidated proportion of loss to the standard by which the value is calculated, that is, to the invoice price, itself being calculated as before stated.

Floating policy on goods

A floating policy may be used when insuring goods for a voyage when the ship or ships expected to carry the goods, and other relevant particulars, are not known at the time the policy is effected. To this end, s 29(1) states:

> A floating policy is a policy which describes the insurance in general terms, and leaves the name of the ship or ships and other particulars to be defined by subsequent declaration.

A floating policy may be valued or unvalued. But, if there is no declaration of value made before the notification of a loss or arrival, the policy must be treated as being unvalued. Thus, s 29(4) affirms that:

> Unless the policy otherwise provides, where a declaration of value is not made until after notice of loss or arrival, the policy must be treated as an unvalued policy as regards the subject matter of that declaration.

However, s 29(4) is prefixed by the proviso 'unless the policy otherwise provides'. In *Union Insurance Society of Canton Ltd v George Wills and Co*, below, the policy did 'otherwise provide', with dire results for the assured.

Furthermore, the Privy Council confirmed that the latter part of s 29(3), which states that: '... an omission or erroneous declaration may be rectified even after loss or arrival, provided the omission or declaration was made in good faith' does not apply to a case in which no declaration has been made, contrary to the terms laid down in the contract of insurance.

Union Insurance Society of Canton Ltd v George Wills and Sons [1915] AC 281, PC

The respondents, George Wills and Co, were merchants with businesses in London and Australia. In February 1911, the respondents effected a floating policy of marine insurance with the appellants, covering all shipments of merchandise up to February 1912. The policy contained a clause which stated: 'Declarations of interest to be made to this society's agent at port of shipment where practicable or agent in London or Perth as soon as possible after sailing of vessel to which the interest attaches.' The respondents' goods were loaded aboard the vessel *Papanui* in the UK, but the ship and all the respondents' goods were lost near St Helena when *Papanui* caught fire. The declaration of interest regarding the insurance on the goods was only forwarded by the respondents to the insurers the day after the loss of the vessel and goods. When the respondents laid claim for an indemnity of £5,225, the insurers refused payment, on the basis that the respondents had failed to comply with what amounted to a promissory warranty.

The Privy Council ruled that the failure by the respondents to make a declaration of interest as soon as possible after the vessel sailed amounted to the breach of a promissory warranty and the insurers were not liable with respect to the loss.

Lord Parmoor: [p 287] ... In the present policy, the word 'warranty' is not used, but their Lordships are of opinion that, on the construction of the contract as a whole, the parties did intend that the promise to make a declaration as soon as possible after sailing of the vessel should be a warranty, and that, in the events that have happened, there is no liability upon the insurers. There is no difficulty in construing the terms of the promise which the assured have made, and there is no question that this promise has not been complied with. The object of the promise is to protect the interests of the insurer.

[p 289] ... In the case of *Stephens v Australasian Insurance Co* [(1872) LR 8 CP 18], it was held that, in accordance with the custom therein stated, and according to the usage of merchants and underwriters as recognised by the courts without formal proof in each case, a declaration of interest, which it is the right of the assured to make without the consent of the underwriters, may be altered even after the loss is known, if it be altered at a time when it can be, and is altered innocently and without fraud. This principle is now recognised by statute, in s 35(3) of the Commonwealth Marine Insurance Act, No 11, 1909, and in the corresponding s 29(3) of the English Act:

> Unless the policy otherwise provides, the declarations must be made in order of despatch or shipment. They must, in the case of goods, comprise all consignments within the terms of the policy, and the value of the goods or other property must be honestly stated, but an omission or erroneous declaration may be rectified even after loss or arrival, provided the omission or declaration was made in good faith.

The provision that an omission or erroneous declaration may be rectified even after loss or arrival, provided the omission or declaration has been made in good faith, does not apply to the circumstances which exist in the present appeal. It is not a case of omission or error in a declaration which may be rectified even after loss or arrival if there is good faith, but a case in which no declaration has been made within the terms of the contract. To extend the provision to a case like the present would be, in effect, to deprive the insurers of the benefits of an express warranty in such cases and to abrogate the principle that the insurers are not liable unless the warranty has been exactly complied with.

The insurable value of any other subject matter

In the event of a subject matter being insured which cannot be deemed to fall within the meaning of ss 16(1), (2) or (3), provision is made under s 16(4) for determining the insurable value of 'any other subject matter'. Section 16(4) states:

> In insurance on any other subject matter, the insurable value is the amount at the risk of the assured when the policy attached, plus the charges of insurance.

CHAPTER 6

UTMOST GOOD FAITH, DISCLOSURE AND REPRESENTATIONS

INTRODUCTION

A contract of marine insurance is *uberrimae fidei* or, as enunciated in s 17 of the Marine Insurance Act, 'a contract based upon the utmost good faith'. The notion of utmost good faith, the cardinal principle governing the marine insurance contract, is a well established doctrine derived from the celebrated case of *Carter v Boehm* (1766) 3 Burr 1905, decided long before the inception of the Act. With the codification of the law, the principle found expression in ss 17–20: in s 17 is presented the general duty to observe the utmost good faith, with the following sections introducing particular aspects of the doctrine, namely, the duty of the assured (s 18) and the broker (s 19) to disclose material circumstances, and to avoid making misrepresentations (s 20).

The obligations to disclose and to abstain from misrepresentations constitute the most significant manifestations of the duty to observe utmost good faith. Both ss 18 and 20 echo the rule that every 'material circumstance' must be disclosed to the insurer 'before the contract is concluded'. Section 17, unlike ss 18, 19 and 20, does not specify when the duty of utmost good faith is to be observed. Whilst ss 18 and 19 spell out the duty of disclosure before the formation of the contract, the Act is silent about any such duty after the conclusion of the contract. For a long time, the overwhelming concern was, whether an assured was under any duty to disclose material information after the conclusion of the contract. The nature and scope of the duty to observe utmost good faith were thus called into question; in particular, whether a continuing duty of disclosure is embraced within s 17.

Hirst J (as he then was), in *Black King Shipping Corporation v Massie, 'Litsion Pride'* [1985] 1 Lloyd's Rep 437, introduced a novel concept in the law when he extended the duty of disclosure to circumstances beyond the conclusion of the contract. *Litsion Pride* has made it patently clear that the duty of utmost good faith is not only overriding, going beyond the obligations set out in the following sections, but that it is also continuing. Hirst J also referred to the duty not to make fraudulent claims as a facet of the duty to observe utmost good faith. Recently, the approach of Hirst J found approval in a number of cases, the most notable of which is *Bank of Nova Scotia v Hellenic Mutual War Risks Association, 'Good Luck'* [1988] 1 Lloyd's Rep 514; [1989] 2 Lloyd's Rep 238; [1991] 2 Lloyd's Rep 191, HL.

The legal effect of a breach of the duty is severe: the only remedy available to the innocent party is avoidance *ab initio*, that is, avoidance from the very beginning, even though the breach may have occurred during the course of the contract. The harshness of the rule is evident, and has been described by the courts as a 'draconian remedy'. As the law of disclosure (s 18) and representation (s 20) both emanate from the doctrine of *uberrimae fidei*, it is only natural that the same remedy should apply to both.

How the 'materiality' of a circumstance is to be judged has also generated controversy in recent years. Fortunately, the matter has now, after much debate, been finally resolved by the House of Lords in *Pan Atlantic Insurance Co Ltd v Pine Top Insurance Co Ltd* [1994] 2 Lloyd's Rep 427, HL. The House also clarified the law relating to the right of avoidance and has, in upholding the 'actual inducement' test, rejected the 'decisive influence' test.

The content and nature of the duty of utmost good faith under s 17, its extent and scope, and the legal effects of its breach, the law of disclosure under s 18, and of representation under s 20, will be examined in this chapter.

UTMOST GOOD FAITH

Nature of the duty

Section 17 of the Act declares that:

> A contract of marine insurance is a contract based on utmost good faith, and if the utmost good faith be not observed by either party, the contract may be avoided by the other party.

A reciprocal duty

Section 17, by the use of the word 'either', has made it amply clear that the duty to observe utmost good faith operates on a bilateral basis. The Act reiterates the sentiments of Lord Mansfield, in *Carter v Boehm* (1766) 3 Burr 1905, where he used the example of an underwriter insuring a ship for a voyage which he privately knows has arrived. He said: [p 1909] '... Good faith forbids either party, by concealing what he privately knows, to draw the other into a bargain.'

Despite the early recognition that the duty is mutual, the underwriters, in *Banque Financière de la Cité SA v Westgate Insurance Co Ltd*,[1] below, attempted to assert that the obligation of utmost good faith need only be observed by the assured, and not the insurer. Though a non-marine insurance case, the judgment is nonetheless relevant, in that it confirms the reciprocal nature of the duty.

---

[1] For convenience, this case shall henceforth be referred to as *'Banque Financière'*. In the court of first instance, it is cited as *Banque Keyser Ullmann SA v Skandia (UK) Insurance Co Ltd and Others* [1987] 1 Lloyd's Rep 69.

Banque Financière de la Cité v Westgate Insurance Co Ltd [1987] 1 Lloyd's Rep 69; [1988] 2 Lloyd's Rep 513; [1990] 2 Lloyd's Rep 377, HL

A group of banks agreed to advance money to four companies represented by a Mr Ballestero. As security for the loans, credit insurance policies were effected and gemstones deposited with the banks. The gemstones proved to be worthless and Mr Ballestero disappeared with the bank's money. Since the policies contained a fraud exclusion clause, the banks were unable to claim on the credit insurances. However, they sought to recover on the grounds of breach of utmost good faith by the insurers in failing to disclose to the assured banks a fraud committed by a Mr Lee, an employee of the brokers.

Both the court of first instance and the Court of Appeal ruled that there was indeed a duty of utmost good faith owed by the insurers to disclose to the bank the fraud of their brokers, and found the underwriters in breach of that duty. In the House of Lords, the decision was reversed on other grounds; however, the mutuality of the duty was not challenged. Steyn J, at first instance, felt that:

> **Steyn J:** [court of first instance, p 93] ... The rationale of the rule imposing a duty of utmost good faith in the insured is that matters material to the risk are, generally, peculiarly in his knowledge. In so far as matters are peculiarly in the insurer's knowledge, as in Lord Mansfield's example of the arrived ship, principle and fairness required the imposition of a similar duty on the insurer. It is difficult to imagine a more retrograde step, subversive of the standing of our insurance law and our insurance markets, than a ruling today that the great judge erred in *Carter v Boehm* in stating that the principle of good faith rests on both parties. I unhesitatingly reject this contention.
>
> **Slade LJ:** [Court of Appeal, p 544] ... there is no doubt that the obligation to disclose material facts is a mutual one imposing reciprocal duties on insurer and insured. In case of marine insurance contracts, s 17 in effect so provides.

Notes

It has to be pointed out that the duty of utmost good faith is owed only between the assured and the insurer, that is, the original parties to the marine insurance contract. Thus, in **Bank of Nova Scotia v Hellenic Mutual War Risks Association (Bermuda) Ltd, 'Good Luck'** [1988] 1 Lloyd's Rep 514,[2] at first instance, it was held that no separate duty of utmost good faith existed between the insurers and the bank, who were the mortgagee and assignee of the policy of insurance. Hence, as the insurer did not, on the facts of the case, owe a duty of utmost good faith to the assured, it followed that no duty was owed to the assignee, since the assignee does not have any better rights than the assignor, who was, in this case, the assured.[3]

---

2 Hereinafter referred to as the *Good Luck* case; the facts of this case are discussed below, p 220.
3 See ss 15 and 50 of the Act.

Hobhouse J: [Court of first instance, pp 546–47] ... The duty of the utmost good faith is an incident of the contract of insurance. It is mutual. The assignee of the benefit of such a contract does not initially owe any duty of the utmost good faith to the insurer, nor on the basis of mutuality is there, initially, any duty owed by the insurer to the assignee. The insurer's duty is to the shipowner, and if that duty is broken as against the shipowner, the assignee can have the benefit of the rights and remedies that arise from such a breach. The rights of the assignee can only arise from obligations to the assignor.

[p 547] ... A different situation may arise where the assignee steps into the shoes of the assignor and takes over the conduct of the contract. Under those circumstances, where the assignor ceases to be the person dealing with the insurer, the duty of the utmost good faith has to be discharged by reference to the assignee. However, this was not the case here ... For the reasons already given, I consider that the mere assignment was not enough to create such a duty.

An overriding and continuing duty

It is somewhat surprising that s 17, being a long founded doctrine, has not attracted the attention of the courts until very recently. The nature and full extent of the duty to observe utmost good faith under marine insurance only received judicial scrutiny in 1985, in *Black King Shipping Corporation v Massie*, *'Litsion Pride'* [1985] 1 Lloyd's Rep 437, below.

Given that the most significant manifestations of *uberrimae fidei* are non-disclosure and misrepresentations, fulfilment of the obligation of utmost good faith was, not unreasonably, for a long time perceived in terms of the duty to disclose and not to misrepresent. However, *Litsion Pride* has clarified that the duty of disclosure stems from the duty of utmost good faith, and not vice versa. The duty of utmost good faith is an independent and an *overriding* duty, with the ensuing sections on disclosure and representations providing mere illustrations of that duty.[4] Section 17, being wider, is all-embracing, and could be described as the umbrella under which the law of non-disclosure and misrepresentation are enveloped. The case has also construed s 17 as having imposed on the parties a *continuing* duty to observe utmost good faith.

As much of the recent development of the law on utmost good faith has germinated from the *Litsion Pride* case, the judgment of Hirst J is cited *in extenso* below.

Black King Shipping Corporation v Massie, 'Litsion Pride' [1985] 1 Lloyd's Rep 437

Litsion Pride was insured under a marine insurance policy which provided that, in the event of the vessel entering a number of specified areas, in particular, ports in the Gulf area during the war, notice was to be given to the

---

[4] See *Container Transport International Inc and Reliance Group Inc v Oceanus Mutual Underwriting Association (Bermuda) Ltd* [1984] 1 Lloyd's Rep 476, CA.

underwriters 'as soon as practicable' and an additional premium was to be adjusted for the duration of the vessel's stay in that area. On 2 August, *Litsion Pride* sailed into the Persian Gulf without declaring the voyage to the underwriters or paying the additional premium, as was obligatory under the terms of the policy. On 9 August, the vessel sank, having been struck by a missile. On 11 August, a telex was sent to the brokers by the shipowners informing them that a letter regarding the imminent entry of *Litsion Pride* into the Gulf had been written, but, by oversight, not sent. The letter was dated 2 August and did not reach the underwriters until after the casualty. The mortgagees, standing in the shoes of the owners, claimed under the policy, but the insurers declined payment on the grounds of breach of the duty of utmost good faith. The policy also contained a clause entitling the insurers to give 14 days' notice of cancellation.

The court ruled in favour of the underwriters, finding on the evidence that the shipowners had sought to support their claim with fraudulent documents, such as the purportedly backdated letter of 2 August. In the view of Hirst J, there was a continuing duty of utmost good faith resting upon the assured, which continued beyond the formation of the contract.

> **Hirst J:** [p 511] ... I now state my conclusions on this very important point. In my judgment, the authorities in support of the proposition that the obligation of utmost good faith in general *continues after the execution of the insurance contract* are very powerful. First, there are the ships' papers cases, which are decisions of the highest authority, and which, in my judgment, clearly found their decision on a general duty of utmost good faith ...
>
> But, the ambit of authority goes much wider than ship's papers (see, for example, the summing up of Willes J in the case of *Britton v The Royal Insurance Co* ...)
>
> The *Style* and *Liberian* cases are also, in my judgment, instances of the same doctrine. I have no doubt whatever that both McNair J and Donaldson J intended their references to utmost good faith in those cases to mean exactly what they said, and I reject Mr Kentridge's argument [for the plaintiffs] that they are to be interpreted as connoting fraud. There was no finding of fraud in either case nor, as far as I can see, even any allegation of fraud, and the facts in both cases are fully consistent with non-fraudulent, though no doubt discreditable, non-disclosure.
>
> Moreover, if the marked difference between pre- and post-contract duty which Mr Kentridge suggests applied, it is quite remarkable that s 17, which both parties accept covers both the pre- and post-contract duty, makes no differentiation between these two stages.
>
> [p 512] ... I consider that it is the better view in accordance with commercial good sense that the insured is required to notify any *relevant* information available from time to time, particularly since – as the evidence shows – this is a field where, during the course of a voyage, ETAs, destinations, etc, are quite likely to change as it proceeds. [Emphasis added.]

... it seems to me manifest that, as part of the duty of utmost good faith, it must be incumbent on the insured to include within it all *relevant* information available to him at the time he gives it; and in any event the self-same duty required the assured to furnish to the insurer any further *material* information which he acquires subsequent to the initial notice as and when it comes to his knowledge, particularly if it is materially at variance with the information he originally gave. [Emphasis added.]

So far as claims are concerned, I consider that the general principle requiring utmost good faith must apply also.

[p 515] In my judgment, 'avoidance' in s 17 means avoidance *ab initio*. Certainly this is the case in relation to pre-contract avoidance ... and I see no reason for putting a different meaning on the word in relation to post-contractual events.

[p 518] ... I am prepared to hold that the duty not to make fraudulent claims and not to make claims in breach of the duty of utmost good faith is an implied term of the policy ...

Notes

As can be seen from the above comments delivered by Hirst J, the duty to observe utmost good faith under s 17 is indeed comprehensive and powerful:

(a) first, the judge elaborated on the nature of the duty, namely, that s 17 is *overriding* and imposes a *continuing* duty on *both* parties to observe utmost good faith;

(b) secondly, the extent and scope of the duty is all-embracing, capable of covering a wide range of subjects, including a continuing duty of disclosure and a duty not to make fraudulent claims. Under the duty to observe utmost good faith, relevant information may have to be disclosed at the following points in time: at the time of the renewal of the policy; when considering cover for reinsurance; when a vessel intends to enter an additional premium area under a trading warranty; when tendering a change of voyage endorsement, and when required by a held covered clause and, possibly, a cancellation clause;

(c) thirdly, the matter of whether conduct which is less than fraudulent is covered by s 17 was also discussed. In this regard, the pointed question is, whether s 17 envisages inadvertent and innocent non-disclosure of relevant information. The question may also be framed as: whether conduct which is innocent, negligent, culpable and discreditable, but not sufficiently serious as to amount to fraud, will cause a breach of s 17;

(d) finally, the effects of a breach of s 17 on the particular claim and/or on the contract (policy) as a whole were also considered under the rule of avoidance. The right of an aggrieved party to sue for damages for a breach of s 17 is another relevant issue.

As each of these aspects of the duty of utmost good faith has been picked up in subsequent cases, it is necessary to examine them in depth.

An overriding duty

The principle that s 17 is an overriding duty was actually formulated a year before *Litsion Pride* by the Court of Appeal in *Container Transport International Inc and Reliance Group Inc v Oceanus Mutual Underwriting Association (Bermuda) Ltd* [1984] 1 Lloyd's Rep 476, CA.[5] Although the decision of the *CTI* case was much criticised, and finally overruled on the important points of materiality and inducement[6] by *Pan Atlantic Insurance Company Ltd v Pine Top Insurance Company Ltd* [1994] 2 Lloyd's Rep 427, HL, the comments made by the judges are, nevertheless, still of vital significance, in that they declare the independent nature of the duty of utmost good faith. As will be seen, all the judges in the *CTI* case were in agreement that there is an independent duty of utmost good faith.

Container Transport International Inc and Reliance Group Inc v Oceanus Mutual Underwriting Association (Bermuda) Ltd [1982] 2 Lloyd's Rep 178; [1984] 1 Lloyd's Rep 476, CA

CTI, a container leasing company, took out insurance with Crum and Forster covering a 'Damage Protection Plan' in respect of their containers. Crum and Forster were unhappy with the terms of the policy, and refused to renew the policy after its expiration. Seeking fresh cover, CTI approached CE Heath and Co and managed to obtain 100% cover, the majority of which was with syndicates at Lloyd's; however, the Lloyd's experience was no better, as they also refused to renew. Finally, the insurance was placed with Oceanus. When CTI put forward their claims for losses they had incurred, Oceanus refused to pay, and sought to avoid the policy, contending that CTI had presented an inaccurate claims record and that they had failed to disclose the refusal by previous underwriters to renew.

The Court of Appeal held that as there was both non-disclosure and misrepresentation, the underwriter was entitled to avoid the policy. Each of the judges took time to embellish the scope of s 17.

Kerr LJ: [p 492] ... The duty of disclosure, as defined or circumscribed by ss 18 and 19, is one aspect of the *overriding* duty of the utmost good faith mentioned in s 17.

Parker LJ: [p 512] ... Finally, it is necessary to mention at this stage that the duty imposed by s 17 goes, in my judgment, further than merely to require fulfilment of the duties under the succeeding sections. If, for example, the insurer shows interest in circumstances which are not material within s 18, s 17 requires the assured to disclose them fully and fairly. Again, if the assured or his broker

---

5 Hereinafter referred to simply as '*CTI*'.
6 These issues are discussed below, p 257.

realised, in the course of negotiations, that the insurer had made a serious arithmetical mistake or was proceeding upon a mistake of fact with regard to past experience he would, under s 17, be obliged to draw attention to the matter. It would ... be the plainest breach of the duty under s 17 not to do so.

Stephenson LJ: [p 525] ... I also conclude that the special sections which follow s 17 must be read in the light of this leading section, and all their references to insurer and assured follow the imposition of the statutory duty of utmost good faith on each party.

A continuing duty

In the *Litsion Pride* case, Hirst J relied heavily on the earlier authorities of *Overseas Commodities Ltd v Style* [1958] 1 Lloyd's Rep 546, and *Liberian Insurance Agency v Mosse* [1977] 2 Lloyd's Rep 560, to support his proposition of a continuing duty to observe utmost good faith. Both these cases were concerned with the application of 'held covered' clause protection, under which cover was to be obtained only if the assured acted with the utmost good faith 'throughout the currency of the policy', as emphasised by McNair J [p 559] in *Overseas Commodities Ltd v Style*.[7]

The issue of a continuing duty of utmost good faith was also considered in the *Good Luck* case, below, by Hobhouse J in the court of first instance and May LJ in the Court of Appeal, but escaped the attention of the House of Lords.

Bank of Nova Scotia v Hellenic Mutual War Risks Association, 'Good Luck' [1988] 1 Lloyd's Rep 514; [1989] 2 Lloyd's Rep 238; [1991] 2 Lloyd's Rep 191, HL

Good Luck was insured against war risks with the defendants' club. Under the cover, it was provided, *inter alia*, that should the vessel enter an additional premium area (APA), prompt notice was to be given to the club. If no notice was given, the club would be entitled to reject any and all claims arising out of events occurring while the vessel was in an APA. The assured shipowners mortgaged *Good Luck* and assigned the policy to the mortgagee bank. The club were given notification of the assignment, and in a letter of undertaking they agreed to inform the bank if the insurance ceased. *Good Luck* entered into a charterparty to trade in the Gulf, an APA, but neither the bank nor the club was informed. Furthermore, when the club eventually became aware of the trading pattern of *Good Luck*, they took no steps to inform the bank. At the time, the shipowners were renegotiating their loans with the bank, the bank knew that *Good Luck* was trading in the Gulf, but had assumed that the shipowners were paying the additional premium, and on this basis they advanced more money. *Good Luck* was struck by a missile and became a constructive total loss. The club rejected the claim, because no notification had been given to them according to the terms of the cover. Subsequently, the

---

7   [1958] 1 Lloyd's Rep 546. For a further discussion on the held covered clause, see Chapter 4, pp 161 and 179.

bank, as assignee, sued the club, claiming, *inter alia,* breach of utmost good faith, because the club failed to disclose to them what they knew at any material time.

The court ruled that the club (the insurer) did not owe the bank a duty of utmost good faith. The letter of undertaking was not a contract of utmost good faith, it was an obligation. The only duty owed by the club was to the assured; there being no separate duty owed to the bank as assignee to the policy. As to the continuing duty of utmost good faith, the comments made by Hobhouse J were supported by May LJ in the Court of Appeal.

> **Hobhouse J:** [court of first instance, pp 545–46] ... Contracts of insurance are contracts of the utmost good faith. The obligation of the utmost good faith is one which arises normally in relation to the making of the contract. This is because that is the situation in which the duty is most usually relevant. But, as stated by Hirst J in the *Litsion Pride* case, the duty exists throughout the contract.
>
> **May LJ:** [Court of Appeal, p 263] ... We do not think it is necessary to question the decision of Hirst J in the *Litsion Pride* case so far as concerns his decision that the obligation of utmost good faith could continue after the contract was made with reference to such a matter as the fixing of the rate of additional premiums.

More recently, in the Court of Appeal, in ***Orakpo v Barclays Insurance Services and Another* [1995] 1 Lloyd's Rep 443, CA,** the same principle was affirmed by Hoffman LJ, who said that: [p 452] 'In principle, insurance is a contract of good faith. I do not see why the duty of good faith on the part of the assured should expire when the contract has been made.'

Scope of the duty to observe utmost good faith

Having determined that the duty to observe utmost good faith is a continuing one, the question is now left open as to the content and extent of that duty.

As was seen, Hirst J, in the *Litsion Pride* case, drew out two main limbs of the duty, namely, the duty to disclose relevant information, and the duty not to make fraudulent claims. Though the categories (and examples) set out are by no means exhaustive, they may be safely regarded as the fountain heads from which most, if not all, of the problems relating to the duty are likely to spring. The scope of the duty to observe utmost good faith is not only ongoing, but also extensive, capable of covering a wide range of events and situations. Thus, it would be a futile exercise to speculate the circumstances which may constitute a breach of that duty. The duty is 'moulded to the moment'[8] and, therefore, whether utmost good faith has or has not been observed is, in each case, a question of fact.

---

8 See *Star Sea* [1995] 1 Lloyd's Rep 659, p 667; [1997] 1 Lloyd's Rep 360, CA, discussed below, p 226.

As the duty to observe utmost good faith is mutual, so must be the duty of disclosure which is derived therefrom: this means that both the assured and the insurer are required, under s 17, to disclose relevant information which is expected of them for compliance with the duty to observe utmost good faith. Thus, in so far as the assured is concerned, it would appear that there is a degree of overlapping of the duty imposed upon him by s 18, to disclose material circumstances 'before the conclusion of the contract', and the duty of the disclosure expected of him by s 17. Under s 17, however, the assured's duty extends far beyond the formation of the contract; hence, that duty is often referred to as the assured's 'post-contractual duty of disclosure'.

In so far as the insurer is concerned, it is noted that, though s 18 does not impose a duty of disclosure upon him, his duty of disclosure is, as the case of *Banque Financière* has demonstrated, derived from s 17.[9]

In summary, the assured's duty of disclosure is governed by both ss 17 and 18, whilst that of the insurer is dedicated only by s 17, the duty to observe utmost good faith. For convenience, the insurer's duty of disclosure under s 17 will be first discussed, to be followed by a study of the assured's post-contractual duty of disclosure. The assured's pre-contractual duty of disclosure under s 18 is separately discussed later.[10]

Reciprocal duty of disclosure under s 17

Scope of the insurer's duty of disclosure

The extent of the insurer's *pre-contractual* duty of disclosure came under scrutiny for the first time in ***Banque Financière* [1988] 1 Lloyd's Rep 513, CA; [1998] 2 Lloyd's Rep 513, HL** (the facts of which were cited in full earlier),[11] where the issue was whether the insurer owed the bank a duty to disclose to them the fact that their (the bank's) agent, a Mr Lee, was dishonest. The scope of the insurer's duty was analysed by both Slade LJ, delivering the judgment of the entire Court of Appeal, and the members of the House of Lords.

> **Slade LJ:** [Court of Appeal, p 544] ... the principal debate in this court has concerned the proper test of materiality when the court is considering the duty of disclosure falling upon the insurer as opposed to the insured. Not surprisingly, counsel have been able to cite very little authority giving direct guidance on this point. The process of adapting the well established principles relating to the duty of the insured to the obverse case of the insurer is not wholly easy.
>
> [p 545] ... In our judgment, the duty falling upon the insurer must at least extend to disclosing all facts known to him which are material either to the nature of the risk sought to be covered or the recoverability of a claim under

---

9   See above, p 215.
10 The scope of the duty of disclosure under s 18 is discussed below, p 246.
11 See above, p 215.

the policy which a prudent insured would take into account in deciding whether or not to place the risk for which he seeks cover with that insurer ...

Lord Bridge: [House of Lords, p 380] ... in my opinion, that Mr Dungate's failure to disclose to the banks the dishonesty of their agent, whatever may be said about it as a matter of business ethics, did not amount to the breach of any legal duty.

Lord Templeman: [p 383] ... It would be strange if, in these circumstances, one party to a contract owed a duty in negligence to the other, to warn the other party of his suspicions of former misconduct by the agent of that other party ...

[p 384] ... No authority was cited for the proposition that a negotiating party owes a duty to disclose to the opposite party information that the agent of the opposite party had committed a breach of the duty he owed to his principal in an earlier transaction.

Lord Jauncey: [p 389] ... What is said in this appeal is that when Dungate [representing the insurers] discovered in early June 1980 that Lee had issued fraudulent covers notes in January of that year he, as insurer, came under a duty to disclose this fact to the banks. I do not consider that the obligation of disclosure extends to such a matter.

... In the present case, the risk to be insured was the inability, otherwise than by reason of fraud, of Ballestero and his companies to repay the loan to the bank. Lee's dishonesty neither increased nor decreased that risk. Indeed, it was irrelevant thereto. It follows that the obligation of disclosure incumbent upon Dungate, as the insurer, did not extend to telling the banks that their agent, Lee, was dishonest ... it is clear that the scope of any such duty would not extend to the disclosure of facts which are not material to the risk insured.

Notes

The above case refers to the insurer's pre-contractual duty of disclosure. For an illustration of his post-contractual duty of disclosure, reference may be made to the *Good Luck* case, discussed below, where the plaintiff (bank) was not the original assured, but the assignee of a policy.[12]

Scope of the assured's post-contractual duty of disclosure

Given that s 17 is placed under the heading of 'Disclosure and Representations', one might be tempted to argue along the lines that, since the ensuing sections are applicable *'before the contract is concluded'*, s 17 must likewise be applicable only in a pre-contract situation. Indeed, there was some suggestion that there was no duty of disclosure owed beyond the formation of the contract.[13] But, according to Hirst J in the *Litsion Pride* case, an assured is

---

12 See above, p 220.
13 See, eg, *Cory v Patton* (1874) LR 9 QB 577; *Lishman v Northern Maritime Insurance Co* (1875) LR 10 CP 179, HL; and *Niger Co Ltd v Guardian Assurance Co and Yorkshire Insurance Co* (1922) 13 LlL Rep 75, HL, all of which are discussed below, p 253.

undoubtedly under a continuing duty to disclose relevant information even after the conclusion of the contract. However, it has to be stressed that this duty does not fall under the scope of the duty of disclosure as perceived in the pre-contractual stage covered by s 18, which is not in question here.

Apart from s 18, there is an overriding duty under s 17, that of *uberrimae fidei*, which embraces also the duty of disclosure of relevant information which comes to the knowledge of the parties, in particular, the assured, *after* the conclusion of the contract.[14] Though the wording of s 17 does not explicitly provide for a continuing duty of disclosure, its wording is also not explicit enough to rule out the conception either. Whilst s 18 is clear as to the application of the duty of disclosure 'before the contract is concluded', s 17 imposes no such time constraints. This should not seem bizarre, as s 17 imposes a much broader duty, of a general nature: the view adopted both in the *Litsion Pride* case and the *CTI* case.

As s 17 was construed as having established an all-prevailing principle, rather than one of restricted application, the duty of post-contractual disclosure which emanates therefrom must also be given the same leeway. After all, the *rationale* for the duty of disclosure, according to Lord Mansfield in *Carter v Boehm* **(1766) 3 Burr 1905**: [p 1911] '... is to prevent fraud, and to encourage good faith. It is adapted to such facts as vary the nature of the contract; which one privately knows, and the other is ignorant of, and has no reason to suspect.'

Later, in *Leon v Casey* **[1932] 2 KB 576, CA**, the same principle was reiterated by the Court of Appeal:

Scrutton LJ: [p 579] ... insurance has always been regarded as a transaction requiring the utmost good faith between the parties in which the assured is bound to communicate to the insurer every material fact within his knowledge not only at the inception of the risk, but at every subsequent state while it continues, up to and including the time when he makes his claim ...

In *Good Luck* **[1988] 1 Lloyd's Rep 514**, Hobhouse J, in the court of first instance, drew our attention to the fact that the ground covered by the pre- and post-contractual duty of disclosure are distinct and separate.

Hobhouse J: [pp 545–46] ... But, as stated by Hirst J in the *Litsion Pride* case, the duty exists throughout the contract. The defendants [the club] before me sought to argue on the basis of cases such as *Niger Co Ltd v Guardian Assurance Co* (1922) 13 LlL Rep 75, and the inclusion of the phrase 'before the contract is concluded' in s 18 of the Act, that there was no duty of disclosure after the contract was concluded. I consider that this argument is a confusion. There is no duty to disclose matters *relevant to the making of the contract* once the contract has been made; the time has then passed within which they must be disclosed. The later disclosure of later discovered facts would serve no useful purpose

---

14 See below, p 226.

Utmost Good Faith, Disclosure and Representations

and, therefore, is not required. By contrast, there can be situations which arise subsequently where the duty of utmost good faith makes it necessary that there should be further disclosure, because the relevant facts are relevant to the later stages of the contract. The *Litsion Pride* case illustrates such a situation in relation to the making and prosecution of a claim.

Interestingly enough, in the recent case of **New Hampshire Insurance Co v MGN Ltd [1997] LRLR 24, CA,** Staughton LJ expressed scepticism over the value of this post-contractual duty of disclosure. His reservation warned of the fact that the assured's post-contractual duty of disclosure, embodied within the good faith principle under s 17, is, when compared with the pre-contractual duty of disclosure under s 18, somewhat limited in scope.

> **Staughton LJ:** [p 58] ... The question whether there is a continuing duty of disclosure in any other circumstances is of considerable importance. We are surprised that, in recent times, it has only been considered in one decision at first instance: *Black King Shipping Corporation v Massie, 'Litsion Pride'* [1985] 1 Lloyd's Rep 437. However, the surprise is tempered when one realises that, in the ordinary way, disclosure would be of little or no benefit to the insurer during the currency of a policy. Unless it happens before the contract is made, or before renewal, or (perhaps) before a claim is paid, disclosure could only fill the insurer with foreboding that he has made a bad bargain, as a loss was likely to occur; he would have no right to cancel the contract of insurance on that account, although we suppose that he might be able to obtain reinsurance.

Disclosure of 'relevant' and 'material' information

Unlike s 18, there is no reference to 'materiality' in s 17; consequently, the assured might well be left in doubt as to the kind of information he is obliged to disclose under s 17. The key words in Hirst J's judgment in **Litsion Pride [1985] 1 Lloyd's Rep 437** are *'relevant'* and *'material'*. He did not, aside from citing illustrations, explain what is meant by 'relevant' information. However, he accepted counsel's argument that: [p 511] '... by analogy with s 18(2) of the Act, that a circumstance is material, if it would influence the judgment of a prudent underwriter in making the relevant decision on the topic to which the misrepresentation or non-disclosure relates.' Thus, the law of 'materiality' for pre-contractual disclosure, as laid down in s 18(2), should (it would appear) also be applied to post-contractual disclosure under s 17. Terms such as 'relevant' and 'material' are incapable of exact definition, for what may be relevant or material in one case may not be so in another. It is a flexible concept which has to be judged in accordance with 'commercial good sense', as Hirst J [p 512] has put it.

In the recent reinsurance case of *Société Anonyme d'Intermédiaires Luxembourgeois v Farex Cie* **[1995] LRLR 116, CA,** the facts of which are complex and need not be set out here, Hoffmann LJ observed that: [p 149] '... s 17 seems to be adequate to deal with cases of genuine bad faith without the need to extend the meaning of "material circumstances" beyond matters relevant to the actual contract of insurance.' This statement seems to suggest that we need not bog ourselves down with rules of materiality, and that the guiding star is the wider good, old-fashioned principle of utmost good faith.

Appropriate to the moment or specific decision points

It is one thing to say that there is a *continuing* duty of disclosure of relevant information and another to say *when* it should arise and end. For a clear exposition of the rule as to when it would arise, reference should be made to ***Manifest Shipping and Co Ltd v Uni-Polaris Insurance Co Ltd and La Réunion Européenne, 'Star Sea'* [1995] 1 Lloyd's Rep 651; [1997] 1 Lloyd's Rep 360, CA**, the facts of which need not concern us here and will be cited later.[15] In the Court of Appeal, Leggatt LJ gave his approval to a passage, which he has described as having correctly stated the law, from *Clarke on the Law of Insurance Contracts*, 2nd edn, 1994, London: LLP, p 708 which reads as follows:

> [p 372] ... As regards insurance contracts, the duty of good faith continues throughout the contractual relationship at a level *appropriate to the moment*. In particular, the duty of disclosure, most prominent prior to contract, revives whenever the insured has an express or implied duty to supply information *to enable the insurer to make a decision*. Hence, it applies if cover is extended or renewed. It also applies when the insured claims insurance money; he must make 'full disclosure of the circumstances of the case' ... the degree of disclosure, however, varies according to the phase in the relationship. It seems that the level of disclosure appropriate to a claim is different from that at the time of contract ... [Emphasis added.]

In so far as the time factor is concerned, the key phrase is 'appropriate to the moment'. Another writer, Schoenbaum, has most aptly described it as a duty which will arise at 'specific decision points'.[16] Similarly, Tuckey J, in the court of first instance in *Star Sea* [1995] 1 Lloyd's Rep 651, p 667, referred to it as a continuing duty which is 'moulded to the moment', and Hobhouse J, in *Good Luck* [1988] 1 Lloyd's Rep 514, observed that [p 545] '... there can be situations which arise subsequently where the duty of utmost good faith makes it necessary that there should be further disclosure because the relevant facts are relevant to the later stages of the contract'.

What is clear from the above is that the duty is a continuing one and, therefore, can arise at any time during the currency of the policy. But whether

---

15 See below, p 235.
16 Schoenbaum, T, 'The duty of utmost good faith in marine insurance law: a comparative analysis of American and English law' (1998) 29 J Maritime Law and Commerce 1, p 32.

it has a life after the expiration of the policy, and for how long thereafter, is another matter altogether which needs to be discussed.[17]

To enable the insurer to make a decision

In terms of content – as to the nature of the information which needs to be disclosed – the criterion can be found in the key phrase 'to enable the insurer to make a decision'. Information relating to extension and renewal of a policy, as pointed out by Clarke, will naturally have an effect on any evaluation to be made regarding the cover. In *Litsion Pride* **[1985] 1 Lloyd's Rep 437**, Hirst J referred to various types of information which would appropriately trigger 'the moment' contemplated by Clarke.

> **Hirst J:** [p 511] ... it seems to me that there is a very close analogy with the position which arose in the *Style* and *Liberian* cases, where the duty was held to apply. The information is material because it is required to enable the underwriter to make a decision as to the rate of AP, as to facultative reinsurance, and ... possibly even as to cancellation under the 14 day notice clause.

Later, in *Banque Financière* **[1990] 2 Lloyd's Rep 377, HL**,[18] an attempt, so it would appear, was made by Lord Jauncey to restrict the scope of the continuing duty of disclosure under s 17, as envisaged by Hirst J in *Litsion Pride* [1985] 1 Lloyd's Rep 437, to the following events:

> **Lord Jauncey:** [p 389] ...There is, in general, no obligation to disclose supervening facts which come to the knowledge of either party after conclusion of the contract ... subject always to such exceptional cases as a ship entering a war zone or an insured failing to disclose all facts relevant to a claim.

In *Star Sea* **[1997] 1 Lloyd's Rep 360, CA**, Leggatt LJ, in the Court of Appeal, summarised the 'decision' test as thus:

> **Leggatt LJ:** [p 370] ... there is force in the argument that the scope of the duty of utmost good faith will alter according to whether underwriters have to make a decision under the policy or the assured decides to make a claim, and may also be affected according to the stage of the relationship at which the scope of the duty becomes material. There is no difference in principle as to the extent of disclosure required between entering into a policy and the renewal of it; in both cases, the scope of the duty of disclosure should be the same.

In the recent case of *Fraser Shipping Ltd v Colton and Others* **[1997] 1 Lloyd's Rep 586**, the full facts of which were cited earlier,[19] the issue of non-disclosure

---

17 See below, p 246.
18 The facts of this case are discussed above, p 215; in the court of first instance, the case was named as *Banque Keyser Ullmann v Skandia* [1987] 1 Lloyd's Rep 69.
19 This case is also discussed, in the context of the law relating to change of voyage and the held covered clause, in Chapter 4, p 154.

of relevant information relating to circumstances surrounding a change of voyage (or the change of destination of an insured voyage) was discussed. On this occasion, when the assured submitted their change of voyage endorsement, they had failed to disclose to their insurers material information, of which they (the assured) were in possession, concerning the hazardous conditions which the insured vessel was likely to encounter at the anchorage of the new destination of Huang Pu to which the vessel was subsequently sent. Potter LJ ruled, *inter alia*, that, in the circumstances of the case, there was a non-disclosure of material facts.

Potter LJ: [p 594] ... (3) *Was the change of voyage endorsement of 25 June 1993 vitiated by non-disclosure of material circumstances?*

Materiality

The duty to disclose the circumstances material to the risk existed at the time the variation was concluded, that is, at the time the endorsement recording the agreement to the change of destination was recorded by the underwriters' scratches ...

A material circumstance within the meaning of s 18 of the MIA is one that, objectively assessed, would have an effect on the mind of a prudent insurer in estimating the risk proposed, without necessarily having a decisive influence on either his acceptance of that risk or the amount of premium demanded ... Section 18(5) of the MIA provides that a 'circumstance' includes any communication made to or information received by the insured. That provision seems to me apt to apply to the content of information and communications received by and from the master of the tug and tow concerning the anchoring of the vessel, the weather and its possible impact on the tug and tow, and the master's views on the future safety of the voyage as varied.

[p 595] ... so far as the defendant underwriters were concerned, until the morning of 25 June 1993, the tug and tow the subject of the insurance were proceeding uneventfully to Shanghai. However, by 25 June, it was apparent to the master and the owners that the change of voyage to Huang Pu involved the vessel having to reduce its draught before it could proceed to its point of delivery, and that meanwhile it was obliged to wait at a hazardous outer anchorage under increasing threats from a typhoon, the precise path of which was unknown but which might well (as, in the event, it did) descend upon Huang Pu. The mounting concern of the master in the face of the difficulties which faced him is made clear by a series of telexes which it is not necessary to detail.

It seems to me that, so enumerated, the materiality of those facts to a prudent insurer speaks for itself, without need for the benefit of independent expert evidence ...

Inducement

[p 596] ... On the question of inducement ... I consider they [the insurers] have discharged the burden of showing that they were induced to agree to the endorsement of the policy on 25 June 1993 by reason of the non-disclosure of

the circumstances set out above. Mr Colton [one of the insurers] was clear that he would not have signed the endorsement as it stood.

[p 597] ... that, if he [Mr Townsend, one of the insurers] had known of the relevant communications concerning the congestion at the anchorage, the bad weather, the tug master's opinion, the various delays, and the fact that there had already been a collision, he would not have agreed to sign the endorsement.

I have no hesitation in holding that, because of the non-disclosure of the circumstances of which the underwriters complain, each of the underwriters was induced to scratch the endorsement on 25 June 1993 on the terms as presented and that the underwriters were entitled to avoid the policy, as varied by that endorsement, on the grounds of non-disclosure.

It is interesting to note that Potter LJ had, throughout his judgment, applied s 18 to the issue at hand, even though the question was, in fact, strictly one of post-contractual non-disclosure falling within the scope of the duty to observe utmost good faith under s 17, rather than pre-contractual non-disclosure under s 18. In this case, the failure to disclose the relevant information can only arise after the conclusion of the contract, as it relates to information pertaining to a change of voyage (and the held covered clause) which by its very nature can only occur after the attachment of the risk.[20] Though not said in so many words, the judge was actually applying the rules on 'materiality' applicable in the case of pre-contractual non-disclosure to what was effectively a breach of the duty to disclosure under s 17.

Notes

Indeed, the range of information to be disclosed after the conclusion of the contract is rather extensive. Naturally, anxiety on the part of the assured is inevitable: uncertain as to the exact extent of his obligation, he may yet be faced with the threat of avoidance in the event of a breach of this duty. Though the duty may be perceived as awesome and menacing, English case law has, however, posited three main 'specific decision points' where the post-contractual duty of disclosure under s 17 will arise:

(a) when the policy is due for enlargement, extension or renewal;

(b) where disclosure is required either expressly or impliedly under a term in the policy, for example, a warranty, a held covered clause and a change of voyage endorsement; and

(c) when the assured is required to inform the insurer that he intends to enter an additional premium area.

Though the list is open-ended, allowing each case to be decided on its own facts, it should nevertheless be borne in mind that the limitation which the

---

20 This issue is discussed in depth in Chapter 4, p 161.

recent cases of *New Hampshire Insurance Co v MGN Ltd* [1997] LRLR 24, CA, below, relating to the right of the insurer under a cancellation clause, and *NSW Medical Defence Union Ltd v Transport Industries Insurance Co Ltd* [1985] 4 NSWL 107, relating to both cancellation and reinsurance (cited with approval by Staughton LJ in the former case), have placed on the scope of this continuing duty of disclosure.

Disclosure and the right to cancel

In the *Litsion Pride* case, Hirst J's comment to the effect that the post-contractual duty of disclosure could apply '... possibly even as to cancellation under the 14 day notice clause' was later capitalised on by counsel acting for the insurer in the *New Hampshire* case, below. Although the policy in question was non-marine, nevertheless, the judicial comments offered are pertinent as they referred to the ruling of the *Litsion Pride* case.

New Hampshire Insurance Co v MGN Ltd [1997] LRLR 24, CA

MGN Ltd effected four 'fidelity' insurance policies underwritten by the New Hampshire Insurance Company to cover losses brought about by the dishonest or fraudulent acts of their employees. Following the death of Robert Maxwell, various companies in the Maxwell Group claimed under the policies in respect of losses incurred by those companies as a result of the dishonest and fraudulent acts of Robert Maxwell himself and his associates. The insurers denied liability on the basis, *inter alia*, that they, the insurers, could avoid the policies because the assureds were in breach of their duty of utmost good faith, in that there had been a continuing duty of disclosure imposed upon the assureds during the currency of the policies which had not been fulfilled.

Counsel for the insurers further argued, *inter alia*, that where there was a continuing cover (not limited in duration) subject to the right of the insurer to cancel on notice, that right could only be valuable and properly exercised if the insurer had full knowledge of the facts relevant to whether he should exercise it or allow the contract to continue.

The Court of Appeal, affirming the decision of Potter J, held that there was no continuing duty of disclosure during the currency of the insurance merely by reason of the insurers' right to cancel. The legal position on this point was best summarised by Potter J; his perception of the ruling of Hirst J in the *Litsion Pride* case was expressed with commendable clarity.

> **Potter J:** [court of first instance, p 48] ... I do not think that Hirst J intended to state that the right of an insurer to terminate on notice would or could *per se* create an obligation of continuing disclosure upon the insured in respect of anything which might render the risk insured more hazardous or onerous since inception.
>
> It seems to me that the continuing obligation of good faith which was accepted to exist in the *Litsion Pride* case was held to arise in connection with the

obligation to supply information in respect of an event which, under the terms of the policy, entitled the insurer to re-assess the risk and fix an AP. The reference by Hirst J to cancellation was made to emphasise the options which were open to the insurer as part of his right to reassess the risk or the happening of the event specified by the policy. It was not made in order to suggest any free standing right in an insurer to re-assess the risk (and thereby create some obligation of further disclosure by the assured) simply for the purposes of deciding whether or not to exercise his right of termination on notice.

Thus, while I accept that the obligation of good faith as between insurer and insured is one which continues throughout the policy, in particular, in relation to the making of claims, it does not, in my view, apply so as to trigger positive obligations of disclosure of matters affecting the risk during the currency of the cover except in relation to some requirement, event or situation provided for in the policy to which the duty of good faith attaches. I do not consider that a simple right of termination on notice constitutes such event or situation.

Staughton LJ: [Court of Appeal, p 60] ... the *Litsion Pride* case was concerned with an express obligation in the policy to supply information if trading in an excluded zone.

[p 61] ... Whilst there are no doubt cases where a defence of non-disclosure is fully justified, there are also, in our experience, some where it is not. We should hesitate to enlarge the scope for oppression [by the underwriter against the assured] by establishing a duty to disclose throughout the period of a contract of insurance, merely because it contains (as is by no means uncommon) a right of cancellation for the insurer.

Notes

It can be seen from the above that the remarks made by Hirst J in the *Litsion Pride* case, in reference to the duty of disclosure vis à vis the right of cancellation, have to be read in their proper context. In the light of the *New Hampshire* case, it is fair to say that an insurer has no right to expect disclosure by the assured of any information which he (the insurer) may consider necessary or relevant to assist him in arriving at a determination of whether or not to exercise the right to cancel. With regard to the matter of reinsurance, it would appear, from the Australian case of **NSW Medical Defence Union Ltd v Transport Industries Insurance Co Ltd [1985] 4 NSWL 107**, that the same principle applies: Rogers J was quick to point out that one should not neglect to note that: [p 112] '... in the *Litsion Pride* case, the duty to act in good faith [was] fastened on to an obligation contained in the policy requiring the insured to supply information.'

Duty not to make fraudulent claims

The duty not to make fraudulent claims – encompassed within the duty to observe utmost good faith referred to by Hirst J in the *Litsion Pride* case – is not a new-fangled idea. As early as 1858, Pollock CB, in **Goulstone v Royal**

Insurance Company (1858) 1 F&F 276, p 279, described a fraudulent claim as one which is 'wilfully false in any substantial respect'. In this case, the assured's property was destroyed by fire. The assured submitted his claim to be more than £200, whereas, in earlier insolvency proceedings, the same property was declared to be of the value of £50. The court ruled in favour of the underwriter based on a finding on the facts that there was a fraudulent claim. Later, in *Britton v Royal Insurance Company* (1866) 4 F&F 905, below, the same subject was broached in relation to a fire insurance policy upon which a fraudulent claim was presented by the assured.

Britton v Royal Insurance Company (1866) 4 F&F 905

The case concerned a fire insurance policy upon household furniture, trade fixtures and stock-in-trade. When the assured's property was destroyed by fire, the insurer declined payment, alleging both arson and fraud, in that the assured had set fire to his house, and had presented a claim which was greater than it actually was.

The court ruled in favour of the insurer, as there was a finding on the facts that the assured had made a fraudulent claim.

> **Willes J:** [p 909] ... The law is, that a person who has made such a fraudulent claim could not be permitted to recover at all. The contract of insurance is one of perfect good faith on both sides, and it is most important that such good faith should be maintained ... It would be most dangerous to permit parties to practise such frauds, and then, notwithstanding their falsehood and fraud, to recover the real value of the goods consumed. And, if there is wilful falsehood and fraud in the claim, the insured forfeits all claim whatever upon the policy.

The above comments, uttered by Willes J, were approved by Hirst J in *Litsion Pride* [1985] 1 Lloyd's Rep 437, the facts of which have already been cited.[21]

> **Hirst J:** [p 512] ... So far as claims are concerned, I consider that the general principle requiring utmost good faith must apply also. That was certainly the view of Willes J in his summing up in the case of *Britton v Royal Insurance* ...
>
> Moreover, in the leading, and now authoritative textbook, *The Law Relating to Fire Insurance,* by Baker Welford and Otter-Barry, 4th edn, 1948, the paragraph under the heading of 'Fraudulent Claims' on p 289 starts:
>
> > Since it is the duty of the assured to observe the utmost good faith in his dealing with the insurers throughout, the claim which he puts forward must be honestly made ...
>
> However, in contrast to the pre-contract situation, the precise ambit of the duty in the claims context has not been developed by the authorities; indeed, no case has been cited to me where it has been considered outside the fraud context in relation to claims ...

---

21 See above, p 216.

[p 513] ... Consequently, I hold that any fraudulent statement which would influence a prudent underwriter's decision to accept, reject or compromise the claim, is material ...

[p 518]...I am prepared to hold that the duty not to make fraudulent claims and not to make claims in breach of the duty of utmost good faith is an implied term of the policy...

Lek v Mathews (1927) 29 LlL Rep 141, HL

The assured made a claim under a theft insurance policy that his collection of stamps had been stolen. Following police investigation, the albums were discovered, still containing some of the stamps. The insurer refused to pay for the partial loss of the stamps, on the grounds that there were a large number of valuable stamps which the assured had never possessed, and also the assured's collection contained counterfeit stamps, which were suspected as such, but nevertheless concealed from the underwriters.

The House ruled in favour of the insurer, in that the assured's claim as to the possession and the value of the stamps was false.

Viscount Sumner: [p 145] ... As to the construction of the false claim clause, I think that it refers to anything falsely claimed, that is, anything not so insubstantial as to make the maxim *de minimis* applicable, and is not limited to a claim which as to the whole is false. It means claims as to particular subject matters in respect of which a right to indemnity is asserted, not the mere amount of money claimed without regard to the particulars or the contents of the claim; and a claim is false not only if it is deliberately invented, but also if it is made recklessly, not caring whether it is true or false, but only seeking to succeed in the claim.

But fraud, or any other breach of what I will assume is continuing duty of utmost good faith in relation to the making of claims, also breaks an implied term of the contract, whether facts exist which would ground a genuine claim.

More recently, the law on the duty not to make fraudulent claims[22] was further discussed in *Orakpo v Barclays Insurance Services* [1995] LRLR 443, CA, and *Transthene Packaging Co Ltd v Royal Insurance (UK) Ltd* [1996] LRLR 32, both of which were involved with non-marine insurance policies.

Orakpo v Barclays Insurance Services [1995] LRLR 443, CA

A building which was insured under a household insurance policy was destroyed by fire. The assured claimed in respect of cost of repairs due to the fire and loss of rent. Although part of the damage was caused by an insured peril, the claim in respect of the rent was found to be grossly exaggerated, in the sense that it was false, and, therefore, fraudulent to a substantial extent.

---

22 See, also, *Continental Illinois National Bank and Trust Co of Chicago and Xenofon Maritime SA v Alliance Assurance Co Ltd, 'Captain Panagos DP'* [1986] 2 Lloyd's Rep 470, discussed below, p 245.

The Court of Appeal ruled that the assured forfeited all his benefits under the policy of insurance, including his claim for loss of the household content.

Hoffman LJ: [p 451] ... In my view, the claim also fails on the ground that it was substantially fraudulent. The relevant principle is stated as follows by Malcolm Clarke in his book, *The Law of Insurance Contracts*, 1989, p 434:

> Since it is the duty of the assured to observe the utmost good faith in his dealing with the insurers throughout, the claim which he puts forward must be honestly made, and if it was fraudulent, he will forfeit all benefit under the policy, whether there is a condition to that effect or not.

This proposition is supported by both principle and authority. In principle, insurance is a contract of good faith. I do not see why the duty of good faith on the part of the assured should expire when the contract has been made. The reasons for requiring good faith continue to exist. Just as the nature of the risk will usually be within the peculiar knowledge of the insured, so will the circumstances of the casualty; it will rarely be within the knowledge of the insurance company. I think that the insurance company should be able to trust the assured to put forward a claim in good faith. Any fraud in making the claim goes to the root of the contract and entitles the insurer to be discharged ...

Sir Roger Parker: [p 452] ... The appellant submits that the law, in the absence of a specific clause, is that an insured may present a claim which is to his knowledge fraudulent to a very substantial extent, but may yet recover in respect of the part of the claim which cannot be so categorised. To accept this proposition involves holding that, although an insurance contract is one of utmost good faith, an assured may present a positively and substantially fraudulent claim without penalty, save that his claim will, to that extent, be defeated on the facts. He may yet, it is said, recover on the honest part of the claim. I would be unable to accept such a proposition without compelling authority, and there is none. To do so would, in my view, require me to hold that utmost good faith applies only to inception or renewal and not to matters subsequent thereto, or, in the alternative, that, whilst the law provides for avoidance of mere representation or non-disclosure on inception or renewal, given only that it is material, it provides no similar remedy for the most heinous fraud in the making of claim on the policy. I can see no ground for so holding.

... It appears to me that it is contrary to reason to allow an insurer to avoid a policy for material non-disclosure or misrepresentation on inception, but to say that, if there is subsequently a deliberate attempt by fraud to extract money from the insurer for alleged losses which had never been incurred, it is only the claim which is forfeit.

Transthene Packaging Co Ltd v Royal Insurance Co (UK) Ltd [1996] LRLR 32

The plaintiff owned a company which manufactured and sold plastic bags, and was insured with the defendant, *inter alia*, against fire and loss of profit resulting from fire. When a fire occurred at the factory, the plaintiff claimed on his policy of insurance, but the insurers refused payment on the basis that:

(a) the fire had been started deliberately by the plaintiff; and (b) the plaintiff had fraudulently claimed for the total loss of equipment, when such was not the case.

The court ruled that the insurers were not liable under the policy, because the plaintiff had fraudulently claimed for losses not incurred. The fire was adjudged to have been started by persons unknown. The judge ruled that the duty of utmost good faith is applicable also at the stage of making the claim.

> **Judge Kershaw QC:** [p 43] ... On that authority [referring to *Orakpo v Barclays Insurance Services*] it seems to me that there is a further reason why an insured cannot escape the duty of utmost good faith when making a claim, even if after the casualty has occurred ...

Manifest Shipping and Co Ltd v Uni-Polaris Insurance Co Ltd and La Réunion Européenne, 'Star Sea' [1995] 1 Lloyd's Rep 651; [1997] 1 Lloyd's Rep 360, CA

Star Sea was owned by Captain Kollakis and his two sons, the Kollakis brothers. The same people owned a shipping fleet of 30 vessels, which included two other ships called *Centaurus* and *Kastora*. All three ships were managed by Kappa Ltd, of which the directors were Captain Kollakis, his two sons, and Mr Nicholaidis, the technical director. Both *Centaurus* and *Kastora* were lost by fire. A report was prepared by an expert regarding the *Kastora* fire, whereby it was stated that the engine room was not properly sealed, because the dampers on board *Kastora* were ineffective. That prevented the fire extinguishing system from working and thus, the fire spread. Subsequently, a fire broke out on board *Star Sea* which rendered the vessel a constructive total loss and the dampers were again found to be defective. The report about the *Kastora* fire had not been shown to the insurers, because it had been mislaid by solicitors and did not appear until after the beginning of the trial. Thus, the Kollakis brothers did not see the report until the trial. When the assured sought to claim under the policy, the insurers alleged breach of utmost good faith for the failure to disclose the contents of the said report, and fraud.[23]

The court ruled in favour of the assured, in that they were innocent and did not act in breach of the duty of utmost good faith. An important aspect of the case lies in the fact that it expressed its disapproval of one aspect of the *Litsion Pride* case, viz, the precise scope of the duty of utmost good faith.

> **Leggatt LJ:** [p 371]...When the assured makes his claim, there is a duty of utmost good faith on both the assured and the insurer ... As Mr Pollock [acting for the insurer] contends, there may be an obligation to disclose matters relevant to the underwriters' decision as to whether or not to settle the claim. It is less clear from the cases whether there is a duty to disclose co-extensive with that which exists before the contract of insurance is entered into, as opposed to

---

23 For further discussion of this case in relation to the issue of unseaworthiness, see Chapter 7, p 322.

a rather different obligation to make full disclosure of the circumstances of the claim. But that distinction matters not.

... When the assured makes his claim, the duty of utmost good faith requires that it should not be made fraudulently; and we are prepared to contemplate that the duty not to present a fraudulent claim subsumes a duty not to prosecute a claim fraudulently in litigation. There is no need to demand more of the assured than that, if the Draconian remedy is to apply.

Utmost good faith

At this juncture, it is perhaps pertinent to be reminded that both the post-contractual duty of disclosure and the duty not to make fraudulent claims stem from the duty to observe 'utmost' good faith. The word 'utmost' must necessarily call for a study of the standard of conduct, namely, the degree or level of good faith expected of the parties. Section 17 seems to exact a high standard of conduct: exemplary and impeccable, almost faultless behaviour is to be observed by the parties in the disclosure of relevant information before and after the formation of the contract, and in the making of a claim. It suggests that any hint of impropriety would not be tolerated. Obviously, fraud would be the most clear-cut and most damning case of a breach of s 17. But whether lesser conduct, committed without an intention to defraud, would also be caught by s 17, has to be considered.

It would appear that judges are, in the main, reluctant to enter into any debate as to whether there are, in fact, different shades of good faith. What is clear, though, is that the duty is a positive one, which is not fulfilled merely by the absence of bad faith. In *CTI* **[1984] 1 Lloyd's Rep 476, CA**, Stephenson LJ expressed his sentiments as follows:

> **Stephenson LJ:** [p 525] ... Section 17 of the Act restates the long established duty of the utmost good faith in contracts of insurance. It is not necessary, even if it were possible, to go into degrees of good faith or the question what degree of good faith may apply to other contracts. It is enough that much more than an absence of bad faith is required of both parties to all contracts of insurance.

In similar vein, Steyn J, in *Banque Financière* **[1987] 1 Lloyd's Rep 69**, remarked that: [p 93] '... reciprocal duties rest on both parties to an insurance contract not only to abstain from bad faith, but to observe in a positive sense the utmost good faith by disclosing all material circumstances.'

The above comments are not particularly helpful; further, they do not provide a satisfactory answer to a nagging problem which had so perturbed Leggatt LJ in *Star Sea* [1997] 1 Lloyd's Rep 360, CA, as to have provoked him to ask the question [p 3] '... whether there is room for an intermediate position between innocence and fraud'.

The intermediate position between innocence and fraud

Case law has firmly established that, in the pre-contractual stage, the assured is in breach even for an innocent non-disclosure of a material circumstance. This principle of law, as will be seen later, is settled beyond doubt.[24] The question which arises is: is the same principle to be applied to the post-contractual duty of disclosure under s 17? In recent years, this matter has occupied a great deal of time in the courts. In *Litsion Pride* **[1985] 1 Lloyd's Rep 437**, Hirst J expressed his view on the subject as follows:

> **Hirst J:** [p 511] ... The *Style* and *Liberian* cases are also, in my judgment, instances of the same doctrine. I have no doubt whatever that both McNair and Donaldson JJ intended their references to utmost good faith in those cases to mean exactly what they said, and I reject Mr Kentridge's argument [for the plaintiffs] that they are to be interpreted as connoting fraud. There was no finding of fraud in either case nor, as far as I can see, even any allegation of fraud, and the facts in both cases are fully consistent with non-fraudulent, though no doubt discreditable, non-disclosure.
>
> ... Moreover, if the marked difference between pre- and post-contract duty which Mr Kentridge suggests applied, it is quite remarkable that s 17, which both parties accept covers both the pre- and post-contract duty, makes no differentiation between these two stages.
>
> [p 512] ... Consequently, I hold that the duty of utmost good faith applied with its *full rigour* in relation to the giving of information of the voyage under the warranty.
>
> However, in contrast to the pre-contract situation, the precise ambit of the duty in the claims context has not been developed by the authorities; indeed, no case has been cited to me where it has been considered outside the fraud context in relation to claims. It must be right, I think, by comparison with the *Style* and *Liberian* cases, to go so far as to hold that the duty in the claims sphere extends to *culpable* misrepresentation or non-disclosure. [Emphasis added.]

Notes

Hirst J was obviously of the view that the standard of conduct should be the same for both pre- and post-contractual duty of disclosure. This is evident from his reliance on the cases of *Style* and *Liberian*, both of which were concerned with the *pre-contractual* duty of disclosure under s 18. As both the pre- and post-contractual duty of disclosure emanate from the same overriding duty of utmost good faith, one could be tempted to argue that the same rule should be applied to both. However, this does not appear to be the case, because the pre-contractual duty demanded of the assured has always been regarded as a separate duty altogether, with its own special rules contained within ss 18 and 19, laying out the precise ambit of the obligation. More significantly, it would appear that the 'absolute' nature of the duty

---

24 See below, p 247.

under s 18 justifies a different treatment. This can be gleaned from the remarks made by Slade J in the Court of Appeal in *Banque Financière* [1988] 2 Lloyd's Rep 513, CA.

> **Slade LJ:** [p 544] ... It is no less clear that where there is an obligation to disclose material facts it is an *absolute* one which is not negatived by the absence of fraud or negligence. The law requires a party to an insurance contract to state not only all those material circumstances within his knowledge which he believes to be material, but those which are in fact so ... Thus, the merely accidental failure to disclose facts, if material facts, will involve a breach of duty.
>
> [p 550] ... in the case of a contract, *uberrimae fidei*, the obligation to disclose a known material fact, is an *absolute* one. It attaches with equal force whether the failure is attributable to:
>
>> ... fraud, carelessness, inadvertence, indifference, mistake, error of judgment or even the failure to appreciate its materiality ... [see Hardy Ivamy's *General Principles of Insurance Law*, 5th edn, 1993, p 156 and the cases there cited].[25]

If further authority be required to show support for this rule, reference should be made, in particular, to the remarks of Scrutton LJ, in *Hoff Trading Company v Union Insurance Society of Canton Ltd* (1929) 45 TLR 466, CA, and the related cases cited later.[26]

Doubtful and exaggerated claims

In relation to the duty not to make fraudulent claims, there is a trilogy of recent authorities, namely, *Orakpo v Barclays Insurance Services* [1995] LRLR 443, CA; *Transthene Packaging Co Ltd v Royal Insurance Ltd* [1996] LRLR 32, and *Star Sea* [1997] 1 Lloyd's Rep 360, CA, which have all approved the rule that an inflated or exaggerated claim, even if false, will not, unless there is evidence of fraud, prevent the assured of the right to recovery under the policy.

Orakpo v Barclays Insurance Services [1995] LRLR 443, CA

The plaintiff, Mr Orakpo, borrowed money on a house from Barclays Bank; a condition of the loan being that the property should be insured. The house consisted of a number of bedsit rooms which were rented out. The property was duly insured with Commercial Union Assurance, the second defendants; the declaration on the proposal form declaring that the property was in a good state of repair. In fact, soon afterwards, Wandsworth Council served notice on Mr Orakpo to the effect that the house was in need of repairs. No

---

25 See Ivamy, ER, *Chalmers: Marine Insurance Act 1906*, 10th edn, 1993, London: Butterworths, p 27: 'Mere silence, and even innocent silence, as to a material fact entitles the insurer to avoid the contract.'

26 See below, p 248.

substantial repairs were carried out and, with time, the property further deteriorated on account of vandalism and a fire. Subsequently, Mr Orakpo claimed on Commercial Union for repairs carried out, as well as loss of rent. The insurers refused the claim, on the basis that, not only was the declaration in the proposal a misrepresentation, the claim itself was fraudulent, in that few of the 13 rooms had ever actually been rented out.

The Court of Appeal ruled that the insurers were not liable. The declaration in the proposal form amounted to a misrepresentation and the plaintiff was also in breach of his duty of utmost good faith in presenting a claim which was, in fact, fraudulent.

Staughton LJ: [p 450] ... Of course, some people put forward inflated claims for the purpose of negotiation, knowing that they will be cut down by an adjuster. If one examined a sample of insurance claims on household contents, I doubt if one would find many which stated the loss with absolute truth. From time to time claims are patently exaggerated ... In such a case, it may perhaps be said that there is, in truth, no false representation, since the falsity of what is stated is readily apparent. I would not condone falsehood of any kind in an insurance claim, but in any event, I consider that the gross exaggeration in this case went beyond what can be condoned or overlooked.

[p 451] ... so I am not convinced that a claim which is knowingly exaggerated in some degree should, as a matter of law, disqualify the insured from any recovery.

Hoffman LJ: [p 451] ... I think that the insurance company should be able to trust the assured to put forward a claim in good faith. Any fraud in making the claim goes to the root of the contract and entitles the insurer to be discharged. One should, naturally, not readily infer fraud from the fact that the insured has made a doubtful or even exaggerated claim. In cases where nothing is misrepresented or concealed, and the loss adjuster is in as good a position to form a view of the validity or value of the claims as the insured, it will be a legitimate reason that the assured was merely putting forward a starting figure for negotiation. But in cases in which fraud in the making of the claim has been averred and proved, I think it should discharge the insurer from all liability.

Sir Roger Parker: [p 452] ... I also agree with the conclusions in both judgments that the appellant knowingly made and persisted in a claim which was false and therefore fraudulent to a substantial extent. I also agree ... that the consequence of this is that the claim must fail in toto ...

In *Transthene Packaging Co Ltd v Royal Insurance Ltd* [1996] LRLR 32, Kershaw J, citing the *Orakpo* case as authority, remarked that: [p 44] '... a known departure from literal and absolute truth in a claim is not necessarily fraud.'

Finally, in **Star Sea [1995] 1 Lloyd's Rep 651; [1997] 1 Lloyd's Rep 360, CA**, Leggatt LJ, though he had accepted that an assured is under a continuing duty of utmost good faith to supply relevant information, was reluctant to welcome any widening of the duty so as to include *culpable* non-disclosure and *discreditable* conduct. The same stance was adopted by Tuckey J, in the court of first instance.

Tuckey J: [Court of first instance, p 668] ... I should make it clear, however, that I do not think that the many authorities to which I have been referred establish that the scope of the duty is any wider than a duty not to make a fraudulent claim, by which is meant that the claim is 'wilfully false in any substantial respect' (*Goulstone v Royal Insurance Co* (1858) 1 F&F 276, p 279). This includes a claim made recklessly, not caring whether it is true or false (*Lek v Mathews* (1927) 29 LlL Rep 141, p 145).

Leggatt LJ: [Court of Appeal, p 369] ... the only authority cited to us in which the word 'culpably' was used was *Litsion Pride* [1985] 1 Lloyd's Rep 437.

[p 371] ... The language of s 17 itself ('if the utmost good faith be not observed') is inconsistent with an entitlement to avoid the whole contract where a party is acting innocently. The real question is whether there is room for an intermediate position between innocence and fraud.

[p 372] ... we come unhesitatingly to the conclusion in the present case that no enlargement of the duty not to make fraudulent claims, so as to encompass claims made 'culpably', is warranted. Such statements as were made in the *Litsion Pride* case to the contrary, were wrong. In our judgment, there is no warrant for any widening of the duty so as to embrace 'culpable' non-disclosure. Either it does not enlarge the scope of fraud, in which case it is not needed, or it does, in which case the extent of the enlargement is unclear and the concept should be rejected.

Notes

The Court of Appeal in *Orakpo v Barclays Insurance Services* **[1995] LRLR 443, CA**, and *Star Sea* **[1997] 1 Lloyd's Rep 360, CA**, have also made it patently clear that an assured will be stripped of his right to recover only if he acted fraudulently. Thus, the making of an exaggerated claim, even if false, would not fall foul of the duty not to make fraudulent claims. Likewise, it must necessarily follow that an innocent, inadvertent, and even 'culpable' or 'discreditable' non-disclosure of relevant information, after the conclusion of the contract, should not defeat the claim of the assured.

End of the continuing duty to observe utmost good faith

Whilst the beginning of the duty to observe utmost good faith is identifiable, the end remains somewhat vague. *Litsion Pride*, unfortunately, did not address the issue, thus leaving a gap in the law. That the duty must end at some time is clear, but this was not considered until *Star Sea* **[1995] 1 Lloyd's Rep 651; [1997] 1 Lloyd's Rep 360, CA**, where Tuckey J, in the court of first instance, proposed the question thus: [p 667] '... does there come a moment when it is no longer appropriate for the duty to continue at any level?' In the Court of Appeal, the question was answered as follows:

Leggatt LJ: [Court of Appeal, p 372] ... In the present case, disclosure is sought not only in aid of the presentation of a claim, but also so as to assist underwriters in their defence or their attempt to limit liability. Although it might in practice be difficult, if it were necessary, to disentangle claim from defence to claim, there is, as the judge remarked, 'no reason why adversaries should be under a duty to provide ammunition to one another'. The mere fact of rejection of the claim by the underwriters would not, in our judgment, bring the duty to an end in relation to the *Star Sea* case. But despite the fact that the pre-contractual duty of disclosure might have survived the contract in respect of any contractual decisions which underwriters continued to make under it, it was, after issue of the writ, supplanted by the procedural regime of the Rules of the Supreme Court, by which alone, for purposes of the action, the obligations of the parties as to discovery were governed.

Notes

It appears from the above that the duty of utmost good faith terminates when a writ is issued. In so stating, the Court of Appeal rejected the stand taken by Tuckey J, in the court of first instance [1995] 1 Lloyd's Rep 651, to the effect that: [p 667] '... once insurers have rejected a claim, the duty of utmost good faith in relation to that claim comes to an end.' The Court of Appeal postponed the cut-off point to the moment of the issuing of the writ, to coincide with the commencement of the process of discovery.

Avoidance of the contract

Sections 17, 18 and 20 are explicit as to the legal effect of the breach of the duty of utmost good faith, non-disclosure and misrepresentation respectively; the contract 'may be avoided' by the party prejudiced by the breach. The use of the word 'may' gives the aggrieved party the option to avoid the contract.

Avoidance ab initio

The said sections leave open the question, from which point in time can the innocent party treat the contract as void? No firm position was established in law until 1985, where again Hirst J, in ***Litsion Pride* [1985] 1 Lloyd's Rep 437**, stirred the waters in one more aspect of the *uberrimae fidei* principle.

> **Hirst J:** [p 515] ... In my judgment, 'avoidance', in s 17, means avoidance *ab initio*. Certainly, this is the case in relation to pre-contract avoidance, and I see no reason for putting a different meaning on the word in relation to post-contractual events ... Section 17 provides that the policy may be avoided, not that it must be avoided.

It must be noted that s 17 specifies no other remedy but 'avoidance' in the event of breach of the duty. Given that, in the light of the *Litsion Pride* case, the aggrieved party can retrospectively, that is, avoid the contract from the beginning, the harshness of the rule is evident. Tuckey J, at first instance, in ***Star Sea* [1995] 1 Lloyd's Rep 651**, remarked:

Tuckey J: [p 667] ... the only specified remedy for breach is avoidance. The courts have held that damages cannot be awarded for such a breach (see *Banque Financière de la Cité SA v Westgate Insurance Co Ltd* [1990] 2 Lloyd's Rep 377). This, therefore, is a draconian remedy ... The English courts have, I think rightly, become more conscious of the draconian nature of this remedy recently. Accordingly, when considering the duration and the scope of the duty, I think it is important for the court to bear in mind the consequences which will follow from its breach.

Notes

At this juncture, it is necessary to mention that the right of avoidance for a breach of s 18, the pre-contractual duty of disclosure, is governed by a different set of rules, those established by the recent authority of the *Pine Top* case [1994] 2 Lloyd's Rep 427; [1995] 1 AC 501, HL. It is sufficient here to mention that by the 'actual inducement' rule, the insurer is, in order to avoid the contract, required to provide proof that he was, by reason of the misrepresentation or the wrongful non-disclosure of a material fact, *induced* to enter into the contract, or to do so on the terms to which he agreed. This aspect of the law is discussed in depth later.[27]

Action for damages for breach of duty to observe utmost good faith

In *Banque Financière* [1988] 2 Lloyd's Rep 513, CA; [1990] 2 Lloyd's Rep 377, HL, an attempt was made to introduce a remedy in damages regarding breach of the duty of utmost good faith on the part of the insurers. The Court of Appeal, overruling the decision of Steyn J, quickly restored the position and declared that avoidance is the only remedy available to the aggrieved party. Though the claim was eventually rejected by the House of Lords, primarily on the ground of causation, nevertheless, the reasoning and comments made by Slade LJ, who delivered the judgment of the Court of Appeal, are pertinent and illuminating. Moreover, they were approved by Lord Templeman in the House of Lords.

> Slade LJ: [Court of Appeal, p 546] ... The first of these routes rests on the submission that the breach of a party to a contract *uberrimae fidei* of his obligation of disclosure is itself capable of giving rise to an action for damages in an appropriate case. This is a novel claim, as yet entirely unsupported by any decision of the courts of this country beyond the judgment of the learned judge. And, indeed, we have been told that, after research, no authority of any common law court has been discovered which supports it.
>
> However, while the 1906 Act and the judgment in many reported cases specifically refer to avoidance of the contract as the remedy for the breach of the obligation to disclose in contracts of insurance, neither the 1906 Act nor any

---

27 See below, p 261.

reported book cited to us suggests that a remedy by way of damages may also be available.

[p 547] ... However the principle *ubi jus ibi remedium* cannot, in our judgment, by itself justify a decision to give the remedy of damages in a novel situation not covered by previous authority, unless this is preceded by an analysis of the origin and nature of the right in question.

... In support of this submission he [Mr Strauss, acting for the bank] referred us first to the wording of s 17 of the 1906 Act. If a contract of marine insurance is 'based upon the utmost good faith' it is, in his submission, natural to treat the fundamental obligation of disclosure as an implied term of the contract ...

[p 548] ... In our judgment, however, the wording of s 17, if anything, goes against, rather than supports, the bank's submission, in as much as it explicitly confers on the other party, in a case where the utmost good faith has not been observed, the right to avoid the contract but makes no mention of damages, as we would have expected if the legislature had regarded the duty as arising out of an implied term of the contract ...

[p 548] ... If the duty of disclosure were founded upon an implied term of the contract of insurance that each party had made full disclosure of all material facts to the other, we could see no reason in principle why the breach of such implied term should not give rise to a claim for damages. In our judgment, however, the weight of authority and of principle is against any such conclusion.

[p 550] ... Nevertheless, we think the clear inference from the 1906 Act is that Parliament did not contemplate that a breach of the obligation would give rise to a claim for damages in the case of such contracts. Otherwise, it would surely have said so.

... A decision that the breach of such an obligation in every case and by itself constitute a tort if it caused damage could give rise to create potential hardship to insurers and even more, perhaps to insured persons. An insured who had in complete innocence failed to disclose a material fact when making an insurance proposal might find himself subsequently faced with a claim by the insurer for a substantially increased premium by way of damages before any event had occurred which gave rise to a claim.

Lord Templeman: [House of Lords, p 387] ... I agree with the Court of Appeal that a breach of the obligation does not sound in damages. The only remedy open to the insured is to rescind the policy and recover the premium. The authorities cited and the cogent reasons advanced by Slade LJ are to be found in the report of the proceedings in the Court of Appeal ...

Notes

The facts in *Banque Financière* were concerned with a pre-contractual non-disclosure culminating in a breach of the duty of utmost good faith under s 17. As the duty under s 17 is a continuing one, the question which may be validly asked is, is the above law, that damages are not an available remedy for pre-contractual non-disclosure, also applicable to a post-contractual non-disclosure? Save for a judicial comment uttered by Slade LJ in the Court of Appeal in *Banque Financière*, to the effect that there could be an exception to the general rule, there is no direct answer to this question. One can only surmise that, as the duties of pre- and post-contractual disclosure both arise from the same source, that of utmost good faith, it would be difficult to find a justification for having different rules applying to each of them. Slade LJ, however, has indicated that a different rule may well apply in a particular circumstance.

> **Slade LJ:** [p 548] ... It may be that, on the particular facts of some cases (though by no means necessarily all), the duty of post-contractual disclosure can be said to arise under the terms of the preceding contract. However, it by no means follows that the duty of pre-contractual disclosure arises under the contract rather than the general law.

In *Good Luck*[28] [1989] 2 Lloyd's Rep 238, CA; [1991] 2 Lloyd's Rep 191, HL, the bank which was suing as an assignee of the insurance policy claimed damages from the club for breach of the post-contractual duty of utmost good faith.[29] The issue arose in the Court of Appeal, where May LJ relied on the judgment of Slade LJ, in the Court of Appeal in *Banque Financière*, to dismiss the claim for damages.

> **May LJ:** [Court of Appeal, p 263] ... We do not think it is necessary to question the decision of Hirst J in the *Litsion Pride* case so far as concerns his decision that the obligation of utmost good faith could continue after the contract was made ... Assuming that the obligation can continue, we see no reason why the source in law of the obligation, or the remedy for its breach, should be different after the contract is made from what it is at the pre-contract stage. We would, therefore, hold that, if the obligation of utmost good faith could be said to have arisen, either in that contract of insurance as a separate obligation owed to the bank as assignees, or in the contract contained in the letter of undertaking, the bank could not establish a claim to damages in respect of any breach of it.

Notes

The core of the judgment is that the duty of disclosure does not arise out of an implied term of the contract; the drift is that, in infringing the duty to observe utmost good faith, the assured has not merely committed a breach of an implied term of the contract, but has 'breached' the *whole* of the contract of insurance which is *uberrimae fidei*. As his conduct has offended the whole policy, the whole has to be discarded.

However, the position has to be compared with that of Hirst J, in *Litsion Pride* [1985] 1 Lloyd's Rep 437, who stated that: [p 518] '...the duty not to make fraudulent claims and not to make claims in breach of the duty of

---

28 The facts of this case are discussed above, p 220.
29 It is to be noted that the Court of Appeal held that no duty of utmost good faith was owed by the club (insurer) to the bank, an assignee.

utmost good faith is an implied term of the policy ...'[30] Though the two views on the basis of the duty appear to be contradictory, it does not make any difference in the end with regard to the remedy of avoidance. Avoidance is a statutory right, and the only redress provided by the Act. Further, the Court of Appeal, in the *Good Luck* case and in *Banque Financière*, has certainly, and most firmly, settled the law that avoidance is the exclusive legal remedy available for a breach of the duty of utmost good faith.

One genuine, one fraudulent claim

In relation to the making of a fraudulent claim, the problem which arises is, whether a fraudulent claim made in respect of one casualty could taint another separate or closely connected but honest claim under the policy. As the remedy for the breach is avoidance *ab initio*, the insurer is entitled to avoid the entire policy; consequently, the legal effect of the breach is not limited only to the tainted claim.

Continental Illinois National Bank and Trust Co of Chicago and Xenofon Maritime SA v Alliance Assurance Co Ltd, 'Captain Panagos DP' [1986] 2 Lloyd's Rep 470; [1989] 1 Lloyd's Rep 33, CA

The vessel was wilfully cast away by her owners by setting her on fire. The issue that arose was whether a good partial loss claim in respect of one casualty, either the grounding or the fire, could be defeated by the assured's fraud or lack of good faith in pursuing a claim for fortuitous loss in respect of another casualty. Though the case was one primarily concerned with the defence of wilful misconduct of the assured,[31] Evans J, at first instance, took time to explain the issue of utmost good faith.

> **Evans J:** [court of first instance, p 511] ... A fraudulent claim, meaning one which is made on the basis that facts exist which constitute a loss by an insured peril, when to the knowledge of the assured those alleged facts are untrue, can be defeated without the assistance of any implied terms. But fraud, or any other breach of what I will assume is continuing duty of utmost good faith in relation to the making of claims, also breaks an implied term of the contract, whether facts exist which would ground a genuine claim. That breach entitles the insurer to avoid the policy *ab initio* under s 17 of the Marine Insurance Act 1906, and on general principles it is likely to be fundamental and so give him also the right to elect whether or not to accept the breach as discharging him from further performance of the contract, at least where other primary obligations remain to be performed ... If there were two separate claims, each independent of the other, then ... that fraud in the making of one could only release insurers from liability in the other if insurers exercise their right to

---

30 See *Captain Panagos DP* [1986] 2 Lloyd's Rep 470, *per* Evans J: [p 551] '... But fraud ... in relation to the making of claims, also breaks an implied term of the contract ...'.
31 See Chapter 9, p 400.

avoid or terminate the contract, subject always to prior affirmation with full knowledge of the facts. Here, however, the two claims are closely connected, notwithstanding their technical separation for the purposes of alternative partial loss claims, and on the present hypothesis, the one claim is defeated by connivance by the assured. In these circumstances, in my judgment, the plaintiffs' fraud in relation to one entitles the defendants to refuse liability in respect of both.

Similarly, in *Orakpo v Barclays Insurance Services* **[1995] LRLR 443, CA**, albeit a non-marine insurance case, a fraudulent claim was submitted under a household insurance policy. Although part of the damage was caused by an insured peril, the claim in respect to the rent was found to be grossly exaggerated in the sense that it was false and, therefore, fraudulent to a substantial extent. The significance of the judgment lies in the fact that the assured could not recover even on the honest part of his claim.

> **Sir Roger Parker:** [p 452] ... The appellant submits that the law, in the absence of a specific clause, is that an insured may present a claim which is to his knowledge fraudulent to a very substantial extent, but may yet recover in respect of the part of the claim which cannot be so categorised. To accept this proposition involves holding that, although an insurance contract is one of utmost good faith, an assured may present a positively and substantially fraudulent claim without penalty, save that his claim will, to that extent, be defeated on the facts. He may yet, it is said, recover on the honest part of the claim. I would be unable to accept such a proposition without compelling authority, and there is none. To do so would, in my view, require me to hold that utmost good faith applies only to inception or renewal and not to matters subsequent thereto, or, in the alternative, that, whilst the law provides for avoidance of mere representation or non-disclosure on inception or renewal, given only that it is material, it provides no similar remedy for the most heinous fraud in the making of a claim on the policy. I can see no ground for so holding.

DUTY OF DISCLOSURE UNDER s 18

Section 18 has imposed a strict and absolute obligation upon the assured to disclose to the insurer every material circumstance *'before the contract is concluded'*. Section 20, on representations, echoes the same rule on the issues of 'materiality' and 'avoidance'. As the same fundamental principles are applicable to both, the ensuing discussion, though focused on non-disclosure, is also applicable to representations.

Nature of the duty

Unlike s 17, s 18 has expressly imposed upon only the assured a positive duty to disclose all material circumstances before the contract is concluded. This means that it is for the assured to take the initiative to reveal to his insurer all material circumstances, and not for the insurer to inquire. What is peculiar about the law of pre-contractual disclosure under s 18 is that breach of the obligation does not depend upon the establishment of dishonesty or fraud, and, therefore, any defence or excuse to the effect that an assured had no intention to conceal or defraud is of no avail. The mere failure to disclose material information is, in itself, sufficient to strip him of his right to recover under the policy. The effect of pre-contractual non-disclosure is indeed harsh on the assured; whilst the assured might innocently or inadvertently fail to disclose, the legal consequence is the same: the insurer is still entitled to avoid the contract. All that the law is interested in is that the withheld information is material; the intention of the assured is irrelevant. As mentioned earlier, the rule is derived from *Carter v Boehm*, below.

Carter v Boehm (1766) 3 Burr 1905

In this case, the contingency insured against was whether Fort Marlborough in Sumatra would be taken by an enemy within the year of the insurance cover. The fort was indeed taken by the French, and the Governor of the said fort claimed under the policy. The underwriters put forward a defence of non-disclosure, contending that the weakness of the fort and the probability of it being attacked were not disclosed.

Lord Mansfield ruled in favour of the assured, the Governor, on the ground that he was under no obligation to disclose those matters which the underwriters could have investigated themselves. The judgment, however, is important, because of the lucid statement of Lord Mansfield regarding the *uberrimae fidei* principle in insurance transactions.[32]

> **Lord Mansfield:** [p 1909] ... Insurance is a contract of speculation. The special facts upon which the contingent chance is to be computed, lie most commonly in the knowledge of the insured only; the underwriter trusts to his representation, and proceeds upon confidence that he does not keep back any circumstances in his knowledge, to mislead the underwriter into a belief that the circumstance does not exist and to induce him to estimate the risque, as if it did not exist.
>
> The keeping back such circumstances is a fraud, and therefore the policy is void.[33] Although the suppression should happen through mistake, without any fraudulent intention; yet still the underwriter is deceived, and the policy is void; because the risque run is really different from the risque understood and intended to be run, at the time of the agreement.

---

32 Lord Mansfield's speech was cited with approval by Mellor J in *Bates v Hewitt* (1867) LR 2 QB 595, p 609, CA. Cockburn CJ added: [p 607] '... And it is also well established law, that it is immaterial whether the omission to communicate a material fact arises from intention, or indifference, or a mistake, or from it not being present to the mind of the assured that the fact was one which it was material to make known.'

33 'Void' should now be read as 'voidable'.

[p 1918] ... The underwriter here, knowing the Governor to be acquainted with the state of the place; knowing that he apprehended danger and must have some grounds for his apprehension; being told nothing of either; signed the policy without asking a question.

Greenhill v Federal Insurance Company Ltd [1927] 1 KB 65, CA

A consignment of celluloid, which had suffered injury by reason of a protracted voyage from New York to Halifax, Nova Scotia, was insured by its owners for a further voyage from Halifax to Nantes without disclosing the fact of the pre-carriage.

The court ruled that the pre-carriage was a fact material to be disclosed to the underwriters by the owners when effecting the policy; therefore, the underwriters were not liable.

Scrutton LJ: [p 76] ... Now, insurance is a contract of the utmost good faith, and it is of the greatest importance to commerce that that position should be observed. The underwriter knows nothing of the particular circumstances of the voyage to be insured. The assured knows a great deal, and it is the duty of the assured to inform the underwriter of everything that he is not taken as knowing, so that the contract may be entered into on an equal footing.

Hoff Trading Co v Union Insurance Society of Canton Ltd (1929) 45 TLR 466, CA

The plaintiffs were a trading firm in Estonia with interests in a Russian railway system. In 1925, for business reasons, the plaintiffs decided to send a large number of bearer shares, which they held in the railway, to their London office. The shares were insured with the defendants for their journey from Estonia to London. The shares were placed in a travelling trunk in the care of a family member of the firm, but were stolen during the journey when that person fell asleep. When a claim was pursued for the loss of the shares, the insurers refused payment, because, they contended, *inter alia*, there had been a non-disclosure by the plaintiffs in that the value put on the shares was not their immediate value, but in fact a value which the plaintiffs thought they were worth.

The Court of Appeal upheld the decision of the trial judge and ruled that there had been a concealment of a fact material to the risk. The fact that the non-disclosure may not have been based upon dishonesty was irrelevant. The statement made by Scrutton LJ was most informative, in that it laid down the rationale of the rule.

Scrutton LJ: [p 467] ... The law required that a contract of insurance must be based on the utmost good faith; and it was really a contract between two parties, one of whom, the intending assured, knew everything, and the underwriter, the other party, knew nothing. In such a contract, it was essential that the two parties should be put on equal terms, and it was the duty of the assured to disclose all matters which it was material for the underwriter to know; and if the valuation proposed to be put on the property insured was more than its real and present valuation, so as to make it a speculative one, it was material that all the facts which went to show that the valuation was speculative should be disclosed to the underwriter.

Joel v Law Union and Crown Insurance Company [1908] 2 KB 863, CA

In a policy of life insurance, the assured had foolishly, but not fraudulently, failed to disclose that she had consulted a doctor for a nervous breakdown. Nevertheless, since the undisclosed circumstance was held to be material, the insurer was entitled to avoid the contract. The important part in this decision is that it emphasises that, if a circumstance is material, that alone is sufficient to disentitle the assured of her right to recover under the policy if it was not disclosed; whether or not the assured regarded the circumstance as material is wholly irrelevant.

> **Fletcher Moulton LJ:** [p 883] ... In policies of insurance, whether marine insurance or life insurance, there is an understanding that the contract is *uberrimae fidei* ... There is an obligation there to disclose what you know, and the concealment of a material circumstance known to you, whether you thought it material or not, avoids the policy. There is, therefore, something more than an obligation to treat the insurer honestly and frankly, and freely to tell him what the applicant thinks it is material he should know. That duty, no doubt, must be performed; but it does not suffice that the application should *bona fide* have performed it to the best of his understanding. There is the further duty that he should do it to the extent that a reasonable man would have done it; and, if he has fallen short of that by reason of his *bona fide* considering the matter not material, whereas the jury, as representing what a reasonable man would think, hold that it was material, he has failed in his duty and the policy is avoided ... The disclosure must be of all you ought to have realised to be material, not of that only which you did in fact realise to be so.
>
> ... Your opinion of the materiality of that knowledge is of no moment. If a reasonable man would have recognised that it was material to disclose the knowledge in question, it is no excuse that you did not recognise it to be so. But the question always is, was the knowledge you possess such that you ought to have disclosed it?

Notes

The golden thread which can be drawn from these judgments is that emphasis is placed upon the 'knowledge of the assured'. Since it is highly unlikely that the insurer is familiar with any special characteristics relating to the subject matter insured, he is wholly dependent on the assured to provide him with the information. Knowledge of facts and circumstances surrounding the risk is at the disposal of assured, thus leaving the underwriter at the mercy (in a manner of speech) of the assured. It is this imbalance of position between the assured, whose knowledge is considerable, and the insurer, who can only know what the assured chooses to disclose, that justifies the strict application of the *uberrimae fidei* principle.

Another important point is the time of estimation of the risk. Given that the crucial time for the insurer to assess the risk accurately is before the contract is concluded, he must have all material information supplied to him in order to gauge the risk properly. Otherwise, should any material fact be kept back from him, the underwriter is deceived: the risk run is different from the risk understood and intended to be run, as was eloquently put by Lord Mansfield in *Carter v Boehm* (1766) 3 Burr 1905, p 1909.

Stephenson LJ, in *CTI* [1984] 1 Lloyd's Rep 476, spoke about: [p 529] '... the need for equality between those bargaining in the marine insurance market ...' It is exactly this need of equality that the *uberrimae fidei* principle seeks to promote. Therefore, the law of disclosure under s 18, though seemingly strict, is to protect the insurer, in that he must be supplied with information relating to any material circumstance before the contract is concluded.

Duty on the assured to disclose

A problem which often arises in shipping law relates to the fact that a ship is, more often than not, owned by a company and not a particular person/persons. A company, of course, cannot act on its own. In the context of marine insurance, the question is, who in the company represents 'the assured'? In *Star Sea* [1997] 1 Lloyd's Rep 360, CA, Leggatt LJ addressed the issue thus: [p 366] '... the question is whose acts should ... count as the acts of the company in the handling of the claim.' The solution to the problem, as other areas of shipping law have advocated, can be found in the rule of attribution.[34]

Who is the assured?

PCW Syndicates v PCW Reinsurers [1996] 1 Lloyd's Rep 241, CA

PCW Underwriting Agencies Ltd, as managing agents, were responsible for underwriting and arranging reinsurance for various Lloyd's syndicates. As it transpired, certain individuals within PCW were fraudulently diverting premiums, which had been paid to them for the benefit of the syndicates, to their own accounts. When losses occurred, some reinsurers contended that they were not liable under the policies which they, the reinsurers, had underwritten because it should have been disclosed to them that fraud was in existence – the moral hazard of fraud being material to the risk insured.

The Court of Appeal ruled that the reinsurers were liable under the policies; it could not be concluded that an assured should know of an agent's behaviour. One of the issues which the court had to consider during the course of its deliberations was: who in a company could be considered when

---

34 The same question also arises in s 39(5) of the Act.

seeking insurance, as having enough relevant knowledge to fall within the meaning of the words 'the assured' when it came to disclosure?

Staughton LJ: [p 253] ... It is, however, necessary to consider ... how s 18 operates when the person seeking insurance is a corporate body. It seems to me that one has to examine this aspect of s 18 ...

It is sometimes said that a company can have no knowledge itself, and can only know things by its servants or agents; others say that there can be knowledge which is in truth that of the company. I do not find it necessary to enter upon that debate (and if I did I would not know how to resolve it). The extent of the knowledge of a company can only be determined by reference to the rule of law which makes the inquiry necessary. That was explained by Lord Hoffman delivering the advice of the Judicial Committee in *Meridian Global Funds Management Asia Ltd v The Securities Commission*, 26 June 1995 (unreported):[35]

> This is always a matter of interpretation: given that it was intended to apply to a company, how was it intended to apply? Whose act (or knowledge, or state of mind) was for this purpose intended to count as the act, etc, of the company?

I can give an example from my own judicial experience. It is an offence to sell a video recording classified '18' to a purchaser who is known to be not 18 but 14 or thereabouts. But whose knowledge is relevant, in particular, if the sale is made in a branch of a supermarket chain? The board of directors, or the check-out girl? The answer is not too difficult (see *Tesco Stores Ltd v Brent LBC* [1993] 2 All ER 718).

The metaphor which has been used to describe knowledge or state of mind or conduct at a high level in a company has been 'the directing mind or will': see *Lennard's Carrying Co Ltd v Asiatic Petroleum Co Ltd* [1915] AC 705 by Viscount Haldane LC, p 713 ('active and directing will ... directing mind'); *HL Bolton (Engineering) Co Ltd v TJ Graham and Sons Ltd* [1957] 1 QB 159 by Denning LJ, p 172; *Tesco Supermarkets Ltd v Nattras* [1972] AC 153 by Lord Reid, p 171.

I can see no reason to restrict knowledge of a company under s 18 to what is known at a high level, by the directing mind and will. I would have thought that knowledge held by employees whose business it was to arrange insurance for the company would be relevant, and perhaps also the knowledge of some other employees.

[p 254] ... By s 18, the person seeking insurance must first disclose what is known to him. If he is a natural person, that means known to him personally; if a company, known to a direct or employee at an appropriate level.

Manifest Shipping and Co Ltd v Uni-Polaris Insurance Co Ltd and La Réunion Européenne, 'Star Sea' [1997] 1 Lloyd's Rep 360, CA

One of the issues in this case was whether a director (a Mr Nicholaidis) with technical expertise, who had seen the report, was to be regarded as the 'assured' for the purpose of conducting the claim. The Court of Appeal held

---

35 Now reported in [1995] 3 All ER 918, PC.

that, as he was not in conduct of the claim and was not the person to whom the solicitors would turn for instructions, he was not 'the assured'.

Leggatt LJ: [p 366] ... In the context of fraud, the first question is who 'the assured' is for the purposes of performance of that duty, namely, the proper conduct of the claim ...

Applying Lord Hoffmann's test from *Meridian Global Funds Management Asia Ltd v Securities Commission* [1995] 2 AC 500, the question is, whose acts should, under his general rules of attribution, count as the acts of the company in the handling of the claim?

[p 367] ... So far as Mr Nicholaidis is concerned, though he had some technical expertise not available elsewhere in the company, there is, in our judgment, no evidence that he was (or formed part of) the company for the purposes of conducting the claim. Though a director of Kappa, the judge found that he had no managerial power. He reported to and was subject to close supervision by the Kollakis brothers. The judge, who had the benefit of seeing the witnesses, made clear that in his judgment that Mr Nicholaidis was not a head man for any purposes.

... As a director of Kappa, his knowledge may be the knowledge of Kappa in those areas where he was concerned, but for Kappa to make a fraudulent claim as the assured it would not be right to add parts of the knowledge of different individuals to test the honesty of Kappa itself. The dishonesty must lie in the mind of an individual making the claim, or in the mind of those for whom the company is vicariously liable. We are satisfied that the relevant individuals making up the 'assured' for purposes of presenting and compromising the insurance claim were the Kollakis brothers.

Before the contract is concluded

Section 18 is explicit, in that it provides that the duty of disclosure on the part of the assured should occur 'before the contract is concluded'.[36] These words have led to the assumption that the duty of disclosure is discharged after the conclusion of the contract. However, as was seen, the duty of pre-contractual duty of disclosure under s 18 is separate and distinct from the post-contractual duty under s 17, as was established by *Litsion Pride* [1985] 1 Lloyd's Rep 437, and its progeny of cases.[37]

The post-contractual duty of disclosure under s 17 is a continuing one, whilst the pre-contractual duty under s 18 terminates with the conclusion of the contract. Moreover, whilst the duty under s 17 is bilateral, that under s 18 is unilateral, imposed only upon the assured, but not the insurer. And, as will

---

36 Section 21 points out that 'A contract of marine insurance is deemed to be concluded when the proposal of the assured is accepted by the insurer, whether the policy be then issued or not ...'. See *Ionides v Pacific Fire and Marine Insurance Co* (1871) LR 6 QB 674, p 684, where Blackburn J stated that: '... the slip is the complete and final contract between the parties.'

37 See above, p 216.

be seen, the content and scope of the duty under s 18 is different from that expected of both parties under s 17.

Niger Company Ltd v Guardian Assurance Company and Yorkshire Insurance Company (1922) 13 LlL Rep 75, HL

In this case, goods were destroyed by fire whilst they were in a warehouse awaiting shipment. The insurers sought to avoid payment on the grounds of non-disclosure concerning unsuitable storage facilities which affected the gravity of the risk, the unsuitability only arising for the first time during the currency of the policy. It was alleged that the matters which ought to have been disclosed by the assured concerned the nature of the store itself, the extent to which the warehouse was used in the ordinary course of business for the deposit of the goods, and the actual quantity of goods so deposited.

The House of Lords ruled in favour of the assured, that there is, under s 18, no continuing duty of disclosure beyond the formation of the contract.

> **Lord Sumner:** [p 82] ... There remains the question of non-disclosure. The object of disclosure being to inform the underwriter's mind on matters immediately under his consideration, *with reference to the taking or refusing of a risk then offered to him*, I think it would be going beyond the principle to say that each and every change in an insurance contract creates an occasion on which a general disclosure becomes obligatory, merely because the altered contract is not the unaltered contract, and, therefore, the alteration is a transaction as the result of which a new contract of insurance comes into existence. This would turn what is an indispensable shield for the underwriter into an engine of oppression against the assured. The authority of *Lishman's* case [see below] is against such a contention and I think it ought to be followed. [Emphasis added.]

Notes

The House of Lords in the *Niger* case relied heavily on the earlier authorities of *Cory v Patton* (1874) LR 9 QB 577, and *Lishman v Northern Maritime Insurance Company* (1875) LR 10 CP 179, HL. In *Cory v Patton* (1874) LR 9 QB 577, goods were shipped and were, by the perils insured against, wholly lost. The insurer declined payment on the basis that a circumstance material to the risk was not disclosed, namely, that the goods on board had met with an accident and misfortune before the loss occurred. The court ruled that the slip is the complete and final contract binding upon the parties. Accordingly, whatever events may subsequently happen, the assured need not communicate to the underwriters material information which only came to his knowledge after the conclusion of the contract.

Similarly, in *Lishman v Northern Marine Insurance Company* (1875) LR 10 CP 179, the assured failed to disclose the loss of the ship after acceptance of the risk by the insurer, but before issuing the policy. The court, applying *Cory v*

Patton, held that the concealment of the loss was not a concealment of a material fact so as to avoid the policy which had already been concluded.

The distinction drawn in **Litsion Pride [1985] 1 Lloyd's Rep 437** by Hirst J, between the continuing post-contractual duty of disclosure under s 17 and the pre-contractual duty of disclosure under s 18, as enunciated by the earlier cases of *Cory v Patton* (1874) LR 9 QB 577 and *Niger Company Ltd v Guardian Assurance Company* [1922] 13 LlL Rep 75, HL, is noteworthy:

> **Hirst J:** [p 511] ... In both cases [referring to the *Cory* and *Niger* cases] the underwriter had already accepted the risk and executed the policy in circumstances where, *ex hypothesi*, the assured had complied fully with his duty of utmost good faith and furnished full disclosure to enable the underwriter to assess the risk. What the underwriter was seeking to do in these two cases was to fix upon the assured a duty to volunteer information *ex post facto* concerning new matter, which had come to light after the conclusion of the policy, and which affected the risk already accepted. The key to these cases is, I think, to be found in the *dictum* of Lord Buckmaster in the *Niger* case that there is no duty on the assured to disclose circumstances arising subsequently which might show that the premium had been accepted at too low a rate. This, in my judgment, does not touch the problem with which the court is concerned in the present case.

In so far as pre-contractual disclosure, namely s 18, is concerned, it may be helpful to be reminded of the fact that the critical test is that only information (as set out in s 18(2)) 'which would influence the judgment of a prudent insurer in fixing the premium, or determining whether he will take the risk' must be disclosed before the conclusion of the contract. As was seen,[38] the type of information to be disclosed under s 17 (post-contractual) is somewhat different, for the risk has already been determined and the premium fixed.[39]

The assured must disclose every material circumstance

Section 18 has placed a limit upon the obligation of disclosure by the assured; the assured is required to disclose only 'material' circumstances. Section 18(4) further provides that 'whether any particular circumstance, which is not disclosed, be material or not is, in each case, a question of fact'. Even so, it is hard for an assured to gauge each time the circumstance that might be considered 'material' by the courts and would need to be revealed. Indeed, it would be commercially impracticable if the assured were required to disclose virtually *everything* to his insurer. This was recognised as early as 1874 by

---

38 See above, p 227.
39 In this regard, it would also be helpful to recall the words of Staughton LJ in *New Hampshire Insurance Co v MGN Ltd* [1997] LRLR 24, p 58, CA, that: '... Unless it happens before the contract is made, or before renewal, or (perhaps) before a claim is paid, disclosure [referring to post-contractual disclosure] could only fill the insurer with foreboding that he made a bad bargain as a loss was likely to occur ...'

Blackburn J, in *Ionides and Another v Pender* **(1874) LR 9 QB 531**, where the assured insured the goods at a value in excess of their real value, without disclosing the overvaluation to the underwriter. The court ruled that the underwriter was entitled to avoid the policy on the basis of non-disclosure. Blackburn J said: [p 539] '... We agree that it would be too much to put on the assured the duty of disclosing everything which might influence the mind of an underwriter. Business could hardly be carried on if this was required.'

Tate and Sons v Hyslop (1885) 15 QBD 368, CA

The plaintiffs effected policies of marine insurance with the defendants on sugar and other merchandise for the carriage of such from ocean-going ships, by way of lighters, to their refinery at Silvertown on the Thames. Insurances of that nature, at a higher premium, gave recourse against lightermen in the event of a loss. However, the plaintiffs failed to inform the insurers that, under an agreement, the lighterman utilised by the plaintiffs was only covered against loss brought about by his, the lighterman's, own negligence. When a loss occurred, the insurers refused payment, because they had not been informed of this special arrangement which, in effect, altered the risk.

The Court of Appeal ruled that the insurers were not liable under the policies. The non-disclosure amounted to the concealment of a material fact which would have influenced the insurers in undertaking the risk and setting the premium.

> **Brett MR:** [p 376] ... The authorities show that the materiality is not as to the risk, but as to whether it would influence the underwriters in entering upon the insurance or the terms on which they would insure.
>
> [p 377] ... What is it that an assured has to disclose? He has to disclose any circumstances which would affect the determination of a prudent and experienced underwriter in insuring, which is known to him, and which is not, or ought not to be, known to the underwriter.
>
> **Bowen LJ:** [p 379] ... What are material facts, have been defined by authority. It is the duty of the assured to communicate all facts within his knowledge which would affect the mind of the underwriter at the time the policy is made, either as to taking the contract of insurance, or as to the premium on which he would take it. The materiality of the fact depends upon whether or no [sic] a prudent underwriter would take the fact into consideration in estimating the premium, or in underwriting the policy. The rule has been clearly laid down over and over again, and is to be found in *Ionides v Pender* and other cases.

The test of materiality

The vexed question is, how is the 'materiality' of a circumstance to assessed; in other words, what criterion is to be used to determine whether a circumstance is, or is not, material. The test of materiality, which has engendered a great deal of debate in the courts over recent years, was finally settled by the House of Lords in *Pan Atlantic Insurance Co Ltd v Pine Top Insurance Co Ltd* [1994] 2 Lloyd's Rep 427, HL, below.[40]

The statutory test of the 'materiality' of a circumstance is contained in s 18(2), which reads:

> Every circumstance is material which would influence the judgment of a prudent insurer in fixing the premium, or determining whether he will take the risk.

The wording of the section leaves no doubt that it is the judgment of a hypothetical prudent insurer which is to be considered; the adoption of an objective, more ascertainable and definable standard is to be expected. However, the section has failed to clarify the degree or manner of influence which the undisclosed information has to have upon the mind or judgment of the prudent insurer.

The hypothetical prudent insurer test

There has never been any uncertainty in marine insurance law as to the use of the test of the hypothetical prudent insurer for the purpose of determining the 'materiality' of a circumstance. As this is never in dispute, suffice it here to quote from the judgment of Lord Mustill in *Pine Top* **[1994] 2 Lloyd's Rep 427, HL.**

> **Lord Mustill:** [p 445] ... I pause for a moment to consider the other conspicuous feature of the earlier law, namely, the presence in the equation of the hypothetical prudent underwriter. Just when and how this feature was added cannot be deduced from the materials now available, but it is at least as old as 1823 ... and may well be much older. It is a fair assumption that at least one reason must have been that the principles stated by Lord Mansfield required fair dealing, and it would have been unfair to the assured to require disclosure of matters which a reasonable underwriter would not have taken into account.

Rejection of the decisive influence test

Prior to the Court of Appeal decision in the *CTI* case, it was thought in some quarters that, to satisfy the test for materiality and to qualify for the right to avoid the contract, the court has to be satisfied that a hypothetical prudent insurer has to be *decisively* influenced by the non-disclosure (or, as the case may be, by the misrepresentation) of the material circumstance.[41] The Court of Appeal in *CTI* was the first to renounce the decisive influence test, and this aspect of the decision was not overruled by the majority of the House of Lords in *Pine Top*, below.

---

40 Hereinafter referred to simply as *'Pine Top'*.
41 See, eg, the judgment of Lloyd J, in the court of first instance, in *CTI* [1982] 2 Lloyd's Rep 178, which was overruled on appeal [1984] 1 Lloyd's Rep 476, CA.

Container Transport International Inc and Reliance Group Inc v Oceanus Mutual Underwriting Association (Bermuda) Ltd [1984] 1 Lloyd's Rep 476, CA

CTI, a container leasing company, effected an insurance with the defendant underwriters to cover damage suffered by their containers. However, CTI failed to inform the insurers that they had been refused insurance cover by other underwriters because of their inaccurate claims record.

The Court of Appeal ruled that the insurers were not liable under the policy because, under s 18(2) of the Act, the non-disclosure would have influenced the 'judgment' of a prudent insurer. The court considered the meaning of the word 'judgment' within the context of s 18.

Kerr LJ: [p 491] ... The point at issue turns mainly on the meaning of 'judgment' in the phrase 'would influence the judgment of a prudent insurer in fixing the premium or determining whether he will take the risk'. The judge [referring to Lloyd J, the trial judge] in effect equates 'judgment' with 'final decision', as though the wording of these provisions had been 'would induce a prudent underwriter to fix a different premium or to decline the risk'.

[p 492] ... This interpretation differs crucially from what I have always understood to be the law ... The word 'judgment' – to quote the Oxford English Dictionary to which we were referred – is used in the sense of 'the formation of an opinion'. To prove the materiality of an undisclosed circumstance, the insurer must satisfy the court on a balance of probability – by evidence or from the nature of the undisclosed circumstance itself – that the judgment, in this sense, of a prudent insurer would have been influenced if the circumstance in question had been disclosed. The word 'influenced' means that the disclosure is one which would have had an impact on the formation of his opinion and on his decision making process in relation to the matters covered by s 18(2).

One must bear in mind that the issue is as to the relevance, and not as to the weight, of any evidence which may be adduced in order to show that an undisclosed circumstance was material ... The section is directed to what would have been the impact of the disclosure on the judgment of the risk formed by a hypothetical prudent insurer in the ordinary course of business ...

He is in a hypothetical position, and evidence to support the materiality of the undisclosed circumstance, from this point of view, is therefore often given by an independent expert witness whose evidence has to be assessed by the court long after the event.

Parker LJ: [p 511] ... The very choice of a prudent underwriter as the yardstick in my view indicates that the test intended was one which could sensibly be answered in relation to prudent underwriters in general. It is possible to say that prudent underwriters in general would consider a particular circumstance as being on the risk and exercising an influence on their judgment towards declining the risk or loading the premium. It is not possible to say, save in extreme cases, that prudent underwriters in general would have acted differently, because there is no absolute standard by which they would have acted in the first place or as to the precise weight they would give to the undisclosed circumstance.

Stephenson LJ: [p 529] ... I conclude from the language of the sub-sections in their context and from the authorities that everything is material to which a prudent insurer, if he were in the proposed insured's place, would wish to direct his mind in the course of considering the proposed insurance with a view to deciding whether to take it up and on what terms, including premium.

Pan Atlantic Insurance Ltd v Pine Top Ltd [1994] 2 Lloyd's Rep 427; [1995] 1 AC 501, HL

Pan Atlantic reinsured their excess of loss with insurers other than Pine Top for the years 1977–79. Pine Top were reinsurers for the first time under the 1980 contract. As Pan Atlantic in 1982 sought a reduced premium, it was natural for Pine Top to be primarily interested in their loss record, before any re-arrangement of premium would be discussed. However, the loss record of Pan Atlantic over the years 1977–79 was misrepresented to Pine Top and there were additional losses sustained by Pan Atlantic between 1980 and 1982 which were not disclosed to them either. Consequently, Pine Top declined any payment of losses, on the grounds of non-disclosure.

The House ruled in favour of the underwriters, in that there was a material non-disclosure and, thus, the insurer was entitled to avoid the contract.[42] The House was concerned with two important points of law, namely, the 'decisive influence' and the 'actual inducement' tests. Only the former will be examined here; the latter will be discussed below, p 261.

Lord Goff: [p 430] ... Underlying the appeal before your Lordships' House have been two questions of principle, of great importance to the law of insurance. The first relates to the test of materiality in cases of non-disclosure, which in the law of marine insurance is to be found in s 18(2) of the Marine Insurance Act 1906 ...

Here, the question for your Lordships is whether, as the appellants (Pan Atlantic) have contended, it must be shown that full and accurate disclosure would have led the prudent insurer either to reject the risk or at least to have accepted it on more onerous terms. This has been called the 'decisive influence' test.

[p 431] ... I turn next to the first question, which is whether the decisive influence test is the appropriate test for deciding whether a fact which has not been disclosed is a material fact. Here, there is a difference of opinion between my two noble and learned friends, Lord Lloyd accepting the decisive influence test and Lord Mustill rejecting it.

On this point, I respectfully prefer the reasoning of Lord Mustill. I do so for the following reasons.

---

42 Although *Pine Top* was a non-marine reinsurance, the point of law was considered as one of construction of ss 18 and 20 of the Act.

First, it seems to me, as it does to Lord Mustill, that the words in s 18(2):

... would influence the judgment of a prudent insurer in ... determining whether he will take the risk ...

denote no more than an effect on the mind of the insurer in weighing up the risk. The sub-section does not require that the circumstance in question should have a decisive influence on the judgment of the insurer; and I, for my part, can see no basis for reading this requirement into the sub-section.

Second ... it seems to me that the decisive influence test faces insuperable practical difficulties, because it ignores the fact that it is the duty of the assured to disclose every material circumstance which is known to him, with the result that the question of materiality has to be considered by the assured before he enters into the contract. At that time, it is not unreasonable to expect that an assured who is aware of, and understands, his duty of disclosure should be able to identify those circumstances, within his knowledge, which would have an impact on the mind of the insurer when considering whether to accept the risk and if so, on what terms he should do so; but it appears to me unrealistic to expect him to be able to identify a particular circumstance which would have a decisive effect. Likewise it seems to me ... that an inquiry after the event as to whether the judgment of a prudent insurer would have been decisively influenced by the relevant circumstance, if disclosed, would in many cases be impracticable, because this must in the nature of things depend upon the reactions of the particular underwriter.

For these reasons ... I would reject the decisive influence test ... In the end, as it seems to me, your Lordships are at liberty to give to the definition of materiality in s 18(2), and indeed to that in s 20(2), an interpretation which accords with the natural and ordinary meaning of the words used, the underlying obligation of good faith and the practicalities of the situation – all of which are, in my opinion, inconsistent with the decisive influence test.

Lord Mustill: [p 434] ... must it be shown that full and accurate disclosure would have led the prudent underwriter to a different decision on accepting or rating the risk; or is a lesser standard of impact on the mind of the prudent underwriter sufficient; and, is [sic] so, what is that lesser standard?

[p 440] ... The main thrust of the argument for Pan Atlantic is that this expression calls for the disclosure only of such circumstances as would, if disclosed to the hypothetical prudent underwriter, have caused him to decline the risk or charge an increased premium. I am unable to accept this argument.

... The next step is to decide what kind of effect the disclosure would have. This is defined by the expression '... influence the mind of the prudent underwriter ...'. The legislature might here have said 'decisively influence'; or 'conclusively influence'; or 'determine the decision'; or all sorts of similar expressions, in which case Pan Atlantic's argument would be right. But the legislature has not done this, and has instead left the word 'influence' unadorned. It therefore bears its ordinary meaning, which is not, as it seems to me, the one for which Pan Atlantic contends. 'Influence the mind' is not the same as 'change the mind'. Furthermore, if the argument is pursued via a purely verbal analysis, it should be observed that the expression used is:

... influence the judgment of a prudent insurer in ... determining *whether* he will take the risk.

To my mind, this expression clearly denotes an effect on the thought processes of the insurer in weighing up the risk, quite different from words which might have been used, but were not, such as 'influencing the insurer to take the risk'.

[p 441] ... I am bound to say that in all but the most obvious cases the 'decisive influence' test faces them with an almost impossible task. How can they tell whether the proper disclosure would turn the scale? By contrast, if all that they have to consider is whether the material are such that a prudent underwriter would take them into account, the test is perfectly workable.

... Accordingly, treating the matter simply as one of statutory interpretation I would feel little hesitation in rejecting the test of decisive influence.

[p 442] ... The materiality or otherwise of a circumstance should be a constant; and the subjective characteristics, actions and knowledge of the individual underwriter should be relevant only to the fairness of holding him to the bargain if something objectively material is not disclosed.

[p 445] ... I can see nothing in them [referring to leading textbooks] to suggest that, before 1906, materiality was understood as extending only to such circumstances as would definitely have changed the underwriter's mind; and they furnish substantial support for the view that the duty of disclosure extended to all matters which would have been taken into account by the underwriter when assessing the risk (that is, the 'speculation') which he was consenting to assume. This is, in my opinion, what the 1906 Act was intending to convey, and what it actually says.

[p 452] ... I propose the following short answers: 1. A circumstance may be material even though a full and accurate disclosure of it would not in itself have had a decisive effect on the prudent underwriter's decision whether to accept the risk, and if so, at what premium.

Lord Slynn of Hadley: [p 454] ... I agree with him [Lord Mustill] that the 'decisive influence' test is to be rejected and that a circumstance may be material for the purposes of an insurance contract (whether marine or non-marine) even though had it been fully and accurately disclosed it would not have had a decisive effect on the prudent underwriter's decision whether to accept the risk, and if so, at what premium ...

Notes

The majority of the House of Lords in *Pine Top* rejected the 'decisive influence' test, and in so doing, also effectively dismissed the 'different decision' test, which asks the question whether a prudent insurer would have reached a 'different decision' if he were supplied with information of the material circumstance.

The case has, however, left unanswered the question of whether there is still room for the application of the rule of 'increased risk'. The opportunity to raise this question arose recently in *St Paul Fire and Marine v McConnell* [1993] 2 Lloyd's Rep 503; [1995] 2 Lloyd's Rep 116, CA, where the issue of materiality was again put to the test by counsel for the defendant, who argued that the 'increase of risk' is the criterion to be applied for determining the materiality of a circumstance. This, together with counsel's other suggestion that the test of materiality laid down by the House of Lords in *Pine Top* is not conclusive,[43] was, however, roundly dismissed by Evans LJ as follows:

> **Evans LJ:** [p 124] ... I would reject Mr Phillips' [acting for the defendants] submission that the fact cannot be material unless the risk is thereby increased, and I would support this conclusion on the wider ground that 'material', like 'relevant', denotes a relationship with the subject matter rather than a prediction of its effect.

Thus, the 'increased risk' test was clearly rejected by the Court of Appeal.

Right of avoidance

The *Pine Top* case clearly established that the materiality of a circumstance alone is not sufficient to confer upon the insurer the right to avoid the contract; it laid down the rule that the insurer has also to satisfy the 'actual inducement' test which is quite separate from the test of the hypothetical prudent insurer, mentioned earlier, employed to ascertain the materiality of a circumstance. There are now two hurdles which the insurer has to satisfy before he would be allowed to avoid the contract: the test of the hypothetical prudent insurer for the 'materiality' or relevance of a circumstance, and the test of 'actual inducement' for the right to avoid the contract.

The actual inducement test

The House of Lords in *Pine Top* **[1994] 2 Lloyd's Rep 427, HL**, may have upheld *CTI* [1984] 1 Lloyd's Rep 476, CA, with regard to the objective test of materiality, but has, in holding that the actual underwriter must be shown to have been induced into the contract (as in the general law of misrepresentation), unanimously overruled its objective test of inducement.[44]

> **Lord Goff:** [p 431] ... I accept that the actual inducement test accurately represents the law ... I conclude that there is to be implied in the Marine Insurance Act 1906 a requirement that a material misrepresentation will only entitle the insurer to avoid the policy if it induced the making of the contract; and that a similar conclusion must be reached in the case of a material non-disclosure. This conclusion is, as I understand it, consistent with the opinion

---

43 Lord Mustill, in *Pine Top* (p 434), questioned whether there was 'a lesser standard of impact on the mind of the prudent underwriter' which could be applied that would satisfy the test of materiality. This was the issue raised by counsel who wished to be informed what this lesser standard was, and its terms.

44 *CTI* is by no means completely overruled by *Pine Top*; save for the issue of inducement, the other parts of the decision of *CTI* still remain intact.

expressed by my noble and learned friend Lord Lloyd, that Parliament, by enacting the law as it did in s 20 of the Act, must have intended to codify the common law on materiality, without touching the common law on inducement.

Lord Mustill: [p 447] ... I turn to the second question which concerns the need, or otherwise, for a causal connection between the misrepresentation or non-disclosure and the making of the contract of insurance ...

[p 452] ... I conclude that there is to be implied in the Act of 1906 a qualification that a material misrepresentation will not entitle the underwriter to avoid the policy unless the misrepresentation induced the making of the contract, using 'induced' in the sense in which it is used in the general law of contract. This proposition is concerned only with material misrepresentations ...

Lord Lloyd: [p 465] ... In the case of a misrepresentation in the ordinary law of contract, it has always been necessary for the party seeking to avoid the contract to show that he relied on the misrepresentation. It seems most unlikely that Parliament, by enacting the second sentence of s 20, intended to exclude this rule of common law, for no apparent reason. It is much more likely that the intention was to codify the common law on materiality, without touching the common law on inducement.

[p 466] ... Whenever an insurer seeks to avoid a contract of insurance or reinsurance on the ground of misrepresentation or non-disclosure, there will be two separate but closely related questions:

(1) Did the misrepresentation or non-disclosure induce the actual insurer to enter into the contact on those terms?
(2) Would the prudent insurer have entered into the contract on the same terms if he had known of the misrepresentation or non-disclosure immediately before the contract was concluded?

If both questions are answered in favour of the insurer, he will be entitled to avoid the contract, not otherwise.

The evidence of the insurer himself will normally be required to satisfy the court on the first question. The evidence of an independent broker or underwriter will normally be required to satisfy the court on the second question. This produces a uniform and workable solution, which has the further advantage, as I see it, of according with good commercial common sense. It follows that the *CTI* case was wrongly decided, and should be overruled.

The actual inducement test and non-disclosure

The actual inducement test may be comfortably applied to a case of misrepresentation, but perhaps not to a wrongful non-disclosure, by reason of the fact that an insurer may have to be called upon to show that he was induced by something which amounted to silence, by something not said. The problem is, can a person be induced to enter into a contract by information, however material, which he has no knowledge of? Lord Mustill in ***Pine Top***

[1994] 2 Lloyd's Rep 427, HL, took time to analyse the position and arrived at the conclusion that the test of actual inducement should also be applied to non-disclosure,[45] as well as misrepresentation of a material circumstance.

> Lord Mustill: [p 452] ... There remain two problems of real substance. The first is whether the conclusion just expressed can be transferred to the case of wrongful non-disclosure. It must be accepted at once that the route via s 91(2) of the Act and the general common law which leads to a solution for misrepresentation is not available here, since there was and is no general common law of non-disclosure. Nor does the complex interaction between fraud and materiality, which makes the old insurance law on misrepresentation so hard to decipher, exist in respect of non-disclosure. Nevertheless, if one looks at the problem in the round, and asks whether it is a tolerable result that the Act accommodates in s 20(1) a requirement that the misrepresentation shall have induced the contract, and yet no such requirement can be accommodated in s 18(1), the answer must surely be that it is not – the more so since in practice the line between misrepresentation and non-disclosure is often imperceptible. If the Act, which did not set out to be a complete codification of existing law, will yield to qualification in one case, surely it must in common sense do so in the other. If this requires the making of new law, so be it. There is no subversion here of established precedent. It is only in recent years that the problem has been squarely faced. Facing it now, I believe that to do justice, a need for inducement can and should be implied into the Act.
>
> [p 453] ... If the misrepresentation or non-disclosure of a material fact did not in fact induce the making of the contract (in the sense in which that expression is used in the general law of misrepresentation), the underwriter is not entitled to rely on it as a ground for avoiding the contract.

In fact, the first traces of the actual inducement test can be found earlier, in *Berger and Light Diffusers Ltd v Pollock* [1973] 2 Lloyd's Rep 442, below.

Berger and Light Diffusers Ltd v Pollock [1973] 2 Lloyd's Rep 442

Moulds which were shipped under an open cover arrived in a rusty condition. The underwriter refused payment, on the grounds of non-disclosure that the bills of lading were claused and that the moulds were overvalued.

The court ruled in favour of the assured, in that the undisclosed circumstances were held not to be material, thus the underwriter was not entitled to avoid the policy. The relevant part of the judgment is to be found in the *dictum* of Kerr J (as he then was).

> Kerr J: [p 463] ... It seems to me, as a matter of principle, that the court's task in deciding whether or not the defendant insurer can avoid the policy for non-disclosure must be to determine as a question of fact whether, by applying the

---

45 See *Fraser Shipping Ltd v Colton and Others* [1997] 1 Lloyd's Rep 586, where Potter LJ had no difficulty whatsoever in applying the actual inducement test to a post-contractual non-disclosure of material facts; this case is discussed at length above, p 228 and in Chapter 4, p 154.

standard of the judgment of a prudent insurer, the *insurer in question* would have been influenced in fixing the premium or determining whether to take the risk if he had been informed of the undisclosed circumstances before entering into the contract. Otherwise, one could in theory reach the absurd position where the court might be satisfied that the insurer in question would in fact not have been so influenced, but that other prudent insurers would have been. It would then be a very odd result if the defendant insurer could nevertheless avoid the policy. I do no think that this is the correct interpretation of s 18, despite the generality of the language used in sub-s 2. [Emphasis added.]

Notes

It is to be noted that Kerr LJ (as he became) changed his mind in the Court of Appeal in *CTI* [1984] 1 Lloyd's Rep 476, CA. His earlier opinion, as expressed in *Berger v Pollock* [1973] 2 Lloyd's Rep 442, was, however, restored by the House of Lords in *Pine Top* [1994] 2 Lloyd's Rep 427, HL, where Lord Mustill thought that: [p 452] '... the instinct of Kerr J in *Berger v Pollock* [1973] 2 Lloyd's Rep 442, was right, and that the adoption of the contrary view by the Court of Appeal in *CTI* [1984] 1 Lloyd's Rep 476 should not now be upheld.

St Paul Fire and Marine v McConnell [1993] 2 Lloyd's Rep 503; [1995] 2 Lloyd's Rep 116, CA

The appellants were a construction company contracted to build the parliament building in the Marshall Islands. They then effected a 'Contractors All Risks' policy with the defendants but, at the time the insurance contract was drawn up, the plans shown to the insurers showed the building to have piled foundations. When subsidence later occurred, the insurers refused payment on the claim because it became evident that the building had been constructed without piled foundations.

The Court of Appeal ruled that there had been a non-disclosure of a material fact and the insurers had been induced into underwriting the policy.

Evans LJ: [p 122] ... The House of Lords decided unanimously in *Pan Atlantic Insurance Co Ltd v Pine Top Insurance Co Ltd* [1994] 2 Lloyd's Rep 427; [1994] 3 WLR 677 that the insurer's right of avoidance arises only when the misrepresentation, or non-disclosure, induced him to make the contract. This is part of the general law of contract and, although not stated expressly, must be regarded as an implied qualification of the right to avoid the contract under the Act ...

... there is only a right to avoid when the misrepresentation or non-disclosure was 'material' and when the actual insurer was induced thereby to enter into the contract ...

[p 124] ... As regards inducement, it is common ground that the insurer must prove that he was induced by the non-disclosure or misrepresentation to enter into a contract on terms which he would not have accepted if all the material

facts had been made known to him, and that the test of 'inducement' is the same as that established by many authorities in the general law of contract.

Marc Rich and Co AG v Portman [1996] 1 Lloyd's Rep 430; [1997] 1 Lloyd's Rep 225, CA

The assured were traders in crude oil, and to perform their sale and purchase contracts they chartered vessels to collect oil from several loading ports. They insured their oil cargoes against loss or damage, and they also insured against incurring liabilities as charterers. The insurance also provided demurrage cover. When demurrage claims arose, the insurers paid some, but declined payment in respect of some other substantial claims on the grounds of non-disclosure. This non-disclosure included the lack of any information regarding demurrage claims (the loss experience), which the assured (as charterers) had previously paid to the shipowners. Furthermore, the assured had failed to disclose adverse port characteristics (such as bad weather or difficult tides) which are likely to give rise to demurrage claims.

The court ruled in favour of the assured in respect of the non-disclosure of the characteristics of the port, in that it was held not to be a material fact. However, the insurer was entitled to avoid liability in respect of the non-disclosure of the loss experience. Longmore J applied the 'actual inducement' test, and ruled that an underwriter has to show that he was induced before he was entitled to avoid the contract.

> **Longmore J:** [p 441] ... In my view, the question whether the actual underwriter was induced to write the relevant risk is to be determined by reference to the actual risks underwritten.
>
> ... In either event, the risk would not have been written on the terms it was. In these circumstances, I hold that insurers have shown that they were induced to write the risk on the terms they did by reason of the non-disclosure of the loss experience.

Presumption of inducement

The 'actual inducement' test has raised a related question, that of the notion of the presumption of inducement. This was considered by Kerr J, in *Berger and Light Diffusers Ltd v Pollock* **[1973] 2 Lloyd's Rep 442**, as follows:

> **Kerr J:** [p 463] ... The burden of establishing the materiality of undisclosed circumstances rests on the defendant ... there are a number of references in reported decisions in which judges have stressed the desirability for the underwriter concerned to go into the witness box, at any rate in cases of doubt.
>
> ... The effect of the non-disclosure may, of course, be so clear that the court will require no evidence, or only little evidence, to decline in favour of the insurer. In doubtful cases, on the other hand, the court may require evidence from the insurers themselves before being able to hold that their right to avoid the policy has been established. In my view, the underwriter concerned should

have been called in the present case, and this should be the practice in all doubtful cases, even if an independent underwriter or broker is called as well.

In *Pine Top* **[1994] 2 Lloyd's Rep 427, HL**, Lord Mustill was clear in his mind that there is such a 'presumption' in favour of the insurer:

> **Lord Mustill:** [p 453]... As a matter of common sense, however, even where the underwriter is shown to have been careless in other respects, the assured will have an uphill task in persuading the court that the withholding or misstatement of circumstances satisfying the test of materiality has made no difference. There is ample material, both in the general law and in the specialist works on insurance, to suggest that there is a presumption in favour of a causative effect.

But, as it was unnecessary in the case for him to elucidate on the issue, the matter was left open to interpretation in the subsequent decisions of *St Paul Fire and Marine v McConnell* [1995] 2 Lloyd's Rep 116, CA, and *Marc Rich and Co AG v Portman* [1997] 1 Lloyd's Rep 225, CA. Both decisions have also indicated that, independent from materiality, the insurer may, in certain circumstances, have to prove inducement.

In *St Paul Fire and Marine v McConnell* **[1995] 2 Lloyd's Rep 116, CA**, a dispute arose because the trial judge accepted the testimony of three of the four underwriters as being sufficient to establish inducement. The fourth underwriter did not testify. Evans LJ, in the Court of Appeal, clarified the issue with the following comment:

> **Evans LJ:** [p 127] ... These respondents are not entitled to avoid their contract unless there is a presumption upon which they can rely to discharge the burden of proving inducement which rests upon them.
>
> The existence of such a presumption is recognised in the authorities: see *Halsbury's Laws*, Vol 31, para 1067, where the law is stated as follows:
>
>> Inducement cannot be inferred in law from proved materiality, although there may be some cases where the materiality is so obvious as to justify an inference of fact that the representee was actually induced, but, even in such exceptional cases, the inference is only a *prima facie* one and may be rebutted by counter-evidence.
>
> The authorities cited include *Smith v Chadwick* (1884) 9 App Cas 187 and, in my judgment, they justify the above statement of the law ... There is no evidence to displace a presumption that Mr Earnshaw [the fourth underwriter] like the other three was induced by the non-disclosure or misrepresentation to give cover on the terms on which he did. In my judgment, these insurers also have discharged their burden of proof.

Except for stating that the burden of proof of inducement lay upon the underwriters, Leggatt LJ, in the Court of Appeal in *Marc Rich and Co AG v Portman* **[1996] 1 Lloyd's Rep 430; [1997] 1 Lloyd's Rep 225, CA**, had little to say about the presumption. No disapproval, however, was expressed by the Court of Appeal over the stand taken by Longmore J, the trial judge, on the matter.

Longmore J: [court of first instance, p 442] ... In most cases in which the actual underwriter is called to give evidence and is cross-examined, the court will be able to make up its own mind on the question of inducement. The presumption will only come into play in those cases in which the underwriter cannot (for good reason) be called to give evidence and there is no reason to suppose that the actual underwriter acted other than prudently in writing the risk. In cases where he is called and the court genuinely cannot make up its mind on the question of inducement, the insurer's defence of non-disclosure should fail, because he will not have been able to show that he had been induced by the non-disclosure to enter into the insurance on the relevant terms. At the end of the day, it is for the insurer to prove that the non-disclosure did induce the writing of the risk on the terms in which it was written.

REPRESENTATIONS

The law of representations also forms part of the obligation of utmost good faith. As mentioned earlier, the same basic principles relating to non-disclosure also apply to representations. Consequently, the test for materiality and for the right of avoidance is the same as for non-disclosure: the hypothetical prudent insurer criterion is applicable to define the 'materiality' of a representation, and the requirement of 'actual inducement' as espoused by the *Pine Top* case [1994] 2 Lloyd's Rep 427 for the right of avoidance. In this respect, s 20(2) echoes the rule enunciated in s 18(2).

Section 20(1) provides that 'every material representation made by the assured ... must be true'. The remedy is also avoidance. This section, though, has to be read together with s 20(4), which defines that 'a representation as to a matter of fact is true, if it be substantially correct, that is to say, if the difference between what is represented and what is actually correct would not be considered material by a prudent insurer'. It is evident by the wording of the Act that the hypothetical prudent insurer criterion is applicable when defining the truth of the representation, quite apart from its materiality.

The authorities regarding representations have been much concerned with the difference between a representation and a warranty; as the law of warranty is outside the scope of this chapter, suffice it here to say that a representation, unlike a warranty, is not a term of the contract. A warranty has to be inserted in the policy and must be strictly and literally complied with, whilst a representation need only be substantially correct.

The case which best distinguishes a representation from a warranty is that of *Pawson v Watson* **(1778) 2 Cowp 785**,[46] where a vessel was captured after

---

46 This case and *De Hahn v Hartley* (1786) 1 TR 343 are discussed in depth in Chapter 7, pp 270 and 271.

sailing on a voyage with different armament and complement of crew than that envisaged in the policy of insurance. The court ruled that the insurers were liable, because the condition in the policy only amounted to a representation, and not a warranty.

> **Lord Mansfield:** [p 788] ... there cannot be a clearer distinction, than that which exists between a warranty which makes part of the written policy, and a collateral representation, which, if false in a point of materiality, makes the policy void;[47] but if not material, it can hardly ever be fraudulent.

References and further reading

Bennett, HN, 'Utmost good faith in the House of Lords' [1995] LQR 181

Bennett, HN, 'Utmost good faith, materiality and inducement' [1996] LQR 405

Boxer, C, '*Pine Top* just emerges above *Atlantic*' [1994] SJ 936

Brooke, H, 'Materiality in insurance contracts' [1985] LMCLQ 437

Cumming, G, '*Uberrimae fidei*: duty of the insurer to the insured' [1992] Litigation 135

Davenport, BJ, 'The duty of disclosure' [1989] LMCLQ 251

Diamond, A, 'The law of marine insurance – has it a future?' [1986] LMCLQ 25

Ellis, H, 'Disclosure and good faith in insurance contracts' (1990) Irish Law Times 45

Hasson, RA, 'The doctrine of *uberrima fides* in insurance law – A critical evaluation' (1969) 32 MLR 615

Hird, NJ, 'Rationality in the House of Lords?' [1995] JBL 608

Hudson, AH, 'Duty of disclosure again' [1991] LMCLQ 19

Muchlinski, PT, 'The insurer's duties of good faith and disclosure' [1988] LMCLQ 27

Schoenbaum, TJ, 'The duty of utmost good faith in marine insurance law: a comparative analysis of American and English law' [1998] JMLC 1

---

47 'Void' should now be read as 'voidable'.

CHAPTER 7

WARRANTIES

INTRODUCTION

It is perhaps necessary at the outset to mention briefly that, unlike contract law, where a warranty amounts to nothing more than a term in a contract, the breach of which sounds in a remedy only for damages, a promissory warranty in marine insurance law is of much greater significance. In marine insurance, a warranty is promissory in nature and is, in fact, a promissory condition precedent, the non-fulfilment of which will automatically discharge the insurer from liability or, as the case may be, further liability, as from the date of breach.

As will be seen, a promissory warranty has also to be differentiated from a so called warranty prefaced with the words 'warranted free from ...', the purpose of which is to except an insurer from liability for a particular loss. The differences between them are crucial, as they also affect questions relating to burden of proof and causal connection.

The Marine Insurance Act 1906 identifies two types of warranty when it states that: 'A warranty may be express or implied'. Such a warranty in insurance law, be it express or implied, is promissory in nature whereby the assured pledges to fulfil the specific condition contained within the contract; failure to do so will automatically discharge the insurer from liability under the policy. To this effect, s 33(1) of the Act affirms:

> A warranty, in the following sections relating to warranties, means a promissory warranty, that is to say, a warranty by which the assured undertakes that some particular thing shall or shall not be done, or that some condition shall be fulfilled, or whereby he affirms or negatives the existence of a particular state of facts.

Section 35(1) avers that: 'An express warranty may be in any form of words ...' Thus, provided that an intention to warrant may be inferred, a promissory warranty may be in standard form, as in the Institute Clauses, or in any form of words which the contracting parties may care to frame their warranty.

This chapter will examine: the nature and characteristics of a promissory warranty; the legal effects of a breach of a promissory warranty; the subject of waiver; some of the more well known examples of express warranties and the rules relating to their construction; and the warranties implied by law.

NATURE OF A WARRANTY

A warranty, as defined by the Act, has specific characteristics, namely:
(a) it must be exactly complied with;
(b) it need not be material to the risk;
(c) there is no remedy for breach;
(d) there is no defence for breach; and
(e) it is a promissory condition precedent.

A warranty must be 'exactly complied with'

That a warranty must be strictly complied with is confirmed by s 33(3) of the Act, which verifies that: 'A warranty ... is a condition which must be exactly complied with ...' In the early cases, the courts were often required to differentiate between what amounted to compliance with a warranty and compliance with a representation. On this issue, in *Pawson v Watson*, below, the court was precise in its summing up of the difference when it pointed out that: 'A warranty inserted in a policy of insurance must be literally and strictly complied with. A representation to the underwriter need only be substantially performed.'[1]

Pawson v Watson (1778) 2 Cowp 785

During the American War of Independence, the British vessel *Julius Caesar* was insured with the defendants for a voyage from England to Halifax, Nova Scotia. Under the policy, she was required to mount 12 guns and be crewed with 20 men. During the voyage, *Julius Caesar* was captured by an American privateer and, at the time of her capture, she had on board six four-pounder guns, four three-pounders, three one-pounders, six half-pounders and 27 crew, of whom only 16 were men; the rest being boys. The insurers refused to indemnify the assured, because the policy had only been underwritten on the basis of the ship having 12 guns and 20 'men' aboard.

The court ruled that the condition only amounted to a representation and not a warranty, because the condition was not a written part of the policy. It was the assured who had volunteered the information with regard to the strength of the ship, and the insurers had made no other inquiries other than that she was a ship of force.

Lord Mansfield: [p 787] ... There is no distinction better known to those who are at all conversant in the law of insurance, than that which exists, between a warranty or condition which makes part of a written policy, and a

---

1 The quotation is taken from the headnotes in *Pawson v Watson* (1778) 2 Cowp 785.

representation of the state of the case. Where it is a part of the written policy, it must be performed: as if there be a warranty of convoy, there it must be a convoy: nothing tantamount will do, or answer the purpose; it must be strictly performed, as being part of the agreement; for there it might be said, the party would not have insured without convoy. ... So that there cannot be a clearer distinction, than that which exists between a warranty which makes part of the written policy, and a collateral representation, which, if false in a point of materiality, makes the policy void; but if not material, it can hardly ever be fraudulent.[2]

By way of contrast, in *De Hahn v Hartley* (1786) 1 TR 343, a policy was underwritten on the basis of the crew of the vessel *Juno* being 50 hands or upwards on departure from Liverpool. In reality, *Juno* left Liverpool with only 46 crew members aboard, although six more did join soon after departure when the pilot was put ashore at Beaumaris in Wales. When, at a later date, *Juno* was captured, the insurers were held to be not liable for the loss because there had been a breach of the warranty to supply a sufficient crew.

> **Lord Mansfield CJ:** [p 345] There is a material distinction between a warranty and a representation. A representation may be equitably and substantially answered: but a warranty must be strictly complied with ... A warranty in a policy of insurance is a condition or a contingency, and unless that be performed, there is no contract. It is perfectly immaterial for what purpose a warranty is introduced; but, being inserted, the contract does not exist unless it be literally complied with.
>
> **Ashurst J:** [p 346] The very meaning of a warranty is to preclude all questions whether it has been substantially complied with; it must be literally so.

The significance of a warranty within the meaning of the Act was illustrated in the much later, post-statute case of *Overseas Commodities Ltd v Style*, below.

Overseas Commodities Ltd v Style [1958] 1 Lloyd's Rep 546

The plaintiffs shipped two consignments of tinned pork from France to London under an all risks policy of insurance underwritten by the defendants. The policy contained a clause which stated that all the tins should be marked by the manufacturers verifying their date of manufacture. When the tins of pork were delivered, many of the tins were found to be rusty or broken and much of the pork was either condemned or sold off cheaply. The plaintiffs claimed on their policy of insurance. However, the insurers rejected the claim on the basis that, as many of the tins did not have the date of manufacture upon them, the plaintiffs were in breach of the warranty.

The court ruled that the words 'for verification' in the clause meant that the tins must be so marked and the lack of such marks on many of the tins amounted to a breach of a warranty and, thus, the underwriters were not liable.

---

2 'Void' should now be read as 'voidable' – see s 20(1) of the Act.

McNair J: [p 557] ... In my judgment, the use of the words 'for verification' point clearly and definitely to the conclusion that tins must be marked in a manner which will identify the actual date of manufacture. Verification, in its ordinary sense, means the establishment of the truth or correctness of a particular fact. There was no evidence before me that the term has any meaning according to the understanding of merchants other than this ordinary meaning. In my judgment, this warranty quite plainly means that the tins must be marked in the stipulated manner; that is, by a manufacturers' code so that the true or correct date of manufacture may be established.

[p 558] ... It has long been well established law that an express warranty requires a strict and literal performance: see, now, s 33(3) of the Marine Insurance Act 1906. As is stated in *Arnould on Marine Insurance*, 14th edn, s 632:

> Every policy, in fact, in which an express warranty is inserted, is a conditional contract, to be binding if the warranty be literally complied with, but not otherwise.

... Being satisfied that, as regards both policies, a substantial number of the tins – well exceeding any tolerance that could be disregarded under the *de minimis* rule – were not marked with a code which enabled the true and correct date of manufacture to be established, I have no option but to hold that the breach of the express warranty affords the underwriters a complete defence in this action.

A warranty need not be material to the risk

Section 33(3) of the Act clearly indicates that, for the insurer to be discharged from liability by a breach of a warranty, it is irrelevant whether the warranty 'be material to the risk or not'.

Such was the case in ***Newcastle Fire Insurance Co v MacMorran and Co (1815) 3 Dow 255***, where a mill which was insured was wrongly described in the proposal as being of the first class. When the assured claimed for a loss by fire, the insurers refused to indemnify the assured on the ground that the incorrect description of the property amounted to a breach of a warranty. In his summing up, Lord Eldon confirmed that materiality was only relevant to a representation, and not to a warranty.

> **Lord Eldon:** [p 262] ... it is a first principle in the law of insurance, on all occasions, that where a representation is material it must be complied with – if immaterial, that immateriality may be inquired into and shown; but that if there is a warranty, it is part of the contract that the matter is such as it is represented to be. Therefore, the materiality or immateriality signifies nothing. The only question is as to the mere fact.

In similar vein, in ***Thomson v Weems* (1884) 9 App Cas 671**, where, on a life insurance policy, a declaration was made which amounted to a breach of a warranty, Lord Blackburn summed up the law generally with respect to warranties in policies of insurance.

Lord Blackburn: [p 683] ... It is competent to the contracting parties, if both agree to it and sufficiently express their intention so to agree, to make the actual existence of anything a condition precedent to the inception of any contract; and if they do so, the non-existence of that thing is a good defence. And it is not of any importance whether the existence of that thing was or was not material; the parties would not have made it a part of the contract if they had not thought it material, and they have a right to determine for themselves what they shall deem material.

In *Farr v Motor Traders Mutual Insurance Society Ltd* [1920] 3 KB 669, CA, the dispute was in relation to an incorrect declaration made by the assured on a proposal form for a policy of insurance on two taxis. Bankes LJ graphically illustrated the importance of a warranty as follows:

Bankes LJ: [p 673] ... The assured answered certain questions in a proposal form, and those questions and answers thereto were made the basis of the contract and were incorporated therein. The only question for decision by the learned judge [at the trial], and by us, is whether the answer to one of the questions constitutes a warranty by the assured. If, as a matter of construction, it can properly be held that the question and answer amount to a warranty, then, however absurd it may appear, the parties have made a bargain to that effect, and if the warranty is broken, the policy comes to an end.

There is no remedy for breach

Once a warranty has been breached, it is irrelevant whether the warranty is later complied with. A breach of a warranty cannot be remedied: s 34(2) of the Act confirms that 'where a warranty is broken, the assured cannot avail himself of the defence that the breach has been remedied ...'. Such were the circumstances in *Forshaw v Chabert*, below.

Forshaw v Chabert (1821) 3 Br&B 159

The vessel *Hope* and the goods aboard her were insured under a voyage policy of insurance at and from Cuba to Liverpool with the stipulation that the crew should consist of 10 men. However, when *Hope* sailed from Cuba, although there were 10 men aboard, two of those men were only contracted to sail as far as Jamaica, where they were replaced by another two. After leaving Jamaica, *Hope* was lost and the underwriters refused to indemnify the owners for the loss on the basis that they had breached the warranty of seaworthiness by sailing from Cuba with an insufficient crew.

The court ruled, reluctantly, in favour of the insurers. The plaintiff was in breach of the warranty when the ship sailed from Cuba and the fact that it was later remedied at Jamaica was immaterial.

Dallas CJ: [p 162] ... Now it is clear that a ship must be seaworthy when she sails; the assured warrants that, and whatever physical necessities may interpose, he is not allowed to deviate from the strict terms of his warranty ...

the ship was not seaworthy when she sailed from Cuba, because the captain ought then to have had 10 men for Liverpool, and not eight for Liverpool and two for Montego Bay ... what arose afterwards cannot have a retrospective effect.

In the later case of *Quebec Marine Insurance Co v Commercial Bank of Canada*, below, the assured based his defence on the fact that the warranty which had been breached had been cured before the loss occurred.

Quebec Marine Insurance Co v Commercial Maritime Bank of Canada (1870) LR 3 PC 234, PC

The appellants were the insurers of the vessel *West* for a voyage at and from Montreal to Halifax, Nova Scotia. After leaving Montreal, the boiler of *West*, which had been defective from the outset, became unmanageable when she entered seawater and she had to seek refuge nearby in order to effect repairs. The repairs were duly made but, soon after resuming her voyage, *West* encountered severe weather and was lost. The appellants refused to indemnify the policy holder on the basis that *West* had originally sailed in an unseaworthy condition, thereby breaching the implied warranty of seaworthiness.

The Privy Council ruled that the assured were in breach of the implied warranty of seaworthiness and the insurers were not liable under the policy, even though the defect was remedied before the loss occurred.

> **Lord Penzance:** [p 243] ... The second ground taken by the respondents [the assured] is founded upon the language attributed to a great authority (Lord Tenterden), in the case of *Weir v Aberdeen*, to the effect that if a defect, though it exists at the time the vessel sailed, and exists to such an extent and is of such a character as to render the vessel unseaworthy, be remedied before any loss arises, the underwriters still remain responsible. This is a proposition of perilous latitude. It is impossible not to see that such a doctrine would tend, if carried to its legitimate consequences, to fritter away the value of this warranty altogether.

There is no defence for breach

Aside from the exceptions mentioned in s 34(1), there is no defence which will excuse a breach of a promissory warranty. Arnould's statement that 'No cause, however sufficient; no motive, however good; no necessity, however irresistible, will excuse non-compliance'[3] with a promissory warranty is categorical. The word 'absolute' is sometimes used to describe this feature of a promissory warranty. There is no provision in the Act or any recent authority

---

3   Arnould, J, *Law of Marine Insurance and Average*, 16th edn, 1981, London: Sweet & Maxwell, Vol 2, para 687.

dealing directly with this principle. However, the law on the subject is well established, and applies to both express and implied warranties.

A promissory warranty must be exactly complied with and any non-compliance, for whatever cause or reason, would constitute a breach. Furthermore, as s 34(1) will only excuse a breach on two grounds, namely 'by reason of a change of circumstances' and 'when compliance with the warranty is rendered unlawful by any subsequent law', it is implicit that there is no other defence available to the assured. The principle is also derived from the fact that a warranty is 'promissory' in nature: as the assured has undertaken that some particular thing 'shall' or 'shall not' be done, or that some condition 'shall' be fulfilled, he is expected not only to honour his promise to the letter, but also to honour them against all eventualities.[4] The nature of a promissory warranty is such that it does not, in the event of a breach, easily lend itself to being forgiven.

The innocence of the assured is immaterial. This can be seen in *Douglas v Scougal* **(1816) 4 Dow 269**, where, in reference to the implied warranty of seaworthiness in a voyage policy, Lord Eldon remarked:

> [p 276] ... It is not necessary to inquire whether the owners acted honestly and fairly in the transaction; for it is clear law that, however just and honest the intentions of the owner may be, if he is mistaken in the fact and the vessel is, in fact, not seaworthy, the underwriter is not liable.

It is clear that even a latent defect rendering a ship unseaworthy will not excuse the breach of the implied warranty of seaworthiness.[5] And according to Arnould: 'Even the direct and irresistible operation of a peril expressly insured against in the policy is no excuse for non-compliance.'[6] Whether this is still the case in the light of the Inchmaree Clause, which insures a loss of or damage to the subject matter insured caused by, *inter alia*, 'any latent defect in the machinery or hull', 'negligence of Master Officers Crew or Pilots' and the 'negligence of repairers', is, it would appear, not totally clear.[7]

A promissory warranty is a promissory condition precedent

Surprisingly, the nature of a promissory warranty and, more significantly, the legal effects of its breach were not debated until recently, when the House of Lords presided over the milestone case of Bank of Nova Scotia v Hellenic Mutual

---

4   In *Hore v Whitmore* (1778) 2 Cowp 784, even an embargo laid on by a British Governor which prevented the insured ship from sailing on a given date was held not to be a valid excuse for the breach of the sailing warranty.
5   See *Mills v Roebuck*, '*Mills Frigate*', reported in a footnote in *Gibson v Small* (1853) 4 HL Cas 352; 10 ER 499, p 501, which is also discussed in Gibb, DEW, *Lloyd's of London*, 1972, London: LLP, p 67.
6   *Op cit*, Arnould, fn 3.
7   This issue is discussed in Chapter 12, p 500.

War Risks Association (Bermuda) Ltd, 'Good Luck' [1991] 2 Lloyd's Rep 191, HL,[8] below. As will be seen, the principles pertaining to the legal effects of a breach of a warranty and to the right of the insurer to waive such a breach are closely related to the fact that a promissory warranty is essentially a promissory condition precedent.

Bank of Nova Scotia v Hellenic Mutual War Risks Association (Bermuda) Ltd, 'Good Luck' [1991] 2 Lloyd's Rep 191, HL

This was an incident which took place during hostilities between Iran and Iraq. *Good Luck* was one of a number of ships owned by the Good Faith Group which was insured with the defendant P & I Club under a war risks policy. The policy included a rule which specified that, should the vessel enter an additional premium area, the insurers should be given prompt notice. The rule further stated that failure to give the club notice of entering into a prohibited area would result in the rejection of all claims. *Good Luck* was mortgaged to the plaintiff bank who were assignees to the policy. The Club had signed a letter of understanding that it would, at all times, inform the bank should the insurance cover 'cease'. Both the Club and the bank knew that *Good Luck* was under charter to an Iranian company but, when the Club discovered that ships of the Good Faith Group were entering prohibited areas, they failed to inform the bank or deter the owners in their actions. When, therefore, *Good Luck* was struck by an Iraqi missile in the Persian Gulf and declared a constructive total loss, the P & I Club refused any indemnity because, they contended, they had been given no notification of the vessel's entry into an additional premium area. The plaintiff bank, in turn, sued the P & I Club for damages for failing to inform them that *Good Luck* had become uninsured. Their claim was premised on: (a) breach of the letter of undertaking given by the Club; (b) breach of a duty of utmost good faith in failing to disclose to the bank what they (the Club) knew; and (c) breach of the duty to speak.

To determine whether the Club had committed a breach of the letter of the undertaking, the court had to ascertain whether the policy had in fact 'ceased', for it was only upon the cessation of the cover that the duty to inform would arise. And to answer this question, it was necessary for the court to ascertain the precise effect of the breach of the warranty.

The House of Lords, in overturning the decision of the Court of Appeal and reinstating the decision of the trial judge, ruled that the P & I Club had failed in their duty to inform the bank that the insurance cover had 'ceased' due to the breach of the warranty. Lord Goff took the opportunity to clarify the status of a warranty and the effects of its breach.

---

8   Hereinafter referred to as the *Good Luck* case.

Lord Goff of Chieveley: [p 202] ... Section 33(3) of the Act reflects what has been described, in successive editions of Chalmers and Owen, *The Marine Insurance Act 1906*, as the inveterate practice in marine insurance of using the term 'warranty' as signifying a condition precedent. As Lord Blackburn said, in *Thomson v Weems* (1884) 9 App Cas 671, p 684:

> In policies of marine insurance, I think it is settled by authority that any statement of a fact bearing upon the risk introduced into the written policy is, by whatever words and in whatever place, to be construed as a warranty, and, *prima facie*, at least that the compliance with the warranty is a condition precedent to the attaching of the risk.

Once this is appreciated, it becomes readily understandable that, if a promissory warranty is not complied with, the insurer is discharged from liability as from the date of the breach of warranty, for the simple reason that fulfilment of the warranty is a condition precedent to the liability or further liability of the insurer. This, moreover, reflects the fact that the rationale of warranties in insurance law is that the insurer only accepts the risk provided that the warranty is fulfilled. This is entirely understandable; and it follows that the immediate effect of a breach of a promissory warranty is to discharge the insurer from liability as from the date of the breach ... Here, where we are concerned with a promissory warranty, that is, a promissory condition precedent, contained in an existing contract of insurance, non-fulfilment of the condition does not prevent the contract from coming into existence. What it does (as s 33(3) makes plain) is to discharge the insurer from liability as from the date of the breach. Certainly, it does not have the effect of avoiding the contract *ab initio*. Nor, strictly speaking, does it have the effect of bringing the contract to an end. It is possible that there may be obligations of the assured under the contract which will survive the discharge of the insurer from liability, as, for example, a continuing liability to pay a premium. Even if, in the result, no further obligations rest on either parties, it is not correct to speak of the contract being avoided; and it is, strictly speaking, more accurate to keep to the carefully chosen words in s 33(3) of the Act, rather than to speak of the contract being brought to an end, though that may be the practical effect.

... But, as I have said, the insurer does not avoid the policy. Moreover, it is only in the sense of repudiating liability (and not of repudiating the policy) that it would be right to describe him [the insurer] as being entitled to repudiate. In truth, the insurer, as the Act provides, is simply discharged from liability as from the date of the breach, with the effect that thereupon he has a good defence to a claim by the assured.

Legal effects of a breach of warranty

Section 33(3) states that if a warranty is not exactly complied with, '... the insurer is discharged from liability as from the date of the breach of warranty, but without prejudice to any liability incurred by him before that date'. In the light of the *Good Luck* case, the word 'automatically' should now be read before the word 'discharged'.

Automatic discharge from liability

That, after the breach of a promissory warranty, the insurer is automatically discharged from liability or further liability, was clearly illustrated by Lord Goff in the *Good Luck* case, cited above.

> **Lord Goff of Chieveley:** [p 202] ... So it is laid down in s 33(3) that, subject to any express provision in the policy, the insurer is discharged from liability as from the date of the breach of warranty. Those words are clear. They show that discharge of the insurer from liability is *automatic* and is not dependent upon any decision by the insurer to treat the contract or the insurance as at an end ... [Emphasis added.]

Lord Goff was at pains to point out that only the insurer's *liability*, and not the contract itself, is terminated by the breach of a promissory warranty. Thus, when a ship enters a prohibited area and breaches a geographical warranty, and then leaves that area, the policy itself remains, to all intents and purposes, intact. It is also apparent that, from the very moment the breach of the warranty is committed, the insurer is discharged from liability or further liability under the policy.

This approach to a breach of a promissory warranty was actually proposed earlier by Kerr LJ, in *State Trading Corporation of India Ltd v M Golodetz Ltd* [1989] 2 Lloyd's Rep 277. Although this case was concerned with a contract of sale wherein a cargo of sugar was totally lost when the vessel carrying it sank, the question arose as to whether a condition in the sale amounted to a condition precedent. Thus, the court was essentially concerned with the same issues as those posed by promissory warranties; it was suggested that a 'new approach' was required, which was later confirmed by Lord Goff in the *Good Luck* case.

More recently, in *Hussain v Brown* [1996] 1 Lloyd's Rep 627, where commercial premises were damaged by fire, the insurers refused to indemnify the owners on the grounds that the proposal form, with respect to the fire alarm system, had been incorrectly completed. This, they argued, amounted to a breach of a warranty. Saville LJ said: [p 630] '... the breach of such a warranty produces an automatic cancellation of the cover, and the fact that a loss may have no connection at all with that breach is simply irrelevant.'

The insurer may waive the breach

Section 34(3) of the Act confirms that the insurer has the right to waive a breach of a warranty. But one may wish to ask the question as to whether it is still possible for an insurer to waive a breach of a warranty when he has, by reason of the breach, already been automatically discharged from liability or further liability as from the date of breach. This point arose as early 1874 in *Provincial Insurance Co of Canada v Leduc*, below, where the precise inquiry was whether a waiver, by way of an acceptance of an abandonment, albeit a constructive acceptance, can be of any avail in the event of a breach of warranty which, at that time, was known to have had the effect of *terminating* the contract.[9] The case is significant in its ruling that a waiver may take the form of an acceptance (actual or constructive) of an abandonment.

Provincial Insurance Co of Canada v Leduc (1874) LR 6 PC 224, PC

A schooner was lost when she entered the St Lawrence, a prohibited area. When the shipowner learned of the loss, a notice of abandonment was served on the insurers, who did not expressly accept the abandonment. In fact, the insurers sent their agent to the scene of the loss, who salved what he could of the cargo and carried out repairs to the vessel. The insurers then successfully claimed a salvage award against the schooner, which was sold on their behalf, but refused to indemnify the assured under the policy because of the breach of the warranty.

The court ruled that the insurers were liable under the policy, as they had constructively accepted the abandonment and, in so doing, waived the breach of the warranty.

> **Sir Barnes Peacock:** [p 242] ... It was contended that the vessel was not insured at the time when she was lost, as the insurance did not extend to a loss in the Gulf of St Lawrence after 15 November, and that an abandonment can be of no avail when there is no insurance. But the vessel was in fact insured; the loss occurred during the time and upon a voyage described in the policy, but there was a breach of one of the warranties or conditions expressed.
>
> [p 243] ... Suppose that, after they [the insurers] had raised the vessel, they had sold her for £10,000 in excess of the salvage expenses, it is clear that the plaintiff could not have turned round and claimed the full amount of the proceeds of the vessel upon the ground that the loss was not caused by a risk insured against, and that he had, consequently, no right to give notice of abandonment. If the plaintiff could not have treated the abandonment as a nullity, surely the defendant cannot be allowed, after acceptance, to rely upon a breach of the warranty or condition of which they had full notice at the time of their acceptance of the abandonment. Estoppels are mutual. If the mouth of one party is closed, so also is that of the other. By the abandonment and the acceptance of the abandonment, the matter is closed. The whole interest of the plaintiff in the thing abandoned was transferred to the defendants, and became their property.

Fortunately, this issue has now been largely resolved by the House of Lords in *Good Luck* **[1991] 2 Lloyd's Rep 191, HL,** where Lord Goff confirmed that the breach of a warranty only discharged the insurer from liability or further liability under the policy, but did not terminate the contract. Any liability

---

9 It is to be noted that, at the time when this case was decided, the law on the effect of a breach of a warranty was still unclear.

which the insurer had incurred under the policy prior to the breach is not discharged.

> **Lord Goff of Chieveley:** [p 202] ... Even if in the result no further obligations rest on either parties, it is not correct to speak of the contract being avoided; and it is, strictly speaking, more accurate to keep to the carefully chosen words in s 33(3) of the Act, rather than to speak of the contract being brought to an end, though that may be the practical effect. When, as s 34(3) contemplates, the insurer waives a breach of a promissory warranty, the effect is that, to the extent of the waiver, the insurer cannot rely upon the breach as having discharged him from liability. This is a very different thing from saying that discharge of the insurer from liability is dependent upon a decision by the insurer. As Kerr LJ said, in *State Trading Corporation of India Ltd v M Golodetz Ltd* [1989] 2 Lloyd's Rep 277, p 287, after referring to the decision of the Court of Appeal in the present case:
>
>> Thus, the correct analysis of a breach of warranty in an insurance contract may be that, the consequence of the breach is that the cover ceases to be applicable unless the insurer subsequently affirms the contract, rather than to treat the occurrence as a breach of the contract by the insured which the insurer subsequently accepts as a wrongful repudiation.
>
> It was no doubt because of the decision of the Court of Appeal in the present case that Kerr LJ expressed himself in tentative terms. But I respectfully agree with his basic approach, as I do with the approach of the judge, which is entirely consistent with the plain meaning of s 33(3) of the Marine Insurance Act 1906.

Notes

In his speech, Lord Goff raised several salient points. It can be seen that the legal effects of a breach of a promissory warranty is intimately connected with the fact that a promissory warranty is a promissory condition precedent, the breach of which would now automatically discharge the insurer from liability or further liability under the policy. As a promissory condition precedent, it does not, in the event of a breach, have the effect of bringing the contract to an end. And, as the contract still remains on foot, there is nothing (not even the consequence of automatic discharge) to prevent an insurer from exercising his right to waive the breach. Should the insurer decide to do nothing, the rule of automatic discharge will take its natural course – upon which he is freed from liability or further liability under the policy. Under the rule of automatic discharge, an insurer does not have to take any steps to discharge himself from liability, but he would have to take overt steps to waive the breach if he wishes to continue to be liable under the policy.

It should be noted here that, under common law, a breach of the warranty of legality cannot be waived.[10]

---

10 See *Gedge and Others v Royal Exchange Assurance Corporation* [1900] 2 QB 214, discussed below, p 334.

The Waiver Clause: cl 5.2 of the ICC (A), (B) and (C)

With respect to cargo, all the Institute Cargo Clauses, in cl 5.2, employ a Waiver Clause, which states:

> The Underwriters waive any breach of the implied warranties of seaworthiness of the ship and fitness of the ship to carry the subject matter insured to destination, unless the Assured or their servants are privy to such unseaworthiness or unfitness.

Provided that neither the Assured nor their servants are privy to such unseaworthiness or unfitness, the Waiver Clause, in essence, negates both ss 39(1) and 40(2) of the Act.[11]

Held covered clause

The severe consequences which the law has imposed upon an assured in the event of a breach of a warranty have led parties to include within their policy a provision such as the 'held covered' clause. As a reprieve, the insurer is not, provided that the terms of the clause are met, immediately discharged from liability by the breach of the specified warranty.

The 'Breach of Warranty' Clause, cl 3 of the ITCH(95), affirms that the policy is:

> Held covered in case of any breach of warranty as to cargo, trade, locality, towage, salvage services or date of sailing, provided notice be given to the Underwriters immediately after receipt of advices and any amended terms of cover and any additional premium required by them be agreed.

With respect to the IVCH(95), the Change of Voyage Clause, cl 2, only covers a breach of warranty 'as to towage or salvage services'. Equivalent 'held covered' clauses are also contained within other Institute Clauses, notably with respect to cargo[12] and freight.[13]

In the case of *Greenock Steamship Co v Maritime Insurance Co Ltd*, [1903] 1 KB 367; aff'd [1903] 2 KB 657, CA, the vessel insured under a voyage policy containing a held covered clause was adjudged unseaworthy when she left Montevideo with insufficient bunkers. The whole philosophy behind the 'held covered' clause was analysed by Bigham J, in the court of first instance, who laid down the rule that, when fixing an additional premium, '... the parties must assume that the breach was known to the parties at the time it happened, and must ascertain what premium it would then have been reasonable to charge'. It is also to be noted that the held covered clause under consideration was of general application, covering *any* breach of warranty.

---

11 See below, p 325.
12 See ICC (A), (B) and (C), cll 5.2 and 10.
13 See ITCF(95), cl 4 and IVCF(95), cl 3.

Immediately after receipt of advices

It is to be recalled that[14] some clarification as to the assured's duty to notify under a held covered clause was provided in *Mentz, Decker and Co v Maritime Insurance Co* [1909] 1 KB 132 and *Liberian Insurance Agency Inc v Mosse* [1977] 2 Lloyd's Rep 560, where the expressions 'due notice' and 'prompt notice' were employed respectively. Though the Institute Hull Clauses specify that notice be given to the underwriters 'immediately' after receipt of advices,[15] nevertheless, the cases are useful for the purpose of illustrating the point that, no matter how promptly or immediately after a breach an insurer must be notified, the law allows for the fact that an assured is only in a position to notify the insurer after he is in receipt of the relevant information concerning the breach. Thus, even if the insurer is informed of the breach only *after* a loss has taken place, that alone will not prevent the assured of the right to be held covered, provided that the notice is promptly or immediately issued after receipt of the advice.

Where a held covered clause is unqualified with respect to the time allowed to give the insurer notice of the breach of a warranty, as was the case in *Greenock Steamship Co v Marine Insurance Co Ltd* [1903] 1 KB 367; [1903] 2 KB 657 and *Thames and Mersey Marine Insurance Co Ltd v Van Laun and Co* [1917] 2 KB 48, HL,[16] the courts have held that the notice must be given within a reasonable time after the discovery of the breach.

EXPRESS WARRANTIES

The form of a warranty

An express warranty must be incorporated into the contract of insurance by means of written words. Oral statements made during negotiations do not amount to warranties; they are representations. Thus, the Act in s 35(1) states:

> An express warranty may be in any form of words from which the intention to warrant is to be inferred.

And, s 35(2) then goes on to affirm that:

> An express warranty must be included in, or written upon, the policy, or must be contained in some document incorporated by reference into the policy.

---

14 For a fuller discussion of the 'held covered' clause, see Chapter 4, p 161.
15 The Breach of Warranty Clause in the Institute Freight Clauses – Time and Voyage, also uses the word 'immediately', but the ICC (A), (B) and (C), in cl 10, employ the word 'prompt'.
16 These two cases are discussed in Chapter 4, pp 161–63.

Thus, a statement made in writing upon a slip or a proposal form or even a covering note, provided that it is then incorporated into the policy, may amount to a warranty. Furthermore, if an oral statement, a representation, is later incorporated in writing into the policy, it may also be construed as a warranty.

The principles laid down with respect to warranties were established long ago, and may be illustrated in two early cases; *Bean v Stupart* **(1778) 1 Dougl 11** and *Pawson v Watson* **(1778) 2 Cowp 786**. In *Bean v Stupart*, where, in the margin of the policy of insurance, were written the words 'Eight ninepounders ... 30 seamen, besides passengers' and the vessel sailed with a crew of 26 men, the owners were held to have breached what amounted to a warranty.

> **Lord Mansfield:** [p 14] ... There is no doubt, but that this is a warranty. Its being written on the margin makes no difference. Being a warranty, there is no doubt but that the underwriters would not be liable, if it were not complied with, because it is a condition on which the contract is founded.

But, in *Pawson v Watson*, where the issue was again the armament of a vessel and the sufficiency of crew, Lord Mansfield held that the condition only amounted to a representation because, *inter alia*, there was no written incorporation into the policy.

> **Lord Mansfield:** [p 786] ... At the trial I was of opinion, that it would be of very dangerous consequence to add a conversation that passed at the time, as part of the written agreement. It is a collateral representation; and if the parties had considered it as a warranty, it would have been inserted in the policy.

It is also emphasised that, as s 35(1) avers that: 'An express warranty may be in any form of words ... ', it is immaterial whether such a warranty is in standard form, as in the Institute Clauses, or is in the words of the contracting parties, provided that '... the intention to warrant is to be inferred.'

Exception clauses

Promissory warranties, though they need not be couched in any particular form of words, are generally prefaced with the word 'warranted'. Indeed, it is unfortunate that the same expression is also employed in marine policies to introduce an exception clause. The use of the phrase 'warranted free from ...'[17] is, thus, misleading, implying that the term could amount to a promissory warranty when it is patently not the case; such a condition or term

---

17 Eg, 'warranted free from particular average' and 'warranted free from capture and seizure'. In *Naviera de Canarias SA v Nacional Hispanica Aseguradora SA, 'Playa de las Nieves'* [1977] 1 Lloyd's Rep 457, HL, Lord Diplock remarked: [p 459] '"Warranted free from claims" of a particular description is the term of art used in a policy of marine insurance to introduce an exceptions clause excluding the liability of the insurer for losses of the kind described ...'

is intended only to relieve the insurer from liability for the specific loss resulting from its breach. But, when a true promissory warranty is infringed, the insurer is discharged from liability or further liability as from the date of breach, unless, of course, the breach has been waived by the insurer.

An exception clause is limited in scope. The insurer is excepted from liability only when the loss is occasioned by the specific excepted risk. Thus, a causal connection is paramount. In each case, it is for the court to decide whether a so called warranty is, or is not, a promissory warranty. Such was the issue in *The Cap Tarifa*, below, and in the recent case of *Transthene Packaging Co Ltd v Royal Insurance Co (UK) Ltd* [1996] LRLR 32.

Simons v Gale, 'Cap Tarifa' [1957] 2 Lloyd's Rep 485; aff'd [1958] 2 Lloyd's Rep 1, PC

The plaintiff loaned money to a third party, who wished to purchase and convert the vessel *Cap Tarifa* to carry cattle; the loan was to be repaid when cattle were actually loaded aboard her at Townsville. The plaintiff insured the loan with the defendants under two policies of insurance, whereby the risk underwritten was that the insurers would be liable under the policies if the cattle were not loaded within 90 days of *Cap Tarifa* leaving Noumea, where she underwent the conversion. However, the policy was claused: 'Warranted animals available for loading and all arrangements for conversion of vessel made at inception of insurance.' The cattle were not loaded within the prescribed time limit, and the plaintiff claimed on his policies, but the underwriters rejected the claim, on the basis that *Cap Tarifa* had not been converted to carry cattle before she left Noumea and, therefore, the plaintiff was in breach of the warranty.

The Supreme Court of Australia ruled that the warranty was a condition and not a promissory warranty. Nevertheless, as the plaintiff had breached the condition, he could not recover under the policy. The court, in its deliberations, was most careful in classifying the status of the term.

> **Walsh J:** [p 490] ... The question as to the onus of proof appears to me to require a consideration of the nature of the warranty. Is it to be regarded as a true condition precedent such that, unless it be fulfilled, no liability can be regarded as ever attaching under the policies? Or should it be regarded as a condition, the breach of which discharges the insurer from a contractual liability which is assumed to have come into operation?
>
> The term 'warranty' is used in different senses and, in insurance law, special considerations are applicable to the problem under discussion, apart from the general principles of contract law. Thus, the familiar distinction between conditions and warranty in the general law of contract is not applicable in the discussion of warranties in policies of insurances ...
>
> [p 491] ... In the present case, it is contended, for the plaintiff, that the warranty is of the latter type of condition, that is, a condition which has no effect on the formation of the contract, but which may operate to discharge or

excuse from liability ... I have come to the conclusion that the plaintiff's contention should be accepted, and that the onus of proof is on the defendant ... I think the warranty under consideration should be regarded as a 'relieving' or 'discharging' provision, rather than one which is a condition precedent to the formation of the contract.

In the *Good Luck* case, cited in full above,[18] Lord Goff was explicit in distinguishing between a promissory warranty and a 'warranty' which amounted to nothing more than an exception of liability for a particular risk.

> **Lord Goff of Chieveley:** [p 201] ... We are here concerned with the nature of warranties in contracts of marine insurance. We have to distinguish between two forms of warranty, viz, those warranties which simply denote the scope of the cover (as in the familiar f c and s clause – warranted free of capture and seizure) and those which are promissory warranties, involving a promise by the assured that the warranty will be fulfilled. It is with the latter type of warranty, which is the subject of ss 33–41 of the Marine Insurance Act 1906, that we are concerned in the present case.

Transthene Packaging Co Ltd v Royal Insurance Co (UK) Ltd [1996] LRLR 32

The plaintiff owned a company which manufactured and sold plastic bags, and was insured with the defendant, *inter alia*, against fire and loss of profit resulting from fire. Included in the policy was a warranty (W1) that oil and greasy waste and used cleaning cloths be kept in metal bins if left overnight on the premises, and a term (condition 6): 'Whether it increases the risk or not (non-compliance) shall be a bar to any claim in respect of such Property.' When a fire occurred at the factory during the day, the plaintiff claimed on his policy of insurance, but the insurers refused payment on the basis that: (a) the plaintiff was in breach of the warranty W1; (b) the fire had been started deliberately by the plaintiff; and (c) the plaintiff had fraudulently claimed for the total loss of equipment when such was not the case.[19]

The court ruled that the insurers we not liable under the policy, because the plaintiffs had fraudulently claimed for losses not incurred. However, the fire was adjudged to have been started by persons unknown and, with respect to the warranty, the defendant insurers had failed to discharge their onus of proof in showing that the warranty had not been complied with.

> **Judge Kershaw QC:** [p 46] ... The case for the defendant is that this is a continuing warranty, breach of which entitled the defendant to terminate the risk and avoid the policy. It is common ground that the use of the word 'warranty' in a policy is not conclusive that the term so described is a continuing warranty ... I agree that, on the ordinary and natural meaning of the words, W1 is a promise for the future. I agree that condition 6 is consistent with that construction, as well as prescribing the consequence of non-compliance with the warranty. I also agree that W1, both on the ordinary and

---

18 See above, p 276.
19 This defence is discussed in Chapter 6, p 234.

natural meaning of its wording and when read in conjunction with condition 6, are inconsistent with the construction for which Mr Wingate-Saul [for the plaintiff] contended, that the warranty is a description of the risk, that is, that it has an 'on-off' effect, so that there is no fire cover while there is a breach of the warranty, but that cover returned when there is no breach.

Burden of proving breach of warranty

Arnould, citing the case of *Bond Air Services Ltd v Hull* [1955] 2 QB 417 as authority, has in a brief and concise statement declared that: 'The burden of proving a breach of a warranty is on the underwriter, and this even where compliance is expressed to be a condition precedent to recovery under the policy.'[20] It is observed that the said case is cited in *Cap Tarifa* [1957] 2 Lloyd's Rep 485, and the issue of burden of proof has recently been broached in *Transthene Packaging Co Ltd v Royal Insurance Co (UK) Ltd* [1996] LRLR 32.

Reverting first to *Cap Tarifa* **[1957] 2 Lloyd's Rep 485**, it can be seen that Walsh J relied heavily upon the reasoning of Lord Goddard, in *Bond Air Services Ltd v Hill* [1955] 1 Lloyd's Rep 498, to support his stand on the subject.

Walsh J: [p 491] ... Lord Goddard CJ [in *Bond Air Services Ltd v Hill* [1955] 1 Lloyd's Rep 498] ... said [p 501]:

> I do not think it can be doubted that, ordinarily, it is for the underwriter to prove a breach of a condition, at least where he is not contending that the policy is void on the ground that there has been a breach of a condition precedent to the formation of the policy. So, too, it is for him to prove an exception. The difference between a condition and an exception is that the former places some duty or responsibility on the assured, while the latter restricts the scope of the policy. That it is for the insurers who allege that the conditions were broken to prove it, has, I think, always been accepted ...
>
> ... I think is axiomatic in insurance law that, as it is always for an insurer to prove an exception, so it is for him to prove the breach of a condition which would relieve him from liability in respect of a particular loss.
>
> ... what I think, certainly for a century and probably for much longer, has always been regarded as a fundamental principle of insurance law, that it is for the insurers who wish to rely on a breach of condition to prove it.

This 'fundamental principle' seems to be stated by his Lordship in the sentence last quoted as being applicable to all cases of breach of condition. But the earlier passages I have quoted from his reasons suggest that it may not apply in relation to a breach of a condition precedent to the formation of

---

20 *Op cit*, Arnould, fn 3, para 686. See, also, O'May, DR, *Marine Insurance*, 1995, p 79: 'The onus of proving breach of warranty lies upon underwriters (*Simons v Gale*, '*Cap Tarifa*'; and Ivamy, ER, *Chalmers' Marine Insurance Act 1906*, 1993, p 51, also citing the *Cap Tarifa* case: 'The onus of proving a breach of warranty lies on the insurer.'

the policy and that it may be limited to cases of breach of a condition which would relieve the insurer from liability.[21]

In *Transthene Packaging Co Ltd v Royal Insurance Co (UK) Ltd* [1996] LRLR 32, Judge Kershaw QC, after ruling that the warranty (W1) was a promissory warranty (and not an exception clause), proceeded to comment on the question of the burden of proof.

> **Judge Kershaw QC:** [p 48] ... I remind myself that the burden is on the defendant [the insurer] to establish the facts which are alleged to constitute breach of warranty. There must be shown to have been materials in the premises overnight which were not in metal receptacles with metal lids and which were oily and/or greasy, or there must have been other combustible trade waste in the premises overnight. The general impression that the premises of a factory were seldom, if ever, in the condition in which one would hope to find a hospital or kitchen is no substitute for proof. On the evidence, I am not satisfied on either of those allegations.

Descriptive warranties

Perhaps the most difficult aspect of distinguishing promissory warranties from other purported warranties is where a 'descriptive warranty' is employed. That is, where the subject matter insured does not exactly match the description of the subject matter in the policy. In such an instance, does the failure by the assured to comply with the exact description of the goods insured in the policy amount to a breach of a promissory warranty?

In *Yorkshire Insurance Co Ltd v Campbell* [1917] AC 218, PC, below, Lord Sumner was of the opinion that any written statement incorporated into the policy which 'qualified' the subject matter insured amounted to a promissory warranty.

Yorkshire Insurance Co Ltd v Campbell [1917] AC 218, PC

The respondent insured a horse with the appellants under a policy of marine insurance for a voyage from Sydney to Fremantle. The policy insured against the usual marine risks as well as the risk of mortality, but also included a written statement which described the horse's pedigree to be 'by Soult out of St Paul (mare), five years'. During the voyage, the horse died of natural causes and the owner of the horse claimed for a total loss. The underwriters refused

---

21 As a note of caution, it has to be pointed out that a distinction has to be made between a condition precedent 'to the formation of the policy' and a condition precedent 'to the liability or further liability' of the insurer under the policy. *Good Luck* [1991] 2 Lloyd's Rep 191, HL, has established beyond doubt that a promissory warranty belongs to the latter category; *per* Lord Goff [p 202]: 'Here, we are concerned with a promissory warranty, that is, a promissory condition precedent, contained in an *existing* contract of insurance; non-fulfilment of the condition does not prevent the contract from coming into existence.' [Emphasis added.]

an indemnity, on the basis that the assured had committed a breach of a promissory warranty, as the horse was not of the pedigree as described in the policy.

The Privy Council ruled that the description amounted to a promissory warranty, because the details of the horse's pedigree were expressly incorporated into the policy. Furthermore, as the parties to the contract had chosen specifically to identify the horse's pedigree, they were qualifying the subject matter insured and, therefore, it amounted to a promissory warranty.

> **Lord Sumner:** [p 221] ... When the applicant for insurance has to subscribe his statements in writing, and then they are made a part of the policy itself, the whole matter is changed. There is now no such question of fact for a jury; these are questions of construction for the court. There stand the statements in writing; they now form the basis and are part of the contract of insurance. The question is what they mean and what is their legal effect.
>
> [p 224] ... *Prima facie*, all the words which the policy contains (except parts of the general form inapplicable to the particular transaction) are words of contract, to which effect must be given. *Prima facie*, words qualifying the subject matter of the insurance will be words of warranty, which, in a policy of marine insurance, operate as conditions ... The Act itself provides that, where the words used express an intention to warrant, they have effect as a condition, which must be exactly complied with, whether material to the risk or not.
>
> [p 225] ... Their Lordships cannot say that such risks [covered by the policy] may not be capable of being affected by the circumstances expressed in the words which the respondent seeks to deprive of significance. The courage, the docility, the endurance of the horse, and the consequent likelihood of its making the voyage and being landed safely, may, for all their Lordships know, be affected one way or the other by the pedigree in question; and, in any case, since the parties have imported this statement into their contract, presumably they thought it material. Again, the words may be material if, in case of loss, the identity of the animal came to be disputed, or if, the vessel being overdue, the underwriters desired to reinsure their line on the horse. Their Lordships are therefore of opinion that effect must be given to the words in question by holding that the assured warranted their truth, in accordance with the intention expressed in the form of words employed, and, as the words turn out to have been unfounded, in fact, the policy is avoided and the appeal must be allowed.

Notes

In *Overseas Commodities v Style* [1958] 1 Lloyd's Rep 546, the insurers of a policy on goods refused to indemnify the assured when cans of pork were damaged because, contrary to the requirement contained in a warranty, the date of the manufacture had not been stamped on all the cans. McNair J was of the opinion that such an omission amounted to the breach of a promissory warranty, because the contract of insurance required that the date of manufacture be verified. However, he felt differently with regard to the identification marks; he held that the requirement relating to identification marks did not amount to a promissory warranty.

McNair J: [p 557] ... In my judgment, the use of the words 'for verification' point clearly and definitely to the conclusion that the tins must be marked in a manner which will identify the actual date of manufacture.

[p 558] ... Being satisfied that, as regards both policies, a substantial number of the tins ... were not marked with a code which enabled the true and correct date of manufacture to be established, I have no option but to hold that the breach of the express warranty affords the underwriters a complete defence in this action ... I myself am not prepared to hold that the words [concerning the identification marks] above quoted in the two policies are words of warranty in the strict sense.

Examples of express warranties

According to s 33(1) of the Act, a promissory warranty is a warranty:

(a) ... by which the assured undertakes that some particular thing shall or shall not be done or that some condition shall be fulfilled; or

(b) whereby he affirms or negatives the existence of a particular state of facts.

Thus, a promissory warranty can apply at the commencement of, or at any time during the currency of the risk. Furthermore, any statements made or denied by the assured which are then expressly incorporated into the policy must be adhered to.

Although an express warranty may be incorporated into a policy by the contracting parties 'in any form of words',[22] the Act and the Institute Hull Clauses specifically identify certain well established conditions which, through custom and usage are known to materially alter the risk, have been accepted as promissory warranties.

To this effect, the Act, the Institute Hull Clauses, and the Institute Warranties have identified:

(a) the warranty of neutrality;[23]

(b) the warranty of good safety;[24]

(c) the towage and salvage warranty;[25]

---

22 Marine Insurance Act 1906, s 35(1).
23 Ibid, s 36.
24 Ibid, s 38.
25 ITCH(95) and IVCH(95), cl 1.1.

(d) the classification clause;[26]

(e) the disbursements warranty;[27] and

(f) geographical warranties.[28]

Warranty of neutrality

The Act, in s 36(1), states:

> Where insurable property, whether ship or goods, is expressly warranted neutral, there is an implied condition that the property shall have a neutral character at the commencement of the risk, and that, so far as the assured can control the matter, its neutral character shall be preserved during the risk.

The Act then goes on, in s 36(2), to confirm that:

> Where a ship is expressly warranted 'neutral', there is also an implied condition that, so far as the assured can control the matter, she shall be properly documented, that is to say, that she shall carry the necessary papers to establish her neutrality, and that she shall not falsify or suppress her papers. If any loss occurs through breach of this condition, the insurer may avoid the contract.

Thus, the Act will imply a warranty that the ship shall be properly documented if the policy incorporates an express promissory warranty of neutrality. In so doing, the Act confirms that it is not sufficient for the ship simply to declare herself neutral; she must be properly documented in order to substantiate that neutrality.

This principle was established as long ago as 1804, in the old case of *Baring v Christie* (1804) 5 East 398. In this instance, during the Napoleonic wars, a neutral American vessel trading to Europe was captured by a French cruiser. Because the documentation regarding the master's place of abode was not strictly complied with, the owners of the cargo aboard the vessel could not claim on their policy, as the warranty of neutrality had been breached. Lord Ellenborough CJ observed that: [p 404] '... the description of the ship in the said policy clearly contains a warranty that she was an American ship, which induces a necessity of her being documented, as American ships are required to be, by the treaties between that State and France ...'

---

26 ITCH(95), cl 4.1 and IVCH(95), cl 3.1.

27 ITCH(95), cl 22 and IVCH(95), cl 20.

28 The Institute Warranties (1/7/76) identify specific global regions which are warranted as prohibited.

Warranty of good safety

Section 38 of the Act states:

> Where the subject matter insured is warranted 'well' or 'in good safety' on a particular day, it is sufficient if it be safe at any time during that day.

This definition of 'good safety' contained within the Act is derived from the old case of *Blackhurst v Cockell*, below.[29]

Blackhurst v Cockell (1789) 3 Term Rep 360

This was an action on a policy on goods which were insured for a voyage from London to Liverpool 'lost or not lost' and 'warranted well 9 December 1784'. The policy was underwritten between one and three o'clock in the afternoon of that day, but the ship was actually lost at about eight o'clock on the same morning. The insurers refused to indemnify the assured.

The court ruled that the underwriters were liable. It was sufficient that the ship was safe at any time during that day for the warranty to be complied with.

> **Lord Kenyon CJ:** [p 361] The single question is whether the warranty at the bottom of the policy means warranted well at the time when the defendant subscribed it, or any time on that day. And we are all of opinion that, if the ship were well at any time of that day, it is sufficient; and the underwriter is consequently liable.

Warranty as to towage and salvage

Both the ITCH(95) and the IVCH(95), in cl 1.1 (the Navigation Clause), warrant that the insured vessel shall not be towed except in specific circumstances, nor shall she undertake salvage services under any previously arranged contract. As such activities would materially alter the risk underwritten, cl 1.1 states:

> ... it is warranted that the Vessel shall not be towed, except as is customary or to the first safe port or place when in need of assistance, or undertake towage or salvage services under a contract previously arranged by the Assured and/or Owners and/or Managers and/or Charterers. This Clause 1.1 shall not exclude customary towage in connection with loading and discharging.

However, it is accepted that towage contracts must sometimes be entered into in accordance with local law and practice and, in particular, where such contracts limit or exempt the liability of pilots, tugs and tug owners. Therefore, cl 1.2 affirms that:

---

29 Rule 3 of the Rules for Construction also employs the term 'good safety' when the policy is for a voyage 'at and from' a particular place.

This insurance shall not be prejudiced by reason of the Assured entering into any contract with pilots or for customary towage which limits or exempts the liability of the pilots and/or tugs and/or towboats and/or their owners when the Assured or their agents accept or are compelled to accept such contracts in accordance with local law or practice.

Thus, where towage is concerned, the main criterion with which the warranty is concerned is whether such towage is customary or not. This very point was raised in *Russell v Provincial Insurance Co Ltd*, below.

Russell v Provincial Insurance Co Ltd [1959] 2 Lloyd's Rep 275

The plaintiff insured his small fishing vessel *Robsim* with the defendants under a policy of insurance, which included a condition which stated: 'No claim shall attach to this policy while the vessel is being towed (except as is customary or when in need of assistance) ...' However, the plaintiff wished to move *Robsim* up the Thames estuary and, as was customary in the region, she was lashed to another boat in order that both boats could be moved at the same time, thus saving fuel and manpower. During the short voyage, *Robsim* grounded and was totally lost. The plaintiff claimed on his policy of insurance, but the underwriters denied liability, on the basis that the condition had been breached, thereby discharging them from liability.

The court ruled in favour of the plaintiff. The act of lashing the two boats together was customary in the trade and, furthermore, it did not amount to towage.

> **McNair J:** [p 280] ... The question is whether, on those findings of fact, the case is brought within the policy conditions ... having regard to the evidence, which I accept, that it is quite common and customary in this trade for these vessels, even though both are perfectly navigable and fit, to proceed in company abreast, economising on fuel by using the two engines and economising in labour by having one man only at the wheel, I think that it is quite wrong on this policy to hold that that operation constitutes towing.

Notes

What is or is not a 'safe port or place' is not defined. According to Lord Porter in *The Troilus* **[1951] 1 Lloyd's Rep 467, p 471, HL**, much depends upon '... the facts of each case, one of which is the facility for repairs at the place in question, and another, the possibility of safely discharging and storing the cargo and sending it on to its destination and the danger of its deterioration'.

It is emphasised that a breach of the Navigation Clause, cl 1.1 of the ITCH(95) within which the towage and salvage warranties lie, would be 'held covered' by cl 3, the Breach of Warranty Clause, provided that the conditions contained within the latter are adhered to.

Identical towage and salvage warranties appear in the equivalent Navigation Clause, cl 1.1. contained within the IVCH(95). However, in this instance, the warranties are 'held covered' by cl 2, the Change of Voyage Clause.

The Classification Clause

Although the Classification Clause in the Institute Hull Clauses, both Time and Voyage, is not actually expressed as a warranty, the importance of the provision is such that it materially affects the risk and, therefore, is likely to be construed as a promissory warranty. Clause 4 of the ITCH(95) provides that:[30]

> 4.1 It is the duty of the Assured, Owners and Managers at the inception of and throughout the period of this insurance to ensure that:
>
>> 4.1.1 the Vessel is classed with a Classification Society agreed by the Underwriters and that her class within that Society is maintained;
>>
>> 4.1.2 any recommendations requirements or restrictions imposed by the Vessel's Classification Society which relate to the Vessel's seaworthiness or to her maintenance in a seaworthy condition are complied with by the dates required by that Society;
>
> 4.2 in the event of any breach of the duties set out in Clause 4.1 above, unless the Underwriters agree to the contrary in writing, they will be discharged from liability under this insurance as from the date of the breach provided that if the Vessel is at sea at such date the Underwriters' discharge from liability is deferred until arrival at her next port.

The wording of cl 4.1 and, in particular, cl 4.2, which spells out the effects the breach has upon the contract, is, it is submitted, sufficiently positive to be read as a term imposing a continuing warranty of the matters referred therein. Construed as such, it would, in the event of its breach, attract the operation of s 33(3), as interpreted by the House of Lords in the *Good Luck* case, to mean that the insurer is automatically discharged from liability or further liability as from the date of breach.

Clause 4.2 provides the insurer with another weapon to his armoury in denying liability for unseaworthiness. Unlike s 39(5), which requires proof of a causal connection between the unseaworthiness and the loss, cl 4.2 couched in terms of a promissory warranty dispenses with this requirement. A breach of cl 4.2 *per se*, with or without proof of a causal link, is sufficient to discharge the insurer from liability or further liability as from the date of the breach.

Notes

The importance of classification and the continuing maintenance of such cannot be overstated. It should not be overlooked that the failure to maintain class may be construed as the non-disclosure of a material fact, as was the case in *Gandy v Adelaide Marine Insurance Co*, below.

---

30 See, also, IVCH(95), cl 3.

Gandy v Adelaide Marine Insurance Co (1871) LR 6 QB 746

The plaintiff's barque *Annie* was registered with Lloyd's as A1 for seven years. When the half time survey became due, the plaintiff declined to have the survey carried out, and informed Lloyd's that he no longer wished the vessel to be registered with them. However, the plaintiff had previously effected a policy of insurance on *Annie* with the defendants, but did not inform them that the classification with Lloyd's had lapsed. Thus, when *Annie* was later wrecked and totally lost, the insurers refused an indemnity under the policy because of the concealment of the change in the ship's status.

The court ruled that the fact that the plaintiff had not retained *Annie* on the register at Lloyd's was material, and should have been communicated to the underwriters. Cockburn CJ highlighted the importance of classification as follows:

> [p 757] ... Now, the degradation of a vessel from her class appears to me important, as necessarily carrying with it the presumption that a deterioration in the condition of the vessel has taken place, a circumstance, of course, calculated materially to influence the decision of the underwriter as to the amount of premium he will require as the consideration for undertaking the risk.
>
> I take it that if an underwriter, not being a subscriber to Lloyd's, who had been in the habit of insuring a vessel represented to him as classed A1 in Lloyd's register, were asked to renew the insurance at a time when the vessel had been degraded from her class – this not being within his knowledge – the degradation of the vessel would be a fact the omission to inform him of which would amount to concealment of a material fact. If so, the refusal to submit to the survey being, as it seems to me, equivalent to degradation, the fact of such a refusal was, in my judgment, a material fact which ought to have been communicated to the underwriter, unless the latter knew, or ought to have known it.

The Disbursements Warranty

It is not uncommon practice for disbursements, managers' commissions and other expenditures to be insured under a marine policy. However, both the Institute Hull Clauses, Time and Voyage, warrant that such disbursements may only be insured up to 25% of the value stated in the policy. The Disbursements Warranties in the ITCH(95) and the IVCH(95) both state:[31]

> 22.1 Additional insurances as follows are permitted:
>> 22.1.1 Disbursements, Managers' Commissions, Profits or Excess or Increased Value of Hull and Machinery. A sum not exceeding 25% of the value stated herein.

---

31 See ITCH(95), cl 22, and IVCH(95), cl 20. See Chapter 3, p 116.

22.1.2 Freight, Chartered Freight, or Anticipated Freight insured for time. A sum not exceeding 25% of the value as stated herein less any sum insured, however described, under 22.1.1.

This limitation on the sum insurable is specifically incorporated into the policy as a result of the *Gunford* case, below.

Thames and Mersey Marine Insurance Co Ltd v 'Gunford' Ship Co Ltd [1911] AC 529, HL

The plaintiff owners of the sailing ship *Gunford* insured her with various underwriters for £19,000, a considerable over-valuation. The gross freight was also insured, as were the disbursements, which were covered by a ppi policy;[32] in addition, the shipping manager effected ppi policies for his own protection. All in all, the insurance cover amounted to £35,800, when the property at risk only amounted to £14,000. When the defendant insurers had underwritten part of the hull insurance, they had been unaware of the existence of the other policies, or of the fact that the master of *Gunford* had not been to sea for 22 years. When *Gunford* was wrecked and totally lost, the defendants refused to indemnify the plaintiff for two reasons: (a) that the vessel was unseaworthy due to the incompetence of the master, and (b) that the non-disclosure by the assured of the existence of the other policies amounted to the concealment of material facts.

The House of Lords ruled that *Gunford* was seaworthy, but the failure by the plaintiff to inform the defendants of the over-insurance amounted to a non-disclosure of a material fact and, therefore, the insurers were not liable.

Lord Alverstone CJ: [p 539] ... I unhesitatingly come to the conclusion that, both from the point of view of fixing the premium and determining whether he would undertake the risk, the over-valuation was a matter material to be considered by the underwriter.

Lord Shaw of Dunfermline: [p 544] ... So far as the effecting of insurances upon freight is concerned, that is sound business, because it is grounded upon a stipulation for true indemnity; but so far as disbursements, wherever they are duplications of freight, are concerned, these, when freight has already been insured, form no part of a contract of indemnity, but the insurance upon them is merely a gamble, discountenanced by sound principle and not enforceable by law.

Geographical warranties

Marine hull policies sometimes specify certain geographical regions within which the ship is prohibited from trading. This raises the question of whether, in prohibiting entry into these areas, there is created a promissory warranty,

---

32 Policy proof of interest, sometimes known as 'honour policies'. Such policies were illegal under the Marine Insurance Act 1745, but are now merely 'void' under the 1906 Act, s 4, as gaming or wagering contracts. See Chapter 1, p 5.

that is, if a prohibited area is entered into, is the insurer discharged from all liability or further liability under the policy from the date of the breach, or is he merely discharged from liability only for any loss which occurs whilst the vessel is actually within the prohibited area?

In the early case of *Colledge v Hardy*, below, the court was in no doubt that a geographical prohibition amounted to a promissory warranty.

Colledge v Hardy (1851) 6 Exch 205

A policy of insurance was effected on a vessel which declared that the assured's vessel was not to sail from an east coast port in Great Britain to Baltic ports beyond Copenhagen between certain dates during the winter. However, the assured's vessel did in fact sail from Newcastle for Flensburg, beyond Copenhagen, during the prohibited period, but was lost before passing Copenhagen. Thus, the issue before the court was: if the geographical prohibition amounted to a promissory warranty, the insurer was discharged from all liability under the policy but, if the prohibition only amounted to an exception, then, as the vessel had not passed Copenhagen, the assured was entitled to recover.

> **Parke B:** [p 211] ... The next question is, whether this provision is to be considered as an exception or a warranty. If it is an exception, the plaintiff is entitled to judgment *non obstante veredicto*, in as much as the plea is bad for not containing an averment that the ship was lost during a prohibited voyage. Upon this part of the case I entertained some doubt, but, on the whole, I think it ought to be construed as a warranty, and not as an exception ... The reason which induces me to construe this as a warranty and not an exception is, that there is no time in which the vessel is to be on the policy again; and the consequence of holding this an exception would be, that the policy would cease during the voyage within the prohibited period, and after that the ship would be again on the policy. But if a voyage to the Baltic was intended to be altogether prohibited during a particular season, it would be singular that the vessel should be again on the policy. The rule must therefore be construed not as an exception, but as a warranty.

Similarly, in *Birrell v Dryer*, below, the House of Lords were in no doubt that a clause in the policy prohibiting entry into the St Lawrence during the prescribed winter months amounted to a promissory warranty.[33]

Birrell and Others v Dryer and Others (1884) 9 App Cas 345, HL

The plaintiffs insured their sailing barque *Chipman* with the defendants under a time policy of insurance which included a geographical prohibition which stated: '... warranted no St Lawrence between 1 October and 1 April.' *Chipman* sailed from Cardiff in September 1878 and delivered her cargo of rails to Prince Edward Island in the Gulf of St Lawrence, leaving there on 14

---

33 See also *Provincial Insurance Co of Canada v Leduc* (1874) LR 6 PC 224.

December. On her homeward voyage, *Chipman* called into another port in the Gulf of St Lawrence for some cargo, but was later lost in the open sea, and her owners claimed on their policy for a total loss. The underwriters refused to indemnify the assured, contending that the prohibition, which had been breached, amounted to a promissory warranty.

The House of Lords, in overturning the decision of the lower court, ruled that the breach amounted to the breach of a promissory warranty, and the underwriters were discharged from all liability.

> **Lord Watson:** [p 353] ... It must, therefore, be taken as an established fact that there was a breach of warranty through the vessel being navigated within the limits of the Gulf of St Lawrence, during the voyage, in the course of which she was lost, if it be held that the warranty applies to the gulf. In that case, it follows that the respondents cannot recover, under the policy, either the average loss accruing during the deviation, or for the total loss which subsequently occurred.

Why a geographical prohibition should be construed as a true promissory warranty and not just a term which limits the scope of the policy depends very much on the construction of the clause. Thus, where there is clearly an intention to warrant that an area is prohibited, the courts have treated any such breach as a breach of a promissory warranty.

Returning to *Birrell v Dryer* **(1884) 9 App Cas 345, HL**, where a vessel sailed into the Gulf of St Lawrence during the prohibited winter months, Lord Watson was of the opinion that a geographical warranty amounted to a promissory warranty because the limits, set by the policy, provided 'a definition of the subject matter of the insurance'.

> **Lord Watson:** [p 354] ... The main object of the clause is to define the limits within which the vessel is to be kept whilst she is navigated under the policy; and that appears to me to be as much the concern of the shipowner as of the underwriters. To define the limits within which the vessel is to be navigated, for the purposes of a time policy, is, in principle, precisely the same thing as to describe the voyage for which a vessel is insured under an ordinary policy. In both cases, it is a definition of the subject matter of the insurance, a term of the contract, the settlement of which must, in my opinion, be regarded, in a case like the present, as the deliberate act of both parties.

But, in the non-marine case of *Re Morgan and Provincial Insurance Co* **[1932] 2 KB 70, CA**, the court were mindful that not every provision in a policy which purports to be a warranty actually amounts to a promissory warranty.[34] In this instance, a lorry was insured on the basis of carrying coal only. During the currency of the policy, the lorry suffered an accident whilst carrying coal but, because the lorry had previously carried a load of timber,

---

34 There are a number of non-marine cases which have taken similar approaches: see *Roberts v Anglo-Saxon Insurance Ltd* (1927) 10 LlL Rep 313; and *Farr v Motor Traders Mutual Insurance Society Ltd* [1920] 3 KB 669.

the insurers contended that that had amounted to a breach of a promissory warranty and that they were discharged from all liability. However, the Court of Appeal found for the plaintiff lorry owner, because the term only 'defined the risk covered'[35] and not the whole subject matter of the insurance.

> **Scrutton LJ:** [p 79] ... In many cases of this class, the question has arisen whether answers in a proposal form are promises that a certain state of things shall continue, or a certain course of conduct shall continue, during the whole period covered by the policy, so that if the particular promise is not kept, the policy is invalidated; or where these promises are merely descriptive of the risk, so that if the accident happens while the promised state of things subsists there is a valid claim, but if the accident happens while the state of things has ceased or been interrupted there is no valid claim; but that, provided the loss occurs while the state of things is in being, the policy is not avoided by the fact that at some other time the state of things has been discontinued or interrupted.
>
> ... No doubt a great deal turns upon the language of the particular policy; but it must be remembered that, in contracts of insurance, the word 'warranty' does not necessarily mean a condition or promise the breach of which will avoid the policy. A warranty that a marine policy is free from particular average certainly does not mean that if there is a partial loss to the insured ship the whole policy is avoided. It merely describes the risk, and means that the only risk being insured against is the risk of a total loss, and that a partial loss is not the subject of the insurance.

In the Australian case of *Wilson v Boag*, below, a geographical limit contained in the policy was held as only restricting the cover of the insurance.

Wilson v Boag [1957] 2 Lloyd's Rep 564, Supreme Court of New South Wales

The plaintiff effected a time policy of insurance on the motor launch *Irene* which stipulated: '... whilst the same *Irene* is used for private and pleasure purposes only on the waters of Port Stephens and within a radius of 50 miles thereof ...' When a loss occurred during a voyage to Sydney, which is 90 miles from Port Stephens, the insurers were held liable under the policy because the point at which the loss actually took place was within the 50 mile limit. In so ruling, the court had decided that the clause did not amount to a promissory warranty, the breach of which would have discharged the insurers from all liability. Instead, the clause was held to be nothing more than a term in the policy which limited the risk covered.

> **Supreme Court of New South Wales:** [p 565] ... On the whole, we are of opinion that the policy here in question should not be construed as a voyage policy attaching only to voyages intended to begin and end within the perimeter and to remain wholly within it. It is to be regarded rather as a time

---

35 Scrutton LJ suggested that the 'so called' geographical warranty in *Birrell v Dryer* (1884) 9 AC 345, HL, was not a promissory warranty but one which 'merely defines the risk insured against'.

policy in which is contained a limitation of the liability of the insurer to loss sustained while the launch is within a defined geographical area.

Notes

Thus, it is of primary importance for the court to establish that what purports to be a warranty is clear in its construction and defines the subject matter of insurance, and not just the risk covered. In the *Good Luck* case, cited in full earlier in the chapter,[36] where a vessel entered a prohibited zone and was struck by a missile, the House of Lords were in no doubt that the entry into the zone amounted to the breach of a promissory warranty and the insurers were discharged from further liability under the policy.

It is also to be noted that a mere intention to sail into a prohibited area does not constitute a breach of a geographical warranty. In *Simpson Steamship Co Ltd v Premier Underwriting Association Ltd* (1905) 10 Com Cas 198; 10 Asp MLC 127, the warranty prohibited the assured from proceeding 'to the east of Singapore'. The insurer contended that the moment the ship lifted her anchor at Cardiff and started on her voyage to Kiao-chau, she was 'proceeding east of Singapore' and was, therefore, in breach of the warranty. This was rejected by Bigham J, who held that: [p 201] 'There was at most merely an intention to proceed east of Singapore, and an intention to commit a breach, of course, does not itself constitute a breach.'

Construction of warranties

Where there is ambiguity in a warranty, it falls upon the court to interpret the warranty in a reasonable manner, and then apply it literally and strictly. Thus, in **Hart v Standard Marine Insurance Co [1889] 22 QBD 499, CA**, where a vessel loaded some 'steel' items and, in so doing, exceeded a tonnage warranty which stated: 'Warranted no iron, or ore, or phosphate cargo, exceeding the net registered tonnage', the court was obliged to decide whether steel items were also precluded by the warranty.

> **Lord Esher:** [p 501] ... what is the ordinary sense in which the words used in this warranty would be accepted by mercantile men engaged in the business of insurance? If the words are capable of two meanings, you may look to the object with which they are inserted, in order to see which meaning businessmen would attach to them ... The learned judge [at the original trial] has held, and I think rightly, that, in this warranty, primarily 'iron' would include 'steel', and it is not enough to displace this to show that, in other mercantile matters, or in the body of the policy, the words would have a distinct meaning. The learned judge was of opinion that there was no evidence to show that in such a warranty there was a usage as to any limited

---

36 See above, p 276.

meaning of the expression 'iron'. The two questions for a jury would be whether such a warranty had become common; if not, there would be an end to the plaintiff's case. The other question would be whether, if the warranty was a common one, the words had acquired by usage a distinct meaning in the warranty. The learned judge was of opinion that the plaintiff had failed to produce evidence on either point, and I think, under the circumstances, he was absolutely right.

A similar reasoned and logical approach had been taken in the much earlier case of *Bean v Stupart* (1778) 1 Dougl 11, where the court, in interpreting a warranty with respect to crewing, was obliged to decide whether 'boys' counted as seamen. Lord Mansfield pointed out that: [p 14] '... the question is, whether, in this warranty, the word 'seamen' was used in the strict literal sense or not. If it was, the warranty has not been complied with. It is a matter of construction.'

The rule of contra proferentum

The courts have, because of the harsh consequences of a breach of a promissory warranty, applied the rule of *contra proferentum* to resolve any ambiguity in the policy. By this rule, an ambiguous clause will be construed to the advantage of the assured, and to detriment of the insurer.

Thus, in the non-marine case of **Simmonds v Cockell [1920] 1 KB 843**, where a house contents policy contained the clause: 'Warranted that the said premises are always occupied', Roche J construed the warranty as meaning, not that the property need literally be occupied at all times, but only continually used as a residence.

> **Roche J:** [p 844] ... if the warranty does not bear the meaning which I have given to it, I should hold that the language used is very ambiguous; and it is a well known principle of insurance law that if the language of a warranty in a policy is ambiguous, it must be construed against the underwriter who has drawn the policy and has inserted the warranty for his own protection.

In the American case of **Winter v Employers Fire Insurance Co [1962] 2 Lloyd's Rep 320**, where a policy on a motor boat provided cover: 'only within the limits of the continental United States of America ...', and a loss occurred 14 miles from the US coast, the court gave the phrase 'continental United States of America' its broadest possible meaning.

> **Tyrie A Boyer J:** [p 323] ... If the foregoing discussion does nothing more, it clearly demonstrates the ambiguity of the phrase or term 'within the limits of the continental United States of America'. The law is well settled that an ambiguity in a policy of marine insurance must be construed most favourably to the insured and most strictly against a forfeiture.
>
> ... As in other policies, marine contracts are strictly construed against the insurer and favourably to the insured, and where two interpretations are possible, that which will indemnify the insured will be adopted. Any

ambiguity in the policy will be resolved against the company ... Any construction of a marine policy rendering it void should be evaded ... If a marine insurance company desires to limit or restrict the operation of the general provisions of its contract by special proviso, exception, or exemption, it should express such limitation in clear and unmistakable language ... And where restrictive provisions are open to two interpretations, that which is most favourable to the insured is adopted.

And, in *Birrell v Dryer* **(1884) 9 App Cas 345, HL**, the policy on a ship contained the words: '... warranted no St Lawrence between 1 October and 1 April.' When the vessel entered the St Lawrence during the prohibited winter season and was later lost in the open sea, the court had to decide whether the geographical warranty covered both the river and the outlying gulf. Thus, the issue of whether there was any ambiguity in the wording of the warranty was raised.

> **Lord Watson:** [p 354] ... Although the rule of construction *contra proferentum* may not apply, I think it was rightly argued for the respondents that, seeing the clause in question occurs in the shape of an exception from a leading term of the policy which gives the vessel leave to navigate in any waters, it can only receive effect in so far as it is plain and unambiguous. But I am not satisfied that there is any ambiguity, such as will avail the respondents, to be found in the clause when it is read as a whole ... in the present case any ambiguity which might otherwise have arisen is expelled by the word 'no'. It is a universal negative, and in my opinion, excludes all navigable waters, salt or fresh, bearing the name of St Lawrence, which can reasonably be held to have been within the contemplation of the parties to the policy.

Recently, in *Transthene Packaging Co Ltd v Royal Insurance Co (UK) Ltd* [1996] LRLR 32,[37] the applicability of the *contra proferentum* rule was endorsed by Judge Kershaw QC, who agreed with counsel for the plaintiff that: [p 47] '... any ambiguity in the policy should be construed *contra proferentum*.' But, as there was no ambiguity in the warranty, it was unnecessary for him 'to resort to that canon of construction in order to determine the legal effect of the warranty'.

IMPLIED WARRANTIES

An implied warranty is a condition of the contract of insurance which is so fundamental to that contract that it is presumed to apply without having to make express provision for such. Thus, the Act sets out four such implied warranties:

(a) the implied warranty of portworthiness, s 39(2);

(b) the implied warranty of seaworthiness, s 39;

---

37 The facts of which have been cited earlier, see above, p 285.

(c) the implied warranty of cargoworthiness, s 40(2); and

(d) the implied warranty of legality, s 41.

The implied warranty of portworthiness

Where a voyage policy of insurance stipulates that the policy attaches 'at and from' a particular place,[38] it is implied that the ship must be in a reasonably fit condition to withstand the ordinary perils of the port in which she is lying at the commencement of the risk. Thus, s 39(2) states:

> Where the policy attaches while the ship is in port, there is also an implied warranty that she shall, at the commencement of the risk, be reasonably fit to encounter the ordinary perils of the port.

This issue was considered in *Dixon v Sadler* (1839) 5 M&W 405, where a vessel was lost in a squall after the master and crew had wilfully removed ballast before entering port, thereby reducing her stability. Although, on this occasion, the policy in question was a time policy, Parke B was disposed to comment on voyage policies of insurance when he stated: [p 414] '... If the assurance attaches before the voyage commences, it is enough that the state of the ship be commensurate to the then risk ...'[39]

However, it is possible to effect insurance specifically against port risks,[40] and such was the case in *Mersey Mutual Underwriting Association Ltd v Poland*, below. The relevance of the case is that it established when 'port risks' ended and when the risks for the sea passage began. Furthermore, in reaching his decision, Hamilton J outlined the risks associated with a port and, therefore, the requirements of portworthiness.

Mersey Mutual Underwriting Association Ltd v Poland (1910) 15 Com Cas 205

The owners of the sailing barque *Sunlight* insured her under a time policy of insurance with the plaintiff underwriters. The plaintiffs then entered into a contract of reinsurance with the defendants, whereby *Sunlight* was covered for port risks until leaving Shannon, in Ireland. Whilst *Sunlight* was leaving Shannon, she struck the bottom and was damaged. The plaintiffs indemnified the owners of *Sunlight* under the standard marine policy and then sought to recover this indemnity from the defendant reinsurers by claiming on their port risks policy. The defendants rejected the claim.

---

38 See Rules for Construction of Policy, r 3.

39 See, also, *Quebec Marine Insurance Co v Commercial Bank of Canada* (1870) LR 3 PC 234, PC, where Lord Penzance further stated: [p 241] '... The case of *Dixon v Sadler*, and the other cases which have been cited, leave it beyond doubt that there is seaworthiness for the port.'

40 See the Institute Time Clauses Hulls, Port Risks (20/7/87) and the Institute Time Clauses Hulls, Ports Risks including Limited Navigation (20/7/87).

The court ruled that the plaintiffs could not recover on the port risks policy as risks associated with the port terminated when *Sunlight* left her moorings.

Hamilton J: [p 209] ... It seems to me that the essential point in the words 'port risks', both in the sense in which they are understood at Lloyd's and the ordinary sense, is, that it is a risk of a character peculiar to a port and which is involved in a vessel being in port for the ordinary purposes for which a vessel is in port, as distinguished from the risks of a vessel on a voyage, subjecting herself to the ordinary perils of navigating on that voyage.

[p 211] ... I think that the risk under a port risk policy ceases when the ship, being fitted and equipped for sea, and possessed of her clearances, crew, and, if necessary, her cargo, commences to navigate upon her voyage, and no longer remains moored in the port in the course of preparing for the voyage.

Notes

It is emphasised that, where a voyage policy of insurance states that the policy is 'from'[41] and not 'at and from' the port in question, there is no requirement for the vessel to be portworthy, as the attachment of the risk only takes place once the sea passage of the voyage has commenced.

The implied warranty of seaworthiness

Section 39(1) of the Act is as explicit in verifying that there is an implied warranty of seaworthiness in a voyage policy, as s 39(5) is in verifying that there is no such implied warranty applicable at any stage of the adventure in a time policy. Because of the nature of a time policy, whereby the risk does not attach at some specific geographical position, as with a voyage policy, it is neither practicable nor reasonable to imply the warranty in such a policy. Nevertheless, this does not mean that seaworthiness is not important in a time policy – it simply means that it has to be approached differently.

The rationale for this difference in the law between a voyage and a time policy was expounded in *Gibson v Small*, below. The House of Lords was not prepared, for practical reasons, to imply a warranty of seaworthiness in a time policy.

Gibson v Small (1853) 4 HL Cas 353

The plaintiffs insured their vessel *Susan* with the defendants under a time policy of insurance 'lost or not lost' for one calendar year. During the passage from Madras to Mauritius, *Susan* encountered severe weather, was seriously damaged and eventually had to put back to Madras. On the day when the policy attached, *Susan* was at sea, badly damaged and seeking refuge in

---

41 See Rules for Construction of Policy, r 2.

Madras to effect repairs. When *Susan* reached Madras, she had, because of the severity of the damage, to be sold, as she was uneconomic to repair. The plaintiffs gave notice of abandonment and claimed for a constructive total loss. The underwriters denied liability, alleging that *Susan* was not seaworthy at the attachment of the risk.

The House of Lords, affirming the decision of the Exchequer Chamber, ruled in favour of the plaintiffs on the basis that, with a time policy, there could be no warranty of seaworthiness, and the insurers were liable under the policy.

> **Parke B:** [p 405] ... It may happen, indeed, in some cases, from the want of proper materials, of skillful artisans, of proper docks in the port of outfit, of sufficient funds or credit, or from the hidden nature of defects, that the owner may not be able to fulfil his duty of making the ship seaworthy at the commencement of the voyage; but the law cannot regard these exceptional cases, *ad ea quae frequentius accidunt jura adaptantur*; and it wisely, therefore, lays down a general rule, which is a most reasonable one in the vast majority of voyage policies, that the assured impliedly contracts to that which he ought to do on and before the commencement of the voyage; that is, to make the ship seaworthy at the commencement of it, and in part, *quoad hoc*, in the preparation for it. The contract contained in the policy imposes on him no duties which were not incumbent on him before. But how different is in general the case of one who insures for a time! He does not necessarily know the position of his vessel at the commencement of the term; if the term commences whilst the vessel is absent from a port, he cannot, generally speaking, cause it thus to be repaired; and no care or expense of himself or agent could secure that object. The ship may have lost anchor, or sails, or rudder; part of the crew may have deserted, or be dead of malignant fever. All these deficiencies, generally speaking, are such that no care or expense could have prevented or cured. How unreasonable, then, would it be for the law to hold that there was in every case added to a policy, which is silent on the subject, a condition which, in most cases, it would be impossible for the assured to fulfil!
>
> ... I therefore come to the conclusion, from these premises, that there is not, in the case of a time policy, an implied warranty or condition that the vessel must be seaworthy at the commencement of the term insured. I feel no doubt that this condition cannot be implied. I am equally clear that there is no implied warranty or condition that the ship insured shall be seaworthy at the date of insurance.

The meaning of 'seaworthiness'

Before proceeding to discuss the nature and the effects of a breach of the implied warranty of seaworthiness in a voyage policy, and the application of the notion in a time policy, it is necessary to examine the legal meaning of the term 'seaworthiness'.

Reasonably fit in all respects to encounter the ordinary perils of the seas

The general and broad definition of seaworthiness is provided by s 39(4) of the Act, which states:

> A ship is deemed to be seaworthy when she is reasonably fit in all respects to encounter the ordinary perils of the seas of the adventure insured.

This concept of seaworthiness enshrined in the Act is derived from the celebrated case of *Dixon v Sadler*, below.[42]

Dixon v Sadler (1839) 5 M&W 405; (1841) 8 M&W 894

The plaintiffs insured the ship *John Cook* and her cargo with the defendants under a time policy of insurance. Whilst approaching Sunderland on passage from Rotterdam, having embarked the pilot, the master and crew discharged part of the ballast, as was the usual practice, in readiness for loading cargo. But, when a sudden, violent squall was encountered, her stability was so reduced that she was blown on her beam ends and wrecked. When the plaintiffs claimed for a total loss, the underwriters rejected the claim, on the basis that she had been rendered unseaworthy by the negligence of the master and crew.

The court ruled that the underwriters were liable for the loss. The shipowner was not responsible for subsequent deficiencies in the vessel caused by the master and crew. The decision in the lower court was later affirmed in the Exchequer Chamber.

> **Parke B:** [p 414] ... In the case of an insurance for a certain voyage, it is clearly established that there is an implied warranty that the vessel shall be seaworthy, by which it is meant that she shall be in a fit state as to repairs, equipment, and crew, and in all other respects, to encounter the ordinary perils of the voyage insured, at the time of sailing upon it.

That, as Parke B suggested, the fitness of a ship should be such as to be able 'to encounter the ordinary perils of the voyage insured' has been confirmed by a number of other leading cases on the subject.[43] Furthermore, the concept is now enshrined in s 39(4) of the Act, although the word 'voyage' has been replaced by the broader expression 'adventure'. However, though this concept lays down the general principle of seaworthiness, the phrases 'reasonably fit' and 'ordinary perils' require closer study.

---

42 Although this case was decided before *Gibson v Small* (1853) 4 HL Cas 353, HL, at a time when the law with respect to seaworthiness in time policies of insurance was still unsettled, nevertheless, the general principles enunciated therein in relation to the meaning of seaworthiness are relevant to all policies, whether for voyage or time.

43 See, eg, *Kopitoff v Wilson* (1876) 3 Asp MLC 163; *Steel v State Line SS Co* (1877) 3 B&S 669; and *Elder Dempster and Co v Paterson, Zochonis and Co* [1924] AC 522.

Standard of reasonable fitness

The standard of reasonable fitness required by s 39(4) of the Act is not one of perfection, whereby the ship and her crew are capable of contending with all aspects or eventualities of the contemplated voyage; the requirement is merely that the vessel be 'reasonably fit' for the use intended.

This requirement of 'reasonable fitness' was particularly well summed up by Roche J in *Rio Tinto Co Ltd v Seed Shipping Co Ltd* **(1926) 24 LlL Rep 316**. Although this was a carriage of goods by sea case involving a charterparty, the pronouncements made on seaworthiness were and remain equally pertinent to marine insurance. In this instance, the charterers of a vessel contended, unsuccessfully, that the loss of a cargo caused by a grounding was the direct result of unseaworthiness, in that the master was physically and mentally unfit to carry out his duties.

> **Roche J:** [p 320] ... The warranty of seaworthiness is an absolute contract, but, at the same time, although it is an absolute contract that the ship in question is reasonably fit for the voyage, and in such reasonable fitness is included and comprised that she is equipped with a captain who is competent and in sufficient good health to command the ship, it is not a contract that the ship is absolutely fit for the voyage, either in herself or in the nature of the health of her commander. As is sometimes said, it is not a contract that the ship is a perfect ship, and it is certainly not a contract that the master is a perfect master or that he is in perfect health. All must be regarded and decided in reference to what shipowners of reasonable skill and care would do under the circumstances, and having regard to proper and reasonable and ordinary standards in these matters.

Ordinary perils of the seas

For a vessel to be seaworthy, she need only be fit to encounter the 'ordinary', and not the extraordinary, perils of the seas.[44] However, that does not mean that the vessel need not be reasonably fit to contend with adverse conditions which may reasonably be expected on a specific voyage at a particular time of the year.[45]

In *Steel v State Line SS Co* **(1877) 3 App Cas 72, HL**, a cargo of wheat was damaged because a port hole was left open. The Lord Chancellor concluded:

> [p 77] ... By '*seaworthy*', my Lords, I do not desire to point to any technical meaning of the term, but to express that the ship should be in a condition to encounter whatever perils of the sea a ship of that kind, and laden in that way, may be fairly expected to encounter in crossing the Atlantic.

---

44 'Perils of the seas' is defined in the Act, Rules for Construction of Policy, r 7.
45 See *The Gaupen* [1926] 24 LlL Rep 355, *per* Hill J: [p 357] '... Now a ship which left in ordinary winter weather on a voyage from Iceland, and lets in such an amount of water as is shown by the engineer's records, is not a seaworthy ship, because she is not in a fit state to encounter the ordinary perils of the voyage.'

And, in *Lloyd Instruments Ltd v Northern Star Insurance Co Ltd, 'Miss Jay Jay'* [1985] 1 Lloyd's Rep 264, where a yacht was damaged crossing the English Channel and her seaworthiness was questioned, at the court of first instance, Mustill J affirmed that: [p 271] '... the vessel must be fit to deal adequately with adverse, as well as favourable weather'.

The prudent uninsured shipowner test

It was suggested, in **Gibson v Small (1853) 4 HL Cas 353, HL**, that seaworthiness should not only be related to the perils which a ship might reasonably encounter on the contemplated voyage, but also that the degree of such seaworthiness should be compared with the measures that would be taken by a prudent uninsured shipowner.

> **Erle J:** [p 384] ... the contract, so construed, contains a condition that the ship insured has the degree of fitness for the service it is engaged in, which is expressed by seaworthiness; it being now settled that the term 'seaworthy', when used in reference to marine insurance, does not describe absolutely any of the states which a ship may pass through, from the repairs of the hull in a dock till it has reached the end of its voyage, but expresses a relation between the state of the ship and the perils it has to meet in the situation it is in; so that a ship, before setting out on a voyage, is seaworthy, if it is fit in the degree which a prudent owner uninsured would require to meet the perils of the service it is then engaged in, and would continue so during the voyage, unless it met with extraordinary damage.

In this regard, it is, perhaps, necessary to cite the more well known test laid down by Channel J in *McFadden v Blue Star Line* [1905] 1 KB 697, which reads as follows: [p 706] '... If the defect existed, the question to be put is, would a prudent owner have required that it should be made good before sending his ship to sea and he known of it? If he would, the ship was not seaworthy within the meaning of the undertaking.'

Seaworthiness is a relative and flexible term

The degree of seaworthiness required by a ship is relative to the circumstances of the case, that is, the place, the type of ship and her cargo are factors which must be taken into consideration.[46]

Furthermore, by their very design, not all ships can be brought up to an equal standard of seaworthiness. In *Burges v Wickham* (1863) 3 B&S 669, where a river steamer, *Ganges*, was insured for a voyage from Liverpool to Calcutta and was lost, the court held that the insurers were liable under the policy because all the necessary information regarding the ship had been passed to

---

46 In *Foley v Tabor* (1861) 2 F&F 663, Erle CJ stated: '... seaworthiness is a word which the import varies with the place, the voyage, the class of ship, or even the nature of the cargo.'

the underwriters. And as every effort had been made to render *Ganges* as fit as possible for the intended voyage and an additional premium had been paid, she was held to be seaworthy in the circumstances of the case.

> **Cockburn CJ:** [p 683] ... there is in every voyage policy an implied warranty of seaworthiness; the term 'seaworthiness' is a relative and flexible term, the degree of seaworthiness depending on the position in which the vessel may be placed, or on the nature of the navigation or adventure on which it is about to embark. It seems to me to follow that, if an insurer agrees, with full knowledge of the facts, to insure a vessel incapable from her size or construction of being brought up to the ordinary standard of seaworthiness, the implied warranty must be taken to be limited to the capacity of the vessel, and will be satisfied if she is made as seaworthy as she is capable of being made.

Specific aspects of seaworthiness

There is much to be taken into consideration when determining whether a ship is reasonably fit to undertake the contemplated adventure. Thus, in order to ascertain her seaworthiness, specific aspects of her preparedness must be examined, namely:

(a) her design and construction;[47]

(b) her machinery, equipment and navigational aids;[48]

(c) the sufficiency and competence of her crew;[49]

(d) the sufficiency and quality of her fuel;[50] and

(e) the stowage of cargo and her stability.[51]

Seaworthiness in stages

It is well established that, where a voyage is insured and the voyage is to be performed in different stages, it is sufficient that the insured vessel be

---

47 See *Anglis and Co v P and O Steam Navigation Co* [1927] 2 KB 456; *The Marine Sulphur Queen* [1973] 1 Lloyd's Rep 88, US CA; *The Torenia* [1983] 1 Lloyd's Rep 210; and *Coltman v Bibby Tankers Ltd, 'Derbyshire'* [1986] 1 WLR 751.

48 See *The President of India* [1963] 1 Lloyd's Rep 1; *The Antigoni* [1991] 1 Lloyd's Rep 209; *The Yamatogawa* [1990] 2 Lloyd's Rep 39; *The Theodegmon* [1990] 1 Lloyd's Rep 52; *The Subro Valour* [1995] 1 Lloyd's Rep 509; *The Maria* (1937) 91 Fed Rep (2d) 819; and *The Irish Spruce* [1976] 1 Lloyd's Rep 63.

49 See *Wedderburn and Others v Bell* (1807) 1 Camp 1; *The Makedonia* [1962] 1 Lloyd's Rep 316; *Standard Oil Co of New York v Clan Line Steamers Ltd* [1924] AC 100; and *Hong Kong Fir Shipping Co v Kawasaki Kisen Kaisha* [1962] 2 QB 26; [1961] 2 Lloyd's Rep 478.

50 See *Louis Dreyfus and Co v Tempus Shipping Co* [1931] AC 726, HL; *Fiumana Società di Navigazione v Bunge and Co Ltd* [1930] 2 KB 47; *Thin v Richards* [1892] 2 QB 141; *McIver and Co v Tate Steamers Ltd* [1903] 1 KB 362; and *Northumbrian Shipping Co v Timm and Son Ltd* [1939] AC 397.

51 See *The Aquacharm* [1982] 1 Lloyd's Rep 7; *The Friso* [1980] 1 Lloyd's Rep 469; *Elder Dempster and Co Ltd v Paterson, Zochonis and Co* [1924] AC 522; and *Smith Hogg and Co v Black Sea and Baltic Insurance Co* [1940] AC 997.

seaworthy at the commencement of each stage of that voyage. That is, the ship need only carry sufficient fuel for each stage of the voyage and be reasonably fit to encounter the ordinary perils contemplated for that stage. Thus, s 39(3) of the Act states:

> Where the policy relates to a voyage which is performed in different stages, during which the ship requires different kinds of or further preparation or equipment, there is an implied warranty that at the commencement of each stage the ship is seaworthy in respect of such preparation or equipment for the purposes of that stage.

The concept of seaworthiness in stages is not a relaxation of the law, but rather a pragmatic approach which recognises that, where a ship passes through different political, geographical or climatic regions, the requirements of seaworthiness regarding weather conditions, equipment, documentation or manning levels may be markedly different. It is, therefore, beholden on the shipowner to ensure that, at the commencement of each stage of the voyage, the ship is reasonably fit to encounter the ordinary perils that may be associated with the stage in question.[52]

Seaworthiness in stages is by no means a new concept; it was discussed in the first half of the 19th century in *Dixon v Sadler* (1841) 5 M&W 895, and some 20 years later in *Biccard v Shepherd* (1861) 14 Moore 491, where the owner of a consignment of copper was unable to recover on his policy of insurance because the ship was overloaded and unseaworthy, the issue was again raised. However, in *Bouillon v Lupton*, below, Willes J drew on those past authorities to define clearly the concept of seaworthiness in stages, and then confirmed that the degree of seaworthiness required may be different for each stage of the voyage.

Bouillon v Lupton (1863) 15 CB (NS) 113

Three river steamers were insured by the plaintiffs with the defendants for a voyage from Lyons, on the River Rhone, down that river to Marseilles and thence across the Mediterranean to Galatz on the River Danube. All three vessels reached Marseilles safely and work was put in hand to prepare them for the sea passage. But, during that sea passage across the Mediterranean, they were all lost. The plaintiffs claimed on their policies of insurance, but the underwriters refused to accept liability and contended, *inter alia*, that all three steamers had departed Marseilles unseaworthy.

The court ruled in favour of the plaintiffs, in that the steamers were seaworthy when they sailed from Lyons and the preparations then made in Marseilles made them once again seaworthy for the sea passage.

---

52 See *Thin v Richards and Co* [1892] 2 QB 141, CA; *The Vortigern* [1899] P 40, CA; and *Greenock SS Co v Maritime Insurance Co Ltd* [1903] 2 KB 657, CA.

Willes J: [p 137] ... the next question is, whether there is in our law of insurance such a case as that of a warranty of seaworthiness applicable in different degrees to two several parts of the voyage insured, arising either from the necessity of the case or from the usage of navigation ... Now, to show that there is such a case, it appears to me only to be necessary to refer to the authority of Lord Wensleydale [previously Parke B] in *Biccard v Shepherd* 14 Moore's PC 471 ... The case is one of the highest authority, seeing that it is the unanimous judgment of the judicial committee of the Privy Council. They felt that there was considerable difficulty in separating a voyage between intermediate ports from the voyage from the port of departure to the port of ulterior destination: but, after much consideration, they held that the sea voyage was to be divided into several periods, and that the warranty of seaworthiness had reference to the condition of the vessel at those several periods. Lord Wensleydale, of whose great authority it is unnecessary to say anything, thus lays down the law: 'Some propositions in the doctrine of implied warranty of seaworthiness, which forms a part of every contract of marine insurance on voyages (for, to time policies it does not apply), are perfectly settled. They are laid down in the case of *Dixon v Sadler* (1840) 5 M&W 514, in which I gave the judgment of the Court of Exchequer ... If the insurance attaches before the voyage commences, it is enough that the state of the ship be commensurate with the then risk; and, if the voyage be such as to require a different complement of men or state of equipment in different parts of it, as if it was a voyage down a canal or river, and thence to and on the open sea, it is enough if the vessel be, at each stage of the navigation in which the loss happens, properly manned and equipped for it. But the assured makes no warranty to the underwriters that the vessel shall continue seaworthy.' Therefore my Lord Wensleydale, evidently contemplating a case of this description, lays it down authoritatively that it is sufficient if the warranty is complied with by the ship being seaworthy at and for each stage of the navigation.

In *Northumbrian Shipping Co Ltd v E Timm and Son* [1939] AC 397, HL, a carriage of goods by sea case, the issue of seaworthiness in stages was again raised. In this instance, because of the insufficiency of bunkers, it was necessary for the ship to put into a port en route and, whilst doing so, she struck a reef which resulted in both ship and cargo being lost. Not surprisingly, the shipowner was held liable under the bill of lading for the loss suffered by the cargo-owner. However, in reaching his decision, Lord Porter summed up the whole philosophy of seaworthiness in stages as follows:

Lord Porter: [p 411] ... *Prima facie* a ship must be seaworthy on sailing from her starting point for the whole voyage upon which she is engaged, but it has long been established that the voyage may be divided into stages, and that it is sufficient if she be satisfactorily equipped for each stage at its commencement. The principle is older than the age of steam. It has been held to apply to such stages as lying in harbour: *McFadden v Blue Star Line*; proceeding down a river: *Bouillon v Lupton*; and passing from one port to another: *Biccard v Shepherd*.

The doctrine was, however, of less importance in the days when vessels proceeded under sail. Once steam propulsion was adopted and bunkers had to be carried, it became important for the shipowner that he should not be compelled to carry so large a quantity of bunkers as to compel him unduly to diminish his cargo or should even force him to avoid certain voyages altogether ... Whatever its origin, the doctrine of stages is now well established, and it is immaterial to consider whether it is a concession granted to the shipowner or a provision for the mutual advantage of the carrier and the cargo-owner.

But, though the voyage may be divided into stages and the obligation of the shipowner confined to providing the proper equipment for each of those stages at its beginning, the force of the obligation has not been diminished. It may well be that the shipowner has the right to predetermine what those stages shall be, at any rate provided he chooses usual and reasonable stages. Once chosen, however, they are those for which the necessary equipment must be furnished.

Last but not least, reference should be made to the case of **Quebec Marine Insurance Co v Commercial Bank of Canada (1870) LR 3 PC 234**, PC, where Lord Penzance, in the Privy Council, observed that:

> [p 241] ... The case of *Dixon v Sadler*, and the other cases which have been cited, leave it beyond doubt that there is seaworthiness for the port, seaworthiness in some cases for the river, and seaworthiness in some cases, as in a case which has been put forward of a whaling voyage, for some definite, well recognised, and distinctly separate stage of the voyage.

The implied warranty of seaworthiness in voyage policies

That there is an implied warranty of seaworthiness in a voyage policy of insurance is confirmed by s 39(1) of the Act, which states:

> In a voyage policy, there is an implied warranty that at the commencement of the voyage the ship shall be seaworthy for the purpose of the particular adventure insured.

The above applies to all voyage policies whether on ship, goods or freight. But, where goods or movables are insured under a voyage policy, the ship in which the insured goods and movables are carried must, at the commencement of the voyage, be both seaworthy and cargoworthy. The latter is stipulated in s 40(2):

> In a voyage policy on goods or other movables, there is an implied warranty that at the commencement of the voyage the ship is not only seaworthy as a ship, but also that she is reasonably fit to carry the goods or other movables to the destination contemplated by the policy.

However, there is no requirement that the goods or movables should themselves be seaworthy, and this is clarified in s 40(1) of the Act:

> In a policy on goods or other movables, there is no implied warranty that the goods or movables are seaworthy.

The ship

Section 39(1) specifically refers to the implied warranty of seaworthiness as being applicable to 'the ship'. In the case of a hull policy, this does not pose any problem, as the subject matter insured is the ship herself. But, in the case of a cargo policy, the difficulty which arises is, what precisely does the word 'ship' relate to; besides the carrying ship, does it also apply to the smaller craft, such as barges or lighters employed during loading or discharging of the carrying ship?

Under common law, this issue was raised in *Lane v Nixon* (1866) LR 1 CP 412, where goods were insured for a voyage from Liverpool to Melbourne, but were then damaged because the lighters carrying the goods ashore were unseaworthy. The court ruled that the implied warranty of seaworthiness could not apply to such lighters; it was not prepared to extend the implied warranty of seaworthiness to lighters and such crafts because the owner of the goods had no means of knowing anything about them or the means of controlling or regulating them.

Unseaworthiness of vessel or craft: cl 5.1 of the ICC (A), (B) and (C)

However, all the Institute Cargo Clauses have, in cl 5.1, specifically excluded recovery for 'loss damage or expense arising from unseaworthiness of vessel or craft' where the assured or their servants are privy to such unseaworthiness. Clause 5.1 states:

> In no case shall this insurance cover loss damage or expense arising from
>
> > unseaworthiness of vessel or craft,
> >
> > unfitness of vessel craft conveyance container or liftvan for the safe carriage of the subject matter insured,
>
> where the assured or their servants are privy to such unseaworthiness or unfitness, at the time the subject matter insured is loaded therein.

Thus, unlike the common law, the Institute Cargo Clauses have ensured that a cargo-owner can only be denied of his right to indemnity for loss, damage or expense arising from unseaworthiness of the vessel or craft, if he or his servants are privy to such unseaworthiness at the time the goods were loaded onto the vessel or craft. The same principle also applies to the second limb of cl 5.1, in relation to the cargoworthiness of the 'vessel, craft, conveyance container, or liftvan'.

At the commencement of the voyage

As in the law of contract of affreightment, the implied warranty of seaworthiness in a voyage policy is applicable only 'at the commencement of the voyage'. This issue was raised in **Dixon v Sadler (1839) 5 M&W 405** by Parke B as follows:

[p 414] ... But the assured makes no warranty to the underwriters that the vessel shall continue seaworthy, or that the master or crew shall do their duty during the voyage; and their negligence or misconduct is no defence to an action on the policy, where the loss has been immediately occasioned by the perils insured against.

Exclusion and waiver of the implied warranty of seaworthiness

The implied warranty of seaworthiness may be negated, either by an express exclusion clause, or by the insurer waiving the breach. In either event, the effect is the same: the assured is able to recover for the loss under the policy in spite of the fact that the warranty has been breached.

Seaworthiness admitted clause

The 'seaworthiness admitted' clause, which replaced the previously named 'allowed to be seaworthy' clause, is now rarely used. As the seaworthiness of the ship was admitted, the insurer was precluded from raising any question on the subject. As there is nothing to prevent an assured from inserting such a clause in a policy, it may be helpful to be aware of the impact it has upon the question of seaworthiness.

The effect of the inclusion of a 'seaworthiness admitted' clause or its equivalent was particularly well illustrated in the old case of *Parfitt v Thompson* (1844) 13 M&W 392, where the clause in the policy on a ship read: 'allowed her to be seaworthy in her hull, tackle, and materials for the voyage ...'. When the vessel was later declared a constructive total loss due in part to her poor condition, the underwriters were held to be bound by their admission and could not dispute her seaworthiness. Pollock CB remarked: [p 395] '... It seems to me that the admission ensures for all purposes and amounts to a dispensation of the usual warranty of seaworthiness.'

Held covered clause

Unlike a 'seaworthiness admitted' clause, a 'held covered' clause does not preempt the insurer's defence of unseaworthiness. The 'held covered' clause simply provides that, in the event of a breach, the insurer is not discharged from liability as long as the assured complies with its terms. These terms usually include informing the underwriter of the breach as soon as is reasonably possible and the payment of an additional premium.

It is important to note that the IVCH(95) does not make provision for unseaworthiness to be held covered.[53] Thus, if the assured wishes to contract

---

53 As was seen, only a breach of warranty as to cargo, trade, locality, towage, salvage services or date of sailing are held covered by ITCH(95), cl 3, the Breach of Warranty Clause. Under the IVCH(95), only a breach of warranty as to 'towage or salvage services' is held covered by the Change of Voyage Clause, cl 2. See above, p 281.

for such a breach to be covered, he would have to make suitable provision or otherwise trust that the insurer might waive such a breach.

In the case of *Greenock Steamship Co v Maritime Insurance Co Ltd*, below, the wording of the held covered clause, to the extent that it covers '*any* breach of warranty', was wide enough to embrace the implied warranty of seaworthiness. But, as the assured was unaware that the warranty of seaworthiness had been breached, he was unable to tender the necessary notice or arrange the additional premium. However, the court was prepared to apply the held covered clause, even though the notice was tendered after loss.

Although the Court of Appeal affirmed the decision of the court of first instance, the higher court only concerned itself with the breach of seaworthiness and made no mention of the held covered clause. This case is notable in that, at first instance, the whole philosophy behind the 'held covered' clause was examined.

Greenock Steamship Co v Maritime Insurance Co Ltd [1903] 1 KB 367; aff'd [1903] 2 KB 657, CA

The plaintiffs insured their steamship *Gulf of Florida* under a voyage policy of insurance 'at and from' Europe to the west coast of South Africa with leave to call into ports on the east coast of South America. The policy included a held covered clause which stated that the assured was: 'held covered in case of any breach of warranty ... at a premium to be hereafter arranged.' *Gulf of Florida* left Montevideo without sufficient bunkers and, as a result, had to burn part of the cargo and her own apparel in order to avoid the danger of her becoming a total loss. Because the plaintiffs had not known that their ship had sailed unseaworthy from Montevideo and thereby breached a warranty, they had been unable to arrange the additional premium. The issue before the court was whether the plaintiffs could claim under the policy.

The court took upon itself the estimation of what the extra premium would have amounted to and, in so doing, ruled that the additional premium would have amounted to more than the loss incurred. Thus, even though the held covered clause applied, the insurers were not required to indemnify the assured for their loss.

> **Bigham J:** [court of first instance, p 374] ... The plaintiffs, however, relied upon another of the appended clauses as affording them a right to recover. The consideration of this clause presents more difficulty. It is as follows: 'Held covered in case of any breach of warranty, deviation and/or any unprovided incidental risk or change of voyage, at a premium to be hereafter arranged.' Now, undoubtedly the warranty of seaworthiness is far and away the most important of the few implied warranties which a shipowner enters into when he insures his ship, and I am satisfied that, if proper effect is to be given to this clause, it must be held to apply to that particular warranty.

... In the present case, the parties ask the court to fix this additional premium, and I am prepared to do it. What might an underwriter fairly require as a premium for insuring a steamer which starts on a voyage short of coal? One of the almost inevitable consequences of such a state of things is that some other fuel will have to be used during the voyage – cargo, or ship's fittings, or spars. Such a sacrifice will constitute a general average loss, for which the underwriter will be responsible to the shipowner. Would it be reasonable to require the underwriter to charge as premium a less sum than the amount of a loss so obviously probable? I think not, and indeed I think the underwriter would reasonably be entitled to charge more, for the short supply of coal would not merely bring about the general average loss I have mentioned (as I did in this very case), but would also materially increase the risk of a total loss of the vessel herself. Thus I come to the conclusion that the additional premium in this case ought to be at least equivalent to the average loss now claimed. It follows that the plaintiffs can recover nothing in this action, for the additional premium more than meets the loss claimed.

Waiver clause: cl 5.2 of the ICC(A), (B), and (C)

However, with respect to cargo, all the Institute Cargo Clauses, in cl 5.2, employ a waiver clause which states:

> The Underwriters waive any breach of the implied warranties of seaworthiness of the ship and fitness of the ship to carry the subject matter insured to destination, unless the Assured or their servants are privy to such unseaworthiness or unfitness.

Provided that neither the assured nor their servants are privy to such unseaworthiness or unfitness, the Waiver Clause, in essence, negates both ss 39(1) and 40(2) of the Act.

Unseaworthiness and the Inchmaree Clause

A ship could well be rendered unseaworthy by a latent defect or by an act of negligence of a ship repairer, master or crew. Loss of or damage to the ship caused by such events are insured under the Inchmaree Clause, cl 6.2 of the ITCH(95).[54] Does this, therefore, mean that, in such cases, the breach of a warranty of seaworthiness, express or implied, is to be overlooked?

As was seen, it is well established in marine insurance law that a breach of a warranty is absolute, meaning that there is no defence for such a breach. Thus, the cause of the unseaworthiness (whether brought about by a latent defect or negligence) is irrelevant; the insurer is discharged from liability even though the assured is not guilty of any fault.

---

54 IVCH(95), cl 4.2. The whole point of the Inchmaree Clause is to provide additional cover for perils which are difficult to discover or anticipate, such as the case of a loss caused by a latent defect or where ship repairers are negligent.

In the light of this, it would appear that some difficulty may be arise in reconciling a breach of the warranty of seaworthiness in a voyage policy (brought about by a latent defect or negligence) with the Inchmaree Clause. The question is, can the Inchmaree Clause function in the event of a breach of the warranty of seaworthiness?

It must be emphasised, however, that, under English law, this dilemma would only arise when the policy of insurance is for a voyage – where there is an implied warranty of seaworthiness. The conflict does not arise in a standard time policy, as there is no implied warranty of seaworthiness in such a policy.[55] But having said that, there is, of course, nothing to prevent the parties from incorporating an express warranty of seaworthiness in a time policy, and thereby creating the same problem as that existing in a voyage policy.

Under American law, unlike English law, there is an implied warranty of seaworthiness applicable to both voyage and time policies of insurance, and it has long been argued in America that the Inchmaree Clause negates the effectiveness of the implied warranty of seaworthiness.[56] The American approach found approval in *Martin Maritime Ltd v Provident Capital Indemnity Fund Ltd, 'Lydia Flag'*, below, where the issue raised was whether, in a time policy of insurance which contained an express warranty of seaworthiness, the assured was precluded from claiming under the Inchmaree Clause for a loss caused by the negligence of repairers; the loss having taken place during the currency of the policy, but the negligence which caused that loss having occurred before the attachment of the policy.

Martin Maritime Ltd v Provident Capital Indemnity Fund Ltd, 'Lydia Flag' [1998] 2 Lloyd's Rep 652

The plaintiffs' vessel *Lydia Flag* was insured under a time policy of insurance. The policy, which was underwritten by the defendants, incorporated the 1983 version of the Institute Time Clauses Hulls which included cover for loss or damage caused by the negligence of repairers (see Inchmaree Cl 6.2.3). However, although it was a time policy, the insurance contained an 'express' warranty of seaworthiness whereby cl 11 stated: 'Warranted that at the inception of this policy the vessel ... shall be in a seaworthy condition and thereafter during the valid period of this policy the insured shall exercise due diligence to keep the vessel seaworthy ...' In August 1996, *Lydia Flag* lost her rudder at Abidjan on the Ivory Coast and it was common ground that the cause of the loss was the negligence of ship repairers who had previously dismantled her rudder in dry dock in Piraeus in December 1995 in order to examine the tail shaft. When the plaintiffs claimed on their policy of insurance

---

55 See *Gibson v Small* (1853) 4 HL Cas 353, p 405, HL.
56 See Deutsch, GD and Hammond, JP, 'Marine insurance policies: the implied warranty of seaworthiness' [1963] Insurance Counsel Journal 94.

under the Inchmaree Clause, the insurers refused liability on the basis that, at the time of the inception of the policy in question, the vessel had been unseaworthy and, therefore, the plaintiffs were in breach of the express warranty.

The hearing instituted, under order 14 of the Rules of Supreme Court, for summary judgment was to determine whether there were any triable issues for which leave to defend may be granted to the defendant insurers. Moore-Bick J awarded judgment in favour of the plaintiffs as there was no evidence, on the question of seaworthiness, sufficient to raise a triable issue. The judge was of the opinion that the correct way of interpreting the Inchmaree Clause was that it provided exceptions to the express warranty of seaworthiness: cover was not lost if 'the unseaworthiness has not resulted from want of due diligence on the part of the owners or managers'.

Moore-Bick J: [p 655] ... In this case, it is accepted that the loss of the rudder was caused by negligence on the part of the repairers. It could just as well, of course, have been caused by some latent defect in the mechanism securing the rudder to the rudder stock. One would be surprised to find that, having taken insurance of this kind and the vessel being unseaworthy by reason of a latent defect at the inception of the policy, the owners would be completely without cover if the vessel was lost as a result, for example, of a collision with another vessel for which no fault could be attached to the owners of the vessel simply because there was a latent defect which had not in any way contributed to the casualty. That leads me to wonder whether a sensible construction can be placed on this policy which would not deprive the owners of cover under circumstances of that kind but would still give some meaning to all the clauses of the policy.

Mr Butcher, on behalf of the plaintiffs, submits that that can be done and that it can be done in the following way. Warranty No 11 is worded in absolute but wholly general terms. Clause 6 [the Inchmaree Clause] of the Institute Time Clauses, on the other hand, deals with certain identified perils which are specifically covered by the policy. He submits that the right way in which to read this policy is to read cl 6 as providing, where appropriate, exceptions upon the general terms of the warranty contained in warranty No 11. There seems to me a great deal to be said in favour of that proposition. I say that because this, as I have already indicated, is a policy under which losses occurring during the currency of the policy as a result of certain points are specifically covered. It would make little sense if the presence of a latent defect, which is a point specifically covered under cl 6.2.2 of the Institute Time Clauses (Hulls), precluded the owners from recovery simply because it rendered the vessel unseaworthy at the inception of the policy.

[p 656] In my judgment, the only sensible way in which to read these clauses together is in the way suggested by Mr Butcher and in those circumstances I am satisfied that cover is not lost in so far as the vessel may be unseaworthy at the inception of the policy as a result of latent defect or negligence, as in this case, of repairers, provided of course that unseaworthiness has not resulted from want of due diligence on the part of the owners or managers.

... There is very little, if any, evidence in the material before me to suggest exactly what was wrong with this vessel when she left the repairers' yard. It is common ground that the loss of the rudder was caused by negligence on the part of the repairers but the precise nature of that negligence and the manner in which it manifested itself and, indeed, the precise manner in which it led to the loss of the rudder, has not been identified. Whether a vessel is seaworthy or not depends essentially on whether she is fit to meet the perils of the voyage upon which she embarks. One test which is often regarded as appropriate is this: 'If the owner had known of the particular deficiency would he have required it to be repaired before the vessel was sent to sea?'

In this case, it is difficult to see precisely what the nature of the deficiency was ...

That being so, it seems to me that the evidence currently before the court is not sufficient to give rise to a triable issue as to whether or not the vessel was in fact unseaworthy at the commencement of the policy and on that ground also I would reject this first limb of the defendants' [insurers] argument.

Notes

It is interesting to note that Moore-Bick J was partial to the view that the perils insured under the Inchmaree Clause were to have priority over the warranty of seaworthiness, even when the warranty was on this occasion specially incorporated (not implied) into the time policy. Though his comments were made in reference to an express warranty of seaworthiness in a time policy, they are nevertheless also relevant to a voyage policy under which there is a similar, albeit implied, warranty of seaworthiness.

In English law, a breach of any promissory warranty discharges the insurer, as from the date of breach, from all further liability under the policy.[57] And, as the implied warranty of seaworthiness under a voyage policy is applicable *at the commencement of the voyage* (at which time the insurer is automatically and immediately discharged from all further liability), it is difficult to envisage how an assured could plead the perils of the Inchmaree Clause or, for that matter, any of the standard perils, as the basis of his claim. Any claim for loss would necessarily have to arise *after* the commencement of the voyage, by which time the insurer has already been discharged from liability. It is submitted that the problem cries out for further debate, as the point of law is significant.

---

57 See *Bank of Nova Scotia v Hellenic Mutual War Risks Association (Bermuda) Ltd, 'Good Luck'* [1991] 2 Lloyd's Rep 191, HL, p 202.

No implied warranty of seaworthiness in time policies

That there is no warranty of seaworthiness required by English law in time policies of insurance was established in *Gibson v Small*,[58] and this principle is further confirmed by s 39(5) of the Act which states:

> In a time policy there is no implied warranty that the ship shall be seaworthy at any stage of the adventure, but where, with the privity of the assured, the ship is sent to sea in an unseaworthy state, the insurer is not liable for any loss attributable to unseaworthiness.

With respect to seaworthiness in a time policy, a different approach, under English law, is taken from that under a voyage policy. This is because the nature of a time policy, under which the policy may often attach whilst a vessel is at sea, is such that it may be impractical to guarantee seaworthiness at the time of attachment.

Under a time policy, by s 39(5), the underwriter is not liable for any loss attributable to such unseaworthiness to which the assured is privy.[59] It is also noteworthy that the Act specifically confirms that, with a time policy, there is no implied warranty of seaworthiness at 'any stage of the adventure'.[60] There are thus three stages to the inquiry: first, the vessel has to be 'unseaworthy' as defined by s 39(4); secondly, the assured has to be 'privy' to such unseaworthiness; and finally, the loss has to be 'attributable to' such unseaworthiness.

The meaning of 'privity'

It was not until 1976 that the meaning of the word 'privity' was thoroughly analysed by high authority, when the *Eurysthenes* case, below, came before the Court of Appeal. Fortunately, all three Law Lords contributed to the definition of the word which Lord Denning, in his summation, described as 'old-fashioned'.

Compania Maritima San Basilio SA v Oceanus Mutual Underwriting Association (Bermuda) Ltd, 'Eurysthenes' [1976] 2 Lloyd's Rep 171, CA

The plaintiffs entered their vessel *Eurysthenes* with the defendant P & I Club to be covered for Class 1 risks under what was later adjudged to be a time policy of insurance. In April 1974, whilst on a voyage from the United States to the Philippines, *Eurysthenes* stranded, and the cargo interests made claims against

---

58 (1853) 4 HL Cas 353, HL, *per* Parke B: [p 406] '... there is not, in the case of a time policy, an implied warranty or condition that the vessel must be seaworthy at the commencement of the term insured.'

59 *Op cit*, Arnould, fn 3, para 719, suggests that the word 'such' should be read before the word 'unseaworthiness'. This is because the insurer is relieved of liability only for the particular (or 'such') unseaworthiness to which the assured is privy.

60 See *Jenkins v Heycock* (1853) 8 Moore PC Cas 350 where, long before the Act, this specific issue was raised.

the plaintiffs. The defendant P & I Club alleged that as, at the time of her sailing, *Eurysthenes* did not have her full complement of deck officers, proper charts, a serviceable echo sounder and an operative boiler, she had been sent to sea unseaworthy. Because there was uncertainty about the exact meaning of the word 'privity', both parties applied to the court for guidance, *inter alia*, on whether, in order to prove privity, it was necessary for the defendants to prove: (a) negligence, and/or (b) knowledge, and/or (c) deliberate or reckless conduct in sending the ship to sea in an unseaworthy state.

The Court of Appeal ruled that the defendant insurers, in order to establish privity, must prove that there had been 'knowledge and concurrence' on the part of the assured in sending the ship to sea in an unseaworthy state, but that this did not necessarily have to amount to wilful misconduct.

> **Lord Denning MR:** [p 179] ... when the old common lawyers spoke of a man being 'privy' to something being done, or an act being done 'with his privity', they meant that he knew of it beforehand and concurred in it being done. If it was a wrongful act done by his servant, then he was liable for it if it was done 'by his command or privity', that is, with his express authority or with his knowledge and concurrence. 'Privity' did not mean that there was any wilful misconduct by him, but only that he knew of the act beforehand and concurred in it being done. Moreover, 'privity' did not mean that he himself personally did the act, but only that someone else did it and that he knowingly concurred in it. Hence, in the later Merchant Shipping Acts, the owner was entitled to limit his liability if the act was done without his 'actual fault or privity'. Without his 'actual fault' meant without any actual fault of the owner personally. Without his 'privity' meant without his knowledge or concurrence. Such is, I think, the meaning we should attach to the word 'privity' in s 39(5). If the ship is sent to sea in an unseaworthy state, with the knowledge and concurrence of the assured personally, the insurer is not liable for any loss attributable to unseaworthiness, that is, to unseaworthiness of which he knew and in which he concurred.
>
> To disentitle the shipowner, he must, I think, have knowledge not only of the facts constituting the unseaworthiness, but also knowledge that those facts rendered the ship unseaworthy, that is, not reasonably fit to encounter the ordinary perils of the sea. And, when I speak of knowledge, I mean not only positive knowledge, but also the sort of knowledge expressed in the phrase 'turning a blind eye'. If a man, suspicious of the truth, turns a blind eye to it, and refrains from inquiry – so that he should not know it for certain – then he is to be regarded as knowing the truth. This 'turning a blind eye' is far more blameworthy than mere negligence. Negligence in not knowing the truth is not equivalent to knowledge of it.
>
> The knowledge must also be the knowledge of the shipowner personally, or his alter ego, or, in the case of a company, its head men or whoever may be considered their alter ego. It may be inferred from evidence that a reasonably prudent owner in his place would have known the facts and have realised

that the ship was not reasonably fit to be sent to sea. But, if the shipowner satisfies the court that he did not know the facts or did not realise that they rendered the ship unseaworthy, then he ought not to be held privy to it, even though he was negligent in not knowing.

Roskill LJ: [p 184] ... In the context of the Act as a whole I think it is clear that 'privity' in this sub-section is not the same as 'wilful misconduct'. Nor is it the same as negligence or fault, whether personal or otherwise. The sub-section says that the underwriter is excused if the ship is sent to sea in an unseaworthy state with the privity of the assured. That must mean that he is privy to the unseaworthiness, and not merely that he has knowledge of facts which may ultimately be proved to amount to unseaworthiness. In other words, if the ship is sent to sea in an unseaworthy state with his knowledge and concurrence and that unseaworthiness is causative of the loss, the time policy does not pay. There must be causative unseaworthiness of which he knew and in which he concurred. Mr Mustill [for the shipowners] at one point of his argument used the phrase 'conscious realisation of the implication of the facts making the ship unseaworthy'. I would accept that phrase as correctly conveying the underlying intention of this sub-section ...

Geoffrey Lane LJ: [p 188] ... For the owners to lose their cover it must be shown that the ship was sent to sea in an unseaworthy condition and that that was done with the privity of the assured. 'Privity' means 'with knowledge and consent'. It has, so far as I can discover, no connotation of fault. It is a neutral word, deriving colour from its surroundings. One can be privy to a good scheme or privy to an evil scheme. The nearest the word gets to a bad connotation is that there are overtones of secrecy in it. But the desirability of secrecy can arise in the case of a good action as well as a bad. Accordingly, I am unable to find any philological basis for Mr Lloyd's contention [for the insurers] that the use of the word 'privity' means that negligence as opposed to actual knowledge of some sort on the part of the assured is enough.

Knowledge of what? Again, the sub-section is clear. It says 'unseaworthiness', not 'facts which in the upshot prove' to amount to 'unseaworthiness'. Accordingly, it seems clear to me that if this matter was *res integra*, the section would mean that the assured only loses his cover if he has consented to or concurred in the ship going to sea when he knew or believed that it was in an unseaworthy condition. I add the word 'believed', to cover the man who deliberately turns a blind eye to what he believes to be true in order to avoid obtaining certain knowledge of the truth. In many cases, no doubt, sending a ship to sea knowing it is unseaworthy will amount to wilful misconduct, but not necessarily so.

The privity issue arose again in *Piermay Shipping Co SA v Chester, 'Michael'* **[1979] 1 Lloyd's Rep 55**, where the vessel was held to have been scuttled. In order to give a graphic illustration of the meaning of 'privity', Kerr J suggested that 'privity' can range from active complicity to passive concurrence, and turned to medieval history to emphasise his point.

Kerr J: [p 66] ... It is clear that consent or privity can range from active complicity to mere passive concurrence. An owner who makes it clear that he would like to see his ship at the bottom of the sea, but does not want to know any more about it, is privy to its sinking in just the same way as Henry II was privy to the murder of Thomas à Becket when he said: 'Will no one rid me of this turbulent priest?'

But, in *Compania Naviera Vascongada v British and Foreign Marine Insurance Co Ltd, 'Gloria'* **(1936) 54 LlL Rep 35**, where a vessel was lost on a voyage from Larne to Port Talbot and the issue of seaworthiness arose, Branson J was clear that a 'mere omission' of a precaution against the possibility of sending a ship to sea in an unseaworthy state did not amount to privity.

> **Branson J:** [p 58] ... I think that if it were shown that an owner had reason to believe that his ship was in fact unseaworthy, and deliberately refrained from an examination which would have turned his belief into knowledge, he might properly be held privy to the unseaworthiness of his ship. But the mere omission to take precautions against the possibility of the ship being unseaworthy cannot, I think, make the owner privy to any unseaworthiness which such precaution might have disclosed.

However, in 1997, a case came before the Court of Appeal which gave their Lordships the opportunity to analyse and further clarify the word 'privity' for the first time in more than 20 years. In so doing, the court drew upon the reasoning of Denning, Roskill and Geoffrey Lane LJJ, in the *Eurysthenes* case, together with that of Kerr J in the *Gloria* case, and then applied that reasoning to the circumstances of the case in question.

Manifest Shipping Co Ltd v Uni-Polaris Insurance Co Ltd and la Réunion Européenne, 'Star Sea' [1995] 1 Lloyd's Rep 651; [1997] 1 Lloyd's Rep 360, CA

Star Sea was a refrigerated cargo vessel owned by the plaintiffs and insured with the defendants under a time policy of insurance. During a voyage from Nicaragua to Zeebrugge with a cargo of bananas, the third engineer accidentally started a fire in the engine room workshop and *Star Sea* was eventually so damaged that she became a constructive total loss. When the plaintiffs claimed on their policy of insurance, the underwriters refused payment on the basis that the vessel had put to sea unseaworthy with the privity of her owners or managers. The insurers contended that, *inter alia*, the engine room dampers, which sealed the engine room in the event of a fire, were faulty, and that the master was ignorant of the proper use of the CO_2 fire extinguishing system. On both issues, the insurers alleged that the owners or managers had turned a blind eye.

The Court of Appeal ruled that the insurers were liable under the policy. Although *Star Sea* put to sea in an unseaworthy state, it was not with the privity of her owners or managers. The owners or managers had not turned a blind eye to the unseaworthiness, because they neither suspected nor believed that the vessel was unseaworthy.

Leggatt LJ: [p 377] ... The emphasis, as we see it, in all judgments even where 'blind eye' knowledge is being alleged, is on some consciousness or suspicion that the ship is unseaworthy which is disregarded so that the person concerned does not know for certain. Lord Denning uses the word 'suspicion;' Lord Roskill accepts that the underlying intention of the sub-section is reflected in the words 'conscious realisation of the implication of the facts' and equates Branson J's words 'believe that his ship was in fact unseaworthy ...' with his own view in the passage which, on one reading, and indeed on the judge's reading, does not expressly refer to a conscious element; Geoffrey Lane LJ uses the word 'believe'.

We, in fact, think that counsel for the defendants got the concept absolutely right when he was putting to witnesses that they 'realised that if the matters were looked into, the crew would be found to be insufficiently trained in matters of firefighting' ... However negligent it may have been not to learn lessons from the previous fires on *Centaurus* or *Kastora* [other company ships], or to fail to give proper instructions in firefighting or whatever, what the defendant underwriters had to establish was a suspicion or realisation in the mind of at least one of the relevant individuals that *Star Sea* was unseaworthy in one of the relevant aspects, and a decision not to check whether that was so for fear of having certain knowledge about it.

Thus on this aspect, and to be precise, to succeed the underwriters would have to establish that one or other of the individuals, Lou Kollakis, George Kollakis or Mr Faraklas [company directors] suspected that the master was incompetent in lacking the knowledge as to how to use CO_2 and that that rendered *Star Sea* unseaworthy, and that he decided not to check, for fear of having certain knowledge, and allowed the ship to go to sea anyway. The judge [Tuckey J at the trial] made no such finding. Indeed, his finding in this area comes down simply to a finding of negligence, albeit negligence in a high degree.

[p 378] ... There is no suggestion that either Lou Kollakis, George Kollakis or Mr Faraklas 'suspected' or 'believed' that in changing the crew of *Star Sea* so as to employ the Greek master, that they might be putting *Star Sea* in the hands of a master incompetent in firefighting and thereby rendering *Star Sea* unseaworthy ... Negligence there may have been in failing to ensure that the master was instructed, but 'suspicion' in the minds of any of the relevant individuals that an incompetent master might be being used was simply not established.

Did Lou Kollakis or George Kollakis or Mr Nicholaidis or Mr Faraklas have 'blind eye' knowledge of the condition of the fire dampers?

Having regard to the fact that privity to both aspects of unseaworthiness is necessary to defeat the plaintiffs' appeal, it is unnecessary to consider this aspect in any detail.[61] Again, however, it is right to say that the judge has not

---

61 It is suggested that the privity of the assured to *any one* aspect of unseaworthiness to which the loss is attributable is sufficient to relieve the insurer from liability under the policy. If the underwriters could have shown that the assured were privy to the second feature of unseaworthiness, the defective condition of the fire dampers, which was also a causative element of the loss, they should have been exonerated from liability. It is believed that the case is pending appeal to the House of Lords.

made any relevant finding that any one of the individuals 'suspected' or 'believed' there might be unseaworthiness caused by defects in the fire dampers ... In this instance, the defendant underwriters' submission ... would seek to suggest that if the judge had applied the right test to the minds of Mr Faraklas and George Kollakis, it might have been proper to conclude that by at least January 1990 there were 'suspicions' as to whether the repairs carried out by outside contractors during the lay-up of *Star Sea* had been effective and that blind eyes were being turned to that possibility. Whether that submission could have been maintained, and whether the further short step of a 'suspicion' as to seaworthiness could be maintained ... would need a detailed analysis of the evidence, which, in the light of our conclusion on the master's competence aspect, is unnecessary. We doubt, however, whether it would ever have been right to substitute our view of the evidence for that of the judge who, as we have said, found negligence to a very high degree, but not the very much more serious finding of sending a ship to sea in an unseaworthy state believing or suspecting that that might be so.

The significance of the words 'attributable to unseaworthiness'

It would appear that s 39(5) need only be invoked when unseaworthiness is not the sole proximate cause of the loss, the reasoning being that, as unseaworthiness is not an insured peril under a standard policy, there can be no recovery under the policy for such a cause of loss. However, where unseaworthiness, to which the assured is privy, is one of two or more proximate causes of loss or where unseaworthiness, to which the assured is privy, is a remote cause of loss, then s 39(5) becomes relevant.

For this reason, the words 'attributable to unseaworthiness' are carefully chosen.[62] By refraining from using the words 'caused by', it is suggested that the Act is effectively diluting the rule of proximate cause of loss in respect to unseaworthiness, when there is privity by the assured. As Roche J submitted, in **George Cohen, Sons and Co v Standard Marine Insurance Co (1925) 21 LlL Rep 30**, where a derelict battleship stranded on the Dutch coast after the tugs attending her departed at the onset of bad weather:

> **Roche J:** [p 36] ... I think the decision of the Court of Appeal in the case of *Thomas v The London and Provincial Marine and General Insurance Co* (1914) 30 TLR 595, is warranty for the proposition that it is enough if a matter of unseaworthiness, being a matter to which the assured is privy, is a cause, or part of the cause, of the loss ... I adopt the principle of *Thomas's* case, as reported in the Court of Appeal, that it is enough if the unseaworthiness to which the assured is privy forms part of the cause of the loss.

---

62 The expression 'attributable to' can also be found in s 55(2)(a). The effect of the use of the term in relation to the defence of wilful misconduct of the assured is discussed in Chapter 9, p 349.

The insurer is not liable for 'such' unseaworthiness to which the assured is privy

Where a ship, under a time policy of insurance, is sent to sea unseaworthy in more than one respect, the insurer is only freed from liability if it can be shown that the loss was attributable to a specific unseaworthiness to which the assured was privy.

Thomas v Tyne and Wear Steamship Freight Insurance Association [1917] KB 938

The vessel in this case was unseaworthy on two counts: insufficient crew and a damaged hull. Because the loss was held to be attributable to the damaged hull to which the owners were not privy, and not to the insufficiency of crew to which the owners were privy, the insurers were adjudged liable under the policy.

> **Atkin J:** [p 941] ... Where a ship is sent to sea in a state of unseaworthiness in two respects, the assured being privy to one and not privy to the other, the insurer is only protected if the loss was attributable to the particular unseaworthiness to which the assured was privy. The other view would be unreasonable.

Notes

Arising out of the same set of facts, in **Thomas v London and Provincial Marine and General Insurance Co (1914) 30 TLR 595, CA**, the trial judge, whose finding was endorsed by the Court of Appeal, arrived at a different finding of fact, that the loss was attributable to unseaworthiness arising from the insufficient crew. As Mr Thomas was found to be privy to this particular aspect of unseaworthiness to which the loss was attributable, the insurers were held not liable for the loss.

The implied warranty of cargoworthiness

That there is no implied warranty that goods or movables should in themselves be seaworthy is confirmed by s 40(1) of the Act, which states:

> In a policy on goods or other movables, there is no implied warranty that the goods or movables are seaworthy.

But, where there is a voyage policy on goods or movables, the ship carrying the goods or movables must be both seaworthy and cargoworthy. To this effect, s 40(2) affirms:

> In a voyage policy on goods or other movables, there is an implied warranty that, at the commencement of the voyage, the ship is not only seaworthy as a ship, but also that she is reasonably fit to carry the goods or other movables to the destination contemplated by the policy.

However, it is to be observed that as the ICC (A), (B) and (C) all include an Unseaworthiness and Unfitness Clause,[63] s 40(2) must be regarded as having been overridden by this Clause.

Bad stowage

Nevertheless, it is still important to distinguish between a ship which is not cargoworthy and one which is merely badly stowed; the implied warranty only applies to cargoworthiness. Cargoworthiness relates to the fitness of the ship to receive the specific cargo insured, whilst bad stowage relates to the manner in which the cargo is placed within or aboard the ship.

This issue has been raised in a number of cases, including **Elder Dempster and Co Ltd v Paterson, Zochonis and Co [1924] AC 522, HL**,[64] a carriage of goods by sea case. In this instance, heavy bags of palm kernels were stowed upon casks of palm oil, resulting in the latter being crushed. As the bills of lading excepted the shipowner from liability for bad stowage, the case turned on whether the damage had been caused by uncargoworthiness or just bad stowage.

> **Viscount Cave:** [p 531] ... There is no rule that, if two parcels of cargo are so stowed that one can injure the other during the course of the voyage, the ship is unseaworthy: *per* Swinfen Eady LJ in *The Thorsa*. Applying these principles to the present case, I have come to the conclusion that the damage complained of was not due to unseaworthiness, but to improper stowage.
>
> [p 532] ... The important thing is that, at the time of loading the palm oil, the ship was fit to receive and carry it without injury; and if she did not do so, this was due not to any unfitness in the ship or her equipment, but to another cause.

The implied warranty of legality

The Act, in s 41, confirms that the legality of an adventure is warranted by stating:[65]

> There is an implied warranty that the adventure insured is a lawful one, and that, so far as the assured can control the matter, the adventure shall be carried out in a lawful manner.

Notably, the section employs the words 'adventure insured' and is unqualified. Thus, the warranty must apply to any subject matter insured and to both voyage and time policies. Furthermore, the rule verifies that not only

---

63 The ICC (A), (B) and (C), cl 5.
64 See, also, *Kopitoff v Wilson* (1876) 1 QBD 377 and *Blackett, Magalhaes and Colombie v National Benefit Assurance Co* (1921) 8 LlL Rep 293, CA.
65 See, also, s 3 of the Act, which confirms that only a lawful marine adventure may be the subject of a contract of insurance.

should the adventure itself be lawful, but also that, as far as the assured can control the matter, its performance must be carried out in a lawful manner.

Is the legality referring to English or foreign law?

As a general rule, a maritime adventure may be said to be legal if it complies with the common law and statutory law of England or, in the event of war, it complies with English policy. Thus, in principle, any illegality must arise out of the contravention of English law,[66] but that does not mean that there is not also a respect for foreign laws. Thus, the question arises, what is the position regarding the warranty of legality when a foreign law is violated?

This very issue of the legality of a contract, although not a contract of insurance, was raised in *Regazzoni v KC Sethia*, below, where the guiding principle was that the breach of a foreign law of a friendly State would render a contract unenforceable if that breach was contrary to English public policy and international comity. It is, therefore, suggested that it would not be unreasonable to apply the same criteria to the legality of a contract of insurance.

Regazzoni v KC Sethia (1944) Ltd [1958] AC 301, HL

The respondents agreed to sell and deliver bags of jute to the appellant; both parties contemplating that the jute would be shipped from India to Genoa for resale in South Africa. At the time of the contract, both parties were aware that the export of jute from India to South Africa was prohibited under Indian law. When the respondents later repudiated the contract, the appellant sued for damages for breach of contract, but the respondents defended their action on the basis that the contract was illegal, and the appellant was aware of that fact.

The House of Lords, in affirming the decision of the Court of Appeal, ruled that the contract was unenforceable, because it was contrary to Indian law; the principle being that to violate the law of a friendly State would be contrary to public policy and international comity.

> **Lord Keith of Avonholm:** [p 327] ... In the present case, I see no escape from the view that to recognise the contract between the appellant and the respondent as an enforceable contract would give a just cause for complaint by the Government of India and should be regarded as contrary to conceptions of international comity. On grounds of public policy, therefore, this is a contract which our courts ought not to recognise ... The Indian law is not a law repugnant to English conceptions of what may be regarded as within the ordinary field of legislation or administrative order even in this

---

66 Traditionally, in order to promote free trade, foreign revenue laws have been ignored unless the breach of such is contrary to English public policy. See *Regazzoni v KC Sethia (1944) Ltd* [1957] AC 301, *per* Lord Somervell, p 330. See, also, *Euro-Diam Ltd v Bathurst* [1988] 2 All ER 23, CA; and *Planche v Fletcher* (1779) 1 Doug KB 251, where Lord Mansfield stated: [p 253] '... The courts in this country do not take notice of foreign revenue law.'

country. It is the illegality under the foreign law that is to be considered, and not the effect of the foreign law on another country.

Lord Somervell of Harrow: [p 329] ... The principle appears clearly from a paragraph in Lord Campbell LC's judgment in *Emperor of Austria v Day and Kossuth*: 'A more specious objection was rested on the class of cases in which it has been held that we take no notice of the "revenue laws" of foreign countries, so that an injunction would certainly be refused to a foreign sovereign who should apply for one to prevent the smuggling of English manufactures into his dominions to the loss of his *fisc*. But, although from the comity of nations, the rule has been to pay respect to the laws of foreign countries, yet, for the general benefit of free trade, "revenue laws" have always made the exception; and this may be an example of an exception proving the rule.' That is the principle rightly applied in *Foster v Driscoll*. It is a principle of our municipal law. Its aim is no doubt to preserve comity with other friendly States, but it is in no sense dependent on proof of universality or reciprocity. In the present case, for reasons which have been stated by your Lordships, the performance of the contract to the knowledge and intention of both parties involved a breach of Indian law. *Prima facie*, that is sufficient to make it unenforceable in our courts.

Furthermore, in *Euro-Diam Ltd v Bathurst*, below, an insurance case, albeit non-marine, the Court of Appeal confirmed that a contract is not rendered wholly illegal by every act of illegality. As the general principles on the law of illegality and s 41 of the Act were discussed, the case cannot be ignored.

Euro-Diam Ltd v Bathurst [1988] 2 All ER 23, CA

The plaintiff supplied a consignment of diamonds to a customer in Germany on a sale or return basis, but falsified the invoice value in order that the customer could avoid German customs duty. When some of the diamonds were stolen in Germany and the plaintiff claimed upon his all risks policy of insurance, the underwriters rejected the claim on the basis, *inter alia*, that, by virtue of s 41 of the Marine Insurance Act, there was an implied warranty of legality in a contract of insurance and the plaintiff's actions, in falsifying the invoices, had tainted his claim with illegality.

The Court of Appeal, in upholding the decision of the trial judge, ruled that the insurers were liable under the policy. Section 41 of the Act was inapplicable to the case, in that it only referred to the legality of an 'adventure', and had no relevance to a non-marine policy on goods alone. Furthermore, the plaintiff's claim was wholly unconnected with the falsified invoice, from which act he stood to gain nothing.

Kerr LJ: [p 28] ... The *ex turpi causa* defence ultimately rests on a principle of public policy that the courts will not assist a plaintiff who has been guilty of illegal (or immoral) conduct of which the courts should take notice. It applies if, in all circumstances, it would be an affront to the public conscience to grant the plaintiff the relief which he seeks because the court would thereby appear to assist or encourage the plaintiff in his illegal conduct or to encourage others in similar acts ... The problem is not only to apply this principle, but also to respect its limits, in relation to the facts of particular cases in the light of the authorities ... Euro-Diam ... did not smuggle the diamonds into Germany and did not themselves make use of the understated invoice; they were not liable for the unpaid tax; and they did not have the goods in their possession at any relevant time.

[p 33] ... The second submission on behalf of the insurers on this appeal was that the policy was subject to a warranty implied by law to the same effect as s 41 of the Marine Insurance Act 1906, viz, that the adventure insured was a lawful one, and that, so far as the assured could control the matter, the adventure must be carried out in a lawful manner. This is not a marine policy. It is a policy on goods and does not insure any adventure: see *Moore v Evans* [1918] AC 185. No implication of a warranty by statute can accordingly arise.

However, where a foreign law is contravened, but that law has not been enforced by the country which had enacted it, there can be no breach of the implied warranty of legality. Such was the case in *Fracis, Times and Co v Sea Insurance Co*, below.

Fracis, Times and Co v Sea Insurance Co (1896) Com Cas 229

A consignment of weapons was insured for a voyage from London to the Persian Gulf under a policy of insurance which covered 'takings at sea, arrests, restraints, and detainments'. At that time, there still existed an old edict which had been issued by the Persian Government prohibiting the importation of weapons into the country, although the edict had not been enforced and the trade in such goods had openly been taking place with the knowledge of the authorities. When the weapons were confiscated by a British warship, purporting to act on behalf of the Persian Government, the court ruled that the insurers were liable for the total loss of the weapons, as the voyage was not illegal.

> **Bingham J:** [p 236] ... As to the second point taken by the defendants – viz, that the adventure was illegal because the import of arms was contrary to the law of Persia, and that, therefore, the policy in respect of it was void, I am of opinion that there is nothing in it. The import of arms was not illegal according to the law of Persia, as that law was administered in practice and enjoined; and the export of arms from England to Persia was certainly not contrary to our law.

The legality of the adventure

It is not always easy to differentiate between what may amount to no more than a breach of a regulation or what, in fact, may render the whole adventure illegal. Thus, as was suggested in *Redmond v Smith*, below, it is important to consider, in each instance, the objective of the legislation which has been contravened.

Redmond v Smith and Another (1844) 7 Man&G 457

The steamer *Brigand* was insured by the plaintiffs with the defendants under a time policy of insurance. During a voyage from Liverpool to London, *Brigand* struck some rocks and was totally lost. When the plaintiffs claimed upon their policy of insurance, the defendants refused to pay and contended that, *inter alia*, as the master and crew had not signed an agreement specifying wages and conditions, the vessel was operating illegally in contravention of an Act of Parliament.

The court ruled that the voyage was not illegal. The breach of the Act only gave the crew a remedy against the master.

Tindall CJ: [p 474] ... it appears to me that 5 & 6 W 4, c 19 [the Act of Parliament] was passed for a collateral purpose only; its intention being to give to merchant seamen a readier mode of enforcing their contracts and to prevent their being imposed upon. The present case is undoubtedly brought within the provisions of the first section of this statute by the allegations contained in the sixth plea. The fourth section enacts that if the master do not comply with the previous requisitions, he shall be liable to a penalty; but it is nowhere said that such non-compliance shall make the voyage illegal; the section merely provides a remedy against the master.

The reluctance of a court to declare a marine adventure illegal, on pragmatic grounds, was well illustrated in the much later American case of *Pacific Queen*, below. In this instance, the United States Court of Appeal was careful not to declare as illegal under the Tanker Act, the practice of a mother ship carrying extra fuel for a fleet of small fishing vessels. The fear was that, as the practice was standard in Alaskan waters, the court did not wish to set a precedent before the whole issue had been looked into by maritime experts.

Pacific Queen Fisheries v Symes, 'Pacific Queen' [1963] 2 Lloyd's Rep 201

Pacific Queen was a large refrigerated wooden hulled vessel which was engaged in freezing and transporting salmon catches from Alaska to ports in Puget Sound, Washington State. Unknown to the insurers, because *Pacific Queen* supplied fuel to the small fishing vessels operating with her, her fuel carrying capacity had been enlarged from 3,000 gallons to 8,000 gallons. During the currency of the policy underwritten by the defendants, *Pacific Queen* suffered a violent explosion caused by the ignition of her fuel and became a constructive total loss. The insurers refused to indemnify the owners for the loss. They contended, *inter alia*, that: (a) she was unseaworthy, and (b) she had been sailing in contravention of the Tanker Act.

The United States Court of Appeal upheld the decision of the district court and ruled that *Pacific Queen* had been sent to sea unseaworthy with the privity of her owners; furthermore, as the owners had not exercised due diligence, the loss was not covered by the Inchmaree Clause. However, the court specifically refrained from ruling the adventure illegal, as it was not the controlling issue of the case. It was not the wish of the court to set a precedent until all the ramifications of the issue had been considered.

Barnes Ct J: [p 214] ... The court [at first instance] concluded that the hauling of gasoline in bulk for the use described above was not the primary purpose of the voyage, but merely an incident thereof. We find the district court's findings and conclusions are detailed and well reasoned, but even were we to assume they were erroneous on this issue alone, and were we to hold that appellants had not violated the Tanker Act [USC, s 391a] because its application as to them was vague and uncertain, this would not require a reversal of the case. With this in mind, we state the following:

We feel there exists a question, under the circumstances here presented, whether or not the bulk gasoline carried by *Pacific Queen* could come within the term 'fuel or stores'. More importantly, other fishing vessels, performing a similar role as that played by *Pacific Queen*, are (or very shortly will be) engaged in fishing adventures. Some carry bulk gasoline for the same purposes as those of *Pacific Queen*. If a loss occurred, this case would be an important and perhaps controlling precedent.

Therefore, we prefer not to make an unnecessary decision on a non-controlling issue until the Merchant Marine Council (an expert body which can hold hearings and consider all ramifications of the question) has determined by regulation whether vessels of *Pacific Queen*'s type and operation should or should not be within the purview of the Tanker and Dangerous Cargo Acts.

Supervening illegality

A marine adventure may well be legal at the outset, but then become illegal during its prosecution by some intervening event, such as the outbreak of war. To comply with s 41, it would, therefore, be necessary for the assured to take such action as was within the bounds of his control in order to continue to comply with the warranty of legality.

Such was the case in **British and Foreign Marine Insurance Co Ltd v Samuel Sanday and Co [1916] P 650, HL,**[67] where goods destined for Germany aboard British ships had to be taken to British ports at the outbreak of the war in 1914 in order to avoid breaking the law. When the owner of the goods claimed for a constructive total loss, the House of Lords decided that the insurers were liable under the policy as the adventure, rather than the goods themselves, had become a constructive total loss; such loss being caused by a peril insured against, namely the 'restraint of princes'.

Lord Parmoor: [p 666] ... By a policy of marine insurance dated 31 July 1914, the respondents insured the said linseed and wheat shipped on the *St Andrew* at and from port or ports of the River Plate and/or tributaries to Hamburg. On 4 August 1914, a declaration was made that a state of war existed between this country and Germany. The effect of the outbreak of war was to interdict, and render illegal, all trading with the enemy without the permission of the Sovereign ... The policy, on which the claim is made, is in the common form of a Lloyd's policy, and the frustration of the contemplated adventure would constitute a constructive total loss of the goods insured in transit, unless an

---

67 See, also, Chapter 3, p 92.

alteration of law has been introduced by the Marine Insurance Act 1906 ... I think that the Act of 1906 has not introduced any alteration of the law, and that there has been a constructive total loss of the goods insured.

Legality in the performance of the adventure

It is not sufficient that the contemplated adventure be of a lawful nature; it has also to be carried out in a lawful manner. Section 41 recognises the fact that the subject matter insured is often far removed from the proximity of the assured. It also acknowledges the fact that the assured may have little control in maintaining the legality in the performance of the adventure when it states: 'so far as the assured can control the matter, the adventure shall be carried out in a lawful manner.'

Such was the issue raised in the old case of *Pipon v Cope* **(1808) 1 Camp 434**.[68] In this instance, the master and crew of a vessel trading in the English Channel were habitually guilty of barratrously committing acts of smuggling. When the vessel was eventually seized by the authorities and then suffered damage during its detention, the insurers were held not liable under the policy, because the owner had made no effort to 'control' the event by taking steps to replace the crew. Lord Ellenborough remarked: [p 436] '... It was the plaintiff's duty to have prevented these repeated acts of smuggling by the crew. By his neglecting to do so, and allowing the risk to be so monstrously enhanced, the underwriters are discharged.'

The effect of a breach of the warranty of legality

In the early case of *Redmond v Smith* **(1844) 7 Man&G 457**, the position under the common law on the question of illegality was summed up by Tindall CJ as follows:

> [p 474] ... A policy on an illegal voyage cannot be enforced; for it would be singular if, the original contract being invalid and therefore incapable to be enforced, a collateral contract founded upon it could be enforced. It may be laid down, therefore, as a general rule, that, where a voyage is illegal, an insurance upon such a voyage is invalid.

Of course, the legal position is now regulated by the Act. The implied warranty of legality is, except in one respect, no different from any other promissory warranty[69] and, as such, is now governed by s 33(3) of the Act, which sums up the effect of a breach of a warranty thus: 'If it [the warranty] be not so complied with, then ... the insurer is discharged from liability as from the date of the breach ...' Thus, there is, under the Act, no longer any question of the contract being 'invalid' or void, only that the insurer is

---

68 Also discussed in Chapter 12, p 523.

69 Unlike the breach of other promissory warranties, a breach of the warranty of legality cannot be waived: see *Gedge and Others v Royal Exchange Assurance Corporation* [1900] 2 QB 214, discussed below, p 334.

discharged from all further liability under the policy.[70] This was the approach taken in the Canadian case of *James Yachts Ltd v Thames and Mersey Marine Insurance Co Ltd*, below.

James Yachts Ltd v Thames and Mersey Marine Insurance Co Ltd [1977] 1 Lloyd's Rep 206

The plaintiff insured his boatyard with the defendants under a 'Builders' Risk' policy of insurance. During the currency of the policy, a fire broke out in the yard, causing considerable damage to boats and equipment stored there. However, when the plaintiff claimed on his policy of insurance, the underwriters refused payment on the basis that, *inter alia*, the policy was illegal, in that the local authority had forbidden the plaintiff a permit to use the premises for industrial purposes.

The court ruled that the activities of the plaintiff were illegal, and the insurers were discharged from liability under the policy.

> **Ruttan J:** [p 212] ... I agree, however, with the defendant that the plaintiff's behaviour extended beyond mere non-disclosure and amounted to the operation of an unlawful business in carrying on the business of boat building when forbidden to do so pursuant to bylaws and regulations of the municipality. Section 43 of the Marine Insurance Act [equivalent to s 41 of the Marine Insurance Act 1906] provides that there shall be an implied warranty that the venture insured is a lawful one and shall be carried out in a lawful manner. The assured's behaviour in carrying on business at 1526 Bay Street was certainly in breach of such implied warranty of legality ... Pursuant to s 35(3) [equivalent to s 33(3) of the Marine Insurance Act 1906], the insurers would be discharged from liability under this policy if they were not already discharged by reason of the insured's non-disclosures.

A breach of the implied warranty of legality cannot be waived

Unlike other warranties which may, under s 34(3), be waived, no such option is open to an insurer in the event of a breach of the warranty of legality; the reason being, that a court will not lend its hand to aid an assured where there is illegality, regardless of whether or not the underwriters have pleaded illegality as a defence. Such was the approach of the court in *Gedge v Royal Exchange Assurance Corporation*, below.

Gedge and Others v Royal Exchange Assurance Corporation [1900] 2 QB 214

By way of a wager, the plaintiff effected a policy of insurance for £400 with the defendants that the steamer *Radnorshire* would arrive at Yokohama before midnight on 31 December 1898; after that date, the duty on goods imported into Japan were set to rise. The plaintiff had no insurable interest in the

---

70 This was confirmed by the House of Lords in *Bank of Nova Scotia v Hellenic Mutual War Risks Association (Bermuda) Ltd, 'Good Luck'* [1991] 2 Lloyd's Rep 191, HL, *per* Goff LJ: [p 202] '... the insurer does not avoid the policy ... the insurer, as the Act provides, is simply discharged from liability as from the date of the breach ...'

venture, but the insurers were unaware at the time of issue that the said policy amounted to nothing more than a ppi policy. When the ship arrived late, the insurers refused to indemnify the assured, not on the basis of illegality, but on the non-disclosure of material facts. In so doing, they had effectively waived the breach of legality by seeking an alternative defence.

The court was not prepared to ignore the issue of the illegality of the policy, even though it was not pleaded by the defence. It was held that the plaintiff could not recover under the policy.

> **Kennedy J:** [p 220] ... This policy then, being an illegal instrument – an assurance which, in the language of Grove J in *Allkins v Jupe*, is contrary to the direction of the statute, and so unlawful in all its incidents that the law will not countenance any part of it – I cannot give judgment upon it in favour of the plaintiffs. Their counsel argued that the illegality was not pleaded by the defendants; in my opinion that makes no difference. *Ex turpi causa non oritur actio*. This old and well known legal maxim is founded in good sense and expresses a clear and well recognised legal principle, which is not confined to indictable offences. No court ought to enforce an illegal contract or allow itself to be made the instrument of enforcing obligations alleged to arise out of a contract or transaction which is illegal, if the illegality is duly brought to the notice of the court, and if the person invoking the aid of the court is himself implicated in the illegality. It matters not whether the defendant has pleaded the illegality or whether he has not. If the evidence adduced by the plaintiff proves the illegality, the court ought not to assist him': *per* Lindley LJ, in *Scott v Brown, Doering, McNab and Co*. 'If', said Lord Mansfield in his judgment in *Holman v Johnson* (which Lindley LJ refers to as an authority immediately after the passage I have just quoted), 'from the plaintiff's own stating or otherwise, the cause of action appears to arise *ex turpi causa* or the transgression of a positive law of this country, there the court says he has no right to be assisted. It is upon that ground the court goes; not for the sake of the defendant, but because they will not lend their aid to such a plaintiff'.

References and further reading

Birds, J, 'The effect of breach of an insurance warranty' [1991] 107 LQR, 540

Clarke, M, 'Breach of warranty in the law of insurance, *The Good Luck*' [1991] LMCLQ 437

Clarke, M, 'Good faith and good seamanship' [1998] LMCLQ 465

Deutsch, GD and Hammond, JP, 'Marine insurance policies: the implied warranty of seaworthiness' [1963] Insurance Counsel Journal 94

Grime, RP, '*The Good Luck* in the House of Lords' [1991] All ER 298

Hodges, S, 'Seaworthiness and safe ship management' [1998] IJIL 162

Mandaraka-Sheppard, A, 'Hull time and voyage clauses: marine perils in perspective', in *The Modern Law of Marine Insurance*, 1996, London, LLP, p 46

CHAPTER 8

THE CAUSE OF LOSS

INTRODUCTION

Section 55(1) of the Marine Insurance Act 1906 encapsulates the general rule of causation to be applied for the purpose of resolving disputes regarding the cause of loss. It states:

> Subject to the provisions of this Act, and unless the policy otherwise provides, the insurer is liable for any loss proximately caused by a peril insured against, but, subject as aforesaid, he is not liable for any loss which is not proximately caused by a peril insured against.

It declares the principle that the liability of the insurer hinges upon the loss or damage being 'proximately' caused by a peril insured against. The general rule of *causa proxima, non remota, spectatur* is well established in insurance law, and unless this is complied with, the insurer bears no liability. It is, therefore, important that the meaning of the word 'proximate' be fully understood as it applies to marine insurance.

Though *causa proxima, non remota, spectatur* is the general principle to be observed, nevertheless, the opening words of the section allow exceptions to the rule. The phrase 'subject to the provisions of the Act' warns that the Act itself may depart from the maxim. This is evident, for example, in ss 39(5) and 55(2)(a), where the term 'attributable to' is employed. With regard to s 39(5), any loss 'attributable to' such unseaworthiness to which the assured is privy is not recoverable. Similarly, any loss or damage 'attributable to' the wilful misconduct of the assured is not recoverable under s 55(2)(a).

Further, the expression 'unless the policy otherwise provides' clearly allows the parties to the contract, by the use of appropriate terminology, to stipulate their own rule of causation if they so desire. A study of some of the standard policies previously and currently in use will reveal that a variety of expressions have been employed. The current versions of the Institute Hulls Clauses, the Institute Cargo Clauses and the Institute Freight Clauses have adopted terms such as 'caused by', 'attributable to', 'reasonably attributable to', 'in consequences thereof', 'consequent on', and 'arising from'. The crux of the question in each case is, are these terms clear enough to displace the general rule of *causa proxima*?

THE RULE OF PROXIMATE CAUSE

Webster's Comprehensive Dictionary of the English Language defines the meaning of the word 'proximate' as 'immediate'. It then defines 'immediate' as meaning 'closeness in time' or 'having a direct bearing'. Thus, the rule of proximate cause may be interpreted in two distinct and different ways, and this dilemma was reflected by the courts until 1918, when *Leyland Shipping Co Ltd v Norwich Union Fire Insurance Society Ltd* [1918] AC 350, HL (henceforth referred to as the *Leyland* case) was decided.

One school of thought which advocated that 'only the *causa proxima* or immediate cause of the loss must be regarded' was endorsed by the court in *Pink v Fleming* (1890) 25 QBD 396. It was thought that, as the test of the last event in the chain was well known, 'people must be taken to have contracted on that footing'. Another point of view was expressed by Lopes LJ, in *Reischer v Borwick* (1894) 2 QB 548, CA, and the relevant parts of his judgment are reproduced below. It is fair to say that the seeds of the current understanding of the rule of *causa proxima* were sown in this case.

The efficient or predominate cause

Reischer v Borwick (1894) 2 QB 548, CA

The plaintiffs insured the paddle tug *Rosa* with the defendants under a policy of marine insurance which included cover for collision damage, but not for loss or damage caused by the perils of the seas. Whilst proceeding along the River Danube, *Rosa* collided with a floating snag, which fouled the port paddle wheel, causing considerable damage to the tug's machinery. This damage included a hole in the cover of the condenser, which allowed water to enter the tug. The captain anchored the tug and effected temporary repairs by plugging the condenser outlet pipes before calling for assistance. When another tug arrived and started towing *Rosa* towards the nearest dock, the plug in the condenser outlet on the port side fell out and the crew were unable to prevent the rush of water which then entered the tug through the hole in the condenser cover. In order to save lives, *Rosa* was beached and abandoned. The plaintiffs claimed damages for the total loss of the tug, but the defendants only agreed to indemnify the plaintiffs for the actual or immediate damage caused by the collision, and not for the subsequent loss.

The Court of Appeal upheld the decision of the trial judge and ruled in favour of the plaintiff owner of the tug. The collision remained the efficient and predominant cause of the loss of *Rosa*.

> **Lopes LJ:** [p 552] ... In cases of marine insurance, it is well settled law that it is only the proximate cause that is to be regarded and all others rejected, although the loss would not have happened without them. Damage received

in collision must, therefore, in this case be the proximate cause of the loss to entitle the plaintiff to recover. The damage received in the collision was the breaking of the condenser, and it was the broken condenser which really caused the proximate loss. The tug was continuously in danger from the time the condenser was broken, and the broken condenser never ceased to be an imminent element of danger, though the danger was mitigated for a time by the insertion of the plug in the outside of the vessel. The cause of the damage to the condenser was the collision, and the consequences of the collision – that is, the broken condenser – never ceased to exist, but constantly remained the efficient and predominating peril to which the damage now sought to be recovered was attributable.

It was contended that the towing of the tug through the water after the collision was the proximate cause of the loss now sought to be recovered. It was, however, admitted that this was a reasonable and proper act in the circumstances. This may have been a concurrent cause, and one without which the loss would not have happened; but in my judgment it is not, but the broken condenser is, the proximate cause.

The *locus classicus* for the present rule of proximate cause is clearly the *Leyland* case, where the House of Lords approved the above decision in *Reischer v Borwick*, and Lord Shaw of Dunfermline affirmed [p 369] that 'the cause which is truly proximate is that which is proximate in efficiency'.

Leyland Shipping Co Ltd v Norwich Union Fire Insurance Society Ltd [1918] AC 350, HL

The plaintiffs (appellants) were the owners of the steamship *Ikaria*, which was insured with the defendant (respondent) underwriters. The policy of insurance covered, *inter alia*, loss by perils of the seas but contained an f c and s clause which stated: 'warranted free of capture, seizure and detention and the consequences thereof or any attempt thereat piracy excepted, and also from all consequences of hostilities or warlike operations whether before or after declaration of war'. After a voyage from South America, *Ikaria* was awaiting a pilot outside Le Havre, when she was struck forward by a torpedo and No 1 hatch filled with water. The crew brought the badly damaged vessel into Le Havre, and she would have been saved if she had been allowed to remain there. However, a gale sprang up, which caused *Ikaria* to range and bump against the quay to such an extent that the port authorities, fearing she would sink and block the quay, ordered her to be taken out and anchored in the outer harbour, near the breakwater. Whilst anchored there, because of the weather conditions and the fact that *Ikaria* was down by the head as a result of the torpedo damage, she grounded at each low tide and, eventually, foundered and was lost. The shipowners claimed that the loss was caused by perils of the seas, but the insurers refused payment.

The House of Lords, in upholding the decisions of both the lower courts, ruled that the loss was not due to perils of the seas; the constant grounding when she was anchored near the breakwater was not a *novus actus interveniens*. The proximate cause of the loss remained the damage caused by the torpedo and, therefore, the underwriters were protected by the warranty against all consequences of hostilities.

Lord Dunedin: [p 363] ... The solution will always lie in settling as a question of fact which of the two causes was what I will venture to call (though I shrink from the multiplication of epithets) the dominant cause of the two. In other words, you seek for the *causa proxima*, if it is well understood that the question of which is *proxima* is not solved by the mere point of order in time.

Lord Shaw of Dunfermline: [p 368] ... In my opinion, my Lords, too much is made of refinements upon this subject. The doctrine of cause has been, since the time of Aristotle and the famous category of material, formal, efficient, and final causes, one involving the subtlest of distinctions ...

To speak of *proxima causa* as the cause which is nearest in time is out of the question. Causes are spoken of as if they were as distinct from one another as beads in a row or links in a chain, but – if this metaphysical topic has to be referred to – it is not wholly so. The chain of causation is a handy expression, but the figure is inadequate. Causation is not a chain, but a net. At each point, influences, forces, events, precedent and simultaneous, meet; and the radiation from each point extends infinitely. At the point where these various influences meet, it is for the judgment as upon a matter of fact to declare which of the causes thus joined at the point of effect was the proximate and which was the remote cause.

What does 'proximate' here mean? To treat proximate cause as if it was the cause which is proximate in time is, as I have said, out of the question. The cause which is truly proximate is that which is proximate in efficiency.

... In my opinion, accordingly, proximate cause is an expression referring to the efficiency as an operating factor upon the result. Where various factors or causes are concurrent, and one has to be selected, the matter is determined as one of fact, and the choice falls upon the one to which may be variously ascribed the qualities of reality, predominance, efficiency. Fortunately, this much would appear to be in accordance with the principles of plain business transaction, and is not at all foreign to the law.

... To apply this to the present case. In my opinion, the real efficient cause of the sinking of this vessel was that she was torpedoed. Where an injury is received by a vessel, it may be fatal or it may be cured: it has to be dealt with. In so dealing with it there may, it is true, be attendant circumstances which may aggravate or possibly precipitate the result, but which are incidents flowing from the injury, or receive from it an operative and disastrous power. The vessel, in short, is all the time in the grip of the casualty. The true efficient cause never loses its hold. The result is produced, a result attributable in common language to the casualty as a cause, and this result, proximate as well as continuous in its efficiency, properly meets, whether under contract or under the statute, the language of the expression 'proximately caused'.

The principle laid down in the *Leyland* case, that the term 'proximate cause' should be construed to mean 'predominant or efficient cause', has been applied in a number of more recent cases, namely, *Board of Trade v Hain SS Co Ltd* [1929] AC 534, HL; *Yorkshire Dale SS Co Ltd v Minister of War Transport, The Coxwold* (1942) 73 LlL Rep 1, HL; *Ashworth v General Accident Fire and Life Assurance Corporation* [1955] IR 268; and *Gray and Another v Barr* [1971] 2 Lloyd's Rep 1, CA.

Board of Trade v Hain SS Co Ltd [1929] AC 534, HL

The steamship *Trevanion* was on requisition charter to the Admiralty and, under the terms of the charterparty, the Admiralty were liable for 'all the consequences of hostilities or warlike operations whether before or after declaration of war'. In December 1918, whilst on a voyage from New York to Portland, *Trevanion* collided with the United States mine-layer *Roanoke* and was badly damaged. The collision was due to the joint negligence of both vessels, and both were equally to blame. Although the armistice for ending the First World War had been declared six weeks earlier, the war had only been suspended, and it was still possible that hostilities could have been revived. The question before the court was whether the damage to *Trevanion* was, or was not, a consequence of warlike operations.

The House of Lords upheld the decision of the Court of Appeal and ruled that, although the collision was due to the negligent navigation of both vessels, this did not displace the fact that *Roanoke* was performing a warlike operation and, therefore, the collision was a consequence of hostilities or warlike operations which remained the proximate cause of the loss. Therefore, the owners of *Trevanion* could recover from the Admiralty.

> **Lord Buckmaster:** [p 538] ... This House has decided that, if a vessel is engaged on warlike operations and none the less by its negligence collides with another vessel, the negligence does not prevent the collision being the result of warlike operations: see *AG v Adelaide SS Co, 'Warilda'*. It is neither necessary nor fitting to discuss or examine the grounds of that judgment, for the law upon this point is authoritative and clear. It follows, therefore, that the negligence of *The Roanoke* does not prevent this collision from being the result of warlike operations. Does, then, the negligence of *Trevanion* produce that result? In my opinion it does not. I think the case of *Reischer v Borwick*, approved by this House in *Leyland Shipping Co v Norwich Union Fire Insurance Society*, shows that it is no answer to a claim under a policy that covers one cause of loss that the loss was also due to another cause that was not so covered. It follows from that that the claim made against *Roanoke*, which, if it stood alone, would have been covered by the policy, is not the less covered because *Trevanion* also contributed to the accident.

In the next case, *Coxwold*, Lord Wright, resorted to common sense when ascertaining the meaning of the phrase 'the real or efficient' cause of the loss.

Yorkshire Dale SS Co Ltd v Minister of War Transport, 'Coxwold' (1942) 73 LlL Rep 1, HL

Coxwold was a small motor vessel of 1,124 gross tons which was on a requisition charter to the Ministry of War Transport during the Norwegian campaign in 1940. On a voyage from Greenock to Narvik, *Coxwold* was sailing in a convoy, at night, which was zigzagging in poor visibility without displaying navigation lights. Due to the poor visibility, *Coxwold* lost contact with the ship ahead and ran aground on the Isle of Skye during a heavy rain squall. At the time of the stranding, the nearby lighthouse was operating on reduced power and was not visible; the ship nearest to *Coxwold* also ran aground. The shipowners laid claim to recover, under the terms of the requisition, for a partial loss. The charterers, the Ministry of War Transport, admitted that, at the time of the stranding, *Coxwold* was engaged on a warlike operation, but denied liability, on the grounds that the loss was not proximately caused by the warlike operation, but by the negligent navigation of the crew.

The House of Lords, in overturning the decision of the Court of Appeal, ruled that the effective and predominant cause of the stranding was the warlike operation on which the vessel was employed.

> **Viscount Simon LC:** [p 6] ... one has to ask oneself what was the effective and predominant cause of the accident that happened, whatever the nature of that accident may be. It is well settled that a marine risk does not become a war risk merely because the conditions of war may make it more probable that the marine risk will operate and a loss will be caused. It is for this reason that sailing without lights, or sailing in convoy, are regarded as circumstances which do not, in themselves, convert marine risks into war risks. But where the facts as found by the judge establish that the operation of a war peril is the 'proximate' cause of the loss in the above sense, then the conclusion that the loss is due to war risks follows.
>
> **Lord Wright:** [p 10] ... Once it is clear, as this House finally held in *Leyland Shipping Company v Norwich Union Fire Insurance Society* [1918] AC 350, that 'proximate' here means, not latest in time, but predominant in efficiency, there is necessarily involved a process of selection from among the co-operating causes in order to find what is the proximate cause in the particular case. In the words of *Phillips on Insurance*, 5th edn, 1867, Cambridge (Mass), Vol II, p 678:
>
> In the case of concurrence of different causes to one of which it is necessary [that is, because of the nature of the contract] to attribute the loss, it is to be attributed to the efficient predominating peril whether it is or is not in activity at the consummation of the disaster.
>
> This choice of the real or efficient cause from out of the whole complex of the facts must be made by applying common sense standards. Causation is to be understood as the man in the street, and not as either the scientist or the metaphysician, would understand it. Cause, here, means what a business or seafaring man would take to be the cause without too microscopic analysis, but on a broad view.

Ashworth v General Accident Fire and Life Assurance Corporation [1955] IR 268, Supreme Court of Ireland

The motor vessel *Mountain Ash* was a converted landing craft which was owned by Captain Ashworth and insured under a time policy of insurance. On a voyage along the Irish coast, calling at various ports, *Mountain Ash* suffered a series of mishaps, including engine failures and a stranding, which caused hull and rudder damage. After leaving Arklow, where the hold of the ship had been pumped out by the local fire brigade, *Mountain Ash* again suffered engine trouble and, because the hold could no longer be pumped out, it was decided to beach her until repairs could be completed. Whilst she was beached, a severe gale sprang up and *Mountain Ash* was so battered by heavy seas that she had to be abandoned as a constructive total loss. The owner claimed on his policy of insurance under the head of 'perils of the seas'.

The Supreme Court of Ireland ruled that the vessel had put to sea in an unseaworthy state with the privity of the owner. In reaching their decision, the court was faced with the problem of having to decide which was the proximate or dominant cause of the loss.

Black J: [p 297] ... Applying this reasoning [the theory of persistence of 'grip'] to the present case, the first cause – the unseaworthiness – made it necessary to beach the ship, thereby placing her in a situation in which she was in continuous danger of being swung round by the waves and made a total constructive loss. The first cause never lost its grip, the operation of the second cause being unpreventable. Therefore, the first cause – the unseaworthiness – was the dominant cause within the meaning of the binding decision in the *Leyland* case.

Notes

***Gray v Barr* [1971] 2 Lloyd's Rep 1, CA**, though a non-marine case, was, nevertheless, involved with insurance law and brushed on the topic of proximate cause. Lord Denning MR summarised the current legal position as follows: [p 5] '... Ever since that case [the *Leyland* case] in 1918, it has been settled in insurance law that the "cause" is that which is the effective or dominant cause of the occurrence, or, as it is sometimes put, what is in substance the cause, even though it is more remote in point of time, such cause has to be determined by common sense ...'

ONE PROXIMATE CAUSE OF LOSS

When there is only one proximate cause of loss, the task for the court is relatively straightforward: it has simply to determine whether that particular cause of loss is, or is not, an insured risk under the policy in question.

Ballantyne v MacKinnon [1896] 2 QB 455, CA

The plaintiff insured the steamship *Progress* with the defendant insurers under a time policy of insurance. *Progress* departed from Hamburg with an insufficient supply of coal, bound for Sunderland. When she was some 41 miles away from her port of destination, under sail and reduced steam power, her captain hailed a steam trawler and was towed into Sunderland. The owners of the steam trawler successfully brought an action in the Admiralty Court for salvage and the plaintiff owner of *Progress* then sought to recover that same amount, by way of an indemnity, from the defendant insurers.

The Court of Appeal upheld the decision of the trial judge and ruled that the loss did not arise from any peril insured against. There was no accident or casualty and any loss arose solely from the insufficiency of coal, which amounted to inherent vice.

> **AL Smith LJ:** [p 460] ... Upon this evidence how can this court find, as we were invited to do by the plaintiff, that the Lord Chief Justice [the trial judge] came to a wrong conclusion upon the question of fact as to the non-existence of a sea peril when the towage services were rendered to *Progress*? There was no weather, no sea on, no accident or casualty of any kind to the ship, no incursion of salt water into the ship, which could have completed the voyage under sail, and no reasonable apprehension of danger ... As before stated, we agree with the Lord Chief Justice when he held upon the evidence before him that the loss sustained was not occasioned by a peril of the sea, for in our judgment the loss complained of arose solely by reason of the inherent vice of the subject matter insured: we mean the insufficiency of coal with which the ship started upon her voyage, the consequence of which was that what in fact did happen must have happened, namely, that the ship ran short of coal, no sea peril bringing this about in any shape or way, or placing the ship in a position of danger thereby.

TWO OR MORE PROXIMATE CAUSES OF LOSS

Proximate causes of equal efficiency

The following case, *Heskell v Continental Express*, although a carriage of goods by sea case, graphically illustrates that it is possible to have more than one proximate cause of loss of equal efficiency: in this case, one cause being the initial breach of contract and the other, an intervening act by another party.

Heskell v Continental Express and Another [1950] 1 All ER 1033

The plaintiff, an export and shipping merchant, sold three bales of poplin to a Persian buyer and instructed Continental Express, the company warehousing the goods at the time, to forward the bales of poplin to the vessel *Mount Orford*

Park at No 9 dock in the port of Manchester. This, Continental Express negligently failed to do. Strick Line Ltd, which had chartered *Mount Orford Park*, allocated space for the bales of poplin and, by their admitted carelessness, issued a bill of lading for the goods that were never actually received. The ship duly arrived in the Persian Gulf without the goods and it was only after a prolonged search that it was discovered that the goods had never been dispatched from the warehouse. It had been assumed, because of the presence of a bill of lading, that the goods had been shipped and then been lost or misdelivered. The plaintiff, who had made recompense to the Persian buyer, mostly for the loss in profit he would have made on the resale of the goods, then laid claim against the two defendants, Continental Express and Strick Line Ltd.

The court ruled that the plaintiff could not recover from Strick Line Ltd as there was no contractual relationship and the issuing of a bill of lading only amounted to a misstatement. However, damages were awarded against Continental Express for a breach of contract, but this only amounted to the fall in the market value during the period the goods were detained. On proximate cause of loss, the court was faced with the problem that the intervening act of the issuing of the bill of lading, and the initial failure of Continental Express to forward the goods to the ship, were equally operative causes of the loss.

> **Devlin J:** [p 1047] ... There are many cases where a loss is foreseeable, but does not in fact occur, because some act intervenes, as a piece of good fortune for the wrongdoer, to prevent the natural and probable consequences of his wrong from operating. Likewise, the intervening act, while not destroying the wrong as a causative event, may contribute to the damage that occurs; the damage is then caused both by the wrong and by the intervening act. That is, I think, what happened here. The issue of the bill of lading could not extinguish the first defendant's breach of duty as a causative event; the breach being continuing is a continuous source of damage. But the two were equally operative causes, in that if either had ceased, the damage would have ceased. If Continental Express had done their duty by informing the plaintiff that they had the goods and by releasing them, the falsity of the bill of lading would have been discovered. Similarly, if it had not been for the false bill of lading and its continuing power of misleading those in whose hands it was, the non-delivery by Continental Express would at once have been discovered.
>
> ... It may be that the term 'a cause' is, whether in tort or in contract, not rightly used as a term of legal significance unless it denotes a cause of equal efficacy with one or more other causes. Whatever the true rule of causation may be, I am satisfied that if a breach of contract is one of two causes, both co-operating and both equal efficacy, as I find in this case, it is sufficient to carry judgment for damages. *Reischer v Borwick* establishes that for the purposes of a contract of insurance it is sufficient if an insured event is, in this sense, a co-operating cause of the loss ... I think, therefore, that Continental Express are responsible in law for the damage which the plaintiff sustained by the fall in value of the goods over the whole period from November 1946 to March 1948.

Notes

If more recent authority be required for the principle that it is possible to have more than one proximate cause of loss, reference may be made to the cases of *Miss Jay Jay* [1987] 1 Lloyd's Rep 32, CA, and *Wayne Tank and Pump Co Ltd v Employers Liability Insurance Corporation Ltd* [1973] QB 57, CA, the judgments of both of which are discussed in depth below. On this issue of a combination of causes, namely, adverse weather and defective design, it is suffice here to capture the words of Lawton LJ in the former case:

> **Lawton LJ:** [p 37] ... What has to be decided in this case is whether on the evidence the unseaworthiness of the cruiser due to the design defects was such a dominant cause that a loss caused by the adverse sea could not fairly and on common sense principles be considered a proximate cause at all. In my judgment, the evidence did not establish anything of the kind. What it did establish was that, but for a combination of unseaworthiness due to design defects and an adverse sea, the loss would not have been sustained. One without the other would not have caused the loss. In my judgment, both were proximate causes.

Two or more proximate causes – no express exclusion in the policy

Lloyd (JJ) Instruments Ltd v Northern Star Insurance Co Ltd, 'Miss Jay Jay' [1987] 1 Lloyd's Rep 32, CA

The yacht *Miss Jay Jay* was insured with the defendants under a time policy of insurance. In July 1980, the yacht made a round trip to France from Hamble and, on her return, it was found that the hull of the yacht was damaged. The owner claimed on his policy of insurance. The underwriters refused payment on the basis that the yacht was unseaworthy due to defective design, for which the manufacturers were liable and not the insurers.

The Court of Appeal ruled that the damage had been caused by a combination of adverse weather and defective design. Both were concurrent and effective causes of the loss, and Lawton LJ elaborated on the law where, under a time policy, there were two proximate causes of loss: an included cause of loss (adverse weather) and a cause of loss (unseaworthiness) which was not expressly excluded by the policy.

> **Lawton LJ:** [p 36] ... If the defects in design and construction had been the sole cause of the loss, then the plaintiff would not have been entitled to claim either at common law (see *Ballantyne v Mackinnon* [1986] 2 QB 455) or because of an express exclusion in the policy. On the facts, as the judge found, the unseaworthiness due to design defects was not the sole cause of the loss. It now seems to be settled law, at least as far as this court is concerned, that, if there are two concurrent and effective causes of a marine loss, and one comes within the terms of the policy and the other does not, the insurers must pay.
>
> ... The plaintiffs were not privy to the defects in design (see s 39(5) of the 1906

Act) nor to the fact that, at the material time, the cruiser was not seaworthy. They had not impliedly warranted that it was (see the same sub-section of the 1906 Act) nor had they failed to take reasonable steps to maintain and keep the cruiser in a proper state of seaworthiness as they were required to do under the policy. The loss was not caused by wear or tear so as to cause 'debility'. Since the defendants did not exclude unseaworthiness or design defects which contributed to the loss without being the sole cause (as they could have done) the plaintiffs' claim falls within the policy provided that what happened in the sea conditions was a proximate cause of the loss.

Notes

It must be emphasised that, when there are two or more proximate causes of loss, the insurer is only liable if there is no express exclusion in the policy. If there is an express exclusion, the insurer is not liable. The following remarks by Lord Sumner in *Samuel v Dumas* (1924) 18 LlL Rep 211 may be helpful in providing a better understanding of the subject: [p 222] '... Where a loss is caused by two perils operating simultaneously at the time of loss and one is wholly excluded because the policy is warranted free of it, the question is whether it can be denied that the loss was so caused, for if not, the warranty operates.'

In *Wayne Tank and Pump Co Ltd v Employers Liability Insurance Corporation Ltd* [1973] QB 57, CA, below, the legal position on this point was summarised as follows: [p 75] '... the law in this respect is the same both for marine and non-marine, namely, that if the loss is caused by two causes effectively operating at the same time and one is wholly expressly excluded from the policy, the policy does not pay.'

Two or more proximate causes – one expressly excluded by the policy

Wayne Tank and Pump Co Ltd v Employers Liability Insurance Corporation Ltd [1973] QB 57, CA

The plaintiffs designed and installed equipment for storing and conveying liquid wax in a factory making plasticine. The plaintiffs effected a public liability policy of insurance with the defendants, which indemnified the assured for 'damages consequent upon ... damage to property as a result of accidents'. The policy excluded the defendant insurers from liability consequent upon 'damage caused by the nature or condition of any goods ... sold or shipped by or on behalf of the insured'. The installation was switched on and left unattended overnight, before it had been tested, with the result that it caught fire and destroyed the factory. The plaintiffs, having paid the factory owners £150,000 in damages, sought to recover their losses under their policy of insurance.

The Court of Appeal, in overturning the decision of the trial judge, ruled that the dominant cause of the loss was the dangerously defective nature of the installation and that, as such a loss was expressly excluded by the policy, the insurers were not liable.

Lord Denning MR: [p 66] ... Those were the two causes of the disaster. The first cause, namely, the dangerous nature of the installation, was plainly within the exception clause. The damage due to it was caused by the nature or condition of the goods supplied by the plaintiffs. Taking that cause alone, the insurance company would be exempt, by reason of the exception clause. The second cause, namely, the conduct of the man in switching on the heating tank and leaving it unattended all night, was not within the exception clause. Taking that cause alone, the insurance company would be liable under the general words and would not be exempted by the exceptions.

So we have the question: what is to happen when there are two causes of the damage – one of which is within the exceptions and the other is not? Up till 1918, there was a strong current of opinion that, in insurance cases, you look at the cause which was the latest in point of time. The Latin maxim was *causa proxima non remota spectatur* ... Since the *Leyland* case it has been settled in insurance law that the 'cause' of a loss is that which is the effective or dominant cause of the occurrence, or, as it is sometimes put, that which is in substance the cause, even though it is more remote in point of time, such cause to be determined by common sense. So I would approach this case by asking which of the two causes was the effective or dominant cause? I should have thought that it was the first cause, the dangerous nature of the installation, and thus within the exception. So the defendants are not liable under this policy.

... That is enough to decide the case. But I will assume, for the sake of argument, that I am wrong about this: and that there was not one dominant cause, but two causes which were equal or nearly equal in their efficiency in bringing about the damage. One of them is within the general words and would render the insurers liable. The other is within the exception and would exempt them from liability. In such a case, it would seem that the insurers can rely on the exception clause ... General words always have to give way to particular provisions.

In *Miss Jay Jay* [1987] 1 Lloyd's Rep 32, CA, Slade LJ expanded on the subject of proximate cause of loss where one cause of loss was expressly excepted by the policy thus:

Slade LJ: [p 40] ... On a common sense view of the facts, both these two causes were, in my opinion, equal, or at least nearly equal, in their efficiency in bringing about the damage. In these circumstances, if the policy had contained a relevant express exception which related to loss caused by the unseaworthiness of the vessel, the plaintiffs' claim might well have been unsustainable.

In the *Leyland* case, which settled the law regarding proximate cause, Lord Dunedin gave the imaginative example of a ship so damaged by a shot from a man-of-war that she eventually sank. In the example, a loss by perils of the seas, when taken in isolation, a loss by perils of the sea was covered by the policy, but a loss caused by the action of a man-of-war was excepted.

> **Lord Dunedin:** [p 363] ... But, the moment that the two clauses have to be construed together it becomes vital to determine under which expression it falls. The solution will always lie in settling as a question of fact which of the two causes was what I will venture to call (though I shrink from the multiplication of epithets) the dominant cause of the two. In other words, you seek for the *causa proxima*, if it is well understood that the question of which is proxima is not solved by the mere point of order in time. In the illustration I have given no one would have the slightest doubt the dominant cause was the shot of the man-of-war. I would also like to remark that this class of competition between causes can only truly arise when you have to deal with an exception.

LOSS CAUSED BY APPREHENSION OF A PERIL

It is well established in insurance law that, where there is apprehension of a peril and action is taken to avoid that peril, the assured cannot recover under the head of that peril should a subsequent loss occur, because the proximate cause of the loss is no longer that peril. This rule has proved, on occasion, to appear unfair and unjust, but the principle of insurance law, which is clearly manifest in s 55(1) of the Marine Insurance Act 1906, remains one of indemnity for loss proximately caused by a peril insured against.

Kacianoff v China Traders Insurance Co Ltd [1914] 3 KB 1121, CA

The plaintiffs (appellants), who were Russian importers, insured a cargo of 4,000 barrels of salt beef with the defendants under a war risks policy of insurance 'at and from' San Francisco to Vladivostok via Nagasaki; the policy included cover against, *inter alia*, capture. The cargo, one of three separate consignments, was to have been carried aboard the British ship *China*. Because of hostilities between Japan and Russia, the first two consignments were captured by blockading Japanese warships and the underwriters informed the plaintiffs that if the cargo aboard *China* was sent to Vladivostok, they would take the position that the plaintiffs had deliberately caused the loss by a peril insured against. Accordingly, the plaintiffs' representatives in San Francisco had the cargo discharged in San Francisco, and eventually, it was sold and forwarded to Shanghai. The plaintiffs claimed on their policy of insurance for the loss in the value of the cargo, having credited the amount realised by the sale in Shanghai. The underwriters rejected the claim.

The Court of Appeal, in upholding the decision of the trial judge, ruled that the loss was not occasioned by the risk insured against. The cargo was never in risk of capture.

> **Lord Reading CJ:** [p 1129] ... The case which is more in point is that of *Hadkinson v Robinson*, in which the court came to the conclusion that the

doctrine of constructive total loss is only applicable to those cases in which it can be proved that the loss is occasioned by one of the perils insured against. In the words of Lord Alvanley CJ: 'It must be a peril acting upon the subject insured immediately, and not circuitously, as in the present case.' Following the principle laid down by these decisions, I put this question: was this loss occasioned by a risk within the policy, that is, was it a loss occasioned by capture? The answer is: certainly not. The vessel never was in risk of capture, because she determined not to undergo the risk, the cargo never underwent the risk, because it was determined to discharge the cargo so as to avoid the risk. Therefore, never having come under the risk and the risk never having begun to operate, no claim can be made on this policy.

Becker, Gray and Co v London Assurance Corporation [1918] AC 101, HL

The appellants (plaintiffs), a firm of British merchants in Calcutta, shipped 218 bales of jute aboard the German ship *Kattenturm*, from Calcutta to Hamburg. The jute was insured under a policy of marine insurance; the clause 'warranted free from capture, seizure, etc' was struck out in consideration of an extra premium. The perils insured against included, *inter alia*, 'arrests, restraint and detainment of all Kings ...'. By the time that *Kattenturm* arrived at Malta, war had broken out between Germany and the western powers and *Kattenturm* put into Sicily, which was then a neutral country, to avoid capture by British or French warships. The voyage was terminated. The appellants gave notice of abandonment of the cargo and claimed upon their policy of insurance.

The House of Lords, in affirming the decision of the Court of Appeal, ruled that the loss was not caused by a peril insured against, but by the voluntary act of the captain putting the vessel into a port of refuge so as to avoid the risk of capture. Therefore, the appellants could not recover.

> **Lord Sumner:** [p 111] ... My Lords, if there is any real distinction to be drawn between a loss by perils insured against and a loss by successfully avoiding them, between a loss by capture and a loss by fear of it, one might think that it arises in this case. It was self-restraint, not restraint of princes, that hindered the captain from putting to sea. I do not say that he ought to have done otherwise, but the plain fact is that he could do as he liked.
>
> ... This is why, as it seems to me, the *causa proxima* rule is not merely a rule of statute law, but is the meaning of the contract writ large. This is also why the reasonableness of the conduct of *Kattenturm*'s captain and the reasonableness of suggesting that he might have done otherwise are alike off the point. So long as his action was voluntary, it was his action and not that of the captain of a British man-of-war, and the policy insures against the second, but against the first only when it amounts to barratry. There is no case here of duress, nor opportunity for saying that his will was not free, except upon grounds too theological to be worth pursuing.

In the case of *The Bamburi* **[1982] 1 Lloyd's Rep 312**, a vessel, insured under a war risks policy of insurance, was detained in port and eventually abandoned because of the outbreak of war between Iraq and Iran. Although the arbitrator ruled that the loss was occasioned by the restraint or detainment of people, Staughton J considered the issue of apprehension of a peril insured against and the unjustness that can sometimes result in an attempt to avoid a peril.

> **Staughton J:** [p 316] ... Common sense suggests that, so long as that situation prevails, the 'detention' of the vessel ought to be a loss by hostilities or warlike operations. However, I do not think I can reach that conclusion consistently with the authorities that I have mentioned, particularly *Kacianoff's* case and the *Becker Gray* case. I find that there has been no loss by hostilities or warlike operations, merely apprehension of loss by those perils. If those were the only perils insured against, it might be thought that this result would be unjust and somewhat absurd. But as there is also cover against restraint or detainment of people it is not, at any rate so far as the shipowners are concerned.

SUBJECT TO THE PROVISIONS OF THIS ACT

Section 55(1) of the Marine Insurance Act 1906, though it states that the rule of *causa proxima* is to be generally applied, nevertheless, points out that this may not always be the case, as exceptions to the norm may well be provided by the Act or by an express term in the policy.

When considering 'the provisions of this Act', ss 39(5) and 55(2)(a) immediately spring to mind, as in both sections, the causative rule is governed by the phrase 'attributable to' where it refers, in the former, to the defence of unseaworthiness with the privity of the assured, and, in the latter, to the wilful misconduct of the assured.

Section 39(5) – loss 'attributable to' unseaworthiness

By s 39(5) of the Act, an insurer is not liable for any loss sustained under a time policy of insurance, when it can be shown that there was privity by the assured to such unseaworthiness. On the issue of causal connection, it is significant to note that s 39(5) states that the insurer is not liable for any loss *'attributable to'* such unseaworthiness to which the assured is privy. It is crucial to note that s 39(5) does not say that an insurer is not liable for any loss *'proximately caused by'* unseaworthiness.

Thomas and Son Shipping Co Ltd v London and Provincial Marine and General Insurance Co Ltd (1914) TLR 595, CA

Dunsley put to sea in a state of unseaworthiness in two respects: (a) she was unseaworthy by reason of insufficiency of crew, to which the assured was privy; and (b) she was unseaworthy by reason of the unfitness of her hull, to which the assured was not privy.

The Court of Appeal, in upholding the decision of the trial judge, ruled that the insufficiency of the crew, in not being capable of dealing with the emergency when it arose, was a proximate cause of that loss. As the plaintiff was privy to this particular unseaworthiness, the underwriters were held not liable.

> **Buckley LJ:** [p 596] ... the first question for decision was whether Mr Thomas was privy to the defect which rendered the vessel unseaworthy for not having on board a sufficient crew; and the second question was whether the insufficiency of the crew was a cause of the loss of the vessel ... there was ample evidence to justify the learned judge in coming to the conclusion that Mr Thomas [the managing owner] had been privy to the vessel's being sent to sea in an unseaworthy state by reason of having an insufficient crew. Then was the insufficiency of the crew a cause of the loss of the vessel? The question was not whether it was the sole cause, but whether it was a cause, *in the sense of being a proximate cause*. The learned judge came to the conclusion that it was, and he could not differ from that conclusion. The appeal would therefore be dismissed. [Emphasis added.]

The above ruling should be compared with that in *Thomas v Tyne and Wear*, discussed below. Both actions had arisen out of the same casualty, but the defendants were different insurers. The respective courts arrived at different decisions, made upon the facts as laid down before them.

Thomas v Tyne and Wear Steamship Insurance Association Ltd [1917] 1 KB 938

The plaintiff was the managing owner of the steamship *Dunsley*, which was insured with the defendants under a time policy of insurance. On a voyage from Port Talbot to Nantes, *Dunsley* stranded in the River Loire, but was refloated after five days. A survey, made by a Lloyd's surveyor, showed *Dunsley* to be seaworthy as long as she was dry-docked as soon as possible in a home port. Having discharged her cargo in Nantes, she loaded another cargo for Rotterdam, but again grounded briefly when passing down the Loire. After reaching Rotterdam and discharging her cargo, it had been intended to send *Dunsley* to Appledore for dry-docking. However, this dry-docking did not take place and, instead, she was sent to Birkenhead with a master and seven crewmen who were said to be both insufficient and inefficient. *Dunsley* sprang a leak off Anglesey, and sank. The plaintiff claimed on his policy of insurance.

The court approved the decision of the arbitrator and ruled that the loss was due to unseaworthiness resulting from the unfitness of the hull, to which the plaintiff was not privy. The other cause of unseaworthiness, the insufficiency of the crew, to which the plaintiff was privy, was held not to be the cause of the loss. Thus, s 39(5) afforded no defence to the insurers.

> **Atkin J:** [p 940] ... The arbitrator found that when the ship left Appledore she was unseaworthy in two respects: she was unfit for the voyage on which she was lost in consequence of damage which she had sustained as the result of strandings during a previous voyage, and secondly, her crew was insufficient. The arbitrator found that the claimant was not privy to the unfitness of the ship, but that she was privy to the insufficiency of the crew. He further found

that the loss of the ship was attributable *solely* to the unfitness of the hull, and not in any degree to the fact of the crew being insufficient. [Emphasis added.]

[pp 940–41] ... I think it [referring to s 39(5)] means that the insurer is not to be liable for a loss attributable to unseaworthiness to which the assured was privy. In the case of insurance under a time policy, the intention was that the assured should be unable to recover in respect of a loss occasioned by his own fault. That was the rule under the law as it existed before the Act ... It was always necessary to show that the loss was the result of some misconduct. Now, the statute has defined the degree of misconduct required as sending the ship to sea in an unseaworthy state with the privity of the assured. Where a ship is sent to sea in a state of unseaworthiness in two respects, the assured being privy to the one and not privy to the other, the insurer is only protected if the loss was attributable to the particular unseaworthiness to which the assured was privy ... There must be judgment for the claimant.

Notes

The focus of the above authority, it is to be observed, was on the question of privity, rather than causal connection. The point of law considered was whether the assured has to be privy to any form of unseaworthiness, or to the specific unseaworthiness to which the loss was attributable. As the unfitness of the hull was held to be the sole (and, therefore, the proximate) cause of loss, the court effectively ruled that, provided that an assured is not privy to the particular unseaworthiness which has caused the loss, an insurer could be made liable for a loss proximately caused by unseaworthiness. It is submitted that, as such a proximate cause of loss is not an insured peril, the loss should not be recoverable regardless of the question of privity on the part of the assured. For further insight into both of these cases, reference should be made to the judgment of Roche J in *George Cohen, Sons and Co v Standard Marine Insurance Co* (1925) 21 LIL Rep 30, below. As observed by Roche J [p 37], on the matter of law, the difference in the outcome of the pair of cases is inconsequential.

George Cohen, Sons and Co v Standard Marine Insurance Co (1925) 21 LIL Rep 30

The plaintiffs insured the obsolete battleship *Prince George* with the defendants under a time policy of insurance which included provision for the battleship to be towed from Chatham to Brake, in Germany, to be broken up. During the towing operation, when *Prince George* was some 30–40 miles off Yarmouth, the weather worsened, and the tow rope to one of the tugs parted. Shortly afterwards, because of the weather, which was described as bad, but not unusual for the time of year, both the tugs departed for the shelter of Yarmouth and left the old battleship to her own devices. The skeleton crew aboard *Prince George*, which had no power available to any of her services, dropped anchor. However, the anchor dragged and the battleship was driven ashore on the Dutch coast. The plaintiffs claimed on their policy of insurance for an actual or constructive loss on the basis that it would have cost more to salvage her than what she was worth. In addition, the Dutch authorities would not sanction such a salvage operation in case the sea defences were damaged. The underwriters refused payment, because they alleged that, *inter alia*, the loss was not due to perils of the seas, but unseaworthiness.

The court ruled that the battleship was a constructive total loss and that the loss was due to the action of the tugs in leaving her unattended in dangerous conditions. This amounted to a loss by perils of the seas. On the issue of unseaworthiness, it was common practice for hulks to be towed for scrapping, and the underwriters were aware of those facts.

> **Roche J:** [p 36] ... I will deal first with regard to whether the vessel was unseaworthy, and next with whether the unseaworthiness was the cause or a cause of the loss. I think the decision of the Court of Appeal in the case of *Thomas v The London and Provincial Marine and General Insurance Co* (1914) 30 TLR 595, is warranty for the proposition that it is enough if a matter of unseaworthiness, being a matter to which the assured is privy, is *a cause*, or *part of the cause*, of the loss. There is sometimes some little confusion about the decision in that case, perhaps because the decision of the Court of Appeal is not, as far as I know, reported in the Law Reports. But a later decision arising out of the same casualty, in which an arbitrator decided on evidence and facts before him differently from the way in which the judge in first instance in the first case in the Court of Appeal had decided in the case reported in the Times Law Reports, is reported at [1917] 1 KB 938. There is no difference at all, I think, between the decision in the arbitrator's case and that of the Court of Appeal in the matter of law, but there is a difference in the findings of fact with which the court was dealing. I adopt the principle of *Thomas's* case, as reported in the Court of Appeal, that it is enough if the unseaworthiness to which the assured is privy forms *part of the cause* of the loss. [Emphasis added.]

Ashworth v General Accident Fire and Life Assurance Corporation [1955] IR 268, Supreme Court of Ireland

The Supreme Court of Ireland ruled that *Mountain Ash* had put to sea in an unseaworthy state with the privity of the owner. As unseaworthiness was held to be the dominant and effective cause of the loss and the assured, under a time policy of insurance, had been privy to the unseaworthiness, the underwriters were not liable under the policy.

> **O'Byrne J:** [p 292] ... As I understand this finding, it means that, though the beaching of the ship was caused by her unseaworthy condition, the subsequent loss was caused by a *novus actus interveniens*, viz, a change in the weather conditions, involving strong winds and heavy seas. I am not to be taken as laying down that, if a storm of unprecedented or unusual violence had arisen and caused the loss, this might not properly be held to be a *novus actus interveniens*. There seems to me to be no foundation for such a finding in the present case. There is not a scintilla of evidence that the wind (and resultant heavy seas) was in any way unusual for the time of the year when the loss

occurred. The ship was beached by reason of her unseaworthy condition and, even after she had been beached, she could have been got off on the next high tide but for that condition. In these circumstances, I am of opinion that the unseaworthy condition of the ship was the dominant and effective cause of the loss.

To complete the picture, the ruling in the following case is included as background information rather than for clarification. It is to be emphasised that it was delivered long before the Marine Insurance Act 1906 was introduced.

In *Dudgeon v Pembroke* **(1877) 2 App Cas 284, HL**, a ship, under a time policy of insurance, was wrecked off Hull due to both perils of the seas and unseaworthiness acting concurrently. The plaintiff was able to recover, because he was held not to be privy to the unseaworthiness.

Lord Penzance: [p 297] ... A long course of decisions in the courts of this country has established that *causa proxima et non remota spectatur* is the maxim by which these contracts are to be construed, and that any loss caused immediately by the perils of the sea is within the policy, though it would not have occurred but for the concurrent action of some other cause which is not within it ... The only exception which has hitherto been established to the underwriters' liability, thus construed, is to be found in the case of *Thompson v Hopper*, where it was alleged that the shipowner himself knowingly and wilfully sent the ship to sea in an unseaworthy state, and that she was lost in consequence.

Reference should also be made to the remarks of AL Smith LJ in *Trinder, Anderson and Co v Thames and Mersey Marine Insurance Co* [1898] 2 QB 114, CA, and of Lord Campbell CJ in *Thompson v Hopper* (1856) 6 E&B 937; (1858) EB&E 1038, uttered in relation to the defence of wilful misconduct, which are reproduced later.[1]

Notes

It has to be said that, for s 39(5) to apply, unseaworthiness does not have to be the sole or 'a' (in the sense of being one of two or more) proximate cause of loss. In the event that unseaworthiness be found to be the sole proximate cause of loss (as in the *Ashworth* case), there should be no need for the court to investigate whether the assured was or was not privy to such a cause of loss. In such a case, the defence of the insurer should be based simply on the fact that unseaworthiness, regardless of the question of privity, is not an insured peril and, on that ground alone, the loss is irrecoverable. This is best explained by Lawton LJ in the *Miss Jay Jay* case, where, in his judgment, the point, though subtle, was made most effectively with a careful choice of words:

---

1   See below, pp 354–55.

[p 36] '... Since the defendants did not exclude unseaworthiness ... which *contributed* to the loss *without being the sole cause* ... the plaintiffs' claim falls within the policy provided that what happened in the sea conditions was *a proximate cause* of the loss.' [Emphasis added.]

Section 39(5), it is suggested, is relevant only in the circumstance when the sole proximate cause of loss or one of the proximate causes of the loss is an insured peril. This is necessary to bring the claim initially under the policy, as a loss which is *prima facie* recoverable. It will then lead us to the next step of the inquiry, namely, to determine whether the assured should be disentitled of his right to recovery by reason of such unseaworthiness to which he is privy and to which the loss is also attributable, either as a remote cause or as another proximate cause of loss. Unlike the *Ashworth* case, the court in the *Miss Jay Jay* case was justified in engaging itself with the question of privity because one of the proximate causes of the loss, namely, perils of the seas, was an insured peril, and the other was unseaworthiness, which was not expressly excluded and to which the assured was found not to be privy.

The above interpretation, it is contended, is dictated by the term 'attributable to', found in s 39(5). The word 'attribute', the meaning of which is given by *Webster's Comprehensive Dictionary* as 'ascribe as belonging to or resulting from', is less demanding and less specific compared to the legalistic term 'proximate'. Should unseaworthiness to which the assured is privy contribute in any way to the loss, the insurer would be exempted from liability. But this question need only arise for consideration when the loss is first brought under the policy by reason of the fact that it is proximately caused by a peril insured against.

Section 55(2)(a) – loss 'attributable to' the wilful misconduct of the assured

The general rule of proximate cause does not apply when the wilful misconduct of the assured is pleaded as a defence. Section 55(2)(a) states: 'The insurer is not liable for any loss attributable to the wilful misconduct of the assured ...'

Thompson v Hopper (1856) 6 E&B 937; (1858) EB&E 1038

The plaintiff effected a time policy of insurance with the defendants upon the vessel *Mary Graham*. After loading a full cargo of coal in Sunderland, *Mary Graham* left harbour with her standing rigging still loose, in order to catch the spring tide at the bar. Once clear of the bar, she anchored, and the captain went ashore on business, leaving the pilot, crew and other personnel to tend to the ship and make ready for the voyage to Constantinople. During the night, an easterly gale blew up, and *Mary Graham* was driven ashore and wrecked. The court later heard from the sole survivor that the anchor cable had parted close to the anchor and the length of cable, still attached, had made the ship unmanageable, and the crew's efforts to release the cable had failed because it was rusted. It was assumed that, at the time of the loss, the standing rigging had been made fast. The question before the court was whether the plaintiffs, the owners of *Mary Graham*, had 'knowingly, wilfully and wrongfully' sent her to sea in an unseaworthy state, and, whether this action was the proximate or remote cause of her loss.

The Appeal Court overturned the decision reached at the original trial and ruled that, although there is no implied warranty of seaworthiness applicable to a time policy of insurance, the plaintiff could not recover when the vessel had knowingly been sent to sea in an unseaworthy state. On the subject of causation, the remarks of Lord Campbell CJ and Cockburn CJ are particularly enlightening.

> **Lord Campbell CJ:** [Court of Queen's Bench, p 949] ... We think that, for this purpose, the misconduct need not be the *causa causans*, but that the assured cannot recover if their misconduct was *causa sine qua non*. In that case, they have brought the misfortune upon themselves by their own misconduct, and they ought not to be indemnified. The very object of insurance is to indemnify against fortuitous losses which may occur to men who conduct themselves with honesty and with ordinary prudence. If the misconduct is the efficient cause of the loss, the assurers are not liable ... The question, therefore, seems to be, not whether the wrongful act or neglect of the assured was the proximate cause or causa causans of the loss, but whether it was a cause without which the loss would not have happened.
>
> **Cockburn CJ:** [Exchequer Chamber, p 1054] ... I am of the opinion that the judgment of the Court of Queen's Bench should be reversed. Although it may no longer be open to dispute that there is no warranty of seaworthiness in a time policy, I concur with the Court of Queen's Bench (and for the reasons set forth in their judgment) in thinking that, if a ship, insured in a time policy, is knowingly sent to sea by the assured in an unseaworthy state, and is lost by means of the unseaworthiness, the assured ought not to be allowed to recover on the policy. And, further, I agree that, to constitute a defence in an action on such a policy, it is not necessary that the unseaworthiness should have been the proximate and immediate cause of the loss, provided it can be shown to have been so connected with the loss as that it must necessarily have led to it.

In *Trinder, Anderson and Co v Thames and Mersey Marine Insurance Co* [1898] 2 QB 114, CA, where a vessel stranded on a reef due to the negligent navigation of the master, who was also a part owner of the ship, the issue of causation was discussed. AL Smith LJ, in referring to the case of *Thompson v Hopper*, emphasised that remote causes of loss were generally of no account unless that remote cause of loss applied to wilful misconduct.

> **AL Smith LJ:** [p 123] ... It cannot be doubted that the legal maxim, *in jure non remota causa sed proxima spectatur*, applies when considering what are the particular perils for which an assurer undertakes to be liable upon a policy of

marine insurance, if such maxim contravenes no principle of insurance law and is not hostile to the manifest intention of the parties: see *per* Lord Campbell in *Thompson v Hopper* ... The risk undertaken by an underwriter upon a policy covering perils of the sea is that, if the subject matter insured is lost or damaged immediately by a peril of the sea, he will be responsible, and, in my judgment, it matters not if the loss or damage is remotely caused by the negligent navigation of the captain or crew, or of the assured himself, always assuming that the loss is not occasioned by the wilful act of the assured. In this last case, the maxim above referred to, *causa proxima non remota spectatur*, does not apply for the reasons pointed out by Lord Campbell in *Thompson v Hopper*, for there, not only does the maxim contravene the principles of insurance law and the manifest intentions of the parties, but it is qualified by another legal maxim, *dolus circuitu non purgatur*.

Notes

It is perhaps necessary to address the dissenting judgment of Lord Sumner of the House of Lords in **Samuel v Dumas (1924) 18 LlL Rep 211, HL**. On the subject of causation in relation to the defence of wilful misconduct of the assured, his rhetoric ran as follows:

> **Lord Sumner:** [p 223] ... The insurer can only be liable for losses covered by perils insured against, and if he is never liable for losses caused by wilful misconduct, why specify the particular case and omit to state the general rule. Why is the language varied and the words 'attributable to' used instead of 'proximately caused by'?

He then proceeded to answer his own question in the following terms: 'It is to be observed that the whole section is framed to state for what an insurer is liable, that is, upon a policy to a person assured by that policy, and is not framed as a definition of proximate or of remote causes.'

This should not come as a surprise, for it is in line with his particular stand on the wider issue, that the entry of seawater, however caused, is a peril of the seas. On this premise, he was able to take comfort in the fact that an innocent claimant (whether he be a cargo-owner or mortgagee), suing as an original assured, would be able to recover under the policy, provided that he himself is not guilty of any wilful misconduct. The act of wilful misconduct committed by a third party, the shipowner, in scuttling the ship should not, according to Lord Sumner's point of view, deny an innocent party of his right to recovery.[2]

---

2 For a fuller discussion of this area of the law, see Chapter 9, p 370.

UNLESS THE POLICY OTHERWISE PROVIDES

Caused by and arising from

Section 55 of the Marine Insurance Act 1906 uses the term 'caused by' in relation to included and excluded losses. This, and the term 'arising from', are also used in the Institute Clauses and, in both instances, it is understood in insurance law to mean 'proximately caused by'.

Coxe v Employers' Liability Assurance Corporation Ltd [1916] 2 KB 629

The deceased, a military officer, was insured with the defendants against accidental death, and included in the policy was a clause which excepted liability for death 'directly or indirectly caused by, arising from, or traceable ... to war'. During the First World War, the deceased was on guard duty on the South Eastern Railway when he was accidentally struck by a train and killed. At the time of the accident, the lighting on the track had been obscured to comply with wartime regulations.

The court confirmed the decision of the arbitrator, and ruled that the death had been caused indirectly by war and recovery under the policy was not possible. The court expanded on the meaning of the words contained within the exceptions clause.

> **Scrutton J:** [p 634] ... The words in the condition 'caused by' and 'arising from' do not give rise to any difficulty. They are words which always have been construed as relating to the proximate cause. I am not sure whether the words 'traceable to' would, of themselves, go any further. They are very vague words, and I should have been disposed to hold, if those were the only words, that, if the defendants choose to employ very vague words of that kind, the words must be read strictly against them and in accordance with the ordinary maxim. But the words which I find it impossible to escape from are 'directly or indirectly'. There does not appear to be any authority in which those words have been considered, and I find it impossible to reconcile them with the maxim causa proxima non remota spectatur. If it were contended that the result of the words is that the proximate cause, whether direct or indirect, is to be looked at, I should reply that the result does not appear to me to be consistent or intelligible. I am unable to understand what is an indirect proximate cause, and, in my judgment, the only possible effect which can be given to those words is that the maxim causa proxima non remota spectatur is excluded and that a more remote link in the chain of causation is contemplated than the proximate and immediate cause.

Attributable to and reasonably attributable to

The legal implication of the use of the term 'attributable to', in s 39(5) of the Marine Insurance Act 1906, when referring to unseaworthiness in a time policy of insurance, and also in s 55(2)(a), in relation to the wilful misconduct of the assured, has already been discussed. The term is also employed in a number of the Institute Clauses, namely the Cargo Clauses (B) and (C), and the War Risks (Cargo), where reference is made to the wilful misconduct of the assured in the exclusion clauses.

In the ICC (B) and (C), the word 'reasonably' is inserted before the phrase 'attributable to'. Whether this adds anything to the meaning of the term is unclear.

Consequences thereof

Although the term 'consequences thereof' would appear to have a broader meaning than the term 'caused by,' there is no authority to show that the general rule of proximate cause is to be disturbed by its use.

Britain SS Co v King, 'Petersham'; Green v British India Steam Navigation Co Ltd, 'Matiana' [1921] 1 AC 99, HL

(a) *Petersham* was on requisition charter to the Admiralty and the charterparty contained a clause which stated that the Admiralty was not liable for any sea risk, but was liable for 'all consequences of hostilities or warlike operations'. In May 1918, *Petersham* collided with another vessel at night and was lost. In accordance with Admiralty regulations, neither vessel was displaying navigation lights at the time of the loss.

(b) *Matiana* was sailing in convoy, north of Tunisia, when she ran upon a reef and became a total wreck. At the time of the stranding, it was dark, and the convoy was zigzagging under the command of a naval officer. Some 11 hours after *Matiana* ran upon the reef, she was struck by a torpedo but, by that time, she was already lost. The policies of insurance included a standard marine policy of insurance with the usual f c and s clause, together with a war risks policy which included a clause which covered loss by 'all consequences of hostilities or warlike operations by or against the King's enemies'.

The House of Lords upheld the decisions of the Court of Appeal in both actions. In the *Petersham* case, the loss was not due to warlike operations in that collision was an ordinary maritime risk and the lack of navigation lights only aggravated that risk. In the *Matiana* case, the loss was not due to the proximate consequence of a warlike operation. *Matiana* stranded because she did not know where she was, and not as a 'consequence of' a warlike operation. Therefore, the loss fell upon the marine risks policy. The court considered the meaning of the words 'consequences of'.

> **Lord Sumner:** [p 131] ... The remaining argument is that, at any rate, each loss is 'attributable' to warlike operations and hence fully within the clause, and the

analogy of a loss by perils of the sea which is held to be irrecoverable when it is attributable to the assured's own wilful act, was put forward. If that means that a loss, not proximately caused by warlike operations but (remotely) attributable to them, is one for which the insurers are liable, in a case like the present, it is contrary to s 55(1) of the Marine Insurance Act 1906, for the policy contains no special provision to this effect, unless the words 'consequences of warlike operations' are pressed beyond anything that they will bear. It is stated, in *Ionides v Universal Marine Insurance Co* (1863) 14 CB (NS) 274, that the word 'consequences' is a compendious description of the words to be excepted, and not a description relating to the loss. Instead of saying what particular results are to be excepted, the word 'consequences' is introduced to denote the class of perils which may result from hostilities.

Liverpool and London War Risks Association Ltd v Ocean SS Co Ltd, 'Priam' [1947] AC 243, HL

The 10,029 ton motor vessel *Priam* was requisitioned by the Minister of War Transport and was insured under a war risks policy which included cover for the '... consequences of hostilities or warlike operations ...'. On a voyage from Liverpool to Alexandria, by way of the Cape of Good Hope, with a cargo of urgently required war supplies, some of which were carried on deck, *Priam* encountered severe weather which caused crated aircraft and an armoured bridge-laying vehicle, carried on the forward well deck, to break loose and smash the No 2 hatch cover, with the result that No 2 hatch was flooded. Although *Priam* was well down by the head due to the ingress of some 2,200 tons of water forward, because of the danger from submarines, the master maintained as much speed as possible and continued zigzagging, which caused further damage, including some weather damage amidships. Before proceeding with the voyage, *Priam* put into Freetown, where repairs were carried out and the cargo in No 2 hatch re-stowed. The owners later claimed on their policy of insurance. The issue before the court was: which damage had been sustained by way of the 'consequences of' hostilities and warlike operations' (war risks) and which damage had been proximately caused by 'perils of the seas' (marine risk).

The House of Lords affirmed the decision of the Court of Appeal and ruled that the damage to No 2 hatch was covered by the war risks policy because the carriage of the war *materiel* on the deck amounted to a special war peril. But all the other damage was only heavy weather damage, and was not covered by the war risks policy. The court considered the significance of the words 'consequences of'.

Lord Porter: [p 265] ... Indeed, to hold that a loss was recoverable if caused by the consequences of consequences of hostilities would, if logically pursued, lead to the conclusion that in an ordinary Lloyd's policy in the form set out in the Marine Insurance Act 1906, losses caused by the consequences of the consequences of capture would be covered since the insured risks are stated to be 'capture', etc, and 'the consequences thereof', a result which is pointed out by Lord Sumner at the end of the judgment quoted above and found unacceptable. My Lords, expressions of opinion to a similar effect might be pointed out in later judgments, and I know of no contrary opinion. I have, however, dealt with the question somewhat at length lest it should be thought that the insurance of the consequences of hostilities or of warlike operations or, for that matter, of capture seizure arrest restraint or detainment by the King's enemies and the *consequences* thereof in any way abrogated or lessened the effect stated in s 55 of the Marine Insurance Act that the insurer is not liable for any loss which is not proximately caused by a peril insured against or that it widens the insurance so as to cover the consequences of consequences.

Consequent on

Clause 15 of the Institute Time Clauses – Freight, the Loss of Time Clause, states:

> This insurance does not cover any claims consequent on loss of time whether arising from a peril of the sea or otherwise.

It would appear, from the following cases, that the term 'consequent on' refers to consequential loss, and does not relate to causation.

Bensaude and Others v Thames and Mersey Marine Insurance Co Ltd [1897] AC 609, HL

The steamship *Peninsular* was contracted to carry a cargo of wheat from Lisbon to West Africa, the freight to be payable on arrival. The owners of *Peninsular* insured the freight payable with the defendants under a time policy of insurance, which included the exception clause 'free from any claim consequent on loss of time, whether arising from a peril of the sea or otherwise'. Shortly after embarking on the voyage, *Peninsular*'s main shaft broke and she returned to her port of loading. The delay was such that the charterers put an end to the charter and the freight was lost. The owners claimed on their policy of insurance.

The House of Lords affirmed the decision of the Court of Appeal and held that the insurers were not liable, as the cause of the loss of freight was the delay which fell within the meaning of the exceptions clause.

> **Lord Herschell:** [p 613] ... The whole basis of the claim, of course, must be the loss of the subject matter insured – that is, the freight. That loss must arise from one of the perils insured against. What is the meaning of saying that the underwriter is not to be liable for any claim consequent upon loss of time? It must mean that although the subject matter insured has been lost, and although it has been lost by a peril insured against, if the claim depends on loss of time in the prosecution of the voyage so that the adventure cannot be completed within the time contemplated, then the underwriter is to be exempt from liability.

Russian Bank for Foreign Trade v Excess Insurance Co Ltd [1918] 2 KB 123

A consignment of barley, shipped aboard the British steamship *Wolverton*, was insured with the defendants; the policy of insurance included cover for the usual perils, including restraint of princes, but excluded the insurers from liability 'for all claims due to delay'. Because of the entry of Turkey into the First World War and the subsequent closing of the Dardanelles, the vessel could not undertake the proposed voyage to Falmouth and *Wolverton* remained at Novorossisk, on the Black Sea, where the cargo was landed. Eventually, *Wolverton* was requisitioned by the Admiralty and the plaintiffs claimed under their policy for a constructive total loss of the barley.

The court ruled that the underwriters were not liable. Although the closing of the Dardanelles was a restraint of princes and a peril insured against, the loss was brought about by the delay which was occasioned by the closure, and such a loss was excluded under the policy.

> **Bailhache J:** [p 128] ... In the Bensaude case there was a peril insured against, namely, of the sea – the propeller shaft broke. Here, there was a peril insured against, namely, restraint of princes – the Dardanelles were closed. In the *Bensaude* case the broken propeller shaft necessitated such delay in the prosecution of the voyage that the adventure was frustrated. Here, the restraint of princes did the same thing. In both cases, it was delay due to a peril insured against, which caused in one case the total loss of the freight, and in the other the constructive total loss of the cargo. The fact that the subject matter insured was in the one case freight and in the other case barley seems to me immaterial.

In *Playa de las Nieves* [1978] AC 853, HL, the facts of which have already been cited in full earlier,[3] Lord Diplock not only delivered a comprehensive explanation of the meaning of the 'Loss of Time' Clause contained within the Institute Time Clauses – Freight, but also expanded on the subject of causation.

> **Lord Diplock:** [p 881] ... My Lords, the fallacy in this argument is that we are not concerned in the instant case with whether the loss of hire was 'proximately caused' by a peril insured against in the sense in which that expression is used in s 55(1) of the Marine Insurance Act 1906. What we are concerned with is the construction of an exceptions clause which does not even use the word 'cause'. It contemplates a chain of events expressed to be either 'consequent on' or 'arising from' one another. It expressly makes the operation of the clause dependent upon the presence in the chain of an intermediate event (viz, 'loss of time') between the loss for which the claim is made (viz, loss of freight) and the event which in insurance law is the 'proximate cause' of that loss (viz, a peril insured against). The intermediate event, 'loss of time', is not in itself a peril, though it may be the result of a peril. That is why the words 'Whether arising from a peril of the sea or otherwise' are not mere surplusage,

---

3   For the facts of this case and a discussion of the Loss of Time Clause, see Chapter 3, p 106.

as was suggested *obiter* by Bailhache J in *Russian Bank for Foreign Trade v Excess Insurance Co Ltd* [1918] 2 KB 123, p 127. They are there to make it plain that the clause is concerned with an intermediate event between the occurrence of a peril insured against and the loss of freight of which the peril was, in insurance law, the proximate cause.

References and further reading

Bennett, H, 'Causation in the law of marine insurance; evolution and codification of the proximate cause doctrine', in *The Modern Law of Marine Insurance*, 1996, London: LLP, p 173

CHAPTER 9

MARINE RISKS

INTRODUCTION

Section 55(2) of the Marine Insurance Act 1906 provides the broad framework for both included and excluded losses, within which the Institute Hull Clauses and the Cargo Clauses are supplementary and not in conflict. In addition, the Rules for Construction, contained in the Act, provide definitions for some of the marine risks: 'perils of the seas', 'pirates', and 'thieves' are given some clarification.

Traditionally, insurable marine risks have included perils of the seas, fire, theft, jettison, and piracy, and, as would be expected, these perils are provided for in cl 6.1 of the ITCH(95) and cl 4.1 of the IVCH(95). But, the Institute Hull Clauses also make provision for other risks, not strictly marine risks as such, but nonetheless risks or hazards associated with the sea and ships. Thus, cl 6.1 of the ITCH(95) and cl 4.1 of the IVCH(95) also include, as insurable risks, loss or damage caused by 'contact with land conveyance, dock or harbour equipment or installation ... earthquake, volcanic eruption or lightning ... accidents in loading, discharging or shifting cargo or fuel'.

The insurable perils contained within the Inchmaree Clause (cl 6.2 of the ITCH(95) and cl 4.2 of the IVCH(95)) are, by definition, additional to the conventional marine risks and, as such, are dealt with separately in another chapter.[1]

With respect to cargo, the ICC (A), being an all risks policy, has no requirement to list the perils insured against. However, both the ICC (B) and (C), in cl 1, enumerate the covered risks, and it is significant that the broad based and long established term 'perils of the seas' is omitted. Instead, the insured perils, usually associated with perils of the seas, are itemised specifically.

Finally, the meaning and significance of the 'all risks' (the ICC (A)) policy of insurance is considered. An all risks policy of insurance provides cover against all marine perils, but does not provide protection against eventualities and certainties. The indemnity provided by the insurer remains an indemnity against fortuitous or unexpected loss or casualty and, thus, does not provide cover, for example, against inherent vice, wear and tear and unseaworthiness. However, of particular significance with an all risks policy is the fact that the

---

1　See Chapter 12.

burden of proof placed upon a claimant is less rigorous, in the sense that he does not have to identify a specific event as the cause of the loss, only that a loss occurred, and that it was a casualty and not a certainty. This, and other aspects of the all risks policy of insurance, is discussed in detail at the end of the chapter.

PERILS OF THE SEAS

Provision for this insurable peril is allowed for in cl 6.1.1 of the ITCH(95) and cl 4.1.1 of the IVCH(95), which state that:

> This insurance covers loss of or damage to the subject matter insured caused by: perils of the seas, rivers, lakes or other navigable waters.

With respect to cargo, the ICC (B) and (C) itemise a list of risks covered and 'perils of the seas' is not specifically mentioned as an insured peril. The ICC (A), being an all risks policy of insurance, has no need to enumerate the perils insured against.

Perils of the sea defined

The statutory definition of 'perils of the seas' can be found in r 7 of the Rules for Construction, the first part of which confines 'perils of the seas' to 'fortuitous accidents or casualties of the seas' and the second states that 'It does not include the ordinary action of the winds and waves.' For the purpose of clarity, it is necessary to divide the ensuing discussion on the subject into its two natural parts.

Fortuitous accidents or casualties of the seas

The fortuitous element and the words 'of the seas' of the first part of the statutory definition have opened up several areas of discussion in case law. First, the requirement of 'fortuity' has, inevitably, generated consideration of matters pertaining to the condition of the ship, such as wear and tear, inherent vice and unseaworthiness: such qualities in a ship would obviously take the fortuitous feature out of the claim of a loss by 'perils of the seas'. Naturally, it has also raised issues pointing to the conduct (or more accurately misconduct) of the master and crew, and of the assured. In this regard, scuttling, if committed with the connivance of the assured, is likely to be pleaded as a defence: as the element of fortuity is, in such a case, negatived by the wilful nature of the act of the assured, the loss is not recoverable. Furthermore, s 55(2)(a) expressly bars indemnity for 'any loss attributable to the wilful misconduct of the assured'. But, should the scuttling be committed without the connivance of the assured, then, the loss would be caused by barratry, and not a peril of the sea. That scuttling is not a peril of the sea is now firmly established by the House of Lords.

Secondly, the phrase 'of the seas' has brought about debate on the question of whether a collision (caused by either the negligence of the master or crew of the insured vessel or by a third party) and other accidents occurring on board ships are 'perils of the seas'. To facilitate a proper understanding of this aspect of the term, judges have drawn the distinction between marine and land risks.

Pre-statute case law has also provided its own definitions of the term; these can be derived, in particular, from the judgments of Lord Bramwell and Lord Herschell in the earlier cases of *Thames and Mersey Marine Insurance Co Ltd v Hamilton, Fraser and Co, 'Inchmaree'* (1887) 12 AC 484, HL, and *Wilson Sons and Co v Owners of Cargo per 'Xantho'* (1887) 12 App Cas 503, HL, respectively. In attempting to give the expression 'fortuitous' a meaning, it can be seen that some of the judges, in both old and recent cases, have unavoidably found themselves having to eliminate from the equation obvious defences, such as delay, inherent vice, wear and tear, unseaworthiness, and the wilful misconduct of the assured. It is observed that *Popham and Willett v St Petersberg Insurance Co* (1904) 10 Com Cas 31 simply endeavours to provide a definition of the term 'perils of the seas' by comparing accidental, fortuitous and unexpected events with ordinary, expected and regular conditions, whereas the recent Canadian case of *CCR Fishing Ltd and Others v Tomenson Inc and Others, 'La Pointe'* [1991] 1 Lloyd's Rep 89 is particularly useful for the purpose of illustrating the variety of defences that may be raised in a claim of a loss by 'perils of the seas'.

Thames and Mersey Marine Insurance Co Ltd v Hamilton, Fraser and Co, 'Inchmaree' (1887) 12 AC 484, HL

In his summation, Lord Bramwell considered other suitable definitions of 'perils of the seas', including two by other eminent judges, before suggesting one himself.[2]

> **Lord Bramwell:** [p 492] ... Definitions are most difficult, but Lord Ellenborough's seems right: '... all cases of marine damage of the like kind with those specially enumerated, and occasioned by similar causes.' I have had given to me the following definition or description of what would be included in the general words: 'Every accidental circumstance not the result of ordinary wear and tear, delay, or of the act of the assured, happening in the course of the navigation of the ship, and incidental to the navigation, and causing loss to the subject matter of insurance.' Probably a severe criticism might detect some faults in this. There are few definitions in which that could not be done. I think

---

2 The facts of this case can be found in Chapter 12, p 491.

the definition of Lopes LJ in *Pandorf v Hamilton* very good: 'In a seaworthy ship damage to goods caused by the action of the sea during transit not attributable to the fault of anybody', is a damage from a peril of the sea.

... I have thought that the following might suffice: 'All perils, losses and misfortunes of a marine character, or of a character incident to a ship as such.'

The following case, *Xantho*, is not actually a marine insurance case but comes, rather, under the head of carriage of goods by sea. Nevertheless, the deliberations of the court and, in particular, those by Lord Herschell on 'perils of the seas', are equally relevant to marine insurance.

Wilson, Sons and Co v Owners of Cargo per 'Xantho' (1887) 12 App Cas 503, HL

The appellants were the owners of the steamship *Xantho*, which sank after a collision, in fog, with another vessel whilst on a voyage from Cronstadt to Hull. The owners lodged their appeal against the cargo-owners on the basis that, *inter alia*, the loss of the ship was due to a collision, which was an excepted peril, namely, a peril of the seas.

The House of Lords, in reversing the decision of the Court of Appeal, decided that collision was, in fact, a peril of the seas and ruled in favour of the appellants.

> **Lord Herschell:** [p 509] ... I think it clear that the term 'perils of the sea' does not cover every accident or casualty which may happen to the subject matter of the insurance on the sea. It must be a peril 'of' the sea. Again, it is well settled that it is not every loss or damage of which the sea is the immediate cause that is covered by these words. They do not protect, for example, against the natural and inevitable action of the winds and waves, which results in what may be described as wear and tear. There must be some casualty, something which could not be foreseen as one of the necessary incidents of the adventure. The purpose of the policy is to secure an indemnity against accidents which may happen, not against events which must happen. It was contended that those losses only were losses by perils of the sea, which were occasioned by extraordinary violence of the winds or waves. I think this is too narrow a construction of the words, and it is certainly not supported by the authorities, or by common understanding.

Popham and Willett v St Petersberg Insurance Co (1904) 10 Com Cas 31

The plaintiffs dispatched five steamers on an expedition to Northern Russia with the intention of exporting goods into Siberia at a low rate of duty. The goods aboard the vessels and the freight were insured under a floating policy of insurance with the defendants. On entering the Kara Sea in July 1899, a large amount of ice was unexpectedly encountered, which caused damage to all the vessels and one, in fact, was wrecked. The vessels then returned to London and the goods were returned to their respective owners. Some of the goods belonging to the plaintiffs were sold, whilst the remainder were warehoused before being sent again to Siberia by rail at a later date, but at a much higher rate of duty. The plaintiffs claimed on their policy of insurance for the loss of goods and freight as well as the extra expenditure brought about by the warehousing and forwarding costs and the increased rate of duty.

The court ruled that the losses incurred were suffered as a consequence of encountering ice in the area at a time of the year when it would not have been expected. The losses were, therefore, losses brought about by a peril insured against, that is, a peril of the seas.

> **Walton J:** [p 34] ... The first question which has been raised is whether the obstruction to these steamers by ice in the Kara Sea was or was not a peril of the seas within the meaning of the policies. It was said to be analogous to the closing of the port by ice in the winter and the obstruction so created to a vessel arriving at her destination at that port. In such a case, the annual regular obstruction of the port by ice in the winter is in no sense an accident; it is part of the ordinary course of things, like the ebb and flow of the tides. It is scarcely necessary to say that difficulties arising merely from the ordinary closing of the port, which is subject to be closed, and is always closed, in the winter months, do not amount to a peril of the seas within the ordinary meaning of a policy of marine insurance. But that was not this case. The obstruction by ice in this case was accidental and unexpected. As far as I can understand, there had been no obstruction to the expedition in either 1897 or 1898. The unexpected prevalence of certain winds and currents in the Arctic Seas in August 1899, created an extraordinary difficulty and danger, for this ice was not only an obstruction, it was also a danger; one vessel was wrecked and the others were more or less damaged. The conclusion which I have come to is that the obstruction and danger and difficulty from the ice which these vessels met with was a peril of the sea, and one of the perils covered by the policies.

CCR Fishing Ltd and Others v Tomenson Inc and Others, 'La Pointe' [1991] 1 Lloyd's Rep 89, Supreme Court of Canada

La Pointe was a black iron hull which had been used in the cod fishing industry and was insured with the defendant insurers. In 1981, *La Pointe* was surveyed and, later in the year, her owners employed some repairers to rectify the faults highlighted in the survey report, with a view to selling her. The following year, without any warning, *La Pointe* developed a list at her moorings and sank in a few hours. The owners claimed that the loss was attributable to a peril of the sea in that, *inter alia*, the loss had been caused by the wrong type of bolts being used on some valve flanges which had later failed. The underwriters rejected the claim, citing ordinary wear and tear as the cause of loss.

The Supreme Court of Canada ruled that the loss was due to the failure of the bolts which had been negligently fitted and was, therefore, fortuitous and a peril of the seas.

> **Mme Justice McLachlin:** [p 91] ... In the case at bar, the loss resulted from the sinking of the ship due to the ingress of seawater. This loss would not have

occurred on land. The requirement that the accident be 'of the sea' is therefore met. The respondents argue that the cause of the loss was corrosion and that could have occurred anywhere, including on land. But, the test is not whether the defect which started the causal chain that led to the loss is one that could occur exclusively at sea, but rather whether the accident itself – in this case, the sinking of the ship – is one which could only occur at sea. Many sinkings result from causes which could occur on land – for example, the piercing of the hull of the ship with a rock could occur on land. No one would suggest that coverage under insurance for 'perils of the sea' would not lie where a ship founders and sinks at sea for that reason. I conclude that this accident was 'of the sea'.

The real issue in this case, as I see it, is whether the cause of the accident was 'fortuitous'. It is fortuitous if it was neither intentional nor inevitable and does not fall within any of the exclusions referred to in s 56 of the Act and the Act's definition of 'perils of the sea'.

... I turn, first, to the question of whether the failure of the bolts can be viewed as 'ordinary wear and tear'. In my view it cannot. There was nothing ordinary about the failure of the cap screws. Their failure was extraordinary, resulting, as the trial judge found, from the negligent act of the repairers who installed them.

The next question is whether the failure of the screws can be considered due to an inherent vice ... The concept of inherent vice in the context of marine insurance refers to loss stemming from qualities inherent in the thing lost. The failure of the cap screws in the case at bar cannot be said to result from purely inherent qualities of the ship. The unfortunate installation of these parts in the ship was a result of the negligence of the repairers, an external cause unrelated to those qualities. The loss was fortuitous, in the sense that it was not the inevitable product of a quality inherent in the vessel. I conclude that even if one were to assume that the proximate cause of the sinking was the failure of the cap screws, that would not assist the respondents, since the cause of the failure was not ordinary wear and tear or inherent vice, but the fortuitous negligence of the repairers.

Notes

In *Hamilton, Fraser and Co v Pandorf and Co* **(1887) 12 App Cas 518,** a carriage of goods by sea case, rats gnawed a hole in a pipe aboard the ship, allowing seawater to escape and damage the cargo of rice. A clause on the bill of lading which excepted 'dangers and accidents of the seas' was held to be applicable and the carrier was not liable.

Lord Fitzgerald: [p 528] ... The accident was fortuitous, unforeseen, and actually unknown until the ship reached her destination and commenced unloading. I do not, however, mean to suggest that to constitute a peril of the sea the accident or calamity should have been of an unforeseen character. The remote cause was in a certain sense the action of the rats on the lead pipe, but the immediate cause of the damage was the irruption of seawater from time to time through the injured pipe caused by the rolling of the ship as she proceeded on her voyage.

Scuttling is not a peril of the sea

Recovery under a policy of marine insurance when there has been wilful misconduct committed by the assured is excluded by s 55(2)(a) of the Marine Insurance Act 1906. By definition, any act of a wilful nature must necessarily remove the basic requirement of fortuity. The absence of fortuity in the event of a loss caused by wilful misconduct of any person (the assured, master or crew) renders the loss irrecoverable as a loss by a peril of the seas.

Similarly, as a barratrous scuttling is an intentional act committed by the master or crew without the connivance of the shipowner, 'barratry' and 'perils of the seas' must, therefore, also be mutually exclusive: a loss caused by a barratrous act, though it may be recoverable under the insurable risk of barratry (if it is an insured risk under the policy in question) is not recoverable as a loss by a peril of the seas.[3]

The case of *Samuel v Dumas* **(1924) 18 LlL Rep 211, HL**, established, in overturning the ruling in *Small v United Kingdom Marine Mutual Insurance Association* [1897] 2 QB 311, CA,[4] that scuttling a ship, with the connivance of the owner, is not a loss recoverable under the head of 'perils of the seas'. In this instance, an innocent mortgagee was barred from recovery, even though he was in no way a party to the conspiracy.

> **Viscount Cave:** [p 215] ... the word 'fortuitous' ... involves an element of chance or ill-luck which is absent where those in charge of a vessel deliberately throw her away ... the expression 'perils of the sea', while it may well include a loss by accidental collision or negligent navigation, cannot extend to a wilful and deliberate throwing away of a ship by those in charge of her.
>
> **Viscount Finlay:** [p 217] ... The scuttling of this vessel occurred on the seas, but it was not due to any peril of the seas; it was due entirely to the fraudulent act of the owner. The scuttling was not fortuitous, but deliberate, and had nothing of the element of accident or casualty about it. Storms are fortuitous; the ordinary action of the waves is not; and the fraudulent scuttling is even more decisively out of the region of accident. The entrance of the seawater cannot, for this purpose, be separated from the act which caused it.

The position of the cargo-owner

The Institute Cargo Clauses do not employ the term 'wilful misconduct'. Instead, cl 4.7 of the ICC (B) and (C) state, as an exclusion, that: 'In no case shall this insurance cover ... deliberate damage to or deliberate destruction of

---

3 For a discussion of the law of barratry, see Chapter 12.
4 Also discussed in Chapter 12, p 530.

the subject matter insured or any part thereof by the wrongful act of any person or persons.' The ICC (A), being an all risks policy, is silent on this matter.

The prickly question which does not appear to have been put before a court for consideration is, whether loss or damage to cargo is recoverable when the carrying ship is scuttled by the shipowner. The wording of cl 4.7 of the ICC (B) and (C) is probably wide enough to exclude such a loss. The ICC (A), however, is for all risks and whether recovery for such a cause of loss may be regarded as a 'risk', is arguable. The fundamental question is: is a cargo-owner, under an all risks policy, insured against the fraudulent casting away of his goods by shipowners? The same dilemma will also arise in the case of cargo which is lost or damaged as a result of a barratrous act.

In the Court of Appeal, in *Samuel v Dumas* [1923] 1 KB 592, CA, Scrutton LJ remarked that he knew of no case (p 620) 'where an owner of goods has recovered for damage to his goods by seawater intentionally admitted by the owner of the ship, either for perils of the sea or barratry'. This comment is correct, for the judge was referring to specific perils under which the element of fortuity is not an essential ingredient.[5] But whether the same may be applied to an all risks policy is, it is submitted, doubtful.

It should be borne in mind that the ICC (A) insure against 'all risks', and not against specified events, such as 'barratry' or 'perils of the seas', and this term has its own special qualities and requirements. Provided that the loss may be regarded as a 'risk' vis à vis the assured cargo-owner and does not fall within any of the exceptions, there is no reason why such a loss should not be allowed. Support for this may be drawn from the judgment of Lord Sumner, albeit the dissenting judge, in *Samuel v Dumas* (1924) 18 LlL Rep 211, HL, who felt that: [p 224] '... it is the business of an underwriter to take risks, and the risk, an inconsiderable one, of the shipowner's wilful misconduct can be considered in the premium as well as the risk of negligent navigation.' He expressed his unease for not allowing recovery for such a loss in the following terms: '... I find it impossible not to be influenced by the consideration that, if a scuttled ship is not proximately lost by perils of the seas, then every cargo-owner, who loses his goods with her, is as uninsured as the scuttling shipowner. Curious results may follow.'

Further reinforcement for this point of view may be drawn from the comments of Goddard LJ, in *London and Provincial Process Ltd v Hudson* [1939] 3 All ER 857, in relation to a cargo claim (brought under an all risks policy)

---

5   It is not a loss caused by 'barratry', because the seawater was intentionally admitted with the connivance of the shipowner, or a loss caused by 'perils of the seas' because of the wilful nature of the misconduct of the shipowner.

resulting from the insolvency of the shipowner.[6] Referring to the general statement of law that there must be an 'accident or fortuitous casualty' before a loss may be recoverable under an all risks policy, the judge added that such a policy covered more than an accidental fire or the destruction of goods by the forces of nature. He was clear in his mind that theft, 'a conscious and wilful act of another person', is recoverable under an all risks policy. It is thus contended that, by parity of reasoning, scuttling, a wilful act committed with or without the connivance of the shipowner, should also be recoverable.

In conclusion, it is safe to say that an innocent mortgagee (suing as an assignee or as original assured under the Institute Hull Clauses) and an owner of cargo which is insured under either the ICC (B) or (C) would not be able to recover for loss or damage caused by scuttling perpetrated with the connivance of the shipowner. The position under an all risks policy (the ICC (A)) is, however, not so clear.

Collision is a peril of the sea

In the case of **Xantho [1887] 12 App Cas 503**, Lord Herschell stated:

> [p 509] ... It is beyond question, that if a vessel strikes upon a sunken rock in fair weather and sinks, this is a loss by perils of the sea. And a loss by foundering, owing to a vessel coming into collision with another vessel, even when the collision results from the negligence of that other vessel, falls within the same category.

Although the *Xantho* case is generally acknowledged as having established the principle that collision is a peril of the sea, there is a much earlier case which also deliberated on this matter.

Smith and Others v Scott (1811) 4 Taunt 126

This was an action upon a policy of insurance on two ships, *Helena* and *Merlin* 'at and from' Honduras to Britain. On the voyage to Britain, *Helena*, through no fault of her own, was run down by another vessel, *Margaret*, as a result of the gross neglect of *Margaret*'s crew. After the collision, the crew of *Helena* boarded *Margaret* and found only one man on deck, and he was asleep. The plaintiff claimed for the loss of *Helena* as being due to a peril of the seas. The insurers cited the loss to be attributable to the gross negligence of the crew of *Margaret* and not perils of the seas.

The jury found for the plaintiff, and Mansfield CJ made some early observations about collision being considered a peril of the seas.

> **Mansfield CJ:** [p 127] ... I do not know how to make this out not to be a peril of the sea. What drove *Margaret* against *Helena*? The sea! What was the cause that

---

6   Insolvency of the shipowner as the basis of a claim under an all risks policy is discussed in Chapter 10, p 445.

the crew of *Margaret* did not prevent her from running against the other, their gross and culpable negligence? But still the sea did the mischief.

Negligence of the master and crew

It should be noted that, in the *Xantho* case, the court only pronounced about a collision where there was negligence on the part of the other vessel. However, s 55(2)(a) of the Marine Insurance Act 1906 clearly does not exclude an insurer's liability where there is negligence aboard the insured vessel when it states that: 'The insurer is not ... unless the policy otherwise provides ... liable for any loss proximately caused by a peril insured against, even though the loss would not have happened but for the misconduct or negligence of the master or crew.' This allows the assured to claim for a loss proximately caused by a peril insured against (perils of the seas), but remotely caused by the negligence of the master or crew.

It is only the provision within the Inchmaree Clause which provides cover for 'the negligence of Master Officers Crew or Pilots' as a proximate cause of the loss: thus, should a loss by collision be held to have been proximately caused by the negligence of the master, officers, crew or pilots, it is recoverable under cl 6.2.2 of the ITCH(95) and cl 4.2.2 of the IVCH(95).

The case of *Walker v Maitland*, below, provides an early, but vivid example of a loss proximately caused by a peril of the sea, but remotely caused by the negligence of the master and crew

Walker v Maitland (1821) 5 B&Ald 171

The sailing ship *Britannia* was chartered for a voyage from St Kitts in the West Indies to Britain. By the custom of the trade, when loading ships at St Kitts, where the cargo was brought from the shore by boat to be loaded into the larger vessel, it fell upon the owner and not the charterer to effect a policy of insurance to cover such loading operations.[7] A sloop called *Vigilant* was duly employed at St Kitts to bring the cargo from shore to ship but, because of the negligence of the crew of the sloop, who were asleep at the time, the sloop was blown ashore and wrecked. Part of the cargo of sugar was lost and the rest was damaged. The owner of *Britannia*, who had effected the policy of insurance, claimed upon it under the head of peril of the seas.

The court ruled in favour of the owner, in that the loss arose immediately from a peril of the sea, but remotely from the negligence of the master and crew.

> **Bayley J:** [p 175] ... Here, the loss arose from the sloop with the goods on board having been beat to pieces by the force of the wind and waves; and the question in this case is, whether the underwriters are exonerated from the loss,

---

7   See, now, ITCH(95), cl 1.4 and IVCH(95).

by proving negligence on the part of the crew, although the damage was occasioned by the perils of the sea. It is the duty of the owner to have the ship properly equipped, and for that purpose, it is necessary that he should provide a competent master and crew in the first instance; but having done that, he has discharged his duty, and is not responsible for their negligence, as between him and the underwriters. If that were not considered to be the law, the question must have frequently arisen, whether there had been proper care and attention by the master and mariners. It is now, however, raised almost for the first time. I am of opinion, that in this case the underwriters were liable.

This principle of negligence by the master and crew is affirmed in *Dixon v Sadler* (1839) 5 M&W 405, where, in his judgment, Parke B stated:

[p 415] ... The great principle established by the more recent decisions, is that, if the vessel, crew, and equipment be originally sufficient, the assured has done all that he has contracted to do, and is not responsible for the subsequent deficiency occasioned by the neglect or misconduct of the master or crew: and this principle prevents many nice and difficult inquiries, and causes a more complete indemnity to the assured, which is the object of the contract of insurance.

The same approach that the loss was proximately caused by a peril of the sea and only remotely caused by the negligence of the crew is also evident in the case of *Davidson and Others v Burnard*, below.

Davidson and Others v Burnard (1868) LR 4 CP 117

The plaintiffs effected a policy of insurance on goods 'at and from' Jamaica to New York aboard *Montezuma*. The day after loading, it was found that seawater had penetrated the hold of the vessel and damaged the goods. A survey confirmed that a discharge pipe in the engine room had inadvertently been left open, with the result that, as the cargo was loaded and the vessel's draught increased, seawater entered *Montezuma* and contaminated the goods. The plaintiffs claimed on their policy of insurance.

The court ruled that the damage done to the goods was due to the negligence of the crew, but was, nevertheless, a peril of the sea and, therefore, the plaintiffs could recover.

Willes J: [p 121] ... Then, unless some distinction can be made between a loss from an accident happening through the negligence of the crew of another vessel and a loss from an accident happening either in the way it has been suggested it did in the present case, from a splinter getting into the valve, or from such negligence of the crew, as was suggested in the report of the survey, the loss would be a loss occasioned by the perils of the sea. As to there being any such distinction between a loss caused by the negligence of the crew of the vessel insured and one caused by the negligence of another vessel, all such distinction has been swept away by the judgment of Lord Wensleydale, as I understand it, in the case of *Dixon v Sadler*. On the whole, it is not necessary, I think, to say whether these goods were damaged by perils of the sea, as the damage to them was clearly caused by perils of the sea or the like within the words of the policy. I wish to add, that my judgment adopts the report of the survey itself, as to the accident probably arising from a negligence referable to leaving cocks and valves open, rather than the evidence suggesting that the accident might have happened by a splinter getting into the valve, and I only referred to that last by way of illustration.

The following case, *The Stranna,* is a carriage of goods by sea case, where, in his deliberation, Scott LJ elaborated on why the negligence of the assured's servants did not lessen the unexpected or fortuitous nature of an accident that was deemed a peril of the seas. The judge also pointed out that the general principles enunciated are also applicable to marine insurance.

The Stranna [1938] 1 All ER 458, CA

Whilst loading a deck cargo of timber, *The Stranna* suddenly heeled over and part of her cargo shot overboard, drifted away in the fog and was never found. The question before the Court of Appeal was whether the loss was by a peril of the sea, an excepted peril in the bill of lading.

The Court of Appeal adjudged that it was a peril of the sea and, therefore, the shipowner was not liable for the loss.

> **Scott LJ:** [p 465] ... In my view, what happened was a loss by a peril of the sea, and none the less so because it was the negligence of those who were concerned with the work of loading the ship that brought the peril into operation. It was argued by Sir Robert Aske that, if the listing of the ship was caused by bad loading, that very fact excluded the idea of a peril of the sea, his contention being that the meaning of that phrase in the English language, or at any rate as judicially defined, restricts it to cases where the damage to ship or cargo by the sea, or seawater, arises through external causes, such as wind and weather, or striking a rock, or where seawater actually gets into the ship. I do not agree. Even apart from the wider expressions in the clause which come after 'perils of the sea', it is, in my opinion, an appropriate use of the English language to say that, on the facts of the present case, the timber was lost by a peril of the sea. The fortuitous aspect of the meaning of the word 'peril' in a contract either of carriage or of insurance is plainly satisfied by the evidence. As the judge points out, so far as the defendants' servants were concerned, the event was wholly unexpected; it was just an unfortunate accident. But it was also a peril of the sea, not merely a peril on the sea. It could not have happened on land. It was a happening which is characteristic of the sea, and of the behaviour of ships.

Notes

In *Baxendale v Fane,* **'Lapwing' (1940) 66 LlL Rep 174,**[8] where a large yacht was damaged on being placed in a dry-dock, no mention was made of

---

8 See Chapter 12, p 503, where this case is discussed in the context of the negligence cover of the Inchmaree Clause.

s 55(2)(a). Though emphasis was placed on the negligence cover of the Inchmaree Clause, nevertheless, recognition was given to the fact that the acting master's negligence provided the necessary fortuity rendering the loss recoverable also under the head of a marine peril. In the words of Hodson J [p 181], 'the intervention of the negligence of those responsible for the docking provides the fortuitous circumstances which entitles the plaintiff to recover under the terms ("perils of the seas and all other perils") of the policy'.

Negligence of the assured acting as master

An assured could well act as the master of his own ship: in such an event, he would, in a manner of speech, be wearing two hats. Although *Westport Coal Co v McPhail* [1898] 2 QB 130, CA was a carriage of goods by sea case, it graphically illustrated the distinction between the duties of the assured as master, and the assured as owner. The principle enunciated in the case is equally pertinent to marine insurance.

Westport Coal Co v McPhail [1898] 2 QB 130, CA

A part owner of *Gainsborough*, serving as master, signed bills of lading for the carriage of a cargo of coal from Westport to San Francisco. *Gainsborough* stranded on a reef due to the negligent navigation of the master, and the plaintiff cargo-owners sued the shipowners for their losses on the basis that the negligence of the part owner (acting as master) precluded the shipowners from seeking the protection of the exception clause which excluded them from liability for the negligence of the master but not of a part owner, albeit acting in the capacity of master.

The Court of Appeal ruled that, as the master's actions in negligently navigating the ship were separate from his liability as part owner the exception clause applied and, therefore, the cargo-owners could not recover their losses under the bill of lading.

> **Collins LJ:** [p 133] ... But, it is at this point that the real difficulty arises. The captain is excused; the owner is not ... it was the negligence of the master in the sphere of his duty as master which caused the loss ... The plaintiffs seek to make him liable by viewing him in two different capacities – that is to say, they distinguish his capacities for the purpose of limiting the exception, but they mix them up again for the purpose of fixing him with liability as owner. But does it follow that because one and the same is captain and part owner, negligence in either capacity is to be deemed negligence in both? Or does not this question involve an examination of what his duty is in each capacity, so as to see whether there was in fact negligence in both? So far as the navigation of the ship is concerned, the duty of the owner, as distinguished from the master, would be to take due care to appoint a competent person; and, therefore, the defendants' co-owners in this case having discharged that duty, and being protected against the master's negligence, are not now charged with negligence as owners.

It seems to us that it would be simpler and more in accordance with common sense to hold that the negligence which caused the damage was exclusively master's, as distinguished from part owner's, negligence, within the meaning of the exception.

Notes

See, also, *Trinder, Anderson and Co v Thames and Mersey Marine Insurance Co* [1898] 2 QB 114, CA, where it was held that the fact that the master was a part owner of the vessel did not prevent the owners from recovery under the negligence cover of the Inchmaree Clause.[9]

Accidents on board ship

The following cases which have distinguished marine risks from land risks illustrate the point that it is not always easy to discern whether a loss or damage sustained by a ship arising from an accident occurring on board ship whilst she is at sea is recoverable as a loss by 'perils of the seas'.

In the case of **Thames and Mersey Marine Insurance v Hamilton, Fraser and Co, 'Inchmaree' [1887] 12 App Cas 484, HL**, Lord Bramwell considered whether an accident to a donkey engine on board the ship constituted a marine risk.

Lord Bramwell: [p 493] ... The damage to the donkey engine was not through its being in a ship or at sea. The same thing would have happened had the boilers and engine been on land, if the same mismanagement had taken place. The sea, waves and winds had nothing to do with it.

In the following case, Lord Buckmaster, in determining between a marine risk and a risk which can happen anywhere, quoted from two other significant cases concerned with this issue, namely, *Xantho* (discussed earlier) and *ED Sassoon v Western Assurance Co* [1912] AC 561.

Grant, Smith and Co v Seattle Construction and Dry Dock Co [1920] AC 162, PC

This was a case originally heard in the courts of British Columbia, and finally brought before the Privy Council. The appellants were a large firm of contractors engaged in the construction of a breakwater at the port of Victoria, British Columbia. To facilitate the building process, the appellants hired a large wooden floating dry-dock, valued at $34,500, from the respondents. Part of the lease agreement was that the appellants would insure the dock for $75,000 against marine risks and fire, which they failed to do. Whilst working near the breakwater, the dry-dock took on a list as it was being submerged, and eventually foundered. The respondents sued the construction company for, *inter alia*, failure to insure the dry-dock against marine risks.

---

9   For a fuller discussion of this aspect of the case in relation to the Inchmaree Clause, see Chapter 12, p 506.

The Privy Council ruled that the loss of the dry-dock was not attributable to a marine risk and, therefore, the respondents were only entitled to recover the actual value of the dry-dock, and not the larger amount stipulated in the proposed contract of insurance.

Lord Buckmaster: [p 170] ... It [the covenant of insurance] was to insure against 'marine risk', which cannot be better described than as against 'the hazards of the sea'. If, while in dock, either while the caissons were being built or while the dock was being submerged, owing to any marine risk the dock had been lost, this loss the policy would have covered; but, in truth, no such risk or peril caused its destruction. The harbour was peculiarly quiet, and it is plain that it was no conditions of wind or wave that caused the dock to capsize. It was destroyed because of its own inherent unfitness for the use to which it was put – an unfitness which the appellants have prevented themselves from raising by reason of their own covenant.

It is not desirable to attempt to define too exactly a 'marine risk' or a 'peril of the sea', but it can at least be said that it is some condition of sea or weather or accident of navigation producing a result which, but for these conditions, would not have occurred.

... The words there occurred in a bill of lading, and the claim arose with regard to the loss of goods covered by the document. But Lord Herschell [in *Wilson, Sons and Co v Owners of Cargo per 'Xantho'*] points out that the phrase has no different meaning whether it occurs in the insurance of the ship or of the goods.

In the case of *ED Sassoon and Co v Western Assurance Co*, a store of opium was lost in a hulk moored in a river by the percolation of water through a leak caused by the rotten condition of the boat. The decay was so covered by copper sheathing that, although the vessel was properly inspected, it was not, and it could not, be detected. It was held by this Board that the loss was not a loss within the phrase 'perils of the sea and all other perils', and Lord Mersey, in delivering the opinion of the Board, states: 'There was no weather, nor any other fortuitous circumstance, contributing to the incursion of the water; the water merely gravitated by its own weight through the opening in the decayed wood and so damaged the opium. It would be an abuse of language to describe this as a loss due to perils of the sea.' Their Lordships can see no difference between the circumstances of this case and the principle there enunciated. It is just as though a vessel, unfit to carry the cargo with which she was loaded, through her own inherent weakness, and without incident or peril of any kind, sank in still water. In such a case, recovery under the ordinary policy of insurance would be impossible. An insurance against 'the perils of the sea and other perils' is not a guarantee that a ship will float, and in the same way, in the present case, had such a policy been effected it would not have covered a loss inevitable in the circumstances due to the unfitness of the structure, and entirely dissociated from any peril by wind and water.

A similar line had been taken some four years earlier in *Stott (Baltic) Steamers Ltd v Marten*, below, where the accident aboard ship was held not to be one peculiarly incident to a ship.

Stott (Baltic) Steamers Ltd v Marten and Others [1916] AC 304, HL

The appellants, who were owners of the steamship *Ussa*, insured her with the respondents under a time policy of marine insurance. Whilst in Liverpool, *Ussa* was loading a large boiler down one of her hatches by means of a floating crane, *Atlas*, which was moored alongside. During the loading process, the boiler touched the hatch coamings of the ship, the weight of the load briefly came off the crane, which then listed with the result that the crane's lifting gear broke, and the boiler fell to the bottom of the ship's hold and damaged her. The shipowners claimed on their policy of insurance, but the underwriters rejected the claim, on the basis that the accident was not a risk peculiarly incident to a ship.

The House of Lords affirmed the decision of the Court of Appeal and found for the respondent insurers. The loss was not recoverable under the head of 'perils of the seas'.

Lord Atkinson: [p 311] ... A peril whose only connection with the sea is that it arises on board ship is not necessarily a peril of the seas nor a peril ejusdem generis as a peril of the sea. The breaking of the chain of a crane, or of a shackle of that chain, if overloaded or subjected to too severe a strain, is not more maritime in character when it occurs on board a ship than when it occurs on land. Nor is the catching of the ends of a lengthy boiler on the coamings when being lowered into the hold of a ship through a hatchway more maritime than would be the catching on land of any piece of machinery on the sides of an opening shorter than itself through which it was being lowered. Neither the winds nor the waves contributed to the accident. Nor did the fact that the ship on which it occurred was waterborne. The listing of *Atlas* to port tended to take up the slack of the chain and to diminish the extent of the drop, and therefore of the strain, when the boiler got free, rather than the contrary. The statement of Lord Ellenborough in *Cullen v Butler* as to the proper construction of general words, such as those used in the present case, in a policy of marine insurance has been many times approved of. He said due effect would be given to them by 'allowing them to comprehend and cover other cases of marine damage of the like kind with those which are specially enumerated and occasioned by similar causes'. By the words 'marine damage', Lord Herschell, in *Thames and Mersey Marine Insurance Co v Hamilton, Fraser and Co*, took Lord Ellenborough to have meant not only damage caused by the sea, but damage of a character to which a marine adventure is subject. In my view, the present case is covered by this last mentioned case.

And, in *Cullen v Butler*, below, the loss of a vessel accidentally sunk by another ship's gunfire was also held not to be a loss caused by a peril of the sea. Nevertheless, the assured recovered under the policy, because of the clause 'all other perils' inserted in the policy.

Cullen v Butler (1816) 5 M&S 461

This was a claim upon an insurance policy on goods lost aboard the ship *Industry* 'at and from' London to the Canary Islands. Whilst on the voyage to the Canary Islands, the captain of another British vessel, *Midas*, mistook her in the dark for an enemy and fired upon her. *Industry* sank, and the cargo was lost. The plaintiff owner claimed that the loss was caused by, *inter alia*, a peril of the sea. The underwriters rejected the claim.

The court ruled for the plaintiff, not under the head of 'perils of the seas', but on another clause in the policy, namely '... all other perils, losses ...'.

Lord Ellenborough CJ: [p 464] ... If it be a loss by perils of the sea, merely because it is a loss happening upon the sea, as has been contended, all the other causes of loss specified in the policy are, upon that ground, equally entitled so to be considered; and it would be unnecessary as to them ever to assign any other cause of loss, than a loss by perils of the sea. But as that has not been the understanding and practice on the subject hitherto, and insomuch as the very insertion of the general or sweeping words, as they are called, in the policy after the special words, imports that the special words were not understood to include all perils happening on the sea, but that some more general words were required to be added, in order to extend the responsibility of the underwriters unequivocally to other risks not included within the proper scope of any of those enumerated perils, I shall think it necessary only to advert shortly to some of the reasons upon which we think that the general words, thus inserted, comprehend a loss of this nature.

Perils of the seas or unseaworthiness?

'Unseaworthiness', like 'ordinary wear and tear', is an obvious defence against a claim for a loss by perils of the seas. As in ordinary wear and tear, there is no element of fortuity in unseaworthiness, and, therefore, a loss so caused is not recoverable as a loss by a peril of the seas. In the following case, *Merchants Trading Co v Universal Marine Insurance Co*, the close relationship between 'perils of the seas' and unseaworthiness' is well illustrated.

Merchants Trading Co v Universal Marine Insurance Co (1870) CP 431, CA

This was a retrial of an action on a voyage policy of insurance 'at and from' the Mersey to Cardiff and thence to Alexandria. The plaintiffs' steamship *Golden Fleece* loaded some coal in the Mersey and then proceeded to Cardiff to load some more. On leaving Cardiff, in order to avoid bad weather, the master anchored *Golden Fleece* off Barry Island, but, whilst in this safe anchorage, there was a sudden ingress of seawater into the starboard bunker, which caused the ship to sink in 35 minutes. The plaintiff owners claimed on their policy of insurance, but the underwriters resisted the claim and contested that the vessel was unseaworthy at the commencement of the voyage and that the loss did not arise from a peril insured against.

The court ruled in favour of the insurers on the basis that *Golden Fleece* was unseaworthy when she left the Mersey and unfit to carry her cargo.

Bovill CJ: [p 432] ... He [Lush J, the trial judge] further explained to the jury that the terms 'perils of the sea' denoted all maritime casualties resulting from the violent action of the elements of the wind and waters, lightning, tempest, stranding, striking on a rock, and so on – all casualties of that description as distinguished from the silent natural gradual action of the elements upon the vessel itself, though the latter properly belonged to wear and tear, and that what the underwriters insured were casualties that might happen, not consequences which must happen, casualties which might occur and were incident to navigation arising from the violent action of the elements upon the ship.

As to the first alleged misdirection, the question at the trial was whether the vessel sank through unseaworthiness or from some extraordinary and unaccountable accident, and the learned judge compendiously expressed this contention in the question which he left to the jury of whether the leak was attributable to injury and violence from without, or to weakness within. It is quite true that the perils mentioned by the learned judge do not include all the risks and perils covered by the policy, but from the nature of the question that was raised in this case, which was as to the cause of the sudden rushing of the water into the vessel, whether it was the inherent weakness of the vessel in consequence of original defects and construction, or neglected rust, or some unaccountable accident resulting in foundering ...

In this case, the fact of her sinking in smooth water and calm weather so immediately after leaving Cardiff Docks, was properly treated as strong evidence of inability to carry her full cargo from Cardiff, which was evidence of unseaworthiness at Cardiff, and under the circumstances and according to the sole discussion raised on both sides of the trial, it was equally strong evidence of unseaworthiness at Birkenhead.

The close relationship between 'perils of the seas' and unseaworthiness was also raised in the three following cases: *Sassoon v Western Assurance*; *Samuel v Dumas* and the *Miss Jay Jay* case.

Sassoon and Co v Western Assurance Co [1912] AC 561, PC

Opium stored in a wooden hulk, moored in a river, was damaged when water leaked through the hull. The poor condition of the hull had been hidden from view by a layer of protective copper sheathing. The plaintiffs claimed for the damage to the opium, citing perils of the sea. The underwriters rejected the claim and questioned the hulk's seaworthiness.

The Privy Council ruled that the damage was not caused by a peril of the sea within the meaning of the policy.

Lord Mersey: [p 563] ... There was no weather, nor any other fortuitous circumstance, contributing to the incursion of the water; the water merely gravitated by its own weight through the opening in the decayed wood and so damaged the opium. It would be an abuse of language to describe this as a loss due to perils of the sea. Although seawater damaged the goods, no peril of the sea contributed either proximately or remotely to the loss.

Samuel v Dumas (1924) 18 LlL Rep 211, HL

The possibility of raising unseaworthiness as a defence to a claim which pleads 'perils of the seas' as the cause of loss was considered by Viscount Finlay in the following manner:

> **Viscount Finlay:** [p 217] ... The view that the proximate cause of the loss when the vessel has been scuttled is the inrush of the seawater, and that is a peril of the sea, is inconsistent with the well established rule that it is always open to the underwriter on a time policy to show that the loss arose not from perils of the seas, but from the unseaworthy condition in which the vessel sailed (see *Arnould on Marine Insurance,* s 799). When the vessel is unseaworthy and the water consequently gets into the vessel and sinks her, it could never be said that the loss was due to the perils of the sea. It is true that the vessel sank in consequence of the inrush of water, but this inrush was due simply to the unseaworthiness. The unseaworthiness was the proximate cause of the loss. Exactly the same reasoning applies to the case of scuttling; the hole is there made in order in order to let in the water. The water comes in and the vessel sinks. The proximate cause of the loss is scuttling, as in the other case of unseaworthiness. The entrance of the water cannot be divorced from the act which occasioned it.

Lloyd (JJ) Instruments Ltd v Northern Star Insurance Co Ltd, 'Miss Jay Jay' [1985] 1 Lloyd's Rep 264, [1987] 1 Lloyd's Rep 32, CA

A yacht, insured under a time policy of insurance which included a clause covering loss by 'external accidental means', was adjudged to have suffered damage to her hull by means of a combination of defective design and adverse weather conditions. The seaworthiness of the ship was questioned by the insurers.

> **Mustill J:** [p 272] ... I now return to the facts of the present case. *Miss Jay Jay* was plainly unseaworthy, but can it be said that the craft suffered from debility in the sense to which I have referred? It seems to me that the answer must be – 'No'. There is no reason to suppose that the boat would have sunk at her moorings, or while under way in a millpond sea. Indeed, she had only recently completed a Channel crossing. Conversely, if one asked whether the loss was due to the fortuitous action of the wind and waves, the answer must be – 'Yes'. True, the weather was not exceptional, but this is immaterial. Whichever of the expert witnesses may be right as to the mechanism of the structural failure, the immediate cause was the action of adverse weather conditions on an ill-designed and ill-made hull. The cases show that this is sufficient to bring the loss within the words of a time policy in the standard form. Since I consider that there is, for present purposes, no material distinction between 'perils of the seas' and 'external accidental means'...

Ordinary action of the winds and waves

The following case from Australia provides a good interpretation of the second part of r 7 of the Rules for Construction, that the term 'perils of the seas' does not include the ordinary action of the winds and waves. This, however, does not mean that the action of the wind and waves must be 'extraordinary' to be considered fortuitous, for the word 'ordinary' qualifies 'action' and not 'winds and waves'.

Skandia Insurance Co v Skoljarev [1979] 142 CLR 375, High Court of Australia

The respondents insured their fishing vessel *Zadar* with the appellants under a time policy of insurance. Soon after leaving Port Lincoln in South Australia, and in calm conditions, *Zadar* suffered a rapid ingress of water into her engine room and sank; the point and cause of entry were unknown. The respondents claimed on their policy of insurance citing the loss as being due to a peril of the sea.

The High Court of Australia dismissed the insurer's appeal, and found for the respondent owners. The loss was attributed to a peril of the sea.

> **Mason J:** [p 384] ... On the other hand, losses due to fortuitous incursions of seawater are attributable to perils of the sea. Such losses comprehend loss or damage caused by foundering in violent weather or by collision with another vessel or with submerged rocks or other obstructions in calm weather. They also include damage done to cargo by the entrance of water through a hole in a pipe gnawed by rats (*Hamilton, Fraser and Co v Pandorf and Co*) or through a valve left open by mistake (*Blackburn v Liverpool, Brazil and River Plate Steam Navigation Co*), and the sinking of a submarine as the result of the negligent cutting of pipes which caused leaks in the skin of the vessel (*George Cohen, Sons and Co v National Benefit Assurance Co Ltd*). As these cases demonstrate, it is enough that an accidental or fortuitous event leads to the admission of seawater into the vessel, thereby causing its loss, or damage to it, even if at all relevant times the sea is calm and the weather is fair. The consequential loss or damage cannot then be attributed to the ordinary action of the wind and waves.
>
> The old view that some extraordinary action of the wind and waves is required to constitute a fortuitous accident or casualty is now quite discredited (the *Xantho* case).

Notes

In *Miss Jay Jay* **[1985] 1 Lloyd's Rep 264; [1987] 1 Lloyd's Rep 32, CA**, Mustill J, in the court of first instance, considered in depth the meaning of r 7 of the Rules for Construction. His interpretation is not in conflict with the *Skandia* case.

> **Mustill J:** [court of first instance, p 271] ... Assuming, therefore, that the cases on 'perils of the seas' may be properly cited in the present context, what principles do they lay down? I think it helpful, when approaching this difficult area of the law, to draw two sets of distinctions. The first relates to weather conditions, which for present purposes may be divided into three categories: (i) 'Abnormally bad weather.' Here the weather lies outside the range of conditions which the assured could reasonably foresee that the vessel might encounter on the voyage in question. (ii) 'Adverse weather': namely, weather

which lies within the range of what could be foreseen, but at the unfavourable end of that range. In effect, the weather is worse than could be hoped, but no worse than could be envisaged as a possibility. (iii) 'Favourable weather': namely, weather which lies within that range, but is not bad enough to be classed as 'adverse'. At the other extreme of the range from 'adverse' weather can be found what may be called 'perfect' weather.

First, as to 'perils of the seas'. The definition contained in r 7 of the Rules for Construction of Policy set out in the first Schedule to the Act excludes 'the ordinary action of the winds and waves'. While it is tempting to deduce from these words that a loss is not recoverable unless it results from weather which is extraordinary (namely, what I have referred to as abnormal weather conditions), this interpretation is mistaken ... The word 'ordinary' attaches to 'action', not to 'wind and waves'. The cases make it quite plain that if the action of the wind or sea is the immediate cause of the loss, a claim lies under the policy notwithstanding that the conditions were within the range which could reasonably have been anticipated. All that is needed is (in the words of Lord Buckmaster in *Grant, Smith and Co v Seattle Construction and Dry Dock Co* [1920] AC 162, p 171) '... some condition of sea or weather or accident of navigation producing a result which, but for these conditions, would not have occurred'.

Perils of the sea or ordinary wear and tear?

Section 55(2)(c) of the Marine Insurance Act 1906 expressly states that, unless the policy otherwise provides, loss or damage caused by ordinary wear and tear is not an insured risk. Additionally, all the Institute Cargo Clauses exclude, in cl 4.2, 'ordinary leakage, ordinary loss in weight or volume, or ordinary wear and tear of the subject matter insured'.

This part of the definition in r 7 was clarified in the case of *Miss Jay Jay* [1985] 1 Lloyd's Rep 264, where Mustill J, in the court of first instance, equated the ordinary action of the winds and waves with wear and tear when he declared that: [p 271] '... The principal object of the definition is to rule out losses resulting from wear and tear.'

Wadsworth Lighterage and Coaling Co v Sea Insurance Co (1929) 15 Com Cas 1, CA

This was a case where a wooden steam barge, with 50 years of service carrying coal on the River Mersey, sank at her moorings, on a calm night. She was later raised and beached. The owners claimed for a total loss under their policy of insurance, basing their claim upon a clause which stated that: '... this insurance is against the risks of total and/or constructive and/or arranged loss, including ... damage to such vessel by collision ... or by fire, lightning, stranding or sinking.' The insurers rejected the claim.

The Court of Appeal, in overturning the decision of the trial judge, ruled that the loss was brought about by ordinary wear and tear, and the insurers were protected from liability by s 55(2)(c) of the Marine Insurance Act 1906.

Scrutton LJ: [p 5] ... The cause is not unexplained; it is obvious that water came through the seams, and if you want to know why water came through the seams it seems to me quite sufficient to say that this is a very old barge which has been bumping about in the Mersey for a long time and it has at last come to the end of its tether.

The learned judge [the trial judge], finding that the sinking of the barge was due to its own inherent weakness, has decided that there is no total loss by perils of the sea though the barge was actually sunk because of the entry of seawater into it. There is no appeal with regard to that; and it seems to me to be in accordance with the law as now laid down in *Samuel v Dumas* that the effect of the entry of seawater into a ship is not in itself a peril of the sea, and in accordance with the provision of s 55(2)(c) of the Marine Insurance Act: 'The insurer is not liable for ordinary wear and tear unless the policy otherwise provides.'

... and, giving the best consideration I can to the matter, this policy does not seem to otherwise provide; it does not seem to me to provide that the insurer is liable for ordinary wear and tear. It would be very unusual that he should be, and I can find no words which do make him liable for ordinary wear and tear.

Unascertainable perils of the seas

Where a loss is alleged to be by a peril of the sea but the claimant is unable to identify the exact cause of the loss, it falls upon him to present, by inference, the reason for the loss. He has to satisfy the court on the balance of probabilities that the loss was so occasioned.[10]

In ***Lamb Head Shipping Co Ltd v Jennings, 'Marel'* [1992] 1 Lloyd's Rep 402**,[11] the vessel was lost in the Mediterranean Sea after a sudden inrush of sea water into her engine room. At the time the ship foundered, the weather conditions were unexceptional and the owners were unable to convince the Court that the cause of the loss was by a peril of the seas. The decision at first instance was later affirmed by the Court of Appeal.

Judge Diamond QC: [p 425] ... The concept of 'perils of the seas' is a wide one embracing any circumstances where there is a fortuitous entry of sea water into a vessel; *Canada Rice Mills Ltd v Union Marine and General Insurance Co Ltd* (1940) 67 Ll L Rep 549; [1941] AC 55. Underwriters take the risk of loss from unascertainable causes; *Ajum Goolam Hossen & Co v Union Marine Insurance Co* [1901] AC 362, p 371. It is therefore, it seems to me, open to an assured to attempt to eliminate the possibility that the vessel was lost from causes not insured by the policy and, if he succeeds in so doing, to rely on that exclusion as raising an inference, to be taken into account with all the other circumstances of the case, that the loss of the vessel was due to an unascertainable peril of the seas.

---

10 See Chapter 11, p 455.
11 On the issue of burden of proof, the *Marel* case is analysed in depth in Chapter 11, p 453.

The concept of perils of the seas though wide does not embrace a case where a vessel has been deliberately sunk; *Samuel v Dumas* (above). The owners, however, for reasons that I have previously given, have eliminated the possibility that the vessel was deliberately cast away with the privity of the owners and the only other remaining possibility of a deliberate sinking is that of barratry, a possibility for which neither side contended and which in any event would be a peril insured by the policy. The owners, therefore, in my judgment, have sufficiently excluded the possibility of causation through a deliberate sinking.

The concept of 'perils of the seas' similarly does not cover a loss caused by the ordinary action of the wind or waves operating on the defective, deteriorated or decayed condition of a vessel since the loss in such a case is to be regarded as being inevitable, as being due to the inherent inability of the vessel to stay afloat ... In the present case, the loss was not caused by the ordinary action of the wind or waves operating on the defective deteriorated or decayed condition of the vessel.

... In these circumstances, the owners have in my judgment successfully eliminated the only two relevant possibilities that the vessel was lost through causes not insured by the policy and the question arises whether I should therefore draw an inference that the vessel was lost through some unascertainable peril of the sea.

... The main reason against drawing such an inference is that, despite having listened to many days of expert evidence, I was not supplied with any suggestion at all as to the mechanism by which an aperture in the vessel's shell plating, at a level of more than 4.5 metres below the still water line, could have been created other than the theory of a contact with a floating container, a theory which I have rejected as being so improbable as to be virtually impossible.

The Institute Cargo Clauses (B) and(C)

The Institute Cargo Clauses do not include 'perils of the seas' as an insurable risk. Instead, the ICC (B) and (C) specifically itemise insurable marine risks which would normally be associated with the dangers inherent to navigation. The ICC (A), being an all risks policy, is silent on this matter.

The ICC (B) and (C) state, in cl 1.1.2, that loss of or damage to the subject matter insured reasonably attributable to: 'vessel or craft being stranded grounded sunk or capsized' and, in cl 1.1.4: 'collision or contact of vessel or conveyance with any external object other than water' is covered.

Stranded

The Marine Insurance Act 1906, in r 14 of the Rules for Construction, states that: 'Where the ship has stranded, the insurer is liable for the excepted losses, although the loss is not attributable to the stranding, provided that when the stranding takes place the risk has attached and, if the policy be on goods, that the damaged goods are on board.' It must be emphasised that r 14 is not intended to be a literal or legal definition of the word 'stranded'. It encapsulates the position under common law where a cargo-owner is allowed to pursue a claim for a loss (even for an excepted loss), if the vessel in which the cargo is carried is 'stranded', without having to show a causal connection between the stranding and the loss sustained. However, the inclusion of the words 'reasonably attributable to' in cl 1.1 of the ICC (B) and (C) has altered the legal position: there must now be a causal link between the loss or damage sustained and the risk covered by the policy.

Furthermore, for a stranding, as opposed to a grounding, to occur, there has to be an element of fortuity in the incident. 'Stranding', in marine insurance terms, is not simply something that happens during the routine navigation or operation of the ship.

M'Dougle v Royal Exchange Assurance Co (1816) 4 Camp 283

This was an action on a voyage policy of insurance on goods which was claused: 'at and from Barnstaple to London being on $474^{1}/_{2}$ quarters of oats valued at £540'; and which further stated, 'in case of particular average, occasioned by the ship being stranded, it was agreed to pay so much thereof as should exceed £5%'. During the course of the voyage, the vessel carrying the goods had to put into the port of New Grimsby and, whilst leaving New Grimsby, the vessel struck a rock and fell on her beam ends. She remained stuck on the rock for about a minute and a half before freeing herself and then proceeding, in a damaged state, to St Ives, where it was found that she had made a great deal of water through damaged planking. The cargo-owners claimed on their policy of insurance, but the question before the court was whether there had been a stranding within the meaning of the clause in the policy.

The court ruled that the event was not a stranding, in that stranding means 'lying on the shore or something analogous to that' and not a mere striking of a rock.

Lord Ellenborough: [p 284] ... I am of opinion that this was not a stranding. *Ex vi termini* stranding means lying on the shore or something analogous to that. To use a vulgar phrase, which has been applied to this subject, if it is 'touch and go' with the ship, there is no stranding. It cannot be enough that the ship lay for a few moments on her beam ends. Every striking must necessarily produce a retardation of the ship's motion. If by the force of the elements she is run aground, and becomes stationary, it is immaterial whether this be on piles, on the muddy bank of the river, or on rocks on the seashore; but a mere striking will not do, wheresoever that may happen. I cannot look to the consequences without considering the causa causans. If the assured mean to be indemnified against a loss arising in this manner, they must introduce a clause making the underwriters liable for a particular average occasioned by the ship striking on a rock. There has been a curiosity in the cases about stranding not creditable to the law. A little common sense may dispose of them more satisfactorily.

Grounded

Arnould states:[12] 'When the vessel took the ground in the ordinary course of navigation, this did not constitute a stranding under the common memorandum.' It is then suggested that: 'The word "grounded" under the new Risks Clause should arguably be construed as referring to events of that character, previously held to be outside of the scope of the word "stranded".'

Magnus and Others v Buttemer (1852) 11 CB 876

Elizabeth called into Sunderland to discharge a cargo of timber and, as there was a delay at the wharf, she moored in the river for some four or five days. When she did go to the wharf to discharge, which took three days, she was moored by the head and the stern but floated and grounded with the rise and fall of the tide, although at no time was she actually dry. The river bed in the vicinity was steep as well as hard and shingly and, every time *Elizabeth* grounded, she took on a list and was later found to be damaged. The owners claimed on their policy of insurance for a loss by a peril of the seas, namely, stranding. The question before the court was whether the grounding, during the normal rise and fall of the tide, constituted a stranding.

The court ruled that it was not a stranding, as there was an absence of fortuity in the incident.

> **Jervis CJ:** [p 881] ... I am of opinion that the loss in this case was not a loss by perils of the sea, but a damage falling within the description of ordinary wear and tear. No doubt, the question is one of importance; but I think it has been very unnecessarily brought before the court; for, the matter seems to have been perfectly understood and settled by the text writers upon this branch of the law. To make the underwriters liable, the injury must be the result of something fortuitous or accidental occurring in the course of the voyage. Here the vessel, upon her arrival at Sunderland, goes up the river, and, in consequence of the rising and falling of the tide, rests upon the river's bed, and receives damage. There was nothing unusual, no peril, no accident. To hold that the assured were covered in such a case, would be virtually making the policy a warranty against wear and tear and ordinary repairs of the vessel.

Sunk and capsized

There is a lack of authority regarding the legal definition of both these terms.

However, in *Bryant and May v London Assurance Corporation* (1866) 2 TLR 591, a ship, *BC Boyesen*, carrying a deck cargo of timber, arrived off Gravesend

---

12 Arnould, J, *Law of Marine Insurance and Average*, 16th edn, 1981, London: Sweet & Maxwell, Vol 3, para 190.

after a voyage from Quebec. She had encountered severe weather off Newfoundland, and also, allegedly, touched the bottom on entering the Thames estuary. By the time she arrived at Gravesend, she was so low in the water that her decks were awash. The owners claimed under a clause in their policy of insurance for losses due to the ship being 'stranded' or 'sunk'. Grove J [p 592] referred to *Johnson's* and *Webster's* dictionaries for definitions and the jury duly found for the defendant underwriters on both points. *Webster's Comprehensive Dictionary of the English Language* defines 'capsize' as 'upset or overturned' and 'sunk' as 'lying at the bottom of a body of water'.

Collision or contact

The ICC (B) and (C), in cl 1.1.4, states that the insurance covers loss or damage to the subject matter insured reasonably attributable to: 'collision or contact of vessel craft or conveyance with any external object other than water'. Arnould[13] affirms that the word 'contact' is understood to be wider in application than 'collision' and that, as in the *Nassau Bay* case, contact with an exploding device, such as a mine, may be deemed to have occurred without the ship actually physically touching anything.

Costain-Blankevoort (UK) Dredging Co Ltd v Davenport, 'Nassau Bay' [1979] 1 Lloyd's Rep 395

This was an appeal by the plaintiffs against the judgment of the Special Commissioners given in favour of the defendants, HM Inspector of Taxes. The plaintiffs were dredging contractors employed by the government of Mauritius. During the course of operations, one of the plaintiff's dredgers, *Nassau Bay*, sucked up a number of 20 mm Oerlikon shells, which exploded and damaged the discharge pipe so severely that it pumped water into the dredger and caused it to sink. The ammunition was presumed to have been dumped in the sea by British Forces at the end of the Second World War. The owners of *Nassau Bay* successfully claimed on their policy of insurance for the loss of the dredger, but HM Inspector of Taxes claimed a balancing charge under the Capital Allowances Act 1968. The dredger's owners resisted liability on the ground that the loss was due to a war risk which excluded balancing charges.

The court confirmed that the loss of the dredger was not as a result of a warlike operation, and found in favour of the Crown (HM Inspector of Taxes). However, Walton J expanded on the meaning of the word 'contact'.

> **Walton J:** [p 406] ... 'Contact' appears to me to mean just that, that any part of the vessel comes into contact with the object concerned; and the mere fact that the typical case of contact is an external contact appears to me to be neither here nor there. I see no reason for limiting the width of the word 'contact' in

---

13 *Op cit*, Arnould, fn 12, para 123.

any way. In many types of mine, the vessel never actually hits anything: the mine explodes acoustically or electrically, and the mine detonates. The precise nature of the 'contact' is therefore a matter of some difficulty, but nobody doubts that it has taken place. So, in the present case: there is no room for doubt that a contact did in fact take place.

Jettison and washing overboard

The ICC (B), in cl 1.2.2, makes provision for loss caused by 'jettison' and 'washing overboard' to be insurable risks; the ICC (C), in cl 1.2.2, only provides for loss caused by 'jettison'. Whilst the term 'washing overboard' is self-explanatory, 'jettison', as it applies to marine insurance, is not. Jettison is a specific insurable marine peril. It is not simply the intentional casting overboard of the subject matter insured, but the intentional casting overboard of the subject matter insured for good reason. In *Butler v Wildman* (1821) 3 B&Ald 398, Bayley J stated: [p 403] '... its true meaning, in a policy of insurance, seems to me to be any casting over board *ex justa causa.*'

Taylor v Dunbar (1869) LR 4 CP 206

The plaintiffs effected a policy of insurance upon 26 packages of dead pigs shipped aboard *Leopard* from Hamburg to London. In addition to perils of the seas, the policy also included a clause which provided cover for 'all other perils, losses and misfortunes'. Because of bad weather, *Leopard* was delayed at the mouth of the River Elbe for a week, by which time the pig carcasses had become so putrid, they were jettisoned. The plaintiff claimed for the loss on his policy of insurance.

The court ruled that the loss was not attributable to a peril of the sea, nor was it a loss covered by 'all other perils, losses and misfortunes'.

> **Keating J:** [p 210] ... The facts stated in the case show beyond a doubt that the proximate cause of the loss of the meat was the delay in the prosecution of the voyage. That delay was occasioned by tempestuous weather: but no case that I am aware of has held that a loss by the unexpected duration of the voyage, though that be caused by perils of the sea, entitles the assured to recover under a policy like this.

Symington and Co v Union Insurance Society of Canton Ltd (1928) 34 Com Cas 23, CA

A fire broke out on a wharf and, as a preventative measure to stop the fire spreading, a quantity of the respondent's goods, a shipment of cork, was thrown into the sea by the authorities and was lost or damaged. As the marine policy of insurance was claused 'warehouse to warehouse', the deliberate action of the authorities was deemed to fall within the meaning of the marine peril of 'jettison'.

> **Scrutton LJ:** [p 30] ... Then next, the goods being within the policy, the risk having attached, while they lay on the quay at Algeciras waiting to be shipped,

were they lost by a peril insured against? ... What happened to them? Some of them were thrown into the sea to save the rest of them and to avoid their destruction by fire. In my view, that risk is covered ... as a peril *ejusdem generis* with jettison. Jettison is throwing into the sea from the ship generally to save some part of the adventure, this jettison from the pier into the sea was also to save some part of the adventure. It was a jettison and appears to me to be covered ... by the general words as being a peril of the same character as jettison.

Entry of sea, lake or river water

Recovery for a loss by this peril is available under the ICC (A), the all risks policy, and the ICC (B), which makes provision in cl 1.2.3. No such provision is made in the ICC (C).

The two cases cited below (*Montoya v London Assurance* and *Cator v Western Insurance Co of New York*) were decided long before the introduction of the Institute Cargo Clauses, but both were concerned with loss or damage caused by the entry of seawater. It is to be noted that, in both instances, it was held that the policies only covered loss or damage proximately caused by the peril insured against.

Montoya and Others v London Assurance Co (1851) 6 Exch 451

The plaintiffs effected two separate policies of insurance with the defendants upon two consignments of hides and tobacco on the same voyage from New Granada to the UK. Both policies included cover for loss or damage caused by perils of the seas. During the voyage, because of severe weather, a considerable quantity of water was shipped aboard the vessel and the hides and some of the tobacco were damaged. The rancid smell of the wet hides further damaged the quality and flavour of yet more of the tobacco. In this action before the court, the plaintiffs were claiming, not for the damage to the cargo directly caused by the entry of the seawater, but only for the tobacco tainted as a consequence of it.

The court ruled that all the losses were due to perils of the seas.

Pollock CB: [p 458] ... It is a matter of no difference whether the whole of the cargo belongs to one person, and consists of one entire package of corn, or whether the cargo consists partly of corn and partly of hides, and is the property of several owners. In both cases, the loss arises from perils of the seas; and it is difficult to see how the loss can be said not to be the immediate result of such perils. Several of the cases put to us on the part of the defendants are, in my opinion, cases of the direct and immediate consequence of perils of the seas, in which the seawater is the immediate cause of the loss. And I think it may be laid down as a general rule, that where mischief arises from perils of the seas, and the natural and almost inevitable consequence of that mischief is to create further mischievous results, the underwriters, in such case, are responsible for the further mischief so occasioned.

Cator v Great Western Insurance Co of New York (1873) 8 LR 8 CP 552

A consignment of 1,711 chests of tea were insured for a voyage aboard *Eurydice* 'at and from' New York to London. During the voyage, due to severe weather, 449 chests of the tea were damaged by seawater. When the consignment was sold, the 1,262 chests of tea, undamaged by the seawater, fetched a much lower price than would have been anticipated. Normally, consignments of tea are sold in the order of the consecutive numbers marked upon the chests. The omission of the damaged chests alerted the traders to the fact that there had been some damage to the consignment and, as a result, suspicions were raised about the quality of the tea in the undamaged chests. The plaintiffs claimed on their policy of insurance not only for the damaged chests of tea but also for the loss in value of the undamaged ones.

The court ruled that the underwriters were only liable for the losses directly caused by the seawater; they were not liable for the loss in value of the undamaged ones. Underwriters only insure for actual damage, not for a suspicion of damage.

> **Bovill CJ:** [p 561] ... it was never intended that the 1,711 packages should be treated as one entire and indivisible subject matter of insurance; and, if not, then there is no practicable division of the packages, except by treating each package as a separate article ... If such a claim as this could be supported, it might next be contended that the underwriters would be responsible if the reputation and value of sound teas were affected by serious damage to the ship, or to other persons' goods in the same ship which were damaged by seawater, or for the loss of markets by delay through the perils of navigation. It appears to us that the underwriters insure against actual damage, and do not in any sense guarantee that the goods shall arrive free from suspicion of damage.

Loss caused by preventive action

The following case illustrates the point that any loss or damage caused by actions taken to prevent a loss caused by an insured peril is recoverable as a loss caused by that insured peril. The same principle, as applied in the case of fire, is discussed below.[14]

Canada Rice Mills Ltd v Union Marine and General Insurance Co Ltd [1941] AC 55, PC

The appellants insured a cargo of rice aboard the motor vessel *Segundo* for a voyage from Rangoon to Vancouver. On arriving in Vancouver, it was found that all the rice had overheated, but the appellants only claimed for the damage done to a portion of the cargo which was of a particularly fine quality. The appellants claimed that the overheating had taken place because, from

---

14 See below, p 395.

time to time, the cargo ventilators had been closed to ensure that, in adverse weather, there was no possibility of damage occurring to the rice. The appellants further claimed that, as the adverse weather was a peril of the sea, the closing of the ventilators was also as a direct result of a peril of the sea. The underwriters rejected the claim, on the basis that the damage to the cargo was caused by inherent vice.

The Privy Council ruled that the damage to the rice had resulted from the closing of the ventilators which, in turn, had been closed to prevent an incursion of seawater. The loss was, therefore, brought about because of a peril of the sea.

> **Lord Wright:** [p 70] ... There remains the second question, whether the damage which was caused not by the incursion of seawater, but by action taken to prevent the incursion, is recoverable as a loss by perils of the sea ... In cases of fire insurance, it has been said that loss caused from an apparently necessary and bona fide attempt to put out the fire, by spoiling goods by water, and in other ways, is within the policy, *per* Kelly CB in *Stanley v Western Insurance Co*. Their Lordships agree with this expression of opinion, and accordingly, are prepared to hold that the damage to the rice, which the jury have found to be due to action necessary and reasonably taken to prevent the peril of the sea affecting the goods, is a loss due to the peril of the sea and is recoverable as such.

FIRE AND EXPLOSION

'Fire' and 'explosion' are both insurable marine risks provided for in cl 6.1.2 of the ITCH(95) and cl 4.1.2 of the IVCH(95). The ICC (B) and (C) make similar provision, whilst ICC (A), being an all risks policy, has no requirement to do so. As both are now standard insured perils, it is unnecessary to differentiate between them.[15]

The Marine Insurance Act 1906, in the Rules for Construction, makes no attempt to define 'fire' or 'explosion' and, therefore, clarification of the meaning and scope of these perils must be gathered from case law. As with other marine perils, s 55(2)(a) of the Act allows recovery of a loss provided that it is not 'attributable to the wilful misconduct of the assured'. Furthermore, unlike 'perils of the seas', the element of fortuity is not a prerequisite to a claim for a loss by fire, and it has been the general proposition that a claim for a loss by fire is recoverable regardless of whether the fire was caused accidentally or deliberately.

---

15 However, should only one of these perils be insured, see below, p 403, for a discussion of the distinguishing features between a 'fire' and an 'explosion'.

Fire

Types of damage covered

The insured peril of 'fire' covers loss or damage caused by fire and by smoke or heating if that smoke or heating emanates from a fire. Furthermore, if steps are taken to prevent fire damage, any loss or damage incurred as a result of that preventative action would also be covered by the policy. Thus, damage caused by water in extinguishing a fire is included in the insured peril.

Heating

However, as illustrated in the following American case, *The Buckeye State*, the insured peril of fire does not cover loss or damage caused by pure and simple heating if that heating is not associated with fire. Nor is it covered if the loss or damage arises as a natural result of inherent vice or the nature of the subject matter insured which loss is expressly excluded by s 55(2)(c) of the Act and cl 4.4 of all the ICC. Though the said case relates to a dispute in a contract of carriage of goods, it is nonetheless useful for the purpose of eliciting the characteristics of a 'fire'.

The Buckeye State (1941) 39 F Supp 344

The plaintiff shipped a cargo of grain aboard the Great Lakes motor vessel *The Buckeye State* from Chicago to Oswego on Lake Ontario. During the voyage, a part of the cargo became very hot and *The Buckeye State* put into Port Huron, where the local fire brigade opened the hatches and doused the cargo with water. There was evidence to show that the crew had negligently left the cargo hold lights on and the heat from some of these lights had raised the temperature of the cargo. The plaintiff cargo-owner pressed a claim for the damage, but the underwriters refused payment, citing inherent vice. The question before the court was thus: if the damage to the cargo had been caused by heating (from the light bulbs), then the shipowner was liable. If the damage was caused by fire, the loss was then attributable to inherent, in which case, the shipowner was not liable.

The court ruled that the cause of the loss was by heating and, therefore, the cargo-owner could recover. However, Knight DJ considered the differences between fire and heating.

> **Knight DJ:** [p 347] ... The sole question for determination here is whether 'fire' or 'heat' caused the damages; if caused by 'fire', the libellant cannot recover; if by 'heat,' the libellant is entitled to recover ... 'Fire' is caused by ignition or combustion, and it includes the idea of visible heat or light. 'No definition of fire can be found that does not include the idea of visible heat or light, and this is also the popular meaning given to the word ... The internal development of heat never at any time became so rapid as to produce a flame or a glow, and

hence ... there was no fire.' *Western Woolen Mill Co v Northern Assurance Co of London* 8 Cir 139 F 637.

... Respondent [shipowner] takes the position that the damage was not caused by any 'electric light', but 'by something burning in the hold and generating a large volume of heat', and that the fire in the grain was 'caused by a condition inherent in the cargo or by foreign substance in the cargo'. There is nothing in the record to show that there was any condition 'inherent in the cargo' which could caused a fire.

Fire damage includes smoke and water damage

The Diamond [1906] P 282

This was a carriage of goods by sea case. *The Diamond* was a small steamer of 468 tons and was engaged in carrying the plaintiff's cargo of bags of flour and bran from Cardiff to Belfast. During the voyage, a stove in the crew's quarters in the forecastle overheated and set fire to some dunnage and nearby cargo. On arrival at Belfast, 4,593 bags of the plaintiff's cargo were found to have been damaged by fire and smoke, and further damage had been caused by water used by the crew in fighting the fire. The owner of *The Diamond* was, provided that he was not guilty of 'actual fault and privity', excluded from liability for damage to cargo caused by fire. The plaintiff claimed that the dangerous nature of the stove made *The Diamond* unseaworthy; furthermore, most of the damage to the cargo had not been caused by fire, but by smoke and the water used to extinguish it.

The court ruled that the damage caused by smoke and water were matters which arose by reason of the fire. And, as there was no evidence of actual fault or privity, the shipowner was held not liable for the loss.

Bargrave Deane J: [p 287] ... Section 502 of the Merchant Shipping Act 1894 deals with the case of a fire happening on board the ship without the actual fault or privity of the owner. Undoubtedly, this cargo was damaged partly by fire, partly by the smoke resulting from the fire, and partly by the water used to put out the fire, and I hold that the water and smoke were matters which occurred by reason of the fire. That is the only reasonable interpretation of the statute.

Fire damage includes damage caused in fighting a fire

In **Stanley v Western Insurance Co (1868) LR 3 Ex 71**, which is not a marine case, the plaintiff ran a business of extracting oil from shoddy (reclaimed wool). A fire, followed by an explosion, destroyed his factory. Because the plaintiff's fire insurance policy expressly excluded damage caused by explosion, the court was mindful of differentiating between the two perils. On damage caused by fighting a fire, Kelly CB stated:

Kelly CB: [p 74] ... I agree that any loss resulting from an apparently necessary and *bona fide* effort to put out a fire, whether it be by spoiling the goods by water, or throwing the articles of furniture out of the window, or even the destroying of a neighbouring house by an explosion for the purposes of checking the progress of the flames, in a word, every loss that clearly and proximately results, whether directly or indirectly, from the fire, is within the policy.

In *Symington and Co v Union Insurance Society of Canton Ltd* **(1928) 34 Com Cas 23, CA**, a shipment of cork on a wharf was wetted to stop a nearby fire from spreading.

> **Scrutton LJ:** [p 31] ... I therefore take the view on the facts found in this case that, there being an existing fire and an imminent peril, the damage caused by water either used to extinguish the fire or prevent it from spreading was a proximate consequence of fire which could be recovered under the general words, it does not matter which for this purpose, as being *ejusdem generis* with fire.

Damage caused by preventive actions

The Knight of St Michael [1898] P 30

The Knight of St Michael was chartered to carry a cargo of 3,206 tons of coal from Newcastle, New South Wales, to Valparaiso. Shortly after sailing, part of the cargo started to heat and 1,706 tons of coal had to be discharged in Sydney. Thus, only a portion of the full cargo was delivered to Valparaiso. The shipowner claimed on his policy of insurance for the loss of freight. The defendant insurers denied liability.

The court ruled that the loss of freight was due to the preventive action of the master. Although none of the cargo was actually lost as the result of fire, it was reasonably certain that, if the voyage had continued, spontaneous combustion would have taken place and the ship and cargo would have been destroyed by fire.

> **Gorrell Barnes:** [p 34] ... Now, I have found that fire did not actually break out, but it is reasonably certain that it would have broken out, and the condition of things was such that there was an actual existing state of peril of fire, and not merely a fear of fire. The case is peculiar, and not exactly analogous to that of any other peril. The danger was present, and, if nothing was done, spontaneous combustion and fire would follow in natural course.
>
> ... Then, does it make any difference that the fire had not actually broken out? I think not in the circumstances. There was imminent danger of fire, and an existing condition of things producing this danger, and if this cannot, strictly speaking, be termed a loss by fire, it is, in my opinion, a loss *ejusdem generis*, and covered by the general words 'all other losses and misfortunes, etc'.

Fire requires no element of fortuity

Unlike 'perils of the seas', fortuity is not an essential element for the peril of 'fire'. In *Alexion Hope* **[1988] 1 Lloyd's Rep 311, CA**, the plaintiffs were the assured under a mortgagees' interest policy of insurance. When a serious fire occurred aboard *Alexion Hope*, the shipowners gave notice of abandonment and claimed for a constructive total loss. The mortgagees' interest insurers refused payment, alleging that the shipowners were guilty of wilful misconduct and connivance, with respect to the loss of the ship. The Court of Appeal ruled in favour of the plaintiffs and the question of fortuity was discussed.

Lloyd LJ: [p 316] ... I go on to consider the meaning of the word 'fire'. As I have already foreshadowed, I agree with the judge that 'fire' in a marine policy is not confined to an accidental or fortuitous fire. It includes a fire started deliberately. Indeed, Mr Hunter, who appeared for the defendants in the court below, conceded that fire in a marine policy covers a fire deliberately started by a stranger to the contract of insurance ... In principle, I find it difficult to draw a distinction between setting something on fire and the fire itself, as the proximate cause of the loss which follows. Different considerations may well be held to apply in the case of perils of the sea, since perils of the sea are defined by r 7 of the Rules of Construction annexed to the Marine Insurance Act as referring *only* 'to fortuitous accidents or casualties of the seas'. There is no such limitation in the case of fire.

Fire may be accidental or deliberate

Gordon v Rimmington (1807) 1 Camp 123

Reliance was on a voyage from Bristol to West Africa and thence to the West Indies. Whilst in West Africa, in the River Gambia, she was chased by a French privateer of superior strength and, to avoid capture, she fired her own guns down her hatchways in order to set fire to herself. Once she was alight, the crew took to the long boat and rowed ashore. The plaintiff, who was not only the owner but also the captain of *Reliance*, claimed on his policy of insurance. The question before the court was whether the loss was a loss by fire within the meaning of the policy.

The court ruled in favour of the plaintiff.

Lord Ellenborough: [p 123] ... Fire is expressly mentioned in the policy, as one of the perils against which the underwriters undertake to indemnify the assured; and if the ship is destroyed by fire, it is of no consequence whether this is occasioned by a common accident, or by lightning, or by an act done in duty to the State. Nor can it make any difference whether the ship is thus destroyed by third persons, subjects of the King, or by the captain and crew acting with loyalty and good faith. Fire is still the *causa causans*, and the loss is covered by the policy.

Negligence of master or crew

Section 55(2)(a) of the Marine Insurance Act 1906 is applicable, just as with any other peril insured, to the marine perils of 'fire' and 'explosion'.

Thus, a loss proximately caused by fire is recoverable even though it may not have occurred but for the negligence of the master or crew.

And even if the negligence of the 'Master Officers Crew or Pilots' is regarded as the proximate cause, the loss is also recoverable by virtue of the negligence cover of the Inchmaree Clause of the ITCH(95) and the IVCH(95), which is, however, subject to the 'due diligence' proviso.[16]

Busk v Royal Exchange Assurance Co (1818) 2 B&Ald 73

A policy of insurance was effected upon *Carolina*, a Russian ship bound, 'at and from' Amsterdam, to St Petersburg. A clause in the policy stated that the assured was protected from 'fire, barratry of the master and mariners ...'. When nearing St Petersburg, *Carolina* became fast in ice and, as was the custom in the trade, the master paid off the crew and left the mate in charge while he went to St Petersburg to settle some accounts. On 9 January, the mate lit a fire in the ship's cabin and, later, went aboard another Russian vessel lying nearby to spend the night there. Early the next morning, the mate was awoken to find that a fire had broken out aboard *Carolina* and she was destroyed. The owners of *Carolina* claimed on their policy of insurance, and the question before the court was whether the loss was covered in view of the mate's actions in lighting the fire and then not remaining on board.

The court ruled that, despite the negligence of the mate, the loss was still by fire.

> **Bayley J:** [p 80] ... In this case, however, the loss is occasioned by fire, against which the assured is protected by the terms of the policy; and, in our law at least, there is no authority which says that the underwriters are not liable for a loss, the proximate cause of which is one of the enumerated risks, but the remote cause of which may be traced to the misconduct of the master and mariners ... We must, therefore, endeavour to collect the meaning of the contracting parties from the terms of the policy itself, and in considering whether the assured claiming for a loss by fire, is to have the claim disallowed, on the ground that the fire was occasioned by the misconduct of the master, we must look to the other terms of the policy, and learn from them, whether the assurers, in other instances, are responsible for the misconduct of the master; and when we find that they make themselves answerable for the wilful misconduct of the master in other cases, it is not too much to say that they meant to indemnify the assured against fire, proceeding from the negligence of the master and mariners. I am therefore of opinion in this case, that the assured are entitled to recover, as for a loss by fire, although that fire was produced by the negligence of the person having the charge of the ship at the time ... The owner certainly is bound, in the first instance, to provide the ship with a competent crew, but he does not undertake for the conduct of that crew in the subsequent part of the voyage ... I therefore think that the plaintiff, upon the facts stated in this case, was entitled to recover ...

---

16 See Chapter 12, p 532.

Notes

In the American case of *Rosa and Others v Insurance Co of the State of Pennsylvania, 'Belle of Portugal'* [1970] 2 Lloyd's Rep 386, where a fishing vessel was lost on account of an electrical fire brought about by the negligence of an electrician, *Busk v Royal Exchange Assurance Co* was cited as the authority and controlling case in the judgment of the court. In the *Belle of Portugal* case, Merrill CJ stated: [p 387] 'Fire, however, is specified as an insured peril in itself. Under English law, the fact that cause of the fire can be traced to the negligence of the captain, crew or agents of the shipowner will not defeat recovery.'

Wilful misconduct of the master or crew

Recovery for a loss by fire under the Institute Hull Clauses and the ICC (A) is permissible even when there is wilful misconduct committed by the master or crew. Such a claim could also be pursued as a loss caused by 'barratry' under the ITCH(95) and the IVCH(95) if the actions of the master and crew were both wrongful and prejudicial to the owners, satisfying the terms of r 11 of the Rules for Construction where barratry is defined.

With regard to the cargo-owner, though fire is an insured peril under cl 1.1.1 of both the ICC (B) and (C), it is to be noted that 'deliberate damage or deliberate destruction of the subject matter insured by the wrongful act of any person or persons' is expressly excluded by cl 4.7. Thus, it would appear that under the ICC (B) and (C), only a loss or damage caused by accidental fire is covered.

Negligence of the assured

Negligence of the assured in the event of fire or explosion is the same as for any other marine peril insured against. Section 55(2)(a) of the Marine Insurance Act 1906 only precludes recovery for any loss attributable to the wilful misconduct, but not the negligence, of the assured.

In *Trinder, Anderson and Co v Thames and Mersey Marine Insurance Co* [1898] 2 QB 114, CA, where a ship was stranded upon a reef due to the negligent navigation of the master who was also a part owner, the subject of negligence by the assured was considered by Smith LJ, who stated: [p 124] 'It is not disputed at the bar that negligence of an assured upon a fire policy, whereby the fire was occasioned which caused the loss, affords no defence to the insurer. Why so? Because loss by fire is what is insured against ...'

Wilful misconduct of the assured

Section 55(2)(a) of the Marine Insurance Act 1906 expressly precludes recovery for any loss 'attributable to the wilful misconduct of the assured'. However, once it has been established by the assured that the loss was occasioned by a peril insured against, it then rests upon the insurer to prove that the loss was attributable to the wilful misconduct of the assured.

In the case of cargo insurances under the ICC (A), (B), and (C), cl 4.1 (and cl 4.7 of the ICC (B) and (C)) bar a cargo-owner from recovery for a loss caused by his own wilful act of misconduct.

Wilful misconduct of a stranger

In **Slattery v Mance [1962] 1 All ER 525**, where a small vessel was destroyed by fire and the insurers alleged wilful misconduct by the assured, Salmon J stated:

[p 526] ... The risk of fire insured against is quite obviously not confined to an accidental fire. If the ship had been set alight by some mischievous person without the plaintiff's connivance, there could be no doubt that the plaintiff would be entitled to recover.

Similarly, in **Alexion Hope [1988] 1 Lloyd's Rep 311, CA**,[17] where a large vessel had been destroyed by fire and it was alleged by the underwriters that there had been wilful misconduct on the part of the assured, Lloyd LJ remarked:

[p 316] ... I agree with the judge that 'fire' in a marine policy is not confined to an accidental or fortuitous fire. It includes a fire started deliberately. Indeed, Mr Hunter, who appeared for the defendants in the court below, conceded that fire in a marine policy covers a fire deliberately started by a stranger to the contract of insurance.

The position of an innocent mortgagee

The case of *Alexion Hope* illustrates the value of the mortgagee's interest policy of insurance[18] when the shipowner is unable to recover because of his own act of wilful misconduct.

Schiffshypothekenbank Zu Luebeck AG v Norman Philip Compton, 'Alexion Hope' [1988] 1 Lloyd's Rep 311, CA

The plaintiffs had lent money to the owners of *Alexion Hope* and were mortgagees of the vessel. The plaintiffs were assignees to the policy on hull and machinery, but had also effected a mortgagee's interest policy with the defendant insurers. In October 1982, a serious fire occurred in the engine room of *Alexion Hope* when she was at Shahjah and, a few days later, she was abandoned as a constructive total loss. The plaintiffs had, first, sought to recover as an assignee to the hull and machinery policy, but payment had

---

17 Also discussed above, p 395
18 See the Institute Mortgagee's Interest Clauses Hulls (30/5/86). For a discussion of the said Clauses, see Hodges, S, 'Mortgagee's interest insurance', in *The Modern Law of Marine Insurance*, 1996, London: LLP, p 251.

been refused by the hull insurers on the basis of wilful misconduct and connivance on the part of the shipowners. In this action, the plaintiffs' claim was upon their mortgagee's interest policy against the mortgagee's interest insurers but, again, payment was refused; the insurers alleging, *inter alia*, wilful misconduct by the vessel's owners.

The Court of Appeal upheld the decision of the trial judge and ruled that the plaintiffs could recover under their mortgagee's interest policy. Lloyd and Purchas LJJ expanded on the benefits of the mortgagee's interest policy of insurance.

> **Lloyd LJ:** [p 313] ... As for the purpose or object of this class of insurance, I think I am entitled to deduce from the language used that it was to protect the plaintiffs, as mortgagees, against the possibility of their security, *Alexion Hope*, proving insufficient in two sets of circumstances: first, if the vessel were to become a total or partial loss, and the mortgagees were to find themselves unable to recover from hull underwriters, as they would ordinarily be able to do, as assignees of the hull policy; and, secondly, if the vessel were to incur liability to a third party, and the vessel's P & I Club were to decline liability on the ground of the shipowner's privity. The circumstances in which the mortgagees might not be able to recover from hull underwriters are not spelled out. But they would presumably include cases where the hull underwriters decline liability on the ground of misrepresentation or non-disclosure, or because the vessel has been wilfully cast away with the connivance of the owners. Inability to recover from hull underwriters on the ground of their insolvency is specifically excluded.
>
> **Purchas LJ:** [p 322] ... Moreover, as between the mortgagee and the mortgagee's interest insurer, it matters not whether the fire was started by an independent agent, or whether by or with the connivance of the shipowner, the master or the crew, or indeed whether it occurred fortuitously.

In contrast, the *Captain Panagos DP* case, below, highlights the problems encountered by an innocent mortgagee when claiming as an assignee to a hull policy of insurance when the assignor, the shipowner, is guilty of wilful misconduct.

Continental Illinois National Bank and Trust Co of Chicago and Xenofon Maritimes SA v Alliance Assurance Co Ltd, 'Captain Panagos DP' [1986] 2 Lloyd's Rep 470; [1989] 1 Lloyd's Rep 33, CA

Captain Panagos DP, a bulk carrier, grounded on the eastern shore of the Red Sea and then caught fire some days later. After being towed to her destination in Iran to discharge her cargo, the owners claimed upon their policy of insurance for a constructive total loss. The hull insurers declined payment on the basis that the claim was fraudulent as the owners had connived to cast the ship away. The mortgagees had already made a claim upon their mortgagee's interest policy, but the indemnity under this policy amounted to considerably less than the insured value in the hull policy. Therefore, they pursued a second claim, with the owners, for the full amount, as assignees, under the hull and machinery policy of insurance.

The Court of Appeal ruled that the owners of *Captain Panagos DP* were guilty of wilful misconduct in conniving with the master to throw away the ship and the mortgagees accepted, from the outset, that they could not recover under the hull policy if the claims made by the owners failed.

Notes

See, also, *Samuel v Dumas* **(1924) 18 LlL Rep 211, HL**,[19] where the steamship *Gregorios* was scuttled and the innocent mortgagee was unable to recover, as an assignee of a hull policy, under barratry or perils of the seas, because of the wilful misconduct of the shipowner.

Exceptions from liability

Although the peril of fire does not require an element of fortuity for a claim to succeed, there are still exceptions to be considered. The Marine Insurance Act 1906 expressly excludes recovery for a loss *attributable to the wilful misconduct of the assured*, as well as *inherent vice or nature of the subject matter insured*. Furthermore, with respect to the cargo-owner, cl 4 of the ICC (A), (B) and (C) itemises a list of exclusions which are not in conflict with the Act. *Boyd v Dubois* is an early case dealing with cargo damaged by fire which broke out because of the inherent vice of the subject matter insured.

Boyd v Dubois (1811) 3 Camp 133

This was an action by a cargo-owner upon a policy of insurance covering a shipment of hemp from London to Devon aboard the vessel *Joseph and Betsy*. Whilst in Torbay, the cargo of hemp caught fire and the plaintiff cargo-owner claimed on his policy of insurance. The underwriters rejected the claim, citing inherent vice, in that the hemp had been loaded in a damp condition and, therefore, had ignited by spontaneous combustion.

The court ruled in favour of the cargo-owner as the underwriters had failed to prove their case.

Lord Ellenborough: [p 133] If the hemp was put on board in a state liable to effervesce, and it did effervesce and generate the fire which consumed it; upon the common principles of insurance law, the assured cannot recover for a loss which he himself has occasioned. But I must positively say, that they were not bound to represent to the underwriters the state of the goods. It would introduce endless confusion and perpetual controversies, if such a duty were to be imposed upon the assured. There was no proof that the fire had originated from the damaged state of the hemp, and the plaintiff had a verdict.

---

19 See above, p 369.

The Knight of St Michael [1898] P 30

In this case, the inherent vice in a cargo of coal did not prevent a shipowner from recovering the freight lost when part of a cargo of coal was discharged to prevent spontaneous combustion taking place. It should be noted that, in the special circumstances of this case, where the master had acted to prevent a loss by fire, there was no bar to the owner recovering the lost freight. However, the cargo-owner would not have been able to recover from his insurer. Gorell Barnes J deliberated on the actions of the master and the subject of inherent vice.

> **Gorell Barnes J:** [p 33] ... If the action had been by the cargo-owners against their underwriters for the loss of the coal, I presume the claim would have been defended on the ground that the loss was due to the inherent vice of the coal; but the position of the shipowners with regard to the freight is different. I find that it was necessary for the safety of the whole adventure for the vessel to put in to Sydney and discharge the coal landed there, and that it was reasonably certain that if she had continued on her direct voyage the temperature of the coal would have continued to rise until spontaneous combustion ensued, and that had she so continued the ship and the cargo would in all probability have been destroyed by fire. I further find that the coal landed at Sydney could not have been reloaded and carried with safety to Valparaiso, and was necessarily and properly sold at Sydney. I also find that no part of the coal was ever actually on fire.

Onus of proof

When a claim is for a loss caused by fire, the claimant only has to show that the loss in fact occurred; there need be no element of fortuity, as was shown in *Slattery v Mance*, below.

Slattery v Mance [1962] 1 All ER 525

The plaintiff owner of the vessel *Treworval Light* brought an action against the defendant insurers claiming, under a policy of marine insurance, a total of £4,500 for the loss of the vessel by fire. The underwriters rejected the claim, on the basis that the plaintiff wilfully caused or connived with the destruction of the vessel.

The court ruled that, on the principle of the common law that he who asserts must prove, it fell upon the defendant underwriters to prove, on the balance of probabilities, that the plaintiff deliberately destroyed *Treworval Light*. The jury was directed accordingly.

> **Salmon J:** [p 526] ... In my judgment, the onus of proof in cases such as the one before me is different from the onus of proof in the 'perils of the sea' cases. The risk of fire insured against is quite obviously not confined to an accidental fire. If the ship had been set alight by some mischievous person without the plaintiff's connivance, there could be no doubt that the plaintiff would be entitled to recover. Of course, the plaintiff cannot recover if he was the person

who fired the ship or was a party to the ship being fired. The result, however, does not depend on the construction of the word 'fire' in the policy, but on the well known principle of insurance law that no man can recover for a loss which he himself has deliberately and fraudulently caused. It is no more than an extension of the general principle that no man can take advantage of his own wrong. In my judgment, once it is shown that the loss has been caused by fire, the plaintiff has made out a *prima facie* case, and the onus is on the defendant to show on a balance of probabilities that the fire was caused or connived at by the plaintiff.

But, where the claim is for a loss by a peril of the sea, as was shown in the *Ikarian Reefer* case, below, the claimant must prove that the loss was, in fact, fortuitous.

National Justice Compania Naviera SA v Prudential Assurance Co Ltd, 'Ikarian Reefer' [1993] 2 Lloyd's Rep 68; [1995] 1 Lloyd's Rep 455, CA

The plaintiffs insured their vessel, *Ikarian Reefer*, with the defendants for US$3 m under a policy of marine insurance which included cover for, *inter alia*, perils of the sea, fire and barratry. Whilst on a voyage from Kiel to Abidjan in ballast, *Ikarian Reefer* ran aground on shoals off the coast of Sierra Leone. Shortly afterwards, fire broke out in the engine room and spread to the accommodation. The plaintiffs claimed for a constructive total loss, citing perils of the seas, fire and barratry as alternative causes of loss. The insurers suspected wilful misconduct by the assured and refused payment.

The Court of Appeal, in overturning the decision of the trial judge, ruled that the loss of the ship was by scuttling, authorised by the owners. Stuart-Smith LJ reflected, succinctly, on the requirements of the plaintiffs and the defendants to prove their respective cases.

> **Stuart-Smith LJ:** [p 508] ... It is unnecessary in the light of our conclusions that both the grounding and the fire were deliberate, and were done with the privity of the owners, to consider this matter further. We merely record briefly the point. If the owners failed to prove that the grounding was fortuitous and therefore a peril insured against, but the underwriters failed to prove that either the grounding or the fire was deliberate, then success or failure would depend upon whether the proximate cause of the constructive total loss was the grounding or the fire. If the former, the underwriters would succeed; if the latter, the owners.

Explosion

Fire or explosion?

Although the Institute Hull Clauses (cl 6.1.2 of the ITCH(95) and cl 4.1.2 of the IVCH(95)), now itemise both 'fire' and 'explosion' as insured perils, this was not always the case. The following authority, though not a marine case, will be useful when it is necessary to differentiate a 'fire' from an 'explosion', namely, where the policy specifies only one of the above as being covered.

Boiler Inspection and Insurance Co of Canada v Sherwin-Williams Co of Canada [1951] AC 319, PC

The respondents were engaged in bleaching turpentine within a tank when, due to internal pressure, the door of the tank was blown off, releasing an explosive mixture which ignited and blew up a large portion of the building. The respondent's insurance with the appellants excluded liability for fire, but covered loss 'from any direct result of an accident'. 'Accident' was then described in the policy as 'a sudden and accidental tearing asunder ...'. The question before the court was whether the loss was due to a fire or explosion.

> The Privy Council ruled that it was a loss caused by explosion, not by fire.
>
> **Lord Porter:** [p 337] ... The Chief Justice found, and their Lordships agree with him, that the incidents from the moment when the first flash was observed until the ultimate explosion took place was all part of one momentary event. The flame was the first stage of an explosion which, in the then condition of the tank and outrush of vapour, necessarily went forward through the next stage, when the speed of the flame increased, until the final stage was reached and the explosion took place.
>
> If this be the true view, it follows that there was no appreciable moment of time between the beginning of the ignition and the explosion. Each was a part of the same event, the ignition being the first and the explosion the final stage of the disaster. There was no separate fire which burnt in the room before the explosion took place. The flame or flash which the witnesses observed was the first stage of an explosion which immediately and inevitably followed. The fact that ignition, and in that sense fire, was an element in the ultimate result is not, in their Lordships' view, destructive of the respondents' claim.
>
> It is true that a flash or flame or fire almost inevitably plays a part in many combustion explosions. But it does not follow that injury from the subsequent explosion is to be attributed to fire. The old flint lock musket required a flash in the pan to ignite the powder and drive out the bullet, but death due to the penetration of the bullet would not naturally be described as death by fire.

Explosion or violent disintegration?

In ***Commonwealth Smelting Ltd and Another v Guardian Royal Exchange Assurance Ltd* [1984] 2 Lloyd's Rep 608**, a furnace blower in a zinc plant, near Bristol, burst apart with such violence that it caused considerable consequential damage to the building in which it was housed. The court had to decide whether the event was, in fact, an 'explosion' within the meaning of the policy. Staughton J resorted to dictionary definitions before concluding:

> [p 612] ... It seems to me that the word 'explosion' is used in these policies to denote the kind of catastrophe described in *Webster*, 1961, and *Encyclopaedia Britannica*: an event that is violent, noisy and is caused by a very rapid chemical or nuclear reaction, or the bursting out of gas or vapour under

pressure. The damage and destruction in this case were not so caused, or at any rate explosion in that sense was not the predominant cause; it was centrifugal disintegration. Accordingly, the claim fails.

VIOLENT THEFT BY PERSONS FROM OUTSIDE THE VESSEL

The Marine Insurance Act 1906, in r 9 of the Rules for Construction, defines 'thieves' as follows: 'The term "thieves" does not cover clandestine theft or a theft committed by any one of the ship's company, whether crew or passengers.' This is not in conflict with either cl 6.1.3 of the ITCH(95) or cl 4.1.3 of the IVCH(95), which make provision for this insurable risk under the terms of 'violent theft by persons from outside the vessel'.

With respect to a cargo-owner, the ICC (B) and (C) do not, in themselves, include theft as an insurable risk, but the Institute Theft, Pilferage and Non-Delivery Clause[20] is available should the assured seek this additional cover, alternatively, the cargo-owner might consider the ICC (A), the all risks policy.

It is noteworthy that, in order to recover under a marine policy of insurance, theft must be 'violent' and committed by 'persons from outside the vessel'.

For theft to have taken place, there must be an element of dishonesty. In *Nishina Trading Co Ltd v Chiyoda Fire and Marine Insurance Co Ltd, 'Mandarin Star'* [1969] 2 All ER 776, the owner of goods aboard *Mandarin Star* was put to a great deal of expense because of a dispute between the owners and charterers of the vessel. Instead of the goods being delivered in Kobe, they were taken to Hong Kong and warehoused, and the cargo-owner had to reclaim them and then forward them to Kobe. He then claimed on his policy of insurance for the additional expenditure. On the subject of theft, Edmund Davies LJ stated:

> [p 780] ... One must certainly import into this civil action the basic conception of theft, which is that it is an offence involving dishonesty. No man – the man on the top of the Clapham omnibus, the man in Lombard Street, the man of ordinary intelligence anywhere – could fail to recognise that, unless dishonesty is shown, no one should be branded as having committed a theft.

Violent theft

For the assured to recover for a loss occasioned by theft, the theft must be of a 'violent' nature. This violence may take the form of violence against the

---

20 See Appendix 18.

person or property. It is not imperative, therefore, that the violence be specifically directed against the person. Clandestine or secret theft, on the other hand, is not covered.

La Fabrique de Produits Chimiques SA v Large [1923] 1 KB 203

The plaintiffs insured three cases of chemicals, each separately, with the defendants, under a policy of marine insurance, warehouse to warehouse, from London to Bordeaux and thence to Switzerland. The policy of insurance included cover for loss by thieves, but was warranted free from particular average. Whilst the goods were in the warehouse, awaiting shipment, two of the cases were stolen and the plaintiffs claimed on their policy of insurance. The insurers rejected the claim on the basis that, first, theft had to include violence and, secondly, the goods were warranted free from particular average (fpa).

The court ruled that the thieves, in breaking into the warehouse, had committed an act of violence and the violence did not have to be against the person. Also, regarding the warranty of fpa, the loss was not a particular average loss of the whole, but a total loss of part (two cases) of the goods insured.

> **Bailhache J:** [p 207] ... It is true that, in a policy of marine insurance pure and simple, the risk of loss by thieves does not cover an ordinary clandestine theft, but only theft accompanied with violence.
>
> I am not sure that in a warehouse to warehouse policy, as in a purely marine policy, the word 'theft' ought to be limited to theft by violence. In my opinion, however, even if in a policy of that kind the word ought to be so limited, the theft which was committed in this case was clearly a theft by violence. Those who took the goods smashed in two sets of doors with crowbars in order to get at them, and in these circumstances it seems to me that they undoubtedly committed theft by violence. I do not think that the expression 'by violence' as used in this connection means that an assault must be committed upon some person. It seems to me, therefore, that even if counsel for the defendant is right in saying that theft from a warehouse must be of the same character as theft from a ship, that is to say a violent and not a clandestine theft, the facts of this case answer to the description of a theft by violence.

Athens Maritime Enterprises Corporation v Hellenic Mutual War Risks Association (Bermuda) Ltd, 'Andreas Lemos' [1982] 2 Lloyd's Rep 483[21]

Local thieves boarded the vessel whilst she was at anchor at Chittagong, Bangladesh, and stole items of equipment, including mooring ropes. It was only when they were challenged by armed members of the crew that the thieves drew knives and then jumped into the sea. On theft and the necessary ingredient of violence, Staughton J commented:

---

21 Also discussed below, p 415.

[p 491] ... What in fact happened was that the theft was complete before they [the thieves] were discovered, or at any rate before any force or threat of force occurred ... The case is, in my judgment, one of clandestine theft which was discovered; force or a threat of force was used by the men to make good their escape.

Notes

In *Dino Services Ltd v Prudential Assurance Co Ltd* [1989] 1 Lloyd's Rep 379, CA, which was not a marine case, the question of entry by 'violent' means during a burglary at a car sales room was considered by Kerr LJ, who then provided comprehensive clarification:

[p 382] ... The word 'violent' is an ordinary English word, which here appears in a common commercial document. It seems to me that there is no reason why its meaning should be in any way different from what any ordinary person would understand. At first sight, I therefore conclude that there should be no need to resort either to a dictionary, or to authorities, to interpret this word; nor to the rule that, this being an insurer's document, it must be construed against them. On that basis, I would take the ordinary meaning of the word 'violent' in this context to be that it is intended to convey that the use of some force to effect entry, which may be minimal, such as the turning of a key in a lock or the turning of a door handle, is accentuated or accompanied by some physical act which can properly be described as violent in its nature or character. An obvious picture that springs to mind is the breaking down of a door or the forcing open of a window, which would be acts of violence directed to the fabric of the premises to effect entry. Or there might be violence to person, such as knocking down someone who seeks to prevent entry, irrespective of whatever may be contained within para (b) of that part of the cover [para (b) of the insurance cover against theft classified directors, partners or employees as being the relevant persons against whom actual or threatened assault or violence would constitute theft].

The ICC (A)

It is important to note that a cargo-owner who has taken up an ICC (A) does not have to prove the requirement within the legal definition of 'theft' that it was committed with violence. In such a policy, his claim is based upon the element of 'risk', and thus, theft committed with or without violence is covered. On this point, reference may be made to the remarks of Walton J, in *Schloss Brothers v Stevens* [1906] 2 KB 665, p 671, cited below.[22]

---

22 See below, p 416.

Persons from outside the vessel

For there to be 'theft', the persons committing that 'theft' must be from outside the vessel, as was shown in *Taylor v Liverpool and Great Western Steam Co*, below.

Taylor v Liverpool and Great Western Steam Co (1874) LR 9 QB 546

This was a carriage of goods by sea case. The plaintiffs shipped five boxes of diamonds from Liverpool to New York aboard the vessel *Nevada*. On arrival in New York, only four boxes of diamonds were delivered; the other box having been stolen during the voyage. The diamonds were insured and the underwriters duly indemnified the plaintiffs for their loss. The plaintiffs (presumably the underwriters by way of subrogation) then pursued the defendant shipowner for the loss. The shipowner resisted the claim on the basis that the bill of lading excepted a loss by 'thieves'.

The court ruled that the word 'thieves' in the exceptions clause was to be interpreted in the same manner as in marine insurance. As the theft was by persons not 'external' or 'outside' the vessel, the shipowners were liable.

> **Lush J:** [p 549] ... The case states that the box was stolen while on board the vessel, either during the voyage or after her arrival in port; but there was no evidence to show whether it was stolen by one of the crew, or by a passenger, or, after her arrival, by some person from the shore. From this statement we must take it as a fact that there were passengers on board. The question is, is that loss within any of the exceptions in the bill of lading, which are the act of God, the Queen's enemies, pirates, robbers, thieves, barratry of the master or mariners, etc? The first question is, does 'thieves' include persons on board the ship, or is it limited, as has been held in cases as to policies of insurance, to persons outside the ship and not belonging to it? The word is ambiguous, and, being of doubtful meaning, it must receive such a construction as is most in favour of the shipper, and not such as is most in favour of the shipowner, for whose benefit the exceptions are framed; for if it was intended to give to it the larger meaning which is now contended for, the intention to give the shipowner that protection ought to have been expressed in clear and unambiguous language. It is not, I think, reasonable to suppose, when the language used is ambiguous, that it was intended that the shipowner should not be liable for thefts by one of the crew or persons on board. The shipowner must protect himself, if he intends this, by the use of unambiguous language.

Similarly, in *Steinman and Co v Angier Line Ltd* **[1891] 1 QB 619, CA**, another carriage of goods by sea case, goods were shipped from Liverpool to Buenos Aires, but were not delivered. It was believed that stevedores, employed to load the ship, had stolen them. A clause in the bill of lading exempted the shipowner from, *inter alia*, liability for loss by 'pirates, robbers, or thieves of whatever kind, whether on board or not, or by land or sea'. The court ruled that the clause did not exempt the shipowner from liability, as the word 'thieves' did not include persons in the service of the ship. Bowen LJ stated:

[p 621] ... Robbery imports violence, but 'theft', which, properly speaking, does not, may be of several kinds. There may be the assailing thief from outside, the thief who 'breaks through and steals'; there may be a thief on board among those who are lawfully on board; there may, lastly, be a thief among the crew. The controversy has principally turned upon the question whether the term 'thieves' ought not to be confined to the first of these categories, viz, the depredators outside the ship ... The exceptions in a bill of lading are not intended to excuse the carrier from the obligation of bringing due skill and care on the part of himself and his servants to bear both upon the stowing and upon the carrying of the cargo. Even in cases within the exceptions, the shipowner is not protected if default or negligence on his part or that of his servants has contributed to the loss ... Upon this ground, I am of opinion on this bill of lading that the mere introduction into the list of exceptions of the words 'thieves of whatever kind', etc, does not relieve the shipowner from liability for the thefts committed by those in the service of the ship.

Institute Theft, Pilferage and Non-delivery Clause

The clause states:

In consideration of an additional premium, it is hereby agreed that this insurance covers loss or damage to the subject matter insured caused by theft or pilferage, or by non-delivery of an entire package, subject always to the exclusions contained in this insurance.

It is important to note that this additional clause covers not only violent theft, but, also, clandestine theft or pilferage, as well as non-delivery of an entire package. Items missing, for example, from within a container would not be covered; the container is the package.

Pilferage or non-delivery?

The *Cleveland Twist Drill* case, below, illustrates the difficulty in determining whether a loss is by pilferage (secret theft) or by non-delivery.

Cleveland Twist Drill Co (GB) Ltd v Union Insurance of Canton (1925) 2 LlL Rep 50, CA

The appellants shipped 89 cases of drills aboard the Cunard ship *Vestalia* from London to New York and thence to Cleveland. The shipment was insured with the respondents under a marine policy of insurance, warehouse to warehouse, which included cover for theft and pilferage. On arrival at New York, only 83 cases were found and, of those, eight were empty and two were part empty. At the original trial, the judge ruled that the loss was due to misdelivery, and the cargo-owners appealed.

The Court of Appeal overturned the decision of the trial judge and found for the appellant cargo-owners. The loss was held to be due to pilferage, a peril insured against.

Scrutton LJ: [p 53] ... The plaintiffs are goods owners who have insured certain machine tools going on a voyage to the United States from warehouse to warehouse, and they have insured them against theft, in the perils insured against, with a clause to cover all risks of theft and pilferage. An insurance against theft by itself is an insurance against robbery by violence and not against secret theft, and it is so laid down in the ninth rule of the schedule to the Marine Insurance Act; but now that underwriters have taken to insuring pilferage as well as theft, and to insuring from warehouse to warehouse as well as on the sea voyage, doubts have been expressed by judges as to whether theft has its original meaning ... It is one of the peculiarities of secret theft that you do not see it happen; and that being so, when the article has disappeared, how are you going to prove that it is a loss by theft as distinct from a loss by wrong delivery, because it is tolerably clear that if what happens is that a ship delivers things to the wrong person, the goods owner cannot recover from the underwriters on a policy against theft. A wrong delivery by accident or mistake or negligence is not theft on the part of the shipowners. No doubt keeping the goods after they are ascertained to be not the goods of the recipient may be theft in the recipient, but it is theft in the recipient after the goods have passed outside the area of the policy, and therefore the mere fact that goods are not delivered, or are delivered to the wrong person, will not found a claim under the policy ... The question therefore is whether in this case there is an equal balance as to whether there was misdelivery or whether there was theft; or whether, upon the proved facts, the balance turns towards theft, in which case the plaintiffs will recover.

We have at once this striking feature, that there is no doubt that thieves were busy with this consignment ... I come to the conclusion that this appeal should succeed, and that the plaintiffs should recover for the six cases which disappeared as well as for the eight of which the contents disappeared and the two of which the contents partly disappeared.

Forestal Land Timber and Railways Co Ltd v Rickards, 'Minden' [1940] 4 All ER 96

The plaintiffs shipped and insured cargo aboard the German freighter *Minden* from South America to Hong Kong or Shanghai. The policy of insurance included a clause covering the assured for '... theft, pilferage and non-delivery ...' Because of war being declared between Germany and Great Britain, and the placing of all German merchant ships under the control of the German Government, *Minden* immediately tried to return to Germany but was intercepted off the Faroe Islands and scuttled by her crew to avoid capture by a British warship. One of the contentions considered by the original trial judge was misdelivery and, on that issue, Hilbery J commented:

[p 110] ... Another alternative contention of the plaintiffs was that, in the circumstances, there was a non-delivery of the cargo, and that non-delivery

was a peril insured against. In truth, the policy does include a typewritten slip in the terms I have already quoted – namely: 'Including damage by hook, oil, theft, pilferage and non-delivery ...' Nevertheless, these general words ('non-delivery' following enumerated perils insured against) cannot be divorced from what has gone before and treated as intended to denominate an entirely new risk. They are limited by the context in which they are found. Such words in such a context are to be construed, not as creating a new or further risk, but as affecting the burden of proof. Where such words occur in such a context, the assured need not prove loss by theft or pilferage. It is enough if he proves non-delivery and gives *prima facie* proof that the goods were not lost in any way other than by theft or pilferage.

PIRACY

Rule 8 of the Rules of Construction of the Act provides a definition for piracy when it states that:

> The term 'pirates' includes passengers who mutiny and rioters who attack the ship from the shore.

Piracy is an insurable risk which is catered for by cl 6.1.5 of the ITCH(95) and cl 4.1.5 of the IVCH(95). Together with barratry, piracy is excepted from the War Risks Exclusion Clause. Thus, having been expressly excluded from the realm of war risks, piracy (and barratry) must be considered a marine risk and not a war risk.

With respect to the cargo-owner, by reason of it being an all risks policy, piracy is covered by the ICC (A) and, as with the Institute Hull Clauses, it is then specifically excepted from the War Exclusion Clause. The ICC (B) and (C) are silent on piracy, and, therefore, the peril is not covered.

Rioters from the shore

Nesbitt v Lushington is an early, but noteworthy, authority, which deliberated on what constitutes an act of piracy.

Nesbitt v Lushington (1792) 4 TR 783

A shipment of wheat and coals, aboard the sailing vessel *Industry*, was insured for a voyage Youghall to Sligo. Whilst proceeding down the coast of Ireland, *Industry* encountered bad weather and sought shelter in Elly Harbour. Whilst there, she was attacked and boarded by persons unknown who weighed the anchor and drove her ashore. These same persons then refused to leave her until the captain had agreed to sell them the cargo of corn at a price about three-quarters of the invoice value; there being a severe shortage of corn in

Ireland at that time. A further 10 tons of the corn was lost as a direct result of the ship being driven ashore, but *Industry* did finally arrive at her intended destination to deliver the cargo of coal. The plaintiff cargo-owner claimed on his policy of insurance which included cover for loss due to '... pirates, rovers, thieves ... takings at sea, restraints, and detainments of all Kings, princes, and people ...'. However, a memorandum, contained within the policy, stated that: '... corn, fish, salt, fruit, flour, and seed, were warranted free from average, unless general, or the ship be stranded ...' The underwriters refused payment.

The court ruled that, although the loss was attributed to piracy, the insurance policy only covered general average losses, not particular average losses and, as the adventure as a whole had not been jeopardised, there was no general average loss. The court further ruled that it anticipated that a claim for the 10 tons of corn, lost directly as a result of the stranding, would be recoverable, but only under the head of stranding, not piracy.

> **Lord Kenyon CJ:** [p 787] ... I think that this loss falls within a capture by pirates: and if a particular average could have been recovered upon this policy, the plaintiffs might have recovered on the count, stating the loss to have happened by piracy: but this being a policy upon corn, the memorandum states that the underwriter will not be liable for any average, unless general, or the ship be stranded; and I am of opinion that this is not a general average; because the whole adventure was never in jeopardy.

Passengers who mutiny

The mutinous acts of passengers may be considered to be acts of piracy, as was illustrated in *Palmer v Naylor*, below.

Palmer and Another v Naylor and Others (1854) 10 Ex 382

This was a claim upon a policy of insurance which covered advances, outfit and provisions with respect to the transportation of Chinese emigrants from China to Peru. The policy included cover against loss by '... pirates, rovers, thieves, etc ...'. During the voyage, the emigrants murdered the captain and some of the crew, and took possession of the ship for the purpose of being put ashore at the nearest point of land, after which, the ship was returned to the mate and the remaining crew. The plaintiff claimed for a total loss of expenses sustained as a result of the emigrants 'piratically murdering the captain and part of the crew, and feloniously stealing and carrying away the ship'. The insurers refused payment stating, *inter alia*, that the actions of the emigrants were only those of persons seeking to escape.

> The court ruled that the actions of the emigrants amounted to piracy.
>
> **Coleridge J:** [p 388] ... In the first place, it cannot be contended that the loss, supposing it to have resulted from the causes stated in the declaration ... was not attributable to the perils stated in the declaration, if it is to be considered

that the acts of the Chinese emigrants or coolies were the proximate, and not merely the remote cause of the loss. The admitted seizure of the vessel by them, the taking her out of the possession and control of the master and crew, and the diverting her from the voyage insured, were either direct acts of piracy or acts so entirely *ejusdem generis*, that, if not reducible to the special words of the policy, they are clearly included within the general words at the end of the peril clause.

... But, if the loss was complete as soon as they had murdered the captain and forcibly taken possession of the vessel, and for a time put an end to the voyage, then the loss is referable proximately to that unlawful act of theirs, and the motive which induced them to commit it; their unwillingness, namely, to be carried to their original destination is immaterial to be considered, because remotely only the cause of what occurred.

Piracy is indiscriminate and not politically motivated

Republic of Bolivia v Indemnity Mutual Marine Insurance Co Ltd [1909] 1 KB 785, CA

This action was brought by the Republic of Bolivia upon a marine policy of insurance on goods, sent up the River Amazon aboard the vessel *Labrea*. The policy covered loss caused by, *inter alia*, '... pirates, rovers, thieves ... takings at sea, arrests, restraints, and detainments of all Kings, princes, and people of what nation ...' but also contained a clause stating that the policy was warranted 'free of capture, seizure ...'. Towards the latter part of the voyage, on the River Acre, which enters Bolivian territory, *Labrea* was seized by another vessel under the command of insurgents, mostly Brazilian. The cargo was lost, and the plaintiffs, the government of Bolivia, claimed on their policy of insurance.

The Court of Appeal, in affirming the decision of the trial judge, ruled that this was not an act of piracy. Pirates plunder indiscriminately for personal gain and not for political reasons. Vaughan Williams LJ, in quoting Pickford J, the trial judge, referred to a well known definition of piracy.

Vaughan Williams LJ: [p 796] ... I adopt what Pickford J says as to the meaning of 'piracy' in the following passage of his judgment: 'I do not think that it can be better expressed than it is in *Hall's International Law*, 5th edn, p 259, where it is said: 'Besides, though the absence of competent authority is the test of piracy, its essence consists in the pursuit of private as contrasted with public ends. Primarily, the pirate is a man who satisfies his personal greed or his personal vengeance by robbery or murder in places beyond the jurisdiction of a State. The man who acts with a public object may do like acts to a certain extent, but his moral attitude is different, and the acts themselves will be kept within well marked bounds. He is not only not the enemy of the human race, but he is the enemy solely of a particular State.' That I think expresses what I have called the popular or business meaning of the word 'pirate', and I find that several, though not all, of the definitions cited in the note on p 260 of the same work bear out that idea. No doubt there are definitions which do not embody that idea, but that, I think, is the common and ordinary meaning; a man who is plundering indiscriminately for his own ends, and not a man who is simply operating against the property of a particular State for a public end, the end of establishing a government, although that act may be illegal and even criminal, and although he may not be acting on behalf of a society which is, to use the expression in *Hall's International Law*, politically organised. Such an act may be piracy by international law, but it is not, I think, piracy within the meaning of a policy of insurance; because, as I have already said, I think you have to attach to 'piracy' a popular or business meaning, and I do not think, therefore, that this was a loss by piracy. I adopt that passage as the basis of my judgment.

In the following case, *Banque Monteca v Motor Union Insurance Co*, the capture of a small vessel was considered to be politically motivated, and not indiscriminate, and was, therefore, an act of seizure and not piracy.

Banque Monteca and Carystuiaki and Another v Motor Union Insurance Co Ltd (1923) 14 LlL Rep 48

The Greek motor schooner *Filia* was insured under a policy of insurance covering war risks. The policy included 'seizure' as an insured risk, but 'piracy' was excepted. Whilst in the Black Sea, *Filia* was captured by Turkish nationalists at knife point and lost to the assured who, at a later date, claimed for the loss on his policy of insurance. The question before the court was whether the loss was by piracy or by seizure.

The court ruled that the loss was by seizure and not piracy. In reaching his decision, the judge again referred to *Hall's International Law* for the definition of piracy.

> **Roche J:** [p 51] ... I think these facts show a marked difference in the two cases, and the difference in the two cases strengthens, rather than destroys, my view that the seizure of *Filia* was so dominantly a military matter as to move it from the position of piracy within the meaning of this clause. Of course, capture or seizure among civilised people is always identified with the form of taking the ship seized before the Prize Court. Osman Agha or the Kemalists did not indulge in that form, but the absence of the legal form does not seem to me to alter the substance of the matter, which is that this purported to be a seizure and capture of an enemy vessel rather than a raid by brigands upon such vessel. For these reasons, I give judgment for the plaintiffs in accordance with their claim.

Piracy requires force

Athens Maritime Enterprises Corporation v Hellenic Mutual War Risks Association (Bermuda) Ltd, 'Andreas Lemos' [1982] 2 Lloyd's Rep 483

This was an action upon a war risks policy of insurance, effected by the shipowners with the defendant association. Whilst at anchor off Chittagong, Bangladesh, a gang of men, armed with knives, boarded *Andreas Lemos* and stole equipment, including mooring ropes. When these men were confronted by armed members of the crew, they drew their knives for protection and fled. The question before the court was whether the loss was attributable to piracy or theft. The association denied liability.

The court ruled that the loss was not attributable to riots, theft or piracy. It was not a loss by piracy, as the gang of men had only used, or threatened to use, force to flee from the ship after the loss had taken place. Furthermore, it could not be theft, within the meaning of the policy as, again, no force had been applied.

> **Staughton J:** [p 491] ... I hold that theft without force or a threat of force is not piracy under a policy of marine insurance ... The association, by the word 'piracy', insures the loss caused to shipowners because their employees are overpowered by force, or terrified into submission. It does not insure the loss caused to shipowners when their nightwatchman is asleep (as might occur, although it did not in this case), and thieves steal clandestinely. The very notion of piracy is inconsistent with clandestine theft.

Again, in the case of *Shell International Petroleum Co Ltd v Caryl Antony Vaughan Gibbs, 'Salem'* [1982] 1 Lloyd's Rep 369, CA, where a large oil tanker was scuttled after illegally discharging her cargo in South Africa, at the Court of Appeal, Lord Denning MR stated: [p 373] 'There were no "pirates" here because there was no forcible robbery. There were no "thieves" here, because there was no violent means.'

ACCIDENTS IN LOADING

This is now an insurable risk provided for by cl 6.1.8 of the ITCH(95) and cl 4.1.8 of the IVCH(95), which state that: 'This insurance covers loss of or damage to the subject matter insured caused by: accidents in loading discharging or shifting cargo or fuel.' The clause was introduced as a direct result of *Stott v Marten*, which is illustrated below.

Due note should be taken that this provision now lies within the general perils clause and not, as was previously the case with the 1983 Institute Hull Clauses, within the Inchmaree Clause. Thus, the provision is no longer subject to the due diligence proviso.

In *Stott (Baltic) Steamers Ltd v Marten and Others* [1916] AC 304, an accident occurred when loading a large boiler down the hatch of a ship which resulted in damage to the ship itself. The loss was not deemed recoverable as a peril of the sea, as it was not an accident unique to the sea. The full facts of the case are recorded above, under perils of the seas.[23]

ALL RISKS: THE ICC (A)

Although the ICC (A) is described as an 'all risks' policy of insurance, the term 'all risks' does not mean 'all eventualities'. Unless the policy provides otherwise, the term 'all risks' means that the assured is covered against all marine perils.

First, in the same manner as the ICC (B) and (C), the ICC (A), in cl 4, itemises exclusions which, in the ordinary course of events, would not be considered to be risks normally associated with a marine adventure. It does not, for example, insure against loss attributable to the wilful misconduct of the assured, nor does it insure against loss caused by inherent vice or ordinary wear and tear.[24] The underwriter, even with an all risks policy, remains an insurer and not a guarantor. Insurance remains an indemnity against a fortuitous or an unexpected loss or casualty; it is not a guarantee against an eventuality.

Secondly, with an all risks policy, the burden of proof placed upon a claimant is less rigorous. Unlike the ICC (B) and (C), a claimant, under an all risks policy, is not required to show how the loss occurred, only that it in fact occurred, and that it was a casualty, not a certainty. The onus is then placed upon the insurer to prove otherwise.

The following two cases, *Schloss Bros v Stevens* and the *Gaunt* case, are good examples of the advantages to be gained by investing in an 'all risks' policy on goods.

Schloss Bros v Stevens [1906] 2 KB 665

This was an action upon an all risks policy of marine insurance on goods insured 'by land and by water' from Savanilla and/or Cartagena to any place or places in the interior of Colombia. During the transit from Savanilla, a port in Colombia, to Medellin, a town in the interior of the country, 14 bales of goods were damaged by damp, accidental wetting and injury by worms. Above all, the damage was attributable to the inordinate delay, in a hostile climate, of one and a half years in getting the goods transported to the interior.

---

23 See above, p 378.
24 Excluded losses are discussed in Chapter 10.

The plaintiffs, the owners of the goods, claimed on their policy of insurance, but the underwriters rejected the claim, on the basis that the damage amounted to ordinary wear and tear.

The court ruled that the all risks policy covered all losses by any accidental cause of any kind, and the underwriters were liable.

> **Walton J:** [p 671] ... Looking at the policy, including the written words and the clauses attached, it covers, in the first place, all losses occurring from any of the perils included in a Lloyd's policy in the ordinary form; it undoubtedly includes other risks – risks of robbery with or without violence, damage by insects, etc – some of which may not be within the ordinary printed words of a Lloyd's policy. It is plain, therefore, that the policy was intended to cover something more than the ordinary risks. For the plaintiffs, it was contended that, during this transit, the policy protected the assured from loss by all risks whatever by any conveyance from the time the goods were taken from on board the import vessel at Savanilla until they were delivered at the consignees' warehouse or elsewhere. The plaintiffs said that the words 'all risks by land and water', etc, meant all risks whatsoever. It is very difficult to arrive at a conclusion with any certainty as to what the intention of the policy is. In considering the construction of such a policy – a marine policy – one is bound to give effect to all well known customs, which are perfectly understood in insurance business, as to the interpretation of such documents; but, after all, the rights of the parties depend upon the language of the contract.
>
> ... I have read this policy as I think it would be reasonably understood by any merchant or insurance broker, and doing so I come to the conclusion that the words 'all risks by land and by water', etc, must be read literally, as meaning all risks whatsoever. I think they were intended to cover all losses by any accidental cause of any kind occurring during the transit. Does the loss suffered in fact come within that category? There must be a casualty. I think the loss was so caused. With regard to the 12 bales, there was an abnormal delay in the transit arising from unusual and accidental causes, which necessarily involved an exposure of the goods to damp. In the case of the 12 bales, therefore, the loss was an accidental loss, and was covered by the policy.

British and Foreign Marine Insurance Co v Gaunt [1921] 2 AC 41, HL

The respondent (plaintiff) was the purchaser of a shipment of wool sent FOB from Chile to England. The policy of insurance was an all risks policy which included cover 'from the sheep's back ... until safely delivered into warehouse in Europe'. On the arrival of the wool at Bradford, it was found that some of the bales were badly damaged by water, and it transpired that this damage had occurred during the transit from the interior of Chile to Punta Arenas on the coast. The wool had been transported in local steamers and then stored in hulks in the harbour at Punta Arenas before being loaded onto the ship bound for Europe. The respondent claimed on his policy of insurance. The underwriters refused payment.

The House of Lords affirmed the decision of the Court of Appeal in favour of the respondent cargo-owner.

Lord Birkenhead LC: [p 46] ... In construing these policies, it is important to bear in mind that they cover 'all risks'. These words cannot, of course, be held to cover all damage however caused, for such damage as is inevitable from ordinary wear and tear and inevitable depreciation is not within the policies. There is little authority on the point, but the decision of Walton J, in *Schloss Bros v Stevens*, on a policy in similar terms, states the law accurately enough. He said that the words 'all risks by land and water' as used in the policy then in question: '... were intended to cover all losses by any accidental cause of any kind occurring during the transit ... There must be a casualty.' Damage, in other words, if it is to be covered by policies such as these, must be due to some fortuitous circumstance or casualty.

Lord Sumner: [p 57] ... There are, of course, limits to 'all risks'. They are risks and risks insured against. Accordingly, the expression does not cover inherent vice or mere wear and tear or British capture. It covers a risk, not a certainty; it is something which happens to the subject matter from without, not the natural behaviour of that subject matter, being what it is, in the circumstances under which it is carried. Nor is it a loss which the assured brings about by his own act, for then, he has not merely exposed the goods to the chance of injury, he has injured them himself. Finally, the description 'all risks' does not alter the general law; only risks are covered which it is lawful to cover, and the onus of proof remains where it would have been on a policy against ordinary sea perils.

Burden of proof

Even with an 'all risks' policy of insurance, the assured must establish a case to show that the loss was caused by a 'casualty' and not an eventuality.

Fuerst Day Lawson Ltd v Orion Insurance Co Ltd [1980] 1 Lloyd's Rep 656

The plaintiffs were purchasers of a shipment of essential oils, used in the perfumery trade, from Djakarta to the UK. The insurance policy with the defendant underwriters was claused: 'anywhere to anywhere', lost or not lost, against all risks. The shipment of 495 drums of essential oils was paid for by letter of credit. When the shipment arrived in the UK, the drums were found to contain mostly water, with just a trace of essential oils on the surface to complete the deception. It later transpired that a even larger shipment of drums of essential oils to the USA, by the same company, at much the same time, had also consisted mostly of water. The plaintiffs claimed on their all risks policy of insurance.[25]

The court ruled for the defendant underwriters. The plaintiffs had failed to discharge their burden of proof in that, on the balance of probabilities, there

---

25 This case is also discussed in Chapter 2, p 55.

was no evidence to show that the shipment of essential oils had ever started out as essential oils. There was the possibility that the drums, from the outset, had been filled with water.

> **Mocatta J:** [p 664] ... I have not, having given careful consideration to the evidence and arguments, been persuaded that the plaintiffs have discharged the burden of proof upon them of establishing on the balance of probabilities that the oil in drums they had agreed to buy from Farmaport ever started on their transit from Farmaport's godown or any other warehouse. I think there is certainly a possibility, to put it no higher, that the drums from the outset contained water with a thin film of essential oils for deception purposes. But whether this be so or not, the burden of proof is upon the plaintiffs to make out their case against the underwriters on the balance of probabilities and this, in my judgment, they have not succeeded in doing. The action accordingly fails, and there must be judgment for the defendants.

In *British and Foreign Marine Insurance Co v Gaunt* [1921] 2 AC 41, HL, wool was shipped from Chile and found to be damaged on arrival at Bradford. The House of Lords, in reaching its decision, deliberated on the question of burden of proof.

> **Lord Birkenhead LC:** [p 47] ... We are, of course, to give effect to the rule that the plaintiff must establish his case, that he must show that the loss comes within the terms of his policies; but where all risks are covered by the policy and not merely risks of a specified class or classes, the plaintiff discharges his special onus when he has proved that the loss was caused by some event covered by the general expression, and he is not bound to go further and prove the exact nature of the accident or casualty which, in fact, occasioned his loss.

> **Lord Sumner:** [p 57] ... I think, however, that the quasi-universality of the description does not affect the onus of proof in one way. The claimant insured against and averring a loss by fire must prove loss by fire, which involves proving that it is not by something else. When he avers loss by some risk coming within 'all risks', as used in this policy, he need only give evidence reasonably showing that the loss was due to a casualty, not to a certainty or to inherent vice or to wear and tear. That is easily done. I do not think he has to go further and pick out one of the multitude of risks covered, so as to show exactly how this loss was caused.

In *Theodorou v Chester* [1951] 1 Lloyd's Rep 204, bales of sponges were shipped from New York to London aboard *American Merchant* under an all risks policy of insurance. On arrival at London, the sponges were found to be contaminated with moisture and dust; the owner claimed on his policy of insurance. The underwriters refused to pay, stating that the damage had occurred for no other reason other than normal transit risks. The court referred to the *Gaunt* case in ruling that the plaintiff could recover because he had shown, on the balance of probability, that the damage to the sponges had been due to an extraneous and accidental cause.

References and further reading

Hazelwood, S, 'The peril of "pirates" all "at sea"' [1983] LMCLQ 283

Hodges, S, 'Mortgagee's interest insurance', in *The Modern Law of Marine Insurance*, 1996, London, LLP, p 251

Muchlinski, PT, 'Mortgagee's interest insurance, *The Alexion Hope*' [1986] LMCLQ 282

O'May, DR, 'The practice of scuttling' [1974] LMCLQ 484

O'May, DR, 'Marine insurance law: can lawyers be trusted?' [1987] LMCLQ 29

CHAPTER 10

EXCLUDED LOSSES

INTRODUCTION

Section 55 of the Marine Insurance Act 1906 provides the framework for all included and excluded losses. Section 55(1) declares the rule of proximate cause as the general principle to be applied for determining the liability of the insurer.[1] Having stated the general position, s 55(2) then enumerates the 'particular' exclusions for which the insurer is not liable. These particular exclusions include, in s 55(2)(a): '... any loss attributable to the wilful misconduct of the assured ...' and, in s 55(2)(b): 'Unless the policy otherwise provides ... any loss caused by delay, although that delay be caused by a peril insured against.' Section 55(2)(c) then deals with the issues of wear and tear and inherent vice. Again, the Act prefaces the exclusion with: 'Unless the policy otherwise provides,' and then goes on to state that '... the insurer is not liable for ordinary wear and tear, ordinary leakage and breakage, inherent vice or nature of the subject matter insured, or for any loss proximately caused by rats or vermin, or by any injury to machinery not proximately caused by maritime perils'.

Notably, the Institute Hull Clauses do not include general exclusions clauses; reliance has, therefore, been placed upon the Act itself to provide the necessary defences for the insurer.

This, however, is not the case with the Institute Cargo Clauses. Clauses 4.1 to 4.5 of all the Institute Cargo Clauses reiterate the general law of exclusions as laid down in the Act, but the ICC (B) and (C) go on, in cll 4.6 to 4.8, to itemise additional exclusions which are not specifically alluded to in the Act. These additional exclusions include cl 4.6: '... insolvency or financial default of the owners managers charterers or operators of the vessel'; cl 4.7: 'deliberate damage to or deliberate destruction of the subject matter insured ...'; and cl 4.8, the radioactivity contamination clause.

Should the assured, under the ICC (B) and (C), wish to be covered against 'deliberate damage' or 'deliberate destruction', then such additional cover is available by way of the Institute Malicious Damage Clause. Clauses 4.6 and 4.7 of the ICC (A) only exclude 'insolvency' and 'contamination from radioactivity'; no mention is made of deliberate damage or deliberate destruction of the subject matter.

---

1   For a discussion of the law of causation, see Chapter 8.

WILFUL MISCONDUCT OF THE ASSURED

Section 55(2)(a) of the Marine Insurance Act 1906 states: 'The insurer is not liable for any loss attributable to the wilful misconduct of the assured ...', and this exclusion is repeated in cl 4.1 of all the Institute Cargo Clauses. It is significant to note that this exclusion is not, as in the cases of s 55(2)(b) and (c), prefaced with the words 'unless the policy otherwise provides'.

Meaning of wilful misconduct

The complexities in this area of the law are twofold.

First, as improper conduct could range from mere negligence, gross or culpable negligence, indifference, reckless disregard, to wilful misconduct, it is necessary to identify the qualities of an act which would amount to 'wilful misconduct'. The following cases: *Papadimitriou v Henderson* [1939] 64 LlL Rep 345; *National Oilwell (UK) Ltd v Davy Offshore Ltd* [1993] 2 Lloyd's Rep 582;[2] *Thompson v Hopper* (1856) 6 E&B 937; (1858) EB&E 1038 and the Australian authority of *Wood v Associated National Insurance Co Ltd* [1985] 1 Qd R 297[3] have endeavoured, in general or specific terms, to draw the line of demarcation between these acts of impropriety. In *Papadimitriou v Henderson*, the characteristics of an act of wilful misconduct was discussed in the context of war, and recently, in *NOW v DOL*, in the context of scuttling, though the policy under consideration was not a marine policy of insurance.

Secondly, a more focused issue – whether a shipowner who has sent an unseaworthy ship to sea with reckless disregard or reckless indifference is guilty of an act of wilful misconduct – has to be examined. The question was specifically considered in *Thompson v Hopper* and the *Wood* case in relation to unseaworthiness under a time policy of insurance, and was discussed in general terms in *NOW v DOL*. This must necessarily refer us to the concept of 'privity' as laid down in s 39(5) of the Act, under which privity or knowledge is sufficient to free the insurer from liability, if the loss is attributable to the particular unseaworthiness to which the assured is privy. The interrelationship between the defences of unseaworthiness with the privity of the assured under s 39(5), and that of wilful misconduct under s 55(2)(a) would, inevitably, have to be considered; more pointedly, would a finding of 'privity' under s 39(5) necessarily lead to a finding of 'wilful misconduct' under s 55(2)(a)? It is to be observed that under both sections, the applicable rule of causation is to be found in the words '*attributable to*'. Thus, any loss attributable to such unseaworthiness to which the assured is privy or any loss

---

2   Hereinafter referred to simply as *NOW v DOL*.
3   Hereinafter referred to as the *Wood* case.

attributable to the wilful misconduct of the assured will prevent recovery under the policy.

Papadimitriou v Henderson [1939] 64 LIL Rep 345

The plaintiffs effected a time policy of insurance with the defendants on freight and on the hull and machinery of *Ellinico Vouno*, a Greek registered vessel. Attached to the policy was a war and strikes clause which covered risks otherwise excluded by the f c and s clause. In May 1938, during the Spanish Civil War, *Ellinico Vouno* sailed from Odessa with a cargo of lorries and spare parts belonging to the Spanish Government and bound for Oran in North Africa. The owners of *Ellinico Vounc* were aware of the presence of hostile warships in the Mediterranean and ordered the vessel to put into Malta to await orders. Whilst passing between Greece and Sicily, *Ellinico Vouno* was intercepted by a Spanish insurgent warship and escorted to Majorca, where the ship and cargo were confiscated and the master and crew returned to Greece. The plaintiffs claimed for an actual or constructive total loss, but the underwriters refused payment on the basis of, *inter alia*, the wilful misconduct of the assured in sending the ship on a voyage where capture was always imminent.

The court ruled in favour of the plaintiff shipowners, in that they were only endeavouring to fulfil a perfectly lawful voyage.

> **Goddard LJ:** [p 349] ... Of course, if it was a case in which the shipowner got warning that a blockade had been established at a particular port or that a ship was lying waiting at a particular point, and the shipowner deliberately sent his ship forward to that point to run the blockade, it may be that there would be, in certain cases, an inference to be drawn that he was not endeavouring to carry out the voyage, but what he was endeavouring to do was to get his ship captured, and that, of course, would be wilful misconduct. In the last war it would have been a serious thing for this country if it was said that every shipmaster who continued his contract voyage to this country, when it was known that there were submarines at large in the Channel or the approaches to the Channel, was guilty of wilful misconduct because there was a risk that his ship would be seized and sunk, whether it was a neutral ship or a British ship. I certainly should be very sorry to lay down any such doctrine, that a shipowner who had dispatched his ship on what was to him a perfectly lawful voyage, should be held guilty of wilful misconduct because he had continued on that voyage and was doing his best to fulfil it, more especially when one finds that when he was asked to order the ship to return, he did order his ship to return. On that point I am quite clear.

The dispute in *AG v Adelaide SS Co Ltd, 'Warilda'* [1923] AC 292, HL,[4] was primarily concerned with the issue of whether, in the case of a collision, the negligent navigation of the master displaced the status or nature of the duty in

---

4   Also discussed in Chapter 14, on War and Strikes Risks.

which the ship was engaged (warlike operations). However, Lord Wrenbury, whilst deliberating over the consequence of such negligence, also considered the effect of wilful misconduct.

Lord Wrenbury: [p 308] ... As regards sea peril, I may perhaps express it by saying that the underwriter insures against the sea peril, however it may happen – including, therefore, negligence of the master. It is otherwise if the loss occurs through the wilful negligence or wilful act of the assured. In that case the loss does not 'happen', but is caused by the assured himself, and, consequently, he cannot recover.

Notes

Whether a negligent act can ever be wilful is, it is submitted, questionable. However, the main controversy is whether an act of reckless disregard or reckless indifference is equivalent to an act of wilful misconduct. The case of *Thompson v Hopper* provides a suitable platform for this discussion, for it centres itself on the act of sending an unseaworthy ship to sea with reckless disregard. Though the judge had tended to merge the specific defence of unseaworthiness (with privity of the assured) with the general defence of wilful misconduct, his comments are, nevertheless, useful for the purpose of providing an insight into the requirements of the latter defence.

Reckless disregard or reckless indifference

The issue raised in *Thompson v Hopper*, below, was whether 'reckless disregard' or 'reckless indifference' fell within the meaning of 'wilful misconduct'. That is, was the meaning of 'wilful misconduct' wide enough to include not just an intentional positive wrongdoing, but also the inaction of an assured in showing disregard or indifference to a wrongdoing? The court concluded that it was.

Thompson v Hopper (1856) 6 E&B 937; (1858) EB&E 1038

The plaintiff effected a time policy of insurance with the defendants upon the vessel *Mary Graham*. After loading a full cargo of coal in Sunderland, she left harbour with her standing rigging still loose, in order to catch the spring tide at the bar. During the night, an easterly gale sprang up and *Mary Graham* was driven ashore and wrecked. The court later heard from the sole survivor that the anchor cable had parted close to the anchor and the length of cable, still attached, had made the ship unmanageable, and the crew's efforts to release the cable had failed, because it was rusted. It was assumed that, at the time of the loss, the standing rigging had been made fast. The question before the court was whether the plaintiffs, the owners of *Mary Graham*, had 'knowingly, wilfully and wrongfully' sent her to sea in an unseaworthy state and whether this action was the proximate or remote cause of her loss.

The Appeal Court overturned the decision reached at the original trial and ruled that, although there is no implied warranty of seaworthiness applicable to a time policy of insurance, the plaintiff could not recover when the vessel had knowingly been sent to sea in an unseaworthy state.

Bramwell B: [p 1045] ... Supposing, I say again, she had been struck by lightning while being there, would the plaintiffs have wilfully caused that? The causing, if in any sense a causing, is a remote causing; it is that the assured sent her to sea unseaworthy, caused her to remain there, and be exposed to a storm if it came, and so caused her to be lost. The maxim, *causa proxima non causa remota spectatur*, applies. This maxim is recognised, but said not to be applicable; that a remote causing by 'improper conduct' of the insured is enough. But a fallacy lurks in that word 'improper'. I agree a man shall not take advantage of his own wrong. But the phrase contains the same fallacy; and the fallacy is made apparent by the inappropriate use of the maxim dolus circuitu non purgator. 'Improper', 'wrong', and *'dolus'*, in the sense in which dolus is used in that maxim, are to my mind inappropriate expressions. There was nothing improper, nothing wrong, no *dolus*, in sending the ship to sea unseaworthy. There is nothing wrongful in sending an unseaworthy ship to sea; though she is insured, there is nothing wrongful in burning her. The wrong is in making a claim founded on such an act.

Willes J: [p 1047] I am of opinion that the judgment ought to be reversed. It appears to me to be founded upon a misapplication of the maxim *dolus circuitu non purgator*. Dolus therein stands for *dolus malus*, and cannot mean simply any thing which may lead to the damage of another: indeed some such acts constitute what has been called *dolus bonus*; and some are *damna absque injuria*. Without entering into a discussion of the precise meaning of *dolus* or *dolus malus* in the civil law, I may say that, if the *dolus*, in the sense in which it is used in the maxim, can exist independent of evil intention, it cannot so exist without either the violation of some legal duty, independent of contract, or the breach of a contract, express or implied, between the parties. To recognise in a court of justice *dolus*, or wrong, or misconduct, as a ground of action or defence, apart from these conditions, would be to confound all certainty in the law.

Notes

Thompson v Hopper has to be read with caution, as it was decided before the Act at a time when the law relating to seaworthiness in a time policy was not well developed. As was seen, under current law, as stated in s 39(5), 'privity' alone of the particular unseaworthiness to which the loss is attributable is sufficient to free the insurer from liability.[5] In such a circumstance, there is no need for the insurer to rely on the wilful misconduct of the assured as a defence, save as an alternative plea should the loss be found not to have been attributable to such unseaworthiness.

---

5   See Chapter 7.

Compared to 'wilful misconduct', 'privity' is obviously a lesser form of blame or misbehaviour (both words used in the broad sense), and, to that extent, easier to prove. But whether the defence be 'privity' under s 39(5) or 'wilful misconduct' under s 55(2)(a), a court need only concern itself with the test of 'attribution', and not the rule of proximate cause, when determining the validity of these defences: any loss attributable to unseaworthiness to which the assured is privy (in the legal sense), or attributable to the wilful misconduct of the assured, will, even though the loss may be proximately caused by an insured peril, strip the assured of his right to recovery under the policy.

Webster's Comprehensive Dictionary of the English Language defines 'reckless' as being 'foolishly heedless of danger' or 'indifferent' to that danger. Although 'reckless indifference' or 'reckless disregard' does not imply intent, as does wilful misconduct, the *Wood* case, an Australian case which reached the Appeal Court, equated the two by showing that reckless indifference may, indeed, amount to wilful misconduct. The same stance, it would appear, was taken in the recent case of *NOW v DOL*.[6]

Wood v Associated National Insurance Co Ltd [1984] 1 Qd R 507; [1985] 1 Qd R 297

Isothel, a diesel powered fishing vessel owned by the plaintiffs, a father and two sons, was insured under a time policy of insurance with the defendants. On Sunday 17 May 1981, *Isothel* left Brisbane bound for Townsville, with one of the sons in command and three other young crewmen. Later that day, after heading northwards for some time, because the bilge pump was not working, *Isothel* anchored off Double Island Point, with the intention of continuing the following morning. This anchorage was, by general consent, unsafe when the wind blew from north of east. The following day, Monday, it was found that the main engine would not start and the son sent a message to his father for assistance. The father, a trained mechanic, arrived later in the day and fixed both the main engine and the bilge pump. Both the father and the son, the skipper of *Isothel*, then departed for Brisbane, leaving the three young crewmen aboard. Whilst in Brisbane, on the Tuesday, the father raised the insurance on *Isothel* by A$20,000 to reflect improvements made to her. Two days later, on Thursday, a gale from the north east sprang up, the three crewmen swam ashore, barely saving their lives, and *Isothel* was wrecked.

The full Court of Appeal upheld the decision of the trial judge and ruled that the plaintiffs had acted with reckless disregard, amounting to wilful misconduct, and that the insurers were not liable for the loss.

---

6   See below, p 428.

McPherson J: [p 305] ... Perhaps the most accurate general statement for present purposes of the conception underlying 'wilful misconduct' is that to be derived from the earlier case of *Orient Insurance Company v Adams* ... that is to say, reckless exposure of the vessel to the perils of navigation knowing that she was not in a condition to encounter them. That raises a further question about the meaning of 'recklessness'. The word is capable of bearing a variety of shades of meaning, depending upon matters such as the likelihood, and consequent foreseeability, of the risk materialising and the degree of attention that is given to that risk ... However, in the present case, the learned trial judge found that the loss of *Isothel* was a probable consequence of the plaintiffs' conduct in leaving her unskippered and with an incompetent crew in the circumstances and for the period for which they did. I have already said that I consider his Honour's finding of fact in that regard to be justified by the evidence. It follows that, whether the criterion adopted is foreseeability of 'possible' or 'probable' consequences, the requirement of recklessness is established by the findings of this case. It is certainly correct to say that the vessel was, on and after Monday 18 May 1981, exposed to perils of the seas, her owners throughout knowing that she was not in a condition to encounter them and being indifferent to the risk that she would not survive those perils.

... There was, in my view, therefore, 'wilful misconduct' in relation to the vessel. The remaining question is whether the loss of *Isothel* can, within the meaning of s 61(2)(a), be said to be 'attributable to' that wilful misconduct. It is for the insured to show that the loss was proximately caused by a peril insured against ... It is difficult to avoid the conclusion that the risk to which *Isothel* was exposed throughout the period was one that the owners would not have run had she not been insured: cf *Thompson v Hopper* (1858) El&Bl 1056, pp 1048–49; 120 ER 796, p 800, *per* Willes J. To the objection that a consideration of that kind is relevant to the element of wilful misconduct rather than to causation, the answer is that it shows the continuing efficacy of wilful misconduct as the operative cause of the loss.

... With an incompetent crew, *Isothel* was deprived of the ordinary protection of a vessel against perils of the sea. That means that the risk of loss by such a peril was transformed, as time progressed and she remained exposed, from a chance to a predictable probability. Because the insured carries the burden of proving that the loss was due to perils of the sea, it is essential to the success of the plaintiffs' claim that it be established on a balance of probabilities 'that the loss was attributable to a fortuitous accident': *Skandia Insurance Co Ltd v Skoljarev* (1979) 142 CLR 375, pp 386–87. The question in each case has been said to be 'whether a fortuitous event has occurred bringing about coverage or application of the policy': see *Northwestern Mutual Life Insurance Co v Linard* 498 F 2d 556, p 563, cited with approval by Mason J in the *Skandia* case: (1979) 142 CLR 386, p 391.

It was the wilful misconduct of the plaintiffs that exposed *Isothel* to the perils of the seas when she was known not to be in a condition fit to encounter them. Once it became predictable that as a matter of probability she would encounter those perils and in her condition not be able to survive them, the element of chance or fortuity was eliminated or substantially reduced and her consequent loss became attributable to the owners' wilful misconduct and not to a peril insured against. The expression 'perils of the sea' in this policy refers only to 'fortuitous accidents or casualties of the seas': see r 7 of the Rules of Construction of Policy forming part of the Second Schedule to the Marine Insurance Act, which Mason J in *Skandia Insurance Co Ltd v Skoljarev* (1979) 142 CLR 375, p 384, said was a codification of the antecedent common law. The loss of The Isothel was due not to a fortuitous accident or casualty of the seas, but to one that was a probable and predictable consequence of the plaintiffs' wilful misconduct.

And, in the case of *NOW v DOL*, below, Colman J considered the meaning of reckless indifference by referring to an older case where wilful misconduct was likened to reckless 'carelessness'.

National Oilwell (UK) Ltd v Davy Offshore Ltd [1993] 2 Lloyd's Rep 582

The plaintiffs, National Oilwell (UK) Ltd, were sub-contracted to supply subsea wellhead components to the defendants, Davy Offshore Ltd. After delivering the components, the plaintiffs pursued a claim upon the defendants for unpaid invoices and the defendants, in turn, counterclaimed for defective parts which had been delayed in delivery. In reality, the defendants' counterclaim was made by their insurers who had settled a claim upon the defendants for these defective parts and were now pursuing the plaintiffs by way of subrogation. Amongst other things, the plaintiffs were accused of wilful misconduct in supplying parts they knew to be defective. Colman J, in delivering the judgment of the court, referred at length to previous cases before deliberating about wilful misconduct and reckless indifference. Initially, reference was made to Lord Alverstone's definition in *Forder v Great Western Railway Co*.

> **Colman J:** [p 621] ... Mr Aikens, on behalf of DOL, has referred me to Lord Alverstone's well known definition of wilful misconduct in the context of terms and conditions of carriage in *Forder v Great Western Railway Co* [1905] 2 KB 532, p 535:
>
>> ... I am quite prepared to adopt, with one slight addition, the definition of wilful misconduct given by Johnson J in *Graham v Belfast and Northern Counties Ry Co* where he says:
>>
>>> Wilful misconduct in such a special condition means misconduct to which the will is party as contradistinguished from accident, and is far beyond any negligence, even gross or culpable negligence, and involves that a person wilfully misconducts himself who knows and appreciates that it is wrong conduct on his part in the existing circumstances to do, or to fail or omit to do (as the case may be), a particular thing, and yet intentionally does, or fails or omits to do it, or persists in the act, failure, or omission regardless of consequences.
>>
>> The addition which I would suggest is, 'or acts with reckless carelessness, not caring what the results of his carelessness may be'.
>
> [p 622] ... Clearly, for the conduct to be characterised as 'misconduct', it must be wrongful in the context of the contractual or other relationship existing at

the relevant time between the parties concerned. That is to say, in the context of a contract, one party must do or omit to do something which is aptly described as misconduct towards the other contracting party. In the context of a policy of insurance on property, the misconduct in question must obviously relate to the subject matter insured and it must also relate to the assured's obligations under the policy. Thus, deliberately to sink an insured ship with a view to claiming on the insurers is clearly misconduct in the context of insurance on that ship. However, deliberately to sink an insured ship because the owner cannot afford to operate it, lay it up or tow it to a scrap yard, but without any intention to claim on the insurers, is clearly not wilful misconduct in the context of the policy. That conduct would, however, become misconduct if a claim in respect of the loss of the ship were presented. Accordingly, the loss of or damage to the insured property in respect of which the assured presents a claim must be shown to have been caused or procured by the assured in order to achieve a loss which he then intends to present to insurers as an insured loss or which subsequently does present to insurers as an insured loss or must be shown to have been permitted to happen in circumstances where the assured was recklessly indifferent whether the subject matter was lost or damaged but where, the loss or damage having thus been sustained, he claims on his insurers in respect of it. In either case, essential elements are that the assured intended to achieve a loss or the damage or that he was recklessly indifferent whether such loss or damage was caused and that his immediate purpose was to claim on his insurers or that he subsequently advanced such a claim.

Although the case of *Compania Maritime San Basilio SA v Oceanus Mutual Underwriting Association (Bermuda) Ltd, 'Eurysthenes'* [1976] 2 Lloyd's Rep 171, CA, is associated with the in depth analysis of 'privity', Lord Denning MR touched briefly on recklessness and wilful misconduct:[7]

[p 177] ... The contest is: what degree of personal involvement is such as to deprive the insurer of his indemnity? The shipowners say that they are only to be deprived of it if they have been guilty of wilful misconduct, in this sense, that they have deliberately or *recklessly* sent the ship to sea knowing she was unfit. [Emphasis added.]

Notes

In a factual situation such as in the *Wood* case, it may be necessary to differentiate between the applicability of the defences of unseaworthiness with the privity of the assured, under s 39(5), and that of wilful misconduct of the assured, under s 55(2)(a). The former defence is of relevance to an insurer only if the loss is found to have been *attributable to* such unseaworthiness to which the assured is privy, and the latter when the loss is *attributable to* the wilful misconduct of the assured. The defences are mutually exclusive, but, in either event, the proximate cause of the loss must be an insured peril before any need to consider these defences can arise.

---

7   This case is also discussed in Chapter 7, p 319.

Should unseaworthiness or wilful misconduct of the assured be held as the proximate cause, the assured would not be able to recover by reason of the fact that neither of these causes is an insured risk. In the light of this, it is advisable to plead these defences in the alternative, for should unseaworthiness be found not to be in any way responsible for the loss, the insurer would naturally wish to rely on the principle enunciated in the *Wood* case (albeit an Australian case), the *obiter dictum* of Lord Denning in the Court of Appeal in the *Eurysthenes* case, and the general comments made in the court of first instance in *NOW v DOL*, that the act of sending an unseaworthy ship to sea with reckless disregard or reckless indifference is capable of amounting to an act of wilful misconduct under s 55(2)(a).

The innocent mortgagee

The position of an innocent mortgagee, as assignee to a policy of insurance on a ship, is far from a happy one when a loss occurs which is attributable to the wilful misconduct of the assignor. This was clearly illustrated in the *Ioanna*, case, below.

Graham Joint Stock Shipping Co Ltd v Merchants' Marine Insurance Co, 'Ioanna' (1923) 17 LlL Rep 44 and 241, HL

The plaintiffs (appellants) were mortgagees claiming upon a policy of insurance as assignees to that policy and not as an independently insured party. The steamship *Ioanna* had been deliberately cast away, off the coast of Spain, with the assent and authority of the owners. The mortgagees then sought to recover moneys advanced by them to the owners on the security of *Ioanna* and another vessel.

The House of Lords upheld the decision of the Court of Appeal in ruling that the mortgagees had no independent interest in the policy and, therefore, could not recover under it. (In the report, the judgment of the House of Lords is preceded by a brief summary of the ruling from the Court of Appeal.)

> [p 45] ... The Court of Appeal, reversing this judgment, held (13 LlL Rep 509) that the appellants had no original or independent interest in the policy and that their interest (if any) was derivative from and dependent on that of the owner, so that they were in no better position to recover for the loss than the owner, and insomuch as the owner had intentionally procured the scuttling of the ship, they could not recover at all.
>
> **Lord Chancellor:** [p 242] ... The premium was paid by the owner, and there was no evidence that the appellants [mortgagees] took any part in the transaction of insurance ... and, if so, the appellants were not independently insured.

Notes

The position of the innocent mortgagee as an assignee to the policy of insurance was also considered in *Samuel v Dumas* [1924] 18 LlL Rep 211, HL, where the ship was scuttled and the innocent mortgagee was unable to recover because of the wilful misconduct of the shipowner, the assignor.[8]

This position was further emphasised by the more recent case of *Continental Illinois National Bank and Trust Co of Chicago and Xenophon Maritimes SA v Alliance Assurance Co Ltd, 'Captain Panagos DP'* [1989] 1 Lloyd's Rep 33, CA, where, again, an innocent mortgagee was unable to recover on an assigned policy of insurance because of the wilful misconduct of the shipowner, the assignor.[9]

These cases should be compared with *Alexion Hope* [1988] 1 Lloyd's Rep 311, CA, where the vessel was wilfully set on fire with the connivance of the shipowners and yet an innocent mortgagee successfully recovered on his policy of insurance: the policy was, in fact, a Mortgagee's Interest Policy and was, therefore, an independent contract between the mortgagee and the mortgagee's interest insurer.[10]

Thus, even though a mortgagee may not himself be guilty of any act of wilful misconduct, his claim (suing as an assignee) could nevertheless be tainted by the wilful misconduct of the shipowner (the assignor).

The position of the cargo-owner

With regard to the position of the cargo-owner, it is to be recalled that the defence of wilful misconduct under s 55(2)(a) and cl 4.1 of all the Institute Cargo Clauses relates to the conduct of the assured, namely, the cargo-owner, not of the shipowner. Thus, neither of these provisions is applicable if the cargo-owner himself has not committed any act of wilful misconduct.

The position of a cargo-owner whose goods have been damaged or lost as a result of the wilful misconduct of the shipowner or of any person is governed by cl 4.7, if the goods are insured under the ICC (B) and (C). In the case of an all risks policy under the ICC (A), the legal position is discussed elsewhere.[11]

---

8   See Chapter 9, p 369 and 370.
9   See Chapter 9, p 400.
10 See Chapter 9, p 399.
11 See Chapter 9, p 369 and 370.

Orders for ship's papers

In the days of sailing ships and poor communications, when it was difficult for underwriters to mount defences without adequate information about a loss, the courts were in the habit of making orders for ship's papers and would stay proceedings until all such information was available to the insurer. In the *Sageorge* case, below, the defendant insurers, having refused to pay a claim, then applied for an order for ship's papers and tried to stay proceedings on this basis. The Court of Appeal and, in particular, Lord Denning MR, deliberated at length on this issue.

Probatina Shipping Co Ltd v Sun Insurance Office Ltd, 'Sageorge' [1974] 1 Lloyd's Rep 369, CA

The plaintiff owners of *Sageorge* insured her with the defendant insurers for £75,000. In April 1972, *Sageorge* stranded on a rocky island off Crete and she became a total loss. The owners furnished their insurers with all the relevant documents and charts before pursuing a claim for a loss by perils of the seas. The insurers refused payment and the owners of *Sageorge* issued a writ and delivered their statement of claim. The underwriters did not deliver their defence. Instead, they asked for an order for ship's papers and a stay in the proceedings so that they could prepare their defence on the basis that the ship was scuttled.

The Court of Appeal upheld the decision of the trial judge and ruled that the defendants were already in possession of a large amount of information and a stay in proceedings would be quite wrong.

> **Lord Denning MR:** [p 371] ... The time has now come for the practice to be revised, even in scuttling cases. It should be brought up to date. It arose in the days of sailing ships when underwriters in Lloyd's Coffee House were completely in the dark as to the loss of the vessel. It is not appropriate in the present day when underwriters at Lloyd's get information as soon as anyone of a loss, and of the circumstances in which it occurred.
>
> ... The singular feature about an order for ship's papers is that it is an order on the plaintiff to give discovery of documents before the defendant delivers his defence. This feature should be retained. In scuttling cases, it may still serve a useful purpose. When a shipowner claims on a policy for a loss by perils of the sea, he will be anxious that the underwriters should admit his claim as soon as may be. He will, therefore, or at any rate should, produce all papers that are relevant to his claim; and, in addition, all other papers that the underwriters reasonably ask to see. If he does not do so, but instead goes ahead with his action, it will be open to the defendants to apply for an order for ship's papers before defence. But the order should not be made automatically. The judge should see whether or not it is a proper case for it. For this purpose, counsel should put before the judge the reasons for it. Counsel will not, of course, disclose any material which would be privileged or which it would be inadvisable to mention. But he should give such reasons as he can properly disclose without embarrassment or giving away too much of his client's case.

Notes

For further cases on the defence of the wilful misconduct of the assured, see: *The Dias* [1972] 2 Lloyd's Rep 60, CA; *Compania Martiartu v Royal Exchange Assurance Corporation, 'Arnus'* [1923] 1 KB 650, CA; *The Spathari* (1924) 21 LlL Rep 265; *Anghelatos v Northern Assurance Co, 'Olympia'* (1924) 19 LlL Rep 255, HL; *The Lakeland* (1927) 28 LlL Rep; *Pateras and Others v Royal Exchange Assurance, 'Sappho'* (1934) 49 LlL Rep 400; *Gloria* (1936) 54 LlL Rep 35; *Tropaioforos* [1960] 2 LlL Rep 469; *Vainqueur* [1973] 2 Lloyd's Rep 275; *Michael* [1979] 2 Lloyd's Rep 1, CA; *Zinovia* [1984] 2 Lloyd's Rep 264; *Elfie A Issaias v Marine Insurance Co Ltd* (1923) 15 LlL Rep 186, CA; *Slattery v Mance* [1962] 1 All ER 525; *Captain Panagos DP* [1986] 2 Lloyd's Rep 470; *Alexion Hope* [1988] 1 Lloyd's Rep 311 CA; and *Ikarian Reefer* [1995] 1 Lloyd's Rep 455, CA, all of which are discussed in connection with the question of burden of proof in Chapter 11.

DELAY

Section 55(2)(b) of the Marine Insurance Act 1906 states:

> Unless the policy otherwise provides, the insurer on ship or goods is not liable for any loss proximately caused by delay, although the delay be caused by a peril insured against.

This exclusion is then reiterated in cl 4.5 of all the Institute Cargo Clauses.

The drastic effects of a loss proximately caused by delay were highlighted in the case of *Pink v Fleming*, below.

Pink v Fleming (1890) 25 QBD 396

This was an action upon a policy of marine insurance on goods, namely, a consignment of citrus fruit. The policy included the following memorandum: 'warranted free from particular average, unless the ship be stranded, sunk, or burnt, or unless damage be consequent on collision with any other ship.' The ship carrying the cargo of fruit came into collision with another vessel and, as a result, had to put into port to effect repairs. Whilst in port, in order to carry out these repairs, some of the fruit had to be discharged temporarily. When the ship finally reached its port of destination, some of the fruit was found to have gone bad due to the delay and the extra handling. The cargo-owners claimed on their policy of insurance.

The court ruled that the damage to the fruit was not recoverable under the policy as the damage was too remote to be considered a consequence of the collision.

> **Lord Esher MR:** [p 397] ... In the case of an action for damages on an ordinary contract, the defendant may be liable for damage, of which the breach is an efficient cause or *causa causans*; but, in cases of marine insurance, only the *causa*

proxima can be regarded. This question can only arise where there is a succession of causes, which must have existed in order to produce the result. Where that is the case, according to the law of marine insurance, the last cause only must be looked to and the others rejected, although the result would not have been produced without them ...The collision may be said to have been the cause, and an effective cause, of the ship's putting into port and of repairs being necessary. For the purpose of such repairs, it was necessary to remove the fruit, and such removal necessarily caused damage to it. The agent, however, which proximately caused the damage to the fruit was the handling, though no doubt the cause of the handling was the repairs, and the cause of the repairs was the collision.

Similarly, in *Taylor v Dunbar* **(1869) LR 4 CP 206,** a cargo of pig carcasses, which had become putrid, had to be jettisoned, because the vessel on which they were carried was delayed due to bad weather. The court ruled that the loss was proximately caused by delay and not by a peril of the sea, and the cargo-owner could not recover. Keating J stated:

> [p 210] ... The facts stated in the case show beyond a doubt that the proximate cause of the loss of the meat was the delay in the prosecution of the voyage. That delay was occasioned by tempestuous weather: but no case that I am aware of has held that a loss by the unexpected duration of the voyage, though that be caused by perils of the sea, entitles the assured to recover under a policy like this.

However, in the case of *Schloss Bros v Stevens* **[1906] 2 KB 665**, where goods being delivered to the interior of Colombia were damaged by an inordinate delay of some one and a half years, the loss was held to be recoverable, because the policy of insurance was an 'all risks' policy. Walton J stated:

> [p 673] ... I have read this policy as I think it would be reasonably understood by any merchant or insurance broker, and in doing so I come to the conclusion that the words 'all risks by land and by water', etc, must be read literally as meaning all risks whatsoever. I think they were intended to cover all losses by any accidental cause of any kind occurring during the transit.

Notes

In *Schloss Bros v Stevens*, the assured was able to recover for the loss for three reasons. First, the policy covered 'all risks', to which the court had given a liberal construction, to mean all risks whatsoever. Secondly, the policy in question, unlike the current version of all the Institute Cargo Clauses, did not have a provision (like cl 4.5) expressly excluding a loss proximately caused by delay. Finally, the excessive or extraordinary nature of the delay in this case brought the claim comfortably under the umbrella of the cover for 'risks'.

It is interesting to note that, under s 55(2) and cl 4.5 of all the Institute Cargo Clauses, the excluded loss of delay is not, as in the case of the exclusion for loss or damage caused by leakage (and breakage in s 55(2)) and wear and tear, qualified with the adjective 'ordinary'. Whether there is any significance in this omission has to be considered. It is relevant to note that s 55(2)(b) and cl 4.5 of all the Institute Cargo Clauses do not specify whether ordinary delay or extraordinary delay, or both, are excluded. The pertinent question is: is a loss or damage caused by expected or ordinary delay insured under a policy incorporating the terms of the ICC (A), (B) and (C), each of which has an express clause excluding simply delay? To put the question in another way, is ordinary (or normal) delay an accidental or fortuitous event contemplated by the term 'risks' under the ICC (A), or it is excluded by cl 4.5?

The said exclusion, it is contended, has to be read in its proper context, namely, in the light of the spirit and scope of the policy in which it is found. In the case of the ICC (B) and (C), cl 4.5 has to be read in the light of the fact that, as the policies are for enumerated risks, the exclusion has to be given its wider meaning, excluding any loss or damage proximately caused by both ordinary and extraordinary delay. In the case of the ICC (A), however, the same exclusion has to be given a meaning consistent with the fact that the policy is for all risks, with the emphasis on the word 'risks'. Thus, if the event (the delay) giving rise to the loss is accidental or fortuitous, it would fall within the expression of 'risk'. And if the delay is expected and normal (as in case of ordinary leakage and wear and tear), then it would be difficult to describe it as a 'risk'. It is thus suggested that cl 4.5 be given a 'tampered' interpretation in line with the general framework of the ICC (A); it could be argued that, read in its proper context, only ordinary delay is excluded by cl 4.5 of the ICC (A).

The Institute Time and Voyage Clauses Freight, under the heading of 'Loss of Time', expressly exclude '... claims consequent on loss of time whether arising from a peril of the sea or otherwise'. In this regard, the issue lies in the term 'consequent on', and this is more appropriately discussed in Chapter 8, on the law of causation.[12]

ORDINARY WEAR AND TEAR

Section 55(2)(c) of the Marine Insurance Act 1906 states that:

> Unless the policy otherwise provides, the insurer is not liable for ordinary wear and tear ...

This exclusion is then repeated in cl 4.2 of all the Institute Cargo Clauses. It is to be recalled that, in the *Miss Jay Jay* case, Mustill J provided clarification that damage sustained as a consequence of the ordinary action of the wind and waves was equivalent to ordinary wear and tear.[13]

---

12 See Chapter 8, p 360.
13 See Chapter 9, p 382.

However, a classic example of a loss brought about by ordinary wear and tear was that of the *Wadsworth Lighterage* case, below.

Wadsworth Lighterage and Coaling Co v Sea Insurance Co (1929) 35 Com Cas 1

A 50 year old wooden steam barge sank at her moorings in the Coburg Dock, Liverpool, and the owners claimed upon their insurers for a total loss. The owners based their claim on a clause which stated that: '... this insurance is against the risks of total and/or constructive and/or arranged loss, including ... damage to such vessel by collision ... or by fire, lightning, stranding or sinking.' The underwriters rejected the claim on the basis that the loss was due to ordinary wear and tear.

The Court of Appeal overturned the decision of the trial judge and ruled that the loss was due to ordinary wear and tear, and the clause in the policy did not cover such a loss.

> **Scrutton LJ:** [p 5] ... The learned judge [at the original trial], finding that the sinking of the barge was due to its own inherent weakness, has decided that there is no total loss by perils of the sea though the barge was actually sunk because of the entry of seawater into it. There is no appeal with regard to that; and it seems to me to be in accordance with the law as now laid down in *Samuel v Dumas* that the effect of the entry of seawater into a ship is not in itself a peril of the sea, and in accordance with the provision of s 55(2)(c) of the Marine Insurance Act: 'The insurer is not liable for ordinary wear and tear unless the policy otherwise provides.'
>
> ... and, giving the best consideration I can to the matter, this policy does not seem to otherwise provide; it does not seem to me to provide that the insurer is liable for ordinary wear and tear. It would be very unusual that he should be, and I can find no words which do make him liable for ordinary wear and tear.

In the more recent case of ***Soya GmbH Mainz Kommanditgesellschaft v White* [1982] 1 Lloyd's Rep 136, CA;** [1983] 1 Lloyd's Rep 122, HL, the full facts of which are quoted below, p 442, a claim was made upon soya beans delivered in a deteriorated condition, and the underwriters mounted a defence based on inherent vice and non-disclosure. At the Court of Appeal, Donaldson LJ quoted at length from para 285 of the second edition of *Arnould on Marine Insurance* (1857):

> [p 145] 285. An important limitation on the underwriter's liability is, that he undertakes to indemnify the assured only against loss caused by the direct and violent operation of the perils insured against, and not against the ordinary wear and tear of the voyage.
>
> No ship can navigate the ocean for any length of time, even under the most favourable circumstances, without suffering a certain degree of decay and diminution in value, which is generally comprised under the term wear and tear; for this, however considerable, if it arises merely from the ordinary operation of the usual casualties of the voyage, the underwriter is never liable: he is only liable when the damage sustained is something beyond this, and has

been caused by the direct and violent operation of one of the perils insured against.

In *Prudent Tankers Ltd SA v Dominion Insurance Co Ltd, 'Caribbean Sea'* **[1980] 1 Lloyd's Rep 338**, a tanker foundered in good weather conditions, and the question before the court was whether the loss was covered by the Inchmaree Clause as a latent defect or was simply due to wear and tear. Goff J stated: [p 347] '... However, the balance of authority indicates that, where the defect is attributable to ordinary wear and tear, there can be no recovery under the Inchmaree Clause.'

ORDINARY LEAKAGE AND BREAKAGE

Section 55(2)(c) of the Marine Insurance Act 1906 states:
> Unless the policy otherwise provides, the insurer is not liable for ... ordinary leakage and breakage.

Clause 4.2 of all the Institute Cargo Clauses repeats this exclusion, but only for leakage, not for breakage. The word 'ordinary' limits the exclusion to leakage or breakage which is not exceptional or fortuitous.

Though the following case, *De Monchy v Phoenix Insurance Co of Hartford and Another*, is not directly relevant for the purpose of explaining the scope of exclusion, it is, nevertheless, useful for highlighting the meaning of the expression 'leakage', which was an insured peril in this case. The policy in question had taken advantage of the opening words of the section ('unless the policy otherwise provides') in providing cover for 'leakage from any cause ...'.

In the subsequent case of *Re Traders and General Insurance Association Ltd*, leakage was also an insured risk under the policy, and the issue which the court was concerned with was whether it covered all forms of leakage, or only leakage caused by a peril insured against.

De Monchy v Phoenix Insurance Co of Hartford and Another (1929) 34 LlL Rep 201, HL

The respondents shipped 100 barrels of turpentine aboard *Cape Town Maru*, from Jacksonville, Florida to Rotterdam under a policy of insurance issued by the appellants. On discharging the drums of turpentine at Rotterdam, it was alleged that the quantity of turpentine, 4,992 gallons, was 115 gallons less than that which was loaded at Jacksonville and the respondents claimed for the shortfall on their policy of insurance. The claim was based on a clause in the policy which stated: 'To pay leakage from any cause, in excess of 1%. On each invoice ... conversion of ... kilograms into American gallons shall be made on the basis of 3.25 kg to the gallon.' The insurers refused payment on the ground that the loss was not established as leakage and the loss could be partly explained by contraction; there being a considerable temperature drop between Jacksonville and Rotterdam.

The House of Lords, in upholding the decision of the lower courts, ruled that, according to the discrepancy in the amount of turpentine loaded and the amount discharged, there had been a physical loss and the plaintiffs were entitled to recover under the terms of the policy.

> **Viscount Dunedin:** [p 204] ... Now, under the claim made up as above mentioned, as first put forward, the answer of the underwriters was simple. They said that no leakage could be held as proved which did not leave signs of it on the cask. That at once raises the question of 'What is the meaning of leakage?' Leakage I take to mean any stealthy escape either through a small hole which might be discernible, or through the pores of the material of which the cask is composed. Turpentine has a very great power of penetration. It even penetrates through metal containers, but it evaporates rapidly, and having penetrated, it leaves no sign or external mark. It is clear, therefore, that if the underwriters' view were right, there would be no leakage except when an actual hole was shown in the cask. The provision as to an average leakage and the elaborate provision as to comparing the contents of the casks on arrival with what they had been at starting, all point clearly to the inadmissibility of such a construction. It is not, therefore, surprising that when the case came into court little or nothing was heard of this defence.
>
> **Lord Atkin:** [p 209] ... The defendants' contention originally was that they were not liable to pay unless the cask or other receptacle in which the turpentine insured was carried showed signs of leakage having taken place. This seems to me quite untenable. Turpentine is very volatile, and substantial leakage may take place without any external sign. I think upon the true construction of the clause the parties intended that if there were any gradual escape of the turpentine from the receptacle from any cause other than wilful damage, the insurers were to pay.

Re Traders and General Insurance Association Ltd (1921) 38 TLR 94

This was a claim by the original insurers upon their re-insurers. Under the policy, a consignment of 289 barrels of soya bean oil was shipped to Genoa. The policy covered loss by perils of the sea and also contained a clause which stated: 'To pay average, including the risks of leakage in excess of 2%. Barrel by barrel over trade ullage.' During the voyage, the vessel carrying the consignment of soya bean oil encountered severe weather and, on arrival at Genoa, a Lloyd's surveyor reported that the barrels were old and second hand and that leakage had taken place because the barrels were not strong enough for their purpose. The plaintiffs rejected this report, and stated that, because new barrels absorbed oil, it was desirable to use old barrels which, on this occasion, had been supplied by a reputable company.

The court ruled in favour of the plaintiffs. On the evidence presented, there was good ground for saying that the loss was caused by perils of the seas. Bailhache J was reported to have held that:

> [p 94] ... the main question raised was whether the word 'leakage' must be read as meaning leakage *simpliciter* or only leakage caused by a peril insured against. In his opinion the word in this policy was intended to cover leakage of any kind, whatever might be the cause of it. Leakage caused by a peril insured against would be covered in any event, and it would have been unnecessary to say anything about it. Apart from the question of construction, he thought that on the evidence there was good ground for saying that the loss was caused by perils of the seas, which were perils insured against. The fair inference was that the bad weather started the damage to the barrels, even though their subsequent handling at Genoa might have increased it. The original insurers made such good use of the report of the surveyor at Genoa that they induced the insured to accept a considerable reduction of his claim, and the compromise made by them was clearly reasonable, and the defendants were therefore liable.

But, in the *Dodwell* case, below, where again there were losses brought about by ordinary leakage and breakage, one of the policies contained an express clause making the insurers liable for such a loss.

Dodwell and Co Ltd v British Dominions General Insurance Co Ltd [1955] 2 LIL Rep 391

The plaintiffs insured a consignment of barrels of oil from Hankow to the UK with the defendant underwriters under two policies of marine insurance; part of the consignment was carried aboard one ship, *Glenstrae*, and the remainder aboard another ship, *Protesilaus*. On arrival in the UK, it was found that there had been a considerable loss of the oil due to leakage; in the case of *Glenstrae*, 12%, and in the case of *Protesilaus*, 60%. The plaintiffs claimed on their policies of insurance, but the insurers resisted the claim, mainly on the basis of non-disclosure.

The court ruled, in both cases, for the plaintiffs. Of particular interest were the different provisions, in the two policies of insurance, with regard to leakage, and Bailhache J's interpretation of the clauses.

> **Bailhache J:** [p 391] ... The policy on *Glenstrae* consignment includes risk of leakage irrespective of the fpa clause, and I think [counsel for the defendants] is probably right when he says that that makes the underwriters liable only for the extra leakage due to sea transit, and that in arriving at the amount to be paid in respect of *Glenstrae* consignment I must eliminate from that amount the normal leakage which would have happened to these barrels if there had been no sea transit at all.
>
> ... I should be glad to decide *Protesilaus* case on the same lines, but in that case the defendants, who I understand make out their own policies, have expressed themselves in this way: 'Including risk of leakage from any cause whatever.' This is not a policy submitted by the broker who makes it out, and signed by the defendants by inadvertence; it is their own policy, and they have expressed

themselves in that way. Having expressed themselves in that way, I think they must be bound by their own chosen expression, and 'leakage from any cause whatever' clearly includes all leakage to which these barrels of oil were subjected.

... So far as *Protesilaus* consignment is concerned, they must pay for the whole of the leakage proved, and so far as *Glenstrae* is concerned, only for the difference between 5% and 12%, the actual leakage. There will be judgment on those lines for the plaintiffs with costs.

INHERENT VICE OR NATURE OF THE SUBJECT MATTER INSURED

Section 55(2)(c) of the Marine Insurance Act 1906 states:

Unless the policy otherwise provides, the insurer is not liable for ... inherent vice or nature of the subject matter insured.

Clause 4.4 of all the Institute Cargo Clauses reiterates this exclusion. It is to be noted that, as in the case of leakage and breakage, it is possible to insure against loss or damage caused by inherent vice. In relation to a hull and machinery policy, the term 'latent defect' is the more appropriate and commonly used expression to describe this exclusion.

Noten BV v Paul Charles Harding [1990] 2 Lloyd's Rep 283, CA

The plaintiffs were Dutch importers of commodities which included industrial leather gloves. Four shipments of leather gloves were made, three in 1982 and the fourth in 1983, all from Calcutta. The shipments were insured, all risks, with the defendants and the policies included clauses excluding cover for 'inherent vice or nature of the subject matter insured'. On arrival in Rotterdam, the gloves were found to be wet, stained, mouldy and discoloured and the plaintiffs claimed upon their policies of insurance. The underwriters refused payment.

The Court of Appeal overturned the decision of the trial judge and ruled that the goods had suffered damage because, at the time of shipment, the gloves had contained excessive moisture and thus fell within the excepted peril of inherent vice.

Bingham LJ: [p 288] ... The goods deteriorated as a result of their natural behaviour in the ordinary course of the contemplated voyage, without the intervention of any fortuitous external accident or casualty. The damage was caused because the goods were shipped wet ... There is nothing to suggest that the position of these containers in the stow was unusual. They were, on the evidence, an entirely normal series of shipments for the time of year. There was, on the evidence, no combination of fortuitous events, and the defendant never undertook to insure the plaintiffs against the occurrence of hot and humid weather in Calcutta during the monsoon.

Inherent vice includes insufficient packing

Clause 4.3 of all the Institute Cargo Clauses takes the broad view of insufficiency of pacing when it states:

> Loss damage or expense caused by insufficiency or unsuitability of packing or preparation of the subject matter insured (for the purpose of this Clause 4.3, 'packing' shall be deemed to include stowage in a container or liftvan, but only when such towage is carried out prior to attachment of this insurance or by the Assured or their servants).

Thus, insufficiency of packing is expanded to include unsuitability of the packing and preparation of the subject matter insured as well as bad stowage in a container or liftvan. However, for damage to be excluded by bad stowage, that stowage must have been carried out by the assured or his servants prior to the attachment of the policy.

Berk and Co v Style [1955] 1 QB 180

The plaintiffs had bought a consignment of kieselguhr FOB from Africa to London. On arrival at London, as the cargo was being transferred to barges, a number of the bags burst open. The plaintiffs incurred considerable expenses in rebagging the kieselguhr and claimed for the loss on their policy of insurance which included cover for 'all risks of loss and/or damage from whatsoever cause arising'.

The court ruled that the expense incurred in rebagging the kieselguhr was not recoverable, as the original packaging was inadequate and the loss, therefore, was due to the inherent vice of the subject matter insured.

> **Sellers J:** [p 183] ... In my judgment, the evidence has established, in the language used in marine insurance, 'inherent vice' in the goods insured, and it was this circumstance (that is, the faulty bags) which brought about the special expenditure of and occasioned by the rebagging on the lighter.
>
> [p 184] ... I quote also the oft-quoted words of Lord Sumner [in *British and Foreign Marine Insurance Co Ltd v Gaunt* [1921] 2 AC 41]: 'There are, of course, limits to "all risks". They are risks and risks insured against. Accordingly, the expression does not cover inherent vice or mere wear and tear or British capture. It covers a risk, not a certainty; it is something which happens to the subject matter from without, not the natural behaviour of that subject matter, being what it is, in the circumstances under which it is carried.'

Gee and Garnham Ltd v Whittall [1955] 2 LlL Rep 562

A consignment of kettles shipped from Hamburg to the UK was found dented and/or water stained on arrival.

The court ruled that the denting was caused by inadequate packing and the water staining was caused by the high moisture content of the wood wool packing. The plaintiffs, therefore, were unable to recover, as the damage was attributable to inherent vice.

Sellers J: [p 569] ... In those circumstances, I have come to the conclusion that the claim here of the underwriters that the damage in the bulk of the cases was due to the inadequate packing even before transit started at all has been made out; and, inadequate packing, of course, brings the case under the plea of inherent vice in the goods. So, on the main claim which is brought, I find in favour of the underwriters. That is with regard to the denting.

... The picture I have of the manufacture and of the supply of wood wool and of cases is that it was getting increasingly difficult in Germany, and it may well be that some of the wood wool was not from such seasoned timber; and that, I think, in so far as any staining is concerned, in general accounted for the moisture which affected the kettles through the tissue paper.

... Therefore, on both those grounds generally, the claim has not been brought home against the underwriters ...

Unless the policy otherwise provides

Even a loss caused by inherent vice can be covered by a policy if a suitable clause is incorporated, as was shown in the *Soya* case, below.

Soya GmbH Mainz Kommanditgesellschaft v White [1982] 1 Lloyd's Rep 136, CA; [1983] 1 Lloyd's Rep 122, HL

In June 1973, the plaintiffs bought three shipments of soya beans, CIF from Indonesia. The shipments were insured under an open cover with the defendant underwriters which had been amended to include soya beans for the first time. When the first shipment aboard *Treviotbank* arrived at Antwerp, it was found that the cargo was damaged and surveyors were called in. Because of this, the shippers of the soya beans ensured that the next two shipments from Indonesia were insured under policies of insurance which included additional cover for loss of or damaged caused by 'heat, sweat and spontaneous combustion (HSSC)'. The other two shipments of soya beans duly arrived, and were also found to be in a heated and deteriorated condition. The plaintiffs claimed on their policy of insurance. The underwriters rejected the claim on the basis of non-disclosure in that they had not been provided with all the material facts regarding the condition of the cargo aboard *Treviotbank*.

The House of Lords ruled, amongst other things, that the inclusion of an HSSC clause made the insurers liable for the loss. Lord Diplock expanded at length on the issues of inherent vice, the HSSC clause and the term 'unless the policy otherwise provides'.

Lord Diplock: [p 125] ... The facts, as I have summarised them for the purpose of determining the question of construction of the HSSC policy in the instant case, assume that the loss resulting from the deterioration of the soya beans during the voyage was proximately caused by the 'inherent vice or nature of the subject matter insured'. This phrase (generally shortened to 'inherent vice') where it is used in s 55(2)(c) refers to peril by which a loss is proximately caused; it is not descriptive of the loss itself. It means the risk of deterioration of the goods shipped as a result of their natural behaviour in the ordinary course of the contemplated voyage without the intervention of any fortuitous external accident or casualty. Prima facie, this risk is excluded from a policy of marine insurance unless the policy otherwise provides, either expressly or by necessary implication, and the question of construction for your Lordships is whether the standard HSSC policy does otherwise provide.

... 'Heat', if it stood alone as a descriptive peril, would be equally apt to describe both the heating of the insured cargo from an external source and its becoming hot as a result of some internal chemical, biological or bacterial process taking place in the cargo itself. But 'heat' does not stand alone; it appears in conjunction with two other perils insured against, 'sweat' and 'spontaneous combustion'. 'Sweat' means the exudation of moisture from within the goods which comprise the cargo to their exterior, as a result of something which happens inside the goods; while 'spontaneous combustion' can refer only to a chemical reaction which takes place inside the goods themselves and results in their becoming incandescent or bursting into flames. Referring as they do to something which can only take place inside the goods themselves, these two expressions in their ordinary and natural meaning appear to me to be clearly intended to be descriptive of particular kinds of inherent vice; and 'heat' appearing in immediate conjunction with them is apt to include heating of the cargo as a result of some internal action taking place inside the cargo itself.

... I would, therefore, hold that the standard HSSC policy does 'otherwise provide', so as to displace the prima facie rule of construction laid down in s 55(2)(c) that the insurer is not liable for 'inherent vice or nature of the subject matter insured'. It does so to the extent that such inherent vice consists of a tendency to become hot, to sweat, or to combust spontaneously. To hold otherwise would, in my opinion, be contrary to commercial common sense.

Notes

In *Berk v Style* [1955] 1 QB 180, we are reminded by Sellers J that [p 187] '... if the plaintiffs had wished to insure against inherent vice – if, indeed, they could have done so at any reasonable premium – they should have used specific words to that effect ...'.

With regard to a hull policy, it is to be noted that any expense incurred to repair or replace a specific piece of equipment or machinery found damaged due to a latent defect within itself would not be recoverable. As to what constitutes a latent defect, see *Sipowicz v Wimble and Others*, 'Green Lion' [1974] 1 Lloyd's Rep 593; *Prudent Tankers Ltd SA v Dominion Insurance Co Ltd*, 'Caribbean Sea' [1980] 1 Lloyd's Rep 338; and *Lloyd (JJ) Instruments Ltd v Northern Star Insurance Co Ltd*, 'Miss Jay Jay' [1987] 1 Lloyd's Rep 32, CA.[14]

---

14 These cases are discussed in Chapter 12.

It is, of course, possible to insure against inherent vice or nature of the subject matter insured; but the Inchmaree Clause, cl 6.2.1 of the ITCH(95) and cl 4.2.1 of the IVCH(95), however, only insures against a loss of or damage to the subject matter insured caused by the latent defect, and not the latent defect itself: see *Oceanic Steamship Co v Faber* [1907] 13 Com Cas 28, CA; *Hutchins Brothers v Royal Exchange Assurance Corporation* [1911] 2 KB 398, CA; and *Scindia Steamships Ltd v The London Assurance* [1937] 1 KB 636, which are discussed in depth in Chapter 12.

RATS AND VERMIN

Section 55(2)(c) of the Marine Insurance Act 1906 states that:

> Unless the policy otherwise provides, the insurer is not liable for ... any loss proximately caused by rats or vermin.

All the Institute Cargo Clauses are silent with respect to this exclusion. It is suggested that the ICC (A), an all risks policy, would provide cover for such a loss: such coverage is expressly permitted by the introductory words. Moreover, the ICC (A) do not specifically exclude such a cause of loss.

Hamilton, Fraser and Co v Pandorf and Co (1887) 12 App Cas 518

This was a carriage of goods by sea case, where rats gnawed a hole in a pipe connecting the bathroom with the sea, which resulted in seawater escaping from the pipe and damaging the rice. The question before the court was whether exceptions clauses contained in the charterparty and the bills of lading protected the shipowner from liability. The clause in the bill of lading excepted liability for loss caused by 'the act of God, the Queen's enemies, fire and every other dangers and accidents of the seas, rivers, and steam navigation of whatever nature and kindsoever'.

The House of Lords ruled that the loss fell within the meaning of the exceptions clauses, and the shipowner was not liable. However, Lord Watson commented at length on the meaning of 'loss proximately caused by rats and vermin' in relation to a policy of marine insurance.

> **Lord Watson:** [p 525] ... If the respondents [cargo-owners] were preferring a claim under a contract of marine insurance, expressed in ordinary terms, I should be clearly of opinion that they were entitled to recover, on the ground that their loss was occasioned by a peril of the sea within the meaning of the contract. When a cargo of rice is directly injured by rats, or by the crew of the vessel, the sea has no share in producing the damage, which in that case, is wholly due to a risk not peculiar to the sea, but incidental to the keeping of that class of goods, whether on shore or on board of a voyaging ship. But in the case where rats make a hole, or where one of the crew leaves a port-hole open, through which the sea enters and injures the cargo, the sea is the immediate

cause of the mischief, and it would afford no answer to the claim of the insured to say that, had ordinary precaution been taken to keep down vermin, or had careful hands been employed, the sea would not have been admitted and there would have been no consequent damage.

INSOLVENCY

Under all the Institute Cargo Clauses (cl 4.6), the insurer is not liable for:

... loss damage or expense arising from insolvency or financial default of the owners managers charterers or operators of the vessel ...

Arnould states:[15]

This is a new exclusion, which was not included in previous versions of the Cargo Clauses. It would appear to have the effect of excluding a category of loss formerly covered under the All Risks Clauses, where the detention or sale of the insured property arising from the insolvency of a third party (including, potentially, the shipowners and others whose insolvency or financial default is referred to in the new cl 4.6) was within the scope of the risks covered.

In the light of this exclusion, the ruling in the case of *London and Provincial Leather Process Ltd v Hudson* [1939] 3 All ER 875, and *Integrated Container Service Inc v British Traders Insurance Co Ltd* [1984] 1 Lloyd's Rep 154, CA may no longer be apposite. Nonetheless, the cases are relevant for the purpose of illustrating the effects of insolvency, a risk no longer covered by the ICC (A).

In the former case, the claimant, under an all risks policy of insurance, was able to recover an indemnity when a quantity of skins were lost when the German company processing them became insolvent.

London and Provincial Leather Process Ltd v Hudson [1939] 3 All ER 857

The plaintiffs sent a large number of undressed lamb skins to Germany to be processed. The skins were insured under a Lloyd's all risks policy for the duration of the carriage and, whilst in Germany, against 'all and every risk whatsoever'. The German company, Popper, that was processing the skins became insolvent and part of the consignment of skins fell into the hands of the administrators, who eventually sold them. The other part of the consignment was in the hands of a subcontractor who refused to release them, on account of money being owed by Popper for work done. The plaintiffs claimed on their policy of insurance, but the underwriters refused payment on the ground that there had been no actual loss under the policy.

---

15 Arnould, J, *Law of Marine Insurance and Average*, 16th edn, 1981, London: Sweet & Maxwell, Vol 3, para 227.

The court ruled in favour of the plaintiffs because the insolvency of the German company was of an accidental or fortuitous character.

Goddard LJ: [p 861] ... I am of opinion that there has been a loss under the policy. The policy insures against all and every risk whatsoever, however arising. Counsel for the underwriter has argued that, before a claim can attach on a policy of insurance, there must be a loss of an accidental or fortuitous character, there must be in some form or another a casualty. There is no doubt that that is a general statement of law. The difficulty at times is to find out in these cases what interpretation one has to put upon the words so often used – 'accident or fortuitous casualty'. It is quite clear that the word [referring to 'casualty'] has a wider meaning than something in the nature of an accidental fire or a destruction of the goods by the forces of nature, such as a flood or hurricane; because it cannot be denied that theft of the goods would be a loss coming within the policy, and that theft is a conscious and wilful act of another person. There is nothing fortuitous and nothing accidental about that. It is accidental and fortuitous in a sense that the assured is deprived by some unexpected acts of his property in the goods or of his possession of the goods. The same is true with regard to embezzlement by an agent.

... Undoubtedly, the goods were lost to the plaintiffs by a happening not analogous to theft, but just as much unexpected, if that is a test to apply, as a theft. I think the circumstances show that the loss fairly falls within the expressions 'a fortuitous occurrence', 'accidental loss' or 'casualty' in the sense, as I have explained earlier in this judgment, in which they have been used in so many insurance cases.

But it was a claim under sue and labour which solved the problem of insolvency in the case below.

Integrated Container Service Inc v British Traders Insurance Co Ltd [1984] 1 Lloyd's Rep 154, CA

The plaintiffs entered into a leasing agreement with Oyama Shipping Co Ltd, whereby Oyama leased 1,016 containers from the plaintiffs for use in the Far East. Part of the agreement was that Oyama would ensure that the containers were insured. In 1975, Oyama ceased trading because of insolvency, and their policy of insurance on the containers lapsed. The plaintiffs then incurred considerable expenses in recovering their containers and claimed on their own all risks policy of insurance. The plaintiffs' insurers settled in principle for any containers actually lost or damaged, but refused payment for the recovery costs of the other containers, as such costs had only been incurred as a commercial undertaking to retrieve items from a bankrupt hirer.

The Court of Appeal ruled that the plaintiffs could recover their expenses as sue and labour, as this expenditure had been properly incurred to avert a loss caused by an insured peril.

Eveleigh LJ: [p 157] ... The plaintiffs had let on hire their containers to a company that was trading effectively and was in a position to maintain the necessary organisation to look after the containers and perform the duties imposed upon them in their capacity as bailees. When, as a result of their insolvency, they ceased to operate, they were no longer bailees capable of taking care of the goods. The containers were effectively abandoned by their custodians. They were consequently exposed to the risk of theft, misuse, enforcement of a lien – in other words, to the risk of loss or damage from some cause or another. We are concerned with a policy which covers all risks. Therefore, if the plaintiffs have established the existence of a threat of loss or damage, no matter if that threat resulted from the insolvency of the lessee, they are entitled to recover moneys laid out to avert a loss which might result from a variety of reasons.

DELIBERATE DAMAGE

Clause 4.7 of the Institute Cargo Clauses (B) and (C) exclude the insurer from:
> ... deliberate damage to or deliberate destruction of the subject matter insured or any part thereof by the wrongful act of any person or persons.

This exclusion is of some significance, as it would exclude loss or damage caused by arson. Ordinarily, under insurance law, recovery for loss or damage caused by fire has not been precluded, even when the fire was started deliberately; the peril of fire requiring no element of fortuity. Further, the words 'any person or persons' are wide enough to include the carrier, the shipowner and the master or crew.

A cargo-owner is not covered for deliberate damage under the ICC (B) or (C). Should he wish to be so covered, he has the option of either taking up the ICC (A) or seek this additional cover under the Institute Malicious Damage Clause, which states:[16]

> In consideration of an additional premium, it is hereby agreed that the exclusion 'deliberate damage to or deliberate destruction of the subject matter insured or any part thereof by the wrongful act of any person or persons' is deemed to be deleted and further, that this insurance cover loss or damage to the subject matter insured caused by malicious acts, vandalism or sabotage, subject always to the other exclusions contained in this insurance.

References and further reading

Mustill, MJ (Sir), 'Fault and marine loss' [1988] LMCLQ 310.

Salter, RJ, 'Wilful misconduct of the assured' [1985] LMCLQ 415

---

16   See Appendix 17.

CHAPTER 11

BURDEN AND STANDARD OF PROOF

INTRODUCTION

Burden of proof is the duty incumbent on a litigant to prove to the court the fact or facts supporting the claim at issue. First, there is the burden on the plaintiff to tender evidence in support of the claim he has put forward. Secondly, there is the persuasive burden, the onus of convincing the court on the facts at issue: this remains constant throughout the trial with any litigant on whom the burden of proof lies, be he plaintiff or defendant.

Whenever a loss or damage occurs under a policy of marine insurance, and a claim is pursued, there falls upon the claimant the duty of presenting evidence to the court to substantiate his claim that the proximate cause of that loss or damage was an insured risk. In so doing, the claimant, who could be a shipowner, cargo-owner, mortgagee or any other interested party, must establish a *prima facie* case to show that the loss or damage was, in fact, caused by the specified peril or perils insured against, and it is only then that the defendant insurer is compelled to offer a defence to counter that claim. Until a *prima facie* case is established by the claimant, the defendant simply refutes the claim on the basis that there is no case to answer.

The subject of burden of proof is necessarily related to the device of presumptions which the common law has, over the years, framed to assist a party in his evidential burden of proof. In the law of marine insurance, the nature and scope of the presumptions of proof of loss by an unascertainable peril of the seas and of unseaworthiness are of particular relevance. Further examples of presumptions are: 'A ship never heard of is presumed to have foundered at sea'; and the statutory presumption, under s 58 of the Act, that a ship missing after a reasonable time with no news of her may be presumed an actual total loss. When and how these presumptions apply will be discussed.

Typically, a claimant may try to establish a *prima facie* case to show that a loss was caused by a peril of the seas, barratry and/or fire, and once that *prima facie* case has been established, the defendant insurer may endeavour to counter that claim either with a simple denial challenging the truth of the plaintiff's account of the cause of loss, or with an affirmative allegation that the loss was caused by the wilful misconduct of the assured.

It is fair to say that, as a general rule, to succeed in a claim for a loss by any insured peril, the burden of proof rests with the claimant to prove that the loss was so caused. However, as will be seen, the law on the burden and standard of proof is rendered that much more contrived and complex by reason of the fact that perils of the seas, barratry and fire each has its own 'ingredients', which would obviously have to be proved by the plaintiff. The plaintiff's burden of proof is thus governed by the inherent characteristics of the peril on which he has chosen to base his claim.

In a claim based on 'perils of the seas' as the proximate cause of loss, the element of fortuity[1] dictates that the plaintiff has to prove that the loss was accidental. And, in the case of fire, neither fortuity nor complicity are essential requirements; this means that the plaintiff does not have to prove that the fire was accidentally caused, nor does he have to prove the absence of complicity. Barratry, on the other hand, is not fortuitous, but contains the element of complicity, namely, that the assured himself did not connive or consent to the barratrous act.

When perils of the seas is pleaded as the proximate cause of loss, the basis of the plaintiff rests critically on the element of fortuity which must be proved to the satisfaction of the court. This means that, to displace the plaintiff's *prima facie* case, the defendant has to adduce evidence sufficient to cast doubts in the mind of the judge that the loss was not fortuitous. Regardless of the nature of the defence, the burden of proof rests throughout with the plaintiff to prove his case on the balance of probabilities, and though wilful misconduct may have been raised, the defendant is clearly not required to offer affirmative (or conclusive) proof that the loss was so caused, neither is he obliged to provide proof even on the balance of probabilities. If, at the end of the day, the court is doubtful or uncertain as to the cause of loss, the plaintiff's action must fail.

In relation to a claim based on fire, the burden of proof thrown upon the plaintiff is considerably lighter. His case is established simply by proof of loss by fire, and, as he is neither required to prove fortuity nor complicity, the burden of proof for the defence of wilful misconduct must surely rest with his opponent. And, according to case law, this has to be proved to a high degree of proof which, though not quite the criminal standard, must match the gravity of the charge.

When wilful misconduct is pleaded in response to a claim based on barratry, the legal position as regards both the burden and standard of proof is less straightforward. Problems have arisen because of the nature of the peril of barratry, which, by definition, envelops the essential element of complicity or, more accurately, the absence of complicity.[2] Two issues arise: first, is the burden on the plaintiff to prove the absence of complicity or on the defendant to prove complicity? Secondly, should the standard of proof for the defendant be higher (the criminal standard) so as to reflect the seriousness of the charge? These rather controversial issues are highlighted in the case extracts.

---

1   Spelt out as an essential requirement in the Rules for Construction, r 7.
2   On the law of barratry, see Chapter 12, p 509.

PROOF OF LOSS BY PERILS OF THE SEAS

The plaintiff's burden of proof

Whenever a claim is pursued for loss under the head of perils of the seas, it falls upon the claimant to show, on the balance of probabilities, that that loss was proximately caused by that peril.

Compania Naviera Santi SA v Indemnity Marine Insurance Co Ltd, 'Tropaioforos' [1960] 2 Lloyd's Rep 469

On 1 December 1957, over a period of five hours, the steamship *Tropaioforos* sank in the Bay of Bengal, in calm weather conditions. The plaintiff owners of the vessel claimed that the loss was due to perils of the seas, in that *Tropaioforos* struck an unknown submerged object which caused sufficient underwater damage to allow her to be sunk by the resulting inrush of seawater. The underwriters refused to pay, and alleged that *Tropaioforos* had been scuttled with the connivance of the owners.

The court ruled that the plaintiff owners of *Tropaioforos* had failed to prove that there had been an accidental loss due to perils of the seas. The insurers' theory of scuttling provided the only explanation for the loss and, therefore, the plaintiffs could not recover under the policy. The court considered the issue of burden of proof.

> **Pearson J:** [p 473] ... As to the burden of proof, the whole question has been reserved in the House of Lords; but, subject to that reservation, it has been established by decisions of the courts of first instance and the Court of Appeal (with some support from dicta in the House of Lords) that the plaintiffs have the burden of proving, in a case such as this, that there was an accidental loss by perils of the seas, although the degree of proof required is only to show a balance of probabilities in favour of an accidental loss by perils of the seas ...

Michalos (N) and Sons Maritime SA v Prudential Assurance Co Ltd, 'Zinovia' [1984] 2 Lloyd's Rep 264

The vessel *Zinovia* ran aground in shallows in the Gulf of Suez and sustained such damage that she was a constructive total loss. The owners claimed on their policy of insurance for a loss caused by perils of the seas, but the insurers alleged that the vessel had been scuttled with the connivance of the owners.

The court ruled that the owners had succeeded in showing that the loss of *Zinovia* was proximately caused by a peril of the sea. The insurers (and cargo-owner) had not satisfied the court (on the high standard of proof required), that the vessel had been deliberately cast away.

> **Bingham J:** [p 271] ... To succeed in their claim for a loss by perils of the sea, the owners must prove that the loss of the vessel was proximately caused by such a peril. There is no doubt that the stranding of the vessel, followed by its

bumping on the bottom, may be a peril of the sea, even though the stranding was the product of negligent navigation ... It is otherwise if the stranding was the result of navigation deliberately calculated to achieve that result, both because the cause of the loss would not, in that event, be fortuitous as any peril of the sea must necessarily be, and also by virtue of s 55(2)(a) of the Marine Insurance Act 1906. But the owners here have this to help them, that the stranding which caused the loss (if fortuitous) was a peril of the sea, and thus the case may be contrasted with cases where a vessel is lost as a result of an ingress of water, when it is necessary to identify the cause of the ingress in order to decide whether that cause was a peril of the sea ... Nonetheless, if, at the end of the case, the court considers loss by perils of the sea to be no more probable than a loss caused by another, uninsured peril, then the owners must fail.

In the *Gloria* case, below, Branson J clarified the position of both parties with regard to the onus of proof when a loss by a peril of the sea is pursued.

Compania Naviera Vascongada v British and Foreign Marine Insurance Co Ltd, 'Gloria' (1934) 54 LlL Rep 35

The plaintiffs insured *Gloria* with the defendants under a time policy of insurance. On a voyage from Larne to Port Talbot, *Gloria* sprang a leak and sank. The plaintiffs claimed that the loss was due to perils of the seas in that *Gloria* had sustained damage whilst leaving Larne and that this, together with the heavy weather experienced during the voyage, had caused the loss. The underwriters rejected the claim citing, *inter alia*, unseaworthiness as the cause of loss.

The court found for the plaintiffs, as they had discharged their onus of showing that the loss was fortuitous, but the defendants, when alleging that *Gloria* had put to sea in an unseaworthy state, had failed to show that there had been privity on the part of the assured.

> **Branson J:** [p 50] ... The law is, in my opinion, clear. The onus of proof that the loss was fortuitous lies upon the plaintiffs, but that does not mean that they will fail if their evidence does not exclude all reasonable possibility that the ship was scuttled. Before that possibility is considered, some evidence in support of it must be forthcoming. Scuttling is a crime, and the court will not find that it has been committed unless it is proved with the same degree of certainty as is required for the proof of a crime. If, however, the evidence is such that the court, giving full weight to the consideration that scuttling is a crime, is not satisfied that the ship was scuttled, but finds that the probability that she was is equal to the probability that her loss was fortuitous, the plaintiffs will fail. With regard to unseaworthiness, on the other hand, the onus is upon the defendants to show that the vessel was unseaworthy when she left Larne – which was her last port – and that the plaintiffs were privy to the fact that she was unseaworthy then.

In the following case, *Popi M*, the House of Lords confirmed that, when a claim is made for a loss by perils of the seas, the burden of proof remains with the plaintiff throughout. That is, even after establishing a *prima facie* case that the loss was by a peril of the sea, the onus of continuing to prove his case, whether or not there is evidence to the contrary put forward by the defence, remains with the plaintiff.

Rhesa Shipping Co SA v Edmunds, 'Popi M' [1985] 2 Lloyd's Rep 1, HL

Popi M was on a voyage from Rouen to the Yemen, and was insured under a time policy of insurance with the defendants and a number of other insurers. When she was steaming through the Mediterranean, off the coast of Algeria and in good weather, the shell plating in the vicinity of the engine room sprang apart, and a large volume of water entered the vessel. The crew abandoned ship and, later that day, *Popi M* sank. The owners claimed on their policy of insurance for a loss by perils of the seas, alternatively, negligence of the crew, but the underwriters refused payment, on the basis that the loss was due to wear and tear.

The House of Lords, in overturning the decisions of both the lower courts, ruled that the reason for the loss of *Popi M* remained in doubt and, therefore, the plaintiffs had failed to discharge the burden of proof which was upon them. The lower courts had not been justified in inferring that the loss had been due to perils of the seas.

> **Brandon LJ:** [p 2] ... In approaching this question, it is important that two matters should be borne constantly in mind. The first matter is that the burden of proving, on the balance of probabilities, that the ship was lost by perils of the sea is, and remains throughout, on the shipowners. Although it is open to underwriters to suggest and seek to prove some other cause of loss, against which the ship was not insured, there is no obligation on them to do so. Moreover, if they choose to do so, there is no obligation on them to prove, even on a balance of probabilities, the truth of their alternative case.
>
> The second matter is that it is always open to a court, even after the kind of prolonged inquiry with a mass of expert evidence which took place in this case, to conclude, at the end of the day, that the proximate cause of the ship's loss, even on a balance of probabilities, remains in doubt, with the consequence that the shipowners have failed to discharge the burden of proof which lay upon them.

Lamb Head Shipping Co Ltd and Others v Jennings, 'Marel' [1992] 1 Lloyd's Rep 403

Marel was lost off the coast of Algeria as a result of the sudden incursion of seawater into the engine room.

At the court of first instance, Judge Diamond QC, citing a number of previous cases, including *Popi M*, as authority, said:

Judge Diamond QC: [p 405] ... First, the burden of proving, on a balance of probabilities, that a ship was lost by perils of the sea is, and remains throughout, on the owners. Whether or not underwriters seek to prove an alternative cause of the loss, if 'an examination of all the evidence leaves the court doubtful what is the real cause of the loss, the assured has failed to prove his case': *La Compania Naviera Martiartu v The Corporation of the Royal Exchange Assurance , 'Arnus'* (1922) 13 LlL Rep 298, p 304, col 2; [1923] 1 KB 650, p 657, *per* Scrutton LJ; *Rhesa Shipping Co SA v Herbert David Edmunds, 'Popi M'* [1985] 1 Lloyd's Rep 1, p 3, col 1; [1985] 1 WLR 948, p 951, *per* Lord Brandon of Oakbrook, giving the leading speech in the House of Lords, with which all the other of their Lordships agreed.

Secondly, it is not sufficient for the owners, in order to discharge the burden of proof which rests on them, merely to prove the incursion of seawater into an insured vessel. This is because an entry of seawater is not in itself a peril of the sea; *Samuel and Co v Dumas* (1924) 18 LlL Rep 211; [1924] AC 431; *Popi M* [1985] 1 Lloyd's Rep 1. That incursion has to be shown to be accidental or fortuitous. If the owners are to discharge successfully the burden of proof which rests on them, it will be necessary for them 'to condescend to particularity in the matter': *Popi M* [1985] 1 Lloyd's Rep 1, p 5, col 1; p 954 A–B.

The third alternative

In the *Popi M* case, the facts of which are cited above, the plaintiff had, at the end of the hearing, failed to persuade the court that, on the balance of probabilities, the loss had been caused by an insured peril. Obviously, whilst doubt remained about the reason for the loss, the court could not find in favour of the plaintiff. Indeed, as the court could not find directly for either party on the facts as presented, it had no choice but to employ a rule, known as the third alternative, to dismiss the plaintiff's claim.

The House of Lords, in overturning the decisions of both the lower courts, ruled that the reason for the loss of *Popi M* remained in doubt and, therefore, the plaintiffs had failed to discharge the burden of proof which was upon them. The lower courts had not been justified in inferring that the loss had been due to perils of the seas. Brandon LJ considered at length the whole issue of burden of proof and the 'third alternative'. In so doing, he invoked Sherlock Holmes and Homer to make his point to good effect.

Brandon LJ: [House of Lords, p 6] ... My Lords, the late Sir Arthur Conan Doyle in his book, *The Sign of Four*, describes his hero, Mr Sherlock Holmes, as saying to the latter's friend, Dr Watson: 'How often have I said to you that, when you have eliminated the impossible, whatever remains, however improbable, must be the truth?' It is, no doubt, on the basis of this well known, but unjudicial, dictum that Bingham J decided to accept the shipowners' theory, even though he regarded it, for seven cogent reasons, as extremely improbable.

In my view, there are three reasons why it is inappropriate to apply the *dictum* of Mr Sherlock Holmes, to which I have just referred, to the process of fact finding which a judge of first instance has to perform at the conclusion of a case of the kind here concerned.

The first reason is one which I have already sought to emphasise as being of great importance, namely, that the judge is not bound always to make a finding one way or the other with regard to the facts averred by the parties. He has open to him the third alternative, of saying that the party on whom the burden of proof lies in relation to any averment made by him has failed to discharge that burden. No judge likes to decide cases on burden of proof if he can legitimately avoid having to do so. There are cases, however, in which, owing to the unsatisfactory state of the evidence or otherwise, deciding on the burden of proof is the only just course for him to take.

[p 7] ... Having regard to the way in which Bingham J expressed the view that he was compelled to choose between the shipowners' submarine theory on the one hand and the underwriters' wear and tear theory on the other, and having regard further to the fact that, when he neared the point of decision in his judgment, he did not discuss or consider the third possibility which was open to him, of simply finding the shipowners' case not proved, I am driven, reluctantly but inescapably, to the conclusion that, on this occasion, even Homer nodded.

... In my opinion, the only inference which could justifiably be drawn from the primary facts found by Bingham J was that the true reason of the ship's loss was in doubt, and it follows that I consider that neither Bingham J nor the Court of Appeal were justified in drawing the inference that there had been a loss by perils of the sea, whether in the form of collision with a submerged submarine or any other form.

Presumption of loss by an unascertainable peril of the seas

When a claimant is unable to present direct evidence showing the precise nature or event of the cause of a loss, such as in the case of a missing ship or when the loss is inexplicable, he may seek the assistance of the court with the request that a presumption of a loss by an unascertainable peril of the seas be drawn in his favour. This plea, if granted, will allow the claimant to present his evidence by way of inference to signify the cause or reason for that loss. But, before a presumption of loss by an unascertainable peril of the sea is allowed, the court has to be satisfied that certain conditions are fulfilled, namely, that the ship was seaworthy when she set sail, and that an uninsured peril did not cause the loss. The purpose of this is to eliminate from the inquiry causes of loss, including unseaworthiness, that are not covered by the policy. It will facilitate the court to make the deduction that, as causes of loss which are not insured have been discounted, the loss must have been caused by an unascertainable peril of the seas.

Compania Martiartu v Royal Exchange Assurance Corporation, 'Arnus' [1923] 1 KB 650, CA; aff'd [1924] AC 850, HL

The plaintiffs were the owners of the steamship *Arnus*, which was insured with the defendants under a time policy of insurance. On a voyage from northern Spain to Rotterdam with a cargo of iron ore, and in calm weather, *Arnus* sank, due, it was contended, to her striking a floating mass of wreckage. The underwriters rejected the claim, alleging that *Arnus* had been deliberately sunk with the connivance of the owners.

The Court of Appeal overruled the decision of the trial judge and held that *Arnus* had been deliberately scuttled with the connivance of the responsible managers of the company. The House of Lords later affirmed that decision. At the Court of Appeal, Bankes LJ considered the issue of presumption of loss by an unascertained peril.

> **Bankes LJ:** [p 655] ... If the assured makes out a *prima facie* case, as the respondents in the present case did, then unless the underwriters displace that prime facie case, the assured is no doubt entitled to rely upon the presumption. On the other hand, if the *prima facie* case, which was the foundation on which the presumption was rested, fails because the underwriters put forward a reasonable explanation of the loss, the superstructure falls with it.

Skandia Insurance Co Ltd v Skoljarev [1979] 142 CLR 375, High Court of Australia

This was a case of a loss of a fishing vessel which sank in calm seas after there was a sudden inrush of seawater into the engine room. The inference sought was that, whatever the cause of the sudden ingress of water, it should be taken as a 'fortuitous accident or casualty of the seas'.

The High Court of Australia ruled that the loss was due to a peril of the seas.

> **Mason J:** [p 390] ... The effect of these decisions [in previous cases] is that it is for the insured to prove a loss by perils of the sea. He will discharge this burden of proof if he gives evidence of a sinking as a result of a fortuitous event. If, in addition to this, there is also evidence of unseaworthiness, the question of what caused the loss must be decided as a question of fact. In speaking of the cause of loss, I refer to the proximate cause of loss (see s 61). It is for this reason that the loss of an unseaworthy ship may be attributed to the perils of the sea.
>
> Although there is nothing in all this to throw the burden of proof of seaworthiness onto the insured, there is one class of case in which the insured will find it necessary to establish seaworthiness in order to prove his case. This is where the insured, having no direct evidence of loss due to a fortuitous event, seeks to establish by inference a case of loss due to an unascertained peril of the sea. To justify this inference, he will seek to exclude the possibility of loss caused by unseaworthiness by calling evidence as to the condition of the ship. In such a case, once evidence is given of seaworthiness, the issue of causation must be decided as a question of fact. Then, the tribunal of fact,

unless it is satisfied that the ship was seaworthy, cannot draw the inference upon which the insured depends in order to make out his case.

[p 393] ... This presumption, or inference as I should prefer to call it, arises from the fact that the immediate cause of the loss is the foundering of the ship and, if that is not due to unseaworthiness at the inception of the voyage, it is difficult to perceive how the foundering could have been caused otherwise than by a fortuitous and unascertained accident of the seas, or perhaps a latent defect. The extensive concept of 'perils of the sea' is an important element in the existence of the presumption.

Elimination of unseaworthiness as a cause of loss

Generally, when unseaworthiness is raised as a defence against a loss by perils of the seas, it falls upon the insurer to prove that the loss was so caused. However, this general rule may be displaced in certain circumstances. When, for example, a vessel is lost in good weather conditions or shortly after sailing, and the plaintiff is unable to show that that loss was caused by a peril insured against, the presumption is raised that the vessel must have sailed in an unseaworthy condition. This effectively shifts the burden of proof to the plaintiff, who must then rebut this presumption of unseaworthiness by adducing evidence to the contrary.

The circumstances under which the presumption of unseaworthiness may be levied against the plaintiff (which he must rebut) were considered in depth in the cases cited below. These cases also illustrate the courses of action available to the plaintiff: he could rest his case on the premise that the circumstances of the case do not justify the drawing of the presumption of unseaworthiness, or rebut the presumption by adducing evidence to prove that his ship was seaworthy when she set sail.

Pickup v Thames and Mersey Marine Insurance Co Ltd (1878) 3 QBD 594, CA

This was an action, on a voyage policy of insurance, for the recovery of freight on a cargo of rice shipped aboard *Diadem* on a voyage from Rangoon to the UK. Eleven days after leaving Rangoon, *Diadem* encountered heavy weather and, such was the concern for her safety after taking in water, the master decided to put back into Rangoon. During the passage back up the Rangoon River, *Diadem* grounded, but was soon refloated. On arrival back in Rangoon, *Diadem* was pronounced unseaworthy. The question before the Court of Appeal was whether the bad weather had caused her leaky condition or whether, at the outset, she had sailed in an unseaworthy condition.

The Court of Appeal decided that there had been a misdirection at the trial and that there should be a new trial. At the trial itself, the jury had been misdirected when they were told that the time which elapsed between sailing from Rangoon and when it had to put back into Rangoon was short enough to create a presumption of unseaworthiness, which then shifted the burden of proving seaworthiness upon the plaintiffs. This was erroneous, in that it gave the jury the impression that the defendant insurers were relieved from proving unseaworthiness, when the weather conditions might also be responsible for the loss. The presumption of unseaworthiness, it would appear, may only be drawn when two conditions are satisfied, namely, that the weather cannot possibly account for the loss and the said period of time is short.

Brett LJ: [p 599] ... A good deal has been said on the argument about 'the burden of proof' and 'presumption'. The burden of proof upon a plea of unseaworthiness to an action on a policy of marine insurance lies upon the defendant, and so far as the pleadings go, it never shifts, it always remains upon him. But when facts are given in evidence, it is often said certain presumptions, which are really inferences of fact, arise, and cause the burden of proof to shift; and so they do as a matter of reasoning, and, as a matter of fact, for instance, where a ship sails from a port, and soon after she has sailed, sinks to the bottom of the sea, and there is nothing in the weather to account for such a disaster, it is a reasonable presumption to be made that she was unseaworthy when she started ... But the question 'What is a short time after sailing?' surely depends on the circumstances; and it is for the jury to say whether under the circumstances of the voyage they think that the time of loss was so soon after sailing that it raises the presumption of unseaworthiness.

Thesiger LJ: [p 603] ... That being so, what is the direction he [the trial judge] gives them? He tells them, perfectly correctly, that upon the issue of seaworthiness, the burden of proof rested upon the underwriters originally. But then he proceeds to tell them that, only 11 days having elapsed since the vessel left Rangoon, and between that time and the time of her return to Rangoon, the burden of proof which originally lay upon the underwriters had shifted, and the burden was thrown upon the plaintiff of showing that the loss of the vessel was due to the causes which had arisen subsequently to her sailing. The meaning of that was obviously this, that the jury must, from the short time that elapsed after her voyage commenced, presume *prima facie* that, instead of the vessel being seaworthy, as they would have presumed without any evidence, they must presume that she was unseaworthy at the commencement, unless such evidence was given on the part of the plaintiff as to satisfy them that the loss was not due to unseaworthiness, but due to perils insured against. Therefore, it appears to me that, although the words 'as a matter of law' may have been used, what the learned judge really intended to say was, that the burden in point of fact had been shifted. But even in this point of view, it seems to me that the learned judge misdirected the jury, and that there was nothing to show or to justify him in saying that the burden of proof, as a matter of fact, had shifted, because at the very same time that it was proved that a short time had elapsed since the vessel had started, it was also proved that there was weather which might possibly account for the loss which took place. Therefore, upon the question of seaworthiness, it seems to me that there was a clear misdirection.

In the following case, *Anderson v Morice*, at the trial at the Court of Common Pleas, Brett J suggested that when a ship sinks in smooth water without any apparent cause, and in the absence of any evidence to the contrary, an irresistible presumption of unseaworthiness would be raised.

Anderson v Morice (1874) LR 10 CP 58; (1876) 1 App Cas 713, HL

The plaintiff, a merchant in London, entered into a contract to purchase a cargo of Rangoon rice, and the seller's agents chartered the vessel *Sunbeam* to carry the cargo. Accordingly, the plaintiff insured the cargo with the defendants under a voyage policy 'at and from' Rangoon to any port in the UK or the Continent. *Sunbeam* duly arrived in the Rangoon River and, after anchoring, commenced loading the cargo of rice from lighters moored alongside. When 8,878 bags of the rice had been loaded, 400 bags still remaining in the lighters, *Sunbeam* suffered a sudden inrush of water aft, with the result that she sank, and all the cargo on board was lost. The plaintiff claimed for a loss caused by a peril of the sea, but the insurers refused payment, citing both unseaworthiness and lack of insurable interest.

The House of Lords, on the question of unseaworthiness, affirmed the findings of the lower courts, that the loss was due to a peril of the sea.[3] There was considerable evidence to show that *Sunbeam* had been well maintained and well run and was, therefore, seaworthy. At the Court of Common Pleas, Brett J was of a mind that the manner of the loss raised a presumption of unseaworthiness.

> **Brett J:** [p 67] ... Dealing, first, with the questions raised as to seaworthiness and loss by a peril insured against, we think that, where the only evidence of fact as to either of those questions is, that the ship sank in smooth water very soon after the attaching of the policy, the significance of such a fact cannot be displaced by mere opinion founded on mere conjecture. We think that the true significance of such evidence is to be termed a presumption, and a shifting of the burden of proof; and that, where such a fact is the only fact in evidence, there being no other evidence as to the condition of the ship, or as to a cause of loss, it is evidence on which a jury ought to find, and should therefore be directed to find, if they believe the evidence, that the ship was unseaworthy at the inception of the risk. But, where there is other evidence of the condition of the ship, or of a cause of the loss, then the fact of the ship sinking in smooth water becomes one of several facts which must all be left to the jury. If from other facts – such as a large amount of repairs recently done, careful surveys recently made, excellent conduct of the ship up to a time immediately preceding the loss, or otherwise – a jury conclude that the ship was seaworthy at the inception of the risk, then the jury may further find that the loss was

---

3 On the issue of insurable interest, the House of Lords, being equally divided, affirmed the decision of the Exchequer Chamber on the basis that, as only part of the cargo had been loaded, risk did not pass to the plaintiffs, and, therefore, they did not have an insurable interest in the goods they had contracted to purchase. For a fuller discussion of this case in relation to the subject of insurable interest, see Chapter 2, p 51.

occasioned by a peril insured against, though they are unable to ascertain or safely conjecture what it was which caused the ship to sink. The immediate visible cause of the loss in such a case is the foundering of the ship. If that was not the result of unseaworthiness existing at the inception of the risk, it is difficult to see, upon the assumption, which is that there is no other evidence as to the loss than the fact of the foundering of the ship, how that could have been caused by anything but some extraordinary, though invisible and unascertained, accident of the seas.

In the *Ajum Goolam* case, cited below, the plaintiffs again succeeded in rebutting the presumption of unseaworthiness, and the defendant underwriters failed to show that the ship had sailed in an unseaworthy condition.

Ajum Goolam Hossen and Co v Union Marine Insurance Co [1901] AC 362, PC

This was an appeal in the form of a consolidated action, brought by cargo-owners to recover for a loss sustained, against their insurers. The shipowners were also made a party to the action, as interveners, on the basis that they were liable for breach of contract, on their bills of lading, should unseaworthiness be proved. The insured cargo consisted of a consignment of 7,059 bags of sugar loaded aboard the steamship *Taif* in Port Louis, Mauritius, bound for Bombay. *Taif* loaded a full cargo of nearly 21,000 bags of sugar, as she had done on previous voyages, but, prior to sailing, the pilot raised concerns about her excessive draught aft and the fact that she was listing to port. The master ordered the aft ballast tank to be pumped out to reduce the trim by the stern. Soon after sailing, having dispensed with the pilot's services, the aft ballast tank was refilled to steady the ship in a confused sea. During the night, because the list to port had increased, the ship's course was altered, and the aft ballast tank was again pumped out. Some two hours later, the list increased dramatically and *Taif* eventually rolled over and was lost.

The Privy Council allowed the appeal and decided that the evidence produced by the plaintiffs had rebutted the presumption of unseaworthiness and, thus, the underwriters had failed in their defence to prove unseaworthiness at the time of the sailing. The loss appeared to have been attributable to the mismanagement of the vessel after she had sailed, rather than to unseaworthiness before she sailed.

Lord Lindley: [p 366] ... The underwriters have the great advantage of the undoubted fact that the vessel capsized and sank in less than 24 hours after leaving port without having encountered any storm of any other known cause sufficient to account for the catastrophe; and there is no doubt that if nothing more were known, they would be entitled to succeed in the action. If nothing more were known, unseaworthiness at the time of sailing would be the natural inference to draw; there would be a presumption of unseaworthiness which a jury ought to be directed to act upon, and which a court ought to act upon if unassisted by a jury. But if, as in this case, other facts material to this inquiry as to the seaworthiness of the ship are proved, those facts must also be considered; and they must be weighed against the unaccountable loss of the ship so soon after sailing, and unless the balance of the evidence warrants the conclusion that the ship was unseaworthy when she sailed, such unseaworthiness cannot be properly treated as established, and the defence founded upon it must fail. The law on this point was finally settled in *Pickup v Thames and Mersey Marine Insurance Co*, which followed *Anderson v Morice*. In these cases, the court pointed out the danger and error of acting on the presumption in favour of unseaworthiness in case of an early loss of which the assured cannot prove the cause; and the court pointed out the necessity of bearing in mind that the defence of unseaworthiness must be overruled unless supported by sufficient weight of evidence in its favour, after duly considering all the evidence bearing on the subject, including, of course, the very weighty evidence with which the underwriters start their case.

[p 371] ... The case is no doubt one of difficulty, and no one can be surprised that the underwriters defended the action on the ground of unseaworthiness. But, as the evidence came out, they were forced from one theory to another, and they have failed to prove their case ... It is supposed that the cargo must have shifted; but this is a mere supposition, and there is no evidence of any bad stowage or other cause to account for any shifting of the cargo. All is conjecture. The real cause of the loss is unknown, and cannot be ascertained from the evidence adduced in this action. But underwriters take the risk of loss from unascertainable causes; and, after carefully weighing all the evidence and bearing in mind the presumption of unseaworthiness on which the undertakers rely, their Lordships have come to the conclusion that unseaworthiness at the time of sailing is not proved.

Skandia Insurance Co Ltd v Skoljarev [1979] 142 CLR 375

In this case, before the High Court of Australia, the facts of which are stated earlier in the chapter,[4] the assured (the respondents) were able to furnish substantial evidence to show that the vessel was seaworthy. As unseaworthiness was discounted as a possible cause of loss, the court was able to draw the inference that an unascertainable peril of the seas must have been responsible for the loss.

Barwick CJ: [p 378] ... As, in this case, the actual cause of the entry of the seawater was not found, there was no room for the view that, if the vessel were unseaworthy, the loss was none the less not due to her unseaworthiness. Thus, as part of the proof of the cause of the loss, the respondents [owners] needed to establish that the vessel was seaworthy when she put to sea. The respondents gave very strong evidence of seaworthiness ... The appellant's [insurer's] sole attack on this evidence was as to the condition of the piping of and associated with the bait tank. The primary judge found positively that that piping was not defective: and that, in any case, its suggested defect could not have caused the entry of water which caused the loss. He did not merely reject the appellant's

---

4　See above, p 456.

case of unseaworthiness; but, in rejecting it and having the positive evidence of seaworthiness, he was in a position to infer that the entry of the water into the hull, in the quantities in which it did enter, was itself a peril of the sea.

Mason J: [p 390] ... there is one class of case in which the insured will find it necessary to establish seaworthiness in order to prove his case. This is where the insured, having no direct evidence of loss due to a fortuitous event, seeks to establish by inference a case of loss due to an unascertained peril of the sea. To justify this inference, he will seek to exclude the possibility of loss caused by unseaworthiness by calling evidence as to the condition of the ship. In such a case, once evidence is given of unseaworthiness, the issue of causation must be decided as a question of fact. Then the tribunal of fact, unless it is satisfied that the ship was seaworthy, cannot draw the inference upon which the insured depends in order to make out his case.

Elimination of all other causes not insured by the policy

When a claim is made under the head of an unascertainable peril of the sea, the court would wish to rule out all the other possible uninsured causes of loss, including unseaworthiness, before allowing the presumption or inference that the loss was due to an unascertainable peril of the sea to be drawn.

In the *Marel* case, cited below, despite ruling out all the other possible uninsured causes of the loss, the plaintiffs were still unable to show that the vessel was seaworthy when she sailed on her final voyage: because of this lack of proof, it was not possible for the court to invoke the presumption of loss by an unascertainable peril of the sea.

Lamb Head Shipping Co Ltd v Jennings, 'Marel' [1992] 1 Lloyd's Rep 402; aff'd [1994] 1 Lloyd's Rep 624, CA

The bulk carrier *Marel* was on a voyage from Salonika in Greece to Ghent in Belgium with a cargo of corn; she was insured, by way of a time policy, with the defendants. The vessel had been well maintained and had recently undergone a classification survey and an ultrasonic test of her shell plating. Whilst passing the south east of Spain, early in the morning, a bump was felt by the crew members and this was followed by a sudden ingress of water into the engine room. The weather conditions were not exceptional and the crew abandoned ship prior to *Marel* sinking by the stern. The owners claimed on their policy of insurance for a loss by perils of the sea.

The two theories put forward by the owners were that she had either collided with a derelict container or that she had been lost due to some extraordinary and fortuitous but unascertained accident. The underwriters rejected the claim leaving the plaintiff owners the burden of proving their case.

The Court ruled that the owners had failed to establish, on the balance of probabilities, that the loss was caused by perils of the seas and their claim, therefore, failed. This ruling was upheld by the Court of Appeal.

> **Judge Diamond QC:** [p 426] ... At this stage, I have reached what I regard as the most difficult and perplexing question raised by the case since there are both strong reasons for drawing the inference in favour of the owners which they ask me to draw and also equally strong reasons against drawing such an inference. The reasons in favour of drawing an inference that the vessel was lost by an unascertainable peril of the seas include the evidence of the ship's witnesses to the 'bump' which they heard or felt, the finding which I have made as to the seaworthiness of the shell plating in way of the engine room, the exclusion of the possibility that the vessel might have been lost through an accidental failure of the sea water pipes within the vessel, or that she might have been deliberately sunk, and the absence of any known explanation for the casualty other than some unascertainable accident. These factors, taken together, point strongly towards the drawing of an inference that there is an aperture in the vessel's shell plating caused by some fortuitous contact with an external object.
>
> The main reason against drawing such an inference is that, despite having listened to many days of expert evidence, I was not supplied with any suggestion at all as to the mechanism by which an aperture in the vessel's shell plating, at a level of more than 4.5 metres below the still water line, could have been created other than the theory of a contact with a floating container, a theory which I have rejected as being so improbable as to be virtually impossible.
>
> ... Since, in my judgment, the owners have failed to establish on the balance of probabilities that the loss was caused by perils of the sea in either of the two ways in which they attempted to do this, it follows that the owner's claim fails and must be dismissed.

At the Court of Appeal, these issues were further clarified by Dillon LJ as follows:

> **Dillon LJ:** [p 629] ... As I see it, the presumption is really founded on the balance of probabilities. If it is known that a ship was seaworthy when she set out, and she has never been seen since and nothing has been heard of her crew, then on the balance of probabilities she must have sunk and, on the balance of probabilities, the sinking must have been due to 'perils of the sea' because she was seaworthy when she set out. The only alternative would be that she was scuttled, but members of a ship's company who scuttle their ship do not normally intend to commit suicide. They expect to be rescued.
>
> But, if it was not shown that the ship was seaworthy when she left on her last voyage, the presumption does not apply since it cannot be held on the balance of probabilities that her presumed sinking was due to perils of the sea rather than to her unseaworthy condition.
>
> In the present case what we do know of the circumstances of the sinking of *Marel* eliminates a number of possible perils of the sea. Thus, she was not overwhelmed by exceptionally bad weather. She did not hit an uncharted reef.. She was not run down and sunk by another vessel. As for the possibility that she sank as a result of collision with an unidentified object, it is shown that it is wholly improbable, and very nearly impossible, that the casualty could have

been caused by the only form of unidentified object which was suggested as a possibility, that is a derelict container.

Therefore, on those facts, there was no room for the presumption. It was for the plaintiffs to prove their case.

Missing ships

Although the three cases cited below, *Green v Brown*; *Koster v Innes* and *Koster v Reed*, are old cases, and may no longer be entirely relevant, they do provide the background, in insurance law, for the reason why there is a presumption of loss by perils of the sea when a ship is known to have sailed: 'A ship never heard of is presumed to be foundered at sea.'

Green v Brown (1743) 2 Str 1199

The ship *Charming Peggy* was insured in 1739, from North Carolina to London, with a warranty against captures and seizures. On the evidence given, *Charming Peggy* sailed out of port on her intended voyage, and was never heard of again. It was put to the court by the plaintiff that, in such a case, the presumption is that she foundered at sea, but the underwriters insisted that, as captures and seizures were excepted, it lay upon the assured to prove that the loss happened in the particular manner declared on.

The jury found for the plaintiff, in that it must be presumed that *Charming Peggy* foundered at sea. From this case was born the phrase 'a ship never heard of is presumed to be foundered at sea'.

> **Lord Chief Justice:** [p 1200] ... it would be unreasonable to expect certain evidence of such a loss, as where everybody on board is presumed to be drowned; and all that can be required is the best proof the nature of the case admits of, which the plaintiff has given; he therefore left it to the jury, who found the loss according to the plaintiff's declaration.

In *Koster v Innes*, below, the plaintiff, a cargo-owner, produced so little evidence to show that the ship had sailed that it could not be presumed that the loss was attributable to the vessel foundering.

Koster v Innes (1825) Ry & Mood 334

This was an action on a policy of marine insurance on goods put on board *La Virgine de la Solitudine* at and from Leghorn to Lisbon. The goods, which consisted of silks, etc, were taken to the vessel and handed over to the captain by a boatman. The boatman claimed that he had been given a receipt for the goods, which were the only goods aboard the ship, but the receipt was not produced as evidence. Another witness, who had given the goods to the boatman, stated that he had seen *La Virgine de la Solitudine* sail and then had heard a few days later that she had been lost; the captain and crew having been saved, but not seen again.

The court held that there was no evidence, not even a bill of lading, to show that the vessel had sailed from Leghorn with the cargo on the insured voyage. Therefore, the presumption that she had foundered, due to a peril insured against, could not be raised.

Lord Abbott CJ: [p 355] I will leave the case to the jury if you wish it, but I have a very strong opinion upon it. The proof offered in support of the plaintiff's case, is less than I can remember or have ever read of. It is necessary that he should establish two things. First, that the vessel sailed from the port of Leghorn on the voyage insured. Secondly, that she was lost, and lost by the particular perils insured against, which the plaintiff has alleged in his declaration to be the cause of the loss. Now, as to the first point, there is no evidence that any bill of lading ever existed, or of any order to send these goods to Lisbon. I think that you have not made out this part of your case, and that it would be very dangerous indeed to allow a party to recover on such evidence. As to the second point, it may perhaps be assumed that there is evidence of the loss, but making such an assumption will be going further than has ever yet been done in cases of this description; but I rely less upon this than on the first point, namely, that there is no evidence that the ship ever sailed for the port of destination.

The above case, *Koster v Innes*, should be compared with the case below, *Koster v Reed*, which concerned the same plaintiff, ship and cargo. On this occasion, the court was convinced by the evidence provided by the plaintiff that the ship had, in fact, sailed.

Koster v Reed (1826) 6 B&C 19

This action, a retrial from a previous hearing, was pursued by the same plaintiff who had failed to recover in *Koster v Innes*, for goods put aboard *La Virgine de la Solitudine* when she foundered soon after leaving Leghorn, bound for Lisbon. On this occasion, the court was convinced by the evidence provided by the plaintiff that the vessel had, in fact, sailed and that her loss was occasioned by perils of the seas. However, Bayley J appears to suggest that, given the circumstances in the case, the fact that the plaintiff was a cargo-owner and not the shipowner had some bearing on the outcome.

Abbott CJ: [p 21] ... The evidence given at the trial was that the vessel, with the goods insured on board, sailed from Leghorn in April 1821, for Lisbon, that she never arrived at that place, and that a few days after her departure from Leghorn, the witness heard that she had foundered at sea, but that the crew were saved. Taking the whole of that account together, it proved a loss by perils of the sea, but we are asked to take half of it only, viz, that the crew survived; and to exclude from our consideration that which related to the loss of the ship. I think we should not be justified in so doing, and that it is impossible for us to say at this distance of time it was incumbent on the plaintiff to send all over Europe in search of the crew of this vessel, whom we must suppose to have been foreigners, the ship being foreign, and trading between foreign ports. For these reasons it appears to me that there was sufficient evidence to be left to the jury, and that the verdict ought not to be disturbed.

Bayley J: [p 22] ... In the present case, the plaintiff was owner of the goods, not of the vessel, and the underwriters might have just as good a means of inquiring about the crew as the plaintiff had. Why, then, is it not as reasonable to call upon them to prove affirmatively that intelligence of the ship had been received, as upon the plaintiff to prove the negative. In the absence of any such evidence, I think it was fair to presume that the ship perished at sea.

Notes

In the case of *Compania Martiartu v Royal Exchange Assurance Corporation, Arnus* [1923] 1 KB 650, CA, where a vessel foundered in calm weather on a voyage from Spain to Rotterdam, Scrutton LJ referred to *Green v Brown* in his summation. However, he pointed out that, where there is evidence to show that there is doubt as to whether the effective cause of the loss was 'within or without the policy', the assured cannot recover.

Scrutton LJ: [p 657] ... The presumption may well be, when nothing is known except that the ship has disappeared at sea, that her loss was by perils of the sea: *Green v Brown*. But when, though it is known that she has sunk, there is evidence on each side as to the cause of the admission of seawater, which leaves the court in doubt whether the effective cause is within or without the policy, the plaintiff, the assured, fails, for he has not proved a loss by perils insured against.

Presumption of an actual total loss – s 58

Whilst on the subject of missing ships, it is pertinent to note that there is a statutory presumption, under s 58 of the Act, to the effect that:

Where the ship concerned in the adventure is missing, and after the lapse of a reasonable time no news of her has been received, an actual total loss may be presumed.

The plaintiff's standard of proof

The standard of proof required upon the plaintiff to prove that the loss was caused by a peril of the seas is the balance of probabilities. Once again, the House of Lords, in the *Popi M* case, has clarified this point beyond doubt. On the issue of the degree of proof, Brandon LJ applied a common sense approach to the problem.

Brandon LJ: [p 6] ... the legal concept of proof of a case on a balance of probabilities must be applied with common sense. It requires a judge of first instance, before he finds that a particular event occurred, to be satisfied on the evidence that it is more likely to have occurred than not. If such a judge concludes, on a whole series of cogent grounds, that the occurrence of an event is extremely improbable, a finding by him that it is nevertheless more likely to have occurred than not, does not accord with common sense. This is especially so when it is open to the judge to say simply that the evidence leaves him in doubt whether the event occurred or not, and that the party on whom the burden of proving that the event occurred lies has therefore failed to discharge such burden.

In the case of *Compania Naviera Santi SA v Indemnity Marine Assurance Co Ltd, 'Tropaioforos'* [1960] 2 Lloyd's Rep 469, Pearson J's view on the subject was couched as follows: [p 473] '... the plaintiffs have the burden of proving, in a case such as this, that there was an accidental loss by perils of the seas, although the degree of proof required is only to show a balance of probabilities in favour of an accidental loss by perils of the seas ...'

Although *National Justice Compania Naviera SA v Prudential Assurance Co Ltd, 'Ikarian Reefer'* **[1995] 1 Lloyd's Rep 455, CA** was a scuttling case, at the Court of Appeal, Stuart-Smith LJ commented on the low order of proof required by a shipowner in having to show how a loss occurred, on the balance of probabilities, in order to prove his case.

Stuart-Smith LJ: [p 459] ... For the shipowners to succeed, the evidence has to establish that the grounding probably was fortuitous; this conclusion can co-exist with a residual possibility that it was deliberate (or, in scientific terms, a low order of probability) because the plaintiffs are required to prove their case on 'balance of probabilities' only.

The defendant's burden of proof

As was seen, when a claim is made under the head of perils of the seas, the plaintiff must first establish a *prima facie* case that the loss was so caused. If he is unable to do this, the defendant will have no case to answer. It is only when a *prima facie* case has been made out that the defendant will then be called upon to refute the claim. He could do this either by:

(a) simply denying or traversing the plaintiff's allegations by calling evidence to show that the loss was not caused by a fortuitous accident – suggesting, perhaps, either unseaworthiness or wear and tear as the cause of loss; or

(b) seeking to present and prove an affirmative allegation that the loss was caused by the wilful misconduct of the assured. Such a serious allegation has, of course, to be specifically and properly pleaded, as he may not, however, at some later stage, surprise the plaintiff with a defence which the plaintiff was not previously made aware of. In the *Dias* case, cited below, this issue of the presentation of the defence was put before the Court of Appeal.

In either event, it should be borne in mind that, regardless of the nature of the defence, the burden of proof remains constantly with the plaintiff to prove, on the balance of probabilities, that the loss was proximately caused by an insured peril.

Palamisto General Enterprises SA v Ocean Marine Insurance Co Ltd, 'Dias' [1972] 2 Lloyd's Rep 60, CA

The plaintiffs were the owners of the steamship *Dias*, which was insured under a time policy of insurance with the defendants. In March 1967, *Dias* suffered a fire in her boiler room which spread to other parts of the ship, and she eventually foundered. The plaintiffs claimed on their policy of insurance, but the underwriters denied liability and alleged that, *inter alia*, the loss was caused by the wilful misconduct of the assured in conniving to cast away the vessel. The appeal was based on the plaintiffs' contention that the particulars put forward by the underwriters were not in accordance with the practice of the Commercial Court over the past 50 years.

The Court of Appeal, by a majority of two to one, allowed the appeal in part, and decided that the practice of the Commercial Court had been wrong.

Cairns LJ: [p 75] ... When a claim is made on marine insurers for the loss of a vessel by perils of the seas and they suspect that the vessel has been scuttled at the behest of the owner, there are two possible courses open to them; they can simply traverse the allegations in the points of claim, or they can make an affirmative allegation of scuttling. If they adopt the former course, they can cross-examine and call evidence to show that the vessel was not lost by a fortuitous accident, but cannot set up an affirmative case that she was cast away with the privity of the owner: *Regina Fur Co Ltd v Bossom* [1958] 2 Lloyd's Rep 425, *per* Lord Evershed MR, p 428; *Roselodge Ltd (formerly 'Rose' Diamond Products Ltd) v Castle* [1966] 2 Lloyd's Rep 113, *per* McNair J, p 119. If scuttling is alleged and the insurers are going to ask the court to find positively that the vessel was scuttled, then they must discharge the onus of proving their allegation; and in considering whether they have discharged it, the court must weigh in the balance the fact that the allegation is one of fraud: *Elfie A Issaias v Marine Insurance Co Ltd* (1923) 15 LlL Rep 186, *per* Lord Sterndale MR, p 187, and Atkin LJ, p 191; *Gloria* (1936) 54 LlL Rep 35, *per* Branson J, p 50; *Regina Fur Co Ltd v Bossom* [1957] 2 Lloyd's Rep 466, *per* Pearson J, p 469. If, where loss by peril of the seas is alleged by the plaintiff and scuttling by the defendant, the court at the end of the day is not satisfied that either story is more probable than the other, then the plaintiff fails: *Martiartu v Royal Exchange* [1923] 1 KB 650; *Tropaioforos* [1960] 2 Lloyd's Rep 469; *Gloria* (1936) 54 LlL Rep 35.

In these circumstances, if the defendant alleges scuttling, it is, in my opinion, not open to him to say: 'I need not have made the allegation at all and therefore I need give no particulars of it.' By making the allegation, he has opened the door for the presentation by himself of an affirmative case of fraud. The question of what particulars he must give of that allegation must depend primarily on the Rules of the Supreme Court.

[p 77] ... The charge of scuttling against a shipowner has all the gravity of a serious criminal charge, and in my view, the question of whether particulars are desirable should be tested on the basis of what is fair to enable an honest

shipowner to meet the charge, rather than on the basis of what would most assist insurers to establish it against a dishonest one.

The defence of wilful misconduct

The defence of wilful misconduct by the assured is the natural and most commonly used defence available to an insurer who wishes to reject a claim for a loss by perils of the seas (and, for that matter, fire and barratry). Once the plaintiff has established a *prima facie* case, it then falls upon the insurer to dispute the cause of loss.

To topple the plaintiff's claim, the defendant has merely to cast sufficient doubts in the mind of the judge as to the cause of loss, and he does not even have to go as far as to prove an affirmative defence. But, should he be in a position to demonstrate that scuttling with the connivance of the assured is an equally probable cause of the loss, the plaintiff would fail in his action: the court is not obliged, should both accounts of the loss be equally probable, to make a choice. Thus, in so saying, the question of the 'third alternative' put forward by Brandon LJ in the *Popi M* case, albeit in a case where wilful misconduct was not an issue, may also be validly raised here. In the ultimate analysis, it is important to be reminded that the burden of proof rests with the plaintiff.

It should make no difference to the issue of burden of proof whether the defence be one of simple denial or the allegation of wilful misconduct, for, at the end of the hearing, the court has to be satisfied that the plaintiff has proved his case, and, on the balance of probabilities, that the loss was accidental. All that the defendant has to do is to displace the *prima facie* case put forward by the plaintiff, either by injecting doubts in the minds of the judge as to the real cause of the loss, or by providing evidence of another reasonably plausible explanation of the loss. This very issue surfaced in *Compania Martiartu v Royal Exchange Assurance Corporation, 'Arnus'* [1923] 1 KB 650, CA, discussed below. It is, however, best explained by Lord Brandon, in *Popi M* [1985] 2 Lloyd's Rep 1, p 2, HL.

It is perhaps necessary to mention that, when the same defence is pleaded in relation to a claim for a loss by barratry, the law as regards the burden of proof on the question of complicity, and the attendant standard of proof, are much more complex and controversial. To avoid confusion, this will be discussed separately, later in the chapter.[5]

Compania Martiartu v Royal Exchange Assurance Corporation, 'Arnus' [1923] 1 KB 650, CA

Arnus sank in calm weather on a voyage from Spain to Rotterdam. The Court of Appeal ruled that the vessel had been deliberately scuttled with the

---

5   See below, p 479.

connivance of the responsible managers. But, in passing judgment, Scrutton LJ also considered the position of the plaintiff in failing to prove that the loss was caused by a peril of the sea.

> **Scrutton LJ**: [p 656] ... I have no hesitation in finding that the admission of water was with the privity of the managing owner, and, therefore, of the company who owned the ship. This view renders it unnecessary finally to discuss the burden of proof, but, in my present view, if there are circumstances suggesting that another cause than a peril insured against was the dominant or effective cause of the entry of seawater into the ship – see *Leyland Shipping Co v Norwich Union Fire Insurance Society* – and an examination of all the evidence and probabilities leaves the court doubtful what is the real cause of the loss, the assured has failed to prove his case ... In this case, I find scuttling, but I do not think it is possible to put the case for the assured higher than by saying the matter is left in doubt, and if that be the true view, in my opinion, the assured fails.
>
> **Bankes LJ**: [p 655] ... if the *prima facie* case ... fails because the underwriters put forward a reasonable explanation of the loss, the superstructure fails with it.

Pateras and Others v Royal Exchange Assurance, 'Sappho' (1934) 49 LlL Rep 400

Sappho was on a voyage from Algeria to Stettin when she struck a rock off the coast of Portugal and was lost. The plaintiffs claimed on their policy of insurance, but the underwriters denied liability, alleging that the ship had been wilfully cast away with the connivance of her owners.

The court ruled that *Sappho* had been scuttled with the connivance of her owners and that the insurers bore no liability. The court considered the position of the plaintiffs should he fail to prove his case.

> **Roche J**: [p 407] ... But substantially, in my view, the rule as to onus of proof is quite correctly stated by Bankes LJ, when the case of *Compania Martiartu* was in the Court of Appeal. It is there reported in [1923] 1 KB 650, and the gist of the matter is that although there is, of course, and must be, a strong presumption against the commission of an act so criminal as wilful throwing away of the ship, yet if the matter is really uncertain as between that explanation of the loss and a fortuitous explanation of the loss, the onus of proof is on the plaintiffs. Here, I have come to a conclusion definitely adverse to the plaintiffs; but at all events I should, as Bankes LJ did in that case, be of opinion that I should find it impossible to say that the plaintiffs had established to my satisfaction that the loss of the vessel was due to a peril covered by the policy, that is to say, that it was fortuitous.

Compania Naviera Vascongada v British and Foreign Marine Insurance Co Ltd, 'Gloria' (1934) 54 LlL Rep 35

Gloria sank on a voyage from Larne to Port Talbot after, it was claimed, sustaining damage leaving Larne and then experiencing heavy weather.

The court decided that the owners had proved that the loss was fortuitous, and Branson J considered the consequences should they have failed.

> **Branson J:** [p 50] ... The law is, in my opinion, clear. The onus of proof that the loss was fortuitous lies upon the plaintiffs, but that does not mean that they will fail if their evidence does not exclude all reasonable possibility that the ship was scuttled. Before that possibility is considered, some evidence in support of it must be forthcoming. Scuttling is a crime, and the court will not find that it has been committed unless it is proved with the same degree of certainty as is required for the proof of a crime. If, however, the evidence is such that the court, giving full weight to the consideration that scuttling is a crime, is not satisfied that the ship was scuttled, but finds that the probability that she was equal to the probability that her loss was fortuitous, the plaintiffs will fail.

In *Palamisto General Enterprises SA v Ocean Marine Insurance Co Ltd, 'Dias'* **[1972] 2 Lloyd's Rep 60, CA**, where a ship was lost after a fire developed in her engine room, Cairns LJ considered the situation if perils of the seas had been pleaded as the cause of loss.

> [p 76] ... If, where loss by perils of the seas is alleged by the plaintiff and scuttling by the defendant, the court at the end of the day is not satisfied that either story is more probable than the other, then the plaintiff fails ...

In *Astrovlanis Compania Naviera SA v Linard, 'Gold Sky'* [1972] 2 Lloyd's Rep 187, a vessel was lost after the shell plating split in the vicinity of the engine room. At the court of first instance, on the issue of burden of proof, Mocatta J [p 192] approved of both *'Gloria'* and *'Dias'*.

In *Michalos (N) and Sons Maritime SA v Prudential Assurance Co Ltd, 'Zinovia'* **[1984] 2 Lloyd's Rep 264**, where a vessel ran aground in the Gulf of Suez and the court ruled that the insurers had not proved that the ship had been deliberately cast away, Bingham J considered the position of the plaintiff should he not have succeeded in proving his case.

> [p 271] ... Nonetheless, at the end of the case, the court considers a loss by perils of the sea to be no more probable than a loss caused by another, uninsured, peril, then the owners must fail.

In *Popi M* **[1985] 2 Lloyd's Rep 1, HL**, the avenues open to the insurer in the presentation of his defence were perceived by Lord Brandon thus:

> [pp 2–3] ... The first matter is that the burden of proving, on the balance of probabilities, that the ship was lost by perils of the sea, is and remains throughout on the shipowners. Although it is open to the underwriter to suggest and seek to prove some other cause of loss, against which the ship was not insured, there is no obligation on them to do so. Moreover, if they chose to do so, there is no obligation on them to prove, even on a balance of probabilities, the truth of their alternative case.

American authorities

In the American case of *Vainqueur*, cited below, District Judge Ward, in his summation, catalogued and clarified the sequence of events, with respect to burden of proof, as they occurred.

Northwestern Mutual Life Insurance Co v Linard, 'Vainqueur' [1973] 2 Lloyd's Rep 275

Vainqueur, which was owned by the Vainqueur Corporation, was insured under a policy of marine insurance, for hull and machinery, by the defendant underwriters. The vessel was operating under a bulk sugar charter between Veracruz and New Orleans when an explosion occurred in her engine room and, within one hour, she sank. The plaintiffs claimed on their policy of insurance, but the insurers rejected the claim, averring that the ship had been sunk deliberately by the assured by means of an explosive device.

The court ruled that the plaintiffs had failed to discharge the burden of proving that the loss fell within the policy and, therefore, they could not recover.

District Judge Ward: [p 282] ... In summation, the court concludes the following:

(1) Vainqueur Corporation had the burden of persuasion throughout this proceeding on the issue of whether the explosion was an insured event.

(2) Vainqueur Corporation also initially had the burden of producing evidence. Vainqueur Corporation met this burden (making out its *prima facie* case) and shifted the burden of producing evidence to the underwriters.

(3) If the underwriters had offered no proof of scuttling, Vainqueur Corporation would have been entitled to a judgment.

(4) Underwriters offered substantial evidence of scuttling, sufficient to meet their burden of producing evidence. At this point, this burden disappeared from the case.

(5) Underwriters' evidence of scuttling was sufficient to rebut a presumption that the loss was by a peril of the sea. Underwriters produced substantial evidence that the loss was by scuttling, not by a peril of the sea or an explosion within the policy coverage.

(6) Although the proof was not sufficient for the court to find that *The Vainqueur* was scuttled, since Vainqueur Corporation had the ultimate burden of persuading the court that the loss was an insured event within the policy, and since the Corporation failed to meet its burden, its cross-claim against underwriters must be dismissed

Another, earlier, American case, *The Lakeland*, is now cited as an example of a case where the defendant offers no defence other than a denial of the circumstances of the loss; there being no affirmative plea of wilful misconduct. The evidence presented by the defence was intended to throw doubt on the plaintiffs' claim for a loss by a peril covered by the policy, suggesting that there was possibly an alternative cause of loss, scuttling.

The Lakeland (1927) 28 LlL Rep 293

This was an American appeal case concerning the Great Lakes steamship *The Lakeland*, which was employed in transporting cars from Detroit to Chicago when she sank in Lake Michigan. The plaintiffs claimed, and the captain testified to the same, that *The Lakeland* had suffered damage when she struck the pier and grounded whilst leaving Chicago and that, when she later encountered heavy weather, she sank. The insurers alleged, although they brought no proof of such, that she had been scuttled by means of a conspiracy with the owners. The insurers' case was based on the denial that *The Lakeland* was lost as a result of any of the hazards covered by the policies, and averred that it was for the plaintiffs to prove their case. At the original trial, the jury had found for the plaintiffs, but the defendants had appealed on the basis that the jury had been misdirected.

The Appeal Court ruled that, at the original trial, the instructions to the jury, in respect of burden of proof, were erroneous and prejudicial to the defendants and, therefore, the case must be retried.

> **Circuit Judge Mack:** [p 295] ... Plaintiffs thus alleged that the loss had resulted from a peril insured against. Defendants had not pleaded and were not required under the policies in this case to plead an affirmative defence; they merely denied plaintiffs' allegations ... The burden of proof established by the proper pleadings, therefore, remained unchanged; it devolved upon plaintiffs to prove, by a preponderance of evidence, that the loss was due to one or the other risk assumed and insured against by defendants under the policies.
>
> Plaintiffs offered substantial evidence to support their allegations, other than those of negligence or barratry in opening the sea-cock; defendants introduced testimony of divers, that they had examined the wreck and found an open sea-cock, as well as evidence of circumstances tending to support their theory of scuttling with connivance of the owners and resulting non-liability under the policies.
>
> The ultimate burden did not shift by reason of the evidence of scuttling presented by the defendants; that evidence was not offered in support of any affirmative defence, because there was none; it was offered to sustain the denial of liability, to raise at least a question in the jury's mind as to whether or not the sinking was in fact due to a peril covered by the policies; it bore only upon the question as to whether or not plaintiffs had affirmatively made out their case of liability under the policies.
>
> ... We think the instructions to the jury in respect to the burden of proof, considered as a whole, were erroneously and materially prejudicial to defendants ... Furthermore, the reference in the charge to a presumption as a rule of law that a loss is covered by the insurance policies in the absence of a plausible or reasonable explanation as to the cause of the sinking, was out of place, both in view of the evidence as to the possible or probable causes and of the restricted nature of the risks covered by the policies.

PROOF OF LOSS BY FIRE

Unlike perils of the seas, fortuity is not an essential element when making a claim for a loss occasioned by fire.[6] Thus, the claimant need only show that the loss was caused by fire, whether started accidentally or deliberately, to establish a *prima facie* case, and throw the burden of proof upon the insurer to prove that there was connivance on the part of the assured, by which the defence of wilful misconduct by the assured could be driven home.

That there is no requirement for the plaintiff to show that there was an element of fortuity in a claim for a loss caused by fire was shown in the case of ***Continental Illinois National Bank and Trust Co of Chicago and Xenofon Maritime SA v Alliance Assurance Co Ltd, 'Captain Panagos DP'* [1986] 2 Lloyd's Rep 470**,[7] where the vessel grounded and suffered a major fire in the Red Sea, which was held to have been a deliberate act brought about with the connivance of the owners. At the court of first instance, Evans J stated:

> [p 511] ... 'Fire', unlike 'perils of the seas', does not itself connote a fortuity; unlike 'barratry', there is no statutory definition which gives grounds for arguing that the possibility of connivance must be disproved. I therefore conclude that the plaintiffs would have proved a loss by fire, if their claim had not been defeated by the defence of owners' connivance.

That the claimant need only establish a *prima facie* case of loss by fire in order to shift the burden of proving complicity by the assured on to the insurers was shown in the following case, *Slattery v Mance*.

Slattery v Mance [1962] 1 All ER 525

The plaintiff owner of the vessel *Treworval Light* brought an action against the defendant insurers, claiming, under a policy of marine insurance, a total of £4,500 for the loss of the vessel by fire. The underwriters rejected the claim, on the basis that the plaintiff wilfully caused or connived with the destruction of the vessel.

The court ruled, on the principle of the common law that he who asserts must prove, that it fell upon the defendant underwriters to prove, on the balance of probabilities, that the plaintiff deliberately destroyed *Treworval Light*. The jury was directed accordingly.

> **Salmon J:** [p 526] ... In my judgment, the onus of proof in cases such as the one before me is different from the onus of proof in the 'perils of the sea' cases. The risk of fire insured against is quite obviously not confined to an accidental fire. If the ship had been set alight by some mischievous person without the plaintiff's connivance, there could be no doubt that the plaintiff would be entitled to recover. Of course, the plaintiff cannot recover if he was the person

---

6   See Chapter 9.
7   This case is also discussed in relation to the peril of 'fire' in Chapter 9, p 400.

who fired the ship or was a party to the ship being fired. The result, however, does not depend on the construction of the word 'fire' in the policy, but on the well known principle of insurance law that no man can recover for a loss which he himself has deliberately and fraudulently caused. It is no more than an extension of the general principle that no man can take advantage of his own wrong. In my judgment, once it is shown that the loss has been caused by fire, the plaintiff has made out a *prima facie* case, and the onus is on the defendant to show, on a balance of probabilities, that the fire was caused or connived at by the plaintiff.

National Justice Compania Naviera SA v Prudential Assurance Co Ltd, 'Ikarian Reefer' [1993] 2 Lloyd's Rep 68, CA

The Court of Appeal ruled that there had been wilful misconduct by the assured when a vessel had been lost due to a combination of grounding and fire. But, at the court of first instance, Cresswell J, with admirable clarity, summarised the legal principles applicable to the burden of proof when claiming for a loss by perils of the seas or fire.

Cresswell J: [p 71] ... The relevant legal principles are as follows:

(1) *Loss by perils of the sea*. The burden of proving, on the balance of probabilities, that a ship was lost by perils of the sea remains throughout on the owners. Although it is open to insurers to suggest and seek to prove some other cause of loss, against which the ship was not insured, there is no obligation on them to do so. Moreover, if insurers choose to do so, there is no obligation on them to prove, even on a balance of probabilities, the truth of their alternative case (*Popi M* [1985] 2 Lloyd's Rep 1, p 2, Lord Brandon).

(2) *Fire*. 'Fire' in a marine policy includes, as a matter of construction, a fire started deliberately by a stranger to the insurance (*Alexion Hope* [1988] 1 Lloyd's Rep 311, p 317, *per* Lloyd LJ).

(3) Where the owners have proved a loss by fire, the burden of proving a deliberate fire and connivance lies upon the insurers. If the evidence leaves the court in doubt, then the assured is entitled to succeed. Thus, the assured in a claim for loss by fire has a lesser burden than one claiming for loss by perils of the sea (who must prove a fortuity), though he is in the same position in this respect as the claimant for loss by barratry (*Captain Panagos DP* [1986] 2 Lloyd's Rep 470, p 510, Evans J).

(4) The assured must prove a loss caused by an insured peril ('fire') and the insurers must prove, if so alleged, that there was a deliberate fire and connivance by the assured and so defeat the claim under s 55(2)(a) of the Marine Insurance Act 1906, which provides that: '... the insurer is not liable for any loss attributable to the wilful misconduct of the assured, but, unless the policy otherwise provides, he is liable for any loss proximately caused by a peril insured against, even though the loss would not have happened but for the misconduct or negligence of the master or crew.' If the evidence shows a loss by fire, which was accidental rather than deliberate, the assured succeeds. If the evidence shows that the fire was deliberately

caused with the connivance of the assured, the assured fails. If the evidence shows a fire deliberately caused by the master or crew (a factual situation co-existing with that required to establish a barratry claim), this is covered by 'fire' and the assured need not prove absence of connivance on his part (*Captain Panagos DP* [1986] 2 Lloyd's Rep 470, pp 510–11, Evans J).

Standard of proof for the defence of wilful misconduct of the assured

When an insurer denies liability for a loss by fire and alleges the defence of complicity and wilful misconduct by the assured, the burden of proof must, on the common law principle of he who asserts must prove, fall on him. It would appear from the brief comment made by Salmon J, in *Slattery v Mance*, that the defendant need only prove his case of the owner's connivance on the balance of probabilities, even though the allegation is effectively a criminal charge. More recent and higher authorities have, however, ruled that, though based on the civil test of balance of probabilities, a higher degree of proof (approaching close to the criminal standard of beyond reasonable doubt) reflecting the gravity of the charge is required. Support for this can be found in the Court of Appeal decision in *Ikarian Reefer* [1993] 2 Lloyd's Rep 68, CA and *Captain Panagos DP* [1989] 1 Lloyd's Rep 33, CA. Neill LJ, in the latter case, remarked:

> [p 41] ... I turn now to the central issues in the case ... (e) that the onus of proving the privity of the owners rests on the insurers; (f) that the burden of proof, though not quite equivalent to that required in a criminal case, is a heavy burden commensurate with the gravity of the matter: see *Bater v Bater* [1951] P 35; *Hornal v Neuberger Products Ltd* [1957] 1 QB 247.

It is perhaps necessary to be reminded of the fact that, unlike barratry, complicity is not an essential feature of a claim based on fire, thus, it is not for the plaintiff to disprove complicity, but for the defendant to prove complicity. Unlike perils of the seas, the plaintiff does not have to prove that the loss was accidental or fortuitous. When compared with a claim for barratry or perils of the seas, the plaintiff enjoys the best of both worlds when fire is pleaded as the cause of loss. It could be said that, once the plaintiff has demonstrated to the court that a fire has caused the loss, he has effectively proved his case on the balance of probabilities. Consequently, for the defendant's rebuttal to be effective, it has to be at a higher level; in other words, he has to do more than merely throw doubts upon the plaintiff's case. Unlike the case of perils of the seas, such a defendant cannot afford to leave the court in any doubt: as the persuasive burden of proof is now in his camp, he has to satisfy the court (at a higher level of proof) that the loss was caused by the wilful misconduct of the assured, otherwise the plaintiff, having already proved his case on the balance of probabilities, is entitled to succeed.

PROOF OF LOSS BY BARRATRY

A loss caused by the insurable peril of barratry may take the form of delay, deviation, intentional breach of a blockade, fire, or scuttling, but, in every instance, it must be without the privity of the shipowner or charterer (as the case may be) because 'barratry', by definition, must be prejudicial to the owner or charterer (see r 11 of the Rules for Construction, Marine Insurance Act 1906).[8]

When a shipowner pleads a loss caused by barratry, the obvious and most effective defence available to the insurer is that the loss occurred with the knowledge and consent of the assured. Thus, it is crucial to any such defence that the complicity of the shipowner be proved, but the question is: on whom does the burden of proof fall? Does it fall upon the shipowner to prove that there was no such complicity, or does it fall upon the insurer to prove that there was? The problem arises because, by the common law principle of he who alleges must prove, it is beholden upon an insurer to prove wilful misconduct. On the other hand, there is an equally fundamental rule of evidence, namely, that the plaintiff must prove the essential ingredients of his claim. And, on this ground, it could be argued that it falls upon the claimant to establish, at the outset, a *prima facie* case that the loss was so occasioned and, in order to do so, non-complicity must be established. Thus, there is a conflict.

This conflict has engendered problems relating to the standard of proof required when complicity by the shipowner is alleged. Indeed, such an accusation effectively embodies not merely a plea of an act of wilful misconduct on the part of the assured, but a criminal charge. Inevitably, this would raise the thorny problem of whether the civil or criminal standard of proof is to be applied. Thus, this part of the chapter will focus on the two main issues which have plagued this area of the law, namely, which party has to prove complicity and the standard of proof required to discharge that obligation. With regard to the former, the two points of view are, for convenience, captioned simply as *'the Issaias rule'* and *'the Martiartu-Michael approach'*.

Onus of proof of complicity

The Issaias rule

In the *Issaias* case, it is to be noted that the fact that the vessel was deliberately cast away by the master and an engineer was not contested. The case hinged on whether there had been complicity in the act of scuttling by the owner.

---

8 On the subject of barratry, see Chapter 12, p 509.

Elfie A Issaias v Marine Insurance Co Ltd (1923) 15 LlL Rep 186, CA

The wooden steamer *Elias Issaias* was on passage from Baltimore to Piraeus when the engines suffered a serious malfunction, and she was found drifting in mid-Atlantic by an English vessel, which took her in tow. During the course of the tow, *Elias Issaias* slowly settled in the water, was abandoned and later sank. The plaintiff shipowner claimed for a total loss by perils of the seas; the underwriters resisted the claim on the grounds that the ship had been wilfully scuttled on the owner's orders. Evidence was put forward that the owner's finances were stretched.

The Court of Appeal upheld the decision of the trial judge in ruling that the ship had been scuttled by the master and engineer with the connivance of the owners. All three judges were of the opinion that the burden of proof, when alleging complicity and wilful misconduct on the part of the shipowner, lay upon the accuser – the underwriter.

> **Lord Sterndale MR:** [p 189] ... It was argued for the defendants that, so soon as scuttling of the ship was proved, the onus of proving that it was not done with his complicity was cast upon the owner, in other words, that proof of scuttling raised a presumption that it took place with his complicity. I cannot assent to this argument; it seems to me to be contrary to the ordinary principles of evidence and also to be contrary to another presumption of English law, that is, that of innocence, which is more fully dealt with within the judgment of Atkin LJ.
>
> **Warrington LJ:** [p 189] ... In the present case, the cause of the loss has been ascertained and is no longer in dispute. *Prima facie* it was an act of barratry and would be one of the perils insured against; and it is for the underwriters to show that the wrongful act of the master was not committed 'to the prejudice' of the owner in as much as it was connived at by him. I apprehend that to cast away a man's ship without his consent is to his prejudice, although the pecuniary effect may be to his advantage.
>
> **Atkin LJ:** [p 191] ... The only issue is whether the owner was privy to the act of the master. I entertain no doubt that the onus of proving this fact rests upon the defendant underwriters. This is not the case of an unexplained loss. I do not think the onus would be altered if it were, if the issue raised was scuttling.

The facts proved by the plaintiff establish a loss either by perils of the sea or by barratry – possibly both, as to which I shall say something later. The charge of privity against the owner makes against him an allegation of what would be a crime if committed in respect of an English ship, and what, in the absence of evidence to the contrary, I am entitled to assume is a crime by Greek law if committed in respect of a Greek ship; and is, in any case, a charge of very serious dishonesty. The plaintiff is entitled to invoke in his favour a principle of English law so well established that it is somewhat surprising to find little reference to it in some recent cases, the principle of presumption of innocence. I will cite from *Stephen on Evidence*, Art 94: 'The burden of proving that any person has been guilty of a crime or wrongful act is on the person who asserts it, whether the commission of such act is or is not directly in issue in the action.'

The Martiartu-Michael approach

In the *Martiartu* case, cited earlier,[9] the whole issue of onus of proof of the defence of wilful misconduct was again raised. Almost in passing, Scrutton LJ put forward an alternative view to that expounded in the *Issaias* case.

Compania Martiartu v Royal Exchange Assurance Corporation, 'Arnus' [1923] 1 KB 650, CA; aff'd (1924) AC 850, HL

> **Scrutton LJ:** [p 657] ... if there are circumstances suggesting that another cause than a peril insured against was the dominant or effective cause of the entry of seawater into the ship – see *Leyland Shipping Co v Norwich Union Fire Insurance Society* – and the examination of all the evidence and probabilities leaves the court doubtful what is the real cause of the loss, the assured has failed to prove his case ... But when, though it is known that she has sunk, there is evidence on each side as to the cause of the admission of seawater, which leaves the court in doubt whether the effective cause is within or without the policy, the plaintiff, the assured, fails, for he has not proved a loss by perils insured against. Not every loss by seawater is a peril of the sea, as is shown by definition in the Marine Insurance Act: when there is evidence on each side suggesting the real cause, the court must determine on the balance of probabilities, as in every case of circumstantial evidence, and not be deterred from finding in favour of the stronger probabilities by the fact that some remote possibility exists the other way.

In the *Michael* case, below, the same approach was taken with respect to onus of proof as that put forward by Scrutton LJ in the *Martiartu* case.

Piermay Shipping Co SA and Brandt's v Chester, 'Michael' [1979] 1 Lloyd's Rep 55; [1979] 2 Lloyd's Rep 1, CA

Michael was insured by her owners with the defendants under a policy of marine insurance which included, *inter alia*, loss by barratry. In January 1973, on a voyage with a cargo of soda ash from Baton Rouge to Venezuela, *Michael* encountered heavy weather and suffered a series of engine breakdowns. After all attempts to repair the engines failed, and with *Michael* drifting helplessly in heavy seas, the master sent out an SOS and the tug Rescue came to her assistance and succeeded in attaching a tow rope. Some hours later, *Michael's* engine room started to flood and, without orders, the tow rope was released. The crew abandoned ship and *Michael* was lost. The owners claimed for a loss by barratry, as it was common knowledge that an engineer had scuttled the ship, but the underwriters denied liability, contending that the owners had consented to the loss.

The Court of Appeal upheld the decision of the trial judge and ruled that the loss had been due to barratry, whereby *Michael* had been sunk deliberately

---

9 See above, p 469.

without the consent or foreknowledge of the owners. At the court of first instance, the subject of proof of complicity was raised, and Kerr J approved of the reasoning in *Spathari* rather than in the *Issaias* case. However, later, the Court of Appeal was careful to point out that, in upholding the judgment of the trial judge, they were not necessarily endorsing his views on that issue, which was formally left open.

> **Kerr J:** [trial judge, p 66] ... What must the owners establish to succeed in barratry? Apart from authority, the answer seems obvious in principle. The owners must establish a loss by the insured peril of barratry, which involves establishing both a deliberate sinking and the absence of the owners' consent. If, at the end of the day, the court is left in doubt whether the owners consented or not, then it seems to me that the claim must fail. This also appears to have been the view of the Court of Session in *Demetriades and Co v Northern Assurance Co, 'Spathari'* (1923) 17 LlL Rep 327, in particular, the judgment of Clerk LJ, p 334. But, as against this, the plaintiffs relied on the decision of the Court of Appeal in *Elfie A Issaias v Marine Insurance Co Ltd* (1923) 15 LlL Rep 186. That was a strange case, which may well have left the insurers justifiably aggrieved in the result.
>
> **Roskill LJ:** [Court of Appeal, p 12] ... But we wish to repeat what we said in giving a brief judgment formally dismissing the appeal, that the fact that we are agreeing with the conclusion reached by the learned judge must not be taken as approval by this court of his views upon the question of burden of proof ... We draw attention to the fact that in the Issaias case, this court regarded the *Martiartu* case as irrelevant. In *Martiartu*, the plaintiffs asserted, but failed to prove, a fortuitous loss. The burden was on them to do so. They succeeded. But in the Issaias case, as the facts were determined in the Court of Appeal, the sinking was held to be, as in the present case it was agreed to be, not fortuitous, but deliberate. The only remaining issue, there as here, was privity. Atkin LJ and the other members of the court clearly thought, and said, that in such a situation the burden of proof was on underwriters and that the assured was entitled to the benefit of the presumption of innocence. We ask, but do not answer, for it is not necessary to do so, whether in these circumstances it was open to the learned judge, or would, indeed, be open to us in this court, not to follow the decision in the Issaias case in the present case, in which deliberate sinking was admitted and the only issue was privity.

The *Spathari* case, an earlier case which is cited below, was also opposed to the *Issaias* rule. The *Spathari* case took the view that, when pleading a loss by barratry, the onus of proving non-complicity lay with the plaintiff.

Demetriades and Co v Northern Assurance Co, 'Spathari' (1923) 17 LlL Rep 65, 327, CA; aff'd (1924) 21 LlL Rep 265, HL

On a voyage from Leith to Samos, *Spathari* sank in moderate weather off the coast of Portugal and the claimants sought to recover for the loss from the defendant insurers. The defendants contended that Demetriades had conceived a fraudulent scheme, whereby he had sold the ship to another person, Borthwick, who registered her under the British flag, filled the ship with cargo, and then over-insured both the ship and the cargo. The chief engineer was then to scuttle the ship. There was little doubt that the chief engineer had, in fact, scuttled the ship, but the question before the court was whether the owners had conspired in the sinking.

The court decided that there had been complicity on the part of the owners and, therefore, they could not recover on their policies of insurance. The question of the burden of proving this complicity was raised by the Court of Appeal.

Clerk LJ: [p 334] ... If the evidence establishes that the ship was scuttled, as I think it clearly does, and leaves it in doubt whether or not the pursuers were parties to the plot, then their actions must fail. That I apprehend to be the result of the case in *La Compania Martiartu v Corporation of the Royal Exchange Assurance* [1923] 1 KB 650. I must own that I find it difficult to reconcile that judgment with the later judgment in *Issaias v Marine Insurance Co Ltd* (1923) 15 LlL Rep 186. If the decisions be irreconcilable, then I prefer the former, and I am prepared to follow it.

Anderson LJ: [p 352] ... The case made in evidence, however, by the pursuers, was that the ship sank by reason of the influx of seawater. There is no doubt that the cause of the sinking of the ship was the inflow of seawater and, if the defenders had led no evidence to explain how that inflow might have been occasioned, the pursuers would have been entitled to decree. They would, in that case, have proved the proximate cause of the sinking, and they would have been entitled to found on the presumption that the unascertained peril which occasioned the inflow of water was a peril covered by the policy. If, however, the evidence led by the defenders is of such potency as to create a doubt which the court is unable to solve as to the cause of the influx of water, the presumption which favours the pursuers is displaced. In this event, the case of *Compania Martiartu* [1923] 1 KB 650 decides that the pursuers cannot succeed if they have failed to prove their case. That case is not easily reconcilable with a later decision of the Court of Appeal, *Elias Issaias* (1923) 15 LlL Rep 186. If these two decisions are inconsistent with one another, I prefer the law laid down in the former case, as it seems to me to rest upon the fundamental rule of proof which denies a pursuer success unless he proves his case.

In the *Zinovia* case, below, although barratry was not pleaded as a cause of loss, the issues of complicity and burden of proof were again broached.

Michalos (N) and Sons Maritime SA v Prudential Assurance Co Ltd, 'Zinovia' [1984] 2 Lloyd's Rep 264

Zinovia ran aground in the Gulf of Suez and the owners claimed on their policy of insurance for a loss caused by a peril of the sea. The underwriters denied liability, and contended that the ship had been deliberately cast away with the complicity of the owners.

The court ruled that the insurers had failed to prove that the vessel had been deliberately cast away. Although, in this case, barratry was not pleaded as a cause of loss, the issue of complicity and barratry was again raised and, although Bingham J cited the *Issaias* case as authority to show that the burden of proving complicity fell upon the insurers, he appeared to be less than enthusiastic about it in principle. Furthermore, in his conclusion, it was significant that he qualified his judgment by saying that the same decision would have been reached regardless of whether the burden of proof of complicity lay upon the plaintiff or the defendant.

> **Bingham J:** [p 272] ... To succeed in a claim for loss by any insured peril, it is necessary for an owner to prove the loss and its causation by that peril. In barratry, this would involve him in proving a deliberate casting away and the absence of consent on his part. In the absence of suspicious circumstances, lack of consent might readily be inferred, and very little in the way of proof might be necessary, but it would still seem to me wrong in principle that the onus should be laid on underwriters of disproving an essential ingredient of the owner's claim. The question is not, however, free of authority. Although the issue arose in the Court of Appeal in the *Elias Issaias case* in a curious way, that decision is, as I understand it, clear authority binding upon me in favour of Mr Hamilton's submission [for the owners]. When the *Michael* case reached the Court of Appeal, this question was not argued and was formally left open, but it was understood by three judges peculiarly well versed in this branch of the law, and at least one member of the Bar was left in no doubt what the result would have been had the argument progressed. I therefore hold that, once the owners have proved a casting away by the deliberate act of the master or crew, it is for the insurers to establish to the high standard required for proof of fraud in civil case that the owners consented to, or connived at, the casting away.
>
> [p 303] ... The owners have, in my judgment, succeeded in showing that the loss of the vessel was proximately caused by a peril of the sea, namely, the grounding of the vessel due to negligent navigation and her subsequent pounding on the bottom. If, contrary to my conclusion, the vessel was deliberately run aground by Mr Kouvaris [the chief officer], or any other member of the crew, the insurers have not proved that the owners in any way consented, or were privy, to that action. If the burden of disproving lay on the owners, I should hold that they had discharged it.

In the case of **Continental Illinois National Bank and Trust Co of Chicago and Xenofon Maritimes SA v Alliance Assurance Co Ltd, 'Captain Panagos DP' [1989] 2 Lloyd's Rep 33, CA**, where a vessel was deliberately run aground in the Red Sea and set on fire with the connivance of the owners, Neill LJ deliberated on the issue of barratry and the proving of complicity.

> **Neill LJ:** [p 40] ... It will also be seen that it is a necessary ingredient of the definition that the wilful act should have been committed 'to the prejudice of the owner'. Accordingly, if the primary contention of the owner of a vessel is that the loss was a loss by barratry, I can see great force in the argument that it is for the owner to prove that the wrongful act was committed 'to his prejudice', and, therefore, that it was committed without his consent or connivance: cf *Shell Petroleum Ltd v Gibbs* [1982] 1 Lloyd's Rep 369, p 373; [1982] QB 946, p 986 C.

In *Compania Naviera Santi SA v Indemnity Marine Assurance Co Ltd, 'Tropaioforos'* [1960] 2 Lloyd's Rep 469, where a vessel sank in calm weather in the Bay of Bengal, and the court ruled that she had been scuttled with the connivance of the owners, Pearson J suggested another reason why the burden of proof should fall upon the plaintiffs.

> **Pearson J:** [p 473] ... In assessing the balance of probabilities, due weight must be given to the consideration that scuttling a ship would be fraudulent and criminal behaviour. No doubt one reason for placing the burden of proof on the shipowners in such a case as this is that they are likely to have all, or almost all, the relevant information, and the insurers are likely to have virtually no information initially. The insurers, for their proof of scuttling, or their suggestion that there is strong ground for thinking that there may have been scuttling, have to rely on such information as they can obtain from discovery of documents, and from cross-examination of ship's witnesses called by the plaintiffs.

A logical approach

A reasoned approach to this conflict, regarding the burden of proof where misconduct is alleged, was considered as long ago as 1924. In the following case, *Olympia*, both the Earl of Birkenhead and Lord Sumner agreed that there was a problem in this area of the law and anticipated the House of Lords clarifying the point at some future date. However, Lord Sumner went further, and put forward a logical explanation and possible solution. He suggested that there was a distinct difference between an insurer having to prove wilful misconduct as a defence against an established *prima facie* case for a loss caused by a peril insured against, such as perils of the sea, as opposed to having to prove wilful misconduct as a defence against a peril, such as barratry, where the absence of complicity on the part of the assured is a prerequisite to such a claim.

Anghelatos v Northern Assurance Co, 'Olympia' [1924] 19 LIL Rep 255, HL

This was an appeal by the owner and mortgagees of the Greek steamer *Olympia*. On a voyage from Newport News to Haifa, with a cargo of 6,000 tons of coal, *Olympia* stranded on rocks, near the Azores, and became a total loss. At the time of her stranding, *Olympia* was 12 miles away from where her last navigational observation would have placed her. The plaintiff, who had a previous history of losing ships, claimed on his policy of insurance, but the insurers denied liability, contending that *Olympia* had been scuttled with the complicity of the owner.

The House of Lords, in affirming the decision of the Court of Appeal, ruled that the loss had been deliberate, and with the connivance of the owner.

> **Earl of Birkenhead:** [p 256] ... It has, for instance, been discussed whether, when a plaintiff produces an insurance policy and gives evidence of the

stranding of the ship, he thereby shifts on to the insurance company the onus of showing that the stranding was not accidental, but was the result of fraudulent connivance. Some difference of judicial opinion has appeared in the courts below. It is said, on the one hand, that if the plaintiff adduces evidence that the ship has been sunk, it is then for the underwriters to discharge effectively the onus of showing that the ship was not accidentally, but dishonestly, sunk. It is said by some judges, on the other hand, that it is for the plaintiff in such cases to show not only that the ship perished, but that the ship perished by the risk insured against. My Lords, it is almost certain that this matter will one day require careful consideration by your Lordships when it arises as an issue which actually requires decision in this house, but, having regard to the view which I have formed, and as I understand your Lordships have all found, this is not such a case. It is not, in other words, for us, differing from our usual practice, to lay down a rule *in abstracto* when the conclusion we have reached absolves us from the necessity of a general pronouncement.

Lord Sumner: [p 262] ... It is unnecessary on this occasion to deal with the onus of proof. In view of what was said by Scrutton LJ, I think it is desirable to say this explicitly: that the question whether *Samuel v Dumas*, a decision of your Lordships' House this year, has not now in any way affected the burden of proof is a question that will have to be seriously considered at some time. It is the case that loss by wilful misconduct by the assured is a mere exception out of a *prima facie* general liability from loss by stranding or by foundering, that I can well understand why the law says that those who allege that exception must prove it, namely, the underwriters, but if it be that the law as I understand it lays down finally that an assured is insured against accidental stranding, but not against designed stranding, then it may well be that the assured only brings himself within the proposition that he has proved a loss by perils insured against, if he proves the circumstances of the loss were circumstances of accidental stranding. I, therefore, think that point should explicitly be kept open for future decision.

In the American case of *The Lakeland* **(1927) 28 LlL Rep 293**, the full facts of which are related earlier in the chapter,[10] the Great Lakes steamer *Lakeland* was lost in Lake Michigan and the insurers, instead of directly accusing the owners of wilful misconduct, limited their defence to denying the cause of the loss, and put forward evidence to suggest that there was reason to believe that there was another reason for the loss, namely, wilful misconduct. At no stage did the insurers mount an affirmative defence. The case illustrates how an insurer may avoid the onus of proving, to a high standard, the wilful misconduct of the assured.

Circuit Judge Mack: [p 296] ... The ultimate burden did not shift by reason of the evidence of scuttling presented by the defendants; that evidence was not offered in support of any affirmative defence, because there was none; it was offered to sustain the denial of liability, to raise at least a question in the jury's mind as to whether or not the sinking was in fact due to a peril covered by the

---

10 See above, p 473.

policies; it bore only upon the question as to whether or not plaintiffs had affirmatively made out their case of liability under the policies ... With the burden resting in the plaintiffs, it was essential for them either affirmatively or inferentially to establish by the preponderance of the evidence that the loss was caused by one of the insured risks.

Standard of proof of complicity

Whilst there has been some controversy in the past about the standard of proof required in establishing complicity or wilful misconduct by an assured, it is now generally accepted, subject to higher authority, that the standard falls within the confines of the civil law, that is, on the balance of probabilities. The degree of proof required must then reflect the gravity of the charge.

Proof beyond reasonable doubt

In the *Issaias* case (1923) 15 LlL Rep 186, CA, where it was admitted that the vessel had been sunk deliberately and the sole question before the court was the issue of privity, the Court of Appeal considered the level of proof required of the accusers (insurers) to be of a criminal standard.

> **Warrington LJ:** [p 189] ... The learned judge has said, and I agree with him in this, that when the defendants charge the plaintiff with the very serious misconduct of conniving at the casting away of his ship, in other words, of being a party to that act, it is incumbent on them to bring his guilt home without reasonable doubt.
>
> **Atkin LJ:** [p 192] ... One might refer to numerous works of authority in support, for example, *Taylor on Evidence*, 11th edn, s 112 and passages were cited. The same article in *Stephen* begins with a proposition which I also think is well established: 'If the commission of a crime is directly in issue in any proceeding, criminal or civil, it must be proved beyond reasonable doubt.' These propositions are the very cornerstone of British justice, and have contributed more than any other to establishing its fame: and I venture to think, despite the uneasiness felt at the suggestion by counsel for the defendants, that they apply even to actions brought against underwriters. The question, therefore, is whether the defendants have succeeded in proving beyond reasonable doubt that the owner was privy to the act of the captain in scuttling the ship – not necessarily by knowing or directing the particular act but by procuring, either by direct order or by hint or suggestion, or by even omitting to prevent a known or suspected intention in some way wilfully to lose the ship.

Proof on the balance of probabilities

However, more recently, in another Court of Appeal decision, it was pointed out that the standard of proof is the civil test of the balance of probabilities.

This was proposed in *National Justice Compania Naviera SA v Prudential Assurance Co Ltd, 'Ikarian Reefer'* [1955] 1 Lloyd's Rep 455, CA.

> **Stuart-Smith LJ:** [p 459] ... On this issue [the alleged deliberate grounding of the vessel], the burden of proof rests unequivocally on the insurers, and the degree or standard of proof which the law requires makes the burden heavier than that which rests upon the shipowners. Although the same 'balance of probabilities' test applies, the standard of proof required is commensurate with the gravity of the allegation made; and no more serious allegation can be made against the master of a ship, a trained and experienced professional who was responsible for its safety and for the lives and welfare of its crew. The court, therefore, must take account of the likelihood or otherwise of the master of this vessel intending deliberately to run his vessel aground (*per* Mustill LJ in *Filiatra Legacy* [1991] 2 Lloyd's Rep 337, pp 365–66).
>
> We do not find it necessary to pursue the question, which may be no more than semantic, whether the burden of proof so described by reference to the balance of probabilities is different in practice from the criminal standard of 'beyond reasonable doubt', and if so, by how much. The burden of proof is not discharged, in our judgment, if the evidence fails to exclude a substantial, as opposed to fanciful or remote possibility that the loss was accidental. But we bear in mind that, on the authorities, the burden which rests upon the insurers is derived from the civil, not the criminal standard, and that its nature is as described above.

No absolute standard of proof

That the standard of proof required could vary was discussed in the cases below; the fact that neither of the cases cited are marine cases does not lessen their relevance. In the *Hornal* case, below, Denning LJ had not only considered the variability of the standard of proof, but had also expressly referred to insurance fraud and the *Issaias* case to assert the point that the criminal standard is too high.

Bater v Bater [1951] P 35

In a petition by a wife for a divorce, on the ground of cruelty, the petitioner appealed, because the trial judge had stated that she must prove her case beyond reasonable doubt.

> **Denning LJ:** [p 36] The difference of opinion which has been evoked about the standard of proof in recent cases may well turn out to be more a matter of words than anything else. It is, of course, true that by our law a higher standard of proof is required in criminal cases than in civil cases. But this is subject to the qualification that there is no absolute standard in either case. In criminal cases, the charge must be proved beyond reasonable doubt, but there may be degrees of proof within that standard.
>
> As Best CJ, and many other great judges have said, 'in proportion as the crime is enormous, so ought the proof to be clear'. So, also, in civil cases, the case may be proved by a preponderance of probability, that there may be degrees of

probability within that standard. The degree depends on the subject matter. A civil court, when considering a charge of fraud, will naturally require for itself a higher degree of probability than that which it would require when asking if negligence is established. It does not adopt so high a degree as a criminal court, even when it is considering a charge of a criminal nature; but still it does require a degree of probability which is commensurate with the occasion.

Hornal v Neuberger Products Ltd [1957] 1 QB 247, CA

The plaintiff bought a used capstan lathe from the defendant who had allegedly stated that the lathe had been reconditioned by a reputable firm of toolmakers. The issue facing the court was whether this statement had, in fact, been made and whether the standard of proof required was the civil test of the balance of probabilities.

The Court of Appeal, in overturning the decision of the trial judge, ruled in favour of the plaintiff, but agreed that the judge had applied the correct standard of proof.

> **Denning LJ:** [p 258] ... Nevertheless, the judge having set the problem to himself, he answered it, I think, correctly. He reviewed all the cases, and held rightly that the standard of proof depends on the nature of the issue. The more serious the allegation, the higher the degree of probability that is required: but it need not, in a civil case, reach the very high standard required by the criminal law ... I have already expressed my views on this subject in *Bater v Bater* and I need not repeat them here. I would only mention the insurance cases on which Mr Samler [for the defendants] especially relied, in which the insured person tried to defraud the insurance company by burning down his house or scuttling his ship. In some of those cases, particularly *Thurtell v Beaumont* and *Issaias v Marine Insurance Co Ltd*, the judges have said that the offence of arson or malicious damage must be as fully proved as a criminal charge: but the latest case in the House of Lords, *Lek v Mathews*, shows that that is putting too high a burden on the insurance company.

That there is no absolute standard of proof is well illustrated in case law, which advocates a variable or flexible standard of proof depending on the gravity of the charge. However, in the *Filiatra Legacy* case, a carriage of goods by sea case, cited below, Mustill LJ expressed reservations about flexible standards of proof, but then went on to suggest that the difference in formulation was of little significance. In similar vein, the problem was described to be 'no more than semantic' in the *Ikarian Reefer* case.

Anonima Petroli Italiana SpA and Neste Oy v Marlucidez Armadora SA, 'Filiatra Legacy' [1991] 2 Lloyd's Rep 337, CA

A cargo of 104,623 tonnes of Iraqi crude oil was loaded in Turkey for Falconara but, on discharge, there was found to be a shortfall of 4,502 tonnes. The plaintiff purchasers of the cargo advanced their claims in tort or bailment relying on negligence or conversion.

The Court of Appeal upheld the appeal by the shipowners and ruled that the purchasers, having alleged a serious crime, had failed to prove their case. The court considered the issue of the standard of proof.

Mustill LJ: [p 365] ... A few sentences ago we made use of the expression 'more likely than not'. This serves to introduce the second feature of the burden of proof, namely, the degree of conviction required of the court before it can find the plaintiffs' case proved, given that such a finding convicts a number of persons of a serious criminal offence. There is no dispute that this is a material factor. One method of taking it into account is that propounded in *Hornal v Neuberger Products Ltd* [1957] 1 QB 247, and perhaps in *R v Secretary of State for the Home Department ex p Khawaja* [1984] AC 74: namely, to postulate a higher burden of proof somewhere between 'sure' and 'balance of probability' where an allegation of criminal conduct is in issue. We ourselves are not altogether comfortable with the idea of flexible burden of proof, and would incline to prefer what we understand to be the view of Slade LJ, in *R v Hampshire CC* [1985] ICR 317, p 329, that, in deciding whether a fact has been proved on balance of probabilities, the likelihood that people such as those involved would band together to commit a crime of the type and magnitude in the manner alleged is one among other factors to be weighed in the balance. We doubt whether the difference in formulation is of any real significance.

References and further reading

Hazelwood, S, 'Marine perils and the burden of proof', in *The Modern Law of Marine Insurance*, 1996, London: LLP, p 143

Muchlinski, PT, 'Proof of scuttling' [1989] LMCLQ 25

CHAPTER 12

THE INCHMAREE CLAUSE

INTRODUCTION

The 'Inchmaree' or 'Negligence' Clause was introduced as a direct result of the case of *Thames and Mersey Marine Insurance Co Ltd v Hamilton, Fraser and Co, 'Inchmaree'* (1887) 12 AC 484, HL, which drew attention to the problems that could arise with some claims made under the auspices of 'perils of the seas'. Often referred to also as the 'additional perils clause',[1] the Clause is now contained within cl 6.2 of the ITCH(95) and cl 4.2 of the IVCH(95).[2] Particular attention is drawn to the due diligence proviso, which applies to the whole of this Clause on additional perils. Should a claim be brought under any one of these perils, the conduct of the 'Assured, Owners, Managers or Superintendents or any of their onshore management' will be called into question.

Noteworthy, also, are the words 'caused by' contained in the Clause. These words ensure that any claim made, for example, under 'bursting of boilers' or 'breakage of shafts', may only be successfully pursued for losses caused by or brought about by such mishaps, and not for any of the damage sustained by the boilers or shafts themselves. The same principle applies to the phrase 'latent defect in the machinery or hull' (cl 6.2.1 of the ITCH(95), and cl 4.2.1 of the IVCH(95)). A claim, for example, for the expenses incurred to replace a specific item of machinery found damaged due to the latent defect within itself would not be recoverable: the underwriter is an insurer, not a guarantor. Such losses would, unless the policy otherwise provides, fall within the exception contained in s 55(2)(c) of the Marine Insurance Act 1906, which states that 'the insurer is not liable for ... inherent vice or nature of the subject matter insured ... or for any injury to machinery not proximately caused by maritime perils'. Clause 6.2 of the ITCH(95) and cl 4.2 of the IVCH(95) have, however, provided otherwise.

A latent defect in hull or machinery could well render a ship unseaworthy, if the extent of the defect was such as to cause her to be incapable of combating the ordinary perils of the seas. In such an event, the Clause will have to be read with s 39 of the Marine Insurance Act 1906. With a voyage policy, s 39(1) clearly states that there is an implied warranty of seaworthiness

---

1 The use of this term is likely to cause confusion, as there is the Institute Additional Perils Clauses, Hulls (1/11/95), which is a separate set of Clauses altogether and may be used only with the ITCH(95): see Appendix 9.
2 For convenience, this clause will hereafter be referred to as the Inchmaree Clause.

which is applicable at the commencement of the insured voyage. Whether the insured peril of latent defect may, therefore, be taken as subordinate to that warranty of seaworthiness, the breach of which will automatically discharge the insurer from liability as from the date of breach,[3] is an interesting question which has yet to be determined by the courts.[4]

There is, however, no such warranty in a time policy: s 39(5) states that '... where, with the privity of the assured, the ship is sent to sea in an unseaworthy state, the insurer is not liable for any loss attributable to seaworthiness'. The very nature of a latent defect is such that it is one not discoverable by the exercise of due diligence. Thus, if the assured were aware of the existence of the defect (rendering the ship unseaworthy) to which the loss is attributable, that defect would not be latent. In such a case, he would not only be unable to rely on the cover for latent defect, but would also fall foul of s 39(5).[5]

The assured is also provided with cover for the 'negligence of Master Officers Crew or Pilots' (under cl 6.2.2 of the ITCH(95) and cl 4.2.2 of the IVCH(95)), which is not incompatible with s 55(2)(a) of the Marine Insurance Act 1906. However, such negligence must be proved to be the proximate cause, or one of the proximate causes, of the loss, for the claim to be successful. Furthermore, the due diligence proviso may also be relevant to a claim for negligence, in so far as it is the responsibility of the assured to ensure that the ship is properly equipped and manned in the broadest sense, so as to ensure that such negligence is minimised.

As would be expected, the Clause does not cover negligence committed by the assured himself. However, the Institute Hull Clauses make specific provision for owners who may also be employed in a seafaring role. To this end, cl 6.3 of the ITCH(95) and cl 4.3 of the IVCH(95) state that 'Masters Officers Crew or Pilots not to be considered Owners within the meaning of this Clause 6 should they hold shares in the vessel'.[6] This allows for an owner or a part owner acting as master (a common occurrence in the coastal trade) to have the protection of the additional perils clause.

The 'negligence of repairers or charterers' is, provided they are not the assured, protected by cl 6.2.3 of the ITCH(95) and cl 4.2.3 of the IVCH(95).

Provision is also made for damage caused by aerial objects: 'contact with aircraft, helicopters or similar objects, or objects falling therefrom' is covered by cl 6.2.5 of the ITCH(95) and cl 4.2.4 of the IVCH(95).

---

3 See s 33(3) and *Bank of Nova Scotia v Hellenic Mutual War Risks Association Ltd, 'Good Luck'* [1991] 2 Lloyd's Rep 191, HL. For a discussion of the legal of a breach of a promissory warranty, see Chapter 7, p 277.

4 See Chapter 7, p 316 and below, pp 500 and 508.

5 See, eg, *Miss Jay Jay* [1987] 1 Lloyd's Rep 32, CA; and *Lemar Towing Co v Fireman's Fund Insurance Co* [1973] AMC 1843, discussed below, p 500 and 505.

6 See ITCH(95), cl 7, Pollution Hazard Clause; IVCH(95), cl 5.

Clause 6.2.4 of the ITCH(95) and cl 4.24 of the IVCH(95) insure against the 'barratry of Master Officers or Crew'. This a major topic within the Inchmaree Clause, and is examined in depth later in the chapter.[7]

The 'additional perils' clause is based upon, and drew its name from, the well known case of *Inchmaree*, below. At the time, a marine policy only provided cover for losses of a 'marine character'; damage or loss caused by the explosion of a boiler, which was not a risk peculiar to the sea, was not covered.

Thames and Mersey Marine Insurance Co Ltd v Hamilton, Fraser and Co, 'Inchmaree' (1887) 12 AC 484, HL

Though a circumstance such as that arising in this case is now an insured peril under the Inchmaree Clause, nevertheless, the case is included, for it provides one with a better insight into the nature of the problem, as it sets the historical background of the Clause and highlights the limitations of the cover of 'perils of the seas'.

Inchmaree was a steamship insured under a time policy, wherein the risks insured against included perils of the seas and '... all other perils, losses and misfortunes that have or shall come to the hurt, detriment, or damage thereof of the aforesaid subject matter of this insurance, or any part thereof'. Whilst lying at anchor awaiting orders, it became necessary to pump up the main boilers by means of the donkey engine. However, a valve in the pipeline between the donkey engine and one of the boilers was closed, due, it was admitted, to the negligence of the engineers, or because it had salted up, even though reasonable care had been taken by the engineers. The result was that the donkey engine became over-pressurised and was damaged. The shipowner claimed on the policy of insurance for the cost of replacing the donkey engine.

The House of Lords, in reversing the decision of the Court of Appeal, ruled that such a loss was not covered by 'perils of the seas' or 'all other perils', and that it was of no account whether the damage was caused accidentally.

Lord Bramwell: [p 491] ... The donkey engine was insured. The adventures and perils which the defendants were to make good, specified a great many particular perils, and 'all other perils, losses and misfortunes that have or shall come to the hurt, detriment or damage of the aforesaid subject matter of insurance, or any part thereof'. Words could hardly be more extensive, and if the question, I ought to say a question on them, arose for the first time, I might perhaps give them their natural meaning, and say they included this case. But the question does not arise for the first time. It has arisen from time to time for centuries, and a limitation has always been put on the words in question.

---

7   See below, p 509.

Definitions are most difficult, but Lord Ellenborough's seems right: 'all cases of marine damage of the like kind with those specifically enumerated, and occasioned by similar causes.' I have had given to me the following definition or description of what would be included in the general words: 'Every accidental circumstance not the result of ordinary wear and tear, delay, or of the act of the assured, happening in the course of the navigation of the ship, and incidental to the navigation, and causing loss to the subject matter of insurance.' Probably, a severe criticism might detect some faults in this. I think the definition of Lopes LJ, in *Pandorf v Hamilton*, very good: 'In a seaworthy ship, damage to goods caused by the action of the sea during transit not attributable to the fault of anybody', is a damage from a peril of the sea.

I have thought that the following might suffice: 'All perils, losses and misfortunes of a marine character, or of a character incident to a ship as such.'

... The damage to the donkey engine was not through it being in a ship or at sea.. The same thing would have happened had the boilers and engines been on land, if the same mismanagement had taken place. The sea, waves and winds had nothing to do with it.

CAUSED BY

The words 'caused by' infer damage brought about or resulting from 'the bursting of boilers, breakage of shafts, or any latent defect in the machinery or hull' and not the damage sustained by the machinery or the hull itself. The following three cases: *Oceanic Steamship Co v Faber*; *Hutchins Brothers v Royal Exchange Assurance Corporation*; and *Scindia Steamships Ltd v London Assurance*, provide an insight into the meaning of the words 'caused by'.

Oceanic Steamship Co v Faber (1907) 13 Com Cas 28, CA

After a voyage from Honolulu, the steamship *Zealandia* dry-docked in San Francisco for maintenance. The vessel was insured under a one year time policy which included 'cover for loss of and/or damage to hull and machinery through ... bursting of boilers, breakage of shafts, or through any latent defect in the machinery or hull ...'. On removing the propeller, a serious crack was detected in the shaft caused by faulty welding some years previously. The shaft was condemned, and the owners claimed on their policy of insurance for a loss caused by a latent defect.

The Court of Appeal ruled that the policy of insurance did not cover the actual machinery within which the latent defect lay, but only losses suffered as a result of (or 'through') the latent defect. This important distinction is emphasised by Fletcher Moulton LJ.

Fletcher Moulton LJ: [p 34] ... Then we come to the words 'or through any latent defect in the machinery or hull'. I am satisfied that that means only actual loss to the machinery or hull, or actual damage to the machinery or hull caused by a latent defect, and that it does not mean condemnation by reason of a patent defect, which is what the plaintiffs contend for. A defect initially latent, but spreading until it becomes a patent defect, is an ordinary incident in all machinery. A person may carefully examine a cylinder cover on one day and find no trace of any defect in it. A week later, he may find a trace of a crack. It is his duty, of course, then to replace it if he can do so. He may be perfectly certain in his mind that the reason that the economic life of that cylinder cover has come to an end is because there was initially something weak in it, and, as is always the case, the weak point is the first to give in. That is a case of a latent defect developing into a patent defect. But it is so ordinary an instance that it is one of the commonest forms in which the economic wearing out of a part of the machinery occurs. I do not believe for one moment that this clause means that the machinery is insured against the existence of latent defects. It only means that, if through their latency those defects have not been guarded against, and actual loss of the hull or machinery, or damage to the hull or machinery, arises from those defects, the insurers will bear the burden of that loss. For these reasons, I think that in the present case there was no loss of shaft or machinery or any other portion of the machinery or of the hull by reason of a latent defect, but that there was simply a condemnation of a shaft, which had shown that it was no longer fit to be used.

Hutchins Brothers v Royal Exchange Assurance Corporation [1911] 2 KB 398, CA

After a voyage to the Black Sea, the vessel *Ellaline* returned to Britain for drydocking and painting. On inspection of the stern frame, a crack was identified, which was later confirmed as a cooling crack caused by faulty workmanship during the casting process. A claim was made by the shipowner for a replacement stern frame. The vessel was insured under a policy which included the Inchmaree Clause.

The court ruled that the cost of a new stern frame was not recoverable, on the basis that the only damage sustained was to the stern frame itself. The damage had been caused by a latent defect during manufacture, and had only been discovered as a result of it being exposed by ordinary wear and tear during the lifetime of the ship.

> **Scrutton LJ:** [p 405] ... In the present case, has any damage to the hull occurred during the currency of the policy through latent defect? The only damage is, in my view, the latent defect itself, which by wear and tear has become patent. But the latent defect did not arrive during the currency of the policy; it existed in 1906, and the underwriter does not insure against wear and tear and its consequences. Has any part of the hull been lost in fact during the currency of the policy? The stern frame has not been lost in fact; it is there as it was before the policy began; the only change is that a previous latent defect has, by wear and tear, become patent.
>
> **Fletcher Moulton LJ:** [p 410] ... It is suggested that this was a 'loss of or damage to hull through a latent defect in the hull' within the meaning of the Inchmaree Clause. It was, in my opinion, nothing of the kind. It was not loss or damage caused by a latent defect but a latent defect itself. To hold that the

clause covers it would be to make the underwriters not insurers, but guarantors, and to turn the clause into a warranty that the hull and machinery are free from latent defects, and, consequently, to make all such defects repairable at the expense of the underwriters. There are no words in the clause which warrant such an interpretation. The fact that it begins with the word 'insurance' negatives, in my opinion, the possibility of its being so interpreted.

BREAKAGE OF SHAFTS

Traditionally, the Inchmaree Clause has always included as covered loss or damage, not only caused by the bursting of boilers, but also by 'the breakage of shafts'. Notably, as with the bursting of boilers, in the event of a shaft breaking, only the loss or damage 'caused by' the breakage of the shaft is covered; damage to the shaft itself does not fall within the liability of the insurer. This was particularly well illustrated in the *Scindia* case, below.

Scindia Steamships Ltd v London Assurance [1937] 1 KB 639

The plaintiff owners of the steamship *Jalavijaya* put her in dry-dock in Bombay to renew some of the wooden lining around the tail end shaft. The vessel was covered by a time policy of insurance, which included an Inchmaree Clause which, in itself, was complicated in its construction. Whilst attempting to remove the propeller, the end of the shaft broke owing to a latent defect, and both the propeller and the end of the shaft fell into the dock and one blade of the propeller was broken off. The owners claimed for both the propeller and the shaft. The defendant underwriters admitted liability for the propeller, but not for the shaft.

The court ruled that the underwriters were not liable for the damage to the shaft; they were only liable for damage caused 'through' the breakage of the shaft, such as the damage sustained by the propeller, and not for damage to the shaft itself.

Branson J: [p 648] ... The facts with regard to the breakage seem to be plain enough. During the operation of wedging off the propeller, the shaft was being subjected to an ordinary operation of repair which any shaft of proper strength and construction would be able to sustain without any difficulty, but, owing to what is described as a 'smooth flaw extending downwards from the top as the shaft then lay' deep into the metal, involving about one-half of the material, the other half of the shaft remained and was broken. It is said on the part of the defendants that that is a latent defect, and, except under those words of this clause which deal with latent defects, damage caused by latent defects is excluded from this clause by virtue of s 55(2)(c) of the Marine Insurance Act 1906. That seems to me to be a sound proposition.

... It is said that 'shafts' are a portion of hull or machinery, being a portion of the machinery, and that loss of or damage to machinery caused through breakage of shafts includes the actual breaking of the shaft itself. That, it seems to me, is a forced construction of the language, and not the ordinary meaning which, reading the clause as a piece of English prose, one would be inclined to put upon it. It follows other clauses in which, obviously, the loss or damage happens to something different from the thing by which the damage is said to be caused. The first clause is 'caused by accidents in loading', and so forth; the next is 'caused through the negligence of master, mariners', and so forth. Both of those clauses obviously envisage, as it seems to me, a state of affairs in which the main cause produces damage which has an effect on something else; and I see no reason why, when after those two clauses, one comes down to the one with which I have particularly to deal, one should read it in any other way. It seems to me, therefore, that the proper reading is that the breakage of the shaft is a loss of or damage to machinery caused by the breakage of the shaft. The breakage of the shaft is the breakage of the shaft, and if, by reason of the breakage of the shaft, the machine is torn to pieces, then one would get damage caused by the breakage of the shaft. But, in this case, the only damage beyond the damage of the propeller, which has been paid for, is the actual damage which happened to the shaft itself, to wit, the breakage of the shaft. To speak of that as damage to the machinery which the breakage of the shaft has caused, seems to me to produce a confusion both of thought and language, which I think should not be introduced into the construction of a clause of this kind.

I therefore think the plaintiffs fail to establish a right to recover under that part of the clause which relates to the breakage of shafts.

LATENT DEFECT IN THE MACHINERY OR HULL

As opposed to normal wear and tear, a latent defect is a flaw in machinery or hull which has not resulted from the want of due diligence by the shipowner or his managers. In the *Wills* case, below, the flaw was in the link of a chain used by a bucket dredger.

Wills and Sons v World Marine Insurance Company Ltd, 'Mermaid' (1911) The Times, 14 March (reported as a note in [1980] 1 Lloyd's Rep 350)

Mermaid was a bucket dredger operated by the plaintiff owners at the port of Aden, and insured by the defendant underwriters; the policy of insurance included an Inchmaree Clause. Whilst the dredger was in motion, a large chain, which controlled the raising and lowering of the bucket ladder, broke, and the dredger was badly damaged. On inspection of the broken link in the chain, it was found to have a defect in the weld. The owners claimed for the cost of repairs to the hull and machinery, the salvage operation in Aden and the cost of the voyage home for those repairs. The underwriters accepted the cost of the salvage operation, but refused to pay the cost of the repairs and the voyage home, on the basis that a prudent owner would have discarded the chain as being unfit for use.

The court ruled that the insurers were liable for an amount to be assessed. The damage to the hull and machinery was caused by a latent defect in a weld in a link of a chain, and not by its usage.

> **Scrutton J:** [p 351] ... Turning now to the Inchmaree Clause, it enables the assured to recover damage to hull or machinery through any latent defect in the machinery, provided such loss or damage has not resulted from want of due diligence by the owners of the ship or by the manager. It was admitted that there was, here, a latent defect in the chain. I find that damage to hull and machinery was caused by this latent defect, and that if the weld had been sound and without defect the link, though worn, would have been of ample strength to stand the strain. I further find that the loss or damage did not result from want of due diligence by the owners or the manager, who were justified in thinking that the chain was sound and of sufficient strength for ordinary perils, and who used all proper care to examine it, and by annealing to keep it in good order. This case appears to me to afford a good example of the legitimate claims which the Inchmaree Clause was intended to cover.

Similarly, in the *Nukila* case, below, the damage to the legs of an accommodation platform were also held to have been caused by latent defects, viz, faulty welds.

Promet Engineering (Singapore) Pte Ltd v Sturge and Others, 'Nukila' [1997] 2 Lloyd's Rep 146, CA

Nukila was an accommodation platform operating in the Java Sea. On a routine inspection, divers found cracks, caused by faulty welding, at the base of all three telescopic legs. It became evident that there were serious fatigue cracks in the feet (spud cans) and also in the legs where they were joined to the spud cans. The platform had to be returned to Singapore, where it had been built, and repair costs amounted to more than S$ 900,000. The owners, Promet Engineering, had insured the platform on the London market under a time policy which incorporated the ITCH(83), including the Inchmaree Clause. The owners claimed for the cost of repairs on the basis of 'damage to the subject matter insured by latent defects in the hull'. The underwriters denied liability, stating that the owners had merely discovered latent defects in the platform legs.

The Court of Appeal, in reversing the decision of the trial judge, ruled that the faulty welds were latent defects which had, in fact, caused damage to the subject matter insured.

> **Hobhouse LJ:** [p 151] ... Insurance covers fortuities, not losses which have occurred through the ordinary incidents of the operation of the vessel. Similarly, the insurance does not cover the cost of maintaining the vessel or running it. As the judge held to be the case in the present action, the cracking occurred as a result of the ordinary working of the platform at sea and the presence of the latent defects in the welds. There was no external accident or cause.

... However, there are further difficulties. A policy of insurance does not cover matters which already exist at the date when the policy attaches. The assured, if he is to recover an indemnity, has to show that some loss or damage has occurred during the period covered by the policy. If a latent defect has existed at the commencement of the period and all that has happened is that the assured has discovered the existence of that latent defect, then there has been no loss under the policy. The vessel is in the same condition as it was at the commencement of the period. Therefore, in any claim under the Inchmaree Clause or any similar clause, the assured has to prove some change in the physical state of the vessel. If he cannot do so, he cannot show any loss under a policy on hull.

[p 152] ... In my judgment, the application of the language of the Inchmaree clause to the facts of the present case is straightforward. At the commencement of the period of cover, there was a latent defect in the welds joining the underside of the top plate of each spud can to the external surface of the leg tube. By that time, that latent defect had also given rise to minute fatigue cracks in the surface of the tube in the way of the weld which could also properly be described as latent defects. Those features during the period of cover caused extensive fractures in the full thickness of the tube extending in places both above and below the defective weld, extensive fractures in the metal of the top plating and bulkheads of the spud cans and other fractures at other locations. This was, on any use of language, damage to the subject matter insured, the hull, etc, of *Nukila*. It was, as the judge found, caused by the condition of *Nukila* at the commencement of the period, that is to say, by the latent defects I have identified. Therefore, subject to authority, the arguments of the owner should be accepted and the claim should succeed.

Meaning of latent defect

In the *Green Lion* case, below, a 'latent defect' was defined as 'one that could not be discovered by any known or customary test'.

Sipowicz v Wimble and Others, 'Green Lion' [1974] 1 Lloyd's Rep 593

In this case from the USA, the plaintiff insured the wooden cutter *Green Lion* with the defendants under a policy of insurance which included an Inchmaree Clause. The vessel sank at her dock in calm weather conditions, and it was subsequently found that the keel and keelson had separated from the hull due to serious corrosion in the fastenings which secured these items in place. The plaintiff owner claimed under the policy, on the grounds that the loss was caused by perils of the seas or by a latent defect.

The court ruled against the plaintiff on both points. It could not be a peril of the sea as the deteriorated state of the fastenings made the loss inevitable, rather than fortuitous. Nor could it be a loss by latent defect, as such a defect is, by definition, one which could not be revealed by a reasonably careful inspection. The plaintiff had been aware of the poor state of the fastenings for some time, including a report made after a condition survey. District Judge Cannella clarified the meaning of 'latent defect'.

> **District Judge Cannella:** [p 598] ... *Green Lion* sank as the result of the incursion of water into her hull. Water was allowed to enter the vessel because the deteriorated metal fastenings which secured the keel and keelson to the hull had weakened and had allowed the separation to occur. These fastenings and the metal assisting frames had deteriorated from age, wear and lack of maintenance, and were not shown to be inherently defective in their original construction. Plaintiff had knowledge of the condition of these metal supports by virtue of the specific recommendations for their repair, reconditioning or replacement contained in the 1966 condition survey report. Plaintiff was further aware of their condition because, as he testified at trial, he had performed certain work in an effort to restore the fastenings. In view of this proof, the loss of *Green Lion* cannot, as a matter of law, be said to have resulted from a latent defect.
>
> A latent defect is a defect which a reasonably careful inspection would not reveal (*Reisman v New Hampshire Fire Insurance Co*). It is not a gradual deterioration, but rather, a defect in the metal itself (*Waterman SS Corporation v United States SR and M Co*). In *Tropical Marine* ..., the court stated that the classic meaning of the term 'latent defect' was as follows:
>
>> A latent defect is one that could not be discovered by any known or customary test ... [and] ... is a hidden defect and generally involves the material out of which the thing is constructed as distinguished from the results of wear and tear ... [It is] a hidden defect ... not manifest, but hidden or concealed, and not visible or apparent; a defect hidden from knowledge as well as from sight ... a defect which reasonably careful inspection will not reveal; one which could not have been discovered by inspection ... by any known and customary test.
>
> ... *Green Lion*'s defective and deteriorated metal fastenings were not, under the above definitions, latent in nature; they were clearly patent. They were observable and had been observed. They were accessible, and access to them had been obtained by the plaintiff, who had made an attempt to restore them. They were not hidden or unknown, but rather, were fully revealed in the 1966 condition survey report. They were not defects inherent in the metal, but were, rather, the result of 27 years of use. As such, the court concludes that the vessel did not sink as the result of a latent defect as that term is employed in the Inchmaree Clause of the instant policies.

And, in the *Caribbean Sea* case, below, a latent defect was considered to include a defect in design which could, in fact, be the proximate cause of a loss.

Prudent Tankers Ltd SA v The Dominion Insurance Co Ltd, 'Caribbean Sea' [1980] 1 Lloyd's Rep 338

The 18,372 ton tanker *Caribbean Sea* was owned by the plaintiffs and insured with the defendants under a hull policy which incorporated the American Institute Hull Clauses, including an Inchmaree Clause. The tanker was employed on a voyage carrying crude oil from Venezuela to Tacoma in the

The Inchmaree Clause

United States via the Panama Canal. On leaving Maracaibo, the tanker grounded lightly whilst avoiding a dredger; the master later lodged a protest at Balboa on the Panama Canal. After leaving the Panama Canal, in fair weather conditions, the tanker started taking in water into the engine room through a damaged main sea suction valve and eventually sank. The owners claimed on their policy of insurance for a total loss, on the grounds that the loss was the result of: (a) the grounding; (b) metal fatigue around the valve; and (c) the negligent navigation of the master. The underwriters resisted the claim citing unseaworthiness and wear and tear as the causes of loss.

The court ruled in favour of the plaintiff owners. It was held that the grounding had been a trivial matter, but the defect in the suction valve constituted a latent defect, and any design faults did not preclude recovery under the policy.

Robert Goff J: [p 345] ... I take first Mr Kentridge's submission [for the insurers] that a defect in design is excluded from the cover provided by the Inchmaree Clause. In considering this question, it is important to appreciate that a defect of design may be relevant in more than one way. It may, for example, in due time result in a defect (for example, a crack) in the material from which the hull or machinery is constructed, which, in its turn, may cause a casualty. On the other hand, it may, because the ship is subjected to work for which it is (by reason of the defect in design) inadequate, result in a casualty without any determinate intermediate defect developing in the material, to which the casualty can be attributed as the proximate cause. Furthermore, in considering whether there was a defect in the hull or machinery which directly caused the loss of or damage to the ship, one is concerned with the actual state of the hull or machinery and not with the historical reason why it has come about that the hull or machinery is in that state. If the hull or machinery is in such a state that there can properly be said to be a defect in it, and such a defect is the proximate cause of the casualty, it would seem to matter not that it had come into existence by virtue of (for example) poor design, or poor construction, or poor repair, unless a casualty so caused is excluded from the cover.

[p 346] ... At all events, however this case is to be interpreted, neither the decision, nor the dictum on which Mr Kentridge relied, has, in my judgment, the effect of excluding a defect in hull or machinery from the cover provided by the Inchmaree Clause merely because the historical reason for such defect was defect in design.

[p 347] ... In the present case, however, the casualty is not simply to be attributed to ordinary wear and tear. The defect upon which the owners rely consisted of the fatigue cracks in the wedge-shaped nozzle; and the presence of these cracks is to be attributed to two factors – the manner in which the ship was designed (viz, the welding of the gussets to the nozzle with fillet welds in proximity to the circumferential weld between the nozzle and the spool piece) and the effect upon the nozzle, in these circumstances, of the ordinary working of the ship. The result of this combination of circumstances was that the

fracture opened up a significant period of time before the end of the natural life of this ship.

... The present case is one where defective (though not negligent) design has had the effect that defects would inevitably develop in the ship as she traded; if such defects develop and have the result that a fracture occurs and the ship sinks, such a loss is not, in my judgment, caused by ordinary wear and tear, and so is not excluded by s 55(2)(c) of the Act.

I am also satisfied that the defect in the present case, consisting as it did of the fatigue cracks in the wedge-shaped nozzle, constituted a latent defect. There was, in fact, no discussion before me of the meaning of the word 'latent' in this context. In contracts of affreightment, a latent defect has been held to be a defect which could not be discovered on such an examination as a reasonably careful skilled man would make: see *Brown v Nitrate Producers SS Co* (1937) 58 LlL Rep 188. In the American cases cited to me, a latent defect has been said to be one which cannot be discovered by any known and customary test: see the dictum from *Parente v Bayville* [1975] 1 Lloyd's Rep 333, which I have already quoted. I prefer the former of these two tests, which appears to me to be more in accordance with commercial sense, taking into account as it does the possibility that a ship may be properly and carefully maintained and yet a defect may not be discovered, although a more meticulous examination would have revealed its existence: a casualty caused by such a defect is surely covered by the Inchmaree Clause. I therefore conclude, on that test, that the loss of the ship in the present case was directly caused by a latent defect in the hull, within the cover provided by the Inchmaree Clause ...

Latent defect and unseaworthiness

A latent defect may cause a vessel to become unseaworthy by rendering her incapable of encountering the ordinary perils of the seas. Whether insurance cover for such a defect would override the implied warranty of seaworthiness in a voyage policy, or an express warranty in a time policy, is not clear.[8]

Both a latent defect in design and unseaworthiness were the issues in the *Miss Jay Jay* case, below. However, in this instance, both were held to be concurrent and effective causes of the loss.

Lloyd (JJ) Instruments Ltd v Northern Star Insurance Co Ltd, 'Miss Jay Jay' [1987] 1 Lloyd's Rep 32, CA

The yacht *Miss Jay Jay* was insured by the owner with the defendants on a 12 month time policy which included cover for '... latent defects in the hull or machinery ...'. In July 1980, the owner took the yacht on a round trip to Deauville in France from Hamble; the weather conditions were generally moderate. On her return to Hamble, it was discovered that she had suffered

---

8   See below, p 508.

some damage to her hull; the bonding between the plastic layers of the hull had separated in places. The owner claimed on his insurance policy; the insurers denied liability, citing defective design and manufacture.

The Court of Appeal upheld the decision of the trial judge, who found in favour of the plaintiff owner; the damage was judged to have been sustained by a combination of adverse weather and defective design. Both were concurrent and effective causes of the loss, and Lawton LJ elaborates on the law in such circumstances, in particular, the right of recovery under a time policy where there are two proximate causes of loss, an included loss (adverse weather), and a loss (unseaworthiness) which has not been expressly excluded by the policy.

> **Lawton LJ:** [p 36] ... The fact, as the judge found, that the sea was not exceptional and could have been anticipated, does not stop the loss from being adjudged to have been caused by 'external accidental means'. It was not caused by 'the ordinary action of the wind and waves' (see r 7 of the Construction Rules in the First Schedule to the Marine Insurance Act 1906), but by the frequent and violent impacts of a badly designed hull upon an adverse sea.
>
> ... If the defects in design and construction had been the sole cause of the loss, then the plaintiff would not have been entitled to claim either at common law (see *Ballantyne v Mackinnon* [1986] 2 QB 455) or because of an express exclusion in the policy. On the facts, as the judge found, the unseaworthiness due to design defects was not the sole cause of the loss. It now seems to be settled law, at least as far as this court is concerned, that, if there are two concurrent and effective causes of a marine loss, and one comes within the terms of the policy and the other does not, the insurers must pay.
>
> ... The plaintiffs were not privy to the defects in design (see s 39(5) of the 1906 Act), nor to the fact that, at the material time, the cruiser was not seaworthy. They had not impliedly warranted that it was (see the same sub-section of the 1906 Act), nor had they failed to take reasonable steps to maintain and keep the cruiser in a proper state of seaworthiness as they were required to do under the policy. The loss was not caused by wear or tear so as to cause 'debility'. Since the defendants did not exclude unseaworthiness or design defects which contributed to the loss without being the sole cause (as they could have done), the plaintiffs' claim falls within the policy, provided that what happened in the sea conditions was a proximate cause of the loss.

Notes

If the ship had, in this case, been insured under a voyage policy, and had suffered from a defect existing at the commencement of the voyage rendering her unseaworthy, the insurer could simply have pleaded a breach of the implied warranty of seaworthiness as his defence. In such an event, there would have been no need for the insurer to involve itself with the legal niceties pertaining to the meaning of the term 'latent defect'. For a case illustrating the interaction between negligence and unseaworthiness (and the due diligence proviso), reference should be made to the American case of *Lemar Towing Co v Fireman's Fund Insurance Co* [1973] AMC 1843, which is discussed later.[9]

NEGLIGENCE OF MASTER OFFICERS CREW OR PILOTS

It is emphasised that this part of the Inchmaree Clause covers a loss proximately caused by 'negligence of Master Officers Crew or Pilots'; whereas the last limb of s 55(2)(a) of the Marine Insurance Act 1906 is only relevant to a case where the loss is 'proximately caused by a peril insured against', but remotely caused by the 'negligence of the master or crew'.

Lind v Mitchell (1928) 45 TLR 54, CA

The plaintiff was the mortgagee of a sailing vessel operating in the area of eastern Canada. On sailing towards Burgeo in Newfoundland, she encountered bad weather and ice, and her side was damaged to such an extent that she started to leak. The captain anticipated a worsening of the weather, and abandoned ship while the conditions were still favourable, and the crew rowed the 15 miles to shore. Before leaving, the captain set fire to the vessel to avoid her becoming a floating derelict and a danger to navigation. She was later found by another ship, still well afloat and not seriously damaged. The mortgagee claimed under the time policy of insurance, which included cover for fire and perils of the seas. There was further cover, under cl 8 of the Institute Time Clauses, for loss of the vessel 'caused' (not 'directly caused') through the negligence of master, mariners, engineers or pilots. Owing to the suspicious circumstances surrounding the loss, the insurers resisted the claim.

The Court of Appeal upheld the decision of the trial judge and ruled that, though the master's abandonment had been unreasonable, it still constituted negligence and the plaintiff mortgagee could recover.

Scrutton LJ: [p 56] ... But in this case, the matter goes higher, I desire to say that I entirely agree with the view of the learned judge below that, suspicious as the case may be, there is no evidence on which one would be justified in finding intentional casting away of the ship, wilful and deliberate misconduct, conduct akin to scuttling by the master. Wilful casting away is a criminal offence and the man who alleges it must prove it, and he must prove it by evidence as if he were alleging a criminal offence.

[p 57] ... Then we have this: there has been negligence of the master, not negligence of the assured. There has been negligence of the master which has resulted in the continuing action of a previously existing peril of the sea. Now,

---

9 See below, p 505.

in my view, that is covered, if it were necessary to cover it, by cl 8 of the Institute Time Clauses. The word 'directly' is left out, and the underwriter insures against loss of the vessel 'caused through the negligence of master, mariners, engineers or pilots'. Now if it were true – and I do not think it is – that, under the existing law, but for that clause you would treat the direct cause of the loss as being the premature abandonment and not the entry of seawater from a previously existing peril, in my view, that clause requires the underwriters to pay where the negligence of the master has caused the loss of the ship.

Sankey LJ: [p 57] ... I think the master was undoubtedly negligent. I think he abandoned the ship prematurely and unreasonably, but I cannot think that those findings amount to something which comes between the negligence for which the insurers are responsible and the criminal negligence for which they are not.

Similarly, in the *Lapwing* case, below, an Inchmaree Clause, covering the 'negligence of Master Officers Crew or Pilots' proved effective. In this instance, even the manager of a boatyard, who acted as master during a dry-docking, was considered to fall within the meaning of 'master' as defined by s 742 of the Merchant Shipping Act 1894, which states: '"Master" includes every person (except a pilot) having command or charge of any ship.'

Baxendale v Fane, 'Lapwing' (1940) 66 LlL Rep 174

The plaintiff, owner of the large yacht *Lapwing*, contracted with a local boatyard to have her dry-docked for cleaning and painting. The boat was insured with the defendants under a time policy which included an Inchmaree Clause. The plaintiff informed their insurers of the intended dry-docking, and was assured that the policy would remain valid. During the dry-docking, the manager of the boatyard, Mr O'Connor, negligently placed her in the dock straddling a large baulk of timber so that when the dock was drained, the yacht strained herself and started to leak badly. *Lapwing* was refloated and repositioned in the dry-dock, but was still inadequately supported. The owner claimed on his policy of insurance for damage caused by a peril of the sea and also relied upon the Inchmaree Clause: '... negligence of Master ...' The insurers refused payment because, they contended, they only insured against 'events that might happen, not events that must happen'.

The court held that the underwriters were liable under the policy on two counts. The yacht had effectively been damaged by stranding during the first attempt to dry-dock her. The negligence of those carrying out the dry-docking provided the fortuitous circumstance necessary to make the damage suffered by the yacht a loss caused by a peril of the sea. Furthermore, as the boatyard manager was acting as 'master' within the meaning of s 742 of the Merchant Shipping Act 1894, the loss was also covered by the Inchmaree Clause under the head of claim which provided cover for a loss 'caused by negligence of Master ...'.

Hodson J: [p 181] ... It is true that it was intended that the vessel should be docked, but not that she should be so negligently docked as to be allowed to sit on a dangerous bottom, and I think that the intervention of the negligence of those responsible for the docking provides the fortuitous circumstances which entitles the plaintiff to recover under the terms of the policy.

... 'Master' has been defined in many statutes. In s 742 of the Merchant Shipping Act 1894, 'Master' includes every person (except a pilot) having command or charge of any ship. I have no doubt that O'Connor was the master of the vessel at the time of the first docking. He was still in charge of her. The fact that he was, at the same time, manager of the yacht works and was the servant of the yacht works, not of the plaintiff, seems to me to make no difference. Indeed, his dual position enables his negligence to be the more clearly established, because he was in a position to know what was the nature of the bottom of the dock in which he was placing the vessel.

... The allegation of negligence against the master was made in the pleadings, and I find that the plaintiff has established that the ship was negligently docked on both occasions. It was not incumbent on him to call the masters or either of them to establish this negligence. The master being in charge of the ship is *prima facie* responsible for the docking of the ship in the proper manner. I have therefore come to the conclusion that the plaintiff is covered under cl 5 of the Institute Yacht Clauses in respect of loss of or damage to hull caused by negligence of the master, whether or not the damage was due to a marine peril.

Notes

It is emphasised that the scope of an Inchmaree Clause could be widened, as it was in the American case of *Rosa and Others v Insurance Company of the State of Pennsylvania, 'Belle of Portugal'*, below, to include the negligence of 'mariners'.

Rosa and Others v Insurance Company of the State of Pennsylvania, 'Belle of Portugal' [1970] 2 Lloyd's Rep 386

The owners insured with the defendants (appellants) the hull of the fishing vessel *Belle of Portugal* and the skiff carried aboard her. The policy included an Inchmaree Clause which stated, *inter alia*, 'This insurance also specially to cover ... loss of or damage to hull or machinery directly caused by the following: ... Negligence of master, charterers, mariners, engineers or pilots'; *Belle of Portugal* sailed from San Diego and was lost at sea due to an electrical fire. The crew took to the skiff and were later picked up by *Port Adelaide*. The crew of *'Port Adelaide'* tried to hoist the skiff aboard, but it was lost. The owners duly claimed for a total loss by fire for *Belle of Portugal* herself, and also for the skiff, due to the negligence of 'mariners'.

The Appeal Court upheld the decision of the trial judge, and ruled for the owners on both issues. Circuit Judge Merrill's observations on the loss of the skiff were brief, but pertinent.

Circuit Judge Charles M Merrill: [p 387] ... Appellant contends that the loss of the skiff was due to the negligence of *Port Adelaide*'s crew; that since such negligence was not insured against in the policy, the insurance company is not liable.

... There is no proof of negligence (other than the testimony of the captain of *Belle of Portugal*, who stated that he was told that the operation of hoisting the skiff was not properly done). Even if there were evidence of negligence, however, the Inchmaree Clause of the insurance policy covers losses due to the negligence of 'mariners'.

Negligence or unseaworthiness?

Negligence should not be confused with incompetence. The Inchmaree Clause provides cover for loss caused by the 'negligence of Master Officers Crew or Pilots', not their incompetence. An incompetent master (or crew) may render a vessel unseaworthy, as was the case in *Lemar Towing Co v Fireman's Fund Insurance Co*, below.

Lemar Towing Co v Fireman's Fund Insurance Co [1973] AMC 1843

The tug *Trudy B* was insured with the defendants and the policy of insurance included an Inchmaree Clause. After departing from the Port of New Orleans for a destination on the West Pearl River, via the inland waterways, she grounded and started taking in water. The captain reported the incident to his employers and was instructed to proceed to a specific shipyard in the vicinity. Before reaching the shipyard, the tug ran into fog and lost its way. When the fog cleared, it was apparent that the tug was quite a distance from her intended position, and the captain had to ask for directions from a passing oyster boat. The captain duly set course as directed but, by now, the ingress of water had worsened, and the tug was listing to port. Shortly afterwards, some rough weather was encountered, and *Trudy B* rolled over and sank. The owners claimed for the loss on their policy of insurance; the underwriters resisted the claim, citing, amongst other things, unseaworthiness due to the incompetence of the crew as their defence.

The court ruled that the crew were incompetent, rendering the tug unseaworthy, and the owners could not recover on their policy of insurance for two reasons: first, they had, by reason of the incompetence of the master, breached the implied warranty of seaworthiness. Secondly, they were unable to satisfy the terms of the due diligence proviso, for the loss or damage had resulted from the want of diligence by the owners in their failing to ascertain the qualification and competence of the master when he was appointed.

District Judge Boyle: [p 660]... It is impliedly warranted that the vessel is seaworthy as of the very moment of the attachment of the insurance; and if the vessel is, in fact, unseaworthy at the time the insurance were to attach, the breach avoids the policy.

... The defendant [insurer] does contend that the crew which manned the vessel on her voyage to the West Pearl was incompetent, thereby rendering the vessel unseaworthy. To escape liability by way of this contention, the underwriter must prove that the shipowner had knowledge of this unseaworthy condition, if in fact it did exist, and that said condition was the proximate cause of the loss.

... We conclude that the crew of *Trudy B*, and particularly its captain, were incompetent at the commencement of the voyage, thus rendering the vessel unseaworthy at that and subsequent times, and that such unseaworthiness proximately resulted from the owner's neglect in failing to determine the qualification and competence of the crew to man the vessel for the intended voyage before its commencement. We further conclude that such unseaworthiness was the proximate cause of the loss of *Trudy B*. And, since the unseaworthiness was caused by the incompetence of the crew, and not by the negligence of the master and crew, the Inchmaree Clause is thus inapplicable.

Notes

Reference should also be made to the *Brentwood* case, examined in detail at the end of this chapter, under the heading of 'the due diligence proviso', where the shipowners were also found to be wanting in their duty.[10]

Negligence of master who is owner or a part owner

In the *Trinder, Anderson* case, below, it was confirmed that a claim for a loss caused by the negligence of a master is not invalidated because the master is also the part owner of the vessel. This principle is maintained and expanded upon by cl 6.3 of the ITCH(95) and cl 4.3 of the IVCH(95), both of which state: 'Master Officers Crew or Pilots not to be considered Owners within the meaning of this Clause 6 should they hold shares in the Vessel.'

Trinder, Anderson and Co v Thames and Mersey Marine Insurance Co [1898] 2 QB 114, CA

The owners of *Gainsborough* effected a policy of insurance with the defendants for a voyage from Sydney to Newcastle, New South Wales, and thence to New Zealand and San Francisco. The master was a part owner in the vessel. During the voyage from New Zealand to San Francisco, with a cargo of coal, she put into Honolulu to replenish her water supply. On nearing Honolulu, the ship stranded on a reef, due to negligent navigation. The ship and cargo were eventually sold, and the owners pressed a claim on the insurers for unpaid freight on the basis of a loss by a peril of the sea through negligent navigation.

---

10 See below, p 532.

The Court of Appeal endorsed the decision of the trial judge, who found for the owners. The fact that the loss was caused by the negligence of the master, who was a part owner of the vessel, did not prevent the owners from recovery under the policy.

AL Smith LJ: [p 123] ... It was held over 50 years ago, in *Dixon v Sadler*, that an assured of ship makes no warranty to the underwriters that the master and crew will do their duty during the voyage, and consequently, their negligence is no defence to an action on a policy when the loss is brought about by their negligent navigation, if the loss is immediately occasioned by the perils of the sea.

... That the negligent navigation of a ship by a person other than the assured affords no defence to an action upon a policy of marine insurance against perils of the sea when the loss is immediately occasioned by a peril of the sea is clear, the reason, in my opinion, being that what is insured against is a peril of the sea, which is none the less a peril of the sea though brought about by negligent navigation. Is there, then, any warranty by a part owner, if he be one of the assured, that he will not personally be guilty of negligent navigation during the voyage covered by the policy? We are not dealing with a loss brought about by the wilful act of an assured. Negligent navigation has never been held to be equivalent to *dolus*, or the 'misconduct' which is spoken by Lord Campbell in *Thompson v Hopper*; nor is it the negligence referred to by Lord Ellenborough in *Bell v Carstairs*, the case of insurance against capture.

[p 124] ... It is not disputed at the bar that negligence of an assured upon a fire policy, whereby the fire was occasioned which caused the loss, affords no defence to the insurer. Why so? Because loss by fire is what is insured against; so, in a marine policy, sea perils are what are insured against. The risk undertaken by an underwriter upon a policy covering perils of the sea is that, if the subject matter insured is lost or damaged immediately by a peril of the sea, he will be responsible, and, in my judgment, it matters not if the loss or damage is remotely caused by the negligent navigation of the captain or crew, or of the assured himself, always assuming that the loss is not occasioned by the wilful act of the assured.

Notes

The Inchmaree Clause, cl 6.3, has clarified that should the 'Master Officers Crew or Pilots' hold shares in the vessel, they are not, for the purposes of the Clause, to be considered the owners of the vessel. Clause 6.3 has deemed irrelevant the fact that a master, officer, crew or pilot may also be the owner or part owner of the insured vessel. The purpose of the Clause is to separate the shipboard duties of a master (officer, crew or pilot) from his obligations and responsibilities as owner or part owner of the insured vessel. Without such a separation, a claim arising out of the negligence or barratrous acts[11] of such shipboard personnel would be tainted. Clause 6.3 ensures that any claim for a loss under the Clause would not be compromised by the fact that the assured, as owner or part owner of the insured vessel, has acted in the capacity of either master, officer, crew or pilot on board his own ship.

NEGLIGENCE OF REPAIRERS OR CHARTERERS

The Inchmaree Clause also provides additional cover against the negligence of repairers or charterers. Clause 6.2.3 of the ITCH(95) states:

6.2 This insurance covers loss or damage to the subject matter insured caused by:

6.2.3 negligence of repairers or charterers, provided such repairers are not an Assured hereunder.

The issue of negligence of 'repairers' arose in the recent case of *Martin Maritime Ltd v Provident Capital Indemnity Fund Ltd, 'Lydia Flag'*.[12] The point of law raised was whether, in a time policy which contained an *express* warranty of seaworthiness, the assured was entitled to recover under the Inchmaree Clause for a loss caused by the negligence of repairers even though, as a result of that negligence, the vessel was shown to be unseaworthy at the inception of the policy. Moore-Bick J was not in any doubt that such a loss is recoverable even though the *express* warranty of seaworthiness had been breached. He said: [p 656] '... I am satisfied that cover is not lost in so far as the vessel may be unseaworthy at the inception of the policy as a result of latent defect or negligence, as in this case, of repairers, provided of course that unseaworthiness has not resulted from the want of due diligence on the part of the owners or managers.'

Thus, it is evident that the same legal issues can also arise in relation to two other heads of the Inchmaree Clause, namely, cl 6.2.1 on 'latent defect in the machinery or hull' and cl 6.2.2 on the 'negligence of Master Officers Crew or Pilots', both causes of which could well render a ship unseaworthy resulting in a breach of the implied warranty of seaworthiness in a voyage policy,[13] or, as the case may be, of an express warranty of seaworthiness in a time policy.[14]

---

11 Clause 6.3 also applies to barratry. See, also, ITCH(95), cl 7, and IVCH(95), cl 5.
12 [1998] 2 Lloyd's Rep 682. This case is also discussed, in greater depth, in Chapter 7, p 316.
13 See s 39(5).
14 Though there is no warranty of seaworthiness implied at any stage of the adventure in a time policy, there is nothing to prevent the parties from incorporating an express warranty of seaworthiness into the policy, as was done in *Martin Maritime Ltd v Provident Capital Indemnity Fund Ltd, 'Lydia Flag'* [1998] 2 Lloyd's Rep 656.

BARRATRY

Rule 11 of the Rules for Construction, Marine Insurance Act 1906, defines barratry to include '... every wrongful act wilfully committed by the master or crew to the prejudice of the owner, or, as the case may be, the charterer'.

'Barratry of Master Officers or Crew' is an insured peril under cl 6.2.4 of the ITCH(95), and cl 4.2.4 of the IVCH (95), which is made subject to the due diligence proviso. Further, it is to be noted that barratry, and piracy, are expressly excluded from the War Exclusion Clause, cl 24.2 of the ITCH(95), and cl 21.2 of the IVCH(95), which free an insurer from '... loss, damage, liability or expense caused by capture, seizure, arrest or detainment (barratry and piracy excepted), and the consequences thereof or any attempt thereat'.

Barratry may be committed by the master or members of the crew or, indeed, by a master who is a part owner.[15] The barratrous act must, by definition, be prejudicial to the owner or the charterer, and in the case of a master who is also a part owner, his co-owners. Thus, any wrongful act committed by the master or crew with the consent of, or connivance with, the shipowner or, as the case may be, the charterer, must preclude barratry as a head of claim. The word 'charterer' read in its proper context includes a demise charterer, any charterer or person who may be regarded as having sufficient control of the ship to make him owner *pro hac vice*.

The use of the term 'wrongful' represents a broadening of the concept of barratry which, in earlier cases, under common law, had inferred either fraud, corruption, criminal conduct, illegality, malfeasance, or neglect of duty. A barratrous act may include deviation, scuttling, smuggling, and the master and crew running off with the ship. In so far as smuggling is concerned, the vessel is put at risk with respect to capture and seizure by customs authorities. This raises issues relating not only to causation, but also as to whether the loss or damage falls within the Marine or the War Clauses: is the loss caused by barratry (a marine risk) and/or seizure (a war risk)? It is significant also to note that any loss, damage, liability or expense, though caused by a barratrous act, could also fall within the scope of one of the Exclusion Clauses, namely, War, Strikes, Malicious Acts and Radioactive Contamination, in which case the loss would not be covered by the ITCH(95) or the IVCH(95), but by the Institute War and Strikes Clauses. A strike-related or a politically motivated barratrous act, for example, could well be ensnared by the Strikes Exclusion Clause.

A cargo-owner would not be able to claim for a loss caused by a barratrous act, unless barratry is specifically insured against. However, under the ICC (A), barratry is a peril insured against by reason that the ICC (A) is an 'all

---

15 See ITCH(95), cl 6.3, and IVCH(95), cl 4.3: see above, p 506.

risks' policy with no specific provision excluding barratry within its General Exclusions Clause. Both the ICC (B) and the ICC (C) are silent with regard to barratry, and it must, therefore, not be an insured peril under these policies. Moreover, the General Exclusions Clause (cl 4.7 of the ICC (B) and ICC (C)) reinforces this, in that barratry would fall within the meaning of the words 'deliberate damage or deliberate destruction of the subject matter insured or any part thereof by the wrongful act of any person or persons,' unless, of course, they are deleted by the incorporation of the Institute Malicious Damage Clause.[16]

The wrongful act committed by the master or crew has to be committed against the interests of the shipowner or the charterer, regardless of whether or not either of them is the assured of the policy under consideration. A cargo-owner and a mortgagee (whether suing as an assignee or as an original assured), for example, would have to prove that the act was prejudicial to the shipowner or the charterer, as the case may be.

A plaintiff, in providing the necessary proof that the loss was caused by the deliberate action of the master or member of the crew, will almost invariably be faced with the defence of wilful misconduct, that he was privy to the loss. Thus, the success or failure of a claim for barratry could well depend on the court being convinced that there was, or was not, privity or connivance on the part of the shipowner or, as the case may be, the charterer. This would lead to the question of the burden of proof, namely, whether it lies with the insurer or the assured to prove complicity or the absence of complicity of the shipowner or the charterer, as the case may be, and the related issue of the standard of proof. As there are clearly two points of view on both these issues, it is more convenient to discuss them elsewhere.[17]

Wrongful act

Barratry is a wrongful act in so far as it embraces fraud, breach of duty and criminal conduct. Indeed, in *Vallejo v Wheeler*, below, Lord Mansfield went so far as describe barratry in the most vivid terms as meaning '... every *species* of fraud, knavery or criminal conduct'.

Vallejo v Wheeler (1774) 1 Cowp 143

A Mr Willes chartered the vessel *Thomas and Matthew* to Darwin for a voyage from London to Seville. Darwin, who was both the charterer and owner of the cargo, appointed Brown as captain. Instead of proceeding direct to Seville, the ship deviated to Guernsey on the captain's account to take on wine and brandy. After leaving Guernsey, the ship sprung a leak, and after suffering

---

16 See Appendix 17.
17 See Chapter 11.

further damage, was unable to proceed with the voyage, which resulted in extensive damage to the cargo. Darwin brought an action against his insurer claiming indemnity for the loss of his cargo by barratry.

The court held that the deviation by the captain was barratrous. The deliberations of Lord Mansfield and Aston J provided an early, but clear, explanation of a barratrous act.

Lord Mansfield LCJ: [p 154] ... The first thing to be considered is, what is meant by barratry of the master. I take the word to have been originally introduced by the Italians, who were the first great traders of the modern world. In the Italian dictionary the word *barratrare* means to cheat, and whatsoever is by the master a cheat, a fraud, a cozening, or a trick, is barratry in him: nothing can be so general. Here, the underwriter has insured against all barratry of the master, and we are not now in a case of the owner or freighter being privy to it; if we were, nothing is so clear as that no man can complain of an act done, to which he himself is a party.

... Darwin was the freighter of the ship, and the goods that were on board were his: if any fraud is committed on the owner, it is committed on Darwin. The question then is, what is the ground of complaint against the master? He had agreed to go on a voyage from London to Seville; Darwin trusts he will set out immediately; instead of which the master goes on an iniquitous scheme, totally distinct from the purpose of the voyage to Seville: that is a cheat, and a fraud on Darwin, who thought he would set out directly ... The moment the ship was carried from its right course it was barratry; and here, the loss was immediately upon it. Suppose the ship had been lost afterwards, what would have been the case of the insured, if not secured against the barratry of the master? He would have lost his insurance, by the fraud of the master; for it was clearly a deviation; and the insured cannot come on the underwriters for a loss, in consequence of a deviation. Therefore, I am clearly of the opinion, this smuggling voyage was barratry in the master.

Aston J: [p 155] ... In the present case, the hulk of the ship belonged to Willes, but he had nothing to do with it, having chartered it to Darwin; the jury, therefore, did right to consider Darwin as the owner *pro hac vice*. Having considered him in that light, the conduct of the master was clearly barratry, for he was acting for his own benefit, and without the consent, or privity, or any intended good to his owner ... Therefore, I am clearly of opinion that this change of the voyage for an iniquitous purpose was barratry; which is not confined to the running away with the ship, but comprehends every species of fraud, knavery or criminal conduct in the master by which the owners or freighters are injured.

Notes

It is to be noted that the action in *Vallejo v Wheeler* was brought not by the shipowner, but by Darwin, the charterer and owner of the damaged goods. It would appear that, for all intents and purposes (though not said in so many words), Darwin, who had the right to appoint the captain, was regarded as having sufficient control of the ship as to make him owner *pro hac vice*; as such the act of the master was, as against him, barratrous.[18] The meaning of the words 'the owner, or, as the case may be, the charterer', appearing in r 11, will be discussed later.[19]

But, an act by a master can also be barratrous even when it is committed with the best of intentions, but is nevertheless prejudicial to the owner. Such was the well known case of *Earle v Rowcroft*, below, where Lord Ellenborough analysed in depth the concept of barratry.

Earle v Rowcroft (1806) 8 East 126

The vessel *Annabella* was employed on a voyage from Liverpool to West Africa to exchange goods for slaves before proceeding to the West Indies. On arriving off West Africa, the master, who was also the supercargo, decided to complete his trading with the Dutch in the area, rather than the British, as the terms were advantageous. Holland, at the time, was at war with Great Britain and *Annabella* was intercepted by a British frigate, claimed as a prize and sent to Jamaica, as such.

The court held that the master's actions in trading with the enemy were barratrous for, although his actions were intended for the benefit of the owners, they were committed without their authority. Lord Ellenborough, in providing the judgment of the court, delivered a classic definition of barratry, and clearly indicated that he considered barratry to be a combination of fraud, neglect of duty and a criminal offence.

> **Lord Ellenborough CJ:** [p 133] ... It has been asked, how is this act of the captain in going to D'Elmina, in order to purchase the cargo for his owners cheaper and more expeditiously, a breach of trust, as between him and them? Now I conceive that the trust reposed in the captain of a vessel obliges him to obey the written instructions of his owners where they give any: and where his instructions are silent, he is, at all events, to do nothing but what is consonant to the laws of the land, whether with or without a view to their advantage: because in the absence of express orders to the contrary, obedience to the law is implied in their instructions. Therefore, the master of a vessel, who does an act in contravention of the laws of his country, is guilty of a breach of the implied orders of his owners.
>
> [p 138] ... we are certainly warranted in pronouncing that a fraudulent breach of duty by the master, in respect to his owners; or, in other words, a breach of duty in respect to his owners, with criminal intent, *ex maleficio*, is barratry. And, with respect to the owner of the ship or goods, whose interest is to be protected by the policy, it can make no difference in the reason of the thing, whether the prejudice he suffers be owing to an act of the master, included by

---

18 See, also, *Small v United Kingdom Marine Mutual Insurance Association* [1897] 2 QB 311, CA.
19 See *Soares v Thornton* (1817) 7 Taunt 627; *Nutt v Bourdieu* (1786) 1 Term Rep 323; and *Salem* [1981] 2 Lloyd's Rep 316, QBD.

motives of advantage to himself, malice to the owner, or a disregard to those laws which it was the master's duty to obey, and which (or it would not be barratry) his owners relied upon his observing. It has been strongly contended on the part of the defendant, that if the conduct of the master, although criminal in respect to the State, were, in his opinion, likely to advance his owner's interest, and intended by him to do so, it will not be barratry. But to this we cannot assent. For it is not for him to judge in cases not entrusted to his direction, or to suppose that he is not breaking the trust reposed in him, but acting meritoriously, when he endeavours to advance the interest of his owners by means which the law forbids, and which his owners also must be taken to have forbidden, not only from what ought to be, and, therefore, must be presumed to have been, their own sense of public duty, but also from a consideration of the risk and loss likely to follow from the use of such means. ... And, in giving this opinion, we do not feel any apprehension that simple deviations will be turned into barratry, to the prejudice of the underwriters; for unless they be accompanied with fraud, or crime, no case of deviation will fall within the true definition of barratry, as above laid down.

However, as was shown in *Everth v Hannam*, below, a court is loth to 'fix a master with barratry', unless it can be shown that the alleged barratrous action was of a criminal nature.

Everth v Hannam (1815) 6 Taunt 375

A vessel was insured for a voyage at and from Jutland to Leith. At the time, Sweden was blockading Norway. During the voyage, the insured vessel sailed close to the Norwegian coast and was arrested by the Swedes, who later condemned the vessel and cargo for violating the blockade. The plaintiff owner of the vessel pleaded that the loss had been caused by the barratrous action of the master in taking the ship near to the Norwegian coast.

The court, however, ruled that, in order to recover for a loss caused by barratry, it was necessary to show that the actions of the master were essentially of a criminal nature. As the evidence was insufficient to prove criminal intent, the actions of the master could not be held to be barratrous and, therefore, the insurers were not liable under the policy.

> **Gibbs CJ:** [p 386] ... On consideration, we think that this is not sufficient to so fix the master with barratry as to entitle the plaintiff to recover, without much more inquiry. The master cannot be fixed with barratry, unless he acts criminally; we cannot raise that charge on the loose expression that he was bound for Leith; he might be so, and yet might have order to touch in Norway.

A more recent interpretation of the word 'barratry' was provided by Mustill J (as he then was), in the celebrated case of *Salem*, below, where the judge described 'barratry' as 'this strange word'.

Shell International Petroleum Co Ltd v Caryl Anthony Vaughan Gibbs, 'Salem'
[1981] 2 Lloyd's Rep 316, [1982] 1 Lloyd's Rep 369, [1983] 1 Lloyd's Rep 342, HL

This was a conspiracy to sell a large shipment of illegal oil to the South African Fuel Fund Association (SFF) by breaking a United Nations embargo then in force against all such imports into South Africa. The conspirators acquired a large tanker, registered her as *Salem*, belonging to the Oxford Shipping Company Inc, and insured her with the defendants under a Lloyd's SG policy. The vessel was then offered on the open market for a voyage from the Persian Gulf to the usual European and Caribbean discharge options. The vessel was duly chartered by Pentoil, and 200,000 tons of crude oil was loaded aboard in Kuwait, ostensibly for the voyage advertised. Soon after leaving Kuwait, Pentoil sold the cargo to the plaintiffs (Shell Oil). On arriving off Durban, the vessel's name was changed to *Lema*, and she entered the port where she discharged all but 15,840 tons of residue. She then loaded seawater as ballast, so as to appear still laden, and sailed towards the west coast of Africa. After receiving payment for the cargo, the ship was scuttled by the crew on the orders of the conspirators. Shell claimed on their insurance policy for the loss, citing, inter alia, barratry as the cause of loss.

Mustill J, at first instance, held that since Oxford Shipping were the owners of *Salem* and were undeniably privy to the dishonest act, the plaintiffs' (Shell Oil's) claim premised on barratry was bound to fail. In a clear and concise speech, all the salient features of barratry were spelt out.

> **Mustill J:** [p 334] ... This strange word [barratry], which has featured in policies of marine insurance since medieval times, originally had the connotation of 'trickery'. It has, however, long been established that the peril must be understood in a much more limited sense. In particular: (1) the policy insures only against barratry 'of the master and mariners'. A fraudulent taking by the carrier himself or by a third party does not fall within this peril; (2) it is not enough to show fraudulent conduct by the master and crew directed against the interests of the person insured. Barratry necessarily involves a damnification of the shipowner whether he or someone else is the person insured under the policy sued upon. The word has this meaning, even in the context of a policy on goods or freight: see *Nutt v Bourdieu* (1786) 1 Term 323, p 330, where Lord Mansfield CJ treated it as clear beyond contradiction that barratry could not be committed against any but the owners of the ship; (3) it follows that if the shipowner is privy to the dishonesty of the crew, there can be no recovery under a policy on either ship or goods. Under a hull policy, the assured fails for two reasons: (a) because the loss is not by barratry, since the act is not contrary to his interests; and (b) because he cannot recover for the consequences of his own wrongful act. Under a policy on goods, the assured fails, for the single reason that there is no loss by barratry.

Mere deviation or barratrous deviation?

It is necessary to distinguish a mere (accidental or negligent) deviation from a barratrous deviation, as may be seen in the two cases of *Ross v Hunter* and *Phyn v Royal Exchange Assurance Co*, below. The distinction is significant. A deviation is not barratrous if it occurred because of the master's ignorance and if there was no fraudulent intent.

Ross v Hunter (1790) 4 Term Rep 33

The vessel *Live Oak* was put up as a general ship in Jamaica by Rati, the captain. The plaintiff, amongst others, shipped goods aboard her for delivery in New Orleans. On arriving at the mouth of the Mississippi, the captain dropped anchor and made inquiries in New Orleans some 100 miles away. On returning, he weighed anchor and proceeded to Havana. It appeared that the captain had slaves aboard on his own account, and on finding it difficult to sell them in New Orleans due to an interdiction by the Spanish Government, he sailed for Havana. There were grounds for believing the ship to be lost, and the plaintiff sued for the loss of his cargo by barratry.

The court ruled that the deviation was barratrous and not a mere deviation; the establishment of ownership being a major factor in the decision.

Lord Kenyon CJ: [p 36] ... [on ownership] The conclusion which the jury have drawn by their verdict is, that this was barratry; and the question now is, whether the evidence be sufficient to support that conclusion? The first point to be considered is, whether Rati can be taken to be the owner of the ship? Now, as to that, he was clearly proved to be the captain; but there was no proof whatever of his being owner. And if that fact were necessary to constitute the defence of the underwriter, the affirmative proof lay upon him.

Buller J: [p 37] ... [on deviation and ownership] Barratry is a question of law which, like other questions of law, arises out of facts, and has been well settled. In one sense of the word, it is a deviation by the captain for fraudulent purposes of his own; and that is the distinction between deviation, as it is generally used, and barratry. Then the question is, whether the captain in this case deviated with a fraudulent view, so as to constitute barratry upon the evidence given in the cause. That will depend upon two questions; first, what it is necessary for a plaintiff to prove upon a declaration for the barratry of the captain, and, secondly, what evidence there was in this case of fraud in the captain. First, it appeared that the ship had been put up as a general ship, ready to take the goods of any person to the port to which he professed to be destined; the owner of goods, therefore, may in such a case be supposed, in general, to be an entire stranger to the ship; he deals with the captain qua captain; he knows him in no other character; he acts under the information of the advertisement, which is usually put forth on those occasions, wherein Rati was in the present instance described to be master. By the terms, too, of the policy, the underwriter contracted to indemnify the plaintiff against the barratry of this very man. In the case, then, of a loss, what is incumbent in the plaintiff to prove? He must prove the subscription of the underwriter, his own interest in the goods, his shipping them on board the vessel described in the policy, and the loss of them in consequence of such an act by the captain as amounts to barratry; that is, that he went out of the course of his voyage for a fraudulent purpose. It was not incumbent on the plaintiff to prove that the captain was not the owner, for that would be calling on him to prove a negative ... Proof of that fact, which operates in discharge of the other party, lies upon him. I agree that, if the captain had freighted the ship for the voyage, he could not be guilty of barratry; but the proof of such a fact lies equally on the defendant. It is then asked, why it should not be presumed that the captain went out of his course by the directions of his owner, if he had any? The reason is plain; because the court cannot presume fraud in another person.

... That brings me to the next question, which, in my opinion, is the most material one here, namely, what was the view of the master when he sunk his anchor at the mouth of the river Mississippi? For if it were done with a fraudulent view, I hold that the very sinking of his anchor was an act of barratry ... It appears that he had some negros on board belonging to himself, which he wished to have disposed of at New Orleans; but finding upon going up thither in his boat, that he should not be able to do so, he returned back again to his ship, and immediately sailed for another port. Then, is it too much to say, that he went to New Orleans for the purpose of his own private advantage, and that the stopping the course of his ship was for a fraudulent purpose? Does it not prove clearly that when he dropped his anchor, he did not intend going to New Orleans, unless it suited his own private advantage? The evidence, too, to be collected from the letters, shows that he was considered as a thief and a criminal, and pursued as such; and that all the persons concerned treated him in the character of master only.

Phyn v Royal Exchange Assurance Co (1798) 7 Term Rep 505

The master of a vessel was instructed by his owners to proceed direct from London to Jamaica, but, on leaving the English Channel, she was carried by strong currents and other circumstances to a position close to Tenerife. Although the route to Jamaica lay to the south west, the master proceeded to the north west, to the island of Santa Cruz, where she dropped anchor. The vessel was detained by the Spanish Government and, after hearing of hostilities breaking out between Britain and Spain, condemned as a prize. The cargo-owners pursued a claim for loss by barratry and capture.

The court ruled against the plaintiffs, asserting that the deviation was not barratrous, in that it was due to the captain's ignorance rather than fraudulent intent.

Grose J: [p 507] The question is, whether this was a barratrous deviation. Now in order to see whether this were or were not barratry, I will refer to the opinion of a very able lawyer, Aston J, who, in the case of *Vallejo v Wheeler*, said that there must be fraud or knavery to constitute barratry: 'Barratry is not confined to the running away with the ship, but comprehends every species of fraud, knavery, or criminal conduct in the master, by which the owners or freighters are injured.' An opinion of Buller J, in *Saloucci v Johnson*, has, however, been cited to show that he thought that fraud was not necessary to constitute a barratry ... and, in a subsequent case, *Ross v Hunter*, where his attention was more immediately called to this subject, he considered that barratry could not exist without fraud: '... in one sense of the word it is deviation by the captain for fraudulent purposes of his own; and that is the distinction between deviation, as is generally used, and barratry.' Therefore, Buller J agreed with Aston J in thinking that fraud is a necessary ingredient in barratry. ... The plaintiff's counsel do not say that the captain did anything fraudulently for purposes of his own against the interest of his owners: and it is enough for me to say that I do not see that any fraud was committed, that we cannot presume fraud, and that the jury have negatived fraud.

Smuggling: barratry and/or seizure?

In dealing with barratrous smuggling cases, the court has to decide whether the loss was proximately caused by the barratrous act of smuggling and/or by the eventual seizure by the authorities resulting therefrom. As many of the earlier policies contained the 'warranted free from capture and seizure' clause, it was necessary for the court to determine whether the loss fell within the cover of the peril of barratry and/or the said exclusion. It is necessary in each case to determine the proximate cause (or causes) of the loss. The modern equivalent of the said clause can be found in the War Exclusion Clause (cl 24.2 of the ITCH(95) and cl 21.2 of the IVCH(95)), which reads as follows: '... capture, seizure, arrest, restraint or detainment (barratry and piracy excepted), and the consequences thereof or any attempt thereat.' This has engendered much discussion on the meaning of the word 'seizure', and the interesting question of whether a barratrous seizure (and a piratical seizure) falls within the exception of this exception, all the more so now that it is possible for a court to hold both barratry and seizure as the proximate causes of the loss. In short, is a barratrous seizure (if found to be a proximate cause of loss) an included, or an expressly excluded, loss under the ITCH(95)?[20]

Another issue which the courts may have to resolve in such cases is whether the loss occurred within the period of the cover, namely, during the currency of the time or voyage policy. On this point, a comparison may be made between the cases of *Cory v Burr* (1883) 8 AC 393, HL, and *Lockyer v Offley* (1786) 1 TR 252, where, in the one case, the actual seizure for the barratrous act took place during the currency of the policy and, in the other, after the expiration of the policy.

Cory v Burr (1883) 8 AC 393, HL

The owners of the vessel *Rosslyn* were signatory to a time policy of insurance, wherein the ordinary perils insured against included 'barratry of the

---

20 See Chapter 14, p 571.

master', but the ship was warranted 'free from capture and seizure and the consequences of any attempts thereat'. Before leaving Gibraltar, the master was paid £30 to take on board 8 tons of tobacco to be smuggled into Spain. The ship was arrested off Cadiz by the Spanish authorities, and the shipowners were compelled to pay a sum of money to recover her. The action by the owners against the underwriters was to recover this expense; the claim being based on the barratrous acts of the master.

The House of Lords affirmed the decisions of the lower courts, in ruling that the loss be imputed to 'capture and seizure' and not to the barratry of the master, and the underwriters were held not liable.

Earl of Selbourne LC: [p 395] ... Everything depends upon the construction of the words of the warranty in the policy, the warranty being 'free from capture and seizure and the consequences of any attempts thereat'.

[p 396] ... The facts of this case show what the nature and effect of such a seizure is. The ship was seized in every sense we can put upon the word 'seize'. It was taken forcible possession of, and that not for a temporary purpose, not as incident to a civil remedy or the enforcement of a civil right, not as security for performance of some duty or obligation by the owners of the ship, but it was carried into effect in order to obtain a sentence of condemnation and confiscation of the ship. To my mind, these facts are properly described by the word 'seizure' in its natural sense, and unless there is something else in the policy to show that the word was meant to bear a different sense not inclusive of such a state of facts, I should have said in the absence of authority that they were included.

Lord Blackburn: [p 399] ... The definition of barratry in the case of *Earle v Rowcroft* has never been departed from. The effect of that case is that the act of a captain, for his own purposes and to serve his own ends, engaging in a smuggling transaction which might tend, and in fact in this case did tend, to the injury of his owners and to the ship being seized, is barratry. When he was off the coast of Spain, he caused the engines to be stopped, to look out for the ship into which he had intended to tranship the tobacco in order that it might be smuggled; and he proceeded 'dead slow' while he was looking out for that vessel. That was a clear case of barratry.

... Now, first of all, was that act of the two Spanish revenue officers in taking and seizing this ship in itself one of those matters which would be covered by the insurance against the enumerated perils? I cannot myself doubt that it was. I cannot doubt that it came quite within the terms 'restraints and detainments of all kings, princes and people', namely the Government of Spain; and their seizing the vessel was, I think, a thing for which the owners might have recovered under that head. But it was also, I think, not at all a remote, but a direct and immediate, consequence of the barratrous act of the captain.

[p 400] ... Now comes the question, does this warranty free the underwriters from that responsibility? That is the main question.

... Now, here they are 'warranted free from capture and seizure and the consequences of any attempts thereat'. It was argued that here they have not been warranted free of barratry. That is true, but the barratry would itself occasion no loss at all to the parties insured. If it had not been that the Spanish revenue officers, doing their duty (they were quite right in that respect), had come and seized the ship, the barratry of the captain in coasting along there, hovering, as we should call it, along the coast, in order that the small smuggling vessel might come and take the tobacco, would have done the assured no harm at all. The underwriters do undertake to indemnify against barratry; they do undertake to indemnify against any loss which is directly sustained in consequence of the barratry; and in the case, as I said before, I think the seizure was as direct a consequence of the barratry as could well be. But still, as Field J says, it was the seizure which brought the loss into existence – it was a case of seizure. Then why should it not be protected by this warranty?

Lord Fitzgerald: [p 405] ... I find the following to be the definition of 'barratry' given by Willes J in *Lockyer v Offley*: 'Barratry is every species of fraud or knavery in the master by which the freighters or owners are injured.' Now it is obvious that, with so large a definition as that, there may be instances of barratry which may be either harmless or effect but a small loss – for instance, a deviation, or wilful delay; but barratry may also consist in a very small matter over which the owners or freighters have no control, the effects or consequences of which may be very serious; and I can well understand that prudence of insurers stipulating: 'We will not be responsible for seizure caused by some barratrous act of the master or crew, rendering not only the ship, but also the cargo, liable to confiscation and seizure.'

If such be the interpretation which is to be put upon the contract, I ask the question, by what was the loss occasioned? I apprehend that there can be but one answer to this question, namely, that the loss arose from the seizure. There was no loss occasioned by the act of barratry. The barratry created a liability to forfeiture or confiscation, but might, in itself, be quite harmless; but the seizure, which was the effective act towards confiscation, and the direct and immediate cause of the loss, was not because the act of the master was an act of barratry, but that it was a violation of the revenue laws of Spain.

Lockyer v Offley (1786) 1 TR 252

During the voyage of the vessel *Hope* from Hamburg to London, the master, on his own account, smuggled brandy ashore in casks. The ship arrived in safety at her moorings on the River Thames, but was seized 26 days later by revenue officers for the offence of smuggling. The plaintiff shipowner laid claim against the underwriters for loss by barratry.

The court held that, though the seizure was consequential upon the wrongful actions committed during the voyage insured, an underwriter was not liable for any loss arising from seizure after she had been 24 hours in port.

Willes J: [p 259] ... [Delivering the judgment of the court] Many definitions of barratry are to be found in the books, but perhaps this general one may comprehend almost all the cases. Barratry is every species of fraud or knavery in the master of the ship by which the freighters or owners are injured; and, in this light, a criminal deviation is barratry, if the deviation be without their consent.

But the general question here is whether, as the loss occasioned by the barratry of the master did not happen during the continuance of the voyage, the insurers are liable? I must own this appears to me to be a novel question, and not to have been decided by any former determinations. But as in all commercial transactions the great object is certainty, it will be necessary for this court to lay down some rule, and it is of more consequence that the rule should be certain, than whether it is established one way or the other.

Difficulties occur on both sides in laying down any rule. The first thing to be observed is, that the policy by the terms of it is an undertaking by the insurer for a limited time, during the voyage from Hamburg to London, till the ship has been moored 24 hours in safety; and the ship was not actually seized till near a month afterwards. But it has been said that under ... the Excise laws, the forfeiture attaches the moment the act is done, and that barratry was committed during the voyage. It may be so as to some purposes, as to prevent intermediate alienations or encumbrances; but I think that the actual property is not altered till after the seizure, though it may be before condemnation.

I will put this case: suppose before the seizure of the ship, she had gone on another voyage, and on her return had been seized, would the Crown be entitled to an account of her earnings, after deducting the expenses of the outfit? Surely not. Till the seizure of the ship, it was not certain that the officers of the Crown knew of the illicit trade carried on by the master, or whether they would take advantage of the forfeiture. It would be a dangerous doctrine to lay down that the insurer should, in all cases, be liable to remote consequential damages. This has been compared to a death's wound received during the voyage, which subjected the ship to a subsequent loss. To this point, the case of *Meretrony and Dunlope* seems very material. That was an insurance on a ship for six months, and three days before the expiration of the time she received her death's wound, but, by pumping, was kept afloat till three days after the time: there the verdict was given for the insured, which was confirmed by the court.

I will put another case: suppose an insurance on a man's life for a year, and some short time before the expiration of the term he receives a mortal wound, of which he dies after the year, the insurer would not be liable.

... And this brings me to that part of the case, which weighs most with the court in favour of the defendant, and to which it does not appear to us that any sufficient answer has been given. It was agreed, in the argument, that the Custom House officers might seize for the forfeiture within three years after the fact committed; and that the Attorney General might file and information at any time whilst the ship was in being. Is the insurer during all this time to continue liable? Suppose the ship had gone several voyages afterwards; and suppose a partial loss paid, and the underwriter's name struck off, shall an action be brought on the policy afterwards? His accounts could never be settled, nor could he be finally discharged, while the ship was in existence. Such a position would be monstrous, and would be attended with infinite inconvenience. There must be some certain and reasonable limitation in point of time laid down by the court, when the insurer shall be released from his engagement. If he be liable for a month, he may be for a year, and so on. And we all think that the law on insurances would be left unsettled, and in much confusion, if any other time were suggested than that prescribed by the policy, namely, the continuance of the voyage, and the ship's being moored 24 hours in safety.

The close relationship between 'barratry' and 'seizure' was never better illustrated than in the important American case of *Hai Hsuan*, below.

Republic of China, China Merchants Steam Navigation Company Ltd and United States of America v National Union Fire Insurance Company of Pittsburgh, Pennsylvania, 'Hai Hsuan' [1958] 1 Lloyd's Rep 351, US CA

Hai Hsuan was one of the seven Liberty Class merchant ships sold by the United States Government to the Nationalist Chinese Government and operated by the China Merchants Steam Navigation Company based in Taiwan. All the vessels were insured 'free from capture and seizure'. After the British Government recognised the Government of Communist China, the master and crews of six of the ships defected in Hong King but, in the case of the seventh vessel, *Hai Hsuan*, which was still at sea, the officers and crew took her to Singapore without the consent of the master. There, they raised the communist flag and refused to hand over the vessel to her owners. The owners (CMSN Co) and the United States Government (mortgagees) claimed for the loss of all seven ships by barratry; the insurers refused liability, saying the losses were due to seizure.

The court of first instance held that the six ships in Hong Kong were lost by barratry, but that *Hai Hsuan* was lost by seizure. The Court of Appeal held that all the losses were by barratry and, in so ruling, gave some interesting insights into the differences between a loss by barratry and by seizure.

> **Circuit Judge Soper:** [p 357] ... Barratry is one of the enumerated perils against which the defendants insured the plaintiff. This is a generic term which includes many acts of various kinds and degrees. It comprehends any unlawful, fraudulent or dishonest act of the master or mariners, and every violation of duty by them arising from gross and culpable negligence contrary to their duty to the owner of the vessel, and which might work loss or injury to him in the course of the voyage insured. A mutiny of the crew and forcible dispossession by them of the master and other officers from the ship is only one form of barratry. Now it is obvious, in a practical point of view, that no reasons existed for exempting this particular mode of committing the act from the general risk of barratry which the underwriters assumed. There was nothing in the nature of the voyage, or the business in which the ship was to engage, which furnished occasion for such exception.
>
> ... Upon careful consideration, we are of the opinion that the exception of a loss by seizure does not include the risk of mutiny of the mariners and the forcible taking of the ship from the control of the officers; or, in other words, that it

does not properly exclude from the operation of the policy a loss by barratry. Certainly the word 'seizure' cannot be applied to any barratrous act of the master. He has, by law, possession and control of the ship. He may, it is true, take her out of her course, or convert her to his own use in violation of this duty to the owners. But he cannot be justly said to seize that which is already in his own keeping. The same is true, to a certain extent, of the mariners. While in the discharge of their duty, they have a qualified possession of the vessel. Subject to the order of the master, it is in their care and custody. If they violate their duty and disobey the master, displace him from command and assume entire control of the vessel, it is a breach of trust rather than a seizure: *Lawton v Sun Insurance Company* 2 Cush 500, p 514. It can be properly described only as a barratry, in like manner as misappropriation of money by a servant or agent to whom it is entrusted is, correctly speaking, embezzlement, and not larceny. Indeed, the word 'seizure', as applied to the contract of insurance, may be said to import the taking possession of a ship or vessel by superior force, or by violence from without, and not a barratrous conversion of her by the officers and crew, or either of them.

[p 358] ... Authority is not wanting for the position that 'seizure', in a contract of insurance, is always to be understood in a restricted and limited sense, as signifying only the taking of a ship by the act of governments or other public authority for a violation of trade, or some rule or regulation instituted as a matter of municipal policy, or in consequence of an existing state of war ... It is sufficient for the decision of the present case to say, that it cannot be interpreted to include the dispossession of the master and other officers from the ship by the mariners, and the barratrous conversion of her by them to their own use.

[p 359] ... and so it has become familiar knowledge to the underwriters of marine insurance and their technical advisers, as pointed out in the opinion of the district court, that according to recognised authority, the term 'seizure' does not include a violent taking of possession of the ship by a mutinous crew.

[p 361] ... The respondent further contends that masters and mariners who change sides in a civil war and take their ships with them cannot be considered to have committed barratry. The answer to this is simply that the characterisation of an act as barratrous is independent of the motives which provoke the act. Barratry cannot be modified by patriotism.

Notes

In the recent American case of *Nautilus Virgin Charters Inc, Hilliard L Lubin and Aileen G Lubin v Edinburgh Insurance Co Ltd* (1981) AMC 2082, a chartered auxiliary ketch, unknown to the owners or their brokers, Nautilus Inc, was used for smuggling purposes and was arrested and detained by the Colombian authorities, when it was found to have on board a quantity of marijuana. When the plaintiffs claimed for a loss due to barratry, *Cory v Burr* was cited as the controlling case.

Alexander Harvey II DJ: [p 2094] ... It must therefore be concluded that, whatever the rule may be elsewhere, in this Circuit *Cory v Burr* is controlling in a case such as this one. Accordingly, this court finds and concludes that the loss of *Teho* was proximately caused by the yacht's seizure by Colombian officials and not by the earlier barratrous acts of McKay, Jr. Since loss by seizure is excluded by the express terms of the insurance policy, plaintiffs are not entitled to recover.

Repeated acts of smuggling

If the crew of a vessel repeatedly carry out barratrous acts, such as smuggling, an owner cannot expect to recover from an insurer what he could easily have prevented by not turning a blind eye.

Pipon v Cope (1808) 1 Camp 434

The vessel *General Doyle* was employed as a Post Office packet between Weymouth and the Channel Islands. The owners had effected a 12 month insurance policy warranted 'free from capture and seizure, and the consequences of any attempt thereof'. On three occasions, the vessel was seized by the Customs authorities in Weymouth when they found quantities of spirits, tobacco and salt concealed in her. On each occasion, the owner pleaded ignorance of the crew's activities and the vessel was duly returned. On the last occasion, the vessel was damaged by another ship whilst moored in Weymouth, after being seized, and the owners laid claim against the insurers for sums expended for these restitutions and for repairs to the vessel.

The court ruled for the defendant underwriters, on the basis that the owners could not be excused by pleading continued ignorance.

> **Lord Ellenborough:** [p 436] ... I can conceive, that as by 'captures' in the warranty, hostile captures are evidently meant, so by 'seizures' must be understood seizures ejusdem generis. But this is a clear case of crassa negligentia on the part of the assured. It was the plaintiff's duty to have prevented these repeated acts of smuggling by the crew. By his neglecting to do so, and allowing the risk to be so monstrously enhanced, the underwriters are discharged. Nor can he recover for the repairs. The ship being under seizure when she was run foul of, he had then ceased to have property in her.

Notes

Repeated acts of smuggling, as in *Pipon v Cope* (1808) 1 Camp 434, have now to be considered in the light of the proviso to cl 6.2 and cl 4.2 of the ITCH(95) and the IVCH(95) respectively, for any loss or damage, though proximately caused by barratry, but resulting from 'the want of due diligence by the Assured, Owners, Managers or Superintendents or any of their onshore management' is not recoverable.

Barratrous scuttling

Although the case of *Elfie A Issaias v Marine Insurance Co* (1923) 15 LlL Rep 186 largely concerned itself with the issue of the burden of proof, it nevertheless provides a good example of a case where barratry, pleaded as the basis of a claim, is met with the allegation of privity and connivance on the part of the shipowner, namely, the defence of wilful misconduct under s 55(2)(a) of the Marine Insurance Act 1906. The decisive consideration is whether the act of the master or crew was committed 'to the prejudice' of the owner without his privity or consent.[21] Such was the issue in the *Elfie A Issaias* case, below.

Elfie A Issaias v Marine Insurance Co (1923) 15 LlL Rep 186, CA

The wooden steamer *Elias Issaias* was on passage from Baltimore to Piraeus when the engines suffered a serious malfunction, and she was found drifting in mid-Atlantic by an English vessel, which took her in tow. During the course of the tow, *Elias Issaias* slowly settled in the water, was abandoned, and later sank. The plaintiff shipowner claimed for a total loss by perils of the seas; the underwriters resisted the claim, on the grounds that the ship had been wilfully scuttled on the owner's orders. Evidence was put forward that the owner's finances were stretched.

The Court of Appeal upheld the decision of the trial judge in ruling that the ship had been scuttled by the master and engineer with the connivance of the owners. Warrington LJ, in his judgment, clarified the word 'prejudice', whilst Atkin LJ expanded on the word 'privity'.

> **Warrington LJ:** [p 189] ... it is for the underwriters to show that the wrongful act of the master was not committed 'to the prejudice' of the owner in as much as it was connived at by him. I apprehend that to cast away a man's ship without his consent is 'to his prejudice', although the pecuniary effect may be to his advantage.
>
> **Atkin LJ:** [p 191] ... We have, then, a case now admitted by the plaintiff to be one where the master, intentionally and successfully, let water into the ship for the purpose of sinking her. Unless done with the privity of the owner, this would be barratry: '... a wrongful act wilfully done by the master or crew to the prejudice of the owner' (Sched 1, r 11 of the Marine Insurance Act 1906); and a loss so caused would be covered by the policy sued on.

The owner or, as the case may be, the charterer

Under r 11 of the Rules for Construction, an act committed by the master or crew, even though wrongful, can only constitute barratry if it was committed to the prejudice of 'the owner or, as the case may be, the charterer'. As the

---

21 See, also, *Salem* [1983] 1 Lloyd's Rep 342; and *Piermay Shipping Co v Chester, Michael* [1979] 2 Lloyd's Rep 1.

word 'charterer' is unqualified, one could be tempted to construe the term to include both the ordinary (time and voyage) charterer and the demise charterer. However, the older cases, decided before the Act, have ruled that, to constitute barratry, the wrongful act has to be committed to the prejudice of the owner or the owner *pro hac vice* of the vessel. This would obviously exclude a mere shipper of goods under a bill of lading (see *Nutt v Bourdieu* (1786) 1 Term Rep 323); an ordinary charterer (see *Hobbs v Hannam* (1811) 3 Camp 93 and *Salem* [1981] 2 Lloyd's Rep 316) and a mortgagee (see *Small v United Kingdom Marine Mutual Insurance Association* (1897) 2 QB 311, CA, and *Samuel v Dumas* (1924) AC 431, HL), all of whom belong to a class of persons who generally do not have sufficient control of the ship so as to make them owner *pro hac vice*. On the other hand, as a charterer by demise (or bareboat charterer) is, for all intents and purposes, recognised as the owner *pro hac vice*, an act of barratry may thus be committed against him, provided, of course, that he has not consented to the commission of the wrongful act (see *Vallejo v Wheeler* (1774) 1 Cowp 143 and *Soares v Thornton* (1817) 7 Taunt 627).

In *Salem* [1981] 2 Lloyd's Rep 316, however, Mustill J, in the court of first instance, envisaged that there might be a third 'intermediate' category of charterer, falling between an ordinary and a demise charterer, who is also covered. In each case, he said, the charterparty contract has to be construed in the light of its commercial context. The word 'charterer' has, therefore, to be interpreted to include not only a charterer by demise, who undisputedly has control and possession of the ship, but also a charterer who may have a sufficient degree of control of the ship to be regarded as the owner of the ship for the particular occasion.

It is to be stressed that, regardless of whether the plaintiff is an innocent cargo-owner or an innocent mortgagee, whether suing as an assignee or as an original assured, it has still to be shown that the wrongful act was committed by the master or crew to the prejudice of the shipowner or, as the case may be, the charterer, which expression is, in its proper historical context, understood to mean one who is the owner *pro hac vice*.

In *Soares v Thornton*, below, an act by the owner of a vessel was considered to be barratrous because the charterer of the vessel was the effective owner during the course of the charter and the act by the owner was prejudicial to the charterer.

Soares v Thornton (1817) 7 Taunt 627

The plaintiffs entered into a charterparty with one Joze de Fontes, described in the charterparty as commander and sole owner of the vessel *Joze and Maria*. During the charter, the vessel put into Deal to repair a leak caused by bad weather. While the ship lay in Deal, Fontes came aboard, took the management of her and, together with the actual captain, deliberately ran her ashore, whereby the ship was lost together with half the cargo. The plaintiff charterers claimed that the loss was by barratry.

The court ruled that the loss was by barratry, in that the charterer was the 'effective owner' during the course of the charter and was not privy to the barratrous acts of the master and Fontes, the original owner; the privity of Fontes did not prevent the wrongful act from being barratrous as against the plaintiffs.

> **Gibbs CJ:** [p 639] ... While she was lying at Deal, full of the plaintiff's goods, and no room for any others, the owner of the ship came aboard, and Gouvea, the captain, assenting, wilfully ran her ashore, and the goods were lost to the plaintiffs. The material question is, whether this is a loss by barratry, and the objection to the plaintiff's recovery is, that it was the owner of the vessel who ran her ashore, and by his act occasioned that; which is supposed to be a loss by barratry. Barratry is an act or fraud not directed against the owner of the goods which are lost, but a fraud against the owner of the ship; and, however innocent may be the owner of the goods, who seeks to recover from the underwriter, yet, if the owner of the ship concurs in the act which caused the loss, it takes from it the character of barratry; for the very definition of barratry is, a fraud by the master and mariners against the owner of the ship. Pursuing this principle, in *Vallejo v Wheeler*, an action which was brought to recover a loss by barratry, wherein it was objected, that as the owner did concur, it could not be barratry, the answer given was, the freighter is, for the time, *pro hac vice*, the owner. You, who have let the ship to freight, are for the time not the owner.
>
> [p 641] ... The freighter had filled her up at Pernau, and the owner's opportunity was passed; and the freighter had a right to require that she should then proceed, without any control of any other person, except himself, to her place of destination. Then, the act of the original owner and master together was a complete act of barratry. If the right or the original owner was then at an end, the right of the freighter must be in existence. The concurrence of the freighter was the only thing that would prevent the act of the master from being an act of principle of *Vallejo v Wheeler*; and though there are some minute circumstances of distinction in this case, we are of the opinion that they do not take it out of that principle, and that the judgment therefore must be for the plaintiff. We cannot regret this result to which the reasoning has conducted us; for it is a very hard thing, when a person has insured his goods, to find himself exposed to loss, to which he supposed his indemnity would extend, but in which he is frustrated.

However, as was shown in *Hobbs v Hannam*, below, the actions of a master, in following the orders of a charterer or a charterer's agent, cannot be held to be barratrous, because the charterer was, in effect, the agent of the owner.

Hobbs v Hannam (1811) 3 Camp 93

The plaintiff owner of the ship *Jane* chartered her to a Mr Woodman and then insured her for the voyage at and from Rio de Janeiro and ports on the River Plate to the UK. According to the terms in the charterparty, the charterer, Mr Woodman, was to indemnify the owner in the event of the ship being lost. However, the charterer entrusted the care of the ship to his associate in

Buenos Aires, who smuggled goods aboard *Jane* with the result that she was seized by the authorities. The plaintiffs claimed for a loss caused by barratry, in that the master of *Jane* should never have put into Buenos Aires.

The court held that the loss could not be imputed to barratry, because the master was obeying the orders of the charterer and the charterer was the agent of the owner of the vessel.

> **Lord Ellenborough:** [p 94] ... I clearly think that the loss is to be imputed to the plaintiff himself. I give the dominion of my ship to the charterer, his acts are my acts: and in this case Kendal [the charterer's associate in Buenos Aires], whose orders the master implicitly obeyed, according to his instructions, was, in point of law, the agent of the plaintiff. Therefore, the loss arose from following his own orders; and there is no pretence of imputing it to barratry.

But, in *Nutt v Bourdieu*, below, the owner of cargo failed in his claim that the loss suffered had been caused by barratry, because he, the cargo-owner, was a mere shipper of goods under bills of lading.

Nutt v Bourdieu (1786) 1 Term Rep 323

A cargo-owner by the name of Hague shipped goods aboard the vessel *Bellona* on a voyage from London to Rochelle; the goods were duly insured. The owner of the ship, Le Grands, joined the ship and sailed with her and the cargo to Bordeaux instead of Rochelle, where the cargo was sold by the agents of Le Grands at Le Grands' instigation; Le Grands also induced the master to falsify the bills of lading. The cargo-owner pursued his insurers for the loss by barratry.

The court ruled that the cargo-owner failed in his claim as barratry can only be committed against the owner of a ship. As Hague was a mere shipper of goods under bills of lading and not a charterer, he could in no way be considered the temporary owner of the ship.

> **Lord Mansfield:** [delivering the opinion of the court, p 330] ... The point to be considered is, whether barratry, in the sense in which it is used in our policies of insurance, can be committed against any but the owners of the ship. It is clear beyond any contradiction that it cannot. For barratry is something contrary to the duty of the master and mariners, which are very particular. An owner cannot commit barratry. He may make himself liable by his fraudulent conduct to the owner of the goods, but not as for barratry. And, besides, barratry cannot be committed against the owner with his consent; for though the owner may become liable for a civil loss by the misbehaviour of the captain, if he consent, yet that is not barratry. Barratry must partake of something criminal, and must be committed against the owner by the master or mariners. In the case of *Vallejo v Wheeler*, the court took it for granted that barratry could only be committed against the owner of the ship.

However, in the *Salem* case, below, Mustill J was clearly of the opinion that a charterer, not necessarily a demise charterer, could conceivably have such control over the master and ship as to be qualified to make a claim under the head of barratry should the master or crew act in a manner prejudicial to his interests.

Shell International Petroleum Co Ltd v Caryl Anthony Vaughan Gibbs, 'Salem' [1981] 2 Lloyd's Rep 316, QB

Mustill J: [p 325] ... There might be cases in which the charterer, although unwilling to become a shipowner in the full sense of the word, or even a demise charterer who had the responsibility to man, equip and supply the vessel, might nevertheless need to have a close degree of direct control over the voyage and over the activities of the master and crew. There was thus recognised a third category of charter, intermediate between the ordinary voyage contract of carriage (*locatio operis vehendarum mercium*) and the bareboat charter (*locatio navis*): namely, a contract for the letting of the ship with master and mariners on board (*locatio navis et operarum magistri*). Under this latter form, the charterer was regarded as having possession and control of the ship, and as being the owner *pro hac vice* of the crew.

[p 326] ... The principles of the law of barratry have been established for so long that a court (and certainly not a court of first instance) should not now seek to disturb them, however inclined it might have been to set off in a different direction if tackling the question afresh ... The court ought, in my judgment, still to apply the principles that there can be barratry only against the owner of the ship, and that 'the owner' includes, for this purpose, those who have a sufficient degree of control to make them owners *pro hac vice*. The latter proposition is indeed recognised in a rather oblique way by r 11 of the Rules of Construction of Policy, contained in the Schedule to the Act ... the established interpretation tells one only that barratry may be committed against one owner *pro hac vice*. It is still necessary to consider whether, in a given case, the charterer is such an owner. This requires the charter to be construed; and construed, like any other contract, in the light of its commercial context. This is the context of today, not of 150 years ago ...

[p 327] ... Instead, the court should take note of the established law that barratry only takes the shape of an act directed against the owner *pro hac vice*, who may on occasion be the charterer, and then go on to construe the individual contact before it, taking all the relevant circumstances into account, in order to decide whether this status was conferred on the particular charterer in question.

Owner or part owner acting as master officer or crew

Whilst it is established that a master as sole owner of a vessel cannot commit barratry against himself, there is nothing in law to prevent a master as part owner committing barratry against another part owner. Nor is there anything to prevent a master as sole owner or part owner committing barratry against a charterer, as was shown in *Jones v Nicholson*, below.

Jones v Nicholson (1854) 10 Exch 28

The defendant chartered the vessel *Helena* to carry a cargo of goods from Montevideo to Valparaiso; the captain was in possession of the ship and was described as the owner (ownership was divided thus: David Moffatt, captain, 34/64ths and George Moffatt 30/64ths). The vessel never arrived in Valparaiso, was presumed lost, and the plaintiff underwriters settled for a total loss. The captain had actually sailed the ship to the Cape of Good Hope where he sold the goods and the ship. When the underwriters realised that *Helena* was not actually lost, they laid claim for the return of their money.

The court ruled that the underwriters could not recover their money, because the charterer had suffered a loss by barratry, notwithstanding the fact that the master was also part owner of the ship.

> **Pollock CB:** [p 37] ... We all agree that the plaintiffs [insurers] are not entitled to recover. The question is precisely the same as if, instead of the underwriters seeking to get back the money paid to the assured, the latter had sought to recover for their loss against the underwriters; and the point which we have to decide is, whether the barratry can be committed by a master, who is also part owner of the vessel. I am of opinion that it can. Some expressions of modern authors to the contrary have been cited; but they are, in truth, no authority whatever, since the doctrine laid down is not supported by any decided case. A master who is sole owner cannot commit barratry, because he cannot commit a fraud against himself, but there is no reason why the fact of a master being part owner should prevent the other part owners from insuring their interest in the ship, or the freighters from insuring their goods. If a master, being part owner, in fraud of the other owners, makes away with the ship, that, in my opinion, is barratry. The whole principle in which the doctrine rests supports that view. I forbear to express my opinion on the points raised: it is sufficient to say that there has been a loss by barratry, which would have entitled the assured to recover from the underwriters, and consequently they cannot recover in this action.

Notes

It should be borne in mind that cl 6.3, discussed earlier,[22] is also applicable to a claim under barratry. As in a claim for loss or damage caused by the negligence of the 'Master Officers Crew or Pilots' under cl 6.2.3, a claim for a loss or damage caused by 'barratry of Master Officers or Crew' is also governed by cl 6.3. The fact that a master, officer or crew may also be the owner or part owner of the insured vessel is irrelevant when considering a claim for a loss or damage caused by barratry or negligence.

---

22 See above, p 506.

The innocent mortgagee

As was seen, barratry, by definition, can only be committed against the owner or a person who is effectively in possession or control of the ship. In most circumstances, a mortgagee would not be considered to be the owner or owner *pro hac vice* within the meaning of the definition and, therefore, would be unable to rely on barratry as a basis for recovery. The two cases of *Small v United Kingdom Marine Insurance Association* and *Samuel v Dumas*, below, graphically illustrate the tenuous position of the mortgagee, particularly if he is merely an assignee of a policy.[23]

Small v United Kingdom Marine Mutual Insurance Association (1897) 2 QB 311, CA, CA

Small advanced moneys to Wilkes, so that Wilkes could become part owner of a ship, and was then appointed her master. Wilkes, as a condition of the loan, mortgaged his shares in the vessel to Small and, together with the other part owners, effected a policy of insurance on the ship which also covered Small's interest as a mortgagee. The insurance policy provided cover against, amongst other things, perils of the seas and barratry of the master and mariners. The vessel was lost and Small, the mortgagee, claimed under the insured peril of barratry, alleging that her master, Wilkes, the mortgagor and part owner, had wilfully cast the ship away. The insurers appealed.

The Court of Appeal upheld the decision of the trial judge in ruling that the mortgagee could claim under a loss by barratry, as he was a signatory and party to the insurance policy and not merely an assignee. He had also played a part in the appointment of Wilkes as master of the ship.

> **Lord Esher MR:** [p 313] ... There is no question of an assignment of the policy. The plaintiffs sue on the footing that Small was a party to the policy. It cannot be disputed, in my opinion, that, if this ship had been lost in a storm, and not by the wilful act of the captain, Small could have recovered upon the policy to the extent of his interest, which had been insured by his authority and on his behalf ... It is clear that Small, as the mortgagee of Wilkes' shares in the ship, had an insurable interest to the amount for which the ship was his security. Therefore, Small was insured by this policy against a loss of the ship by perils of the sea or other perils insured against to the extent of his interest as mortgagee. For this purpose, the interest of the mortgagor and mortgagee are distinct interests; the mortgagee does not claim his interest through the mortgagor, but by virtue of the mortgage, which has given him an interest distinct from that of the mortgagor. If the case rested there, the mortgagee would not be in possession of the ship, and would have nothing to do with sailing her, and the captain and crew would be the captain and crew of the mortgagor and his co-owners only ... But, on the other hand, if the captain

---

23 For the position of a mortgagee suing as an assignee of a policy, see *Graham Joint Stock Shipping Co Ltd v Merchants Marine Insurance Co Ltd* (1923) 17 LlL Rep 44 and 241, HL, discussed in Chapter 10, p 430.

were the captain of the mortgagee, then he would be guilty of such misconduct towards the person who employed him as is called barratry. In this case, the judge has found that before the policy was effected, Small had entered into an arrangement with Wilkes in which he was to find the money required, and take a mortgage of Wilkes' shares in the ship as security, and Wilkes was to be captain of the ship; and he appears to have held that Small took part in placing Wilkes in the position of captain. The consent of the co-owners would, I suppose, be necessary to the arrangement that Wilkes was to be the captain, and I think the inference is that they did consent to it. If that were so, then he was in reality the captain of the mortgagee and the co-owners. If he were the captain of the mortgagee, then the wrongful act alleged against him would be barratry as against the person who so appointed him captain; and, accordingly, the learned judge below treated the case as one of barratry. In that view of the case, the mortgagee would be covered by the insurance against a loss by barratry of the master.

AL Smith LJ: [p 315] ... In my judgment, Small was entitled to sue on this policy in his own name, and being so entitled, how did the wrongful act of Wilkes affect him? It is suggested that, because the wrongful act of Wilkes would be a defence to an action by him, therefore, it is a defence to the plaintiff's action. But the answer is that Small was entitled to sue on this policy in his own name and on his own account and had nothing to do with Wilkes ... I think the learned judge was right in holding upon the evidence that Small had taken part in the appointment of Wilkes as captain of the ship. If so, the act of Wilkes was barratrous as against Small, just as it was as against the co-owners, and this is a peril insured against. On that footing, too, the loss was covered by the policy.

Samuel v Dumas (1924) 18 LlL 211, HL

The new owners of the steamship *Gregorios* secured a mortgage on the vessel in favour of P Samuel and Co, bankers, and, accordingly, the ship became security for the advance. The mortgagee, Samuel, instructed the shipowner to effect an all risks insurance policy on the ship, and this was duly done with Dumas and other underwriters. Four months later, whilst on a voyage from Philipeville to the Tyne, *Gregorios* foundered in calm weather off the coast of Spain. It transpired that she had been scuttled by the master and some members of the crew with the connivance of the owners, but not the mortgagee. The mortgagee claimed that the losses were due to barratry, or perils of the seas.

The House of Lords, in upholding the decision of the Court of Appeal, ruled against the mortgagee. Although the mortgagee had an insurable interest, a claim under barratry would fail, as the captain was not in the service of the mortgagee; nor could it be peril of the seas, as such a loss must be fortuitous and scuttling was not.[24]

---

24 This aspect of the case, that scuttling is not a peril of the sea, is discussed in Chapter 9, p 369.

Viscount Finlay: [p 216] ... The action was brought, as I have said, on behalf of the owner and on behalf or the mortgagee. Any claim on behalf of the owner is, of course, out of the question, as it was he who scuttled the ship. Can the innocent mortgagee recover – can he, in virtue of his independent right as one of the assured under the policy, claim in respect of the loss of the vessel? This will be found to resolve itself into the inquiry whether the loss can be considered as a loss by perils of the sea. The loss was not by barratry, as the captain, in destroying the vessel, was acting under the orders of the owner, and the captain was not in the service of the mortgagee. It follows that, to recover, the mortgagee must show that the sinking of the vessel by the entrance of the seawater which followed from the scuttling can be considered as a loss by perils of the sea, as otherwise, the loss would not be from a peril covered by the policy.

[p 217] ... The scuttling of this vessel occurred on the seas, but it was not due to any peril of the seas; it was due entirely to the fraudulent act of the owner. The scuttling was not fortuitous, but deliberate, and had nothing of the element of accident or casualty about it.

Notes

In the *Small* case, the fact that Small, the mortgagee, had a say (as part of the mortgage arrangement) in the appointment of Wilkes as master was seen as sufficient to 'elevate' his position from that of a mere mortgagee to that of owner *pro hac vice*. As owner *pro hac vice*, the court was able to regard the wrongful act of Wilkes (acting as master) as barratrous as against Small. This, perhaps, is the intermediate third category of charterers envisaged by Mustill J in the *Salem* case.[25] In *Samuel v Dumas*, there was no such arrangement in the mortgage contract. It is submitted that, as the wrongful act committed by the master, Wilkes, was barratrous against his co-owner, the legal requirement 'to the prejudice of the owner' was fulfilled.

It is also to be noted that the decision of the Court of Appeal in the *Small* case, pertaining to the plea of perils of the seas, that any entry of seawater into a ship is a peril of the seas, is now overruled by the House of Lords in *Samuel v Dumas*.

THE DUE DILIGENCE PROVISO

The due diligence proviso, which applies to all of cl 6.2 of the ITCH(95) and cl 4.2 of the IVCH(95), states that it will provide cover only if the loss or damage has 'not resulted from want of due diligence by the Assured, Owners, Managers or Superintendents or any of their onshore management'.

---

25 See above, p 525, and *Vallejo v Wheeler* (1774) 1 Cowp 143, where a charterer who was also the owner of the cargo had a right to appoint the captain.

The insertion of the words 'or Superintendents or any of their onshore management', in 1995, was to bring the clause in line with the spirit of the International Management Code for the Safe Operation of Ships and for Pollution Prevention (the ISM Code) which, though it only came into force on 1 July 1998, was adopted on 4 November 1993 and incorporated on 19 May 1994 into SOLAS 1974 as Chapter IX. The primary objective of the ISM Code is, as declared in its preamble, 'to provide an international standard for the safe management and operation of ships and for pollution prevention'.

The proviso effectively places an umbrella of corporate responsibility upon the shoulder of the shipowner. It is not possible to delegate this duty to exercise due diligence to the master or, for that matter, any other of her seagoing personnel; this is clearly illustrated in the Canadian case of *Coast Ferries Ltd v Century Insurance Company of Canada and Others, 'Brentwood'* [1973] 2 Lloyd's Rep 232, CA. Neither is it possible for the shipowner to escape responsibility by delegating the task to a ship manager, superintendents, or any of their shore-based employees, such as the 'designated person(s)' the appointment of whom is required by Art 4 of the ISM Code.[26]

Coast Ferries Ltd v Century Insurance Company of Canada and Others, 'Brentwood' [1973] 2 Lloyd's Rep 232, CA

Brentwood was a converted car carrier employed in the coastal trade out of Vancouver. The owners insured her with the defendants under a time policy which included cover, subject to an average warranty, for loss or damage directly caused by the '... negligence of Master, Charterers other than the Assured, Mariners, Engineers or Pilots; provided such loss or damage has not resulted from want of due diligence by the Assured, the Owners or Managers of the vessel, or any of them ...'. Whilst at sea on 23 October 1969, during the early hours of the morning, *Brentwood* started taking in water and the master and crew abandoned her. The master later reboarded her and beached her. The owners claimed for the repair costs on their policy of insurance, citing the negligence of the master as the basis of their claim. The insurers resisted, claiming that the owners were privy to the master's negligence. *Brentwood* had apparently put to sea in a badly loaded condition and was down by the head to such an extent that water from her bow wave had entered the ventilators until she had lost stability and rolled over.

The trial judge found for the owners, affirming that the unseaworthiness was caused by incorrect loading, for which the master was to blame, but the owners were not. The Court of Appeal reversed the decision and ruled that, although the loading was indeed the responsibility of the master, the owners

---

26 Article 4 states: 'To ensure the safe operation of each ship and to provide a link between the Company and those on board, every Company, as appropriate, should designate a person or persons ashore having direct access to the highest level of management. The responsibility and authority of the designated person or persons should include monitoring and safety and pollution prevention aspects of the operation of each ship and to ensure that adequate resources and shore-based support are applied, as required.'

had not convinced the court that the master had been provided with enough information about minimum freeboard and trim to operate in safety. Davey J expanded on the court's reasoning when considering the lack of 'due diligence' shown by the owner.

> **Davey J:** [p 233] ... I am not prepared to disturb the finding that the proximate cause of the casualty was the unseaworthiness of the vessel due to improper loading, or that the improper loading was due to the negligence of the master. The underwriters are therefore liable under the policies unless the owner was privy to the master's negligence within the meaning of s 41(5) of the Marine Insurance Act, or the loss or damage resulted from want of due diligence by the owner under cl 2 of the policy.
>
> The learned trial judge held that the improper loading was not due to want of due diligence by the owner. It had employed a competent and fully qualified master, and left the entire operation of loading to him, as it was entitled to do, and had not retained in its own hands any responsibility for that operation. He also held that the master was not privy to the negligence of the master. The learned judge also held that the onus of proving that the owner was not guilty of want of due diligence, or privy to the negligence of the master, was upon the owner, but that the owner had discharged that onus. I do not need to express my opinion on whom the burden of proving those matters rested, since I am, with respect, fully satisfied on the evidence that the owner was wanting in due diligence in seeing that the vessel was properly loaded.
>
> ... But, when the owner left full responsibility for the loading to the master, it became its duty to furnish the master with sufficient information about minimum freeboard and trim for the vessel (among other data) to enable the master to exercise sound judgment in loading in the light of his skill and experience. The owner did not do so. Therein lay its want of due diligence.
>
> [p 234] ... Mr Allan [a naval architect employed by the owner] found it incredible that a master would load the vessel so that it had a rake of 1 ft down by the head with a freeboard at the stem of only 18 in. From that, it would appear that an experienced master without any loading instructions should have seen the folly of so loading the vessel. But in my respectful opinion, that does not excuse the lack of diligence of the owner in not supplying proper loading instructions. It emphasises the need for them.
>
> I would allow the appeal and dismiss the action.

Notes

As to which party has to bear the burden of proof of the requirement of the proviso, that the 'loss or damage has not resulted from the want of due diligence by the Assured, Owners, Managers or Superintendents or any of their onshore management', is still unclear.

References and further reading

Pitts, GR, 'Barratry as a covered risk in marine insurance: problems and perspective' [1983] JMLC 131

Hazelwood, SJ, 'Barratry – the scuttler's easy route to the "golden prize"' [1982] LMCLQ 383

CHAPTER 13

THE 3/4THS COLLISION LIABILITY CLAUSE

INTRODUCTION

The purpose of the 3/4ths Collision Liability Clause, more frequently referred to as the Running Down Clause, is to provide a shipowner with some insurance cover for third party liability in the event of a collision.[1] It is necessary, at the outset, to note that two distinct types of loss may arise as a result of a collision.

First, it is to be recalled that the damage suffered by the insured vessel is recoverable as a loss by 'perils of the seas', as defined in r 7 of the Rules for Construction read with the celebrated case of *Wilson, Sons and Co v Owners of Cargo per 'Xantho'* [1887] 12 App Cas 503.[2] Such a loss, if arising as a result of the 'negligence of Master Officers Crew or Pilots' in navigation, is also recoverable under cl 6.2.2 of the ITCH(95).[3]

The second type of loss, known as third party liability, incurred by the assured in the form of damages payable to the owner of the other vessel, is also recoverable under this Clause. Such a consequential loss was not, however, prior to the decision of *De Vaux v Salvador* [1836] 4 Ad&E 420, by reason of its remoteness, considered as a loss by a peril of the sea. The Running Down Clause was thus introduced to provide a shipowner with cover for such a monetary loss resulting from a collision of his vessel with another vessel.

By cl 8 of the ITCH(95),[4] underwriters agree to indemnify the assured to the amount of 3/4ths of the damage inflicted upon the other vessel in the event of a collision; the other 1/4th being borne by the assured. But, in practice, the shipowner is usually a member of a Protection and Indemnity Club, who will meet the shortfall in the third party cover. It is significant to note that in no circumstances will the underwriters' liability for damages amount to more than 3/4ths of the insured value of the vessel insured.[5]

---

1 This is not in conflict with the Marine Insurance Act 1906, which states, in ss 3(1) and 3(2)(c): 'Subject to the provisions of this Act, every lawful marine adventure may be the subject of a contract of marine insurance. In particular, there is a marine adventure where: any liability to a third party may be incurred by the owner of, or other person interested in or responsible for, insurable property, by reason of marine perils.'
2 See Chapter 9, pp 366 and 371.
3 Corresponding IVCH(95), cl 8.2.2.
4 IVCH(95), cl 6.
5 See ITCH(95), cl 8.2.2, and IVCH(95), cl 6.2.2.

However, they have also agreed to pay 3/4ths of the assured's legal costs when contesting liability or taking proceedings to limit their liability.[6] This commitment by the underwriters is dependent upon their prior written consent, and is only intended to cover the costs of the assured when defending a claim, and not when the assured pursues a claim against a third party. Furthermore, unlike a claim for damages, there is, under this head of claim, no limit to the underwriter's liability in relation to the insured value of the vessel.

Clause 8.4 of the ITCH(95)[7] lists the exclusions to the 3/4ths Collision Liability Clause. A new exclusion can be found in cl 8.4.5, which has been incorporated to complement cl 7, the Pollution Hazard Clause.[8] Whereas the Pollution Hazard Clause allows recovery for loss or damage sustained by the assured's vessel caused by the actions of governmental authority taken in order to prevent or mitigate damage to the environment, the purpose of cl 8.4 is to exclude the insurer from liability for certain types of loss, the most notable of which is contained in cl 8.4.5, which relates to any sum which the Assured may have incurred in respect of pollution, contamination or damage to the environment, or threat thereof. Suffice it here to mention that there are exceptions within the exceptions contained in cl 8.4.5.[9]

It is also to be noted that the 3/4ths Collision Liability Clause is subordinate to the provisions contained within the Paramount Clause, cll 24 to 27 of the ITCH(95) and cll 21 to 24 of the IVCH(95).

The Sister Ship Clause, cl 9 of the ITCH(95) and cl 6 of the IVCH(95), is included to ensure that, when a collision occurs between two ships belonging to the same owner, the relationship between the two parties, although actually one and the same, may be considered as being no different from that between strangers. Without this provision, any claim made by one vessel against the other would be out of the question, because, under common law, it is not possible for a person to sue himself. In addition, the Clause ensures that any such claims made against sister ships are referred to a sole arbitrator.

It is significant to note that the 3/4ths Collision Liability Clause is based upon settlement by cross-liabilities, and not single liability.[10] Under the concept of cross-liability, when two ships collide, a level of blame is apportioned between the two ships, which then determines the amount each ship will pay as a proportion of the total damage sustained by both vessels.

In practice, when a collision occurs, the assured's underwriter is liable for the full amount (up to the insured value) of the loss suffered by the assured's

---

6 See ITCH(95), cl 8.3, and IVCH(95), cl 6.3.
7 Corresponding IVCH(95), cl 6.4.
8 Corresponding IVCH(95), cl 5.
9 See below, p 553.
10 See ITCH(95), cl 8.2.1, and IVCH(95), cl 6.2.1.

vessel *plus*, under the 3/4ths Collision Liability Clause, 3/4ths of a proportionate amount of the damage suffered by the other vessel, that amount being dependent upon the degree of blame attached to the assured's vessel. If, for example, the assured is 100% to blame, then the underwriter's liability is 3/4ths of the total damage sustained by the other vessel. If the assured is 50% to blame, then the underwriter's liability becomes 3/4ths of 50% of the total damage sustained by the other vessel.

The assured's underwriter can then, by way of subrogation, recover from the owner (or his underwriter) of the other vessel a proportion (depending on the degree of blame apportioned) of the damage sustained by the assured's vessel. If the assured is 100% to blame, the amount recoverable is 0%; if the assured is 50% to blame, the amount recoverable by the assured's underwriter is 50% of the total damage sustained by the assured's vessel; if the assured is blameless, then the amount recoverable is 100% of the total damage sustained by the assured's vessel.

When cargo insured under the ICC (A) is damaged as result of a collision, the loss is recoverable by virtue of the policy being for all risks. Loss of, or damage sustained by, cargo insured under the ICC (B) and ICC (C) are, however, recoverable under cl 1.1.4 which states:

> This insurance covers ... loss of or damage to the subject matter insured reasonably attributable to collision or contact of vessel, craft, or conveyance with any external object other than water.

The meaning of the word 'contact' was recently considered, albeit briefly, and in a different context, in connection with an express warranty, in *Costain-Blankevoort (UK) Dredging Co Ltd v Davenport, 'Nassau Bay'* [1979] 1 Lloyd's Rep 395.[11] And, should the vessel or craft, in which the cargoes are carried, 'strand, ground, sink, or capsize' as a result of a collision, cl 1.1.2 of the ITCH(95) and IVCH(95) may also be invoked.

THE 3/4THS COLLISION LIABILITY CLAUSE

Clause 8 of the ITCH(95) and cl 6 of the IVCH(95) state:

> The Underwriters agree to indemnify the Assured for 3/4ths of any sum or sums paid by the Assured to any other person or persons by reason of the Assured becoming legally liable by way of damages for ... where such payment by the Assured is in consequence of the Vessel hereby insured coming into collision with any other vessel.

---

11 See Chapter 9, p 388.

Particular attention is drawn to the words 'collision', 'in consequence of', 'vessel,' 'by way of damages', 'paid by', and 'payment by'. The courts have deliberated to some length on their correct application and interpretation.

Collision

Although the following case is strictly one relating to carriage of goods by sea, concerning the litigation between a cargo-owner and a carrier over contractual matters, the affirmation by the House of Lords that 'collision' is a peril of the sea is equally pertinent to marine insurance. It should be noted that, in the *Xantho* case, the court only pronounced about a collision where there was negligence on the part of the other vessel. In this regard, reference should be made to s 55(2)(a) of the Marine Insurance Act 1906, which, clearly, does not exclude an insurer from liability when there is negligence aboard the assured's vessel. Section 55(2)(a) states:

> ... unless the policy otherwise provides, he is liable for any loss proximately caused by a peril insured against, even though the loss would not have happened but for the misconduct or negligence of the master or crew.

Wilson, Sons and Co v Owners of Cargo per 'Xantho' (1887) 12 App Cas 503

The appellants were the owners of the steamship *Xantho*, which sank after a collision, in fog, with another vessel whilst on a voyage from Cronstadt to Hull. The owners lodged their appeal against the cargo-owners on the basis that, *inter alia*, the loss of the ship was due to a collision which was, in this case, an excepted peril, namely, a peril of the sea.

The House of Lords, in reversing the decision of the Court of Appeal, decided that collision was, in fact, a peril of the sea and ruled in favour of the appellants.

> **Lord Herschell:** [p 509] ... It is beyond question, that if a vessel strikes upon a sunken rock in fair weather and sinks, this is a loss by perils of the sea. And a loss by foundering, owing to a vessel coming into collision with another vessel, even when the collision results from the negligence of that other vessel, falls within the same category.

Furthermore, as was illustrated in the *Niobe* case, below, the 3/4ths Collision Liability Clause covers loss or damage sustained by a third party vessel even when that loss or damage is caused by a tug towing the insured vessel.

M'Cowan v Baine and Johnson and Others, 'Niobe' [1891] AC 401, HL

The respondent owners of the sailing ship *Niobe* insured her with the appellant underwriter (David M'Cowan) for a voyage from the Clyde, under tow, to South Wales and thence to Singapore. Included in the policy of insurance was a clause providing indemnity to the assured should the insured vessel be involved in a collision. During the voyage to Cardiff, the tug towing

Niobe collided with and sank another vessel, the owners of which recovered damages from both the tug and *Niobe*. The owners of *Niobe* then pressed a claim against their insurers to recoup their proportion of the payment. The insurers declined to pay, on the basis that the tug, and not *Niobe*, had actually been in the collision, and that the policy of insurance did not cover losses brought about by the actions of the tug.

The House of Lords, affirming the decision of the lower court, ruled that the tug and *Niobe* were one and the same within the meaning of the policy and the insurers were liable for the loss caused by the tug whilst *Niobe* was being towed.

> **Earl of Selborne:** [p 403] ... The words of this contract are: 'If the ship hereby insured shall come into collision with any other ship or vessel, and the insured shall, in consequence thereof, become liable to pay to the persons interested in such other ship or vessel, or in the freight thereof, or in the goods or effects on board thereof, any sum or sums of money, not exceeding the value of the ship hereby assured.' If a ship cannot be said to 'come into collision with any other ship' except by direct contact, causing damage, between the two hulls (including, under the term hull, all parts of a ship's structure), there was in this case no such contact, and the appellants ought to succeed.
>
> But I cannot adopt so narrow a construction of those words. I should hold them to extend to cases in which the injury was caused by the impact, not only of the hull of the ship insured, but of her boats or steam launch, even if those accessories were not (as in this case) insured as being, in effect, parts of the ship. I should also hold them to cover an indirect collision, through the impact of the ship insured upon another vessel or thing capable of doing damage, which might by such impact be driven against the ship suffering damage. I should take the same view, as against insurers in similar terms, of a tug towing one or more barges (in which case, the barge owners would not be liable for a collision) if damage to any vessel were caused by the barge or barges being driven against it through the improper navigation of the tug, although there might have been no impact of the tug itself upon the injured vessel. And, after full consideration, it seems to me to be no more than a reasonable extension of the same principle to include within them such a case as the present.
>
> Where a ship in tow has control over, and is answerable for, the navigation of the tug, the two vessels – each physically attached to the other for a common operation, that of the voyage of the ship in tow, for which the tug supplies the motive power – have been said, by high authority, to be for many purposes properly regarded as one vessel.

Notes

The above case illustrates the point that actual bodily contact between the insured vessel and the third vessel is not necessary to invoke the 3/4ths Collision Liability Clause.

In **Union Marine Insurance Co v Borwick** [1895] 2 QB 279, though the clause in question was much wider in scope than the standard Running Down

Clause (as it included, *inter alia*, damage sustained through collision with 'harbours or wharves or piers or stages or similar structures'), nevertheless, the remarks of Mathew J are cited, as they are useful for a better understanding of the term 'collision'.

> **Mathew J:** [p 281] ... the only question for my decision is, whether the facts which occurred in the cases of these two vessels amounted to loss or damage through collision ... I cannot distinguish collision with from striking against. It has been contended on behalf of the defendant that, in order to constitute a collision, the upper works of the ship must strike some one of the things referred to in the clause in the contract, and that there were not collisions in the present case, because it appears that it was the keels of these two vessels which struck against the toe of the breakwater. According to the view which I have expressed as to the meaning of the words, that argument must be unavailing; and I am therefore satisfied that this was a case of damage by collision ...

In the early case of ***Woodrop-Sims* (1815) 2 Dods 83**, two ships, *Industry* and *Woodrop-Sims*, collided off the South Foreland and, in his judgment, Sir W Scott expanded on the principle of the apportionment of blame:

> [p 85] ... There are four possibilities under which an accident of this sort may occur. In the first place, it may happen without blame being imputable to either party; as where the loss is occasioned by a storm, or any other vis major: in that case, the misfortune must be borne by the party on whom it happens to light; the other not being responsible to him in any degree. Secondly, a misfortune of this kind may arise where both parties are to blame; where there has been a want of due diligence or of skill on both sides: in such a case, the rule of law is that the loss must be apportioned between them, as having been occasioned by the fault of both of them. Thirdly, it may happen by the misconduct of the suffering party only; and then the rule is, that the sufferer must bear his own burden. Lastly, it may have been the fault of the ship which ran the other down; and, in this case, the injured party would be entitled to an entire compensation from the other.

In consequence of

The liability of the insurer under the 3/4ths Collision Liability Clause can only arise where the payments made by the assured is 'in consequence of' the insured vessel coming into collision with any other vessel. The significance of the words 'in consequence of' was highlighted in *France, Fenwick and Co v Merchants Marine Insurance Co Ltd*, below.

France, Fenwick and Co v Merchants Marine Insurance Co Ltd [1915] 3 KB 290

The plaintiff owners of the 5,000 ton steamship *Cornwood* insured her with the defendant underwriters under a policy of insurance incorporating the Institute Time Clauses. Whilst proceeding up the River Seine, *Cornwood* signalled to overtake a slower moving vessel, *Rouen*. During the overtaking manoeuvre, *Cornwood* struck *Rouen* a glancing blow, which did little actual damage, but did result in *Rouen* veering off course and colliding with an oncoming vessel, *Galatee*, which was seriously damaged. The owners of *Cornwood* accepted liability, and claimed on their policy of insurance for the damage done to both the other vessels; the insurers rejected the claim for damage done to *Galatee* on the basis that there had been no physical contact between *Cornwood* and *Galatee*.

The Court of Appeal upheld the decision of the trial judge and ruled for the owners. The collision between *Rouen* and *Galatee* was a 'consequence' of the original slight collision, and the insurers were liable.

> **Swinfen Eady LJ:** [p 299] ... The question raised by this appeal turns upon the construction and true effect of part of the Running Down Clause in The Institute Time Clauses which is attached to a policy of insurance. By the terms of that clause, it was agreed that if the ship insured should come into collision with any other ship or vessel 'and the assured shall in consequence thereof become liable to pay, and shall pay by way of damages to any other person or persons any sum or sums not exceeding in respect of any one such collision the value of the ship hereby insured', then the company will pay. The material words that have to be construed and dealt with in this clause are the words 'in consequence thereof'.
>
> [p 301] ... In my opinion, according to the true construction of a clause such as the present, an assured may become liable to pay damages in consequence of a collision between his ship and another ship, although the damage is not immediately and directly caused by the actual impact between the two colliding vessels ... Under these circumstances, I am of the opinion that the damage occasioned to *Galatee* arose in consequence of the collision between *Cornwood* and *Rouen*, although not the direct and immediate consequence of the impact – although one ship was not, by the force of the impact, driven directly against the other. The collision, with what has to be taken as part of the collision – the attendant incidents of the collision – produced the subsequent result. For these reasons, I am of opinion that the judgment below was right, and that the appeal should be dismissed.

Vessel

An assured can only claim under the 3/4ths Collision Liability Clause for any sum or sums which he has paid for the 'loss of or damage to any other vessel or property on any other vessel'. The Clause may be invoked only when a collision occurs with a 'vessel'. What constitutes a 'vessel' within the meaning of the 3/4ths Collision Liability Clause is most important, for the insurer is clearly not liable for damage or loss arising as a result of collision with any 'object' other than a 'vessel'.

A number of cases are presented, to illustrate not only the problem of determining what exactly constitutes a 'vessel', but also, the relationship between hull insurers and P & I Clubs. As will be seen, one of the criteria which has been employed by the courts for the purpose of determining whether a particular 'object' is or is not a 'vessel' is the test of navigability, proposed in *Chandler v Blogg*. This test was, however, rejected by Greer J, in *Pelton SS Co v North of England Protection and Indemnity Association*, also cited below.

Chandler v Blogg [1898] 1 QB 32

This was a case where the original insurers laid a claim against the reinsurers. The steamship *Newburn* collided with a sunken sailing barge in the Thames. The sailing barge had only recently been sunk, and was later raised and returned to service. The original insurers claimed an indemnity from the reinsurers under the Running Down Clause; the reinsurers rejected the claim, on the basis that a sunken barge was not a 'vessel' within the meaning of the policy.

The court ruled that the sunken barge was a 'vessel' in that it was inherently navigable.

> **Bingham J:** [p 35] ... I am disposed to agree with Mr Walton's contention [for the defendant], that 'collision', when used alone, without other words, means two navigable things coming into contact. In the present case, *Lizzie* was a barge, which happened to have been sunk, and therefore could not have been navigated at the moment when that which the plaintiff contends was a collision took place. If one takes the case of a vessel at anchor, which has taken the ground at low water, it is clear that she cannot be navigated until the tide rises and floats her. Or take the case of a vessel, the rudder of which has been unshipped, she cannot be navigated until her rudder has been shipped again. Yet in neither of the cases which I have suggested could it properly be said that there was not a vessel, or that the vessel was not navigable. I am of opinion that, although *Lizzie* could not have been navigated during a period of a few hours, that is, until she was raised and floated, nevertheless, she was a vessel, and was navigable, within the meaning of the definition which has been suggested, and therefore, what took place comes within Mr Walton's own definition of a collision. The result is that there will be judgment for the plaintiff for his claim in respect of the damage caused to *Newburn* by the collision with *Lizzie*.

Pelton SS Co v North of England Protection and Indemnity Association (1925) 22 LlL Rep 510

The steamship *Zelo* struck the wreck of the Finnish steamship *Merkur* in Barry Roads; *Merkur* had sunk some four months earlier and was in the process of being salvaged. Because of the circumstances of the collision, the hull insurers had previously refused to accept any liability for damages under the Running Down Clause, and the owners of *Zelo* now pursued the P & I Club for the full amount. The P & I Club asserted that any claim could only be met under the terms of the Running Down Clause and, therefore, their liability was 1/4th of the full amount. The test of the case was whether the sunken ship was still a ship within the meaning of the Running Down Clause.

The court ruled that the wreck was still a ship and any claim would have to be within the terms of the Running Down Clause, and the P & I Club was only liable for 1/4th of the damage.

> **Greer J:** [p 512] ... A ship, like any other thing, remains entitled to its description until facts are established which show it has become disentitled to its ordinary name or description. Just as a man may be moribund without ceasing to be a man if the doctors are hopeful that they will be able to secure his recovery by treatment, so I think a ship may remain a ship or vessel even though she be damaged and incapable of being navigated, if she is in such a position as would induce a reasonably minded owner to continue operations of salvage; and if she would, in the ordinary use of the English language, be still described as a ship or vessel, though described as one which was in serious danger of ceasing to be a ship or vessel. In my judgment, the salvors at the time of the loss had a reasonable expectation that they would be able to salve the vessel.
>
> [p 513] ... It seems to me, with great respect, that navigability cannot be the test as to whether the thing is or is not a ship or vessel. I mean navigability at the time of collision, because in this case, *Chandler v Blogg,* above, the vessel was not navigable at the time of collision. It does not seem to me you can test whether a vessel at the bottom is or is not a ship or vessel by saying she will be navigable immediately she comes to the surface. You must apply some other test; and I cannot find any better test than the question whether or not any reasonably minded owner would continue salvage operations in the hope of completely recovering the vessel by those operations and subsequent repair.

Merchants Marine Insurance Co v North of England Protection and Indemnity Association (1926) 32 Com Cas 165, CA

The owners of the steamship *Fernhill* were members of the defendant's association. In 1924, *Fernhill* collided with a large pontoon crane in the harbour at Rochfort in France, due to the negligence of the pilot. The French authorities sued the shipowners, who, together their insurers, accepted liability under French law. The shipowners then assigned the policy of insurance to their insurers, who, in turn, pursued the P & I Club for the full amount of damages on the basis that a pontoon crane was not a ship or 'vessel' within the meaning of the Running Down Clause contained in the hull policy and, therefore, the full liability lay with the P & I Club.

The Court of Appeal found for the hull insurers in ruling that the pontoon crane was not a ship, and did not fall within the definition of the Running Down Clause.

> **Bankes LJ:** [p 169] ... it seems to me that one has to consider not only the structure of the floating crane, but the purposes for which it is capable of being used and the purposes for which, taking its life history, it has been used, and to come to a conclusion upon what would ultimately be an inference from the facts.

[p 170] ... It is in fact a platform upon which a crane is fixed, and permanently fixed. It has no motive power of its own. I do not attach much importance to that, but it is an incident. It is not capable of being steered; it has no rudder. I think that again is only an incident, but I think it rather an important incident. It is undoubtedly capable of being moved, but it is obviously so unseaworthy that it can only be moved short distances, or comparatively short distances, and only when the weather is exactly favourable. It is a most unwieldy structure ... The conclusion I come to is that for the purpose of the construction of this rule, it is more accurately described as a floating platform for the crane than a ship or vessel.

Bennett SS Co v Hull Mutual SS Protecting Society [1914] 3 KB 57, CA

The plaintiff shipowners were members of the defendant's Mutual Protecting Society (P & I Club). The plaintiff's vessel anchored outside Boulogne in fog, and it was later found she had fouled some fishing nets, but had made no actual contact with the fishing vessel. The shipowners made restitution to the owners of the fishing vessel and then pursued the P & I Club for the full amount. The P & I Club admitted liability for 1/4th of the damage, on the basis that the collision was with another ship within the meaning of the Running Down Clause and that the other 3/4ths lay with the hull insurers.

The Court of Appeal, in upholding the decision of the lower court, ruled that the fishing nets were not part of the ship; the claim, therefore, did not fall within the Running Down Clause and the P & I Club was liable for the full amount.

> **Phillimore LJ:** [p 61] ... Whenever any part of the tackle of a vessel is being used in connection with the vessel, although it may be outside the ambit of the hull, as the anchor or a boat towing astern or working ahead to warp the vessel, it may just as well be said to be a part of the vessel when there is a collision with it as if it were still on board the vessel itself. Upon that ground, the case of *In re Margetts and Ocean Accident and Guarantee Corporation* was properly decided. Nets, however, are not a part of the ship in that sense, nor are they things which it is necessary for her to have without which she could not prudently put to sea.

Notes

In *Wells v Owners of Gas Float Whitton No 2* [1897] AC 337, a claim for salvage on a gas float, shaped like a boat, which had broken free in a storm, was rejected by the court, which held that it was not a ship, part of a ship's apparel or cargo.

However, in *The St Macher* (1939) 65 LlL Rep 119, where an incomplete ship was launched and collided with a tug, not actually towing her, she was held to be a 'ship' within the meaning of s 742 of the Merchant Shipping Act 1894.

In *Re Margetts and Ocean Accident and Guarantee Corporation* [1901] 2 KB 57, a collision with the anchor of another vessel was held to be a collision with that vessel. And, in *Polpen Shipping Co Ltd v Commercial Union Assurance Co Ltd* [1943] 1 All ER 162, Atkinson J observed: [p 165] '... I should say a vessel was any hollow structure intended to be used in navigation, that is, intended to do its real work upon the sea or other waters, and which is capable of free and ordered movement from one place to another.' A flying boat was, in this case, held not to be a vessel.

It is difficult to lay down any fixed or reliable criteria which may be applied in all cases for the purpose of determining whether or not a particular object or thing is or is not a vessel. It is fair to say that the 'navigability' of the object is perhaps one of many considerations, for much depends upon the purpose for which the item is being used and whether its real work is upon the sea or other waters.

By way of damages

The very objective of the 3/4ths Collision Liability Clause is, as its name suggests, to indemnify the assured for third party 'liabilities' which he has incurred as a consequence of a collision with a vessel or vessels. The liability incurred has to be 'by way of damages'. This implies that the claim to which the assured is liable (to the third party) must be in tort. Any liabilities brought about by a breach of contract or statute do not fall within the 3/4ths Collision Liability Clause, and are excluded. This point is well illustrated in the cases of *Furness Withy and Co v Duder* and *Hall Bros SS Co v Young*, below.

Furness Withy and Co v Duder [1936] 2 KB 461

The plaintiffs insured the passenger liner *Monarch of Bermuda* with the defendant underwriters under a policy of marine insurance which contained a Running Down Clause. When approaching the island of Bermuda, the Admiralty tug *St Blazey* was engaged under a contract of towage to assist the liner to dock. During the docking procedure, and due entirely to the negligence of the tug, the tug sustained damage. The plaintiffs, as owners of the towed vessel, paid for the damage to the tug under the terms of the towage contract and then, by way of a test case, pursued their insurers for reimbursement. The underwriters resisted the claim.

The court ruled in favour of the insurers. The owners of the passenger liner could not recover the expenditure from their insurers; it was held that the Running Down Clause only applies to liabilities in tort, and not to liabilities in contract, such as a contract of towage.

Branson J: [p 466] ... The argument of the plaintiffs is that, in view of the incident of their having in the circumstances to contract with the tug owners under terms which made them as owners of the ship responsible to the tug owners for any damage which the tug might sustain while engaged in towing the ship, or which the tug might do to third persons whilst so employed, these words in the policy are sufficiently wide to cover the damages which they have had to pay to the Admiralty under the contract between themselves and the Admiralty.

[p 467] ... I think the clause means that, where in consequence of a collision there arises a legal liability upon the shipowners to pay a sum which can properly be described as damages for a tort, then the underwriters will indemnify them. The expression 'become liable to pay ... by way of damages' indicates, to my mind, a liability which arises as a matter of tort, and not as a matter of contract.

I do not think I need pursue the matter further, except perhaps to add that if one were to hold that this language in the Running Down Clause was sufficient to cover any sort of liability which a shipowner might undertake by way of contract if and when his ship got into collision, the obligation of the underwriters would, I suppose, only be limited by the pity which the shipowner might be willing to extend to them.

Hall Bros SS Co v Young [1939] 1 KB 748, CA

The steamship *Trident* was insured with the defendants, under a policy of marine insurance incorporating the Institute Time Clauses, which included a Running Down Clause. When *Trident* arrived at Dunkirk from the River Plate, she stopped to take on board a pilot. As the pilot boat approached, the pilot boat's steering gear broke down and she collided with *Trident*. Both vessels were damaged but, even though *Trident* was in no way to blame, under French law, she was liable for any damage sustained by the pilot vessel except when the pilot was guilty of gross negligence. The owners duly paid the pilotage authorities, and then attempted to reclaim their expenditure from their insurers. The insurers refused the indemnity.

The Court of Appeal, affirming the decision of the trial judge, found for the insurers. The insurers were only liable under the Running Down Clause for damages in tort, and not for an expenditure brought about by a statutory liability.

Sir Wilfred Greene MR: [p 760] ... The obligation which arises is an obligation to make good the damage suffered by the pilot vessel in the circumstances stated, whether or not there is a collision, whether or not the vessel insured is to blame, whether or not the pilot himself is negligent, provided that his negligence is not the type of negligence described as *'faute lourde'*. It has nothing in the world to do with any duty on the vessel itself, but it is a provision under which the vessel is compelled to bear a particular charge irrespective of any question of duty imposed upon it. In the present case, the liability would have arisen equally if the pilot vessel, without touching *Trident*, had been swamped by sea owing to the failure of its steering gear. It so happened that that failure led, not to the pilot boat being swamped, but to its colliding with *Trident*. But the liability would have been precisely the same in either case. Looking at the terms of the French law – without doing what the learned judge found it unnecessary to do, and I find it unnecessary to do, namely, to express any concluded opinion as to the true category in which this class of payment ought to be put – one thing which is, to my mind, quite clear is this, that it cannot be put into the category of 'damages' within the meaning of this particular clause. It is based on an entirely different conception, and the liability which arises under it is not a liability to avoid collision, it is not an obligation to navigate carefully or to do acts of that kind; it is merely a liability to make a payment of that particular character; it has no reference whatsoever to any act or default on the part of the vessel insured.

... The result, in my opinion is, in a sentence, that the very special liability imposed by Art 7 of the French law of 28 March 1928 is not one which, upon the true construction of the Running Down Clause, falls under the head of a sum which the assured became liable to pay by way of damages in respect of the collision. Whatever else it may be, it is in its nature outside the word 'damages' as used in that clause. In my opinion, the learned judge was perfectly right in his conclusion, and the appeal must be dismissed with costs.

Paid by the assured (pay to be paid rule)

The 3/4ths Collision Liability Clause may, as stipulated in its introductory cl 8.1, only be invoked when the assured himself has actually paid the third party. The concept stems from the 'pay to be paid' rule, well known in the world of P & I insurance. The relevance of the Third Parties (Rights Against Insurers) Act 1930[12] to the 'pay to be paid' rule may, at first sight, appear to be unclear. Its relevance, however, was clarified in the *Nautilus* case, which has settled beyond doubt that the said Act is applicable to cl 8. Recently, in the case of *The Fanti and The Padre Island*, below, the connection between the 'pay to be paid' rule and the Third Parties (Rights Against Insurers) Act 1930 again came under scrutiny, this time by the House of Lords.

Third Parties (Rights Against Insurers) Act 1930

The case of *Re Nautilus SS Co* (1935) 52 LlL Rep 183, CA has clarified that the Third Parties (Rights Against Insurers) Act 1930 applies to the Running Down Clause.

Re Nautilus SS Co (1935) 52 LlL Rep 183, CA

A collision took place in Chile, in 1925, between *Pear Branch*, belonging to the Nautilus Company, and another vessel. As a result, *Pear Branch* was arrested and the appellants, agents for the Nautilus Company in Chile, put forward a

---

12 See Appendix 3.

bond as surety for outstanding liabilities claimed by the other vessel. In 1931, the Nautilus Company was the subject of a winding up order, and placed into liquidation. The agents pressed a claim for the money still owing to them, arguing that any money still held by the insurers for third party liability should go to them, and not become part of the assets of the liquidator.

The Court of Appeal ruled that the Third Parties (Rights Against Insurers) Act 1930 was applicable to the Running Down Clause, but then had to determine, as the Act was not retrospective, whether the date of the collision or the date of the winding up order was apposite. The court decided that the pertinent date was the date of the winding up order, and, therefore, the Act was applicable, and the agents won their claim.

> **Lord Hanworth MR:** [p 187] ... as creditors their rights have to be determined not earlier than 13 October 1931, and at that date this statute [Rights Against Insurers Act 1930] had become operative to say what is to happen in respect of the sum payable by the insurers to the insured arising out of a liability of the insured to the third party.

A recent case which highlighted the principle of 'pay to be paid', as well as the Third Parties (Rights Against Insurers) Act 1930, is *The Fanti and The Padre Island*.

The Fanti and The Padre Island [1990] 2 Lloyd's Rep 191, HL

This was an appeal to the House of Lords by two independent third party claimants seeking redress against Protection and Indemnity Associations. In both cases, the question put before the court was whether the rights of a third party as against an insurer were still strictly subject to an original term in the policy, namely the 'pay to be paid' rule.

(a) The owners of *The Fanti* were members of the Newcastle Protection and Indemnity Association; the policy of insurance included the usual prerequisite of 'pay to be paid'. That is, the insurer was not liable to indemnify the assured until the assured had, in fact, made payment himself. In 1983, *The Fanti*, whilst on a voyage from Rostock to Nigeria, began to take in water and was escorted into Portuguese waters by a salvage tug. Both the ship and the cargo were abandoned to the salvors. As no payment had been made to the salvors by the owners of *The Fanti*, the salvors successfully petitioned for a winding up order against the owners and then pressed a claim themselves against the P & I Club under the Third Parties (Rights against Insurers) Act 1930. The insurers refused payment.

(b) In the second case, the owners of *The Padre Island* entered their vessel with the defendant Club, the West of England Mutual Assurance Association. Again, the policy of insurance contained the usual 'pay to be paid' proviso to the clause, which stated that the Club undertook to 'protect and indemnify members in respect of losses or claims which they as owners of the entered vessel shall have become liable to pay and shall have in fact paid ...' In this case, the claimants had successfully pressed cargo claims against the owners of *The Padre Island* and, on non-payment, had an order made for the winding up of the shipowners. The cargo claimants then pressed their claim against the P & I Club under the Third Parties (Rights Against Insurers) Act 1930. Again, the insurers refused payment.

The House of Lords ruled in favour of both the P & I Clubs on the basis that the 'pay to be paid' proviso was a term of the contract of insurance that had not been adhered to. It would not, therefore, be reasonable to confer on a third party to that policy of insurance conditions which were more favourable than the original contract intended.

> **Lord Goff of Chieveley:** [p 198] ... The central question is one which has troubled maritime lawyers, in the City of London and in the Temple, ever since the enactment of the Third Parties (Rights Against Insurers) Act 1930 ('the 1930 Act'). It is whether the Act confers upon a third party, who has a claim against an insolvent shipowner whose ship is entered in a P & I Club, under rules covering the relevant risk, an effective right to proceed directly against the club for the loss or damage suffered by him despite the presence of a condition of prior payment in the club's rules. It is a matter of common knowledge that many opinions have been written by distinguished maritime lawyers on this subject, and in those opinions differing views have been expressed. I believe that I am right in saying that those opinions have focused primarily upon the impact of s 1(3) of the 1930 Act, and upon the question whether a condition of prior payment in the club's rules is rendered of no effect by that sub-section because it indirectly alters the rights of the parties under the contract of insurance embodied in the rules upon the happening of an event specified in s 1(1) of the 1930 Act.
>
> [p 199] ... I start from the position that what is transferred to and vested in the third party is the member's right against the club. That right is, at best, a contingent right to indemnity, the right being expressed to be conditional upon the member having in fact paid the relevant claim or expense. If that condition is not fulfilled, the member had no present right to indemnity, and the statutory transfer of his right to a third party cannot put the third party in any better position than the member. It is as simple as that.
>
> [p 200] ... What is transferred under the statute is the right. That right is expressed to be conditional upon the happening of a certain event; and the right as transferred remains so conditional. It is, in my opinion, misleading to describe that event as a 'burden', since this is the language of obligation and appears to connote a duty which is transferred with the right. But there is no duty on the member to make prior payment; there is simply a contractual term that, if he does not do so, he has no right to be indemnified. The statutory transferee of the member's right is in no better position than the member; and so, if the condition is not fulfilled, he too has no right to be indemnified.

LEGAL COSTS

Clause 8.3 of the ITCH(95) and cl 6.3 of the IVCH(95) state:

> The Underwriters will also pay three-fourths of the legal costs incurred by the Assured or which the Assured may be compelled to pay in contesting liability or taking proceedings to limit liability, with the prior written consent of the Underwriters.

The clause lays down the contractual terms under which the underwriter will indemnify the assured for legal costs incurred in defending an action for damages. It does not refer to legal costs incurred by the assured in making a claim against a third party. The case of *Xenos v Fox* [1869] LR 4 CP 665, below, illustrates the limited scope of an earlier version of Running Down Clause which did not have a provision for the reimbursement of legal costs; it also shows the irrelevance of the Sue and Labour Clause.

Xenos v Fox (1869) LR 4 CP 665

The plaintiffs insured the steamship *Smyrna* with the defendants under a policy of marine insurance. The Running Down Clause included protection for damages incurred, but was silent with respect to legal costs. *Smyrna* was navigating a branch of the Danube when she collided with the steam tug *Mars*, which was badly damaged and later sank. The owners of *Mars* sued the owners of *Smyrna*, who resisted the claim. The court in Turkey dismissed the suit, leaving each party to bear their own costs. The owners of *Mars* appealed against the judgment twice, but, on each occasion, the appeal was dismissed, with the costs being apportioned to both parties. The plaintiffs claimed that they had defended these claims with the written consent of their insurers, and, in an attempt to recoup their losses, sued their own insurers in the English courts for a proportion of the costs incurred.

The Court of Appeal affirmed the decision of the trial judge and ruled that the costs of defending an action were not recoverable from the insurers either under the terms of the Running Down Clause or the Sue and Labour Clause included in the policy. The written consent was considered immaterial; the insurers were only liable for damages, not the legal costs.

> **Cockburn CJ:** [p 667] ... The Suing and Labouring Clause has no application whatever to the facts of this case. That Clause applies to a loss or misfortune happening to the thing insured. Nor has it any relation to the Running Down Clause. The Running Down Clause is a distinct contract, under which the underwriters engage to pay a proportion of any damages which may be awarded against the assured in a suit for a collision which may be defended with their previous consent in writing. That is express ... But the parties have not so contracted, and we cannot do it for them. It can hardly be said that the expenses in question were incurred by reason of the consent of the

underwriters to the suit being defended. That assent was given only with reference to the special terms of the Running Down Clause. If damages had been recovered by the owners of *Mars* against the plaintiff, that would have brought the case within the Clause.

EXCLUSIONS

Clause 8.4 of the 3/4ths Collision Liability Clause lists the exclusions to the liability of the insurer for damage sustained by the Assured in relation to a claim arising from a collision. Clause 8.4 states:

8.4 Provided always that this Clause 8 shall in no case extend to any sum which the Assured shall pay for or in respect of:

8.4.1 removal or disposal of obstruction, wrecks, cargoes or any other thing whatsoever;

8.4.2 any real or personal property or thing whatsoever except other vessels or property on other vessels;

8.4.3 the cargo or other property on, or the engagements of, the insured Vessel;

8.4.4 loss of life, personal injury or illness;

8.4.5 pollution or contamination, or threat thereof, of any real or personal property or thing whatsoever (except other vessels with which the insured Vessel is in collision or property on such other vessel) or damage to the environment, or threat thereof, save that this exclusion shall not extend to any sum which the Assured shall pay for or in respect of Salvage remuneration in which the skill and efforts of the salvors in preventing or minimising damage to the environment as is referred to in Art 13, para 1(b) of the International Convention on Salvage 1989 have been taken into account.

As cll 8.4.2, 8.4.3 and 8.2.4 are, by and large, self-explanatory, very little need be said about them; liability for loss of life, personal injury or illness has always been the province of P & I insurance.

Removal or disposal of obstructions, wrecks, cargoes or any other thing whatsoever – cl 8.4.1

The cases of *The North Britain* [1894] P 77 and *Tatham, Bromage and Co v Burr, 'Engineer'* [1898] AC 382, HL, cited below, are concerned with the cost of wreck removal. In *The North Britain*, Lindley LJ, in explaining the meaning of a proviso to an earlier version of the Running Down Clause, used almost the precise words presently found in cl 8.4.1. Clause 8.4.1 is, however, wider in scope, excluding not only the cost of the removal and disposal of obstructions and wrecks, but also of 'cargoes and any other thing whatsoever'.

The North Britain [1894] P 77

The owners of *The North Britain* insured her with the defendant underwriters under a hull policy of insurance which included a Running Down Clause incorporating a proviso which excepted the insurer from liability for the removal of obstructions under statutory powers. In February 1891, *The North Britain* collided with the British steamer *Paraguay* in the River Scheldt and the latter vessel was sunk. The Belgian authorities removed the wreck under statutory powers, as it was an impediment to navigation. The owners of both vessels, in cross-actions, admitted liability for the damage done to the other vessel. The owners of *The North Britain* then claimed on their insurers for the third party damages to *Paraguay*, including the cost of her removal, on the basis that the proviso only applied, in the case of a collision, to the assured vessel and not the other vessel. The underwriters rejected the claim.

The Court of Appeal overturned the decision of the trial judge and ruled that the proviso applied to the circumstances of the case, and the insurers were held not liable for the costs of the wreck removal.

> **Lindley LJ:** [p 83] ... Now, upon that, two views are presented to the court. One is that this proviso only applies to sums which the owners of the ship insured may become liable to pay directly for removal of obstructions caused by itself – the ship insured. The other is that which is contended by the defendants [insurers] in this particular case, that it covers whatever the plaintiffs may be called upon to pay, even to the other ship with which the collision has taken place, if that other ship has been ordered to pay for the removal of the obstruction. The case is one of some little difficulty; but when we look at it, and at the object of the clause, it appears to me that the construction which is put by the underwriters is the correct one.
>
> [p 84] ... The true meaning of the proviso is that 'this clause shall in no case extend to any sum which the assured shall have to pay for removal of obstruction consequent on such collision'.

Similarly, in the *Engineer* case, below, there was a proviso to the Running Down Clause stating that the insurers were not liable 'for the removal of obstructions under statutory powers'. The House of Lords considered the meaning of the proviso.

Tatham, Bromage and Co v Burr, 'Engineer' [1898] AC 382, HL

The appellants, owners of the steamship *Engineer*, effected a time policy of insurance with the respondents. The Running Down Clause within the policy included a proviso which stated that '... this clause shall in no case extend to any sum which the assured may become liable to pay or shall pay for removal of obstructions under statutory powers ...'. In April 1896, *Engineer* collided with the steamship *Harraton* in the River Tees; *Engineer* was damaged and *Harraton* sank, becoming a constructive total loss. The Tees Conservatory Commissioners duly removed the sunken wreck under their statutory powers and the expense fell upon the owners of both ships, who had agreed that both were at fault. The appellant owners of *Engineer* paid their share of these expenses to the owners of *Harraton*, and then attempted to recoup this expenditure from their insurers, who refused payment.

The House of Lords ruled for the insurers, in that the proviso excluded the insurer's liability for the removal of obstructions to navigation under statutory powers.

> **Earl of Halsbury LC:** [p 386] ... My Lords, I certainly am not desirous of hearing this discussion prolonged, because for some time I have arrived at a very clear conclusion in my mind, and I confess I adopt the paraphrase of this contract which the then Davey LJ put upon it in *The North Britain* [1894] P 77, p 89. He says the clause means something of this kind: 'I will reimburse you, the injuring vessel, the bill which you have to pay the injured vessel for damages; but, mind, I am not to be called upon to pay, directly or indirectly, for the removal of obstructions under statutory powers.' That I believe to be a proper reading of the language which was actually used by the parties.

Notes

The wording of cl 8.4.1 does not restrict the exclusion, as did the clauses in the cases, to the removal of wrecks under statutory powers. Its wording is plain and wide enough to exclude any expense incurred or payable by the assured in respect of the removal or disposal of obstructions, wrecks, cargoes or any other thing whatsoever.

Pollution, contamination and damage to the environment – cl 8.4.5

The above exclusion, cl 8.4.5 of the ITCH(95), has to be read with cl 7, the Pollution Hazard Clause, which also deals with pollution and environmental damage. At first sight, the clauses may appear to be contradictory, but, in fact, they cover different ground. Clause 7 relates to damage sustained by the insured Vessel, whereas cl 8.4.5 relates to any other property or thing, aside from the insured Vessel and 'other vessels'(and property on such other vessels) which the insured Vessel has collided with.

The Pollution Hazard Clause allows recovery for loss of or damage 'to the Vessel' resulting directly from any action taken by any governmental authority to prevent or mitigate a pollution hazard or damage to the environment. Clause 8.4.5, on the other hand, excludes the assured from recovery for any sum which has been incurred or may have to be incurred in respect of:

(a) pollution or contamination (or threat thereof) of 'any real or personal property or thing whatsoever'; or

(b) damage to the environment, or threat thereof.

There are two exceptions contained within the exclusions in cl 8.4.5. Clause 8.4.5 does not exclude the insurer from liability in respect of:

(a) pollution or contamination (or threat thereof) of other vessels (or property on such other vessels) with which the insured Vessel is in collision; and

(b) salvage remuneration in which the skill and efforts of the salvors in preventing or minimising damage to the environment (as referred to in Art 13(1)(b) of the International Convention on Salvage 1989) have been taken into account. This provision is consistent with the line taken by the 1995 amendments, for the insurer is, in any event, liable for such an 'enhanced award' by virtue of cl 10.6.

O'May is astute in pointing out that: 'In effect, therefore, the exclusion does not infringe upon the cover against damages which is afforded under cll 8.1.1 to 8.1.3.'[13]

THE SISTER SHIP CLAUSE

The Sister Ship Clause (cl 9 of the ITCH(95) and cl 6 of the IVCH(95)) is included to ensure that, when a collision takes place between two vessels belonging to the same owner, claims made by one ship upon the other are not barred. The common law does not permit a person to sue himself. The case of *Simpson v Thomson*, below, emphasised this very point.

Simpson v Thomson (1877) 3 App Cas 279

In February 1876, the steamship *Dunluce Castle*, on passage from London to Leith, was run down and destroyed by the steamship *Fitzmaurice*, which admitted liability. Both vessels belonged to the same owner, Mr Burrell, and were, therefore, sister ships. Mr Burrell, as the owner of *Fitzmaurice*, the vessel at fault, then paid a sum of money into the court as fixed by statute, leaving all those who had a claim against him to establish against that sum. However, the underwriters, after paying Mr Burrell a large sum of money in settlement of the total loss of *Dunluce Castle*, sought to join the cargo-owners and others as a major claimant on the fund deposited by Mr Burrell. The cargo-owners and other claimants objected.

The court, in reversing the decision of the trial judge, ruled that the insurers had no right to lay claim to any of the fund. The insurers, in claiming the rights of the person insured after payment for a total loss, could not then make a claim on that very same person who also owned the ship at fault.

---

13 O'May, DR, *Marine Insurance*, 1993, London: Sweet & Maxwell, p 240.

Lord Chancellor: [p 284] ... I know of no foundation for the right of underwriters, except the well known principle of law, that where one person has agreed to indemnify another, he will, on making good the indemnity, be entitled to succeed to all the ways and means by which the person indemnified might have protected himself against or reimbursed himself for the loss. It is on this principle that the underwriters of a ship that has been lost are entitled to the ship in specie if they can find and recover it; and it is on the same principle that they can assert any right which the owner of the ship might have asserted against a wrongdoer for damage for the act which has caused the loss. But this right of action for damages they must assert, not in their own name, but in the name of the person insured, and if the person insured be the person who has caused the damage, I am unable to see how the right can be asserted at all.

References and further reading

Michael, K and Congdon, S, 'Third party rights against insurers' [1989] LMCLQ 495

CHAPTER 14

WAR AND STRIKES RISKS

INTRODUCTION

It was not until 1898 that, after a general meeting of Lloyd's, it was decided that marine risks and war risks should be underwritten under separate policies. The result is that, now, war risks are excluded from standard marine policies and are provided for under separate cover. Thus, a vessel may now be insured specifically against war and strikes risks under the Institute War and Strikes Clauses Hulls (IWSC(H)(95)), Time and Voyage.[1] Freight may, similarly, be insured against war and strikes risks under one policy,[2] but, with cargo, insurance cover against war risks is separate from cover against strikes risks.[3]

That war and strikes risks may be insured under a policy of marine insurance is confirmed by s 3 of the Act, which states:

> 'Maritime perils' means the perils consequent on, or incidental to, the navigation of the sea, that is to say, perils of the seas, fire, war perils, pirates, rovers, thieves, captures, seizures, restraints, and detainments of princes and peoples, jettisons, barratry, and any other perils, either of the like kind or which may be designated by the policy.

In the past, in order to exclude war risks, a standard policy would include an f c and s (free from capture and seizure) clause. During the First and Second World Wars, the principle behind war risks insurance was that the assured could only recover for a loss under the war risks policy if that loss could have been recovered under the marine policy, but was then excluded by the f c and s clause.[4]

However, f c and s clauses had, for a long time, been considered unsatisfactory, and the low regard in which they were held was eloquently summed up by Mocatta J, in *Panamanian Oriental Steamship Corporation v Wright* [1970] 2 Lloyd's Rep 365. In this instance, a vessel was confiscated at Saigon for carrying unmanifested goods. The policy of insurance was in

---

1 See Appendix 19. As the main clauses of IWSC(H)(95) – Time and Voyage, are identical, the abbreviation 'IWSC(H)(95)' will be used when referring to both the Institute War and Strikes Clauses, Time and Voyage.
2 See the Institute War and Strikes Clauses Freight (Time) and the Institute War and Strikes Clauses (Voyage).
3 The Institute War Clauses Cargo (IWC(C)(82)) and the Institute Strikes Clauses Cargo (ISC(C)(82)).
4 See O'May, DR, *Marine Insurance*, 1993, London: Sweet and Maxwell, p 254.

standard form, with the f c and s clause deleted, but incorporated the Institute War and Strikes Clauses (Hulls – Time).

> **Mocatta J:** [p 372] ... It is probably too late to make an effective plea that the traditional methods of insuring against ordinary marine risks and what are usually called war risks should be radically overhauled. The present method, certainly as regards war risks insurance, is tortuous and complex in the extreme. It cannot be beyond the wit of underwriters, and those who advise them, in this age of law reform, to devise more straightforward and easily comprehended terms of cover.

Fortunately, after further criticism in 1978 by UNCTAD, that the method used to distinguish war risks from marine risks was, at the very least, unsatisfactory, the London market radically reformed the structure of their policies. New and separate Institute Clauses were introduced for both marine risks and war risks; the cargo clauses taking effect in January 1982, hull and freight clauses following in October 1983.[5] Significantly, the system was harmonised, whereby the war risks policy covered the same risks as those which have been excluded from cover by the marine risks policy.

The f c and s clause

The f c and s clause was a clause inserted into a marine risks policy which excluded marine risks insurers from war and strikes risks. The war and strikes risks covered by the war risks insurer were similar, but not necessarily identical, to those excluded by the f c and s clause from the policy for marine risks.

Problematically, the mere fact that certain risks, namely, the non-marine risks, were excluded by the f c and s clause from the cover for marine risks did not mean that they were automatically insured under the war risks policy. That is to say, the risks excluded by the marine risks policy were not necessarily covered by the war risks policy.

The current regime of insurance cover provided by marine and war risks policies is much simpler: the war and strikes risks excluded by the War and Strikes Exclusion Clauses of the ITCH(95) and the IVCH(95) are now mirrored verbatim by the risks covered by the IWSC(H)(95).

The Paramount and the Exclusion Clauses

Both the ITCH(95) and the IVCH(95) incorporate exclusion clauses which except the insurer from liability under the marine risks policy from specific enumerated perils. The four exclusion clauses, namely: War Exclusion; Strikes

---

5   Containers were not catered for until 1987.

Exclusion; Malicious Acts Exclusion; and the Radioactive Contamination Exclusion Clauses are governed by the paramount clause.[6] The paramount clause declares that the exclusion clauses '... shall override anything contained in this insurance inconsistent therewith'. Thus, the paramount clause serves to override any endorsements contained within or attached to the policy, including any express warranty which may be inconsistent with the exclusion clauses.[7]

Thus, where war and strikes risks are excluded from a marine risks policy, as with the ITCH(95) and the IVCH(95), it is not possible to seek cover for such risks without taking out a separate policy for those risks. There is, however, no paramount clause in the ICC (A), (B) and (C), which means that its War Exclusion Clause, cl 6, has no paramount status.

The paramount clause of the ITCH(95) and the IVCH(95) not only excludes the marine risks insurer from liability for loss or damage arising from the excluded perils, but also excludes him from liability for any 'expense' caused by those perils. No such equivalent cover for 'expense' is provided under the War and Strikes Clauses, Hull, Cargo or Freight. Thus, the war and strikes risks cover is, in this respect, narrower than the marine risks exclusions.

Dual causes of loss – marine risk and war risk

In time of war, the courts have not always found it easy to differentiate between a loss caused by marine risks and a loss caused by war risks. This causes problems when the vessel is insured under both marine risks and war risks policies of insurance: in the event of a collision or a stranding, it is often difficult to determine whether the collision or stranding was caused by a navigational error, which would be covered by the marine risks policy, or it was brought about by the hazardous nature of a warlike operation, which would be covered by the war risks policy.

The rule of proximate cause

The courts have sought to resolve the issue by employing the principle set out in s 55 of the Act, the rule of proximate cause.[8] In *Yorkshire Dale Steamship Co Ltd v Minister of War Transport, 'Coxwold'* **(1942) 73 LlL Rep 1, HL**,[9]

---

6   See ITCH(95), cll 24–27, and IVCH(95), cll 21–24.
7   The paramount clause could even override the insurer's liability under the 3/4ths Collision Liability Clause and the Sue and Labour Clause.
8   For an in depth analysis of the rule of proximate cause, see Chapter 8.
9   See, also, the speech of Viscount Simon, p 6. His comments on this issue are reproduced in Chapter 8, p 340.

where a vessel stranded whilst sailing in convoy, the House of Lords decided that the proximate cause of the loss was the warlike operation and, therefore, the Minister of War Transport, who requisitioned the ship, was liable, not the marine risks insurers. Lord MacMillan summed up the problems raised.

> **Lord MacMillan:** [p 7] ... This division of liability has given rise to many perplexing cases in which the minister on the one hand and the shipowner or his insurers on the other hand have been at issue as to whether a particular casualty was due to warlike operations or to the ordinary perils of navigation, each naturally seeking to place the casualty in the category for which the other is under liability. The minister accepts the position that he must be treated as if he had granted a marine insurance policy covering the risks which he has undertaken. Consequently, under s 55 of the Marine Insurance Act 1906, he is liable for any loss proximately caused by warlike operations. The adverb 'proximately' does not greatly assist the solution of the problem, but it at least serves to emphasise that it is the predominant and determining cause that is to be sought.

More recently, a case came before the South African Court of Appeal which provided a graphic example of the law of proximate cause. In *Incorporated General Insurances Ltd v AR Shooter T/A Shooter's Fisheries, 'Morning Star'* **[1987] 1 Lloyd's Rep 401, SA CA**, the fishing vessel *Morning Star* was arrested and detained by the People's Republic of Mozambique for illegal fishing. As the owner was unable to pay the resulting fine, *Morning Star* was confiscated.

The owner of *Morning Star* duly claimed upon his policy of insurance, which incorporated war risks, on the basis that the loss had been caused by the 'arrest, restraints and detainments of all kings ...', a peril insured against. But the court ruled that the insurers were not liable under the policy, because the proximate cause of the loss was not the arrest or detainment, but the failure by the assured to pay the fine.

> **Galgut AJA:** [p 406] ... I am, with respect, unable to agree with the finding of the court a quo that the loss of the trawler was due to a continuous process. The Mozambican tribunal imposed a fine. Had that fine been paid, the loss would not have resulted. In my view, the confiscation did not result from the arrest of the trawler, it resulted from the failure to pay the fine. That failure was, therefore, the proximate cause of the confiscation of the trawler. The fact that the plaintiff was unable to pay the fine is irrelevant. The issue is not his ability to pay the fine. The issue is what caused the confiscation. That, as we have seen, was the fact that the fine was not paid. That was not a peril covered by the risk clause. In the result, the appeal [by the insurers] must succeed.

Why, therefore, if it is simply the rule of proximate cause which determines whether the marine risks insurer or the war risks insurer is liable for the loss, is it necessary to ensure that the war and strikes exclusion clauses contained within the marine risks policy are made paramount? The answer lies with the *Warilda* case, below, where a collision took place in wartime and it was shown that a standard f c and s clause, excluding liability for war risks, did not exclude third party liability for collision damage. Thus, although the proximate cause of the loss was the warlike operation, the f c and s clause was limited in its scope and did not except all liability under the marine policy.

In *AG v Adelaide Steamship Co Ltd, 'Warilda'* [1923] AC 292, HL, a hospital ship, *The Warilda*, was requisitioned by the Admiralty under the standard form of charter (T 99). The vessel was insured against marine risks and the Admiralty, under the terms of the charter, were liable for any losses proximately caused by war risks. Whilst steaming across the English Channel with wounded soldiers, at full speed with her navigation lights switched off, *Warilda* was involved in a collision with another ship for which *Warilda* was deemed solely to blame. The House of Lords ruled that the Admiralty were liable for the loss because, at the time of the collision, *Warilda* was engaged in a warlike operation, and the f c and s clause in the marine risks policy excluded war risks.

However, subsequently, in another action before the House of Lords, regarding the damage caused to the other vessel, the court ruled that the liability for the collision damage remained with the marine risks insurer. This was because the f c and s clause did exclude collision liability.

As O'May points out, the ruling in this case heralded the arrival of the paramount clause:[10]

> ... It followed from this finding that such damages were not excluded by the f c and s clause and had to be paid by the marine underwriters under the Running Down Clause, which was not, at that time, made subject to the f c and s clause. It was surprising that a revision of the clauses was made thereafter to ensure that all terms of the marine cover, including the Running Down Clause, were caught by the f c and s exclusion. To avoid a repetition of *Warilda* situation, the Institute Clauses for hull and cargo are expressly made subject to the War Exclusion. By stating that the War Exclusion in the Hull Clauses is paramount and overrides anything inconsistent contained 'in this insurance', not just in the Institute Clauses, it means that any typewritten or other attached clauses or endorsements to the policy and clauses will likewise be overridden, in the absence of a clearly expressed contrary intention.

WAR RISKS

The specific war risks covered by the Institute War and Strikes Clauses (Hulls) (IWSC(H)(95)) are enumerated in cll 1.1, 1.2 and 1.3; these risks mirror the war risks excluded by cl 24 of the ITCH(95).[11] Identical war risks are also covered

---

10 *Op cit*, O'May, fn 4, p 259.
11 See, also, IVCH(95), cl 21.

by cll 1.1, 1.2 and 1.3 of the Institute War Clauses (Cargo) (IWC(C)(82))[12] and, yet again, those war risks mirror the war risk exclusions contained within cl 6 of the ICC (A), (B) and (C).

The war risks covered are annotated thus:

1.1 war civil war revolution rebellion insurrection, or civil strife arising therefrom, or any hostile act by or against a belligerent power;

1.2 capture seizure arrest restraint or detainment, and the consequences thereof or any attempt thereat;

1.3 derelict mines torpedoes bombs or other derelict weapons of war.

Clause 1.1: War civil war revolution rebellion insurrection, or civil strife arising therefrom, or any hostile act by or against a belligerent power

The war risks covered by cl 1.1 of both the IWSC(H)(95) and the IWC(C)(82) are graded in a descending order of gravity, which may be subdivided thus:

(1) war;

(2) civil war, revolution, rebellion, insurrection;

(3) civil strife arising therefrom; and

(4) any hostile act by or against a belligerent power.

War

Webster's Comprehensive Dictionary of the English Language defines war as: 'A contest between or among nations or States ... carried on by force and with arms.' Thus, in general terms, it involves hostilities between belligerent States, but it is not necessary for a formal declaration of war to have been made. Conversely, a formal declaration of war is not conclusive evidence that a state of war exists; whether a state of war actually exists at a particular time is a question of fact.

That there is no technical definition of the word 'war' was confirmed by Sir Wilfred Greene MR, in *Kawasaki Kisen Kabushiki Kaisha of Kobe v Bantham Steamship Co Ltd* **[1939] 2 KB 544, CA**. In this instance, a clause in a charterparty gave the charterers the liberty to cancel the charterparty '... if war breaks out involving Japan'. The Court of Appeal was, wisely, unwilling even to attempt to define 'war', but it was prepared to confirm that a state of war could exist without there being a declaration of war.

Sir Wilfred Greene MR: [p 556] ... I asked for any authority in which, for the purpose of the municipal law of this country, 'war' is in any way defined. No

---

12 See Appendix 20.

such authority could be suggested ... to say that English law recognises some technical and ascertainable description of what is meant by 'war' appears to me to be a quite impossible proposition ... Nobody would have the temerity to suggest in these days that war cannot exist without a declaration of war ... I do not propose to be the first to lay down a definition of 'war' in a so called technical sense.[13]

Civil war revolution rebellion insurrection

The above events relate to strife or internal conflict which takes place within one nation or State. At one end of the scale, civil war implies open armed conflict between organised factions, whilst, at the other end of the scale, insurrection may amount to nothing more than an 'organised resistance to established government'.[14]

The leading authority regarding definitions of the words contained within the war and strikes clauses is the non-marine case of *Spinney's v Royal Insurance Co*, below.

Spinney's (1948) Ltd v Royal Insurance Co [1980] 1 Lloyd's Rep 406

The plaintiffs were merchants and retailers in Beirut who insured their properties with the defendants under policies of insurance containing a special condition which stated: 'This insurance does not cover any loss or damage occasioned by or through or in consequence directly or indirectly of any of the following occurrences: (a) ... civil war; (b) ... civil commotion assuming the proportions of or amounting to a popular rising ... insurrection, rebellion, revolution military or usurped power ...' In January 1976, shops and warehouses belonging to the plaintiffs were looted and damaged by a group or groups of persons, and the plaintiffs claimed on their policies of insurance for their losses. The underwriters refused payment.

The court ruled that the insurers were excluded from liability under the policies, because the losses fell within the meaning of the special condition clause. Although, the judge reasoned, the situation in Beirut did not amount to a civil war, the disturbances were 'assuming the proportions of a popular rising'. In reaching his decision, Mustill J (as he then was) was obliged to analyse the meaning of all the exceptions contained within the special condition clause.

---

13 The word 'war' does not appear in f c and s clause. The most commonly used term is 'warlike operations', and the meaning of these words is analysed later in the chapter, p 566.
14 The definition contained within *Webster's Comprehensive Dictionary of the English Language*.

Mustill J:

Civil war

[p 429] ... What are these characteristics of an armed conflict which make it a war, albeit of an internal character? I do not propose to attempt any general definition of a civil war. It does, however, seem to me that a decision on whether such a war exists will generally involve a consideration of three questions:

(1) Can it be said that the conflict was between opposing sides?
(2) What were the objectives of the 'sides' and how did they set about pursuing them?
(3) What was the scale of the conflict, and of its effect on public order and on the life of the inhabitants?

As regards the first element, I find it difficult to visualise a war of any kind which is not fought between sides ... it must, to my mind, be possible to say of each fighting man that he owes allegiance to one side or another, and it must also be possible to identify each side by reference to a community of objective, leadership and administration. It does not necessarily follow that the objectives of all those on any one side must be identical. There may be considerable differences and even animosities between allies. But there must be some substantial community of aim, which the allies have banded together to promote by the use of force. Nor, in my view, need there always be only two sides. Two factions might fight one another, and also the State, in order to seize power. This would still be a civil war. But if the factions are too numerous, the struggle is no more than a melee, without the clear delineation of combatants which is one of the distinguishing features of a war.

The second matter for consideration is the nature of the objectives for which the sides are fighting. The classical opinion of the international lawyers is that the parties must be either the existing authorities and a faction striving to seize complete dominion over the whole or part of the State; or two factions striving against each other to seize power, with the existing rulers either fighting both factions at once, or standing impotently by ... But, where the term is used in ordinary speech, I am not convinced that a desire to seize or retain the reins of State is the only motive which can ever put the contestants into a state of civil war. If all the above requirements are satisfied, I believe that there would be a civil war if the objective was not to seize complete political power, but (say) to force changes in the way in which power is exercised, without fundamentally changing the existing political structure.

Finally, there is the character and scale of the conflict, and its effect on public order and on the life of the inhabitants ... I would include: the number of combatants; the number of casualties, military and civilian; the amount and nature of the armaments employed; the relative sizes of the territory occupied by the opposing sides; the extent to which it is possible to delineate the territories so occupied; the degree to which the populace as a whole is involved in the conflict ...

Rebellion; insurrection

[p 436] ... As regards 'rebellion', I adopt the definition in the *Oxford English Dictionary* (Murray): ... *'organised resistance to the ruler or government of one's country; insurrection, revolt'* [emphasis added]. To this I would add that the purpose of the resistance must be to supplant the existing rulers, or at least to deprive them of authority over part of their territory.

The dictionary defines 'insurrections' in a similar manner, but also suggests the notion of an incipient or limited rebellion. I believe that this reflects the distinction between two exceptions as they are used in the present clause, subject to the rider that a lesser degree of organisation may also mark off an insurrection from a rebellion. But, with each exception, there must be action against the government with a view to supplanting it.

The definitions suggested by Mustill J in the Spinney's case were later referred to by Saville J, in **National Oil Co of Zimbabwe (Private) Ltd v Sturge [1991] 2 Lloyd's Rep 281**, where it was held that losses sustained by an oil company could not be recovered under a marine risks policy of insurance (incorporating only the Institute Strikes Clauses) when installations were blown up by the Mozambique National Resistance, because the policy excepted losses caused by, amongst other things, 'insurrection'. The judge, however, suggested that the words 'civil war', 'rebellion', and 'insurrection' should be given their 'business' meaning rather than, presumably, their technical meaning.

Saville J: [p 282] ... In the context of a commercial contract such as the policy under discussion, the expressions 'civil war', 'rebellion' and 'insurrection' bear their ordinary 'business' meaning. In this context, 'civil war' means a war with the special characteristics of being civil – that is, being internal rather than external – see *Spinney's (1948) Ltd v Royal Insurance Co Ltd* [1980] 1 Lloyd's Rep 406, p 429. 'Rebellion' and 'insurrection' have somewhat similar meanings to each other. To my mind, each means an organised and violent internal uprising in a country with, as a main purpose, the object of trying to overthrow or supplant the government of that country, though 'insurrection' denotes a lesser degree of organisation and size than rebellion – see *Home Insurance v Davila* (1954) 212 F 2d 731.

Notes

Unfortunately, there appears to be little in the way of authority regarding a definition of the word 'revolution'. Although, it is submitted, 'revolution' has a similar meaning to 'rebellion', the word 'revolution' suggests a more widespread uprising than 'rebellion', which may be localised.[15]

---

15 *Webster's Comprehensive Dictionary of the English Language* defines 'revolution' as: 'The overthrow and replacement of a government or political system by those governed.' O'May (*op cit*, fn 4, p 261) describes revolution as 'a rebellion which succeeds or substantially succeeds'.

Civil strife arising therefrom

It is emphasised that the insurable risk of 'civil strife', excluded by a marine policy and covered under war risks, is only that civil strife which has arisen from 'war, civil war, revolution, rebellion or insurrection'. O'May suggests that: [p 262] 'It may be that these additional words "civil strife arising therefrom" add little to the enumerated perils ... but ... the phrase may be significant enough, in practice, to embrace an event which arises from the war, civil war, revolution, rebellion or insurrection, though it is geographically separated from the main action.'

Any hostile act by or against a belligerent power

This provision insures one of the risks, namely, 'hostilities', contained within the f c and s clause, which warranted that the marine risks insurer was: '... free ... from the consequences of hostilities and warlike operations.' Clause 24.1 of the ITCH(95) excludes a marine risks insurer thus:[16] 'In no case shall this insurance cover loss damage liability or expense caused by ... any hostile act by or against a belligerent power.' Correspondingly, cl 1.1 of the IWSC(H)(95) and of the IWC(C)(82) provide the necessary war risk cover excluded by the marine policy. Though the f c and s clause is no longer in use in the present regime of exclusion of war risks from the marine cover, nevertheless, a brief historical account of its ambit and degree of influence is useful for a proper understanding of this aspect of the law.

The f c and s clause – consequences of hostilities and warlike operations

Prior to the introduction of the paramount war risks exclusion clause, a marine risks insurer employed the f c and s clause to exclude war risks from the cover for marine risks. By far the most important exclusion contained within the f c and s clause was the provision that the marine risks insurer was: 'Warranted free of ... the consequences of hostilities and warlike operations.' Invariably, the courts, often the House of Lords, had to decide what did, or did not, amount to 'hostilities' and 'warlike operations'.

Loss or damage suffered as a consequence of 'hostilities' – previously excluded by the f c and s clause (and now by cl 24.1, the War Exclusion of the ITCH(95)) from the marine cover) – is now covered by cl 1.1 of the IWSC(H)(95). Thus, case law which previously provided an interpretation of the meaning of 'hostilities' under the f c and s clause is still relevant under the present cover for loss caused by any 'hostile' act. The same, however, cannot be said of the cases which have defined 'warlike operations', as such a cause of loss or damage is not an insured risk under the IWSC(H)(95): consequently,

---

16 See, also, IVCH(95), cl 21.1.

the old cases,[17] which have awarded a meaning to the expression 'warlike operations' in the context of the f c and s clause, are, therefore, not directly relevant to the present scheme of things.

That the insured risk of an act of 'hostility' is not as wide a term as 'warlike operations' was noted by Mustill J (as he then was) in *Spinney's (1948) Ltd v Royal Insurance Co Ltd* [1980] 1 Lloyd's Rep 406, cited above, who remarked: [p 437] '... Warlike operations has a wider meaning [than hostilities], and includes such operations as belligerents have recourse to in war, even though no state of war exists' (*Arnould on Marine Insurance*, 15th edn, para 904).

As a result of the experience gained in two major conflicts, the insurance industry expressed concern that, in time of war, many of the liabilities usually associated with marine risks had effectively been transferred to war risks insurers by the phrase 'consequences of hostilities and warlike operations' contained within the f c and s clause. It was felt that the scope of the exclusion of 'warlike operations' was too wide, with the effect that the marine risks insurer appeared to bear little liability. A loss incurred by a stranding, for example, caused by negligence, could fall upon the war risks insurer if the vessel was carrying war *materiel*.

After the ruling in the *Coxwold* case,[18] where a small vessel ran aground whilst in convoy, and the loss was held to be as a direct result of a warlike operation and not a marine risk, the f c and s clause was restructured in order to redress the balance. However, it was only a question of time before the whole concept of the war exclusion under the f c and s clause was re-addressed. The result was the demise of the f c and s clause in the early 1980s, and the introduction of the paramount war risks exclusion clause (contained within the ITCH(95)), which it has now replaced.

Hostile act

Although there is little in the way of modern authority clarifying the meaning of 'hostile act', some guidance is provided by past cases, where the word 'hostilities' was employed under the f c and s clause.

There is, for example, little doubt that the words 'hostile act' may be considered in the same light as 'hostilities'; the word, employed in the old f c and s clause, has been much commented on. In ***Britain Steamship Co Ltd v King, 'Petersham' and 'Matiana'*** **[1921] 1 AC 99, HL**, where two vessels were lost during the First World War, but not on account of 'warlike operations',

---

17 See, eg, *Britain Steamship Co v King, 'Petersham'* [1921] 1 AC 99, HL; *Yorkshire Dale SS Co Ltd v Minister of War Transport, 'Coxwold'* (1942) 73 LlL Rep 1, HL; *Clan Line Steamers Ltd v Liverpool and London War Risks Association Ltd* (1943) 73 LlL Rep 165; and *Athel Line Ltd v Liverpool and London War Risks Insurance Association Ltd* [1946] 1 KB 117, CA. As some of these cases are still relevant for the purpose of determining the meaning of 'consequences thereof' (appearing in the f c and s clause), they are discussed in Chapter 8, see p 358.

18 See Chapter 8.

the House of Lords was of the opinion that the word 'hostilities' could be read as 'acts of hostility' and, as such, did not require the existence of a state of war to be applicable.

> **Lord Wrenbury:** [p 133] ... All the decisions have, I think, proceeded, and in my judgment have rightly proceeded, upon the footing that the word 'hostilities' does not mean 'the existence of a state of war', but means 'acts of hostility' or (to use the noun substantive which follows) 'operations of hostility'.

But, the question arises, what sort of organisation may be ascribed as being a belligerent power and who, in perpetrating hostile acts, may be considered to be acting on behalf of that belligerent power? This question was answered, in part, in *Atlantic Mutual Insurance Co v King*, below. In this instance, the court was of the opinion that 'hostile acts' meant hostile acts 'by persons acting as the agents of Sovereign Powers or of such organised and considerable forces as are entitled to the dignified name of rebels ...'. Whilst the word 'belligerent' was not actually used, it is presumed that, for there to be a hostile act, both the sovereign power and the rebels would necessarily have had to be belligerent towards one another.

Atlantic Mutual Insurance Co v King [1918] 1 KB 307

Goods placed aboard the vessel *Tennyson*, bound from Bahia to New York, were reinsured by the plaintiffs with the defendants under a marine risks policy of insurance. The policy contained an f c and s clause which stated: 'Warranted free from all consequences of hostilities or warlike operations whether before or after the declaration of war.' Five days out of Bahia, an explosion occurred in the hold of *Tennyson* and the goods, the subject matter of the reinsurance, were burned. It transpired that the explosion had been caused by a bomb placed aboard the vessel by a man named Niewerth, a German subject resident in Bahia, aided by an accomplice. The question before the court was whether a hostile act by a German civilian could be construed as a hostile act by a sovereign power.

The court ruled that the reinsurers were not liable under the marine risks policy. The Act by a civilian, in following the policy of his government, amounted to a hostile act within the meaning of the f c and s clause.

> **Bailhache J:** [p 310] ... the plaintiffs say rightly, as I think, that the word 'hostilities', as used in the clause, means hostile acts by persons acting as the agents of Sovereign Powers, or of such organised and considerable forces as are entitled to the dignified name of rebels as contrasted with mobs or rioters, and does not cover the act of a mere private individual acting entirely on his own initiative, however hostile his action may be.
>
> [p 313] ... I do not, however, think that the word 'agent' in this connection is limited to the strictness in which the words 'agent' and 'principal' are used in business transactions. I am disposed to think that a man is acting, in such a case as this, as the agent of his government when knowing that the settled and concerted policy of that government is to avail itself of the efforts of all its

subjects, whether naval, military, or civilian, to destroy enemy life and property as occasion offers, he uses such opportunity as presents itself in furtherance of that policy.

Clause 1.2: Capture seizure arrest restraint or detainment, and the consequence thereof or any attempt thereat

The IWSC(H)(95), in cl 1.2, states that:
> ... this insurance covers loss of or damage to the Vessel caused by ... capture seizure arrest restraint or detainment, and the consequences thereof or any attempt thereat.

The same risks are covered by the IWC(C)(82), except that the provision is qualified in that 'capture seizure arrest restraint or detainment, and the consequences thereof or any attempt thereat' is only covered when the loss or damage arises from 'risks covered under 1.1 above'.

Capture and seizure

The words 'capture' and 'seizure' are imported into cl 1.2 from the now defunct f c and s clause.[19] That 'capture' is confined to capture by an enemy or belligerent, whereas 'seizure' has a much wider meaning, in that it could include any act of forcible possession, by lawful authority or otherwise, was confirmed by Lord Fitzgerald in *Cory v Burr* **(1883) 8 App Cas 393, HL**. In this instance, a vessel was seized by the Spanish authorities because of the barratrous acts of the master in smuggling tobacco. As the policy of insurance contained an f c and s clause, the House of Lords was obliged to analyse the meaning of both 'capture' and 'seizure'.

> **Lord Fitzgerald:** [p 405] ... In the construction of this warranty, it is observable that 'capture' and 'seizure' do not mean the same thing. 'Capture' would seem properly to include every act of seizing or taking by an enemy or belligerent. 'Seizure' seems to be a larger term than 'capture', and goes beyond it, and may reasonably be interpreted to embrace every act of taking forcible possession either by a lawful authority or by overpowering force.

The issues of 'capture' and 'seizure' were again raised in the *Robinson Gold Mining* case, below.

Robinson Gold Mining Co and Others v Alliance Insurance Co [1901] 2 KB 919

The plaintiffs insured a shipment of gold, destined for Britain or France from South Africa, with the defendants under a policy which insured against, amongst other risks: '... arrests, restraints, and detainments of all kings,

---

19 These same words are also employed in s 3 of the Act which states: '"Maritime perils" means the perils consequent on, or incidental to, the navigation of the sea, that is to say ... captures, seizures, restraints, and detainments of princes and peoples ...'

princes, and people.' However, the policy also contained an f c and s clause, warranting the insurance cover 'free of capture, seizure, and detention, and the consequences thereof'. The gold was 'requisitioned' or, in the words used by the court, 'constitutionally seized' by South African commandos, acting on behalf of the government who, rightly as it turned out, feared the outbreak of the Boer war in 1899. The plaintiffs claimed on their policy of insurance for the loss of the gold, but the underwriters declined to pay, on the basis that the warranty which excluded a loss caused by 'seizure' relieved them from liability.

The court ruled that the insurers were not liable under the policy. Even if the requisition amounted to the restraint of princes, an insured risk, the policy also contained an f c and s clause, and the 'constitutional seizure' of the gold by officers of the government amounted to 'seizure' within the meaning of the f c and s clause. Therefore, the insurers were excluded from liability.

Phillimore J: [p 923] ... I have no doubt that the gold was, in each case, forcibly taken by officers of the South African Republic within the territory of the South African Republic ... I have further no doubt that the gold was legally seized according to the laws in force in the South African Republic; I shall perhaps best explain my meaning by saying that it was constitutionally seized.

[p 925] ... This brings us to two questions: Was the taking of this gold an arrest, restraint, or detainment of rulers? If so, was it also a capture, seizure, or detention, or a consequence of warlike operations?

I am in some doubt about the first point. Restraint of princes and rulers is often more exercised by a government against the citizens of another State. It generally arises in a war, or at least as an act of retorsion, such as embargo or blockade. It is not a restraint of princes when a ship or cargo is arrested by civil process at the suit of a subject.

... Was this taking a capture, seizure, or detention within the terms of the clause of exception? It has been suggested that these words point to hostile taking, and to hostile taking only. That is probably true of capture. But seizure is an additional word.

[p 926] ... 'Seizure' signifies 'the taking of a ship by the act of governments or other public authority for a violation of the laws of trade, or some rule or regulation instituted as a matter of municipal police, or in consequence of an existing state of war'. This is the language of Bigelow CJ, in *Greene v Pacific Mutual Insurance Co*. In *Cory v Burr* the seizure was not, as it was at first contended before me, an act of mere force; it was a legal seizure ... The cases I have cited further show that seizure is not confined to hostile acts. Nor is the word 'detention'.

[p 927] ... The argument may be put this way: there is no arrest or restraint of princes except by capture, seizure or detention; the most outlying case of restraint of princes, *Rodocanachi v Elliott*, being a case of detention. In other words, if the risk is one covered in the body of the policy, it is necessarily excluded by the clause of exception – a clause which probably excludes this risk and some others.

Similarly, in *Forestal Land, Timber and Railways Co Ltd v Rickards, 'Minden'* [1940] 4 All ER 96, where cargo was lost when the German vessel carrying it was scuttled in order to avoid capture, at first instance, Hilbery J stated: [p 109] '... Capture is a taking by the enemy as prize in time of open war with intent to deprive the owners of their property in the goods. It is a belligerent act.'

Are barratrous and piratical seizures covered by marine or war risks?

Essential to both 'capture' and 'seizure' is the act of taking forcible possession. But 'seizure' is a broad concept, and such an act need not necessarily be confined to external forcible possession. Thus, in *Kleinwort v Shepard* (1859) E&E 447, the taking over of a ship by emigrants, effectively an act of piracy, was adjudged to be 'seizure'. But, in the American case of **Republic of China, China Merchants Steam Navigation Co Ltd and United States of America v National Union Fire Insurance Company Of Pittsburgh, Pennsylvania, 'Hai Hsuan'** [1958] 1 Lloyd's Rep 351, where Communist Chinese crews took control of Nationalist Chinese vessels, the court was in no doubt that such action by a crew could not amount to seizure as it applied to an f c and s clause. It amounted to barratry. The court, in reaching its decision, distinguished the *Kleinwort* case.

> **Circuit Judge Soper:** [p 359] ... No case has come to our attention in which the barratrous conduct of either the master or the crew of a vessel has been held to be within the capture and seizure exclusion clause of a marine insurance policy. In *Kleinwort v Shepard* (1859) 1 E&E 447, coolie passengers took control of a ship and made off with her. The court, in holding that the resulting loss came within the exclusion of 'capture and seizure', inquired, argumentatively, whether it would not also be a seizure if a crew, intending to turn pirates, should murder the master and run away with the ship. But this was mere *dictum* ... The single point decided was that the passengers on board the ship, owing no duty of loyalty to the owner and being incapable of committing barratry, had effected a 'seizure' of the vessel within the excluding clause.

It is emphasised that barratry and piracy are specifically excepted from the paramount War Exclusion Clause of the ITCH(95) and the IVCH(95). To that effect, cl 24.2 of the ITCH(95) states:

> In no case shall this insurance cover loss damage liability or expense caused by ...
>
> 24.2 capture seizure arrest restraint or detainment (barratry and piracy excepted) and the consequences thereof or any attempt thereat.

The words in brackets have clarified the point that barratry and piracy remain as marine risks, insured under the ITCH(95). Recovery under the marine risks policy is only possible if barratry or piracy is the proximate cause of the loss. However, the question which arises is, can there be recovery under the marine risks policy if a barratrous act, such as smuggling, results in the seizure of the vessel, and that consequent seizure (not barratry) by the authorities is then adjudged to be 'the' proximate cause of loss?[20]

It is observed that the exception in brackets in the War Exclusion Clause reads as 'barratry and piracy excepted', and not 'barratrous or piratical seizure excepted'. Given a literal and strict construction, it could be argued that only a loss proximately caused by barratry and piracy is excluded from the War Exclusion Clause, and any loss proximately caused by seizure, even if the seizure were to result from a barratrous or piratical act, is not excluded from the War Exclusion Clause.

A loss held to be proximately caused by a seizure arising from a barratrous act of smuggling would not be recoverable under the IWSC(H)(95), for such a loss would also be caught by the exclusion clause contained within cl 5.1.4 of the IWSCH(H)(95), which states that: 'This insurance excludes ... arrest restraint detainment confiscation or expropriation under quarantine regulations or by reason of infringement of any customs or trading regulations.' Nor, it is submitted, could such seizure be deemed a hostile seizure appropriate to a war risks policy.

There is, of course, nothing to prevent a court from holding both barratry and seizure (or, as the case may be, piracy and seizure) to be the proximate causes of loss. 'Barratry' is an included risk under cl 6.2.4 of the ITCH(95) and 'seizure' is a specifically excluded risk under cl 24.2 of the ITCH(95). In such an event, where one proximate cause of loss is included and another proximate cause of loss is specifically excluded, it has been held that the loss is not recoverable under the policy.[21] Naturally, this will only hold true if cl 24.2 is given a wide interpretation as excluding all forms of seizure, including barratrous and piratical seizures (but not barratry and piracy), from the marine cover.

The Institute Cargo Clauses

It should also be noted that, with respect to cargo, neither barratry or piracy are insurable risks under the ICC (B) and (C), and, thus, there is no requirement to except them specifically from the War Exclusion Clause. On the other hand, barratry and piracy are both covered under the ICC (A), by reason of its being an all risks policy. Why, therefore, only piracy, and not barratry, is specifically excepted from the War Exclusion Clause, cl 6.2, in the ICC (A), is not clear.

---

20 See *Cory v Burr* (1883) 8 AC 393, HL and *Nautilus Virgin Charters Inc Hilliard L Lubin and Aileen G Lubin v Edinburgh Insurance Co Ltd* (1981) AMC 2082; in both cases, seizure was held to be the proximate cause of loss. Cf *Republic of China Merchants Steam Navigation Co Ltd and United States of America v National Union Fire Insurance Co of Pittsburgh, Pennsylvania, 'Hai Hsuan'* [1958] 1 LIL Rep 351. These cases are discussed in Chapter 12.
21 See *Wayne Tank and Pump Co Ltd v Employers Liability Insurance Co Ltd* [1973] QB 57, CA; and *Miss Jay Jay* [1987] 1 Lloyd's Rep 32, CA; both cases are discussed in depth in Chapter 8.

Arrest restraint or detainment

Rule 10 of the Rules for Construction affirms that:

> The term 'arrests, etc, of kings, princes, and people' refers to political or executive acts, and does not include a loss caused by riot or by ordinary judicial process.

Thus, the rule makes it clear that the provision 'arrest restraint or detainment' is only applicable to the political or executive acts of governments or authorities. Furthermore, it was confirmed, in the case of *Miller v Law Accident Insurance Co*, below, that 'force' is not a prerequisite for a claim under the head of 'detainment'.

Force is not a requirement

Miller v Law Accident Insurance Co [1903] 1 KB 712, CA

The plaintiff shipped live cattle aboard the steamer *Bellevue* bound for Buenos Aires from Liverpool. The cattle were insured with the defendants under a policy which provided cover against 'arrests, restraints, and detainments of all kings, princes, and people of what nation, condition, or quality soever ...'. However, also included in the policy was an f c and s clause, which warranted the policy 'free of capture, seizure, or detention ...'. When *Belleview* arrived at Buenos Aires, the authorities refused to allow the cattle into the country, because they were diseased. The cattle were, therefore, put on board another vessel bound for Montevideo, where they were sold at a considerable loss. The plaintiff claimed on his policy of insurance, but the insurers refused payment on two counts: (a) the covered perils of 'arrest, restraint or detainment' required force, and none had been used; and, furthermore (b) if the plaintiffs could rely on the perils of 'arrest, restraint or detainment', the use of the word 'detention' in the f c and s clause equally excluded recovery under the warranty.

The Court of Appeal, in affirming the decision of the lower court, ruled that the f c and s clause excluded the insurers from liability under the policy. The court also confirmed that 'force' was not a prerequisite of 'arrest, restraint, or detainment', and, furthermore, 'detention' meant the same as 'detainment'.

> **Mathew LJ:** [p 721] ... It was argued for the defendants that the loss thus occasioned was not due to 'arrest, restraint, or detainment' within the meaning of the policy. The words, it was contended [by the insurers], implied the use of direct force, and none had in fact been employed ... If actual force was not used, it was because there was no opposition. The master submitted to the orders of the administration. The result to the assured was the same as if force had been used, and, even if the defendants were right in their interpretation of the words in question, the loss was *ejusdem generis* with the perils described in the policy ... I am of opinion that, but for the warranty, the underwriters would be responsible for the loss in question ... But the policy contains the

warranty against 'capture, seizure, or detention', commonly called at Lloyd's the f c and s clause; and it was argued for the defendants that their liability under the earlier part of the policy was cancelled. The warranty goes beyond 'arrest' and 'restraint'. 'Capture' and 'seizure' are stronger expressions ... It seems to me sufficient to point out that the word 'detention' in the warranty cannot be distinguished from the word 'detainment' in the earlier in the policy. The loss, in my judgment, is within the warranty, and the underwriters are not liable in this action.

Some years later, in 1916, an even higher court had cause to reflect on the meaning of 'restraint'. In *British and Foreign Marine Insurance Co Ltd v Samuel Sanday and Co* **[1916] P 650, HL**, the House of Lords deemed cargo aboard two British vessels bound for Hamburg to be a constructive total loss when the declaration of war frustrated the whole adventure by making its continuance illegal.

> **Lord Wrenbury:** [p 672] ... It is not necessary that force should be employed, or even that force should be immediately available for employment. Every State ultimately enforces obedience to its laws by force. Restraint is equally imposed when obedience is given by reason of the existence of force in reserve as when it is given by reason of force employed. Neither is it necessary that there should be any specific action upon the goods themselves. The master was restrained, and the venture was restrained, by the fact that illegality supervened as the immediate result of the declaration of war. In my opinion, there was in this case restraint falling within the words 'restraint of kings, princes, and people'.

The issue of the meaning of 'detainment' again arose in the *Wondrous* case, below. In this instance, the underwriters of a war risks policy, the IWSC(H)(95), used as their defence the exclusion of liability under the policy for 'detainment' brought about by an infringement of customs regulations (cl 5.1.4). The case is interesting because three judges, Hobhouse J, at first instance, Lloyd LJ and McCowan LJ, on appeal, saw the issue differently and, for that reason, extracts of the reasoning of each judge are reproduced.

Ikerigi Compania Naviera SA and Others v Palmer and Others, 'Wondrous' [1991] 1 Lloyd's Rep 400; [1992] 2 Lloyd's Rep 566, CA

The plaintiffs chartered their vessel *Wondrous* to an Iranian company to carry a full cargo of 30,000 tons of molasses from Bandar Abbas in Iran to North European or Mediterranean ports. The plaintiffs then effected insurance policies with the defendants, including one covering loss of hire; the policy incorporated war risks.[22] On arriving at Bandar Abbas, *Wondrous* was delayed from sailing for 18 months because the charterers were unable to pay the port

---

22 The policy on loss of hire also included another vessel, *Welcomer*; there was also a policy on freight covering both *Wondrous* and *Tropez Comfort*, but the Court of Appeal decided that there was no loss of freight because the freight was, finally, earned and paid.

dues and freight tax. When *Wondrous* did eventually sail with her cargo for Denmark, she first had to be towed to another port to repair her engines, which had become inoperable; the overall losses were considerable. The plaintiffs claimed on their policy of insurance, but the underwriters refused payment. The main issue before the court was whether the detainment fell within the meaning of 'detainment' as applicable to the war risks policy.

The Court of Appeal ruled that the detainment of *Wondrous*, in failing to pay customs dues, did not fall within the meaning of 'detainment' as applicable to the IWSC(H); McCowan LJ did not concur with this reasoning. At first instance, Hobhouse J had decided that the plaintiffs could not recover under the policy because the detention itself, the proximate cause of the loss, was brought about by an infringement of customs regulations, thereby excluding the liability of the war risks insurer. At the Court of Appeal, Lloyd and Nourse LJJ saw it as no detainment at all within the meaning of the policy. But, McCowan LJ, dissenting, was in no doubt that the vessel had been detained.

Hobhouse J: [court of first instance, p 417] ... However, the exclusion clause 4.1.5 [equivalent to exclusion cl 5.1.4 of the IWSC(H)(95)], loss arising from detainment by reason of the infringement of any customs regulations, does fully apply in this case. In one sense, the vessel was not detained at all; as previously stated, she was not physically restrained. What happened was that she was not able to comply with the customs regulations and, therefore, if she had attempted to sail, she would have been physically detained for infringement of those customs regulations. The words 'restraint' and 'detainment' have to be given a wide commercial interpretation (see, for example, *The Bamburi* [1982] 1 Lloyd's Rep 315) but, by the same token, the exclusion must be read in the same way. In a commercial sense she was detained by reason of infringement of customs regulations. She was only detained because, if she tried to leave, she would have been infringing customs regulations and would have been stopped by force; therefore the reason for her detention was infringement of customs regulations.

Lloyd LJ: [Court of Appeal, p 572] ... I agree with that reasoning [Hobhouse J's reasoning above]. The judge again correctly emphasises that the detention was conditional. If the vessel had tried to leave, without having obtained customs clearance, she would have been forcibly detained. I do not suggest that the threat of detainment was any less real or effective on that account. But the threat of detainment depended on prior infringement ... On the above ground, I would hold in agreement with the judge that *if* there was a detainment within the meaning of cl 1.2 [the perils insured against], then there was an infringement within the meaning of cl 4.1.5 [the perils excluded]. But, putting it in my own words, I would prefer to say that, reading the two clauses together, there was no detainment within the meaning of cl 1.2 at all ... It was common ground that if there was no detainment within the meaning of cl 1.2, the plaintiffs' claim under the policy must fail.

McCowan LJ: [Court of Appeal, dissenting, p 577] ... I have no difficulty in concluding that the vessel was detained in this case, in the sense that a man under house arrest could be properly described as detained, since, although free within his house, he would immediately be apprehended if he tried to leave it. I would not have thought it necessary to give 'a wide commercial interpretation' to arrive at the same conclusion in respect of *Wondrous*. What puzzles me is how the judge [Hobhouse J] arrives at his conclusion that 'in a commercial sense she was detained by reason of infringement of customs regulations', when she did not attempt to leave the port (any more than a man under house arrest who made no attempt to leave it could be said to have infringed the terms upon which he was permitted to remain under house arrest). No authority has been put before this court to support a suggestion that 'infringement' has to be given a special sense in commercial cases ... 'Was the vessel guilty of an infringement?' I fail to see how, in common sense, the answer could be other than 'No'.

Political or executive acts

Interestingly, it was another customs infringement, albeit in different circumstances, which brought about the 'arrest, restraint or detainment' of a vessel in the *Anita* case, below. On this occasion, however, the issue was whether the decree of a special court to confiscate the vessel was *bona fide*. Lord Denning MR was in no doubt that the onus of proving that the court was other than *bona fide* lay with the plaintiff shipowner.

Furthermore, regarding an infringement of customs or trading regulations, Lord Fenton Atkinson was at pains to point out why it was important to differentiate between an 'arrest, restraint or detainment' by a puppet court as opposed to a *bona fide* court. An 'arrest, restraint or detainment' ordered by a puppet court amounted to a political act and would, therefore, be covered by the war risks policy (cl 1.2).[23] But, if the 'arrest, restraint or detainment' was ordered by a *bona fide* court of law, then the war risks insurer could rely on the exclusion cl 5.1.4 to avert liability.[24]

Panamanian Oriental Steamship Corporation v Wright, 'Anita' [1971] 2 All ER 1028, CA

The plaintiff owners of the steamship *Anita* insured her with the defendants under a time policy of insurance. The policy was in the usual Lloyd's Form, with the f c and s clause deleted and incorporating the Institute War and Strikes Clauses (Hulls – Time). In March 1966, during the Vietnam War, *Anita* arrived at Saigon where, on inspection by customs authorities, a large quantity of prohibited articles were found on board. A 'special' court in Saigon eventually acquitted the master of smuggling charges, but some of the

---

23 Rules for Construction, r 10 confirms that: 'The term arrests ... (including restraint and detainment) refers to political or executive acts.'
24 Because of the '... infringement of any customs or trading regulations'.

crew were fined or imprisoned and *Anita* was confiscated. The vessel was accepted as a constructive total loss, but, when the plaintiffs claimed on their war risks policy, the insurers refused payment because, they contended, they were excluded from liability on account of the vessel infringing customs regulations (see cl 5.1.4 of the IWSC(H)(95)).

The Court of Appeal overturned the decision of the trial judge and ruled that the confiscation of *Anita* amounted to an 'arrest, restraint or detainment'. But, because the plaintiffs had failed to prove that the 'special' court had acted without jurisdiction, the underwriters were able to rely on the exception which excluded them from liability for 'arrest, restraint or detainment' when customs or trading regulations were infringed.

> **Lord Denning MR:** [p 1032] ... I cannot agree with the judge about the burden of proof. The position in law was this: at the outset, of course, the owners had the task of proving that the loss came within the perils insured against, in particular 'restraint of people' or, alternatively, 'barratry'. If the owners succeeded on that issue, the underwriters had the task of bringing the case within the exception clause ... But, in the course of the case, the underwriters adduced evidence to show that these transistors were smuggled on board and that the ship was confiscated for smuggling by order of a Vietnamese court. That evidence shifted the *legal* 'burden of proof' on that issue on to the owners ... Once the legal burden was thus shifted back on to the owners, it was for them to adduce sufficient evidence to displace the sentence of confiscation. It was for them to show that the special court acted without jurisdiction and under political direction. They did not do so. So the underwriters can rely on the exception.
>
> **Fenton Atkinson LJ:** [p 1034] The result of this case depends, as I see it, on the answer to the question: was the decision of the special court to order confiscation of The Anita a bona fide and independent exercise of its powers ... If the answer is 'Yes', then in my view the owners' loss arose by reason of the infringement of customs regulations and the underwriters are entitled to rely on the exception in cl 4(1)(e). If, on the other hand, the answer is 'No', because the special court was not acting *bona fide* as an independent judicial body, but merely acting as a puppet court following the directions of the government, or knowingly exceeding its powers, then the loss arose by reason of a political or executive act and in my view was, therefore, covered by cl 1 of the Institute War and Strikes Clauses (Hulls – Time).
>
> ... In my view, the underwriters, on whom the onus lay to bring the case within the exception, showed a blatant case of smuggling, or, perhaps more correctly, a strong prima facie case of an infringement of customs regulations followed by a proper hearing by a lawfully constituted tribunal to which this court should be slow indeed to attribute bad faith.
>
> [p 1035] ... For my part, I do not think that the owners' evidence went far enough to cast any real doubt on the good faith of this special court, and I think on a balance of probabilities it was established by the underwriters that the special court acted in good faith and independently, and that they proved a restraint by reason of infringement of customs regulations.

Loss caused by 'riot or ordinary judicial process' is excluded

Under r 10 of the Rules for Construction, '... a loss caused by riot or by ordinary judicial process' is not recoverable under the insurable risk of 'arrest, restraint or detainment'. With respect to 'riot', this is of little significance, as loss or damage caused by riot is insurable under cl 1.4 of the IWSC(H)(95) and cl 1.1 of the ISC(C)(82).

However, the meaning of a loss by 'ordinary judicial process' needs some clarification, not least because cl 5.1.5 of the IWSC(H)(95) specifically excludes the war risks insurer from liability from such when it states:

> This insurance excludes ... the operation of ordinary judicial process, failure to provide security or to pay any fine or penalty or any financial cause.

The exclusion relates largely to financial matters, and, not unreasonably, the 'operation of ordinary judicial process', which is intended to protect the insurer from any liability arising from litigation where, for example, a ship is arrested by the Admiralty Court on behalf of creditors and then appraised and sold. The logic behind this was expressed by the judge in the court of first instance in *Panamanian Oriental Steamship Corporation v Wright, 'Anita'* **[1970] 2 Lloyd's Rep 365**, thus:

> **Mocatta J:** [p 377] ... In my opinion, the words 'ordinary judicial process' in r 10 refer to the employment of courts of law in civil proceedings. If a rationale be required for this, it is that, in such cases, the State is merely providing a service to litigants, rather than exercising its own power through the courts for its own purposes.

... and the consequences thereof or any attempt thereat

It was well established long ago, in *Ionides v Universal Marine Insurance Co*, below, that the phrase 'consequences of' does not modify the rule of proximate cause now laid down in s 55 of the Act.

Ionides v Universal Marine Insurance Co (1863) 14 CB(NS) 259

During the American Civil War, the Federal vessel *Linwood* ran aground on the coast of North Carolina, an area in Confederate control. Because of both bad weather and the interference of Confederate soldiers, the ship was lost, together with most of the cargo of coffee. The coffee had been insured under a policy of insurance containing an f c and s clause which, *inter alia*, warranted the policy 'free from all consequences of hostilities'. A major issue before the court was whether the words 'consequences of' broadened the scope of the warranty regarding hostilities.

> **Willes J:** [p 289] ... It has been argued that the ordinary rules of insurance law are not applicable to this policy, by reason of the words of the warranty 'all consequences of hostilities' ... I apprehend it is a fallacy to say that a larger sense is to be given to this exception by reason of the use of the word

'consequences' than if the word had been 'effects'. In construing the exception, we can only look to the proximate consequences of hostilities. The introduction of the word 'all' really makes no difference; for, no rule of grammar is more universally applicable than this, that words general and words universal are all one. The words 'all consequences of hostilities' refer to the totality of causes, not to their sequence, or their proximity or remoteness.

With respect to the phrase 'any attempts thereat', the addition of these words is to ensure that where a loss is incurred as a result of an attempt to capture, seize, arrest, restrain or detain the subject matter insured, the insurer is still liable. Any loss or damage sustained in avoiding the same would also be covered by the war risks insurer.

The Detainment Clause

Clause 3 of the IWSC(H)(95) states:

> In the event that the Vessel shall have been the subject of capture seizure arrest restraint detainment confiscation or expropriation, and the Assured shall thereby have lost the free use and disposal of the Vessel for a continuous period of 12 months, then for the purpose of ascertaining whether the Vessel is a constructive total loss the Assured shall be deemed to have been deprived of the possession of the Vessel without any likelihood of recovery.

The object of the clause is to assist an assured to determine how long a vessel must be detained before it can be declared a constructive total loss. Thus, the clause must be read in conjunction with s 60(2)(i) of the Act. It is emphasised that the Detainment Clause only applies where the assured is deprived of possession on account of 'capture seizure arrest restraint detainment confiscation or expropriation'.[25]

In ***The Bamburi* [1982] 1 Lloyd's Rep 312**,[26] where a vessel was deemed to be a constructive total loss after being detained in Iraq after the outbreak of the Iran/Iraq war, the court was of the opinion that a reasonable time for such a detention, in order to establish irretrievable loss, was 12 months from the date of the notice of abandonment.

> **Staughton J:** [p 321] ... Viewing the question as one of principle, I have to bear in mind that the insurance is against loss of the vessel, and not against delay or loss of earnings. Against that background, for what period is it reasonable that the owner should be required to wait to get his vessel back ... Doing the best I can, I judge a reasonable time to be 12 months from the notice of abandonment, without taking into account any period of detainment before the notice.

---

25 Confiscation and expropriation are discussed later in the chapter, p 587.
26 *The Bamburi* is also discussed in the context of a constructive total loss in Chapter 16, p 643.

However, there is another phrase contained in the Detainment Clause which must be considered, namely, 'without any likelihood of recovery'.[27] For an assured to show that recovery is unlikely is no easy task. In *Rickards v Forestal Land, Timber and Railways Co Ltd, 'Minden'* **[1941] 3 All ER 62, HL**, where goods were lost aboard a German vessel when she was scuttled in order to avoid capture, Lord Wright had occasion to consider the meaning of both 'uncertain' and 'unlikely'. Although this very point was also raised with respect to constructive total loss, the words Lord Wright employed are equally relevant to the Detainment Clause.

> **Lord Wright:** [p 81] ... There is a real difference in logic between saying that a future happening is uncertain and saying that it is unlikely. In the former, the balance is even. No one can say one way or the other. In the latter, there is some balance against the event ... If, on the test of uncertainty, the scales are level, any degree of unlikelihood would seem to shift the balance, however slightly. It is not required that the scale should spring up and kick the beam.

Perhaps the position of the assured under the Detainment Clause is best summed up by O'May (*Marine Insurance*, 1993, p 276):

> ... The burden on the assured to establish an actual total loss by irretrievable deprivation is a heavy one. Though a ship be seized, there may still be the possibility that she will be subsequently recovered. Arrest, restraint and detainment may, depending on the surrounding circumstances, be transitory in nature and ephemeral in duration. Even in the case of confiscation and expropriation, there may be grounds for the belief that the order of confiscation may be rescinded.

Clause 1.3: Derelict mines torpedoes bombs or other derelict weapons of war

It is to be noted that an 'explosion' which is not proximately caused by any of the above is covered by the marine risks policy.[28]

This clause would have had marked effect upon the outcome of the case of *Costain-Blankevoort (UK) Dredging Co Ltd v Davenport, 'Nassau Bay'* [1979] 1 Lloyd's Rep 395, had it been in use at the time. In this instance, a dredger was lost off Mauritius when it dredged up derelict 20 mm shells which had been dumped by British forces at the end of the Second World War. However, the loss was not considered a war risk, because, at the time, the f c and s clause was still in use and the court ruled that the dredger was not lost as a consequence of a warlike operation. The outcome, it is suggested, would have been different under the present IWSC(H)(95), cl 1.3.

---

27 See Chapter 16, p 643.
28 See ITCH(95), cl 6.1.2 and IVCH(95), cl 4.1.2.

STRIKES RISKS

The strikes risks insured by the IWSC(H)(95) are enumerated thus:[29]

This insurance covers loss of or damage to the Vessel caused by ...

3.1 strikers, locked-out workmen, or persons taking part in labour disturbances, riots or civil commotions;

3.2 any terrorist or any person acting maliciously or from a political motive;

3.3 confiscation or expropriation.

As with the war risks, the risks covered by the strikes clauses mirror those risks excluded by the Strikes Exclusion Clause contained within the marine risks policy (cl 25 of the ITCH(95) and cl 22 of the IVCH(95)).

Attention is also drawn to the ICC (A), (B) and (C), cl 7, the Strikes Exclusion Clause. It is noticeable that there is an additional exclusion, namely, cl 7.2, which is not mirrored in the ISC(C)(82).[30] Clause 7.2 states: 'In no case shall this insurance cover loss damage or expense ... resulting from strikes, lock-outs, labour disturbances, riots or civil commotions', whereas the cover provided in cl 1.1 of the ISC(C)(82) is worded as: 'strikers, locked-out workmen, or persons taking part in labour disturbances, riots or civil commotions.'

Clause 1.4: Strikers locked-out workmen or persons taking part in labour disturbances riots or civil commotions

Strikers locked-out workmen or persons taking part in labour disturbances

For a legal definition of 'strike', the case of **Williams Brothers (Hull) Ltd v Namlooze Vennootschap WH Berghuys Kolenhandel (1915) 21 Com Cas 253**, is helpful in that it provides a good benchmark. In this instance, the owners of two vessels chartered to carry coal from Hull to Rouen were held not liable, under the charterparty, for delay in delivery when the crews refused to sail after the German Government had threatened to sink all neutral ships in the North Sea. The charterparty contained a clause which stated: '... the owners shall not be liable for any delay ... due to a strike or lock-out of seamen ...'. During the course of its deliberations, the court saw reason to define the word 'strike'.

> **Sankey J**: [p 257] ... The only matter I have to consider is the meaning of the word 'strike'. It is true that in the older cases the definition which has been given by various learned judges as to what constitutes a strike has chiefly turned upon the question of wages. It has been said that a demand by workmen for increase of wages or a refusal by workmen to accept diminution

---

29 See, also, ISC(C)(82), cll 1.1 and 1.2.
30 See Appendix 21.

of wages is itself a strike. I think those definitions rather show the danger, if I may be allowed to say so, of attempting to give an exhaustive definition of the word 'strike', because it is obvious that, since those cases were decided, many circumstances have arisen which would constitute, or might be held to constitute, a strike. A strike does not depend merely upon the question of wages. At the same time, I do not think it would be possible to say that abstention of a workman from mere fear to do a particular thing or perform a particular contract would necessarily constitute a strike. I think the true definition of the word 'strike', which I do not say is exhaustive, is a general concerted refusal by workmen to work in consequence of an alleged grievance.

The definition in the above case was approved of by the Court of Appeal and then developed in the *New Horizon* case, below.

Tramp Shipping Corporation v Greenwich Marine Inc, 'New Horizon' [1975] ICR 261, CA

This was a dispute between a shipowner and a charterer, concerning laytime, when a vessel was delayed in discharging its cargo of soya beans because French crane and sucker drivers, who were in dispute with their employers over conditions, refused to work a night shift and then stopped work altogether. A clause in the charterparty stated that any time lost by reason of a strike was not to be counted as laytime and the issue before the court was whether the stoppage of work amounted to a strike.

The Court of Appeal ruled that the charterers were not liable for the laytime, because the action by the French workers amounted to a strike.

Lord Denning MR: [p 266] ... If I may amplify it a little [the definition of strike by Sankey J], I think a strike is a concerted stoppage of work by men done with a view to improving their wages or conditions, or giving vent to a grievance or making a protest about something or other, or supporting or sympathising with other workmen in such endeavour. It is distinct from a stoppage which is brought about by an external event, such as a bomb scare or by apprehension of danger.

Stephenson LJ: [p 266] ... In my judgment, it [a strike] is a species of stoppage. There cannot be a strike without a cessation of work by a number of workmen agreeing to stop work; and the question is, what kind of concerted stoppages are properly called strikes today? It must be a stoppage intended to achieve something or to call attention to something, as Lord Denning MR has said: a rise in wages, improvement in conditions, support for other workers or for political changes; an expression of sympathy or protest ... In my view, there can be a strike where the concerted stoppage lasts for some hours, but work will be resumed when they have elapsed.

With respect to the term 'lock-out', a good general definition is provided by Smith and Wood which, on p 185, considers both 'lock-out' and 'strike' within the same industrial relations framework:[31]

---

31 See Smith, IT and Wood, JC, *Industrial Law*, 4th edn. 1989, London: Butterworths.

... A lock-out involves the closing of a place of employment, the suspension of work or the refusal by an employer to continue to employ any number of his employees. A strike involves cessation of work by a body of employees acting in combination, a concerted refusal to continue work. In the case of both strikes and lock-outs, these actions must be in consequence of a dispute and in each case the aim of the action must be to coerce the employees or employers, as the case may be, to accept or not to accept terms or conditions of, or affecting, employment.

Unfortunately, there is no authority defining the meaning of the term 'labour disturbances'. However, it is suggested that a 'labour disturbance' may well have a broader scope than a strike or lock-out. Whilst a strike or lock-out is an organised industrial dispute between employees and employers over pay and conditions, there is no such limitation placed upon a labour disturbance which may be conducted by persons from outside the workplace, whose motives may have little or nothing to do with pay and conditions. Such a disturbance may, for example, be politically inspired by 'persons', for example, activists, seeking a forum for their grievances.

Riots

The word 'riot' has a fixed meaning in criminal law, which was spelled out in *Field v The Receiver of Metropolitan Police* **[1907] 2 KB 853**. In this instance, a number of youths created a disturbance in Canning Town, London, and succeeded in demolishing a wall. In an appeal from the county court, the judge ruled that the damage done by knocking down the wall was not caused by riotous behaviour. In coming to his decision, Phillimore J deduced that there must be five necessary elements for a disturbance to constitute a riot.

Phillimore J: [p 860] ... In *R v Cunninghame Graham*, Charles J, largely relying upon the passages in Hawkins, instructed the jury that 'a riot is a disturbance of the peace by three persons at the least, who, with intent to help one another against any person who opposes them in the execution of some enterprise or other, actually execute that enterprise in a violent and turbulent manner to the alarm of the people'.

From these passages we deduce that there are five necessary elements of a riot: (1) numbers of persons, three at least;[32] (2) common purpose; (3) execution or inception of the common purpose; (4) an intent to help one another by force if necessary against any person who may oppose them in the execution of their common purpose; (5) force or violence not merely used in demolishing, but displayed in such a manner as to alarm at least one person of reasonable firmness and courage.

---

32 The Public Order Act 1986, which came into force on 1 April 1987, has increased the number from three to 12 or more persons: s 10(2) of the 1986 Act expressly provides that rr 8 and 10 of the Rules for Construction of the Marine Insurance Act 1906 be construed in accordance with the definition of riot contained within the 1986 Act.

But, in the American case of *Pan American World Airways Inc v The Aetna Casualty and Surety Co* [1974] 1 Lloyd's Rep 207, SDNY; [1975] 1 Lloyd's Rep 77, which later went to appeal, the court was faced with deciding whether the hijacking of an insured Boeing 747 was excepted under the policy because, inter alia, the exclusion clause included loss or damage by 'riot'. When considering the word 'riot', the district court gave the word 'riot' its popular meaning, rather than its more technical interpretation still applicable in English criminal law. Indeed, the judge was critical of the definition of 'riot' as used in the English courts, and rejected it.

> **District Judge Frankel:** [p 232] ... The definitions [based on the one by Phillimore J, in *Field v The Receiver of Metropolitan Police*] give serious trouble at the outset, and probably would not serve even if there were sound reason to use them ... the notion of a flying riot in geographic instalments cannot be squeezed into the ancient formula. Among its other attributes, as the cases reflect, a riot is a local disturbance, normally by a mob, not a complex, travelling conspiracy of the kind in this case.
>
> [p 233] ... There are other difficulties, however. There is substantial basis for the view that: (1) the strained definition urged for the exclusion is not 'the' common law definition of 'riot', for insurance or other purposes; (2) the historic definition, if it were really the proper one to use, would not apply anyhow to the facts; and (3) the guides of ordinary English usage should be followed in any event ... On a more compelling note, it was, in fact, exceedingly rare, even in olden times, for insurance or any other purposes, that numbers of actors as small as we have in this case were deemed capable of mounting a riot. In distinguishing riots from other kinds of violent crimes by groups of people, the courts tended regularly, as everyone does, to speak of 'disorder' and 'the tumult', along with 'the terrorising, the putting in fear, the violence, [and] the unlawful acts [as] ... the essential things'.
>
> [p 234] ... Other illustrations of current usage have been called to the court's attention, but it seems unnecessary to lengthen this discussion. The court concludes that if assemblages numbering as few as three could ever make 'riots', for insurance purposes, they do not today.

However, the issue of riot came up before an English court again in 1982. This time, it was a marine insurance case and the court, in the *Andreas Lemos* case, below, had little hesitation in adopting the definition of riot in its technical, criminal sense.

Athens Maritime Enterprises Corporation v Hellenic Mutual War Risks Association (Bermuda) Ltd, 'Andreas Lemos' [1982] 2 Lloyd's Rep 483

Items of the ship's apparel were stolen by a gang of persons from ashore, whilst the ship lay at anchor outside Chittagong, Bangladesh. As the ship was insured under both a marine risks policy and a war risks policy of insurance, it was important for the court to establish under which policy the loss had taken place. In considering whether the loss was caused by 'riot', Staughton J, in considering the American interpretation of riot as compared with the

English legal definition, injected a degree of humour into his reasoning in order to make his point.

> **Staughton J:** [p 491] ... If one takes the word in its current and popular meaning, nobody but a Sloane Ranger would say of this casualty: 'It was a riot.' The word today means the sort of civil disturbance which has recently occurred in Brixton, Bristol or Wormwood Scrubs. Mr Saville [for the insurers] referred me, in this connection, to the case of *Pan American World Airways v The Aetna Casualty and Surety Co* [1974] 1 Lloyd's Rep 207, decided in the United States District Court for the Southern District of New York. There, an aircraft had been hijacked and blown up by members of the Popular Front for the Liberation of Palestine. The insurers denied liability on the ground that this was a loss by 'riots', and therefore excluded. District Judge Frankel expressed some forthright criticism of English jurisprudence on this point, and declined to depart from the current and ordinary meaning of the word. That approach attracts considerable sympathy, at any rate from me, and at any rate in theory. But, on further examination, it cannot be adopted for an English policy of marine insurance. Take, for example, the word 'rovers'. Its only current and popular meaning is, I suppose, a species of motor car, such as Fords or Vauxhalls.
>
> [p 492] ... Kerr LJ said, in the *Shell Petroleum* case (pp 376 and 778):
>
>> As it has been said many times in many authorities, in construing the various archaic expressions which are still to be found in this form of policy, one cannot go by their ordinary meaning in our language today, but one must treat them as terms of art and interpret them in accordance with their original meaning.
>
> I therefore adopt, for this purpose, the definition of riot provided in *Field v The Receiver of Metropolitan Police* [1907] 2 KB 853 by Phillimore J, p 860 ...

In fact, the House of Lords had taken a similar view, many years earlier, regarding the word 'riot' in *Bolands Ltd v London and Lancashire Fire Insurance Co Ltd* [1924] 19 LlL Rep 1, HL, a non-marine insurance case concerning an armed robbery, where Lord Atkinson stated: [p 4] '... I see no reason at all why the word "riot" should not include its technical meaning as clearly as burglary or housebreaking do.'

Civil commotions

In the case of ***Levy v Assicurazioni Generali*** **[1940] 3 All ER 427, PC,**[33] a non-marine insurance case, merchandise which was stored in a warehouse in Palestine caught fire and was damaged. At the time, in that part of the world, there was much unrest and enmity between Jews and Palestinian Arabs and

---

[33] This case is also notable in respect of 'burden of proof'. Luxmoore LJ: [p 432] '... It [the onus of proof] was placed upon the appellant [assured] by the express terms of the contract. There can be no doubt that, as a matter of agreement between parties, the onus of proof of any particular fact or of its non-existence may be placed on either party, in accordance with the agreement made between them ...'

the insurers refused to pay the subsequent claim because the policy of insurance contained an exception clause which stated: 'This insurance does not cover any loss or damage ... proximately or remotely occasioned by ... mutiny, riot, civil commotion, insurrection, rebellion, revolution ...'

The Privy Council ruled that there was no civil commotion in existence at the time when the fire occurred, and the insurers were liable under the policy.

> **Luxmoore LJ:** [p 431] ... [quoting *Welford and Otter-Barry's Fire Insurance*, 3rd edn, p 64] 'Civil commotion'. This phrase is used to indicate a stage between a riot and civil war. It has been defined to mean an insurrection of the people for general purposes, though not amounting to rebellion; but is probably not capable of any precise definition. The element of turbulence or tumult is essential; an organised conspiracy to commit criminal acts, where there is no tumult or disturbance until after the acts, does not amount to civil commotion. It is not, however, necessary to show the existence of any outside organisation at whose instigation the acts were done.[34]

However, it is emphasised that the term 'civil commotion' in the above case was directly related to a war exclusion clause, and not to a strikes clause, as is the case under cl 1.4 of the IWSC(H)(95) and cl 1.1 of the ISC(C)(82). It is submitted that, in interpreting such a term, the context in which it is used is of paramount importance and the definition of 'civil commotion' quoted by Luxmoore LJ in the *Levy* case may not be altogether relevant to its meaning in the context of a strikes clause. As Brown suggests:[35]

> [p 39] ... Civil commotions: this generic term defies specific definition. It is intended to extend the strikes, etc, exclusion in cl 25.1 to embrace any sort of public disorder where no armed conflict becomes involved. Where the same situation develops into an armed conflict, loss, damage, liability or expense caused thereby is excluded by the term 'civil strife' in cl 24.1.

Thus, in the context of a strikes clause, it is probable that 'civil commotion' should be read as some form of public disorder and not as insurrection, which is just short of rebellion. In ***Spinney's (1948) Ltd v Royal Insurance Co Ltd* [1980] 1 Lloyd's Rep 406**, where premises in Beirut were broken into during a period of political strife, Mustill J was careful, when considering whether the loss was caused by 'civil commotion', to point out that the meaning of 'civil commotion' depended on two criteria, the context in which it was used and the decisions of the courts. In this instance, the clause excluding civil commotion amounted to a war exclusion which stated: 'Condition 6. This insurance does not cover any loss or damage occasioned by ... (b) ... civil commotion assuming the proportions of or amounting to a popular rising ... insurrection, rebellion, revolution ...'

---

34 This definition was based upon the definition given by Lord Mansfield in *Langdale v Mason* (1780) 2 Park on Insurance 965, where he stated: '... I think a civil commotion is this; an insurrection of the people for general purposes, though it may not amount to a rebellion, where there is a usurped power.'

35 Brown, RH, *The Institute Time Clauses Hulls 1995*, 1996, London: Witherby, Pt 1, p 39.

Mustill J: [p 437] ... If there were no authority on the matter and 'civil commotion' were to be construed according to its natural meaning, the application of the words to the present case could scarcely be a question for serious argument. If the violence, death and destruction prevailing in Lebanon did not amount to a civil commotion, the words would be meaningless. Whatever their precise connotation, they must be wide enough to cover the event which I have described. The only issue is whether the context in which they are used, or the decisions of the courts, require them to be given some narrower technical meaning.

The context does not call for a contrary view. Certainly the nature of the positive cover and of the other exceptions in sub-cl (b) shows that civil commotion connotes something considerably more serious than a mere leaderless mob. But, even so construed, the words are apt to cover the present case.

Clause 1.5: Any terrorist or any person acting maliciously or from a political motive

Because of the prevalence in recent years of terrorism and violent actions carried out for political motives, cl 1.5 extends the traditional cover to loss or damage caused by any terrorist or person acting maliciously or from a political motive. Clause 1.5 of the IWSC(H)(95) provides cover for, *inter alia*, what is excluded by cll 25.2 and 26 of the ITCH(95).

However, it should be noted that the ISC(C)(82) does not provide cover for loss or damage caused by 'any person acting maliciously', even though it is effectively excluded under the marine risks policy for cargo by way of cl 4.7 of the ICC (B) and (C).[36] The ICC (A), being an all risks policy, makes no such exclusion.

Thus, a policyholder under the ICC (B) and (C), who wishes to avail himself of cover for malicious damage, should, for an additional premium, incorporate the Institute Malicious Damage Clause.[37]

Clause 1.6: Confiscation or expropriation

Clause 1.6 of the IWSC(H) states that: '... this insurance covers loss of or damage to the Vessel caused by ... confiscation or expropriation'.[38]

---

36 The ICC (B) and (C), cl 4.7 states: 'In no case shall this insurance cover ... deliberate damage to or deliberate destruction of the subject matter insured or any part thereof by the wrongful act of any person or persons.'
37 See Appendix 17.
38 There is no equivalent cover for 'confiscation or expropriation' in ISC(C)(82).

It is emphasised that, whilst 'confiscation or expropriation' are insured risks under the IWSC(H)(95), they are subject to the exclusion clauses 5.1.3 and 5.1.4 also contained in the IWSC(H)(95).

Webster's Comprehensive Dictionary of the English Language defines 'confiscation' as: 'appropriated as forfeited to the public use or treasury, usually as a penalty', and 'expropriation' as: '... the act of taking land [property][39] for the public use by right of eminent domain.' Thus, 'confiscation or expropriation' is distinguished from 'seizure', in that confiscation or expropriation has a confined meaning based strictly upon the right of a Sovereign State to appropriate property within its own territory for its own benefit. This difference was confirmed long ago by Lord Ellenborough in *Levin v Allnutt*, below.

Levin v Allnutt (1812) 15 East 267

During the Napoleonic wars, goods aboard the vessel *Theseus* were insured for a voyage at and from London to Baltic ports. The policy was warranted 'free from confiscation by the government in the ship's port or ports of discharge'. When *Theseus* arrived outside Pillau, in Prussia, she was boarded by both Prussian soldiers and the crew of a French privateer, which resulted in the ship and cargo being condemned as French prizes. The insurers refused to indemnify the cargo-owner for the loss because, they contended, the loss fell under the exclusion of confiscation in the port of discharge.

The court ruled that the insurers were liable under the policy. For it to have been confiscation, the Prussian Government would have had to appropriate the goods for their own purposes. As it was, they had only permitted the French to run away with the property.

> **Lord Ellenborough CJ:** [p 269] ... There was no confiscation in the case, which must be an act done in some way on the part of the government of the country where it takes place, and in some way beneficial to that government; though the proceeds may not, strictly speaking, be brought into its treasury. But here, the Prussian Government only permitted the French to run away with the property. If underwriters wish to guard against such a risk generally, they insert a clause to be freed from seizure, generally, in the port of discharge, according to the common practice in these cases, and not merely to be free from confiscation, which is a more confined meaning.

The Detainment Clause also applies to confiscation and expropriation

As with capture, seizure, arrest, restraint and detainment, 'confiscation or expropriation' are subject to the Detainment Clause.[40] Thus, if a vessel is

---

39 The word 'property' has been added in order for the definition to be made more relevant to marine insurance.
40 See above, p 579.

confiscated or expropriated and the assured is deprived of its free use and disposal for a continuous period in excess of 12 months, he may claim for a constructive total loss, provided that there is no likelihood of recovery.

EXCLUSIONS UNDER THE IWSC(H)(95)

Although many of the exclusions contained within the IWSC(H)(95) are self-explanatory, there are four clauses, namely cll 5.1.2 to 5.1.5, which are of particular relevance. As cll 5.1.4 and 5.1.5 have already been discussed in some detail,[41] only the significance of cll 5.1.2 and 5.1.3 will now be considered.

Clause 5.1.2: Requisition and pre-emption

Clause 5.1.2 of the IWSC(H)(95) states:
> This insurance excludes ... requisition, either for title or use, or pre-emption.

Requisition

Any loss suffered by the owner of a vessel as a result of requisition by government in time of emergency or national need, usually in time of war or hostilities, is not recoverable from the war risks insurer. If the exclusion was not included, it is conceivable that that any loss suffered by the owner of a requisitioned vessel could be recovered from the war risks insurer by way of the insured risk of 'seizure'.

There is no legal definition of the word 'requisition' but, in *The Broadmayne*, *The Sarpen*, *France Fenwick and Co Ltd v The King* and *The Steaua Romana*, below, the courts have shed some light on the practical effects of 'requisition'.

The Broadmayne [1916] P 64, CA

The tanker *The Broadmayne* was under requisition charter to the Admiralty when she stranded outside Harwich harbour. The tug *Revenger* gave assistance, succeeded in towing *The Broadmayne* into harbour and then claimed a salvage award against the ship and freight. The Court of Appeal confirmed that the tug owners had every right to pursue a claim against the owners of *The Broadmayne*, but had no right of arrest against the vessel whilst she was under 'requisition', as that amounted to an action against the Crown.

---

41 See above, pp 574 and 578.

Pickford LJ: [p 73] ... That [requisition] is really nothing more than a hiring of the ship, and the effect of the requisition is that His Majesty has the power to make the owner of the ship come to that hiring agreement. The owner of the ship has no alternative as to whether he will accept the proposition of hiring or not, but the vessel is, after all, a hired ship. It does not take the property of the ship out of the owner and vest it in the Crown, and therefore this vessel is not, for all purposes, in the same position as a vessel which is the property of the Crown. You cannot take proceedings in rem against a ship which is the property of the Crown, because the result of doing so is to attempt to bring the King as a defendant into his own court just as much as if you were to try to serve a writ in personam upon him personally ... Here, the vessel remains the property of her previous owners – the American Oil Company, I think they were. She still remains their property, and is liable to satisfy claims upon them subject to the right of the Crown not to have its prerogative interfered with, and not to have its interest in any way deteriorated.

The Sarpen [1916] P 306, CA

In 1914, the Norwegian steamship *The Sarpen* ran aground on the Isles of Orkney and the steam tug *Simla*, which was under requisition to the Admiralty, rendered salvage services to *The Sarpen* and succeeded in towing her into Kirkwall harbour. Because vessels 'belonging to Her Majesty' were not eligible for salvage awards under s 557 of the Merchant Shipping Act 1894, for a salvage award to be granted to *Simla*, it had to be shown that 'requisition' amounted to a form of hiring, not ownership by the Crown.

Pickford LJ: [p 316] ... But to bring the salving vessel within the section [s 557 of the Merchant Shipping Act 1894], she must belong to the Crown. It is not enough that she is chartered by the Crown, which has the sole directing power over her, and that she cannot render salvage services without the Crown's consent. She does not necessarily belong to the Crown in that case any more than a vessel under charter not by way of demise to any one else belongs to the charterer ... I do not deny that there may be a requisition under such terms as to give the Crown the dominion as well as the control of the ship, and it may be that, in such a case, she may be said to belong to the Crown, although not in the ordinary sense belonging to it. But I am of the same opinion that I expressed in *The Broadmayne*, that the word 'requisition' does not necessarily connote such a state of things; it means that the Crown has the right to require the services of the ship without the consent of the owner, but it does not define the terms upon which the Crown may see fit to take those services.

[p 318] ... In my opinion, where there is a hiring under requisition, as in this case, on terms to be settled after the hiring, the question of whether the requisitioned ship is a ship belonging to the Crown cannot be ascertained until those terms are settled. I do not think in this case there was a taking over of the absolute dominion of the vessel subject to being afterwards altered at the will of the Crown, but a taking over on terms which the Crown had not then settled and which, when settled, might or might not confer such dominion. In this case there were not, in my opinion, materials before the court on which it could

come to the conclusion that *Simla* was a ship belonging to His Majesty, and I think, therefore, that the plaintiffs are entitled to an award.

France Fenwick and Co Ltd v The King [1927] 1 KB 458

The insured vessel arrived in London during a national coal strike, and had her cargo of coal requisitioned by the government under the Emergency Powers Act 1920. Lord Wright had occasion to discuss the background to requisition as well as confirming that the mere direction of a vessel to another port did not amount to requisition. For a ship to be requisitioned, there had to be 'effective and positive dominion or control constituted by a definite order under the Regulations'.

> **Lord Wright:** [p 465] ... The word 'requisition' appears from the *Oxford Dictionary* to have been adopted from the French, and as early as 1837 was used by Carlyle as meaning 'to require anything to be furnished for military purposes'. It came, however, into official prominence during the Great War ... it was employed in several of the War Emergency Regulations ... The nature of the requisition of vessels under the Admiralty Proclamation was explained by Pickford LJ in *The Broadmayne* and in *The Sarpen* ... He [Pickford LJ] obviously would regard as a requisition a case where the Government, having taken possession of a cargo, kept it in the ship at their disposal, but he held that, in the contest before him, a mere direction to the ship to proceed to a particular port, the order being assumed to be lawful, did not constitute a requisition.
>
> [p 467] ... I cannot find it suggested, still less decided, in any case, that a mere direction by the Government to a ship to go to a place, or, *a fortiori*, a mere negative direction, such as not to unload without permission, can constitute a requisition or a requirement that a vessel should be placed at the Government's disposal within such a regulation as the present ... I think, however, that the rule can only apply (if it does apply) to a case where property is actually taken possession of, or used by, the Government, or where, by order of a competent authority, it is placed at the disposal of the Government.

The Steaua Romana; The Oltenia [1944] P 43

Two Rumanian ships were requisitioned by the Kenyan Government at the outbreak of the Second World War under the Defence of the Realm Regulations in force in the colony. One year later, when Rumania entered the war as an ally of Germany, the two vessels were de-requisitioned, seized as prizes by the British Government, and then requisitioned again. The plaintiffs were a Belgian company, based in Britain, who had leased radio equipment, first, to the Rumanian owners of the ships and then to the British Government under the initial requisition. They questioned the right of the British Government to condemn the radio equipment when the ships were later seized as prizes and requisitioned again.

The court ruled that the Government had no such right, but, in reaching that decision, Lord Merriman considered what 'requisition' meant in practice.

Lord Merriman: [p 48] ... it should be remembered that the word 'requisition' is not a term of art, and, as Pickford LJ explained in *The Broadmayne*, does not connote the same state of things in every particular case. Requisitioning may be, and usually is, nothing more than a hiring of the ship which does not take the property in the ship out of the owner, though the owner has no alternative whether he will accept the proposition of hiring or not, or it may involve a taking over of the absolute dominion of the vessel, though this may not be ascertained in any given case until the terms are finally settled ... in the colloquial sense, all requisitioned ships, whether or not the property is actually acquired, may be described as 'ministry owned'.

Pre-emption

Webster's Comprehensive Dictionary of the English Language defines pre-emption as 'the right or act of purchasing before others'. Thus, under cl 5.1.2, the underwriter is excluded from any liability for loss or expense which may be brought about by the exercise of this prior right. The reason for its inclusion in the clause was considered by O'May (*Marine Insurance*, 1993, p 273):

> ... 'Pre-emption' is a term used in the American Institute Clauses, and relates to the situation common in the United States where, in return for government subsidy, the owner grants the right to the Government to take over the ship in time of national emergency. It contemplates a prior contractual right to take over ownership or use and is probably covered by 'requisition'. To avoid the danger of narrow and irrelevant distinctions being made, both terms, 'requisition' and 'pre-emption', are used in the Institute and American Institute Clauses.

Notes

There is another different interpretation of the meaning of pre-emption, which may or may not still be relevant. In ***The Zamora* [1916] 2 AC 77, PC**, where the Swedish steamship Zamora, a neutral vessel, was intercepted by a British cruiser and both ship and cargo seized as prizes, the court considered the historical background to pre-emption. According to Lord Parker of Waddington:

> [p 105] ... The right of pre-emption appears to have arisen in the following manner: according to the British view of international law, naval stores were absolute contraband, and if found on a neutral vessel bound for an enemy port, were lawful prize. Other countries contended that such stores were only contraband if destined for the use of the enemy government. Under these circumstances, the British Government, by way of mitigation of the severity of its own view, consented to a kind of compromise. Instead of condemning such stores as lawful prize, it bought them out and out from their neutral owners, and, in this practice, after forming the subject of many particular treaties, at last came to be recognised as fully warranted by international law ... It is obvious, therefore, that this 'right of pre-emption' differs widely from the right to requisition the vessels or goods of neutrals, which is exercised without

prejudice to, and does not conclude or otherwise affect, the question whether the vessel or goods should or should not be condemned as prize.[42]

Clause 5.1.3: Capture seizure arrest ... by or under the order of the government ... of the country in which the vessel is owned or registered

The other relevant exclusion contained within the IWSC(H)(95) is cl 5.1.3, which states:

This insurance excludes ...
Capture seizure arrest detainment confiscation or expropriation by or under the order of the government or any public or local authority of the country in which the Vessel is owned or registered.

It is significant to note that, though cl 1.2 of the IWSC(H)(95) provides cover for a loss caused by 'capture seizure arrest restraint or detainment ...', it does not, by reason of cl 5.1.3, provide cover for the same if it were to arise 'by or under the order of the government or any public or local authority of the country in which the Vessel is owned or registered'. The circumstances under which cll 1.2 and 5.1.3 apply are different. In the case of the former, there must be present the element of hostility or war; whereas, in the latter, the loss sustained by the assured has arisen not as a result of an act of a 'foreign' country, but as a result of an order issued by 'the government or any public or local authority of the country in which the Vessel is owned or registered'. This may be described as a 'domestic' problem between the assured and 'the country in which the Vessel is owned or registered'. The exclusion has taken into account the fact that the country of ownership and registry of the vessel may not be the same. An example of a loss falling within cl 5.1.3 is when the flag State or the country in which the vessel is owned seizes or detains a vessel for non-compliance with its statutory laws on operating standards, for example, manning levels.

O'May has suggested that cl 5.1.3 also provides the insurer with protection against liability, additional to cl 5.1.2, in the event of requisition. He goes on to say (*Marine Insurance*, 1993, p 274) that: '... to avoid argument that a requisition by government may not in certain circumstances be apt to fall within "seizure", the two exceptions are used.'

The exclusion appears to be logical, in that no war risks insurer would wish to shoulder responsibility for the loss of a vessel by seizure and the like resulting not from an act of war or hostility, but from an 'internal' matter between the assured and the country in which the vessel is owned or registered.

---

42 See Bennett, H, *The Law of Marine Insurance*, 1996, London: Clarendon, p 216.

INSTITUTE WAR CLAUSES (CARGO) AND INSTITUTE STRIKES CLAUSES (CARGO)

As the war and strikes perils insured by the IWC(C)(82) and the ISC(C)(82), respectively, are the same those found in the hull policy, the IWSC(H)(95), the law described above is also relevant to the said cargo clauses covering war and strikes risks. Thus, discussion need only centre upon the Frustration Clause, which is relevant to the cargo policy only.

The frustration clause

Clause 3.7 of the IWC(C)(82) and cl 3.8 of the ISC(C)(82) state that:
> In no case shall this insurance cover ...
> any claim based upon loss of or frustration of the voyage or adventure.

The origin of the frustration clause lies with the milestone case of *British and Foreign Marine Insurance Co Ltd v Samuel Sanday and Co* [1916] 1 AC 650, HL,[43] where two British vessels were unable to deliver goods, belonging to British merchants, to Hamburg because of the outbreak of war between Britain and Germany. Although the goods were physically undamaged and were in the possession of their owners, they were held to be a constructive total loss because the whole adventure had been frustrated by a peril insured against, the restraint of princes.

Thus, the frustration clause is now inserted into both the IWC(C)(82) and the ISC(C)(82) to ensure that the decision in the *Sanday* case is not permitted to apply.[44]

Background to the frustration clause

It is noticeable that the frustration clause now employed by both the IWC(C)(82) and the ISC(C)(82) is unqualified and extremely brief; this was not always the case. Originally, following the ruling in the *Sanday* case, the frustration clause was worded thus:
> Warranted free of any claim based upon loss of, or frustration of, the insured voyage or adventure, caused by arrests, restraints, or detainments of kings, princes or people.

---

43 A discussion of this case in the context of 'loss of voyage' as an insured peril under a cargo policy can be found in Chapter 3, p 91.
44 There is no frustration clause contained within IWSC(H)(95) because the concept of loss caused by the frustration of the adventure only applies to cargo. See *Doyle v Dallas* (1831) 1 M&Rob 48.

Surprisingly, the original frustration clause was narrow in scope in that it only excluded the insurer from loss based upon the frustration of the voyage or adventure when that frustration was caused by the 'arrests, restraints, or detainments of kings, princes or people'. By widening the scope of the frustration clause, as it now stands, the insurer is excluded from loss based upon the frustration of the voyage or adventure caused by any of the perils insured against.

However, it is stressed that the frustration clause is only applicable to any loss 'based upon loss of or frustration of the voyage or adventure'. Where the frustration clause is concerned, it is the voyage or adventure which is the subject matter of the insurance, and the clause does not apply to claims made by an assured for loss or damage to the goods themselves. This point was emphasised in the *Rickards* case, below, where three separate cases, dealing with similar issues, were heard by the House of Lords at one sitting.

Rickards v Forestal Land, Timber and Railways Co Ltd; Robertson v Middows Ltd; Kann v WH Howard Bros and Co Ltd [1941] 3 All ER 62, HL

In three separate instances, goods aboard three German ships, *Minden*, *Wangoni* and *Halle*, were lost to their owners at the advent of the Second World War. *Minden* was scuttled off the Faroe Islands to avoid capture by a British warship, *Wangoni* returned to Germany with the cargo still on board, and *Halle* was scuttled off the coast of Africa to avoid capture by a French warship. In all three cases, the policies of insurance contained frustration clauses, and the insurers contended that they were excused liability because, effectively, the voyages had been frustrated the moment war was declared and the German Government took over control of all merchant shipping.

The House of Lords ruled that, in all three instances, there had been a constructive total loss of the goods brought about by the actions of the German Government, and the insurers were liable under the policies. The frustration clause did not exclude the underwriters from liability, because the clause only applied to the voyage or adventure when the goods were not lost to their owners. The frustration clause would not apply when the goods were totally or partially lost, because, in such circumstances, the claim would be based on the physical loss or damage to the goods themselves, not on the loss of the adventure.

> **Viscount Simon LC:** [p 66] ... If any and every claim for loss of goods by war peril is rendered futile by the insertion of the frustration clause, the policy, so far as loss by war perils is concerned, is perfectly useless. Such a result is no doubt possible if clear and apt words are used, with the result that the underwriter takes away with one hand what he gives with the other, but it seems to me that the fallacy in the argument arises from assuming that every loss of goods is 'based upon loss of adventure'. I agree with the Court of Appeal in thinking that the proper interpretation of the frustration clause is not

'free of any claim which on the facts might be based on loss of the insured voyage', and that its proper meaning must be 'free from any claim which is in fact based, because it can only be based, upon loss of the insured voyage'.

Lord Wright: [p 84] ... It is not necessary to multiply examples of cases in which the loss claimed was loss of the venture. To cases of that type the frustration clause has a clear and precise application. In my opinion, however, it cannot be applied to a case where the assured is claiming for loss of, or damage to, the actual physical things or chattels. He is entitled to resist the application of the clause on the ground that the primary subject matter is the goods, and that the adventure is merely ancillary or accessory. A claim in respect of the loss of the adventure is an added benefit granted to the assured over and above his interest in the goods themselves. The exception is expressly by its language limited to the loss of, or frustration of, the insured voyage or adventure. Its language cannot, in my opinion, be twisted to make it exclude a claim for actual loss of, or damage to, the goods themselves.

[p 85] ... what I may call the adventure interest is notionally severable from what I may call the goods or chattel interest. It seems clear, on that footing, that it is only the latter [should read 'former'][45] which is affected by the frustration clause. The assured can claim for the loss of the goods or things or chattels without being harmed by the frustration clause. This conclusion is fortified by the history of the clause, which was undoubtedly invented from a desire to abrogate the effect of the *Sanday* case, where only the adventure was affected by the peril, the goods being unaffected.

Notably, the frustration clause uses the words *based upon* as opposed to *caused by* when it states that: 'In no case shall this insurance cover ... any claim based upon loss of or frustration of the voyage or adventure.' It is suggested that the words 'based upon' have been carefully chosen to ensure that the clause has a wide remit which is not constrained by the rule of proximate cause, because it is likely that the proximate cause of loss would be an insured peril rather than the frustration of the voyage or adventure which results from it.[46]

In *Atlantic Maritime Co Inc v Gibbon* [1953] 2 Lloyd's Rep 294, CA, the insurers of a time policy on freight, which incorporated the Institute War and Strikes Clauses containing a frustration clause, were successful in avoiding a claim when the vessel was ordered out of Taku Bar by the Nationalist Chinese Navy during the civil war with the Communists. Despite the proximate cause of the loss being held to be the restraint of princes, a peril insured against, the underwriters were deemed not liable under the policy because the loss fell within the meaning of the frustration clause, that is, the frustration of the adventure was caused by '... arrests restraints or detainments of kings princes

---

45 There appears to be an error or misquotation in the text. Unless the word 'latter' is replaced by 'former', it makes no sense.
46 In *Rickards v Forestal Land, Timber and Railway Co Ltd* [1941] 3 All ER 62, HL, Lord Porter equated the words 'based on' with 'founded upon' when he stated: [p 99] '... No doubt it can be said that "based upon" bears the same meaning as "founded upon".'

people or persons attempting to usurp power'. Sir Raymond Evershed MR remarked that: [p 307] '... If, then, I am right in saying that the real, efficient cause of this loss was the restraint of princes, I have already said that it seems to me clearly, as a matter of language, covered by the frustration exception.'

References and further reading

Miller, MD, *Marine War Risks*, 2nd edn, 1994, London: LLP

CHAPTER 15

ACTUAL TOTAL LOSS

INTRODUCTION

The Marine Insurance Act 1906 classifies two types of loss, partial loss[1] and total loss (s 56(1)); total loss being further subdivided into actual total loss and constructive total loss (s 56(2)).[2]

Notice of Claim and Tenders Clause

All claims for loss, partial or total, are subject to the Notice of Claim and Tenders Clause within the Institute Hulls Clauses (cl 13 of the ITCH(95) and cl 11 of the IVCH(95)). This clause is a new provision which, unlike its predecessor,[3] specifies that:

> In the event of an accident whereby loss or damage may result in a claim under this insurance, notice must be given to the Underwriters promptly after the date on which the Assured, Owners, or Managers become or should have become aware of the loss or damage and prior to survey so that a surveyor may be appointed if the Underwriters so desire.

Prompt notice

Presumably, prompt notice is notice which is given as soon as is reasonably practicable in the circumstances and is, therefore, a question of fact (s 88), but it is emphasised that the prompt notice relates to the time when the 'Assured, Owners or Managers become or should have become aware of the loss or damage and prior to survey'. As to the effect of prompt notice not being given, Arnould submits that '... failure to give notice, under the new cl 13.1, cannot of itself amount to a breach of utmost good faith: but if the assured acts dishonestly in this regard, that may well be a breach of the continuing duty of good faith'.[4]

Furthermore, the Notice of Claim and Tenders Clause also introduces a time bar, which stipulates:

> If notice is not given to the Underwriters within 12 months of that date unless the Underwriters agree to the contrary in writing, the Underwriters will be

---

1 See Chapters 17 and 18.
2 See Chapters 15 and 16.
3 ITCH(83), cl 10, and IVCH(83), cl 8.
4 Arnould, J, *Law of Marine Insurance and Average*, 16th edn, 1981, London: Sweet & Maxwell, Vol 3, para 128.

automatically discharged from liability for any claim under this insurance in respect of or arising out of such accident or the loss or damage.

Automatic discharge from liability

Failure of the assured, who need not necessarily be the shipowner, but may well be a mortgagee, to ensure that notice of loss or damage is given to the underwriter within the prescribed time limit of 12 months would result in the underwriter being automatically discharged from liability. But it should be noted that the failure to provide notice within the time limit only discharges the underwriter from liability for the loss or damage arising out of that specific event or accident. Unlike a warranty, which uses similar language, failure to give notification within the time limit does not absolve the underwriter from other liabilities within the policy. The policy, as a whole, remains intact, and only the liability for the particular loss in question is displaced. Naturally, the underwriter is free to waive the breach if he so wishes, but such a waiver must be confirmed in writing.[5]

DEFINITION OF ACTUAL TOTAL LOSS

With respect to actual total loss, s 57(1) of the Marine Insurance Act 1906 applies to any subject matter insured within a policy of marine insurance, and this may include, amongst others, ship, goods, freight, profits and commissions, wages and disbursements when it states:

> Where the subject matter insured is destroyed, or so damaged as to cease to be a thing of the kind insured, or where the assured is irretrievably deprived thereof, there is an actual total loss.

Furthermore, actual total loss, within the meaning of the definition, may be construed in three distinct ways, namely:

(a) when the subject matter is totally destroyed,

(b) when the subject matter is so damaged as to cease to be a thing of the kind insured, and

(c) when the assured is irretrievably deprived thereof.

Roux v Salvador was an early case which pre-empted and influenced the provisions laid down within s 57(1) of the Act.

Roux v Salvador (1836) 3 Bing NC 266

The plaintiff shipped a cargo of 1,000 salted hides aboard *Roxalane* from Valparaiso to Bordeaux. The hides were insured with the defendants under a

---

5 See ITCH(95), cl 13.1.

voyage policy of insurance, which covered the usual perils, but was warranted free of particular average unless the ship be stranded. On the voyage from Valparaiso, by way of Cape Horn, *Roxalane* encountered severe weather and had to put into Rio de Janeiro for repairs. Accordingly, all the cargo was landed, and it was then that the hides were found to have been so wetted by seawater that they could not be taken onwards to Bordeaux because they would, through further putrefaction, have lost their character as hides. They were, therefore, sold in Rio de Janeiro for a quarter of their true value. The plaintiff claimed on his policy of insurance for a total loss brought about by the damage and eventual sale of the hides in Rio de Janeiro.

The court ruled that the plaintiff could recover for a total loss, as the goods were both perishable and out of the control of the assured.

> **Lord Abinger CB:** [p 278] ... If the goods are of an imperishable nature, if the assured become possessed or can have control of them, if they still have an opportunity of sending them to their destination, the mere retardation of their arrival at their original port may be of no prejudice to them beyond the expense of re-shipment in another vessel. In such a case, the loss can be but a partial loss, and must be so deemed, even though the assured should, for some real or supposed advantage to themselves, elect to sell the goods where they have been landed, instead of taking measures to transmit them to their original destination. But if the goods once damaged by the perils of the sea, and necessarily landed before the termination of the voyage, are, by reason of that damage, in such a state, though the species not be utterly destroyed, that they cannot with safety be re-shipped into the same or any other vessel; if it be certain that, before the termination of the original voyage, the species itself would disappear, and the goods assume a new form, losing all their original character; if, though imperishable, they are in the hands of strangers not under the control of the assured; if by any circumstance of their existing *in specie* at that forced termination of the risk, is of no importance. The loss is, in its nature, total to him who has no means of recovering his goods, whether his inability arises from their annihilation or from any other insuperable obstacle.
>
> [p 285] ... The underwriter engages, that the object of the assurance shall arrive in safety at its destined termination. If, in the progress of the voyage, it becomes totally destroyed or annihilated, or if it be placed, by reason of the perils against which he insures, in such a position, that it is wholly out of the power of the assured or the underwriter to procure its arrival, he is bound by the very letter of his contract to pay the sum insured.

TYPES OF ACTUAL TOTAL LOSS

Where the subject matter is totally destroyed

In any claim for total loss, the question must arise as to the condition of the subject matter insured or how severely it must be damaged before it may be considered as totally destroyed and, therefore, recoverable as an actual total loss. It should be noted that, in many of the early cases, prior to the introduction of the Marine Insurance Act 1906, there was often little effort made to differentiate between actual and constructive total loss. The courts were mainly concerned with distinguishing a total loss from a partial loss.

Actual total loss of a ship – a total wreck

In **Cambridge v Anderton (1824) 2 B&C 691**, where a vessel was badly damaged in the St Lawrence and later sold, Abbott CJ introduced a colourful, but apt, phrase, the principle of which is no less appropriate now, in order to differentiate between a partial and a total loss.

> **Abbott CJ:** [p 692] ... If the subject matter of insurance remained a ship, it was not a total loss, but if it were reduced to a mere congeries of planks, the vessel was a mere wreck, the name which you may think fit to apply to it cannot alter the nature of the thing.

In *Bell v Nixon*, below, which was also concerned with the loss of a ship, the court again had to consider the degree of damage required to determine whether the vessel was a total loss. The significance of a notice of abandonment was also raised.

Bell v Nixon (1816) Holt NP 423

Dorset was insured by the plaintiffs, with the defendants, under a voyage policy of insurance from Hull to Quebec. After running into severe weather, *Dorset* put into Limerick, a port in Ireland which had few facilities, in order to gain shelter and effect repairs. A survey, carried out at Limerick, showed *Dorset* to be considerably damaged and, as it was impossible to carry out the necessary repairs where she was or move her to a more suitable port, she was condemned and broken up. The plaintiffs claimed for a total loss under their policy of insurance, but the insurers contested the claim, on the basis that the ship still existed *in specie* and, furthermore, they had not received a notice of abandonment.

The court ruled that, on the 'slight evidence' given, the plaintiffs had given notice of abandonment and, therefore, they could recover for a total loss. However, the court discussed the issue of notice of abandonment and the actual condition of the vessel when she was abandoned.

> **Dallas J:** [p 424] ... The assured has a right to abandon under certain circumstances; and, in some cases, he may claim a total loss without abandonment. But, if the case be doubtful, the assured ought not to take upon himself to determine for the underwriters; to break up the ship; and to call upon them for a total loss. I think that he should, in this instance, have communicated to the underwriter the state of the vessel. The ship is proved to have been in that condition that it was necessary to have a survey. Examination and judgment were therefore applied to determine what it was expedient to do. The arguments by which this ship is represented to be a wreck

proceed upon a fallacy. She was not a wreck. Her timbers were together; she existed as a ship specifically, both when she was surveyed, and when she was sold; and it is not because there was no dock at Limerick to receive her, and because she is found to contain rotten timber upon breaking up, that she is to be represented as a wreck. If her planks and apparel had been scattered in the sea it would have been another question ... but the plaintiffs ultimately had a verdict on two points: (1) that a notice of abandonment had been given to the underwriters, of which fact the plaintiffs gave some slight evidence; (2) that the vessel was not unseaworthy.

Although the *Blairmore* case, below, is concerned with constructive total loss, the issue of what constituted an actual total loss was also raised. The opinion voiced by Lord Halsbury that, for a vessel to be a total loss, she need only be sunk, has since been clarified in the case of *Captain JA Cates Tug and Wharfage Co Ltd v Franklin Insurance Co*, also cited below.[6]

Sailing Ship Blairmore Co Ltd v Macredie [1898] AC 593, HL

The sailing ship *Blairmore* was moored in San Francisco Bay, awaiting employment, when she was struck by a squall and sank; the owners gave notice of abandonment to the insurers, and claimed that the ship was a constructive total loss in that her repaired value would be less than the cost to raise and right her. At their own expense, the underwriters then had *Blairmore* raised and righted, and then contended that their expenditure, when determining a constructive total loss, need not be taken into consideration. The owners continued to pursue their claim for a total loss, but the underwriters refused payment. The question before the court was whether the underwriters, in taking action themselves, could change a total loss into a partial loss.

The House of Lords allowed the appeal by the shipowners, and ruled that the underwriters could not take it upon themselves to change their liability from a total loss to a partial loss.

> **Earl of Halsbury LC:** [p 598] ... I myself should say a ship was totally lost when she goes to the bottom of the sea, though modern mechanical skill may bring her up again; and I think, in construing a contract now for many years a common contract, no one could doubt that that contract was intended by the parties to contemplate the loss of a ship as comprehending the case of her being sunk.
>
> **Lord Watson:** [p 603] ... In the admitted circumstances of this case, I do not think it is a matter of necessary inference that *Blairmore*, when she went to the bottom of the sea on 9 April 1896, became immediately an actual total loss. She did not become, in the strict sense of the term, a total wreck, seeing that she was not reduced to the condition of a mere congeries of wooden planks or of pieces of iron which could not without reconstruction be restored to the form

---

6   See below, p 604.

of a ship, and that she had sunk in a depth of water which admitted of her being raised to the surface and repaired.

In the case of *Captain JA Cates Tug and Wharfage Co Ltd v Franklin Insurance Co*, below, the issue raised in the *Blairmore* case by Lord Halsbury, that 'a ship was totally lost when she goes to the bottom of the sea', was clarified.

Captain JA Cates Tug and Wharfage Co Ltd v Franklin Insurance Co [1927] AC 698, PC

The tug *Radius*, which was insured by the defendants, was sunk after a collision at Vancouver and the owners, who were the appellants, gave notice of abandonment which was not accepted by the insurers. Salvors were then employed by the insurers and the tug was raised at a moderate cost. Most estimates for repair were below the tug's insured value, but the owners had not considered this fact when they abandoned. Another issue for consideration was that the salvors had tentatively made an offer to buy the tug from the insurers, and it was alleged that this showed that the insurers had accepted the abandonment.

The Privy Council ruled that there was no actual or constructive total loss, and the insurers were not precluded from denying the acceptance of the abandonment. Viscount Sumner, however, took the opportunity to clarify Lord Halsbury's remarks, made previously in the *Blairmore* case.

> **Viscount Sumner:** [p 704] ... What Lord Halsbury said [in the *Blairmore* case] was not necessary to the decision, nor was it part of the reasoning on which the decision of the House was based, and it expresses only his opinion at that time on the particular fact which the case presented – namely, that this ship had been sunk in a squall in 60 fathoms, while laid up in ballast in San Francisco Bay in the year 1896. The physical possibility of raising a sunken ship depends not only on the place where she lies, her size and injuries, and the available facilities for salvage work, but also on the existing state of the salvors' art, which, since 1896, has made very considerable advances. Lord Halsbury's remark must not be taken as meaning that any ship is an actual total loss whenever she is under water, nor even when she is submerged in such circumstances as to present to salvors a problem of some difficulty.

Barker v Janson, below, raised another issue, that of whether a policy of insurance can attach when there is already a claim in place for total loss. In this instance, after an accident, the notice of abandonment was not given in time for there to be a constructive total loss, and the loss, therefore, was adjudged to be a partial loss. Thus, when another policy of insurance, a valued time policy, was effected in ignorance of the previous casualty, it was held to have attached, because the ship still existed as a ship and there was no intended fraud.

Actual Total Loss

Barker v Janson (1868) LR 3 CP 303

The plaintiffs were the owners of the vessel *Sir William Eyre*, which was insured for a voyage from England to New Zealand but, on her arrival at New Zealand, she was driven ashore and severely damaged. Because there were no facilities in New Zealand to repair her, she sailed for Calcutta and, after a survey, the underwriters settled for a partial loss. But, before they knew of the first accident, the plaintiffs had effected another policy of insurance on *Sir William Eyre* and, during the currency of this second policy, a time policy, the vessel was wholly destroyed by a cyclone whilst moored in the river at Calcutta. The plaintiffs claimed on their second policy of insurance also, but the underwriters refused payment, contending that, *inter alia*, at the time that the new policy was issued, *Sir William Eyre* was no longer a ship.

The court ruled that the policy had attached, and the underwriters were liable for the second claim. During the course of the trial, Willes J deliberated on what constituted an actual total loss.

> **Willes J:** [p 305] ... If a ship is so injured that it cannot sail without repairs, and cannot be taken to a port at which the necessary repairs can be executed, there is an actual total loss, for that has ceased to be a ship which never can be used for the purposes of a ship; but if it can be taken to port and repaired, though at an expense far exceeding its value, it has not ceased to be a ship, and unless there is a notice of abandonment, there is not even a constructive total loss.

The issue of what constituted an actual total loss was raised in the recent case of *Fraser Shipping Ltd v Colton*, below.

Fraser Shipping Ltd v Colton and Others [1997] 1 Lloyd's Rep 586

The semi-submersible heavy lift vessel *Shakir III* was insured for actual total loss only for a voyage under tow, from Jebil Ali to either Shanghai or Huang Pu. In the event, the vessel was towed to Huang Pu, where a typhoon was encountered and *Shakir III* was driven aground and stranded. The plaintiff owners of the vessel claimed under their policy, on the basis that the vessel was an actual total loss in that it was a wreck, and, as s 57(1) states, had 'ceased to be a thing of the kind insured'. The insurers refused to indemnify the owners, contending, *inter alia*, that *Shakir III* was not in fact an actual total loss.[7]

> **Potter LJ:** [p 591] ... In asserting that the vessel became an actual total loss, Mr Milligan [for the owners] made submissions under both limbs of the definitions in s 57(1).
>
> First, he submitted that, by reason of the state into which the vessel was rendered upon grounding, it ceased to be 'a thing of the kind insured'. In short, he said that it ceased to be a 'vessel' and became a wreck. That is, it seems to me, an unduly simplistic approach. It is true that 'a thing of the kind insured' involves consideration of a broad generic description of the subject matter of

---

7 The issues of change of voyage and non-disclosure of material facts which also arose in this case are discussed in Chapter 4, p 154, and Chapter 6, p 227, respectively.

the insurance in each case. However, it seems clear from the authorities that the particular characteristics of that subject matter must be elucidated to some extent for the purpose of the doctrine: cf *George Cohen Sons and Co v Standard Marine Insurance Co Ltd* (1925) 21 LlL Rep 30, p 31, *per* Roche J:

> The thing insured was an obsolete battleship called *Prince George* which had been acquired by the plaintiffs for the purpose of being broken up in Germany.

Taking a similar approach to this case, the vessel was a semi-submersible heavy lift carrier which had been decommissioned and was being towed, as a dead ship, for break-up in a Chinese port.

... The highest evidence goes as a result of the distant and incomplete examination which occurred is that the vessel was 'almost in two', but the photographs and weight of the evidence before me show that it was not, in fact, in two and still retained its original appearance and character as a single vessel, so that it seems to me that the possibility (or indeed the probability) that, in the course of salvage, it would have to be separated into two halves for towage goes more to the economics of salvage than to the question of whether the vessel had lost its essential character.

As to the definition of actual total loss, whether the plaintiff were 'irretrievably deprived' of the vessel prima facie depends upon whether, by reason of the vessel's situation, it was wholly out of the power of the plaintiffs or the underwriters to procure its arrival. It seems to me that this, in turn, depends upon whether the vessel could have been physically salved or not. The undisputed evidence in this respect was to the effect that it was feasible to salvage the vessel subject to accessibility and cost.

The aspect of accessibility and cost are again by no means certain, for the reason that, in the period following the stranding, neither the plaintiffs nor the defendant underwriters progressed beyond a preliminary assessment of the position in the light of the limited value of the vessel and the uncertain attitude of the Chinese authorities. However, there was no reason, nor was there evidence before me to suppose, that salvage would not have been permitted; rather the position was that, as a result of previous experience, all concerned feared that the cost of salvage were likely to prove prohibitive by reason of penal charges and/or Chinese insistence that the salvage be carried out by a local salvage company.

[p 593] ... In the light of the commercial realities, as well as the defendants' willingness ... to entertain the claim as one for actual total loss, Mr Milligan's submissions under this head have been attractive in may respects. Nonetheless, I feel obliged to find that the vessel was not an actual total loss within the period of the policy.

Presumption of an actual total loss of a ship: missing ship

When a vessel is known to have sailed and no further word is heard of her, then, after a reasonable lapse of time, she may be presumed to have been lost due to the perils of the seas and the owners may lay a claim for actual total loss under s 58 of the Act. That a reasonable time is a question of fact is stipulated in s 88 of the Marine Insurance Act 1906.

The presumption that the ship was lost by a peril of the seas was raised in the case of **Green v Brown (1743) 2 Str 1199**, where evidence was given to indicate that the vessel *Charming Peggy* was observed leaving North Carolina for London and was never heard of again. The Chief Justice raised the presumption:

> [p 1200] ... it would be unreasonable to expect certain evidence of such a loss, as where everybody on board is presumed to be drowned; and all that can be required is the best proof the nature of the case admits of, which the plaintiff has given; he therefore left it to the jury, who found the loss according to the plaintiff's declaration.

However, in *Houstman v Thornton*, below, the presumption was again raised, but only allowed on the basis that, should the vessel later be discovered, it would be for the benefit of the underwriters; she having, in effect, been abandoned.

Houstman v Thornton (1816) Holt NP 242

This was an action on a policy of insurance on ship and cargo 'at and from' Havannah to Holland or Flanders. Evidence showed that the insured vessel left Havannah in the middle of August 1815, and was never heard of again. The question before the court was whether it could be presumed, on the time elapsed since sailing, that the vessel had been lost.

The court ruled that the loss could be presumed, but only on the proviso that, should she be discovered later, it would be for the benefit of the underwriters.

> **Gibbs CJ:** [p 242] ...There is no fixed rule of law with regard to the time, after which a missing ship shall be reputed to be lost. It is, in all cases, a question of presumption to be governed by the circumstances of the particular case.
>
> [p 243] ... When the circumstances are laid before the court and jury, the presumption will be governed by them. It is to be presumed that this ship is lost, in as much as she has not been heard of for nine months. If she be discovered afterwards, it will be for the benefit of the underwriters. She is, in fact, abandoned, and will belong to them.

Actual total loss of goods – lost or missing goods

With regard to goods which are lost or missing, the presumption can only arise if the ship carrying them is presumed lost. Thus, if goods are lost, but the ship that was carrying them is still in existence, the court will have to be convinced on clear evidence that the missing goods were utterly destroyed by an insured peril. If such were not the case, it would be all too easy, on a protracted voyage, to cast the goods away and claim for a total loss. Thus, the courts look upon missing goods with an element of suspicion. In *Dyson v Rowcroft,* below, only the utter destruction of a cargo of fruit satisfied the court.

Dyson and Others v Rowcroft (1802) 3 B&T 474

The plaintiffs effected a policy of insurance on a cargo of fruit, 'at and from' Cadiz to London aboard the vessel *Tartar,* with the defendants, to the value of £225. During the voyage, *Tartar* experienced severe weather and had to put into Santa Cruz for shelter. However, the cargo of fruit had been damaged by seawater and it stank to such a degree that the authorities at Santa Cruz prohibited it from being landed, and, as a result, it had to be thrown overboard. *Tartar,* also, had been so damaged that she was unable to continue the voyage, and was sold. The question before the court was whether the cargo-owner could recover for an actual total loss.

The court ruled that the throwing overboard of the fruit was a necessity which produced total annihilation of the commodity and was, therefore, a total loss.

> **Lord Alvanley CJ:** [p 476] ... The question is, what is a total loss? I admit that the circumstances of cases like the present are generally suspicious. If the voyage be protracted, deterioration necessarily takes place; and it becomes the interest of the captain and mariners to turn the injury into a total loss. But this is a matter for the consideration of the jury. We ought, indeed, to look at the case with some suspicion, where there is so much temptation to throw the cargo overboard. But, here, it is found that the necessity of so doing arose from seawater shipped during the course of the voyage; and that the commodity was in such a state that it could not be suffered to remain on board consistently with the health of the crew. In consequence of this necessity, therefore, the commodity was annihilated, by being thrown overboard. Had it not been so annihilated, it would have been annihilated by putrefaction; and is it not as much lost by the assured by being thrown overboard, as if the captain had waited until it had arrived at complete putrefaction? ... I must now take it, that the circumstances under which the cargo in this case stood, were such that sea-damage had so operated as to make it impossible for the captain to keep it any longer on board. Whether the cause of the loss were direct or indirect, it produced a total annihilation of the commodity.

That a cargo-owner cannot recover for an actual total loss, even when the injured goods have been seriously reduced in quality and value, is clearly illustrated in *Anderson v Royal Exchange Assurance Co,* below.

Anderson v Royal Exchange Assurance Co (1805) 7 East 38

A cargo of wheat, aboard the ship *Fanny,* was insured with the defendants for a voyage from Waterford to Liverpool. The policy contained the stipulation that it was 'free from all average on corn, flour ... unless general or otherwise specially agreed'. There was no such special agreement. Whilst leaving

Waterford, *Fanny* struck a rock, was run ashore and the whole cargo of wheat was damaged by the ingress of water. Some of the wetted wheat was removed, taken ashore and kiln-dried; the remainder being sold as pig food or discarded. Some three or four weeks after the casualty, the plaintiffs served the insurers with notices of abandonment, but the underwriters refused to accept these, contending that the loss was not total, but partial. The plaintiffs' claim was based on a total loss of the whole cargo or a total loss of that part of the cargo which was not kiln-dried.

The court ruled in favour of the underwriters on two counts. The notice of abandonment was out of time and, at the time of the abandonment, the cargo was no longer a total loss.

> **Lord Ellenborough CJ:** [p 42] ... Now here it was three weeks or near a month before the abandonment; and all the intermediate time the assured took to the ship and cargo, and worked at it as upon their own account; and did not elect to abandon till a considerable part of the cargo was taken out. It has been determined in a variety of cases that a party must abandon within a reasonable time, otherwise he waives his right ... We can only pronounce on the case presented to us, and, on that case, as it appears to us at present, we are of opinion that the abandonment was out of time. It was not in fact, as it turned out, a total loss; but during the time it was submersed in the water, it might have been treated as such: they did not, however, treat it as a total loss at that time, but continued labouring on the vessel on their own account for some time afterwards, from 31 January till 18 February, and had succeeding in preserving part of it, and did not elect to abandon till they found that it would not answer to keep the cargo; and when they did abandon it was no longer in fact a total loss.

Cease to be a thing of the kind insured

The fact that the subject matter insured may be an actual total loss but still exist *in specie* is a principle well established in insurance law. Naturally, this principle is unlikely to be applicable to, for example, a ship[8] or freight, but it is highly relevant to cargo, particularly a cargo which is perishable and which may easily become 'unmerchantable'.

Such was the case in *Asfar v Blundell*, below, which is the leading authority on the notion that a commodity may continue to exist after having lost its merchantable character. Lord Esher MR approached the issue on a commercial basis, and suggested that the test as to whether a commodity had become a total loss should be based on its merchantable condition and whether an honest businessman would buy or sell it.

---

8 But, see *Fraser Shipping Ltd v Colton and Others* [1997] 1 Lloyd's Rep 586, discussed above, p 605.

Asfar and Co v Blundell and Another [1896] 1 QB 123, CA

The plaintiffs chartered the steamship *Govino* for a voyage from the Persian Gulf to London, and she was duly loaded with a mixed cargo, under various bills of lading, freight being payable on 'right delivery'. The plaintiffs then insured their profit on the charter with the defendants. However, on arriving in the Thames, *Govino* was in collision with another vessel and sank. She was later raised and docked, but a large portion of the cargo, consisting of dates, was condemned as unfit for human consumption. The dates, therefore, could not be delivered according to the terms of the bill of lading and were sold and exported to be distilled into spirits. The plaintiffs paid the chartered freight and then claimed from their insurers for the loss of profits brought about by the non-delivery of the dates.

The Court of Appeal upheld the decision of the trial judge and ruled that there had been a total loss of the consignment of dates, and the plaintiffs were entitled to recover the difference between the chartered freight and the total amount of bill of lading freight that would have been received had the whole cargo, including the dates, been delivered in London.

> **Lord Esher MR:** [p 127] ... There is a perfectly well known test which has, for many years, been applied to such cases as the present – that test is whether, as a matter of business, the nature of the thing has been altered. The nature of a thing is not necessarily altered because the thing itself has been damaged; wheat or rice may be damaged, but may still remain the things dealt with as wheat or rice in business. But if the nature of the thing is altered, and it becomes for business something else, so that it is not dealt with by business people as the thing which it originally was, the question for determination is whether the thing insured, the original article of commerce, has become a total loss. If it is so changed in its nature by the perils of the sea as to become an unmerchantable thing, which no buyer would buy and no honest seller would sell, then there is a total loss.

Similarly, in *Roux v Salvador* **(1836) 3 Bing NC 266**, cited earlier,[9] where a consignment of hides was so wetted by seawater that they had to be sold during the course of the voyage, Lord Abinger stated:

> [p 279] ... But, if the goods once damaged by the perils of the sea, and necessarily landed before the termination of the voyage, are, by reason of that damage, in such a state, though the species not be utterly destroyed, that they cannot with safety be re-shipped into the same or any other vessel ... if by any circumstance of their existing in specie at that forced termination of the risk, is of no importance. The loss is, in its nature, total to him who has no means of recovering his goods, whether his inability arises from their annihilation or from any other insuperable obstacle.

---

9 See above, p 600.

However, in *Francis v Boulton*, cited below, where a consignment of rice was damaged by seawater, because the rice was adjudged to be still merchantable, the loss was held to be a partial loss and not a total loss.

Francis v Boulton [1895] 1 Com Cas 217

The plaintiff's lighter was loaded with bags of rice which were insured with the defendants but warranted 'free from particular average, unless the vessel or craft be stranded, sunk, on fire, or in collision ...'. During the course of her passage up the Thames, the lighter came into collision with the steamer *Ulleswater* and was sunk. The lighter was refloated and, on the advice of the Salvage Association, the plaintiff had the rice kiln-dried and then sold at a considerable loss as river damaged. After failing to succeed in an action against the owners of *Ulleswater*, the plaintiff and the underwriters brought this action in order to settle the dispute between them as to whether there had been a total or partial loss.

The court ruled that the loss was a partial loss, as the rice was still merchantable, in that it could still be conditioned and kiln-dried.

> **Matthew J:** [p 221] ... With respect to the first question – viz, whether there was a total loss of the goods – reliance was placed on the evidence of the plaintiff and Mr Frost [from the Salvage Association], who described the rice when it had been immersed for two tides as unmerchantable as sound rice, smelling offensively, and as unfit for food. But, as against this, the defendant relied upon the fact that the offer for the purchase of the damaged rice had been refused, and that Frost and the plaintiff had sanctioned the kiln-drying of the rice as the best course to be taken in the interest of all concerned ... I am of opinion that there was not a total loss of the rice, and that the loss was partial only. The case is distinguished from *Asfar v Blundell* by the fact that the rice was capable of being conditioned, and that when kiln-dried it was sold as rice, and fetched about a third of its sound value.

Obliteration of marks

A cargo-owner may suffer a loss on account of cargo being delivered in a merchantable condition, but unidentifiable because the markings have been obliterated. However, such a loss may only be construed as a partial loss, and, to that effect, s 56(5) of the Marine Insurance Act 1906 states:

> Where goods reach their destination *in specie*, but by reason of obliteration of marks, or otherwise, they are incapable of identification, the loss, if any, is partial, and not total.

Spence and Another v Union Marine Insurance Co Ltd [1868] LR 3 CP 427

This was an action by the plaintiff owners of 43 bales of cotton shipped aboard *Caroline Nasmyth* at Mobile, bound for Liverpool, and insured by the defendants. The plaintiffs' 43 bales were included in one consignment of 532 bales, shipped under one bill of lading. Near the Florida Keys, *Caroline Nasmyth* stranded on a reef and was wrecked and, although much of the cargo was landed at Key West, it was damaged, with many of the identifying marks obliterated. Later, the majority of the cargo was forwarded to Liverpool, but, of the 43 bales of cotton owned by the plaintiff, only two could be identified. The plaintiffs gave notice of abandonment for the other 41 bales, and claimed for a total loss of those bales, but the underwriters contended that the loss was only partial.

The court ruled that there was no total loss, only a partial loss.

Bovill CJ: [p 435] ... The principal question in the case was, whether there was a total loss of the whole of the plaintiffs' 41 bales which were not delivered.

[p 437] ... We must, thus, necessarily consider what is the effect of the obliteration of marks upon various goods of the same description which are shipped in one vessel, and which, without any fault of the owners, become so mixed that one part is undistinguishable from another ... In our law, there are not many authorities to be found upon this subject; but, as far as they go, they are in favour of the view, that, when goods of different owners become by accident so mixed together as to be indistinguishable, the owners of the goods so mixed become tenants in common of the whole, in the proportions which they have severally contributed to it ... It has long been settled in our law, that, where goods are mixed so as to become undistinguishable, by the wrongful act or default of one owner, he cannot recover, and will not be entitled to his proportion, or any part of the property, from the other owner: but no authority has been cited to show that any such principle has ever been applied, nor indeed could it be applied, to the case of an accidental mixing of the goods of two owners; and there is no authority or sound reason for saying that the goods of several persons which are accidentally mixed together thereby absolutely cease to be the property of their several owners. The goods being before they are mixed the separate property of the several owners, unless, which is absurd, they cease to be the property by reason of the accidental mixture, when they would not so cease if the mixture were designed, must continue to be the property of the original owners; and, as there would be no means of distinguishing the goods of each, the several owners seem necessarily to become jointly interested, as tenants in common, in the bulk. This is the rule of the Roman Law as stated in *Mackeldey's Modern Civil Law*, under the title *Commixtio et Confusio*, in the special part, Book 1, s 270.

[p 438] ... We are, thus, by authorities in our own law, by the reason of the thing, and by the concurrence of foreign writers, justified in adopting the conclusion that, by our own law, the property in the cotton of which the marks were obliterated did not cease to belong to the respective owners; and, that, by the mixture of the bales, and their becoming undistinguishable by reason of the action of the sea, and without the fault of the respective owners, these parties become tenants in common of the cotton, in proportion to their respective interests. This result would follow only in those cases where, after the adoption of all reasonable means and exertions to identify or separate the goods, it was found impracticable to do so.

We cannot assume that the whole of the plaintiffs' 41 bales were amongst those that were destroyed, any more than we can assume that they all formed part of the 1,645 which were brought home; and we see no means of determining the extent of the interest of the several owners, except by adopting a principle of proportion, and which would, we think, be equally applicable in determining the plaintiffs' portion of the 231 bales that were totally lost as of the 1,645 which arrived in this country, though without marks ... Upon the main question, therefore, that was argued before us, we think that there was not an actual total loss of the plaintiffs' 41 bales of cotton. We think also there was not a constructive total loss of those bales.

Irretrievably deprived thereof

Section 57(1) of the Marine Insurance Act 1906 makes provision for one final category of actual total loss, namely, where the assured is 'irretrievably deprived' of the subject matter insured. This is to allow the assured to recover when, through no fault of his own, he is deprived of his property even though it still exists in specie. Such a deprivation may take the form of seizure or appropriation by a third party or, possibly, by the actions of a barratrous crew.

Assured irretrievably deprived of ship

The question of what constitutes 'irretrievable deprivation' of a ship was raised in the cases of *George Cohen, Sons and Co v Standard Marine Insurance Co Ltd* and *Marstrand Fishing Co Ltd v Beer, 'Girl Pat'*.[10]

George Cohen, Sons and Co v Standard Marine Insurance Co Ltd (1925) 21 LlL Rep 30

The obsolete battleship, *Prince George*, was wrecked on the Dutch coast when the tugs which were towing her sought shelter from bad weather, in Yarmouth, leaving the battleship unattended and in danger of drifting. Although the court ruled that she was a constructive total loss brought about by perils of the seas, another plea had been entered, on the basis that the owners had been 'irretrievably deprived' of the battleship because of the exorbitant cost of any salvage operation, and also because the Dutch authorities would not sanction such an operation, in case the sea defences were damaged as a result.

On the issue of 'irretrievable deprivation', the court ruled that such was not the case, as the battleship was still physically intact and the edict by the Dutch authorities was not final.

---

10 See, also, *Fraser Shipping Ltd v Colton and Others* [1997] 1 Lloyd's Rep 586, discussed above, p 605.

Roche J: [p 33] ... It is not contended that this ship was destroyed. She is there still. It is not and could not be contended that she is so damaged as to cease to be a thing of the kind insured, but it is suggested that the assured is irretrievably deprived thereof, and that, accordingly, she is an actual total loss. Of course, if that is so, as the section provides in accordance with the common law, no notice of abandonment need be given. My reasons for deciding that the plaintiffs have not been irretrievably deprived thereof are as follows ... I am of opinion that this vessel physically could be got off. It would be a matter of great elaboration and difficulty, but, at all events, putting the matter at the highest, I am not satisfied that she could not. On the whole, I think that she could ... In these circumstances, there has been no irretrievable deprivation which a court can find by reason of physical impossibility.

There is another matter in this connection which has to be considered. It is said that the assured is irretrievably deprived of *Prince George* because the authorities charged with the management of these sea defences would not allow her to be moved or the works which are necessary for her removal to be undertaken ... I am satisfied, since both the Dutch advocate called by the plaintiffs, and the Dutch advocate called by the defendants agreed on it, that the decision of the Dyke Reeve Board, however influential it is, and however likely to strongly influence the court, is not conclusive ... in those circumstances, I am not satisfied that there was such a certainty of deprivation as to amount to the deprivation being irretrievable. Accordingly, I decide that there is not actual total loss.

In the *Girl Pat* case, cited below, it was ruled that the taking of a ship by a barratrous crew was not, in itself, sufficient evidence to show that there had been an irretrievable loss so as to constitute an actual total loss. Porter J was also of the opinion that the older cases failed to differentiate between actual and constructive total loss, and, further, that capture or seizure would normally amount to constructive total loss and not actual total loss.

Marstrand Fishing Co Ltd v Beer, 'Girl Pat' [1937] 1 All ER 158

The master of the fishing vessel *Girl Pat*, instead of proceeding to fishing grounds in the North Sea, decided to run away with her and called into Dover to load provisions for a substantial voyage. As nothing further was heard of her for six weeks, the owners served a notice of abandonment on their insurers, which they accepted as equivalent to a writ, but not as an abandonment. She was later known to have put into the Channel Islands before sailing via Spain and West Africa to Georgetown in British Guiana, where she was arrested. The owners then claimed for either an actual or constructive total loss by barratry, which the underwriters continued to contest.

The court ruled that actions of the master were barratrous, but barratry was not, in itself, sufficient evidence of an irretrievable loss so as to constitute an actual total loss. Furthermore, as the court was unsure whether *Girl Pat* was or was not recoverable, there could be no constructive total loss.

Porter J: [p 163] ... First of all, with regard to an actual total loss, it is said that barratry is analogous to capture, and that capture is an actual total loss, though that loss may be redeemed by a recapture. I doubt if this ever was the true question. I think it was always a question of fact whether capture was an actual total loss or merely a possible constructive total loss. Capture followed by condemnation no doubt was actual total loss, but that was because the vessel had in fact been condemned; the war was supposed to last indefinitely, and, therefore, there was no chance within any reasonable time of the ship being restored. The capture alone I do not think was ever necessarily an actual total loss. It is possible that if the vessel had been carrying contraband and that condemnation was certain, she might be held to be an actual total loss, but I do not think it certain, even then, that that result would follow. Normally, I think that capture is a constructive total loss, and the confusion which has arisen, with regard to whether it is an actual or constructive total loss, arose merely because, in the earlier cases, the distinction between those two classes of loss was not kept clear ... The class of case I am referring to is *Dean v Hornby* and *Stringer v English and Scottish Marine Insurance Co*. However that may be, whether under the old law capture was or was not an actual or constructive total loss, the case is now governed by ss 56–60 of the Marine Insurance Act 1906. The Act provides, in s 57, amongst its definitions of 'actual total loss', 'if the vessel be irretrievably lost'. In my view, no one could say here that the vessel was irretrievably lost to her owners. Under the Marine Insurance Act, loss by barratry is necessarily an actual total loss, and in this case I find there was no actual total loss.

Assured irretrievably deprived of goods

In the following case, *Stringer v English and Scottish Marine Insurance Co Ltd*, goods shipped aboard a vessel which was seized as a prize and ultimately sold were held to be an actual total loss. Although, in this particular case, the claim for a loss caused by seizure was, initially, pursued as a partial loss, the sale of the goods changed the circumstances to such an extent that the plea could be changed to one of actual total loss. The court explained that, unless circumstances of the loss have changed, it is not permissible to amend a plea for a partial loss to a total loss.

Stringer and Others v English and Scottish Marine Insurance Co Ltd (1869) LR 4 QB 676

During the time of the American Civil War, the plaintiffs shipped goods aboard the brig *Dashing Wave* from Liverpool to Mexico, under a policy of insurance underwritten by the defendants. When *Dashing Wave* arrived at her destination, which was close to the American border, she was intercepted and seized by officers of the Union Navy, which was blockading Confederate ports at the time. *Dashing Wave* was taken to New Orleans as a prize, and the plaintiffs gave notice of abandonment and claimed for a partial loss. More than 18 months after her capture, because of the deteriorating condition of both ship and cargo, the court in New Orleans ordered both to be sold, and the plaintiffs changed their claim to one of total loss.

The court ruled that the sale of the goods changed the character of the loss from a partial loss to a total loss, and the plaintiffs could recover for such.

Blackburn J: [p 688] ... The assured having elected to treat the seizure and detention as a partial and not a total loss, and proceeded with the suit on their account, were bound by this election, and could not afterwards turn round and treat the same seizure and detention as a total loss ... To allow the assured to change his election whilst the circumstances remain the same would enable the assured to treat the property as his as long as there was a prospect of profit from the rise in the market, and as the property of the insurers, as soon as there was a certainty of loss, which would be inequitable: *qui sentit commodum sentire debet et onus*. But that election, though binding as long as the circumstances remain the same, does not prevent the assured from claiming for a total loss, if a change in circumstances occurs which makes the loss actually total.

[p 690] ... We think, therefore, that the appeal on 1 July did not amount to a change of facts as would justify the assured in changing their election, and consequently, that the assured could not, by the notice of abandonment on 12 September 1864, make the loss by seizure and detention a total loss after having elected to treat it as partial only. But we think the sale by the Prize Court stands on a very different footing.

[p 692] ... We come, therefore, to the conclusion of fact, that the assured could not, by any means, which they could reasonably be called on to adopt, have prevented the sale by the American Prize Court, which at once put an end to all possibility of having the goods restored *in specie*, and consequently entitled the assured to come upon their insurers for a total loss.

Assured irretrievably deprived of the voyage or adventure

It would appear from the following remarks of the Earl of Loreburn in the *Sanday* case, below, that it is possible for an assured of cargo to recover for an actual total loss under this head of claim if it can be shown that there was a frustration of the voyage or adventure to be undertaken by the cargo insured.[11]

British and Foreign Marine Insurance Co Ltd v Samuel Sanday and Co [1915] 1 AC 650, HL

A British firm of corn merchants shipped two consignments of linseed and wheat from Argentina to Hamburg aboard two British ships. Before either ship reached Hamburg, hostilities broke out between Great Britain and

---

11 This case, and the principle that a loss of voyage or adventure is an insured peril under a policy on goods, are discussed in Chapter 3, p 92.

Germany, and both vessels were ordered into British ports. The cargo-owners warehoused the goods, and served notice of abandonment on their underwriters for a constructive total loss.

The House of Lords ruled that the cargo-owners had suffered a constructive total loss of the goods brought about by the actual total loss of the adventure. In reaching his decision, Earl Loreburn analysed the Act in trying to establish whether, with respect to goods, there was anything within it which precluded recovery for an actual total loss of the adventure.

> **Earl Loreburn:** [p 657] ... Section 57(1) says 'where the assured is irretrievably deprived' of the subject matter insured there is an actual total loss. Now here, the subject matter insured, as the law stood in 1906, included the adventure and not merely the goods, and the party assured was irretrievably deprived of it because all prospect of safe arrival on the voyage to Germany was hopelessly frustrated by the outbreak of war. Therefore, the assured party reasonably abandoned, because actual total loss appeared to be unavoidable ... The argument, however, is that the 'subject matter insured' on such a policy no longer included the adventure. There is not a line in the Act which says so, and, if it were relevant, many reasons might be urged against the probability of so inconvenient a change being made. But it is conclusive to point out that s 26 says: 'The subject matter insured must be designated in a marine policy with reasonable certainty', and, further: 'In the application of this section regard shall be had to any usage regulating the designation of the subject matter insured.' ... The words of this policy have for generations been understood and held by judges to designate not merely the goods, but also the adventure. So far from abrogating this designation of subject matter, I should have thought the Act took pains to preserve it and others like it.

ACTUAL TOTAL LOSS OF FREIGHT

Freight may be paid in advance or upon delivery and, if it is to be paid on delivery, it is payable in full at the time of such delivery, even if there is a shortfall or damage to the goods. Any claim for such a shortfall or damage lies separate from the freight payable, and should not be settled by an adjustment to that freight payable. If the freight is payable in advance, including chartered freight, it may be insured by the person who has paid the freight.[12]

Actual total loss of freight caused by an actual or constructive total loss of ship and/or goods

Where there is an actual or constructive total loss of ship and/or goods caused by a peril insured against, then there is also an actual total loss of freight.

---

12 See Chapter 3, p 110.

In *Iredale v China Traders Insurance Co*, below, it was ruled that freight was recoverable, because the cargo became an actual total loss when it overheated and had to be off-loaded and sold. The insurers argued that the loss was a general average loss, not a total loss.

Iredale and Another v China Traders Insurance Co [1900] 2 QB 519, CA

Lodore was chartered to carry a cargo of coal from Cardiff to British Columbia and the chartered freight was insured by the shipowners with the defendants. During the course of the voyage, the cargo started to overheat, and *Lodore* put into Buenos Aires, where the cargo was condemned as unsafe and was sold. The voyage having been abandoned, the owners claimed for an actual total loss of the chartered freight, but the insurers refused payment, contending that the sale of the coal represented a general average sacrifice made by the cargo-owners, for which the shipowners were liable to contribute as general average.

The Court of Appeal upheld the decision of the trial judge, and ruled that the loss (by reason of sale) was not a general average sacrifice, but a total loss, and, therefore, the freight was also a total loss and recoverable under the policy.

> **AL Smith LJ:** [p 521] ... The sale of the cargo, which, in my opinion, constituted the abandonment of the voyage, was not a general average sacrifice which forms the subject of a general average contribution, for the common danger had ceased, and the ship and cargo had been in safety for about a month ... I am of opinion that there was no general average sacrifice in this case, and consequently, the right to a general average contribution never arose, and that this appeal must be dismissed with costs. I agree with Bingham J's inference of fact that at Buenos Aires the coal was hopelessly lost.

That freight is recoverable as an actual total loss when the cargo itself is totally lost, due to a peril insured against, is well illustrated in *Rankin v Potter*, below.[13]

Rankin v Potter (1873) LR 6 HL 83, HL

The plaintiffs (respondents) were the mortgagees in possession of the vessel *Sir William Eyre*, which had been chartered for a voyage from Calcutta to Liverpool or London. The shipowners had then insured the chartered freight with the defendants (appellants). When *Sir William Eyre* arrived at Calcutta, she was surveyed because of a grounding that had taken place previously, and it was found that the cost of repairs would have exceeded her value. The plaintiffs claimed for a total loss of chartered freight occasioned by perils of the seas, but the underwriters refused payment on the basis that the shipowner had become bankrupt and it was that which had caused the

---

13 This case is also discussed, in the context that voyage chartered freight is a subject matter of a marine policy of insurance, in Chapter 3, p 100.

charterer to withdraw from the charter. Shortly afterwards, whilst moored in the river at Calcutta, *Sir William Eyre* was destroyed in a cyclone.

The Court of Exchequer Chamber ruled, later affirmed by the House of Lords, that there was a total loss of freight occasioned by a peril of the seas. It was also held that, when there was a constructive total loss of the vessel concerned, there was no requirement for a notice of abandonment to be given in respect of the total loss of freight.

> **Brett J:** [p 99] ... There may be an actual total loss of freight under a general policy on freight, if there be an actual total loss of ship, or an actual total loss of the whole cargo. An actual total loss of ship will occasion an actual total loss of freight, unless, when the ship is lost, cargo is on board, and the whole or a part of such cargo is saved, and might be sent on in a substituted ship so as to earn freight. An actual total loss of the whole cargo will occasion an actual total loss of freight, unless such loss should so happen as to leave the ship capable, as to time, place, and condition, of earning an equal or some freight by carrying other cargo on the voyage insured.
>
> It has become a question in this case whether there may not be on a general policy on freight another kind of actual total loss, namely, by such damage to the ship as one would justify notice of abandonment, and make thereupon a constructive total loss of ship under a policy on ship, although there be no loss of cargo, or an average loss of cargo without means of sending on the cargo. In such a state of things, the ship may or may not be insured; if the ship be insured, due notice of abandonment of ship may or may not have been given. If the ship is not insured, what must happen upon the assumption? The assumption is that a prudent owner will not repair. Then the ship will not be repaired. If not repaired, it will remain a wreck or be sold as a wreck. It cannot, therefore, sail on the voyage insured in the policy on freight. There is no freight, no chance of freight, to abandon to the underwriter on freight. It has never been suggested that the ship should be abandoned to the underwriter on freight. There is nothing then which can be abandoned to him of which he could take possession or from which he could derive profit.

When goods are delivered in such a condition as to be unmerchantable, there is no requirement for the freight to be paid. Thus, a constructive total loss of goods may occasion an actual total loss of freight. This was well illustrated in *Asfar v Blundell* [1896] 1 QB 123, CA, cited in full earlier.[14] In this instance, the ship carrying a consignment of dates was sunk in the Thames after a collision with another vessel, and the dates were not destroyed, but were deemed unfit for human consumption. Because the dates had become unmerchantable as dates, no freight was payable on delivery as they were, effectively, a constructive total loss.

> **Kay LJ:** [p 132] ... I think, therefore, that the learned judge below was right when he said: 'Total destruction is not necessary, destruction of the merchantable character of the goods is sufficient; and ... I hold that the plaintiffs were not entitled to receive freight in respect of these dates.'

---

14 See above, p 610.

Therefore, the bill of lading freight on the dates not being recoverable, the plaintiffs made no profit whatever on the whole adventure.

Actual total loss of freight caused by a loss of voyage or adventure

Where the payment of freight is conditional upon the delivery of the cargo, a loss of the voyage concerned through delay or frustration will also result in an actual total loss of the freight. This is a point illustrated in *Jackson v Union Marine Insurance Co Ltd*, below.

Jackson v Union Marine Insurance Co Ltd (1873) 2 Asp M C 435

Spirit of the Dawn got onto rocks before reaching her loading port at Newport. She only got off four months later; but in the meantime, the charterer abandoned her and procured another ship to carry the cargo. The assured shipowner claimed that there had been a total loss of freight, as the delay was so serious as to bring the charterparty to an end in the commercial sense. Both the Court of Common Pleas and the Exchequer Chamber held that the assured shipowner was entitled to recover for a total loss of freight under the freight policy.

> **Bramwell B:** [pp 441 and 444] ... The jury have found that the voyage the parties had contemplated had become impossible, that a voyage undertaken after the ship was sufficiently repaired, would have been a different voyage ... a voyage for which, at the time of the charter, the plaintiff had not in intention engaged the ship, nor the charterer the cargo ... It was argued that the doctrine of *causa proxima spectatur non remota* applied: that the proximate cause of the loss of freight here was the refusal of the charterer to load. But, if I am right, the voyage, the adventure was frustrated by the perils of the seas, both parties were discharged ... The freight is lost unless the charterer chooses to go on.

Notes

Underwriters now circumvent the outcome of the *Jackson* case by using the Loss of Time Clause in freight policies.[15] See, for example, cl 11 of the IVCF(95) and cl 15 of the ITCF(95), which now each expressly provide that 'this insurance does not cover any claim consequent on loss of time whether arising from a peril of the sea or otherwise'.

---

15 The Loss of Time Clause is discussed in Chapter 3, p 106.

RECOVERY FOR A PARTIAL LOSS

Section 56(4) of the Marine Insurance Act 1906 states:
> Where the assured brings an action for a total loss and the evidence proves only a partial loss, he may, unless the policy otherwise provides, recover for a partial loss.

Thus, an assured who fails in his claim to recover for a total loss is not barred from recovering for a partial loss, unless the policy otherwise provides, for example, by being warranted free from particular average for the peril which caused the loss. Such an exception is commonplace, and can be found in *Boon and Cheah v Asia Insurance Co Ltd*, below, where the plaintiff, pleading the *de minimis* rule, made a claim for a total loss because the policy was warranted free from particular average.

Boon and Cheah v Asia Insurance Co Ltd [1975] 1 Lloyd's Rep 452, Malaysian High Court

The plaintiffs shipped 668 large steel pipes aboard a barge to be towed from Prai to Brunei. The pipes were insured with the defendants for $938,702, but were warranted free from particular average. During the voyage, all but 12 of the pipes were lost, and even those were damaged. Because the shipment was not covered for partial loss, the plaintiffs, relying on the *de minimis* rule, claimed that the loss was either a constructive or an actual total loss.

The Malaysia High Court ruled that in the circumstances of the case, the de minimis rule could not be applied, and, therefore, the loss was not an actual total loss.

> **Raja Azlan Shah J:** [p 460] ... In my judgment, 12 pipes measuring a total of 360 ft, weighing 36 tons, costing $14,400 and insured at $16,000, affect far too high a proportion of the whole consignment of 668 pipes to be capable of being dismissed as a matter of de minimis. It may well be that in the case of a single pipe or two out of the whole consignment, the rule would apply, but I fail to see how it is possible to hold that 12 pipes can be ignored or treated as trifling and to be brushed aside. I find, therefore, on the facts before me that a consignment of 668 pipes is not totally lost when 12 pipes making it up are not lost.

CHAPTER 16

CONSTRUCTIVE TOTAL LOSS

DEFINITIONS OF CONSTRUCTIVE TOTAL LOSS

The concept of constructive total loss, whereby the subject matter insured is effectively lost to the assured, but is not actually destroyed, is unique to marine insurance. This concept is outlined within s 60 of the Marine Insurance Act 1906, which defines, in s 60(1), constructive total loss as follows:

> Subject to any express provision in the policy, there is a constructive total loss where the subject matter insured is reasonably abandoned on account of its actual total loss appearing to be unavoidable, or because it could not be preserved from actual total loss without an expenditure which would exceed its value when the expenditure had been incurred.

Section 60 is a complete definition

Although s 60(2) appears to qualify the general provisions laid down in s 60(1), this is not the case. In *Robertson v Petros M Nomikos Ltd*, below, the House of Lords confirmed that the two sub-sections within s 60 contained two separate definitions, which may be applied to different conditions of fact.

Robertson v Petros M Nomikos Ltd [1939] AC 371, HL

The plaintiffs (respondents) were the owners of a tanker which was chartered to carry crude oil from the Caribbean to Europe; the chartered freight being insured with the defendant (appellant) underwriters. Prior to proceeding to her port of loading under the charterparty, the tanker suffered an explosion and fire whilst undergoing boiler repairs in Rotterdam. Because of the conditions laid down in the hull policy, the owners did not claim for a constructive total loss, although they could have done so. Instead, they chose to claim for a partial loss on that policy and did not abandon. They then claimed on their policy covering the chartered freight for a total loss, but the underwriters refused payment, on the basis that, under a term in the freight policy, such a claim was invalid unless the vessel was, in fact, a constructive total loss.

The House of Lords, in affirming the decision of the Court of Appeal, ruled that the vessel had been a constructive total loss, and that a notice of abandonment, with respect to a hull policy, was not intended to show that there was a constructive total loss, but rather that the assured intended to claim for such. Furthermore, no such notice of abandonment was required to claim for a total loss of freight, and, therefore, the plaintiffs could recover under their policy on chartered freight.

> **Lord Wright:** [p 382] ... The objective definition of a constructive total loss is found in the preceding section of the Act [s 60]. Some difficulty has been found in interpreting that section, because it consists of two parts. Sub-section 2 is purely objective; it gives the two cases of constructive total loss of ship, the first being deprivation of possession, the second the cost of repairs. This is completely consistent with s 61. But s 60(1) is said to be inconsistent, because it makes the constructive total loss depend on the condition that the subject matter is reasonably abandoned for either of the reasons stated. This, I think, does not qualify the definition in sub-s 2. The two sub-sections contain two separate definitions, applicable to different conditions of circumstances.
>
> **Lord Porter:** [p 392] ... That s 60 is intended to be a complete and not a partial definition appears to follow from the wording of s 56, when it says: 'Any loss other than a total loss, *as hereinafter defined*, is a partial loss.' But, it does not follow that the first sub-section [in s 60] lays down the general rule, whereas the second gives certain particular instances already covered by the general rule. Indeed, whatever may be the case with regard to sub-s 2(i), sub-sub-ss (ii) and (iii) do not appear to be covered in terms by the definition in sub-s 1.
>
> But in any case, unless there is some reason to the contrary, a definition must be held to include the whole of the wording, and if particular instances are given which include matters which are outside the more general definition, that is no reason for supposing that their application is limited by the more general words. They do not merely illustrate – they add to the terms of the definition. Section 60 does not confine constructive total loss to cases where the subject matter of insurance has been abandoned, though, in some circumstances, there may be no constructive total loss unless abandonment has taken place.

Rickards v Forestal Land, Timber and Railways Co Ltd [1941] 3 All ER 62, HL

A German vessel was scuttled by the master and crew off the Faroe Islands in order to avoid capture by a British warship. The cargo-owners successfully claimed for a constructive total loss caused by the actions of the German Government in taking over control of all German shipping.

> **Lord Wright:** [p 79] ... Some aspects of the section [s 60] have been recently discussed in this House in *Robertson v Petros M Nomikos*. In particular, the difficulty of fitting together the two sub-sections of s 60 and reading them together with s 61 was there considered. I think the view which this House arrived at was that the two sub-sections contain two separate definitions, which may be applied to different conditions of fact. Thus, an assured can base his claim on the terms of sub-s (2), which give an objective criterion in each case, ship, goods or freight, not only more precise than, but substantially different from, that in sub-s (1). Sub-section (2), as compared with sub-s (1), is thus additional, and not merely illustrative.

But, in *Irvin v Hine*, below, a claim for constructive total loss was based on the proposition that the complete definition contained in s 60 did not preclude other claims which were valid under common law.

Irvin v Hine [1949] 1 KB 555

A trawler was severely damaged after stranding on a rock and the owner gave notice of abandonment to the insurers, which was refused. The owner's claim that the trawler was a constructive total loss was based on the fact that, due to the wartime restrictions then in place, he could not obtain a licence in a reasonable time in order to repair the vessel. The owner accepted that the claim was not tenable under any of the heads specified in s 60, but contended that the claim was justified under the common law, and that the claim was not inconsistent with the provisions of s 60, and was also valid under s 91(2), which preserved the application of the rules of the common law provided they were consistent with the express provisions of the Act.

The court ruled that the loss was a partial loss, and, in so ruling, clarified the interpretation of s 60, which was held to be a complete definition.

> **Devlin J:** [p 567] ... Section 56(1) provides: '... Any loss other than a total loss, as hereinafter defined, is a partial loss.' That seems, as Lord Porter pointed out in *Robertson v Nomikos* [1939] 2 All ER 734, to mean that the definition of constructive total loss in s 60 must be complete. If any loss outside s 57 (which defines actual total loss) and s 60 were to be held to be a total loss, it could not be a partial loss, as that would be inconsistent with the express provision of s 56. I see no answer to this argument, except possibly that it puts too literal a construction on the words of s 56. That makes it material to consider whether such a construction is out of harmony with the object of s 60, as shown in its marginal note, and with the general purpose of the Act. The marginal note is 'Constructive total loss defined'. This is in keeping with the words of s 56, 'total loss, as hereinafter defined', and shows that s 60 is intended to contain a definition. I have used the words 'complete definition', as Lord Porter did, as a convenient and expressive term. I dare say it is not meticulously accurate, for, strictly speaking, a definition must be complete, else it is not a definition at all. The question really is whether s 60 is a definition section, defining constructive total loss as a whole, and not merely categories of it, or whether, as counsel for the plaintiff in terms argued, all it does is to lay down the main characteristics of a constructive total loss. This argument gives no weight to the word 'defined', both in s 56 and in the marginal note to s 60. I think that that word shows conclusively that s 60 is intended to define a constructive total loss, which is the same as saying that s 60 circumscribes completely the conception of constructive total loss.

Loss of voyage or adventure

Although it is established that, within the Act, s 60 is a complete definition of constructive total loss, it was shown, first in *Rodocanachi v Elliott* (1874) LR 9

CP 518, and later in *British and Foreign Marine Insurance Co v Samuel Sanday and Co* [1916] 1 AC 650, HL (hereinafter referred to as the *Sanday* case), that there was another form of constructive total loss which existed under common law before the Act. Unlike insurance on a ship, it has long been established by the law merchant that, when hostilities exist, goods may be lost to an assured not just by physical damage, but also by the very existence of the hostile conditions themselves, which may lead to the voyage or adventure being terminated prematurely.

The Marine Insurance Act 1906 makes no express reference to this type of loss whereby an owner of goods might suffer loss or damage because of the termination of the whole venture or voyage caused by an insured peril. Since the *Sanday* case, cited below, which is the leading authority on this subject, it is now firmly established that a claim for constructive total loss of goods may be brought when the voyage or adventure is abandoned or frustrated. The House of Lords in that case was in agreement that this form of constructive total loss must remain valid, as it is not in conflict with the provisions of the Act and is also admissible under s 91(2).

However, as mentioned earlier, it was the case of *Rodocanachi v Elliot*, below, which first raised the issue, some years before the passing of the Act.

Rodocanachi v Elliott (1874) LR 9 CP 518

A cargo of silks was shipped from the Far East to Marseilles by sea, and thence by rail and sea to Boulogne and London. At the time the consignment of silks was passing through Paris, the German army invaded France and besieged the city. The owners of the goods served notice of abandonment upon the insurers, and laid claim for a constructive total loss.

The court ruled in their favour on the basis that there was a constructive total loss caused by 'the restraint of princes', a peril insured against.

> **Keating J:** [p 667] ... There are few English cases to be found of English goods blockaded in a foreign port; but there are several cases where the question has arisen as to the goods which are prevented by a blockade from getting in. It seems to me that goods which are within a besieged or a blockaded town or port, stand precisely in the same position as goods detained under an embargo. It is true that, in the one case, the detention is the act of the sovereign of the State in which the goods are, and in the other it is the act of the enemy. But in both a restraint is placed upon the owner of the goods by a sovereign power. That is precisely the case. It is found that it was impossible, in consequence of the German armies having closely invested Paris, to remove the silks from the railway station there. I apprehend that was a loss which was covered by these policies. The goods were for an indefinite time lost to the assured. If, therefore, the case of a besieged town is analogous to that of a blockaded port, as I think it is, the assured were clearly entitled to abandon.

British and Foreign Marine Insurance Co Ltd v Samuel Sanday and Co [1915] 1 AC 650, HL

A British firm of corn merchants shipped two consignments of linseed and wheat aboard the British steamships *St Andrew* and *Orthia* from Argentina to Hamburg. The consignments were insured by the defendants and, in both cases, the usual f c and s clauses were deleted and an increased premium was paid by the cargo-owners. Before the ships reached Hamburg, hostilities broke out between Germany and Great Britain, and both vessels were ordered into British ports. The cargo-owners warehoused their goods and served notice of abandonment on their insurers.

The House of Lords, affirming the decisions of both the lower courts, ruled that there was a constructive total loss of the goods by a peril insured against, brought about by the destruction of the adventure, and the cargo-owners could recover.

> **Earl Loreburn:** [p 657] ... So far I see nothing in the Act to alter the law, but I do see that under the old decisions there is a constructive total loss. The argument, however, is that the 'subject matter insured' on such a policy no longer included the adventure. There is not a line in the Act which says so, and, if it were relevant, many reasons might be urged against the probability of so inconvenient a change being made ... The words of this policy have, for generations, been understood and held by judges to designate not merely the goods, but also the adventure. So far from abrogating this designation of subject matter, I should have thought the Act took pains to preserve it and others like it.
>
> I will merely in a sentence refer to s 91(2) of the Act, which preserves the rules of the common law, including the law merchant, save in so far as they are inconsistent with the express provisions of this Act. It seems to me that Parliament was triply guarded against the danger that the Act should be construed in the sense urged upon us by Sir Robert Finlay [for the insurers]. It has refrained from saying that the old rule shall be altered. It has twice warned us that we are to regard and preserve rules and usages in terms that are applicable to this rule. Accordingly, I take with me the conclusion that the adventure was a subject matter insured, when I proceed to inquire whether or not the loss of it is to be compensated under the clause protecting the assured against restraint by kings or princes.
>
> **Lord Wrenbury:** [p 672] ... Before the Marine Insurance Act 1906, authority is uniform that, where goods are insured at or from one port to another, the insurance is not confined to an indemnity to be paid in case the goods are injured or destroyed, but extends to an indemnity to be paid in case the goods do not reach their destination. This may be variously described as an insurance of the venture, or an insurance of the voyage, or an insurance of the market, as distinguished from an insurance of the goods simply and solely. Goods delivered at the port of destination may be of value very different from their value at the port of loading. The underwriter's obligation is to pay money in the event of the goods failing to arrive at their destination uninjured by any perils insured against. Bramwell B, in *Rodocanachi v Elliott*, says: 'It is well

established that there may be a loss of the goods by a loss of the voyage in which the goods are being transported, if it amounts, in the words of Lord Ellenborough, "to a destruction of the contemplated adventure".' The insurance is on the venture, and the loss of the venture is a constructive total loss of the goods.

I cannot find that the Act of 1906 has in any way altered this. On the contrary, it seems to me to have preserved it. The Act is expressed by its title to be an Act to codify the law relating to marine insurance. Attention has been called to certain particulars in which, nevertheless, the Act alters the law. That is true. But it remains that the Act is a codifying Act. That being so, I should look more carefully in a codifying Act to see whether any existing law is altered by express words, and should not hold that the Act is going beyond codification unless it puts the matter beyond dispute. I can find nothing which upon this matter has any such effect.

(Atkinson LJ, pp 661–63, and Parmoor LJ, pp 667–68, pursued the same argument.)

Notes

It must be emphasised that, in a claim based on loss of voyage or adventure, the assured is not deprived of control or possession of the goods in the legal sense; such deprivation of possession would come under s 60(2)(i). And it is further emphasised that the principle of 'loss of voyage', laid down in the *Sanday* case, is only applicable to goods, and not to a ship (see *Doyle v Dallas* (1831) 1 M&Rob 48, cited below).

Doyle v Dallas (1831) 1 M&Rob 48

The plaintiff was the owner and master of the vessel *Triton*, which was anchored off Buenos Aires when she fouled a discarded anchor lying on the sea-bed, which pierced her hull, and she sank. *Triton* had been contracted to carry a cargo back to England, but, although she was sold by the plaintiff and later raised by the purchaser, she was still pronounced unfit for the contracted voyage. The plaintiff claimed for a (constructive) total loss of the ship and included the loss of voyage as a reason for the claim. The insurers were only prepared to settle for a partial loss.

The court ruled that *Triton* was not a total loss, but the issue of loss of voyage was raised with regard to it having any bearing on the constructive total loss of a ship.

Lord Tenterden CJ: [p 55] ... The loss of the voyage will not, in my opinion, make a constructive total loss of the ship. Some cases have been so decided; but as the thing insured remained *in specie*, I do not think that amounted to a total loss. The best thing for the underwriters must be done, not merely for the owner; and as they indemnify only against the loss of the ship, the loss of the voyage would not injure them.

*The frustration clause – Institute War Clauses (Cargo)
and Institute Strikes Clauses (Cargo)*

Following the ruling in the *Sanday* case, above, the frustration clause was introduced into cl 3.7 of the Institute War Clauses (Cargo) (IWC(C)(82)) and cl 3.8 of the Institute Strikes Clauses (Cargo) (ISC(C)(82)); it states:

> In no case shall this insurance cover ... any claim based upon loss of or frustration of the voyage or adventure.

Attention is drawn to the fact that this frustration clause only appears in the IWC(C)(82) and the ISC(C)(82), and not in the ICC (A), (B) or (C), reflecting that the principle of loss of voyage or adventure no longer applies during conditions of strife. However, should a planned adventure, under normal circumstances of trade, be frustrated, for example, by a vessel no longer being capable of prosecuting the voyage and there being no alternative method of continuing the venture, the principle laid down in the *Sanday* case would still be applicable.

TYPES OF CONSTRUCTIVE TOTAL LOSS

Section 60 of the Marine Insurance Act 1906 defines, in two sub-sections, the meaning of constructive total loss and the manner in which it may occur. The two sub-sections are separate: s 60(2) does not qualify s 60(1). Section 60(1) relates in general terms to the subject matter insured, be it ship, goods or freight, whereas s 60(2) is more specific. Section 60(2)(i) is applicable to ship or goods only, whilst s 60(2)(ii) is concerned with damage to a ship; and s 60(2)(iii) only with damage to goods.

To acquire an understanding of how these provisions apply in practice and how the language within s 60 may be interpreted, reference must be made to past authorities, where the construction of the section, and the words within it, were carefully analysed.

Reasonable abandonment of the subject matter insured

There are two distinct and separate elements to s 60(1), when it states:

> Subject to any express provision, there is a constructive total loss where the subject matter insured is reasonably abandoned on account of its actual total loss appearing to be unavoidable, or because it would not be preserved from actual total loss without an expenditure which would exceed its value when the expenditure had been incurred.

Although the term 'reasonable abandonment' is common to both elements of s 60(1), 'abandonment' in the context of a ship may mean actually leaving the ship or giving it up for lost. The former is the physical act of vacating the property, the latter is a decision based on economics and business expediency. Scott LJ remarked in graphic terms that one can be expressed 'in boats', the other in 'a letter'.

Naturally, where goods are concerned, it is only possible to give them up for lost. It is to be noted that in relation to goods, the provisions in s 60(1) are reiterated, almost verbatim, in cl 13 of all the Institute Cargo Clauses, as follows:

> No claim for Constructive Total Loss shall be recoverable hereunder unless the subject matter insured is reasonably abandoned either on account of its actual total loss appearing to be unavoidable, or because the cost of recovering, reconditioning and forwarding the subject matter to the destination to which it is insured would exceed its value on arrival.

Meaning of abandonment

Although the *Lavington Court* case, cited below, was not a marine insurance case, the issue of what constituted the abandonment of a ship arose under a wartime charter, and is equally relevant to marine insurance.

Court Line Ltd v R, 'Lavington Court' [1945] 78 LlL Rep 390, CA

The motor vessel *Lavington Court*, owned by the plaintiffs (respondents), was chartered to the Ministry of War Transport when she was torpedoed, in the Atlantic, whilst sailing in convoy. The master and crew abandoned her on 18 July 1942, the day she was torpedoed, but she did not sink until 1 August, two weeks later, by which time she had been taken in tow by a naval vessel. The Crown submitted that the charterparty ended on 18 July, when abandonment took place, and not on 1 August, when she actually sank.

The Court of Appeal affirmed the decision of the lower court (Stable J dissenting), and ruled that there was no constructive total loss at the time of the abandonment, because, at that time and with the naval authorities later trying to save her, there was nothing to show that a total loss was unavoidable. The fact that the insurers had settled for a total loss occurring on 18 July did not affect the plaintiffs' rights under the charterparty.

Scott LJ was of the opinion that the word 'abandoned', as used in s 60(1), should be interpreted in two different ways.

> **Scott LJ:** [p 396] ... The word 'abandon', as was said in *Bradley v Newsom, Sons and Co* [1939] AC 16, has, in the English legal use, several different meanings. It is used in three different senses in the very group of sections which deal with constructive total loss. Indeed, it is used in two different senses in the first sub-section of s 60. When the ship is spoken of as 'abandoned on account of its actual total loss appearing to be unavoidable', the word is used in nearly the same sense as when, according to the law of salvage, the ship is left by master and crew in such a way as to make it a 'derelict', which condition confers on

salvors a certain, but not complete, exclusiveness of possession, and a higher measure of compensation for salvage services. But to constitute the ship a 'derelict', it must have been left: (a) with that intention (*animo derelinquendi*) (*The John and Jane* 4 C Rob 216); (b) with no intention of returning to her; and (c) with no hope of recovering her. Obviously, that sense of the word is frequently inappropriate to the second case to which the first sub-section applies, namely, because it could not be preserved from total loss (that is, an economic test) 'without an expenditure which would exceed its value when the expenditure had been incurred'.

Another distinction between those two alternative grounds in sub-s (1) for claiming a constructive total loss is that, in the latter case, the financial estimate is one which normally would be made by the owner; whereas the forecast of the probability of actual total loss would, at any rate a century ago, nearly always have to be made by the master on the spot; and even in these days of easy and quick wireless communication, the decision would very often devolve on the master. The making of the financial estimate is, of course, merely an exercise of business judgment and discretion. The abandonment which follows after it may be expressed in a letter, and not in boats, as in the first alternative; or be a mere mental decision by the owner that he will exercise the option which s 61 allows him.

On the other hand, Du Parcq LJ was disinclined to give the word 'abandoned' two separate meanings within s 60, and suggested that the true meaning of 'abandon' was 'to give up for lost'. In effect, by equating the meaning of 'abandon' to the phrase 'give up for lost', Du Parcq LJ introduced a phrase which was broad enough to encompass both interpretations put forward by Scott LJ, and, thus, both judges arrived at the same solution by different routes.

> **Du Parcq LJ:** [p 399] ... The word 'abandoned' in s 60 cannot, in my opinion, be given one sense in relation to the first, and another in relation to the second limb of sub-s (1). The same word is sometimes used more than once in a section, with different meanings, but I cannot believe that the same word, used once, can be intended to mean more than one thing. I agree with Tucker J that the word 'abandon' must refer to something done by the shipowner or his agent with his authority, and I would add that the master may often be an agent of necessity. I understand 'abandon' to mean 'give up for lost', and when I say give up for lost I mean that the owners are renouncing all their rights in the ship except the right to recover insurance. This meaning fits both limbs of the sub-section. Of course, the master may, in this sense, abandon the ship on behalf of the owners, but, in order to prove that he has done so, it is not enough to show that he and the crew left the ship temporarily to her fate, or that, having left her, he had grave doubt whether she would be recovered or ultimately saved. It must, I think, be made clear that he so acted as to show an intention to renounce all the owner's (his principal's) rights in the ship, their right to property as well as to possession.

Notes

It must be emphasised that, whether the abandonment be of ship or goods, the assured is, under s 60(1) (and cl 13 of all the ICC), not deprived of control or possession of the subject matter insured; the case of a deprivation of possession falls under s 60(2)(i).

Actual total loss appearing unavoidable

There is a constructive total loss when the abandonment takes place 'on account of an actual total loss appearing to be unavoidable'. What may be deemed to be 'unavoidable' was an issue raised in *Lind v Mitchell* **(1928) 45 TLR 54, CA**, where a master abandoned a sailing ship after she was damaged by ice, and a gale was expected.

> **Scrutton LJ:** [p 56] ... Next, one comes to a question of fact; was this, in the language of s 60(1) of the Act, which deals with constructive total loss, a reasonable abandonment of the ship 'on account of its actual total loss appearing to be unavoidable'; that is to say, total loss probable from the leak appearing, judged to be unavoidable, and therefore a reasonable abandonment of the vessel which it is reasonably thought will anyhow be lost by perils of the sea? Now I am satisfied that the abandonment was unreasonable.

In *Read v Bonham* **(1821) 3 Brod&B 147**, a ship sailed from Calcutta in a seaworthy state but, due to severe weather, had to return to Calcutta, where she was sold by the master, after a survey, in the best interests of all parties, because of the exorbitant cost of repairs. As the owners had claimed for a constructive total loss, it was necessary to consider the issue of whether her total loss was unavoidable.

> **Park J:** [p 155] ... The verdict was clearly right on the first point; for a case of stronger necessity to justify the sale of a ship has seldom been made out. The captain could not procure money for repairs, and it was not to be expected that he should let the ship rot. Did he then act as a fair man ought? He went to the very person whom he thought authorised to act in the business (that person, indeed, denied any authority to accept an abandonment); but he was called in to the survey, and the ship was sold, as the most advisable way of disposing of her when the result of the survey was known.

However, in *Court Line Ltd v R, 'Lavington Court'* **(1945) 78 LlL Rep 390, CA**, where the vessel was torpedoed during the war and the question before the court was when, in relation to the total loss becoming unavoidable, the abandonment actually took place, the court sought to qualify the meaning of 'unavoidable'.

> **Stable J:** [p 401] ... The word 'unavoidable' is undoubtedly a strong word, and it may be said in one sense that nothing is unavoidable until it has actually happened. In my judgment, in considering the meaning of avoidability in relation to some future event, one cannot assign such an absolute meaning to the word as inevitable in the sense of something which must in the course of

nature happen. To attempt to give a definition of the word applicable in all circumstances is, I think, likely to do more harm than good. It is sufficient to say that I think the word connotes a very high degree of probability, with the additional element that there is no course of action, project or plan, present at the time or place in the mind of the person concerned which offers any reasonable possibility of averting the anticipated event.

An expenditure which would exceed its value

Abandonment of ship

The abandonment of a ship for the above reason would now, in the light of advances made in communications, be the prerogative of the owners rather than the master. Such an abandonment is brought about because the subject matter insured cannot be preserved from being an actual total loss without incurring an expenditure in excess of her value. The abandonment is based on economic expediency.

A shipowner, whose ship has been so severely damaged that the cost of repairing the damage would exceed the value of the ship when repaired, could, besides s 60(2)(ii), rely on the general wording of this limb of s 60(1) (read with s 61) to base his claim.

In *Court Line Ltd v R, 'Lavington Court'* **[1945] 78 LlL Rep 390, CA**, cited in full earlier in this chapter,[1] Scott LJ expanded on the issue of economic abandonment, astutely describing it as one made by means of a letter rather than a lifeboat.

> **Scott LJ:** [p 397] ... Another distinction between those two alternative grounds in sub-s (1) for claiming a constructive total loss is that, in the latter case, the financial estimate is one which normally would be made by the owner; whereas the forecast of the probability of actual total loss would, at any rate a century ago, nearly always have to be made by the master on the spot; and even in these days of easy and quick wireless communication, the decision would very often devolve on the master. The making of the financial estimate is, of course, merely an exercise of business judgment and discretion. The abandonment which follows after it may be expressed in a letter, and not in boats, as in the first alternative; or be a mere mental decision by the owner that he will exercise the option which s 61 allows him.

Abandonment of goods

It should be noted that, under s 60(1) of the Act and cl 13 of all the Institute Cargo Clauses, a cargo-owner may abandon goods and claim for a constructive total loss even though the insured goods are not in fact a total loss. According to cl 13, an assured may abandon the cargo if the cost of

---

1   See above, p 630.

recovering, reconditioning and forwarding the goods has become uneconomic (see *Farnworth v Hyde* (1866) LR 2 CP 204 and *Vacuum Oil Co v Union Insurance Society of Canton* (1926) 25 LlL Rep 546, CA, cited below).

Commercial viability of recovering, reconditioning and forwarding the goods

In general terms, with respect to goods, the second part of s 60(1), read with cl 13, may apply to the situation where goods, by reason of an insured peril, have been prevented from reaching their intended destination and the cost of ensuring their delivery becomes prohibitive. In other words, it is not economically viable to recover, recondition and forward the goods to their proper destination.

In this regard, a distinction has to be drawn between a commercial viability and the physical impossibility of forwarding the goods to their proper destination. The latter, which has already been discussed, is the *Sanday* principle. And, provided the loss of voyage or adventure caused by an insured peril has occurred in peacetime conditions, a claim for a constructive total loss could be brought under the Institute Cargo Clauses by reason of the absence of the frustration clause, which appears only in the War and the Strikes Clauses.

The two following cases: *Farnworth v Hyde*, a pre-statute case, and *Vacuum Oil Co v Union Insurance Society of Canton*, a post-statute case, are included to give examples of what expenses may be included when ascertaining a claim for constructive total loss where the deciding factor is commercial viability.

Farnworth v Hyde (1866) LR 2 CP 204

Avon was carrying the insured cargo from Quebec to Liverpool when she was driven ashore in the St Lawrence by severe weather and ice. The ship and cargo had to remain *in situ* until the following spring, when both were sold at auction. In order to recover for a constructive total loss, it had to be shown that the cost of recovering the cargo would have been more than the cargo was worth when recovered. Thus, the question before the court was what expenses were to be included when calculating the cost of recovery.

The court determined that the cost of recovery should include all the extra expenses incurred consequent on the loss by perils of the seas. That is, the cost of landing, drying, warehousing and re-shipping the goods, but not including the freight payable if the goods were forwarded in the original ship or one substituted by the original shipowners; such freight remains payable by the cargo owners at destination. On that calculation, there was no constructive total loss.

> **Channel B:** [p 225] ... where goods are in consequence of the perils insured against lying at a place different from the place of their destination, damaged, but in such a state that they can at some cost be put into a condition to be carried to their destination, the jury are to determine whether it is practically

possible to carry them on, that is, according to the well known exposition in *Moss v Smith*, whether to do so will cost more than they are worth; and that, in determining this, the jury should take into account all the extra expenses consequent on the perils of the sea, such as drying, landing, warehousing, and reshipping the goods, and that they ought not to take into account the fact that if they are carried in the original bottom, or by the original shipowner in a substituted bottom, they will have to pay the freight originally contracted to be paid; that being a charge to which the goods are liable when delivered, whether the perils of the sea affect them or not. And we also agree that *Rosetto v Gurney* correctly decides that, where the original bottom is disabled by perils of the seas, so that the shipowner is not bound to carry the goods on, and he does not choose to do so, the jury are not to take into account the whole of the cost of transit from the place of distress to the place of destination, which must be incurred by the goods owner if he carries them on, but only the excess of that cost above that which would have been incurred if no peril had intervened.

Vacuum Oil Co v Union Insurance Society of Canton [1926] 25 LlL Rep 546, CA

The sailing vessel *Agios Georgios* was carrying a cargo of tins of petroleum from Alexandria to Cyprus when she went ashore and was lost. The tins of petroleum, however, floated, and many were saved although, in many cases, the contents were contaminated. The question before the court was whether, given the circumstances, the loss was total or partial.

The Court of Appeal, in affirming the decision of the trial judge, ruled that there had been a constructive total loss but, as no notice of abandonment had been given, the plaintiffs could not claim on their policy of insurance.

> **Atkin LJ:** [p 553] ... I think it is unnecessary to consider the other alternatives, as to the new tins, which seems to me to involve a calculation which no businessman, indeed, nobody but an underwriter trying to show that there was no constructive loss, would have contemplated for a moment. It involved going to the expense of making a very large number of new tins, and then finding some vessel which would transport them at a very large cost to Tripoli, the total cost of getting to Tripoli amounting to something like £1,200, and then it involved the question of chartering a ship which arrived at such a time as would coincide with the time when the tins had arrived and the refilling was ready, and then transporting the goods in that vessel to the port of destination, Cyprus, at which time, when they did arrive, they still would be subject to the fact that it was salved oil, and a very possible chance of the oil being mixed with seawater and fresh water. It appears to me quite plain that there was a constructive total loss in this case; but, unfortunately for the assured, it is not sufficient on the policy of insurance to show that you in fact lost all your goods. On a constructive total loss you have also to give a notice of abandonment.

Deprivation of possession of ship or goods

Section 60(2)(i) is applicable to ship or goods where it states:

In particular, there is a constructive total loss:

(i) Where the assured is deprived of the possession of his ship or goods by a peril insured against; and

    (a) it is unlikely that he can recover the ship or goods, as the case may be; or

    (b) the cost of recovering the ship or goods, as the case may be, would exceed their value when recovered ...

Meaning of deprived of possession

It is generally accepted that s 60(2)(i) is primarily concerned with losses likely to have been caused by the capture or seizure of a ship or goods by a belligerent State or other hostile act. Such deprivation of possession may ultimately bring about what amounts to a constructive total loss. That is, the assured no longer has control of the ship or goods insured and it is unlikely that the ship or goods can be recovered, or the cost of such recovery would exceed their value when recovered. It is conceivable that such a deprivation of possession could occur in other circumstances where, for example, a ship is impounded for a breach of regulations or taken away by a barratrous crew, but, in general, the cases illustrating the effects of s 60(2)(i) relate to capture and seizure brought about by hostilities or political strife.

That the whole doctrine of constructive total loss was originally based on the effects of capture and seizure was clearly illustrated in *Moore v Evans*, below. Although it was not a marine case, Atkinson LJ, in his summation, considered it necessary to explain the concept, origin and purpose of constructive total loss.

Moore v Evans [1918] AC 185, HL

The plaintiffs were a London firm of jewellers which dispatched insured pearls to trading customers in Belgium and Germany on the basis of sale or return. The property in the goods remained with the plaintiffs until the jewels were sold. When war broke out between the western powers and Germany invaded Belgium, it became impossible for the plaintiffs to recover their goods, and they claimed on their policy of insurance.

The House of Lords, affirming the decision of the Court of Appeal, ruled that the plaintiffs could not recover as their policy (non-marine) covered the goods, and not the adventure. Atkinson LJ took pains to show that the principle of constructive total loss did not apply to ordinary contracts of insurance, and then proceeded to explain the whole background to constructive total loss, including a most seemly quote from the classic work of *Marshall on Marine Insurance*.

Atkinson LJ: [p 193] ... Marine insurance grew out of the necessities of maritime trade and commerce. It dealt with the hazardous enterprise of the navigation of the sea by ships carrying cargo for reward. The law dealing with it is a branch of the law maritime as well as of the law merchant. It is founded upon the practices of merchants who were themselves for long the expounders of its principles, which principles general convenience had established in order to regulate the dealings of merchants with each other in all countries. Its utility, according to *Marshall on Marine Insurance*, 3rd edn, Vol I, pp 3 *et seq*, cannot be better expressed than in the words of the preamble of a very early statute, 43 Eliz c 12, which recites that by means of policies of insurance: 'it cometh to pass upon the loss or perishing of any ship, there followeth not the undoing of any man, but the loss lighteth rather easily upon many than heavily upon few, and rather upon them that adventure not than on those that do adventure, whereby all merchants, especially the younger sort, are allured to venture more willingly and more freely.'

[p 194] ... So, also, as soon as these marine policies came to be regarded as indemnities and not wagering policies, the law of constructive total loss based upon notice of abandonment was shaped and moulded by decisions of Lord Mansfield about the middle of the 18th century. The doctrine had its origin in cases of the capture. *Goss v Withers* and *Hamilton v Mendes* were both cases of capture and recapture, and were apparently based upon the principle that the assured should not be obliged to wait till he had definitely ascertained whether his ship had been recaptured or not, but might upon capture proceed at once and, after notice of abandonment, recover his capital, the value of his ship, from the underwriters, provided he was not aware of her recapture when he commenced his action.

Notes

The link between capture and this type of constructive total loss was referred to in ***Polurrian Steamship Co Ltd v Young* [1915] 1 KB 922, CA** (hereinafter referred to as the *Polurrian* case) cited in full later in this chapter,[2] where a neutral vessel was detained for six weeks and her owners claimed for a constructive total loss. Warrington J, when he was considering the meaning of the phrase 'unlikelihood of recovery', confirmed that s 60(1) and 60(1)(a) – introduced into the Act to replace 'uncertainty of recovery' – were related to constructive total loss by capture.

Warrington J: [p 937] ... Whence the statute derived the phrase 'unlikely that he can recover' as expressing a necessary condition of the assured's right to recover for a constructive total loss by capture I do not know. I have referred to many of the reported capture cases, and I have been unable to find it used judicially in any of them.

---

2   See below, p 638.

But, in *The Bamburi* [1982] 1 Lloyd's Rep 312, where a vessel was indefinitely detained in Iraq because of the outbreak of hostilities between Iraq and Iran, Staughton J was obliged to interpret the meaning of 'deprivation of possession' in a broad sense, when the owners claimed for a constructive total loss even though there were still crew members aboard.

> **Staughton J:** [p 316] ... The concept of possession in English law was never simple, whether under the Larceny Act 1916, or elsewhere. It is admitted that if possession has its narrowest legal significance in the present case, the claimants have not been deprived of it. There are still four crew members on board the ship, who are there by virtue of the claimants' title; there is no Iraqi presence on board; and neither the Iraqi nor the Iranian government asserts any right to, interest in or claim over the vessel.
>
> On the other hand, it is alleged, and I find, that the owners have been wholly deprived of the free use and disposal of their vessel. All movement of the ship is prohibited. There is not even an opportunity similar to that afforded to the owners of ships trapped in the Suez canal some years ago, of organising races in the Great Bitter Lake on Sunday afternoons. She must remain as idle as a painted ship.

Meaning of unlikely

In the *Polurrian* case, below, the court deliberated on the fact that, when the 1906 Act was codified, the previously used phrase of 'uncertainty of recovery' was replaced by the phrase 'unlikelihood of recovery'. Warrington J was of the opinion that the change in phraseology was to the detriment of the assured in that 'unlikelihood' is a more severe test than 'uncertainty'.

Polurrian Steamship Co Ltd v Young [1915] 1 KB 922, CA

The neutral steamship *Polurrian* was owned by the plaintiffs and insured by the defendants 'against the risk of capture seizure and detention'. In 1912, during the war between Greece and Turkey, *Polurrian* sailed with a cargo of Welsh coal for Constantinople but, when nearing her destination, she was captured and detained by a Greek warship for carrying contraband. The plaintiffs claimed for a constructive total loss; the defendants admitted detainment, but not capture.

The Court of Appeal upheld the decision of the trial judge, and ruled that, although the recovery of *Polurrian* was uncertain, it was not unlikely.

> **Warrington J:** [p 936] ... One may, I think, without disrespect, express some regret about the two expressions 'reasonably abandoned on account of its actual total loss appearing to be unavoidable' and 'unlikely that he can recover the ship' should be used apparently to describe the same position of things; for in my view, at any rate, it is one thing to predicate that a total loss of a thing reasonably appears to be unavoidable and another to predicate that its recovery is unlikely. Taking, however, the latter and, as it seems to me, the less severe test of the right to treat a capture as constituting a constructive total loss,

I think that the statute has modified the pre-existing law to the disadvantage of the assured. One is always properly afraid of incompleteness in attempting a definition; but I venture to say that the test of 'unlikelihood of recovery' has now been substituted for 'uncertainty of recovery'.

[p 937] ... Addressing myself, however, to the best of my ability to the question which this s 60 directs me to consider, my conclusion is that whilst I hold that on 26 October – the crucial date, because the date of commencement of the plaintiffs' action – the recovery of *Polurrian* by her owners was quite uncertain, I do not feel myself justified in holding that the balance of probabilities has been proved to me so clearly against her recovery that I can say that such recovery was 'unlikely'. This being so, the plaintiffs have failed to make out their case, and this appeal must be dismissed.

In *Court Line Ltd v R, 'Lavington Court'* **[1945] 78 LlL Rep 390**, where a vessel was torpedoed in the Atlantic but did not sink for a considerable period after the attack, the court was faced with deciding when abandonment actually took place. During these deliberations, the issue of unlikelihood of recovery was raised, and Stable J referred to the *Polurrian* case when he described the word 'unlikely' to lie somewhere between uncertainty and inevitability.

Stable J: [p 402] ... In order to substantiate a constructive total loss under this sub-section, the Crown must establish that the shipowner was deprived of the possession of the ship and that it was at the time of such deprivation unlikely that he could recover her ... The word used is 'unlikely', not 'uncertain', and seems to connote a degree of probability, somewhere between mere uncertainty on the one hand and inevitability on the other (see *Polurrian Steamship Company v Young* [1915] 1 KB 922, pp 937, 938).

Whether recovery of a vessel was likely or unlikely was looked upon from a logical point of view in *Marstrand Fishing Co Ltd v Beer* **[1937] 1 KBD 158**, where the master of a fishing vessel ran away with her for his own purposes and the owners claimed for a constructive total loss caused by barratry.

Porter J: [p 165] ... I cannot say that, in my view, on the balance of probabilities, she was more likely to be lost than recovered. To my mind, it is a case exactly on all fours with that of *Polurrian*, her recovery being uncertain, but not unlikely. If I had been asked to say: 'Is she more likely to be lost than to be recovered?' I should have felt obliged to reply: 'I do not know.' ... For my part, I am left in complete darkness as to whether *Girl Pat* was likely or unlikely to be recovered, and I must hold that she was never a constructive total loss, and that her owners cannot recover.

The same reasoned and logical approach was also used in *Rickards v Forestal Land, Timber and Railways Co* **[1941] 3 All ER 62, HL**, where a cargo-owner based his claim on actual or constructive total loss: the actual total loss being due to the vessel carrying the cargo being scuttled in order to avoid capture; the constructive total loss occurring because, when the vessel left Rio de Janeiro, the cargo was already effectively lost to the owners, because the ship had already been put under the orders of the German Government. Wright LJ took time to compare the term 'unlikely' with that of 'uncertain'.

> **Wright LJ:** [p 81] ... There is a real difference in logic between saying that a future happening is uncertain and saying that it is unlikely. In the former, the balance is even. No one can say one way or the other. In the latter, there is some balance against the event. It is true that there is nothing in the Act to show what degree of unlikelihood is required. If, on the test of uncertainty, the scales are level, any degree of unlikelihood would seem to shift the balance, however slightly. It is not required that the scale should spring up and kick the beam. In the present case, in my opinion, it is unlikely that the goods would be recovered. The odds were all against it. When *Minden* sailed from Rio under the orders of the German Government, it was, I think, not merely uncertain that she would evade the British blockade. It was, in my opinion, unlikely.

Objective test of unlikelihood of recovery

The test of whether a ship or goods are unlikely to be recovered is an objective test based upon the viewpoint of a reasonable man, and not that of the assured. This issue was discussed at some length in *Marstrand Fishing Co Ltd v Beer* [1937] 1 All ER 158, below, where it was also confirmed that the date on which such an objective test should be made was the date on which the writ was issued to enforce the abandonment.

Marstrand Fishing Co Ltd v Beer [1937] 1 All ER 158

The owners of the fishing vessel *Girl Pat* pursued a claim for constructive total loss when the master and crew of the vessel absconded with her for their own purposes. Effectively, the owners had been deprived of possession of the vessel, but the question before the court was whether this deprivation amounted to a constructive total loss.

The court ruled that it was not a constructive total loss, and, in so ruling, analysed in depth the meaning of the phrase 'unlikely to be recovered' as well as referring to the *Pollurian* case for authority. Porter J decided that the test of 'unlikely to be recovered' should be objective, and the date when that objective test should be made was the date when the writ, enforcing the abandonment, was made.

> **Porter J:** [p 164] ... Then comes the question: was the ship a constructive total loss? There is the test set out in *Polurrian SS Co Ltd v Young*, which was actually, of course, the test set out in s 60(2)(i): is the recovery of the vessel unlikely? It is also, I think, conceded – and, at any rate, it has been determined by the *Polurrian* case – that 'unlikely' means that the balance of probabilities is against the vessel being recovered, and also that the person to whom it must appear that the vessel is unlikely to be recovered is not the individual concerned, but is the reasonable man. But that leaves the question: by what information must the person concerned judge? Of course, in giving notice of abandonment, he can only act on such information as he has, and indeed, he

may act on a reasonable guess, and can recover, providing in fact the recovery of the vessel was unlikely: *George Cohen, Sons and Co v Standard Marine Insurance Co Ltd.* In determining whether, in fact, the loss was a constructive total loss, two matters must be determined: (i) at what date must the judgment be exercised? and (ii) is the accuracy of that judgment to depend upon the facts known to the person forming the judgment at the time he does so, or is it to depend upon the true facts existing at that time? As to the first question, at what date must the judgment be formed, I think the *Polurrian* case determines the question; it is the date of the issue of the writ, or the notional issue of the writ; that is to say, the date at which the underwriters agree to treat the matter as if it had been an issue ... The second question, namely, on what must the person making the claim be taken to have acted, depends upon s 60(1), (2) of the Act. If the decision depended upon s 60(2), then the question is: Was the recovery on the proper date unlikely or not? *Prima facie*, that means: was the recovery unlikely on the true facts as then existing and not upon the facts as known to the assured? But it may be said that s 60(2) is a particular instance of which s 60(1) is the general expression, and, if so, the meaning of the general must govern that of the particular which is an instance or example of it. Even if this be so, the phrase in s 60(1) – that is, that there is a constructive total loss when the subject matter insured is reasonably abandoned on account of its actual total loss appearing to be unavoidable – may mean because, on the facts as known, the vessel's loss appears unavoidable, or because, on the true facts, the loss appears unavoidable. I prefer the latter of those two constructions: (a) because the particular instance in s 60(2) would seem to point to the true facts being the criterion; and (b) because that was, I think, the view accepted in the *Polurrian* case. If that be an accurate view, the word 'appears' is used because the future of the vessel is still unknown, and her loss must still be described as appearing unavoidable, since certainty can never be predicted of the future ... If the decision were to depend on the apparent facts, an owner, whose credible information was that the ship had been driven ashore in such circumstances that her loss appeared to be unavoidable, could give notice of abandonment, issue his writ, and recover, though it was found the next day that the vessel was safe and sound in harbour. To accept that a constructive total loss had occurred in such a case, would be, I think, to hold, as Mr Willink said [for the insurers], that the insurance had been effected, not against loss, but against bad news.

Notes

In *Kuwait Airways Corporation v Kuwait Insurance Co SAK* **[1996] 1 Lloyd's Rep 664**, following the invasion of Kuwait by Iraq, aircraft and spares belonging to Kuwait Airways were plundered by the invading forces and the airline made a prompt claim upon their war risk insurers. One of the issues before the court was whether all the losses arose out of one 'occurrence', and Rix J reflected upon the objective test in marine insurance for constructive total loss in order to clarify the point:

> **Rix J:** [p 686] ... The matter must be scrutinised from the point of view of an informed observer placed in the position of the insured. I would suggest that

as in the case of analysing a situation for the purpose of deciding whether a constructive total loss has occurred, the scrutiny must be performed on the basis of the true facts as at that time and not simply on the facts as they may have appeared at that time (see *Polurrian Steamship Co Ltd v Young* [1915] 1 KB 922, *Marstrand Fishing Co Ltd v Beer* [1936] 56 LlL Rep 163); and that, as in the case of frustration, the probabilities as to the true facts as at that time may be tested by reference to subsequent events (see *Bank Line Ltd v Arthur Capel and Co* [1919] AC 435, p 454).

Period of deprivation of possession

Subject to any express provision in the policy,[3] the length of time that an assured may be deprived of his ship or goods beyond which recovery may be deemed to be unlikely is not one of perpetuity, but is based upon a test of reasonableness as set out in s 88 of the Act. A reasonable length of time is dependent upon the facts of the case and is, therefore, variable. Whether this span of time starts from the date of the casualty, or from the date of the notice of abandonment (or the issuing of the writ), is not settled.

From the date of the casualty?

In *Irvin v Hine* [1950] 1 KB 555, a trawler was severely damaged and the owner claimed for a constructive total loss as he was unable to repair her in a reasonable time because, on account of the wartime restrictions then in place, he could not obtain a licence to do so. Devlin J suggested that the time would normally be expected to run from the time of the casualty.

> **Devlin J:** [p 567] ... I think that the reasonable time is to be judged prospectively from the time of the casualty; and that the prospect of indefinite delay negatives the likelihood of return within a reasonable time.

From the date of the notice of abandonment?

But, in *Polurrian Steamship Co Ltd v Young* [1915] 1 KB 922, CA, where a vessel was seized by the Greek authorities for breaking an embargo on coal shipments to Turkey, Warrington J suggested that the time ran from the date of the writ.

> **Warrington J:** [p 935] ... But if the taking of the vessel, lawful or unlawful, out of the possession of the owner was, at the date of the commencement of the owner's action to enforce his notice of abandonment, a taking which still continued in operation, and the owner's loss of the use and disposal of the ship, once total, was at that date one which might be permanent, and was, at any rate, of uncertain continuance, the owner who had duly given notice of

---

3   The Detainment Clause, cl 3, in IWSC(H)(95) (for Time and Voyage) expressly stipulates 12 months to be the period the assured needs to be deprived of possession for there to be a constructive total loss, provided there is still no likelihood of recovery.

abandonment was held by English law entitled to recover upon his insurance for a constructive total loss.

Similarly, in *The Bamburi* **[1982] 1 Lloyd's Rep 312**, where a vessel was detained in Iraq because of the outbreak of hostilities, Staughton J followed much the same approach as that taken by Warrington J in the *Polurrian* case when he suggested that the time ran from no earlier date than the notice of abandonment or when the writ was issued.

> **Staughton J:** [p 321] ... In my opinion, time is counted from no earlier date than the notice of abandonment. It is then, under the Act, that a vessel must be a constructive total loss for the notice to be valid. It is then that recovery must be unlikely within a reasonable time. (I have said no earlier, because a possible view is that the correct date is when the action is commenced. There is no difference in the present case; nor in most other cases, since if abandonment is declined it is the usual practice of underwriters, so far as my knowledge goes, to agree to place the insured in the same position as if a writ had been issued.)

The Detainment Clause

Because deprivation of possession or detainment is normally associated with hostilities or industrial strife, the provision covering such an eventuality is contained within cl 3 of the Institute War and Strikes Clauses Hulls – Time and Voyage. The clause states:

> In the event that the Vessel shall have been the subject of capture seizure arrest restraint detainment confiscation or expropriation, and the assured shall thereby have lost the free use and disposal of the Vessel for a continuous period of 12 months, then for the purpose of ascertaining whether the Vessel is a constructive total loss the Assured shall be deemed to have been deprived of the possession of the Vessel without any likelihood of recovery.

There is no mention within the clause of when the 12 month time period is to commence, and following the pronouncements in the aforementioned three cases: *Irvin v Hine*; the *Polurrian* case; and *The Bamburi*, it still remains unsettled whether that time runs from the time of the casualty or from the time of the serving of the notice of abandonment.

Cost of recovering the ship or goods

Section 60(2)(i)(b) states that there is a constructive total loss:

> (i) where the assured is deprived of possession of his ship or goods by a peril insured against; and ...
>
> (b) the cost of recovering the ship or goods, as the case may be, would exceed their value when recovered ...

It is significant to recall that, under this limb, the subject matter insured is in the hands of a third party, and the economic consideration is the cost that is to be incurred in 'recovering' the property.

In relation to a claim for a constructive total loss of cargo, the authority which is squarely on point is *Stringer v English and Scottish Marine Insurance Co* **(1869) LR 4 QB 699; (1870) LR 5 QB 599**, where the assured could have recovered possession of their goods if they were prepared to pay the Prize Court about 150 to 180% more than the value of the goods. The court applied the 'prudent uninsured owner' criterion in support of their decision that the assured were not at fault in not preventing the sale of the cargo. The seizure, which ultimately led to the enforced sale, was held to have occasioned the total loss of the goods. The remarks of Blackburn J, whose judgment was affirmed by the Exchequer Chamber, were couched in the following manner:

> **Blackburn J:** [p 691] ... They might have prevented the sale by giving security, and generally, we think that it would be a reasonable thing to give security rather than allow the goods to be sold. But, in this case, from the peculiar nature of the American currency at the time, those who became sureties must have bound themselves in the event of condemnation to pay the value of the goods estimated in paper dollars at a time when gold was at from 150 to 180 premium; and it was not improbable that they might be called upon to pay when gold was at par, thus being liable to pay from 150 to 180% more than the value of the goods.
>
> [p 692] We come, therefore, to the conclusion of fact, that the assured could not by any means, which they could reasonably be called on to adopt, have prevented the sale by the American Prize Court, which at once put an end to all possibility of having the goods restored in specie, and consequently entitled to assured to come upon their insurers for a total loss.

Damage to ship

Section 60(2)(ii) of the Act states, as a general principle, that there is a constructive total loss:

> In the case of damage to a ship, where she is so damaged by a peril insured against that the cost of repairing the damage would exceed the value of the ship when repaired.

Unlike s 60(2)(i), the assured remains in control and possession of the ship and the claim for a constructive total loss is based upon an economic decision. This decision would normally, in the present day, be made by the owner, whereas in the past, when communications were limited, it was often made by the master or other agent of the owner. It is also implied, as the wording suggests, that the ship is actually repairable.

In the early case of *Roux v Salvador* **(1836) 3 Bing NC 266**, which was concerned with the total loss of a consignment of hides, the principle that there was a constructive total loss when it was uneconomic to carry out repairs was already apparent.

Lord Abinger CB: [p 286] ... There may be some other peril which renders the ship unnavigable, without any reasonable hope of repair, or by which the goods are partly lost, or so damaged, that they are not worth the expense of bringing them, or what remains of them, to their destination. In all these or any similar cases, if a prudent man not insured, would decline any further expense in prosecuting an adventure, the termination of which will probably never be successfully accomplished, a party insured may, for his own benefit, as well as that of the underwriter, treat the case as one of a total loss, and demand the full sum insured.

In *Moss v Smith*, below, Maule J applied the same principle of constructive total loss to a ship although, at that time, such a loss was often still referred to as a total loss and not specifically as a constructive total loss.

Moss and Others v Smith and Another (1850) 9 CB 94

The plaintiffs were the mortgagees of the vessel *Alfred*, which had been insured with the defendants for a voyage from Valparaiso to England. Soon after sailing, with a cargo of guano, *Alfred* encountered severe weather and had to return to Valparaiso, where, after various surveys, she was sold; the cargo being forwarded on other vessels. The plaintiffs claimed for a (constructive) total loss.

The court ruled that there had been no constructive total loss, because the cost of repairing the ship later proved to be considerably less than her repaired value.

Maule J: [p 103] ... it may be that it may be physically possible to repair the ship, but at enormous cost: and there also the loss would be total; for, in matters of business, a thing is said to be impossible when it is not practicable; and a thing is impracticable when it can only be done at an excessive or unreasonable cost. A man may be said to have lost a shilling, when he has dropped it into deep water; though it might be possible, by some very expensive contrivance, to recover it. So, if a ship sustains such extensive damage, that it would not be reasonably practicable to repair her – seeing that the expense of repairs would be such that no man of common sense would incur the outlay – the ship is said to be totally lost.

The value of the ship when repaired

The salient factor in determining whether a ship is a constructive total loss on economic grounds is, at the end of the day, the repaired value of that ship. This value, naturally, determines the actions of the assured when considering the expense of repairs, and it also has much bearing on the decision of a court which may, at some later stage, be called upon to adjudicate on the matter. On what, then, is the repaired value of the ship to be based?

The market value of the vessel

Under common law, whether the policy be valued or unvalued, the true or market value, and not the insured value, of the ship is taken as the repaired value for the purpose of determining whether there was a constructive total loss (see *Irving v Manning* (1847) 1 HL Cas 287). This principle has been continued in the Act itself which, in s 27(4), confirms that the insured value is 'not conclusive for the determining whether there has been a constructive total loss'. But, having said that, the opening phrase of s 27(4) – 'Unless the policy otherwise provides' – allows the parties to the contract to specify their own figure or value, which is to be taken as the repaired value of the vessel.

Although in *Irving v Manning*, below, there was an agreed value on the vessel, the court considered both valued and unvalued policies, and confirmed that, in both instances, the figure used when claiming for a constructive total loss was still her market value. The case is relevant to a policy which has not (otherwise) specified a figure which is to be taken as the repaired value of the vessel.

Irving v Manning (1847) 1 HL Cas 287, HL

The ex-East Indiaman *General Kydd* was insured under a valued policy for a voyage 'at and from' China to Madras and back when she was damaged by storms and, after a survey, abandoned by her owners, who claimed for a constructive total loss. The claim was based on the fact that the cost of repairs would have amounted to more than her market value, which was less than her insured value. The insurers refused payment.

The House of Lords affirmed the decisions of the lower courts, and ruled that the vessel was a constructive total loss in that the market value was the relevant value when comparison was made with the cost of repairs.

> **Patteson J:** [p 304] ... If this had not been the case of a valued policy, it is clear that on the facts found there was a total loss; for a vessel is totally lost, within the meaning of the policy, when it becomes of no use or value as a ship to the owner, and is as much so as if the vessel had gone to the bottom of the sea, or had been broken to pieces, and the whole or great part of the fragments had reached the shore as wreck; and the course has been in all cases in modern times to consider the loss as total where a prudent owner, uninsured, would not have repaired. In an open policy, therefore, the assured would have been entitled to recover for a total loss, the amount to be ascertained by evidence. What difference arises from the circumstances that the policy is a valued policy?
>
> [p 306] ... the question of loss, whether total or not, is to be determined just as if there was no policy at all; and the established mode of putting the question, when it is alleged that there has been, what is perhaps improperly called, a constructive total loss of a ship, is to consider the policy altogether out of the question, and to inquire what a prudent uninsured owner would have done in

the state in which the vessel was placed by the perils insured against. If he would not have repaired the vessel, it is deemed to be lost. When this test has been applied, and the nature of the loss has been thus determined, the quantum of compensation is then to be fixed. In an open policy, the compensation must be then ascertained by evidence. In a valued one, the agreed total value is conclusive; each party has conclusively admitted that this fixed sum shall be that which the assured is entitled to receive in case of a total loss.

The insured value

Clauses 19.1 and 17.1 of the ITCH(95) and the IVCH(95) respectively, have taken advantage of the opening words of s 27(4) by providing otherwise, when they state that:

> In ascertaining whether the vessel is a constructive total loss, the insured value shall be taken as the repaired value and nothing in respect of the damaged or break-up value of the Vessel or wreck shall be taken into account.

In this instance, cll 19.1 and 17.1 have departed from the common law rule and have chosen the insured value as the figure to be taken as the repaired value of the vessel, as there is nothing within the Act to prevent the parties to the insurance from contracting in a manner in which they please.

Such was the case in *Sailing Ship Holt Hill Co v United Kingdom Marine Association*, below, where a clause in the policy stated that, when determining a constructive total loss, the cost of repairs must amount to more than 80% of the insured hull value. However, the court decided that the clause was so worded that it did not affect the repaired value of the ship.

Sailing Ship Holt Hill Co v United Kingdom Marine Association [1919] 2 KB 789

The plaintiffs insured the sailing vessel *Holt Hill* with the defendants under a policy of insurance which provided cover for total and constructive total loss, but included a clause which stated: 'No vessel insured in this association shall be deemed to be a constructive total loss unless the cost of repairing the damage caused by perils insured against shall amount to 80% of the value in the ordinary hull 'all risks' policy – say, £12,500'. *Holt Hill* was seriously damaged in bad weather, and abandoned by her master and crew; the plaintiffs served notice of abandonment on the insurers and claimed for a constructive total loss. The vessel was eventually salved, and it was estimated that the cost of repairs amounted to more than 80% of the £12,500, but very much less than her true repaired value.

The court ruled that she was not a constructive total loss. The clause only applied to the cost of repairs, and did not substitute a new repaired value for the actual repaired value.

> **Rowlatt J:** [p 793] ... This reading of the clause does great and manifest violence to the language, but if it can be collected from the general purport of

the policy or from the nature of the transaction that such was the intention, it would be justifiable to extract the affirmative proposition out of the negative as contended for. It seems to me, however, that there is no reason whatever why the clause should not mean just what it says. If this is so, the position is that the underwriters are to pay if the ship is a constructive total loss as defined by the general law now found in the Marine Insurance Act 1906 – namely, if the cost of repairs exceeds the value of the ship when repaired, with a proviso by way of guarding against overvaluation, that the cost of repairs amounts to 80% of the value in the 'all risks' policy. In fact, if this is what the parties intended, I do not see what form of words they could have chosen better calculated to express that intention than those which they have used. On the other hand, if they had desired to substitute the agreed figure of £10,000 for the repaired value, the direct and plain language of the well known Institute Clause was ready to hand as a precedent. There is no tradition of obscurity in defining the position in this respect. I do not know whether underwriters usually pay when the condition provided for in the clause is satisfied without agitating the question of the actual repaired value, but I cannot read the clause as compelling them to do so.

Can freight payable be included in the repaired value of the ship?

It is reasonable to assume that, if the market value is to be taken as the repaired value of the ship when considering a claim for a constructive total loss, that value should include all the market forces affecting the decision to abandon. This is because, in making that choice, a prudent owner, if uninsured, would consider all the commercial factors involved before making his election to repair or abandon and one of these factors would be the freight payable.

In *MacBeth and Co Ltd v Maritime Insurance Co Ltd* **[1908] AC 144, HL**, where a vessel was badly damaged in the Firth of Clyde and was abandoned as a constructive total loss, the issue of the true value of the ship was raised.

> **Lord Robertson:** [p 149] ... In ascertaining whether there is a constructive total loss, one has to hold an inquest, as it were, and consider whether the ship shall be repaired or shall be abandoned. I do so, first of all, because I do not see how there can be such a thing as a constructive total loss without this being done; and, secondly, because it has for long been laid down by very high authorities that the criterion is the presumable judgment of the owner, on the footing of this being uninsured and acting in his own interests.

In *Kemp v Halliday* **(1866) 6 B&S 623**, cited in full later in this chapter,[4] where the repaired value of a salved ship was an issue, the court acceded to the fact that freight payable should be taken into consideration.

> **Blackburn J:** [p 745] ... as I understand the statement in the case, the cost of raising the submerged ship and cargo, though it would have been excessive having regard to the value of the unrepaired ship alone, was reasonable having

---

4   See below, p 652.

regard to the value of the ship and cargo and freight, which were jointly saved by this expenditure from a common jeopardy.

As things stand, however, the question of freight payable being considered as a component of the market value of the ship is now hypothetical, in the light of the fact that cl 19.1 of the ITCH(95) and cl 17.1 of the IVCH(95) have made provision for the insured value of the ship to be taken as the repaired value.

The cost of repairing the damage

To qualify as a constructive total loss, the cost of repairs must exceed the market value or, as the case may be, the insured value.[5] However, if the vessel is so damaged that she may be considered little more than a wreck, the question arises as to whether the value of that wreck should be included in the balance sheet by adding its value to the cost of repairs. In so doing, the wreck is treated as an asset which becomes the property of the insurer should the loss be deemed total.

Is the value of the wreck to be taken into account?

In *MacBeth and Co Ltd v Maritime Insurance Co Ltd* [1908] AC 144, HL, which came before the courts after the introduction of the Act, but was not governed by it, as the casualty occurred before the legislation was on the statute book, the House of Lords decided that the value of the wreck should be included in the calculation.

But, in *Hall v Hayman*, below, which was a post-statute case, Bray J took a narrow, but, in many ways, more logical approach when deciding what amounted to a repair cost. He reasoned that the value of the wreck was not an 'expenditure' as such, and, therefore, was not an expenditure as laid down in s 60(1) of the Act. Thus, the value of the wreck could not be taken into account when determining the cost of repairs.

Hall v Hayman [1912] 2 KB 5

This was a reinsurance case whereby the plaintiffs reinsured the steamship *King Edward* with the defendants under a time policy of insurance which included cover only for total loss. *King Edward* was severely damaged by a gale in the St Lawrence, as a result of which she was sold by her owners to a purchaser, who later repaired her. The plaintiffs, having settled on the original policy of insurance for a constructive total loss, then claimed on the reinsurers on the basis that the cost of repairs, which included the unrepaired wreck, exceeded the repaired value.

The court ruled that there was no constructive total loss, and that the value of the wreck could not be added to the repair costs. The 1906 Act had

---

5 See ITCH(95), cl 19.1, and IVCH(95), cl 17.1, discussed above, p 647.

superseded the common law, and the word 'expenditure' in s 60(1) could no longer include the value of the wreck.

> **Bray J:** [p 13] ... It seems to me that the word 'expenditure' as there used is a word having a plain meaning, denoting an expenditure of money, and I cannot construe it as including the value of the wreck. The supposed expenditure is by the owner of the ship, and the value of the wreck is not an expenditure by the owner ... It seems to me that sub-s 2(ii) is clear, and is inconsistent with what is now admitted to have been the common law or the law merchant before the Act as laid down by the House of Lords in *MacBeth and Co v Maritime Insurance Co*. It is said, however, that in contrasting the words 'expenditure' and 'the cost of repairing the damage', I ought to have regard to what Lord Collins said in that case, that 'she' – the wreck – 'is a necessary factor in the formation of the repaired ship which it is proposed to bring into being; at whose cost, it may be asked, except that of her owner, is she contributed to the new entity which is to be formed by the process of reparation?' Lord Collins, however, was not construing the Marine Insurance Act 1906; he was endeavouring to reconcile certain decisions and certain language used by judges in former cases, and to show that those decisions and that language were consistent with the decision he was giving. One does not look at the language of a judge in quite the same way as one looks at the words of an Act of Parliament ... The rule, therefore, of the common law, that the value of the wreck ought to be added to the estimated cost of repairs in determining whether the ship can be treated as a constructive total loss, is, in my opinion, inconsistent with the express provision of s 60 and can no longer be treated as the law.

Notes

It should be noted that cl 19.1 of the ITCH(95) and cl 17.1 of the IVCH(95) have now resolved the matter by expressly excluding the value of the wreck, when they state:

> ... nothing in respect of the damaged or break-up value of the Vessel or wreck shall be taken into account.

How complete must the repairs be?

In estimating the extent of the repairs required, it would appear that, in the older cases, it was not necessary for the vessel to be repaired to such a standard as to be able to complete the contemplated voyage. The reasoning behind this was that it was the ship that was insured, and not the voyage.

Reid v Darby [1808] 10 East 143

The master of a vessel sold her in the West Indies because she was in such a leaky condition that she was unable to complete the return voyage across the Atlantic. Because of an outstanding account, the master did not pass on the proceeds of the sale to the owner. The action was then brought by the original owner against the purchaser to recover the value of the ship.

The court ruled that the master had no authority to sell the ship as a constructive total loss, as she still existed and was navigable, and, therefore, capable of being registered.

Lord Ellenborough: [p 157] ... But supposing that it could be fully made out in argument, that the captain was warranted by an adequate authority, express or implied, from his owner to sell the ship, in the case of necessity like that which has occurred; still, in as much as the ship specifically subsists, and is capable of being used as such for purposes of navigation, and has in fact continued to be so used; we are of opinion that it must be regarded as an object of registration, under Lord Liverpool's Act ...

This same principle was followed in *Doyle v Dallas* (1831) 1 M&Rob 48,[6] where it was ruled that a vessel which was damaged was not a constructive total loss, because she was later repaired and used as a coasting vessel. The fact that she was no longer fit to undertake the contracted ocean voyage was immaterial. The ship was insured, not the voyage.

However, in ***North Atlantic Steamship Co Ltd v Burr* (1904) 9 Com Cas 164**, the policy of insurance contained a clause identical to that now contained within the Institute Hulls Clauses (cl 19.1 of the ITCH(95) and cl 17.1 of the IVCH(95)) which stated: 'The insured value to be taken as the repaired value in ascertaining whether the vessel is a constructive total loss.' When the steamship *Monadnock* was abandoned by her owners as a constructive total loss caused by perils of the seas, it was ruled by the court not to be so, because the cost of repairs was less than her repaired value. The question before the court, taking into account the wording in the clause, was: to what extent did the repairs have to go, when calculating whether she was a constructive total loss?

Kennedy J: [p 165] ... the repaired value meant the repaired value with reference to that particular vessel as she was at the time of insurance. The repairs, the cost of which had to be considered, did not mean reconstruction. But the clause did mean that the vessel should be repaired so as not to be merely seaworthy, but, as far as repairs could effect it, a vessel of the same classification and as nearly as possible the same thing as that which was valued.

Estimating the cost of repairs – s 60(2)(ii)

The second limb of s 60(2)(ii) provides some guidance as to what may or may not be included in the cost of repairs. It touches in general terms upon three items of expenses which have to be considered when assessing whether a vessel is, or is not, a constructive total loss. It states:

In estimating the cost of repairs, no deduction is to be made in respect of general average contributions to those repairs payable by other interests, but

---

6 See above, p 628.

account is to be taken of the expense of future salvage operations and of any future general average contributions to which the ship would be liable if repaired ...

There are two distinct constituents to this sub-section, namely:

(a) 'general average contributions to those repairs payable by other interests'; and

(b) 'the expense of future salvage operations and of any future general average contributions to which the ship would be liable if repaired'.

There is little doubt that interpretation of the sub-section presents serious problems. Strictly speaking, one should, in accordance with the rule set out in *Bank of England v Vagliano* [1891] AC 107, before referring to case law, first analyse the wording of the section to ascertain its natural meaning.[7] However, on this occasion, it is necessary, in order to gain some insight into the controversies involved, to examine the case of *Kemp v Halliday*, below. The facts of the case will provide the proper setting and background to the provision.

Kemp v Halliday (1865) 34 LJ (QB) 233; (1866) LR 1 QB 520

The plaintiff was the owner of the vessel *Chebucto*, which was insured with the defendants under a valued policy of insurance on a voyage from Liverpool to Rio de Janeiro. At the outset of the voyage, *Chebucto* encountered severe weather and had to put into Falmouth for the safety of the ship and cargo and, in so doing, sustained a general average loss. In order to carry out repairs, part of the cargo had to be discharged, but, whilst the repairs were being carried out, a violent storm hit Falmouth and the ship, with the portion of cargo still aboard her, sank at her moorings. The plaintiff claimed for a constructive total loss, although the ship's agents, acting on their own initiative, later raised the vessel together with the remaining cargo left on board.

The case turned on whether, in estimating the cost of repairs, the cost of raising and salvaging the sunken vessel and her cargo amounted to a general average act and whether, if it was a general average act, the general average contributions payable by cargo interests should or should not be deducted from the total cost of repairs.

The Exchequer Chamber affirmed the decision of the lower court and ruled that *Chebucto* was not a constructive total loss. It held that the raising and salving of the vessel amounted to a general average act, because both ship and cargo were in imminent danger of becoming a total loss. However, the general average contributions which became payable by cargo interests in order to raise and salve both ship and cargo were deducted from the cost of

---

[7] Note, also, s 91(2): 'The rules of the common law including the law merchant, save in so far as they are inconsistent with the express provision of this Act, shall continue to apply to contracts of marine insurance.'

repairs. This was the pragmatic approach taken by Blackburn J at the court of first instance and later upheld by the Exchequer Chamber. Notably, at first instance, Shee J disagreed with Blackburn J's reasoning, but later withdrew his opposition.

Blackburn J: [Court of Queen's Bench, p 241] ... The plaintiff claimed as for a total loss: the underwriters paid money into court as for a partial loss, and it appears to have been agreed between the parties that the payment was sufficient unless the loss was total. It appears also to have been agreed between them that, if the fact that there would be a claim for contribution against the cargo on board the submerged vessel, which cargo would be raised by the same operation as raised the hull and which would be saved along with the hull, was to be taken into account, there was no total loss. It seems also to have been agreed between the parties that, if the fact that part of the sea damage which necessitated the repairs and was the subject of general average was to be taken into account, there was no total loss.

[p 242] ... It is first necessary to consider whether, if the shipowner had, in this case, raised the ship and cargo as Messrs Broad and Son did [the ship's agents acting on their own initiative], they would have been entitled to charge that expense as general average against the portion of cargo raised by its expenditure as well as against the hull.

In order to give rise to a charge as general average, it is essential that there should be a voluntary sacrifice to preserve more subjects than one exposed to a common jeopardy; but an extraordinary expenditure incurred for that purpose is as much a sacrifice as if, instead of money being expended for the purpose, money's worth were thrown away. It is immaterial whether the shipowner sacrifices a cable or an anchor to get the ship off a shoal, or pays the worth of it to hire those extra services which get her off. It is quite true, that so long as the expenditure by the shipowner is merely such as he would incur in the fulfilment of his ordinary duty as shipowner, it cannot be general average; but the expenditure in raising a submerged vessel with cargo is extraordinary expenditure, and is, if incurred to save the cargo as well as the ship (which *prima facie* is the object of such an expenditure), chargeable against all the subjects in jeopardy saved by this expenditure.

[p 246] ... I should observe that I think, in the present case, the question whether there was a total loss at the time when the ship lay submerged, and that whether there was a total loss when she lay moored at Falmouth in the custody of Messrs Broad and Sons [after being raised], are identically the same. Whilst the ship lay submerged, it was a question of calculation what the cost of raising her would be; but, before the trial, Messrs Broad and Sons had, by experiment, ascertained what it was, and the assured could have got their ship by adopting their act, and paying them for what they had done; and then the assured would have been exactly in the same position as if they had themselves originally raised her.

In considering whether it was reasonable to raise the ship and cargo in the present case, I think that every circumstance tending to increase or diminish the necessary outlay, and every circumstance tending to increase or diminish the benefit to be derived from that outlay, ought to be taken into account; and, amongst those, the fact that cargo would be saved by the operation, and would contribute to the expense, seems to me a very important element.

Erle CJ: [Exchequer Chamber, p 527] ... We do not lay down a rule that all claims for contribution to the ship from any other interest ought to be taken into account in determining whether the ship was worth raising. But we hold that the plaintiff, in considering whether the submersion of his ship containing cargo as stated in the case was a constructive total loss, was bound to take into his estimate the fact that cargo would be saved by the operation which raised the ship, and would contribute to the expense thereof, and the circumstances which would go to increase or diminish the outlay required for raising and repairing the ship, and the circumstances which would go to increase or diminish the benefit to be derived from that outlay, are elements in calculating whether the cost of raising would exceed the value when saved.

We infer from the statement in the case that there was a common peril of destruction imminent over the ship and cargo as they lay submerged, that the most convenient mode of saving either ship or cargo or both was by raising the ship together with the cargo, that the expense required for such raising would be an extraordinary expense for the common benefit of both, that the cargo would be liable for a general average contribution towards that expense, and that the shipowner would have a lien on the cargo to secure the payment of that general average.

If these facts are properly inferred from the statement of the special case, it follows that the plaintiff in calculating the cost of raising was bound to take into his estimate the contribution which would become due to him from the cargo secured to him by a lien thereon, and if so, the special case provides that the defendant should succeed. If the case had not been so stated and we had to apply the common rule, we should consider that a prudent owner uninsured would calculate on the amount of the general average contribution inseparably connected with the raising of the ship, and safely secured, with as much reliance as he could calculate on the value of the ship itself when repaired; it being clear that all the items both of cost and of value on which the owner is to make his calculation when electing between repairing or abandoning are subject to contingency and matter of conjecture only.

In this decision, we have adopted the principle on which Blackburn J relied below, and we refer to his judgment for a more ample statement of that principle in the application of it to this case.

Has s 60(2)(i) overruled Kemp v Halliday?

It is by no means easy, when construing s 60(2)(i) of the Act, to determine whether the principles laid down in *Kemp v Halliday* have been overruled.

Two salient points were raised in this case: first, *Kemp v Halliday* is concerned only with general average contributions in the nature of expense for salvage operations (or, in the words of Blackburn J, for *'raising'* the vessel) payable by other interests. Such expenses, according to the case, have to be deducted from the cost of repairs when determining whether the vessel was a constructive total loss. Secondly, it would appear from the case that the same principle applies whether the vessel was, or was not, in fact raised from where she lay submerged; in other words, it is the *liability* of the other interests to contribute which is to be considered. If the ship was not in fact salved, the question would be, what the cost *would have been*, had salvage been undertaken? Whether or not the shipowner had in fact received any contributions from these other interests is irrelevant.

General average contributions payable by other interests

The term 'general average contribution' is defined in s 66 of the Act to include any 'extraordinary sacrifice or expenditure ... reasonably made or incurred in time of peril for the purpose of preserving the property imperilled in the common adventure'. It is wide enough to embrace expense for salvage operations incurred for the purpose of saving the whole adventure from imminent danger. Any interests which have benefited from the expenditure are required, by s 66(3), to make a contribution to the party on whom it falls. And for the purpose of determining whether a vessel is a constructive total loss, s 60(2)(ii) has declared that: 'In estimating the cost of repairs, no deduction is to be made in respect of general average contribution to those repairs payable by other interests.'

As was seen, the common law, as enunciated in *Kemp v Halliday*, would not allow a shipowner to include within the cost of repairs expense for salvage operations (though in the nature of general average) payable by other interests. On this issue, s 60(2)(ii) is capable of admitting to two interpretations.

First, it may be read side by side with the rule in *Kemp v Halliday* to mean that all forms of general average contributions, *with the exception of expense for raising the ship*, payable by other interests may be added to the cost of repairs. Read in this light, *Kemp v Halliday* is not overruled by s 60(2)(ii), but is allowed to operate as an exception, albeit of the common law, to the general rule. Arnould would prefer not to see *Kemp v Halliday* overruled by the sub-section, and holds the view that: '... the true position is ... that contributions by third parties to the cost of salvage must be deducted when deciding whether the vessel is a constructive total loss.'[8]

Such a construction does not, however, explain why expense for *salvage operations* payable by other interests should be treated differently from other forms of general average contributions. Moreover, the section itself makes no distinction between general average contribution in the nature of salvage and other forms of general average payable by other interests.

---

8   Arnould, J, *Law of Marine Insurance and Average*, 16th edn, 1981, London: Sweet & Maxwell, Vol 2, para 1202.

Secondly, this limb to s 60(2)(ii) may be construed to have overruled the principle in *Kemp v Halliday*, in that all forms of general average contributions, without exception, payable by other interests may now be included in the cost of repairs. The wording of the section is generous enough to support such a construction. One author has explained the rationale for the rule contained in s 60(2)(ii) as follows:

> The estimated cost of repairs cannot be reduced by any prospective recovery from a third party, for example, from a negligent vessel with which the insured vessel is involved in collision, and this extends to contributions from other parties in the adventure towards the insured vessel's general average damage. This is because the Act is merely concerned with whether a constructive total loss situation actually exists, and not with the question of who will ultimately be responsible for paying for the loss.[9]

Such an interpretation, though it is in line with the expansive wording of the sub-section, would go against the grain of the prudent uninsured shipowner criterion which was applied by both Blackburn J and Erle CJ. Surely, an uninsured shipowner would take into account 'every circumstance tending to increase or diminish the necessary outlay, and every circumstance tending to increase or diminish the benefit to be derived from that outlay'.[10] And the fact that cargo would be saved by the operation, and would contribute to the expense, must be an important factor to be taken into consideration.

As the term 'general average contributions ... payable by other interests' is not qualified with the word 'future' (as it is in the case of that payable by the ship), it may be interpreted to cover not only future general average contributions payable by other interests to which liability will attach, but also general average contributions to which liability had already attached.

As can be seen, s 60(2)(ii) is not at all happily worded. It is beset with problems, whether it be construed with or without *Kemp v Halliday* in the picture. Arnould feels that: '... the scales are so nicely balanced that it scarcely seems possible to prefer one view or the other.'[11] The case was decided more than 130 years ago, and, thus, further clarification from the courts is required to resolve this controversy.

Expense of future salvage operations and of future general average contributions to which the ship would be liable

Section 60(2) states that any expense of 'future' salvage operations and of 'future' general average contributions to which the ship would be liable may be taken into account when calculating the repair costs. The statutory enactment is silent on whether such expenses which have already been

---

9 Goodacre, JK, *Marine Insurance Claims*, 3rd edn, 1996, London: Witherby, p 972.
10 *Per* Blackburn J, p 246.
11 *Op cit*, Arnould, fn 8.

incurred by the shipowner may be taken into account for the purpose of determining whether the vessel was a constructive total loss. As they pertain to expenses to which the ship is (as opposed to 'would be') liable, it may be assumed that they may also be added to the cost of repairs for the purpose of determining whether the vessel was a constructive total loss.

As the expense of salvage operations and the associated general average contributions are both qualified by the word 'future' (and 'would') in s 60(2)(ii), it is not unreasonable to wish to ascertain from which point in time the future may be measured. Presumably, that point of time would be the time of the casualty in question, as suggested by Arnould:

> If notice of abandonment is rightly given, the loss dates back to the casualty, and the test for ascertaining whether there is a constructive total loss ought presumably to be applied, actually or notionally, at the same date.[12]

Damage to goods

With respect to goods, whilst s 60(1) deals with the general concept of constructive total loss and s 60(2)(i) with deprivation of possession, s 60(2)(iii) is specifically directed at physical damage to the goods, where it states that there is a constructive total loss:

> ... in the case of damage to goods, where the cost of repairing the damage and forwarding the goods to their destination would exceed their value on arrival.

It should be noted that cl 13 of the ICC (A), (B) and (C) reiterates this provision, but changes the wording of 'repairing the damage and forwarding the goods' to 'reconditioning and forwarding the subject matter'. There is no significance in this minor alteration of the phraseology, but what the word 'forwarding' actually entails is not so easy to resolve. It is not clear whether the costs incurred in forwarding the goods to their destination are covered in full, or whether only the additional costs in forwarding are so covered.

Meaning of forwarding

In the pre-statute case of *Farnworth v Hyde* **(1866) LR 2 CP 204**, cited in full above, p 634, goods had to be forwarded from Canada to England after the vessel carrying them was badly damaged in severe weather. The court decided that only the additional cost of freight was to be included in the calculation when the goods were forwarded by a carrier other than the original contracting carrier. The rationale behind this ruling was that freight is generally paid on delivery and, therefore, has not yet been expended.

---

12 *Op cit*, Arnould, fn 8, para 1203.

Channel B: [p 225] ... if they [the goods] are carried in the original bottom, or by the original shipowner in a substituted bottom, they will have to pay the freight originally contracted to be paid; that being a charge to which the goods are liable when delivered, whether the perils of the sea affect them or not. And we also agree that *Rosetto v Gurney* correctly decides that, where the original bottom is disabled by perils of the seas, so that the shipowner is not bound to carry the goods on, and he does not choose to do so, the jury are not to take into account the whole of the cost of transit from the place of distress to the place of destination, which must be incurred by the goods' owner if he carries them on, but only the excess of that cost above that which would have been incurred if no peril had intervened.

Whether the introduction of the Act has changed this interpretation is uncertain, and there is nothing in the Act, or in cl 13 of the Institute Hull Clauses, to suggest that it has.

An assured in possession of his goods which are damaged by an insured peril may base his claim for indemnity for a constructive total loss under either the second part of s 60(1), read with cl 13, or under s 60(2)(iii). If he is not in possession of his goods, he would have to plead s 60(2)(i)(b) as the basis of his claim.

EFFECTS OF CONSTRUCTIVE TOTAL LOSS

Abandonment of subject matter insured

Outlining the general concept of abandonment when there is a constructive total loss, s 61 states:

> Where there is a constructive total loss, the assured may either treat the loss as a partial loss, or abandon the subject matter insured to the insurer and treat the loss as if it were an actual total loss.

Furthermore, s 62(1) then goes on to state that:

> Subject to the provisions of this section, where the assured elects to abandon the subject matter insured to the insurer, he must give notice of abandonment. If he fails to do so, the loss can only be treated as a partial loss.

It is emphasised that a constructive total loss can exist without the notice of abandonment being given, but, in general, the notice is a precondition to such a claim. If no such notice of abandonment is given, the assured may only claim for a partial loss.[13] In ***Western Assurance Company of Toronto v Poole* [1903] 1 KB 376**, discussed in full earlier in the context of reinsurance,[14] it was

---

13 A notice of abandonment is not a precondition for a constructive total loss of freight, as there is nothing to abandon to the insurers. In *Rankin v Potter* (1873) LR 6 HL 83, Brett J stated: '... on a policy on freight in general terms there need be no abandonment of freight, and no notice of abandonment is required ...'

14 See Chapter 2, p 64.

held that a shipowner may elect not to give notice of abandonment, and may, instead, sue for a partial loss.

> **Bigham J:** [p 384] ... Of course, the owner is not compellable to give any notice of abandonment; there is nothing in his policy which obliges him to divest himself of his property in the ship; and this is true whatever the extent of the damage may be. He can always keep his ship and claim for a partial loss, even though the cost of repairs may amount to 100% of the insured value. But if he elects to take this course, his claim is a claim for a partial loss only.

Meaning of abandonment

For a claim to be made for constructive total loss, the assured must abandon the ship or goods to the insurer by way of a notice of abandonment. In the context of the notice of abandonment, the meaning of 'abandon' is not the same as in the case of an abandonment of the subject matter insured as provided for in ss 57 and 60 of the Act. With a notice of abandonment, the abandonment is to the insurer, and constitutes the transfer of the subject matter insured from the assured to the insurer in return for a full indemnity.

Abandonment, in this context, was raised in ***Rankin v Potter* (1873) LR 6 HL 83**, where a vessel was so damaged in Calcutta that the charterer withdrew and there was a total loss of freight.

> **Brett J:** [p 101] ... The end to be obtained by abandonment would seem to be the preservation of the cardinal principle of marine insurance, the principle of indemnity, and to that end to prevent the assured from having at the same time payment in full of the sum insured, a thing of value, in his hands.

> **Blackburn J:** [p 119] ... In cases of marine insurance, the regular mercantile mode of letting the underwriters know that the assured mean to come upon them for a complete indemnity, is by giving notice of abandonment, which is a very different thing from the abandonment or cession itself. This notice, when given, is conclusive, that the assured is still in a situation to determine his election, has determined to come upon the underwriters for a total loss, the consequence of which is that everything is ceded (to avoid the use of the ambiguous word 'abandoned') to the underwriters. Abbott CJ, in *Cologan v London Assurance*, says: 'I do not consider an abandonment as having the effect of converting a partial into a total loss ... The abandonment, however, excludes any presumption which might have arisen from the silence of the assured that they still mean to adhere to the adventure as their own.'

In ***Kaltenbach v MacKenzie* (1878) 3 CPD 467**, where a vessel was abandoned in Saigon as a constructive total loss but no notice of abandonment was given, the court deliberated on the meaning and significance of abandonment.

> **Cotton LJ:** [p 479] ... When, as in the present case, the assured elects to treat the loss as a total loss, he is bound to transfer to the underwriters the subject matter insured. The general rule is that he must, as soon as he has the information which enables him to make his election, give notice to the underwriters that he has so elected. That rule is founded upon two grounds:

when the assured has once elected to treat the loss as a total loss, the underwriters can insist upon his abiding by the election, so as to enable them to take the benefit of any advantage which may arise from the thing insured. Therefore, the object of notice, which is entirely different from abandonment, is that he may tell the underwriters at once what he has done, and not keep it secret in his mind, to see if there will be a change of circumstances.

Notice of abandonment

The concept of notice of abandonment is unique to marine insurance, and is the means by which the assured may inform his insurer of his intention to renounce his rights in the property insured. The necessity of such a process was well illustrated by Brett LJ, in *Kaltenbach v MacKenzie*, below.

Kaltenbach v MacKenzie (1878) 3 CPD 467, CA

This was an appeal by the defendants against an earlier decision in the Court of Common Pleas. The vessel *Amiral Protet* was owned by the plaintiff, a merchant residing in Zurich, and insured with the defendants. On a voyage from Saigon to Hong Kong, *Amiral Protet* struck a shoal and was so damaged that she had to return to Saigon where, after she was surveyed, she was condemned as a constructive total loss on account of the repair costs being greater than her repaired value. She was later sold and put back into service. The plaintiff claimed for a constructive total loss, but the underwriters refused payment on the basis that they had received no notice of abandonment.

The court allowed the appeal, and ruled in favour of the insurers. There was some evidence to show that the underwriters had received a notice of abandonment, but even if they had, it was too late to be accepted. The court examined the reasoning behind the notice of abandonment, and why it was essential in marine insurance cases.

> **Brett LJ:** [p 471] ... With regard to the notice of abandonment, I am not aware that in any contract of indemnity, except in the case of contracts of marine insurance, a notice of abandonment is required. In the case of marine insurance where the loss is an actual total loss, no notice of abandonment is necessary; but in the case of constructive total loss it is necessary, unless it be excused. How, then, did it arise that a notice of abandonment was imported into a contract of marine insurance? Some judges have said that it is a necessary equity that the insurer, in the case of a constructive total loss, should have the option of being able to take such steps as he may think best for the preservation of the thing abandoned from further deterioration. I doubt if that is the origin of the necessity of giving a notice of abandonment. It seems to me to have been introduced into contracts of marine insurance – as many other stipulations have been introduced – by the consent of the shipowner and underwriter, and so to have become part of the contract, and a condition precedent to the validity of a claim for a constructive total loss. The reason why it was introduced by the shipowner and underwriter is on account of the

peculiarity of marine losses. These losses do not occur under the immediate notice of all the parties concerned. A loss may occur in any part of the world. It may occur under such circumstances that the underwriter can have no opportunity of ascertaining whether the information he received from the assured is correct or incorrect. The assured, if not present, would receive notice of the disaster from his agent, the master of the ship. The underwriter in general can receive no notice of what has occurred, unless from the assured, who is the owner of the ship or the owner of the goods, and there would, therefore, be a great danger if the owner of the ship or of goods – that is, the assured – might take any time that he pleased to consider whether he would claim for a constructive total loss or not – there would be great danger that he would be taking time to consider what the state of the market might be, or many other circumstances, and would throw upon the underwriter a loss if the market were unfavourable, or take to himself the advantage if the market were favourable.

Cotton LJ: [p 480] ... the object of notice, which is entirely different from abandonment, is that he may tell the underwriters at once what he has done, and not keep it secret in his mind, to see if there will be a change of circumstances. There is another reason: the thing in various ways may be profitably dealt with, as the ship was in this case. Therefore, the second reason for requiring notice of abandonment to be given to the underwriters is, that they may do, if they think fit, what in their opinion is best, and make the most they can out of that which is abandoned to them as the consequence of the election which the assured has come to.

Notice of abandonment applies only to the 'claim' for constructive total loss

Although there appears to have been some confusion in the past, it is emphasised that the notice of abandonment is a prerequisite of a 'claim' for a constructive total loss of a ship or goods. It is not an essential element of the constructive total loss itself.

In the pre-statute case of **Kaltenbach v MacKenzie (1878) 3 CPD 467, CA**, cited above, notice of abandonment was adjudged to be a 'condition precedent' to a claim for a constructive total loss.

Brett LJ: [p 478] ... It is the notice which is the symbol of the abandonment. That notice must be given within a particular time. In this case, it is obvious it was not. Therefore, although it must be assumed there were circumstances which entitled the assured to treat the loss as a total loss, and although it must be taken that at some time or other he did give notice of abandonment, yet in my opinion the evidence was beyond dispute that he did not give notice of abandonment at the proper time, and the giving notice in proper time, unless some excuse exists, is a condition precedent.

But, in *Roura and Forgas v Townend*, below, the insurers raised the issue of whether the notice of abandonment was an essential element of constructive total loss in general, rather than simply as a condition precedent to a 'claim' for constructive total loss by the owner of a ship or goods. Their reasoning was that, if the notice of abandonment was an essential element of a constructive total loss, the claim on chartered freight would fail, because no notice of abandonment had been given.

Roura and Forgas v Townend [1919] 1 KB 189

The plaintiffs chartered the Spanish vessel *Igotz Mendi* to carry a cargo of jute from Calcutta to Valencia. As they anticipated a large profit on the venture, the plaintiffs insured this profit on the charter with the defendants. Before *Igotz Mendi* arrived in Calcutta, she was captured, and the charter never materialised. But, because the actual fate of *Igotz Mendi* was a long time in being established, the plaintiffs were late in claiming on their policy of insurance for the loss of the chartered profit, and the insurers refused payment, on the basis that, *inter alia*, there had been no notice of abandonment.

The court decided that, with respect to chartered profit, the notice of abandonment was not an essential element of the constructive total loss, and the plaintiffs could recover.

> **Roche J:** [p 194] ... With regard to notice of abandonment by the shipowner, there was no dispute that, in general, such a notice is necessary. The point of debate was whether the giving of such notice is an integral element of a constructive total loss, or is rather a condition precedent to a claim by the owner of ship and goods based upon such a loss.
>
> ... A condition precedent to a right of action may well be dispensed with in a proper case, but such dispensation would seem to be a nugatory and indeed impossible process to apply to an essential element of a thing itself. As regards the present action, the scope of the defendants' argument is curious and far-reaching. Their counsel, when pressed on the point, did not shrink, and in this they were entirely logical, from the conclusion that here, since the shipowners were uninsured, and since in that state of facts no notice of abandonment by them was possible, there never could be a constructive total loss of this ship and the risk never attached. I do not find myself in agreement with the defendants' reasoning or their conclusions, and I accordingly decide against their contention on this part of the case.

However, any confusion about the role of the notice of abandonment was finally resolved by Lord Wright and Lord Porter in *Robertson v Petros M Nomikos Ltd* **[1939] AC 371, HL**. In this case, which is cited in full above, p 623, the plaintiffs had claimed for the total loss of chartered freight when the tanker in question was badly damaged by a boiler explosion and was unable to carry out the insured charter.

> **Lord Wright:** [p 381] ... In my opinion, notice of abandonment is not an essential ingredient of a constructive total loss. The appellant's argument confuses two different concepts, because it confuses constructive total loss with the right to claim for a constructive total loss. The right to claim, except in certain cases, depends on due notice of abandonment under s 62 of the Act. The distinction is explicitly stated in s 61 of the Marine Insurance Act, which is

as follows: 'Where there is a constructive total loss, the assured may either treat the loss as a partial loss, or abandon the subject matter insured to the insurer, and treat the loss as if it were an actual total loss.' The section makes it clear that the right to abandon only arises when there is a constructive total loss in fact. That is the necessary precondition to a right to abandon. The frame of the section makes it impossible to treat the right to abandon as identical with the constructive total loss. It is a superimposed right of election where there is a constructive total loss. Nor is it even a necessary ingredient of a constructive total loss, because though there is a constructive total loss, the assured may still treat it as a partial loss.

Lord Porter: [p 393] ... Having regard to the wording in s 61, abandonment may be a condition or consequence of recovery and not a condition precedent to the existence of a total loss, whether actual or constructive. A constructive total loss may exist, but if the assured wishes to take advantage of it, he must give notice of abandonment, at any rate in a case where there would be any possibility of benefit to the insurer. If he does give notice and the underwriters accept the abandonment, or if the assured recover as for a total loss, the property insured thereby becomes the property of the underwriters.

Exceptions to the requirement of a notice of abandonment

Notice of abandonment is not always a necessary precondition to a claim for a constructive total loss. There are instances where such a notice of abandonment would amount to nothing more than a pointless exercise or, in the words of three judges in one case, an 'idle ceremony'.[15] To this effect, s 62(7) of the Act states:

Notice of abandonment is unnecessary where, at the time when the assured receives information of the loss, there would be no possibility of benefit to the insurer if notice were given to him.

In addition, s 62(9) also states:

Where an insurer has reinsured his risk, no notice of abandonment need be given by him.

It is emphasised that, although s 62(7) appears simply to codify the common law as it was, it is suggested that the inclusion of the words 'no possibility of benefit to the insurer' has effectively widened the scope of application. It is now possible to claim for a constructive total loss of a ship or goods without giving a notice of abandonment, provided that that ship or those goods are of 'no benefit' to the insurer (see the *Litsion Pride* case, below, p 665).

However, in general, s 62(7) reflects the pre-statute authority that a notice of abandonment was unnecessary when there was nothing to abandon to the

---

15 See *Rankin v Potter* (1873) LR 6 HL 83, pp 111, 121 and 129.

insurer. This was clearly illustrated in ***Rankin v Potter* (1873) LR 6 HL, 83**, where a claim was advanced for a constructive total loss of chartered freight.

> **Brett J:** [p 99] ... It has never been suggested that the ship should be abandoned to the underwriter on freight. There is nothing then which can be abandoned to him of which he could take possession or from which he could derive profit.

But, on a cautionary note, in ***Kaltenbach v MacKenzie* (1878) 3 CPD 467, CA**, where a vessel was sold in Saigon after a survey and the plaintiff later suggested that a notice of abandonment was unnecessary because there was no longer anything to abandon, Brett LJ pointed out that, in this case, there actually was something to abandon, namely, the proceeds of the sale.

> **Brett LJ:** [p 474] ... In *Rankin v Potter*, the law was established that where at the time when the assured receives information which would otherwise oblige him to give notice of abandonment, at the same time he hears that the subject matter of the insurance has been sold so as to pass the property away, in as much as there was nothing of the subject matter of the insurance which he could abandon, notice of abandonment was not necessary. No doubt the reason given for this was that notice at that time and under such circumstances would be a mere idle ceremony; it could be of no use. That was the point decided in *Rankin v Potter*. In those particular circumstances, it was held that notice of abandonment need not be given, because there was nothing to abandon. That, in one sense, is true; but if goods had been sold, it is obvious there must be something to abandon, that is, the proceeds of the sale; the money which is the proceeds of the sale, when the insurance is settled, is abandoned; but where there is nothing of the subject matter of insurance to abandon, there is no ship to abandon, there are no goods to abandon, notice of abandonment under those circumstances was said to be futile.

In the post-statute case of ***Vacuum Oil Co v Union Insurance Society of Canton* (1926) 25 LlL Rep 546**, a cargo of tins of oil were declared a constructive total loss, but a claim for such was not valid, because there had been no notice of abandonment by the assured. An issue which arose was the wording contained in s 62(7) of the Act, namely, 'no possibility of benefit to the insurer'.

> **Bankes LJ:** [p 549] ... Now, in construing that section [s 62 of the Act] it must be borne in mind what the state of the law was at the time of the passing of the statute; and when the statute speaks of no possibility of benefit, it does not mean, as Mr Schiller suggests [for the cargo-owners], that in the events which have happened, the underwriter would have been no better off. What it means, as I understand it, and as I understand the law existing at the time when the statute was passed, is that when the circumstances are such that the underwriter, if the goods had been abandoned and he had had the absolute control over them, could have exercised that control and done what he thought best under the circumstances ... That is what I understand is aimed at by the words 'possibility of benefit'. But here, on the facts, it is perfectly obvious that the position of things was this, that if notice of abandonment had been given within a reasonable time, the underwriter had the fullest opportunity of

dealing with these goods: they were in existence in specie, they were being reconditioned for the purpose of sale for the benefit of whom it might concern, and they were in a condition in which, if notice of abandonment had been given within a reasonable time, there was every possibility of benefit to the insurer within the meaning of this sub-section, because there were the goods, and he could do what he liked with them.

More recently, in **Black King Shipping Corporation v Massie, 'Litsion Pride'** [1985] 1 Lloyd's Rep 437,[16] where a vessel was sunk by a missile during the war between Iraq and Iran, and part of the defence was that a notice of abandonment was not given, Hirst J was of the opinion that a notice of abandonment was immaterial in the circumstances. There was no possibility of benefit to the underwriters, in that they could not salvage the wreck because of the hostilities which were still taking place.

> **Hirst J:** [p 478] ... I hold that there was no possibility of benefit to the underwriters if notice of abandonment had been given, since any notion of salvage was completely impracticable by reason of the place where, and the wartime circumstances in which, this vessel was sunk.

Notice of abandonment when the ship or cargo is sold of necessity

Although it is now unlikely that a master would sell a vessel and her cargo without communicating with the owners, in times past this was often the case. Thus, it was possible for a constructive total loss to occur where the master, as agent of necessity, felt justified in selling the vessel and cargo because it was to the benefit of all concerned. In that instance, the notice of abandonment was a necessary prerequisite to the claim, but, where the sale was shown to be unjustified, the notice of abandonment was worthless.

In *Kaltenbach v MacKenzie* (1878) 3 CPD 467, where the ship was damaged near Saigon and then sold after a survey, Brett LJ was of the opinion that a constructive total loss must exist before a sale or notice of abandonment may be effected.

> **Brett LJ:** [p 476] ... A sale cannot make a total loss; notice of abandonment cannot enable the assured to recover for a total loss unless the sale was justifiable by the circumstances, and the circumstances were such as to justify a person in claiming for a total loss. The constructive total loss, in other words, must exist before the sale or the notice of abandonment; the circumstances must be such as to justify it.

---

16 This case is also discussed in Chapter 6, p 216, in relation to the doctrine of utmost good faith.

Notice of abandonment must be given in 'a reasonable time'

Section 62(3) of the Act states:

> Notice of abandonment may be given with reasonable diligence after the receipt of reliable information of the loss, but where the information is of a doubtful character, the assured is entitled to a reasonable time to make inquiry.

Thus, if the assured is in receipt of reliable information concerning the nature of the loss and the reason for it, he must be reasonably diligent in ensuring that the notice of abandonment is passed quickly to the insurer. But, when the assured is in some doubt about the information received, he is given a reasonable time to investigate the circumstances of the loss before giving such notice.[17]

In *Kaltenbach v MacKenzie* **(1878) 3 CPD 467**, above, Brett LJ deliberated at length on the time the assured may take in giving the notice of abandonment.

> **Brett LJ:** [p 472] ... Notice of abandonment, therefore, being a part of the contract, questions arose as to the time when that notice should be given. The first question which arose was whether the notice must be given at the first moment that the assured heard of the loss, or at some subsequent period. It was, however, decided that it is not at the moment of the first hearing of the loss that notice of abandonment must be given, but that the assured must have a reasonable time to ascertain the nature of the loss with which he is made acquainted; if he hears merely that his ship is damaged, that may not be enough to enable him to decide whether he ought to abandon or not; he must have certain and accurate information as to the nature of the damage. Now, sometimes, the information which he receives discloses at once the imminent danger of the subject matter of insurance becoming and continuing a total loss; as, for instance, if he hears his ship is captured in time of war; it must be obvious to everybody, unless the ship is recaptured, it would be a total loss; or if he hears that the ship is stranded, and her back is broken, although she retains her character as a ship, if he gets information upon which any reasonable man must conclude that there is very imminent danger of her being lost, the moment he gets that information he must immediately give notice of abandonment. The law that has been laid down is, that immediately the assured has reliable information of such damage to the subject matter of insurance as there is imminent danger of its becoming a total loss, then he must at once, unless there is some reason to the contrary, give notice of abandonment; but if the information which he first receives is not sufficient to enable him to say whether there is that imminent danger, then he has a reasonable time to acquire full information as to the state and nature of the damage done to the ship.

---

17 Section 88 of the Act states: 'Where by this Act any reference is made to reasonable time, reasonable premium, or reasonable diligence, the question what is reasonable is a question of fact.'

But, in *Rickards v Forestal Land, Timber and Railways Co Ltd* [1941] 3 All ER 52, HL, where the cargo aboard a German ship was lost when she was scuttled to avoid capture, Lord Wright suggested that a 'reasonable time' did not include giving the assured time to see how things panned out in order to decide what best suited his interests.

> **Lord Wright:** [p 79] ... If the assured elects to avail himself of this option [constructive total loss], he must do so by giving notice of abandonment within a reasonable time after the receipt of sufficient information. He is not allowed to await events to see how things turn out or to decide what may best suit his interests. If he duly elects to abandon on good grounds, the risk is ended, because the assured can recover as for a total loss, and the salvage vests in the underwriter.

Form of notice of abandonment

Section 62(2) of the Act states:

> Notice of abandonment may be given in writing, or by word of mouth, or partly in writing and partly by word of mouth, and may be given in any terms which indicate the intention of the assured to abandon his insured interest in the subject matter insured unconditionally to the insurer.

In the old case of *Parmeter v Todhunter* (1808) 1 Camp 540, a vessel and her cargo were sold after being captured and then recaptured. The assured gave no express notice of abandonment when he claimed for a constructive total loss. Although the policy was on freight, the goods still existed, and the court ruled that it could not be a constructive total loss unless notice of abandonment was given. Lord Ellenborough laid down guidelines for the form in which abandonment should take place.

> **Lord Ellenborough:** [p 542] There is no implied abandonment by a demand of a total loss. It would be very well to prevent parol abandonments entirely; but if they are allowed, I must insist upon their being express. An implied parol abandonment is too uncertain, and cannot be supported. The abandonment must be express and direct, and I think the word 'abandon' should be used to render it effectual.

Acceptance of the notice of abandonment

Section 62(5) of the Act states:

> The acceptance of an abandonment may be either express or implied from the conduct of the insurer. The mere silence of the insurer after notice is not an acceptance.

The assured may, at any time, withdraw his notice of abandonment if he so wishes, but the insurer, once he has accepted the notice, cannot withdraw, and is bound by his acceptance. For that reason, and others, a notice of abandonment is rarely accepted by the insurers when it is first issued, and it is the normal practice of insurers merely to acknowledge receipt of the notice and inform the assured that he will be placed in the same position as if a writ had been issued.

In *Pesquerias y Secaderos de Bacalao de Espana SA v Beer* (1946) 79 LlL Rep 417, where Spanish trawlers were seized at the outset of the Spanish Civil War and abandoned as constructive total losses, Atkinson J, at the court of first instance, put forward the position of the assured whilst awaiting the acceptance of the abandonment by the insurers when he stated:

> **Atkinson J:** [p 433] ... until it [the notice of abandonment] is accepted, the assured has the right to look for intervening events which may restore in whole or in part his former situation, and may limit his claim accordingly if it suits him better to claim as for a partial loss.

However, it is emphasised that, under cl 11.3 of the ITCH(95) and cl 9.3 of the IVCH(95), both the assured and the insurer may take measures to mitigate any damage without altering their status. The clause states:

> Measures taken by the Assured or the Underwriters with the object of saving, protecting or recovering the subject matter insured shall not be considered as a waiver or acceptance of abandonment or otherwise prejudice the rights of either party.

ADEMPTION OF LOSS

Ademption of loss is where the subject matter insured is restored to the assured before the action for a claim is commenced, thereby changing the basis of that claim. This could happen when a seizure takes place and the subsequent claim for a constructive total loss is precluded by the return of the subject matter to the assured. However, once the action has commenced, the claim persists in full. Thus, it is imperative that a cut-off date for ademption be established, after which the claim for constructive total loss persists regardless of a change in circumstances.

This issue was raised in *Ruys v Royal Exchange Assurance Corporation*, below, where Collins J decided that the cut-off date for ademption was the date when the action commenced, and that date was the date of the issuing of the writ.

Ruys v Royal Exchange Assurance Corporation [1897] 2 QB 135

During the war between Italy and Abyssinia, the plaintiffs insured the ship *Doelwyk* with the defendants under a war risks policy of insurance and dispatched her with a cargo of arms for the King of Abyssinia. *Doelwyk* was captured by an Italian cruiser, and the plaintiffs gave notice of abandonment. One week after the notice of abandonment, the plaintiffs commenced the court action by issuing the writ, but, soon afterwards, *Doelwyk* was released into the safe keeping of the underwriters as the war had come to an end. The question before the court was whether, after the date of the issuing of the writ and the commencement of the action, the rights of the parties should be altered by the return of the insured ship.

The court ruled that the return of the ship after the commencement of the action did not disentitle the plaintiffs from claiming for a constructive total loss.

> **Collins J:** [p 137] ... After the date of the writ, the vessel was taken before a prize court at Rome, which on 8 December following, pronounced that she was lawful prize. The war, however, being then over, it did not decree the confiscation of the ship or cargo, and she has since been taken over under an arrangement with the underwriters for the benefit of all concerned. Can the defendants rely on these facts occurring after action as diminishing their liability, or must the rights of the parties be ascertained as at the date of the writ? The state of the authorities appears to be as follows. In *Hamilton v Mendes*, news of the capture and recapture of the ship reached the assured at the same time. He thereupon gave notice of abandonment, which the underwriters rejected. Lord Mansfield held that he could not recover. He says: 'The plaintiff's demand is for an indemnity. His action then must be founded upon the nature of his damnification as it really is at the time the action is brought. It is repugnant, upon a contract of indemnity, to recover as for a total loss when the final event has decided that the damnification in truth is an average, or perhaps no loss at all.' Later on he says: 'I desire it may be understood, that the point here determined is that the plaintiff upon a policy can only recover an indemnity according to the nature of his case *at the time of the action brought*, or, at most, at the time of his offer to abandon.'
>
> [p 142] ... I have now, I think, exhausted the authorities. The text-writers, without exception so far as I know, treat it as settled law that the rights of the parties must be ascertained as at the date of the action brought ... But, the object of litigation being to settle disputes, it is obvious that some date must be fixed upon when the respective rights of the parties may be finally ascertained, and the line of the writ may be regarded as a line of convenience which has been settled by uniform practice for at least 70 years (see this point well treated: Arnould, 6th edn, Vol I, p 15).

A year later, in *Sailing Ship Blairmore Co Ltd v Macredie, 'Blairmore'* [1898] AC 593, Lord Herschell agreed that the cut-off date for ademption was when the action commenced, but he did not confirm that that date was the date of the issuing of the writ.

> **Lord Herschell:** [p 610] ... I take it, then, that the general rule applicable is, according to the law of this country, that if in the interval between the notice of abandonment and the time when legal proceedings are commenced, there has been a change in circumstances reducing the loss from a total to a partial one, or, in other words, if at the time of action brought, the circumstances are such that a notice of abandonment would be justifiable, the assured can only recover for a partial loss.

Similarly, in ***Polurrian Steamship Co v Young* [1915] 1 KB 922, CA**, where a neutral ship was seized by the Greek authorities for carrying contraband, Warrington J again agreed that the cut-off date for ademption was the commencement of the action, but, again, failed to confirm that that date was the date of the issuing of the writ.

> **Warrington J:** [p 935] ... But, if the taking of the vessel, lawful or unlawful, out of the possession of the owner was, at the date of the commencement of the owner's action to enforce his notice of abandonment, a taking which still continued in operation, and the owner's loss of the use and disposal of the ship, once total, was at that date one which might be permanent, and was, at any rate, of uncertain continuance, the owner who had duly given notice of abandonment was held by English law entitled to recover upon his insurance for a constructive total loss.

But, in ***Rickards v Forestal Land, Timber and Railways Co Ltd* [1941] 3 All ER 52, HL**, where the cargo aboard a German ship was lost when she was scuttled to avoid capture, the House of Lords confirmed that the issuing of the writ by the plaintiff to enforce his claim for a constructive total loss was the date that the action may be said to have commenced.

> **Lord Wright:** [p 80] ... By the English common law, the date of giving notice of abandonment was not treated as the decisive date, which was taken to be the date of issuing the writ in the action.

Notes

Although many countries have used the date of the issuing of the notice of abandonment as the cut-off date for ademption (see *Sailing Ship Blairmore Co v Macredie, 'Blairmore'* [1898] AC 593, *per* Lord Herschell, p 609), the law of England has maintained that the date of the issuing of the writ is the relevant date. In practice, this makes little difference, as it is the normal practice of the underwriters, on receiving the notice of abandonment, to put the assured in the same position as if a writ had been issued (see *Panamanian Oriental SS Corp v Wright, 'Anita* '[1970] 2 Lloyd's Rep 355, p 379; *The Bamburi* [1982] 1 Lloyd's Rep 312, p 314).

The waiver clause

Clause 11.3 of the ITCH(95) and cl 9.3 of the IVCH(95) ensure that the position of the parties remains the same regardless of whether one party chooses to make any effort to alter the status of the subject matter insured. It states:

> Measures taken by the Assured or the Underwriters with the object of saving, protecting or recovering the subject matter insured shall not be considered as a waiver or acceptance of abandonment or otherwise prejudice the rights of either party.

This provision within the Institute Hulls Clauses is in line with the ruling in the *Blairmore* case, above, where an attempt by the insurers to change a total loss into a partial loss by undertaking salvage operations on their own account, without the consent of the shipowner, was held not to have any effect on the claim.

CHAPTER 17

PARTIAL LOSS – 1

PARTICULAR AVERAGE LOSS

Introduction

The subject of partial loss is, for the purpose of clarity, dealt with in two chapters. This chapter will consider the nature of particular average loss, and Chapter 18 will consider extraordinary expenses, such as salvage charges, general average and particular charges, commonly referred to as sue and labour. Particular average losses are losses which are directly sustained by the subject matter insured caused by an insured peril, generally described as losses which lie where they fall. Salvage charges, general average and particular charges, on the other hand, are extraordinary expenses incurred in an emergency, as a consequence of damage caused by an insured peril. Though salvage charges are, strictly speaking, particular average losses and are recoverable as such[1] – as a loss caused by the peril which has necessitated the expenditure – they are, nonetheless, extraordinary expenses and, therefore, may be more conveniently discussed together with general average and particular charges to which comparisons would have to be made.

Meaning of partial loss

A partial loss is any loss other than a total loss, and, to this effect, s 56(1) of the Marine Insurance Act states:

> A loss may be either total or partial. Any loss other than a total loss, as hereinafter defined, is a partial loss.

A partial loss may include a particular average loss, a general average loss and particular charges. Thus, there are two distinct types of partial loss:

(a) a particular average loss, where the subject matter insured is injured by a peril insured against and the loss falls directly upon the person who has suffered that loss;

(b) extraordinary expenses arising from the casualty which may include a general average loss, salvage charges and particular charges (sue and labour).

---

1 See MIA 1906, s 65(1).

Thus, a partial loss may arise out of any of the above and, typically, may be described as a partial loss by way of particular average damage.

Meaning of particular average loss

Section 56(1) of the Marine Insurance Act 1906 states that: 'Any loss other than a total loss, as hereinafter defined, is a partial loss.' Section 64(1) then goes on to affirm that:

> A particular average loss is a partial loss of the subject matter insured, caused by a peril insured against, and which is not a general average loss.

It is emphasised that 'particular average' is not simply another name for a partial loss. A particular average loss is a form of partial loss, but does not include a general average loss or particular charges.

Particular average is separate from general average

A particular average loss is a loss which falls directly upon the party who has suffered that loss. A general average loss, on the other hand, is one where the loss falls initially upon the party who has incurred the loss, but is, ultimately, borne proportionately by all the parties interested in the adventure who have benefited from the general average expenditure or sacrifice. Those who have stood to gain have to make a contribution known as a general average contribution.

The difference between a particular average loss and a general average loss was summed up in *Hingston v Wendt*, below.

Hingston v Wendt (1876) 1 QBD 367

The German brigantine *Theodor* stranded near to Dartmouth in Devon, and the master put the plaintiff, a local shipping agent, in charge of the stranded vessel for the benefit of all concerned. Although *Theodor* could not be saved, the plaintiff accrued considerable expenses in removing the cargo, and later sought to recover that expenditure from the defendant, who was the bill of lading holder at the time of the casualty.

The court ruled that the plaintiff could recover his expenditure, as his actions had been 'analogous to general average and salvage, in both of which there was a lien'. The court saw fit to differentiate between general average and particular average.

> **Blackburn J:** [p 371] ... In insurance law, the phrase 'general average' is commonly used to express what is chargeable on all, ship, cargo, and freight, and 'particular average', to express a charge against some one thing.

Particular average does not include particular charges

Section 64(2) of the Act defines 'particular charges' thus:

> Expenses incurred by or on behalf of the assured for the safety or preservation of the subject matter insured, other than general average and salvage charges, are called particular charges. Particular charges are not included in particular average.

Particular charges are expenses incurred in trying to minimise damage or loss already sustained by the subject matter insured. Whereas particular average is a loss or damage brought about by a peril insured against, a particular charge is the expenditure then incurred in mitigating that loss or damage. Particular charges do not include general average expenditures, because these are recoverable by way of contribution from the other interested parties; nor do they include any salvage charges which are incurred, because such charges are recoverable as part of the particular average loss which necessitated the salvage.

Unlike a particular average loss which may be directly recoverable as a loss caused by a peril insured against, any particular charges incurred, consequent on that loss, are recoverable as 'sue and labour' under s 78.

Particular average includes salvage charges

Salvage charges, which are non-contractual in nature and incurred on a 'no cure, no pay' basis (s 65(2)), are included within the umbrella of a 'particular average' loss. This is because the right to salvage developed independently of contract as part of the 'law maritimes', under which salvors offer their services voluntarily, and must be successful in order to be paid. Such salvage charges are then recoverable under s 65(1) as having been incurred in preventing a loss by perils insured against.

Any charges for salvage incurred on a strictly contractual basis are not recoverable as a particular average loss, and must, thus, be recovered either as a particular charge (under the auspices of sue and labour), or as general average according to the circumstances of the case.

PARTIAL LOSS OF A SHIP

When damage occurs to a ship, the loss sustained by her owner may be total, actual or constructive, or partial. Whilst total loss is self-descriptive and usually easy to establish, there is often a fine dividing line separating a constructive total loss from a partial loss.

When a vessel is so damaged that the cost of repairs is less than the 'repaired value'[2] of that ship, any claim would be for a partial loss. On the other hand, if the cost of repairs were to exceed the repaired value of the ship, the ship could be declared a constructive total loss and any claim could be based as such. However, in such an event, even though the shipowner may have the right to claim for a constructive total loss, he has, by virtue of s 61, also the option to claim for a particular loss should he so wish.[3]

However, it is emphasised that, even when a partial loss occurs, the insurer is, regardless of whether the policy is warranted free of particular average, still liable for salvage charges, particular charges and other expenses properly incurred under the sue and labour clause. On this point, s 76(2) states:

> Where the subject matter insured is warranted free from particular average, either wholly or under a certain percentage, the insurer is nevertheless liable for salvage charges, and for particular charges and other expenses properly incurred pursuant to the provisions of the suing and labouring clause in order to avert a loss insured against.

Measure of indemnity

With any claim for a partial loss, there are always a number of options open to the assured under the law of marine insurance, and, depending upon the option chosen, the amount that may then be claimed under the policy represents 'the measure of indemnity'.

The options available to an assured in the event of a partial loss and the measure of indemnity applicable were discussed in the pre-statute case of **Pitman v Universal Marine Insurance Co (1882) 9 QBD 192**, where a vessel was damaged and then sold in her damaged state.[4]

> **Brett LJ:** [p 208] ... The following propositions are all, I think, recognised as true in insurance law. The insured is not under any circumstances bound to sell his ship. The assured may under any circumstances sell his ship. He is entitled under any circumstances to repair his ship. He is not bound under any circumstances to repair his ship. In none of these respects does any question arise as to whether a prudent owner uninsured would act in the like manner. All this is so, because there is nothing in the contract of insurance which takes away from the assured the absolute power and right to do with his own property what he will. The assured, therefore, can always, whatever be the amount of damage done to his ship, repair her. If he does repair and keep the

---

2 Under s 27(3) and common law, the market value is to be taken as the repaired value, whereas, under the ITCH(95) and IVCH(95), the insured value is to be compared with the cost of repairs. See Chapter 16, p 647.

3 See *Western Assurance Co of Toronto v Poole* [1903] 1 KB 376.

4 This case is discussed in depth later in this chapter, p 693.

ship, there cannot be a total loss; the loss must then be a partial or average loss leaving open the question of how such loss is to be adjusted.

Cotton LJ: [p 215] ... As a general rule, where there is a partial loss in consequence of injury to a vessel by reason of perils insured against, the insured is entitled to recover the sum properly expended in executing the necessary repairs, or, if the work has not been done, the estimated expense of the necessary repairs ...

Surprisingly, s 69 of the Act only allows for three methods of computing the measure of indemnity for a partial loss:

(a) a ship which has been wholly repaired;

(b) a ship which has been only partially repaired; and

(c) a ship which has not been repaired and has not been sold in her damaged state during the risk.

The fourth scenario, namely 'a ship which has not been repaired, but has been sold in her damaged state during the risk', referred to in the *Pitman* case, above, is not mentioned in the Act but is, obviously, still relevant.

Thus, when examining the subject of measure of indemnity, all four methods of computation should be taken into account, and the task may be simplified by dividing any such measure of indemnity into two distinct categories: repaired and unrepaired damage.

The Deductible Clause

Clause 12.1 of the ITCH(95) states:[5]

No claim arising from a peril insured against shall be payable under this insurance unless the aggregate of all such claims arising out of each separate accident or occurrence (including claims under cll 8, 10 and 11) exceeds the deductible amount agreed in which case this sum shall be deducted. Nevertheless the expense of sighting the bottom after stranding, if reasonably incurred specially for that purpose, shall be paid even if no damage be found. This Clause 12.1 shall not apply to a claim for total or constructive total loss of the Vessel or, in the event of such a claim, to any associated claim under cl 11 arising from the same accident or occurrence.

The intention of the Deductible Clause is to exclude small claims below a certain value from the policy. This effectively means that the assured is self-insured up to the agreed value in return for which his premium is adjusted. It is stressed that the Deductible Clause is an 'excess' clause, whereby the insurer has no liability until the threshold set by the policy is surpassed. It is also emphasised that the Deductible Clause is applicable to all types of partial loss, including third party damage (3/4ths collision liability), general average, salvage and sue and labour which are connected with such a loss.

---

5 Equivalent IVCH(95), cl 10.1.

Repaired damage

When an insured vessel is damaged, the owner may elect to repair all, or just part of the damage sustained.

Should he decide to repair all of the damage, the measure of indemnity applicable is covered by s 69(1), which states that:

> Where a ship is damaged, but is not totally lost, the measure of indemnity, subject to any express provision in the policy, is as follows:
>
> (1) where the ship has been repaired, the assured is entitled to the reasonable cost of the repairs, less the customary deductions, but not exceeding the sum insured in respect of any one casualty.

On the other hand, should the owner decide to repair only part of the damage sustained, the relevant measure of indemnity falls under s 69(2), which affirms that:

> (2) where the ship has been only partially repaired, the assured is entitled to the reasonable cost of such repairs, computed as above, and also to be indemnified for the reasonable depreciation, if any, arising from the unrepaired damage, provided that the aggregate shall not exceed the cost of repairing the whole damage, computed as above.

Thus, the measure of indemnity for repaired damage is computed in the same way, regardless of whether the vessel is wholly repaired or partly repaired.

Reasonable cost of repairs

It is well established in insurance law that the owner of a ship is entitled to recover the reasonable cost of repairs. Furthermore, case law has clarified what may now be included in those costs of repairs.

Expenses of docking

The expense of dry-docking can be considerable, and it is now established that, when determining the extent of the loss, such expenditure may be added to the costs of repair. Such was the issue in the *Vancouver* case, below, where the question before the court was whether dry-docking expenses could be apportioned between the shipowner and the insurers when both routine maintenance and repairs to insured damage were carried out at the same time.

Marine Insurance Co v China Transpacific SS Co, 'Vancouver' (1886) 11 App Cas 573, HL

On a voyage from Hong Kong to San Francisco, the steamship *Vancouver* encountered severe weather, as a result of which she sustained slight damage, including a leak, the source of which could not be identified. Whilst in San Francisco, *Vancouver* was dry-docked to have her hull scraped and painted, and it was only during this dry-docking that it was found that the cause of the leak was a fractured stern-post. The owners claimed on their policy of insurance for the whole of the cost for dry-docking, or a proportion of the cost. As the policy was warranted 'free from average under 3%', the inclusion of the dry-dock charges was vital to the claim.

The House of Lords, affirming the decision of the Court of Appeal, decided that the dry-dock charges should be apportioned between the routine maintenance carried out by the owners and the repair costs for which the insurers were liable. The additional cost of the apportioned dry-docking charges then ensured that the underwriters were liable for a particular average loss, as the total amount of repair costs then amounted to more than 3% of the insured value.

> **Lord Esher MR:** [p 576] ... If you find that the loss to the assured would have been less than 3% as compared with the value in the policy, the underwriter is not liable at all. If you find that the loss exceeds 3%, then the condition is fulfilled, and the underwriter has to pay the whole of the average loss. Therefore the question here must be, what was the loss to the assured in respect of the sea damage, considering it as if the 3% clause was not in the policy; that is, we must arrive at what was the real loss first ... The difficulty in this case arises thus: in order to repair the damage to the stern-post, it was in fact necessary that the ship should go into dry-dock. The ship had a foul bottom, which had not been caused by perils of the sea. It was equally necessary that she should go into dock for the purpose of curing that defect, if it was to be cured, and she did in fact go into the same dry-dock for that purpose.
>
> [p 578] ... Supposing the ship had gone in and had only cleaned her bottom, for every day she was in the dock for that purpose she would have had to pay the whole sum. If the ship had gone into the dock for the purpose of repairing the stern-post only, she would, for every day she was in, have to pay the whole of the dock dues. The use of the dock whilst both these transactions were going on board the ship at the same time, was not increased or diminished in the least by the increase of the work done on the ship during the same time ... The dock dues were certainly part of the cost of the repairs if nothing else happens; the cost of the repairs is the cost of the workmen upon the ship, and the materials, and the payments for the use of the dock, which is a necessary preliminary to being able to do the other work. Therefore, if half of these dock expenses during the common days is paid by the shipowner in respect of the repairs to the stern-post, that half is part of the cost of repairing the stern-post, in other words, is part of the cost of repairing the loss which was occasioned by the sea peril; and if that half is to be so attributed, then what this shipowner paid for repairs was larger than 3% of the value of the ship in the policy. The condition is satisfied, and the underwriter is liable to pay the amount of the average loss.

The question of apportionment of dry-docking expenses was again raised in *Ruabon Steamship Co Ltd v London Assurance*, below.

Ruabon Steamship Co Ltd v London Assurance [1900] AC 6, HL

During a voyage, *Ruabon*, which was owned by the appellants, suffered damage for which the respondent underwriters were liable. In order to undertake the necessary repairs, *Ruabon* was placed in dry-dock, and the owners then added the costs of the dry-docking and a Lloyd's survey to the cost of repairs claimed under the policy. The underwriters rejected the costs, and contended that the cost of the dry-docking should be apportioned between themselves and the assured.

The court ruled that the survey fees could not be charged to the underwriters, as no classification survey was necessary. However, the cost of the dry-docking could be added to the cost of repairs for which the underwriters were liable. The insurers were held liable for dry-docking fees as part of the cost of repairs. But the owners, who had other work, additional to the repair work, done on the ship, were held liable for their proportion of the dry-docking fees.

> **Lord Brampton:** [p 17] ... *Ruabon* was dry-docked solely to enable the underwriters to effect the repairs for which they were liable and with no other object, and no other repair was, in fact, done or required to be done on the ship; the survey of Lloyd's surveyor was in no way necessary for any purpose connected with the work performed on the vessel, and was only made to entitle the owners to reclassification at Lloyd's and need not have been made at that moment, or at any particular time, so long as it was made within the time limited by Lloyd's rules, which had then nine months to run ... Assuming, however, that the expense of another dry-docking was in this way saved, and to that extent the owners were benefited, I think that circumstance is immaterial, and does not warrant a claim for contribution towards the dock dues imperatively incurred on the underwriters' account in the discharge of their obligations. I think that such contribution can only be insisted upon in those cases where work is done to the vessel itself, by two or more persons, each separately and simultaneously engaged under different obligations in doing portions of it, dry-docking being necessary for each.

Bottom treatment

Clause 15 of the ITCH(95)[6] is inserted to ensure that a claim for repairs does not, in general, cover treatment of the ship's bottom unless the treatment is preparatory to the repairs or as a result of those repairs. Clause 15 is careful to specify the type of bottom treatment covered by the policy:

> In no case shall a claim be allowed in respect of scraping, gritblasting and/or other surface preparation or painting of the Vessel's bottom except that:
>
> 15.1 gritblasting and/or other surface preparation of new bottom plates shore and supplying and applying any 'shop' primer thereto;
>
> 15.2 gritblasting and/or other surface preparation of:

---

6 See, also, IVCH(95), cl 13.

the butts or area of plating immediately adjacent to any renewed or refitted plating damaged during the course of welding and/or repairs;

areas of plating damaged during the course of fairing, either in place or ashore;

15.3 supplying and applying the first coat of primer/anti-corrosive to those particular areas mentioned in 15.1 and 15.2 above,

shall be allowed as part of the reasonable cost of repairs in respect of bottom plating damaged by an insured peril.

These provisions are in keeping with the precept of reasonable cost, whereby the insurer is only liable for the cost of repairs pursuant to the damage caused by a peril insured against.

To this effect, in *Field Steamship Co Ltd v Burr* [1899] 1 QB 579, CA, where, after a collision, a shipowner tried to claim from a hull underwriter for expenses incurred in dealing with damaged cargo, AL Smith LJ remarked: [p 586] '... All he [the insurer] has to do under his contract is to make good to the insured shipowner the deterioration occasioned to the hull and machinery of his ship by a sea peril, and nothing more.'

Crew's wages and provisions

Clause 16 of the ITCH(95) states that:[7]

No claim shall be allowed, other than in general average, for wages and maintenance of the Master, Officers and Crew or any member thereof, except when incurred solely for the necessary removal of the Vessel from one port to another for the repair of damage covered by the Underwriters, or for trial trips for such repairs, and then only for such wages and maintenance as are incurred whilst the Vessel is underway.

The provision, therefore, is again based upon the underwriters accepting liability for any reasonable expenditure incurred in crew's wages for the 'specific' purpose of moving a vessel to a place where the insured damage may be repaired. From past authorities, it is clear that it is not possible to recover crew's wages or expenditure on provisions as part of the cost of repairs.

Robertson v Ewer (1786) 1 Term Rep 127

The plaintiff insured his ship *Dumfries* with the defendants under a voyage policy of insurance from London to the coast of Africa and thence to the West Indies. The policy included a clause which stated that cover was included for '... detainments of kings, princes, and people of what nation soever'. When *Dumfries* arrived at Barbados with a cargo of slaves, she was prevented from sailing to Jamaica by an embargo on all shipping. The master of *Dumfries*

---

7 See, also, IVCH(95), cl 14.

ignored the embargo and sailed, but was chased down and brought back by the naval sloop *Salamander*. The crew were taken off the ship and dispersed amongst his Majesty's ships of war, and the slaves had to be taken ashore because of an outbreak of smallpox. For all these reasons, *Dumfries* was detained in Barbados for over two months, and the owners claimed on their policy of insurance for crew's wages and provisions.

The court ruled that crew's wages and provisions were not part of the insurance cover. Buller J also referred specifically to the instance where a ship may be detained whilst undergoing repairs to insured damage.

> **Lord Mansfield CJ:** [p 132] There is no authority to show that, on this policy, the insured can recover for such a loss; but it is contrary to the constant practice. On a policy on a ship, sailors' wages or provisions are never allowed in settling the damages. The insurance is on the body of the ship, tackle, and furniture; not on the voyage or crew.
>
> **Buller J:** [p 132] I take it to be perfectly well settled that the insured cannot recover seamen's wages or provisions on a policy on the body of the ship; those are not the subject of the insurance. The case put by the plaintiff's counsel proves the rule. For, if the ship had been detained in consequence of any injury which she had received in a storm, though the underwriter must have made good that damage, yet the insured could not have come upon him for the amount of wages or provisions during the time that she was so repairing.

In **De Vaux v Salvador (1836) 4 Ad&E 420**, where a vessel suffered collision damage and was detained in Calcutta awaiting arbitration, the court again ruled out crew's wages and provisions as part of the shipowner's claim.

> **Lord Denman CJ:** [p 430] ... We think it clear, on authority, that the former item [the claim for crew's wages and provisions] ought not to be allowed. As long ago as 1769, in *Fletcher v Poole* (1 Park, Ins Ch Ii, 7th edn, p 89), the point was decided by Lord Mansfield at *Nisi Prius*. The doctrine has been cited in the textbooks ever since that period, and is expressly recognised by Buller J, in *Robertson v Ewer* (1 TR 132).

In **Helmville Ltd v Yorkshire Insurance Co Ltd, 'Medina Princess' [1965] 1 Lloyd's Rep 361**, where the owners of a vessel claimed for both a partial and constructive total loss when they alleged that her engines had been badly damaged by negligence, Roskill J affirmed that the leading cases precluded recovery of crew's wages as part of the cost of repairs when he declared:

> **Roskill J:** [p 523] ... the decisions in *Robinson v Ewer* (1786) 1 TR 182; (1786) 99 ER 1111, and *de Vaux v Salvador* (1836) 4 A&E 420; (1836) 111 ER 845, place insuperable difficulties in the way of the plaintiffs' recovering crew's wages during repairs as part of the cost of repairs. Moreover, there is nothing to show that such crew would have done any work the cost of which would have been recoverable from hull underwriters. This part of the claim has been wholly disallowed.

Partial Loss – 1

Surveyor's fees

It is well established that surveyor's fees, provided that they are reasonable, may be included in the cost of repairs. But, in *Agenoria Steamship Co Ltd v Merchants' Marine Insurance Co Ltd*, below, the cost of sending a surveyor from England to Australia for relatively minor repairs was considered unreasonable, and the claim was adjusted accordingly.

Agenoria Steamship Co Ltd v Merchants' Marine Insurance Co Ltd (1903) 8 Com Cas 212

On a voyage from Australia to New Zealand, the steamship *Elmville* was damaged by both bad weather and striking a reef and, after being temporarily repaired in Auckland, she was dispatched to Melbourne, where she was repaired permanently. When the owners claimed on their policy of insurance, they included in their claim the cost of sending a surveyor from England to represent them. The underwriters contended, *inter alia*, that the repairs could have been done in an equally efficient manner without the additional cost.

The court decided that the owners were entitled to the cost of a surveyor, but that a local one would have sufficed in the circumstances. Thus, the owners could only claim £100, and not the £756 claimed for sending a surveyor from England.

> **Kennedy J:** [p 214] ... The effect of the evidence upon my mind is that the question of the chargeability to the underwriters of the cost of a surveyor sent out from this country by the owners in connection with the damage repairs of an insured vessel at a foreign port as their representative is rightly held in practice to depend in each case upon the particular circumstances.
>
> [p 215] ... It seems to me in these circumstances I cannot properly saddle the underwriters, after their clear protest against the adoption of such a course, with the expense of £756 for a superintendent of £4,000 of work ...

Similarly, in *Helmville Ltd v Yorkshire Insurance Co Ltd*, *'Medina Princess'* **[1965] 1 Lloyd's Rep 361**, where the owners of a vessel claimed for both a partial and constructive total loss when they alleged that her engines had been badly damaged by negligence, the surveyors' fees were held to be part of the reasonable cost of repairs.

> **Roskill J:** [p 523] ... Mr Brandon [for the insurers] accepted, on the authority of *Agenoria Steamship Co Ltd v Merchants' Marine Insurance Co Ltd*, that reasonable fees for classification surveyors and other surveyors were properly allowable as part of the cost of repairs. Those surveyors' fees which I have allowed have been allowed on the strength of that authority.

Temporary repairs and costs incurred for towage to a suitable port for repairs

Again, in *Helmville Ltd v Yorkshire Insurance Co Ltd*, *'Medina Princess'* **[1965] 1 Lloyd's Rep 361**, where the vessel was incapacitated due to machinery damage at Djibouti in the Gulf of Aden, the court ruled that the cost of repairs did not include the crew's wages or expenses incurred in discharging cargo, but they did include the damage to the machinery, dry-docking charges, surveyors' fees and the cost of a tow to Karachi where the necessary repairs could be carried out. Reference was also made to temporary repairs.

> **Roskill J:** [p 520] ... Devlin J [in *Irvin v Hine*] had to consider both constructive total loss (which he rejected) and partial loss (which he accepted). The learned judge quite clearly and specifically admitted the cost of temporary repairs and of towage as part of the cost of repairs for the purposes of s 69(3) ... I have arrived at my conclusion without further reference to *Armar*, above [an American case [1954] 2 Lloyd's Rep 95] to which I have already referred. I ought, however, to observe that the learned judge in that case included the cost of both towage and temporary repairs for partial loss purposes. It follows that, on my findings of fact, towage from Djibouti to Karachi would have been necessary in order to repair the ship.

Expenses consequential on or arising out of the damage sustained

Both the Act and the Institute Hull Clauses are silent on the matter of consequential losses, but it appears unlikely that an underwriter would be liable for losses or expenditure arising out of particular average damage, unless that additional loss or expenditure could be reasonably considered as part of the cost of repairs.

Thus, in *Field v Burr* **[1899] 1 QB 571**, where a shipowner tried to claim from a hull underwriter for expenses incurred, after a collision, in dealing with damaged cargo, AL Smith LJ remarked:

> **AL Smith LJ:** [p 585] ... Whether the cargo be sound, or partially damaged, or putrid, it has to be discharged at the port of destination by the shipowner, if it is to be got out of the ship at all. With this, the underwriter of hull and machinery has nothing to do. Whether the cargo be such that the consignee was bound to receive it or not is, in my opinion, as regards the liability of an underwriter upon hull and machinery, wholly immaterial. What has he to do with it? ... All he has to do under his contract is to make good to the insured shipowner the deterioration occasioned to the hull and machinery of his ship by a sea peril, and nothing more.

But, in *Agenoria Steamship Co Ltd v Merchants' Marine Insurance Co Ltd* **(1903) 8 Com Cas 212,** where the shipowners accrued bank charges for an overdraft which they had to obtain in order to send money overseas to pay for repairs, the court decided that such bank charges could be considered as part of the reasonable cost of repairs.

> **Kennedy J:** [p 216] ... There are two other questions involving principle. The first of these is £64 17s 6d for 'Bankers' charges on amounts remitted to New Zealand and overdrafts'. I have, on the whole, decided to allow this to the owners. It appears to me to be right in reason, and as far as I can find any authority, in accordance with the English usage to treat as part of the cost of

repairs of damage in a foreign port expenses reasonably and properly incurred in providing for payment there, as well as the mere cost of transmitting the funds to the foreign port.

Less customary deductions

It is now accepted that when a claim is made for particular average damage, the assured is entitled to replace the damaged subject matter with new materials or equipment. This concept of 'new for old' is reflected in cl 14 of the ITCH(95) which states: 'Claims payable without deduction new for old.'[8]

However, this has not always been the case, and the phrase 'less customary deductions', which is included in s 69(1) of the Act, was originally included to accommodate the old two-thirds rule. Under that rule, the indemnity amounted to two-thirds of the actual cost of replacement materials and equipment, thereby reflecting the benefit gained by the assured in replacing old with new.

Not exceeding the sum insured

When claiming for the costs incurred in repairing a vessel which has suffered particular average damage, there is nothing in the Act or the Institute Hull Clauses to prevent an assured, even upon a claim for a partial loss, from recovering an indemnity amounting to the full value insured under the policy, and it is for this reason, and others, that he may elect to repair rather than abandon a vessel as a constructive total loss.

In *Goole and Hull Steam Towing Co Ltd v Ocean Marine Insurance Co Ltd* **[1927] 29 LlL Rep 242**, the court ruled that the assured could claim up to the full insured value of the ship from his insurers, and any liability then owed by the third party by way of collision damage was then subrogated to the insurers. The assured could not, as he wished to do, recover part of the loss from the third party and then claim the outstanding balance (up to the full insured value) from his hull insurers.

> **MacKinnon J:** [p 245] ... accordingly, as is laid down in s 69, he [the assured] is entitled in respect of such particular average to the reasonable cost of repairs not exceeding the sum insured in respect of any one casualty. When the underwriters, in respect of a particular average loss, have paid the assured the indemnity agreed under this provision, when in particular they have paid a sum not exceeding the insured amount, in this case £4,000, I think the underwriters are entitled to say: 'we have paid the agreed indemnity for the whole of the particular average loss you have sustained, and not merely for a part of it', they are therefore entitled to be subrogated, or to take credit, for the whole sum which the assured may recover from a third party in respect of that particular average damage.

---

8 See, also, IVCH(95), cl 12.

Unrepaired damage

When a claim is pursued for a partial loss, the measure of indemnity for unrepaired damage is covered in the Act by ss 69(2) and 69(3).

Unrepaired damage and ship not sold

The first part of s 69(2) is concerned with a vessel which has only been partially repaired, whilst the latter part of the provision, dealing specifically with that portion of the damage which has not been repaired, states that the assured is:

> ... also to be indemnified for the reasonable depreciation, if any, arising from the unrepaired damage, provided that the aggregate amount shall not exceed the cost of repairing the whole damage, computed as above.

Thus, although the assured may have chosen not to repair the whole of the damage, he is still entitled to recover under the policy for any unrepaired damage. However, the claim for the unrepaired damage, when added to the cost of the repaired damage, must not exceed the amount that it would have cost, had the vessel been totally repaired.

Section 69(3) then goes on to make provision for the situation where a ship has not been repaired at all, nor sold during the period of the attachment of the risk, when it states:

> Where the ship has not been repaired, and has not been sold in her damaged state during the risk, the assured is entitled to be indemnified for the reasonable depreciation arising from the unrepaired damage, but not exceeding the reasonable cost of repairing such damage, computed as above.

Reasonable depreciation

The Act refers to 'reasonable depreciation' in both s 69(2) and s 69(3), and this is clarified to some extent by cl 18.1 of the ITCH(95), which states:[9]

> The measure of indemnity in respect of claims for unrepaired damage shall be the reasonable depreciation in the market value of the Vessel at the time this insurance terminates arising from such unrepaired damage, but not exceeding the reasonable cost of repairs.

As a general principle, the concept of depreciation for unrepaired damage, as provided for in s 69(2) and (3) of the Act, was well illustrated in ***Goole and Hull Steam Towing Co Ltd v Ocean Marine Insurance Co Ltd* (1927) 29 LIL Rep 242**, where the steamship *Goole* suffered damage after a collision on the Thames.

---

9   See, also, IVCH(95), cl 16.1.

MacKinnon J: [p 245] ... Now, as regards partial loss of ship by particular average loss, the convention is that you are to estimate the depreciation not in the way that depreciation is estimated in the case of goods, because it is impracticable, but you are to estimate the depreciation in terms of the cost of repairs. The assured need not actually do the repairs; if he does not do them, then you are to estimate the cost, instead of taking what he spent upon them; and accordingly, as is laid down in s 69, he is entitled in respect of such particular average to the reasonable cost of repairs not exceeding the sum insured in respect of any one casualty.

When during the risk is the measure of indemnity computed?

The time at which the measure of indemnity is calculated was considered in **Helmville Ltd v Yorkshire Insurance Co Ltd, 'Medina Princess' [1965] 1 Lloyd's Rep 361**, the full details of which are cited later in the chapter,[10] where Roskill J was of the opinion that the relevant time could only be at the termination of the risk.

Roskill J: [p 516] ... The first matter in dispute under s 69(3) is as to the point of time at which the plaintiffs' measure of indemnity falls to be determined ... Sub-section (3) is silent as to the point of time at which the measure of indemnity is to be ascertained and quantified. But, I think that help is to be derived from the opening words of the sub-section, namely:

Where the ship has not been repaired, and has not been sold in her damaged state during the risk ... [Emphasis added.]

The ship may be repaired at any time after the casualty and during the risk. If she is then wholly repaired, sub-s (1) operates. If she is then partly repaired, sub-s (2) operates. But if 'during the risk', which I construe as meaning 'during the period between the casualty and the expiry of the policy whether by effluxion of time or otherwise' she is neither repaired nor sold, then sub-s (3) comes into operation. Until the moment when the risk expires, the ship might be repaired, or indeed might be sold. The section is silent as to the position if the ship is sold unrepaired, and I need not trouble with that contingency. But, it is only when the risk is ended that it can be predicted for certain that neither repair nor sale will take place during the risk. That, in my judgment, is the moment at which sub-s (3) operates and requires that the measure of indemnity shall be ascertained and quantified.

The issue was also raised recently in **Kusel v Atkin, 'Catariba' [1997] 2 Lloyd's Rep 749**, where a large catamaran suffered successive unrepaired particular average losses.

Colman J: [p 756] ... That leaves the question: when should the depreciation be calculated? There are only two possible times: the time of the casualty and the termination of cover. However, the structure of s 69 leads conclusively to the latter point of time. On its proper construction, sub-s (1) must relate to damage repaired during the currency of the cover. Conversely, sub-ss (2) and (3) must

---

10 See below, p 690.

refer to damage unrepaired during the currency of the cover. One can therefore only determine into which sub-section a given case falls by looking at the position at the moment when cover ceases. It must, therefore, be that the exercise of quantification of indemnity is taken to be carried out at that time. Hence, the depreciation must be calculated at that point of time, for the Act could not have been intended to introduce a dislocation between the time of categorisation and the time at which depreciation is to be assessed. That conclusion would be consistent with the operation of s 77(2) of the MIA, under which the claim for unrepaired damage merges with a subsequent total loss.

The time for ascertainment of depreciation under s 69(3) was considered by Roskill J in the *Medina Princess* case ... He, too, concluded that as a matter of construction, the time for calculation of depreciation was the time of termination of cover.

The computation of reasonable depreciation

Valued policy

In a valued policy, the measure of indemnity is governed by the depreciation value, the market or true value before and after the damage, the insured value of the ship, and the reasonable cost of repairs.

Whilst the task of estimating the cost of repairs is an exercise in costing, the exact method of computing depreciation was often raised in the courts. The method now generally used is, first, to determine the depreciation in terms of a percentage. This figure is arrived at by taking the market value of the ship before and after the damage. The measure of indemnity is then calculated by multiplying the percentage of depreciation with the insured value of the ship. The ultimate sum, however, for which the insurer is liable must not exceed the reasonable cost of repairs or the insured value of the ship, whichever is the lower.

The problems encountered in computing depreciation were well illustrated in *Irvin v Hine*, below, where, after various methods of computation were put forward, the court decided that only two were possibly relevant, one of which was the percentage method now most favoured.

Irvin v Hine [1949] 1 KB 555

A trawler was badly damaged after stranding, and the owner, after failing in his claim for a constructive total loss, then claimed for a partial loss. As the trawler had not been repaired or sold during the risk, the court turned to s 69(3) of the Act as being applicable to the case and, in quantifying the depreciation, illustrated the difficulties in so doing.

Both the assured and the underwriters produced alternative methods of computing the depreciation which were considered by Devlin J.

Devlin J: [p 572] ... I assess the cost of repairs due to the stranding at £4,620. I now return to s 69, sub-s 3, of the Act. By its provisions, I have first to ascertain the reasonable depreciation arising from the unrepaired damage. That requires a comparison between the value of the vessel immediately before the damage, and the value in her damaged condition. The value in her damaged condition is taken by both sides to be £685. There is a dispute about the ascertainment of her undamaged value, both on the law and on the facts. Counsel for the underwriters contended that the value to be ascertained for this purpose was her true value, which he put at £2,000, and not her conventional [insured] value of £9,000 ... he contended that the extent to which the ship had depreciated in value should be ascertained by a comparison between her true undamaged value and her true damaged value. This would show that she had depreciated in value by approximately two-thirds. This proportion should then be applied to her conventional [insured] value, thus arriving at a figure (subject, of course, to the overriding maximum of the cost of repairs) of about £6,000.

[p 573] ... Section 27, sub-s 4, provides that the value fixed by the policy is conclusive of the insurable value of the subject intended to be insured, whether the loss be total or partial. Consequently, I think that, unless the underwriters' alternative contention is right [method (ii)], the effect of s 69, sub-s 3, is that the true damaged value must be subtracted from the conventional [insured] undamaged value [method (i)]. This is indeed what was contended on behalf of the assured. It produces a figure of over £8,000. It is unnecessary for me to decide whether this contention of the assured is to be preferred to the alternative contention of the underwriters. For both methods produce a higher figure than that which I have taken as the cost of repairs; and there is no doubt that that the latter figure is overriding.

Notes

Method (i): Insured value less damaged value: £9,000 – £685 = £8,215.

Method (ii): Depreciation (true undamaged value less true damaged value) applied as a proportion of the insured value:

$$\frac{£2,000 - £685}{£2,000} \times £9,000 = £5,918.$$

It was not necessary in *Irvin v Hine* to choose between methods (i) and (ii) because, in both instances, the computation resulted in amounts greater than the estimated cost of repairs, which was the overriding figure. As the court had not expressed particular preference for one or the other method of computation as being applicable under s 69(3) of the Act,[11] the case cannot be cited with confidence as 'the' authority which has settled the law on the

---

11 In the pre-statute case of *Pitman v Universal Marine Insurance Co* (1882) 9 QB 192, a similar system was suggested by Lindley J at the court of first instance, when he suggested that: [p 201] '... the correct mode of ascertaining the proportion of loss to be made good by the underwriter appears to be to compare the value of the sound ship at the port of distress with her value there when damaged, and to apply this proportion to her real value at the commencement of the risk if the policy be open, or to her agreed value if, as in the present case, the policy be valued.'

subject. Nevertheless, method (ii) has become the system which has since received approval by the court for determining the measure of indemnity in the event of depreciation.

In *Elcock v Thomson* **[1949] 2 All ER 381**, a non-marine case, the court settled on, effectively, the same percentage system for computing the depreciation as method (ii) in *Irvin v Hine*, although it was presented in a slightly different manner. In this instance, a mansion was partially damaged by fire, and the court was faced with calculating the liability of the insurers.

After referring at length to ss 69(3) and 27(3) of the Marine Insurance Act for some guidance on this matter, Morris J concluded that the most appropriate way of computing the depreciation of the property was by applying the percentage of the actual depreciation against the insured or agreed value. That is, the actual value of the mansion before the fire was £18,000, whilst its actual value after the fire was £12,600; representing a 30% drop in value. As the insured value of the mansion was £106,850, the underwriters' liability to the assured, subject to any other provisions in the policy, was 30% of £106,850, which amounted to £32,055.

In arriving at that figure, the court was of the opinion that, as in *Irvin v Hine*, the agreed or insured value of the subject matter was the figure on which any claim must be assessed.

> **Morris J:** [p 386] ... the statutory provisions of the Marine Insurance Act 1906 do not apply in this case, but, if those provisions are to be looked at in order to seek guidance on principle, then I am not prepared to accept the validity of the contentions of counsel for the defendant. Section 69(3) of the Act uses the words 'is entitled to be indemnified for the reasonable depreciation'. Those words do not fix the measure of such indemnity. They do not lay it down that the parties' agreed valuation is to be ignored. They certainly do not provide that s 27(3) of the Act is to be disregarded. Indemnification for reasonable depreciation must, in my judgment, take into account any agreed valuation. Such agreed valuation is the corpus out of which depreciation takes place, and by reference to which the depreciation must be measured.

In the *Medina Princess* case, below, the question of the computation of depreciation arose again and, although mention was made of an American case, *Armar*, which had used method (ii) as proposed in *Irvin v Hine*, the matter was held in abeyance, awaiting a decision from higher authority.

Helmville Ltd v Yorkshire Insurance Co Ltd, 'Medina Princess' [1965] 1 Lloyd's Rep 361

Medina Princess was insured by the plaintiff owners with a number of underwriters, including the defendants, under hull policies which included the Institute Hull Clauses. The full insured value was £350,000. On a voyage from Bremen to China with a cargo of flour, *Medina Princess* put into Djibouti, in the Gulf of Aden, because of serious engine problems. In order to rectify those problems, she would have had to be towed to Karachi where there were suitable facilities. Because the owners estimated that the repair costs would have amounted to more than her insured value, they laid claim for a constructive total loss or, alternatively, a partial loss.

The court ruled that the damage to the machinery was caused by the negligence and mal-operation of the officers and crew but, as the estimated cost of repairs amounted to less than the ship's insured value, the plaintiffs could only recover for a partial loss. The cost of repairs included the damage to the machinery, the anticipated towing charges to Karachi, dry-docking expenses and surveyors' fees, but excluded crew's wages and expenses incurred in discharging cargo. Again, the issue of computation of depreciation under s 69(3) was raised.

> **Roskill J:** [p 515] ... *Medina Princess* has neither been completely nor partially repaired. Nor has she been sold. Accordingly, neither sub-ss (1) or (2) of s 69 applies. As she has been neither repaired nor sold, sub-s (3) alone is relevant, though the two previous sub-sections may cast light upon the true construction of sub-s (3).
>
> *Prima facie*, the measure of indemnity under sub-s (3) is the depreciation arising from the unrepaired damage. But Mr Brandon [for the insurers] agreed that that was not the measure here because, on the finding I have made that the damaged value of the ship was virtually nil, the depreciation (whether calculated by reference to the agreed value of £350,000 or the true sound value of about £65,000) must be almost 100%. Hence, he accepted (rightly, I think) that the ceiling of reasonable cost of repairs must, upon the footing that the ship was not a constructive total loss, come into play ... I should perhaps mention that, since the decision in *Irvin v Hine*, above, this question [of computing depreciation] has arisen in a case decided in the Supreme Court of the State of New York. In *Armar* [1954] 2 Lloyd's Rep 95, p 101; [1954] AMC 1674, p 1685, Rabin J applied the second of the two alternatives. In so doing, the learned judge was seeking to apply the law of England ... The problem to which I have just referred has never been decided in England. Its solution must wait until the occasion for its decision arises. I only mention it, lest it otherwise be thought that it had been overlooked.

Valued and unvalued policies compared

When the policy is unvalued, there is no yardstick in the policy with which the level of depreciation may be related other than the true value of the ship. In such a case, the measure of indemnity is the proportionate fall in value of the ship, before and after the damage occurred, as applied to the 'insurable value'[12] or the cost of repairs, whichever is the lower.

---

12 See s 16(1) of the Act for the definition of 'insurable value'.

Kusel v Atkin, 'Catariba' [1997] 2 Lloyd's Rep 749

A large catamaran suffered successive and serious damage, but, because no notice of abandonment was given, the loss was deemed to be a partial one. During the course of its deliberations, the court considered the effect of s 69 as a whole, and then compared the measure of indemnity applicable to both an unvalued and valued policy in the case of an unrepaired partial loss.

> **Colman J:** [p 755] ... The section has the purpose of stating the measure of indemnity for partial losses. In so doing, it states the law subject to any express provision of the policy. In other words, it sets out the common law and recognises that the parties can, in terms of the policy, agree to modify or exclude the measure of indemnity which would otherwise apply under the common law. The measure of indemnity is expressed by reference to three distinct factual situations by the three sub-sections: (1) where the ship has been repaired; (2) where the ship has been partially repaired; and (3) where the ship has not been repaired. Common to each of the three sections is the limitation that the measure of indemnity is not to exceed the sum insured. That is expressly provided by sub-s (1) and the provision is then applied by reference in both sub-ss (2) and (3) by the words 'computed as above'.
>
> The measure of indemnity in respect of an unrepaired partial loss is based upon the reasonable cost of repairing the damage. The *Castellain v Preston* (1883) 11 QBD 380 indemnity principle works in this way. If the partial loss has diminished the sound value of the vessel, the assured has sustained a loss measured by the reduction in value unless he could have mitigated that loss by restoring the value of the vessel by means of repairs costing less than the reduction in value. In that case, the true loss is obviously the cost of the repairs that he would carry out, and not the reduction in value.
>
> Where, however, the value of the vessel has been fixed by the policy, depreciation must clearly be calculated not by reference exclusively to the sound value, but by reference to the insured value. That is because the parties have, by their contract, agreed to treat the insured value as the yardstick for all loss measurements for which the value of the vessel is a relevant factor, except for the calculation of a constructive total loss. That is the effect of s 27(3) and (4) of the MIA.

Unrepaired damage and ship is sold during the risk

The Act makes no mention of the situation where, after the vessel has suffered damage amounting to a partial loss, she is then sold during the currency of the risk. That an assured would consider selling his ship in such circumstances is far from remote, and there is a well known precedent for such in the *Pitman* case, below.

The loss is fixed by the sale

In the *Pitman* case, one of the issues raised was whether, in selling the ship, the assured had effectively 'fixed' his loss. That is, in selling the ship, the damaged value was fixed by the sale price and the depreciation was, therefore, calculated by subtracting the sale price from the sound value and then applying that proportion to the insured value of the ship. There was no requirement to estimate the damaged value of the ship, because that had already been fixed by the sale price.

Another point which was raised was the ceiling of the indemnity. Since the introduction of the Act, the precise wording in s 69(3) has ensured that the measure of indemnity is either the cost of repairs or the depreciation, whichever is the lower.[13]

Pitman and Another v Universal Marine Insurance Co (1882) 9 QBD 192, CA

The plaintiffs insured their vessel *Thracian* with the defendants under a time policy of insurance valued at £3,700. On a voyage from Singapore to Moulmein in Burma to take on a cargo of teak, *Thracian* grounded and was seriously damaged. She was then taken into Moulmein, where the plaintiffs decided to abandon her and gave notice of such intent to the insurers. The underwriters refused to accept the notice of abandonment, and requested that the ship be repaired. The plaintiffs did not press their notice of abandonment, but, instead of carrying out repairs, they sold the ship in its unrepaired state for £3,897. The question before the court was a matter of principle: whether the plaintiffs were entitled to recover the cost of repairs, or the difference between the actual sound value of the ship and the net proceeds of the sale, expressed as a proportion of the insured value.

The Court of Appeal affirmed the decision of the trial judge (Brett LJ dissenting) and decided that the cost of repairs could not be taken into consideration if the ship was sold, but disagreed with the trial judge over the method of ascertaining the depreciation in value. The Court of Appeal were of the opinion that the depreciation was the difference between the sound value and the sale price, and the liability of the underwriters was the proportion of that drop in value as measured against the agreed valuation in the policy.

> **Cotton LJ:** [p 218] ... The authorities, therefore, in my opinion, do not support the contention of the plaintiffs that the estimated cost of repairs ... is necessarily the measure of the sum to be recovered by the insured, and the reasoning and expressions used by the judges in the cases tend strongly to show that the estimated cost of repairs which have not been executed is a method, but not under all circumstances the only method, of estimating the deterioration of the vessel ... In this state of the authorities, I am of opinion that the estimated cost of repairs, less the usual allowance ... is not under all circumstances the sum which the insured is to recover. Where, as in the present case, there is not a constructive total loss, he is not as against the insurers entitled to sell so as to bind them by the loss resulting therefrom; but when he elects to take this course, as in the present case, he, as against himself,

---

13 Subject, in a valued policy, to s 27(3) of the Act.

fixes his loss, that is, he cannot as against the underwriters, say that the depreciation of the vessel exceeds that which is ascertained by the result of the sale. Probably, the most accurate way of stating the measure of what, under such circumstances, he is to recover, is that it will be the estimated cost of repairs less the usual deduction, not exceeding the depreciation in value of the vessel as ascertained by the sale.

Successive particular average losses

As it is possible for the subject matter insured to suffer more than one accident or loss during the currency of the policy, the Act, in s 77(1), makes provision for such when it states:

> Unless the policy otherwise provides, and subject to the provisions of this Act, the insurer is liable for successive losses, even though the total of such losses may exceed the sum insured.

A shipowner has, of course, the right to elect whether to repair or not to repair any of the losses sustained. The wording of s 77(1) does not clarify whether it refers to repaired or unrepaired successive losses. Further, on first reading, there appears to be a conflict between ss 69(3) and 77(1). Two main points arise from s 69(3): first, the assured is entitled to be indemnified for the reasonable depreciation arising from any *unrepaired* damage, and, secondly, the sum recoverable must not exceed the reasonable cost of repairing such damage. But, as was seen, the upper limit of the amount recoverable is either the reasonable cost of repairs or the insured value, whichever is the lower. Section 77(1), however, declares, in general terms, that the sum recoverable for successive losses may even exceed the sum insured. Has s 77(1) removed the insured value as the limit of recovery? The first task, obviously, is to determine the scope of s 77(1), namely, whether it applies to repaired or unrepaired successive losses.

It is clear that, where there are unrepaired losses, successive or otherwise, the method of computation remains as provided for in s 69(3): the measure of indemnity for unrepaired damage is computed at the termination of the cover as the fall in real value expressed as a percentage of the insured value.[14]

The above issues, surprisingly, only surfaced recently, in the *Catariba* case, discussed below.

Kusel v Atkin, 'Catariba' [1997] 2 Lloyd's Rep 749

The plaintiff was the owner of the large catamaran *Catariba*, which was insured under a time policy of insurance with the defendant, a member of a Lloyd's syndicate, for £625,000. The policy expressly incorporated the Institute

---

14 See, also, *Helmville Ltd v Yorkshire Insurance Co Ltd, 'Medina Princess'* [1965] 1 Lloyd's Rep 361, *per* Roskill J, p 516.

Yacht Clauses, which contained the provision that: 'The Underwriters shall not be liable in respect of unrepaired damage for more than the insured value at the time this insurance terminates.' In August 1995, *Catariba* ran aground in the British Virgin Islands (the first casualty), but salvors succeeded in saving her by towing her to a nearby island and beaching her. In September 1995, the island where *Catariba* was beached was struck by a hurricane, and the vessel was severely damaged (the second casualty). At the time of the expiration of the policy, no repairs had been carried out in respect of either the first or second casualty, and it was agreed that the cumulative cost of repairs would have exceeded her insured value.

The questions before the court were, *inter alia*: (a) Was she a constructive total loss or a partial loss? (b) Was the measure of indemnity for two successive unrepaired losses limited by the insured value of the vessel? (c) Did the clause in the policy limit the measure of indemnity for successive losses to the depreciation in value at the termination of the policy?

The court ruled that: (a) *Catariba* was not a constructive total loss, as the letter sent by the plaintiff amounted to a request for advice rather than a notice of abandonment; (b) the measure of indemnity for a valued policy, under s 69 of the Marine Insurance Act, for unrepaired losses was based on the reasonable depreciation of the vessel as a proportion of the insured value; (c) the measure of indemnity was limited by the depreciation in value at the time of the termination of the policy, even with successive losses.

> **Colman J:** [p 756] ... One, therefore, arrives at the position where, if there were successive partial losses which are unrepaired at the point of time when the cover terminates, the measure of indemnity has to be assessed by reference to the depreciation *at that time*. But what is meant by depreciation? In particular, does one investigate the actual damaged value of the vessel, with all its unrepaired damage, or does one separate the consequences of the successive partial losses by asking what would have been the damaged value of the vessel if each one of the partial losses *alone* had been sustained, then aggregating the separate amounts of depreciation to arrive at a total depreciation. To these questions, the answer is, in my judgment, very clear. Once it is accepted that the measure of indemnity is to be assessed as at the termination of the cover, it must also follow that the pecuniary loss in respect of which the indemnity applies is the *actual* reduced value of the vessel *at that time*.
>
> [p 757] ... Just as a partial loss which is left unrepaired is, for the purposes of the measure of indemnity, superseded or obliterated by a subsequent total loss, so successive partial losses, unrepaired at the date of termination of cover, must, by analogy, be treated as having caused to the assured only such actual pecuniary loss as is measured by reference to the cumulative depreciation of the vessel's value at the time of termination of cover. By the express terms of s 69(3), that measure of indemnity may in turn be capped by whichever is the lower of the reasonable cost of repairing the damage and the insured value of the vessel.

That being, in my judgment, the effect of s 69 of the MIA, what is the effect of s 77(1)? In particular, does it override s 69(3) so as to remove the limit of recovery by reference to the insured value? It clearly does not. It has to be read consistently with s 69(3). The two provisions are not in conflict. Sub-section (1) relates to successive losses in respect of which the total measure of indemnity specified by the Act could exceed the insured value. That would be the case where successive partial losses were sustained and repaired before the termination of cover, as provided for under s 69(1). Although no one partial loss could give rise to a right of indemnity in excess of the insured value, the aggregate of more than one such partial loss could do so. It is to that eventuality that s 77(1) is directed. In other words, the sub-section can consistently with s 69(3) only refer to the successive repaired losses. I therefore conclude that, on the underlying assumption that there is no constructive total loss, the aggregate amount which the plaintiff would be entitled to recover in respect of two successive losses identified is, by the operation of s 69(3) of the MIA, limited to the insured value of the vessel less any amounts for which the plaintiff must give credit.

The heavy weather clause

When considering the issue of successive losses, the 'heavy weather clause' contained within the Institute Hulls clauses cannot be ignored. Clause 12.2 of the ITCH(95) states:[15]

> Claims for damage by heavy weather occurring during a single sea passage between two successive ports shall be treated as being due to one accident. In the case of such heavy weather extending over a period not wholly covered by this insurance, the deductible to be applied to the claim recoverable hereunder shall be the proportion of the above deductible that the number of days of such heavy weather falling within the period of this insurance bears to the number of days of heavy weather during the single sea passage. The expression 'heavy weather' in this Clause 12.2 shall be deemed to include contact with floating ice.

The Clause provides that successive damage suffered during one sea passage may, for the purposes of making a claim, be combined together and treated as one loss. Thus, any amount deductible would only apply to the combined claim and, should the policy only cover a part of the sea passage, then the amount deductible is calculated on the proportionate basis of the number of heavy weather days experienced during the currency of the policy as compared with the number of heavy weather days experienced during the single sea passage. It is emphasised that, although the term 'heavy weather' is not defined, it does include contact with floating ice.

---

15 See, also, IVCH(95), cl 10.2.

Merger of losses

Section 77(2) of the Act states:

> Where, under the same policy, a partial loss, which has not been repaired or otherwise made good, is followed by a total loss, the assured can only recover in respect of the total loss.

An unrepaired partial loss is not recoverable when followed by a total loss

The doctrine of merger of claims is applicable where an 'unrepaired' partial loss is followed by a total loss under the same policy. Under those circumstances, the insurer is only liable for the total loss. Thus, if a ship suffers damage which is not repaired and then, at a future date, is totally lost, and both incidents fall within the currency of the same policy, the assured may only claim for the total loss. This principle is reiterated in cl 18.2 of the ITCH(95), in the following terms:[16]

> In no case shall the Underwriters be liable for unrepaired damage in the event of a subsequent total loss (whether or not covered under this insurance) sustained during the period covered by this insurance or any extension thereof.

The reasoning behind the merger of losses for unrepaired damage when it is followed by a total loss is that the liability for the partial loss cannot accrue until the termination of the policy, by which time it is 'swallowed up' by the total loss.[17] It is, therefore, emphasised that the merger of claims only applies to unrepaired damage, and not to repaired damage. The doctrine of merger of losses was considered as long ago as 1810 in *Livie v Janson*, below.

Livie v Janson (1810) 12 East 648

The ship *Liberty* was owned by the plaintiff and insured with the defendants under a voyage policy of insurance 'at and from' New York to London, but was warranted free from 'American condemnation'. In January 1809, *Liberty* sailed from New York in breach of an American embargo, but was damaged by ice whilst leaving. The crew abandoned her and the American authorities impounded her. The plaintiff claimed that the loss, whether partial or total, had been caused by perils of the seas, and that the subsequent seizure by the American authorities did not make the earlier loss any the less relevant.

The court ruled that there was ultimately a total loss caused by an excepted peril and the assured could not recover for the total loss or any previous loss, as the previous loss had become immaterial.

---

16 See, also, IVCH(95), cl 16.2.
17 *Per* Viscount Finlay, *British and Foreign Insurance Co Ltd v Wilson Shipping Co Ltd* [1921] 1 AC 188, p 202.

Lord Ellenborough CJ: [p 652] As there is some novelty in the point, we will look further into it; though as it appears to me this case falls within the general principle, that causa proxima et non remota spectatur. It therefore seems to me useless to be seeking about for odds and ends of previous partial losses which might have happened to a ship in the course of her voyage, when at last there was one overwhelming cause of loss which swallowed up the whole subject matter.

[p 654] ... The object of a policy is indemnity to the assured; and he can have no claim to indemnity where there is ultimately no damage to him from any peril insured against. If the property, whether damaged or undamaged, would have equally been taken away from him, and the whole loss would have fallen upon him had the property been ever so entire, how can he be said to have been injured by its having been antecedently damaged? ... The object of insurance is that the thing insured shall arrive safe at the place of destination, and if it do not arrive at all, in consequence of any of the perils insured, the assured shall recover as for a total loss: and that if it arrive damaged, a proportional compensation shall be paid for the damage; because in that case the proprietor receives the thing pro tanto in a worse condition than he ought to have done: but of what consequence to him is the intermediate condition of the thing, if he be never to receive it again? If, before the completion of the voyage, it be, as to him and his interests, in a state of utter annihilation, what is it to him whether it had been damaged or not in an anterior part of the voyage, before it became annihilated?

[p 656]... we are of opinion that such prior partial injury forms in this case no claim upon the underwriters of this policy; and consequently that the postea must be delivered to the defendant.

Similarly, in *Knight v Faith* (1850) 15 QB 509, where a vessel was unknowingly damaged and later sold by her master when the full extent of her injuries were apparent, Lord Campbell CJ, in order to distinguish *Livie v Janson* from the case being heard, stated:

Lord Campbell CJ: [p 518] ... In *Livie v Janson*, the policy was on a ship for a voyage from New York to London, warranted free from American condemnation, and after a partial loss by sea damage, the ship was seized and condemned by the American Government. The assured, in the event which happened, were not in any degree prejudiced by the partial loss, which only rendered the ship less valuable to the American Government, the assured being in the same situation as if the partial loss had never occurred.

The same issue of the doctrine of merger of losses was again raised in the post-statute case of *British and Foreign Insurance Co Ltd v Wilson Shipping Co Ltd*, below.

British and Foreign Insurance Co Ltd v Wilson Shipping Co Ltd [1921] 1 AC 188, HL

The ship *Eastlands* was on charter to the Admiralty when she was torpedoed and became a total loss. During the preceding months, the ship had suffered some damage, some of which had remained unrepaired. When the Admiralty recompensed the owners for the total loss, the compensation amounted to £80,230, that being the damaged value of the ship at the time. The owners insisted that the compensation would have been £82,000 if the ship had, in fact, been repaired and they laid claim for the outstanding £1,770 from their insurers, who declined to pay.

The House of Lords overturned the decision of the Court of Appeal and ruled that the underwriters were not liable for the additional £1,770. The unrepaired damage was followed by a total loss during the currency of the same policy, and the smaller loss merged into the larger.

> **Lord Birkenhead LC:** [p 199] ... The true rule is capable of statement in the following proposition. When a vessel, insured against perils of the sea, is damaged by one of the risks covered by the policy and before that damage is repaired she is lost, during the currency of the policy, by a risk which is not covered by the policy, then the insurer is not liable for such unrepaired damage.

A repaired partial loss is recoverable when followed by a total loss

That a repaired loss is recoverable when followed by a total loss is well established, in that any such indemnity is for expenditure that has, in fact, been incurred. This was illustrated in the early case of *Le Cheminant v Pearson*, below.

Le Cheminant v Pearson (1812) 4 Taunt 367

During the Napoleonic wars, the vessel *Nooytstill* was insured by her owners with the defendants under a voyage policy of insurance 'at and from' Jersey to ports in Norway and back to London. During the currency of the policy, *Nooytstill* suffered weather damage which, through sue and labour, was repaired. She was later seized by a Danish privateer as prize. Her owners claimed for both the cost of repairing the weather damage and the total loss.

The court ruled that the insurers were liable for both.

> **Lord Mansfield CJ:** [p 380] ... in practice I know of cases in the Court of King's Bench, where such expenses have been recovered as an average loss, without making any distinction whether it was recoverable as an average loss from damage repaired, or within the words of the permission to 'sue, labour, and travail, etc'; and as no such distinction has been made, we find it safer to adhere to the practice which has obtained, and to call it all average damage; and therefore the rule must be discharged as to the whole sum.

The issue of previous repaired damage being recoverable after a subsequent total loss was again touched upon in *British and Foreign Insurance Co Ltd v Wilson Shipping Co Ltd* [1921] 1 AC 188, the facts of which are cited above.

> **Viscount Finlay:** [p 202] ... If the damage resulting from the sea perils had been repaired, the amount disbursed for that purpose would have been recoverable

on the policy in spite of the subsequent loss. But if the repairs have not been executed, the liability cannot accrue until the termination of the risk under the policy, and if, before that happens, there is a total loss, the partial loss is 'swallowed up' in the total.

A constructive total loss followed by an actual total loss

That an earlier serious loss, which could amount to a constructive total loss, does not necessarily preclude recovery for a subsequent actual total loss, was illustrated in *Woodside v Globe Marine Insurance Co*, below. When the insurers argued that the actual total loss had merged into the previous constructive total loss, the court ruled that the earlier loss did not impair the subsequent actual total loss. However, it is emphasised that, in this instance, the owners had not given notice of abandonment with respect to the previous constructive total loss which, as a result, was deemed a partial loss.

Woodside v Globe Marine Insurance Co Ltd [1896] 1 QB 105

The plaintiffs' vessel *Bawnmore* was insured under a time policy of insurance with the defendants, against loss or damage by fire. During the currency of the policy, *Bawnmore* was driven ashore on the coast of Oregon and stranded; some 36 hours later, she was completely destroyed by fire. The plaintiffs claimed for an actual total loss by fire. The insurers denied liability, and argued that, at the time of the fire, *Bawnmore* was already a constructive total loss by stranding, which was not covered by the policy. The insurers further argued that the subsequent actual total loss by fire had merged into the previous constructive total loss.

The court ruled that the plaintiffs could recover for the actual total loss by fire. The plaintiffs had given no notice of abandonment for the loss by stranding, which meant that, for insurance purposes, the loss was a partial one. Thus, the claim on the subsequent actual total loss by fire was not impaired by the previous loss.

> **Matthew J:** [p 107] ... For the defendants it was argued that, if the fire had occurred first, and the damage had not been repaired, the underwriters would not have been liable. The damage by fire, it was said, was, as it were, merged in the previous total loss. The assured must be treated as if they had been indemnified and had received the value of their ship, and they ought not to be permitted to recover twice over for what was one loss.
>
> I am of opinion that the plaintiffs are entitled to judgment. The loss by stranding would only become total if the assured gave timely notice of abandonment. If none were given, the loss would be a particular average, and it would seem clear law that a particular average loss, however serious, could not impair the right of the assured to recover for a subsequent total loss ...

Merger of losses must be under the same policy

For there to be a merging of losses, both such losses must fall within the currency of the same policy of insurance. To this effect, the merging of losses under s 77(2) of the Act is qualified by the statement: 'Where, under the same policy ...' and cl 18.2 of the ITCH(95) by '... sustained during the period covered by this insurance or any extension thereof'.[18]

Thus, the doctrine of merger of losses does not apply when a partial loss is succeeded by a total loss under different policies of insurance. This was made evident in *Lidgett v Secretan*, below, where two such losses occurred to a ship which was insured with the same underwriter, but under different policies.

Lidgett v Secretan (1871) LR 6 CP 616

The plaintiffs insured their vessel *Charlemagne* under two policies of insurance with the defendants. Both were voyage policies: the first policy was for the outward voyage 'at and from London to Calcutta and for 30 days after arrival', the second policy was for the homeward voyage 'at and from Calcutta to London'. On her outward voyage, *Charlemagne* struck a reef and, to get her off, part of the cargo had to be jettisoned. On arrival in Calcutta, *Charlemagne* was placed in dry-dock for repairs and, whilst she was in dry-dock, she caught fire and was totally destroyed. At the time of the fire, the first policy had expired and the second policy had attached. The plaintiffs claimed under the first policy for the whole of the loss, including dock dues and the like, caused by the ship striking the reef. They also claimed for the total loss by fire under the second policy.

The court ruled that the plaintiffs could recover for the vessel's depreciation at the end of the risk in consequence of the damage sustained on the outward voyage, on the basis that the depreciation took no account of the repairs already completed; the indemnity would also include dock fees and the like. They could also recover under the second policy without reference to their claim under the first policy. In their summations, Willes J only touched briefly on the doctrine of merger, and tended to concentrate on the measure of indemnity, whilst Montague Smith J paid particular attention to the issue of merger of losses.

Willes J: [p 620] ... The doctrine of merger cannot apply to such a case as this. The reason for applying it where the partial loss and the total loss occur during the continuance of the same risk is obvious: the parties never intended that the insurers should be liable for more than a total loss in any event.

Montague Smith J: [p 630] ... It was contended on the part of the defendant that the particular average under the first policy is merged in the subsequent total loss under the second policy. It seems to me that the loss occurring after the expiration of the first policy, and when the second policy had attached,

---

18 See, also, IVCH(95), cl 16.2.

gives nothing in which the partial loss can be merged. No doubt, where both the partial and total loss occur during the same voyage, and during the period covered by the same policy, the former is merged in the latter. That is so on obvious principles of justice. The underwriter insures against accidents happening during the voyage; and the whole voyage must be regarded before it can be ascertained whether and to what extent the assured are damnified. But I am at a loss to see how anything which may occur after the expiration of the risk can alter or affect the rights of the parties. In *Knight v Faith*, there is a portion of Lord Campbell's judgment which supports this view. He says: 'The insurers have not paid, and they deny their liability to pay a total loss; and they are not at liberty to allege that the partial loss is merged in a total loss from which they are exempt.' In the present case, the underwriters under the second policy have nothing whatever to do with the partial loss under the first policy. It is a mere accident that there was a second policy; and the rights of the assured on the first policy stand precisely as if the second had never been entered into.

The death blow theory

Where a vessel suffers damage during the currency of the policy, but later becomes a total loss after the policy has expired, the doctrine of merger cannot apply. In this instance, there is only one cause of loss; the initial damage has eventually caused the total loss. This, known as the death blow theory, was apparent in *Knight v Faith*, below.

Knight v Faith (1850) 15 QB 509

Pusey Hall was insured by the plaintiffs with the defendants under a time policy of insurance. Whilst entering Santa Cruz, in Patagonia, *Pusey Hall* grounded, but was subsequently refloated. One month later, after the policy of insurance had expired, the ship was surveyed, and it was found that the damage previously received, during the currency of the policy, had been so severe that she had to be sold for a pittance where she lay; there being no facilities there to repair her. The plaintiffs claimed for a constructive total loss or, alternatively, a partial loss. The underwriters denied liability for the constructive total loss, as there had been no notice of abandonment, and argued that they were not liable for the partial loss, because that loss had merged into the total loss.

The court ruled that there was no constructive total loss, as no notice of abandonment had been given. However, there was a partial loss for which the underwriters were liable; the question of merger did not arise, as there was only one loss.

> **Lord Campbell CJ:** [p 518] ... But, here, the insurers have not paid, and they deny their liability to pay a total loss; and they are not at liberty to allege that the partial loss is merged in a total loss, from which they are exempt. In *Livie v Janson*, the policy was on a ship for a voyage from New York to London,

warranted free from American condemnation, and after a partial loss by sea damage, the ship was seized and condemned by the American Government. The assured, in the event which happened, were not in any degree prejudiced by the partial loss, which only rendered the ship less valuable to the American Government, the assured being in the same situation as if the partial loss had never occurred. But, here, the owners of *Pusey Hall* suffered an injury to their property when the ship grounded near Santa Cruz, and that has continued a prejudice to them ever since ... Nor was there a supervening loss by the sale of the ship; for there is no such loss known in insurance law as a sale by the master, unless it be barratrous; and a *bona fide* sale by the master can only affect the insurers when it becomes necessary by prior damage, arising from a peril for which they were answerable.

We, therefore, think that in this case the ship insured sustained a partial loss, for which the assured ought to be indemnified. But they have left us entirely in the dark as to the amount of that indemnity ... There having been no notice of abandonment, although the ship subsisted as a ship, we cannot proceed upon the supposition that she could not be repaired; and the partial loss must be calculated on the same principles as if she had actually been repaired and proceeded on her voyage, or had foundered at sea without having been repaired soon after the policy expired ... We think that the proper course would be to refer it to an arbitrator to ascertain the amount of the partial loss, and the verdict for the plaintiffs should be reduced to this amount: but if both parties will not agree to the course which we recommend, we shall direct a new trial, and the amount of the damages may be ascertained by a jury.

... Nor do I think that *Lockyer v Offley* is an authority against the plaintiffs; for there, the proximate cause of the loss was the seizure by the government, which occurred after the policy had expired, while the proximate cause of the loss here was the grounding off Santa Cruz while the ship was still protected by the policy, and immediately and directly some damage arose, by which the value of the subject matter was lessened.

Notes

In *Knight v Faith*, above, the case of *Lockyer v Offley* (1786) 1 TR 252[19] was referred to and distinguished. In *Lockyer v Offley*, where the insurance was, in fact, a voyage policy, the barratrous act of smuggling by the master, during the currency of the policy, resulted in the seizure of the ship after the expiration of cover. In this instance, there were two different incidents: barratry and seizure. The assured could not claim for the loss by barratry, as the intervening act of seizure by the authorities had broken the chain of causation.

---

19 For a fuller discussion of this case in relation to barratry, see Chapter 12, p 519.

PARTIAL LOSS OF GOODS

Other than when a total loss occurs, goods may be lost or damaged in a variety of ways. There may be:
(a) a total loss of part of the goods;
(b) the whole of the goods may be partially damaged;
(c) part of the goods may be partially damaged; or
(d) the goods have become unidentifiable because of the obliteration of marks.

Although it may appear inappropriate to include 'a total loss of part of the goods' under the heading of partial loss, it is so done in order to distinguish this specific type of loss from a total loss of the whole of the goods.

A total loss of part of the goods

When goods of the same specie are insured under a single valuation, it is not unusual for the individual components of cargo within the consignment to be valued separately within the whole. That is, a valuable consignment of cargo, such as barrels of wine, may, for example, be insured and valued under one policy, but, within the policy, each barrel may be considered as a separate entity and insured as such. In those circumstances, the loss of one barrel would constitute a total loss of that barrel within the consignment. Thus, for a total loss of a part of the goods to take place, each item or portion of the cargo must be clearly identifiable and valued within the policy.[20]

However, the same principle may apply to a consignment of goods which are of a different specie, but are still insured under a single valuation. In this instance, each item may be of a different value and the proportionate value of each item in relation to the full valuation must be expressed in the policy. That is, there must be an apportionment of valuation, and this is provided for in s 72(1) of the Act, namely:

> Where different species of property are insured under a single valuation, the valuation must be apportioned over the different species in proportion to their respective insurable values, as in the case of an unvalued policy. The insured value of any part of a species is such proportion of the total insured value of the same as the insurable value of the part bears to the insurable value of the whole, ascertained in both cases as provided by this Act.

But, where the value of the different species of goods has not been apportioned in the policy, the method of apportionment is provided for in s 72(2), which states:

---

20 Typically, 100 barrels of wine valued at £10,000, each barrel valued at £100.

Where a valuation has to be apportioned, and particulars of the prime cost of each separate species, quality, or description of goods cannot be ascertained, the division of the valuation may be made over the net arrived sound values of the different species, qualities, or descriptions of goods.

Thus, it is only when apportionment has taken place that there may be a total loss of a part. If no such apportionment has taken place, any loss must be a partial loss, and the true relevance of this differentiation can only be seen if the goods are warranted 'free from particular average'. To that effect, s 76(1) of the Act states:

Where the subject matter insured is warranted free from particular average, the assured cannot recover for a loss of part, other than a loss incurred by a general average sacrifice, unless the contract contained in the policy be apportionable; but, if the contract be apportionable, the assured may recover for a total loss of any apportionable part.

The importance of goods being apportioned was graphically illustrated in *Duff v Mackenzie*, below.

Duff v Mackenzie (1857) 3 CB (NS) 16

This was an action brought in respect of the loss of a master's personal effects, which were insured with the defendants for £100, but the policy was warranted free from all average. When the plaintiff's vessel *Lion* was destroyed by fire, the master succeeded in saving about one-third of his effects, the remainder being lost. The master sought to be indemnified for his loss by his insurers, but the insurers denied liability, on the basis that the effects were only insured for a total loss.

The court ruled that the master could recover under the policy, as the personal effects that had been lost had been totally lost. That is, the effects were all different and, therefore, could be itemised as individual total losses and easily apportioned as such.

Williams J: [p 29] ... The articles which constitute the 'master's effects' have no natural or artificial connection with each other, but, of necessity, must be essentially different in their nature and kind, in their value, in the use to be made of them, and the mode in which they would be disposed on board. The word 'effects' is obviously employed to save the task of enumerating the nautical instruments, the chronometer, the clothes, books, furniture, etc, of which they happened to consist. And, although it is stipulated by the warranty that these effects shall be free of all average – or, in other words, that the insurer shall not be liable for any amount of sea-damage to them short of a total loss – we think, looking at the nature of the subject of insurance, and the terms of this exemption, it is doing no violence to the language used, to hold that he is not to be exempted from liability for a total loss of any of the articles of which the 'effects' consist ... The more strict construction leads to the very harsh and absurd consequences, that, if the assured happens to be successful in rescuing any portion of the articles insured – even the clothes he may be wearing – from the perils of the sea, he will thereby incur the penalty of forfeiting his insurance on the rest, though they are all totally lost. This result is so startling that we find it impossible to believe the parties could have intended it. And, it may be added, that the contract, so construed, would be quite at variance with the object for which, as it is well known, the memorandum as to average was introduced into policies, viz, that, since it may be difficult to ascertain the true cause of the damage which goods of certain kinds, such as those usually specified in the memorandum, receive in the course of a voyage – whether it arose from the nature of the articles themselves, or from the perils insured against – the insurers thereby expressly provide, that, as to some kinds of goods, they will not be answerable for any average or partial loss, and, as to others, that they will not be liable for such loss not amounting to a certain percentage on the goods.

The measure of indemnity for a total loss of a part of the goods

The measure of indemnity for a total loss of a part is provided for by the Act in ss 71(1) and 71(2).

Where the policy is valued, the measure of indemnity is the value of the goods lost expressed as a proportion of the insured value and, to this effect, s 71(1) states:

> Where part of the goods, merchandise or other movables insured by a valued policy is totally lost, the measure of indemnity is such proportion of the sum fixed by the policy as the insurable value of the part lost bears to the insurable value of the whole, ascertained as in case of an unvalued policy.

Where the policy is unvalued, the measure of indemnity is the value of the goods lost expressed as a proportion of the insurable value. Section 71(2) affirms:

> Where part of the goods, merchandise, or other movables insured by an unvalued policy is totally lost, the measure of indemnity is the insurable value of the part lost, ascertained as in case of a total loss ...

A partial loss of the whole or part of the goods

When there is a partial loss and there is damage to the whole or part of the goods, the measure of indemnity is provided for in s 71(3) of the Act, which states that:

> Where the whole or any part of the goods or merchandise insured has been delivered damaged at its destination, the measure of indemnity is such proportion of the sum fixed by the policy in the case of a valued policy, or of the insurable value in the case of an unvalued policy, as the difference between the gross sound and damaged values at the place of arrival bears to the gross sound value ...

Partial Loss – 1

The principles contained within s 71(3) were originally laid down in two old cases: *Lewis v Rucker* and *Johnson v Sheddon*, below.

Lewis v Rucker (1761) 2 Burr 1167

The plaintiffs insured their goods under a valued policy with the defendants for a voyage from the West Indies to Hamburg. Included in the consignment were hogsheads of sugar 'warranted free from particular average under £3%, unless general, or the ship be stranded'. On arrival in Hamburg, the hogsheads of sugar were found to have been damaged by seawater and had to be sold immediately for a price below their undamaged value. That is, the undamaged price at Hamburg would have been £23 7s 8d per hogshead, whilst the damaged price was actually £20 0 8d. However, the plaintiffs claimed that if the sugar had not been damaged, they would have stored it until the price had risen to £30 per hogshead, and that that was the price from which the measure of indemnity should be calculated.

The court ruled that the measure of indemnity must be such as to put the assured in the same position as he would have been had the goods been delivered sound, and speculative profit could not be considered as part of the indemnity. Thus, the measure of indemnity was the difference between the damaged and the undamaged value of the goods at the port of delivery, computed as a proportion of the value specified in the policy.

Lord Mansfield CJ: [p 1169] ... I will first state the rule by which the defendant and jury have gone ... The defendant [the insurer] takes the proportion of the difference between the sound and damaged at the port of delivery, and pays that proportion upon the value of the goods specified in the policy; and has no regard to the price in money which either the sound or damaged goods bore in the port of delivery.

[p 1172] ... The nature of the contract is 'that goods shall come safe to the port of delivery; or if they do not, to indemnify the plaintiff to the amount of the prime cost, or the value in the policy'. If they arrive, but lessened in value through damage received at sea, the nature of an indemnity speaks demonstrably, that it must be in putting the merchant in the same condition, (relation being had to the prime cost or value in the policy) which he would have been if the goods had arrived free from damage; that is, by paying such proportion, or aliquot part of the prime cost, or value in the policy, as corresponds with the proportion, or aliquot part of the diminution in value occasioned by the damage ... But, if speculative destinations of the merchant, and the success of such speculations are to be regarded, it would introduce the greatest injustice and inconvenience. The underwriter knows nothing of them. The orders here were given after the signing of the policy. But the decisive answer is, that the underwriter has nothing to do with the price; and that the right of the insured to a satisfaction, where goods are damaged, arises immediately upon their being landed at the port of delivery. We are of opinion that the plaintiffs are not entitled to have the price for which the damaged sugars were sold, made up to £30 per hogshead: and it seems to us as plain as

any proposition in Euclid, that the rule by which the jury have gone is the right measure.

Section 71(4) then goes on to define the meaning of 'gross value',[21] which is based on the ruling in *Johnson v Sheddon*, below. The question put before the court was whether the difference between the sound value and the damaged value should be calculated on the basis of gross prices or net prices. That is, the gross price of the goods which would include freight, landing charges, etc, or the net price, which would be the bare price of the goods themselves.

Johnson v Sheddon (1802) 2 East 581

The plaintiff insured a cargo of brimstone with the defendants for a voyage from Sicily to Hamburg. When the cargo arrived in Hamburg, it was found to be damaged by seawater, and the plaintiff suffered a partial loss. The question before the court was whether the measure of indemnity should be calculated on the basis of the difference between the respective sound and damaged net values, or the respective sound and damaged gross values.

The court ruled that the indemnity should be based on the difference between the respective sound and damaged gross values, although the underwriter should not be liable for any charges due after the arrival of the goods at their port of destination. Lawrence J highlighted the problems which would arise with the use of net values.

> **Lawrence J:** [p 583] ... Lord Mansfield, in laying down the rule, speaks of the price of the thing at the port of delivering as the means of ascertaining the damage; by which he must mean the whole sum, which is to be paid for the thing. For the net proceeds are not the price, but so much of the price as remains after the deduction of certain charges. Lord Mansfield cannot mean the price before the mast, leaving the purchaser liable to the payment of further sums; for such payment is in effect but a part of the price; it is not an equivalent for the thing sold; for if the purchaser were not liable to the duties and charges, he would give as much more as the amount of those charges comes to. The price of a thing is what it costs a man; and if, in addition to a sum to be paid before the mast, other charges are to be borne, that sum and the charges constitute the cost.
>
> [p 586] ... Another objection is that, if the net produce be taken, it may happen that you can have no data to calculate by, which will be the case if the gross produce of the sound commodity should only pay the charges; and leave no net proceeds; for then there can be no difference between the net proceeds of the sound and damaged; in proportion to which it is contended that the underwriter is to pay.

---

21 Section 71(4): 'Gross value' means the wholesale price or, if there be no such price, the estimated value, with, in either case, freight, landing charges, duty paid before hand; provided that, in the case of goods or merchandise customarily sold in bond, the bonded price is deemed to be the gross value. 'Gross proceeds' means the actual price obtained at a sale where all charges on sale are paid by the sellers.

Part of the goods are partially damaged

This form of loss may be considered as being the type of loss most naturally associated with a partial loss of goods. The meaning is self-explanatory, and such a loss is provided for, in general, by s 71 of the Act.

Goods that are not identifiable

When goods, which are *in specie*, are unidentifiable when they reach their destination, because, for example, their identifying marks have been obliterated, it is not possible for them to be appropriated to their owner. In these circumstances, it is accepted that any such loss may only be recoverable as a partial loss. To this effect, s 56(5) of the Act states:

> Where goods reach their destination *in specie*, but by reason of obliteration of marks, or otherwise, they are incapable of identification, the loss, if any, is partial, and not total.

This principle was established in *Spence v Union Marine Insurance Co Ltd* (1868) LR 3 CP 427. Whether the loss be total or partial, the same principle applies in relation to the obliteration of marks.[22]

Computing the measure of liability

When a partial loss of goods occurs, the measure of indemnity, as with a ship, is based upon the depreciation suffered, that is, the difference between the gross sound value and the gross damaged value at the destination. If the policy is valued, the percentage drop in value must then be multiplied against the insured value in order to establish the true measure of indemnity in relation to the policy itself.

That, when establishing the fall in value of the damaged goods, the sound and damaged values are those values applicable at the 'point of arrival' was illustrated in *Whiting v New Zealand Insurance Co*, below.

Whiting v New Zealand Insurance Co (1932) 44 LlL Rep 179

The plaintiffs insured two consignments of ladies' panama hats with the defendants aboard two different vessels sailing from Kobe to London. On arrival in London, 893 dozen hats were found to be mouldy. One of the questions before the court was the measure of indemnity, and at what point the fall in value was to be established.

---

22 For a fuller discussion of this case and s 56(5), see Chapter 15, p 611.

The court decided that the measure of indemnity should be based upon the difference between the 'arrived' sound value and the 'arrived' damaged value.

> **Roche J:** [p 180] ... I now pass to the question of amount. There is really no dispute about the proper measure which governs the case. It is under s 71(3) of the Marine Insurance Act 1906, the difference between the gross sound and the damaged values of the goods in question. I think that means at the place and time of arrival. Of course, the price at the time of arrival may not be able to be gauged by any immediate testing of the market, but I think it means market or other value of the goods at that place and time.

When the policy in question is an unvalued policy, there being no valuation fixed by the policy, the depreciation is then relative to the 'insurable value', and reference must be made to s 16(3) of the Act in order to establish what that insurable value may include. Section 16(3) states that:

> In insurance on goods and merchandise, the insurable value is the prime cost of the property insured, plus the expense of and incidental to shipping and the charges of insurance upon the whole ...

Thus, with an unvalued policy, the 'insurable value', as referred to in s 16(3), is the 'prime' or invoice price of the goods, plus expenses incurred in shipping the goods, as well as the cost of insurance; that insurable value being established when the risk attaches (see s 16(4)).

The meaning of 'insurable value' was explained long ago, in **Usher v Noble (1810) 12 East 639**, where goods were lost after the vessel carrying them sank in the Thames. The issue before the court was the establishment of the measure of indemnity and the 'insurable value' of the goods in an unvalued policy.

> **Lord Ellenborough:** [p 646] ... It is admitted that the assured is entitled to an indemnity, and no more; but by what standard of value the indemnity sought should be regulated is the question. In the case of a valued policy, the valuation in the policy is the agreed standard: in case of an open policy, the invoice price at the loading port, including premiums of insurance and commission, is, for all purposes of either total or average loss, the usual standard of calculation resorted to for the purpose of ascertaining this value.

PARTIAL LOSS OF FREIGHT

Freight is the money earned by the employment of the ship. It may take the form of ordinary freight, which is the money earned for transporting goods to an agreed destination, or it may be the money earned by chartering the ship itself, in which case the freight is paid for the usage of the ship.[23]

---

23 See Chapter 3, p 96.

In either case, the freight that is expected to be earned may be insured by the shipowner, but it is emphasised that only the freight which is at risk may be thus insured, that is, with ordinary or bill of lading freight, only the freight which is payable on delivery is insurable. This would include pro rata freight, but would exclude advance freight, as the latter, by definition, has already been paid and is not at risk.

A partial loss of freight may occur in a variety of ways, namely:
(a) there may be a total loss of part of the cargo;
(b) there may be a total loss of the whole of the cargo, but the ship still earns some freight by carrying alternative goods;[24]
(c) the ship is totally lost, but some freight is still earned by sending any goods saved in a substitute ship.

The different ways in which freight may be lost was discussed in ***Rankin v Potter* (1873) LR 6 HL 83**, where there was a total loss of chartered freight when the chartered vessel was, through previous damage, found to be a constructive total loss.

> **Brett J:** [p 98] ... There is a partial loss of freight under a general policy on freight ... under certain circumstances, if there be a total loss of part of the cargo; or if in the case of total loss of the ship the cargo be sent on a substituted ship; or if in case of a total loss of the cargo the ship earns some freight in respect of other goods carried on the voyage insured.

Total loss of part of the cargo

Under common law, ordinary freight is payable in full when the goods are delivered at the proper destination, regardless of whether there is a shortfall in the quantity delivered or whether they are damaged. Thus, there cannot be a partial loss of freight when there is a shortfall in delivery or part of a consignment is damaged. However, the terms of the contract of carriage may well alter the position of the common law. For example, the conditions in the contract of carriage may be such that freight is payable only for the proportion of cargo delivered undamaged. Under such a contract, should some of the cargo be damaged, there would be a corresponding reduction in the freight payable, and if that freight had been insured, there would have been a partial loss of that freight. Such were the circumstances in *Griffiths and Others v Bramley-Moore and Others* (1878) 4 QB 70, CA, discussed earlier,[25] where the shipowners effected a policy of insurance which provided cover for '... only the one-third loss of freight in consequence of sea-damage as per charterparty ...'.

---

24 This can only occur with chartered freight.
25 See Chapter 3, p 102.

Another example of a variation in the terms of payment of freight can be found in *Price v Maritime Insurance Co Ltd*, below. In this instance, the contract of carriage was not governed by English law, but by Italian law, under which distance freight was payable even when only a part of the cargo was delivered: the loss of freight was deemed to be a partial loss.

Price and Another v Maritime Insurance Co Ltd [1901] 2 KB 412, CA

The master of the Italian ship *Cinque* received a loan from a bank in Florida and pledged the ship and freight as security. The bank then insured the advance with the defendants under a policy of insurance which was claused as being 'free of all average'. During the voyage from Pensacola to Southampton, *Cinque* encountered severe weather and, whilst trying to put into the Azores for shelter, was driven ashore and became a constructive total loss. Part of the cargo of timber was saved and forwarded to the purchasers, who then paid £790 distance freight, permissible under Italian law, to the master. The bank, which received none of the distance freight paid, then sought to recover under their policy, but the insurers refused payment, on the basis that there had not been a total loss of the subject matter insured as part of the freight had been paid.

The Court of Appeal, in affirming the judgment of Bigham J, ruled that there had not been a total loss of the subject matter insured. The subject matter insured in the advance included the freight, and the freight had only suffered a partial loss.

> **AL Smith MR:** [p 416] ... What happened subsequently was this. The ship got as far as the Azores on her voyage, and then became a constructive total loss, and, had it not been that the Italian law applied, there would have been a total loss of the freight; but by reason of the provisions of that law, distance freight was earned by the ship, and paid, to the amount of £790. Under these circumstances, can it be said that there was a total loss of the subject matter of insurance? The liability of the master and the charge on the ship have been no doubt lost, but it cannot be said that charge on the freight was totally lost. Consequently there was, at the most, only a partial loss. And, as the insurance was only against total loss, the action must fail.

Chartered freight – substituted cargo

When a vessel is chartered, the freight that is payable under that charterparty may be insured, but, unlike ordinary freight, the chartered freight is the freight payable on the whole adventure, be it voyage or time.

Thus, if an intended cargo is not carried or is lost, it may be substituted by an alternative cargo and, should the freight on that substituted cargo amount to less than that originally insured, the assured will have suffered a partial loss.

In *Rankin v Potter* (1873) LR 6 HL, 83, where there was a total loss of chartered freight, Brett J suggested: [p 99] '... An actual total loss of the whole cargo will occasion an actual total loss of freight, unless such loss should so happen as to leave the ship capable, as to time, place, and condition, of earning an equal or some freight by carrying other cargo on the voyage insured.'

Goods carried in a substituted ship

As, under common law, freight on goods is payable on delivery, it is still possible to earn that freight if the goods are carried on a substituted ship. That is, should the assured be unable to fulfil the contract of carriage by carrying the goods himself, he may choose to forward the goods by other means and still earn the freight on delivery.

Again, in *Rankin v Potter* (1873) LR 6 HL 83, where the whole issue of freight was considered in depth by Brett J, the question of the substitution of the ship was raised. Brett J observed that: [p 99] '... An actual total loss of ship will occasion an actual total loss of freight, unless, when the ship is lost, cargo is on board, and the whole or part of such cargo is saved, and might be sent on a substituted ship so as to earn freight.'

Expenses incurred in substituting a ship are recoverable as sue and labour

Although a policy may be warranted free from particular average and there is a partial loss of freight, the cost of providing a substitute ship can be recovered as sue and labour. To this effect, s 76(2) of the Act states:

> Where the subject matter insured is warranted free from particular average, either wholly or under a certain percentage, the insurer is nevertheless liable for salvage charges, and for particular charges and other expenses properly incurred pursuant to the provisions of the suing and labouring clause in order to avert a loss insured against.

Furthermore, s 78(1) states:

> Where the policy contains a suing and labouring clause, the engagement thereby entered into is deemed to be supplementary to the contract of insurance, and the assured may recover from the insurer any expenses properly incurred pursuant to the clause, notwithstanding that the insurer may have paid for a total loss, or that the subject matter may have been warranted free from particular average, either wholly or under a certain percentage.

The principles now contained within the Act were established in the case of *Kidston v Empire Marine Insurance Co Ltd*, below.

Kidston and Others v Empire Marine Insurance Co Ltd (1866) LR 1 CP 535

The plaintiffs were the owners of *Sebastapol*, which was chartered for a voyage from Peru to the UK with a cargo of guano. The chartered freight was then insured by the plaintiffs with the defendants for £5,000. Although the policy contained the usual sue and labour clause, it was warranted free from particular average. On the voyage by way of Cape Horn, *Sebastapol* was so damaged by bad weather that she had to put into Rio de Janeiro, where she was declared a constructive total loss. The master then chartered another vessel, *Caprice*, for £2,467 11s 10d, to carry the guano to the UK, which was so done. When the plaintiffs had paid the owners of *Caprice* the chartered sum, they then claimed on their insurers for the expenses incurred in chartering *Caprice* as well as cargo handling fees. The underwriters denied liability, contending that the policy was warranted free from particular average.

The court ruled that the plaintiffs could recover under sue and labour; the term particular average did not include expenses incurred in saving the subject matter insured for which the underwriters were liable, and that such expenses were allowed under the name of particular charges.

> **Willes J:** [p 541] ... As to the first question [whether the expenses incurred were of a character to be within the sue and labour clause], it was hardly disputed that the expenses incurred were of a character to be within the clause. Without incurring them, the subject matter of the insurance never would have had any complete existence. They were incurred in order to earn it; and they represented so much labour beyond and besides the ordinary labour of the voyage, rendered necessary for the salvation of the subject matter of insurance, by reason of a damage and loss within the scope of the policy, the immediate effect of which was that the subject matter insured would also be lost, or rather would never come into existence, unless such labour was bestowed.
>
> [p 542] ... As to the second head – whether the occasion upon which the expenses were incurred was such as to be within the suing and labouring clause ...
>
> [p 544] ... In this case, there is no abandonment, and may be no prospect of one; and yet it is the duty of the master to use all reasonable means to preserve the goods, and obviously for the interest of the underwriters to encourage him in the performance of that duty by contributing to the expense incurred. Not only the generality of the words, but also the subject matter to which they relate, therefore, point to the application of the clause to all cases in which the underwriter is saved from liability to loss, whether partial or total, and whether an abandonment does or may possibly take place or not.
>
> There remains to be considered, thirdly, whether the application of the suing and labouring clause is excluded in this particular case by the warranty against particular average ...
>
> [p 546] ... In our opinion, quite apart from usage, the true construction of the policy, as reconciling and giving effect to all its provisions, is, that the warranty against particular average, does no more than limit the insurance to total loss

of the freight by the perils insured against, without reference to extraordinary labour or expense which may be incurred by the assured in preserving the freight from loss, or rather from never becoming due, by reason of the operation of perils insured against; and that the latter expenses are specially provided for by the suing and labouring clause, and may be recovered thereunder.

[p 552] ... we have, for the reasons already given, come to the conclusion that there was a danger of the total loss of the freight by reason of the loss of the ship by perils insured against; that the measures taken by the plaintiff to avert that loss, and the expense incurred therein, were taken and incurred for the benefit of the underwriters, in averting a loss for which they would have been liable; and so that they were within the suing and labouring clause, and that the underwriters are liable to contribute thereto. It is satisfactory, however, to think, that, in arriving at this conclusion upon the meaning of the contract into which the defendants have entered, we are deciding also in accordance with the approved usage of commerce.

Measure of indemnity

The measure of indemnity for a partial loss of freight is described in s 70 of the Act, which states:

> Subject to any express provision in the policy, where there is a partial loss of freight, the measure of indemnity is such proportion of the sum fixed by the policy in the case of a valued policy, or of the insurable value in the case of an unvalued policy, as the proportion of freight lost by the assured bears to the whole freight at the risk of the assured under the policy.

Thus, when the policy is valued, the measure of indemnity is the proportionate loss of freight as compared with the value fixed by the policy, but when the policy is unvalued, the measure of indemnity is the proportionate loss of freight as compared with the insurable value. This method of computation is in line with the methods used generally in marine insurance.

> The insurable value of freight is defined in s 16(2) of the Act as follows:
>
> In insurance on freight, whether paid in advance or otherwise, the insurable value is the gross amount of the freight at the risk of the assured, plus the charges of insurance.

However, reference must also be made to the Institute Clauses Freight. Clause 14.1 of the ITCF(95) states:[26]

> The amount recoverable under this insurance for any claim for loss of freight shall not exceed the gross freight actually lost.

---

26 See, also, IVCF(95), cl 10.1.

That the indemnity for freight is based upon the gross freight was established as long ago as 1822, in *Palmer v Blackburn*, below.

Palmer v Blackburn (1822) 1 Bing 61

Juliana was on a voyage from the East Indies to London when she was totally lost just before the termination of her voyage; as a result, the plaintiffs suffered a total loss of freight. When the plaintiffs claimed for indemnity on the total loss of freight, the insurers suggested that their liability only amounted to the net freight, that is, the full or gross freight less any charges the plaintiff would normally have had to pay if the vessel had arrived safely: seamen's wages, pilotage, light dues, tonnage duty and dock dues.

The court ruled that the indemnity was to be adjusted on the gross freight. The quotation outlining the principle is taken from the headnote of the case.

> **Dallas CJ** *dubitante*: [p 61] ... The general principle of insurance, that the assured shall, in the case of loss, recover no more than an indemnity, may be controlled by a mercantile usage clearly established to the contrary: and usage, that the loss in an open policy on freight shall be adjusted on the gross, and not on the net amount of the freight, is a legal usage.

The issue of what may or may not be included in 'gross freight' was raised in *United States Shipping v Express Assurance Corporation*, below. However, the court was of the opinion that gross freight could only include charges directly related to the insurance premium.

United States Shipping v Express Assurance Corporation [1907] 1 KB 259

The plaintiffs time chartered the vessel *Hero* and then, as chartered owners, subchartered her to an American railway company for the carriage of coal from Baltimore to Colon in central America. The plaintiffs had insured any freight, including chartered freight, with the defendants under a time policy of insurance. During the currency of the subcharter, *Hero* was part way through discharging her cargo of coal in Colon when she was lost due to a peril of the seas. The coal, which was still on board, was also lost and there was a total loss of freight. The plaintiffs claimed on their policy of insurance for a partial loss of freight. The questions before the court were: (a) in addition to the premium on the policy, could the plaintiffs recover the commission of £16 which had been paid to secure the charterparty with the railway company? (b) whether £54, representing two days' hire, which still had to run under the charterparty and which was lost when *Hero* sank, should be deducted from the claim.

The court ruled that neither the hire saved nor the commission paid in securing the charterparty could be taken into account under the policy.

> **Channel J:** [p 262] ... I think that if there had been evidence before me in this case of a custom to include a commission paid on getting a charterparty or on

getting freight, I might have allowed the commission claimed, but in the absence of any evidence of custom, I think I am bound to hold that the commission is not recoverable under the policy, unless it is a commission upon getting a premium.

With regard to the defendants' contention that the amount of two days' hire, £54, must be deducted from the claim, there are no decisions of the courts here upon the point, but it does appear that some trustworthy text-writers take the view that, where a charterer loses freight by reason of perils of the sea and by the same event is saved payment in the way of hire, then, notwithstanding the rule as to gross freight, the amount of hire which has been saved may be deducted; and if the question is looked at logically and as a matter of principle, that is clearly right, because insurance is only an indemnity ... If the principle of indemnity were carefully adhered to, an account would have to be taken in every case showing exactly what had been lost and exactly what had been saved, and the account would be an extremely difficult one to take, and to get rid of that difficulty, the rule has been adopted that an insurance on freight is to be an insurance, not upon the net amount, but on the gross amount of freight receivable. That being the rule, the defendants are not in my opinion entitled to say that, although the plaintiffs have lost a certain amount of freight, they have by the same cause been saved the cost of two days' hire which would have been incurred if the cargo had not been lost. That is, in effect, asking that an account should be taken, but the rule shows that that is not to be done.

The Franchise Clause

Clause 12 of the ITCF(95) states:[27]

> This insurance does not cover partial loss, other than general average loss, under 3%, unless caused by fire, sinking, stranding or collision with another vessel. Each craft and/or lighter to be deemed a separate insurance if required by the Assured.

It is emphasised that, unlike the Deductible Clause in a policy on a ship,[28] whereby the insurer bears no liability until the percentage threshold is passed, with the Franchise Clause on freight, the insurer bears the loss in full once the prescribed threshold is passed.

References and further reading

Anderson, C, 'Liability for successive losses in marine insurance contracts: a comparative view' [1985] JMLC 553

---

27 See, also, IVCF(95), cl 9.
28 See above, p 677.

CHAPTER 18

PARTIAL LOSS – 2

SALVAGE, GENERAL AVERAGE AND SUE AND LABOUR

Introduction

Salvage charges, general average and sue and labour are all forms of loss incurred at a time of emergency; though somewhat closely interwoven, they also remain distinct and separate in so far as their recoverability under a policy of marine insurance is concerned. They all come under the umbrella of 'partial loss'.[1] And, though a 'particular average loss' is also partial loss, the Act has not included all forms of partial losses within the realm of 'particular average'. This is made clear by s 64(1), which declares that: 'A particular average loss is a partial loss of the subject matter insured, caused by a peril insured against, and which is not a general average loss', and by s 64(2), which states that: 'Particular charges are not included in particular average.' Thus, though general average and particular charges are partial losses, they are not particular average losses.[2] Salvage charges are also partial losses, but as they have not been expressly excluded from the province of 'particular average', they are particular average losses.[3]

Warranted free from particular average

The above categorisation is significant should a policy contain a 'warranted free from particular average' clause (sometimes referred to simply as the fpa clause), which is, in fact, an exception clause and not a promissory 'warranty' in the true marine insurance sense of the term. Though the expression 'particular average' is used, it is commonly understood to mean that all *partial losses* are not covered by the policy.[4] The question which thus arises is, are salvage charges, general average and particular charges (sue and labour) recoverable under a policy containing a 'warranted from free particular average' clause? If the words 'particular average' in the warranty are given a broad construction to mean partial losses, then, salvage, general average and

---

1 The main heading of the Act reads as follows: 'Partial Losses (Including Salvage and General Average and Particular Charges)'.
2 See, also, Rules for Construction of Policy, r 13.
3 See, also, s 65(1).
4 Regrettably, the terms 'particular average' and 'partial loss' are often used interchangeably.

particular charges (which are all partial losses) should not be recoverable under a policy containing such a warranty. But, if 'particular average' is given its strict meaning, then, only salvage charges are caught by the warranty, and are, therefore, not recoverable under such a policy.

Though 'salvage charges' were considered by the common law as irrecoverable in a policy containing a free from particular average warranty,[5] the position under the Act is different, for s 76(2) of the Act states that:

> Where the subject matter insured is warranted free from particular average, either wholly or under a certain percentage, the insurer is nevertheless liable for salvage charges, and for particular charges and other expenses properly incurred pursuant to the provisions of the suing and labouring clause in order to avert a loss insured against.

As a 'particular charge' is not a particular average loss (as is made clear by s 64(2)), there is no real need for the above section to reiterate that the insurer is liable for 'particular charges' in a policy containing such a warranty. As such a loss is clearly not a particular average loss, it does not come within the purview of the warranty.

In relation to general average, the Act has, through s 76(1), expressly declared that: 'Where the subject matter of insurance is warranted free from particular average, the assured cannot recover for a loss of part, other than a loss incurred by a general average sacrifice ...' Such a declaration, save for the purpose of clarification, is also unnecessary, as a general average loss has been expressly excluded from the definition of 'particular average' by s 64(1), and is, therefore, not affected by warranty.

To sum up, when a policy is warranted 'free from particular average', the assured is prohibited from claiming for a particular average loss. It does not, however, prevent him from claiming other expenses, such as general average and sue and labour (neither of which is a particular average loss), and salvage charges, which, by s 76(2), are expressly said to be recoverable from the insurer.

In relation to sue and labour, the case of **Kidston v Empire Marine Insurance Co Ltd (1866) LR 1 CP 535** may be cited to illustrate the point. On this occasion, the assured successfully claimed under the head of sue and labour, even though the policy on freight was warranted free from particular average. After the ship was badly damaged, the assured incurred costs for chartering a substitute vessel to transport the cargo to the UK.

> **Willes J:** [p 546] ... In our opinion, quite apart from usage, the true construction of the policy, as reconciling and giving effect to all its provisions, is, that the warranty against particular average, does no more than limit the insurance to

---

5 See *Dixon v Whitworth* (1880) 4 Asp MLC 326, CA, discussed later. The ruling by the Court of Appeal that the salvage charges were not recoverable by reason of the warranty must now be regarded as having been negated by s 76(2) of the Act.

total loss of the freight by the perils insured against, without reference to extraordinary labour or expense which may be incurred by the assured in preserving the freight from loss, or rather from never becoming due, by reason of the operation of perils insured against; and that the latter expenses are specially provided for by the suing and labouring clause, and may be recovered thereunder.

SALVAGE CHARGES

Introduction

The philosophy behind this concept was adequately summed up as long ago as 1793 by Lord Eyre CJ, in *Nicholson v Chapman*, below, where the court had to differentiate between salvage and a claim for preserving mislaid property.

Nicholson v Chapman (1793) 2 H Bl 254

A considerable quantity of timber, owned by the plaintiff, was placed in a dock on the bank of the Thames. However, the fastenings gave way, and the timber was carried by the tide to Putney, where it was recovered by the defendant. The defendant then refused to hand over the timber to the plaintiff until a suitable salvage award had been made by the plaintiff. The plaintiff refused such payment.

The court ruled that this was not a case of salvage, and then went on to show why it was not.

> **Lord Eyre CJ:** [p 257] ... The taking of goods left by the tide upon the banks of a navigable river, communicating with the sea, may in a vulgar sense be said to be salvage; but it has none of the qualities of salvage, in respect of which the laws of all civilised nations, the laws of Oleron, and our own laws in particular, have provided that a recompense is due for the saving, and that our law has also provided that this recompense should be a lien upon the goods which have been saved. Goods carried by sea are necessarily and unavoidably exposed to the perils which storms, tempest and accidents (far beyond the reach of human foresight to prevent) are hourly creating, and against which, it too often happens that the greatest diligence and the most strenuous exertions of the marine cannot protect them. When good are thus in imminent danger of being lost, it is most frequently at the hazard of the lives of those who save them, that they are saved. Principles of public policy dictate to civilised and commercial countries, not only the property, but even the absolute necessity of establishing a liberal recompense for the encouragement of those who engage in so dangerous a service.
>
> Such are the grounds upon which salvage stands ... but see how very unlike salvage is to the case now under consideration ... the timber is found lying upon the banks of the rivers, and is taken into the possession, and under the care of the defendants, without any extraordinary exertions, without the least

personal risk, and in truth, with very little trouble. It is therefore a case of mere finding, and taking care of the thing found ... for the owner.

Definition of salvage charges

The term 'salvage charges' is defined in s 65(2) of the Act thus:

> 'Salvage charges' means the charges recoverable under maritime law by a salvor independently of contract. They do not include the expenses of services in the nature of salvage rendered by the assured or his agents, or any person employed for hire by them, for the purpose of averting a peril insured against. Such expenses, where properly incurred, may be recovered as particular charges or as a general average loss, according to the circumstances under which they were incurred.

That salvage charges are recoverable under a policy of insurance is confirmed by cl 10.1 of the ITCH(95), which states:

> This insurance covers the Vessel's proportion of salvage, salvage charges ... reduced in respect of any under-insurance ...[6]

A similar provision is made with respect to goods in cl 2 of the ICC (A), (B) and (C), which affirm that:

> This insurance covers general average and salvage charges, adjusted or determined according to the contract of affreightment and/or governing law and practice, incurred to avoid or in connection with the avoidance of loss from any cause except those excluded in cll 4, 5, 6 and 7 [the exclusion clauses] or elsewhere in this insurance.

Section 65(1) of the Act clearly places salvage charges as an integral part of any particular average loss when it states:

> Subject to any express provision in the policy, salvage charges incurred in preventing a loss by perils insured against may be recovered as a loss by those perils.

Thus, salvage charges are recoverable as part of the claim for the particular average loss.

Meaning of independently of contract

Section 65(2) of the Act defines 'salvage charges' as 'charges recoverable under the maritime law by a salvor independently of contract'. In so stating, the Act is differentiating between what may be termed as true salvage and the hiring of assistance in time of need.

When the Act employs the term 'independently of contract', it is referring to an agreement of salvage which has its roots in maritime law and not in

---

6   See, also, IVCH(95), cl 8.1.

contract. The principle behind this concept is clearly illustrated by Lowndes and Rudolf, who suggests that:

> Where the Marine Insurance Act defines 'salvage charges' as meaning '... the charges recoverable under maritime law by a salvor independently of contract', it does not require that the salvage services should be performed without a contract, but is simply restating the far more fundamental concept that the right to an award of salvage is independent of whether there was a contract or not.[7]

The LOF salvage agreement

To this end, Lloyd's Open Form (LOF) 1995[8] specifically describes itself as an 'agreement', rather than a contract, and, as it operates in accordance with the principles of the law maritimes on a 'no cure – no pay' basis, it is presumed that such an agreement would fall within the definition of 'salvage charges' as contained within the Act.

Some indirect confirmation that salvage under a Lloyd's Open Form would be construed as 'salvage charges' can be found in the case of *'Raisby'*, below. Although this was not an insurance case, it is, nevertheless, relevant, in that it involved salvage under a voluntary agreement which was not unlike the terms contained within a Lloyd's Salvage Agreement.

The Raisby (1885) 10 PD 114

The defendants were the owners of the steamship *Raisby* which, on a voyage from Bombay to Dunkirk, became disabled in the Bay of Biscay. The plaintiffs' steamer *Gironde* went to her assistance, and the following document was signed by the two captains: 'At my request, the captain of the steamship *Gironde*, of Cardiff, will tow my ship, the steamship *Raisby*, of London, to St Nazaire, that being the nearest port, for repairs. The matter of compensation to be left to arbitrators at home, to be appointed by the respective owners.' Thereupon, *Gironde* towed *Raisby* to St Nazaire, where she was repaired, before continuing to Dunkirk and delivering her cargo. Having succeeded in claiming a salvage award against the ship and freight, the plaintiffs were unsuccessful in their action in the French courts against the cargo-owners. Thus, the present action against the defendant owners of *Raisby* was for the unresolved salvage award owed by the cargo-owners for which the plaintiffs considered them responsible under the salvage agreement.

The court ruled that the agreement amounted to salvage proper and not to contractual salvage as such. Therefore, there could be no question of general

---

7 Lowndes, R and Rudolf, GR, *The Law of General Average and the York-Antwerp Rules*, 11th edn, 1990, London: Sweet & Maxwell, p 252.
8 See Appendix 23.

average contributions by the cargo-owners, and the shipowner was not liable for any salvage award which was directly owed by the cargo-owners.

> **Sir James Hannen:** [p 116] ... It seems to me that no primary liability rests on the ship or its owners to pay for the salvage of the cargo. It is laid down in *Abbott on Shipping*, title Salvage: 'With respect to the parties liable to pay salvage, and the interest in respect of which it is payable, the rule is that the property actually benefited is alone chargeable with the salvage recovered.' ... The so called agreement, however, does not purport to extend the liability of the shipowners, or, indeed, to fix any liability on any one, except in so far as such liability may be created by the acknowledgment which it contains that the captain of *Raisby* had requested the captain of *Gironde* to tow his ship to St Nazaire. This part of the document in no way alters the position of the matter from what it would have been if the captain of *Raisby* had simply accepted the services of *Gironde*, in which case it has not been contended that a claim would have been maintained against the ship or its owners for salvage of the cargo ... It appears to me, therefore, that the plaintiffs altogether fail to show any liability on the part of the defendants to pay for the salvage of the cargo.

Notes

Thus, only expenses for salvage which are incurred independently of contract are recoverable under the denomination of 'salvage charges' under the Act.[9] Typically, these would include salvage services rendered on a 'no cure, no pay' basis. Any salvage which is contractual and amounts to the 'hiring' of assistance is not a 'salvage charge', but may constitute a particular charge (which may be recouped under the auspices of sue and labour), or general average, according to the circumstances under which they were incurred.

True salvage, namely, salvage which arises independently of contract, is only applicable to maritime property, and this would include a ship, her apparel or cargo. For such salvage to be earned, the efforts of the salvor must be voluntary and successful. Furthermore, true salvage establishes a lien on the property salved. The whole concept of salvage is to encourage the preservation of maritime property, including life, and any remuneration for such services is dependent on those services being given voluntarily, leading to a successful salving of the property.

Life salvage

Traditionally, an award for life salvage was not provided for under the common law, until the Merchant Shipping Act of 1854 made suitable provision. That provision remains in force under s 544 of the Merchant Shipping Act 1894, which states:

---

9   See *op cit*, Lowndes and Rudolf, fn 7.

Where services are rendered wholly or in part within British waters in saving life from any British or foreign vessel, or elsewhere in saving life from any British vessel, there shall be payable to the salvor by the owner of the vessel, cargo, or apparel saved, a reasonable amount of salvage, to be determined in case of dispute in manner hereinafter mentioned.

Although, at first sight, s 544 still appears to link life salvage with the salvage of property, this is not, in fact, the case. Under statute, an award can be made for life salvage, even when it is made independently of salvage services to property. This was made abundantly clear by Lord Esher MR, in *Nourse v Liverpool Sailing Ship Owners Mutual Protection and Indemnity Association*, below. It is further emphasised that the statutory provision places the liability for life salvage upon the owner of the ship or the cargo saved, and not the insurer; a policy of insurance is a separate matter. As regards insurance, the court concluded that an insurer bore no liability for life salvage.

Nourse v Liverpool Sailing Ship Owners Mutual Protection and Indemnity Association (1879) 4 App Cas 755, CA

In March 1895, the sailing vessel *Arno* was in grave peril in mid-Atlantic when the master and crew were rescued by the steamer *Normannia*; *Arno* herself being salved later by another vessel. In due course, the Admiralty granted an award of life salvage to the owner, master and crew of *Normannia*, and the plaintiff owner of *Arno* paid the award before attempting to recover the amount so paid from their P & I Association. The defendant P & I Association rejected the claim, on the basis that, under cl 18 of their rules, they were not liable for any payment '... in respect of any loss which is capable of being insured against by the usual form of Lloyd's policy ...' and that, under the clause, life salvage was the liability of the hull insurer, and not the P & I Association.

The Court of Appeal affirmed the decision of the trial judge, and ruled that a Lloyd's policy did not cover life salvage. Furthermore, Lord Esher MR was of the opinion that an award for life salvage under statute did not have to be accompanied by the salvage of property.

> **Lord Esher MR:** [p 22] ... The reward given by the statute for saving life is independent of any salvage services rendered in respect of property, whereas, under the maritime law, salvors never could recover anything in respect of life saved unless they had also rendered salvage services in respect of property. Although it is called salvage, the reward given by statute is not like ordinary salvage. It is a new head of salvage altogether. The statute can have no effect, as it appears to me, on the meaning of the ordinary form of Lloyd's policy, because the life salvage for which it provides is a new head of salvage altogether, which was not in existence when the form first came into use, and could not have been in the contemplation of its framers. For these reasons, I think that the loss for which the plaintiff claims is not within the meaning, as it is not within the terms, of an ordinary Lloyd's policy, and therefore is not

within r 18 of the defendants' rules. In my opinion, the judgment of Matthew J was right, and should be affirmed.

However, in the much later case of *Bosworth (No 3)*, below, where the crew were saved at the same time as the ship and cargo were saved, but by another vessel, the court was of the opinion that the life salvage could be included within the meaning of s 65(1) of the Act, even though it involved 'a little stretching of the language'. Whether a court would take a similar wide view where life salvage stood entirely alone is much more debatable.

Grand Union Shipping Limited v London SS Owners' Mutual Insurance Association Ltd, 'Bosworth' (No 3) [1962] 1 Lloyd's Rep 483

On a voyage from Edinburgh to Norway, *The Bosworth* encountered severe weather and was in danger of sinking. Two trawlers and a merchant ship came to her aid, and she was eventually towed into Aberdeen. However, one of the trawlers, *Wolverhampton Wanderers*, was damaged whilst saving the entire crew, and her owners successfully claimed a life salvage award from the Admiralty Court. Having paid out this salvage award, the owners of *Bosworth* then sought to recoup this expenditure from their insurers, who denied liability for the life salvage and suggested that the whole salvage award for the ship and cargo should have been apportioned between the three salving vessels.

The court ruled against any such apportionment, and decided that *Wolverhampton Wanderers* was entitled to recover for the 'enhanced' award of saving life under the Lloyd's policy because she had been involved in the saving of the ship and cargo.

> **McNair J:** [p 490] ... It needs possibly a little stretching of the language to say that a salvage award in so far as it reflects an element of life salvage gives rise to a charge incurred in preventing a loss by perils insured against. I think the answer to that is that by the practice of the Admiralty Court an award made in these circumstances is treated as being, and is in fact, an award for services rendered to the ship and cargo.
>
> The matter, I think, however, is made quite plain by the decision of the Court of Appeal in the case of *Nourse v Liverpool Sailing Ship Owners' Mutual Protection and Indemnity Association* [1896] 2 QB 16. In that case, the sailing vessel *Arno*, which was entered in the defendants' association, had been in great peril in the mid-Atlantic, and her master and crew were rescued by the steamship Normannia. Later, quite independently of that operation, *Arno* herself was picked up by another vessel, *Merrimac*, and brought into Liverpool by a salvage crew. The owners of *Normannia* recovered against the ship an award for true life salvage under the Merchant Shipping Act 1894. That is all they could recover, because they had not helped to save the ship or cargo at all. The question at issue in the case was whether such an award was payable under a Lloyd's policy in the usual form, because, if it was, the liability was excluded from the club cover. It was held by Matthew J that it was not, on the ground that the award in that case was not a true maritime salvage award, but

was a special award under the terms of the Merchant Shipping Act 1894 ... I think it is clearly implicit in his judgment that if the award in that case had been, like *Wolverhampton Wanderers'* award in this case, a true maritime salvage award for saving ship and cargo, enhanced by consideration of life salvage, he would have held that was recoverable under a Lloyd's policy.

An enhanced award for preventing or minimising environmental damage

Clause 10.5 of the ITCH(95) categorically allows recovery from the insurer for the Vessel's proportion of salvage charges. However, it fails to mention whether any additional sum included in the salvage award apportioned for preventing or minimising damage to the environment under Art 13(1)(b) of the International Convention on Salvage 1989 may be included in the claim. The position is clarified in cl 10.6 as follows:

> Clause 10.5 shall not however exclude any sum which the Assured shall pay to salvors for or in respect of salvage remuneration in which the skill and efforts of the salvors in preventing or minimising damage to the environment as is referred to in Art 13(1)(b) of the International Convention on Salvage 1989 have been taken into account.

Thus, any enhancement of the award made under Art 13 is recoverable by the assured.

Incurred in preventing a loss by perils insured against

Like all forms of partial loss, salvage charges are only recoverable if, to quote s 65(1) of the Act, they are '... incurred in preventing a loss by perils insured against ...'. This principle is reinforced by cl 10.4 of the ITCH(95), which states:

> No claim under this cl 10 shall in any case be allowed where the loss was not incurred to avoid or in connection with the avoidance of a peril insured against.[10]

The principle that salvage charges are recoverable provided that they are incurred in preventing a loss by a peril insured against was confirmed by Lord Blackburn in *Aitchison v Lohre* (1879) 4 App Cas, HL, who said that: [p 765] '... The amount of such salvage occasioned by a peril has always been recovered, without dispute, under an averment that there was a loss by that peril ...'

That salvage is not recoverable when it does not arise from a peril insured against was clearly illustrated in *Ballantyne v Mackinnon*, below.

Ballantyne v Mackinnon (1896) 2 QB 455, CA

The plaintiff was the owner of the steamship *Progress*, which was insured with the defendants under a time policy of insurance. On a voyage from Hamburg

---

10 See, also, IVCH(95), cl 8.4.

to Sunderland, *Progress* ran short of coal, and was towed into port by a trawler which was later granted a salvage award of £350. The plaintiffs paid the award, and then sought to recover the sum from their insurers.

The Court of Appeal upheld the decision of the trial judge, and ruled that the underwriters were not liable for the salvage charges, as they had not arisen from a peril insured against.

AL Smith LJ: [p 459] ... The Lord Chief Justice says [in the court of first instance]:

> It was admitted by the plaintiff that there was no weather which rendered salvage assistance necessary, and that the need of assistance of the trawler and the tug was occasioned by the want of coal ... Can it be said on the facts here stated that the salvage services were at all rendered necessary, or the salvage expenses incurred by reason of any peril insured against? In my judgment it cannot ... that condition arose directly from the absence of fuel, and no damage or peril of the sea supervened. In other words, it was the unseaworthiness of the ship which caused the need – if need there were – of salvage aid, and no peril of the sea caused or contributed to the necessity for the aid.

> [p 461] ... As before stated, we agree with the Lord Chief Justice when he held upon the evidence before him that the loss sustained was not occasioned by a peril of the sea, for in our judgment the loss complained of arose solely by reason of the inherent vice of the subject matter insured: we mean the insufficiency of coal with which the ship started upon her voyage ...

The same criterion was applied in ***Pyman Steamship Co v Lords Commissioners of the Admiralty* [1919] 1 KB 49, CA**. Although this was not an insurance case, the issue of salvage was raised with respect to a wartime requisition charter. On this occasion, the vessel in question broke her propeller shaft in severe weather close to a minefield. Salvage services were needed so that she could be towed to safety, away from the adjacent minefield, as well as to avert further damage by perils of the seas. Under the charterparty, the Admiralty were liable for 'the consequences of hostilities or warlike operations', but not sea risks; they were obliged to pay only for the proportion of salvage consequent on the war risk.

Warrington LJ: [p 54] ... Payments made to avert a peril may be recovered as a loss by the peril.

Scrutton LJ: [p 55] ... Ever since the decision in *Aitchison v Lohre*, and long before that, it has been a commonplace in mercantile law that sums paid to avert a peril may be recovered as upon a loss by that peril, and as soon as it is established that this sum of £3,000 was paid partly to avert a sea peril and partly to avert a peril from enemy mines, it follows that there has been one loss by sea perils and another by war perils. The parties have agreed that the appellants shall not be liable for loss by sea perils, and shall be liable for loss by war perils.

Exclusions

Clause 10.1 of the ITCH(95) states that:

> This insurance covers the Vessel's proportion of salvage, salvage charges and/or general average, reduced in respect of any under-insurance ...[11]

But the ITCH(95) then goes on to affirm, in cl 10.5, that:

> No claim under this cl 10 shall in any case be allowed for or in respect of:
>
> 10.5.1 special compensation payable to a salvor under Art 14 of the International Convention on Salvage 1989 or under any other provision in any statute, rule, law or contract which is similar in substance;
>
> 10.5.2 expenses or liabilities incurred in respect of damage to the environment, or the threat of such damage, or as a consequence of the escape or release of pollutant substances from the Vessel, or the threat of such escape or release.[12]

Thus, the policy excludes the insurer from liability for environmental damage, but no such exclusion applies to salvage efforts made in order to prevent or minimise such environmental damage. This is clarified in cl 10.6,[13] which has been discussed earlier.[14]

Salvage charges and sue and labour compared

The line between salvage charges, sue and labour, and general average is subtle, but distinct, and, to this effect, s 65(2) of the Act states that salvage charges do not:

> ... include the expenses of services in the nature of salvage rendered by the assured or his agents, or any person employed for hire by them, for the purpose of averting a peril insured against. Such expenses, where properly incurred, may be recovered as particular charges or as a general average loss, according to the circumstances under which they were incurred.

Section 65(2) is included in the Act following the ruling in *Aitchison v Lohre*, below, where it was held that salvage could not be included within the concept of sue and labour. The reasoning behind the decision was that the sue and labour clause within the policy is not intended to encompass true salvage. The sue and labour clause has been inserted for the benefit of the insurer in so far as it is intended to encourage the shipowner to avert or minimise losses and then be recompensed for such expenses incurred. Sue and labour,

---

11 See, also, IVCH(95), cl 8.1.
12 See, also, IVCH(95), cl 8.5.
13 See, also, IVCH(95), cl 8.6.
14 See above, p 727.

therefore, is distinct from true salvage, and usually takes the form of the hiring of assistance, which is then recoverable by way of particular charges.

Aitchison v Lohre (1879) 4 App Cas 755

The plaintiffs' vessel *Crimea* was insured with the defendants for £1,200, her value being £2,600. The policy contained the usual sue and labour clause. After running into difficulties, *Crimea* was rescued by the steamship *Texas* which was later granted a salvage award by the Irish Court of Admiralty amounting to £800. Because the measure of indemnity, including the cost of repairs and the salvage award, was limited by the insured value of £1,200, less one-third new for old, the owners sought to recover the £800 salvage award as sue and labour, as the latter was recoverable over and above the insured value.

The House of Lords ruled that the £800 award was salvage and not sue and labour. Therefore, the insurers were only liable for the cost of repairs, and any salvage expenses, up to the insured value of the vessel. The court then considered the whole relationship between salvage and sue and labour.

Lord Blackburn: [p 764] ... With great deference to the judges of the Court of Appeal, I think that general average and salvage do not come within either the words or the object of the suing and labouring clause, and that there is no authority for saying that they do. The words of the clause are that in case of any misfortune it shall be lawful 'for the assured, their factors, servants, and assigns, to sue, labour, and travel for, in, and about the defence, safeguard, and recovery of' the subject of insurance, 'without prejudice to this insurance, to the charges whereof we the insurers will contribute'. And, the object of this is to encourage and induce the insured to exert themselves, and, therefore, the insurers bind themselves to pay in proportion any expense incurred, whenever such expense is reasonably incurred for the preservation of the thing from loss, in consequence of the efforts of the assured or their agents. It is all one whether the labour is by the assured or their agents themselves, or by persons whom they have hired for the purpose, but the object was to encourage exertion on the part of the assured; not to provide an additional remedy for the recovery, by the assured, of indemnity for a loss which was, by the maritime law, a consequence of the peril.

[p 765] ... The owners of *Texas* did the labour here, not as agents of the assured, and being paid by them wages for their labour, but as salvors acting on the maritime law.

Lord Cairns LC: [p 766] ... I will only make one observation with regard to salvage expenses. It appears to me to be quite clear that if any expenses were to be recoverable under the suing and labouring clause, they must be expenses assessed upon the *quantum meruit* principle. Now salvage expenses are not assessed upon the *quantum meruit* principle; they are assessed upon the general principle of maritime law, which gives to the persons who bring in the ship a sum quite out of proportion to the actual expense incurred and the actual service rendered, the largeness of the sum being based upon this consideration

– that if the effort to save the ship (however laborious in itself, and dangerous in its circumstances) had not been successful, nothing whatever would have been paid. If the payment were to be assessed and made under the suing and labouring clause, it would be payment for service rendered, whether the service had succeeded in bringing the ship into port or not.

Lord Hatherley: [p 768] ... it is equally clear, as it seems to me, that the suing and labouring clause was inserted by the underwriters for the purpose of securing the benefit of any pains that the shipowner might be inclined to take in preserving, for their benefit, as much as he possibly could preserve. But that does not apply to a case like the present, where the salvage seems to have been an ordinary sort of salvage, namely, a ship perceiving another at a distance and in a state of distress comes to the rescue, no bargain being made. We were expressly told in the case that no bargain was made as to any remuneration which should be given, but it was rescued upon the simple and common principle of salvage.

However, one year later, in *Dixon v Whitworth*, below, a claim for salvage was again pursued as sue and labour because the policy of insurance was warranted 'free from particular average'. Because salvage is a form of particular average loss, any claim for such would, under the common law, have been negated by the said clause.

Dixon v Whitworth (1880) 4 Asp MLC 326, CA

The appellants constructed a barge to transport an obelisk from Alexandria to London, and then insured both with the defendant underwriters against total loss only. Because of severe weather conditions in the Bay of Biscay, the barge was cast loose by the towing vessel, but was later rescued by another vessel. The salving vessel was awarded £2,000 by the Admiralty Court, which was duly paid by the appellants, who then sought to recover that sum from their insurers under the sue and labour clause in the policy. The underwriters denied liability, contending that the award had been for salvage, which, being a form of particular average, was not covered by the policy, which only insured the vessel against a total loss.

The Court of Appeal ruled that the rescue amounted to salvage charges, and not sue and labour, and, as the salvage charges were a type of particular average loss, the appellants could not recover, as, under the policy, only total losses were insured.

Notes

It is to be noted that *Dixon v Whitworth* was decided before the Act, and, therefore, has now to be read in the light of s 76(2), where salvage charges, though they are particular average losses, are, nevertheless, recoverable even in a policy containing a free from particular average warranty.

As distinct from true salvage, which is the award made by the court for salvage services rendered as a voluntary act on the basis of 'no cure, no pay', sue and labour is an extraordinary expenditure incurred to prevent or minimise loss. It is quite separate from salvage and, because those who sue and labour do so as the agents of the assured, it cannot be said to be voluntary.

Primarily, sue and labour is a duty placed upon the assured under a policy of marine insurance to act in a responsible manner by ensuring that loss or damage to the subject matter insured is averted or minimised and, by so doing, lessens the liability of the insurer. Thus, any claim for sue and labour represents an expenditure which has taken place for the benefit of the underwriter, and such a claim may be recovered separately and independently from other partial losses under the head of particular charges.

Expenses incurred for suing and labouring are recoverable in addition to other claims for damage or loss, and, because of this, such a claim may be added to the primary claim, even though the insured value of the policy may then be surpassed.

Salvage charges and general average compared

When a salvor acts voluntarily and independently of contract on a 'no cure, no pay' basis, the award granted is known as salvage charges. In such an event, the shipowner and cargo are then directly and severally liable to the salvor for any salvage award granted.[15]

But, where assistance is hired under contract, the remuneration is on a *quantum meruit* basis, and is quite separate from true salvage. That is, when assistance is hired, there is a general average expenditure made by the ship for which all the other parties to the adventure are liable to make a contribution by way of general average.

Lowndes and Rudolf (*The Law of General Average and the York-Antwerp Rules*, 11th edn, 1990) clearly illustrate the difference between salvage and general average by way of citing an example:

> It is also to be noted that in engaging the services of the tugs on a salvage basis, the master was not performing a general average act, for he was not thereby sacrificing or committing the property or purses of just one or a few of the parties to the adventure to suffer an immediate loss which would then be shared by all the parties benefited on a pro rata basis via the general average distribution system. In engaging the tugs on a salvage basis, the master was committing each and every one of the parties to the adventure with a liability to settle directly with the salvors for their own individual proportion of any

---

15 See *The Raisby* (1885) 10 PD 114, *per* Sir James Hannen, p 118.

award, and the general average distribution system does not need to be called in aid for any re-allocation of the award.

In *The Raisby*, cited in full above,[16] the whole claim was based on whether the services rendered amounted to true salvage or a general average expenditure. If it was a general average expenditure, the shipowner would have been liable to the salvor for the general average contribution of the cargo-owner, but if it was true salvage, the cargo-owner was independently liable for his portion of the salvage award and the shipowner had no responsibility for such. Thus, it was shown that, with salvage, the interested parties are separately and directly liable to the salvor; there is no 'common fund', as is the case with general average, from which the salvor may draw his remuneration.

> **Sir James Hannen:** [p 118] ... Here, the defendants [the shipowners] have not paid anything in respect of the salvage of the cargo, nor have they entered into any agreement to pay it. As I have pointed out, the liability both as to the parties responsible and as to the amount is left at large, to be determined in due course of law, and that is, as it appears to me, that the plaintiffs must seek their remedy for salvage of cargo, as distinct from ship, from those who have had the benefit of that salvage.

However, in *Anderson, Tritton and Co v Ocean SS Co* (1884) 5 Asp MLC 401, there was an agreement between shipowners that all vessels running into danger on the Yangtze River paid a fixed sum for assistance, regardless of success or failure. In this instance, it was agreed that the cost of the assistance amounted to a general average expenditure, and the owners of both the ship and the cargo were liable to contribute.

> **Lord Blackburn:** [p 404] ... The master has, I think, authority to make for his owners all disbursements which are proper for the general purposes of the voyage ... I think that the disbursement, in so far as it is a disbursement for the salvation of the whole adventure from a common imminent peril, may properly be charged to general average.

Salvage and general average under the York-Antwerp Rules

The subtle differences between salvage and general average, which exist under the common law and the Marine Insurance Act 1906, are removed when the York-Antwerp Rules are incorporated into the contract of affreightment.[17] To that end, Rule VI(a), which applies to all salvage, contractual or otherwise, states:

> Expenditure incurred by the parties to the adventure in the nature of salvage, whether under contract or otherwise, shall be allowed in general average

---

16 See above, p 723.
17 See Appendix 22.

provided that the salvage operations were carried out for the purpose of preserving from peril the property involved in the common maritime adventure.

The relevant Institute Clauses, namely: Hull,[18] Cargo,[19] and Freight,[20] all make provision for the incorporation of the York-Antwerp Rules into the contract of affreightment.

GENERAL AVERAGE

Introduction

The concept of general average is an ancient one, and is totally independent of other branches of the law. This is because, historically, it has grown up in its own right under the common law of the sea, with its roots dating back to classical Greece and probably earlier, to the Phoenician traders.

The rationale behind general average is logical. A loss may take the form of physical damage or expenditure, which may be accidental or intentional. Where it is accidental, it is only right that the loss should lie where it falls, but where the loss, whether in the nature of an expenditure or sacrifice, is incurred intentionally, and such a loss is beneficial to others, then those who have benefited should share that loss. Thus, where parts of a ship or cargo are sacrificed, or expenses are incurred by a ship in order to preserve the property of others who are parties to the common adventure, then that act is said to be a general average act, and the loss incurred is then spread 'generally' amongst the beneficiaries. It, therefore, stands to reason that general average can only exist when there is more than one interested party in the marine adventure.

General average is a unique concept, and the property of a participant in a marine adventure may, at any time, become liable for a contribution for such, should he derive benefit from the general average act. Although this liability is insurable, it is emphasised that the parties to a marine adventure remain bound by the principles of general average, regardless of whether they are, or are not, insured. This was clearly illustrated in *The Brigella* **(1893) PD 189**, the full details of which are cited later in the chapter.[21]

Gorrell Barnes J: [p 195] ... Whichever way it is looked at, the obligation to contribute in general average exists between the parties to the adventure, whether they are insured or not. The circumstance of a party being insured can have no influence upon the adjustment of general average, the rules of which,

---

18 See ITCH(95), cl 10 and IVCH(95), cl 8.
19 See ICC (A), (B) and (C), cl 2.
20 See ITCF(95), cl 11 and IVCH(95), cl 8.
21 See below, p 751.

as I have in effect shown above, are entirely independent of insurance. If a contributing party is insured, he can claim an indemnity against his underwriter in respect of the contribution which he has been compelled to pay in general average, but that is all.

That insurance cover against liability in general average does not alter that liability, but only provides an indemnity, for it was illustrated long ago by Abbott CJ in *Simonds v White* **(1824) 2 B&C 805**, where a ship lost her anchor cable whilst endeavouring to free herself from a reef. When the ship reached her destination, the cargo-owner had a general average charge levied against him for part of the cost of replacing the anchor cable.

Abbott CJ: [p 811] ... The principle of general average, namely, that all whose property has been saved by the sacrifice of the property of another shall contribute to make good his loss, is of very ancient date, and of universal reception among commercial nations. The obligation to contribute, therefore, depends not so much upon the terms of any particular instrument, as upon a general rule of maritime law.

Since the introduction of the Marine Insurance Act 1906, the liability for general average, under the common law of the sea, has been replaced by statute. The Act, in s 66, in no way changes the situation regarding insurance; any insurance remains nothing more than indemnity for such.

This was summed up by Bailhache J in *Brandeis Goldschmidt and Co v Economic Insurance Co Ltd* (1922) 38 TLR 609, where a cargo-owner was unable to recover under a policy of insurance covering general average contributions, because there had been no average adjustment as expressly required by the policy. Bailhache J observed that: [p 610] '... The liability in general average before 1906 arose at common law, and since the Act of 1906 by statute. It did not arise under the policy, but the policy might contain express provisions, modifying or excluding it.'

Definition of general average loss

Although the whole concept of general average has its origins in the common law of the sea, the insurance of such losses is regulated by both statute and the contract of insurance itself. Thus, where insurance is concerned, the statutory umbrella is provided by s 66 of the Act, but the contract of insurance, be it hull[22] or cargo,[23] may then incorporate the York-Antwerp Rules 1994. The said Rules will only apply to the contract of insurance if they are incorporated into the contract of affreightment. The Act, in s 66(1), defines a 'general average loss' as:

---

22 See ITCH(95), cl 10.2 and IVCH(95), cl 8.2.
23 See ICC (A), (B) and (C), cl 2.

... a loss caused by or directly consequential on a general average act. It includes a general average expenditure as well as a general average sacrifice.

Section 66(2) then provides the statutory definition of a 'general average act':

> There is a general average act where any extraordinary sacrifice or expenditure is voluntarily and reasonably made or incurred in time of peril for the purpose of preserving the property imperilled in the common adventure.

Thus, for there to be a general average act, certain criteria must be met. The act must be:

(a) 'extraordinary';

(b) 'voluntarily and reasonably' made;

(c) 'in time of peril'; and

(d) for the purpose of preserving property imperilled in the 'common adventure'.

The statutory definition is, in itself, a codification of the principles laid down in past cases, of which *Birkley v Presgrave*, below, is particularly noteworthy.

Birkley v Presgrave (1801) 1 East 220

The plaintiffs' vessel was entering Sunderland harbour with a cargo of the defendant's corn on board when she was hit by a violent squall. In order to save the ship and cargo, the master endeavoured to tie her up to the south pier. In this, he was successful but, during the process of manoeuvring the ship and saving the cargo, extra personnel were required for assistance. An anchor and its cable were deliberately sacrificed for safety reasons, and some hawsers were also lost. The owners claimed a general average contribution from the defendant cargo-owner.

The court ruled that the actions of the master amounted to general average acts, for which the defendant was liable by way of a contribution.

> **Lord Kenyon CJ:** [p 227] ... With respect to the other question, all ordinary losses and damage sustained by the ship happening immediately from the storm or perils of the sea must be borne by the shipowners. But, all those articles which were made use of by the master and crew upon the particular emergency, and out of the usual course, for the benefit of the whole concern, and the other expenses incurred, must be paid proportionately by the defendant as general average.
>
> **Lawrence J:** [p 228] All loss which arises in consequence of extraordinary sacrifices made or expenses incurred for the preservation of the ship and cargo come within general average, and must be borne proportionately by all who are interested. Natural justice requires this.

A more comprehensive definition of general average was provided by Blackburn J, in *Kemp v Halliday* (1865) 34 LJQB 233,[24] a case which concerned a ship, loaded with cargo, which put into Falmouth for repairs, but which later sank in a squall. The ship was later raised, and both ship and cargo were salved. The court was then faced with deciding who was liable in general average. Thus, the issue of general average was analysed in some depth.

> **Blackburn J:** [p 242] ... In order to give rise to a charge as general average, it is essential that there should be a voluntary sacrifice to preserve more subjects than one exposed to a common jeopardy; but an extraordinary expenditure incurred for that purpose is as much a sacrifice as if, instead of money being expended for the purpose, money's worth were thrown away. It is immaterial whether the shipowner sacrifices a cable or an anchor to get the ship off a shoal, or pays the worth of it to hire those extra services which get her off. It is quite true, that so long as the expenditure by the shipowner is merely such as he should incur in the fulfilment of his ordinary duties as shipowner, it cannot be general average; but the expenditure in raising a submerged vessel with cargo is extraordinary expenditure, and is, if incurred to save the cargo as well as the ship (which, prima facie, is the object of such an expenditure), chargeable against all the subjects in jeopardy saved by this expenditure.

With respect to general average and the definitions contained within the Act, Roche J summed up the application of the different sub-sections briefly, but succinctly, in *Green Star Shipping Co Ltd v London Assurance* [1933] 1 KB 378, where the vessel suffered a fire and then sank after a collision. The court was of the opinion that general average expenses had been incurred.

> **Roche J:** [p 387] ... s 66 has some bearing upon the matter. Sub-sections 1–3 define or formulate the rules of general average as between the parties to the contract of affreightment. The rest of the sub-sections deal with the rights of the assured or liabilities of the insurers. Sub-sections 6 and 7 call for no comment. Sub-section 5 deals with the case where the assured has not made an expenditure, but has paid or is liable to pay a contribution to another party's expenditure. Sub-section 4 deals with two cases: general average expenditure and general average sacrifice.

The Act, however, cannot be considered in isolation, because the York-Antwerp Rules 1994 also provide a definition in Rule A:

> There is a general average act when any extraordinary sacrifice or expenditure is intentionally and reasonably made or incurred for the common safety for the purpose of preserving from peril the property involved in a common maritime adventure.

Although the phraseology is slightly different in that, in particular, the word 'voluntary', as used in the Act, is replaced by the word 'intentionally', the principles embodied in both are not in conflict.

---

24 This case is fully discussed in relation to a constructive total loss in Chapter 16, p 652.

The law of general average was probably best summed up by Lord Denning MR, in *Australian Coastal Shipping Commission v Green* **[1971] 1 All ER 353**, the full facts of which are cited later.[25]

Lord Denning MR: [p 355] ... We so rarely have to consider the law of general average that it is as well to remind ourselves of it. It arises when a ship, laden with cargo, is in peril on the sea, such peril indeed that the whole adventure, both ship and cargo, is in danger of being lost. If the master then, for the sake of all, throws overboard some of the cargo, so as to lighten the ship, it is unjust that the owner of the goods so jettisoned should be left to bear all the loss of it himself. He is entitled to a contribution from the shipowner and the other cargo-owners in proportion to their interests. See the exposition by Lord Tenterden quoted in *Hallett v Wigram* and *Burton v English*. Likewise, if the master, for the sake of all, at the height of a storm, cuts away part of the ship's tackle (as in *Birkley v Presgrave*), or cuts away a mast (as in *Atwood v Sellar and Co*), or, having sprung a leak, puts into a port of refuge for repairs and spends money on them (as in *Svendsen v Wallace Bros*), it is unfair that the loss should fall on the shipowner alone. He is entitled to contribution from the cargo-owners for the loss or expenditure to which he has been put. In all such cases, the act done by the master is called a 'general average act', and the loss incurred is called a 'general average loss'.

General average sacrifice and general average expenditure

There are two distinct forms of general average loss, and this is emphasised by the wording in s 66(1), which states that: 'A general average loss ... includes a general average expenditure as well as a general average sacrifice.' This is confirmed in Rule A of the York-Antwerp Rules 1994, in the following terms: 'There is a general average act when any extraordinary sacrifice or expenditure is intentionally and reasonably made or incurred ...'

Thus, the casting away of cargo or a portion of a ship in time of peril would constitute a general average sacrifice, whilst the engaging of assistance, such as a tow, in order to avert a loss by a peril insured against, would amount to a general average expenditure. Both are general average losses, but brought about in different ways.

Caused by or directly consequential on

The Act, in s 66(1), refers to a general average loss as a loss which is 'caused by' or is 'directly consequential on' a general average act. In similar vein, Rule C of the York-Antwerp Rules[26] states that general average losses, damages or expenses must be as 'the direct consequence of' the general average act. The

---

25 See below, p 739.
26 The first part of Rule C states: 'Only such losses, damages or expenses which are the direct consequence of the general average act shall be allowed as general average.'

implication of the words 'directly consequential on' was clarified by Lord Denning MR, in *Australian Coastal Shipping Commission v Green*, below.

Australian Coastal Shipping Commission v Green and Others [1971] 1 All ER 353, CA

Two separate cases, involving similar issues, came before the Court of Appeal. Both were claims for general average losses against the same underwriter, but under different policies.

(a) *Bulwarra* was in port in New South Wales when a storm struck and put the ship in imminent danger. A tug was engaged to tow *Bulwarra* to safety, but, during the operation, a tow rope broke and wrapped itself around the tug's propeller. Although *Bulwarra* reached safety, the tug drifted aground and became a total loss. The tug's owners unsuccessfully claimed against *Bulwarra*'s owners under the contact of towage (UKSTC), but, in putting up a defence, legal costs were incurred. *Bulwarra*'s owners then claimed those legal costs from their insurers as a general average expenditure.

(b) *Wangara* stranded on a voyage from Melbourne to Auckland, and two tugs were engaged to tow her to safety. During the operation, a tow rope parted and fouled a tug's propeller. Both *Wangara* and the stricken tug were successfully rescued, the latter being towed by a local pilot vessel, which was then granted a salvage award. The tug's owners then claimed to be indemnified by *Wangara*'s owners under the terms of the contract of towage (UKSTC). *Wangara* was held liable, and her owners then claimed for this loss to be indemnified by their underwriters as a general average loss.

The Court of Appeal ruled that, in both instances, the losses were general average losses. The towage contracts amounted to general average acts, and the expenses incurred were in direct consequence of those general average acts.

> **Lord Denning MR:** [p 357] ... The 'general average act' was, I think, the contract made by the plaintiffs with the tug. In each case, the vessel was in dire peril and the plaintiffs called on the tug for help ... The next question is: what was the general average loss? If the towline had not parted, and the tug had completed her task in safety, the hiring charge would certainly have been a general average expenditure. But the towline did part. It wrapped itself round the propeller of the tug. The result was that, in the case of *Bulwarra*, the tug became a total loss; and, in the case of *Wangara*, the tug was salved at great expense. The plaintiffs have become bound under the indemnity clause to indemnify the tugowners. Is this expenditure, under the indemnity clause, a 'general average loss'?
>
> [p 358] ... In these circumstances, I propose to go back to the concept, as I understand it, in 1924, when the York-Antwerp Rules were made. 'Direct consequences' denote those consequences which flow in an unbroken sequence from the act; whereas 'indirect consequences' are those in which the

sequence is broken by an intervening or extraneous cause ... If the master, when he does the 'general average act', ought reasonably to have foreseen that a subsequent accident of the kind might occur – or even that there was a distinct possibility of it – then the subsequent accident does not break the chain of causation. The loss or damage is the direct consequence of the original general average act. A good instance was given by Lord Tenterden in his book on *Shipping*:

> So, if, to avoid an impending danger, or to repair the damage occasioned by a storm, the ship be compelled to take refuge in a port to which it was not destined, and into which it cannot enter without taking out a part of her cargo, *and the part taken out to lighten the ship on this occasion happen to be lost in the barges employed to convey it to the shore,* this loss also, being occasioned by the removal of the goods for the general benefit, must be repaired by general contribution.

If, however, there is a subsequent incident which was only a remote possibility, it would be different. Thus, Lowndes gave the illustration of a sailing vessel, where the master cuts away the mast and thus reduces her speed; and afterwards she is captured by the enemy. Her loss is not the direct consequence of the general average act. It is due to the intervening capture. In both cases before us, the master, when he engaged the tug, should have envisaged that it was distinctly possible that the towline might break and foul the propeller. When it happened, therefore, it did not break the chain of causation.

General average contribution

The whole concept of a loss by general average is based upon the fact that the other parties to the common adventure who have benefited from the general average act will contribute towards that loss. This liability to contribute is confirmed by s 66(3) of the Act, which states:

> Where there is a general average loss, the party on whom it falls is entitled, subject to the conditions imposed by maritime law, to a rateable contribution from the other parties interested, and such contribution is called a general average contribution.

Sacrifice or expenditure must be 'extraordinary'

For there to be a general average loss, there must be an 'extraordinary' sacrifice or expenditure which is made for the benefit of all the parties to the common adventure. The former is a physical act, whilst the latter is a financial outlay, but both are losses in general average. The sacrifice may take the form of cargo or ship's apparel being deliberately cast away for the benefit of the whole venture.

In *Birkley v Presgrave* (1801) 1 East 220, the deliberate act of the master of a vessel cutting the cable of his bow anchor in a storm, in order to avert danger, was adjudged to be an 'extraordinary' sacrifice.

> **Lord Kenyon CJ:** [p 227] ... all ordinary losses and damage sustained by the ship happening immediately from the storm or perils of the sea must be borne by the shipowners. But all those articles which were made use of by the master and crew upon the particular emergency, and out of the usual course, for the benefit of the whole concern, and the other expenses incurred, must be paid proportionately by the defendant as general average.

However, unlike a physical sacrifice, it is often much more difficult to determine what, in general average, may be considered to be a relevant extraordinary expenditure. On this very point, in the Exchequer Chamber, Erle CJ raised the issue in *Kemp v Halliday* (1866) LR 1 QB 520, where a vessel which sank in Falmouth harbour was later salved and the issue of general average was foremost.

> **Erle CJ:** [p 527] ... We infer from the statement in the case that there was a common peril of destruction imminent over ship and cargo as they lay submerged; that the most convenient mode of saving either ship or cargo, or both, was by raising the ship together with the cargo; that the expense required for such raising would be an extraordinary expense for the common benefit of both; that the cargo would be liable to a general average contribution towards the expense; and the shipowner would have a lien on the cargo to secure the payment of that general average.

One year later, in *Wilson v Bank of Victoria*, below, the issue of what constituted an extraordinary expenditure arose again.

Wilson and Another v Bank of Victoria (1867) LR 2 QB 203

The plaintiffs' vessel *Royal Standard*, whilst on a voyage from Australia to England, hit an iceberg in the southern ocean and her masts and rigging were so damaged that she had to continue to Rio de Janeiro under steam alone and, in so doing, exhausted her stocks of coal. Because of the cost of permanent repairs in Rio de Janeiro, the master carried out temporary repairs, replenished the bunkers and continued the voyage to England under steam alone. The *Royal Standard*'s owners then sought to recover some of the cost of the coal from the cargo-owners by way of a general average contribution.

The court ruled that the expenditure on coal was not an extraordinary expenditure, but was really an expenditure which could have been envisaged as part of the operation of a vessel equipped with auxiliary power.

> **Blackburn J:** [p 212] ... The shipowners, by their contract with the freighters, are bound to give the services of their crew and their ship, and to make all disbursements necessary for this purpose. In the case of such a vessel as this, which is equipped with an auxiliary screw, their contract (1) includes the use of that screw, and consequently the disbursements necessary for fuel for the steam engine. Now, the disaster which occurred in this case, no doubt, caused

the engine to be used to a much greater extent than would generally occur on such a voyage, and so caused the disbursement for coals to be extraordinarily heavy; but it did not render it an extraordinary disbursement. The case is similar to that of an ordinary sailing vessel, in which, owing to disasters, the voyage is unusually protracted, and consequently the owner's disbursements for provisions, and for the wages of his crew, if they are paid by the month, are extraordinarily heavy. It is not similar to that of the master hiring extra hands to pump when his crew are unable to keep the vessel afloat, or any other expenditure which is not only extraordinary in its amount, but is incurred to procure some service extraordinary in its nature. We think, therefore, that there is no right to charge this item to general average, and, consequently, that the rule to enter the verdict for the defendants must be made absolute.

In *Société Nouvelle d'Armement v Spillers and Bakers Ltd*, below, Sankey J reflected on what amounts to a general average expenditure. He was also of the opinion that: '... there must be expenditure abnormal in kind or degree, and it must have been incurred on an abnormal occasion for the preservation of property.'[27]

Société Nouvelle d'Armement v Spillers and Bakers Ltd [1917] 1 KB 865

The plaintiffs were the owners of the French sailing vessel *Ernest Legouve*, which was chartered by the defendants to carry a cargo of barley from San Francisco to Sharpness in the Bristol Channel. On arriving off Queenstown on the south coast of Ireland, where *Lusitania* had recently been lost, and because the weather was calm and there was the constant threat of enemy submarines in the area, the master hired a tug to tow the vessel all the way to Sharpness. The *Ernest Legouve*'s owners then sought to recover part of the cost of the tow by way of a general average contribution from the cargo-owners.

The court ruled that the loss was not a general average loss. The risk of being attacked by enemy submarines was not an extraordinary and abnormal peril that would be encountered during a war.

Sankey J: [p 870] ... Extraordinary expenditure must to some extent be connected with an extraordinary occasion. For example, an abnormal user of the engines and an abnormal consumption of coal in endeavouring to refloat a steamship stranded in a position of peril is an extraordinary sacrifice and an extraordinary expenditure: see *The Bona*. A mere extra user of coal, however, in order to accelerate the speed of a vessel would not be a general average act. Again, suppose the master, instead of hiring a tug, had purchased guns and hired a crew of gunners at Queenstown on the chance that he might be attacked by a submarine. I doubt if the expenses of the guns and gunners could have been recovered as a general average expenditure: see *Taylor v Curtis* ... It is not sufficient to say that the expenditure was incurred to benefit the property; it must be proved that it was abnormal in kind or degree and incurred to preserve the property.

---

27   *Per* Sankey J, p 871.

Partial Loss – 2

The extraordinary expenditure or sacrifice must be for the whole adventure

For there to be a general average loss caused by an extraordinary sacrifice or expenditure, that sacrifice or expenditure must be for the benefit of the whole adventure, and not just for the benefit of one interest.

In ***Hingston v Wendt* (1876) 1 QBD 367**, where the cargo was salved from the sunken wreck of a sailing vessel by an agent of the master, the court held that, although the agent held a lien on the cargo, the act of saving the cargo alone, though analogous to general average, was not in fact so.

> **Blackburn J:** [p 370] ... The plaintiff, a ship agent at Dartmouth, was put in possession of the wrecked vessel and cargo by the captain, with, as we understand the case, authority from the captain to do, as his agent, what was for the benefit of all concerned. The plaintiff did the work, and expended the money sued for in discharging the cargo, and he brought it to a place of safety, where he kept possession of it. The hull remained on shore, and ultimately broke up. And was sold as a wreck. We think we must take it on the statement to be the fact, that this expenditure was not incurred on behalf of the master as agent of the shipowner, performing on his contract to carry on the cargo to its destination and earn freight, but was an extraordinary expenditure for the purpose of saving the property at risk; and had the expenditure been for the purpose of saving the whole venture, ship as well as cargo, it would have constituted a general average, to which the owners of each part of the property saved must have contributed rateably, and the captain, and the plaintiff, as his agent, would have had a lien or right to retain each part of the property saved till the amount of the contribution due in respect of it was paid or secured.

Voluntarily and reasonably made

Section 66(2) of the Act affirms that 'there is a general average act where any extraordinary sacrifice or expenditure is voluntarily and reasonably made in time of peril ...'. However, Rule A of the York-Antwerp Rules 1994 states that 'there is a general average act when, and only when, any extraordinary sacrifice or expenditure is intentionally and reasonably made ...'.

Reasonably made

The Act, in s 66(2), qualifies both a general average sacrifice and a general average expenditure being 'reasonably made'. Presumably, this infers that the master of a vessel must act reasonably when making a sacrifice for which others will eventually be partly liable. Similarly, any expense incurred must be governed by the same criteria of reasonableness. The issue of excessive or unreasonable expenditure was raised in *Anderson, Tritton and Co v Ocean Steamship Co*, below.

Anderson, Tritton and Co v Ocean Steamship Co (1884) 5 Asp MLC 401, HL

An arrangement existed between two shipping companies, the Ocean Steamship Company and the China Navigation Company, both of whom operated up the Yangtze River. This arrangement was such that, should either company's vessels need assistance, the other company would provide that assistance for a fixed fee of £2,500. Thus, when the steamship *Achilles* ran aground in the river, *Shanghai* came to her assistance and towed her off for the fixed sum previously agreed. When the Ocean Steamship Company, the owners of *Achilles*, sought to recover from the cargo-owners in general average, the cargo-owners objected to the payment, as they contended that the price had been fixed by the owners and not the master, and that the fee was unreasonable.

The House of Lords reversed the decision of the Court of Appeal and ruled that, although the assistance amounted to general average, the sum charged was unreasonable and, with respect to the cargo-owners, should be reduced.

> **Lord Blackburn:** [p 404] ... I have come to the conclusion that, on the evidence given at the trial, it was not a simple issue whether the whole sum actually paid by the shipowners to the owners of *Shanghai* was chargeable to general average, and, if that was not made out, that nothing was to be recovered. I do not think that it would follow merely from the shipowner having become liable to pay and having paid that sum, that the whole of it was chargeable to general average. I think it might well be that, on this evidence, the proper conclusion was that something differing from that sum might be chargeable, and I think that, till it is ascertained whether any sum was chargeable, and what that sum was, the case is not ripe for decision.
>
> ... And though I quite agree that there is some evidence here that *Achilles* and her cargo were both in danger, and were both saved by the services of *Shanghai*, and though I also agree that it is not a question of law whether the amount of the sum charged as a disbursement was exorbitant or not, still I cannot find that any question as to the amount was submitted to the jury. It seems to me that if such a question had been submitted to a jury, there is much in the evidence that might make it very doubtful whether the jury would think this sum properly chargeable against the owners of the goods if uninsured.

Reasonableness under the York-Antwerp Rules 1994

Rule A of the York-Antwerp Rules 1994 uses the words 'intentionally and reasonably made' to qualify a general average act,[28] and the Rule Paramount states, in no uncertain terms, that: 'In no case shall there be any allowance for sacrifice or expenditure unless reasonably made or incurred.' Read with the

---

28 Rule A states: 'There is a general average act when, and only when, any extraordinary sacrifice or expenditure is intentionally and reasonably made or incurred for the common safety for the purpose of preserving from peril the property involved in a common maritime adventure.'

Rule of Interpretation, the position is now clear, that even the numbered Rules are now also subject to the test of reasonableness.[29] The above clarification was rendered necessary because of the decision in *Corfu Navigation Co and Bain Clarkson Ltd v Mobil Shipping Co Ltd, 'Alpha'* [1991] 2 Lloyd's Rep 515, in which Hobhouse J held that, unlike the lettered Rules, the numbered Rules (in this case, Rule VII)[30] were not subject to the test of reasonableness. The position now is that all the Rules, lettered and numbered, are governed by the test of reasonableness.

Intentionally made

Despite the difference in wording between the Act and the York-Antwerp Rules, it is suggested that the principle behind general average remains fundamentally unchanged, but there is little authority in insurance law to confirm this. However, in *Papayanni and Jeromia v Grampian Steamship Co Ltd*, below, where a vessel was intentionally scuttled on the orders of a harbour master, the court still decided that it amounted to a general average sacrifice. The insurers' argument that it could not be general average, as the scuttling was not voluntary, was disregarded on the basis that the scuttling had still been for the benefit of the whole adventure. Although this was not an insurance case, it is suggested that it is still relevant.

Papayanni and Jeromia v Grampian Steamship Co Ltd (1896) 1 Com Cas 448

The plaintiffs shipped a consignment of cargo with the defendants in their vessel *Birkhall* under bills of lading which incorporated the York-Antwerp Rules 1890; Rule III of which stated: 'Extinguishing fire on shipboard: Damage done to ship and cargo, or either of them, by water or otherwise ... in extinguishing a fire on board the ship, shall be made good as general average.' During the voyage, a fire developed in *Birkhall*'s bunkers and she was, in the interests of all concerned, put into a nearby port for assistance. However, the harbour master ordered *Birkhall* to be scuttled in the interest of safety, and the plaintiffs' consignment of goods were effectively destroyed. The plaintiffs then claimed a general average contribution from the defendants.

The court ruled that, although the scuttling was intentional, it still amounted to a voluntary act for the benefit of all, and, therefore, the plaintiffs were entitled to recover in general average.

> **Mathew J:** [p 452] ... The evidence shows that what was done was in the interest of ship and cargo. There is no evidence that there was any other motive for scuttling the ship. The captain, who had not parted with the

---

29 Whereas the 'lettered' Rules set out general principles upon which general average shall be adjusted, the 'numbered' Rules refer to specific events of a general average act, eg, r I refers to 'Jettison of Cargo', and r VII to 'Damage to Machinery and Boilers'.

30 As the test of reasonableness appears in r A and not in r VII, under which the claim was premised, Hobhouse J held that the conduct of the master in attempting to refloat the vessel, though unreasonable, did not defeat the claim.

possession of his ship, did not object. There seems to be clear evidence that he sanctioned what was done. The loss must be adjusted as a general average sacrifice.

In time of peril

A loss may be claimed in general average if the general average act which caused that loss was carried out 'in time of peril'. That the peril must be real and actually exist, rather than simply believed to exist, was demonstrated in *Joseph Watson and Son v Firemen's Fund Insurance Co of San Francisco*, below.

Joseph Watson and Son Ltd v Firemen's Fund Insurance Co of San Francisco [1922] 2 KB 355

The plaintiffs shipped a number of barrels of rosin aboard the steamship *Sophie Frankel* under a policy of insurance underwritten by the defendants. The policy included cover against general average loss. During the voyage, the captain thought he saw – what was later proved mistakenly – smoke issuing from a cargo hold and, as a result, had high pressure steam directed down the hatch in order to extinguish the supposed fire. In the process, the plaintiffs' rosin was damaged and a claim was lodged against their insurers for a general average loss. The underwriters declined payment, on the basis that no peril actually existed within the meaning of the Act and, therefore, they were not liable.

The court ruled that the plaintiffs could not recover. There had been no real peril, only a supposed peril. Furthermore, although the plaintiffs were insured against fire, the insurance only covered real fire, and not an imaginary fire.

Rowlatt J: [p 358] ... It has been contended that there is a 'peril' within the Marine Insurance Act 1906 in every case where the captain believes that it exists. I do not think so. Cases were cited to me which showed that much depends upon the view taken at the time by the captain or person in authority, as opposed to that taken by those who, after the event, had a better opportunity of forming a correct judgment. But it seems to me that there is an ambiguity in the contention which they were cited to support. It is one thing to say that where a peril in fact existed one must take the view of the captain formed at the time the peril existed as to what would be the outcome of that peril, and must not say to him, 'If you had held on you would have found that all would have come right', or something of that sort. It is another thing to say that one must take the captain's view whether the state of facts existed which are alleged to have constituted the peril ... The words of the Marine Insurance Act 1906 do not justify me in saying that there is a peril whenever it looks as if there was a peril.

Partial Loss – 2

The peril need not be immediate

It is now well established that a loss may be a general average loss even when the peril insured against is neither imminent nor immediate. In the case of *Société Nouvelle d'Armement v Spillers and Bakers Ltd* **[1917] 1 KB 865**, a sailing ship unsuccessfully claimed that a lengthy tow from Ireland to the Bristol Channel was a general average loss, because the weather was calm and there was a risk of enemy submarines in the area. In his summation, Sankey J was of the opinion that, as the word 'peril' in the Act was unqualified, it was 'not desirable to define the degree of danger or the amount of peril necessary'. That, he suggested, was a question of fact.

> **Sankey J:** [p 871] ... The word 'peril' is used in the statutory definition [referring to s 66(2)] without any qualification, although in many of the definitions given of general average it is stated that the peril must be imminent, which means that it must be substantial and threatening and something more than the ordinary peril of the seas: see *Covington v Roberts*. It is not desirable, even if it were possible, to define the degree of danger or the amount of peril necessary. That is a question of fact depending alike on time and circumstance, upon which each judge must form his own conclusion. In some cases, as for example where a ship is stranded or sinking, the question approaches a certainty and the decision presents no difficulties. It is far otherwise where, as here, the question depends to some extent on a contingency and quits the realms of certainty for those of conjecture.

But, in *Vlassopoulos v British and Foreign Marine Insurance Co*, below, Roche J went much further and concluded that, under the Act, it was not necessary for a ship to be 'in the grip of danger' for there to be a general average loss.

Vlassopoulos v British and Foreign Marine Insurance Co [1929] 1 KB 187

The appellants were the owners of the steamship *Makis*, which was insured with the defendants under a policy of insurance which, with respect to general average, was governed by the York-Antwerp Rules 1924. During a voyage from Bordeaux to Cardiff, the ship's propeller was fouled by wreckage and she put into Cherbourg for repairs. As no dry dock was available, *Makis* had to be tipped over onto her side in order to carry out repairs and, for this to be accomplished, some of the cargo had to be removed. The owners claimed on all these expenses as general average. The question before the court was whether this claim could be considered as general average, as neither *Makis*, nor her cargo, was at any time in immediate danger.

The court ruled that the claim amounted to general average, as everything that had been done had been for the benefit of the venture. The fact that the ship and cargo were not in immediate danger did not lessen the validity of the claim.

> **Roche J:** [p 199] ... The only special matter which has to be dealt with in this connection is that the arbitrator has found, in para 6(p) [in the arbitrator's

report] in connection with the ... casualty, that neither *Makis* nor her cargo or freight was, in fact, in any immediate danger. I suppose that he had been asked to find that by the underwriters, and having made the finding, he attributed some legal consequences to it, and it may be that is the reason why he has held that this is not general average. If that was his reason, it is, in my judgment, erroneous in law. It is erroneous because it is to attach an unwarranted weight to the word 'immediate'. The earlier findings amount to this: that the ship was in the grip of danger. The finding in para 6(p) could only mean under those circumstances that the ship, though in the grip of danger, was not actually in the grip or nearly in the grip of a disaster that might result from the danger. That is not necessary in order to constitute a general average act. It is not necessary that the ship should be actually in the grip, or even nearly in the grip, of the disaster that may arise from a danger. It would be a very bad thing if shipmasters had to wait until that state of things arose in order to justify them doing an act which would be a general average act.

The common adventure

It cannot be over-emphasised that the term 'common adventure' is unique to general average. Unless the sacrifice or expenditure is made for the benefit of all who are party to the adventure, the loss cannot be in general average. Any extraordinary expenditure which is not beneficial to all the parties to the venture would amount to a particular charge (sue and labour). Thus, the words 'common adventure' distinguish general average from sue and labour.

When one party owns both ship and cargo

It is not unusual for one party to have a pecuniary interest in more than one facet of a marine adventure. A shipowner, or charterer, may also own the cargo, and it therefore stands to reason that he must also be the party who is interested in the earning of the freight. But, the whole principle behind the concept of general average is the mutual sharing of a loss by the other parties to the venture. Thus, the question arises, can there be a general average loss when the interested parties to the common adventure are one and the same?

When dealing with this issue, it is convenient to separate general average in its pure sense from the insurance of such. They are different. This is because, when a general average loss is uninsured, and the property in the common adventure is owned by one person, the issue of contributions owed is an exercise in futility. That is, there would be no point in declaring a general average loss, because any contributions deriving from such a loss would be paid by and received by the same person.

However, the insurance of a general average loss is an entirely different matter. Here, the insurer is not concerned with who owns the property, but only that he has to indemnify the assured. The issue of whether there could be a general average loss when the parties to the common adventure were one and the same was raised in *Montgomery and Co v Indemnity Mutual Marine Insurance Co*, below.[31]

Montgomery and Co v Indemnity Mutual Marine Insurance Co [1902] 1 KB 734

The plaintiffs were the owners of both the sailing ship *Airlie* and the cargo of nitrate aboard her. The cargo was insured with the defendants. On the voyage from the west coast of South America to the UK, *Airlie* ran into difficulties, and, in order to save both the ship and cargo, the mainmast was cut away. The plaintiffs then sought to recover an indemnity from the defendants to cover the cost of the general average contribution which became due to the ship. The question before the court was, whether there could be a general average loss, with respect to a policy of insurance, when the assured was the owner of both the ship and cargo.

The Court of Appeal affirmed the decision of the trial judge, and ruled that there could be a general average loss when the assured was the owner of both the ship and the cargo.

Vaughan Williams LJ: [p 740] ... It seems to us that the question, whether contribution is of the essence of a general average loss or a mere incident of it, must depend upon the occasion which is a condition of such an act. It is not, we think, true to say that it is only the danger to the ship, freight, or cargo which necessitates and justifies sacrifice by the master of either a portion of the cargo or a portion of the ship. This may be done in fear of death, and if it is done upon a proper occasion, all must contribute to the loss. If there be one owner of ship, freight, and cargo he will bear it all. If there be several, each will contribute according to the value of his interest. The object of this maritime law seems to be to give the master of the ship absolute freedom to make whatever sacrifice he thinks best to avert the perils of the sea, without any regard whatsoever to the ownership of the property sacrificed; and, in our judgment, such a sacrifice is a general average act, quite independently of unity or diversity of ownership.

[p 743] ... As I understand it, the rule, as to what constitutes a general average or not, is founded upon the consideration, whether it is for the benefit of all, who are, as may be, interested in the accomplishment of the voyage; or only for the benefit of a particular party. Suppose a person to be owner of the ship and cargo, and, of course, ultimately of the freight also; and he should insure the ship, cargo, and freight in three different policies, by different offices; if a jettison should be made, or a mast cut away, or any other sacrifice be made for the common benefit of all concerned in the voyage; there can be no doubt that this would be a case of general average, and the underwriters on ship, cargo, and freight must all contribute as for a general average. What possible difference in such a case could it make, that the same underwriters were underwriters in one policy on the ship, cargo, and freight? ... To be sure, if the owner stands as his own insurer throughout, the question degenerates into a mere distinction, for it is a pure speculative inquiry. Not so, when there is an

---

31 See, also, *Oppenheimer v Fry* (1863) 3 B&S 873.

insurance; for in such a case, the underwriters are *pro tanto* benefited by the sacrifice or other act done; and they are in a just sense bound to contribute towards it.

Notes

The Court of Appeal was in no doubt that a claim in general average was legitimate in such circumstances. Vaughan Williams LJ was of the opinion that the 'principle' of general average was not precluded by there being only one participant in the common adventure. The basis of this reasoning was that a general average act and the ensuing loss was a question of fact, and the contributions which then became liable from the beneficiaries of that general average act were only 'incident' to and not the 'essence' of the act. Hitherto, it was thought that general average could not exist when the parties to the adventure were one and the same, because it was not possible to sue oneself for that contribution.

The principle laid down in the *Montgomery* case has since been adopted by the Act in s 66(7), which affirms that:

> Where a ship, freight, and cargo, or any two of those interests, are owned by the same assured, the liability of the insurer in respect of general average losses or contributions is to be determined as if those subjects were owned by different persons.

Vessel not under charter and in ballast

When a vessel is not under charter and is in ballast, there is no common adventure, as there is only the one interested party to that adventure, namely, the shipowner. However, where insurance is concerned, the Institute Hull Clauses make special provision for voyages made in ballast by allowing such voyages to be treated as though they are being conducted under a contract of affreightment which incorporated the York-Antwerp Rules 1994. The effect of this is to fictionalise a voyage where a loss incurred by a general average act could still be recoverable even though the vessel is in ballast and there is no common adventure. Clause 10.3 of the ITCH(95) states:

> When the vessel sails in ballast, not under charter, the provisions of the York-Antwerp Rules 1994 (excluding Rules XI(d), XX and XXI) shall be applicable, and the voyage for this purpose shall be deemed to continue from the port or place of departure until the arrival of the Vessel at the first port or place thereafter other than a port or place of refuge or a port or place of call for bunkering only ...

Vessel under charter and in ballast

When a vessel is under charter, there is immediately created a common adventure as between the shipowner and the charterer and, should that charter include the voyage in ballast to the port of loading, that common adventure exists even before any cargo is loaded. This was illustrated in

Carisbrook SS Co Ltd v London and Provincial Marine and General Insurance Co Ltd, below.

Carisbrook SS Co Ltd v London and Provincial Marine and General Insurance Co Ltd (1901) 6 Com Cas 291

The plaintiffs insured their vessel *Yestor* with the defendants under a time policy of insurance. The charterparty allowed for *Yestor* to sail from Fleetwood to Savannah and thence to Liverpool, Manchester or Bremen. On arriving at Savannah, *Yestor* grounded, and she was so damaged that repairs had to be effected to her propeller and engine. The plaintiffs claimed on their policy of insurance for a particular average loss by perils of the seas, but the underwriters contended that the loss was general average, and that a contribution for chartered freight should be deducted from the claim.

The court ruled that the loss was in general average, and that, therefore, there should be a contribution in respect of the chartered freight. Although the vessel was in ballast, the charterparty was for the round trip, outward and homeward.

> **Mathew J:** [p 295] ... In the course of the voyage to Savannah, the vessel stranded, and a general average sacrifice was made to which, it is said, the homeward freight must contribute. Now, there cannot be a question to my mind that the vessel, while on the outward voyage, was earning the homeward freight. The charterparty obliged her to go to Savannah and to bring the cargo home, and she was discharging that obligation when the disaster occurred. It happened, therefore, in the course of the voyage contemplated by the charterparty. The vessel eventually reached Savannah, took the cargo on board, brought it home, and became entitled to the freight. In that state of things, it appears to me both on principle and according to reason that the homeward freight should contribute in general average, because everything points to the freight as the object for which the sacrifice was made. It was the owners' interest, to secure the arrival of the ship at her port of loading to take her cargo on board, deliver the cargo, and receive the freight in consideration of the services by the ship in going out and bringing the cargo home.

The *Carisbrook* case should be compared with *The Brigella* (1893) P 189, below, where the charterparty was for the homeward voyage only.

The Brigella (1893) P 189

The plaintiff owners of *The Brigella* effected a policy of insurance with the defendants on chartered homeward freight. On the outward voyage from Liverpool to Delaware, in ballast, *The Brigella* put into Holyhead to repair weather damage, the expenditure for which was levied on the ship and freight by way of general average. The owners then claimed on their insurers for the proportion of that expenditure which had been charged against freight.

The court ruled that the owners could not recover under their policy. The money expended at Holyhead could not be considered as general average, as the vessel was in ballast and the chartered freight was for the homeward voyage only. Therefore, there could be no common adventure, as the only party to the adventure was the ship.

> **Gorrell Barnes J:** [p 197] ... I have already pointed out that in the present case there were no expenses incurred to avert a loss of the joint interests, but only certain expenses incurred in order to repair the ship, or owing to the delay in effecting those repairs. There was no general average loss, or even any loss or expenditure common to both interests.

Avoidance of a peril insured against

It should be noted that, in marine insurance, an insurer is liable for general average when a general average sacrifice or expenditure is made in order to avoid a peril insured against. He is liable for any contribution which becomes due as a result of the avoidance of a peril insured against. To this effect, s 66(6) of the Act states:

> In the absence of express stipulation, the insurer is not liable for any general average loss or contribution where the loss was not incurred for the purpose of avoiding, or in connection with the avoidance of, a peril insured against.

In like vein, cl 10.4 of the ITCH(95) declares:

> No claim under this cl 10 shall in any case be allowed where the loss was not incurred to avoid or in connection with the avoidance of a peril insured against.[32]

The true meaning of s 66(6) was clarified, to some extent, in *Joseph Watson and Son Ltd v Firemen's Fund Insurance Co of San Francisco* **[1922] 2 KB 355**, where a claim was made when goods were damaged when the crew of a vessel filled a hold with steam in order to extinguish a fire which, it turned out, did not exist. The plaintiff owner of the goods sought to give s 66(6) a wide interpretation by reading it as meaning the avoidance of an assumed or mistaken peril. The court, however, applied the strict and narrow interpretation of the sub-section, and ruled that s 66(6) only applied to a peril insured against, and that that peril must exist in fact.

> **Rowlatt J:** [p 359] ... It has been contended that this was a loss incurred 'for the purpose of avoiding, or in connection with the avoidance of, a peril insured against' within the meaning of s 66(6) of the Act. But I do not think this was a loss of that kind, and I am of opinion that the effect of the sub-section is to bring in losses collateral to the main process of avoiding a peril insured against, and that it does not touch losses incurred in a mistaken attempt to avoid a peril in fact non-existent.

The ICC (A), (B) and (C) also make provision for general average, where cl 2 states:

---

32   See, also, IVCH(95), cl 8.2.

> This insurance covers general average ... incurred to avoid or in connection with the avoidance of loss from any cause except those excluded in cll 4, 5, 6 and 7, or elsewhere in this insurance.

Recovery for general average under the Institute Cargo Clauses is for the avoidance of loss from 'any cause', and not only for the perils insured against. Thus, in so far as general average is concerned, the cover that is provided is, in effect, for 'all risks' other than those specifically excepted by exclusion cll 4, 5, 6 and 7.

A general average act must be successful

If, in making the general average sacrifice or expenditure, no property in the venture is saved, there would be no forthcoming contributions, because nobody has benefited from the general average act. Unless there is a degree of success, there can be no surviving property upon which the value of contributions may be established. Whether the success needs to be total or only partial is not entirely clear, but if, it is suggested, some portion of the property survives, there is some element of success, and, thus, something tangible on which contributions may be levied. If this were not the case, the loss would be in particular average, and any such loss would lie where it fell.

It is not inconceivable that, after incurring expenses in endeavouring to save a ship and cargo, one or both of them may then be totally lost. A shipowner who has suffered a total loss of his ship and has incurred general average expenses to salve both ship and cargo could well find himself out of pocket when nothing is salved, or when the expenditure exceeds the proceeds of the property salved. General average contributions, unlike sue and labour, are not, under the common law, recoverable in addition to a total loss. And, to alleviate a shipowner of his predicament, cl 11.5 of the ITCH(95) allows a claim to be made in general average even when the property insured is subsequently totally lost.

Clause 11.5 of the ITCH(95): pro rata share

Clause 11.5 states:[33]

> When a claim for total loss of the Vessel is admitted under this insurance and expenses have been reasonably incurred in saving or attempting to save the

---

33 See, also, IVCH(95), cl 9.5. Though the clause appears under the heading of 'Duty of Assured (Sue and Labour)', it is, however, from its wording, applicable to general average, but not sue and labour expenses. It does not apply to sue and labour because the expenses are incurred for the benefit of both 'the Vessel and other property'. Moreover, as can be seen from cll 11.1 and 11.6, sue and labour expenses are recoverable in addition to the total loss of the subject matter insured. Whether cl 11.5 is applicable to salvage charges is questionable, as salvage charges are paid on the basis of 'no cure, no pay'. However, read with cl 11.2, it would appear that it could also be relevant to salvage charges.

Vessel and other property and there are no proceeds, or the expenses exceed the proceeds, then this insurance shall bear its pro rata share of such proportion of the expenses, or of the expenses in excess of the proceeds, as the case may be, as may reasonably be regarded as having been incurred in respect of the Vessel, excluding all special compensation and expenses as referred to in cl 10.5; but if the Vessel be insured for less than its sound value at the time of the occurrence giving rise to the expenditure, the amount recoverable under this clause shall be reduced in proportion to the under-insurance.

The words 'the Vessel and other property' suggest a general average scenario where a common adventure is at risk. It is also to be noted that the clause begins with phrase: 'When a claim for total loss of the Vessel is admitted under this insurance ...' This necessarily means that the insurers are liable for a total loss of the subject matter insured, and the question is now confined to whether they are also liable for the expenses incurred by way of general average, even though 'there are no proceeds, or the expenses exceed the proceeds'.

The insurer's liability under cl 11.5 is, however, limited on a pro rata basis, to a proportion of the total expenditure made in time of peril; that proportion being based on the value of subject matter insured as compared with the value of the whole. Any under-insurance would also have to be taken into consideration.

The liability of the insurer

Distinction between general average sacrifice and expenditure

The liability of the insurer is different for a general average sacrifice as compared with a general average expenditure. When the loss amounts to a sacrifice, the insurer is liable directly to the assured for the full amount, whereas, when the loss is by way of an expenditure, the insurer's liability is to the general average fund, and only amounts to a proportion of that loss. Section 66(4) of the Act illustrates the difference thus:

> Subject to any express provision in the policy, where the assured has incurred a general average expenditure, he may recover from the insurer in respect of the proportion of the loss which falls upon him; and, in the case of a general average sacrifice, he may recover from the insurer in respect of the whole loss without having enforced his right of contribution from the other parties liable to contribute.

Similarly, cl 10.1 of the ITCH(95) states:

> This insurance covers the Vessel's proportion of salvage, salvage charges and/or general average, reduced in respect of any under-insurance, but in case of general average sacrifice of the Vessel the Assured may recover in respect of

the whole loss without first enforcing their right of contribution from other parties.[34]

It is emphasised that the phrase 'reduced in respect of any under-insurance' is of considerable importance, as was illustrated in the case of *Steamship 'Balmoral' Co Ltd v Marten* [1902] AC 511, HL, below. The principle is applicable to salvage and general average.

Steamship 'Balmoral' Co Ltd v Marten [1902] AC 511, HL

The steamship *Balmoral* was insured by the appellants with the respondents under a time policy of insurance. Whilst on a voyage from Philadelphia to London, *Balmoral* broke her tail shaft in a severe gale and accepted the voluntary assistance of *Amroth Castle*. Later, two tugs were engaged to tow her into London. The owners of *Amroth Castle* received a salvage award, and the cost of hiring the two tugs was put down as a general average expenditure. The ship's liability to the salvage award and her contribution towards the general average expenditure were based on the true value of the vessel. When the owners of *Balmoral* sought to be indemnified for these expenditures, the insurers contested the amount of the claims.

The House of Lords ruled that the insurer's liability only amounted to the same percentage of the loss as the value in the policy bore to the real value. As the insured value of the ship was 33/40ths of her true value, the indemnity could only amount to 33/40ths of the total claim.

> **Lord Shand:** [p 516] ... In questions of salvage and general average, which at once give rise to claims of indemnity under an insurance policy, the value of the ship is necessarily a material element, for the value of the ship will, with the circumstances in which the salvage services have been given, enter deeply into the question of the remuneration to be given. Of course, that value in a question with salvors must be the real value at the time when the salvage services are rendered. Accordingly, in this case, the ship was taken at her full value, and the owner had to pay a larger sum than if the value had been £33,000 only [the insured value]. It seems to me that when he claims full relief by way of indemnity, the underwriter in his defence is simply asking that effect shall be given to his stipulation in the policy, that in all questions of indemnity the ship shall be valued at £33,000 only. It follows that he is liable to pay only the proportion which the value in the policy bears to the actual value on which the statement has been made up.

General average sacrifice

A general average sacrifice is a physical and tangible loss and, therefore, may be identified and quantified with relative ease. The insurer's liability to the assured is direct and in full, and any contributions owed by the other parties

---

34 See, also, IVCH(95), cl 8.1.

to the assured may, by way of subrogation, be recovered by the insurer. This principle was laid down in *Dickinson v Jardine*, below.

Dickinson v Jardine (1868) LR 3 CP 639

The plaintiffs shipped 641 chests of tea aboard the vessel *Canute* from Foochow to London, and insured them with the defendants under a valued policy of insurance. During the voyage, *Canute* struck a reef, and, in order to lighten ship and free herself, 607 of the chests of tea were jettisoned. The vessel, having freed herself of the reef, continued her voyage to London and delivered the remainder of the cargo. The plaintiffs claimed for a general average loss in full. However, the insurers, instead of paying the full value of the cargo which was jettisoned, only paid the plaintiffs a sum which equated to the value of their contribution to the whole of the general average loss, on the basis that the plaintiffs could recover the remainder of their loss from the other contributors. The plaintiffs submitted that the insurers were liable for the whole loss that they had suffered by way of jettison.

The court ruled that the insurers were directly liable to the plaintiffs for the whole loss they had suffered by way of the general average sacrifice. It was then for the insurers to recoup the contributions from the other parties by way of subrogation.

Bovill CJ: [p 642] I am of opinion that the plaintiffs are entitled to recover the whole of the amount claimed by them. I think the rule is correctly stated in *Phillips on Insurance*, 3rd edn, Vol 2, s 1348, as follows: 'It is not a condition that the assured on goods must claim contribution of the other parties for a jettison before he can demand indemnity from his underwriters. He may demand it of them in the first instance.' ... In this case, the goods were insured against jettison, amongst other risks, and the goods were jettisoned, and I think the plaintiffs are entitled, therefore, to recover the sum insured. It is true that there is a remedy against the owners of the ship and the remainder of the cargo, if they ultimately arrive safely at their destination, for part of the loss. But this does not affect the plaintiffs' right against the underwriters, who will then be entitled to stand in their place, and recover contributions from the other parties who are liable.

Montague Smith J: [p 644] ... I think the goods jettisoned were totally lost to the assured within the terms of the policy, and the underwriters are therefore liable to pay for the value of the goods. It is said that the loss is not total, because there are other parties who are bound to contribute to the loss, and the plaintiffs are therefore already partially indemnified: that in one sense is so, but the assured have made a contract with the underwriters that they shall be paid the sum insured in certain events which have happened, and they are entitled to look to that contract for their indemnification independently of their other rights.

General average expenditure

Unlike a general average sacrifice, a general average expenditure does not entail the physical loss of the whole or part of the subject matter insured. It only amounts to an extraordinary expenditure that is made in a time of peril for the benefit of all who are party to the common adventure.

The Act, in s 66(4), states that: 'Subject to any express provision in the policy ... where the assured has incurred a general average expenditure, he may recover from the insurer in respect of the proportion of the loss which falls upon him ...' Unfortunately, there is an element of ambiguity in this phrase: does the word proportion apply to only the amount of the contribution owed by the assured, or does it have a wider meaning, in that the underwriters' liability is literally for all the loss which falls upon the assured? This is important. Should a shipowner be unable, for whatever reason, to recover the contributions from cargo-owners after making an extraordinary expenditure, can he then be indemnified for the unpaid contributions from the cargo-owners as well as his own?

In the pre-statute case of *The Mary Thomas*, below, the outcome of which had some bearing on s 66(4), the shipowner was unable to recover unpaid contributions from the cargo-owners, but this was only because of an express clause in the policy.

The Mary Thomas (1894) P 108, CA

The plaintiffs effected two time policies of insurance with the defendants; one on the hull and machinery of *The Mary Thomas*, and the other on freight. The hull policy contained a clause which stated: 'General average and salvage charges payable according to foreign statement, or per York-Antwerp Rules, if in accordance with the contract of affreightment.' Whilst passing Malta on the way to Rotterdam, *The Mary Thomas* stranded on a reef. Part of the cargo was removed in order to get off the reef, whilst the remainder was discharged in Valetta, so as to carry out repairs. Once she was repaired, *The Mary Thomas* reloaded her cargo, which was safely taken to Rotterdam. An average statement was prepared in Rotterdam according to Dutch law, and the defendants paid their proportion on hull and freight. The plaintiffs, having failed in the Dutch courts to recover general average contributions from the consignees of the cargo, then sought to recover those contributions from the defendants on their hull policy.

The Court of Appeal, in affirming the decision of the trial judge, ruled that the defendants were only liable for the proportion of the expenditure which fell upon the ship and freight. They were not liable for the proportion that had not been paid by the cargo-owners, because of the express clause in the hull policy, which confirmed that the average adjustment in Holland was conclusive.

Lindley LJ: [p 123] ... The proportions allocated to ship and freight respectively have been paid by the underwriters; but the proportion allocated to cargo cannot be recovered by the shipowners from the cargo-owners, and have been lost therefore, by them. They now seek to recover them from their own underwriters. The question thus raised turns on the contract of insurance ... For the purpose of this case the clause may be read short, thus: 'General average payable according to foreign statement.' ... The average adjustment was made at Rotterdam, and the adjuster, as already mentioned, treated these expenses as general average expenses ... But, the shipowners contend that that they are entitled to these expenses, either as partial losses or under the suing and labouring clause; and that the adjustment has nothing to do with, and in no way affects, claims in respect of partial losses, or claims under the suing and labouring clause.

[p 124] ... Expenses so treated cannot be treated as something else by those who have agreed to be bound by his decision ... The assured is attempting by an ingenious process to convert his underwriters on ship and freight into guarantors for the payment by the cargo-owners of those portions of the expenses which the average adjuster has allocated to them, but which they will not pay. I am not prepared to say that the expenses in question were not general average expenses according to English law. Most, I think, were, but some may not have been. However, this may be, they were all general average expenses by the law of Holland, and were so treated by the foreign average adjuster.

But, in the post-statute case of *Green Star Shipping Co Ltd v London Assurance*, below, there was no express clause in the policy of insurance, and, thus, the court had the opportunity of clarifying the scope of s 66(4). Roche J was of the opinion that s 66(4) should be interpreted widely; 'the proportion of loss' being read as all the general average losses that fall upon the assured, including the non-payment of contributions by cargo interests.

Green Star Shipping Co Ltd v London Assurance and Others [1933] 1 KB 378

The plaintiffs' vessel *Andree* was loading cargo in New York, under a contract of affreightment which incorporated the York-Antwerp Rules, when a fire broke out and the cargo had to be discharged, thus incurring general average expenses. After being repaired, *Andree* reloaded some of the cargo and set sail, but was so damaged in a collision with another vessel that she sank. Again, the cargo had to be discharged, and again, general average expenses were incurred. The cargo interests only paid the salved value of the cargo by way of general average contributions, and, thus, there was a shortfall in those contributions. *Andree* was insured under two hull policies which contained the Institute Time Clauses, and there was also P & I cover which undertook to indemnify its members for the cargo's proportion of general average which was not recoverable. The question before the court was which of the policies was liable for the shortfall in the cargo contributions.

The court ruled that, under s 66(4) of the Act, the hull insurers, and not the P & I Club, were liable for the unpaid cargo contributions.

> **Roche J:** [p 387] ... I have arrived at the conclusion that the parties liable for the balance are the hull underwriters. This question to my mind presents very great difficulty and is also, in my view, one bare of authority. Its decision seems to me to depend upon the terms and meaning of s 66(4) of the Marine Insurance Act 1906.
>
> [p 389] ... As to the more general application of the decision in the case of *The Mary Thomas*, I do not regard that decision as supporting these defendants' contention. It was a case where the foreign adjusters, whose adjustment both Gorrell Barnes J and the Court of Appeal held to be binding, had apportioned a certain amount to cargo as its contribution. The Dutch courts had held that the shipowner could not recover that contribution, because his servant, the master of the vessel, had been negligent. The English courts held that the shipowners could not go behind the foreign adjustment and recover from the underwriters what they had failed to recover from the cargo-owners.
>
> [p 391] ... The intention of an insurance contract in the present form seems to me to be that as regards general average the contract of affreightment and the contract of insurance shall in respect of the matters now in question proceed upon the same basis and principles. Accordingly, if a shipowner, being the assured under a policy in the present form, incurs expenditure for general average and the cargo's contribution falls short of what is hoped or expected by reason of the diminution or extinction of its value before the adventure terminates, then I think that loss falls into the category of the proportion of the loss which falls upon the assured, the shipowner, and is within the meaning of those words in s 66(4) of the Marine Insurance Act.

Notes

In ***Brandeis Goldschmidt and Co v Economic Insurance Co Ltd* (1922) 38 TLR 609**, where an owner of goods was unable to recover a general average contribution from his insurer because no average statement had been made out, Bailhache J summed up the difference between recovery for a general average sacrifice and a general average expenditure in just a few words.

> **Bailhache J:** [p 610] ... The law applicable was to be found in s 66 of the Marine Insurance Act 1906. A general average sacrifice was different from general average expenditure, and if there had been a sacrifice here, the underwriters would have been immediately liable, independently of the statute and notwithstanding cl 4, read with sub-s 5 of s 66 of the Act, could only be enforced when there had been an adjustment.

Average adjustment

When a cargo-owner ships goods under a contract of affreightment, he effectively agrees that, should there be a general average loss, it is the shipowner's prerogative, under the contract, to stipulate the law and practice of any adjustment in general average. Under common law, it is accepted that such an adjustment takes place at the port of destination, or where the goods are delivered.

Foreign average adjustment

This principle, under the common law, was clearly illustrated in **Simonds v White (1824) 2 B&C 805**, where, after a general average sacrifice by the ship, the cargo-owner was forced to accept that the adjustment had to be based on Russian law, as the port of destination was St Petersburg.

> **Abbott CJ:** [p 811] ... There are, however, many variations in the laws and usages of different nations as to the losses that are considered to fall within this principle [general average]. But in one point all agree; namely, the place at which the average shall be adjusted, which is the place of the ship's destination or delivery of her cargo.
>
> [p 813] ... The shipper of goods, tacitly, if not expressly, assents to general average, as a known maritime usage, which may, according to the events of the voyage, be either beneficial or disadvantageous to him. And, by assenting to general average, he must be understood to assent also to its adjustment, and to its adjustment at the usual and proper place; and to all this it seems to us, to be only an obvious consequence to add, that he must be understood to consent also to its adjustment according to the usage and law of the place at which the adjustment is to be made.

However, in the even earlier case of *Power v Whitmore*, below, which was cited in *Simonds v White*, Lord Ellenborough was of the opinion that a foreign adjustment need not be binding in certain circumstances. In this instance, the court was plainly of the opinion that the average adjustment in Portugal so favoured the merchant that it would be unreasonable to bind an insurer to it.

Power v Whitmore (1815) 4 M&S 141

The plaintiff was a Portuguese merchant who insured some goods for a voyage from London to Lisbon with the defendants. During the voyage, the vessel carrying the goods suffered damage, and put into Cowes for repairs. On arriving in Lisbon, an average statement was prepared, which included, as general average, the cost of the repairs at Cowes as well as the crew's wages and provisions during the delay. When the plaintiff claimed an indemnity from the defendants for the cost of his contribution, they refused to pay, on the basis that the adjustment was wrong in law.

The court ruled in favour of the defendant insurers. The foreign adjustment was not binding, because it was clearly not English law nor the general usage of merchants.

> **Lord Ellenborough:** [p 150] ... Now, without pronouncing what might have been the effect of a statement in this case ... that it was the known and invariable usage amongst merchants at Lisbon, the port of discharge, to treat

losses and expenses of the kind and description which are specified in the case, as the subjects of general average, we cannot but observe that the case contains no allegation of fact whatsoever on this head, but merely states a decree of a court at Lisbon which proceeds upon the assumption of this supposed fact as its foundation. And although by the comity which is paid by us to the judgment of other courts abroad of competent jurisdiction we give a full and binding effect to such judgments ... yet we feel that we should carry that principle of comity further than reasonably ought to be done, or ever hitherto has in practice been done, if we should draw from the recitals of facts and usages which are contained in those judgments, general evidence of the existence of such facts and usages, and allow them to be available for all causes, and purposes, and consider them as applicable to, and obligatory upon other persons than the immediate parties to those judgments, in which these recitals occur. Here the underwriters have a right to insist, as this defendant does insist, that the general average to which their indemnity is confined, is general average as it is understood in England where this contract of indemnity was formed.

But, in *Harris v Scaramanga*, below, the court confirmed that a foreign adjustment was binding.[35] However, Brett J did not wholly disagree with the ruling in *Power v Whitmore* when he suggested that the insurers were bound by the foreign adjustment, provided that the adjustment was '*bona fide* made'.

Harris v Scaramanga (1872) LR 7 CP 481

The plaintiffs insured a cargo of rye with the defendants for a voyage from Taganrog, on the Black Sea, to Bremen. The policy contained a foreign average statement. During the voyage, the vessel carrying the cargo suffered weather damage, and had to put into a port of refuge twice to carry out repairs. On each occasion, the master raised the money for the repairs by putting up a bottomry bond on ship, freight and cargo. On arriving in Bremen, an average statement was prepared, but the master was unable to pay the contribution owed by the ship and freight to the bond holders. The ship was, therefore, sold, but the amount still fell short of the required contribution. So, the average adjuster added the outstanding balance to the cargo which the plaintiffs then claimed from their insurers. The insurers refused to pay the additional amount.

The court ruled that the underwriters were bound by the average statements that had been made and, therefore, the plaintiffs could recover.

Brett J: [p 495] ... The next point to be determined is, whether, under such circumstances, underwriters of an ordinary English policy [containing no foreign adjustment clause] would be liable. That raises the question as to how far underwriters of such a policy on an insured voyage to terminate at a

---

35 See, also, *De Hart v Compania Anonima De Seguros 'Aurora'* [1903] 2 KB 503, CA, *per* Romer LJ, p 509, the full text of which is cited later in this chapter, p 762.

foreign port are bound by a foreign general average adjustment made at that port of destination. Now, I think it is clearly established that, upon such a policy, English underwriters are bound by the foreign adjustment as an adjustment, if made according to the law of the country in which it was made. They are bound although the contributions are apportioned between the different interests in a manner different from the English mode, or though matters are brought into or omitted from general average, which would not be so treated in England. I further incline to think, notwithstanding the case of *Power v Whitmore*, that underwriters, if they are not absolutely bound to accept the foreign adjustment as rightly made, if *bona fide* made, must assume it to be rightly made, if *bona fide* made, until the contrary be proved. It seems to be stated as a general principle of insurance law that 'when a general average is *fairly stated in a foreign port* [emphasis added], and the assured is obliged to pay his proportion of it, he may recover the amount from the insurer, *though the average may have been settled differently from what it would have been at the home port*' (2 Phillips on Insurance 1414, citing *Depan v Ocean Insurance Co*).

The foreign adjustment clause and cl 10.2 of the ITCH(95)

The foreign adjustment clause, now replaced by the adjustment clause (cl 10.2) in the Institute Hull Clauses,[36] typically stated: 'To pay general average as per foreign statement, if so made up.' That such a clause was binding was confirmed in *De Hart v Compania Anonima de Seguros, 'Aurora'*, below.[37] However, Romer LJ expressed concern that a hull insurer could be unaware of special terms contained within the contract of affreightment, but which would, nevertheless, affect his liability. The judge also appeared to be of the opinion that, because of the wording in the Institute adjustment clause, such a clause was not necessarily binding and could be re-evaluated depending on the circumstances.

De Hart v Compania Anonima de Seguros, 'Aurora' [1903] 2 KB 503

The plaintiff insured his ship with the defendants under a time policy of insurance which included both the Institute Time Clauses and a foreign adjustment clause with respect to general average. The vessel was then chartered to a third party to carry a cargo of timber to Antwerp; the charterparty included a clause which stated: 'In case of average ... jettison of deck cargo for the common safety shall be allowable as general average.' During the voyage, for the common safety of all, part of the deck cargo of timber was jettisoned, and, on arrival at Antwerp, an average statement was drawn up. Although Belgian law did not normally allow the jettisoning of

---

36 See ITCH(95), cl 10.2, and IVCH(95), cl 8.2.
37 See, also, *The Mary Thomas* (1893) P 108, CA, per Lindley LJ [p 123]. '... It is admitted that his adjustment is final and conclusive as an adjustment of general average: *Harris v Scaramanga* is conclusive on the point.'

deck cargo to be considered as general average, it did recognise the terms of the charterparty, and, thus, included the lost deck cargo as general average. The insurers refused to indemnify the plaintiff for his contribution.

The court ruled that the underwriters were bound by the average statement, provided that the statement was made up in good faith and was not special or unusual in character.

> **Romer LJ:** [p 509] ... Now there are two clauses in the policy of insurance dealing with the same subject matter; they only differ in this, that in the clause in the body of the policy the words are, 'General average payable according to foreign statement if so made up', whereas the words 'if so made up' are omitted in the corresponding clause in what are called the Institute Time Clauses; but it is clear to my mind that the two clauses should be read together, and I have no hesitation, therefore, in coming to the conclusion that in this policy the foreign statement which is meant is the foreign statement if so made up. Now I think that, by agreeing that general average shall be payable according to foreign statement if so made up, the parties have in effect agreed to be bound by the foreign statement if made up as it exists in fact, subject only to two observations which I am about to make. In the first place I think that, in order to bind the parties, the statement so made up must have been made up in good faith; but it is not suggested here by the appellants that the statement has not been made up in good faith. In the second place, I should like to make a reservation for further consideration if the case I am about to mention should hereafter arise; that is to say, if the statement were made up according to the law of the port which recognised the special terms of the contract of affreightment, I doubt if the parties to the policy of insurance in a case like the present would be bound by the statement if the contract of affreightment imported terms as to general average of a special and unusual character, which could not reasonably have been contemplated by the parties to the policy of insurance. If such a case arises, I should like to further consider it, but such a case does not arise here.

However, the foreign adjustment clause has now been replaced by the Institute adjustment clause, and it should be noted that, in deference to Romer LJ's fears in the *De Hart* case that an insurer could be unaware of detrimental terms in the contract of affreightment, the new clause overrides such terms. Clause 10.2 of the ITCH(95) states:[38]

> Adjustment to be according to the law and practice obtaining at the place where the adventure ends, as if the contract of affreightment contained no special terms upon the subject; but where the contract of affreightment so provides the adjustment shall be according to the York-Antwerp Rules.

Whether the Institute adjustment clause is equally binding on the parties as the foreign adjustment clause it replaced was considered by Roche J in *Green Star Shipping Co Ltd v London Assurance* **[1931] 1 KB 378**. In this instance,

---

38 See, also, IVCH(95), cl 8.2.

the policy of insurance incorporated the Institute Time Clauses Hulls and the contract of affreightment provided for general average according to the York-Antwerp Rules. After the vessel in question suffered two general average losses, there was a shortfall in cargo contributions, for which the hull insurers were held liable, and one of the issues before the court was whether the average adjustment in New York was binding. Roche J was mindful of the opinion of Romer LJ in the *De Hart* case, above, when he concluded that the Institute adjustment clause was also not strictly binding.

> **Roche J:** [p 389] ... As to the contention that the New York adjustment is binding and cannot be reviewed, it was held in *Harris v Scaramanga; De Hart v Compania Anonima de Seguros, 'Aurora'*, and *The Mary Thomas*, that the foreign adjustments were binding, because the contracts provided that general average was payable according to (or per) foreign statements. Here there is no such stipulation, but merely cl 9 of the Institute Clauses [now cl 10.2 of the ITCH(95)], and it seems clear from the language of Romer LJ in *De Hart's* case, that had the Institute clauses stood alone, the foreign adjustments would not have been held to be binding. In my judgment there is nothing in the present case making the New York adjusters' views or statement binding upon the parties as to the effect of provisions of the York-Antwerp Rules or as to any matter now in controversy.

SUE AND LABOUR

Introduction

Sue and labour is an extraordinary expenditure made in time of peril to avert or minimise any loss or damage to the subject matter insured. Because such an expenditure is incurred for the safety or preservation of the subject matter insured, it may be claimed under the separate head of a 'particular charge', as defined in s 64(2). Unlike general average, sue and labour is not something which is carried out for the benefit of a common adventure, it is carried out specifically for the singular benefit of the subject matter insured.

Definition of sue and labour

Section 78(3) defines 'sue and labour' as: 'Expenses incurred for the purpose of averting or diminishing any loss ...' Section 78(4) imposes a 'duty' upon the 'assured and his agents, in all cases to take such measures as may be reasonable for the purpose of averting or minimising a loss'. And, in a similar vein, cl 11.1 of the ITCH(95) states:[39]

---

39 See, also, IVCH(95), cl 9.1.

In case of any loss or misfortune it is the duty of the assured and their servants and agents to take such measures as may be reasonable for the purpose of averting or minimising a loss which would be recoverable under this insurance.

But the duty to sue and labour is equally applicable to cargo. Therefore, the ICC (A), (B) and (C), in cl 16, all confirm that:

It is the duty of the Assured and their servants and agents in respect of loss recoverable hereunder:

16.1 to take such measures as may be reasonable for the purpose of averting or minimising such loss; and

16.2 to ensure that all rights against carriers, bailees or other third parties are properly preserved and exercised,

and the Underwriters will, in addition to any loss recoverable hereunder, reimburse the Assured for any charges properly and reasonably incurred in pursuance of these duties.

Unlike the Act and the Institute Hull Clauses, the Institute Cargo Clauses incorporate an additional and important provision, namely cl 16.2, commonly referred to as the 'bailee' clause. Because cargo-owners usually ship their goods under a contract of carriage involving a third party, the clause is inserted to ensure that the assured preserves the rights of the insurer, under subrogation, against such a third party.[40]

It is interesting to note that there is no sue and labour clause in any of the Institute Freight Clauses. This, of course, raises the question of whether an assured of freight is, in the absence of such a clause, under a duty to sue and labour, and should he do so, whether the expense so incurred is recoverable from the insurer.

The principle behind sue and labour was summed up by Willes J in *Kidston v Empire Marine Insurance Co Ltd* **(1866) LR 1 CP 535**, as follows:

Willes J: [p 543] ... The meaning [of the sue and labour clause] is obvious, that, if an occasion should occur in which by reason of a peril insured against unusual labour and expense are rendered necessary to prevent a loss for which the underwriters would be answerable, and such labour and expense is incurred accordingly, the underwriters will contribute, not as part of the sum insured in case of loss or damage, because it may be that a loss or damage for which they would be liable is averted by the labour bestowed, but as a contribution on their part as persons who have avoided detriment by the result in proportion to what they would have had to pay if such detriment had come to a head for want of timely care.

Expenses incurred for suing and labouring are recoverable under cl 11.2 of the ITCH(95),[41] which states that:

---

40 This clause is discussed at length later in this chapter, p 790.
41 See IVCH(95), cl. 9.2.

... the Underwriters will contribute to charges properly and reasonably incurred by the Assured their servants or agents for such measures ...

Under the ICC (A), (B) and (C), cl 16 provides that:

... the underwriter will, in addition to any loss recoverable hereunder, reimburse the Assured for any charges properly and reasonably incurred in pursuance of these duties.

The assured and his agents

The Act, in s 78(4), refers to sue and labour as a duty imposed upon 'the assured and his agents', but both the Institute Hull and Cargo Clauses add the word 'servants' to their clauses. Presumably, this addition is to leave no doubt that employees, such as the master and crew, are included within the general provision.

This very issue was raised in the case of *Astrovlanis Compania Naviera SA v Linard, 'Gold Sky'* **[1972] 2 Lloyd's Rep 187**, where salvors were deliberately kept away from a sinking ship after an alleged scuttling. Mocatta J, at the court of first instance, was of the opinion that the word 'agents' did not include the master and crew.

> **Mocatta J:** [p 221] ... in s 78(4), the words used are: 'It is the duty of the assured and his agents.' The word 'agents' is capable of a wide range of different meanings depending upon the context and circumstances in which it is used. The master of a ship is primarily the servant of her owner; his authority as master is strictly limited and in general he only has wide powers as an agent to bind his principal and employer in cases where he has to act as agent of necessity. Whilst the master of *Gold Sky*, had he entered into a Lloyd's salvage agreement with Captain Emblem of *Herkules*, would no doubt by so doing have bound the plaintiffs, I do not think that it necessarily follows that, in the absence of instructions from his owners, the master of a vessel must be taken to be included within the words 'the assured and his agents' in s 78(4), so that a failure by the master to take such measures as may be reasonable will militate against his owners' claim against insurers. I think the words 'his agents' should in the context and to avoid an acute conflict between two sub-sections of the Act be read as inapplicable to the master and crew, unless expressly instructed by the assured in relation to what to do or not to do in respect of suing and labouring.

Mocatta J's reasoning on the construction of s 78(4) has not met with universal approval and, in the main, should be considered as flawed. In *State of The Netherlands v Youell*, below, the relevance of s 78(4) was again raised and the whole issue of agency, within the meaning of the section, was discussed. During those deliberations, Phillips LJ, in the Court of Appeal, was moved to say: [p 245] '... It will be apparent that my name must be added to the list of those who have felt unable to accept the analysis of the nature and effect of s 78(4) reached Mocatta J in *Gold Sky* [1972] 2 Lloyd's Rep 187.' More importantly, he then went on to add:

> **Phillips LJ:** [p 243] ... it is apparent that the duty to sue and labour to avert or minimise consequences of a marine peril was, in 1906, a long established incident of international maritime law arising in the contract of a marine adventure where the shipowner necessarily delegated authority to agents, and, in particular, to his master.
>
> [p 245] ... The duty of agents to sue and labour referred to in s 78(4) is a duty that arises in relation to a maritime adventure by reason of the delegation to master, crew and other agents of the conduct of that adventure.

It would appear from the above remarks that the master and crew, whether or not acting as agents of necessity or specially instructed to sue and labour, are nevertheless 'agents' of the assured for the purpose of s 78(4).

Shipbuilders

State of The Netherlands v Youell and Hayward and Others [1998] 1 Lloyd's Rep 236, CA

The plaintiffs, the Dutch navy, were the purchasers of two submarines which were being built in the shipyard of RDM, a Dutch company. The submarines were both insured, under different policies, with the defendants. In the course of construction and during sea trials, the submarines suffered debonding and cracking in their paintwork, and the plaintiffs claimed on their policies of insurance. The insurers denied liability, on the basis that the damage had not occurred as the result of an insured peril; their contention being that there had been wilful misconduct on the part of the navy and the builders in knowingly and recklessly applying an excessive coating of primer. The insurers also claimed that the builders, as agents of the assured, had failed to avert or minimise loss within the meaning of s 78(4).

The Court of Appeal, in affirming the decision of the trial judge, ruled that there was no misconduct as, within the meaning of the Act, misconduct implied a state of mind coupled with a more direct physical cause of loss.

Furthermore, s 78(4) did not apply to the builders – as they were not agents of the assured, they were under no duty to sue and labour.

> **Phillips LJ:** [p 245] ... The duty of agents to sue and labour referred to in s 78(4) is a duty that arises in relation to a maritime adventure by reason of the delegation to master, crew and other agents of the conduct of that adventure. I can see no scope for the application of such a duty in relation to an assured who insures as the purchaser of ships under a shipbuilding contract.
>
> **Buxton LJ:** [p 247] ... it [the meaning of agency] is certainly made explicit in the very first words of Bowstead and Reynolds (16th edn):
>
>> Agency is the fiduciary relationship which exists between two persons, one of whom expressly or impliedly consents that the other should act on his behalf so as to affect his relations with third parties ...

In that formulation, I venture to draw attention in particular to the words 'so as to affect his relations with third parties'. Whatever a builder agrees to do for the employer when entering into an orthodox building contract, such as the present, he does not agree to act for the employer in respect of the principal's relations or dealings with third parties. Indeed, before this case, and the attempt to apply s 78(4) to it, I do not think that anyone would have thought that a builder was his employer's agent *in respect of his completion of the building contract*. The matter might be different if complaint were made of the builder's conduct towards third parties, but that is not this case. Nor, if such latter agency were in issue, would it be an agency that had anything to do with s 78(4).

Reinsurers

Thus, it is emphasised, the courts apply a strict interpretation to the meaning of the words 'the assured and their servants and agents'. This was further illustrated in *Uzielli v Boston Marine Insurance Co*, below. In this instance, although the words contained in the sue and labour clause were slightly different, expenses incurred as sue and labour were held not recoverable, as the party concerned in that sue and labour, the original insurers, were not the 'factors, servants or assigns' of the reinsurer.

Uzielli v Boston Marine Insurance Co (1884) 15 QBD 11, CA

The owners of a ship insured her under a time policy of insurance. The sue and labour clause contained within the policy applied to '... the assured, their factors, servants, and assigns ...'. The underwriters then took out a reinsurance policy with a French company who, in turn, reinsured itself with the defendants. Whilst the policy was in force, the insured vessel ran aground and was abandoned to the original insurers. But, the original insurers then took it upon themselves to refloat the ship at considerable expense before selling her. The French reinsurers became liable to the original insurers, and, thus, sought to recover an indemnity from the defendants. One of the issues before the court was whether the defendants were liable for the expenditure incurred by the original insurer in refloating the ship.

The Court of Appeal ruled that, although the defendants were liable under their policy of reinsurance for a constructive total loss, they were not liable for any of the expenditure incurred in refloating the vessel; as the original insurers were not the 'factors, servants, and assigns' of the assured (the French reinsurers who were the plaintiffs in the case), the expenditure incurred did not fall within the scope of the sue and labour clause.

> **Lord Brett MR:** [p 17] ... I myself should be inclined to give to that clause [the sue and labour clause] all the width that I could: I should be inclined to hold that it gave the assured in this policy power to sue and labour for the benefit of the adventure; I think that the assured would have sufficient interest in the ship to entitle them to do so. But in this case the suing and labouring for the

safeguard and preservation of the ship was not by the assured under this policy, but by other underwriters. Those other underwriters were not either the 'factors', the 'servants', or the 'assigns' of the re-assured.

Furthermore, in *Crouan v Stanier* **[1903] 1 KB 87**, where a vessel struck a reef and her owner abandoned her as a constructive total loss, the insurers, having incurred considerable expenditure in refloating her on their own account, were unable to offset that expenditure against the claim. This was because the insurers were effectively trying to reclaim from the assured what they, the underwriters, would have been liable for under the policy if the owners had sued and laboured.

> **Kennedy J:** [p 90] ... What the underwriters did they had a right to do for themselves under the policy, without prejudice to their contention that there was no constructive total loss; they, as well as the assured, had the right to work and try to preserve the property. The assured refused to take any further step in the matter; the underwriters then did what the assured might have done himself, and the cost of which, if he had done it, he would have been entitled to recover from the underwriters; therefore, the underwriters are, in substance, under their claim for work and labour done for the assured, asking me to give them money which might be recovered back from them by the assured under the suing and labouring clause of the policy. I ought not, I think, to treat the cost of work and labour of preserving the vessel as the cost of work and labour done for the assured on any implied contract for payment by him, because if it were so done for him, and at his request, he would have a right under the policy to ask repayment from the underwriters of any sum that was given by such a judgment.

Salvors

In *Aitchison v Lohre* **(1879) 4 App Cas 755, HL**, Lord Blackburn was of the opinion that any expenditure incurred in salvage could not be recovered as sue and labour, as salvors, acting independently of contract, could not be considered as 'agents' of the assured.

> **Lord Blackburn:** [p 765] ... The owners of *Texas* [the salving vessel] did the labour here, not as agents of the assured, and being to be paid by them wages for their labour, but as salvors acting on the maritime law, which, as explained by Eyre LCJ in *Nicholson v Chapman*, already cited, gives them a claim against the property saved by their exertions, and a lien on it, and that quite independently of whether there is an insurance or not; or whether, if there be a policy of insurance, it contains the suing and labouring clause or not. The amount of such salvage occasioned by a peril has always been recovered, without dispute, under an averment that there was a loss by that peril; see *Cary v King*; and I have not been able to find any case in which it was recovered under a count for suing and labouring.

To avert or minimise a loss

Dillon LJ, in describing sue and labour as 'a stitch in time', summed up the concept most adeptly.[42] But, it is emphasised, sue and labour applies equally to averting a loss as well as minimising one, provided that, in both instances, the type of loss is covered by the policy.

The practical application of a sue and labour clause is particularly well illustrated in *The Pomeranian*, below.

The Pomeranian (1895) P 34

The plaintiffs insured a consignment of 125 head of cattle with the defendants for a voyage from New York to Glasgow aboard *The Pomeranian*. The policy was for all risks, including mortality, and it also contained a sue and labour clause. Soon after leaving New York, *The Pomeranian* encountered severe weather and put into Halifax, Nova Scotia, for repairs. Because of this delay, extra fodder had to be purchased for the cattle, and the plaintiffs later claimed this additional expense under sue and labour. The insurers denied liability, contending that the cattle had not been in any peril at the time the expense was incurred.

The court ruled that the plaintiffs could recover their expenditure as sue and labour. There had been a real danger that the cattle would have been totally lost if the extra fodder had not been purchased.

> **Gorrell Barnes J:** [p 352] ... if the animals had been necessarily landed during repairs, it is hardly contended that the underwriters would not be liable for the expense of hiring places to keep them in, and I do not understand why, if extra cost was incurred in feeding them on shore, to prevent mortality, the underwriters should not be liable for such extra cost. The shipowners were entitled to carry the cattle on; and if they did so, and no more food was supplied, it is obvious that there would be a risk of total loss from mortality. This condition of things would be brought about by perils enumerated in the policy; and in my opinion the expense incurred to prevent this loss comes within the suing and labouring clause ... There was under the circumstances a danger of total loss unless the expense was incurred, and it seems reasonable to hold that for this extra expense the underwriters are liable.

In relation to a policy on freight, the point is illustrated in *Kidston v Empire Marine Insurance Co Ltd* (1866) LR 1 CP 535; (1867) LR 2 CP 357, the facts of which are set out later.[43] For the present purpose, it is sufficient to say that, though the cargo was safely forwarded to its destination and freight was thereby earned, the assured of the freight was nevertheless entitled to recover the cost they had incurred in warehousing and forwarding the goods under the suing and labouring clause in the policy.

---

42 See *Integrated Container Service Inc v British Traders Insurance Co Ltd* [1984] 1 Lloyd's Rep 154, CA, *per* Dillon LJ, p 163.
43 See below, p 776.

But, in *Irvin v Hine* [1950] 1 KB 555, the failure by the assured to have a vessel put into dry dock to be surveyed after a stranding was held not to be a breach of the duty to sue and labour. Devlin J ruled that even if a survey had been carried out, it would not have averted or minimised the loss.

> **Devlin J:** [p 571] ... It is common ground that any accurate estimate of the extent of the damage could not be obtained without a survey of the ship in dry dock, which was never carried out. The underwriters contend that it was the assured's duty, under s 78(4), to cause such a survey to be made, and that as he was in breach of his duty the claim cannot be sustained. Section 78(4) requires the assured to take such measures as may be reasonable for the purpose of averting or minimising a loss. A survey in dry dock in the circumstances of this case would not have averted or minimised the loss, but merely ascertained its extent. Its cost would, I think, be part of the cost incurred by the assured in proving his claim.

Notes

In *Kuwait Airways v Kuwait Insurance Co SAK* [1996] 1 Lloyd's Rep 664, the issue was raised as to whether legal costs incurred in minimising a loss could be included as sue and labour. Rix J was of the opinion that solicitors' costs would only be applicable as sue and labour if those costs were incurred whilst endeavouring to recover the property. But costs incurred in pursuing damages would not be appropriate under sue and labour, as the insurers stood to gain no benefit.

> **Rix J:** [p 698] ... The submission is made that at any rate so far as the recovery action seeks damages rather than the specific return of the aircraft, or primarily seeks damages, the expenses incurred cannot be in the nature of sue and labour. It seems to me that that is correct.

Whilst on the question of legal costs, it is necessary here to mention the case of *Netherlands Insurance Co (Est 1845) Ltd v Karl Ljungberg and Co A/B* [1986] 2 Lloyd's Rep 19, PC, the judgment of which is cited later.[44] In this instance, the Privy Council held that an assured was entitled to recover from his insurers the legal expenses (for proceedings instituted to prevent a time bar) he had incurred, in so far as they related to the preservation or exercise of rights in respect of loss or damage for which the insurers are liable under the policy. By reason of the bailee clause (cl 16.2 of the ICC), the assured and their agents were duty bound 'to take such measures to ensure that all rights against carriers, bailees or other third parties are properly preserved and exercised'.

Cargo insurance – transhipment and forwarding

In addition to sue and labour, the assured of cargo is given further protection by both the Institute Cargo Clauses and the Act when, by a peril insured

---

[44] See below, p 790.

against, the voyage is interrupted and cargo has to be transhipped and forwarded to its destination. The first part of cl 12 of the ICC (A), (B) and (C) states:

> Where, as a result of the operation of a risk covered by this insurance, the insured transit is terminated at a port or place other than that to which the subject matter is covered under this insurance, the Underwriters will reimburse the Assured for any extra charges properly and reasonably incurred in unloading storing and forwarding the subject matter to the destination to which it is insured hereunder.

Furthermore, cl 8.3 of the ICC (A), (B) and (C) affirm that:

> This insurance shall remain in force ... during ... forced discharge, reshipment or transhipment ...

The same is reiterated in s 59 of the Act, which provides:

> Where, by a peril insured against, the voyage is interrupted at an intermediate port or place, under such circumstances as, apart from any special stipulation in the contract of affreightment, to justify the master in landing and reshipping the goods or other movables, or in transhipping them, and sending them on to their destination, the liability of the insurer continues, notwithstanding the landing or transhipment.

The loss to be averted or minimised must be covered by the policy

Section 78(3) of the Act outlines the general principles under which expenses incurred by suing and labouring may be indemnified, when it states:

> Expenses incurred for the purpose of averting or diminishing any loss not covered by the policy are not recoverable under the suing and labouring clause.

In cl 11.1 of the ITCH(95), the same point is made with the words '... which would be recoverable under this insurance', and in cl 16 of the ICC (A), (B) and (C), with the words '... in respect of loss recoverable hereunder'.

Thus, sue and labour is recoverable only if it is incurred to avert or diminish a loss which is an insured risk under the policy.

This was particularly well illustrated in the case of ***The Pomeranian* (1895) P 34**, where a vessel carrying livestock suffered weather damage and had to put into a port of refuge. The ensuing delay, a risk not normally covered by a policy,[45] meant that extra fodder had to be bought for the cattle, and the expenditure on such was deemed recoverable under the sue and labour clause because the policy on live cattle contained a clause which stated: '... including all risk of shipping, and until safely landed. Against all risks, including mortality and jettison arising from any cause whatsoever.'

---

45 See s 55(2)(b); *Weissburg v Lamb* (1950) 84 LlL Rep 509 and *Meyer v Ralli* (1876) CPD 358.

Gorrell Barnes J: [p 352] ... The policy by its special terms differs from an insurance under which the underwriter is not liable for delay, or any other cause affecting the subject matter of insurance. It was admitted that if there was a proper supply of food at the commencement of the voyage, and the vessel were delayed by bad weather so long that the food became exhausted, and the animals died from starvation, the underwriters would be liable.

But, there can be no recovery by way of sue and labour where the loss that is averted or diminished is not covered by the policy. Thus, in *Berk v Style* [1956] 1 QB 181, where expenses were incurred in rebagging kieselguhr, the court ruled that, as the loss was occasioned by inherent vice – a risk not insured under the policy – the claim for sue and labour must fail.

Under an all risks policy, however, the suing and labouring clause can have a very wide scope. In *Integrated Container Service Inc v British Traders Insurance Co Ltd*,[46] below, the insolvency of a company to which containers had been leased was adjudged to have put the assured's property at risk and money expended in recovering those containers was, therefore, held to be recoverable under the suing and labouring clause.

Integrated Container Service Inc v British Traders Insurance Co Ltd [1984] 1 Lloyd's Rep 154, CA

The plaintiffs leased 1,016 containers to Oyama Ltd, a far eastern company, which became insolvent and had to cease trading. Because Oyama Ltd owed money by way of port dues and warehousing, the plaintiffs were concerned that their property was put at risk to those third parties. Therefore, the plaintiffs, who had insured their containers under an all risks policy, recovered the containers at considerable expense, and claimed an indemnity from their insurers under the sue and labour clause. The insurers settled in principle for those containers actually lost or damaged, but refused to indemnify the assured for the expenses incurred in recovering the undamaged ones, as, they argued, they were not at risk from a peril insured against.

The Court of Appeal ruled that, as the policy covered all risks, the insurers were liable, as the insolvency of the lessee put the containers at risk and any expenditure made in diminishing that risk was recoverable as sue and labour.

Eveleigh LJ: [p 158] ... From the point of view of insurers, they wish to encourage the assured to act expeditiously in an emergency where there is a risk of their having to meet a claim. The nature and degree of the risk will of course vary. It will determine what measures are reasonable to avert it. I therefore think that the sue and labour clause entitles the assured to recover the cost of such measures as were reasonably taken for the purpose of averting or minimising a loss when there was a risk that insurers might have to bear that loss.

---

46 See Chapter 10, p 446, where the case is discussed in relation to insolvency as an insured risk under ICC (A).

Dillon LJ: [p 162] ... The policy is against all risks, and I can see no reason why the risk of lawful sale by a third party should be excluded. The plaintiffs effectively lose their containers whether the sale is lawful under a lien – port regulations or a process of judicial execution – or unlawful.

Sue and labour to avert a particular average loss

Expenses incurred in suing and labouring are, unless the policy otherwise provides, recoverable regardless of whether the loss that is being averted or minimised is partial or total. But, as was seen,[47] a policy may well contain a 'free from particular average' warranty, in which case only a total loss is insured. Such a warranty, therefore, raises two questions, which, it is significant to note, are separate and distinct.

First, is an expenditure incurred for suing and labouring recoverable under a policy which insures only a total loss? This, as was seen,[48] does not pose a problem, as s 76(2) has now clarified that the insurer is nevertheless liable for 'expense properly incurred pursuant to the provisions of the suing and labouring clause in order to avert a loss insured against', even when the subject matter insured is warranted free from particular average, either wholly or under a certain percentage. The second question relates to the point of whether an extraordinary expenditure incurred to avert or minimise a *particular average loss* is recoverable.

The latter issue was raised in three cases during the 1860s, all of which are cited below. The first two, *Great Indian Peninsula Railway Co v Saunders*, and *Booth v Gair*, concluded that, where a policy contained an fpa clause, any expenditure incurred for suing and labouring to prevent a loss other than a total loss is not recoverable. Because of the said warranty, the assured could only recover under sue and labour if that sue and labour were rendered to avert or prevent a total loss.

Great Indian Peninsula Railway Co v Saunders (1862) 2 B&S 266

The plaintiffs insured a consignment of iron rails with the defendants under a policy of insurance which was warranted 'free from particular average'. The policy also contained the usual clause authorising the assured to: '... sue, labour, and travel for ... the defence, safeguard and recovery of the goods.' Though the vessel carrying the rails became a constructive total loss, the rails were all saved. However, the plaintiffs incurred charges for freight, in order to convey the rails to their proper destination. They then sought to recover the freight charges incurred from the defendants, under the suing and labouring clause.

---

47 See above, p 719.
48 See above, p 720.

The court ruled that, as the policy was warranted free from particular average, and there was no risk of the rails becoming a total loss, the plaintiffs could not recover under the policy. As the expense was incurred to avert or minimise a partial loss, a loss not covered by the policy, the plaintiffs' claim was not recoverable.

Erle CJ: [p 272] ... This is an insurance on goods 'warranted free from particular average' – in effect an insurance against a total loss.

[p 273] ... but the cargo was landed and delivered to the plaintiffs who were the owners of it, and by them taken to its destination in a state undamaged by sea in any way ... But Mr James [for the plaintiffs] ably argues that the plaintiffs are entitled to recover this money; not as compensation for loss of the goods within the general language of the policy; but as the expense of forwarding them to their destination in other vessels, under what has been called 'the labour and travel clause' which empowers the assured to sue, labour, and travel to save the thing assured from impending loss. The substantial ground, however, on which I decide this case is entirely beside his able argument. The expenses that can be recovered under the suing, labouring and travelling clause are expenses incurred to prevent impending loss within the meaning of the policy. Now, here, the goods were given up to the plaintiffs in perfect safety; and the question is, were these expenses incurred to prevent a *total* loss? Had the owners a right when the goods were given into their possession to turn the transaction into a total loss? Certainly not, for they had the goods *in specie*, and consequently that £825 11s 7d [freight] had no reference to suing, labouring or travelling in order to prevent such a loss. [Emphasis added.]

Booth v Gair (1863) 33 LJCP 99

The plaintiffs insured a cargo of bacon from New York to Liverpool, aboard the vessel *Plantagenet*, with the defendants, under a policy of insurance which was warranted 'free from particular average'. The policy also authorised the plaintiffs to 'sue, labour, and travel for ... the defence, safeguard and recovery of the said goods and merchandises ...'. During the voyage, *Plantagenet* suffered severe weather damage, and, after putting into Bermuda, the undamaged portion of the cargo of bacon was forwarded to Liverpool in other ships, but the plaintiffs had to pay the freight. This they now sought to recover from the defendants under the suing and labouring clause.

The court, citing the *Great Indian Peninsula Railway* case, came to the conclusion that there was no substantial distinction between the two cases and ruled that, as there was no risk of the cargo becoming a total loss, the only risk covered by the policy, any expenses incurred in suing and labouring were not recoverable.

Erle CJ: [p 101] ... The plaintiff claimed in this action from the underwriters the expenses incidental to this transhipment of the cargo ... But we are unable to find any substantial distinction between the two cases. There [the *Great Indian*

Peninsula Railway case], the goods were returned to the assured at the port of loading in an undamaged state, and sent on by him; here, they were perishable goods landed at a port on the voyage in a damaged state, and sent on by the master. What the master did in this case was in discharge of his duty in ordinary course, and there was no peril creating a risk of a total loss from which the underwriter was saved by the expenses in question ... If the assured intended to confine the warranty to partial loss from damage to the cargo and to leave the underwriters liable for expenses of transhipment, in our opinion this policy does not express that intention.

In the third case, *Kidston v Empire Marine Insurance Co Ltd*, the court arrived at a different decision, as the expenses incurred were to avert a *total* loss. The case may be distinguished from the other two by the policy being on freight, and the expense for suing and labouring was incurred to prevent a total loss of freight.

Kidston v Empire Marine Insurance Co Ltd (1866) LR 1 CP 535; (1867) LR 2 CP 357

The plaintiff owners of *Sebastopol* effected a policy on freight with the defendants for a voyage from the west coast of South America to the UK. The policy was warranted free from particular average, but contained the usual suing and labouring clause. During the voyage by way of Cape Horn, *Sebastopol* was severely damaged by storms, and had to put into Rio de Janeiro, where she was condemned and sold. The cargo, however, was forwarded safely to its destination, and the plaintiffs claimed the cost of warehousing the goods and procuring an alternative ship as sue and labour.

The court ruled that the free from particular average warranty did not prevent recovery for expenses incurred for suing and labouring, and as there would have been a total loss of freight at Rio if the goods had not been forwarded, the plaintiffs were entitled to recover the sum claimed under the suing and labouring clause of the policy.

> **Kelly CB:** [p 364] ... We are of opinion, however, that upon the ship Sebastopol becoming a wreck at Rio, and the goods having been landed there, in as much as no freight *pro rata itineris* could be claimed, a total loss of freight had arisen, and that the expenses incurred in forwarding the goods to England by another ship were charges within the suing and labouring clause, incurred for the benefit of the underwriters to protect them against a claim for total loss of freight, to which they would have been liable but for the incurring of these charges, and that consequently the amount is recoverable under that clause in the policy.
>
> [p 366] ... that upon the facts of this case there was a total loss of the freight when the ship had become a wreck, and the goods had been landed at Rio; and that the cost incurred by the master in shipping the goods by *Caprice*, and causing them to be conveyed to this country, is a charge within the express terms of the suing and labouring clause, and that the amount, or the due proportion of it, is recoverable under that clause against the underwriters.

The cases of *Great Indian Peninsular Railway Company v Saunders* and of *Booth v Gair* have been pressed upon the attention of the court, as showing that a loss of this nature is a partial loss only, and cannot be recovered against the underwriters by reason of the warranty against particular average. But, these were cases of insurance upon goods, to which the *pro rata* doctrine has no application, and where, the whole or a great portion of the goods still existing in specie, it was impossible to hold that a total loss had arisen.

[p 367] We think, therefore ... that on the destruction of the ship and the landing of the cargo at Rio there was a total loss of the freight, unless it could be averted by the forwarding of the cargo by another ship to Great Britain; that the forwarding of the cargo by *Caprice* was a particular charge within the true meaning of the suing and labouring clause, and not the conversion of total loss into a partial loss, which brought the case within the warranty against particular average; and that the due proportion of that particular charge, that charge being thus within the suing and labouring clause, and incurred for the benefit of the underwriters to preserve the subject of the insurance, and to prevent a total loss, is recoverable under the policy in this action.

Measures as may be reasonable

Section 78(4) of the Act verifies that it is 'the duty of the assured and his agents, in all cases, to take such measures as may be reasonable for the purpose of averting or minimising loss'.

The test of reasonableness required was best summed up by Eveleigh LJ, in **Integrated Container Service Inc v British Traders Insurance Co Ltd [1984] 1 Lloyd's Rep 154, CA**, where the plaintiff successfully claimed, under a suing and labouring clause, for expenses incurred in recovering containers when the lessee had become insolvent.

> **Eveleigh LJ:** [p 158] ... The duty under s 78 is '... to take such measures as may be reasonable for the purpose of averting or minimising a loss ...'. Those words seem to me to impose a duty to act in circumstances where a reasonable man intent upon preserving his property, as opposed to claiming from insurers, would act. Whether or not the assured can recover should depend upon the reasonableness of his assessment of the situation and the action taken by him. It should not be possible for insurers to be able to contend that, upon an ultimate investigation and analysis of the facts, a loss, while possible or even probable, was not 'very probable'. As the right to recover expenses is a corollary to the duty to act, in my opinion the assured should be entitled to recover all extraordinary expenses reasonably incurred by him where he can demonstrate that a prudent assured person, mindful of an obligation to prevent a loss, would incur expense of an unusual kind. In my opinion, this is the effect of the sue and labour clause, and I do not think that authority compels me to hold otherwise.

Notes

In the much older case of ***Stringer v English and Scottish Marine Insurance Co Ltd* (1869) LR 4 QB 676**, a ship and cargo were seized during the American Civil War, and the Prize Court in New Orleans insisted that the goods would be sold unless their full value was deposited with the court. Blackburn J ruled that the plaintiffs had not failed in their duty to sue and labour by not depositing the sum of money with the court, because an expenditure of such a proportion in the circumstances would have been unreasonable.

> **Blackburn J:** [p 691] ... It appears that the assured might have prevented the sale by depositing the full value of the goods, but we think it can seldom be reasonable to require an assured to deposit the *full* value of the subject matter in a foreign court and country; and consequently that, without reference to the peculiarity arising from the state of the American currency, the assured were not bound to adopt that alternative.

Much more recently, in *Stephen AP v Scottish Boatowners Mutual Insurance Association, 'Talisman'* [1989] 1 Lloyd's Rep 535, HL, a fishing vessel was insured with a P & I Club which included in its rules the requirement that the assured shall take reasonable care during the risk to maintain the vessel in a seaworthy condition, and an usual provision that: 'The Association shall not be liable for any claim for loss or damage when the assured making such claim has not used all reasonable endeavours to save his vessel from such loss or damage'. When the vessel sank, and it was shown that the skipper had failed to close the seacocks because he thought it was necessary for them to be open whilst operating the bilge pumps, Lord Keith, in finding against the Club, considered the tests to be applied for determining the 'reasonableness' of the skipper's conduct. Lord Keith [p 540] applied the objective test of how 'an ordinarily competent skipper, in the circumstances in which the pursuer [owner-skipper] was placed', would reasonably have acted, and rejected the criterion of how 'a more knowledgeable individual, viewing the situation dispassionately' might have assessed the situation.

Cargo insurance – duty under cl 16.2

In addition to the duty imposed upon a cargo-owner under s 78(4) of the Act and cl 16.1 of the ICC (A), (B) and (C), a cargo-owner is bound by cl 16.2 of the ICC (the Bailee Clause) to: '... ensure that all rights against carriers, bailees or other third parties are properly preserved and exercised.' It is significant to note that both the above provision and the general duty to sue and labour encapsulated in cl 16.1 are subject to the reimbursement obligation by which the underwriters undertake to 'reimburse the Assured any charges properly and reasonably incurred in pursuance of these duties'.[49]

A cargo-owner who enters into a contract of carriage with a third party is generally bound, by his contract of insurance, to ensure that the rights of the insurer, by way of subrogation, are 'properly' safeguarded. This issue was raised in the cases of *Netherlands Insurance Co (Est 1845) Ltd v Karl Ljungberg and Co A/B* and *Vasso*, below, where the nature and extent of the obligation imposed by cl 16 and the consequences for a failure to perform that obligation were examined.

The inclusion of the right to claim reimbursement in cl 16, which now qualifies both cll 16.1 and 16.2, has removed many of the legal problems encountered in *Netherlands Insurance Co (Est 1845) Ltd v Karl Ljungberg and Co A/B* [1986] 2 Lloyd's Rep 19, PC.[50] As the undertaking of reimbursement in this case was not expressly made applicable to the bailee clause, the Privy Council had no choice but to imply such a term into the contract in order to allow the assured recovery of the expenses he had incurred pursuant to the bailee clause.

Noble Resources Ltd v George Albert Greenwood, 'Vasso' [1993] 2 Lloyd's Rep 309

The plaintiffs insured their cargo of 57,513 tonnes of iron ore, which was loaded aboard the bulk carrier *Vasso*, with the defendants under a policy of insurance which incorporated the Institute Cargo Clauses (A). During the voyage from South Africa to China, *Vasso* sprung a leak and sank; both the ship and cargo were totally lost. The plaintiffs claimed on their policy of insurance, but the defendants refused to pay, on the basis that the assured had failed in their duty under cl 16 of the ICC (A) to apply for a Mareva injunction in order to restrain the shipowner from removing any insurance proceeds from their hull policy, valued at US$6.5 m, from the jurisdiction. This, the plaintiffs had failed to do.

The court ruled that the plaintiffs' failure to apply for a Mareva injunction did not amount to a failure by the assured in their duty imposed by cl 16. Furthermore, as the insured had submitted, cl 16 should not be construed as a contractual warranty. The duty imposed by cl 16 was essentially a duty to sue and labour which was contractual in nature, the breach of which gave rise to a liability in damages.

> **Hobhouse J:** [p 313] ... The subject matter of cl 16, as of s 78, is to make express the duty of the assured to minimise or avoid a loss and provide for the assured

---

49 Whereas an earlier edition (1963) of the Institute Cargo Clauses (all risks), cl 9, did not expressly provide that the insurer reimburse the assured for any expenses he might incur for the purpose of preserving their rights of action.

50 Also discussed later in relation to the question of whether an express reimbursement clause is essential for the right of recovery under the policy: see below, p 789.

to be indemnified against the expenses that he so incurs. Neither cl 16 nor s 78 has any role in defining the scope of the primary cover. It states a collateral duty which arises once an insured peril has begun to take effect and confers collaterally an additional indemnity in connection with the performance of that duty. Neither under the statute, nor under the clause, is the assured required to act unreasonably or to undertake any step other than one which could reasonably be expected to result in the avoidance or reduction of the loss. The word 'reasonable' is included in 16.1 and the word 'properly' is included in 16.2. Accordingly, on the facts of the present case, the mere failure to apply for a Mareva injunction does not, without more, establish any failure to perform the duty imposed by cl 16 (or s 78). The assured, and ... their agent, acted reasonably and properly. On the correct construction of the clause, more has to be shown than merely that some step was not taken. Underwriters have to show that the step was a proper one which a reasonable assured, having regard to the interests of himself and the insurers and to the provisions of the policy, should have taken.

[p 314] ... The duty [under cl 16] is essentially a duty to sue and labour. The breach of that duty may cause loss to the insurer, in which case the insurer will have a claim for damages against the assured in respect of such breach of duty in so far as the insurer has been caused loss. Where the failure of the assured is a failure to exercise or preserve some right against a third party to which the insurer is entitled to be subrogated, the loss to the insurer will be equivalent to the value of the lost right against the third party. This would be the position both under s 78 and under cl 16. The duty is a contractual duty, breach of which gives rise to liability in damages. In certain circumstances, those damages may be equivalent to the full amount of the assured's claim. Where the subrogated right against the third party would have provided the insurer with a full reimbursement, the damages for the breach of the duty would, when set off against the liability of the insurer to the assured, eliminate that liability and provide the insurer with a defence to the claim upon the policy.

Supplementary cover

That sue and labour is unique and additional to normal insurance cover is confirmed by s 78(1) of the Act, which states that '... the engagement [to sue and labour] thereby entered into is deemed to be supplementary to the contract of insurance ...'. Further, the phrase 'in addition', appearing in cl 11.6 of the ITCH(95)[51] and cl 16 of the ICC (A), (B) and (C), also clarifies the point. An assured may, thus, recover for the total loss of the subject matter insured *and* any expense incurred in suing and labouring to avert or minimise that loss.

The amount that may be recovered for suing and labouring has traditionally been subject to a test of reasonableness, which is still the case,

---

51 See IVCH(95), cl 9.6.

and, presumably, the ceiling of such a claim is the insured value of the property. To remove any doubt, the Institute Hulls Clauses now expressly limit any claim under sue and labour to the insured value of the policy where they state:[52]

> The sum recoverable under this cl 11 shall be in addition to the loss otherwise recoverable under this insurance but shall in no circumstances exceed the amount insured under this insurance in respect of the Vessel.

But, no such express limit is stipulated by the Institute Cargo Clauses. Nevertheless, the test of reasonableness still applies as was illustrated in *Lee v Southern Insurance Co*, below.

Lee and Another v Southern Insurance Co (1870) LR 5 CP 397

The plaintiffs were insurance brokers who, on behalf of the owners of the vessel *Charles*, effected a policy of insurance on freight for a voyage from the Cameroons to Liverpool. The policy included a sue and labour clause. Whilst sailing up the Irish Sea, *Charles* encountered severe weather and was stranded on the Welsh coast, near Pwllheli. The cargo of palm oil was off-loaded and forwarded to Liverpool by rail at a cost of more than £200. *Charles* was later repaired, and it was estimated that she could have carried the palm oil to Liverpool for £70. The insurers refused to indemnify the assured for the expense incurred in forwarding the cargo by rail, because, they argued, it was unreasonable.

The court ruled that the expense incurred in forwarding the palm oil was unreasonable, and the insurers were, therefore, only liable for £70, the amount it would have cost to send the cargo by sea.

> **Bovill CJ:** [p 403] ... It seems to me that it was necessary to incur expense for the purpose of earning the freight; but that the whole of the expense actually incurred (£212 15s 1d) was not properly incurred. The inference which I draw from the facts stated is, that £70 is the proper measure of the liability of the underwriters on freight. That, it is found, would have been the cost of carrying the oil in lighters to St Tidswell's Roads and there reloading it on board *Charles*. It is true that the plaintiffs did not actually incur expense for that purpose; but they incurred a much larger expense in forwarding the goods and earning the freight; and, upon the whole, I am of opinion that £70 is the sum which they are entitled to recover.

Similarly, in ***Wilson Brothers Bobbin Co Ltd v Green* [1917] 1 KB 860**, where a cargo of timber had to be forwarded from Norway to Garston, Liverpool, after the vessel carrying it was turned back by German warships, Bray J stated:

> [p 864] ... The goods were at Grimstadt, the port of destination was Garston, and the goods could not safely be got to Garston without incurring the expense of storage at Grimstadt and the cost of forwarding, and therefore, in my

---

52 See ITCH(95), cl 11.6 and IVCH(95), cl 9.6.

opinion, these were expenses (I will leave out the word 'proper' for the moment) incurred in endeavouring to avert that loss. [The learned judge then dealt with the evidence, and came to the conclusion that if the plaintiffs had acted with reasonable diligence, they could have had a ship ready to load the cargo at Grimstadt for carriage to this country by 15 April 1915, at a lower rate of freight than they in fact paid, and that the expense of storage and forwarding, a proportion of which they were entitled to recover from the defendant, must be calculated upon that footing.]

Breach of the duty to sue and labour

The assured of a policy on ship, cargo or freight may, at best, be guilty of negligence or, at worst, wilful misconduct, should he fail to instruct his servants or agents to sue and labour in order to avert or minimise a loss. Such was the case in *Currie v Bombay Native Insurance Co*, below.

Currie and Co v Bombay Native Insurance Co (1869) LR 3 PC 72

The plaintiffs (appellants) insured with the defendants, for total loss only, a cargo of timber aboard the vessel *Northland* for a voyage from Moulmein in Burma to Madras. Whilst leaving Moulmein, *Northland* grounded, and was eventually wrecked. The master, who was a part owner of the vessel, but uninsured, was apparently left in charge of affairs by the assured of cargo. The master made great efforts to save the ship, but did nothing to preserve the cargo which was eventually sold *in situ*. When the plaintiffs (assured of cargo) claimed on their policy of insurance for a total loss, the underwriters refused payment, on the ground that there was no total loss of the cargo.

The Privy Council ruled that at no time could the cargo be considered as a total loss. Nevertheless, the court considered what the position would have been if the cargo had not been sold, but had become totally lost by reason of a failure on the part of the master to minimise the loss.

> **Lord Chelmsford:** [p 80] ... It was the duty of the Assured, or of the Captain of *Northland* (to whom everything appears to have been left), to take some steps in accordance with the recommendation of the Surveyors to try and save the cargo. But towards this object, the Captain literally did nothing.
>
> [p 81] ... if previously a portion of it, at least, might have been saved by the exertions of the Captain acting for the assured, and he chose not to make the slightest attempt to save it, how can the assured recover from the Underwriters a loss which was made total by their own negligence ... In this case, his tenderness to the ship might have arisen from his being a part owner uninsured; but, at all events, there was no reason why she should have been spared if her sacrifice were necessary to the safety of the cargo. She was a hopeless wreck, and was sold at the auction in that character and by that description.

[p 82] ... This omission of the Captain to take any steps towards saving the cargo, at a time when it was probable that his endeavours would be successful, in their Lordships' judgment, precludes the Assured from claiming for a total loss of the cargo into whatever condition it might have been brought afterwards.

Unfortunately, since the passing of the Act in 1906, there has been little in the way of authority to indicate what would be the effect of a breach of duty to sue and labour under s 78(4), although Eveleigh LJ went some way towards clarifying the issue, in *Integrated Container Service Inc v British Traders Insurance Co Ltd* **[1984] 1 Lloyd's Rep 154, CA**, cited above:[53]

Eveleigh LJ: [p 157] ... While it is not possible to state with certainty all the adverse consequences which will be suffered by an assured who fails to perform his duty under the sue and labour clause, there is no doubt that he incurs a risk of his claim for loss or damage being rejected in whole or in part if it can be shown that he failed to act when he should have done.

However, the words of Eveleigh LJ should be read with the comments of Phillips LJ in *State of The Netherlands v Youell* **[1998] 1 Lloyd's Rep 236, CA**, the facts of which were briefly stated earlier.[54] The insurers refused payment, unsuccessfully, on the ground that the shipbuilders had not fulfilled their duties under s 78(4) to minimise the loss.

Phillips LJ: [p 244] ... I revert to the fact that there has been no example of s 78(4) providing underwriters with a defence to a claim since 1906. This, of itself, seems clear indication that the section does not impose a conventional contractual duty which displaces, after a casualty has occurred, the general principle embodied in s 55(2)(a).

The conflict between ss 55(2)(a) and 78(4)

Both the Act, in s 78(4), and the ITCH(95), in cl 11.1, impose a duty upon the assured, his servants and agents to sue and labour in order to avert or minimise a loss.[55] Failure to do so would, in general, be considered as negligence. However, the Act, in s 55(2)(a), states that the insurers will remain liable under the policy regardless of the negligence of the master and crew.[56] Thus, there appears to be an anomaly. This very problem has been discussed in a number of prominent cases,[57] some recently, from which a picture has begun to emerge.

In *Astrovlanis Compania Naviera SA v Linard, 'Gold Sky'* **[1972] 2 Lloyd's Rep 187**, where the master and crew of a sinking vessel refused help

---

53 See above, p 777.
54 The facts are set out in full below, p 784.
55 See, also, IVCH(95), cl 9.1.
56 See, also, ITCH(95), cl 6.2.2 and IVCH(95), cl 4.2.2.
57 All of which are discussed in *State of The Netherlands v Youell* [1997] 2 Lloyd's Rep 440.

from salvors, Mocatta J tried to resolve the anomaly between ss 55(2)(a) and 78(4) by suggesting that the word 'agents' did not include the master and crew.

> **Mocatta J:** [p 221] ... On my construction of s 78(4), the master here was not the agent of the plaintiffs [the assured], since there is no evidence that he was instructed by them to refuse salvage assistance, and I do not feel able to draw the inference that he was so instructed.

A more convincing approach to resolve this anomaly is proposed by Arnould,[58] where it is suggested that s 55(2)(a) only applies to the negligence of the master and crew prior to a casualty, whereas the duty to sue and labour under s 78(4) is only relevant after the casualty. In this way, s 78(4) comes into operation only after the peril has struck and it is then, and only then, that it will have precedence over s 55(2)(a). Nevertheless, under this approach, there remains, under s 78(4), a 'positive obligation that is owed by the assured to the underwriters, breach of which sounds in damages'.[59]

Yet another solution to the problem is, as Arnould proposes, to approach the issue as one of causation. This, Arnould suggests, is probably the most satisfactory means of settling the conflict, particularly where the negligence of the 'Master Officers Crew and Pilots' is an insured risk under cl 6.2.2 of the ITCH(95).[60] By treating the effects of non-compliance in s 78(4) as, principally, issues of causation, the dispute may be resolved. In this way, if the master negligently fails in his duty to sue and labour, and that negligence becomes the proximate cause of the loss, the underwriter has a defence, but that defence is only sustainable if the policy does not insure against such negligence.

The issue was finally analysed in depth in the case of *State of The Netherlands v Youell* [1998] 1 Lloyd's Rep 236, CA, below. The significance of this case is that it traced the background to the problem, emphasised the relevant cases, and outlined the differing points of view, before coming to a reasoned conclusion. A great deal of the text from the reasoning of Phillips LJ is reproduced, as it includes, in chronological order, both the opinions and decisions reached in leading cases on the issue and the submissions of respected text writers.

State of The Netherlands v Youell [1998] 1 Lloyd's Rep 236, CA

After two submarines were completed for the Dutch navy by the shipbuilders RDM, it was found that there were serious defects in the bonding and paintwork. The navy claimed under their policies of insurance to be

---

58 Arnould, J, *Law of Marine Insurance and Average*, 16th edn, 1997, London: Sweet & Maxwell, Vol 3, para 770.
59 *Per* Phillips LJ, *State of The Netherlands v Youell* [1998] 1 Lloyd's Rep 236, p 243, CA.
60 See, also, IVCH(95), cl 4.2.2.

indemnified for the costs of rectification, but the underwriters refused payment, on the basis that both the navy and RDM were guilty of misconduct. Furthermore, the insurers contended that RDM, as agents of the assured, had failed in their duty, under s 78(4), to sue and labour and minimise the loss.

The Court of Appeal, in affirming the decision of the trial judge, ruled that there was no misconduct as, within the meaning of the Act, misconduct implied a state of mind coupled with a more direct physical cause of loss. Furthermore, s 78(4) did not apply to the builders, as they were not agents of the assured.

Phillips LJ: [pp 243–45] ... The express reference to the duty in s 78(4) provoked discussion as to the consequences of a breach of that duty which have persisted to this day ... In a climate which has seen English common law preoccupied with the development of the law of obligations, there has more recently been a tendency to treat s 78(4) as imposing a positive obligation owed by the assured to the underwriters, breach of which sounds in damages – see, for example, *Gold Sky* [1972] 2 Lloyd's Rep 187, p 221 and *Vasso* [1993] 2 Lloyd's Rep 309, p 314.

If the approach in these cases is correct, then it would seem to follow that, whenever agents of the assured, by negligence or misconduct, fail to take steps which would avert or minimise the consequences of an assured peril, underwriters can, by defence or counterclaim, avoid liability for such consequences. Thus, in effect, the policy would exclude liability for loss attributable to negligence or misconduct of the assured's agents after, but not before, the casualty.

The case that comes nearest to supporting such a proposition is one cited by the first edition of *Chalmers*, in a footnote to s 78(4). *Currie and Co v The Bombay Native Insurance Co* (1869) LR 3 PC 72 involved a 'total loss only' policy on a cargo of timber. The carrying ship stranded in circumstances where some, at least, of the timber, could readily have been salved. The captain did nothing ... The Privy Council considered, however, what the position would have been had the cargo become a total loss ... As to this, they said, through Lord Chelmsford, p 81:

... if, previously, a portion of it, at least, might have been saved by the exertions of the Captain acting for the assured, and he chose not to make the slightest attempt to save it, how can the assured recover from the Underwriters a loss which was made total by their own negligence.

The previous editors of *Arnould* considered that this *dictum* was 'certainly too wide', but the editors of the current edition do not agree – see para 770. They support the following statement in relation to a sue and labour clause in the 2nd edition of *McArthur*, p 263, a passage also referred to by *Chalmers*:

Although the terms of the clause with reference to the action contemplated are simply permissive, there can be no doubt that it is the duty of the assured, in case of accident, to make every reasonable exertion to save the property; and should any loss be directly caused by a failure to perform that duty, it will not be recoverable under the policy.

The conclusion that the current edition of *Arnould* draws, in para 770, is as follows:

> The most satisfactory approach to this problem is, in our opinion, to treat the issue as one of causation; if a negligent response to a casualty is the proximate cause of loss, or converts a partial into a total loss under a policy against total loss only, the underwriter has a complete defence, and if the negligent conduct is the proximate cause of part of the loss under a policy covering particular average losses, the underwriter has a defence *pro tanto*, unless in either case the negligence itself constitutes an insured peril. This approach would at least afford a means of resolving the apparent conflict between s 78(4) and s 55(2)(a) of the Marine Insurance Act 1906, although it, too, is not free from objection.

This passage was approved by Colman J in *National Oilwell (UK) Ltd v Davy Offshore Ltd* [1993] 2 Lloyd's Rep 582. At p 618, he said this of s 78(4):

> It goes no further than the obvious proposition that if, after the advent of an insured peril, or when the advent of an insured peril was obviously imminent, the assured or his agent failed to act to avert or minimise loss in circumstances where any prudent uninsured would have done so, the chain of causation between the insured peril and the loss will be broken. Clearly, if the insured peril is not the proximate cause of the loss, the assured cannot recover.

In the instant case, p 458, col 2 of [1997] 2 Lloyd's Rep, Rix J expressed a similar view. He compared the duty to sue and labour to the duty to mitigate loss in response to a breach of duty in contract or tort. He concluded:

> ... Thus, a loss proximately caused by perils of the seas, but remotely caused (as where the master is guilty of poor navigation) or merely contributed to (as in *Lind v Mitchell*) by the negligence of master or crew, is recoverable: but a loss which ought to have been averted or minimised and was proximately caused by the master's failure to take reasonable steps in the face of a casualty could not be made the basis for recovery.

I revert to the fact that there has been no example of s 78(4) providing underwriters with a defence to a claim since 1906. This, of itself, seems clear indication that the section does not impose a conventional contractual duty which displaces, after a casualty has occurred, the general principle embodied in s 55(2)(a). The approach of treating a breach of the duty in s 78(4) as material only in the context of causation provides a satisfactory explanation for the insignificance that s 78(4) has had in practice, if, in practice, negligence after the casualty will rarely be held to break the chain of causation. Such an approach was evidenced by no less an authority than Lord Justice Scrutton in *Lind v Mitchell*. In that case, the insured vessel was holed by contact with ice, and then abandoned by her master and crew unreasonably and in unusual circumstances. Underwriters' primary defence was that the vessel had been deliberately cast away, but this failed on the facts. The court went on to consider, however, the effect of the negligent abandonment. The policy covered against negligence of the master and crew, but Scrutton LJ held that, even if this were not the case, a claim would lie under the policy. He indicated, p 75, that he considered the direct cause of the loss was the collision with the ice and not the subsequent abandonment. He also indicated that s 55(2)(a) showed that there would be recovery, notwithstanding the negligent abandonment. Whilst it is not clear whether underwriters invoked s 78, the approach of a commercial judge of the standing of Scrutton LJ is a cogent indication of the true state of the law ...

Having considered the authorities and, perhaps more significantly, the lack of them, I align myself with Colman J, Rix J and *Arnould* in concluding that the principle embodied in s 55(2)(a) applies before and after a casualty and that the duty referred to in s 78(4) will only have significance in the rare case where breach of that duty is so significant as to be held to displace the prior insured peril as the proximate cause of the loss. Even in that rare case, however, the breach of s 78(4) is unlikely in practice to afford a defence to underwriters. This is because such breach is likely to constitute a separate insured peril under the express cover that has, for many years, been given by the standard forms of policies of marine insurance against negligence of the master, officers and crew – see *Arnould*, 16th edn, p 701.

Notes

The last cited paragraph from the judgment of Phillips LJ in *State of The Netherlands v Youell* **[1998] 1 Lloyd's Rep 236, CA**, to the effect that the conflict between ss 55(2)(a) and 78(4) will rarely pose a problem, is correct in so far as the Institute Hull Clauses (both for time and voyage) and the ICC (A) are concerned. As the former provide cover for loss or damage to the subject matter insured caused by the 'negligence of Master, Officers or Crew ...', the dispute is unlikely to arise. The latter being for 'all risks', any loss is covered even if it was proximately caused by the negligence of the assured or his agents in failing to sue and labour. The ICC (B) and (C) insure against only enumerated risks; and if cargo under such a policy is held to be proximately caused by a failure on the part of the assured and his agents to sue and labour, the assured would not be able to recover under the policy, as such a cause of loss is not an insured risk under the said Clauses.

The best way to deal with the problem is, perhaps, to follow the sequence suggested by Phillips LJ:

[p 245] ... The normal approach will be to identify the proximate cause of the loss, to consider whether it is a peril insured against, and where the issue arises, to consider whether the loss is attributable to the wilful misconduct of the assured or otherwise falls under an exclusion under the terms of the cover.

An assured and his agents could fail to sue and labour for a number of reasons, ranging from mere negligence to wilful omission. Should the case be one of mere negligence on the part of his agents or servants, then, as was seen above, the conflict in the law is between ss 55(2)(b) and 78; in this regard, the matter may be resolved simply by determining what the proximate cause of the loss was. However, should the conduct of the assured himself amount to more than a simple case of negligence and constitute a blatant refusal, without good cause, to sue and labour, then, his conduct (or rather misconduct) could attract the operation of s 55(2)(a) – the defence of wilful misconduct of the assured.[61]

A failure to sue and labour, in the absence of reasonable justification, could, it is suggested, also be construed as evidence of bad faith on the part of the assured. Though the defence of a breach of utmost good faith has never been raised in relation to suing and labouring, there does not appear to be any reason why this cannot be pleaded as a defence to a claim for a loss of or damage to the subject matter insured. The recent spate of litigation in the area of law on the doctrine of *uberrimae fidei* contained in s 17 of the Act has demonstrated a new trend – that insurers have now increasingly become less shy and more ready to invoke the plea of bad faith as a defence to a claim.[62] Such a plea, if upheld, would confer the insurer with the right to avoid the contract.

When is the cut-off date for suing and labouring?

The question of whether it was possible to recover for expenditure under sue and labour after the subject matter insured had already become a total loss was raised in the case of **Kuwait Airways Corporation v Kuwait Insurance Co SAK [1996] 1 Lloyd's Rep 644**, where aircraft and spares belonging to Kuwait Airways were plundered by invading Iraqi forces. On this issue, the court saw no reason in principle why such a claim should be rejected, and then went on to suggest that the cut-off date for claiming under sue and labour was the date of the issuing of the writ to commence proceedings.

> Rix J: [p 696] ... This is the so called 'shelf-life' point. It was expressed in the order in the following terms: does the sue and labour clause have any application to expenses incurred after the occurrence of a total loss or total losses claimed by the assured and/or admitted and/or paid by the insurers? Can any of the expenses be recovered to the extent that they were incurred after the date of the writ? ... I do not see why the making of a total loss claim should bring the right to sue and labour to an end. It does not in the marine context. The date of payment ushers in the right of subrogation. It might be said that at that date, if the right to sue and labour were still extant, it made way for the insurer's right of subrogation: but that point has not been pressed. The date of issue of a writ for a constructive total loss, however, is a familiar date in the case of marine insurance ... it seems to me to emphasise the point made by Collins J [in *Roura and Fourgas v Townend*] that it is at the time of issue of proceedings that the rights of the parties must be viewed as crystallised.

---

61 It is to be stressed that, under s 55(2)(a), any loss 'attributable to' the wilful misconduct of the assured is not recoverable.
62 See Chapter 6.

Since, therefore, recovery after action brought does not affect the total loss indemnity to which an assured is entitled as of that date, that also seems to me to be an appropriate date at which to find that an assured's right (and correlative duty under s 78(4) of the Marine Insurance Act) comes to an end.

Is an express clause essential to a right of reimbursement?

The duty to sue and labour and the right of the assured to claim for reimbursement for suing and labouring are separate issues. Section 78(4), which states that: 'It is the duty of the assured and his agents, in all cases, to take such measures as may be reasonable for the purpose of averting or minimising a loss', may be construed as a statutory duty to sue and labour. The phrase 'in all cases' supports the view that an assured is duty bound, even in the absence of a suing and labouring clause in a policy, to take reasonable measures to avert or minimise a loss. Ivamy,[63] on the other hand, adopts the view that, as all the other three sub-sections of s 78 expressly refer to the 'suing and labouring clause' within the policy, it would not be unreasonable to assume that s 78(4) must be read likewise.

A policy may or may not contain a sue and labour clause; such a clause, if incorporated, may or may not contain a provision on the subject of the right of reimbursement. Under the Act, the right to be indemnified for such an expense is governed by s 78(1), the opening words of which seem to suggest that only in the case where the policy contains a suing and labouring clause may the assured recover from the insurer any expenses properly incurred pursuant to the clause. The question which thus arises is, is an assured under a policy which does not contain a suing and labouring clause and/or a reimbursement obligation entitled to be indemnified for any expenditure he has incurred to avert or minimise a loss covered by the policy?

The above was first raised in the Australian case of *Emperor Goldmining Co Ltd v Switzerland General Insurance Co Ltd*, below. In this instance, the court was of the opinion that an express clause was not a prerequisite to a claim under sue and labour, because s 78(4) of the Act applied regardless of the existence of such a clause. The reasoning behind the decision was that it would be illogical to assume that s 78(4) of the Act would impose a duty to sue and labour at the assured's own expense unless there was an express sue and labour clause incorporated in the policy.

Emperor Goldmining Co Ltd v Switzerland General Insurance Co Ltd [1964] 1 Lloyd's Rep 348, Supreme Court of New South Wales

The plaintiffs insured a cargo of explosives and general goods with the defendants for a voyage from Sydney to Fiji; the policy did not contain a suing

---

63 Ivamy, ER, *Marine Insurance*, 1985, London: Butterworths, p 451.

and labouring clause. Soon after leaving Sydney, the vessel carrying the cargo was found to be leaking badly, and she had to return and be put into a dock for examination. In order for this to be done, the cargo had to be off-loaded, stored and eventually forwarded to Fiji aboard another ship. The plaintiffs claimed for all the additional expenditure as sue and labour, but the underwriters declined to pay, contending that such expenses were not expressly covered by the policy.

The Supreme Court of New South Wales ruled that the plaintiff could recover the expenditure as sue and labour. Although the policy contained no express sue and labour clause, the court found it impossible to read the duty to sue and labour as imposed by the Marine Insurance Act as a duty to be carried out by the assured at his own expense.

> **Manning J:** [p 354] ... Section 84(4) [equivalent to s 78(4) of the Marine Insurance Act 1906] plainly imposes on the assured a duty to take such measures as are reasonable for the purpose of averting or minimising a loss. I am unable to read this provision as a duty to be carried out by the assured at his own expense, in the absence of a suing and labouring clause in the policy ... Having regard to the conclusion at which I have arrived, substantially, the whole of the plaintiff's claim succeeds.

Notes

The above decision obviously regarded s 78(4) as imposing a statutory duty to sue and labour for which the assured should naturally be reimbursed, even though the policy in question did not contain an express provision on suing and labouring. Perceived as a legal or statutory duty, the Australian judge, driven by conscience, had found it difficult to deny the assured of the right to be reimbursed for his felicitous efforts.

The issue raised in the above case of whether an expense incurred in suing and labouring would be indemnified by the insurer has been the subject of a number of recent cases. This contention came before the Privy Council in an marine insurance case in *Netherlands Insurance Co (Est 1845) Ltd v Karl Ljungberg and Co A/B*, and the Court of Appeal, in a non-marine case, in 1997 in *Yorkshire Water Services Ltd v Sun Alliance and London Insurance plc and Others*, where the plaintiffs, Yorkshire Water Services Ltd, claimed an indemnity from their insurers on that very basis.

Netherlands Insurance Co (Est 1845) Ltd v Karl Ljungberg and Co A/B [1986] 2 Lloyd's Rep 19, PC

The respondents were the consignees of a shipment of plywood which was insured with the appellants. The respondents were assignees to the policy which incorporated, within the Institute Cargo Clauses All Risks 1963, both a sue and labour clause and a bailee clause, the latter imposing a duty on the assured to preserve the rights of the insurers against third parties. On discharge, some of the plywood was found to be missing or damaged, and, in order to preserve the time bar imposed by the contract of carriage and thereby likewise preserve the insurers' rights against the carrier, the cargo consignees instituted proceedings against the carrier in Japan. The cargo consignees then sought to recover the cost of those proceedings in Japan from their insurers under the bailee clause. The case turned on the issue that, whilst it was expressly provided in the sue and labour clause that the insurers would reimburse the assured for any expenses incurred by suing and labouring, no such express provision applied to the bailee clause.

The Privy Council ruled that the insurers were liable to indemnify the cargo consignees for the expenses incurred in starting proceedings in Japan. The implied duty of reimbursement by the insurers applied to both the sue and labour clause and the bailee clause.

> **Lord Goff:** [p 22] It can, of course, be said, as indeed it was said on behalf of the appellants [insurers], that the fact that the sue and labour clause makes express provision for reimbursement of the assured by the insurers, whereas the bailee clause does not do so, militates against the implication of a term in the bailee clause to the same effect ...
>
> [p 23]: The respondents [assured] placed in the forefront of their submissions the proposition that the obligation of the assured under the bailee clause properly to preserve and exercise all rights against carriers was an obligation imposed upon them for the benefit of the insurers. Their Lordships do not feel able to accept that, as a general proposition, the mere fact that an obligation is imposed upon one part to a contract for the benefit of the other carried with it an implied term that the latter shall reimburse the former for his costs incurred in the performance of the obligation. But the fact that, in the present case, the relevant obligation is, their Lordships consider, a material factor which may be taken into account; and when that fact is considered together with all the other facts which their Lordships have set out, they consider that a term must be implied in the contract in order to give business efficacy to it, that expenses incurred by an assured in performing his obligations under the second limb of the bailee clause (in the form now under consideration) shall be recoverable by him from the insurers in so far as they relate to the preservation or exercise of rights in respect of loss or damage for which the insurers are liable under the policy.

Yorkshire Water Services Ltd v Sun Alliance and London Insurance plc and Others [1997] 2 Lloyd's Rep 21, CA

The plaintiffs were insured with the defendants under public liability policies of insurance. When the retaining walls of the plaintiffs' sewage works collapsed and polluted the river Colne, the plaintiffs expended over £4 m in alleviating the damage and then claimed an indemnity for such under their policies. The policies contained clauses which stated: 'that the assured at his own expense shall ... take reasonable precautions to prevent any circumstances ...' But, the plaintiffs contended that: 'every contract of insurance carries an implied term that the insured will make reasonable efforts to prevent or minimise loss which may fall on the insurer', and, therefore, they were entitled to be indemnified.

The Court of Appeal, in affirming the decision of the trial judge, ruled that the express terms in the policies confirmed that the work done in alleviating damage was at the plaintiffs' expense and not the underwriters. But, the court went on to point out that the mere fact that an obligation was imposed upon a party for the benefit of another did not mean that expenses incurred in fulfilling that obligation need be indemnified.

> **Stuart-Smith LJ:** [p 31] ... I do not think much, if any, assistance can be derived from this case [referring to *Netherlands Insurance Co (Est 1845) Ltd v Karl Ljungberg and Co A/B*] in the plaintiff's favour. It is clear that the mere fact that an obligation is imposed on one party for the benefit of another is not sufficient for the implication of a term that the latter will reimburse the expenses of performing it.
>
> **Otton LJ:** [p 32] ... The judge [at the trial] declined to imply the first term [which the plaintiffs implied] that the assured will make reasonable efforts to prevent or minimise loss which may fall to the insurer. He did not consider that, strictly speaking, such a duty is a term, since it is no more than the corollary of the principle that losses which are reasonably avoidable are not recoverable in the law of contract, and is thus expressed as 'the duty to mitigate'. He pointed out that none of the textbook writers suggest that there is such a term. In my view the judge was correct. There was no basis for implying such a term by operation of law.
>
> [p 33] ... I am further satisfied that there is no need to imply the proposed term. It is not necessary to give business efficacy to the contract ... If such a term were implied, it would create a new area of indemnity in addition to those expressed by the policy and for which (Mr Crowther wryly observed) the assured has not paid any additional premium for the loss he seeks to include.
>
> Mr Griffiths [acting for the plaintiffs] presented an argument based on the law of marine insurance. This is conveniently summarised in MacGillivray and Parkington, *Insurance Law*, 8th edn, p 840, para 1877:
>
>> *Cost of averting or minimising damage.* It has always been the law in marine insurance that the assured can recover the cost of averting or minimising a peril insured against because there is a duty as well as a right for the assured to 'sue and labour' in respect of the property insured ... If, of course, there is an equivalent of a sue and labour clause, the insurer can undoubtedly recover this sort of expense.
>
> [p 34]: I have come to the conclusion that this decision [referring to *Netherlands Insurance Co (Est 1845) Ltd v Karl Ljungberg and Co A/B*] is of little relevance or assistance in the present case. Unlike the present policy which stipulated at the 'insured's expense', there was no provision about who was to bear the cost either of 'averting or minimising a loss' or of insuring that 'all risks against carriers – are properly preserved'. Moreover, the insurers in the other case conceded that the sue and labour clause obliged them to reimburse the insured for complying with its duty under that part of the clause. Not surprisingly, the Privy Council then had little difficulty in implying a similar term in the second part of the clause ...

Finally, with regard to the passage cited from MacGillivray and Parkington it is only necessary to point out, first, that the example given to support the author's suggestion concerns a property insurance and not a public liability policy. Secondly, the last sentence suggests an express sue and labour clause, and not an implied one.

Notes

It would appear that whether the duty to sue and labour be statutory or contractual, there is no rule under English law that an assured has the automatic right to be indemnified for any expenditure he may incur for suing and labouring. The preponderant view, it would seem, is that there is generally no implication in insurance law that an insurer is bound to indemnify an assured for mitigating a loss. Thus, unless there is an express clause in a policy to the effect that the assured shall be indemnified for suing and labouring, it must be assumed that expenses incurred in averting or minimising a loss are not, as a general rule, recoverable under the policy.

In so far as the Institute Hulls Clauses (for Time and Voyage) and all the Institute Cargo Clauses are concerned, the above question is academic, as each of the said Clauses has incorporated its own sue and labouring clause with an express obligation of reimbursement. However, in the case of the Institute Freight Clauses (both for Time and Voyage), the protracted question raised is still very much alive because there is no sue and labour provision in the Freight Clauses and s 78(4), if given a wide interpretation, imposes a duty to sue and labour in all polices including freight. It therefore appears that unless an English court adopts the view as expressed in *Emperor Goldmining Co Ltd v Switzerland General Insurance Co Ltd* or is prepared (for reason of business efficacy) to imply a right of reimbursement as a term of the policy, as in the case of *Netherlands Insurance Co (Est 1845) Ltd v Karl Ljungberg and Co A/B*, an assured on a policy of freight may well find himself out of pocket for any expenses incurred in averting or minimising a loss of freight.

No claim for salvage charges – no s/c

Just as it is possible for an insurer expressly to undertake to indemnify an assured for suing and labour, it is also possible for him expressly to except liability for the same. A policy may well contain a clause stating that 'no claim to attach to this policy for salvage charges', abbreviated as 'no s/c'. In common parlance, the abbreviation is taken to mean 'no salvage charges'. In **Western Assurance Company of Toronto v Poole [1903] 1 KB 376**, the facts of which were cited in full earlier in relation to the matter of insurable interest,[64] the policy of insurance contained two conflicting clauses: a printed clause

---

64 See Chapter 2, p 64, and Chapter 16, p 658.

declaring the usual undertaking by the insurer to contribute to suing and labouring charges and a written clause, 'no s/c'. Bigham J explained how the conflict was to be resolved and, in the process, explained the meaning of the term 'no s/c'.

> **Bigham J:** [p 389] ... On the slip appear the letters 'no s/c,' which it is agreed to mean 'no salvage charges'. In pursuance of this slip the policy now sued on was issued, in which the printed words of the suing and labouring clause were not struck out. But it was proved before me that other underwriters on the same slip had issued a policy in which the words were struck out. The plaintiffs apparently accepted both policies without objection. Was one policy right and the other wrong? I think not; for, in my opinion, both parties knew quite well that the words were inapplicable to the contract they were making, and thought that it was of no importance whether they were left in or struck out. Salvage charges may, no doubt, in some connection mean claims for volunteer salvage services. But it is quite common to use the words for the purpose of describing those expenses which come within the scope of suing and labouring expenditure; and several witnesses of great experience were called before me to say, and they did say very plainly, that used in a policy such as this they were always understood to bear that meaning.
>
> [p 390] ... I am quite satisfied that if I were to allow the plaintiffs to recover under the suing and labouring clause I should be inventing and giving effect to a contract which the parties never intended to make ... And if this be so, it was a useless form to insert the words 'no claim for salvage charges', unless they were intended to exclude claims under the suing and labouring clause.

References and further reading

Eggers, PM, 'Sue and labour and beyond: the assured's duty of mitigation' [1998] LMCLQ 228

Hudson, NG, 'The insurance of average disbursements' [1987] LMCLQ 443

O'Sullivan, BP, 'The scope of the sue and labour clause' [1990] JBL 545

Rose, FD, 'Failure to sue and labour' [1990] JBL 190

Rose, FD, 'Aversion and minimisation of loss', in *The Modern Law of Marine Insurance*, 1996, London: LLP, p 215

APPENDIX 1

MARINE INSURANCE ACT 1906
[6 Edw 7 Ch 41]

ARRANGEMENT OF SECTIONS

MARINE INSURANCE

Section
1 Marine insurance defined
2 Mixed sea and land risks
3 Marine adventure and maritime perils defined

INSURABLE INTEREST

4 Avoidance of wagering or gaming contracts
5 Insurable interest defined
6 When interest must attach
7 Defeasible or contingent interest
8 Partial interest
9 Re-insurance
10 Bottomry
11 Master's and seamen's wages
12 Advance freight
13 Charges of insurance
14 Quantum of interest
15 Assignment of interest

INSURABLE VALUE

16 Measure of insurable value

DISCLOSURE AND REPRESENTATIONS

17 Insurance is *uberrimae fidei*
18 Disclosure by assured
19 Disclosure by agent effecting insurance
20 Representations pending negotiation of contract
21 When contract is deemed to be concluded

The Policy

Section
- 22 Contract must be embodied in policy
- 23 What policy must specify
- 24 Signature of insurer
- 25 Voyage and time policies
- 26 Designation of subject matter
- 27 Valued policy
- 28 Unvalued policy
- 29 Floating policy by ship or ships
- 30 Construction of terms in policy
- 31 Premium to be arranged

Double Insurance

- 32 Double insurance

Warranties, &c

- 33 Nature of warranty
- 34 When breach of warranty excused
- 35 Express warranties
- 36 Warranty of neutrality
- 37 No implied warranty of nationality
- 38 Warranty of good safety
- 39 Warranty of seaworthiness of ship
- 40 No implied warranty that goods are seaworthy
- 41 Warranty of legality

The Voyage

- 42 Implied condition as to commencement of risk
- 43 Alteration of port of departure
- 44 Sailing for different destination
- 45 Change of voyage
- 46 Deviation
- 47 Several ports of discharge
- 48 Delay in voyage
- 49 Excuses for deviation or delay

Appendix 1

ASSIGNMENT OF POLICY

50 When and how policy is assignable
51 Assured who has no interest cannot assign

THE PREMIUM

52 When premium payable
53 Policy effected through broker
54 Effect of receipt on policy

LOSS AND ABANDONMENT

55 Included and excluded losses
56 Partial and total loss
57 Actual total loss
58 Missing ship
59 Effect of transhipment, etc
60 Constructive total loss defined
61 Effect of constructive total loss
62 Notice of abandonment
63 Effect of abandonment

PARTIAL LOSSES (INCLUDING SALVAGE AND GENERAL AVERAGE AND PARTICULAR CHARGES)

64 Particular average loss
65 Salvage charges
66 General average loss

MEASURE OF INDEMNITY

67 Extent of liability of insurer for loss
68 Total loss
69 Partial loss of ship
70 Partial loss of freight
71 Partial loss of goods, merchandise, etc
72 Apportionment of valuation
73 General average contributions and salvage charges
74 Liabilities to third parties
75 General provisions as to measure of indemnity
76 Particular average warranties
77 Successive losses
78 Suing and labouring clause

Rights of Insurer on Payment

79 Right of subrogation
80 Right of contribution
81 Effect of under insurance

Return of Premium

82 Enforcement of return
83 Return by agreement
84 Return for failure of consideration

Mutual Insurance

85 Modification of Act in case of mutual insurance

Supplemental

86 Ratification by assured
87 Implied obligations varied by agreement or usage
88 Reasonable time, etc, a question of fact
89 Slip as evidence
90 Interpretation of terms
91 Savings
92 Repeals
93 Commencement
94 Short title
    Schedules

CHAPTER 41

An Act to codify the Law relating to Marine Insurance

[21 December 1906]

BE it enacted by the King's most Excellent Majesty, by and with the advice and consent of the Lords Spiritual and Temporal, and Commons, in this present Parliament assembled, and by the authority of the same, as follows:

MARINE INSURANCE

1. Marine insurance defined

A contract of marine insurance is a contract whereby the insurer undertakes to indemnify the assured, in manner and to the extent thereby agreed, against marine losses, that is to say, the losses incident to marine adventure.

2. Mixed sea and land risks

(1) A contract of marine insurance may, by its express terms, or by usage of trade, be extended so as to protect the assured against losses on inland waters or on any land risk which may be incidental to any sea voyage.

(2) Where a ship in course of building, or the launch of a ship, or any adventure analogous to a marine adventure, is covered by a policy in the form of a marine policy, the provisions of this Act, in so far as applicable, shall apply thereto; but, except as by this section provided, nothing in this Act shall alter or affect any rule of law applicable to any contract of insurance other than a contract of marine insurance as by this Act defined.

3. Marine adventure and maritime perils defined

(1) Subject to the provisions of this Act, every lawful marine adventure may be the subject of a contract of marine insurance.

(2) In particular there is a marine adventure where—

(a) Any ship goods or other moveables are exposed to maritime perils. Such property is in this Act referred to as 'insurable property';

(b) The earning or acquisition of any freight, passage money, commission, profit, or other pecuniary benefit, or the security for any advances, loan, or disbursements, is endangered by the exposure of insurable property to maritime perils;

(c) Any liability to a third party may be incurred by the owner of, or other person interested in or responsible for, insurable property, by reason of maritime perils.

'Maritime perils' means the perils consequent on, or incidental to, the navigation of the sea, that is to say, perils of the seas, fire, war perils, pirates, rovers, thieves, captures, seizures, restraints, and detainments of princes and peoples, jettisons, barratry, and any other perils, either of the like kind or which may be designated by the policy.

INSURABLE INTEREST

4. Avoidance of wagering or gaming contracts

(1) Every contract of marine insurance by way of gaming or wagering is void.

(2) A contract of marine insurance is deemed to be a gaming or wagering contract—
- (a) Where the assured has not an insurable interest as defined by this Act and the contract is entered into with no expectation of acquiring such an interest; or
- (b) Where the policy is made 'interest or no interest', or 'without further proof of interest than the policy itself', or 'without benefit of salvage to the insurer', or subject to any other like term:

Provided that, where there is no possibility of salvage, a policy may be effected without benefit of salvage to the insurer.

5. Insurable interest defined

(1) Subject to the provisions of this Act, every person has an insurable interest who is interested in a marine adventure.

(2) In particular a person is interested in a marine adventure where he stands in any legal or equitable relation to the adventure or to any insurable property at risk therein, in consequence of which he may benefit by the safety or due arrival of insurable property, or may be prejudiced by its loss, or damage thereto, or by the detention thereof, or may incur liability in respect thereof.

6. When interest must attach

(1) The assured must be interested in the subject matter insured at the time of the loss though he need not be interested when the insurance is effected:

Provided that where the subject matter is insured 'lost or not lost', the assured may recover although he may not have acquired his interest until after the loss, unless at the time of effecting the contract of insurance the assured was aware of the loss, and the insurer was not.

(2) Where the assured has no interest at the time of the loss, he cannot acquire interest by any act or election after he is aware of the loss.

7. Defeasible or contingent interest

(1) A defeasible interest is insurable, as also is a contingent interest.

(2) In particular, where the buyer of goods has insured them, he has an insurable interest, notwithstanding that he might, at his election, have rejected the goods, or have treated them as at the seller's risk, by reason of the latter's delay in making delivery or otherwise.

8. Partial interest

A partial interest of any nature is insurable.

9. Re-insurance

(1) The insurer under a contract of marine insurance has an insurable interest in his risk, and may re-insure in respect of it.

(2) Unless the policy otherwise provides, the original assured has no right or interest in respect of such re-insurance.

10. Bottomry

The lender of money on bottomry or *respondentia* has an insurable interest in respect of the loan.

11. Master's and seamen's wages

The master or any member of the crew of a ship has an insurable interest in respect of his wages.

12. Advance freight

In the case of advance freight, the person advancing the freight has an insurable interest, in so far as such freight is not repayable in case of loss.

13. Charges of insurance

The assured has an insurable interest in the charges of any insurance which he may effect.

14. Quantum of interest

(1) Where the subject matter insured is mortgaged, the mortgagor has an insurable interest in the full value thereof, and the mortgagee has an insurable interest in respect of any sum due or to become due under the mortgage.

(2) A mortgagee, consignee, or other person having an interest in the subject matter insured may insure on behalf and for the benefit of other persons interested as well as for his own benefit.

(3) The owner of insurable property has an insurable interest in respect of the full value thereof, notwithstanding that some third person may have agreed, or be liable, to indemnify him in case of loss.

15. Assignment of interest

Where the assured assigns or otherwise parts with his interest in the subject matter insured, he does not thereby transfer to the assignee his rights under the contract of insurance, unless there be an express or implied agreement with the assignee to that effect.

But the provisions of this section do not affect a transmission of interest by operation of law.

INSURABLE VALUE

16. Measure of insurable value

Subject to any express provision or valuation in the policy, the insurable value of the subject matter insured must be ascertained as follows—

(1) In insurance on ship, the insurable value is the value, at the commencement of the risk, of the ship, including her outfit, provisions and stores for the officers and crew, money advanced for seamen's wages, and other disbursements (if any) incurred to make the ship fit for the voyage or adventure contemplated by the policy, plus the charges of insurance upon the whole:

The insurable value, in the case of a steamship, includes also the machinery, boilers, and coals and engine stores if owned by the assured, and, in the case of a ship engaged in a special trade, the ordinary fittings requisite for that trade:

(2) In insurance on freight, whether paid in advance or otherwise, the insurable value is the gross amount of the freight at the risk of the assured, plus the charges of insurance:

(3) In insurance on goods or merchandise, the insurable value is the prime cost of the property insured, plus the expenses of and incidental to shipping and the charges of insurance upon the whole:

(4) In insurance on any other subject matter, the insurable value is the amount at the risk of the assured when the policy attaches, plus the charges of insurance.

DISCLOSURE AND REPRESENTATIONS

17. Insurance is *uberrimae fidei*

A contract of marine insurance is a contract based upon the utmost good faith and, if the utmost good faith be not observed by either party, the contract may be avoided by the other party.

18. Disclosure by assured

(1) Subject to the provisions of this section, the assured must disclose to the insurer, before the contract is concluded, every material circumstance which is known to the assured, and the assured is deemed to know every circumstance which, in the ordinary course of business, ought to be known by him. If the assured fails to make such disclosure, the insurer may avoid the contract.

(2) Every circumstance is material which would influence the judgment of a prudent insurer in fixing the premium, or determining whether he will take the risk.

(3) In the absence of inquiry the following circumstances need not be disclosed, namely—
- (a) Any circumstance which diminishes the risk;
- (b) Any circumstance which is known or presumed to be known to the insurer. The insurer is presumed to know matters of common notoriety or knowledge, and matters which an insurer in the ordinary course of his business, as such, ought to know;
- (c) Any circumstance as to which information is waived by the insurer;
- (d) Any circumstance which it is superfluous to disclose by reason of any express or implied warranty.

(4) Whether any particular circumstance, which is not disclosed, be material or not is, in each case, a question of fact.

(5) The term 'circumstance' includes any communication made to, or information received by, the assured.

19. Disclosure by agent effecting insurance

Subject to the provisions of the preceding section as to circumstances which need not be disclosed, where an insurance is effected for the assured by an agent, the agent must disclose to the insurer—

(a) Every material circumstance which is known to himself, and an agent to insure is deemed to know every circumstance which in the ordinary course of business ought to be known by, or to have been communicated to, him; and

(b) Every material circumstance which the assured is bound to disclose, unless it come to his knowledge too late to communicate it to the agent.

20. Representations pending negotiation of contract

(1) Every material representation made by the assured or his agent to the insurer during the negotiations for the contract, and before the contract is concluded, must be true. If it be untrue the insurer may avoid the contract.

(2) A representation is material which would influence the judgment of a prudent insurer in fixing the premium, or determining whether he will take the risk.

(3) A representation may be either a representation as to a matter of fact, or as to a matter of expectation or belief.

(4) A representation as to matter of fact is true, if it be substantially correct, that is to say, if the difference between what is represented and what is actually correct would not be considered material by a prudent insurer.

(5) A representation as to a matter of expectation or belief is true if it be made in good faith.

(6) A representation may be withdrawn or corrected before the contract is concluded.

(7) Whether a particular representation be material or not is, in each case, a question of fact.

21. When contract is deemed to be concluded

A contract of marine insurance is deemed to be concluded when the proposal of the assured is accepted by the insurer, whether the policy be then issued or not; and, for the purpose of showing when the proposal was accepted, reference may be made to the slip or covering note or other customary memorandum of the contract, although it be unstamped.

The Policy

22. Contract must be embodied in policy

Subject to the provisions of any statute, a contract of marine insurance is inadmissible in evidence unless it is embodied in a marine policy in accordance with this Act. The policy may be executed and issued either at the time when the contract is concluded, or afterwards.

23. What policy must specify

A marine policy must specify—

(1) The name of the assured, or of some person who effects the insurance on his behalf;

(2) The subject matter insured and the risk insured again;

(3) The voyage, or period of time, or both, as the case may be, covered by the insurance;

(4) The sum or sums insured;

(5) The name or names of the insurers.

24. Signature of insurer

(1) A marine policy must be signed by or on behalf of the insurer, provided that in the case of a corporation the corporate seal may be sufficient, but nothing in this section shall be construed as requiring the subscription of a corporation to be under seal.

(2) Where a policy is subscribed by or on behalf of two or more insurers, each subscription, unless the contrary be expressed, constitutes a distinct contract with the assured.

25. Voyage and time policies

(1) Where the contract is to insure the subject matter 'at and from', or from one place to another or others, the policy is called a 'voyage policy', and where the contract is to insure the subject matter for a definite period of time the policy is called a 'time policy'. A contract for both voyage and time may be included in the same policy.

(2) Subject to the provisions of section eleven of the Finance Act, 1901, a time policy which is made for any time exceeding twelve months is invalid.

26. Designation of subject matter

(1) The subject matter insured must be designated in a marine policy with reasonable certainty.

(2) The nature and extent of the interest of the assured in the subject matter insured need not be specified in the policy.

(3) Where the policy designates the subject matter insured in general terms, it shall be construed to apply to the interest intended by the assured to be covered.

(4) In the application of this section regard shall be had to any usage regulating the designation of the subject matter insured.

27. Valued policy

(1) A policy may be either valued or unvalued.

(2) A valued policy is a policy which specifies the agreed value of the subject matter insured.

(3) Subject to the provisions of this Act, and in the absence of fraud, the value fixed by the policy is, as between the insurer and assured, conclusive of the insurable value of the subject intended to be insured, whether the loss be total or partial.

(4) Unless the policy otherwise provides, the value fixed by the policy is not conclusive for the purpose of determining whether there has been a constructive total loss.

28. Unvalued policy

An unvalued policy is a policy which does not specify the value of the subject matter insured, but, subject to the limit of the sum insured, leaves the insurable value to be subsequently ascertained, in the manner herein-before specified.

29. Floating policy by ship or ships

(1) A floating policy is a policy which describes the insurance in general terms, and leaves the name of the ship or ships and other particulars to be defined by subsequent declaration.

(2) The subsequent declaration or declarations may be made by indorsement on the policy, or in other customary manner.

(3) Unless the policy otherwise provides, the declarations must be made in the order of dispatch or shipment. They must, in the case of goods, comprise all consignments within the terms of the policy, and the value of the goods or other property must be honestly stated, but an omission or erroneous declaration may be rectified even after loss or arrival, provided the omission or declaration was made in good faith.

(4) Unless the policy otherwise provides, where a declaration of value is not made until after notice of loss or arrival, the policy must be treated as an unvalued policy as regards the subject matter of that declaration.

30. Construction of terms in policy

(1) A policy may be in the form in the First Schedule to this Act.

(2) Subject to the provisions of this Act, and unless the context of the policy otherwise requires, the terms and expressions mentioned in the First Schedule to this Act shall be construed as having the scope and meaning in that schedule assigned to them.

31. Premium to be arranged

(1) Where an insurance is effected at a premium to be arranged, and no arrangement is made, a reasonable premium is payable.

(2) Where an insurance is effected on the terms that an additional premium is to be arranged in a given event, and that event happens but no arrangement is made, then a reasonable additional premium is payable.

DOUBLE INSURANCE

32. Double insurance

(1) Where two or more policies are effected by or on behalf of the assured on the same adventure and interest or any part thereof, and the sums insured exceed the indemnity allowed by this Act, the assured is said to be over-insured by double insurance.

(2) Where the assured is over-insured by double insurance—

(a) The assured, unless the policy otherwise provides, may claim payment from the insurers in such order as he may think fit, provided that he is not entitled to receive any sum in excess of the indemnity allowed by this Act;

(b) Where the policy under which the assured claims is a valued policy the assured must give credit as against the valuation for any sum received by him under any other policy without regard to the actual value of the subject matter insured;

(c) Where the policy under which the assured claims is an unvalued policy he must give credit, as against the full insurable value, for any sum received by him under any other policy;

(d) Where the assured receives any sum in excess of the indemnity allowed by this Act, he is deemed to hold such sum in trust for the insurers, according to their right of contribution among themselves.

WARRANTIES, &C

33. Nature of warranty

(1) A warranty, in the following sections relating to warranties, means a promissory warranty, that is to say, a warranty by which the assured undertakes that some particular thing shall or shall not be done, or that some condition shall be fulfilled, or whereby he affirms or negatives the existence of a particular state of facts.

(2) A warranty may be express or implied.

(3) A warranty, as above defined, is a condition which must be exactly complied with, whether it be material to the risk or not. If it be not so complied with, then, subject to any express provision in the policy, the insurer is discharged from liability as from the date of the breach of warranty, but without prejudice to any liability incurred by him before that date.

34. When breach of warranty excused

(1) Non-compliance with a warranty is excused when, by reason of a change of circumstances, the warranty ceases to be applicable to the circumstances of the contract, or when compliance with the warranty is rendered unlawful by any subsequent law.

(2) Where a warranty is broken, the assured cannot avail himself of the defence that the breach has been remedied, and the warranty complied with, before loss.

(3) A breach of warranty may be waived by the insurer.

35. Express warranties

(1) An express warranty may be in any form of words from which the intention to warrant is to be inferred.

(2) An express warranty must be included in, or written upon, the policy, or must be contained in some document incorporated by reference into the policy.

(3) An express warranty does not exclude an implied warranty, unless it be inconsistent therewith.

36. Warranty of neutrality

(1) Where insurable property, whether ship or goods, is expressly warranted neutral, there is an implied condition that the property shall have a neutral character at the commencement of the risk, and that, so far as the assured can control the matter, its neutral character shall be preserved during the risk.

(2) Where a ship is expressly warranted 'neutral' there is also an implied condition that, so far as the assured can control the matter, she shall be properly documented, that is to say, that she shall carry the necessary papers to establish her neutrality, and that she shall not falsify or suppress her papers, or use simulated papers. If any loss occurs through breach of this condition, the insurer may avoid the contract.

37. No implied warranty of nationality

There is no implied warranty as to the nationality of a ship, or that her nationality shall not be changed during the risk.

38. Warranty of good safety

Where the subject matter insured is warranted 'well' or 'in good safety' on a particular day, it is sufficient if it be safe at any time during that day.

39. Warranty of seaworthiness of ship

(1) In a voyage policy there is an implied warranty that at the commencement of the voyage the ship shall be seaworthy for the purpose of the particular adventure insured.

(2) Where the policy attaches while the ship is in port, there is also an implied warranty that she shall, at the commencement of the risk, be reasonably fit to encounter the ordinary perils of the port.

(3) Where the policy relates to a voyage which is performed in different stages, during which the ship requires different kinds of or further preparation or equipment, there is an implied warranty that at the commencement of each stage the ship is seaworthy in respect of such preparation or equipment for the purposes of that stage.

(4) A ship is deemed to be seaworthy when she is reasonably fit in all respects to encounter the ordinary perils of the seas of the adventure insured.

(5) In a time policy there is no implied warranty that the ship shall be seaworthy at any stage of the adventure, but where, with the privity of the

assured, the ship is sent to sea in an unseaworthy state, the insurer is not liable for any loss attributable to unseaworthiness.

40. No implied warranty that goods are seaworthy

(1) In a policy on goods or other moveables there is no implied warranty that the goods or moveables are seaworthy.

(2) In a voyage policy on goods or other moveables there is an implied warranty that at the commencement of the voyage the ship is not only seaworthy as a ship, but also that she is reasonably fit to carry the goods or other moveables to the destination contemplated by the policy.

41. Warranty of legality

There is an implied warranty that the adventure insured is a lawful one, and that, so far as the assured can control the matter, the adventure shall be carried out in a lawful manner.

THE VOYAGE

42. Implied condition as to commencement of risk

(1) Where the subject matter is insured by a voyage policy 'at and from' or 'from' a particular place, it is not necessary that the ship should be at that place when the contract is concluded, but there is an implied condition that the adventure shall be commenced within a reasonable time, and that if the adventure be not so commenced the insurer may avoid the contract.

(2) The implied condition may be negatived by showing that the delay was caused by circumstances known to the insurer before the contract was concluded or by showing that he waived the condition.

43. Alteration of port of departure

Where the place of departure is specified by the policy, and the ship instead of sailing from that place sails from any other place, the risk does not attach.

44. Sailing for different destination

Where the destination is specified in the policy, and the ship, instead of sailing for that destination, sails for any other destination, the risk does not attach.

45. Change of voyage

(1) Where, after the commencement of the risk, the destination of the ship is voluntarily changed from the destination contemplated by the policy, there is said to be a change of voyage.

(2) Unless the policy otherwise provides, where there is a change of voyage, the insurer is discharged from liability as from the time of change, that is to say, as from the time when the determination to change it is manifested; and it is immaterial that the ship may not in fact have left the course of voyage contemplated by the policy when the loss occurs.

46. Deviation

(1) Where a ship, without lawful excuse, deviates from the voyage contemplated by the policy, the insurer is discharged from liability as from the time of deviation, and it is immaterial that the ship may have regained her route before any loss occurs.

(2) There is a deviation from the voyage contemplated by the policy—

(a) Where the course of the voyage is specifically designated by the policy, and that course is departed from; or

(b) Where the course of the voyage is not specifically designated by the policy, but the usual and customary course is departed from.

(3) The intention to deviate is immaterial; there must be a deviation in fact to discharge the insurer from his liability under the contract.

47. Several ports of discharge

(1) Where several ports of discharge are specified by the policy, the ship may proceed to all or any of them, but, in the absence of any usage or sufficient cause to the contrary, she must proceed to them, or such of them as she goes to, in the order designated by the policy. If she does not there is a deviation.

(2) Where the policy is to 'ports of discharge', within a given area, which are not named, the ship must, in the absence of any usage or sufficient cause to the contrary, proceed to them, or such of them as she goes to, in their geographical order. If she does not there is a deviation.

48. Delay in voyage

In the case of a voyage policy, the adventure insured must be prosecuted throughout its course with reasonable dispatch, and, if without lawful excuse it is not so prosecuted, the insurer is discharged from liability as from the time when the delay became unreasonable.

49. Excuses for deviation or delay

(1) Deviation or delay in prosecuting the voyage contemplated by the policy is excused—

(a) Where authorised by any special term in the policy; or

(b) Where caused by circumstances beyond the control of the master and his employer; or

(c) Where reasonably necessary in order to comply with an express or implied warranty; or

(d) Where reasonably necessary for the safety of the ship or subject matter insured; or

(e) For the purpose of saving human life, or aiding a ship in distress where human life may be in danger; or

(f) Where reasonably necessary for the purpose of obtaining medical or surgical aid for any person on board the ship; or

(g) Where caused by the barratrous conduct of the master or crew, if barratry be one of the perils insured against.

(2) When the cause excusing the deviation or delay ceases to operate, the ship must resume her course, and prosecute her voyage, with reasonable dispatch.

Assignment of Policy

50. When and how policy is assignable

(1) A marine policy is assignable unless it contains terms expressly prohibiting assignment. It may be assigned either before or after loss.

(2) Where a marine policy has been assigned so as to pass the beneficial interest in such policy, the assignee of the policy is entitled to sue thereon in his own name; and the defendant is entitled to make any defence arising out of the contract which he would have been entitled to make if the action had been brought in the name of the person by or on behalf of whom the policy was effected.

(3) A marine policy may be assigned by indorsement thereon or in other customary manner.

51. Assured who has no interest cannot assign

Where the assured has parted with or lost his interest in the subject matter insured, and has not, before or at the time of so doing, expressly or impliedly agreed to assign the policy, any subsequent assignment of the policy is inoperative:

Provided that nothing in this section affects the assignment of a policy after loss.

The Premium

52. When premium payable

Unless otherwise agreed, the duty of the assured or his agent to pay the premium, and the duty of the insurer to issue the policy to the assured or his agent, are concurrent conditions, and the insurer is not bound to issue the policy until payment or tender of the premium.

53. Policy effected through broker

(1) Unless otherwise agreed, where a marine policy is effected on behalf of the assured by a broker, the broker is directly responsible to the insurer for the premium, and the insurer is directly responsible to the assured for the amount which may be payable in respect of losses, or in respect of returnable premium.

(2) Unless otherwise agreed, the broker has, as against the assured, a lien upon the policy for the amount of the premium and his charges in respect of effecting the policy, and, where he has dealt with the person who employs him as a principal, he has also a lien on the policy in respect of any balance on any insurance account which may be due to him from such person, unless when the debt was incurred he had reason to believe that such person was only an agent.

54. Effect of receipt on policy

Where a marine policy effected on behalf of the assured by a broker acknowledges the receipt of the premium, such acknowledgment is, in the absence of fraud, conclusive as between the insurer and the assured, but not as between the insurer and broker.

LOSS AND ABANDONMENT

55. Included and excluded losses

(1) Subject to the provisions of this Act, and unless the policy otherwise provides, the insurer is liable for any loss proximately caused by a peril insured against, but, subject as aforesaid, he is not liable for any loss which is not proximately caused by a peril insured against.

(2) In particular—
  (a) The insurer is not liable for any loss attributable to the wilful misconduct of the assured, but, unless the policy otherwise provides he is liable for any loss proximately caused by a peril insured against even though the loss would not have happened but for the misconduct or negligence of the master or crew;
  (b) Unless the policy otherwise provides, the insurer on ship or goods is not liable for any loss proximately caused by delay, although the delay be caused by a peril insured against;
  (c) Unless the policy otherwise provides, the insurer is not liable for ordinary wear and tear, ordinary leakage and breakage, inherent vice or nature of the subject matter insured, or for any loss proximately caused by rats or vermin, or for any injury to machinery not proximately caused by maritime perils.

56. Partial and total loss

(1) A loss may be either total or partial. Any loss other than a total loss, as hereinafter defined, is a partial loss.

(2) A total loss may be either an actual total loss, or a constructive total loss.

(3) Unless a different intention appears from the terms of the policy, an insurance against total loss includes a constructive, as well as an actual, total loss.

(4) Where the assured brings an action for a total loss and the evidence proves only a partial loss, he may, unless the policy otherwise provides, recover for a partial loss.

(5) Where goods reach their destination in specie, but by reason of obliteration of marks, or otherwise, they are incapable of identification the loss, if any, is partial, and not total.

57. Actual total loss

(1) Where the subject matter insured is destroyed, or so damaged as to cease to be a thing of the kind insured, or where the assured is irretrievably deprived thereof, there is an actual total loss.

(2) In the case of an actual total loss no notice of abandonment need be given.

58. Missing ship

Where the ship concerned in the adventure is missing, and after the lapse of a reasonable time no news of her has been received, an actual total loss may be presumed.

59. Effect of transhipment, etc

Where, by a peril insured against, the voyage is interrupted at an intermediate port or place, under such circumstances as, apart from any special stipulation in the contract of affreightment, to justify the master in landing and re-shipping the goods or other moveables, or in transhipping them, and sending them on to their destination, the liability of the insurer continues, notwithstanding the landing or transhipment.

60. Constructive total loss defined

(1) Subject to any express provision in the policy, there is a constructive total loss where the subject matter insured is reasonably abandoned on account of its actual total loss appearing to be unavoidable, or because it could not be preserved from actual total loss without an expenditure which would exceed its value when the expenditure had been incurred.

(2) In particular, there is a constructive total loss—

(i) Where the assured is deprived of the possession of his ship or goods by a peril insured against, and (a) it is unlikely that he can recover the ship or goods, as the case may be, or (b) the cost of recovering the ship or goods, as the case may be, would exceed their value when recovered; or

(ii) In the case of damage to a ship, where she is so damaged by a peril insured against that the cost of repairing the damage would exceed the value of the ship when repaired.

In estimating the cost of repairs, no deduction is to be made in respect of general average contributions to those repairs payable by other interests, but account is to be taken of the expense of future salvage operations and of any future general average contributions to which the ship would be liable if repaired; or

(iii) In the case of damage to goods, where the cost of repairing the damage and forwarding the goods to their destination would exceed their value on arrival.

61. Effect of constructive total loss

Where there is a constructive total loss the assured may either treat the loss as a partial loss, or abandon the subject matter insured to the insurer and treat the loss as if it were an actual total loss.

62. Notice of abandonment

(1) Subject to the provisions of this section, where the assured elects to abandon the subject matter insured to the insurer, he must give notice of abandonment. If he fails to do so the loss can only be treated as a partial loss.

(2) Notice of abandonment may be given in writing, or by word of mouth, or partly in writing and partly by word of mouth, and may be given in terms which indicate the intention of the assured to abandon his insured interest in the subject matter insured unconditionally to the insurer.

(3) Notice of abandonment must be given with reasonable diligence after the receipt of reliable information of the loss, but where the information is of a doubtful character the assured is entitled to a reasonable time to make inquiry.

(4) Where notice of abandonment is properly given, the rights of the assured are not prejudiced by the fact that the insurer refuses to accept the abandonment.

(5) The acceptance of an abandonment may be either express or implied from the conduct of the insurer. The mere silence of the insurer after notice is not an acceptance.

(6) Where a notice of abandonment is accepted the abandonment is irrevocable. The acceptance of the notice conclusively admits liability for the loss and the sufficiency of the notice.

(7) Notice of abandonment is unnecessary where, at the time when the assured receives information of the loss, there would be no possibility of benefit to the insurer if notice were given to him.

(8) Notice of abandonment may be waived by the insurer.

(9) Where an insurer has re-insured his risk, no notice of abandonment need be given by him.

63. Effect of abandonment

(1) Where there is a valid abandonment the insurer is entitled to take over the interest of the assured in whatever may remain of the subject matter insured, and all proprietary rights incidental thereto.

(2) Upon the abandonment of a ship, the insurer thereof is entitled to any freight in course of being earned, and which is earned by her subsequent to the casualty causing the loss, less the expenses of earning it incurred after the casualty, and, where the ship is carrying the owner's goods, the insurer is entitled to a reasonable remuneration for the carriage of them subsequent to the casualty causing the loss.

PARTIAL LOSSES (INCLUDING SALVAGE AND GENERAL AVERAGE AND PARTICULAR CHARGES)

64. Particular average loss

(1) A particular average loss is a partial loss of the subject matter insured, caused by a peril insured against, and which is not a general average loss.

(2) Expenses incurred by or on behalf of the assured for the safety or preservation of the subject matter insured, other than general average and salvage charges, are called particular charges. Particular charges are not included in particular average.

65. Salvage charges

(1) Subject to any express provision in the policy, salvage charges incurred in preventing a loss by perils insured against may be recovered as a loss by those perils.

(2) 'Salvage charges' means the charges recoverable under maritime law by a salvor independently of contract. They do not include the expenses of services in the nature of salvage rendered by the assured or his agents, or any person employed for hire by them, for the purpose of averting a peril insured against. Such expenses, where properly incurred, may be recovered as particular charges or as a general average loss, according to the circumstances under which they were incurred.

66. General average loss

(1) A general average loss is a loss caused by or directly consequential on a general average act. It includes a general average expenditure as well as a general average sacrifice.

(2) There is a general average act where any extraordinary sacrifice or expenditure is voluntarily and reasonably made or incurred in time of peril for the purpose of preserving the property imperilled in the common adventure.

(3) Where there is a general average loss, the party on whom it falls is entitled, subject to the conditions imposed by maritime law, to a rateable contribution from the other parties interested, and such contribution is called a general average contribution.

(4) Subject to any express provision in the policy, where the assured has incurred a general average expenditure, he may recover from the insurer in respect of the proportion of the loss which falls upon him; and, in the case of a general average sacrifice, he may recover from the insurer in respect of the whole loss without having enforced his right of contribution from the other parties liable to contribute.

(5) Subject to any express provision in the policy, where the assured has paid, or is liable to pay, a general average contribution in respect of the subject insured, he may recover therefor from the insurer.

(6) In the absence of express stipulation, the insurer is not liable for any general average loss or contribution where the loss was not incurred for the purpose of avoiding, or in connexion with the avoidance of, a peril insured against.

(7) Where ship, freight, and cargo, or any two of those interests, are owned by the same assured, the liability of the insurer in respect of general average losses or contributions is to be determined as if those subjects were owned by different persons.

MEASURE OF INDEMNITY

67. Extent of liability of insurer for loss

(1) The sum which the assured can recover in respect of a loss on a policy by which he is insured, in the case of an unvalued policy to the full extent of the

insurable value, or, in the case of a valued policy to the full extent of the value fixed by the policy, is called the measure of indemnity.

(2) Where there is a loss recoverable under the policy, the insurer, or each insurer if there be more than one, is liable for such proportion of the measure of indemnity as the amount of his subscription bears to the value fixed by the policy in the case of a valued policy, or to the insurable value in the case of an unvalued policy.

68. Total loss

Subject to the provisions of this Act and to any express provision in the policy where there is a total loss of the subject matter insured—

(1) If the policy be a valued policy, the measure of indemnity is the sum fixed by the policy.

(2) If the policy be an unvalued policy, the measure of indemnity is the insurable value of the subject matter insured.

69. Partial loss of ship

Where a ship is damaged, but is not totally lost, the measure of indemnity subject to any express provision in the policy, is as follows—

(1) Where the ship has been repaired, the assured is entitled to the reasonable cost of the repairs, less the customary deductions, but not exceeding the sum insured in respect of any one casualty;

(2) Where the ship has been only partially repaired, the assured is entitled to the reasonable cost of such repairs, computed as above, and also to be indemnified for the reasonable depreciation, if any, arising from the unrepaired damage, provided that the aggregate amount shall not exceed the cost of repairing the whole damage, computed as above;

(3) Where the ship has not been repaired, and has not been sold in her damaged state during the risk, the assured is entitled to be indemnified for the reasonable depreciation arising from the unrepaired damage, but not exceeding the reasonable cost of repairing such damage, computed as above.

70. Partial loss of freight

Subject to any express provision in the policy, where there is a partial loss of freight, the measure of indemnity is such proportion of the sum fixed by the policy in the case of a valued policy, or of the insurable value in the case of an unvalued policy, as the proportion of freight lost by the assured bears to the whole freight at the risk of the assured under the policy.

71. Partial loss of goods, merchandise, etc

Where there is a partial loss of goods, merchandise, or other moveables, the measure of indemnity, subject to any express provision in the policy, is as follows—

(1) Where part of the goods, merchandise or other moveables insured by a valued policy is totally lost, the measure of indemnity is such proportion of the sum fixed by the policy as the insurable value of the part lost bears to the insurable value of the whole, ascertained as in the case of an unvalued policy;

(2) Where part of the goods, merchandise, or other moveables insured by an unvalued policy is totally lost, the measure of indemnity is the insurable value of the part lost, ascertained as in case of total loss;

(3) Where the whole or any part of the goods or merchandise insured has been delivered damaged at its destination, the measure of indemnity is such proportion of the sum fixed by the policy in the case of a valued policy, or of the insurable value in the case of an unvalued policy, as the difference between the gross sound and damaged values at the place of arrival bears to the gross sound value;

(4) 'Gross value' means the wholesale price or, if there be no such price the estimated value, with, in either case, freight, landing charges, and duty paid beforehand; provided that, in the case of goods or merchandise customarily sold in bond, the bonded price is deemed to be the gross value. 'Gross proceeds' means the actual price obtained at a sale where all charges on sale are paid by the sellers.

72. Apportionment of valuation

(1) Where different species of property are insured under a single valuation, the valuation must be apportioned over the different species in proportion to their respective insurable values, as in the case of an unvalued policy. The insured value of any part of a species is such proportion of the total insured value of the same as the insurable value of the part bears to the insurable value of the whole ascertained in both cases as provided by this Act.

(2) Where a valuation has to be apportioned, and particulars of the prime cost of each separate species, quality, or description of goods cannot be ascertained, the division of the valuation may be made over the net arrived sound values of the different species, qualities, or descriptions of goods.

73. General average contributions and salvage charges

(1) Subject to any express provision in the policy, where the assured has paid, or is liable for, any general average contribution, the measure of indemnity is the full amount of such contribution, if the subject matter liable to contribution is insured for its full contributory value; but, if such subject matter be not insured for its full contributory value, or if only part of it be insured, the indemnity payable by the insurer must be reduced in proportion to the under insurance, and where there has been a particular average loss which constitutes a deduction from the contributory value, and for which the insurer is liable, that amount must be deducted from the insured value in order to ascertain what the insurer is liable to contribute.

(2) Where the insurer is liable for salvage charges the extent of his liability must be determined on the like principle.

74. Liabilities to third parties

Where the assured has effected an insurance in express terms against any liability to a third party, the measure of indemnity, subject to any express provision in the policy, is the amount paid or payable by him to such third party in respect of such liability.

75. General provisions as to measure of indemnity

(1) Where there has been a loss in respect of any subject matter not expressly provided for in the foregoing provisions of this Act, the measure of indemnity shall be ascertained, as nearly as may be, in accordance with those provisions, in so far as applicable to the particular case.

(2) Nothing in the provisions of this Act relating to the measure of indemnity shall affect the rules relating to double insurance, or prohibit the insurer from disproving interest wholly or in part, or from showing that at the time of the loss the whole or any part of the subject matter insured was not at risk under the policy.

76. Particular average warranties

(1) Where the subject matter insured is warranted free from particular average, the assured cannot recover for a loss of part, other than a loss incurred by a general average sacrifice unless the contract contained in the policy be apportionable; but, if the contract be apportionable, the assured may recover for a total loss of any apportionable part.

(2) Where the subject matter insured is warranted free from particular average, either wholly or under a certain percentage, the insurer is nevertheless liable for salvage charges, and for particular charges and other expenses properly incurred pursuant to the provisions of the suing and labouring clause in order to avert a loss insured against.

(3) Unless the policy otherwise provides, where the subject matter insured is warranted free from particular average under a specified percentage, a general average loss cannot be added to a particular average loss to make up the specified percentage.

(4) For the purpose of ascertaining whether the specified percentage has been reached, regard shall be had only to the actual loss suffered by the subject matter insured. Particular charges and the expenses of and incidental to ascertaining and proving the loss must be excluded.

77. Successive losses

(1) Unless the policy otherwise provides, and subject to the provisions of this Act, the insurer is liable for successive losses, even though the total amount of such losses may exceed the sum insured.

(2) Where, under the same policy, a partial loss, which has not been repaired or otherwise made good, is followed by a total loss, the assured can only recover in respect of the total loss:

Provided that nothing in this section shall affect the liability of the insurer under the suing and labouring clause.

78. Suing and labouring clause

(1) Where the policy contains a suing and labouring clause, the engagement thereby entered into is deemed to be supplementary to the contract of insurance, and the assured may recover from the insurer any expenses properly incurred pursuant to the clause, notwithstanding that the insurer may have

paid for a total loss, or that the subject matter may have been warranted free from particular average, either wholly or under a certain percentage.

(2) General average losses and contributions and salvage charges, as defined by this Act, are not recoverable under the suing and labouring clause.

(3) Expenses incurred for the purpose of averting or diminishing any loss not covered by the policy are not recoverable under the suing and labouring clause.

(4) It is the duty of the assured and his agents, in all cases, to take such measures as may be reasonable for the purpose of averting or minimising a loss.

RIGHTS OF INSURER ON PAYMENT

79. Right of subrogation

(1) Where the insurer pays for a total loss, either of the whole, or in the case of goods of any apportionable part, of the subject matter insured, he thereupon becomes entitled to take over the interest of the assured in whatever may remain of the subject matter so paid for, and he is thereby subrogated to all the rights and remedies of the assured in and in respect of that subject matter as from the time of the casualty causing the loss.

(2) Subject to the foregoing provisions, where the insurer pays for a partial loss, he acquires no title to the subject matter insured, or such part of it as may remain, but he is thereupon subrogated to all rights and remedies of the assured in and in respect of the subject matter insured as from the time of the casualty causing the loss, in so far as the assured has been indemnified, according to this Act, by such payment for the loss.

80. Right of contribution

(1) Where the assured is over-insured by double insurance, each insurer is bound, as between himself and the other insurers, to contribute rateably to the loss in proportion to the amount for which he is liable under his contract.

(2) If any insurer pays more than his proportion of the loss, he is entitled to maintain an action for contribution against the other insurers, and is entitled to the like remedies as a surety who has paid more than his proportion of the debt.

81. Effect of under insurance

Where the assured is insured for an amount less than the insurable value or, in the case of a valued policy, for an amount less than the policy valuation, he is deemed to be his own insurer in respect of the uninsured balance.

RETURN OF PREMIUM

82. Enforcement of return

Where the premium or a proportionate part thereof is, by this Act, declared to be returnable—

(a) If already paid, it may be recovered by the assured from the insurer; and

(b) If unpaid, it may be retained by the assured or his agent.

83. Return by agreement

Where the policy contains a stipulation for the return of the premium, or a proportionate part thereof, on the happening of a certain event, and that event happens, the premium, or, as the case may be, the proportionate part thereof, is thereupon returnable to the assured.

84. Return for failure of consideration

(1) Where the consideration for the payment of the premium totally fails, and there has been no fraud or illegality on the part of the assured or his agents, the premium is thereupon returnable to the assured.

(2) Where the consideration for the payment of the premium is apportionable and there is a total failure of any apportionable part of the consideration, a proportionate part of the premium is, under the like conditions, thereupon returnable to the assured.

(3) In particular—
- (a) Where the policy is void, or is avoided by the insurer as from the commencement of the risk, the premium is returnable, provided that there has been no fraud or illegality on the part of the assured; but if the risk is not apportionable, and has once attached, the premium is not returnable;
- (b) Where the subject matter insured, or part thereof, has never been imperilled, the premium, or, as the case may be, a proportionate part thereof, is returnable:

    Provided that where the subject matter has been insured 'lost or not lost' and has arrived in safety at the time when the contract is concluded, the premium is not returnable unless, at such time, the insurer knew of the safe arrival;
- (c) Where the assured has no insurable interest throughout the currency of the risk, the premium is returnable, provided that this rule does not apply to a policy effected by way of gaming or wagering;
- (d) Where the assured has a defeasible interest which is terminated during the currency of the risk, the premium is not returnable;
- (e) Where the assured has over-insured under an unvalued policy, a proportionate part of the premium is returnable;
- (f) Subject to the foregoing provisions, where the assured has overinsured by double insurance, a proportionate part of the several premiums is returnable:

    Provided that, if the policies are effected at different times, and any earlier policy has at any time borne the entire risk, or if a claim has been paid on the policy in respect of the full sum insured thereby, no premium is returnable in respect of that policy, and when the double insurance is effected knowingly by the assured no premium is returnable.

MUTUAL INSURANCE

85. Modification of Act in case of mutual insurance

(1) Where two or more persons mutually agree to insure each other against marine losses there is said to be a mutual insurance.

(2) The provisions of this Act relating to the premium do not apply to mutual insurance, but a guarantee, or such other arrangement as may be agreed upon, may be substituted for the premium.

(3) The provisions of this Act, in so far as they may be modified by the agreement of the parties, may in the case of mutual insurance be modified by the terms of the policies issued by the association, or by the rules and regulations of the association.

(4) Subject to the exceptions mentioned in this section, the provisions of this Act apply to a mutual insurance.

SUPPLEMENTAL

86. Ratification by assured

Where a contract of marine insurance is in good faith effected by one person on behalf of another, the person on whose behalf it is effected may ratify the contract even after he is aware of a loss.

87. Implied obligations varied by agreement or usage

(1) Where any right, duty, or liability would arise under a contract of marine insurance by implication of law, it may be negatived or varied by express agreement, or by usage, if the usage be such as to bind both parties to the contract.

(2) The provisions of this section extend to any right, duty, or liability declared by this Act which may be lawfully modified by agreement.

88. Reasonable time, etc, a question of fact

Where by this Act any reference is made to reasonable time, reasonable premium, or reasonable diligence, the question what is reasonable is a question of fact.

89. Slip as evidence

Where there is a duly stamped policy, reference may be made, as heretofore, to the slip or covering note, in any legal proceeding.

90. Interpretation of terms

In this Act, unless the context or subject matter otherwise requires—

'Action' includes counter-claim and set off;

'Freight' includes the profit derivable by a shipowner from the employment of his ship to carry his own goods or moveables, as well as freight payable by a third party, but does not include passage money;

'Moveables' means any moveable tangible property, other than the ship, and includes money, valuable securities, and other documents;

'Policy' means a marine policy.

91. Savings

(1) Nothing in this Act, or in any repeal effected thereby, shall affect—

(a) The provisions of the Stamp Act 1891, or any enactment for the time being in force relating to the revenue;

(b) The provisions of the Companies Act 1862, or any enactment amending or substituted for the same;

(c) The provisions of any statute not expressly repealed by this Act.

(2) The rules of the common law including the law merchant, save in so far as they are inconsistent with the express provisions of this Act, shall continue to apply to contracts of marine insurance.

92. Repeals

The enactments mentioned in the Second Schedule to this Act are hereby repealed to the extent specified in that schedule.

93. Commencement

This Act shall come into operation on the first day of January one thousand nine hundred and seven.

94. Short title

This Act may be cited as the Marine Insurance Act 1906.

SCHEDULES

FIRST SCHEDULE

Section 30

FORM OF POLICY

Lloyd's S.G. policy

Be it known that   as well in   own name as for and in the name and names of all and every other person or persons to whom the same doth, may, or shall appertain, in part or in all doth make assurance and cause
and them, and every of them, to be insured lost or not lost, at and from

Upon any kind of goods and merchandises, and also upon the body, tackle, apparel, ordnance, munition, artillery, boat, and other furniture, of and in the good ship or vessel called the
whereof is master under God, for this present voyage,
or whosoever else shall go for master in the said ship, or by whatsoever other name or names the said ship, or the master thereof, is or shall be named or called; beginning the adventure upon the said goods and merchandises from the loading thereof aboard the said ship

upon the said ship, &c.

and so shall continue and endure, during her abode there, upon the said ship, &c. And further, until the said ship, with all her ordnance, tackle, apparel, &c, and goods and merchandises whatsoever shall be arrived at

upon the said ship, &c, until she hath moored at, anchor twenty-four hours in good safety; and upon the goods and merchandises, until the same be there discharged and safely landed. And it shall be lawful for the said ship, &c, in this voyage, to proceed and sail to and touch and stay at any ports or places whatsoever

with prejudice to this insurance. The said ship, &c, goods and merchandises, &c, for so much as concerns the assured by agreement between the assured and assurers in this policy, are and shall be valued at

Touching the adventures and perils which we the assurers are contented to bear and do take upon us in this voyage: they are of the seas, men of war, fire, enemies, pirates, rovers, thieves, jettisons, letters of mart and countermart, surprisals, takings at sea, arrests, restraints, and detainments of all kings, princes, and people, of what nation, condition, or quality soever, barratry of the master and mariners, and of all other perils, losses, and misfortunes, that have or shall come to the hurt, detriment, or damage of the said goods and merchandises, and ship, &c, or any part thereof. And in the case of any loss or misfortune it shall be lawful to the assured, their factors, servants and assigns, to sue, labour, and travel for, in and about the defence, safeguards, and recovery of the said goods and merchandises, and ship, &c, or any part thereof, without prejudice to this insurance; to the charges whereof we, the assurers, will contribute each one according to the rate and quantity of his sum herein assured. And it is especially declared and agreed that no acts of the insurer or insured in recovering, saving, or preserving the property insured shall be considered as a waiver, or acceptance of abandonment. And it is agreed by us, the insurers, that this writing or policy of assurance shall be of as much force and effect as the surest writing or policy of assurance heretofore made in Lombard Street, or in the Royal Exchange, or elsewhere in London. And so we, the assurers, are contented, and do hereby promise and bind ourselves, each one for his own part, our heirs, executors, and goods to the assured, their executors, administrators, and assigns, for the true performance of the premises, confessing ourselves paid the consideration due unto us for this assurance by the assured, at and after the rate of

IN WITNESS whereof we, the assurers, have subscribed our names and sums assured in London.

NB–Corn, fish, salt, fruit, flour and seed are warranted free from average, unless general, or the ship be stranded – sugar, tobacco, hemp, flax, hides and skins are warranted free from average, under five pounds per cent, and all other goods, also the ship and freight, are warranted free from average, under three pounds per cent, unless general, or the ship be stranded.

Appendix 1

Rules for Construction of Policy

The following are the rules referred to by this Act for the construction of a policy in the above or other like form, where the context does not otherwise require—

1. Lost or not lost

Where the subject matter is insured 'lost or not lost', and the loss has occurred before the contract is concluded, the risk attaches unless, at such time the assured was aware of the loss, and the insurer was not.

2. From

Where the subject matter is insured 'from' a particular place, the risk does not attach until the ship starts on the voyage insured.

3. At and from [Ship]

(a) Where a ship is insured 'at and from' a particular place, and she is at that place in good safety when the contract is concluded, the risk attaches immediately.

(b) If she be not at that place when the contract is concluded, the risk attaches as soon as she arrives there in good safety, and, unless the policy otherwise provides, it is immaterial that she is covered by another policy for a specified time after arrival.

(c) Where chartered freight is insured 'at and from' a particular place, and the ship is at that place in good safety when the contract is concluded the risk attaches immediately. If she be not there when the contract is concluded, the risk attaches as soon as she arrives there in good safety.

(d) Where freight, other than chartered freight, is payable without special conditions and is insured 'at and from' a particular place, the risk attaches pro rata as the goods or merchandise are shipped, provided that if there be cargo in readiness which belongs to the shipowner, or which some other person has contracted with him to ship, the risk attaches as soon as the ship is ready to receive such cargo.

4. From the loading thereof

Where goods or other moveables are insured 'from the loading thereof,' the risk does not attach until such goods or moveables are actually on board, and the insurer is not liable for them while in transit from the shore to ship.

5. Safely landed

Where the risk on goods or other moveables continues until they are 'safely landed,' they must be landed in the customary manner and within a reasonable time after arrival at the port of discharge, and if they are not so landed the risk ceases.

6. Touch and stay

In the absence of any further license or usage, the liberty to touch and stay 'at any port or place whatsoever' does not authorise the ship to depart from the course of her voyage from the port of departure to the port of destination.

7. Perils of the seas

The term 'perils of the seas' refers only to fortuitous accidents or casualties of the seas. It does not include the ordinary action of the winds and waves.

8. Pirates

The term 'pirates' includes passengers who mutiny and rioters who attack the ship from the shore.

9. Thieves

The term 'thieves' does not cover clandestine theft or a theft committed by any one of the ship's company, whether crew or passengers.

10. Restraint of princes

The term 'arrests, etc, of kings, princes, and people' refers to political or executive acts, and does not include a loss caused by riot or by ordinary judicial process.

11. Barratry

The term 'barratry' includes every wrongful act wilfully committed by the master or crew to the prejudice of the owner, or, as the case may be, the charterer.

12. All other perils

The term 'all other perils' includes only perils similar in kind to the perils specifically mentioned in the policy.

13. Average unless general

The term 'average unless general' means a partial loss of the subject matter insured other than a general average loss, and does not include 'particular charges'.

14. Stranded

Where the ship has stranded, the insurer is liable for the excepted losses, although the loss is not attributable to the stranding, provided that when the stranding takes place the risk has attached and, if the policy be on goods, that the damaged goods are on board.

15. Ship

The term 'ship' includes the hull, materials and outfit, stores and provisions for the officers and crew, and, in the case of vessels engaged in a special trade, the ordinary fittings requisite for the trade, and also, in the case of a steamship, the machinery, boilers and coals and engine stores, if owned by the assured.

16. Freight

The term 'freight' includes the profit derivable by a shipowner from the employment of his ship to carry his own goods or moveables, as well as freight payable by a third party, but does not include passage money.

17. Goods

The term 'goods' means goods in the nature of merchandise, and does not include personal effects or provisions and stores for use on board.

In the absence of any usage to the contrary, deck cargo and living animals must be insured specifically, and not under the general denomination of goods.

SECOND SCHEDULE

Section 92

ENACTMENTS REPEALED

Session and Chapter	Title or Short Title	Extent of Repeal
19 Geo 2 c 37.	An Act to regulate insurance on ships belonging to the subjects of Great Britain, and on merchandizes or effects laden thereon.	The whole Act.
28 Geo 3 c 56.	An Act to repeal an Act made in the twenty-fifth year of the reign of his present Majesty, intituled 'An Act for regulating Insurances on Ships, and on goods, merchandizes, or effects,' and for substituting other provisions for the like purpose in lieu thereof.	The whole Act so far as it relates to marine insurance.
31 & 32 Vict c 86.	The Policies of Marine Assurance Act 1868.	The whole Act.

APPENDIX 2

MARINE INSURANCE (GAMBLING POLICIES) ACT 1909

An Act to prohibit gambling on loss by maritime perils [20 October 1909]

BE it enacted by the King's most Excellent Majesty, by and with the advice and consent of the Lords Spiritual and Temporal, and Commons, in this present Parliament assembled, and by the authority of the same, as follows—

1. Prohibition of gambling on loss by maritime perils

(1) If—

    (a) any person effects a contract of marine insurance without having any bona fide interest, direct or indirect, either in the safe arrival of the ship in relation to which the contract is made or in the safety or preservation of the subject matter insured, or a bona fide expectation of acquiring such an interest; or

    (b) any person in the employment of the owner of a ship, not being a part owner of the ship, effects a contract of marine insurance in relation to the ship, and the contract is made 'interest or no interest', or 'without further proof of interest than the policy itself', or 'without benefit of salvage to the insurer,' or subject to any other like term,

the contract shall be deemed to be a contract by way of gambling on loss by maritime perils, and the person effecting it shall be guilty of an offence, and shall be liable, on summary conviction, to imprisonment, with or without hard labour, for a term not exceeding six months or to a fine not exceeding [level 3 on the standard scale], and in either case to forfeit to the Crown any money he may receive under the contract.

(2) Any broker or other person through whom, and any insurer with whom, any such contract is effected shall be guilty of an offence and liable on summary conviction to the like penalties if he acted knowing that the contract was by way of gambling on loss by maritime perils within the meaning of this Act.

(3) Proceedings under this Act shall not be instituted without the consent in England of the Attorney General, in Scotland of the Lord Advocate, and in Ireland of the Attorney General for Ireland.

(4) Proceedings shall not be instituted under this Act against a person (other than a person in the employment of the owner of the ship in relation to which the contract was made) alleged to have effected a contract by way of gambling on loss by maritime perils until an opportunity has been afforded him of showing that the contract was not such a contract as aforesaid, and any information given by that person for that purpose shall not be admissible in evidence against him in any prosecution under this Act.

(5) If proceedings under this Act are taken against any person (other than a person in the employment of the owner of the ship in relation to which the contract was made) for effecting such a contract, and the contract was made 'interest or no interest,' or 'without further proof of interest than the policy itself,' or 'without benefit of salvage to the insurer,' or subject to any other like term, the contract shall be deemed to be a contract by way of gambling on loss by maritime perils unless the contrary is proved.

(6) For the purpose of giving jurisdiction under this Act, every offence shall be deemed to have been committed either in the place in which the same actually was committed or in any place in which the offender may be.

(7) Any person aggrieved by an order or decision of a court of summary jurisdiction under this Act, may appeal to [the Crown Court].

(8) For the purposes of this Act the expression 'owner' includes charterer.

(9) Sub-section (7) of this section shall not apply to Scotland.

2. Short title

This Act may be cited as the Marine Insurance (Gambling Policies) Act, 1909, and the Marine Insurance Act, 1906, and this Act may be cited together as the Marine Insurance Acts 1906 and 1909.

NOTES

Sub-section (1): words omitted repealed by virtue of the Criminal Justice Act 1948, s 1(2); words in square brackets substituted by virtue of the Criminal Justice Act 1982, ss 37, 38, 46.

Sub-section (7): amended by the Courts Act 1971, s 56, Sched 9, Part 1.

APPENDIX 3

THIRD PARTIES (RIGHTS AGAINST INSURERS) ACT 1930

An Act to confer on third parties rights against insurers of third-party risks in the event of the insured becoming insolvent, and in certain other events [10th July 1930]

1. Rights of third parties against insurers on bankruptcy etc of the insured

(1) Where under any contract of insurance a person (hereinafter referred to as the insured) is insured against liabilities to third parties which he may incur, then—

(a) in the event of the insured becoming bankrupt or making a composition or arrangement with his creditors; or

(b) in the case of the insured being a company, in the event of a winding-up order being made, or a resolution for a voluntary winding-up being passed, with respect to the company, or of a receiver or manager of the company's business or undertaking being duly appointed, or of possession being taken, by or on behalf of the holders of any debentures secured by a floating charge, of any property comprised in or subject to the charge;

if, either before or after that event, any such liability as aforesaid is incurred by the insured, his rights against the insurer under the contract in respect of the liability shall, notwithstanding anything in any Act or rule of law to the contrary, be transferred to and vest in the third party to whom the liability was so incurred.

(2) Where an order is made under section one hundred and thirty of the Bankruptcy Act, 1914, for the administration of the estate of a deceased debtor according to the law of bankruptcy, then, if any debt provable in bankruptcy is owing by the deceased in respect of a liability against which he was insured under a contract of insurance as being a liability to a third party, the deceased debtor's rights against the insurer under the contract in respect of that liability shall, notwithstanding anything in the said Act, be transferred to and vest in the person to whom the debt is owing.

(3) In so far as any contract of insurance made after the commencement of this Act in respect of any liability of the insured to third parties purports, whether directly or indirectly, to avoid the contract or to alter the rights of the parties thereunder upon the happening to the insured of any of these events specified in paragraph (a) or paragraph (b) of sub-section (1) of this section or upon the making of an order under section one hundred and thirty of the Bankruptcy Act, 1914, in respect of his estate, the contract shall be of no effect.

(4) Upon a transfer under sub-section (1) or sub-section (2) of this section, the insurer shall, subject to the provisions of section three of this Act, be under

the same liability to the third party as he would have been under to the insured, but—

(a) if the liability of the insurer to the insured exceeds the liability of the insured to the third party, nothing in this Act shall affect the rights of the insured against the insurer in respect of the excess; and

(b) if the liability of the insurer to the insured is less than the liability of the insured to the third party, nothing in this Act shall affect the rights of the third party, against the insured in respect of the balance.

(5) For the purposes of this Act, the expression 'liabilities to third parties,' in relation to a person insured under any contract of insurance, shall not include any liability of that person in the capacity of insurer under some other contract of insurance.

(6) This Act shall not apply—

(a) where a company is wound up voluntarily merely for the purposes of reconstruction or of amalgamation with another company; or

(b) to any case to which sub-sections (1) and (2) of section seven of the Workmen's Compensation Act 1925, applies.

2. Duty to give necessary information to third parties

(1) In the event of any person becoming bankrupt or making a composition or arrangement with his creditors, or in the event of an order being made under section one hundred and thirty of the Bankruptcy Act, 1914, in respect of the estate of any person, or in the event of a winding-up order being made, or a resolution for a voluntary winding-up being passed, with respect to any company or of a receiver or manager of the company's business or undertaking being duly appointed or of possession being taken by or on behalf of the holders of any debentures secured by a floating charge of any property comprised in or subject to the charge it shall be the duty of the bankrupt, debtor, personal representative of the deceased debtor or company, and, as the case may be, of the trustee in bankruptcy, trustee, liquidator, receiver, or manager, or person in possession of the property to give at the request of any person claiming that the bankrupt, debtor, deceased debtor, or company is under a liability to him such information as may reasonably be required by him for the purpose of ascertaining whether any rights have been transferred to and vested in him by this Act and for the purpose of enforcing such rights, if any, and any contract of insurance, in so far as it purports, whether directly or indirectly, to avoid the contract or to alter the rights of the parties thereunder upon the giving of any such information in the events aforesaid or otherwise to prohibit or prevent the giving thereof in the said events shall be of no effect.

(2) If the information given to any person in pursuance of sub-section (1) of this section discloses reasonable ground for supposing that there have or may have been transferred to him under this Act rights against any particular insurer, that insurer shall be subject to the same duty as is imposed by the said sub-section on the persons therein mentioned.

(3) The duty to give information imposed by this section shall include a duty to allow all contracts of insurance, receipts for premiums, and other relevant documents in the possession or power of the person on whom the duty is so imposed to be inspected and copies thereof to be taken.

3. Settlement between insurers and insured persons

Where the insured has become bankrupt or where in the case of the insured being a company, a winding-up order has been made or a resolution for a voluntary winding-up has been passed, with respect to the company, no agreement made between the insurer and the insured after liability has been incurred to a third party and after the commencement of the bankruptcy or winding up, as the case may be, nor any waiver, assignment, or other disposition made by, or payment made to the insured after the commencement aforesaid shall be effective to defeat or affect the rights transferred to the third party under this Act, but those rights shall be the same as if no such agreement, waiver, assignment, disposition or payment had been made.

4. Application to Scotland

In the application of this Act to Scotland—

(a) the expression 'company' includes a limited partnership;

(b) any reference to an order under section one hundred and thirty of the Bankruptcy Act 1914, for the administration of the estate of a deceased debtor according to the law of bankruptcy, shall be deemed to include a reference to an award of sequestration of the estate of a deceased debtor, and a reference to an appointment of a judicial factor, under section one hundred and sixty-three of the Bankruptcy (Scotland) Act 1913, on the insolvent estate of a deceased person.

5. Short title

This Act may be cited as the Third Parties (Rights Against Insurers) Act 1930.

APPENDIX 4

In all communications please quote
the following reference

Lloyd's Marine Policy

The Assured is requested to **read this Policy** and, if it is incorrect, return it immediately for alteration to:

FOR CARGO INSURANCES ONLY

In the event of loss or damage which may result in a claim under this Insurance immediate notice must be given to the Lloyd's Agent at the port or place where the loss or damage is discovered in order that he may examine the goods and issue a survey report

Lloyd's Marine Policy

We, The Underwriters, hereby agree, in consideration of the payment to us by or on behalf of the Assured of the premium specified in the Schedule, to insure against loss damage liability or expense in the proportions and manner hereinafter provided. Each Underwriting Member of a Syndicate whose definitive number and proportion is set out in the following Table shall be liable only for his own share of his respective Syndicate's proportion.

This insurance shall be subject to the exclusive jurisdiction of the English Courts, except as may be expressly provided herein to the contrary.

In Witness whereof the General Manager of Lloyd's Policy Signing Office has subscribed his Name on behalf of each of Us.

LLOYD'S POLICY SIGNING OFFICE
General Manager

MAR 91

SCHEDULE

POLICY NUMBER

NAME OF ASSURED

VESSEL

VOYAGE OR PERIOD OF INSURANCE

SUBJECT-MATTER INSURED

AGREED VALUE
(if any)

AMOUNT INSURED HEREUNDER

PREMIUM

CLAUSES. ENDORSEMENTS. SPECIAL CONDITIONS AND WARRANTIES

THE ATTACHED CLAUSES AND ENDORSEMENTS FORM PART OF THIS POLICY

Definitive numbers of the Syndicates and proportions

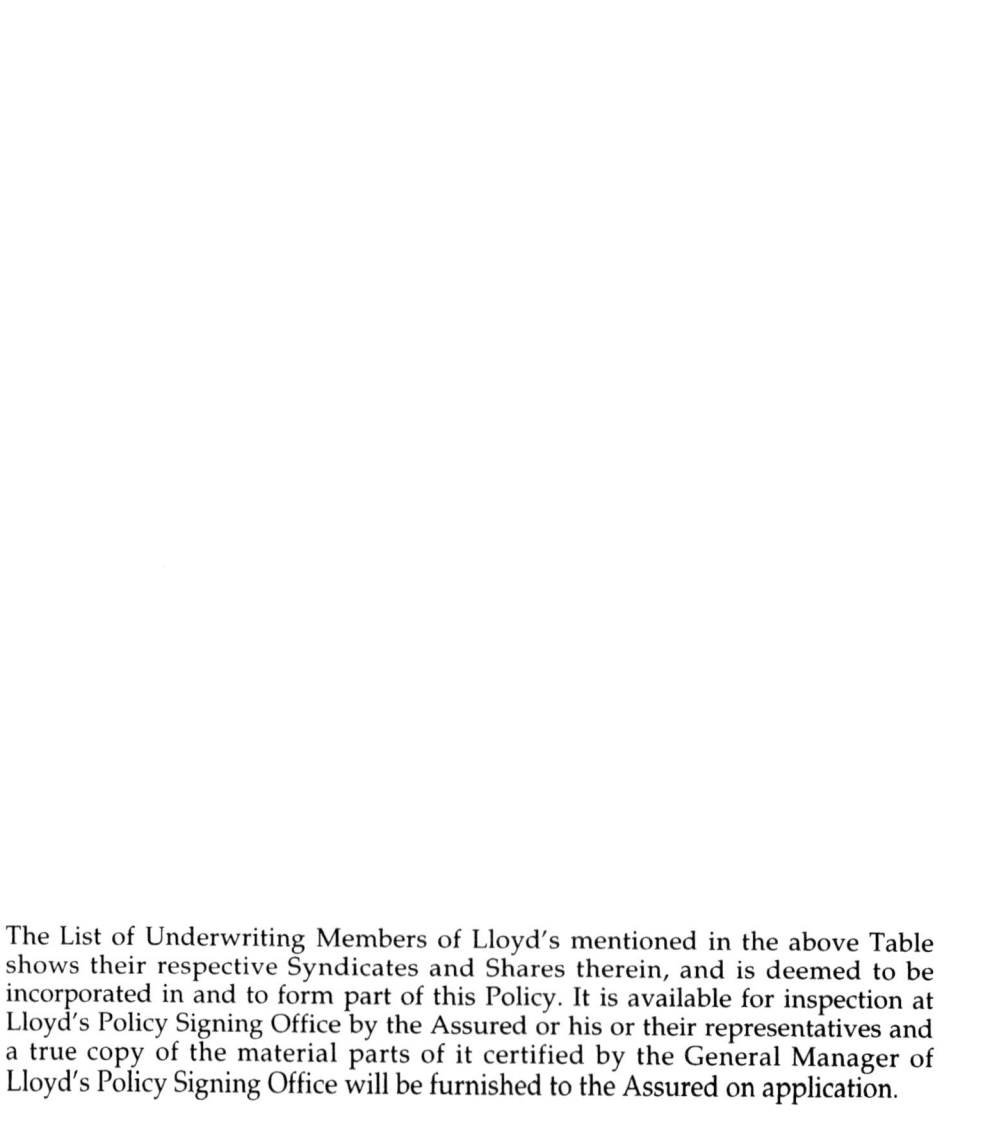

The List of Underwriting Members of Lloyd's mentioned in the above Table shows their respective Syndicates and Shares therein, and is deemed to be incorporated in and to form part of this Policy. It is available for inspection at Lloyd's Policy Signing Office by the Assured or his or their representatives and a true copy of the material parts of it certified by the General Manager of Lloyd's Policy Signing Office will be furnished to the Assured on application.

APPENDIX 5

In all communications please quote
the following reference

**The Institute of London
Underwriters**

Companies Marine Policy[1]

This Policy is subscribed by Insurance
Companies
Members of The Institute of London
Underwriters
49, Leadenhall Street,
London, EC3A 2BE

---

1 Permission to reproduce the Institute Clauses was granted by the International Underwriting Association.

THE INSTITUTE OF LONDON UNDERWRITERS

COMPANIES' MARINE POLICY

WE, THE COMPANIES, hereby agree, in consideration of the payment to us by or on behalf of the Assured of the premium specified in the Schedule, to insure against loss damage liability or expense in the proportions and manner hereinafter provided. Each Company shall be liable only for its own respective proportion.

This insurance shall be subject to the exclusive jurisdiction of the English Courts, except as may be expressly provided herein to the contrary.

IN WITNESS whereof the General Manager and Secretary of The Institute of London Underwriters has subscribed his name on behalf of each Company.

....
General Manager and Secretary
The Institute of London Underwriters

This Policy is not valid unless it bears the embossment of the Policy Department of The Institute of London Underwriters.

MAR 91

SCHEDULE

POLICY NUMBER

NAME OF ASSURED

VESSEL

VOYAGE OR PERIOD OF INSURANCE

SUBJECT MATTER INSURED

AGREED VALUE
(if any)

AMOUNT INSURED HEREUNDER

PREMIUM

CLAUSES, ENDORSEMENTS, SPECIAL CONDITIONS AND WARRANTIES

THE ATTACHED CLAUSES AND ENDORSEMENTS FORM PART OF THIS POLICY

Institute of London Underwriters – Companies Marine Policy [Mar 91]

COMPANIES' PROPORTIONS

For use by the Policy Department

of

The Institute of London Underwriters

APPENDIX 6

1/11/95

(FOR USE ONLY WITH THE CURRENT MAR POLICY FORM)

INSTITUTE TIME CLAUSES
HULLS

This insurance is subject to English law and practice

1 NAVIGATION

1.1 The Vessel is covered subject to the provisions of this insurance at all times and has leave to sail or navigate with or without pilots, to go on trial trips and to assist and tow vessels or craft in distress, but it is warranted that the Vessel shall not be towed, except as is customary or to the first safe port or place when in need of assistance, or undertake towage or salvage services under a contract previously arranged by the Assured and/or Owners and/or Managers and/or Charterers. This Clause 1.1 shall not exclude customary towage in connection with loading and discharging.

1.2 This insurance shall not be prejudiced by reason of the Assured entering into any contract with pilots or for customary towage which limits or exempts the liability of the pilots and/or tugs and/or towboats and/or their owners when the Assured or their agents accept or are compelled to accept such contracts in accordance with established local law or practice.

1.3 The practice of engaging helicopters for the transportation of personnel, supplies and equipment to and/or from the Vessel shall not prejudice this insurance.

1.4 In the event of the Vessel being employed in trading operations which entail cargo loading or discharging at sea from or into another vessel (not being a harbour or inshore craft) no claim shall be recoverable under this insurance for loss of or damage to the Vessel or liability to any other vessel arising from such loading or discharging operations, including whilst approaching, lying alongside and leaving, unless previous notice that the Vessel is to be employed in such operations has been given to the Underwriters and any amended terms of cover and any additional premium required by them have been agreed.

1.5 In the event of the Vessel sailing (with or without cargo) with an intention of being (a) broken up, or (b) sold for breaking up, any claim for loss of or damage to the Vessel occurring subsequent to such sailing shall be limited to the market value of the Vessel as scrap at the time when the loss or damage is sustained unless previous

Institute Time Clauses – Hulls (1995) [ITCH(95)]

notice has been given to the Underwriters and any amendments to the terms of cover, insured value and premium required by them have been agreed. Nothing in this Clause 1.5 shall affect claims under Clauses 8 and/or 10.

2 CONTINUATION

Should the Vessel at the expiration of this insurance be at sea and in distress or missing, she shall, provided notice be given to the Underwriters prior to the expiration of this insurance, be held covered until arrival at the next port in good safety, or if in port and in distress until the Vessel is made safe, at a pro rata monthly premium.

3 BREACH OF WARRANTY

Held covered in case of any breach of warranty as to cargo, trade, locality, towage, salvage services or date of sailing provided notice be given to the Underwriters immediately after receipt of advices and any amended terms of cover and any additional premium required by them be agreed.

4 CLASSIFICATION

4.1   It is the duty of the Assured, Owners and Managers at the inception of and throughout the period of this insurance to ensure that

4.1.1   the Vessel is classed with a Classification Society agreed by the Underwriters and that her class within that Society is maintained,

4.1.2   any recommendations requirements or restrictions imposed by the Vessel's Classification Society which relate to the Vessel's seaworthiness or to her maintenance in a seaworthy condition are complied with by the dates required by that Society.

4.2   In the event of any breach of the duties set out in Clause 4.1 above, unless the Underwriters agree to the contrary in writing, they will be discharged from liability under this insurance as from the date of the breach provided that if the Vessel is at sea at such date the Underwriters' discharge from liability is deferred until arrival at her next port.

4.3   Any incident condition or damage in respect of which the Vessel's Classification Society might make recommendations as to repairs or other action to be taken by the Assured, Owners or Managers must be promptly reported to the Classification Society.

4.4   Should the Underwriters wish to approach the Classification Society directly for information and/or documents, the Assured will provide the necessary authorization.

5 TERMINATION

This Clause 5 shall prevail notwithstanding any provision whether written typed or printed in this insurance inconsistent therewith.

Unless the Underwriters agree to the contrary in writing, this insurance shall terminate automatically at the time of

5.1 change of the Classification Society of the Vessel, or change, suspension, discontinuance, withdrawal or expiry of her Class therein, or any of the Classification Society's periodic surveys becoming overdue unless an extension of time for such survey be agreed by the Classification Society, provided that if the Vessel is at sea such automatic termination shall be deferred until arrival at her next port. However where such change, suspension, discontinuance or withdrawal of her Class or where a periodic survey becoming overdue has resulted from loss or damage covered by Clause 6 of this insurance or which would be covered by an insurance of the Vessel subject to current Institute War and Strikes Clauses Hulls – Time such automatic termination shall only operate should the Vessel sail from her next port without the prior approval of the Classification Society or in the case of a periodic survey becoming overdue without the Classification Society having agreed an extension of time for such survey,

5.2 any change, voluntary or otherwise, in the ownership or flag, transfer to new management, or charter on a bareboat basis or requisition for title or use of the Vessel, provided that, if the Vessel has cargo on board and has already sailed from her loading port or is at sea in ballast, such automatic termination shall if required be deferred, whilst the Vessel continues her planned voyage, until arrival at final port of discharge if with cargo or at port of destination if in ballast. However, in the event of requisition for title or use without the prior execution of a written agreement by the Assured, such automatic termination shall occur fifteen days after such requisition whether the Vessel is at sea or in port.

A pro rata daily net return of premium shall be made provided that a total loss of the Vessel, whether by insured perils or otherwise, has not occurred during the period covered by this insurance or any extension thereof.

6 PERILS

6.1 This insurance covers loss of or damage to the subject matter insured caused by

6.1.1 perils of the seas rivers lakes or other navigable waters

6.1.2 fire, explosion

6.1.3 violent theft by persons from outside the Vessel

6.1.4 jettison

6.1.5 piracy

6.1.6 contact with land conveyance, dock or harbour equipment or installation

6.1.7 earthquake volcanic eruption or lightning

6.1.8 accidents in loading discharging or shifting cargo or fuel.

6.2 This insurance covers loss of or damage to the subject matter insured caused by

Institute Time Clauses – Hulls (1995) [ITCH(95)]

    6.2.1   bursting of boilers breakage of shafts or any latent defect in the machinery or hull

    6.2.2   negligence of Master Officers Crew or Pilots

    6.2.3   negligence of repairers or charterers provided such repairers or charterers are not an Assured hereunder

    6.2.4   barratry of Master Officers or Crew

    6.2.5   contact with aircraft, helicopters or similar objects, or objects falling therefrom

    provided that such loss or damage has not resulted from want of due diligence by the Assured, Owners, Managers or Superintendents or any of their onshore management.

  6.3   Masters Officers Crew or Pilots not to be considered Owners within the meaning of this Clause 6 should they hold shares in the Vessel.

7 POLLUTION HAZARD

This insurance covers loss of or damage to the Vessel caused by any governmental authority acting under the powers vested in it to prevent or mitigate a pollution hazard or damage to the environment, or threat thereof, resulting directly from damage to the Vessel for which the Underwriters are liable under this insurance, provided that such act of governmental authority has not resulted from want of due diligence by the Assured, Owners or Managers to prevent or mitigate such hazard or damage, or threat thereof. Master Officers Crew or Pilots not to be considered Owners within the meaning of this Clause 7 should they hold shares in the Vessel.

8 3/4ths COLLISION LIABILITY

  8.1   The Underwriters agree to indemnify the Assured for three-fourths of any sum or sums paid by the Assured to any other person or persons by reason of the Assured becoming legally liable by way of damages for

    8.1.1   loss of or damage to any other vessel or property on any other vessel

    8.1.2   delay to or loss of use of any such other vessel or property thereon

    8.1.3   general average of, salvage of, or salvage under contract of, any such other vessel or property thereon,

    where such payment by the Assured is in consequence of the Vessel hereby insured coming into collision with any other vessel.

  8.2   The indemnity provided by this Clause 8 shall be in addition to the indemnity provided by the other terms and conditions of this insurance and shall be subject to the following provisions:

    8.2.1   where the insured Vessel is in collision with another vessel and both vessels are to blame then, unless the liability of one or both vessels becomes limited by law, the indemnity under this Clause 8 shall be calculated on the principle of cross-liabilities as if the respective Owners had been compelled to pay to each other such proportion of each other's damages as may have been properly allowed in ascertaining the balance or sum payable by or to the Assured in consequence of the collision,

8.2.2 in no case shall the Underwriters' total liability under Clauses 8.1 and 8.2 exceed their proportionate part of three-fourths of the insured value of the Vessel hereby insured in respect of any one collision.

8.3 The Underwriters will also pay three-fourths of the legal costs incurred by the Assured or which the Assured may be compelled to pay in contesting liability or taking proceedings to limit liability, with the prior written consent of the Underwriters.

EXCLUSIONS

8.4 Provided always that this Clause 8 shall in no case extend to any sum which the Assured shall pay for or in respect of

8.4.1 removal or disposal of obstructions, wrecks, cargoes or any other thing whatsoever

8.4.2 any real or personal property or thing whatsoever except other vessels or property on other vessels

8.4.3 the cargo or other property on, or the engagements of, the insured Vessel

8.4.4 loss of life, personal injury or illness

8.4.5 pollution or contamination, or threat thereof, of any real or personal property or thing whatsoever (except other vessels with which the insured Vessel is in collision or property on such other vessels) or damage to the environment, or threat thereof, save that this exclusion shall not extend to any sum which the Assured shall pay for or in respect of salvage remuneration in which the skill and efforts of the salvors in preventing or minimising damage to the environment as is referred to in Article 13 paragraph 1(b) of the International Convention on Salvage, 1989 have been taken into account.

9 SISTERSHIP

Should the Vessel hereby insured come into collision with or receive salvage services from another vessel belonging wholly or in part to the same Owners or under the same management, the Assured shall have the same rights under this insurance as they would have were the other vessel entirely the property of Owners not interested in the Vessel hereby insured: but in such cases the liability for the collision or the amount payable for the services rendered shall be referred to a sole arbitrator to be agreed upon between the Underwriters and the Assured.

10 GENERAL AVERAGE AND SALVAGE

10.1 This insurance covers the Vessel's proportion of salvage, salvage charges and/or general average, reduced in respect of any underinsurance. but in case of general average sacrifice of the Vessel the Assured may recover in respect of the whole loss without first enforcing their right of contribution from other parties.

10.2 Adjustment to be according to the law and practice obtaining at the place where the adventure ends, as if the contract of affreightment contained no special terms upon the subject; but where the contract of affreightment so provides the adjustment shall be according to the York-Antwerp Rules.

10.3 When the Vessel sails in ballast, not under charter, the provisions of the York-Antwerp Rules 1994 (excluding Rules XI(d), XX and XXI) shall be applicable, and the voyage for this purpose shall be deemed to continue from the port or place of departure until the arrival of the Vessel at the first port or place thereafter other than a port or place of refuge or a port or place of call for bunkering only. If at any such intermediate port or place there is an abandonment of the adventure originally contemplated the voyage shall thereupon be deemed to be terminated.

10.4 No claim under this Clause 10 shall in any case be allowed where the loss was not incurred to avoid or in connection with the avoidance of a peril insured against.

10.5 No claim under this Clause 10 shall in any case be allowed for or in respect of

10.5.1 special compensation payable to a salvor under Article 14 of the International Convention on Salvage, 1989 or under any other provision in any statute, rule, law or contract which is similar in substance

10.5.2 expenses or liabilities incurred in respect of damage to the environment, or the threat of such damage, or as a consequence of the escape or release of pollutant substances from the Vessel, or the threat of such escape or release.

10.6 Clause 10.5 shall not however exclude any sum which the Assured shall pay to salvors for or in respect of salvage remuneration in which the skill and efforts of the salvors in preventing or minimising damage to the environment as is referred to in Article 13 paragraph 1(b) of the International Convention on Salvage, 1989 have been taken into account.

11 DUTY OF ASSURED (SUE AND LABOUR)

11.1 In case of any loss or misfortune it is the duty of the Assured and their servants and agents to take such measures as may be reasonable for the purpose of averting or minimising a loss which would be recoverable under this insurance.

11.2 Subject to the provisions below and to Clause 12 the Underwriters will contribute to charges properly and reasonably incurred by the Assured their servants or agents for such measures. General average, salvage charges (except as provided for in Clause 11.5), special compensation and expenses as referred to in Clause 10.5 and collision defence or attack costs are not recoverable under this Clause 11.

11.3 Measures taken by the Assured or the Underwriters with the object of saving, protecting or recovering the subject matter insured shall not be considered as a waiver or acceptance of abandonment or otherwise prejudice the rights of either party.

11.4 When expenses are incurred pursuant to this Clause 11 the liability under this insurance shall not exceed the proportion of such expenses that the amount insured hereunder bears to the value of the Vessel as stated herein or to the sound value of the Vessel at the time of the occurrence giving rise to the expenditure if the sound value exceeds that value. Where the Underwriters have admitted a claim for total loss and property insured by this insurance is saved, the foregoing provisions shall not apply unless the expenses of suing and labouring exceed the value of such property saved and then shall apply only to the amount of the expenses which is in excess of such value.

11.5 When a claim for total loss of the Vessel is admitted under this insurance and expenses have been reasonably incurred in saving or attempting to save the Vessel and other property and there are no proceeds, or the expenses exceed the proceeds, then this insurance shall bear its pro rata share of such proportion of the expenses, or of the expenses in excess of the proceeds, as the case may be, as may reasonably be regarded as having been incurred in respect of the Vessel, excluding all special compensation and expenses as referred to in Clause 10.5; but if the Vessel be insured for less than its sound value at the time of the occurrence giving rise to the expenditure, the amount recoverable under this clause shall be reduced in proportion to the under-insurance.

11.6 The sum recoverable under this Clause 11 shall be in addition to the loss otherwise recoverable under this insurance but shall in no circumstances exceed the amount insured under this insurance in respect of the Vessel.

12 DEDUCTIBLE

12.1 No claim arising from a peril insured against shall be payable under this insurance unless the aggregate of all such claims arising out of each separate accident or occurrence (including claims under Clauses 8, 10 and 11) exceeds the deductible amount agreed in which case this sum shall be deducted. Nevertheless the expense of sighting the bottom after stranding, if reasonably incurred specially for that purpose, shall be paid even if no damage be found. This Clause 12.1 shall not apply to a claim for total or constructive total loss of the Vessel or, in the event of such a claim, to any associated claim under Clause 11 arising from the same accident or occurrence.

12.2 Claims for damage by heavy weather occurring during a single sea passage between two successive ports shall be treated as being due to one accident. In the case of such heavy weather extending over a period not wholly covered by this insurance the deductible to be applied to the claim recoverable hereunder shall be the proportion of the above deductible that the number of days of such heavy weather falling within the period of this insurance bears to the number of days of heavy weather during the single sea passage. The expression 'heavy weather' in this Clause 12.2 shall be deemed to include contact with floating ice.

12.3 Excluding any interest comprised therein. recoveries against any claim which is subject to the above deductible shall be credited to the Underwriters in full to the extent of the sum by which the aggregate of the claim unreduced by any recoveries exceeds the above deductible.

12.4 Interest comprised in recoveries shall be apportioned between the Assured and the Underwriters, taking into account the sums paid by the Underwriters and the dates when such payments were made, notwithstanding that by the addition of interest the Underwriters may receive a larger sum than they have paid.

13 NOTICE OF CLAIM AND TENDERS

13.1 In the event of accident whereby loss or damage may result in a claim under this insurance, notice must be given to the Underwriters promptly after the date on which the Assured, Owners or Managers become or should have become aware of the loss or damage and prior to survey so that a surveyor may be appointed if the Underwriters so desire. If notice is not given to the Underwriters within twelve months of that date unless the Underwriters agree to the contrary in writing, the Underwriters will be automatically discharged from liability for any claim under this insurance in respect of or arising out of such accident or the loss or damage.

13.2 The Underwriters shall be entitled to decide the port to which the Vessel shall proceed for docking or repair (the actual additional expense of the voyage arising from compliance with the Underwriters' requirements being refunded to the Assured) and shall have a right of veto concerning a place of repair or a repairing firm.

13.3 The Underwriters may also take tenders or may require further tenders to be taken for the repair of the Vessel, Where such a tender has been taken and a tender is accepted with the approval of the Underwriters, an allowance shall be made at the rate of 30% per annum on the insured value for time lost between the despatch of the invitations to tender required by the Underwriters and the acceptance of a tender to the extent that such time is lost solely as the result of tenders having been taken and provided that the tender is accepted without delay after receipt of the Underwriters' approval. Due credit shall be given against the allowance as above for any amounts recovered in respect of fuel and stores and wages and maintenance of the Master Officers and Crew or any member thereof, including amounts allowed in general average, and for any amounts recovered from third parties in respect of damages for detention and/or loss of profit and/or running expenses, for the period covered by the tender allowance or any part thereof. Where a part of the cost of the repair of damage other than a fixed deductible is not recoverable from the Underwriters the allowance shall be reduced by a similar proportion.

13.4 In the event of failure by the Assured to comply with the conditions of Clauses 13.2 and/or 13.3 a deduction of 15% shall be made from the amount of the ascertained claim.

14 NEW FOR OLD

Claims payable without deduction new for old.

15 BOTTOM TREATMENT

In no case shall a claim be allowed in respect of scraping gritblasting and/or other surface preparation or painting of the Vessel's bottom except that

15.1 gritblasting and/or other surface preparation of new bottom plates ashore and supplying and applying any 'shop' primer thereto,

15.2 gritblasting and/or other surface preparation of: the butts or area of plating immediately adjacent to any renewed or refitted plating damaged during the course of welding and/or repairs, areas of plating damaged during the course of fairing, either in place or ashore,

15.3 supplying and applying the first coat of primer/anti-corrosive to those particular areas mentioned in 15.1 and 15.2 above,

shall be allowed as part of the reasonable cost of repairs in respect of bottom plating damaged by an insured peril.

16 WAGES AND MAINTENANCE

No claim shall be allowed, other than in general average, for wages and maintenance of the Master Officers and Crew or any member thereof, except when incurred solely for the necessary removal of the Vessel from one port to another for the repair of damage covered by the Underwriters, or for trial trips for such repairs, and then only for such wages and maintenance as are incurred whilst the Vessel is under way.

17 AGENCY COMMISSION

In no case shall any sum be allowed under this insurance either by way of remuneration of the Assured for time and trouble taken to obtain and supply information or documents or in respect of the commission or charges of any manager, agent, managing or agency company or the like, appointed by or on behalf of the Assured to perform such services.

18 UNREPAIRED DAMAGE

18.1 The measure of indemnity in respect of claims for unrepaired damage shall be the reasonable depreciation in the market value of the Vessel at the time this insurance terminates arising from such unrepaired damage, but not exceeding the reasonable cost of repairs.

18.2 In no case shall the Underwriters be liable for unrepaired damage in the event of a subsequent total loss (whether or not covered under this insurance) sustained during the period covered by this insurance or any extension thereof.

Institute Time Clauses – Hulls (1995) [ITCH(95)]

    18.3   The Underwriters shall not be liable in respect of unrepaired damage for more than the insured value at the time this insurance terminates.

19 CONSTRUCTIVE TOTAL LOSS

    19.1   In ascertaining whether the Vessel is a constructive total loss, the insured value shall be taken as the repaired value and nothing in respect of the damaged or break-up value of the Vessel or wreck shall be taken into account.

    19.2   No claim for constructive total loss based upon the cost of recovery and/or repair of the Vessel shall be recoverable hereunder unless such cost would exceed the insured value. In making this determination, only the cost relating to a single accident or sequence of damages arising from the same accident shall be taken into account.

20 FREIGHT WAIVER

In the event of total or constructive total loss no claim to be made by the Underwriters for freight whether notice of abandonment has been given or not.

21 ASSIGNMENT

No assignment of or interest in this insurance or in any moneys which may be or become payable thereunder is to be binding on or recognised by the Underwriters unless a dated notice of such assignment or interest signed by the Assured, and by the assignor in the case of subsequent assignment, is endorsed on the Policy and the Policy with such endorsement is produced before payment of any claim or return of premium thereunder.

22 DISBURSEMENTS WARRANTY

    22.1   Additional insurances as follows are permitted:

    22.1.1 *Disbursements, Managers' Commissions, Profits or Excess or Increased Value of Hull and Machinery.* A sum not exceeding 25% of the value stated herein.

    22.1.2 *Freight, Chartered Freight or Anticipated Freight, insured for time.* A sum not exceeding 25% of the value as stated herein less any sum insured, however described, under 22.1.1.

    22.1.3 *Freight or Hire, under contracts for voyage.* A sum not exceeding the gross freight or hire for the current cargo passage and next succeeding cargo passage (such insurance to include, if required, a preliminary and an intermediate ballast passage) plus the charges of insurance. In the case of a voyage charter where payment is made on a time basis, the sum permitted for insurance shall be calculated on the estimated duration of the voyage, subject to the limitation of two cargo passages as laid down herein. Any sum insured under 22.1.2 to be taken into account and only the excess thereof may be insured, which excess shall be reduced as the freight or hire is advanced or earned by the gross amount so advanced or earned.

22.1.4 *Anticipated Freight if the Vessel sails in ballast and not under Charter.* A sum not exceeding the anticipated gross freight on next cargo passage, such sum to be reasonably estimated on the basis of the current rate of freight at time of insurance plus the charges of insurance. Any sum insured under 22.1.2 to be taken into account and only the excess thereof may be insured.

22.1.5 *Time Charter Hire or Charter Hire for Series of Voyages.* A sum not exceeding 50% of the gross hire which is to be earned under the charter in a period not exceeding 18 months. Any sum insured under 22.1.2 to be taken into account and only the excess thereof may be insured, which excess shall be reduced as the hire is advanced or earned under the charter by 50% of the gross amount so advanced or earned but the sum insured need not be reduced while the total of the sums insured under 22.1.2 and 22.1.5 does not exceed 50% of the gross hire still to be earned under the charter. An insurance under this Section may begin on the signing of the charter.

22.1.6 *Premiums.* A sum not exceeding the actual premiums of all interests insured for a period not exceeding 12 months (excluding premiums insured under the foregoing sections but including, if required, the premium or estimated calls on any Club or War etc. Risk insurance) reducing pro rata monthly.

22.1.7 *Returns of Premium.* A sum not exceeding the actual returns which arc allowable under any insurance but which would not be recoverable thereunder in the event of a total loss of the Vessel whether by insured perils or otherwise.

22.1.8 *Insurance irrespective of amount against:* Any risks excluded by Clauses 24, 25, 26 and 27 below.

22.2 Warranted that no insurance on any interests enumerated in the foregoing 22.1.1 to 22.1.7 in excess of the amounts permitted therein and no other insurance which includes total loss of the Vessel P.P.I., F.I.A. or subject to any other like term, is or shall be effected to operate during the currency of this insurance by or for account of the Assured, Owners, Managers or Mortgagees. Provided always that a breach of this warranty shall not afford the Underwriters any defence to a claim by a Mortgagee who has accepted this insurance without knowledge of such breach.

23 RETURNS FOR LAY-UP AND CANCELLATION

23.1 To return as follows:

23.1.1 pro rata monthly net for each uncommenced month if this insurance be cancelled by agreement,

23.1.2 for each period of 30 consecutive days the Vessel may be laid up in a port or in a lay-up area provided such port or lay-up area is approved by the Underwriters

(a) .... per cent net not under repair

(b) .... per cent net under repair.

Institute Time Clauses – Hulls (1995) [ITCH(95)]

23.1.3 The Vessel shall not be considered to be under repair when work is undertaken in respect of ordinary wear and tear of the Vessel and/or following recommendations in the Vessel's Classification Society survey, but any repairs following loss of or damage to the Vessel or involving structural alterations, whether covered by this insurance or otherwise shall be considered as under repair.

23.1.4 If the Vessel is under repair during part only of a period for which a return is claimable, the return shall be calculated pro rata to the number of days under 23.1.2 (a) and (b) respectively.

23.2 PROVIDED ALWAYS THAT

23.2.1 a total loss of the Vessel, whether by insured perils or otherwise, has not occurred during the period covered by this insurance or any extension thereof

23.2.2 in no case shall a return be allowed when the Vessel is lying in exposed or unprotected waters, or in a port or lay-up area not approved by the Underwriters

23.2.3 loading or discharging operations or the presence of cargo on board shall not debar returns but no return shall be allowed for any period during which the Vessel is being used for the storage of cargo or for lightering purposes

23.2.4 in the event of any amendment of the annual rate, the above rates of return shall be adjusted accordingly

23.2.5 in the event of any return recoverable under this Clause 23 being based on 30 consecutive days which fall on successive insurances effected for the same Assured, this insurance shall only be liable for an amount calculated at pro rata of the period rates 23.1.2(a) and/or (b) above for the number of days which come within the period of this insurance and to which a return is actually applicable. Such overlapping period shall run, at the option of the Assured, either from the first day on which the Vessel is laid up or the first day of a period of 30 consecutive days as provided under 23.1.2(a) or (b) above.

The following clauses shall be paramount and shall override anything contained in this insurance inconsistent therewith.

24 WAR EXCLUSION

In no case shall this insurance cover loss damage liability or expense caused by

24.1 war civil war revolution rebellion insurrection, or civil strife arising therefrom, or any hostile act by or against a belligerent power

24.2 capture seizure arrest restraint or detainment (barratry and piracy excepted), and the consequences thereof or any attempt thereat

24.3 derelict mines torpedoes bombs or other derelict weapons of war.

25 STRIKES EXCLUSION

In no case shall this insurance cover loss damage liability or expense caused by

25.1   strikers, locked-out workmen, or persons taking part in labour disturbances, riots or civil commotions

25.2   any terrorist or any person acting from a political motive.

26 MALICIOUS ACTS EXCLUSION

In no case shall this insurance cover loss damage liability or expense arising from

26.1   the detonation of an explosive

26.2   any weapon of war

and caused by any person acting maliciously or from a political motive.

27 RADIOACTIVE CONTAMINATION EXCLUSION CLAUSE

In no case shall this insurance cover loss damage liability or expense directly or indirectly caused by or contributed to by or arising from

27.1   ionising radiations from or contamination by radioactivity from any nuclear fuel or from any nuclear waste or from the combustion of nuclear fuel

27.2   the radioactive, toxic, explosive or other hazardous or contaminating properties of any nuclear installation, reactor or other nuclear assembly or nuclear component thereof

27.3   any weapon of war employing atomic or nuclear fission and/or fusion or other like reaction or radioactive force or matter.

APPENDIX 7

1/11/95

(FOR USE ONLY WITH THE CURRENT MAR POLICY FORM)

INSTITUTE VOYAGE CLAUSES
HULLS

This insurance is subject to English law and practice

1 NAVIGATION

1.1 The Vessel is covered subject to the provisions of this insurance at all times and has leave to sail or navigate with or without pilots, to go on trial trips and to assist and tow vessels or craft in distress, but it is warranted that the Vessel shall not be towed, except as is customary or to the first safe port or place when in need of assistance, or undertake towage or salvage services under a contract previously arranged by the Assured and/or Owners and/or Managers and/or Charterers. This Clause 1.1 shall not exclude customary towage in connection with loading and discharging.

1.2 This insurance shall not be prejudiced by reason of the Assured entering into any contract with pilots or for customary towage which limits or exempts the liability of the pilots and/or tugs and/or towboats and/or their owners when the Assured or their agents accept or are compelled to accept such contracts in accordance with established local law or practice.

1.3 The practice of engaging helicopters for the transportation of personnel, supplies and equipment to and/or from the Vessel shall not prejudice this insurance.

1.4 In the event of the Vessel being employed in trading operations which entail cargo loading or discharging at sea from or into another vessel (not being a harbour or inshore craft) no claim shall be recoverable under this insurance for loss of or damage to the Vessel or liability to any other vessel arising from such loading or discharging operations, including whilst approaching, lying alongside and leaving, unless previous notice that the Vessel is to be employed in such operations has been given to the Underwriters and any amended terms of cover and any additional premium required by them have been agreed.

2 CHANGE OF VOYAGE

Held covered in case of deviation or change of voyage or any breach of warranty as to towage or salvage services, provided notice be given to the

Underwriters immediately after receipt of advices and any amended terms of cover and any additional premium required by them be agreed.

3 CLASSIFICATION

3.1 It is the duty of the Assured, Owners and Managers at the inception of and throughout the period of this insurance to ensure that

3.1.1 the Vessel is classed with a Classification Society agreed by the Underwriters and that her class within that Society is maintained,

3.1.2 any recommendations requirements or restrictions imposed by the Vessel's Classification Society which relate to the Vessel's seaworthiness or to her maintenance in a seaworthy condition are complied with by the dates required by that Society.

3.2 In the event of any breach of the duties set out in Clause 3.1 above, unless the Underwriters agree to the contrary in writing, they will be discharged from liability under this insurance as from the date of the breach provided that if the Vessel is at sea at such date the Underwriters' discharge from liability is deferred until arrival at her next port.

3.3 Any incident condition or damage in respect of which the Vessel's Classification Society might make recommendations as to repairs or other action to be taken by the Assured, Owners and Managers must be promptly reported to the Classification Society.

3.4 Should the Underwriters wish to approach the Classification Society directly for information and/or documents, the Assured will provide the necessary authorization.

4 PERILS

4.1 This insurance covers loss of or damage to the subject-matter insured caused by

4.1.1 perils of the seas rivers lakes or other navigable waters

4.1.2 fire, explosion

4.1.3 violent theft by persons from outside the Vessel

4.1.4 jettison

4.1.5 piracy

4.1.6 contact with land conveyance, dock or harbour equipment or installation

4.1.7 earthquake volcanic eruption or lightning

4.1.8 accidents in loading discharging or shifting cargo or fuel.

4.2 This insurance covers loss of or damage to the subject-matter insured caused by

4.2.1 bursting of boilers breakage of shafts or any latent defect in the machinery or hull

4.2.2 negligence of Master Officers Crew or Pilots

Institute Voyage Clauses Hulls (1995) [IVCH(95)]

- 4.2.3 negligence of repairers or charterers provided such repairers or charterers are not an Assured hereunder
- 4.2.4 barratry of Master Officers or Crew
- 4.2.5 contact with aircraft, helicopters or similar objects, or objects falling therefrom

  provided such loss or damage has not resulted from want of due diligence by the Assured, Owners, Managers or Superintendents or any of their onshore management.

- 4.3 Master Officers Crew or Pilots not to be considered Owners within the meaning of this Clause 4 should they hold shares in the Vessel.

5 POLLUTION HAZARD

This insurance covers loss of or damage to the Vessel caused by any governmental authority acting under the powers vested in it to prevent or mitigate a pollution hazard or damage to the environment, or threat thereof, resulting directly from damage to the Vessel for which the Underwriters are liable under this insurance, provided that such act of governmental authority has not resulted from want of due diligence by the Assured, Owners or Managers to prevent or mitigate such hazard or damage, or threat thereof. Master Officers Crew or Pilots not to be considered Owners within the meaning of this Clause 5 should they hold shares in the Vessel.

6 3/4ths COLLISION LIABILITY

- 6.1 The Underwriters agree to indemnify the Assured for three-fourths of any sum or sums paid by the Assured to any other person or persons by reason of the Assured becoming legally liable by way of damages for
- 6.1.1 loss of or damage to any other vessel or property on any other vessel
- 6.1.2 delay to or loss of use of any such other vessel or property thereon
- 6.1.3 general average of, salvage of, or salvage under contract of, any such other vessel or property thereon, where such payment by the Assured is in consequence of the Vessel hereby insured coming into collision with any other vessel.
- 6.2 The indemnity provided by this Clause 6 shall be in addition to the indemnity provided by the other terms and conditions of this insurance and shall be subject to the following provisions:
- 6.2.1 where the insured Vessel is in collision with another vessel and both vessels are to blame then, unless the liability of one or both vessels becomes limited by law, the indemnity under this Clause 6 shall be calculated on the principle of cross-liabilities as if the respective Owners had been compelled to pay to each other such proportion of each other's damages as may have been properly allowed in ascertaining the balance or sum payable by or to the Assured in consequence of the collision,
- 6.2.2 in no case shall the Underwriters' total liability under Clauses 6.1 and 6.2 exceed their proportionate part of three-fourths of the insured value of the Vessel hereby insured in respect of any one collision.

6.3 The Underwriters will also pay three-fourths of the legal costs incurred by the Assured or which the Assured may be compelled to pay in contesting liability or taking proceedings to limit liability, with the prior written consent of the Underwriters.

EXCLUSIONS

6.4 Provided always that this Clause 6 shall in no case extend to any sum which the Assured shall pay for or in respect of

6.4.1 removal or disposal of obstructions, wrecks, cargoes or any other thing whatsoever

6.4.2 any real or personal property or thing whatsoever except other vessels or property on other vessels

6.4.3 the cargo or other property on, or the engagements of, the insured Vessel

6.4.4 loss of life, personal injury or illness

6.4.5 pollution or contamination, or threat thereof, of any real or personal property or thing whatsoever (except other vessels with which the insured Vessel is in collision or property on such other vessels) or damage to the environment, or threat thereof, save that this exclusion shall not extend to any sum which the Assured shall pay for or in respect of salvage remuneration in which the skill and efforts of the salvors in preventing or minimising damage to the environment as is referred to in Article 13 paragraph 1(b) of the International Convention on Salvage 1989 have been taken into account.

7 SISTERSHIP

Should the Vessel hereby insured come into collision with or receive salvage services from another vessel belonging wholly or in part to the same Owners or under the same management, the Assured shall have the same rights under this insurance as they would have were the other vessel entirely the property of Owners not interested in the Vessel hereby insured, but in such cases the liability for the collision or the amount payable for the services rendered shall be referred to a sole arbitrator to be agreed upon between the Underwriters and the Assured.

8 GENERAL AVERAGE AND SALVAGE

8.1 This insurance covers the Vessel's proportion of salvage, salvage charges and/or general average, reduced in respect of any under-insurance, but in case of general average sacrifice of the Vessel the Assured may recover in respect of the whole loss without first enforcing their right of contribution from other parties.

8.2 Adjustment to be according to the law and practice obtaining at the place where the adventure ends, as if the contract of affreightment contained no special terms upon the subject; but where the contract of affreightment so provides the adjustment shall be according to the York-Antwerp Rules.

Institute Voyage Clauses Hulls (1995) [IVCH(95)]

8.3 When the Vessel sails in ballast, not under charter the provisions of the York-Antwerp Rules 1994 (excluding Rules XI(d), XX and XXI) shall be applicable, and the voyage for this purpose shall be deemed to continue from the port or place of departure until the arrival of the Vessel at the first port or place thereafter other than a port or place of refuge or a port or place of call for bunkering only. If at any such intermediate port or place there is an abandonment of the adventure originally contemplated the voyage shall thereupon be deemed to be terminated.

8.4 No claim under this Clause 8 shall in any case be allowed where the loss was not incurred to avoid or in connection with the avoidance of a peril insured against.

8.5 No claim under this Clause 8 shall in any case be allowed for or in respect of

8.5.1 special compensation payable to a salvor under Article 14 of the International Convention on Salvage, 1989 or under any other provision in any statute, rule, law or contract which is similar in substance

8.5.2 expenses or liabilities incurred in respect of damage to the environment, or the threat of such damage, or as a consequence of the escape or release of pollutant substances from the Vessel, or the threat of such escape or release.

8.6 Clause 8.5 shall not however exclude any sum which the Assured shall pay to salvors for or in respect of salvage remuneration in which the skill and efforts of the salvors in preventing or minimising damage to the environment as is referred to in Article 13 paragraph 1(b) of the International Convention on Salvage, 1989 have been taken into account.

9 DUTY OF ASSURED (SUE AND LABOUR)

9.1 In case of any loss or misfortune it is the duty of the Assured and their servants and agents to take such measures as may be reasonable for the purpose of averting or minimising a loss which would be recoverable under this insurance.

9.2 Subject to the provisions below and to Clause 10 the Underwriters will contribute to charges properly and reasonably incurred by the Assured their servants or agents for such measures. General average, salvage charges (except as provided for in Clause 9.5), special compensation and expenses as referred to in Clause 8.5, and collision defence or attack costs are not recoverable under this Clause 9.

9.3 Measures taken by the Assured or the Underwriters with the object of saving, protecting or recovering the subject-matter insured shall not be considered as a waiver or acceptance of abandonment or otherwise prejudice the rights of either party.

9.4 When expenses are incurred pursuant to this Clause 9 the liability under this insurance shall not exceed the proportion of such expenses that the amount insured hereunder bears to the value of the Vessel as stated herein, or to the sound value of the Vessel at the time of the occurrence giving rise to the expenditure if the sound value exceeds that value. Where the Underwriters have admitted a claim for total loss and property insured by this insurance is saved, the foregoing provisions shall not apply unless the expenses of suing and labouring exceed the value of such property saved and then shall apply only to the amount of the expenses which is in excess of such value.

9.5 When a claim for total loss of the Vessel is admitted under this insurance and expenses have been reasonably incurred in saving or attempting to save the Vessel and other property and there are no proceeds, or the expenses exceed the proceeds, then this insurance shall bear its pro rata share of such proportion of the expenses, or of the expenses in excess of the proceeds, as the case may be, as may reasonably be regarded as having been incurred in respect of the Vessel, excluding all special compensation and expenses as referred to in Clause 8.5; but if the Vessel be insured for less than its sound value at the time of the occurrence giving rise to the expenditure, the amount recoverable under this clause shall be reduced in proportion to the under-insurance.

9.6 The sum recoverable under this Clause 9 shall be in addition to the loss otherwise recoverable under this insurance but shall in no circumstances exceed the amount insured under this insurance in respect of the Vessel.

10 DEDUCTIBLE

10.1 No claim arising from a peril insured against shall be payable under this insurance unless the aggregate of all such claims arising out of each separate accident or occurrence (including claims under Clauses 6, 8 and 9) exceeds the deductible amount agreed in which case this sum shall be deducted. Nevertheless the expense of sighting the bottom after stranding, if reasonably incurred specially for that purpose shall be paid even if no damage be found. This Clause 10.1 shall not apply to a claim for total or constructive total loss of the Vessel or, in the event of such a claim, to any associated claim under Clause 9 arising from the same accident or occurrence.

10.2 Claims for damage by heavy weather occurring during a single sea passage between two successive ports shall be treated as being due to one accident. In the case of such heavy weather extending over a period not wholly covered by this insurance the deductible to be applied to the claim recoverable hereunder shall be the proportion of the above deductible that the number of days of such heavy weather falling within the period of this insurance bears to the number of days of heavy weather during the single sea passage. The expression 'heavy weather' in this Clause 10.2 shall be deemed to include contact with floating ice.

10.3 Excluding any interest comprised therein, recoveries against any claim which is subject to the above deductible shall be credited to the Underwriters in full to the extent of the sum by which the aggregate of the claim unreduced by any recoveries exceeds the above deductible.

10.4 Interest comprised in recoveries shall be apportioned between the Assured and the Underwriters, taking into account the sums paid by the Underwriters and the dates when such payments were made, notwithstanding that by the addition of interest the Underwriters may receive a larger sum than they have paid.

11 NOTICE OF CLAIM AND TENDERS

11.1 In the event of accident whereby loss or damage may result in a claim under this insurance, notice must be given to the Underwriters promptly after the date on which the Assured, Owners or Managers become or should have become aware of the loss or damage and prior to survey and so that a surveyor may be appointed if the Underwriters so desire.

If notice is not given to the Underwriters within twelve months of that date, unless the Underwriters agree to the contrary in writing, the Underwriters will be automatically discharged from liability for any claim under this insurance in respect of or arising out of such accident or the loss or damage.

11.2 The Underwriters shall be entitled to decide the port to which the Vessel shall proceed for docking or repair (the actual additional expense of the voyage arising from compliance with the Underwriters' requirements being refunded to the Assured) and shall have a right of veto concerning a place of repair or a repairing firm.

11.3 The Underwriters may also take tenders or may require further tenders to be taken for the repair of the Vessel. Where such a tender has been taken and a tender is accepted with the approval of the Underwriters, an allowance shall be made at the rate of 30% per annum on the insured value for time lost between the despatch of the invitations to tender required by the Underwriters and the acceptance of a tender to the extent that such time is lost solely as the result of tenders having been taken and provided that the tender is accepted without delay after receipt of the Underwriters' approval.

Due credit shall be given against the allowance as above for any amounts recovered in respect of fuel and stores and wages and maintenance of the Master Officers and Crew or any member thereof, including amounts allowed in general average, and for any amounts recovered from third parties in respect of damages for detention and/or loss of profit and/or running expenses, for the period covered by the tender allowance or any part thereof.

Where a part of the cost of the repair of damage other than a fixed deductible is not recoverable from the Underwriters the allowance shall be reduced by a similar proportion.

11.4 In the event of failure by the Assured to comply with the conditions of Clauses 11.2 and/or 11.3 a deduction of 15% shall be made from the amount of the ascertained claim.

12 NEW FOR OLD

Claims payable without deduction new for old.

13 BOTTOM TREATMENT

In no case shall a claim be allowed in respect of scraping gritblasting and/or other surface preparation or painting of the Vessel's bottom except that

13.1 gritblasting and/or other surface preparation of new bottom plates ashore and supplying and applying any 'shop' primer thereto,

13.2 gritblasting and/or other surface preparation of:

the butts or area of plating immediately adjacent to any renewed or refitted plating damaged during the course of welding and/or repairs,

areas of plating damaged during the course of fairing, either in place or ashore,

13.3 supplying and applying the first coat of primer/anti-corrosive to those particular areas mentioned in 13.1 and 13.2 above,

shall be allowed as part of the reasonable cost of repairs in respect of bottom plating damaged by an insured peril.

14 WAGES AND MAINTENANCE

No claim shall be allowed, other than in general average, for wages and maintenance of the Master Officers and Crew or any member thereof, except when incurred solely for the necessary removal of the Vessel from one port to another for the repair of damage covered by the Underwriters, or for trial trips for such repairs, and then only for such wages and maintenance as are incurred whilst the Vessel is under way.

15 AGENCY COMMISSION

In no case shall any sum be allowed under this insurance either by way of remuneration of the Assured for time and trouble taken to obtain and supply information or documents or in respect of the commission or charges of any manager, agent, managing or agency company or the like, appointed by or on behalf of the Assured to perform such services.

16 UNREPAIRED DAMAGE

16.1 The measure of indemnity in respect of claims for unrepaired damage shall be the reasonable depreciation in the market value of the Vessel at the time this insurance terminates arising from such unrepaired damage, but not exceeding the reasonable cost of repairs.

16.2 In no case shall the Underwriters be liable for unrepaired damage in the event of a subsequent total loss (whether or not covered under this insurance) sustained during the period covered by this insurance or any extension thereof.

16.3 The Underwriters shall not be liable in respect of unrepaired damage for more than the insured value at the time this insurance terminates.

17 CONSTRUCTIVE TOTAL LOSS

17.1 In ascertaining whether the Vessel is a constructive total loss, the insured value shall be taken as the repaired value and nothing in respect of the damaged or break-up value of the Vessel or wreck shall be taken into account.

17.2 No claim for constructive total loss based upon the cost of recovery and/or repair of the Vessel shall be recoverable hereunder unless such cost would exceed the insured value. In making this determination only the cost relating to a single accident or sequence of damages arising from the same accident shall be taken into account.

18 FREIGHT WAIVER

In the event of total or constructive total loss no claim to be made by the Underwriters for freight whether notice of abandonment has been given or not.

19 ASSIGNMENT

No assignment of or interest in this insurance or in any moneys which may be or become payable thereunder is to be binding on or recognised by the Underwriters unless a dated notice of such assignment or interest signed by the Assured, and by the assignor in the case of subsequent assignment, is endorsed on the Policy and the Policy with such endorsement is produced before payment of any claim or return of premium thereunder.

20 DISBURSEMENTS WARRANTY

20.1 Additional insurances as follows are permitted:

20.1.1 *Disbursements, Managers' Commissions, Profits or Excess or Increased Value of Hull and Machinery.* A sum not exceeding 25% of the value stated herein.

20.1.2 *Freight, Chartered Freight or Anticipated Freight, insured for time.* A sum not exceeding 25% of the value as stated herein less any sum insured, however described, under 20.1.1.

20.1.3 *Freight or Hire, under contracts for voyage.* A sum not exceeding the gross freight or hire for the current cargo passage and next succeeding cargo passage (such insurance to include, if required, preliminary and an intermediate ballast passage) plus the charges of insurance. In the case of a voyage charter where payment is made on a time basis, the sum permitted for insurance shall be calculated on the estimated duration of the voyage, subject to the limitation of two cargo passages as laid down herein. Any sum insured under 20.1.2 to be taken into account and only the excess thereof may be insured, which excess shall be reduced as the freight or hire is advanced or earned by the gross amount so advanced or earned.

20.1.4 *Anticipated Freight if the Vessel sails in ballast and not under Charter.* A sum not exceeding the anticipated gross freight on next cargo passage, such sum to be reasonably estimated on the basis of the current rate of freight at time of insurance plus the charges of insurance. Any sum insured under 20.1.2 to be taken into account and only the excess thereof may be insured.

20.1.5 *Time Charter Hire or Charter Hire for Series of Voyages.* A sum not exceeding 50% of the gross hire which is to be earned under the charter in a period not exceeding 18 months. Any sum insured under 20.1.2 to be taken into account and only the excess thereof may be insured, which excess shall be reduced as the hire is advanced or earned under the charter by 50% of the gross amount so advanced or earned but the sum insured need not be reduced while the total of the sums insured under 20.1.2 and 20.1.5 does not exceed 50% of the gross hire still to be earned under the charter. An insurance under this Section may begin on the signing of the charter.

20.1.6 *Premiums.* A sum not exceeding the actual premiums of all interests insured for a period not exceeding 12 months (excluding premiums insured under the foregoing sections but including, if required, the premium or estimated calls on any Club or War etc. Risk insurance) reducing pro rata monthly.

20.1.7 *Returns of Premium.* A sum not exceeding the actual returns which are allowable under any insurance but which would not be recoverable thereunder in the event of a total loss of the Vessel whether by insured perils or otherwise.

20.1.8 *Insurance irrespective of amount against*: Any risks excluded by Clauses 21, 22, 23 and 24 below.

20.2 Warranted that no insurance on any interests enumerated in the foregoing 20.1.1 to 20.1.7 in excess of the amounts permitted therein and no other insurance which includes total loss of the Vessel P.P.I., F.I.A., or subject to any other like term, is or shall be effected to operate during the currency of this insurance by or for account of the Assured, Owners, Managers or Mortgagees. Provided always that a breach of this warranty shall not afford the Underwriters any defence to a claim by a Mortgagee who has accepted this insurance without knowledge of such breach.

The following clauses shall be paramount and shall override anything contained in this insurance inconsistent therewith.

21 WAR EXCLUSION

In no case shall this insurance cover loss damage liability or expense caused by

21.1 war civil war revolution rebellion insurrection, or civil strife arising therefrom, or any hostile act by or against a belligerent power

21.2 capture seizure arrest restraint or detainment (barratry and piracy excepted), and the consequences thereof or any attempt thereat

21.3 derelict mines torpedoes bombs or other derelict weapons of war.

22 STRIKES EXCLUSION

In no case shall this insurance cover loss damage liability or expense caused by

- 22.1 strikers, locked-out workmen, or persons taking part in labour disturbances, riots or civil commotions
- 22.2 any terrorist or any person acting from a political motive.

23 MALICIOUS ACTS EXCLUSION

In no case shall this insurance cover loss damage liability or expense arising from

- 23.1 the detonation of an explosive
- 23.2 any weapon of war and caused by any person acting maliciously or from a political motive.

24 RADIOACTIVE CONTAMINATION EXCLUSION CLAUSE

In no case shall this insurance cover loss damage liability or expense directly or indirectly caused by or contributed to by or arising from

- 24.1 ionising radiations from or contamination by radioactivity from any nuclear fuel or from any nuclear waste or from the combustion of nuclear fuel
- 24.2 the radioactive, toxic, explosive or other hazardous or contaminating properties of any nuclear installation, reactor or other nuclear assembly or nuclear component thereof
- 24.3 any weapon of war employing atomic or nuclear fission and/or fusion or other like reaction or radioactive force or matter.

APPENDIX 8

1/11/95

(FOR USE ONLY WITH THE CURRENT MAR POLICY FORM)

INSTITUTE TIME CLAUSES
HULLS

RESTRICTED PERILS

This insurance is subject to English law and practice

1 NAVIGATION

1.1 The Vessel is covered subject to the provisions of this insurance at all times and has leave to sail or navigate with or without pilots, to go on trial trips and to assist and tow vessels or craft in distress. but it is warranted that the Vessel shall not be towed, except as is customary or to the first safe port or place when in need of assistance, or undertake towage or salvage services under a contract previously arranged by the Assured and/or Owners and/or Managers and/or Charterers. This Clause 1.1 shall not exclude customary towage in connection with loading and discharging.

1.2 This insurance shall not be prejudiced by reason of the Assured entering into any contract with pilots or for customary towage which limits or exempts the liability of the pilots and/or tugs and/or towboats and/or their owners when the Assured or their agents accept or are compelled to accept such contracts in accordance with established local law or practice.

1.3 The practice of engaging helicopters for the transportation of personnel, supplies and equipment to and/or from the Vessel shall not prejudice this insurance.

1.4 In the event of the Vessel being employed in trading operations which entail cargo loading or discharging at sea from or into another vessel (not being a harbour or inshore craft) no claim shall be recoverable under this insurance for loss of or damage to the Vessel or liability to any other vessel arising from such loading or discharging operations, including whilst approaching, lying alongside and leaving, unless previous notice that the Vessel is to be employed in such operations has been given to the Underwriters and any amended terms of cover and any additional premium required by them have been agreed.

1.5 In the event of the Vessel sailing (with or without cargo) with an intention of being (a) broken up, or (b) sold for breaking up, any claim for loss of or damage to the Vessel occurring subsequent to such sailing shall be limited to the market value of the Vessel as scrap at the time when the loss or damage is sustained, unless previous notice has been given to the Underwriters and any amendments to the terms of cover, insured value and premium required by them have been agreed. Nothing in this Clause 1.5 shall affect claims under Clauses 8 and/or 10.

2 CONTINUATION

Should the Vessel at the expiration of this insurance be at sea and in distress or missing, she shall, provided notice be given to the Underwriters prior to the expiration of this insurance, be held covered until arrival at the next port in good safety, or if in port and in distress until the Vessel is made safe, at a pro rata monthly premium.

3 BREACH OF WARRANTY

Held covered in case of any breach of warranty as to cargo, trade, locality, towage, salvage services or date of sailing, provided notice be given to the Underwriters immediately after receipt of advices and any amended terms of cover and any additional premium required by them be agreed.

4 CLASSIFICATION

4.1 It is the duty of the Assured, Owners and Managers at the inception of and throughout the period of this insurance to ensure that

4.1.1 the Vessel is classed with a Classification Society agreed by the Underwriters and that her class within that Society is maintained.

4.1.2 any recommendations requirements or restrictions imposed by the Vessel's Classification Society which relate to the Vessel's seaworthiness or to her maintenance in a seaworthy condition are complied with by the dates required by that Society.

4.2 In the event of any breach of the duties set out in Clause 4.1 above, unless the Underwriters agree to the contrary in writing, they will be discharged from liability under this insurance as from the date of the breach provided that if the Vessel is at sea at such date the Underwriters' discharge from liability is deferred until arrival at her next port.

4.3 Any incident condition or damage in respect of which the Vessel's Classification Society might make recommendations as to repairs or other action to be taken by the Assured Owners or Managers must be promptly reported to the Classification Society.

4.4 Should the Underwriters wish to approach the Classification Society directly for information and/or documents, the Assured will provide the necessary authorisation.

5 TERMINATION

This Clause 5 shall prevail notwithstanding any provision whether written typed or printed in this insurance inconsistent therewith.

Unless the Underwriters agree to the contrary in writing, this insurance shall terminate automatically at the time of

5.1 change of the Classification Society of the Vessel, or change, suspension, discontinuance, withdrawal or expiry of her Class therein, or any of the Classification Society's periodic surveys becoming overdue unless an extension of time for such survey be agreed by the Classification Society, provided that if the Vessel is at sea such automatic termination shall be deferred until arrival at her next port. However where such change, suspension, discontinuance or withdrawal of her Class or where a periodic survey becoming overdue has resulted from loss or damage covered by Clause 6 of this insurance or which would be covered by an insurance of the Vessel subject to current Institute War and Strikes Clauses Hulls – Time such automatic termination shall only operate should the Vessel sail from her next port without the prior approval of the Classification Society or in the case of a periodic survey becoming overdue without the Classification Society having agreed an extension of time for such survey,

5,2 any change, voluntary or otherwise, in the ownership or flag, transfer to new management, or charter on a bareboat basis, or requisition for title or use of the Vessel. provided that, if the Vessel has cargo on board and has already sailed from her loading port or is at sea in ballast, such automatic termination shall if required be deferred. whilst the Vessel continues her planned voyage, until arrival at final port of discharge if with cargo or at port of destination if in ballast. However, in the event of requisition for title or use without the prior execution of a written agreement by the Assured, such automatic termination shall occur fifteen days after such requisition whether the Vessel is at sea or in port. A pro rata daily net return of premium shall be made provided that a total loss of the Vessel, whether by insured perils or otherwise, has not occurred during the period covered by this insurance or any extension thereof.

6 PERILS

6.1 This insurance covers loss of or damage to the subject matter insured caused by

6.1.1 perils of the seas rivers lakes or other navigable waters

6.1.2 fire, explosion

6.1.3 violent theft by persons from outside the Vessel

6.1.4 jettison

6.1.5 piracy

6.1.6 contact with land conveyance, dock or harbour equipment or installation

6.1.7 earthquake volcanic eruption or lightning

6.1.8 accidents in loading discharging or shifting cargo or fuel.

Institute Time Clauses Hulls – Restricted Perils (1995)

- 6.2 This insurance covers loss of or damage to the subject matter insured caused by
- 6.2.1 any latent defect in the machinery or hull
- 6.2.2 negligence of Pilots provided such Pilots are not a Master, Officer or Member of the Crew of the Vessel
- 6.2.3 negligence of repairers or charterers provided such repairers or charterers are not an Assured hereunder
- 6.2.4 contact with aircraft. helicopters or similar objects, or objects falling therefrom provided that such loss or damage has not resulted from want of due diligence by the Assured, Owners, Managers or Superintendents or any of their onshore management.
- 6.3 Masters Officers Crew or Pilots not to be considered Owners within the meaning of this Clause 6 should they hold shares in the Vessel.

7 POLLUTION HAZARD

This insurance covers loss of or damage to the Vessel caused by any governmental authority acting under the powers vested in it to prevent or mitigate a pollution hazard or damage to the environment or threat thereof resulting directly from damage to the Vessel for which the Underwriters are liable under this insurance provided that such act of governmental authority has not resulted from want of due diligence by the Assured, Owners or Managers to prevent or mitigate such hazard or damage, or threat thereof. Master Officers Crew or Pilots not to be considered Owners within the meaning of this Clause 7 should they hold shares in the Vessel.

8 3/4ths COLLISION LIABILITY

- 8.1 The Underwriters agree to indemnify the Assured for three-fourths of any sum or sums paid by the Assured to any other person or persons by reason of the Assured becoming legally liable by way of damages for
- 8.1.1 loss of or damage to any other vessel or property on any other vessel
- 8.1.2 delay to or loss of use of any such other vessel or property thereon
- 8.1.3 general average of, salvage of, or salvage under contract of, any such other vessel or property thereon, where such payment by the Assured is in consequence of the Vessel hereby insured coming into collision with any other vessel.
- 8.2 The indemnity provided by this Clause 8 shall be in addition to the indemnity provided by the other terms and conditions of this insurance and shall be subject to the following provisions:
- 8.2.1 where the insured Vessel is in collision with another vessel and both vessels are to blame then, unless the liability of one or both vessels becomes limited by law, the indemnity under this Clause 8 shall be calculated on the principle of cross-liabilities as if the respective Owners had been compelled to pay to each other such proportion of each other's damages as may have been properly allowed in

ascertaining the balance or sum payable by or to the Assured in consequence of the collision,

8.2.2 in no case shall the Underwriters' total liability under Clauses 8.1 and 8.2 exceed their proportionate part of three-fourths of the insured value of the Vessel hereby insured in respect of any one collision.

8.3 The Underwriters will also pay three-fourths of the legal costs incurred by the Assured or which the Assured may be compelled to pay in contesting liability or taking proceedings to limit liability, with the prior written consent of the Underwriters.

EXCLUSIONS

8.4 Provided always that this Clause 8 shall in no case extend to any sum which the Assured shall pay for or in respect of

8.4.1 removal or disposal of obstructions. wrecks, cargoes or any other thing whatsoever

8.4.2 any real or personal property or thing whatsoever except other vessels or property on other vessels

8.4.3 the cargo or other property on, or the engagements of, the insured Vessel

8.4.4 loss of life, personal injury or illness

8.4.5 pollution or contamination. or threat thereof. of any real or personal property or thing whatsoever (except other vessels with which the insured Vessel is in collision or property on such other vessels) or damage to the environment, or threat thereof, save that this exclusion shall not extend to any sum which the Assured shall pay for or in respect of salvage remuneration in which the skill and efforts of the salvors in preventing or minimising damage to the environment as is referred to in Article 13 paragraph 1(b) of the International Convention on Salvage 1989 have been taken into account.

9 SISTERSHIP

Should the Vessel hereby insured come into collision with or receive salvage services from another vessel belonging wholly or in part to the same Owners or under the same management, the Assured shall have the same rights under this insurance as they would have were the other vessel entirely the property of Owners not interested in the Vessel hereby insured; but in such cases the liability for the collision or the amount payable for the services rendered shall be referred to a sole arbitrator to be agreed upon between the Underwriters and the Assured.

10 GENERAL AVERAGE AND SALVAGE

10.1 This insurance covers the Vessel's proportion of salvage, salvage charges and/or general average, reduced in respect of any under-insurance. but in case of general average sacrifice of the Vessel the Assured may recover in respect of the whole loss without first enforcing their right of contribution from other parties.

Institute Time Clauses Hulls – Restricted Perils (1995)

10.2 Adjustment to be according to the law and practice obtaining at the place where the adventure ends, as if the contract of affreightment contained no special terms upon the subject; but where the contract of affreightment so provides the adjustment shall be according to the York-Antwerp Rules.

10.3 When the Vessel sails in ballast, not under charter. the provisions of the York-Antwerp Rules 1994 (excluding Rules XI(d), XX and XXI) shall be applicable, and the voyage for this purpose shall be deemed to continue from the port or place of departure until the arrival of the Vessel at the first port or place thereafter other than a port or place of refuge or a port or place of call for bunkering only. If at any such intermediate port or place there is an abandonment of the adventure originally contemplated the voyage shall thereupon be deemed to be terminated.

10.4 No claim under this Clause 10 shall in any case be allowed where the loss was not incurred to avoid or in connection with the avoidance of a peril insured against.

10.5 No claim under this Clause 10 shall in any case be allowed for or in respect of

10.5.1 special compensation payable to a salvor under Article 14 of the International Convention on Salvage, 1989 or under any other provision in any statute, rule, law or contract which is similar in substance.

10.5.2 expenses or liabilities incurred in respect of damage to the environment, or the threat of such damage, or as a consequence of the escape or release of pollutant substances from the Vessel, or the threat of such escape or release.

10.6 Clause 10.5 shall not however exclude any sum which the Assured shall pay to salvors for or in respect of salvage remuneration in which the skill and efforts of the salvors in preventing or minimising damage to the environment as is referred to in Article 13 paragraph 1(b) of the International Convention on Salvage, 1989 have been taken into account.

11 DUTY OF ASSURED (SUE AND LABOUR)

11.1 In case of any loss or misfortune it is the duty of the Assured and their servants and agents to take such measures as may be reasonable for the purpose of averting or minimising a loss which would be recoverable under this insurance.

11.2 Subject to the provisions below and to Clause 12 the Underwriters will contribute to charges properly and reasonably incurred by the Assured their servants or agents for such measures. General average, salvage charges (except as provided for in Clause 11.5), special compensation and expenses as referred to in Clause 10.5 and collision defence or attack costs are not recoverable under this Clause 11.

11.3 Measures taken by the Assured or the Underwriters with the object of saving, protecting or recovering the subject matter insured shall not be considered as a waiver or acceptance of abandonment or otherwise prejudice the rights of either party.

11.4 When expenses are incurred pursuant to this Clause 11 the liability under this insurance shall not exceed the proportion of such expenses that the amount insured hereunder bears to the value of the Vessel as stated herein, or to the sound value of the Vessel at the time of the occurrence giving rise to the expenditure if the sound value exceeds that value. Where the Underwriters have admitted a claim for total loss and property insured by this insurance is saved, the foregoing provisions shall not apply unless the expenses of suing and labouring exceed the value of such property saved and then shall apply only to the amount of the expenses which is in excess of such value.

11.5 When a claim for total loss of the Vessel is admitted under this insurance and expenses have been reasonably incurred in saving or attempting to save the Vessel and other property and there are no proceeds, or the expenses exceed the proceeds, then this insurance shall bear its pro rata share of such proportion of the expenses, or of the expenses in excess of the proceeds, as the case may be, as may reasonably be regarded as having been incurred in respect of the Vessel, excluding all special compensation and expenses as referred to in Clause 10.5; but if the Vessel be insured for less than its sound value at the time of the occurrence giving rise to the expenditure, the amount recoverable under this clause, shall be reduced in proportion to the under-insurance.

11.6 The sum recoverable under this Clause 11 shall be in addition to the loss otherwise recoverable under this insurance but shall in no circumstances exceed the amount insured under this insurance in respect of the Vessel.

12 DEDUCTIBLE

12.1 No claim arising from a peril insured against shall be payable under this insurance unless the aggregate of all such claims arising out of each separate accident or occurrence (including claims under Clauses 8, 10 and 11) exceeds the deductible amount agreed in which case this sum shall be deducted. Nevertheless the expense of sighting the bottom after stranding, if reasonably incurred specially for that purpose, shall be paid even if no damage be found. This Clause 12.1 shall not apply to a claim for total or constructive total loss of the Vessel or, in the event of such a claim, to any associated claim under Clause 11 arising from the same accident or occurrence.

12.2 Claims for damage by heavy weather occurring during a single sea passage between two successive ports shall be treated as being due to one accident. In the case of such heavy weather extending over a period not wholly covered by this insurance the deductible to be applied to the claim recoverable hereunder shall be the proportion of the above deductible that the number of days of such heavy weather falling within the period of this insurance bears to the number of days of heavy weather during the single sea passage. The expression heavy weather in this Clause 12.2 shall be deemed to include contact with floating ice.

12.3 Excluding any interest comprised therein, recoveries against any claim which is subject to the above deductible shall be credited to the Underwriters in full to the extent of the sum by which the aggregate of the claim unreduced by any recoveries exceeds the above deductible.

12.4 Interest comprised in recoveries shall be apportioned between the Assured and the Underwriters, taking into account the sums paid by the Underwriters and the dates when such payments were made, notwithstanding that by the addition of interest the Underwriters may receive a larger sum than they have paid.

13 NOTICE OF CLAIM AND TENDERS

13.1 In the event of accident whereby loss or damage may result in a claim under this insurance, notice must be given to the Underwriters promptly after the date on which the Assured, Owners or Managers become or should have become aware of the loss or damage and prior to survey so that a surveyor may be appointed if the Underwriters so desire. If notice is not given to the Underwriters within twelve months of that date unless Underwriters agree to the contrary in writing, the Underwriters will be automatically discharged from liability for any claim under this insurance in respect of or arising out of such accident or the loss or damage.

13.2 The Underwriters shall be entitled to decide the port to which the Vessel shall proceed for docking or repair (the actual additional expense of the voyage arising from compliance with the Underwriters' requirements being refunded to the Assured) and shall have a right of veto concerning a place of repair or a repairing firm.

13.3 The Underwriters may also take tenders or may require further tenders to be taken for the repair of the Vessel. Where such a tender has been taken and a tender is accepted with the approval of the Underwriters, an allowance shall be made at the rate of 30% per annum on the insured value for time lost between the despatch of the invitations to tender required by the Underwriters and the acceptance of a tender to the extent that such time is lost solely as the result of tenders having been taken and provided that the tender is accepted without delay after receipt of the Underwriters' approval.

Due credit shall be given against the allowance as above for any amounts recovered in respect of fuel and stores and wages and maintenance of the Master Officers and Crew or any member thereof, including amounts allowed in general average, and for any amounts recovered from third parties in respect of damages for detention and/or loss of profit and/or running expenses, for the period covered by the tender allowance or any part thereof.

Where a part of the cost of the repair of damage other than a fixed deductible is not recoverable from the Underwriters the allowance shall be reduced by a similar proportion.

13.4 In the event of failure by the Assured to comply with the conditions of Clauses 13.2 and/or 13.3 a deduction of 15% shall be made from the amount of the ascertained claim.

14 NEW FOR OLD

Claims payable without deduction new for old.

15 BOTTOM TREATMENT

In no case shall a claim be allowed in respect of scraping gritblasting and/or other surface preparation or painting of the Vessel's bottom except that

15.1 gritblasting and/or other surface preparation of new bottom plates ashore and supplying and applying any 'shop' primer thereto,

15.2 gritblasting and/or other surface preparation of:

the butts or area of plating immediately adjacent to any renewed or refitted plating damaged during the course of welding and/or repairs,

areas of plating damaged during the course of fairing, either in place or ashore,

15.3 supplying and applying the first coat or primer/anti-corrosive to those particular areas mentioned in 15.1 and 15.2 above,

shall be allowed as part of the reasonable cost of repairs in respect of bottom plating damaged by an insured peril.

16 WAGES AND MAINTENANCE

No claim shall be allowed, other than in general average, for wages and maintenance of the Master Officers and Crew or any member thereof, except when incurred solely for the necessary removal of the Vessel from one port to another for the repair of damage covered by the Underwriters, or for trial trips for such repairs, and then only for such wages and maintenance as are incurred whilst the Vessel is under way.

17 AGENCY COMMISSION

In no case shall any sum be allowed under this insurance either by way of remuneration of the Assured for time and trouble taken to obtain and supply information or documents or in respect of the commission or charges of any manager, agent, managing or agency company or the like, appointed by or on behalf of the Assured to perform such services.

18 UNREPAIRED DAMAGE

18.1 The measure of indemnity in respect of claims for unrepaired damage shall be the reasonable depreciation in the market value of the Vessel at the time this insurance terminates arising from such unrepaired damage, but not exceeding the reasonable cost of repairs.

Institute Time Clauses Hulls – Restricted Perils (1995)

18.2 In no case shall the Underwriters be liable for unrepaired damage in the event of a subsequent total loss (whether or not covered under this insurance) sustained during the period covered by this insurance or any extension thereof.

18.3 The Underwriters shall not he liable in respect of unrepaired damage for more than the insured value at the time this insurance terminate.

19 CONSTRUCTIVE TOTAL LOSS

19.1 In ascertaining whether the Vessel is a constructive total loss, the insured value shall be taken as the repaired value and nothing in respect of the damaged or break-up value of the Vessel or wreck shall be taken into account.

19.2 No claim for constructive total loss based upon the cost of recovery and/or repair of the Vessel shall be recoverable hereunder unless such cost would exceed the insured value. In making this determination only the cost relating to a single accident or sequence of damages arising from the same accident shall be taken into account.

20 FREIGHT WAIVER

In the event of total or constructive total loss no claim to be made by the Underwriters for freight whether notice of abandonment has been given or not.

21 ASSIGNMENT

No assignment of or interest in this insurance or in any moneys which may be or become payable thereunder is to be binding on or recognised by the Underwriters unless a dated notice of such assignment or interest signed by the Assured, and by the assignor in the case of subsequent assignment, is endorsed on the Policy and the Policy with such endorsement is produced before payment of any claim or return of premium thereunder.

22 DISBURSEMENTS WARRANTY

22 1 Additional insurances as follows are permitted:

22.1.1 *Disbursements, Managers' Commissions, Profits or Excess or Increased Value of Hull and Machinery.* A sum not exceeding 25% of the value stated herein.

22.1.2 *Freight, Chartered Freight or Anticipated Freight, insured for time.* A sum not exceeding 25% of the value as stated herein less any sum insured, however described, under 22.1.1.

22.1.3 *Freight or Hire, under contracts for voyage.* A sum not exceeding the gross freight or hire for the current cargo passage and next succeeding cargo passage (such insurance to include, if required, a preliminary and an intermediate ballast passage) plus the charges of insurance. In the case of a voyage charter where payment is made on a time basis, the sum permitted for insurance shall be calculated on the estimated duration of the voyage, subject to the limitation of two cargo passages as laid down herein. Any sum insured under 22.1.2 to be taken into account and only the excess thereof may be insured, which excess shall be reduced as the freight or hire is advanced or earned by the gross amount so advanced or earned.

22.1.4 *Anticipated Freight if the Vessel sails in ballast and not under Charter.* A sum not exceeding the anticipated gross freight on next cargo passage, such sum to be reasonably estimated on the basis of the current rate of freight at time of insurance plus the charges of insurance. Any sum insured under 22.1.2 to be taken into account and only the excess thereof may be insured.

22.1.5 *Time Charter Hire or Charter Hire for Series of Voyages.* A sum not exceeding 50% of the gross hire which is to be earned under the charter in a period not exceeding 18 months. Any sum insured under 22.1.2 to be taken into account and only the excess thereof may be insured, which excess shall be reduced as the hire is advanced or earned under the charter by 50% of the gross amount so advanced or earned but the sum insured need not be reduced while the total of the sums insured under 22.1.2 and 22.1.5 does not exceed 50% of the gross hire still to be earned under the charter. An insurance under this Section may begin on the signing of the charter.

22.1.6 *Premiums.* A sum not exceeding the actual premiums of all interests insured for a period not exceeding 12 months (excluding premiums insured under the foregoing sections but including, if required, the premium or estimated calls on any Club or War etc Risk insurance) reducing pro rata monthly.

22.1.7 *Returns of Premium.* A sum not exceeding the actual returns which are allowable under any insurance but which would not be recoverable thereunder in the event of a total loss of the Vessel whether by insured perils or otherwise.

22.1.7 *Insurance irrespective of amount against:*

Any risks excluded by Clauses 24, 25, 26 and 27 below.

22.2 Warranted that no insurance on any interests enumerated in the foregoing 22.1.1 to 22.1.7 in excess of the amounts permitted therein and no other insurance which includes total loss of the Vessel P.P.I., F.I.A. or subject to any other like term, is or shall be effected to operate during the currency of this insurance by or for account of the Assured, Owners, Managers or Mortgagees. Provided always that a breach of this warranty shall not afford the Underwriters any defence to a claim by a Mortgagee who has accepted this insurance without knowledge of such breach.

23 RETURNS FOR LAY-UP AND CANCELLATION

23.1 To return as follows:

23.1.1 pro rata monthly net for each uncommenced month if this insurance be cancelled by agreement,

Institute Time Clauses Hulls – Restricted Perils (1995)

23.1.2 for each period of 30 consecutive days the Vessel may be laid up in a port or in a lay-up area provided such port or lay-up area is approved by the Underwriters

    (a) .... per cent net not under repair

    (b) .... per cent net under repair.

23.1.3 The Vessel shall not be considered to be under repair when work is undertaken in respect of ordinary wear and tear of the Vessel and/or following recommendations in the Vessel's Classification Society survey but any repairs following loss of or damage to the Vessel or involving structural alterations whether covered by this insurance or otherwise shall be considered as under repair.

23.1.4 If the Vessel is under repair during part only of a period for which a return is claimable, the return shall be calculated pro rata to the number of days under 23.1.2 (a) and (b) respectively.

23.2 PROVIDED ALWAYS THAT

23.2.1 a total loss of the Vessel, whether by insured perils or otherwise, has not occurred during the period covered by this insurance or any extension thereof

23.2.2 in no case shall a return be allowed when the Vessel is lying in exposed or unprotected waters or in a port or lay-up area not approved by the Underwriters

23.2.3 loading or discharging operations or the presence of cargo on board shall not debar returns but no return shall be allowed for any period during which the Vessel is being used for the storage of cargo or for lightering purposes

23.2.4 in the event of any amendment of the annual rate, the above rates of return shall be adjusted accordingly

23.2.5 in the event of any return recoverable under this Clause 23 being based on 30 consecutive days which fall on successive insurances effected for the same Assured this insurance shall only be liable for an amount calculated at pro rata of the period rates 23.1.2(a) and/or (b) above for the number of days which come within the period of this insurance and to which a return is actually applicable. Such overlapping period shall run, at the option of the Assured, either from the first day on which the Vessel is laid up or the first day of a period of 30 consecutive days as provided under 23.1.2(a) or (b) above.

The following clauses shall be paramount and shall override anything contained in this insurance inconsistent therewith.

24 WAR EXCLUSION

In no case shall this insurance cover loss damage liability or expense caused by

24.1 war civil war revolution rebellion insurrection or civil strife arising therefrom or any hostile act by or against a belligerent power

24.2 capture seizure arrest restraint or detainment (piracy excepted) and the consequences thereof or any attempt thereat

24.3 derelict mines torpedoes bombs or other derelict weapons of war.

25 STRIKES EXCLUSION

In no case shall this insurance cover loss damage liability or expense caused by

25.1 strikers, locked-out workmen, or persons taking part in labour disturbances, riots or civil commotions

25.2 any terrorist or any person acting from a political motive.

26 MALICIOUS ACTS EXCLUSION

In no case shall this insurance cover loss damage liability or expense arising from

26.1 the detonation of an explosive

26.2 any weapon of war and caused by any person acting maliciously or from a political motive.

27 RADIOACTIVE CONTAMINATION EXCLUSION CLAUSE

In no case shall this insurance cover loss damage liability or expense directly or indirectly caused by or contributed to by or arising from

27.1 ionising radiations from or contamination by radioactivity from any nuclear fuel or from any nuclear waste or from the combustion of nuclear fuel

27.2 the radioactive, toxic, explosive or other hazardous or contaminating properties of any nuclear installation, reactor or other nuclear assembly or nuclear component thereof

27.3 any weapon of war employing atomic or nuclear fission and/or fusion or other like reaction or radioactive force or matter.

APPENDIX 9

1/11/95

(FOR USE ONLY WITH THE CURRENT MAR POLICY FORM)

INSTITUTE ADDITIONAL PERILS CLAUSES – HULLS

(For use only with the Institute Time Clauses Hulls 1/11/95)

1 In consideration of an additional premium this insurance is extended to cover
    1.1   the cost of repairing or replacing
    1.1.1 any boiler which bursts or shaft which breaks
    1.1.2 any defective part which has caused loss of or damage to the Vessel covered by Clause 6.2.1 of the Institute Time Clauses – Hulls 1/11/95.
    1.2   loss of or damage to the Vessel caused by any accident or by negligence, incompetence or error of judgment of any person whatsoever.
2 Except as provided in 1.1.1 and 1.1.2, nothing in these Additional Perils Clauses shall allow any claim for the cost of repairing or replacing any part found to be defective as a result of a fault or error in design or construction and which has not caused loss of or damage to the Vessel.
3 The cover provided in Clause 1 is subject to all other terms, conditions and exclusions contained in this insurance and subject to the proviso that the loss or damage has not resulted from want of due diligence by the Assured, Owners or Managers, Masters Officers Crew or Pilots not to be considered Owners within the meaning of this Clause should they hold shares in the Vessel.

APPENDIX 10

1/1/82

INSTITUTE CARGO CLAUSES (A)

RISKS COVERED

1   This insurance covers all risks of loss of or damage to the subject matter insured except as provided in Clauses 4, 5, 6 and 7 below.

2   This insurance covers general average and salvage charges, adjusted or determined according to the contract of affreightment and/or the governing law and practice, incurred to avoid or in connection with the avoidance of loss from any cause except those excluded in Clauses 4, 5, 6 and 7 or elsewhere in this insurance.

3   This insurance is extended to indemnify the Assured against such proportion of liability under the contract of affreightment 'Both to Blame Collision' Clause as is in respect of a loss recoverable hereunder. In the event of any claim by shipowners under the said Clause the Assured agree to notify the Underwriters who shall have the right, at their own cost and expense, to defend the Assured against such claim.

EXCLUSIONS

4   In no case shall this insurance cover

    4.1   loss damage or expense attributable to wilful misconduct of the Assured

    4.2   ordinary leakage, ordinary loss in weight or volume, or ordinary wear and tear of the subject matter insured

    4.3   loss damage or expense caused by insufficiency or unsuitability of packing or preparation of the subject matter insured (for the purpose of this Clause 4.3 'packing' shall be deemed to include stowage in a container or liftvan but only when such stowage is carried out prior to attachment of this insurance or by the Assured or their servants)

    4.4   loss damage or expense caused by inherent vice or nature of the subject matter insured

    4.5   loss damage or expense proximately caused by delay, even though the delay be caused by a risk insured against (except expenses payable under Clause 2 above)

    4.6   loss damage or expense arising from insolvency or financial default of the owners managers charterers or operators of the vessel

    4.7   loss damage or expense arising from the use of any weapon of war employing atomic or nuclear fission and/or fusion or other like reaction or radioactive force or matter.

Institute Cargo Clauses (A) [ICC (A)]

5 5.1 In no case shall this insurance cover loss damage or expense arising from

unseaworthiness of vessel or craft,

unfitness of vessel craft conveyance container or liftvan for the safe carriage of the subject matter insured,

where the Assured or their servants are privy to such unseaworthiness or unfitness, at the time the subject matter insured is loaded therein.

5.2 The Underwriters waive any breach of the implied warranties of seaworthiness of the ship and fitness of the ship to carry the subject matter insured to destination, unless the Assured or their servants are privy to such unseaworthiness or unfitness.

6 In no case shall this insurance cover loss damage or expense caused by

6.1 war civil war revolution rebellion insurrection, or civil strife arising therefrom, or any hostile act by or against a belligerent power

6.2 capture seizure arrest restraint or detainment (piracy excepted), and the consequences thereof or any attempt thereat

6.3 derelict mines torpedoes bombs or other derelict weapons of war.

7 In no case shall this insurance cover loss damage or expense

7.1 caused by strikers, locked-out workmen, or persons taking part in labour disturbances, riots or civil commotions

7.2 resulting from strikes, lock-outs, labour disturbances, riots or civil commotions

7.3 caused by any terrorist or any person acting from a political motive.

DURATION

8 8.1 This insurance attaches from the time the goods leave the warehouse or place of storage at the place named herein for the commencement of the transit, continues during the ordinary course of transit and terminates either

8.1.1 on delivery to the Consignees' or other final warehouse or place of storage at the destination named herein,

8.1.2 on delivery to any other warehouse or place of storage, whether prior to or at the destination named herein, which the Assured elect to use either

8.1.2.1 for storage other than in the ordinary course of transit or

8.1.2.2 for allocation or distribution,

or

8.1.3 on the expiry of 60 days after completion of discharge overside of the goods hereby insured from the oversea vessel at the final port of discharge,

whichever shall first occur.

8.2 If, after discharge overside from the oversea vessel at the final port of discharge, but prior to termination of this insurance, the goods are to be forwarded to a destination other than that to which they are insured hereunder, this insurance, whilst remaining subject to termination as provided for above, shall not extend beyond the commencement of transit to such other destination.

8.3 This insurance shall remain in force (subject to termination as provided for above and to the provisions of Clause 9 below) during delay beyond the control of the Assured, any deviation, forced discharge, reshipment or transhipment and during any variation of the adventure arising from the exercise of a liberty granted to shipowners or charterers under the contract of affreightment.

9 If owing to circumstances beyond the control of the Assured either the contract of carriage is terminated at a port or place other than the destination named therein or the transit is otherwise terminated before delivery of the goods as provided for in Clause 8 above, then this insurance shall also terminate unless prompt notice is given to the Underwriters and continuation of cover is requested when the insurance shall remain in force, subject to an additional premium if required by the Underwriters, either

9.1 until the goods are sold and delivered at such port or place, or, unless otherwise specially agreed, until the expiry of 60 days after arrival of the goods hereby insured at such port or place, whichever shall first occur, or

9.2 if the goods are forwarded within the said period of 60 days (or any agreed extension thereof) to the destination named herein or to any other destination, until terminated in accordance with the provisions of Clause 8 above.

10 Where, after attachment of this insurance, the destination is changed by the Assured, held covered at a premium and on conditions to be arranged subject to prompt notice being given to the Underwriters.

CLAIMS

11 11.1 In order to recover under this insurance the Assured must have an insurable interest in the subject matter insured at the time of the loss.

11.2 Subject to 11.1 above, the Assured shall be entitled to recover for insured loss occurring during the period covered by this insurance, notwithstanding that the loss occurred before the contract of insurance was concluded, unless the Assured were aware of the loss and the Underwriters were not.

12 Where, as a result of the operation of a risk covered by this insurance, the insured transit is terminated at a port or place other than that to which the subject matter is covered under this insurance, the Underwriters will reimburse the Assured for any extra charges properly and reasonably incurred in unloading storing and forwarding the subject matter to the destination to which it is insured hereunder.

Institute Cargo Clauses (A) [ICC (A)]

This Clause 12, which does not apply to general average or salvage charges, shall be subject to the exclusions contained in Clauses 4, 5, 6 and 7 above, and shall not include charges arising from the fault negligence insolvency or financial default of the Assured or their servants.

13 No claim for Constructive Total Loss shall be recoverable hereunder unless the subject matter insured is reasonably abandoned either on account of its actual total loss appearing to be unavoidable or because the cost of recovering, reconditioning and forwarding the subject matter to the destination to which it is insured would exceed its value on arrival.

14 14.1 If any Increased Value insurance is effected by the Assured on the cargo insured herein the agreed value of the cargo shall be deemed to be increased to the total amount insured under this insurance and all Increased Value insurances covering the loss, and liability under this insurance shall be in such proportion as the sum insured herein bears to such total amount insured.

In the event of claim the Assured shall provide the Underwriters with evidence of the amounts insured under all other insurances.

14.2 **Where this insurance is on Increased Value the following clause shall apply:**

The agreed value of the cargo shall be deemed to be equal to the total amount insured under the primary insurance and all Increased Value insurances covering the loss and effected on the cargo by the Assured, and liability under this insurance shall be in such proportion as the sum insured herein bears to such total amount insured.

In the event of claim the Assured shall provide the Underwriters with evidence of the amounts insured under all other insurances.

BENEFIT OF INSURANCE

15 This insurance shall not inure to the benefit of the carrier or other bailee.

MINIMISING LOSSES

16 It is the duty of the Assured and their servants and agents in respect of loss recoverable hereunder

16.1 to take such measures as may be reasonable for the purpose of averting or minimising such loss, and

16.2 to ensure that all rights against carriers, bailees or other third parties are properly preserved and exercised

and the Underwriters will, in addition to any loss recoverable hereunder, reimburse the Assured for any charges properly and reasonably incurred in pursuance of these duties.

17 Measures taken by the Assured or the Underwriters with the object of saving, protecting or recovering the subject matter insured shall not be considered as a waiver or acceptance of abandonment or otherwise prejudice the rights of either party.

AVOIDANCE OF DELAY

18 It is a condition of this insurance that the Assured shall act with reasonable despatch in all circumstances within their control.

LAW AND PRACTICE

19 This insurance is subject to English law and practice.

NOTE—*It is necessary for the Assured when they become aware of an event which is 'held covered' under this insurance to give prompt notice to the Underwriters and the right to such cover is dependent upon compliance with this obligation.*

APPENDIX 11

1/1/82

INSTITUTE CARGO CLAUSES (B)

RISKS COVERED

1. This insurance covers, except as provided in Clauses 4, 5, 6 and 7 below,
    1.1 loss of or damage to the subject matter insured reasonably attributable to
    1.1.1 fire or explosion
    1.1.2 vessel or craft being stranded grounded sunk or capsized
    1.1.3 overturning or derailment of land conveyance
    1.1.4 collision or contact of vessel craft or conveyance with any external object other than water
    1.1.5 discharge of cargo at a port of distress
    1.1.6 earthquake volcanic eruption or lightning,
    1.2 loss of or damage to the subject matter insured caused by
    1.2.1 general average sacrifice
    1.2.2 jettison or washing overboard
    1.2.3 entry of sea lake or river water into vessel craft hold conveyance container liftvan or place of storage,
    1.3 total loss of any package lost overboard or dropped whilst loading on to, or unloading from, vessel or craft.
2. This insurance covers general average and salvage charges, adjusted or determined according to the contract of affreightment and/or the governing law and practice, incurred to avoid or in connection with the avoidance of loss from any cause except those excluded in Clauses 4, 5, 6 and 7 or elsewhere in this insurance
3. This insurance is extended to indemnify the Assured against such proportion of liability under the contract of affreightment 'Both to Blame Collision' Clause as is in respect of a loss recoverable hereunder. In the event of any claim by shipowners under the said Clause the Assured agree to notify the Underwriters who shall have the right, at their own cost and expense, to defend the Assured against such claim.

EXCLUSIONS

4. In no case shall this insurance cover
    4.1 loss damage or expense attributable to wilful misconduct of the Assured
    4.2 ordinary leakage, ordinary loss in weight or volume, or ordinary wear and tear of the subject matter insured

Appendix 11

- 4.3 loss damage or expense caused by insufficiency or unsuitability of packing or preparation of the subject matter insured (for the purpose of this Clause 4.3 'packing' shall be deemed to include stowage in a container or liftvan but only when such stowage is carried out prior to attachment of this insurance or by the Assured or their servants)
- 4.4 loss damage or expense caused by inherent vice or nature of the subject matter insured
- 4.5 loss damage or expense proximately caused by delay, even though the delay be caused by a risk insured against (except expenses payable under Clause 2 above)
- 4.6 loss damage or expense arising from insolvency or financial default of the owners managers charterers or operators of the vessel
- 4.7 deliberate damage to or deliberate destruction of the subject matter insured or any part thereof by the wrongful act of any person or persons
- 4.8 loss damage or expense arising from the use of any weapon of war employing atomic or nuclear fission and/or fusion or other like reaction or radioactive force or matter.

5
- 5.1 In no case shall this insurance cover loss damage or expense arising from unseaworthiness of vessel or craft, unfitness of vessel craft conveyance container or liftvan for the safe carriage of the subject matter insured, where the Assured or their servants are privy to such unseaworthiness or unfitness, at the time the subject matter insured is loaded therein.
- 5.2 The Underwriters waive any breach of the implied warranties of seaworthiness of the ship and fitness of the ship to carry the subject matter insured to destination, unless the Assured or their servants are privy to such unseaworthiness or unfitness.

6 In no case shall this insurance cover loss damage or expense caused by
- 6.1 war civil war revolution rebellion insurrection, or civil strife arising therefrom, or any hostile act by or against a belligerent power
- 6.2 capture seizure arrest restraint or detainment, and the consequences thereof or any attempt thereat
- 6.3 derelict mines torpedoes bombs or other derelict weapons of war.

7 In no case shall this insurance cover loss damage or expense
- 7.1 caused by strikers, locked-out workmen, or persons taking part in labour disturbances, riots or civil commotions
- 7.2 resulting from strikes, lock-outs, labour disturbances, riots or civil commotions
- 7.3 caused by any terrorist or any person acting from a political motive.

DURATION

8
- 8.1 This insurance attaches from the time the goods leave the warehouse or place of storage at the place named herein for the commencement

Institute Cargo Clauses (B) (ICC (B)]

of the transit, continues during the ordinary course of transit and terminates either

8.1.1 on delivery to the Consignees' or other final warehouse or place of storage at the destination named herein,

8.1.2 on delivery to any other warehouse or place of storage, whether prior to or at the destination named herein, which the Assured elect to use either

8.1.2.1 for storage other than in the ordinary course of transit or

8.1.2.2 for allocation or distribution,

or

8.1.3 on the expiry of 60 days after completion of discharge overside of the goods hereby insured from the oversea vessel at the final port of discharge, whichever shall first occur.

8.2 If, after discharge overside from the oversea vessel at the final port of discharge, but prior to termination of this insurance, the goods are to be forwarded to a destination other than that to which they are insured hereunder, this insurance, whilst remaining subject to termination as provided for above, shall not extend beyond the commencement of transit to such other destination.

8.3 This insurance shall remain in force (subject to termination as provided for above and to the provisions of Clause 9 below) during delay beyond the control of the Assured, any deviation, forced discharge, reshipment or transhipment and during any variation of the adventure arising from the exercise of a liberty granted to shipowners or charterers under the contract of affreightment.

9 If owing to circumstances beyond the control of the Assured either the contract of carriage is terminated at a port or place other than the destination named therein or the transit is otherwise terminated before delivery of the goods as provided for in Clause 8 above, then this insurance shall also terminate unless prompt notice is given to the Underwriters and continuation of cover is requested when the insurance shall remain in force, subject to an additional premium if required by the Underwriters, either

9.1 until the goods are sold and delivered at such port or place, or, unless otherwise specially agreed, until the expiry of 60 days after arrival of the goods hereby insured at such port or place, whichever shall first occur,

or

9.2 if the goods are forwarded within the said period of 60 days (or any agreed extension thereof) to the destination named herein or to any other destination, until terminated in accordance with the provisions of Clause 8 above.

10 Where, after attachment of this insurance, the destination is changed by the Assured, held covered at a premium and on conditions to be arranged subject to prompt notice being given to the Underwriters.

CLAIMS

11 11.1 In order to recover under this insurance the Assured must have an insurable interest in the subject matter insured at the time of the loss.

    11.2 Subject to 11.1 above, the Assured shall be entitled to recover for insured loss occurring during the period covered by this insurance, notwithstanding that the loss occurred before the contract of insurance was concluded, unless the Assured were aware of the loss and the Underwriters were not.

12 Where, as a result of the operation of a risk covered by this insurance, the insured transit is terminated at a port or place other than that to which the subject matter is covered under this insurance, the Underwriters will reimburse the Assured for any extra charges properly and reasonably incurred in unloading storing and forwarding the subject matter to the destination to which it is insured hereunder.

This Clause 12, which does not apply to general average or salvage charges, shall be subject to the exclusions contained in Clauses 4, 5, 6 and 7 above, and shall not include charges arising from the fault negligence insolvency or financial default of the Assured or their servants.

13 No claim for Constructive Total Loss shall be recoverable hereunder unless the subject matter insured is reasonably abandoned either on account of its actual total loss appearing to be unavoidable or because the cost of recovering, reconditioning and forwarding the subject matter to the destination to which it is insured would exceed its value on arrival.

14 14.1 If any Increased Value insurance is effected by the Assured on the cargo insured herein the agreed value of the cargo shall be deemed to be increased to the total amount insured under this insurance and all Increased Value insurances covering the loss, and liability under this insurance shall be in such proportion as the sum insured herein bears to such total amount insured.

In the event of claim the Assured shall provide the Underwriters with evidence of the amounts insured under all other insurances.

    14.2 Where this insurance is on Increased Value the following clause shall apply:

The agreed value of the cargo shall be deemed to be equal to the total amount insured under the primary insurance and all Increased Value insurances covering the loss and effected on the cargo by the Assured, and liability under this insurance shall be in such proportion as the sum insured herein bears to such total amount insured.

In the event of claim the Assured shall provide the Underwriters with evidence of the amounts insured under all other insurances.

BENEFIT OF INSURANCE

15 This insurance shall not inure to the benefit of the carrier or other bailee.

MINIMISING LOSSES

16 It is the duty of the Assured and their servants and agents in respect of loss recoverable hereunder

    16.1   to take such measures as may be reasonable for the purpose of averting or minimising such loss, and

    16.2   to ensure that all rights against carriers, bailees or other third parties are properly preserved and exercised and the Underwriters will, in addition to any loss recoverable hereunder, reimburse the Assured for any charges properly and reasonably incurred in pursuance of these duties.

17 Measures taken by the Assured or the Underwriters with the object of saving, protecting or recovering the subject matter insured shall not be considered as a waiver or acceptance of abandonment or otherwise prejudice the rights of either party.

AVOIDANCE OF DELAY

18 It is a condition of this insurance that the Assured shall act with reasonable despatch in all circumstances within their control.

LAW AND PRACTICE

19 This insurance is subject to English law and practice.

NOTE—*It is necessary for the Assured when they become aware of an event which is 'held covered' under this insurance to give prompt notice to the Underwriters and the right to such cover is dependent upon compliance with this obligation.*

APPENDIX 12

1/1/82

INSTITUTE CARGO CLAUSES (C)

RISKS COVERED

1 This insurance covers, except as provided in Clauses 4, 5, 6 and 7 below,

    1.1   loss of or damage to the subject matter insured reasonably attributable to

    1.1.1   fire or explosion

    1.1.2   vessel or craft being stranded grounded sunk or capsized

    1.1.3   overturning or derailment of land conveyance

    1.1.4   collision or contact of vessel craft or conveyance with any external object other than water

    1.1.5   discharge of cargo at a port of distress,

    1.2   loss of or damage to the subject matter insured caused by

    1.2.1   general average sacrifice

    1.2.2   jettison.

2 This insurance covers general average and salvage charges, adjusted or determined according to the contract of affreightment and/or the governing law and practice, incurred to avoid or in connection with the avoidance of loss from any cause except those excluded in Clauses 4, 5, 6 and 7 or elsewhere in this insurance.

3 This insurance is extended to indemnify the Assured against such proportion of liability under the contract of affreightment 'Both to Blame Collision' Clause as is in respect of a loss recoverable hereunder. In the event of any claim by shipowners under the said Clause the Assured agree to notify the Underwriters who shall have the right, at their own cost and expense, to defend the Assured against such claim.

EXCLUSIONS

4 In no case shall this insurance cover

    4.1   loss damage or expense attributable to wilful misconduct of the Assured

    4.2   ordinary leakage, ordinary loss in weight or volume, or ordinary wear and tear of the subject matter insured

    4.3   loss damage or expense caused by insufficiency or unsuitability of packing or preparation of the subject matter insured (for the purpose of this Clause 4.3 'packing' shall be deemed to include stowage in a container or liftvan but only when such stowage is carried out prior to attachment of this insurance or by the Assured or their servants)

Institute Cargo Clauses (C) [ICC (C)]

4.4 loss damage or expense caused by inherent vice or nature of the subject matter insured

4.5 loss damage or expense proximately caused by delay, even though the delay be caused by a risk insured against (except expenses payable under Clause 2 above)

4.6 loss damage or expense arising from insolvency or financial default of the owners managers charterers or operators of the vessel

4.7 deliberate damage to or deliberate destruction of the subject matter insured or any part thereof by the wrongful act of any person or persons

4.8 loss damage or expense arising from the use of any weapon of war employing atomic or nuclear fission and/or fusion or other like reaction or radioactive force or matter.

5 5.1 In no case shall this insurance cover loss damage or expense arising from unseaworthiness of vessel or craft, unfitness of vessel craft conveyance container or liftvan for the safe carriage of the subject matter insured,

where the Assured or their servants are privy to such unseaworthiness or unfitness, at the time the subject matter insured is loaded therein.

5.2 The Underwriters waive any breach of the implied warranties of seaworthiness of the ship and fitness of the ship to carry the subject matter insured to destination, unless the Assured or their servants are privy to such unseaworthiness or unfitness.

6 In no case shall this insurance cover loss damage or expense caused by

6.1 war civil war revolution rebellion insurrection, or civil strife arising therefrom, or any hostile act by or against a belligerent power

6.2 capture seizure arrest restraint or detainment, and the consequences thereof or any attempt thereat

6.3 derelict mines torpedoes bombs or other derelict weapons of war.

7 In no case shall this insurance cover loss damage or expense

7.1 caused by strikers, locked-out workmen, or persons taking part in labour disturbances, riots or civil commotions

7.2 resulting from strikes, lock-outs, labour disturbances, riots or civil commotions

7.3 caused by any terrorist or any person acting from a political motive.

DURATION

8 8.1 This insurance attaches from the time the goods leave the warehouse or place of storage at the place named herein for the commencement of the transit, continues during the ordinary course of transit and terminates either

8.1.1 on delivery to the Consignees' or other final warehouse or place of storage at the destination named herein,

8.1.2 on delivery to any other warehouse or place of storage, whether prior to or at the destination named herein, which the Assured elect to use either

8.1.2.1 for storage other than in the ordinary course of transit or

8.1.2.2 for allocation or distribution,

or

8.1.3 on the expiry of 60 days after completion of discharge overside of the goods hereby insured from the oversea vessel at the final port of discharge, whichever shall first occur.

8.2 If, after discharge overside from the oversea vessel at the final port of discharge, but prior to termination of this insurance, the goods are to be forwarded to a destination other than that to which they are insured hereunder, this insurance, whilst remaining subject to termination as provided for above, shall not extend beyond the commencement of transit to such other destination.

8.3 This insurance shall remain in force (subject to termination as provided for above and to the provisions of Clause 9 below) during delay beyond the control of the Assured, any deviation forced discharge, reshipment or transhipment and during any variation of the adventure arising from the exercise of a liberty granted to shipowners or charterers under the contract of affreightment.

9 If owing to circumstances beyond the control of the Assured either the contract of carriage is terminated at a port or place other than the destination named therein or the transit is otherwise terminated before delivery of the goods as provided for in Clause 8 above, then this insurance shall also terminate unless prompt notice is given to the Underwriters and continuation of cover is requested when the insurance shall remain in force, subject to an additional premium if required by the Underwriters, either

9.1 until the goods are sold and delivered at such port or place, or, unless otherwise specially agreed, until the expiry of 60 days after arrival of the goods hereby insured at such port or place, whichever shall first occur, or

9.2 if the goods are forwarded within the said period of 60 days (or any agreed extension thereof) to the

destination named herein or to any other destination, until terminated in accordance with the provisions of Clause 8 above.

10 Where, after attachment of this insurance, the destination is changed by the Assured, held covered at a premium and on conditions to be arranged subject to prompt notice being given to the Underwriters.

CLAIMS

11 11.1 In order to recover under this insurance the Assured must have an insurable interest in the subject matter insured at the time of the loss.

11.2 Subject to 11.1 above, the Assured shall be entitled to recover for insured loss occurring during the period covered by this insurance,

Institute Cargo Clauses (C) [ICC (C)]

notwithstanding that the loss occurred before the contract of insurance was concluded, unless the Assured were aware of the loss and the Underwriters were not.

12 Where, as a result of the operation of a risk covered by this insurance, the insured transit is terminated at a port or place other than that to which the subject matter is covered under this insurance, the Underwriters will reimburse the Assured for any extra charges properly and reasonably incurred in unloading storing and forwarding the subject matter to the destination to which it is insured hereunder.

This Clause 12, which does not apply to general average or salvage charges, shall be subject to the exclusions contained in Clauses 4, 5, 6 and 7 above, and shall not include charges arising from the fault negligence insolvency or financial default of the Assured or their servants.

13 No claim for Constructive Total Loss shall be recoverable hereunder unless the subject matter insured is reasonably abandoned either on account of its actual total loss appearing to be unavoidable or because the cost of recovering, reconditioning and forwarding the subject matter to the destination to which it is insured would exceed its value on arrival.

14 14.1 If any Increased Value insurance is effected by the Assured on the cargo insured herein the agreed value of the cargo shall be deemed to be increased to the total amount insured under this insurance and all Increased Value insurances covering the loss, and liability under this insurance shall be in such proportion as the sum insured herein bears to such total amount insured.

In the event of claim the Assured shall provide the Underwriters with evidence of the amounts insured under all other insurances.

14.2 Where this insurance is on Increased Value the following clause shall apply:

The agreed value of the cargo shall be deemed to be equal to the total amount insured under the primary insurance and all Increased Value insurances covering the loss and effected on the cargo by the Assured, and liability under this insurance shall be in such proportion as the sum insured herein bears to such total amount insured.

In the event of claim the Assured shall provide the Underwriters with evidence of the amounts insured under all other insurances.

BENEFIT OF INSURANCE

15 This insurance shall not inure to the benefit of the carrier or other bailee.

MINIMISING LOSSES

16 It is the duty of the Assured and their servants and agents in respect of loss recoverable hereunder

  16.1 to take such measures as may be reasonable for the purpose of averting or minimising such loss,
  and

16.2 to ensure that all rights against carriers, bailees or other third parties are properly preserved and exercised

and the Underwriters will, in addition to any loss recoverable hereunder, reimburse the Assured for any charges properly and reasonably incurred in pursuance of these duties.

17 Measures taken by the Assured or the Underwriters with the object of saving, protecting or recovering the subject matter insured shall not be considered as a waiver or acceptance of abandonment or otherwise prejudice the rights of either party.

AVOIDANCE OF DELAY

18 It is a condition of this insurance that the Assured shall act with reasonable despatch in all circumstances within their control.

LAW AND PRACTICE

19 This insurance is subject to English law and practice.

NOTE—*It is necessary for the Assured when they become aware of an event which is 'held covered' under this insurance to give prompt notice to the Underwriters and the right to such cover is dependent upon compliance with this obligation.*

APPENDIX 13

1/11/95

(FOR USE ONLY WITH THE CURRENT MAR POLICY FORM)

INSTITUTE TIME CLAUSES
FREIGHT

This insurance is subject to English law and practice

1 **NAVIGATION**

    1.1   The Vessel has leave to dock and undock, to go into graving dock, to sail or navigate with or without pilots, to go on trial trips and to assist and tow vessels or craft in distress, but it is warranted that the Vessel shall not be towed, except as is customary or to the first safe port or place when in need of assistance, or undertake towage or salvage services under a contract previously arranged by the Assured and/or Owners and/or Managers and/or Charterers. This Clause 1 shall not exclude customary towage in connection with loading and discharging.

    1.2   This insurance shall not be prejudiced by reason of the Assured entering into any contract with pilots or for customary towage which limits or exempts the liability of the pilots and/or tugs and/or towboats and/or their owners when the Assured or their agents accept or are compelled to accept such contracts in accordance with established local law or practice.

    1.3   The practice of engaging helicopters for the transportation of personnel, supplies and equipment to and/or from the Vessel shall not prejudice this insurance.

2 **CRAFT RISK**

Including risk of craft and/or lighter to and from the Vessel.

3 **CONTINUATION**

Should the Vessel at the expiration of this insurance be at sea and in distress or missing, the subject matter insured shall, provided notice be given to the Underwriters prior to the expiration of this insurance, be held covered until arrival of the Vessel at the next port in good safety, or if in port and in distress until the Vessel is made safe, at a pro rata monthly premium.

4 **BREACH OF WARRANTY**

Held covered in case of any breach of warranty as to cargo, trade, locality, towage, salvage services or date of sailing, provided notice be given to the Underwriters immediately after receipt of advices and any amended terms of cover and any additional premium required by them be agreed.

5 CLASSIFICATION

5.1 It is the duty of the Assured, Owners and Managers at the inception of and throughout the period of this insurance to ensure that

5.1.1 the Vessel is classed with a Classification Society agreed by the Underwriters and that her class within that Society is maintained,

5.1.2 any recommendations requirements or restrictions imposed by the Vessel's Classification Society which relate to the Vessel's seaworthiness or to her maintenance in a seaworthy condition are complied with by the dates required by that Society.

5.2 In the event of any breach of the duties set out in Clause 5.1 above, unless the Underwriters agree to the contrary in writing, they will be discharged from liability under this insurance as from the date of the breach, provided that if the Vessel is at sea at such date the Underwriters' discharge from liability is deferred until arrival at her next port.

5.3 Any incident condition or damage in respect of which the Vessel's Classification Society might make recommendations as to repairs or other action to be taken by the Assured, Owners or Managers must be promptly reported to the Classification Society.

5.4 Should the Underwriters wish to approach the Classification Society directly for information and/or documents, the Assured will provide the necessary authorization.

6 TERMINATION

This Clause 6 shall prevail notwithstanding any provision whether written typed or printed in this insurance inconsistent therewith.

Unless the Underwriters agree to the contrary in writing, this insurance shall terminate automatically at the time of

6.1 change of the Classification Society of the Vessel, or change, suspension, discontinuance, withdrawal or expiry of her Class therein, or any of the Classification Society's periodic surveys becoming overdue unless an extension of time for such survey be agreed by the Classification Society, provided that if the Vessel is at sea such automatic termination shall be deferred until arrival at her next port. However where such change, suspension discontinuance or withdrawal of her Class or where a periodic survey becoming overdue has resulted from loss or damage covered by Clause 7 of this insurance or which would be covered by an insurance of the Vessel subject to current Institute Time Clauses Hulls or Institute War and Strikes Clauses Hulls-Time such automatic termination shall only operate should the Vessel sail from her next port without the prior approval of the Classification Society or in the case of a periodic survey becoming overdue without the Classification Society having agreed an extension of time for such survey,

6.2 any change, voluntary or otherwise, in the ownership or flag transfer to new management, or charter on a bareboat basis, or requisition for title or use of the Vessel, provided that, if the Vessel has cargo on board and has already sailed from her loading port or is at sea in ballast, such automatic termination shall if required be deferred, whilst the Vessel continues her planned voyage, until arrival at final port of discharge if with cargo or at port of destination if in ballast. However, in the event of requisition for title or use without the prior execution of a written agreement by the Assured, such automatic termination shall occur fifteen days after such requisition whether the Vessel is at sea or in port.

A pro rata daily net return of premium shall be made provided that a total loss of the Vessel, whether by insured perils or otherwise, has not occurred during the period covered by this insurance or any extension thereof.

7 PERILS

7.1 This insurance covers loss of the subject matter insured caused by

7.1.1 perils of the seas rivers lakes or other navigable waters

7.1.2 fire, explosion

7.1.3 violent theft by persons from outside the Vessel

7.1.4 jettison

7.1.5 piracy

7.1.6 contact with land conveyance, dock or harbour equipment or installation

7.1.7 earthquake volcanic eruption or lightning

7.1.8 accidents in loading discharging or shifting cargo or fuel.

7.2 This insurance covers loss of the subject matter insured caused by

7.2.1 bursting of boilers breakage of shafts or any latent defect in the machinery or hull

7.2.2 negligence of Master Officers Crew or Pilots

7.2.3 negligence of repairers or charterers provided such repairers or charterers are not an Assured hereunder

7.2.4 barratry of Master Officers or Crew

7.2.5 contact with aircraft, helicopters or similar objects or objects falling therefrom

provided that such loss has not resulted from want of due diligence by the Assured, Owners. Managers or Superintendents or any of their onshore management.

7.3 Masters Officers Crew or Pilots not to be considered Owners within the meaning of this Clause 7 should they hold shares in the Vessel.

8 POLLUTION HAZARD

This insurance covers loss of the subject matter insured caused by any governmental authority acting under the powers vested in it to prevent or mitigate a pollution hazard or damage to the environment, or threat thereof, resulting directly from a peril covered by this insurance, provided that such act of governmental authority has not resulted from want of due diligence by the Assured, Owners or Managers to prevent or mitigate such hazard or damage, or threat thereof. Masters Officers Crew or Pilots not to be considered Owners within the meaning of this Clause 8 should they hold shares in the Vessel.

9 FREIGHT COLLISION

9.1 It is further agreed that if the Vessel shall come into collision with any other vessel and the Assured shall in consequence thereof become liable to pay and shall pay by way of damages to any other person or persons any sum or sums in respect of the amount of freight taken into account in calculating the measure of the liability of the Assured for

9.1.1 loss of or damage to any other vessel or property on any other vessel

9.].2 delay to or loss of use of any such other vessel or property thereon

9.1.3 general average of, salvage of, or salvage under contract of, any such other vessel or property thereon, the Underwriters will pay the Assured such proportion of three-fourths of such sum or sums so paid applying to freight as their respective subscriptions hereto bear to the total amount insured on freight, or to the gross freight earned on the voyage during which the collision occurred if this be greater.

9.2 Provided always that:

9.2.1 liability of the Underwriters in respect of any one such collision shall not exceed their proportionate part of three-fourths of the total amount insured hereon on freight, and in cases in which, with the prior consent in writing of the Underwriters, the liability of the vessel has been contested or proceedings have been taken to limit liability, they will also pay a like proportion of three-fourths of the costs, appertaining proportionately to the freight portion of damages. which the Assured shall thereby incur or be compelled to pay:

9.2.2 no claim shall attach to this insurance:

9.2.2.1 which attaches to any other insurances covering collision liabilities

9.2.2.2 which is or would be, recoverable in the terms of the Institute 3/4ths Collision Liability Clause if the Vessel were insured in the terms of such Institute 3/4ths Collision Liability Clause for a value not less than the equivalent in pounds sterling, at the time of commencement of this insurance, of the Vessel's limit of liability calculated in accordance with Article 6.1(b) of the 1976 Limitation Convention,

9.2.3 this Clause 9 shall in no case extend or be deemed to extend to any sum which the Assured may become liable to pay or shall pay for or in respect of

9.2.3.1 removal or disposal, under statutory powers or otherwise, of obstructions, wrecks, cargoes or any other thing whatsoever

9.2.3.2 any real or personal property or thing whatsoever except other vessels or property on other vessels

Institute Time Clauses Freight (1995) [ITCF(95)]

9.2.3.3 pollution or contamination, or threat thereof, of any real or personal property or thing whatsoever (except other vessels with which the insured Vessel is in collision or property on such other vessels) or damage to the environment, or threat thereof, save that this exclusion shall not extend to any sum which the Assured shall pay for or in respect of salvage remuneration in which the skill and efforts of the salvors in preventing or minimising damage to the environment as is referred to in Article 13 paragraph 1(b) of the International Convention on Salvage, 1989 have been taken into account

9.2.3.4 the cargo or other property on or the engagements of the Vessel

9.2.3.5 loss of life, personal injury or illness.

10 SISTERSHIP

Should the Vessel named herein come into collision with or receive salvage services from another vessel belonging wholly or in part to the same Owners, or under the same management, the Assured shall have the same rights under this insurance as they would have were the other vessel entirely the property of Owners not interested in the Vessel named herein; but in such cases the liability for the collision or the amount payable for the services rendered shall be referred to a sole arbitrator to be agreed upon between the Underwriters and the Assured.

11 GENERAL AVERAGE AND SALVAGE 143

11.1 This insurance covers the proportion of general average, salvage and/or salvage charges attaching to freight at risk of the Assured, reduced in respect of any under-insurance.

11.2 Adjustment to be according to the law and practice obtaining at the place where the adventure ends, as if the contract of affreightment contained no special terms upon the subject; but where the contract of affreightment so provides the adjustment shall be according to the York-Antwerp Rules.

11.3 No claim under this Clause 11 shall in any case be allowed where the loss was not incurred to avoid or in connection with the avoidance of a peril insured against.

11.4 No claim under this Clause 11 shall in any case be allowed for or in respect of

11.4.1 special compensation payable to a salvor under Article 14 of the International Convention on Salvage, 1989 or under any other provision in any statute, rule, law or contract which is similar in substance

11.4.2 expenses or liabilities incurred in respect of damage to the environment, or the threat of such damage, or as a consequence of the escape or release of pollutant substances from the Vessel, or the threat of such escape or release.

11.5 Clause 11.4 shall not however exclude any sum which the Assured shall pay to salvors for or in respect of salvage remuneration in which the skill and efforts of the salvors in preventing or minimising damage to the environment as is referred to in Article 13 paragraph 1(b) of the International Convention on Salvage, 1989 have been taken into account.

12 FRANCHISE

This insurance does not cover partial loss, other than general average loss, under 3% unless caused by fire, sinking, stranding or collision with another vessel. Each craft and/or lighter to be deemed a separate insurance if required by the Assured.

13 ASSIGNMENT

No assignment of or interest in this insurance or in any moneys which may be or become payable thereunder is to be binding on or recognised by the Underwriters unless a dated notice of such assignment or interest signed by the Assured, and by the assignor in the case of subsequent assignment, is endorsed on the Policy and the Policy with such endorsement is produced before payment of any claim or return of premium thereunder.

14 MEASURE OF INDEMNITY

14.1 The amount recoverable under this insurance for any claim for loss of freight shall not exceed the gross freight actually lost.

14.2 Where insurances on freight other than this insurance are current at the time of the loss, all such insurances shall be taken into consideration in calculating the liability under this insurance and the amount recoverable hereunder shall not exceed the rateable proportion of the gross freight lost, notwithstanding any valuation in this or any other insurance.

14.3 In calculating the liability under Clause 11 all insurances on freight shall likewise be taken into consideration.

14.4 Nothing in this Clause 14 shall apply to any claim arising under Clause 16.

15 LOSS OF TIME

This insurance does not cover any claims consequent on loss of time whether arising from a peril of the sea or otherwise.

16 TOTAL LOSS

16.1 In the event of the total loss (actual or constructive) of the Vessel named herein the amount insured shall be paid in full, whether the Vessel be fully or partly loaded or in ballast, chartered or unchartered.

16.2 In ascertaining whether the Vessel is a constructive total loss, the insured value in the insurances on hull and machinery shall be taken as the repaired value and nothing in respect of the damaged or break-up value of the Vessel or wreck shall be taken into account.

16.3 Should the Vessel be a constructive total loss but the claim on the insurances on hull and machinery be settled as a claim for partial loss, no payment shall be due under this Clause 16.

17 RETURNS FOR LAY-UP AND CANCELLATION

17.1 To return as follows:

17.1.1 pro rata monthly net for each uncommenced month if this insurance be cancelled by agreement,

17.1.2 for each period of 30 consecutive days the Vessel may be laid up in a port or in a lay-up area provided such port or lay-up area is approved by the Underwriters

    (a) .... per cent net not under repair

    (b) .... per cent net under repair.

17.1.3 The Vessel shall not be considered to be under repair when work is undertaken in respect of ordinary wear and tear of the Vessel and/or following recommendations in the Vessel's Classification Society survey, but any repairs following loss of or damage to the Vessel or involving structural alterations. whether covered by this insurance or otherwise shall be considered as under repair.

17.1.4 If the Vessel is under repair during part only of a period for which a return is claimable, the return shall be calculated pro rata to the number of days under 17.1.2(a) and (b) respectively.

17.2 PROVIDED ALWAYS THAT

17.2.1 a total loss of the Vessel, whether by insured perils or otherwise, has not occurred during the period covered by this insurance or any extension thereof

17.2.2 in no case shall a return be allowed when the Vessel is lying in exposed or unprotected waters, or in a port or lay-up area not approved by the Underwriters

17.2.3 loading or discharging operations or the presence of cargo on board shall not debar returns but no return shall be allowed for any period during which the Vessel is being used for the storage of cargo or for lightering purposes

17.2.4 in the event of any amendment of the annual rate, the above rates of return shall be adjusted accordingly

17.2.5 in the event of any return recoverable under this Clause 17 being based on 30 consecutive days which fall on successive insurances effected for the same Assured, this insurance shall only be liable for an amount calculated at pro rata of the period rates 17.1.2(a) and/or (b) above for the number of days which come within the period of this insurance and to which a return is actually applicable. Such overlapping period shall run, at the option of the Assured, either from the first day on which the Vessel is laid up or the first day of a period of 30 consecutive days as provided under 17.1.2(a) or (b) above.

The following clauses shall be paramount and shall override anything contained in this insurance inconsistent therewith.

18 WAR EXCLUSION

In no case shall this insurance cover loss damage liability or expense caused by

18.1 war civil war revolution rebellion insurrection, or civil strife arising therefrom, or any hostile act by or against a belligerent power

18.2 capture seizure arrest restraint or detainment (barratry and piracy excepted), and the consequences thereof or any attempt thereat

18.3 derelict mines torpedoes bombs or other derelict weapons of war.

19 STRIKES EXCLUSION

In no case shall this insurance cover loss damage liability or expense caused by

19.1 strikers, locked-out workmen, or persons taking part in labour disturbances, riots or civil commotions

19.2 any terrorist or any person acting from a political motive.

20 MALICIOUS ACTS EXCLUSION

In no case shall this insurance cover loss damage liability or expense arising from

20.1 the detonation of an explosive

20.2 any weapon of war

and caused by any person acting maliciously or from a political motive.

21 RADIOACTIVE CONTAMINATION EXCLUSION CLAUSE

In no case shall this insurance cover loss damage liability or expense directly or indirectly caused by or contributed to by or arising from

21.1 ionising radiation from or contamination by radioactivity from any nuclear fuel or from any nuclear waste or from the combustion of nuclear fuel

21.2 the radioactive, toxic, explosive or other hazardous or contaminating properties of any nuclear installation, reactor or other nuclear assembly or nuclear component thereof

21.3 any weapon of war employing atomic or nuclear fission and/or fusion or other like reaction or radioactive force or matter.

APPENDIX 14

1/11/95

(FOR USE ONLY WITH THE CURRENT MAR POLICY FORM)

INSTITUTE VOYAGE CLAUSES
FREIGHT

This insurance is subject to English law and practice

1 NAVIGATION

1.1 The Vessel has leave to dock and undock, to go into graving dock, to sail or navigate with or without pilots, to go on trial trips and to assist and tow vessels or craft in distress, but it is warranted that the Vessel shall not be towed, except as is customary or to the first safe port or place when in need of assistance, or undertake towage or salvage services under a contract previously arranged by the Assured and/or Owners and/or Managers and/or Charterers. This Clause 1 shall not exclude customary towage in connection with loading and discharging.

1.2 This insurance shall not be prejudiced by reason of the Assured entering into any contract with pilots or for customary towage which limits or exempts the liability of the pilots and/or tugs and/or towboats and/or their owners when the Assured or their agents accept or are compelled to accept such contracts in accordance with established local law or practice.

1.3 The practice of engaging helicopters for the transportation of personnel, supplies and equipment to and/or from the Vessel shall not prejudice this insurance.

2 CRAFT RISK

Including risk of craft and/or lighter to and from the Vessel.

3 CHANGE OF VOYAGE

Held covered in case of deviation or change of voyage or any breach of warranty as to towage or salvage services, provided notice be given to the Underwriters immediately after receipt of advices and any amended terms of cover and any additional premium required by them be agreed.

4 PERILS

4.1 This insurance covers loss of the subject matter insured caused by

4.1.1 perils of the seas rivers lakes or other navigable waters

4.1.2 fire, explosion

4.1.3 violent theft by persons from outside the Vessel

4.1.4 jettison

4.1.5 piracy

4.1.6 contact with land conveyance, dock or harbour equipment or installation

4.1.7 earthquake volcanic eruption or lightning

4.1.8 accidents in loading discharging or shifting cargo or fuel.

4.2 This insurance covers loss of the subject matter insured caused by

4.2.1 bursting of boilers breakage of shafts or any latent defect in the machinery or hull

4.2.2 negligence of Master Officers Crew or Pilots

4.2.3 negligence of repairers or charterers provided such repairers or charterers are not an Assured hereunder

4.2.4 barratry of Master Officers or Crew

4.2.5 contact with aircraft, helicopters or similar objects, or objects falling therefrom

provided that such loss has not resulted from want of due diligence by the Assured, Owners, Managers or Superintendents or any of their onshore management.

4.3 Masters Officers Crew or Pilots not to be considered Owners within the meaning of this Clause should they hold shares in the Vessel.

5 POLLUTION HAZARD

This insurance covers loss of the subject matter insured caused by any governmental authority acting under the powers vested in it to prevent or mitigate a pollution hazard or damage to the environment, or threat thereof, resulting directly from a peril covered by this insurance, provided that such act of governmental authority has not resulted from want of due diligence by the Assured, Owners and Managers to prevent or mitigate such hazard or damage, or threat thereof. Masters Officers Crew or Pilots not to be considered Owners within the meaning of this Clause 5 should they hold shares in the Vessel.

6 FREIGHT COLLISION

6.1 It is further agreed that if the Vessel shall come into collision with any other vessel and the Assured shall in consequence thereof become liable to pay and shall pay by way of damages to any other person or persons any sum or sums in respect of the amount of freight taken into account in calculating the measure of the liability of the Assured for

6.1.1 loss of or damage to any other vessel or property on any other vessel

6.1.2 delay to or loss of use of any such other vessel or property thereon

6.1.3 general average of, salvage of or salvage under contract of, any such other vessel or property thereon, the Underwriters will pay the Assured such proportion of three-fourths of such sum or sums so paid applying to freight as their respective subscriptions hereto bear

Institute Voyage Clauses Freight (1995) [IVCF(95)]

to the total amount insured on freight, or to the gross freight earned on the voyage during which the collision occurred if this be greater.

6.2 Provided always that:

6.2.1 liability of the Underwriters in respect of any one such collision shall not exceed their proportionate part of three-fourths of the total amount insured hereon on freight, and in cases in which, with the prior consent in writing of the Underwriters, the liability of the Vessel has been contested or proceedings have been taken to limit liability, they will also pay a like proportion of three-fourths of the costs, appertaining proportionately to the freight portion of damages, which the Assured shall thereby incur or be compelled to pay;

6.2.2 no claim shall attach to this insurance:

6.2.2.1 which attaches to any other insurances covering collision liabilities

6.2.2.2 which is, or would be, recoverable in the terms of the Institute 3/4ths Collision Liability Clause if the Vessel were insured in the terms of such Institute 3/4ths Collision Liability Clause for a value not less than the equivalent in pounds sterling, at the time of commencement of this insurance, of the Vessel's limit of liability calculated in accordance with Article 6.1(b) of the 1976 Limitation Convention,

6.2.3 this Clause 6 shall in no case extend or be deemed to extend to any sum which the Assured may become liable to pay or shall pay for in respect of:

6.2.3.1 removal or disposal, under statutory powers or otherwise, of obstructions, wrecks, cargoes or any other thing whatsoever

6.2.3.2 any real or personal property or thing whatsoever except other vessels or property on other vessels

6.2.3.3 pollution or contamination, or threat thereof, of any real or personal property or thing

whatsoever (except other vessels with which the insured Vessel is in collision or property on such other vessels) or damage to the environment, or threat thereof, save that this exclusion shall not extend to any sum which the Assured shall pay for or in respect of salvage remuneration in which the skill and efforts of the salvors in preventing or minimising damage to the environment as is referred to in Article 13 paragraph 1(b) of the International Convention on Salvage, 1989 have been taken into account

6.2.3.4 the cargo or other property on or the engagements of the Vessel

6.2.3.5 loss of life, personal injury or illness.

7 SISTERSHIP

Should the Vessel named herein come into collision with or receive salvage services from another vessel belonging wholly or in part to the same Owners or under the same management, the Assured shall have the same rights under this insurance as they would have were the other vessel entirely the property of Owners not interested in the Vessel named herein; but in such cases the liability for the collision or the amount payable for the services rendered shall be referred to a sole arbitrator to be agreed upon between the Underwriters and the Assured.

8 GENERAL AVERAGE AND SALVAGE

8.1 This insurance covers the proportion of general average, salvage and/or salvage charges attaching to freight at risk of the Assured, reduced in respect of any under-insurance.

8.2 Adjustment to be according to the law and practice obtaining at the place where the adventure ends. as if the contract of affreightment contains no special terms upon the subject, but where the contract so provides the adjustment shall be according to the York-Antwerp Rules.

8.3 No claim under this Clause 8 shall in any case be allowed where the loss was not incurred to avoid or in connection with the avoidance of a peril insured against.

8.4 No claim under this Clause 8 shall be in any case allowed for or in respect of

8.4.1 special compensation payable to a salvor under Article 14 of the International Convention on Salvage, 1989 or under any other provision in any statute, rule, law or contract which is similar in substance;

8.4.2 expenses or liabilities incurred in respect of damage to the environment, or the threat of such damage, or as a consequence of the escape or release of pollutant substances from the Vessel, or the threat of such escape or release.

8.5 Clause 8.4 shall not however exclude any sum which the Assured shall pay to salvors for or in respect of salvage remuneration in which the skill and efforts of the salvors in preventing or minimising damage to the environment as is referred to in Article 13 paragraph 1(b) of the International Convention on Salvage, 1989 have been taken into account.

9 FRANCHISE

This insurance does not cover partial loss, other than general average loss, under 3% unless caused by fire, sinking, stranding or collision with another vessel. Each craft and/or lighter to be deemed a separate insurance if required by the Assured.

10 MEASURE OF INDEMNITY

10.1 The amount recoverable under this insurance for any claim for loss of freight shall not exceed the gross freight actually lost.

10.2 Where insurances on freight other than this insurance are current at the time of the loss, all such insurances shall be taken into consideration in calculating the liability under this insurance and the amount recoverable hereunder shall not exceed the rateable proportion of the gross freight lost, notwithstanding any valuation in

Institute Voyage Clauses Freight (1995) [IVCF(95)]

this or any other insurance. In calculating the liability under Clause 8 all insurances on freight shall likewise be taken into consideration.

10.4   Nothing in this Clause 10 shall apply to any claim arising under Clause 12.

11 LOSS OF TIME

This insurance does not cover any claim consequent on loss of time whether arising from a peril of the sea or otherwise.

12 TOTAL LOSS

12.1   In the event of the total loss (actual or constructive) of the Vessel named herein the amount insured shall be paid in full, whether the Vessel be fully or partly loaded or in ballast, chartered or unchartered.

12.2   In ascertaining whether the Vessel is a constructive total loss, the insured value in the insurances on hull and machinery shall be taken as the repaired value and nothing in respect of the damaged or break-up value of the Vessel or wreck shall be taken into account.

12.3   Should the Vessel be a constructive total loss but the claim on the insurances on hull and machinery be settled as a claim for partial loss, no payment shall be due under this Clause 12.

13 ASSIGNMENT

No assignment of or interest in this insurance or in any moneys which may be or become payable thereunder is to be binding on or recognised by the Underwriters unless a dated notice of such assignment or interest signed by the Assured, and by the assignor in the case of subsequent assignment, is endorsed on the Policy and the Policy with such endorsement is produced before payment of any claim or return of premium thereunder.

The following clauses shall be paramount and shall override anything contained in this insurance inconsistent therewith.

14 WAR EXCLUSION

In no case shall this insurance cover loss damage liability or expense caused by

14.1   war civil war revolution rebellion insurrection, or civil strife arising therefrom, or any hostile act by or against a belligerent power

14.2   capture seizure arrest restraint or detainment (barratry and piracy excepted), and the consequences thereof or any attempt thereat

14.3   derelict mines torpedoes bombs or other derelict weapons of war.

15 STRIKES EXCLUSION

In no case shall this insurance cover loss damage liability or expense caused by

15.1   strikers, locked-out workmen, or persons taking part in labour disturbances, riots or civil commotions

15.2   any terrorist or any person acting from a political motive.

16 MALICIOUS ACTS EXCLUSION

In no case shall this insurance cover loss damage liability or expense arising from

16.1   the detonation of an explosive

16.2   any weapon of war and caused by any person acting maliciously or from a political motive.

17 RADIOACTIVE CONTAMINATION EXCLUSION CLAUSE

In no case shall this insurance cover loss damage liability or expense directly or indirectly caused by or contributed to by or arising from

17.1   ionising radiations from or contamination by radioactivity from any nuclear fuel or from any nuclear waste or from the combustion of nuclear fuel

17.2   the radioactive, toxic, explosive or other hazardous or contaminating properties of any nuclear installation, reactor or other nuclear assembly or nuclear component thereof

17.3   any weapon of war employing atomic or nuclear fission and/or fusion or other like reaction or radioactive force or matter.

APPENDIX 15

1/5/61

INSTITUTE DUAL VALUATION CLAUSE

(a) Insured value for purposes of Total Loss (Actual or Constructive) ....£..............................

(b) Insured value for purposes other than Total Loss ....£..............................

In the event of a claim for Actual or Constructive Total Loss (a) shall be taken to be the insured value and payment by the Underwriters of their proportions of that amount shall be for all purposes payment of a Total Loss.

In ascertaining whether the vessel is a Constructive Total Loss (a) shall be taken as the repaired value and nothing in respect of the damaged or break-up value of the vessel or wreck shall be taken into account.

No claim for Constructive Total Loss based upon the cost of recovery and/or repair of the Vessel shall be recoverable hereunder unless such cost would exceed the insured value as in (a).

In no case shall Underwriters' liability in respect of a claim for unrepaired damage exceed the insured value as in (a).

Additional insurances allowed under the Disbursements Clause to be calculated on the amount of the insured value as in (a).

APPENDIX 16

1/7/76

INSTITUTE WARRANTIES

1. Warranted no:
    (a) Atlantic Coast of North America, its rivers or adjacent islands,
       (i) north of $52°\ 10'$ N Lat and west of $50°$ W Long;
       (ii) south of $52°\ 10'$ N Lat in the area bounded by lines drawn between Battle Harbour/Pistolet Bay; Cape Ray/Cape North; Port Hawkesbury/Port Mulgrave and Baie Comeau/Matane between 21st December and 30th April both days inclusive.
       (iii) west of Baie Comeau/Matane (but not west of Montreal) between 1st December and 30th April both days inclusive.
    (b) Great Lakes or St Lawrence Seaway west of Montreal.
    (c) Greenland Waters.
    (d) Pacific Coast of North America its rivers or adjacent islands north of $54°\ 30'$ N Lat, or west of $130°\ 50'$ W Long
2. Warranted no Baltic Sea or adjacent waters east of $15°$ E Long:
    (a) North of a line between Mo ($63°\ 24'$ N Lat) and Vasa ($63°\ 06'$ N Lat) between 10th December and 25th May bdi.
    (b) East of a line between Viipuri (Vyborg) ($28°\ 47'$ E Long) and Narva ($28°\ 12'$ E Long) between 15th December and 15th May bdi.
    (c) North of a line between Stockholm ($59°\ 20'$ N Lat) and Tallinn ($59°\ 24'$ N Lat) between 8th January and 5th May bdi.
    (d) East of $22°$ E Long, and south of $59°$ N Lat between 28th December and 5th May bdi.
3. Warranted not North of $70°$ N Lat other than voyages direct to or from any port or place in Norway or Kola Bay.
4. Warranted no Bering Sea, no East Asian waters north of $46°$ N Lat and not to enter or sail from any port or place in Siberia except Nakhodka and/or Vladivostock.
5. Warranted not to proceed to Kerguelen and/or Croset Islands or south of $50°$ S Lat, except to ports and/or places in Patagonia and/or Chile and/or Falkland Islands, but liberty is given to enter waters south of $50°$ S Lat, if en route to or from ports and/or places not excluded by this warranty.
6. Warranted not to sail with Indian Coal as cargo:
    (a) between 1st March and 30th June, bdi.
    (b) between 1st July and 30th September, bdi, except to ports in Asia, not West of Aden or East of or beyond Singapore.

APPENDIX 17

1/8/82

INSTITUTE MALICIOUS DAMAGE CLAUSE

In consideration of an additional premium, it is hereby agreed that the exclusion 'deliberate damage to or deliberate destruction of the subject-matter insured or any part thereof by the wrongful act of any person or persons' is deemed to be deleted and further that this insurance covers loss of or damage to the subject-matter insured caused by malicious acts vandalism or sabotage, subject always to the other exclusions contained in this insurance.

APPENDIX 18

1/12/82

INSTITUTE THEFT, PILFERAGE AND NON-DELIVERY CLAUSE

(For use only with Institute Clauses)

In consideration of an additional premium, it is hereby agreed that this insurance covers loss of or damage to the subject-matter insured caused by theft or pilferage, or by non-delivery of an entire package, subject always to the exclusions contained in this insurance.

APPENDIX 19

1/11/95

(FOR USE ONLY WITH THE CURRENT MAR POLICY FORM)

INSTITUTE WAR AND STRIKES CLAUSES

HULLS – TIME

This insurance is subject to English law and practice

1 PERILS

Subject always to the exclusions hereinafter referred to, this insurance covers loss of or damage to the Vessel caused by

1.1 war civil war revolution rebellion insurrection, or civil strife arising therefrom, or any hostile act by or against a belligerent power

1.2 capture seizure arrest restraint or detainment. and the consequences thereof or any attempt thereat

1.3 derelict mines torpedoes bombs or other derelict weapons of war

1.4 strikers, locked-out workmen, or persons taking part in labour disturbances, riots or civil commotions

1.5 any terrorist or any person acting maliciously or from a political motive

1.6 confiscation or expropriation.

2 INCORPORATION

The Institute Time Clauses – Hulls 1/11/95 (including 3/4ths Collision Liability Clause amended to 4/4ths) except Clauses 1.4, 2, 3, 4, 5, 6, 12, 22,1.8, 23, 24, 25, 26 and 27 are deemed to be incorporated in this insurance in so far as they do not conflict with the provisions of these clauses.

Held covered in case of breach of warranty as to towage or salvage services provided notice be given to the Underwriters immediately after receipt of advices and any additional premium required by them be agreed.

3 DETAINMENT

In the event that the Vessel shall have been the subject of capture seizure arrest restraint detainment confiscation or expropriation, and the Assured shall thereby have lost the free use and disposal of the Vessel for a continuous period of 12 months then for the purpose of ascertaining whether the Vessel is a constructive total loss the Assured shall be deemed to have been deprived of the possession of the Vessel without any likelihood of recovery.

4 NOTICE OF CLAIM AND TENDERS

In the event of accident whereby loss or damage may result in a claim under this insurance, notice must be given to the Underwriters promptly after the date on which the Assured, Owners or Managers become or should have become aware of the loss or damage and prior to survey so that a surveyor may be appointed if the Underwriters so desire. If notice is not given to Underwriters within twelve months of that date unless the Underwriters agree to the contrary in writing, the Underwriters will be automatically discharged from liability for any claim under this insurance in respect of or arising out of such accident or the loss or damage.

5 EXCLUSIONS

This insurance excludes

5.1   loss damage liability or expense arising from

5.1.1   the outbreak of war (whether there be a declaration of war or not) between any of the following countries:

United Kingdom, United States of America, France, the Russian Federation, the People's Republic of China

5.1.2   requisition, either for title or use, or pre-emption

5.1.3   capture seizure arrest restraint detainment confiscation or expropriation by or under the order of the government or any public or local authority of the country in which the Vessel is owned or registered

5.1.4   arrest restraint detainment confiscation or expropriation under quarantine regulations or by reason of infringement of any customs or trading regulations

5.1.5   the operation of ordinary judicial process, failure to provide security or to pay any fine or penalty or any financial cause

5.1.6   piracy (but this exclusion shall not affect cover under Clause 1.4),

5.2   loss damage liability or expense directly or indirectly caused by or contributed to by or arising from

5.2.1   ionising radiations from or contamination by radioactivity from any nuclear fuel or from any nuclear waste or from the combustion of nuclear fuel

5.2.2   the radioactive, toxic, explosive or other hazardous or contaminating properties of any nuclear installation, reactor or other nuclear assembly or nuclear component thereof

5.2.3   any weapon of war employing atomic or nuclear fission and/or fusion or other like reaction or radioactive force or matter.

5.3   loss damage liability or expense covered by the Institute Time Clauses – Hulls 1/11/95 (including 3/4ths Collision Liability Clause amended to 4/4ths) or which would be recoverable thereunder but for Clause 12 thereof,

- 5.4 any claim for any sum recoverable under any other insurance on the Vessel or which would be recoverable under such insurance but for the existence of this insurance,
- 5.5 any claim for expenses arising from delay except such expenses as would be recoverable in principle in English law and practice under the York-Antwerp Rules 1994.

6 TERMINATION

- 6.1 This insurance may be cancelled by either the Underwriters or the Assured giving 7 days notice (such cancellation becoming effective on the expiry of 7 days from midnight of the day on which notice of cancellation is issued by or to the Underwriters). The Underwriters agree however to reinstate this insurance subject to agreement between the Underwriters and the Assured prior to the expiry of such notice of cancellation as to new rate of premium and/or conditions and/or warranties.
- 6.2 Whether or not such notice of cancellation has been given this insurance shall TERMINATE AUTOMATICALLY
- 6.2.1 upon the outbreak of war (whether there be a declaration of war or not) between any of the following countries:

  United Kingdom, United States of America, France, the Russian Federation, the People's Republic of China
- 6.2.2 in the event of the Vessel being requisitioned, either for title or use.
- 6.3 In the event either of cancellation by notice or of automatic termination of this insurance by reason of the operation of this Clause 6, or of the sale of the Vessel, pro rata net return of premium shall be payable to the Assured.

This insurance shall not become effective if, subsequent to its acceptance by the Underwriters and prior to the intended time of its attachment, there has occurred any event which would have automatically terminated this insurance under the provisions of Clause 6 above.

APPENDIX 20

1/1/82

INSTITUTE WAR CLAUSES (CARGO)

RISKS COVERED

1 This insurance covers, except as provided in Clauses 3 and 4 below, loss of or damage to the subject matter insured caused by

    1.1   war civil war revolution rebellion insurrection, or civil strife arising therefrom, or any hostile act by or against a belligerent power

    1.2   capture seizure arrest restraint or detainment, arising from risks covered under 1.1 above, and the consequences thereof or any attempt thereat

    1.3   derelict mines torpedoes bombs or other derelict weapons of war.

2 This insurance covers general average and salvage charges, adjusted or determined according to the contract of affreightment and/or the governing law and practice, incurred to avoid or in connection with the avoidance of loss from a risk covered under these clauses.

EXCLUSIONS

3 In no case shall this insurance cover

    3.1   loss damage or expense attributable to wilful misconduct of the Assured

    3 2   ordinary leakage, ordinary loss in weight or volume, or ordinary wear and tear of the subject matter insured

    3.3   loss damage or expense caused by insufficiency or unsuitability of packing or preparation of the subject matter insured (for the purpose of this Clause 3.3 'packing' shall be deemed to include stowage in a container or liftvan but only when such stowage is carried out prior to attachment of this insurance or by the Assured or their servants)

    3.4   loss damage or expense caused by inherent vice or nature of the subject matter insured

    3.5   loss damage or expense proximately caused by delay, even though the delay be caused by a risk insured against (except expenses payable under Clause 2 above)

    3.6   loss damage or expense arising from insolvency or financial default of the owners managers charterers or operators of the vessel

    3.7   any claim based upon loss of or frustration of the voyage or adventure

    3.8   loss damage or expense arising from any hostile use of any weapon of war employing atomic or nuclear fission and/or fusion or other like reaction or radioactive force or matter.

Institute War Clauses (Cargo) (1982) [IWC(C)(82)]

4   4.1   In no case shall this insurance cover loss damage or expense arising from

unseaworthiness of vessel or craft,

unfitness of vessel craft conveyance container or liftvan for the safe carriage of the subject matter insured,

where the Assured or their servants are privy to such unseaworthiness or unfitness, at the time the subject matter insured is loaded therein.

    4.2   The Underwriters waive any breach of the implied warranties of seaworthiness of the ship and fitness of the ship to carry the subject matter insured to destination, unless the Assured or their servants are privy to such unseaworthiness or unfitness.

DURATION

5   5.1   This insurance

       5.1.1   attaches only as the subject matter insured and as to any part as that part is loaded on an oversea vessel

and

       5.1.2   terminates, subject to 5.2 and 5.3 below, either as the subject matter insured and as to any part as that part is discharged from an oversea vessel at the final port or place of discharge,

or

on expiry of 15 days counting from midnight of the day of arrival of the vessel at the final port or place of discharge,

whichever shall first occur;

nevertheless,

subject to prompt notice to the Underwriters and to an additional premium, such insurance

       5.1.3   reattaches when, without having discharged the subject matter insured at the final port or place of discharge, the vessel sails therefrom,

and

       5.1.4   terminates subject to 5.2 and 5.3 below, either as the subject matter insured and as to any part as that part is thereafter discharged from the vessel at the final (or substituted) port or place of discharge,

or

on expiry of 15 days counting from midnight of the day of re-arrival of the vessel at the final port or place of discharge or arrival of the vessel at a substituted port or place of discharge, whichever shall first occur.

    5.2   If during the insured voyage the oversea vessel arrives at an intermediate port or place to discharge the subject matter insured for on-carriage by oversea vessel or by aircraft, or the goods are discharged from the vessel at a port or place of refuge, then, subject to 5.3 below and to an additional premium if required, this insurance continues until the expiry of 15 days counting from midnight of the day of arrival of the vessel at such port or place, but thereafter reattaches as the subject matter insured and as to any part as that part is loaded on an on-carrying oversea vessel or aircraft. During the period of 15 days the insurance remains in force after discharge only whilst the subject matter insured and as to any part as that part is at such port or place. If the goods are on-carried within the said period of 15 days or if the insurance reattaches as provided in this Clause 5.2

5.2.1 where the on-carriage is by oversea vessel this insurance continues subject to the terms of these clauses,

or

5.2.2 where the on-carriage is by aircraft, the current Institute War Clauses (Air Cargo) (excluding sendings by Post) shall be deemed to form part of this insurance and shall apply to the on-carriage by air.

5.3 If the voyage in the contract of carriage is terminated at a port or place other than the destination agreed therein, such port or place shall be deemed the final port of discharge and such insurance terminates in accordance with 5.1.2. If the subject matter insured is subsequently reshipped to the original or any other destination, then provided notice is given to the Underwriters before the commencement of such further transit and subject to an additional premium, such insurance reattaches

5.3.1 in the case of the subject matter insured having been discharged, as the subject matter insured and as to any part as that part is loaded on the on-carrying vessel for the voyage;

5.3.2 in the case of the subject matter not having been discharged, when the vessel sails from such deemed final port of discharge; thereafter such insurance terminates in accordance with 5.1.4.

5.4 The insurance against the risks of mines and derelict torpedoes, floating or submerged, is extended whilst the subject matter insured or any part thereof is on craft whilst in transit to or from the oversea vessel, but in no case beyond the expiry of 60 days after discharge from the oversea vessel unless otherwise specially agreed by the Underwriters.

5.5 *Subject to prompt notice to Underwriters, and to an additional premium if required*, this insurance shall remain in force within the provisions of these Clauses during any deviation, or any variation of the adventure arising from the exercise of a liberty granted to shipowners or charterers under the contract of affreightment

(For the purpose of Clause 5

'arrival' shall be deemed to mean that the vessel is anchored, moored or otherwise secured at a berth or place within the Harbour Authority area. If such a berth or place is not available, arrival is deemed to have occurred when the vessel first anchors, moors or otherwise secures either at or off the intended port or place of discharge 'oversea vessel' shall be deemed to mean a vessel carrying the subject matter from one port or place to another where such voyage involves a sea passage by that vessel)

6 Where, after attachment of this insurance, the destination is changed by the Assured, *held covered at a premium and on conditions to be arranged subject to prompt notice being given to the Underwriters.*

7 **Anything contained in this contract which is inconsistent with Clauses 3.7, 3.8 or 5 shall, to the extent of such inconsistency, be null and void.**

CLAIMS

8 8.1 In order to recover under this insurance the Assured must have an insurable interest in the Insurable subject matter insured at the time of the loss.

    8.2 Subject to 8.1 above, the Assured shall be entitled to recover for insured loss occurring during the period covered by this insurance, notwithstanding that the loss occurred before the contract of insurance was concluded, unless the Assured were aware of the loss and the Underwriters were not.

9 9.1 If any Increased Value insurance is effected by the Assured on the cargo insured herein the Increased agreed value of the cargo shall be deemed to be increased to the total amount insured under this Value insurance and all insurances covering the loss, and liability under this insurance shall be in such proportion as the sum insured herein bears to such total amount insured.

In the event of claim the Assured shall provide the Underwriters with evidence. of the amounts insured under all other insurances.

    9.2 **Where this insurance is on Increased Value the following clause shall apply:**

The agreed value of the cargo shall be deemed to be equal to the total amount insured under the primary insurance and all Increased Value insurances covering the loss and effected on the cargo by the Assured, and liability under this insurance shall be in such proportion as the sum insured herein bears to such total amount insured.

In the event of claim the Assured shall provide the Underwriters with evidence of the amounts insured under all other insurances.

BENEFIT OF INSURANCE

10 This insurance shall not inure to the benefit of the carrier or other bailee.

MINIMISING LOSSES

11 It is the duty of the Assured and their servants and agents in respect of loss recoverable hereunder

    11.1 to take such measures as may be reasonable for the purpose of averting or minimising such loss,

and

11.2 to ensure that all rights against carriers, bailees or other third parties are properly preserved and exercised

and the Underwriters will, in addition to any loss recoverable hereunder, reimburse the Assured for any charges properly and reasonably incurred in pursuance of these duties.

12 Measures taken by the Assured or the Underwriters with the object of saving, protecting or recovering the subject matter insured shall not be considered as a waiver or acceptance of abandonment or otherwise prejudice the rights of either party.

AVOIDANCE OF DELAY

13 It is a condition of this insurance that the Assured shall act with reasonable despatch in all circumstances within their control.

LAW AND PRACTICE

14 This insurance is subject to English law and practice.

NOTE—*It is necessary for the Assured when they become aware of an event which is 'held covered' under this insurance to give prompt notice to the Underwriters and the right to such cover is dependent upon compliance with this obligation.*

APPENDIX 21

1/1/82

INSTITUTE STRIKES CLAUSES (CARGO)

RISKS COVERED

1   This insurance covers, except as provided in Clauses 3 and 4 below, loss of or damage to the subject matter insured caused by
    1.1   strikers, locked-out workmen, or persons taking part in labour disturbances, riots or civil commotions
    1.2   any terrorist or any person acting from a political motive.
2   This insurance covers general average and salvage charges, adjusted or determined according to the contract of affreightment and/or the governing law and practice, incurred to avoid or in connection with the avoidance of loss from a risk covered under these clauses.

EXCLUSIONS

3   In no case shall this insurance cover
    3.1   loss damage or expense attributable to wilful misconduct of the Assured
    3.2   ordinary leakage, ordinary loss in weight or volume, or ordinary wear and tear of the subject matter insured
    3.3   loss damage or expense caused by insufficiency or unsuitability of packing or preparation of the subject matter insured (for the purpose of this Clause 3.3 'packing' shall be deemed to include stowage in a container or liftvan but only when such stowage is carried out prior to attachment of this insurance or by the Assured or their servants)
    3.4   loss damage or expense caused by inherent vice or nature of the subject matter insured
    3.5   loss damage or expense proximately caused by delay, even though the delay be caused by a risk insured against (except expenses payable under Clause 2 above)
    3.6   loss damage or expense arising from insolvency or financial default of the owners managers charterers or operators of the vessel
    3.7   loss damage or expense arising from the absence shortage or withholding of labour of any description whatsoever resulting from any strike, lockout, labour disturbance, riot or civil commotion
    3.8   any claim based upon loss of or frustration of the voyage or adventure
    3.9   loss damage or expense arising from the use of any weapon of war employing atomic or nuclear fission and/or fusion or other like reaction or radioactive force or matter

Appendix 21

3.10 loss damage or expense caused by war civil war revolution rebellion insurrection, or civil strife arising therefrom, or any hostile act by or against a belligerent power.

4 4.1 In no case shall this insurance cover loss damage or expense arising from

unseaworthiness of vessel or craft,

unfitness of vessel craft conveyance container or liftvan for the safe carriage of the subject matter insured,

where the Assured or their servants are privy to such unseaworthiness or unfitness, at the time the subject matter insured is loaded therein.

4.2 The Underwriters waive any breach of the implied warranties of seaworthiness of the ship and fitness of the ship to carry the subject matter insured to destination, unless the Assured or their servants are privy to such unseaworthiness or unfitness.

DURATION

5 5.1 This insurance attaches from the time the goods leave the warehouse or place of storage at the place named herein for the commencement of the transit, continues during the ordinary course of transit and terminates either

5.1.1 on delivery to the Consignees' or other final warehouse or place of storage at the destination named herein,

5.1.2 on delivery to any other warehouse or place of storage, whether prior to or at the destination named herein, which the Assured elect to use either

5.1.2.1 for storage other than in the ordinary course of transit or

5.1.2.2 for allocation or distribution,

or

5.1.3 on the expiry of 60 days after completion of discharge overside of the goods hereby insured from the oversea vessel at the final port of discharge,

whichever shall first occur.

5.2 If, after discharge overside from the oversea vessel at the final port of discharge, but prior to termination of this insurance, the goods are to be forwarded to a destination other than that to which they are insured hereunder, this insurance, whilst remaining subject to termination as provided for above, shall not extend beyond the commencement of transit to such other destination.

5.3 This insurance shall remain in force (subject to termination as provided for above and to the provisions of Clause 6 below) during delay beyond the control of the Assured, any deviation forced discharge, reshipment or transhipment and during any variation of the adventure arising from the exercise of a liberty granted to shipowners or charterers under the contract of affreightment.

Institute Strikes Clauses (Cargo) (1982) [ISC(C)(82)]

6   If owing to circumstances beyond the control of the Assured either the contract of carriage is terminated at a port or place other than the destination named therein or the transit is otherwise terminated before delivery of the goods as provided for in Clause 5 above, then this insurance shall also terminate unless prompt notice is given to the Underwriters and continuation of cover is requested when the insurance shall remain in force, subject to an additional premium if required by the Underwriters, either

   6.1   until the goods are sold and delivered at such port or place, or, unless otherwise specially agreed, until the expiry of 60 days after arrival of the goods hereby insured at such port or place, whichever shall first occur,

   or

   6.2   if the goods are forwarded within the said period of 60 days (or any agreed extension thereof) to the destination named herein or to any other destination, until terminated in accordance with the provisions of Clause 5 above.

7   Where, after attachment of this insurance, the destination is changed by the Assured, *held covered at a premium and on conditions to be arranged subject to prompt notice being given to the Underwriters.*

CLAIMS

8   8.1   In order to recover under this insurance the Assured must have an insurable interest in the subject matter insured at the time of the loss.

   8.2   Subject to 8.1 above, the Assured shall be entitled to recover for insured loss occurring during the period covered by this insurance, notwithstanding that the loss occurred before the contract of insurance was concluded, unless the Assured were aware of the loss and the Underwriters were not.

9   9.1   If any Increased Value insurance is effected by the Assured on the cargo insured herein the agreed value of the cargo shall be deemed to be increased to the total amount insured under this insurance and all Increased Value insurances covering the loss, and liability under this insurance shall be in such proportion as the sum insured herein bears to such total amount insured.

   In the event of claim the Assured shall provide the Underwriters with evidence of the amounts insured under all other insurances.

   9.2   **Where this insurance is on Increased Value the following clause shall apply:**

   The agreed value of the cargo shall be deemed to be equal to the total amount insured under the primary insurance and all Increased Value insurances covering the loss and effected on the cargo by the Assured, and liability under this insurance shall be in such proportion as the sum insured herein bears to such total amount insured.

   In the event of claim the Assured shall provide the Underwriters with evidence of the amounts insured under all other insurances.

BENEFIT OF INSURANCE

10 This insurance shall not inure to the benefit of the carrier or other bailee.

MINIMISING LOSSES

11 It is the duty of the Assured and their servants and agents in respect of loss recoverable hereunder

    11.1   to take such measures as may be reasonable for the purpose of averting or minimising such loss,

            and

    11.2   to ensure that all rights against carriers, bailees or other third parties are properly preserved and exercised

            and the Underwriters will, in addition to any loss recoverable hereunder, reimburse the Assured for any charges properly and reasonably incurred in pursuance of these duties.

12 Measures taken by the Assured or the Underwriters with the object of saving, protecting or recovering the subject matter insured shall not be considered as a waiver or acceptance of abandonment or otherwise prejudice the rights of either party.

AVOIDANCE OF DELAY

13 It is a condition of this insurance that the Assured shall act with reasonable despatch in all circumstances within their control.

LAW AND PRACTICE

14 This insurance is subject to English law and practice.

NOTE—*It is necessary for the Assured when they become aware of an event which is 'held covered' under this insurance to give prompt notice to the Underwriters and the right to such cover is dependent upon compliance with this obligation.*

APPENDIX 22

YORK-ANTWERP RULES 1994

Rule of Interpretation

In the adjustment of general average the following Rules shall apply to the exclusion of any Law and Practice inconsistent therewith.

Except as provided by the Rule Paramount and the numbered Rules, general average shall be adjusted according to the lettered Rules.

Rule Paramount

In no case shall there be any allowance for sacrifice or expenditure unless reasonably made or incurred.

Rule A

There is a general average act when, and only when, any extraordinary sacrifice or expenditure is intentionally and reasonably made or incurred for the common safety for the purpose of preserving from peril the property involved in a common maritime adventure.

General average sacrifices and expenditures shall be borne by the different contributing interests on the basis hereinafter provided.

Rule B

There is a common maritime adventure when one or more vessels are towing or pushing another vessel or vessels, provided that they are all involved in commercial activities and not in a salvage operation.

When measures are taken to preserve the vessels and their cargoes, if any, from a common peril, these Rules shall apply.

A vessel is not in common peril with another vessel or vessels if by simply disconnecting from the other vessel or vessels she is in safety; but if the disconnection is itself a general average act the common maritime adventure continues.

Rule C

Only such losses, damages or expenses which are the direct consequence of the general average act shall be allowed as general average.

In no case shall there be any allowance in general average for losses, damages or expenses incurred in respect of damage to the environment or in consequence of the escape or release of pollutant substances from the property involved in the common maritime adventure.

Demurrage, loss of market, and any loss or damage sustained or expense incurred by reason of delay, whether on the voyage or subsequently, and any indirect loss whatsoever, shall not be admitted as general average.

Rule D

Rights to contribution in general average shall not be affected, though the event which gave rise to the sacrifice or expenditure may have been due to the fault of one of the parties to the adventure; but this shall not prejudice any remedies or defences which may be open against or to that party in respect of such fault.

Rule E

The onus of proof is upon the party claiming in general average to show that the loss or expense claimed is properly allowable as general average.

All parties claiming in general average shall give notice in writing to the average adjuster of the loss or expense in respect of which they claim contribution within 12 months of the date of the termination of the common maritime adventure.

Failing such notification, or if within 12 months of a request for the same any of the parties shall fail to supply evidence in support of a notified claim, or particulars of value in respect of a contributory interest, the average adjuster shall be at liberty to estimate the extent of the allowance or the contributory value on the basis of the information available to him, which estimate may be challenged only on the ground that it is manifestly incorrect.

Rule F

Any additional expense incurred in place of another expense which would have been allowable as general average shall be deemed to be general average and so allowed without regard to the saving, if any, to other interests, but only up to the amount of the general average expense avoided.

Rule G

General average shall be adjusted as regards both loss and contribution upon the basis of values at the time and place when and where the adventure ends.

This rule shall not affect the determination of the place at which the average statement is to be made up.

When a ship is at any port or place in circumstances which would give rise to an allowance in general average under the provisions of Rules X and XI, and the cargo or part thereof is forwarded to destination by other means, rights and liabilities in general average shall, subject to cargo interests being notified if practicable, remain as nearly as possible the same as they would have been in the absence of such forwarding, as if the adventure had continued in the original ship for so long as justifiable under the contract of affreightment and the applicable law.

The proportion attaching to cargo of the allowances made in general average by reason of applying the third paragraph of this Rule shall not exceed the cost which would have been borne by the owners of cargo if the cargo had been forwarded at their expense.

Rule I – Jettison of Cargo

No jettison of cargo shall be made good as general average, unless such cargo is carried in accordance with the recognised custom of the trade.

Rule II – Loss or Damage by Sacrifices for the Common Safety

Loss of or damage to the property involved in the common maritime adventure by or in consequence of a sacrifice made for the common safety, and by water which goes down a ship's hatches opened or other opening made for the purpose of making a jettison for the common safety, shall be made good as general average.

Rule III – Extinguishing Fire on Shipboard

Damage done to a ship and cargo, or either of them, by water or otherwise, including damage by beaching or scuttling a burning ship, in extinguishing a fire on board the ship, shall be made good as general average; except that no compensation shall be made for damage by smoke however caused or by heat of the fire.

Rule IV – Cutting away Wreck

Loss or damage sustained by cutting away wreck or parts of the ship which have previously carried away or are effectively lost by accident shall not be made good as general average.

Rule V – Voluntary Stranding

When a ship is intentionally run on shore for the common safety, whether or not she might have been driven on shore, the consequent loss or damage to the property involved in the common maritime adventure shall be allowed in general average.

Rule VI – Salvage Remuneration

(a) Expenditure incurred by the parties to the adventure in the nature of salvage, whether under contract or otherwise, shall be allowed in general average provided that the salvage operations were carried out for the purpose of preserving from peril the property involved in the common maritime adventure.

Expenditure allowed in general average shall include any salvage remuneration in which the skill and efforts of the salvors in preventing or minimising damage to the environment such as is referred to in Article 13 paragraph 1(b) of the International Convention on Salvage, 1989 have been taken into account.

(b) Special compensation payable to a salvor by the shipowner under Article 14 of the said Convention to the extent specified in paragraph 4 of that Article or under any other provision similar in substance shall not be allowed in general average.

Rule VII – Damage to Machinery and Boilers

Damage caused to any machinery and boilers of a ship which is ashore and in a position of peril, in endeavouring to refloat, shall be allowed in general average when shown to have arisen from an actual intention to float the ship for the common safety at the risk of such damage; but where a ship is afloat no loss or damage caused by working the propelling machinery and boilers shall in any circumstances be made good as general average.

Rule VIII – Expenses lightening a Ship when Ashore, and Consequent Damage

When a ship is ashore and cargo and ship's fuel and stores or any of them are discharged as a general average act, the extra cost of lightening, lighter hire and reshipping (if incurred), and any loss or damage to the property involved in the common maritime adventure in consequence thereof, shall be admitted as general average.

Rule IX – Cargo, Ship's Materials and Stores used for Fuel

Cargo, ship's materials and stores, or any of them, necessarily used for fuel for the common safety at a time of peril shall be admitted as general average, but when such an allowance is made for the cost of ship's materials and stores the general average shall be credited with the estimated cost of the fuel which would otherwise have been consumed in prosecuting the intended voyage.

Rule X – Expenses at Port of Refuge, etc

(a) When a ship shall have entered a port or place of refuge or shall have returned to her port or place of loading in consequence of accident, sacrifice or other extraordinary circumstances which render that necessary for the common safety, the expenses of entering such port or place shall be admitted as general average; and when she shall have sailed thence with her original cargo, or a part of it, the corresponding expenses of leaving such port or place consequent upon such entry or return shall likewise be admitted as general average.

When a ship is at any port or place of refuge and is necessarily removed to another port or place because repairs cannot be carried out in the first port or place, the provisions of this Rule shall be applied to the second port or place as if it were a port or place of refuge and the cost of such removal including temporary repairs and towage shall be admitted as general average. The provisions of Rule XI shall be applied to the prolongation of the voyage occasioned by such removal.

(b) The cost of handling on board or discharging cargo, fuel or stores whether at a port or place of loading, call or refuge, shall be admitted as general average, when the handling or discharge was necessary for the common safety or to enable damage to the ship caused by sacrifice or accident to be repaired, if the repairs were necessary for the safe prosecution of the voyage, except in cases where the damage to the ship is discovered at a port or place of loading or call without any accident or other extraordinary circumstances connected with such damage having taken place during the voyage.

The cost of handling on board or discharging cargo, fuel or stores shall not be admissible as general average when incurred solely for the purpose of restowage due to shifting during the voyage, unless such restowage is necessary for the common safety.

(c) Whenever the cost of handling or discharging cargo, fuel or stores is admissible as general average, the costs of storage, including insurance if reasonably incurred, reloading and stowing of such cargo, fuel or stores shall likewise be admitted as general average. The provisions of Rule XI shall be applied to the extra period of detention occasioned by such reloading or restowing.

But when the ship is condemned or does not proceed on her original voyage, storage expenses shall be admitted as general average only up to the date of the ship's condemnation or of the abandonment of the voyage or up to the date of completion of discharge of cargo if the condemnation or abandonment takes place before that date.

Rule XI – Wages and Maintenance of Crew and other expenses bearing up for and in a port of refuge, etc

(a) Wages and maintenance of master, officers and crew reasonably incurred and fuel and stores consumed during the prolongation of the voyage occasioned by a ship entering a port or place of refuge or returning to her port or place of loading shall be admitted as general average when the expenses of entering such port or place are allowable in general average in accordance with Rule X(a).

(b) When a ship shall have entered or been detained in any port or place in consequence of accident, sacrifice or other extraordinary circumstances which render that necessary for the common safety, or to enable damage to the ship caused by sacrifice or accident to be repaired, if the repairs were necessary for the safe prosecution of the voyage, the wages and maintenance of the master, officers and crew reasonably incurred during the extra period of detention in such port or place until the ship shall or should have been made ready to proceed upon her voyage, shall be admitted in general average

Fuel and stores consumed during the period of detention shall be admitted as general average, except such fuel and stores as are consumed in effecting repairs not allowable in general average.

Port charges incurred during the extra period of detention shall likewise be admitted as general average except such charges as are incurred solely by reason of repairs not allowable in general average.

Provided that when damage to the ship is discovered at a port or place of loading or call without any accident or other extraordinary circumstance connected with such damage having taken place during the voyage, then the wages and maintenance of master, officers and crew and fuel and stores consumed and port charges incurred during the extra detention for repairs to damages so discovered shall not be admissible as general average, even if the repairs are necessary for the safe prosecution of the voyage.

When the ship is condemned or does not proceed on her original voyage, the wages and maintenance of the master, officers and crew and fuel and stores consumed shall and port charges be admitted as general average only up to the date of the ship's condemnation or of the abandonment of the voyage or up to the date of completion of discharge of cargo if the condemnation or abandonment takes place before that date.

(c) For the purpose of this and the other Rules wages shall include all payments made to or for the benefit of the master, officers and crew, whether such payments be imposed by law upon the shipowners or be made under the terms of articles of employment

(d) The cost of measures undertaken to prevent or minimise damage to the environment shall be allowed in general average when incurred in any or all of the following circumstances:

(i) as part of an operation performed for the common safety which, had it been undertaken by a party outside the common maritime adventure, would have entitled such party to a salvage reward;

(ii) as a condition of entry into or departure from any port or place in the circumstances prescribed in Rule X(a);

(iii) as a condition of remaining at any port or place in the circumstances prescribed in Rule X(a), provided that when there is an actual escape or release of pollutant substances the cost of any additional measures required on that account to prevent or minimise pollution or environmental damage shall not be allowed as general average;

(iv) necessarily in connection with the discharging, storing or reloading of cargo whenever the cost of those operations is admissible as general average.

Rule XII – Damage to Cargo in Discharging, etc

Damage to or loss of cargo, fuel or stores sustained in consequence of their handling. discharging, storing, reloading and stowing shall be made good as general average, when and only when the cost of those measures respectively is admitted as general average.

Rule XIII – Deduction from Cost of Repairs

Repairs to be allowed in general average shall not be subject to deductions in respect of 'new for old' where old material or parts are replaced by new unless the ship is over fifteen years old in which case there shall be a deduction of one third. The deductions shall be regulated by the age of the ship from the 31st December of the year of completion of construction to the date of the general average act, except for insulation, life and similar boats, communications and navigational apparatus and equipment, machinery and boilers for which the deductions shall be regulated by the age of the particular parts to which they apply.

The deductions shall be made only from the cost of the new material or parts when finished and ready to be installed in the ship.

No deduction shall be made in respect of provisions, stores, anchors and chain cables.

Drydock and slipway dues and costs of shifting the ship shall be allowed in full

The costs of cleaning, painting or coating of bottom shall not be allowed in general average unless the bottom has been painted or coated within the twelve months preceding the date of the general average act in which case one-half of such costs shall be allowed.

Rule XIV – Temporary Repairs

Where temporary repairs are effected to a ship at a port of loading, call or refuge, for the common safety, or of damage caused by general average sacrifice, the cost of such repairs shall be admitted as general average.

Where temporary repairs of accidental damage are effected in order to enable the adventure to be completed, the cost of such repairs shall be admitted as general average without regard to the saving, if any, to other interests, but only up to the saving in expense which would have been incurred and allowed in general average if such repairs had not been effected there.

No deductions 'new for old' shall be made from the cost of temporary repairs allowable as general average.

Rule XV – Loss of Freight

Loss of freight arising from damage to or loss of cargo shall be made good as general average, either when caused by a general average act, or when the damage to or loss of cargo is so made good.

Deduction shall be made from the amount of gross freight lost, of the charges which the owner thereof would have incurred to earn such freight, but has, in consequence of the sacrifice, not incurred.

Rule XVI – Amount to be made good for Cargo Lost or Damaged by Sacrifice

The amount to be made good as general average for damage to or loss of cargo sacrificed shall be the loss which has been sustained thereby based on the value at the time of discharge, ascertained from the commercial invoice rendered to the receiver or if there is no such invoice from the shipped value The value at the time of discharge shall include the cost of insurance and freight except insofar as such freight is at the risk of interests other than the cargo.

When cargo so damaged is sold and the amount of the damage has not been otherwise agreed, the loss to be made good in general average shall be the difference between the net proceeds of sale and the net sound value as computed in the first paragraph of this Rule.

Rule XVII – Contributory Values

The contribution to a general average shall be made upon the actual net values of the property at the termination of the adventure except that the value of cargo shall be the value at the time of discharge, ascertained from the commercial invoice rendered to the receiver or if there is no such invoice from the shipped value. The value of the cargo shall include the cost of insurance and freight unless and insofar as such freight is at the risk of interests other than the cargo, deducting therefrom any loss or damage suffered by the cargo prior to or at the time of discharge. The value of the ship shall be assessed without taking into account the beneficial or detrimental effect of any demise or time charterparty to which the ship may be committed.

To these values shall be added the amount made good as general average for property sacrificed, if not already included, deduction being made from the freight and passage money at risk of such charges and crew's wages as would not have been incurred in earning the freight had the ship and cargo been totally lost at the date of the general average; deduction being also made from the value of the property of all extra charges incurred in respect thereof subsequently to the general average act, except such charges as are allowed in general average or fall upon the ship by virtue of an award for special compensation under Article 14 of the International Convention on Salvage, 1989 or under any other provision similar in substance.

In the circumstances envisaged in the third paragraph of Rule G, the cargo and other property shall contribute on the basis of its value upon delivery at original destination unless sold or otherwise disposed of short of that destination, and the ship shall contribute upon its actual net value at the time of completion of discharge of cargo.

Where cargo is sold short of destination, however, it shall contribute upon the actual net proceeds of sale, with the addition of any amount made good as general average.

Mails, passengers' luggage, personal effects and accompanied private motor vehicles shall not contribute in general average.

Rule XVIII – Damage to Ship

The amount to be allowed as general average for damage or loss to the ship, her machinery and/or gear caused by a general average act shall be as follows:

(a) When repaired or replaced,

The actual reasonable cost of repairing or replacing such damage or loss, subject to deductions in accordance with Rule XIII;

(b) When not repaired or replaced,

The reasonable depreciation arising from such damage or loss, but not exceeding the estimated cost of repairs. But where the ship is an actual total loss or when the cost of repairs of the damage would exceed the value of the ship when repaired, the amount to be allowed as general average shall be the difference between the estimated sound value of the ship after deducting therefrom the estimated cost of repairing damage which is not general average and the value of the ship in her damaged state which may be measured by the net proceeds of sale, if any.

Rule XIX – Undeclared or Wrongfully Declared Cargo

Damage or loss caused to goods loaded without the knowledge of the shipowner or his agent or to goods wilfully misdescribed at time of shipment shall not be allowed as general average, but such goods shall remain liable to contribute, if saved.

Damage or loss caused to goods which have been wrongfully declared on shipment at a value which is lower than their real value shall be contributed for at the declared value, but such goods shall contribute upon their actual value.

Rule XX – Provision of Funds

A commission of 2 per cent on general average disbursements, other than the wages and maintenance of master, officers and crew and fuel and stores not replaced during the voyage, shall be allowed in general average.

The capital loss sustained by the owners of goods sold for the purpose of raising funds to defray general average disbursements shall be allowed in general average.

The cost of insuring general average disbursements shall also be admitted in general average.

Rule XXI – Interest on Losses made good in General Average

Interest shall be allowed on expenditure, sacrifices and allowances in general average at the rate of 7 per cent per annum, until three months after the date of issue of the general average adjustment, due allowance being made for any payment on account by the contributory interests or from the general average deposit fund.

Rule XXII – Treatment of Cash Deposits

Where cash deposits have been collected in respect of cargo's liability for general average, salvage or special charges, such deposits shall be paid without any delay into a special account in the joint names of a representative nominated on behalf of the shipowner and a representative nominated on behalf of the depositors in a bank to be approved by both. The sum so deposited, together with accrued interest, if any, shall be held as security for payment to the parties entitled thereto of the general average, salvage or special charges payable by cargo in respect to which the deposits have been collected, Payments on account or refunds of deposits may be made if certified to in writing by the average adjuster. Such deposits and payments or refunds shall be without prejudice to the ultimate liability of the parties.

APPENDIX 23

LOF 1995

LLOYD'S

STANDARD FORM OF
SALVAGE AGREEMENT

(APPROVED AND PUBLISHED BY THE COUNCIL OF LLOYD'S)

NO CURE – NO PAY

On board the..
Dated...................................

IT IS HEREBY AGREED between Captain...
for and on behalf of the Owners of the '...'
her cargo freight bunkers stores and any other property thereon (hereinafter collectively called 'the Owners') and...for and on behalf of ....
(hereinafter called 'the Contractor') that:

1. (a) The Contractor shall use his best endeavours:

    (i) to salve the '..' and/or her cargo freight bunkers stores and any other property thereon and take them to .... or to such other place as may hereafter be agreed either place to be deemed a place of safety or if no such place is named or agreed to a place of safety and

    (ii) while performing the salvage services to prevent or minimize damage to the environment.

   (b) Subject to the statutory provisions relating to special compensation the services shall be rendered and accepted as salvage services upon the principle of 'no cure – no pay'.

   (c) The Contractor's remuneration shall be fixed by Arbitration in London in the manner hereinafter prescribed and any other difference arising out of this Agreement or the operations thereunder shall be referred to Arbitration in the same way.

   (d) In the event of the services referred to in this Agreement or any part of such services having been already rendered at the date of this Agreement by the Contractor to the said vessel and/or her cargo freight bunkers stores and any other property thereon the provisions of this Agreement shall apply to such services.

(e) The security to be provided to the Council of Lloyd's (hereinafter called 'the Council') the Salved Value(s) the Award and/or any Interim Award(s) and/or any Award on Appeal shall be in .... currency.

(f) If Clause 1(e) is not completed then the security to be provided and the Salved Value(s) the Award and/or Interim Award(s) and/or Award on Appeal shall be in Pounds Sterling.

(g) This Agreement and Arbitration thereunder shall except as otherwise expressly provided be governed by the law of England, including the English law of salvage.

PROVISIONS AS TO THE SERVICES

2. *Definitions*: In this Agreement any reference to 'Convention' is a reference to the International Convention on Salvage 1989 as incorporated in the Merchant Shipping (Salvage and Pollution) Act 1994 (and any amendment thereto). The terms 'Contractor' and 'services'/'salvage services' in this Agreement shall have the same meanings as the terms 'salvor(s)' and 'salvage operation(s)' in the Convention.

3. *Owners Cooperation*: The Owners their Servants and Agents shall co-operate fully with the Contractor in and about the salvage including obtaining entry to the place named or the place of safety as defined in Clause 1. The Contractor may make reasonable use of the vessel's machinery gear equipment anchors chains stores and other appurtenances during and for the purpose of the salvage services free of expense but shall not unnecessarily damage abandon or sacrifice the same or any property the subject of this Agreement.

4. *Vessel Owners Right to Terminate*: When there is no longer any reasonable prospect of a useful result leading to a salvage reward in accordance with Convention Article 13 the owners of the vessel shall be entitled to terminate the services of the Contractor by giving reasonable notice to the Contractor in writing.

PROVISIONS AS TO SECURITY

5. (a) The Contractor shall immediately after the termination of the services or sooner notify the Council and where practicable the Owners of the amount for which he demands salvage security (inclusive of costs expenses and interest) from each of the respective Owners.

(b) Where a claim is made or may be made for special compensation, the owners of the vessel shall on the demand of the Contractor whenever made provide security for the Contractor's claim for special compensation provided always that such demand is made within two years of the date of termination of the services.

(c) The amount of any such security shall be reasonable in the light of the knowledge available to the Contractor at the time when the demand is made. Unless otherwise agreed such security shall be provided (i) to the Council (ii) in a form approved by the Council and (iii) by persons firms or corporations either acceptable to the Contractor or resident in the United Kingdom and acceptable to the Council. The Council shall not be responsible for the sufficiency (whether in amount or otherwise) of any security which shall be provided nor the default or insolvency of any person firm or corporation providing the same.

(d) The owners of the vessel their Servants and Agents shall use their best endeavours to ensure that the cargo owners provide their proportion of salvage security before the cargo is released.

6. (a) Until security has been provided as aforesaid the Contractor shall have a maritime lien on the property salved for his remuneration.

(b) The property salved shall not without the consent in writing of the Contractor (which shall not be unreasonably withheld) be removed from the place to which it has been taken by the Contractor under Clause 1(a). Where such consent is given by the Contractor on condition that the Contractor is provided with temporary security pending completion of the voyage the Contractor's maritime lien on the property salved shall remain in force to the extent necessary to enable the Contractor to compel the provision of security in accordance with Clause 5(c).

(c) The Contractor shall not arrest or detain the property salved unless:

(i) security is not provided within 14 days (exclusive of Saturdays and Sundays or other days observed as general holidays at Lloyd's) after the date of the termination of the services or

(ii) he has reason to believe that the removal of the property salved is contemplated contrary to Clause 6(b) or

(iii) any attempt is made to remove the property salved contrary to Clause 6(b).

(d) The Arbitrator appointed under Clause 7 or the Appeal Arbitrator(s) appointed under Clause 13(d) shall have power in their absolute discretion to include in the amount awarded to the Contractor the whole or part of any expenses reasonably incurred by the Contractor in:

(i) ascertaining demanding and obtaining the amount of security reasonably required in accordance with Clause 5.

(ii) enforcing and/or protecting by insurance or otherwise or taking reasonable steps to enforce and/or protect his lien.

PROVISIONS AS TO ARBITRATION

7. (a) Whether security has been provided or not the Council shall appoint an Arbitrator upon receipt of a written request made by letter telex facsimile or in any other permanent form provided that any party requesting such appointment shall if required by the Council undertake to pay the reasonable fees and expenses of the Council and/or any Arbitrator or Appeal Arbitrator(s).

(b) Where an Arbitrator has been appointed and the parties do not proceed to arbitration the Council may recover any fees costs and/or expenses which are outstanding.

8. The Contractor's remuneration and/or special compensation shall be fixed by the Arbitrator appointed under Clause 7. Such remuneration shall not be diminished by reason of the exception to the principle of 'no cure – no pay' in the form of special compensation.

REPRESENTATION

9. Any party to this Agreement who wishes to be heard or to adduce evidence shall nominate a person in the United Kingdom to represent him failing which the Arbitrator or Appeal Arbitrator(s) may proceed as if such party had renounced his right to be heard or adduce evidence.

CONDUCT OF THE ARBITRATION

10. (a) The Arbitrator shall have power to:

(i) admit such oral or documentary evidence or information as he may think fit

(ii) conduct the Arbitration in such manner in all respects as he may think fit subject to such procedural rules as the Council may approve

(iii) order the Contractor in his absolute discretion to pay the whole or part of the expense of providing excessive security or security which has been unreasonably demanded under Clause 5(b) and to deduct such sum from the remuneration and/or special compensation

(iv) make Interim Award(s) including payment(s) on account on such terms as may be fair and just

(v) make such orders as to costs fees and expenses including those of the Council charged under Clauses 10(b) and 14(b) as may be fair and just.

(b) The Arbitrator and the Council may charge reasonable fees and expenses for their services whether the Arbitration proceeds to a hearing or not and all such fees and expenses shall be treated as part of the costs of the Arbitration.

(c) Any Award shall (subject to Appeal as provided in this Agreement) be final and binding on all the parties concerned whether they were represented at the Arbitration or not.

INTEREST & RATES OF EXCHANGE

11. *Interest*: Interest at rates per annum to be fixed by the Arbitrator shall (subject to Appeal as provided in this Agreement) be payable on any sum awarded taking into account any sums already paid:

(i) from the date of termination of the services unless the Arbitrator shall in his absolute discretion otherwise decide until the date of publication by the Council of the Award and/or Interim Award(s) and

(ii) from the expiration of 21 days (exclusive of Saturdays and Sundays or other days observed as general holidays at Lloyd's) after the date of publication by the Council of the Award and/or Interim Award(s) until the date payment is received by the Contractor or the Council both dates inclusive.

For the purpose of sub-clause (ii) the expression 'sum awarded' shall include the fees and expenses referred to in Clause 10(b).

12. *Currency Correction*: In considering what sums of money have been expended by the Contractor in rendering the services and/or in fixing the amount of the Award and/or Interim Award(s) and/or Award on Appeal the Arbitrator or Appeal Arbitrator(s) shall to such an extent and in so far as it may be fair and just in all the circumstances give effect to the consequences of any change or changes in the relevant rates of exchange which may have occurred between the date of termination of the services and the date on which the Award and/or Interim Award(s) and/or Award on Appeal is made.

PROVISIONS AS TO APPEAL

13. (a) Notice of Appeal if any shall be given to the Council within 14 days (exclusive of Saturdays and Sundays or other days observed as general holidays at Lloyd's) after the date of the publication by the Council of the Award and/or Interim Award(s).

(b) Notice of Cross-Appeal if any shall be given to the Council within 14 days (exclusive of Saturdays and Sundays or other days observed as general holidays at Lloyd's) after notification by the Council to the parties of any Notice of Appeal. Such notification if sent by post shall be deemed received on the working day following the day of posting.

(c) Notice of Appeal or Cross-Appeal shall be given to the Council by letter telex facsimile or in any other permanent form.

(d) Upon receipt of Notice of Appeal the Council shall refer the Appeal to the hearing and determination of the Appeal Arbitrator(s) selected by it.

(e) If any Notice of Appeal or Cross-Appeal is withdrawn the Appeal hearing shall nevertheless proceed in respect of such Notice of Appeal or Cross-Appeal as may remain.

(f) Any Award on Appeal shall be final and binding on all the parties to that Appeal Arbitration whether they were represented either at the Arbitration or at the Appeal Arbitration or not.

CONDUCT OF THE APPEAL

14. (a) The Appeal Arbitrator(s) in addition to the powers of the Arbitrator under Clauses 10(a) and 11 shall have power to:

(i) admit the evidence which was before the Arbitrator together with the Arbitrator's notes and reasons for his Award and/or Interim Award(s) and any transcript of evidence and such additional evidence as he or they may think fit.

(ii) confirm increase or reduce the sum awarded by the Arbitrator and to make such order as to the payment of interest on such sum as he or they may think fit.

(iii) confirm revoke or vary any order and/or Declaratory Award made by the Arbitrator.

(iv) award interest on any fees and expenses charged under paragraph (b) of this clause from the expiration of 21 days (exclusive of Saturdays and Sundays or other days observed as general holidays at Lloyd's) after the date of publication by the Council of the Award on Appeal and/or Interim Award(s) on Appeal until the date payment is received by the Council both dates inclusive.

(b) The Appeal Arbitrator(s) and the Council may charge reasonable fees and expenses for their services in connection with the Appeal Arbitration whether it proceeds to a hearing or not and all such fees and expenses shall be treated as part of the costs of the Appeal Arbitration.

PROVISIONS AS TO PAYMENT

15. (a) In case of Arbitration if no Notice of Appeal be received by the Council in accordance with Clause 13(a) the Council shall call upon the party or parties concerned to pay the amount awarded and in the event of non-payment shall subject to the Contractor first providing to the Council a satisfactory Undertaking to pay all the costs thereof realize or enforce the security and pay therefrom to the Contractor (whose receipt shall be a good discharge to it) the amount awarded to him together with interest if any. The Contractor shall reimburse the parties concerned to such extent as the Award is less than any sums paid on account or in respect of Interim Award(s).

(b) If Notice of Appeal be received by the Council in accordance with Clause 13 it shall as soon as the Award on Appeal has been published by it call upon the party or parties concerned to pay the amount awarded and in the event of non-payment shall subject to the Contractor first providing to the Council a satisfactory Undertaking to pay all the costs thereof realize or enforce the security and pay therefrom to the Contractor (whose receipt shall be a good discharge to it) the amount awarded to him together with interest if any. The Contractor shall reimburse the parties concerned to such extent as the Award on Appeal is less than any sums paid on account or in respect of the Award or Interim Award(s).

(c) If any sum shall become payable to the Contractor as remuneration for his services and/or interest and/or costs as the result of an agreement made between the Contractor and the Owners or any of them the Council in the event of non-payment shall subject to the Contractor first providing to the Council a satisfactory Undertaking to pay all the costs thereof realize or enforce the security and pay therefrom to the Contractor (whose receipt shall be a good discharge to it) the said sum.

(d) If the Award and/or Interim Award(s) and/or Award on Appeal provides or provide that the costs of the Arbitration and/or of the Appeal Arbitration or any part of such costs shall be borne by the Contractor such costs may be deducted from the amount awarded or agreed before payment is made to the Contractor unless satisfactory security is provided by the Contractor for the payment of such costs.

(e) Without prejudice to the provisions of Clause 5(c) the liability of the Council shall be limited in any event to the amount of security provided to it.

GENERAL PROVISIONS

16. *Scope of Authority*: The Master or other person signing this Agreement on behalf of the property to be salved enters into this Agreement as agent for the vessel her cargo freight bunkers stores and any other property thereon and the respective Owners thereof and binds each (but not the one for the other or himself personally) to the due performance thereof.

17. *Notices*: Any Award notice authority order or other document signed by the Chairman of Lloyd's or any person authorised by the Council for the purpose shall be deemed to have been duly made or given by the Council and shall have the same force and effect in all respects as if it had been signed by every member of the Council.

18. *Sub-Contractor(s)*: The Contractor may claim salvage and enforce any Award or agreement made between the Contractor and the Owners against security provided under Clause 5 or otherwise if any on behalf of any Sub-Contractors his or their Servants or Agents including Masters and members of the crews of vessels employed by him or by any Sub-Contractors in the services provided that he first provides a reasonably satisfactory indemnity to the Owners against all claims by or liabilities to the said persons.

19. *Inducements prohibited*: No person signing this Agreement or any party on whose behalf it is signed shall at any time or in any manner whatsoever offer provide make give or promise to provide demand or take any form of inducement for entering into this Agreement.

For and on behalf of the Contractor	For and on behalf of the Owners of property to be salved
....	....
(To be signed by the Contractor personally or by the Master of the salving vessel or other person whose name is inserted in line 4 of this Agreement)	(To be signed by the Master or other person whose name is inserted in line 4 of this Agreement)

INTERNATIONAL CONVENTION ON SALVAGE 1989

The following provisions of the Convention are set out below for information only.

Article 1

Definitions

(a) *Salvage operation* means any act or activity undertaken to assist a vessel or any other property in danger in navigable waters or in any other waters whatsoever

(b) *Vessel* means any ship or craft, or any structure capable of navigation

(c) *Property* means any property not permanently and intentionally attached to the shoreline and includes freight at risk

(d) *Damage to the environment* means substantial physical damage to human health or to marine life or resources in coastal or inland waters or areas adjacent thereto, caused by pollution, contamination, fire, explosion or similar major incidents

(e) *Payment* means any reward, remuneration or compensation due under this Convention

Article 6

Salvage Contracts

1. This Convention shall apply to any salvage operations save to the extent that a contract otherwise provides expressly or by implication

2. The master shall have the authority to conclude contracts for salvage operations on behalf of the owner of the vessel. The master or the owner of the vessel shall have the authority to conclude such contracts on behalf of the owner of the property on board the vessel

Article 8

Duties of the Salvor and of the Owner and Master

1. The salvor shall owe a duty to the owner of the vessel or other property in danger:

    (a)   to carry out the salvage operations with due care;

    (b)   in performing the duty specified in subparagraph (a), to exercise due care to prevent or minimize damage to the environment;

    (c)   whenever circumstances reasonably require, to seek assistance from other salvors; and

    (d)   to accept the intervention of other salvors when reasonably requested to do so by the owner or master of the vessel or other property in danger; provided however that the amount of his reward shall not be prejudiced should it be found that such a request was unreasonable

2. The owner and master of the vessel or the owner of other property in danger shall owe a duty to the salvor:

    (a)   to co-operate fully with him during the course of the salvage operations;

    (b)   in so doing, to exercise due care to prevent or minimize damage to the environment; and

    (c)   when the vessel or other property has been brought to a place of safety, to accept redelivery when reasonably requested by the salvor to do so

Article 13

Criteria for fixing the reward

1. The reward shall be fixed with a view to encouraging salvage operations, taking into account the following criteria without regard to the order in which they are presented below:

(a) the salved value of the vessel and other property;

(b) the skill and efforts of the salvors in preventing or minimizing damage to the environment;

(c) the measure of success obtained by the salvor;

(d) the nature and degree of the danger;

(e) the skill and efforts of the salvors in salving the vessel, other property and life;

(f) the time used and expenses and losses incurred by the salvors;

(g) the risk of liability and other risks run by the salvors or their equipment;

(h) the promptness of the services rendered;

(i) the availability and use of vessels or other equipment intended for salvage operations;

(j) the state of readiness and efficiency of the salvor's equipment and the value thereof

2. Payment of a reward fixed according to paragraph 1 shall be made by all of the vessel and other property interests in proportion to their respective salved values

3. The rewards, exclusive of any interest and recoverable legal costs that may be payable thereon, shall not exceed the salved value of the vessel and other property

Article 14

Special Compensation

1. If the salvor has carried out salvage operations in respect of a vessel which by itself or its cargo threatened damage to the environment and has failed to earn a reward under Article 13 at least equivalent to the special compensation assessable in accordance with this Article, he shall be entitled to special compensation from the owner of that vessel equivalent to his expenses as herein defined

2. If, in the circumstances set out in paragraph 1, the salvor by his salvage operations has prevented or minimized damage to the environment, the special compensation payable by the owner to the salvor under paragraph I may be increased up to a maximum of 30% of the expenses incurred by the salvor. However, the Tribunal, if it deems it fair and just to do so and bearing in mind the relevant criteria set out in Article 13, paragraph 1, may increase such special compensation further, but in no event shall the total increase be more than 100% of the expenses incurred by the salvor

3. Salvor's expenses for the purpose of paragraphs 1 and 2 means the out-of-pocket expenses reasonably incurred by the salvor in the salvage operation and a fair rate for equipment and personnel actually and reasonably used in the salvage operation, taking into consideration the criteria set out in Article 13, paragraph 1(h), (i) and (j)

4. The total special compensation under this Article shall be paid only if and to the extent that such compensation is greater than any reward recoverable by the salvor under Article 13

5. If the salvor has been negligent and has thereby failed to prevent or minimize damage to the environment, he may be deprived of the whole or part of any special compensation due under this Article

6. Nothing in this Article shall affect any right of recourse on the part of the owner of the vessel.

INDEX

3/4ths Collision
  Liability Clause
    in consequence of, ... 540–41
    cross-liabilities, ... 536
    damages, ... 545–47
    defined, ... 537–38
    exclusions, ... 551–54
    Institute Cargo
      Clauses (ICC), ... 537
    Institute Time
      Clauses Hulls
      (ITCH(95)), ... 127, 535, 536,
                                         550, 842–43,
                                           866–67
    Institute Voyage
      Clauses Hulls
      (IVCH(95)), ... 550, 854–55
    legal costs, ... 536, 550–51
    paid by assured, ... 547–49
    perils of the seas, ... 535
    pollution, ... 553–54
    removal of
      obstructions, ... 551–53
    Sister Ship Clause, ... 554–55
    subrogation, ... 537
    third party liability, ... 535, 545–47
    vessels, ... 541–45

Ab initio avoidance
  (breach, utmost good
    faith duty), ... 213–14, 241–42
Abandonment
  actual total loss, ... 632–33
  constructive total loss, ... 658–68
  deprivation
    of possession, ... 642–43
  effect of, ... 813
  expenditure
    exceeding value, ... 633–34
  goods, ... 632, 633–35
    commercial viability
      of recovering,
      reconditioning and
      forwarding, ... 634–35

  meaning, ... 630–32, 659–60
  notice of
    acceptance, ... 667–68
    'claims', ... 661–63
    defined, ... 660–61, 812–13
    exceptions to
      requirement, ... 663–65
    form of, ... 667
    given in 'a
      reasonable time', ... 666–67
    sale of ship or cargo
      of necessity, ... 665
    property, ... 22
    reasonable, ... 629–35
    ships, ... 629–30, 632
Accidents
  on board ship, ... 376–79
  fortuitous, ... 364–69
  loading, ... 415–16
Actual total loss
  abandonment, ... 632–33
  automatic discharge
    from liability, ... 600
  cease to be a thing of
    the kind insured, ... 609–11
  defined, ... 600–01
  destruction of
    subject matter, ... 601–09
  freight, ... 617–20
  goods, ... 607–09,
                                     615–16, 617–20
  irretrievably
    deprived thereof, ... 613–17
  Notice of Claim
    and Tenders Clause
    (Institute Hulls Clauses), ... 599–600
  obliteration
    of marks, ... 611–13
  partial loss, ... 621, 699
  prompt notice, ... 599–600
  ships, ... 602–07, 613–15,
                                       617–20, 700

voyage or
 adventure, ...616–17,
                         620, 625–29
see, also, Constructive total loss;
Partial loss; Total loss
Ademption of loss, ...668–71
Advance freight, ...110–11, 801
Adventure, marine
 common, ...748–50
 defined, ...83, 799
 loss of, ...91–93, 616–17,
                         620, 625–29
Agency commission,
 Institute Hull
  Clauses, ...847, 859, 871
All risks policies, ...363, 416–19, 434
 burden of proof, ...418–19
Animals, living, ...88–91
Anticipated freight, ...848, 849,
                              872, 873
Assignment of
 interests, ...82, 215–16,
                              431, 801
 Institute Freight
  Clauses, ...897, 904
 Institute Hull Clauses, ...848, 860, 872
Assured, the
 3/4ths Collision
  Liability Clause, ...547–49
 bankruptcy, ...828–29, 830
 disclosure
  requirements, duties, ...250–55,
                              802–03
 loss of voyage
  or adventure, ...616–17
 negligence, ...375–76, 398
 subrogation, ...23–25, 31–34
 sue and labour, ...766–67, 844–45,
                         856–57, 868–69
 valued policies, ...190–91
 voyage policies, ...173–75
 wilful misconduct, ...354–56,
                              422–33

see, also, Insurable interest
Attachment
 insurable interest, ...76–82
 see, also, Voyage policies
Attorney, power of, ...47–50

Ballast, ...750, 849, 873
Bankruptcy of insured, ...828–29, 830
Barratry
 cargo, lost or
  damaged, ...370
 charterers, ...508, 524–28
 defined, ...509–10
 deviation, ...515–17
 Inchmaree Clause
  (Institute Hulls
   Clauses), ...509–32
 innocent mortgagee, ...530–32
 Institute Cargo Clauses, ...509–10
 Issaias rule, ...477–78
 marine risks, ...571–72
 Martiartu-Michael
  approach, ...479–85
 onus of proof
  of complicity, ...477–85
 owners, ...506–08, 524–29
 proof of loss, ...477–88
  on balance
   of probabilities, ...485–86
  beyond
   reasonable doubt, ...485
  no absolute
   standard of, ...486–88
 repairers, ...508
 scuttling, ...369, 371, 524
 seizure, ...517–24
 smuggling, ...509, 517–24
 standard of proof
  of complicity, ...485–88
 war risks, ...571–72
 wilful misconduct, ...450
 wrongful acts, ...510–14

Index

Bills of lading, ...97–99
Bottom treatment,
   Institute Hull Clauses, ...847, 859, 871
Bottomry,
   insurable interest,.............75, 801
Breach of warranty
   see Warranties
Burden of proof
   all risks policies, ...418–19
   defendants,
      perils of the seas, ...467–73
   due diligence proviso, ...534
   excessive over-
      valuation, ...200
   fire damage, ...450, 476
   meaning, ...449
   plaintiffs,
      perils of the seas, ...451–66
   proximate cause rule, ...450
   warranties, ...286–87
   see, also, Proof of loss

Capture
   constructive total loss, ...637
   insurable interest,..............74–75
   seizure,...................569–71, 593
Cargoworthiness,................325–26
Causa proxima, non
   remota, spectatur, ...335, 425
Causes of loss
   apprehension of
      perils, ...347–49
   efficient, ...336–41, 342–44
   misconduct
      of assured, ...354–56, 422–33
   predominate, ...336–41
      attributable to and
         reasonably
         attributable to, ...357–58
      caused by and
         arising from, ...357
      consequences
         thereof, ...358–60

      consequent to, ...360–62
   unseaworthiness,
      attributable to, ...349–54
   see, also, Proximate cause rule
Change of Voyage Clause
   Institute Voyage
      Clauses Freight, ...900
   Institute Voyage
      Clauses Hulls
      (IVCH(95)), ...153–55,
                                 281, 852–53
Charter, profit on, ...114–15
Charter hire,...................103–05,
                                 849, 873
Chartered freight, ...99–110,
                                 848, 872
Charterers
   barratry,.................508, 524–28
   negligence, ...508
Classification Clause
   Institute Hull
      Clauses,..................133–34, 165,
                               293–94, 840,
                               853, 864
   Institute Time
      Clauses Freight, ...893
Co-assured, rights of
   subrogation against, ...31–34
Collision
   3/4ths Collision
      Liability Clause, ...538–40
   freight, ...895–96
   Institute Time
      Clauses Freight, ...895–96
   as peril of the sea, ...371–72, 538
Commission, ...115–16
Companies, marine policy, ...835–38
Company ventures
   insurable interest,..............68–72
   subject matter insured, ...120
Condition precedent,
   promissory, ...269, 275–80

943

Constructive total loss
  abandonment, ...632–33
  ademption, ...668–71
  capture, ...637
  defined, ...623–25, 812
  effects, ...658–68, 812
  freight, ...617–20
  general average, ... 655–57
  goods, ...617–20,
    636–44, 657–58
  Institute Hulls
    Clauses, ...848, 860, 872
  loss of voyage
    or adventure, ...625–29
  reasonable abandonment
    of subject matter
    insured, ...629–35
  ships
    damage to, ...644–57
    deprivation
      of possession, ...636–44
    loss of freight, ...617–20
    repairs to, ...645–57
    unrepaired damage
      (partial loss), ...700
    waiver clause (Institute
      Hull Clauses), ...670–71
  see, also, Actual total loss;
    Partial loss; Total loss
Containers and packing
  materials, ...91
Contingent interests, ...39, 51–58,
  60–62, 800
Continuation Clause
  Institute Time
    Clauses Freight, ...892
  Institute Time
    Clauses Hulls (ITCH(95)), ...127–28,
    840, 864
Contra proferentum rule, ...300–01
Contracts, concluded, ...803

Contribution, right to, ...9–14
Craft risk, Institute
  Freight Clauses, ...892, 900

Deck cargoes, ...88–91
Deductible Clause
  (Institute Hull
  Clauses), ...677, 845–46,
    857–58, 869–70
Defeasible interests, ...39, 51–58,
  60–62, 800
Delay
  excluded loss, ...444–35
  Institute Cargo
    Clauses (ICC), ...434–35,
    881, 886, 891
  voyage policies, ...164–65,
    173–75, 809
Deliberate damage, ...447
Depreciation
  of ships, ...686–87, 688–92
Deprivation of
  possession, ...636–44
Detainment Clause
  (IWSC(H)(95)), war risks, ...579–80,
    643, 910
Deviation
  barratry, ...515–17
  voyage policies, ...155–64
Disbursements
  ballast, ...849, 873
  defined, ...116–17
  over-insurance, ...118–19
  ship agents,
    incurred by, ...117–19
Disbursements
  Warranty Clause,
  Institute Hull
    Clauses, ...119, 294–95,
    848–49, 860–61,
    872–73

Index

Disclosure requirements
  agents effecting
    insurance, ... .803
  appropriate
    to the moment, ...226–27
  assured, duties of, ...250–55, 802–03
  cancellation rights, ...230–31
  continuing duty, ... .226
  insurers, ...222–23,
                                227–30
  material information, ...225–26,
                                254–55, 293
  materiality tests
    actual inducement, ... .214, 261–65
    decisive influence, ... .214, 256–61
    defined, ...255–61
    hypothetical prudent
      insurer test, ... .256
    'increased risk', ... .260, 261
    presumption of
      inducement, ...265–67
  nature of duty, ...246–67
  over-valuation, ...194–203
  post-contractual
    duty, ...223–25, 252
  pre-contractual
    duty, ... .237, 246, 252
  reciprocal duty, ...222–23
  relevant information, ...225–26
  specific decision points, ...226–27
  see, also, Fraudulent claims;
  Representations; Utmost good faith
Dolus malus, ... .425
Double insurance
  contribution rights, ... .818
  defined, ... .806
  disbursements, ...118–19
  indemnity contracts, ...9–14
Doubtful claims, ...238–41
Due diligence proviso,
  Inchmaree Clause
  (ITCH(95)), ... .490, 532–34

Equitable proprietary
  interests, subrogation, ...27–31
Exaggerated claims, ... .233, 238–41
Exception clauses,
  express warranties, ...283–87
Excluded losses
  delay, ...433–35
  deliberate damage, ... .447
  inherent vice, ...440–44
  insolvency, ...445–47
  insufficient packing, ...441–42
  latent defects, ... .440, 443
  nature of subject
    matter insured, ...440–44
  ordinary leakage
    and breakage, ...437–40
  ordinary wear and tear, ...435–37
  proximate cause rule, ... .430
  rats and vermin, ...444–45
  wilful misconduct
    of assured, ...422–33
Exclusions
  3/4ths Collision
    Liability Clause, ...551–54
  Institute Cargo
    Clauses (ICC), ... .421, 877–78,
                                882–83, 887–88
  Institute Time
    Clauses Hulls (ITCH(95)), ... .421
  Institute Voyage
    Clauses Hulls
    (IVCH(95)), ... .421,
                                855–56, 862
  Institute War and
    Strikes Clauses Hulls
    (IWSC(H)(95)), ...589–03, 911
  insufficient packing, ...441–42
  salvage charges, ... .729
Explosion, insured
  peril, ... .392, 403–05

Express warranties
   Classification Clause
     (Institute Time
     Clauses Hulls), ...293–94
   construction, ...299–300
   contra proferentum, ...300–01
   descriptive, ...287–89
   Disbursements
     Warranties (Institute
     Hull Clauses), ...294–95
   examples, ...289–93
   exception clauses, ...283–87
   form, ...282–93, 807
   geographical, ...295–99
   good safety, ...291, 807
   neutrality, ...290–91, 807
   towage and salvage, ...291–93
Extension clauses,
   time policies, ...122–24

F c and s clauses
   (free from capture
   and seizure), ...557, 558,
                            566–67
Fire damage
   accidental or
     deliberate, ...396–98
   exceptions from
     liability, ...401–02
   fortuity, ...395–96
   fraudulent claims, ...232, 233–36
   heating, ...393–94
   innocent mortgagee, ...399–401
   negligence of assured, ...398
   onus of proof, ...402–03
   preventative
     actions causing, ...395
   proof of loss, ...474–76
     burden of proof, ...450, 476
   smoke and water, ...394–95
   wilful misconduct, ...398–99, 476

Floating policies, ...203, 211–12, 805
Fortuity
   accidents, ...364–69
   fire damage, ...364–69
   perils of the seas, ...364–69, 450
Forwarding of goods, ...657–58
Fpa clause (warranted
   free from particular
   average), ...719–20
Franchise, Institute
   Freight Clauses, ...717, 897, 903
Fraudulent claims
   fire damage, ...232, 233–36
   genuine claims
     connected, ...245–46
   innocence and fraud, ...237
   over-valuation, ...2–3, 191–94
   ppi policies, ...7
   utmost good faith, ...231–38, 239
   see, also, Barratry; Doubtful claims;
   Exaggerated claims
Free from capture
   and seizure
   (f c and s clauses), ...557, 558
Freight
   actual total loss, ...617–20
   advance, ...110–12, 801
   anticipated, ...848, 849, 872, 873
   bill of lading, ...97–99
   chartered, ...99–110, 848, 872
   collision, ...895–96, 901–02
   constructive
     total loss, ...617–20
   contingent or
     defeasible interest in, ...39, 60–62
   defined, ...94–96,
                              710, 820
   gross, ...95–96, 207
   insurable values, ...207

Index

loss of hire, ...105–06, 108–10
'loss of time' clause, ...106–08,
    897, 904
net, ...95–96, 207
ordinary, ...97–99
owners, ...59–60, 112
partial loss
    chartered vessels, ...712–13
    defined, ...711, 815
Franchise Clause,
    Institute Time
        Clauses Freight,   717
        measure of indemnity, ...715–17
        substituted cargo, ...712–13
        substituted ships, ...713–14
        total loss of
            part of the cargo, ...711–12
    passage money, ...96
    payable by third party, ...96–99
    time, ...103–05
    voyage contracts, ...100–03,
        848, 872–73
    waiver clauses, ...848, 860, 872
    see, also, Institute Time Clauses Freight;
    Institute Voyage Clauses Freight
Frustration clause
    (Institute War
    Clauses), ...93,
    594–97, 629

Gambling legislation, ...826–27
Gaming and wagering
    avoidance, ...800
    defined, ...3–4, 76
    indemnity contracts, ...3–8
    insurable interest, ...39
    valued policies, ...187
    'without benefit
        of salvage', ...8

General average
    adjustment, ...759–60
    foreign, ...760–64
    ballast, in, ...750
    caused by or directly
        consequential on, ...738–40
    chartered vessels, ...750–52
    common adventure, ...748–50
    constructive total loss, ...655–57
    contribution, ...740
    defined, ...735–38, 814
    expenditure, ...738, 754, 757–59
    extraordinary, ...740–43
    history, ...734
    Institute Freight
        Clauses, ...896–97, 903
    Institute Hull
        Clauses, ...753–54,
        843–44,
        855–56, 867–68
    insurers, ...754–55
    intentionally made, ...745–46
    perils, ...746–48
        insured against, ...752–53
    rationale, ...734
    reasonably made, ...743–44
    sacrifice, ...738, 754–56
        extraordinary, ...740–43
    salvage
        charges compared, ...732–34, 816
    ships, repair of, ...655–57, 674
    successful acts, ...753–55
    voluntarily made, ...743–44
    York-Antwerp Rules, ...733–34, 738,
    744–45
    see, also, Particular average loss
Geographical limits,
    time policies, ...124–25
Geographical
    warranties, ...295–300
Gifts, subrogation, ...34
Goods
    abandonment, ...632, 633–35

actual total loss, ...607–09,
                        615–16, 617–20
constructive
   total loss, ...617–20,
                        636–44, 657–58
containers and
   packing materials, ...91
contingent and
   defeasible interests in, ...51–58
deck cargo, .88–91
defined, ...87
floating policies, ...211–12
forwarding of, ...657–58
frustration clause, ...93, 594–97
Institute Cargo
   Clauses (ICC), ...88, 170–84
Institute War
   Clauses, ...93,
                        594–97, 913–17
insurable interests
   of owners, ...50–59
insurable values, ...207–12
living animals, ...88–91
loss of adventure, ...91–93
measure of
   indemnity, ...706, 709–10
partial interest in, ...59
partial loss
   computing measure
     of liability, ...709–10
   defined, .815–16
   not identifiable, ...709
   total loss of part of, ...704–06
   whole or part of, ...706–08, 709
'prime cost', ...208, 209
profit on, .113–14
voyage policies, ...170–81
Goods owners,
   insurable interest, ...50–59

Heat, sweat and
   spontaneous combustion
   (HSSC) clause, ...442–43
Helicopters, time policies, ...126
Honour policies
   see Ppi (policy proof of interest) policies
Hull policies
   see Institute Time Clauses Hulls;
   Institute Voyage Clauses Hulls

ICC
   see Institute Cargo Clauses (ICC)
Implied warranties
   see Cargoworthiness; Legality;
   Portworthiness; Seaworthiness
Inchmaree Clause (ITCH(95))
   barratry, .509–32
   breakage of shafts, ...494–95
   caused by, ...492–94
   due diligence proviso, ...490, 532–34
   latent defect in
     machinery or hull, ...444, 495–502
   marine risks, ...315–18,
                        363, 375, 444
   negligence, ...490, 502–08
   perils of the seas, ...491
   seaworthiness, implied
     warranty of, ...315–18,
                            363, 375
Indemnity contracts
   double insurance, ...9–14
   gaming and wagering, ...3–8
   imperfection of, ...2–3
   insurance as, ...1–3, 39
   over-insurance, ...14–15
   return of premium, ...15–17
   right to contribution, ...9–14
   subrogation, ...17–38
   see, also, Measure of indemnity; Ppi
   (policy proof of interest) policies
Inherent vice,
   excluded losses, ...440–44

Index

Inland voyages,
  deck cargoes, ... 89
Innocent mortgagee
  barratry, ... 530–32
  fire damage, ... 399–401
  wilful misconduct, ... 430–31
Insolvency
  excluded losses, ... 445–47
  see, also, Bankruptcy of insured
Institute Cargo Clauses (ICC)
  3/4ths Collision
    Liability Clause, ... 537
  all risks policies, ... 363,
                                    416–19, 434
  barratry, ... 509–10
  claims, ... 879–80,
                                    885, 889–90
  delay, ... 434–35, 881,
                                    886, 891
  deliberate damage, ... 447
  duration, ... 878–79,
                                    883–84, 888–89
  exclusions, ... 421, 877–78,
                                    882–83, 887–88
  goods, damage to, ... 657
  inherent vice, ... 440
  Institute Malicious
    Damage Clause, ... 421
  loss minimisation, ... 880, 886, 890–91
  perils of the seas, ... 369, 371, 385–92
  risks covered, ... 88, 877, 882, 887
    war risks, ... 572
  violent theft, ... 407, 909
  voyage policy on goods, ... 170–84
  Waiver Clause, warranties, ... 281
Institute Dual
  Valuation Clause, ... 906
Institute Freight Clauses
  see Institute Time Clauses Freight;
  Institute Voyage Clauses Freight
Institute Hull Clauses
  see Institute Time Clauses
  Hulls(ITCH(95)); Institute Voyage
  Clauses Hulls (IVCH (95))

Institute of London
  Underwriting Companies
  Marine Policy Form (MAR 91), ... 87
Institute Malicious
  Damage Clause, ... 421, 447, 908
Institute Strikes
  Clauses (Cargo), ... 594–97, 629,
                                    918–21
Institute Time
  Clauses Freight, ... 717, 892–99
Institute Time Clauses
  Hulls (ITCH(95))
  3/4ths Collision
    Liability Clause, ... 127, 535,
                                    536, 550,
                                    842–43, 866–67
  adjustment clause, ... 762–64
  agency commission, ... 847, 871
  assignment of
    interests, ... 848, 872
  barratry, ... 509–32
  bottom treatment, ... 847, 871
  Breach of Warranty
    Clause, ... 281, 840, 864
  cancellation
    returns, ... 849–50, 873–74
  Classification
    Clause, ... 133–34,
                                    293–94, 840, 864
  constructive
    total loss, ... 848, 872
  Continuation
    Clause, ... 127–28,
                                    840, 864
  Deductible Clause, ... 677,
                                    845–46, 869–70
  defined, ... 87
  Disbursements
    Warranty Clause, ... 119, 294–95,
                                    848–49, 872–73
  fire risks, ... 392
  general average, ... 753–54,
                                    843–44, 867–68

949

general exclusions
   clauses, ...421
heavy weather clause, ...696
Inchmaree Clause, ...315–18,
                              363, 375, 444
lay-up returns, ...849–50, 873–74
loading accidents, ...415
malicious acts exclusion, ...851, 875
Navigation
   Clause, ...125–27,
                              291, 292,
                              839–40, 863–64
new for old, ...847, 871
Notice of Claim and
   Tenders Clause, ...599–600,
                              846–47, 870–71
Paramount Clause, ...536
perils, ...841–42,
                              865–66, 876
Pollution Hazard
   Clause, ...536, 553–54,
                              842, 866
radioactive contamination
   exclusion clause, ...851, 875
Ranging Clause, ...126–27
salvage charges, ...727, 729,
                              843–44, 867–68
Scrapping Voyage
   Clause,   125
Sister Ship Clause, ...554–55,
                              843, 867
Termination Clause
change of ownership
   or flag, ...132,
                              840–41, 865
classification, ...129–32,
                              840–41, 865
unrepaired
   damage, ...847–48, 871–72
wages and
   maintenance, ...847, 871
waiver clauses, ...670–71, 848, 872

War and Strikes Clauses, ...558,
                              559, 850–51,
                              874–75
   see, also, Time policies
Institute Voyage
   Clauses Freight, ...900–05
Institute Voyage
   Clauses Hulls (IVCH(95))
3/4ths Collision
   Liability Clause, ...550, 854–55
agency commission, ...859
assignment of interests, ...860
barratry, ...509
bottom treatment, ...859
Change of Voyage
   Clause, ...153–55,
                              281, 852–53
Classification
   Clause, ...165, 853
constructive total loss, ...860
deductible amounts, ...857–58
defined, ...87
Disbursement
   Warranty Clause, ...119, 860–61
fire risks, ...392
freight waiver, ...860
general average, ...855–56
general exclusions
   clauses, ...421, 855–56
loading accidents, ...415
malicious acts
   exclusions, ...862
Navigation Clause, ...125, 126, 852
new for old, ...859
Notice of Claim and
   Tenders Clause, ...599–600,
                              858–59
Paramount Clause, ...536
perils included, ...853–54
pollution hazards, ...854
radioactive
   contamination
      exclusion, ...862

Index

salvage, ...855–56
Sister Ship Clause, ...554–55, 855
sue and labour, ...856–57
unrepaired damage, ...859–60
unseaworthiness, ...313–14
wages and maintenance, ...859
waiver clauses, ...670–71
war and
    strikes risks, ...558, 559,
                                861–62
see, also, Voyage policies
Institute War
    Clauses (Cargo), ...93, 594–97,
                                629, 913–17
Institute War and
    Strikes Clauses Hulls
    (IWSC(H)(95)), ...557, 558,
                                581, 910–12
    exclusions, ...589–03, 911
Institute warranties, ...907
Insurable interest
    advance freight, ...110–11, 801
    assignees
        see Assignment of interests
    bottomry and
        respondentia, ...75, 801
    captors, ...74–75
    company ventures, ...68–72
    contingent and
        defeasible interests, ...39, 51–58,
                                60–62, 800
    defined, ...39–46, 800
    'factual
        expectancy test', ...41
    freight owners, ...59–60
    gaming and
        wagering contracts, ...4–8, 39
    goods owners, ...50–59
    insurers, ...62–65
    'moral certainty', ...41
    mortgagors and
        mortgagees, ...65–67, 801

power of attorney, ...47–50
shareholders' interests, ...67–72
ship agents, ...72–74
ship owners, ...46–50
wages, ...801
when interest
    must attach, ...76–82, 800
Insurable values
    see Unvalued policies
Insurance
    as indemnity contract, ...1–3, 39
    marine, defined, ...1
    mutual, ...820
    ratification of contracts, ...820
Insurers
    breach of warranty, ...278–80
    disclosure
        requirements, ...222–23, 227–30
    general average, ...754–55
    insurable interest, ...62–65
    subrogation rights, ...818
    unseaworthiness, ...325
ITCH (95)
    see Institute Time Clauses Hulls
IVCH (95)
    see Institute Voyage
        Clauses Hulls
IWSC(H)(95) (Institute
    War and Strikes
    Clauses Hulls), ...557, 558,
                                581, 589–93

Latent defect,
    machinery or hull
        inherent vice, ...440, 443, 444
        meaning, ...495–500
        unseaworthiness, ...489, 500–02
Lay-up returns
    Institute Time
        Clauses Freight, ...898
    Institute Time
        Clauses Hulls (ITCH(95)), ...849–50,
                                873–74

951

Leakage and breakage,
excluded losses, ... 437–40
Legality, implied
warranty of
adventure, the, ...329–31, 332
breach, ...332–34
defined, ... 326–27, 808
English or foreign law, ...327–29
supervening
illegality, ...331–32
Lloyd's, salvage
agreement, .931–40
Lloyd's Marine
Policy (MAR 91), ...87, 831–34
Lloyd's Open Form (LOF), ...723–24
Loading accidents, ...415–16
Loss
see Ademption of loss; Causes of loss;
Mitigation of loss; Partial loss; Proof of
loss; Proximate cause rule; Total loss
Loss of adventure, ...91–93,
616–17,
620, 625–29
Loss of time, Institute
Freight Clauses, ...106–08,
897, 904
Loss of voyage, ...616–17,
620, 625–29
Losses
excluded
see Excluded losses
merger of, ...697–99,
701–03
successive, ...817

Malicious acts exclusion, ...908
Institute Freight
Clauses, ...899, 905
Institute Hull Clauses, ...851, 862, 875
see, also, Institute Malicious
Damage Clause

MAR 91 form (Institute
of London Underwriting
Companies Marine
Policy Form), ...87
Marine adventure, ...83, 91–93,
329–31,
332, 799
Marine insurance, defined, ...1, 799
Marine risks
all risks policies, ...363, 416–19, 434
barratry, ...571–72
defined, ...363–64
explosion, ...392, 403–05
fire, ...392–403
Inchmaree Clause
(ITCH(95)), ...315–18,
363, 375, 444
loading accidents, ...415–16
negligence, ...372–76, 398
perils of the seas, ...364–92
persons outside the
vessel, theft by, ...408–09
pilferage, ...409–11, 909
piracy, ...411–15,
571–72
violent disintegration, ...404–05
violent theft, ...405–11
see, also, Strikes risks; War risks
Master, negligence of, ...372–75,
376, 490,
502–08
Material information
see Disclosure requirements
Measure of indemnity
defined, ...814–15
freight, ...715–17
Institute Freight
Clauses, ...897, 903–04
goods, .706, 709–10
partial loss, ...715–17
ships, ...676–77,
687–88, 815

Index

total loss, ...815
 see, also, Indemnity contracts
Merger of losses, ...697–99,
 701–03
Misconduct, wilful
 see Wilful misconduct
Mitigation of loss, ...26–27
Mixed sea and land risks, ...799
Mixed (time and
 voyage) policies, ...181–84
Mortgages, insurable
 interest, ...65–67, 801
Movables, ...93, 325
Mutiny by passengers, ...412–13

Navigation Clause
 Institute Hulls
  Clauses, ...125–27, 291,
   292, 839–40,
   852, 863–64
 Institute Time
  Clauses Freight, ...892
 Institute Voyage
  Clauses Freight, ...900
Negligence
 assured, ...375–76, 398
 charterers, ...508
 fire damage, ...398
 Inchmaree Clause
  (ITCH(95)), ...490, 502–08
 marine risks, ...372–76, 398
 masters, .372–75,
   376, 490, 502–08
 proximate causes
  of loss, ...490
 repairers, ...508
 sue and labour, ...782
 unseaworthiness, ...505–06
 wilful misconduct, ...424
New for old, Institute
 Hull Clauses, ...847, 859, 871

'No cure – no pay',
 salvage, ...723, 724,
   931–40
No s/c (no salvage
 charges), ...793–94
Non-delivery clauses, ...409–11, 909
Notice of Claim
 and Tenders Clause, ... 599–600,
   846–47, 858–59,
   870–71, 911

'Open' policies
 see Unvalued policies
Ordinary wear
 and tear, ...383–84,
   435–37, 495
Over-insurance, ...9, 14–15,
   118–19
Over-valuation
 non-disclosure, ...200–03
 burden of proof
  over 'materiality', ...200
 common notoriety
  or knowledge, ...197
 fraud, ...2–3, 192
  absence of, ...191–94
 non-disclosure of
  material circumstance, ...194–203
 sound business reasons, ...192–94
 'utmost good
  faith', breach of
  duty to observe, ...194
Owners
 barratry, ...506–08, 524–29
 freight, ...59–60, 112
 goods, ...50–59

P & I (Protection and
 Indemnity) insurance, ...535, 541,
   543, 544, 547
Packing, insufficient
 (exclusions), ...441–42

Paramount Clause
   (ITCH(95) and IVCH(95)), ...536,
                                   558–59
Partial loss
   defined, ...673–74
   freight, ...710–17, 815
   general average, ...719, 734–64
   goods, ...704–10, 815–16
   particular
      average loss, ...673–75, 694–96,
                            719–21, 774–77, 813
   recovery for, ...621
   salvage, ...721–34
   ships, ...675–703, 815
   subrogation, ...25–27
   sue and labour, ...720–21,
                                729–32, 764–94
   see, also, Actual total loss; Constructive
   total loss; Total loss
Particular
   average losses, ...673–75,
                                  694–96, 719–21,
                                  774–77, 813
Particular
   average warranties, ...817
Particular charges, ...675, 720
Passage money, ...96
Pay to be paid rule, ...547–49
Perils
   apprehension of, ...347–49
   explosions, ...403–04
   general average, ...746–48, 752–53
   Institute Freight
      Clauses, ...894, 900–01
   Institute Hull
      Clauses, ...841–42, 853,
                            863, 865–66, 876
   Institute War and
      Strikes Clauses, ...910
Perils, maritime, defined, ...799

Perils of the seas
   3/4ths Collision
      Liability Clause, ...535
   accidents on
      board ship, ...376–79
   cargo-owner,
      position of, ...369–71
   collision, ...371–72
   fortuitous accidents, ...364–69
   Inchmaree Clause
      (ITCH(95)), ...491
   Institute Cargo
      Clauses (ICC)
      collision or contact, ...388–89
      entry of sea, lake,
         or river water, ...390–91
      grounded, ...387
      jettison or washing
         overboard, ...389–90
      preventative action
         causing losses, ...391–92
      stranded, ...385–87
      sunk and capsized, ...387–88
   marine risks, ...364–92
   negligence of master
      and crew, ...372–75
      assured acting as master, ...375–76
   ordinary action of
      wind and waves, ...381–83
   ordinary wear
      and tear, ...383–84
   proof of loss, ...451–73
   scuttling, ...369, 371, 524
   unascertainable, ...384–85
   unseaworthiness, ...379–81
Pilferage or non-
   delivery,....................409–11, 909
Piracy
   indiscriminate, ...413–14
   marine risks, ...571–72
   not politically motivated, ...413–14
   passengers who

mutiny, ...412–13
  requiring force, ...415
  rioters from the shore, ...411–12
  war risks, ...571–72
Policies, marine, ...804–05
Pollution Hazard Clause
  Institute Freight
    Clauses, ...894–95, 901
  Institute Hull
    Clauses, ...536, 553–54,
                    842, 854, 866
Portworthiness,
  implied warranty of, ...302–03
Possession,
  deprivation of, ...636–44
Ppi (policy proof of
  interest) policies
  gaming and
    wager contracts, ...5–8
  over-insurance, ...14–15
  subrogation, no
    right of, ...18–19
Pre-emption, IWSC(H)(95)
  exclusion, ...592–93
Premiums,
  arrangement of, ...805, 873
Premiums,
  disbursements, ...849
Premiums, return of, ...15–17, 132–33,
                  818–19, 849, 873
'Privity' doctrine, ...319–24,
                  351, 425–26, 429
Profit
  charter, ...114–15
  goods, ...113–14
  insurance
    considerations, ...112–13
Proof of loss
  barratry, ...477–88
  fire, ...450, 474–76
  perils of the seas
    missing ships, ...464–66

presumption of
  actual total loss, ...466
standard of
  proof, plaintiffs, ...466–67
unascertainable, ...455–57,
                      462–64
unseaworthiness, ...457–62
within the policy, ...466
see, also, Burden of proof
Property, abandonment of, ...22
Protection and
  Indemnity insurance
  (P & I), ...535, 541,
                    543, 544, 547
Proximate cause rule
  burden of proof, ...450
  efficient or
    predominate cause, ...336–41
  excluded losses, ...430
  marine and war risks, ...559–61
  negligence, ...490
  no express exclusions, ...344–45
  one expressly
    excluded, ...345–47
  one proximate cause, ...341–42
  two or more
    proximate causes, ...342–47

Radioactive contamination
  exclusion clause
  Institute Freight
    Clauses, ...899, 905
  Institute Hull
    Clauses, ...851, 862, 875
Ratification of insurance, ...820
Rats, excluded losses, ...444–45
Reckless disregard
  or indifference, ...424–30
Recovery (of ship
  or goods)
  cost, ...643–44

uncertainty, ...637–38
unlikelihood, ...638–41
Repair of ships
   bottom treatment, ...680–81
   completion of, ...650–51
   constructive total loss, ...645–57
   crew's wages
      and provisions, ...681–82
   customary deductions, ...685
   Deductible Clause
      (ITCH(95)), ...677, 845–46,
                                 869–70
   docking, ...678–80
   estimation of cost, ...651–55
   expenses, ...684–85
   freight, ...648–49
   future salvage operations, ...656–57
   general average
      contributions, ...655–57, 674
   insured values, ...647–48
   market values, ...646–47
   measure of
      indemnity, ...676–77,
                             687–88, 815
   not exceeding
      sum insured, ...685
   partial loss, ...678–85
   reasonable cost, ...678–80
   repaired value, ...645
   surveyor's fees, ...683
   temporary, ...683–84
   towage, ...683–84
   wrecks, ...649–50
   see, also, Ships; Unrepaired damage,
   ships
Repairers, negligence, ...508
Representations, ...267–68, 803
Requisition,
   IWSC(H)(95) exclusion, ...589–92
Res nullius
   (abandoned to the world), ...22, 25
Respondentia,
   insurable interest, ...75, 801

Rioting, ...411–12
Risks
   see Marine risks; Mixed sea and land
   risks; War risks
Running Down Clause
   see 3/4ths Collision Liability Clause

Salvage
   future operations, ...656–57
   general average
      compared, ...732–34, 816
   Institute Freight
      Clauses, ...896–97, 903
   Institute Hull
      Clauses, ...727, 729,
                         843–44, 855–56,
                                 867–68
   particular average, ...675
   ships, repair of, ...656–57
   see, also, Towage and salvage warranties
Salvage charges
   defined, ...722–29, 814
   enhanced awards
      for preventing
      environmental damage, ...727
   exclusions, ...729
   general average
      compared, ...732–34, 816
   incurred in preventing
      a loss by perils insured
      against, ...727–28
   independently of
      contract, ...722–23
   life salvage, ...724–27
   LOF agreement, ...723–24
   'no cure – no pay'
      basis, .723, 724,
                                 931–40
   sue and labour, ...729–32,
                                 793–94
   York-Antwerp Rules, ...733–34,
                                 922–30
Scuttling, ...369, 371, 524

Index

Seamen's wages, ...119
Seaworthiness
  commencement
    of voyage, ...312–13, 318
  exclusion and waiver, ...313
  held covered clause, ...313–15
  Inchmaree Clause, ...315–18, 363, 375
  ordinary perils
    of the seas, ...305, 306–07
  'privity', ...319–24, 351,
    425–26, 429
  prudent uninsured
    shipowner test,.................307
  reasonable fitness, ...305–06
  relative and flexible term, ...307–08
  seaworthiness
    admitted clause,................313
  ship, the, ...312
  stages,........................308–11
  time policies, ...303, 319, 490
  voyage policies, ...311, 489–90
  waiver clause (ICC), ...315
  warranty defined, ...807–08
  see, also, Unseaworthiness
Seizure
  barratry,......................517–24
  capture, ...569–71, 593
Shafts, breakage of, ...494–95
Shareholders,
  insurable interests,..............67–72
Ship agents
  disbursements, ...117–18
  insurable interests, ...72–74
Ship and furniture policies, ...86
Ship owners,
  insurable interest,...............46–50
Shipbuilders, sue and labour, ...767–68
Ships
  abandonment, ...629–30, 632
  actual total loss, ...602–07,
    613–15, 617–20
  constructive
    total loss,...........617–20, 636–57

  damage to, ...644–57,
    675–703
  defined, ...85
  depreciation, ...686–87,
    688–92
  floating policies, ...203, 805
  insurance
    considerations, ...85–87,
    206–07, 647–48
  market values, ...646–47
  measure of
    indemnity, ...676–77,
    687–88, 815
  missing, ...812
  partial loss, ...675–703, 815
  repair of, ...645–57,
    674, 676–85
  transhipment, ...812
  voyage policies, ...138–46
Sister Ship Clause
  3/4ths Collision
    Liability Clause, ...554–55
  Institute Freight
    Clauses, ...896, 902–03
  Institute Hull
    Clauses, ...554–55, 843,
    855, 867
Smuggling
  barratry,.................509, 517–24
  repeated acts, ...523
Stealing
  see Theft
Stowage, bad, ...326
Strikes risks
  civil commotions, ...585–87
  confiscation, ...587–89
  expropriation, ...587–89
  Institute Freight
    Clauses, ...899, 904
  Institute Hull
    Clauses, ...558, 559,
    851, 862, 875
  labour disturbances, ...583

lock-out, ...581–83
riots, ...583–85
risks covered, ...581
terrorism, ...587
Subject matter insurable
  commission, ...115–16
  company ventures, ...120
  designation in
    marine policy, ...804
  disbursements, ...116–19
  freight, ...93–112
  goods, ...87–93
  liability to
    third parties, ...120
  movables, ...93
  profit, ...112–15
  seamen's wages, ...119
  ships, ...85–87
Subrogation
  3/4ths Collision
    Liability Clause, ...537
  abandonment of
    property, ...22
  automatic transfer
    of ownership, ...22–23
  co-assured,
    rights against, ...31–34
  defined, ...17–18
  gifts, ...34
  insurers, ...818
  limited
    indemnified amounts, ...26
  mitigation of loss, ...26–27
  ownership remains
    with assured, ...23–25
  partial loss, ...25–27
  ppi policies, ...18–19
  proprietary
    interests, ...19–22, 27–31
  res nullius, ...25
  rights of insurers, ...818
  total loss, ...19–25
  under-insurance, ...37–38

voluntary payments, ...34
waiver clauses, ...35–37
Successive losses, ...817
Sue and labour
  assured and
    his agents, ...766–67,
                              844–45,
                         856–57, 868–69
  averting or
    minimising a loss, ...770–74
  avoidance measures, ...777–78
  particular average, ...774–77
  breach of duty, ...782–88
  cargo insurance, ...778–80
  cut-off date, ...788–89
  defined, ...732,
                          764–66, 817–18
  Institute Hull
    Clauses, ...844–45, 856–57
  negligence, ...782
  partial loss, ...720–21,
                          729–32, 764–94
  particular average, ...720–21
  reimbursement
    rights, ...789–93
  reinsurers, ...768–69
  salvage charges, ...729–32, 793–94
  salvors, ...769
  shipbuilders, ...767–68
  supplementary
    cover, ...780–82

Termination of
  insurance
  goods, ...175–81
  Institute Time
    Clauses Freight, ...893–94
  Institute Time
    Clauses Hulls, ...129–32,
                            840–45, 865
  Institute War and
    Strikes Clauses, ...912
  ships, ...165–70

Index

Terminology, policies, ...805
Theft, violent, ...405–09
Third parties
  3/4ths Collision
    Liability Clause, ...535, 545–47
  duty to give
    information to, ...829–30
  freight payable by, ...96–99
  liability to
    collision damage, ...120
  3/4ths Collision
    Liability Clause, ...535, 545–47
  measures of indemnity, ...816
  rights, bankruptcy
    of insured, ...828–29
  under-insurance, ...37–38
Time charter hire, ...103–05,
                      849, 873
Time policies
  at all times, ...125
  defined, ...804
  definite period
    of time, ...121–22
  extension clauses, ...122–24
  geographical limits, ...124–25
  helicopters, use of, ...126
  return of premium, ...132–33
  seaworthiness, ...303,
                      319, 490
  towage and
    salvage warranties, ...125–26,
                      281, 291–93
  trading operations,
    loading and discharging, ...126–27
  see, also, Institute Time Clauses Hulls
  (ITCH(95))
Total loss
  Institute Freight
    Clauses, ...897–98, 904
  measure of
    indemnity, ...815
  missing ships, ...466
  subrogation, ...19–25

see, also, Actual total loss; Constructive
  total loss; Partial loss
Towage and
  salvage warranties, ...125–26,
                      281, 291–93
Trading operations,
  time clauses, ...126–27

Uberrimae fidei
  see 'utmost good faith'
Under-insurance, ...37–38, 818
Unlikelihood, recovery
  of ship or goods, ...638–41
Unrepaired damage,
  ships
    actual total loss, ...700
    constructive total loss, ...700
    death blow theory, ...702–03
    Institute Time
      Clauses Hulls (ITCH(95)), ...847–48,
                      871–72
      heavy weather clause, ...696
    Institute Voyage
      Clauses Hulls (IVCH(95)), ...859–60
    measure of
      indemnity, ...687–88
    merger of losses, ...697–99,
                      701–03
    not sold, ...686
    reasonable
      depreciation, ...686–87,
                      688–92
    repaired partial
      losses recoverable, ...699–700
    sold, ...692–94
    successive particular
      average losses, ...694–96
Unseaworthiness
  elimination as
    cause of loss, ...457–62
  implied warranties, ...312, 315–18,
                      324, 325
  insurers, ...325

latent defect, ...489, 500–02
  loss attributable to, ...349–54
  negligence, ...505–06
  perils of the seas, ...379–81
Unvalued policies
  defined, ...206, 805
  depreciation, ...691–92
  insurable values
    freight, ...207
    goods and merchandise, ...207–12
    measure, ...801–02
    other subject matter, ...212
    ships, ...206–07
'Usage', meaning, ...89–91
'Utmost good faith',
  duty to observe
    assignees, ...215–16
  breach
    avoidance, ...213–14,
                            241–46
    damages,
      action for, ...242–45
    one genuine,
      one fraudulent
        claim, ...245–46
    continuing, ...216–19, 220–21
    end of, ...240–41
    defined, ...194, 213,
                            236, 802
    excessive over-
      valuation, ...194
    fraudulent claims, ...231–38, 239
    overriding, ...216–20
    reciprocal, ...214–16
    scope of, ...221–22
    see, also, Disclosure requirements;
    Representations

Valuation, apportionment of, ...816
Valued policies
  agreed value
    is conclusive, ...186–91

binding on assured, ...190–91
  definition and
    purpose, ...185–86, 805
  depreciation, ...688–92
  excessive
    over-valuation, ...191–203
  floating, ...203
  gaming and wagering, ...187
  'intended' to
    be insured, ...186–87
  scrapping voyages, ...191
  subject matter insured
    not at risk, ...203–05
Vessels, ...
  3/4ths Collision
    Liability Clause, ...541–45
Violent disintegration, ...404–05
Violent theft, ...405–09
Void policies
  excessive over-
    valuation, ...194
  gambling and
    wagering, ...3–8, 39
  ppi, ...18
  utmost good faith,
    breach of requirement, ...213–14
Voluntary payments,
  subrogation, ...34
Voyage, loss of, ...616–17,
                          620, 625–29
Voyage contracts,
  freight, ...100–03, 848,
                            872–73
Voyage policies
  defined, ...804
  goods, ...170–81
    attachment of
      insurance, ...171–73
    delay beyond
      control of assured, ...173–75
    insurance
      remaining in force, ...173–75

Index

termination
  of insurance, ...175–81
  see, also, Institute Cargo
    Clauses (ICC)
seaworthiness, ...311, 489–90
ships, ...134–70
  attachment, ...135–46
  alteration of
    departure port, ...136–37, 808
    good safety, ...144–46
    named ports, ...139–44
  particular places,
    at and from, ...135–46
  sailing for a different
    destination, ...137–38, 808
  change of voyage, ...151–55, 808
  delay in voyage, ...164–65, 809
  deviation, acts of, ...155–64, 809
  course of voyage, ...156–58
  held covered, ...161–64
  intention, immaterial, ...158–59
  lawful excuses, ...160
  legal effect of, ...161
  without lawful excuse, ...159–60
  implied condition
    as to commencement
      of risk, ...146–49
  'lawful excuse', ... 147–48,
                                      159–60
  overlapping of, ...149–51
  ports of discharge, ...809
  termination of
    insurance, ...165–70
  see, also, Institute Voyage Clauses Hulls
    (IVCH(95))

Wagering
  see gaming and wagering
Wages, seamen, ...119
Wages and maintenance,
  Institute Hull Clauses, ...847,
                                      859, 871

Waiver clauses
  ademption of loss, ...670–71
  freight, ...848,
                                      860, 872
  seaworthiness, ...281, 315
  subrogation, ...35–37
War risks
  arrest restraint or
    detainment, ...573
  barratry, .571–72
  belligerent power, ...566
  capture and seizure, ...569–71
  civil war revolution
    rebellion insurrection, ...563–65
  civil strife, .566
  derelict mines, ...580
  Detainment Clause
    (IWSC(H)(95)), ...579–80, 643, 910
  f c and s clause, ...566–67
  force is not a
    requirement, ...573–76
  hostile acts, ...567–69
  Institute Cargo Clauses, ...572
  Institute Freight Clauses, ...899, 904
  Institute Hull
    Clauses, ...851, 861, 874–75
  political or
    executive acts, ...576–79
  war defined, ...562–63
  see, also, Marine risks; Mixed sea and
    land risks; Strikes risks
Warranted free from
  particular average
    (fpa clause), ...719–20
Warranties
  breach
    automatic discharge
      of insurers, ...278
    burden of proof, ...286–87
    excused, .806
    geographical, ...299
    Institute Time
      Clauses Freight, ...892

stitute Time
  Clauses Hulls (ITCH(95)), ...281,
                              840, 864
  legal effects, ...277–78
  no defence for, ...274–75
  no remedy for, ...273–74
  waivers by insurers, ...278–80
compliance with, ...270–72
express, ...269,
                          282–301, 807
geographical, ...295–300
held covered
  clause, ...281–82, 313–15
  see, also, Change of Voyage Clause
implied, ...301–34, 807
Institute, ...907
material to risk, ...272–73
nationality, ...807
nature of, ...806
particular average, ...817
promissory, ...269,
                          275–80, 283
representations
  compared, ...267–68
Waiver Clause, ICC, ...281, 315

Wilful misconduct
  barratry, ...450
  by assured, ...354–56,
                                 422–33
  cargo owner,
    position of, ...431
  causes of loss, ...354–56
  dolus circuitu
    non purgator, ...425
  excluded losses, ...422–33
  fire damage, ...398–99
    standard of proof, ...476
  innocent mortgagee, ...430–31
  meaning, ...422–33
  negligence, ...424
  orders for ship's
    papers, ...432
  reckless disregard
    or indifference, ...424–30
  sue and labour, ...782
Wrongful acts,
  barratry, ...510–14

York-Antwerp Rules, ...733–34, 738,
                          744–45, 922–30